MUSIC

CAVALCADE

1620 - 1969

*A Chronology of
Vocal and
Instrumental
Music Popular in
the United States*

Third Edition

BY

JULIUS MATTFELD

WITH AN INTRODUCTION BY

ABEL GREEN, Editor of *Variety*

PRENTICE-HALL, INC., *Englewood Cliffs, N.J.*

PREFACE

Methinks I have been thirty years
a collector.—Charles Lamb: *The
Essays of Elia.*

The purpose of this compilation is to provide a chronological check
list of music which enjoyed a degree of popularity in the United States
from the time of the Pilgrims to the present day. The project grew out
of a music librarian's card file of notes and newspaper clippings which
had accumulated over a long period of years as a reference for answer-
ing recurrent questions. The nature of these inquiries has undoubtedly
affected the character of the material which is presented here in book
form.

The compilation makes no pretense at being definitive. As already
stated, the assembled data represents a librarian's selection. The choice
covers hymns, secular and sacred songs, choral compositions, and instrumental and orchestral works. For practical reasons only such music
as is, for the most part, available in print today has been included. Many
of the secular songs tabulated before 1900 are traceable to sources
through the two-volume "Song Index," edited by Minnie Earl Sears (The
H. W. Wilson Co.; New York, 1926-34). Brief bibliographies of collections containing music of the period under consideration also will be
found at appropriate places in the compilation.

The listings are based on the year of publication or of copyright, and
are derived from the earliest editions accessible to the compiler. No effort
has been made to follow the subsequent history of an entry through the
channels of the music publishing industry. To have done so would have

Variety Music Cavalcade, Third Edition, by Julius Mattfeld
Copyright © 1971 by the Estate of Julius Mattfeld
© 1962, 1952, by Julius Mattfeld • Copyright under International and Pan
American Copyright Conventions • All rights reserved. No part of this book
may be reproduced in any form or by any means, except for the inclusion of
brief quotations in a review, without permission in writing from the publisher •
ISBN 0-13-940718-9 • Library of Congress Catalog Card Number: 70-129240
• Printed in the United States of America *T* • Prentice-Hall International, Inc.,
London • Prentice-Hall of Australia, Pty. Ltd., Sydney • Prentice-Hall of
Canada, Ltd., Toronto • Prentice-Hall of India Private Ltd., New Delhi •
Prentice-Hall of Japan, Inc., Tokyo •

Second printing..........June, 1971

entailed endless labor, particularly in this area of confusing copyright renewals, transfers, and split assignments.

Omissions? There are plenty, as the compiler knows. They are the lacunae that disturb every bibliographer's sense of detail—the inevitable disappointment attending his most careful efforts. In a work of this category, each perusal reveals one or more so-called "glaring" omissions. "Not in—" is a familiar phrase of criticism, bibliographically speaking, and is as applicable, alas, to this book as to the productions of every pioneer researcher. Some—indeed, many—titles have inevitably escaped the compiler's attention. As the always quotable Charles Lamb said of the omissions in his autobiographical sketch, "To any Body—Please to fill up these blanks."

This compilation is already familiar in several guises. It was first published in the "*Variety* Radio Directory, 1938-39." A portion of the compilation, from 1814 to 1889, was incorporated shortly thereafter, without publishers' names and historical commentaries, in Edward B. Marks' reminiscences "They All Had Glamour" (Messner; New York, 1944).

The "Musical-Historical Cavalcade" next appeared in *Variety* in a serial reprint which began in 1948 and extended over a period of two years. In this, its second form, it was republished, with additions which brought the compilation up to and including 1950, in the weekly issues of *Variety* —hence the name of the present book. Now, greatly expanded and with further additions, annotations, and new historical paragraphs, the material is issued in the format of a volume.

In conclusion, it is the pleasant duty of the compiler to acknowledge gratefully the assistance of institutions and many interested persons. Were it not for such institutions as the New York Public Library; the Columbia Broadcasting System; the Union Theological Seminary, New York; and the Grosvenor Library, Buffalo, much of the material gathered together in the following pages would not have been possible in the present form. To them, their chiefs and employees, the compiler expresses his appreciation for all assistance. No less helpful have been the suggestions, often unsolicited, of friends and unknown correspondents.

J. M.

FOREWORD TO SECOND EDITION

This edition of VARIETY MUSIC CAVALCADE carries the chronicle of musical titles and historic events to the close of the year 1961. New material has been inserted in the pages before 1950; and some factual and typographical errata have been corrected. Limitations of space have governed the nature of the revisions and additions. In consequence, many rock 'n' roll songs, which enjoyed a temporary vogue, have been omitted; a sufficient number, however, are included to highlight the period.

J. M.

New York, 1962

INTRODUCTION: THE MUSIC BIZ

By ABEL GREEN
Editor of *Variety*

During the last decade or so, the music business has been "rocked" by a revolution, probably more profound than in any other facet of American life. A new wave of youngsters has taken over with its own talent, its own concepts, and its own techniques, all keyed to swiftly changing patterns of the last third of the 20th century.

The torch has been passed from the hands of the Irving Berlins, Rodgers & Hammersteins, Cole Porters and the other grandmasters of popular music into the hands of The Beatles, The Rolling Stones, the Bob Dylans, the Jimmy Webbs, the Laura Nyros, the Otis Reddings, the "soul" writers, and other representatives of "the new sound." In the process, the music business has not only become louder and bolder, it has also become considerably larger than it ever was before.

Cassettes and Cartridges In 1960, the record industry grossed about $500,000,000. Now augmented by tape cartridges and cassettes, the current gross of the record industry is over the $1.5 billion mark. And coming over the horizon are the audio-visual tape cartridges designed for the home entertainment market. This new technology promises to have a major impact on the music business of the decade ahead.

During the decade of the 1960s, a spectacular imprint was made by the youngsters who, whether working solo, like Dylan, or in combos, like The Beatles, broke with the past and did their own thing.

They set the Generation Gap to music, with "hip" youngsters lined up on one side and their "square" elders on the other. In place of the old "moon-June-spoon" sentiments that saturated the old popular hits, contemporary songs can be understood as manifestos in behalf of a new morality. The youngsters who write and perform today's music won't conform to the standards of the past and speak up about their own ideas about politics, sex, and narcotics.

Yesteryear's goldfish-swallowers and phonebooth-crowders have given way to flower children. Panty raids have given way to communes, physical encounters, sleep-ins and even gay-ins.

Raccoon coats from the Stone Age were replaced by blue suede shoes; white bucks and black denim trousers; in turn now eclipsed by bare feet, cowboy hats, Fu-Manchu mustachios, long hair, love beads, Indian hairbands, Navajo talismen, and Afro coiffs.

From the earlier "leerics" of the 1950s, with their double-entendre, the four-letter words now spell out the facts of life. Hash, pot, acid, groupies are part of the new music scene, and with the relaxation of moods and mores, forbidden words have become part of the rhetoric, so much so that many radio stations must screen new record releases very closely.

The drug scene, mod fashions, flower children ("often potted," aver the captious critics), the Generation Gap, Liverpool Sound, Nashville Sound, Vietnam, groovy, Gurus, sitars, rock festivals, protest songs, love, peace, campus revolts, soul, cajun—all have their roots and/or reflections in the pop scene.

When rock and roll music swept over the nation in the mid-1950s, there was a general conviction in the music industry that it was only a passing fad, a seasonal sensation. But after 15 years, the "fad" has refused to pass. Rock, in fact, has become the dominant sound in popular music throughout the world. Like other manifestations of the youth rebellion, rock music simply won't go away.

With the death in 1968 of Dr. Julius Mattfeld, a dedicated musicologist and the original compiler of the VARIETY MUSIC CAVALCADE (music from the Pilgrims to the mid-20th century), Herm Schoenfeld, music editor of *Variety,* compiled the supplementary decade which complements this third edition. He also authored the Historical Notes, and in choosing the galaxy of top tunes that has distinguished the post-Rock Generation, he has also done a broader selection.

Alfred Cain, editor for Prentice-Hall on this edition, sagely includes the previous Introduction by Abel Green as an historical contrast to the new "Rock Generation" summation of the new Music Biz.

INTRODUCTION TO 1962 EDITION

The music biz is a multi-million dollar business. It has been variously estimated at $500,000,000 per annum, including everything from the over $33,000,000 royalty melon of the American Society of Composers, Authors & Publishers, the $12,700,000 from Broadcast Music Inc. (BMI, the competitive collection agency to ASCAP) to the astronomic fees for filmusical scores and synchronization rights, television and radio programs, not counting individual music publisher and songwriter earnings.

When Irving Berlin made film deals for "Annie Get Your Gun" for $500,000, and $600,000 for the screen rights to an "Easter Parade," he dwarfed the $125,000 paid by Metro for a biopic of the careers of Lorenz Hart and Richard Rodgers ("Words and Music"), or the Warner Bros. deal for George M. Cohan's "Yankee Doodle Dandy" ($125,000 and a percentage). But a decade or so later Warners committed itself to $5,500,000 (plus percentage) for a seven-year deal for Lerner & Loewe's "My Fair Lady," not to mention the $1,000,000-$2,000,000 film right sales to such click legit musicals as Frank Loesser's "Guys and Dolls," Rodgers and Hammerstein's "The King and I," "South Pacific," and "Oklahoma!"; Meredith Willson's "Music Man" and, again, Alan Jay Lerner and Frederick Loewe's "Camelot."

Still another music biz evolution of vast importance, perhaps as rebuttal to or because of rock 'n' roll and the Twist and kindred manifestations, has been the upbeat of the LP.

Payola, which had made the disk jockey king of Tin Pan Alley, became more discreet under Federal Communications Commission threat to suspend the licenses of those radio stations which knowingly or otherwise countenanced subsidy for plugging records. While payola is as time dishonored in the music biz as is the tradition of songplugging, the evolution of the single record business catapulted into stardom in recent years such song stylists as Elvis Presley, Paul Anka, Connie Francis, Pat Boone, Joni James, Bobby Darin, Frankie Avalon, Fabian, Rosemary Clooney, Guy Mitchell, Frankie Laine, Tony Martin, Patti Page, Dinah Shore, Doris Day, et al.

Latterly the LP, or longplaying (33 rpm), album has become the favored merchandising medium of the record business because of its greater economic potential as a musical package, and found audience acceptance with "the kids" (the rock 'n' roll set) as well as the more adult disk buyers.

The maturer bunch go for the popular standards in packaged albums, along with the yesteryear musicomedy and operetta perennials, the Original Cast and Original Soundtrack albums of the legit and film scores.

This in turn skyrocketed bidding for the OC (Original Cast) album rights so that a diskery such as Columbia, for example, in the one season (1961-62) had more than $1,000,000 invested in "advances" to the show's producers and authors.

Considering that Col's parent CBS Inc. had pyramided a $350,000 investment in "My Fair Lady" into millions and the show's global box-office gross has gone over $58,000,000, that was no great risk. Col also hit the jackpot with Lerner & Loewe's sequential musical "Camelot," but "took a bath" with its $300,000 investment in "Kean."

Columbia was not alone. Before RCA Victor hit the jackpot with "How to Succeed in Business Without Really Trying" and "Milk and Honey," it had some big red ink losses in Frank Loesser's "Greenwillow," for example; "Saratoga" (musicalization of Edna Ferber's "Saratoga Trunk"); and "Wildcat." The last loss was more in the form of a commitment of $100,000 for advertising and promotion rather than an actual stake in the financing of the show, since some producers and songwriters would rather trade off their rights for the extra ballyhoo in merchandising the albums because of resultant stimulus to the boxoffice. Capitol, which got strongly into the show album bidding, likewise hit and missed. Cap hits were "Fiorello," "The Unsinkable Molly Brown" and "Music Man," latter two by Meredith Willson, and Richard Rodgers' "No Strings."

It may have been because of the increasing acceptance of dialog-and-song, in the OC Albums, that the upsurge of the comedians-on-wax grew into such bestselling proportions, *viz.*, the albums of Mort Sahl, Shelley Berman, Bob Newhart, Bill Dana ("Jose Jiminez"), et al. Also, the "live" performances of such nitery and concert favorites as Lena Horne, Harry Belafonte, Marlene Dietrich, Noel Coward, Dinah Shore, Tony Martin, Jane Morgan, Kingston Trio, The Limeliters, Ella Fitzgerald, Judy Garland, Frank Sinatra, Dean Martin and Sammy Davis, Jr., were taped direct from Carnegie Hall, the Cocoanut Grove and sundry Las Vegas and Miami Beach plusheries, etc.

The band business, at one time a $50,000,000 industry, has long since given way to "groups," even with the upbeat of the Twist which requires nothing more than an up-front "personality kid," guitar, organ, piano and drums.

TV repeated the Hollywood technique of stringing songsmiths' careers into video "specials," much as biopix were based (or are being planned) on the life and times and songs of tunesmiths and music men such as Berlin, Porter, Gershwin, Cohan, Rodgers and Hart, Kern, Arlen, Joe E. Howard ("I Wonder Who's Kissing Her Now"), Kalmar & Ruby ("Three Little Words"), two Jolson biopix, Stephen Foster, Paul Dresser, Eddie Cantor, Marilyn Miller, Will Rogers, Helen Morgan, Ruth Etting, Sophie

Tucker, Blossom Seeley ("Somebody Loves Me"), Ted Lewis, Ben Bernie, Paul Whiteman ("King of Jazz"), Jane Froman ("With A Song In My Heart"), "The Great Caruso" (Mario Lanza), Fred Fisher ("Oh You Beautiful Doll"), Gus Kahn ("I'll See You In My Dreams"), Glenn Miller, Benny Goodman, Vincent Lopez, et al.

So, too, have these and other more contemporary tunesmiths been "saluted" on TV, with attendant revitalization of their catalogs for renewed plugs and "performance credits," the latter so important in the ASCAP pattern of quarterly royalty melons.

As this writer's favorite wife once observed, "Songwriters have the most wonderful obits—everything they leave behind not only lives after them but ofttimes becomes even more vivid with the passing years. And not only that—the most casual reprise of their life's accomplishments even make their death notices create living nostalgic scenes anew because of the indelible association of the popular music with some personal event."

Showmen have built entire productions on that premise. Million-dollar filmusicals come off the Hollywood production line based on durable works, either from contemporary American sources or the older and richer Continental originations that embrace anything from Johann Strauss to Oskar Straus, from Josef J. Lanner to Franz Lehár to Robert Stolz.

HISTORICAL MUSICAL MILESTONES

Irving Berlin once told this writer that the history of America could be traced through its music. This book by musicologist Julius Mattfeld attests to that fact. Certainly none can dispute that our contemporary history is reflected by the tunes that America—and the world—whistles, hums, plays, or dances to.

Not only does history but the moods, manners, modes and mores of the land come to mind, whether it's "Break the News to Mother," of the Spanish-American War, or such banal oddities of more recent vintage as "Goodbye Mama, I'm Off to Yokohama."

"Save Your Kisses Till the Boys Come Home" and "Till We Meet Again" of World War I found a counterpart 35 years later with "Praise the Lord and Pass the Ammunition." "Over There" became "God Bless America" one world war later. Pacifism of 1914, exemplified by "Don't Take My Darling Boy Away" and "I Didn't Raise My Boy to Be a Soldier," gradually gave way in 1915 to "I'd Be Proud to Be the Mother of a Soldier" ("it would be a different story if they trampled on Old Glory—then I'd be proud to be the mother of a soldier!"). And later to "America I Love You," "I'm Proud of You Laddie," "Soldier Boy I Kiss Before You Go," "What Kind of an American Are You?" "America Needs You Like a Mother—Would You Turn Your Mother Down?" "Sister Susie's Sewing Socks for Soldiers (Sailors)," "Liberty Bell It's Time to Ring Again," George M. Cohan's "There's Only One Little Girl and One Little Flag for Me" (this preceded his immortal "Over There"), finally capped by "America, Here's My Boy," "So Long Mother," "That's a Mother's Liberty Loan," "There's a Vacant Chair in Every Home Tonight," "There Is a Service Flag Flying at Our House," "Say a Prayer for the Boys Over There."

The nation's dance styles, naturally, are highlighted by its music, be it the first real impetus to jazz in 1911, via Irving Berlin's "Alexander's Ragtime Band," along with the "Bunny Hug" and "Grizzly Bear" dances of the period; right through the "Castle Walk" (Irene and Vernon Castle) of the pre-Prohibition "lobster palace" period. This was the golden era of Reisenweber's, Churchill's, Rector's, Maxim's, the Pre-Catelan and Mouquin's, Murray's Roman Gardens and Jack's; of Broadway's glittering period when Victor Herbert, Karl Hoschna, Louis A. Hirsch, Otto Harbach, Jerome Kern, Guy Bolton, P. G. Wodehouse, Henry Blossom, Harry B. Smith, Harold Atteridge, Rida Johnson Young, Anne Caldwell, Robert B. Smith, Gene Buck and Gustave Kerker ruled the Broadway boards.

THE PIONEER JAZZISTS

Then came the era of the Chicago "coon-shouters," exemplified by Sophie Tucker ("Angle Worm Wriggle," which got the Windy City gendarmerie after her) and Blossom Seeley ("Doing the Toledo"). Also up to Chicago came jazz, which was first spelled jass or jaz, blended by a admixture of shimmy dancing (Bee Palmer, Gilda Gray, Frank Hale, Joe Frisco), later giving way to the hula (Doraldina). Before these came such New Orleanists as the Original Dixieland Jazz Band (Nick LaRocca), King Oliver and Sidney Becket, but it wasn't long before, also out of the West, came the more melodic strains of Art Hickman and Paul Whiteman. The latter's symphonic syncopation, in 1924, at the now historic Aeolian Hall (N. Y.) concert, was to be the interpreting medium which made a lady out of jazz—referring, of course, to George Gershwin's "Rhapsody In Blue," which Whiteman premiered.

The golden era of musical comedy brought forth the young modern composers of the mid-1920s, the Gershwins (George and Ira), Vincent Youmans, Richard Rodgers, Lorenz (Larry) Hart, B. G. DeSylva, Lew Brown and Ray Henderson, Leo Robin, Herbert and Dorothy Fields, Irving Caesar, Arthur Schwartz, Howard Dietz, and the perennial Irving Berlin. They were the relatively conservative interpreters of the passing show business scene in the hectic F. Scott Fitzgerald period. Among other mores of the fabulous Jazz Age were the Varsity Drag, the Charleston (prime disciples: George Raft and another nitery hoofer, Ruby Stevens, later to be know as Barbara Stanwyck), and the Black Bottom.

This era of wonderful nonsense, with its mobs and slobs of all degrees, created the slinking gown; the "it" girl (Clara Bow); the "sheik" type (Valentino) and the attendant "shebas"; the somnolent sirenesque lost weekends, only this time Elinor Glynn called them "Three Weeks"; the flappers and their flippers; the raccoon coats and hip flasks.

WALL STREET LAYS AN EGG

"Wall Street Lays An Egg" is now an historic *Variety* headline, referring to the Oct. 29, 1929, financial debacle. And as the Jazz Age was cacophonously pyramiding itself to the big fawdown, Rudy Vallee was romantically soothing the savagery of the period with his megaphone heigh-ho'ing and vagabond loving. The Ignoble Experiment of Volsteadism gave way to banks closing. Theatre givaways increased to bolster the lagging b.o. (for boxoffice, to borrow another *Variety* term). And as beer parlors put in more and more skee-ball and pinball games to bolster the bar biz, the radio industry boomed with its peak stay-at-home audiences.

The candid camera craze first started to click, along with homepuzzles, put-and-take games, "knock-knock" and kindred divertissements of the period that swept the land, much as gin rummy and canasta, the rhumba, cha-cha and the Twist in later, lusher years were destined to do.

The two-for-five applesellers on the streets of every big city, and the breadlines (with attendant gags about "we have two lines: one for white and one for rye") were typical of a short but dread early FDR period. The theme song was "Brother, Can You Spare a Dime?"

Benny Goodman and Artie Shaw with their swing; Louis (Satchmo) Armstrong with his jive; Frank Sinatra with his lazy-daisy crooning of "All or Nothing At All"; the ensuing jump and jive period and the abortive bebop that never came off, continued an ever-changing pattern, even through the post-Pearl Harbor war period.

Just as the Big Apple, the Lambeth Walk, the Lindy Hop and the jitterbug, the shag and the hucklebuck gave young and old alike a chance to "shine," the midcentury saw the rhumba and the conga give way to the cha-cha, pachanga and the meringue, of which the cha-ca remains most durable.

And from the Latin beat the kids evolved their own "big beat" tastes for rock 'n' roll which, for all its cacophony and public derision, remains durable because of its appeal to the youngsters.

There was a period when moralists and realists alike looked askance at the "leer-ics" (this writer's coinage for the pseudo-lyrics, many with double-entendre connotation). But the r&r aficionados contended that the prime appeal to the youngsters was "the beat" while the words were for the birds. That was not to be so easily accepted but, in the evolution of rock 'n' roll, the country & western (hillbilly) tempos combined into a "rockabilly" beat. Just as, in time, the cha-cha became enhanced with a rock 'n' roll accent that resulted in a rock-a-cha-cha.

None the less, as if in repudiation of all this cacophony, "singalongs" became inordinately popular, sparked by Mitch Miller's top-rated TV show and resultant big album sellers.

The popular standards created new bonanzas for the old-line publishers whose durable ballads, both pop and musicomedy, remained evergreen with the kids, the young marrieds and adults alike.

That American musical tastes have constantly moved upward is evidenced by the extension of the "middlebrow" category. Strictly longhair or highbrow styles of show business also extended their audience appeal. Broadway legit musicals are more adult. From England first came "Red Shoes" and later "Tales of Hoffmann" to sell ballet to the film masses. Metro walked in at the right time with Mario Lanza and "The Great Caruso" for a boxoffice mopup.

POPULARIZING THE CLASSICS

European refugees marveled at "how intelligent and how wonderfully musical are the American people—everywhere you go you hear them whistle and hum the old masters," but they soon learned that Tin Pan Alley was more and more frankly borrowing from classic sources. In former years it was a challenge to transmute Chopin and Strauss, Beethoven and Tchaikowsky into "popular" acceptance. Somebody even wrote a kidding-on-the-square pop, "Everybody's Makin' Money But Tchaikowsky." A yesteryear songsmith, Fred Fisher, in the early days of the "Hollywood gold rush," wanted to know why he wasn't tapped to write a film score. Told that the Hollywood moguls wanted the top Broadway songwriters—Porter, Kern, Berlin, Harry Warren, Hammerstein, Romberg, Friml, Al Dubin—he exclaimed with righteous indignation. "When you get Fisher you get all of these and besides, in addition, you get Strauss, Bach, Beethoven, Grieg, Chopin and almost every great composer you can mention."

Thus, "Over The Waves" became Lanza's "The Loveliest Night of the Year"; the "Anniversary Waltz" is an old Rumanian folk song. The Spanish tango "Adios Muchachos" becomes "I Get Ideas." Any number of Strauss waltzes are now in the pop catalog, and even Bizet made the Hit Parade when Oscar Hammerstein II reshuffled the whole thing into "Carmen Jones."

ECONOMICS OF THE MUSIC BIZ

From the creative end of the music biz, the quarterly dividends that the American Society of Composers, Authors and Publishers pays off its writer and publisher members speaks a Fort-Knox-style musical jingle through the pyramiding royalty melons.

The $33,191,987 divided by ASCAP in 1962 is a far cry from what Victor Herbert envisioned in 1914 when he took his plaint to attorney Nathan Burkan that if Shanley's Restaurant, then a class Broadway dining rendezvous, publicly performs his (Herbert's) operetta music—as he happened to hear one night—then why doesn't the restaurateur pay for it? After a series of now historic test suits, up to the U. S. Supreme Court, the plugs no longer were deemed to be an adequate payoff to the tunesmiths. The performances came after the fact that pop music, as it is created and exploited off the Tin Pan Alley production line, has a definite commercial value.

And where songwriters like Irving Berlin, Cole Porter, George Gershwin, Jerome Kern, et al., felt that an $18,000 and $20,000 annual melon was a right handsome by-product for their wares, it was not until another U. S. consent decree, in 1949, that the really productive writers were to realize undreamed-of fruits of their writing labors. The Government edicted a per-point payoff system, with result that the more popularly performed writers and publishers, as logged by the major networks, got more than others.

As a result, the prolific Berlin's and Porter's ASCAP income is around the $90,000-$100,000 annual take; Rodgers and Hammerstein around $75,000; the Gershwin, Kern and Larry Hart estates around $50,000 per annum; and contemporary songwriters like Lerner and Loewe, Johnny Mercer, Ira Gershwin, Jimmy McHugh, Jule Styne, Frank Loesser, the Youmans and Romberg estates, Rudolf Friml, Sammy Cahn, Dorothy Fields, Harry Warren, among others, are in the $30,000-$50,000 brackets, just from the public performances for profit of their past and present works—in most cases past.

This is the irony of the music business as presently constituted. One name songsmith conceded that "if I had to compete in the current rat race for plugs, 'getting that record,' and all the attendant chicanery, skulduggery and payola as exists in the present pattern of our business, I'd starve because I could never compete with the presentday crop of eager-beavers. In the traditional days of the music business, a publisher went to work on a 'plug song,' if he thought it could be exploited into a hit. Sure we had our own special brand of deviousness to get favored attention, either from a headliner or plugging a song at the bike races, in Coney Island and Brighton Beach to the masses, behind the piano counters at McCrory's and Woolworth's chainstores, but it's nothing like the intrigue that obtains today."

This is where the values of the yesteryear "solid" songs stand these old-line songsmiths in good stead. They're their lifetime annuities and beyond, for benefit of their estates. That is why all creative writers (literary as well as songsmiths) have been petitioning for a new Copyright Act to replace the now obsolescent Copyright Act of 1909 with its 2¢ statutory fee for phonograph records, for example, never foreseeing the $500,-000,000 jukebox industry as it exists today. Both ASCAP and BMI have long petitioned Congress for a tithe on the performance of each platter as they grind endlessly in candystores, taverns, juke-joint danceries and the like. Incidentally, a prime fear is that many of the "solid" songs' full 56-year terms of copyright are about to expire before any such protection to their songs is ever enacted.

Thus, it was after much weighting of all values (continuing performances, longevity, reactivation from time to time) that *Variety* came up with this listing, in alphabetical order, of the "Golden 100":

"After You've Gone," "Ah, Sweet Mystery of Life," "Alexander's Ragtime Band," "All Alone," "All the Things You Are," "Always," "A Pretty Girl Is Like a Melody," "April in Paris," "April Showers," "As Time Goes By," "Ballin' the Jack," "Begin the Beguine," "Bewitched, Bothered and Bewildered," "Blue Moon," "Blues in the Night," "Body and Soul," "Chicago," "Come Rain or Come Shine," "Dancing in the Dark," "Darktown Strutters' Ball," "Dinah," "Easter Parade," "Exactly Like You," "For Me and My Gal," "Get Happy," "God Bless America," "Goodnight Sweetheart," "Great Day," "Happy Days Are Here Again," "Heartaches," "How Deep is the Ocean?" "How High the Moon," "I Believe," "I Can't Give You Anything But Love," "I Could Have Danced All Night," "I Get a Kick Out of You," "I Got Rhythm," "I'll Be Seeing You," "I'll See You in My Dreams," "I'm in the Mood for Love," "It Might as Well Be Spring," "I've Got the World on a String," "I've Got You Under My Skin," "I Wonder Who's Kissing Her Now," "Just One of Those Things," "Kiss Me Again," "La Vie en Rose," "Let Me Call You Sweetheart," "Love Me or Leave Me," "Lover," "Lover Come Back to Me," "Marie," "My Blue Heaven," "My Funny Valentine," "My Heart Stood Still," "My Melancholy Baby," "Night and Day," "Old Black Magic," "Ol' Man River," "On the Sunny Side of the Street," "Over the Rainbow," "Peg o' My Heart," "Pennies from Heaven," "Poor Butterfly," "Rudolph, the Rednosed Reindeer," "School Days," "September Song," "Shine on Harvest Moon," "Smoke Gets in Your Eyes," "Somebody Loves Me," "Some Enchanted Evening," "Some of These Days," "Sometimes I'm Happy," "Stardust," "St. Louis Blues," "Stormy Weather," "Summertime," "Swanee," "Sweet Sue," " 'S Wonderful," "Take Me Out to the Ball Game," "Tea for Two," "Tenderly," "The Birth of the Blues," "The Man I Love," "The Nearness of You," "These Foolish Things," "Tiger Rag," "Wait 'Til the Sun Shines Nellie," "Waiting for the Robert E. Lee," "What a Difference a Day Makes," "What Is This Thing Called Love?" "White Christmas," "Who?" "With a Song in My Heart," "Without a Song," "You Go to My Head," "You'll Never Walk Alone," "You Made Me Love You," "Zing Went the Strings of My Heart."

GLOBAL HITS

Such is the global impact of the pop music business today that, for example, a "Volare" of a few seasons back or a "Never On Sunday" (incidentally, the first time a foreign, in this case Greek, song ever copped an Academy Award as the best motion picture song), must be reckoned with. In their concentrated performances, international recording versions, global performances and sales, in multiple languages, these add up to a quick fancy score that has taken most of the list herewith many accumulative years to achieve.

It should be established here quickly that some of these are "seasonal" songs. This means "Easter Parade," "Rudolph the Rednosed Reindeer," "White Christmas" and the like.

Some 34,000,000 platters of "White Christmas," including Bing Crosby's own 20,000,000-sales mark, along with the 33,000,000 disks of "Rudolph," can't be ignored. Both, also, have enjoyed sales into the millions of pianoforte copies, multiple band and vocal arrangements, and the like.

Not "strictly popular" but seasonal or patriotic standards, such as John

Philip Sousa's "Stars and Stripes Forever," Berlin's "God Bless America,"
Reginald DeKoven's "Oh Promise Me," Carrie Jacobs Bond's "I Love
You Truly" both of which, along with Berlin's (there's that man again!)
"Always" are the staples at weddings and anniversaries.

INGREDIENTS FOR DURABILITY

The elements of what makes for "most popular" are frequently im-
measurable, such as the mass appeal to the man-in-the-street (whistle
while you work, etc.); the accumulative millions of sheet music, the different folio and orchestral, vocal, band, barbershop quartet, choral and
kindred arrangements; the countless radio performances by hinterland
radio stations (not fully logged by either ASCAP or BMI for per-plug
payoffs); and the general longevity of the copyright. Obviously, the older
the tune, if it remains fresh in memory and enjoys repetitive renditions,
the greater its values–performance income, record and music sales, synchronization and other mechanical reproduction usages, and the like.

It is generally conceded in that euphemistical orbit called Tin Pan
Alley—no longer tinpanny nor an alley, nor has it been for decades—that
"St. Louis Blues" and "Stardust" are neck-and-neck for the two most
recorded pops. Each has some 800-900 different American disk versions,
and their waxings by foreign artists, on global labels, also runs into scores
of different interpretations.

"Auld Lang Syne" gets repeated performance in niteries, dancehalls
and for everything ranging from politico to sentimental occasions. FDR
put "Home On The Range" on the musical map, and President Truman
dittoed "The Missouri Waltz." New York Mayor Wagner's theme song
is the "Carousel" excerpt by Rodgers & Hammerstein, "You'll Never
Walk Alone," which is a favorite also at graduations and similar fraternal
occasions, as is "Auld Lang Syne."

A number of songs survived flop shows and became perennials. "Begin
The Beguine" and "Just One Of Those Things" meant little in the original
"Jubilee," a moderately successful Broadway musical despite the fact
that librettist Moss Hart and songsmith Cole Porter went on a round-the-
world cruise to write it.

In the same idiom as "Jubilee," Berlin likes to point out that despite
the cast presence of such musicomedy favorites as Marilyn Miller, Helen
Broderick, Clifton Webb and Ethel Waters in "As Thousands Cheer," his
1933 Music Box Revue was chiefly panned for its score. "Heat Wave,"
"Not For All The Rice In China" and other tunes in his 14-song score
were "liked" by the critics but eventually it was "Easter Parade" which
survived as the standard.

Cole Porter's "Night and Day" dates back to the 1932 orignial stage
source, "The Gay Divorce." "When it was filmed later, Hollywood chose
to add an "e" and the title became "Divorcee," and the tune has been
an evergreen for virtually a third-of-a-century.

Hoagy Carmichael's 1929 "Star Dust," originally an instrumental, also
was a slow starter but really took off after Mitchell Parish added a lyric.

"Star Dust," "Beguine," "Tea For Two" and "St. Louis Blues" are the most prolifically recorded tunes in pop song history.

W. C. Handy's "St. Louis Blues," from its original 1914 cradling in Memphis, is of the same pure American jazz strain as "Alexander's Ragtime Band" and will remain symbolic of the wealth of American Negro music that has become part of our musical heritage.

"Tea for Two," circa 1924, by Irving Caesar (words) and Vincent Youmans (music), from a modest Broadway musical, "No No Nanette," has been the perennial boy-meets-girl "double number." Countless "bench acts" in vaudeville—the dapper juvenile, usually *avec* strawhat and cane, and the sweet ingenue, usually in flouncy lace and *avec* parasol—have glorified this dream of young love. And almost 40 years later it got a big play as a cha-cha.

"Tenderly" had an inauspicious start but snowballed with increasing impact, first as a particular favorite of the nitery chanteuses, and in recent years this Jack Lawrence-Walter Gross ballad has been reprised in countless albums and versions, instrumental and vocal.

As this Top Pops roster indicates, legit has been the springboard of some of the richer heritages of the American popular music scene and the following will achieve similar distinction. Some already have. Among them are "Some Enchanted Evening," "People Will Say We're In Love," "I Could Have Danced All Night," "June Is Busting Out All Over," "On The Street Where You Live," "Mack The Knife" ("Moritat"), "Summertime," "If I Loved You," "All The Things You Are," "There's No Business Like Show Business," "Where Or When," "Makin' Whoopee." In fact, a glance at the VARIETY MUSIC CAVALCADE will produce dozens of tunes by Porter, Romberg, Friml, Gershwin, Berlin, Rodgers and Hart, Youmans, Rodgers and Hammerstein, Lerner and Loewe, Hirsch, Stamper, Hubbell, Dietz and Schwartz, Loesser, DeSylva, Brown and Henderson, Merrill and others which would also qualify in this category.

Smash ballads that have lasted are of the calibre of "Till We Meet Again," "Memories," "Poor Butterfly," "My Buddy," "Beautiful Ohio," "Three O'Clock In The Morning," "When You and I Were Young Maggie," "Sidewalks of New York," "Down by the Old Mill Stream," "Isle of Capri," "South of the Border," "Paradise," among many more.

Periodically revived have been such perennial pops as "California Here I Come," "Avalon," "Remember?" "That Old Gang of Mine," "Laura," "Winter Wonderland" (another Christmas perennial), "Santa Claus Is Coming to Town," "Third Man Theme," and many others. This list, too, is far from complete.

The global cycle, especially post-World War II, spawned such international favorites as "La Vie en Rose," "The Seine," "Autumn Leaves," "At Last," "Lisbon Antigua," "April in Portugal," "Torero," "Cia Cia Bambino," "Under Paris Skies," "A Paris," "Poor People of Paris," "Never on Sunday," "Volare" and others. The last-named tune was so popular at one stage that the Brill Bldg. denizens dubbed it "Mussolini's revenge." (In another era, when the John Golden-Raymond Hubbell ballad was equally overly familiar, a couple of Tin Pan Alleyites whipped up an "answer" song, "I'd Like To Catch The Guy Who Wrote 'Poor Butterfly.'"

The music business is replete with cycles and frequently a social evolution, as with the Latin dance vogue, creates greater receptivity for such old and new standards as "Siboney," "Granada," "Green-Eyes," "Amapola," "Amor," "Peanut Vendor," "Rum and Coca-Cola," "You Belong To My Heart," "Brazil," "Bahia," "Frenesi," "Besame Mucho," "Malaguena" and the like.

Pop music also traditionally reflects the moods and mores of the times. It may be the religiosos, such as "I Believe" and "He's Got The Whole World In His Hands." It may be George M. Cohan's "Over There," "Yankee Doodle Dandy," "Mary's a Grand Old Name."

INSTRUMENTALS

It includes great instrumentals. Right up there with "St. Louis Blues" would be "Nola," "12th St. Rag," "Livery Stable Blues," "Memphis Blues," "Kitten On The Keys," "Canadian Capers," "Indianola," "Ragging the Scale," "In the Mood," "Mood Indigo," "Canadian Sunset," "Deep Purple," among others. And, on a grander scale, Gershwin's "Rhapsody in Blue" and Grofé's "Grand Canyon Suite."

When historians hark back to the frenetic '50s with its plethora of country music and rock 'n' roll, representative of that era will be such items as "Tennessee Waltz," "Blue Suede Shoes," "Rock Around The Clock," "Earth Angel," "Hound Dog," ("Purple People Eater," "Splish-Splash" and "Itsy Bitsy Teenie Weenie Yellow Polka Dot Bikini" for example). And then came the Twist.

STILL OTHERS

And still others come to mind as durable standards, big sellers in their heyday, and constantly being revived and reprised, for this or that interpretation, album, filmusical synchronization, video period song, etc. Among these include other titles as "Carolina Moon," "The Best Things In Life Are Free," "Charmaine," "Diane," "Jeannine (I Dream of Lilac Time)," "Ramona," "My Wonderful One," "I'm Forever Blowing Bubbles," "I'm Always Chasing Rainbows," "Paradise," "Pagan Love Song," "Singing in the Rain," "Dardanella," "And the Band Played On," "My Wild Irish Rose," "You Were Meant For Me," "Who's Afraid of the Big Bad Wolf?" "Whistle While You Work," "Brother, Can You Spare A Dime?" "I Got Plenty of Nuttin'," "It's A Good Day," "I'm Looking Over a Four-Leaf Clover," "Bye-Bye Blackbird," "Avalon," "Whispering," "Breezin' Along with the Breeze," just to name a few of the memorable perennials.

From "Ja-Da" and "Yacki-Hula, Hicky-Dula" and "Lily of the Valley" to "Who Put the Bomp in the Bomp," there have been flash-in-the-pan novelties which enjoy extraordinary concentrated vogue and some, in time, also become musical symbols of their times. So with these, as with the

6,000-odd members of ASCAP and the far-flung affiliates of BMI, who might well point to this or that of their pet bestsellers as "belonging" in this roster, it must be stressed anew that the above are samplings of standards. For reasons already detailed it is impossible to include *every* standard, else it becomes a catalog of songs. It is unrealistic also not to recognize that a cavalcade such as this is fallible, through omission, and perhaps even by commission of including certain titles and slighting some others.

In today's $33,000,000 ASCAP performance rights melon, about $28,000,000 of it comes from television and radio usages, divided as follows: $18,000,000 from TV and $10,000,000 from radio. BMI collects $12,700,000 from the broadcasters.

ASCAP income is divided equally between publishers and authors. Taking the above figure, over $16,000,000 goes into the writers' pool, and a ditto amount into the publishers'.

Each segment concerns itself with their own methods of payoff but, over-all, the value of the catalogs and the frequency of performance is the secret ingredient along with the wealth and maturity of each catalog, be it writer or publisher.

Thus, the Warner Bros.' Music Publishers Holding Corp. (Witmark, Remick, Harms and affiliated subsidiaries) realizes around $2,000,000 annually. The MGM-20th Century-Fox partnership in The Big Three (Robbins, Feist and Miller Music) collects around $1,750,000 annually; and the third biggest group, the "class" showtune pool controlled by Max and Louis Dreyfus (Chappell, et al.) collects around $1,500,000 per annum. Consdering that it can cost $1,000 a day for the average big league music publisher to operate this is no disproportionate yield.

NOSTALGIA'S BIG PAYOFF

Nostalgia is big boxoffice with the successive years. As history creates stress—martial, political or economic—Americans increasingly long to hark back. The mauve decade constituted the "good ole days" as they looked to the Prohibition era. In turn, the Volsteadian period, for all its gangsterism and bootlegging, now looks better than today's nervousness over the world's future in the face of the Communistic threat.

The songs of the days of our years tend to punctuate history in the making. "Bicycle Built for Two" gives way to "In My Merry Oldsmobile" and "Come Josephine in My Flying Machine." "Hello Central Give Me Heaven" (when Alexander Graham Bell's invention was still a novelty) has given way to radio and TV and Outer Space Songs. The change is only a variation of the theme to fit the modern pattern.

In the tradition that a good song will never down, Kurt Weill and Maxwell Anderson's "September Song" survived "Knickerbocker Holiday" from whence it stemmed with result that Walter Huston's identification with the ballad, especially after his appealing cracked-voice interpretation on a Decca platter caught on, found it to be as big boxoffice as the legit shows in which he toured. Huston had to come out between acts of whatever vehicle he played to sing "September Song" so that it became as much a b.o. lure as the play.

Television, radio, film and other producers who initially urged this VARIETY MUSIC CAVALCADE be published in book form stress that the old "solid" songs are the real nuggets of the music business. Thus, a strain of "By the Sea" sets an Atlantic City or bathing beauty scene much as Irving Berlin's "A Pretty Girl Is Like A Melody" is the thematic for a fashion or beauty parade, Gus Edwards' "School Days," Jack Norworth and Albert Von Tilzer's "Take Me Out To the Ballgame" or Berlin's "Alexander's Ragtime Band" or any of the old faves become automatic audience identifications of the place or the time.

Durable in memory are such linkings as Al Jolson's "Mammy," Eddie Cantor's "Making Whoopee," Maurice Chevalier's "Valentina," Sir Harry Lauder's "Roamin' In The Gloamin'," Sophie Tucker's "Some of These Days," Paul Whiteman's "Rhapsody in Blue," Ted Lewis' "Me and My Shadow," Vincent Lopez's "Nola," Eva Tanguay's "I Don't Care." Ruth Etting's "Shine on Harvest Moon," Judy Garland's "Over the Rainbow," Bert Williams' "You Cannot Make Your Shimmy Shake on Tea," Harry Richman's "Puttin' On The Ritz," Bing Crosby's "When the Blue of the Night Meets the Gold of the Day," Rudy Vallee's "Vagabond Lover," Kate Smith's "When the Moon Comes Over the Mountain," Russ Columbo's "I'm a Prisoner of Love," Morton Downey's "Carolina Moon," or Joe Frisco's "Darktown Strutters' Ball."

In the midst of the 1930s depression when the late Jack Kapp and Milton Rackmil founded Decca Records (with the sales appeal of a 35¢ pricetag) it was Kapp's counsel to Bing Crosby that he would produce an all-inclusive catalog of recordings that "will make yours (Crosby's) the most listened to voice around the world for all time."

It was a realistic vision as Crosby not only "cut" pops and musical comedy excerpts but he ranged the musical scene from hillbilly (now called country and western) to "race" (now called rhythm and blues), from Stephen Foster ballads to gospel paeans.

There were times when independent radio stations devoted hours on end to nothing but Crosby, as many now do to Sinatra, and there were instances also where Crosby-on-wax would oppose himself when he was on a prime radio show, and ditto later when on TV. Kapp insisted this would tend to enhance the Groaner and not pall. He was correct.

"TOP 40" EVIL

The "top 40" evil, if evil it was, created a payola scramble and race to "get on the sheet," as the tradepaper charts were called. Payola to five or six deejays in strategic spots, plus other subsidies and under-the-counter deals, including record distributors and dealers to "push" this or that song title, effected a spurious "getting on the sheet." The local distributors would spread false "information" to the local radio stations and deejays, and even to the tradepapers, that there were "calls'" for this or that title. Actually, because the distributor had been given a "box of free records" (100 to 250), which cost him nothing, and which he sold to his local retailers at a 100 percent profit, some were willing to become part of such conspiracy. Such are the intratrade machinations of some segments of the music biz, yet this all conspired to possibly help create a "call" for this or that disk.

It is no secret that in the more sacrosanct precincts of TV and radio programming, the insecure "program directors" with agencies in sleekly polished, chromium-and-mahogany Madison Avenue offices, leaned on these "top 40" charts for *their* song components, when in doubt. By nature of the breed they're in doubt more often than not.

To the credit of certain enterprising disk jockeys—and not all were "on the take"—it was their adventure in projecting new artists and unknown songs that contributed to bringing certain songs and singers to the fore. It is said that Bill Randle thus was instrumental, for example, in helping showcase Presley who was then with an obscure Memphis-based label, Sun Records.

This dates back to many intra-music biz stunts, such as the North Carolina deejay who liked an oldie, "Heartaches," so much that he played it nightly on his clear channel station and made the nation take notice. From time to time other exhibitionistic platter-chatterers repeated the same stunt with disks of their own choice, whether because of genuine affection for the performer or mercenary "inspiration," yclept payola. In reverse, a stunt by Ted Steel, an ex-disk jockey who became general manager of WINS, New York, edicted a "good music" marathon of Frank Sinatra recordings, playing them from Saturday midnight until Tuesday morning. It got national attention. He finally ran out of Sinatras but not only his own switchboard lit up into the early Sunday A.M. but the metropolitan newspapers' information bureaus received calls from those who "couldn't get through to WINS" to relay their endorsement of this "good music" policy. Two weeks later, KRAK, in Sacramento, repeated the same stunt with similar favorable results.

Paradoxically, despite rebellion against "the top 40" and "the charts," other music biz proponents decry the FCC bogey that seems to have cast a shadow over the independent radio stations which, heretofore, daringly exposed new songs and singers, groups and instrumentalists, but which now were being hidebound by "station management committee" programming methods, so that they, in turn, were falling into a trite, stylized record routining.

The pyramiding values of a "standard" may be gathered from the nearly 1,000 different photograph platters of such perennials as "St. Louis Blues" and "Stardust," and it is nothing for a good evergreen to attain 300-400 different domestic recordings. As each new dance vogue, for example, comes into being, W. C. Handy or the Hoagy Carmichael durables have been given polka, march, cha-cha, mambo, conga, "twist," progressive, Dixieland and any other jazz treatment imaginable. Not to mention the individual vocal and/or dance styles of the sundry veteran headliners and the upstart newcomers who invariably add this or that tune to their repertoires for their penchant for the "beat" treatment. It was Bobby Darin's driving "beat" that finally made "Moritat" ("Mack the Knife" from Bertolt Brecht-Kurt Weill's "Threepenny Opera") a mass disclick.

Thus it is a royalty windfall to author and publisher alike when a "Tea for Two Cha-Cha" catches on or some vocal group revives "Smoke Gets in Your Eyes." The average songsmith and publisher takes the common-sense viewpoint that individual artistic interpretations are permissible. Of late, however, there has been marked objection by all concerned to the manner in which certain "party" disk artists have parodied some of the top favorites. This is valid cause for complaint in that the commercial value of a wholesome ballad can be perverted into a double-entendre meaning as some of the free-wheeling nitery and "party" disk "artists" have para-phrased or parodied the original lyrics into distorted ribaldry.

One reason for this revised edition of VARIETY MUSIC CAVALCADE has been the constant search by newcomer artists for a catalog of prime yester-year favorites which they can give modern treatment.

The VARIETY MUSIC CAVALCADE, since selling out its initial edition, has been photostated page-by-page by many a Hollywood film studio and a radio-and-TV programming department all over the land, because it has been so painstakingly compiled by Julius Mattfeld.

The proponents of the "solid" songs—the roster of which is highlighted particularly in the twentieth century copyrights in this VARIETY MUSIC CAVALCADE—are concerned about where the standards of tomorrow will come from. They scoff at the current crop of pops. Irving Berlin, who should know about those things, doesn't agree. "If the public buys 'em that makes it a 'good' song. Instead of griping, maybe we should eat away from the Lindy's and Brown Derby sphere of influence and explore folk music in the making and we Broadway and Hollywood weisenheimers don't know it—yet!"

                                                                    A.G.

CONTENTS

ABBREVIATIONS

The following are symbols employed in the musical listings:

arr.	*arranged*
ATTB	*alto, two tenors and bass*
ca.	*circa (about)*
cop.	*copyright*
l.	*unnumbered leaves*
m.	*music*
n.d.	*no date*
op.	*opus*
orch.	*orchestral*
pseud.	*pseudonym*
SATB	*sop., alto, tenor and bass*
w.	*words*
f°	*folio*
4°	*quarto*
8°	*octavo*
12°	*duodecimo*

Square-brackets [ ] indicate supplied information from other sources
than the sheet music.
Titles in parentheses ( ) denote the name of stage productions.
The dash — in titles indicates parenthetical sub-titles.
Unless otherwise specified, the place of publication is New York.

MUSIC OF THE PILGRIMS

Fisher, William Arms

Ye Olde New England Psalm-Tunes, 1620-1820. With historical sketch, biographical notes, and hints on performance. Boston: Oliver Ditson Co. [cop. 1930.] xvi, 56 p. 4°.

Pratt, Waldo Seldon

The Music of the Pilgrims; a description of the psalm-book brought to Plymouth in 1620. Boston: Oliver Ditson Co. [1921.] 80 p. incl. facsims. 8°. (Contains tunes.)

AMERICAN COLONIAL PERIOD
(See also under caption: Before 1800.)

a) COLLECTIONS

Belcher, Supply

Choruses from The Harmony of Maine, 1794, for mixed or male voices in three and four parts. Edited by Oliver Daniel. New York: Music Press, Inc. [cop. 1948.] 23 p. 4°. (Contains nine choruses.)

Buchman, Carl

Seven Songs of the Early Republic.   Edited by Richard Franko Goldman. New settings by Carl Buchman. New York: Mercury Music Corp. [cop. 1942.] (Contents: 1. Brother Soldiers, All Hail! 2. Jefferson and Liberty. 3. The Green Mountain Farmer. 4. America, Commerce and Freedom. 5-7, unpublished.)

Endicott, Samuel

Melodies of Revolutionary Times. Harmonized by Samuel Endicott. Boston: Charles W. Homeyer & Co., cop. 1918. 4 nos. 4°. (Contents: 1. He Stole My Tender Heart Away. 2. The Charms of Floremel. 3. Sheep in Clusters. 4. The Heavy Hours.)

1

Endicott, Samuel

Three Melodies of Revolutionary Times. Harmonized by Samuel Endicott. Boston: Charles W. Homeyer & Co., cop. 1918. 7 p. 4°. (Contents: 1. Queen Mary's Farewell to France. 2. He Stole My Tender Heart. 3. The Bee.)

Engel, Carl

Music from the Days of George Washington. Collected and provided with an introduction by Carl Engel. The music edited by W. Oliver Strunck. With a preface by Hon. Sol Bloom. Washington, D. C.; George Washington Bicentennial Commission [cop. 1931 by Sol Bloom]. ix, 61 (1) p. 4°.

Fisher, William Arms

The Music That Washington Knew. With an historical sketch. A program of authentic music, vocal and instrumental, with historical and biographical data. Boston: Oliver Ditson Co., Inc. [cop. 1931.] xxiv, 44 p. 4°. (The music is arranged mostly for chorus and piano—for an orchestral arrangement, see below. "Fifteen old-time dances," arr. by N. Clifford Page, are appended, p. 33-40.)

The Music That Washington Knew. Edited by William Arms Fisher. [For orchestra.] Orchestrated by August Damm. Boston: Oliver Ditson Co., Inc., cop. 1931. f°.

Goldman, Richard Franko, and Roger Smith

Landmarks of Early American Music, 1760-1800. A collection of thirty-two compositions compiled, arranged, and edited by Richard Franko Goldman and Roger Smith for orchestra or band or smaller instrumental groups or mixed chorus (SATB) with or without accompaniment. New York: G. Schirmer, Inc. [cop. 1943.] 101 p. 4°. (Contents: Part 1. Psalm-tunes, hymns, and chorales. Part 2. Patriotic and historical music.)

Hopkinson, Francis

Colonial Love Lyrics. Six songs by Francis Hopkinson (1737-1791). Edited and augmented by Harold V. Milligan. Boston: The Arthur P. Schmidt Co. [cop. 1919.] 29 p. f°.

The First American Composer. Six songs by Francis Hopkinson (1737-1791). Edited and augmented by Harold V. Milligan. Boston: The Arthur P. Schmidt Co., cop. 1918. 33 p. f°.

Howard, John Tasker

A Program of Early American Piano Music. Collected, edited, and arranged by John Tasker Howard. New York: J. Fischer & Bro. [cop. 1931.] 2 l., 36 p. f°.

Howard, John Tasker, and Eleanor S. Bowen

Music Associated with the Period of the Formation of the Constitution and Inauguration of George Washington. Edited and compiled by John Tasker Howard and Eleanor S. Bowen. With a preface by Hon. Sol Bloom. Washington, D. C.: United States Sesquicentennial Commission [1937]. 35 p. 4°.

Kimball, Jacob

Jacob Kimball's Down East Spirituals. Editor, Oliver Daniel. New York: Music Press, Inc. [cop. 1949.] 23 p. 4°. (Contains ten choruses for SATB.)

Milligan, Harold Vincent

Pioneer American Composers. A collection of early American songs. Edited and augmented by Harold Vincent Milligan. Boston: The Arthur P. Schmidt Co., cop. 1931. 35 p. f°.

Schmid, Adolf

From the Days of George Washington. Suite of marches. Arranged [for orchestra] by Adolf Schmid. New York: G. Schirmer, Inc., cop. 1931. 4°.

Siegmeister, Elie

Songs of Early America, 1620-1830. Compiled and arranged by Elie Siegmeister. New York: Edward B. Marks Music Corp., cop. 1944. 56 p. 4°. (Contains sixteen hymns, ballads, and songs, arr. for SATB.)

b) INDIVIDUAL

Adams and Liberty, or, The Boston Patriotic Song. w., Robert Treat Paine. m., tune: "To Anacreon in Heaven" [subsequently the air of "The Star-Spangled Banner"]. Boston: Thomas & Andrews [1798].

Alknomook. The Death Song of the Cherokee Indian. w., m., anon. G. Gilfert [1799-1801]. (The title is also spelled Alkmoonok. The words were used by Royall Tyler, to whom they have been ascribed, in his comedy "The Contrast," 1790, and, "as altered from the old Indian song," by Mrs. Ann Julia Hatton in her libretto to James Hewitt's ballad opera "Tammany," 1794.)

The Battle of the Kegs. w., Francis Hopkinson. m., a variant of the tune: "Yankee Doodle." (The words were published in 1778, during the American Revolution, and satirized the British who, on learning of certain "infernal machines" devised by David Bushnell to destroy enemy shipping at Philadelphia, fired on all floating objects on the Delaware River in the belief that armed rebels were hidden therein.)

The Battle of Trenton. A sonata for piano. m., James Hewitt. New York: James Hewitt [1797]. (An American counterpart to Kotzwara's piece "The Battle of Prague"—see under the caption: Before 1800.)

Chester. ["Let Tyrants Shake Their Iron Rod."] Hymn. w., m., William Billings. Boston: Draper and Folsom, 1778 (in: William Billings, "The Singing Master's Assistant," p. 12).

Coronation. Hymn tune. m., Oliver Holden. Boston: Isaiah Thomas and Ebenezer T. Andrews, 1793 (in: Oliver Holden, "Union Harmony, or, Universal Collection of Sacred Music," vol. 1). (To this tune are now sung the words of Edward Perronet, "All Hail the Power of Jesus' Name!" written in 1780.)

Hail, Columbia. w., Joseph Hopkinson. m., tune: "The President's March" (see below), ascribed to Philip Phile. Philadelphia: B. Carr [1798]. (The words were written for the poet's friend, actor Gilbert Fox, and were sung by him as the finale to Boaden's comedy "The Italian Monk," given for the actor's benefit at the New Theatre, Philadelphia, April 25, 1798. The song was an instantaneous success and widely reprinted under the title "New Federal Song," as it was first called. The writer of the verses should not be confused with Francis Hopkinson.)

Liberty Song; or, Come, Join Hand in Hand. w., Mrs. Mercy Warren (wife of Col. James Warren of Plymouth, Mass.). m., tune: "Heart of Oak," by William Boyce.

The Liberty Song—"In Freedom We're Born." w., John Dickinson. m., tune: "Heart of Oak," by William Boyce. (Published by Mein and Fleming, Boston, 1768; Hall and Sellars, Philadelphia, 1768, without music; and again by Mein and Fleming, Boston, 1769, in "Bickerstaff's Boston Almanac.")

The President's March. m., ascribed to Philip Phile. (Composed in 1789—see above: "Hail, Columbia," 1798.)

Yankee Doodle. w., anonymous—of American origin. m., traditional —of English origin: sufficiently popular to have been published, in an early version, in Glasgow, 1782. (The tune was already familiar in America as early as 1790; was used by Benjamin Carr in his frequently played orchestral medley, "Federal Overture," composed in 1794; and was published as a song by G. Willig, Philadelphia, 1798.)

BEFORE 1800

Artaxerxes. English ballad opera; libretto and music, Thomas Augustine Arne. (Produced at Covent Garden Theatre, London, 1762, and popular in England. The overture and various vocal solos, particularly "Water Parted from the Sea," were frequently performed in concerts in America from 1765 onward.)

Auld Lang Syne. w., Robert Burns (adapted). m., traditional Scottish tune. London: Preston & Son [1799] (in: George Thomson, "A Select Collection of Original Scotish [sic] Airs for the Voice," no. 68). (The song and its title were already popular in Burns's day, being then sung to another tune—"a mediocre air," Burns called it. The poet re-cast the original words, adding the second and third stanzas. The present, and familiar, melody appears to be a synthesis of several Scottish tunes.)

[Auld Robin Gray.] When the Sheep Are in the Fauld. w., anon. m., "original favourite air." [London, 1780?] (Copy in British Museum. The song became popular and was soon reprinted by other London publishers and in the American colonies. The words were written in 1772 by Lady Anne Barnard, née Lindsay; the autograph also is in British Museum. The music of the above "original favourite air" was composed by a clergyman, the Rev. William Leeves, and first publicly acknowledged by him in 1812.)

Away with Melancholy. Duet. w., anon. m., Wolfgang Amadeus Mozart. (The music is adapted from the finale of Act I of Mozart's opera "Die Zauberflöte." The piece in this form was first published in London during the early 1790s, and was widely reprinted in America from 1797 onward. It was found until recently in the older type of school songbooks.)

The Battle of Prague. Piano solo (usually with additional instruments). m., Franz Kotzwara. London: Longman and Broderip [1793?]; and others with later imprints. (George Schetky, a Philadelphia singer, violoncellist, and composer, arranged the piece for "full band," i.e., for full orchestra. In its original form it was long a parlor favorite in America.)

Drink to Me Only with Thine Eyes. w., Ben Jonson. m., traditional (sometimes attributed to Colonel R. Mellish and erroneously to others). London: J. Oswald [1762?] (copy in British Museum).

Heart of Oak (Harlequin's Invasion). w., David Garrick. m., William Boyce. ("Harlequin's Invasion" was a pantomime, produced in London, 1759.)

Hope Told a Flattering Tale. w., Peter Pindar [pseud. of John Wolcott]. m., Giovanni Paisiello. London: T. Skillern [1793]. (The words were adapted to a popular Italian duet, "Nel Cor Più Non Mi Sento," in Paisiello's opera "La Molinara," produced in Naples, 1788. The song was popularized in England by the famous Mme. Mara, who sang it to a harp accompaniment composed by Joseph Mazzinghi, in a revival of Arne's "Artaxerxes," listed above. In 1795 the young Beethoven composed variations on the melody as did other composers of the period. The song is found as a solo in nearly all operatic and song collections today.)

Iphigénie en Aulide. French opera; m., Christoph Willibald von Gluck. (Produced in Paris, 1774. The overture to this opera was frequently played in orchestral concerts in America from 1793 onward.)

La Marseillaise. w., m., Claude Joseph Rouget de l'Isle (1760-1836). (The song, now the French national anthem, was composed by a young French military engineer at Strassburg in 1792, on the French declaration of war against Austria. An American edition of the song, with French and English words, was published in 1793, by Carr & Co., Philadelphia; subsequent reprints appeared in New York and Boston.)

The Lass of Richmond Hill. w., Leonard McNally. m., James Hook. London: Preston & Son [1790?]. (The words were first published in the "Morning Herald," London, Aug. 1, 1789.)

The Lass with the Delicate Air. See below: **Young Molly Who Lives at the Foot of the Hill.**

Life Let Us Cherish. w., anon. m., Hans Georg Naegeli (1773-1836). Baltimore: J. Carr, 1796. (The song is an adaptation of the German "Freut euch des Lebens," first published in Germany about 1794. It became a favorite in America and was published also under the title "Snatch Fleeting Pleasures.")

Mary's Dream; or, Sandy's Ghost. w., anon. m., John Relfe. (The song was published anonymously in London during the early 1790s and was reprinted in America from 1793 onward in Philadelphia, Boston, and Northampton, Mass.)

My Lodging It Is on the Cold Ground. w., m., traditional. London: Baker and Galabin, 1775 (in: "Vocal Music, or The Songster's Companion").

My Mother Bids Me Bind My Hair. w., Mrs. Anne Hunter, née Home. m., Joseph Haydn. (This one of the six "Original Canzonettas," published in 1794 during the first of Haydn's two visits to London. Reprinted by B. Carr's Musical Repository, Philadelphia, 1799.)

O! Dear! What Can the Matter Be? w., m., anon [London] R. Birchall [1792?] (copy in British Museum.)

The Request—*better known as:* Tell Me, Babbling Echo. w., —(?) Clarke. m., Gerard Vogler. London: J. and G. Vogler [1775?].

Robin Adair. w., Lady Caroline Keppel. m., Irish tune: "Eileen Aroon." (The words were written about 1750 and addressed to a young Irish surgeon whom the poetess married in 1758 and who later became Surgeon-General to George III of England.)

Rule, Britannia! (Alfred). w., James Thomson; sometimes attributed to David Mallet. m., Thomas Augustine Arne. ("Alfred" was a masque, performed at the Prince of Wales' residence, Cliefden House, at Maidenhead, England, Aug. 1, 1740.)

Sally in Our Alley. w., m., Henry Carey. [London, 1715?] (copy in British Museum).

Sigh No More, Ladies. Glee for three voices. w., William Shakespeare (in: "Much Ado About Nothing"). m., Richard John Samuel Stevens. (Frequently sung in concerts in America during the 1790s.)

Softly Rise, O Southern Breeze (Solomon). w., Edward Moore. m., William Boyce. ("Solomon" was a serenata, produced at London, 1743.)

Tell Me, Babbling Brook. See above: The Request.

To Anacreon in Heaven. w., Ralph Tomlinson. m., attributed to (1) John Stafford Smith; (2) Samuel Arnold. (Written and composed in London between 1770 and 1776; published between 1780 and 1783. Subsequently the tune of "The Star-Spangled Banner"—see 1814.)

Tobacco's but an Indian Weed. w., m., anon. London: William Pearson, 1699 (1700) (in: "Wit and Mirth; or, Pills to Purge Melancholy").

[Tom Bowling.] **Poor Tom; or, The Sailor's Epitaph.** w., m., Charles Dibdin. London: The author, 1790.

The Wayworn Traveller (The Mountaineers). w., G. Colman. m., Samuel Arnold. Philadelphia: B. Carr & Co. Musical Repository [1794]. (The song comes from a ballad opera, produced in London, 1793, and was published in America in February, 1794. The opera was performed at Hartford, Conn., 1795, and long remained in the repertory of early American theatrical companies.)

The Wearing of the Green. w., m., anon., of Irish origin. (The words, aaapted to a traditional tune, date from 1797.)

Within a Mile of Edinburgh (Harlequin and Faustus). w., adapted from Thomas D'Urfey. m., James Hook [London, 1794]. (Copy in British Museum. The words were derived from D'Urfey's "Within a Furlong of Edinburgh Town." The song was introduced in William Shield's stage piece "Harlequin and Faustus," produced at Covent Garden Theatre, London, 1793, and reprinted in America from 1795 onward.)

Ye Banks and Braes o' Bonnie Doon. w., Robert Burns. m., tune: "The Caledonian Hunt's Delight." Edinburgh: J. Johnson, 1792 (in his: "The Scots Musical Museum," No. 374). (This version is Burns's third revision of the song.)

Young Molly Who Lives at the Foot of the Hill—*better known as:* **The Lass with the Delicate Air.** w., anon. m., Michael Arne [not Thomas Augustine Arne]. [London, 1760?; London, 1762] (in: "Universal Magazine," vol. 31, p. 95).

*   *   *   *   *

For a detailed record of the printed and manuscript music of this period, consult—

Sonneck, Oscar George Theodore

A Bibliography of Early Secular American Music (18th century). Revised and enlarged by William Treat Upton. [Washington, D. C.:] The Library of Congress, 1945. xvi, 616 p. 8°.

First blood of the American War of Independence shed—Westminster (Vt.) Massacre (1775).

Tom Paine published "Common Sense" in Philadelphia, in behalf of the American cause. Declaration of Independence signed. "By order and in behalf of the Congress, John Hancock, President, Attest, Charles Thompson, Secretary" (1776).

Stars and Stripes flag adopted. Articles of Confederation and Perpetual Union adopted by Continental Congress, ratified by the 13 states, and announced by the Congress as formally ratified (1777).

Bank of Philadelphia chartered (first in United States) (1780).

First successful daily paper in the United States, the "Pennsylvania Packet and Daily Advertiser," appeared in Philadelphia (1784).

First United States Congress met, New York City (1789).

Washington inaugurated 1st President in Federal Hall, New York City (1789).

United States Congress established the mint, in Philadelphia (1792).

First balloon ascent made in America (1793).

AROUND 1800

De Filippi, Amedeo

Our Earliest American Songs. Edited and arranged by Philip Weston [pseud. of Amedeo De Filippi]. New York: Concord Music Pub. Co., Inc. [cop. 1941.] 6 nos. f° (The composers represented are B. Carr, J. Hewitt, F. Hopkinson, A. Reinagle, W. Selby.)

Dolph, Edward Arthur

"Sound Off!" Soldier Songs from the Revolution to World War II [edited by] Edward Arthur Dolph; music arranged by Philip Egner; illustrated by Lawrence Schick. New York: Farrar & Rinehart, Inc. [cop. 1942.] xxvii, 3-621 p. illus. 4°.

Downes, Olin, and Elie Siegmeister

A Treasury of American Song. New York: Howell, Soskin & Co. [cop. 1940 by Elie Siegmeister and Olin Downes.] 351 p. f°.

Howard, John Tasker

A Program of Early and Mid-nineteenth Century American Songs. Collected, edited, and arranged by John Tasker Howard. New York: J. Fischer & Bro. [cop. 1931.] 3 l., 51 p. f°.

Johnson, Margaret, and Travis Johnson

Early American Songs from the Repertoire of the "Song-Spinners," arranged and edited with piano accompaniments and historical notes by Margaret and Travis Johnson. New York: Associated Music Publishers, Inc. [cop. 1943.] v, 271 p. 8°. (Contains 64 songs.)

Luther, Frank

Americans and Their Songs. New York: Harper & Bros. [cop. 1942 by Frank Luther.] xiv, 323 p. 8°. (Contains words and music.)

Sandburg, Carl

The American Songbag. New York: Harcourt, Brace & Co. [cop. 1927.] xxiii, 495 p. 4°. (Contains words and music with piano accompaniment.)

Vernon, Grenville

Yankee Doodle-Doo. A collection of songs of the early American stage. Compiled with an introduction and notes by Grenville Vernon. New York: Payson & Clarke Ltd. [cop. 1927.] 165 p. illus. 4°. (Contains 36 tunes.)

ࢡ 1 8 0 0

The American Star. w., John McCreery. m., tune: "The Wounded Hussar," by D. C. Hewitt. J. Hewitt's "Musical Repository" [1799-1800]. (The song became widely popular during the War of 1812, and is found, from 1810 onward, in many songsters of the period.)

The Blue Bell of Scotland. w., m., anon. (This song of the late eighteenth century became equally popular in America. It was published here by B. Carr, Baltimore, 1800, "as lately revived in England by Mrs. Jordan," in "The Musical Journal for the Piano Forte," vol. 2, no. 25; and was subsequently reprinted in Philadelphia, New York, and Boston. The song is usually called incorrectly "The Blue Bells of Scotland." Mrs. Dorothea, or Dorothy, Jordan, née Bland, 1762-1816, was a noted Irish actress who appeared at Drury Lane Theatre, London.)

Crazy Jane. w., Matthew Gregory Lewis. m., John Davy, G. Gilfert [1800]. (The song was published a year or two earlier by Clementi & Co., London. It became a great favorite in America, was immediately reprinted in Boston and Philadelphia, and at once provoked a flood of imitations.)

The United States comprised 16 States. The census showed a population of 5,308,483 (as against 3,929,214 in 1790). John Adams, Federalist, of Massachusetts, was second President (inaugurated 1797); his opponent, Thomas Jefferson, was Vice-President. A state of war existed between the United States and France, created by mutual distrust abroad and partisan interests at home. Although war was undeclared, the United States Navy captured or destroyed 84 French vessels. In Europe, Napoleon was rising to power. Now follow some events of 1800.

The seat of the national government was transferred from Philadelphia to Washington, D. C., when the north wing of the Capitol was finished.

President Adams and his wife, Abigail, were the first occupants of the uncompleted President's Palace (now the White House).

Congress appropriated $5,000 "for the purchase of such books as may be necessary for the use of Congress at the said City of Washington," thus establishing (April 24) the Library of Congress.

The Sixth Congress (2nd Session) was the first to convene (Nov. 17) in Washington.

In the national election, Thomas Jefferson and Aaron Burr, who had jockeyed the hitherto unpolitical Tammany Society of New York into a political machine, received equal electoral votes. The House of Representatives, influenced strongly by Alexander Hamilton, the former Secretary of the Treasury who hated Burr, chose after many ballots Jefferson as President and Burr as Vice-President.

Mason Locke Weems, Episcopal clergyman of Mt. Vernon, Va., published about this time his "Life and Memorable Actions of George Washington." The subject of this idealized account died the previous year. The celebrated but fictitious cherry-tree episode first appeared in the so-called Fifth Edition of the book (1806).

William Dunlap was the country's leading playwright.

American women novelists published a host of romantic best-sellers. (Among these authors were Sarah Wentworth Morton, Sarah Sayward, Barrell Keating Wood, Susannah Haswell Rowson, and Hannah Webster Foster, whose novel "The Coquette" went through 13 editions.)

The Mount Vernon Gardens in New York on Broadway and Leonard Street opened (July 9) as a regularly organized summer theatre, perhaps the first in the United States.

₿≈ 1801

The United States rounded out its first twenty-five years.

Thomas Jefferson, Republican, of Virginia, was inaugurated 3rd President—the first to be inaugurated in Washington.

Dolly Payne Madison, wife of the newly appointed Secretary of State, James Madison, became the first social leader in the White House as hostess for President Jefferson, a widower since 1782.

To curb piracy and stop the paying of tribute money by American shippers to the Barbary pirates, President Jefferson instituted naval action against their States (Morocco, Algiers, Tripoli, and Tunis). (The operations were carried on intermittently until 1815.)

Governor James Monroe, of Virginia, later 5th President, proposed the founding of a Negro colony in Africa for American slaves. (Monrovia, capital of Liberia, established in 1847, was named after him.)

In Massachusetts woollen-milling was begun, with Arthur Schofield's mill a leading exponent of the industry. Meantime the Berkshire Hills region became a noted sheep country.

The first United States pleasure yacht, a 22-ton sloop called "Jefferson," was built for Captain George Crowninshield, Jr.,

The New York "Evening Post" was founded by Alexander Hamilton. (Published today as "The New York Post.")

The completion of the Bank of Pennsylvania (1799-1801), designed by the English-born architect Benjamin Henry Latrobe, set the fashion of Greek temples for bank buildings.

Benedict Arnold, aged 60, died (June 14) in exile in London.

੩੶ 1802

The U. S. Military Academy opened (July 4) at West Point, N. Y., with 10 cadets.

Frederick Graff of Philadelphia burned anthracite (hard coal) in a large stove—a startling novelty, inasmuch as anthracite was considered fit for use only by blacksmiths.

In Saratoga, N. Y., a hotel was built, and the spa was started on its career as a society resort.

Nathaniel Bowditch published "The New American Practical Navigator," commonly called "Bowditch's Navigator," of which more than 60 editions have since been printed.

Self-styled "Lord" Timothy Dexter, eccentric wealthy landowner of Newburyport, Mass., brought out a volume, "A Pickle for the Knowing Ones," remarkable for its absence of punctuation and for its queer, phonetic spelling.

A public demonstration of an early type of upright piano, called the "cottage piano," was held in Philadelphia at the Franklin Institute. The instrument was patented by John Isaac Hawkins. It is said that President Jefferson was interested in obtaining one for his home in Monticello, Va.

The United States entered its fourth depression since 1790; it lasted three years.

੩੶ 1803

He Who His Country's Liv'ry Wears (The Glory of Columbia, Her Yeomanry). w., William Dunlap. m., Victor Pellesier. ("The Glory of Columbia" was a patriotic play with music, produced at the Park Theatre,

New York, July 4, 1803. The words and the tune are reproduced in Grenville Vernon, "Yankee Doodle-Doo," Payson & Clarke Ltd., New York, cop. 1927, p. 73-76; the following entry, p. 71-73.)

When a Woman Hears the Sound of the Drum and Fife (The Glory of Columbia, Her Yeomanry). See preceding entry.

Ohio was admitted (Mar. 1) as the 17th State.

Former U. S. Minister to France, James Monroe, and present minister, Robert R. Livingston, exceeded their instructions and purchased (Apr. 31) from Napoleon for the sum of $15,000,000, or about four cents per acre, the entire Louisiana area in North America. This comprised all the French possessions west of the Mississippi. The purchase, ratified (Oct. 31) by Congress, added territory to the United States for 13 subsequent states. The United States took possession (Dec. 30) at New Orleans with a simple ceremony, the simultaneous lowering and raising of the national flags.

John Marshall, Chief Justice of the Supreme Court, in the case of Marbury vs. Madison laid down the principle that the Supreme Court can render an act of Congress void when, in the Court's opinion, it violates the Constitution.

Congress voted $2,500 to Captains Meriwether Lewis, private secretary to President Jefferson, and William Clark to explore a land route to the Pacific. (They set out from St. Louis with 32 men in May, 1804, and returned in Sept., 1806. The journey covered 8,500 miles.)

Robert Fulton, American inventor, launched a primitive steamboat in France on the Seine.

William Wirt, Virginia lawyer, published "Letters of the British Spy," ten essays on contemporary Southern life that gained a wide reading public.

Benjamin Crehore of Milton, Mass., is said to have made the first pianoforte in the U. S.

The Charleston, S. C., "News and Courier" was founded as a daily newspaper. (Still published.)

ৼ 1804

Canadian Boat Song. Glee for three voices. w., Thomas Moore. [m., French-Canadian tune: "Dans Mon Chemin."] [London: J. Carpenter, 1804.) (The words were written during Moore's visit to Canada in 1803 to a tune that was sung by the boatman who rowed the poet down the St. Lawrence.)

Stephen Decatur became a national hero when he recaptured and destroyed the grounded United States frigate "Philadelphia." It had been seized by Barbary pirates in the harbor of Tripoli.

The 12th Amendment (procedure of choosing the President and Vice-President) was ratified (Sept. 25).

Alexander Hamilton was killed (July 12) in a duel with Aaron Burr on the Palisades above Weehawken, N. J. Hamilton fired into the air. The duel resulted from Hamilton's bitter criticism of Burr during the latter's unsuccessful candidacy for the governorship of New York. With this event duels went into disfavor in this country.

John Stevens, of Hoboken, N. J., experimented with a steamboat equipped with twin-screw propellers.

John James Audubon began drawing and classifying the birds and flowers in Kentucky.

Georg Rapp and 600 co-religionists of a pietist sect from Württemberg, Germany, established in Pennsylvania a communal town called Harmony —the forerunner of numerous socialized communities in the United States. (The Rappists also founded settlements at New Harmony on the Wabash, Ind., 1814, and at Economy, Pa., 1825.)

Rhode Island College, founded at Providence in 1764, was renamed Brown University in honor of its benefactor Nicholas Brown.

John Pickering, Judge of the District Court of New Hampshire, became the first man to be removed from office by impeachment when he was found guilty of drunkenness and other charges. (It was the second impeachment in American history; the first occurred in 1797.)

Modern printer's ink was brought into use at Philadelphia by Jacob Johnston.

In the same city, Oliver Evans appeared on Market Street in a scow mounted on wheels and powered by a steam engine.

᚛ 1805

All's Well (The English Fleet in 1342). Duet. w., Thomas John Dibdin. m., John Braham. ("The English Fleet in 1342" was "an historical comic opera," produced at the Theatre-Royal, Covent Garden, London, 1805; the libretto was published in the same year. The duet "All's Well" became a popular vocal piece, and was reprinted during the first quarter of the century in America by Firth & Hall, New York, and by G. E. Blake and J. G. Klemm, both of Philadelphia. Another popular song from the same work was "The Origin of Gunpowder," beginning "When Vulcan forg'd the bolts of Jove," which was reprinted by W. Dubois, New York, around 1820.)

The Bay of Biscay O! (Spanish Dollars). w., Andrew Cherry. m., John Davy. ("Spanish Dollars" was an English ballad opera, produced at Covent Garden Theatre, London, 1805.)

The Origin of Gunpowder. See above: "All's Well."

President Thomas Jefferson began his second term.

Robert Fulton experimented unsuccessfully with torpedoes.

A precocious 14-year-old lad attracted the attention of New York literati with a theatrical journal, "The Thespian Mirror." He was John Howard Payne, the future poet of "Home, Sweet Home" (1823).

The Pennsylvania Art Academy was founded, but the replica of Venus de Medici was such a shock that it had to be shown discreetly.

At Yale University courses in chemistry were started under Benjamin Silliman.

New England men of letters formed the "Boston Athenaeum" as a literary club. (It is the scene of Hawthorne's story "The Ghost of Doctor Harris.")

Lorenzo da Ponte, famous Italian librettist of Mozart's operas "Don Giovanni" and "Così fan tutte," settled in New York City. He engaged in Italian operatic enterprises and became a teacher of Italian at Columbia College (now Columbia University).

₹∾ 1806

American shipping was hampered by the war between England and France inasmuch as each nation had different sea laws. However, American blockade runners got such high prices for their wares that they considered the situation tolerable. Meanwhile, in retaliation against Great Britain's maritime restrictions, Congress passed a Non-Importation Act limiting the importation of certain British commodities. The Act was never actually enforced.

Pike's Peak was discovered (Nov. 15) by Lieutenant Zebulon Montgomery Pike during an expedition to locate the source of the Mississippi.

An approximately 60-year-long "War of the Dictionaries," chiefly concerned with pronunciation, began between the lexicographers Joseph Worcester and Noah Webster. Webster brought out a "Compendious Dictionary of the English Language" which was a forerunner of his monumental two-volume work in 1828. The rivalry finally resolved itself in favor of Webster in 1864, twenty-one years after his death, when a group of scholars published a revised edition of his dictionary.

William Colgate, English-born soapmaker's apprentice, opened a modest soap-making shop in New York.

⧫ 1807

The Harp That Once, Thro' Tara's Halls. w., Thomas Moore. m.,
tune: "Gramachree." London: J. Power's Music & Instrument Warehouse
[1807] (in: Thomas Moore, "A Selection of Irish Melodies," No. 1, p. 23).

Rich and Rare Were the Gems She Wore. w., Thomas Moore. m.,
tune: "The Summer Is Coming." London: J. Power's Music & Instrument
Warehouse [1807] (in: Thomas Moore, "A Selection of Irish Melodies,"
No. 1, p. 41).

Wide-spread resentment prevailed when the British frigate "Leopard"
fired a broadside off Cape Henry (June 12) at the American man-of-war
"Chesapeake," which had refused to halt and be searched for deserters
from the Royal Navy. Five men were killed and 16 were wounded. Of
four alleged deserters, three proved to be American citizens. England
made full restitution.

In consequence of the French and British interdicts against one another, Congress passed the Embargo Act closing American ports to foreign trade. The Act aroused much indignation, which is reflected in
Bryant's poem "The Embargo."

Aaron Burr was arrested in Mississippi for complicity in a plot to establish a Southern empire in Louisiana and Mexico. He went on trial for
treason (May 23) at Richmond, Va., but was acquitted (Sept. 1).

Robert Fulton's first practical steamboat, the "Clermont," made (Aug.
17) a trial run of 154 miles up the Hudson River from New York to
Albany in 32 hours. The boat created such curiosity that the New York
Legislature passed a bill making it a crime for anyone to tamper with the
vessel. (Fulton's undertaking was financed by Robert R. Livingston, of
the Louisiana Purchase deal, and gave both men conjointly a monopoly
on the river's traffic. The steamboat was named after Livingston's estate.)

The first lifeboat station in the United States was built at Cohasset,
Mass.

A Connecticut poet, Joel Barlow, published an attempt at an American
Miltonic epic in 10 "books." It was called "The Columbiad," and re-
counted in heroic didactic couplets a vision that is unfolded by a "radi-
ant seraph" before the eyes of an imprisoned and dying Columbus. The
poem ended with a prophetic picture of universal brotherhood, "all regions in the leagues of peace."

William Hill Brown, author of "the first American novel" ("The Power
of Sympathy," 1789), published his second book of fiction, "Ira and Isa-
bella, or, The Natural Children."

New York City became popularly known as Gotham, when it was so dubbed, after an imaginary English village proverbial for its follies, in the humorous "Salmagundi" pamphlets written by Washington Irving, William Irving, and James Kirke Paulding.

₹⤳ 1808

Believe Me if all Those Endearing Young Charms. w., Thomas Moore. m., tune: "My Lodging Is on the Cold Ground." London: J. Power's Music & Instrument Warehouse [1808] (in: Thomas Moore, "A Selection of Irish Melodies," No. 2, p. 99).

Jessie, the Flow'r o' Dumblane. w., Robert Tannahill. m., Robert Archibald Smith. [Edinburgh, 1808?]

Let Erin Remember the Days of Old. w., Thomas Moore. m., tune: "The Red Fox." London: J. Power's Music & Instrument Warehouse [1808] (in: Thomas Moore, "A Selection of Irish Melodies," No. 2, p. 85).

Congress prohibited the importation of African slaves into the United States; smuggling of Negroes, however, continued. (Great Britain also abolished slave trade in the same year.)

John Jacob Astor, a German immigrant in 1784 who had prospered, established the American Fur Company which soon acquired a monopoly on Canadian fur.

Because of the shipping embargo wheat dropped from $2 to 75¢ per bushel.

A temperance society was founded at Saratoga, N. Y.

The American Academy of Fine Arts was founded in New York.

The Théâtre St. Philippe, seating 700 and built at a cost of $100,000, opened (Jan. 30) in New Orleans.

"The Indian Princess, or, La Belle Sauvage," a play by James Nelson Barker with music by John Bray, was produced (Apr. 6) in Philadelphia at the New Theatre and given (June 14) in New York at the Park Theatre. (A riot ruined the Philadelphia performance because "a large party" or section of the audience objected to the presence in the cast of an actor named Webster. The play was also performed in London in 1820. It is the earliest known dramatization of the story of Pocahontas.)

Pepin and Breschard opened (in June) in New York their extravagantly advertised "New Circus, Corner of Broadway and Anthony Streets," which had "received the most unbounded applause and approbation of the inhabitants of Boston."

⅋ 1809

James Madison, Republican, of Virginia, was inaugurated 4th President.

The first inaugural ball was held in Washington, with the experienced Dolly Madison presiding.

The unpopular Embargo Act (1807) was repealed and replaced by a Non-Intercourse Act that prohibited commercial shipping to Great Britain and France.

The "Phoenix," an American steamboat built by John Stevens, sailed (June 8) from New York to Philadelphia.

Some 30 daily newspapers circulated throughout the nation.

Washington Irving published his burlesque account, "A History of New York from Beginning of the World to the End of the Dutch Dynasty," purportedly the work of a Dutch-American scholar, Dietrich Knickerbocker.

John Howard Payne, precocious, playwriting, theatre-minded genius, aged 18, enjoyed a brief and exciting three months' acting career in New York and Boston. He made (Feb. 24) his debut in New York at the Park Theatre as the handsome Scottish "Young Norval," with sword, shield, head plumes, and kilts. He played in quick order the beloved rhetorical roles in "Mahomet," "The Mountaineers," "Barbarossa," "Tancred," "Pizarro in Peru," "Douglas," "Jane Shore," "Romeo and Juliet," "Hamlet," and Edgar in "King Lear." Summarizing his talents, W. W. Clapp, Jr., wrote ("Record of the Boston Stage"): "In general his action was elegant, his attitudes bold and striking, and his most prominent defects were those of pronunciation." (There was then, however, no future for an American actor, and in 1813 Payne went to London where he remained until 1832, working mainly as a literary hack and becoming the poet of "Home, Sweet Home.")

During Payne's interval in Boston, the Park Theatre in New York mounted (Mar. 20) with elaborate scenery and stage machinery a splendid "Arabian Nights" spectacle, "The Forty Thieves." It played eight nights consecutively, and held the boards for many years in revivals.

Thomas Paine, aged 72, died (June 8) in New York; he was buried on his New Rochelle farm when interment in consecrated ground was refused.

⅋ 1810

According to the census there were now 109 cotton mills in New England just 20 years after Samuel Slater introduced the first one—and became the father of the factory system in the U. S.

John Scudder's long-famed still life, "American Museum," eventually to become the property of P. T. Barnum, opened (in Apr.) in New York. Here were to be seen 12 wax figures (one of the recently deceased Daniel Lambert, the English Mammoth, who weighed 739 pounds and whose body measured 9 feet 4 inches in circumference), a stuffed tortoise (7 feet 6 inches long), 70 quadrupeds, 100 preserved reptiles, 150 Indian weapons and articles, 250 stuffed birds, 1,200 submarine objects, besides other curiosa—and an organ.

Mary Ann Duff, young English tragedienne, made her American debut as Juliet in Boston. (She was one of the outstanding figures on the American stage until her retirement in 1838. Her husband, John Duff, was a recognized and versatile actor.)

George Frederick Cooke, 54-year-old veteran English actor, came to the U. S. and was admired during the next two years as a popular tragedian in New York, Boston, Philadelphia, Baltimore, and Providence. (He died of alcoholism Sept. 26, 1812, in New York and was buried in the strangers' vault in St. Paul's churchyard. There the great Edmund Kean, during his first New York season [1820-21] erected in Cooke's memory the first monument in the United States to an actor.)

William B. Wood made (Nov. 12) his New York début as an actor at the Park Theatre in the popular play "The Foundling of the Forest." (Born in Montreal and raised in New York, Wood was long an important figure in the American theatre as an actor and as a manager in Philadelphia.)

The musical sensation of the year was the Pandean Band of Italian Music "from Drury Lane and Covent Garden," which made (Oct. 29) its first appearance in New York at the Park Theatre and was heard in most amusement places until 1817.

Fashionable ladies used rouge and pearl powder, and dresses were fuller. The population of the United States was 7,239,881.

ৡ 1811

The Battle of the Wabash. w., Joseph Hutton. m., tune: "To Anacreon in Heaven" (subsequently the air of "The Star-Spangled Banner"). Philadelphia: G. E. Blake, n.d. (Published previously in song-sheets without publisher's imprints.)

The Death of Nelson (The American). w., m., John Braham. "The American" was a musical play produced at the Lyceum Theatre, London, 1811,

Rebellious Indians in a conspiracy organized in defiance of the United States government by Tecumseh, Shawnee chief, were defeated (Nov. 7)

during his absence in the disastrous Battle of the Wabash (or Tippecanoe) by William Henry Harrison, governor of Indiana Territory. The victory was celebrated in a popular ballad (see above: "The Battle of the Wabash") and earned Harrison the sobriquet Tippecanoe, which became the slogan of his presidential campaign in 1840.

The world's first steam ferryboat began operation (in Oct.) between New York and Hoboken. (It was built by John Stevens, after whom is named the Stevens Institute of Technology, Hoboken, N. J., founded in 1870.)

Henry Clay, Virginia-born statesman of Kentucky, was elected to the House of Representatives, and became its first prominent Speaker (1811-20, 1823-25).

Fire destroyed the theatre in Richmond, Va., with a loss of 70 lives— the first major catastrophe of its kind in American theatrical history. Since the fire was regarded by the pious as an act of divine punishment, a law was enacted prohibiting public amusements for four years.

Earthquakes were reported in the Mississippi Valley in December.

The United States was building up a war fever against Great Britain, fanned by the "war hawk" elements in Congress which were headed by Henry Clay and John Caldwell Calhoun. Tension was aggravated by the alarms of western farmers who were being harassed by Indians said to be abetted by England through Canada.

₿₷ 1812

The American Star. See 1800.

Rousseau's Dream. m., arr. from Jean Jacques Rousseau by Johann Baptist Cramer (in his: "Air with Variations for the Pianoforte"). London: Chappell & Co. [1812.] (The music is an adaptation of a song in Rousseau's one-act opera "Le Devin du Village," produced at Fontainebleau, 1752. The melody was adapted as a hymn in Thomas Walker's "Companion to Dr. Rippon's Tunes," London, 1825, and has appeared since then in many hymnbooks. Cramer's variations were reprinted in America by G. Graupner, Boston, soon after their publication in London.)

For some songs of the War of 1812-15, consult—

Colcord, Joanna C. Songs of American sailormen. New York: W. W. Norton & Co., Inc. [cop. 1938.]

Dolph, Edward Arthur. "Sound Off!" New York: Farrar & Rinehart, Inc. [cop. 1942.]

Louisiana was admitted (Apr. 30) as the 18th State.

The enthusiastic efforts of Henry Clay and John C. Calhoun finally led the United States to declare (June 18) its second war on Great Britain, although the latter had withdrawn its maritime restrictions two days earlier. The hostilities gained momentum slowly and lasted officially until the end of 1814 (actually Jan. 8, 1815). Throughout the Americans were more successful on sea than on land. They had also to engage the Creek Indians of Alabama, under the Shawnee chief Tecumseh, who had joined ranks with the British.

In New York, a mass meeting was held (Aug. 19) in protest against the war.

The term "gerrymander" came into use when Benjamin Russell, ardent Federalist editor of the Boston "Centinel," so described the lizard-like appearance of the map of the new voting districts in Essex County, Mass., alleged to have been re-aligned by Democratic Governor Elbridge Gerry to favor his party then in power. The word was coined from "salamander."

Joel Barlow, aged 58, American poet and lawyer, died (Dec. 24) from exposure near Vilna, Poland, during Napoleon's retreat from Moscow. Barlow was on a diplomatic mission to the emperor from President Madison.

The American Antiquarian Society was founded at Worcester, Mass.

The Walnut Street Theatre in Philadelphia opened with Sheridan's comedy "The Rivals." (The building is still standing, the oldest extant theatre in the United States.)

As a result of the war, the United States became entangled in the sixth depression since 1790; it lasted three years.

⁊✺ 1813

The Minstrel Boy. w., Thomas Moore. m., tune: "The Moreen." London; J. Power's Music & Instrument Warehouse [1813] (in: Thomas Moore, "A Selection of Irish Melodies," No. 5, p. 23).

'Tis the Last Rose of Summer. w., Thomas Moore. m., tune: "The Groves of Blarney." London: J. Power's Music & Instrument Warehouse [1813] (in: Thomas Moore, "A Selection of Irish Melodies," No. 5, p. 15).

President Madison began his second term.

The War of 1812 continued. American naval successes spread from Newfoundland to Brazil and across the Atlantic to the Azores. During the land defeat of the British on the Thames River in Canada, the Indian chief Tecumseh, now a brigadier general with the enemy, was killed (Oct. 15).

Two historic utterances signalized the war events of the year. Commander James Lawrence, fatally wounded while his frigate "Chesapeake" engaged the British "Shannon" in a bitter 15-minute encounter (June 15) off the shore of Boston, cried: "Don't give up the ship" (though the "Chesapeake" did later surrender with 145 killed and wounded). The words were inscribed on a flag unfurled at the Battle of Lake Erie by Commodore Oliver Hazard Perry, who defeated (Sept. 10) the British navy and announced his victory with the words: "We have met the enemy and they are ours." (The slogans are often incorrectly interchanged.)

The earliest known printed reference to the United States by the nickname "Uncle Sam" is believed to have occurred (Sept. 7) in the "Troy Post."

The "Boston Daily Advertiser" was founded and became the first successful daily newspaper in New England. (Ceased publication in 1929.)

The Baptist Burmese Mission was founded.

The Théâtre d'Orléans in New Orleans, La., was rebuilt at a cost of $180,000; it had grilled loges for people in mourning.

৪৵ 1814

Love Has Eyes. w., Charles Dibdin. m., Sir Henry Rowley Bishop. (Composed in 1814. The writer of the words should not be confused with his more famous father of the same name. The son's full name was Charles Isaac Mungo Dibdin.)

The Star-Spangled Banner. w., Francis Scott Key. m., tune: "To Anacreon in Heaven," arranged by Thomas Carr. Baltimore: Carrs [sic] Music Store [1814].

Strike the Cymbal. Sacred chorus for SATB. w., Rev. William Slaughton (?); adapted by Benjamin Carr in 1812 from an Italian operatic chorus, "Viva Enrico," by Vincenzo Puccitta—usually misspelled Pucitta, or Puccita; sung under Carr's direction in a concert in St. Augustine's Church, Philadelphia, Pa., April 13, 1814.

The War of 1812 entered its final stages.

In the North, the Americans frustrated (Sept. 11) an attempted invasion from Canada via Lake Champlain. In the South, however, they had been routed (Aug. 24) at Bladensburg, Md., and had lost the nation's capital to the British who burned the Capitol, the Library of Congress, the White House, and other public buildings.

The tide of the war turned when the British Chesapeake fleet unsuccessfully bombarded Fort McHenry, near Baltimore, for 25 hours in the night of Sept. 13-14. During the engagement the future national anthem of the United States was born. Francis Scott Key, 33-year-old Baltimore lawyer, who witnessed the scene from a British man-of-war on which he was detained while on a legal mission, wrote the words of "The Star-Spangled Banner."

Meanwhile, 26 disgruntled New England merchantmen were meeting in convention (1814-15) at Hartford, Conn., in protest against "Mr. Madison's War." Motions were entertained for secession or a separate peace with England, and against the admission of new States to the Union.

A treaty of peace between the United States and Great Britain, terminating the War of 1812, was signed (Dec. 24) at Ghent, Belgium. The news did not reach the United States until two weeks later (after the decisive American victory at New Orleans).

At Middlebury, Vt., Emma Willard opened a female seminary for the study of philosophy, history, mathematics, and the sciences—subjects hitherto unavailable to women.

The Massachusetts Historical Society printed the Burwell Papers, a contemporary manuscript account of Bacon's Rebellion (1676). (They are now preserved by the Virginia Historical Society.)

ࣷ 1815

On the Banks of Allan Water. w., Matthew Gregory Lewis. m., ["Lady C. S."], arr. by Charles Edward Horn. London: J. Power [ca. 1815].

Unaware that the war with England was terminated, Major General Andrew Jackson fifteen days later (Jan. 8) defeated the powerful British land and naval forces in a needless battle at Chalmette, outside New Orleans, in which 2,000 British were killed. There were seven American fatalities.

As an aftermath of the war (Apr. 6), a guard at Dartmoor Prison, Princetown, England, killed seven and wounded about 60 of the 1,700 American naval prisoners confined there during the War of 1812. It was reported that those killed were attempting to escape. England made liberal restitution to the families of the victims. The incident is known as the Dartmoor Massacre.

The United States renewed naval operations against the Barbary States to suppress piracy. Algiers declared war, but capitulated before the speedy action of Admiral Stephen Decatur. At a banquet in his honor, he delivered the famous toast: "Our country! In her intercourse with foreign nations may she be always right; but our country, right or wrong."

President Madison pardoned Jean Lafitte, French-American pirate and smuggler, for his bravery and help at the Battle of New Orleans. (He later resumed piracy, operating out of Galveston, Tex., and was driven away by government troops after his gang had damaged American property.)

To re-establish the Library of Congress, burned by the British in 1814, Congress purchased Jefferson's library of 6,457 volumes for $23,950.

The Handel and Haydn Society, a long-famous choral organization, was founded (Mar. 30) in Boston.

Civic improvements of the year included gaslights in Boylston Hall, Boston; municipal gas lighting for Baltimore, and the completion of the Fairmount waterworks in Philadelphia.

The government raised funds by taxing watches, hats, caps, boots, umbrellas, etc.

"The North American Review" was founded in Boston as a monthly literary magazine.

Benjamin Franklin's newspaper, "The Pennsylvania Gazette," started 1792, came to an end.

John Singleton Copley, aged about 78, Boston painter, died (Sept. 9) in London. (Copley Square in Boston is named after him. His son John Singleton Copley, Lord Lyndhurst, was three times Lord Chancellor of England.)

₹≫ 1816

The Second Bank of the United States was established in Philadelphia and chartered for 21 years with $35,000,000 capital. (Its predecessor, chartered in 1791, had failed five years before, and the nation's currency was in virtual chaos with 245 state corporations individually issuing their own money.)

Indiana was admitted (Dec. 11) as the 19th State.

The National Colonization Society of America was organized to settle free American Negroes in Africa. (The first attempt was made south of Sierra Leone in 1820.)

United States manufacturing broke into full stride, due to the stimulus of the war which had excluded English products and encouraged national self-sufficiency.

The American Bible Society was founded (May 6) in New York for the distribution of the Scriptures.

"Guy Mannering" was the hit play of Boston with Mrs. Powell, a popular actress, playing the role of Meg.

Jacob Hyer and Tom Beasley fought the first ring prizefight in American history.

Of grave concern to the United States was the formation of the Holy Alliance by Russia, Austria, and Prussia at Paris (Sept. 26, 1815) and proclaimed at Frankfort (Feb. 2, 1816). One of its most drastic pronouncements was the demand for the abolition of the republics then being established on the principles of the United States Constitution by the revolting Spanish colonies in South America under Simon Bolivar. This demand caused the formulation of the Monroe Doctrine.

₰ 1817

Mary's Tears. w., Thomas Moore. m., Oliver Shaw. Providence, R. I.: O. Shaw [1817] (2nd edition).

James Monroe, Republican, of Virginia, was inaugurated 5th President, beginning a period that was called the "Era of Good Feeling" by the "Boston Journal."

The United States and Great Britain signed (Apr. 28-29) the Rush-Bagot Treaty, which eliminated forts and limited naval armaments on the Great Lakes.

Mississippi was admitted (Dec. 10) as the 20th State.

The United States began military operations against the Seminole Indians in Florida, then under Spanish rule.

Thousands of settlers moved west, and the prairies were dotted with log cabins.

The first steamboat appeared in St. Louis.

With the double distinction of being the first state university and the first to introduce co-education, the University of Michigan opened at Detroit. (It removed to Ann Arbor in 1837.)

Harvard University Law School was established.

William Cullen Bryant published "Thanatopsis," written at age of 16, in "The North American Review," Boston. (The poem lacked the present opening 17 lines and closing 15, which first appeared in the author's collected "Poems," 1821.)

Charles Benjamin Incledon, noted English tenor then 54 years of age, sang with great acclaim in American cities (1817-18).

Benjamin West finished his immense painting (25 feet x 15 feet) "Death on the Pale Horse," illustrating Revelation, chap. vi, in the Pennsylvania Academy, Philadelphia.

A season of English drama was given at the Théâtre St. Philippe in New Orleans, although half of the audience understood no English.

₰ 1818

Hark! the Vesper Hymn Is Stealing. Part song for SATB with piano acc. w., Thomas Moore. m., tune: "Russian Air," arr. by Sir John Stevenson. London: J. Power [1818] (in: Thomas Moore. "A Selection of Popular National Airs," No. 1, p. 54-48).

Oft in the Stilly Night. w., Thomas Moore. m., Scotch Air, arr. by Sir John Stevenson. London: J. Power [1818] (in: Thomas Moore, "A Selection of Popular National Airs," No. 1, p. 51-53).

Silent Night, Holy Night—*original German title:* **Stille Nacht; Heilige Nacht.** w., Joseph Mohr. m., Franz Gruber. (First sung on Christmas Eve, 1818, at Oberndorf, Bavaria, with guitar accompaniment. The English translation by which the song is known today dates from the 1870s —see 1871.

Exceeding orders, Andrew Jackson, military hero of the War of 1812, suppressed the uprising (1817-18) of the Seminole Indians in Florida— an act which involved the United States in serious diplomatic exchanges with Spain and Great Britain.

Congress standardized the national flag, prescribing 13 horizontal stripes (7 red and 6 white) and a blue field with one white star for each state. (At the time, the flag contained 15 stripes and 15 stars.)

Illinois was admitted (Dec. 3) as the 21st State.

Charles Bulfinch succeeded Benjamin Latrobe as architect of the Capitol at Washington, D. C. (He held the post until the completion of the building in 1830. Bulfinch's design has been the model for state capitols throughout the United States.)

The great Edmund Kean acted in London a blank-verse play by a struggling American poet, "Brutus, or, The Fall of Tarquin" by John Howard Payne.

Pigs were so common in the streets of New York that the "Evening Post" started a crusade against them.

James William Wallack, the elder, London-born tragedian, made his American debut (Sept. 7) as Macbeth in New York at the Park Theatre. Meanwhile T. A. Cooper, member of an English theatrical company in New Orleans, was said to have received the fabulous sum of $333 per night.

Josiah White and Erskine Hazard formed the Lehigh Navigation Company to mine coal near Mauch Chunk, Pa.

The system of pensioning war veterans and their widows and children was established.

Silversmith and engraver Paul Revere of the historic "midnight ride" died (May 18) in his native Boston. He was 83.

࿐ 1819

Lo! Here the Gentle Lark. w., William Shakespeare. m., Sir Henry Rowley Bishop. (The words are extracted from Shakespeare's long poem in six-line stanzas, "Venus and Adonis," published in London, 1593—probably the poet's first printed work. The music was composed for a production of Shakespeare's play "The Comedy of Errors," London, 1819. The title of the song is often spelled incorrectly "Lo! Hear the Gentle Lark.")

Sicilian Hymn. w., m., anon. Boston: West, Richardson & Lord, 1819 [cop. Oct. 26, 1816] (in: "Templi Carmina . . . or, Bridgewater Collection of Sacred Music," 7th edition, p. 182). (The tune is better known in connection with the Latin hymn to the Virgin "O sanctissima, O piissima," and with the German Christmas song "O du fröhliche, O du selige." The Latin words and music were collected by Johann Gottfried von Herder and published in his "Stimmen der Völker in Liedern," edited by Johann von Müller, Tübingen, 1807, p. 175. In the above American publication, the music was set to the words "Lord, dismiss us with Thy blessing" and retained a place in subsequent editions of "Templi Carmina." Around the 1820s, E. Riley, New York, brought out a sheet music edition, adapted to the words "Guide me, O Thou great Jehovah" under the title "Sicilian Mariner's Hymn." Asahel Nettleton included the music, set to the words "While the heralds of salvation," in his "Zion's Harp," S. S. Jocelyn, New Haven, Conn., 1824. The music is still found in hymnbooks today.)

Chief Justice John Marshall of the Supreme Court set the precedent in the Dartmouth College Case that the Supreme Court is the tribunal for reviewing laws passed by state legislatures.

On Washington's Birthday, Spain ceded Florida to the United States. No money was paid but the United States assumed and settled American claims against Spain to the amount of $5,000,000.

Alabama was admitted (Dec. 14) as the 22nd State, making now 11 slave States and 11 free States.

The S.S. "Savannah," a sailing packet of 350 tons equipped with a steam engine and iron paddle wheels, was the first American vessel to cross the Atlantic mainly under steam propulsion. She sailed (May 22) from Savannah, Ga., for New York and proceeded (July 15) to Liverpool, making the crossing in 26 days (the whole trip taking 31 days). (The date, May 22, was proclaimed National Maritime Day in 1935.)

The University of Virginia, at Charlottesville, was founded in accordance with Jefferson's plans and built according to his architectural designs.

Harvard University Divinity School was established.

Ludwig van Beethoven was already sufficiently known in the New England part of the world so that a choral organization in Portland, Me., called itself the "Beethoven Musical Society." (The great composer was then living in Vienna, writing his 9th Symphony, and still had eight years of life ahead.)

The remains of Thomas Paine were removed from their New Rochelle, N. Y., burial plot by William Cobbett, English journalist and radical, for re-interment in England. (Cobbett's plan to erect a monument was never realized, and the whereabouts of Paine's bones are now unknown.)

A group of German Separatists under Joseph Bäumeler (Bimeler) established the Zoar Community in Tuscarawas County, O.

James Long, Natchez, Miss., merchant, led a filibustering expedition into Texas, then a Mexican State, and declared a republic. The notorious pirate, Jean Lafitte, was appointed governor. (Long was shot in 1832 on his way to Mexico City.)

Washington Irving's classic "The Sketch Book of Geoffrey Crayon," containing the stories "Rip Van Winkle" and "The Legend of Sleepy Hollow," was the literary event of the year.

Emma Hart Willard, Vermont-born pioneer in women's education, submitted to DeWitt Clinton, Governor of New York, a "Plan for Improving Female Education."

"The Philadelphia Register and National Recorder" appeared as a weekly journal. (Subsequently published under various names, it became a monthly called "The Eclectic Magazine," which ceased publication in 1907.)

The French corset, a two-piece affair, laced up the back, and considered standard feminine equipment until the 1900s, came into use.

The seventh depression since 1790 now set in, and like most of its predecessors it lasted three years.

༂❧ 1820

Bid Me Discourse. w., William Shakespeare. m., Sir Henry Rowley Bishop. (The words are extracted from Shakespeare's poem "Venus and Adonis"—see under the caption: 1819, "Lo! Here the Gentle Lark." The song was composed for a production of "Twelfth Night" in London, 1820.)

Hail to the Chief. w., Sir Walter Scott. m., James Sanderson. E. Riley [ca. 1820]. (The song was published earlier in London. The words are from Scott's narrative poem, "The Lady of the Lake," published in 1810. The composer was a self-taught English violinist and the conductor of the Surrey Theatre, London, who wrote many songs for local theatrical productions during the 1790s and the early years of the nineteenth century.)

John Peel—*also known as:* **D'ye Ken John Peel.** w., John Woodcock Graves. m., traditional. (Written about 1820. John Peel was born in 1776 and died in 1854. For a portrait and brief biographical sketch consult Percy A. Scholes, "The Oxford Companion to Music," London, 1943, 2nd ed.)

Maine was admitted (Mar. 15) as the 23rd State.

Congress passed (Mar. 3) Henry Clay's Missouri Compromise bill, permitting slavery in Missouri but in no other state west of the Mississippi and north of 36° 30′.

President Monroe congratulated the newly established republics in South America (Venezuela, Paraguay, Argentina, Chile, Colombia).

Capt. Nathaniel Brown Palmer explored the Antarctic regions.

The first American missionaries visited Hawaii.

In New York, the Mechanics and Tradesmen, and Mercantile libraries were established.

Men considered watch fobs an essential piece of haberdashery.

An English translation of Carlo Botta's Italian "History of the War of Independence of the United States of America" (1809) appeared and remained a standard book until superseded by George Bancroft's "History of the United States" (1834-76).

The Musical Fund Society of Philadelphia was founded to help indigent musicians and to give concerts of choral and orchestral music. (The Society gave its first concert Apr. 24, 1821, playing Beethoven's 1st Symphony interspersed, as was the custom, with vocal and other solos, and celebrated its centenary May 4, 1920, with a masque reproducing a "Jenny Lind Concert in 1850.")

Edwin Forrest, American tragedian, made his debut in Philadelphia at the Walnut Street Theatre.

Edmund Kean, English actor, came to the United States and was acclaimed in New York, Boston, and Philadelphia.

Deaths of the year included: Benjamin West, aged 82 (Mar. 11) in London, American painter (his large paintings were dubbed "ten-acre" canvases) and second president of the Royal Academy; and Daniel Boone, aged 86 (Sept. 20), in St. Charles County, Mo., quasi-legendary frontiersman.

In the national elections, President Monroe was re-elected, receiving all but one vote, which was cast by the staunchly independent Federalist John Quincy Adams of Massachusetts, son of the second President, so that Washington would not be deprived of the honor of being the only unanimously elected President.

The total population of the country now was 9,638,453, with New York State assuming the lead it has held ever since. Westward migrations had shifted the center of population to Moorfield, W. Va.

⪼ 1821

Invitation to the Dance—*original German title:* Aufforderung zum Tanze. Piano solo. m., Carl Maria von Weber, op. 65. Berlin: Schlesinger [1821]. (Composed in 1819.)

President James Monroe began his second term. He was the first President to be inaugurated on the fifth of March instead of the traditional fourth because the latter date fell on a Sunday.

Missouri was admitted (Aug. 10) as the 24th State.

Russia prohibited by imperial ukase all navigation and fishing within 100 miles of the northwestern coast of Alaska—a step toward the Monroe Doctrine (1823).

The Santa Fe Trail, extending from Independence, Mo., to Santa Fe, N. M., was mapped out (1821-22) by William Becknell.

Junius Brutus Booth, English actor, made his American debut as Richard III at Petersburg, Va. (He made his first New York appearance in the same role in 1822, and settled in the United States. He was the father of John Wilkes Booth who shot Lincoln in 1865.)

Connecticut-born James Gates Percival published his "Poems." He was esteemed by his contemporaries as a great poet until the ascendancy of William Cullen Bryant, and the long Spenserian epic, "Prometheus," included in the volume was regarded the equal of Byron's "Childe Harold." (Percival was an eccentric, unstable person, who lived awhile by his own choice in the New Haven State Hospital, but was nonetheless a man of varied attainments. He was a journalist in South Carolina, New York, and in his native State, taught chemistry at West Point, and served as state geologist of Connecticut [1835-42] and Wisconsin [1854-56]. He died in 1856.)

James Fenimore Cooper published in the usual two-volume format of the time his immediately popular novel "The Spy." (Franz Schubert, the great German composer, enjoyed Cooper's novels in German translations.)

In New York a new and rebuilt Park Theatre, which replaced an older structure of the same name which was erected in 1798 and destroyed in 1820, opened (Sept. 1) its doors to fashionable theatregoers with Mrs. Elizabeth Inchbald's English comedy "Wives as They Were and Maids as

They Are," followed by the American John Howard Payne's charming success, "Thérèse, the Orphan of Geneva."

Negro singers and actors in New York gave for their own people who were not admitted to the white theatres several performances at the African Grove, even essaying a version of "Richard III" with "a dapper wooly-haired waiter at the City Hotel" in the role of the king. Neighbors, however, soon objected to the noise, and two of the actors were "taken up by the watch." Undaunted, they resumed their performances at the Pantheon, corner of Mercer and Bleecker streets, again giving "Richard III" with one Hewlett who continued to appear in New York and Brooklyn for a number of years as a singer and impersonator.

Ladies' shoes insinuated themselves into view beneath decidedly shorter skirts; Nile green was a fashionable color; and jewelry was made chiefly of polished steel.

₰ 1822

The Fortune I Crave (The Deed of Gift). w., Samuel Woodworth. m., air: "The Cottage on the Moor." ("The Deed of Gift" was a play with music, produced at the Boston Theatre, Mar. 25, 1822. The words and the tune are reprinted in Grenville Vernon, "Yankee Doodle-Doo," New York, 1927, p. 109-10.)

The Harp of Love (The Spy). w., Charles Powell Clinch. m., traditional air. ("The Spy," a play with music, adapted from James Fenimore Cooper's recent novel, was produced in New York at the Park Theatre, Mar. 1, 1822. The words and the tune are reprinted in Grenville Vernon, "Yankee Doodle-Doo," New York, 1927, p. 99-100.)

Stephen Fuller Austin of Virginia established the first American settlement in Texas, then under Mexican rule, on land inherited from his father.

Daniel Treadwell of Boston constructed the first American printing press to be operated by steam.

Lowell Mason brought out in Boston the long-popular oblong "Boston Handel and Haydn Society Collection of Church Music," which went through many revisions and editions.

The novelist James Fenimore Cooper and his circle of literary friends formed about this time the informal Bread and Cheese Club in New York.

A "Grand Orchestra of Androides," consisting of "seven Automaton Figures as large as life, who perform on Twelve different instruments," was an attraction in New York at the Saloon of Apollo.

₰ 1823

Home, Sweet Home. (Clari, or, The Maid of Milan). w., John Howard Payne. m., "Sicilian Air" [arranged by Sir Henry Rowley Bishop]. [London: D'Almaine & Co., 1823.] (See below.)

Rose of Lucerne, or, The Swiss Toy Girl. w., anon. m., John Barnett. [London, 1823.] (Date from John Duff Brown, "Biographical Dictionary of Musicians," Paisley, 1886.)

President Monroe, replying to the pronouncements of the Holy Alliance (1816), proclaimed (Dec. 2) the principles known as the Monroe Doctrine, "that the American continents, by the free and independent condition which they have assumed and maintained, are henceforth not to be considered as subjects for future colonization by European powers."

The "Virginia" was the first steamboat to sail up the Mississippi on a run of 729 miles to Fort Snelling, Minn. The journey took approximately 19 days (Apr. 21-May 10).

Sir Henry Rowley Bishop's 3-act opera "Clari, or, The Maid of Milan," to a libretto by the American poet John Howard Payne, containing "Home, Sweet Home" (above), was produced in London at Covent Garden Theatre, May 8, and given in New York at the Park Theatre, Nov. 12.

Equestrian spectacles and dramas, imported from Astley's London Amphitheatre, began their long vogue on American stages. Among the outstanding shows of this type were "Timour the Tartar" and "El Hyder."

The "Troy (N.Y.) Sentinel" printed (Dec. 23) an anonymous poem, "A Visit from St. Nicholas," which became better known under the title " 'Twas the Night before Christmas," by Clement Clarke Moore, a learned Biblical scholar of New York City.

₰ 1824

The 67-year-old Marquis de Lafayette revisited the United States by invitation of Congress, which voted him a gift of $200,000 and a land grant of 24,000 acres and conferred American citizenship on him and his descendants in perpetuity. He made a triumphal tour of all 24 States before returning to France (1825).

The American Sunday School Union came into being inasmuch as the Sunday School was one of the chief educational mediums, secular as well as religious, at this time. (In 1872 uniform Sunday School lessons were established, but by that time the Sunday School was mainly religious.)

John Trumbull, American painter, completed his four large pictures (each 12 feet x 18 feet) for the rotunda of the Capitol at Washington, D. C. (They were begun in 1817 and represent the Signing of the Declaration of Independence, Surrender of Cornwallis, Surrender of General Burgoyne, and Washington Resigning His Commission. Trumbull died in 1825.)

"The Springfield Republican" was founded as a weekly newspaper in Springfield, Mass. (Still published; issued as daily since 1844.)

The greatest billiard player in the land was one Higham, "The Albany Pony," who appeared in New York City from his native Albany, N. Y., and embarked on a long series of victories.

The Camp Street Theatre opened (Jan. 1) as the first English-language playhouse in New Orleans.

The veteran actor Joseph Jefferson, the elder, closed (Aug. 5) his glorious stage career in New York at the new Chatham Theatre, "overpowered with the good wishes of every one present," as newspapers reported.

"The Saw Mill, or, A Yankee Trick," an "opera" by Micah Hawkins with music by James Hewitt, was produced (Nov. 29) at the same theatre.

Johann Nepomuk Maelzel, Bavarian mechanical genius, associated with Beethoven in the performance of the latter's battle symphony "Wellington's Victory" and maker of his ear trumpet, came to New York apparently during this year. His Panharmonicon, a mechanical monstrosity capable of imitating 206 musical instruments, was exhibited (Dec. 14) for some time in a large hall in Reed Street. (Maelzel's movements in America are vague. He also visited the West Indies. From 1826 until 1834, either he or a relative, one "W. Maelzel," according to newspaper advertisements, displayed other automatons of his invention such as a chess player, a trumpeter, slack-rope dancers, and a mechanical panorama "The Conflagration of Moscow." Maelzel was found dead, July 31, 1838, in his berth on the American brig "Otis.")

ह~ 1825

Buy a Broom? w., m., anon. Firth & Hall [ca. 1825]. (The song is an adaptation of the German "O Du Lieber Augustin." According to Wulf Stratowa, "Oesterreichische Lyrik aus Neun Jahrhunderten," Vienna, 1848, p. 355, Augustin was an itinerant bagpiper, probably one Marx Augustin, who is said to have survived the plague in 1679 and the Turkish occupation of Vienna in 1683, and died on an Austrian highway, Oct. 10, 1705.)

Cherry Ripe. w., Robert Herrick (1591-1674). m., Charles Edward Horn. (The song was published in London about 1825 and widely reprinted in the United States.)

Love's Eyes (The Forest Rose). w., Samuel Woodworth. m., Scottish air: "Roy's Wife," arr. by John Davies. ("The Forest Rose" was a ballad opera produced in New York at the Chatham Theatre, Oct. 7, 1825, and enjoyed a considerable vogue both in its original form and later in a dramatic version. The words and the tune are reprinted in Grenville Vernon, "Yankee Doodle-Doo," New York, 1927, p. 112-13.)

The Meeting of the Waters of Hudson and Erie. w., m., Samuel Woodworth. E. Riley, cop. 1825. (See below.)

A Wet Sheet and a Flowing Sea. w., Allan Cunningham. [m., tune: "Le Petit Tambour."] London: John Taylor, 1825 (in: Allan Cunningham, "The Songs of Scotland, Ancient and Modern," vol. 4, p. 208-09).

John Quincy Adams, Republican, of Massachusetts, was inaugurated 6th President. He was the first President to serve only one term.

In New York State, the Erie Canal, extending from Buffalo to Albany and connecting Lake Erie with the Hudson River, was completed after 32 years at a cost of $7,000,000 and opened (Oct. 26) with appropriate ceremonies by Governor De Witt Clinton. (The first boat sailed from Buffalo on the opening day and arrived in New York City on Nov. 4.)

Lafayette laid the cornerstone of the Bunker Hill Monument, opposite Boston, on the 50th anniversary of the battle (June 17). (The monument was completed in 1843.)

John Elgar built the first American iron steamboat, "Codorus," in York, Pa.

The first Norwegian immigrants arrived (Oct. 9) on the sloop "Restaurationen." (The 100th anniversary of the event was celebrated in 1925 by the issuance of two commemorative postage stamps by the United States Post Office Department.)

The murder of Kentucky Solicitor-general Col. Solomon P. Sharp was a nation-wide sensation and became the subject of pamphlets, ballads, plays ("Conrad and Eudora" by Thomas Holley Simms, 1832; "Politian" by Edgar Allan Poe, 1835-36; "Octavia Brigaldi" by Charlotte Barnes, 1837) and novels ("Greyslaer" by Charles Fenno Hoffman, 1840; "Beauchampe" by William Gilmore Simms, 1842). Sharp had seduced Ann Cook who married an attorney, Jeroboam O. Beauchamp. She persuaded her husband to murder Sharp. After several unsuccessful attempts, Beauchamp, in disguise, stabbed Sharp to death (Nov. 5). Beauchamp's trial was marked by perjury and corruption, and resulted in his conviction.

During the night before his execution, Ann gained admittance to the jail and both swallowed laudanum. When it failed of effect, they stabbed themselves. Ann died; Beauchamp was carried to the gallows and hanged.

The "Boston Traveler" was founded as a daily newspaper.

Italian opera was introduced (Nov. 29) in the United States at the Park Theatre in New York by Manuel Garcia and his 17-year-old daughter Maria Felicita Garcia (afterward the famous singer Malibran). The opening opera was Rossini's "Il Barbiere di Siviglia," in which Garcia had created the tenor role at the world première (Rome, 1816). The performance grossed $2,980. As was the European custom, librettos were sold at the theatre (price 37¾ cents). Joseph Bonaparte, ex-King of Spain; James Fenimore Cooper, American novelist; and Lorenzo da Ponte, Mozart's librettist, were in the audience. (The season ran to Sept. 30, 1826.)

Frances Wright, Scottish-born reformer and author, founded the Nashoba Community, Tenn., for the education and eventual emancipation of Negro slaves. (The rigors of the climate and the hardship of frontier life caused her to abandon the project in 1828. She freed 30 Negroes in her care and settled them in Haiti.)

The United Tailoresses of New York became the first American trade union for women only.

Jefferson Medical College was founded in Philadelphia. (Still in existence.)

The Kappa Alpha Society, second American college Greek letter fraternity, was founded (Nov. 26). (The first was Phi Beta Kappa, organized Dec. 5, 1776, at William and Mary College, Williamsburg, Va.)

Gift annuals, containing stories, poetry, and engravings, became the vogue. (Contributions from many well-known writers and poets appeared in them. One of the first books of this kind was "The Atlantic Souvenir," which was issued annually until 1832.)

Fitz-Greene Halleck's poem, "Marco Bozzaris," written on the death of the Greek patriot, was printed in the "New York Review."

The Chatham Theatre, New York, re-opened (May 6) as the first American playhouse to be illuminated by gas. (It was followed in 1826 by the Lafayette Amphitheatre and the Bowery Theatre.)

ૐ 1826

Araby's Daughter. w., Thomas Moore. m., George Kiallmark. Boston: James L. Hewitt & Co. [ca. 1826.] (Published earlier in London. The words are derived from "The Fire-Worshippers," the third of the four tales which comprise Moore's "Lalla Rookh," published in London, 1817. The music was adapted later to Samuel Woodworth's poem "The Old Oaken Bucket"—see below.)

The Dashing White Sergeant. w., General Burgoyne. m., Sir Henry Rowley Bishop. (Composed in 1826.)

The Hunters of Kentucky. w., Samuel Woodworth (in his: "Melodies, Duets, Trios, Songs, and Ballads," p. 221-23). m., tune: "Miss Bailey." James M. Campbell, 1826. (The words were written in honor of the Kentucky riflemen at the Battle of New Orleans, Jan. 8, 1815, for the tenor Arthur Keene who came to America in 1817. The title of the tune is usually quoted as "Miss Bailey's Ghost." The song was also published as sheet music during this period by T. Birch, New York, n.d., arr. by William Blondell, and by other publishers.)

I'd Be a Butterfly. w., m., Thomas Haynes Bayly. (The song was written and composed in Chessel, England, in 1826. An American edition was published by E. Riley, New York, during the 1820s.)

Meet Me by Moonlight Alone. w., m., Joseph Augustine Wade. London: F. T. Latour [1826]. (The song was popularized by the celebrated Mme. Lucia Elizabeth Vestris.)

[The Old Oaken Bucket.] **The Bucket.** w., Samuel Woodworth (in his: "Melodies, Duets, Trios, Songs, and Ballads," p. 12-13). m., tune: "Jessie, the Flower of Dumblane" (see 1808). (Woodworth's volume contained no music, but, for the most part, specified the tunes. The above song was published as sheet music by C. Bradlee, Boston, ca. 1833, and others. The words are now sung to the tune of "Araby's Daughter" by George Kiallmark—see above.)

The United States was 50 years old. Its semicentennial (July 4) was marked by the death of two former Presidents—John Adams, aged 91, in New York, and Thomas Jefferson, aged 83, in Monticello, Va.

The American Society for the Promotion of Temperance was founded (Feb. 13) in Boston.

Jedediah Strong Smith, New York-born fur trader, led the first exploring expedition (1826-27) over the Sierra Nevada from Salt Lake along a route that later formed part of the Overland Trail, the traffic artery of the 1849 gold rush.

Josiah Holbrook, Connecticut-born educational reformer, founded in Millbury, Mass., the first "American Lyceum," a system of popular adult education. (One hundred branches were established during the next two years. After 1890 the movement was gradually absorbed into the Chautauqua system.)

The first experimental steam locomotive was built by John Stevens of Hoboken, N. J.

The disappearance and alleged murder of one William Morgan, a Mason of New York who had published the secrets of Freemasonry, brought into existence the political Anti-Masonic Party. (During the presidential campaign of 1831 the party stoutly opposed Henry Clay, the Republican nominee and a Mason. It merged with the Whig Party in 1834.)

Sing Sing, New York State penitentiary at Ossining on the Hudson, was built by convicts.

American colonists in Texas announced their independence from Mexico and named their settlements the Republic of Fredonia.

The first season of Italian opera in the United States at the Park Theatre, New York, ended (Sept. 30) after 10 months of presentation. Some 80 performances of nine operas by Rossini, Mozart, Zingarelli, and Garcia were given. "Il Barbiere di Siviglia" was sung completely 24 times.

James Henry Hackett, who abandoned a successful mercantile career to become the first outstanding native American actor, made (Mar. 1) his stage debut in New York at the Park Theatre. He played Justice Woodcock in Arne's well-known ballad opera "Love in a Village" with his wife, the former actress Miss Leesugg, whom he married in 1819. He was followed (June 23) at the same theatre by a 20-year-old rival, Edwin Forrest, who began his career as a popular American tragedian as Othello.

James Fenimore Cooper published his best-seller, "The Last of the Mohicans," the second of the Leather-Stocking Tales, which derive their name from the long deerskin leggings worn by the hero Natty Bumppo.

The first New York performance of Shakespeare's play "A Midsummer Night's Dream" was given (Nov. 9) at the Park Theatre.

࿊ 1827

The Coal Black Rose. w., m., anon. Firth & Hall [ca. 1827]; P. Maverick [ca. 1829]. (Popularized by the Negro minstrel George Washington Dixon at Albany, N. Y., about 1827. The song was attributed to one White Snyder in the Maverick edition.)

The Merry Swiss Boy. Tyrolese song. w., translated by William Ball. m., arranged by Ignaz Moscheles (in his: "Tyrolese Melodies"). London: Willis & Co. [1827?]

The Minstrel's Return from the War. w., m., James Hill Hewitt. James Hewitt [ca. 1827]. (The composer was the son of the well-known New York publisher. The song is reprinted in John Tasker Howard's "Program of Early and Mid-Nineteenth Century American Songs," New York, 1931, p. 28-30.)

My Long-Tail Blue. w., m., anon. Atwill's Music Saloon [ca. 1827]; J. L. Hewitt [ca. 1827]. (Popularized by the Negro minstrels George Washington Dixon and William Pennington.)

The United States made an unsuccessful attempt to purchase Texas from Mexico.

The New York State Legislature abolished (July 4) slavery in the State.

In Gurleyville, Conn., the first successful silk mill was established, and a veritable craze developed in the Connecticut and Willimantic valleys for raising mulberry trees to feed the silkworms.

Madame Francisque Hutin, "of the Opera House, Paris," introduced (Feb. 7) French ballet for the first time on the American stage in New York at the Bowery (then New York) Theatre, and flabbergasted the first nighters by her flimsy attire. She was followed (Mar. 1) at the same theatre by M. and Mme. Achille, also "from the Opera House, Paris," and presently (June 27) by the later incomparable Mlle. Celeste, then a young danseuse. The new style of dancing eliminated from the stage the prevalent English type.

French art being the major attraction of the time, the French Opera Company from New Orleans gave seasons of opera in New York, Philadelphia, and other cities.

"The Youth's Companion" was founded in Boston as a weekly magazine for young people. (Long a popular publication to which Tennyson, Hardy, Kipling, Louisa Alcott, Whittier, Theodore Roosevelt, Robert Louis Stevenson, Jules Verne, Jack London, Woodrow Wilson, and others contributed, it ceased publication after 102 years in 1929.)

Audubon began the publication (1827-38) of his elephant folio edition of drawings, "The Birds of America."

The United States complained about the eighth depression since 1790; running true to form, it lasted three years.

1828

Oh! No, We Never Mention Her. w., m., Thomas Haynes Bayly. E. Riley [1828]. (Published earlier in London. The tune and the words were later reprinted under the title "O No, I Never Mention Her" in a small song collection "The Musical Carcanet," Collins & Hanay, New York, 1832, p. 11.)

Tyrolese Evening Hymn. w., Felicia Dorothea Hemans. m., Augusta Browne (Garrett). Boston: C. Bradlee, cop. 1828.

Congress passed an obnoxious tariff bill, raising prices up to 44 per cent. Popularly called the Tariff of Abominations, it was beneficial to no one and particularly harmful to the South. It helped to pattern the events that were to lead to the Civil War.

In protest against the tariff, Vice-President John Caldwell Calhoun of South Carolina resigned. A defender of slavery and the theory of states' rights, he declared in his "South Carolina Exposition" that the "United States is not a union of the people, but a league or compact between sovereign states, any of which has the right to judge when the compact is broken and to pronounce any law null and void which violates its conditions."

On the nation's anniversary (July 4), President John Quincy Adams turned the first earth of the Chesapeake and Ohio Canal, an artificial waterway 184 miles long from Washington, D. C., to Cumberland, Md. (The construction was completed in 1850.)

On the same day, the Baltimore & Ohio Railroad inaugurated the first passenger service with horse-drawn cars over wooden rails covered with iron.

Mechanics in Philadelphia organized a workingmen's party.

Varnish was first introduced in the United States. So, too, damask linen and straw paper.

Peter Cooper founded his famous iron works in Baltimore.

After the collapse of the Nashoba Community (1825-28) in Tennessee, Frances Wright continued to disturb the American peace of mind with her lectures on women's rights, birth control, emancipation of Negroes, equal distribution ot wealth, and sundry other then startling topics. (She left the United States in 1830, only to return in 1836 and resume her activities.)

Noah Webster published his mammoth two-volume philological work, "An American Dictionary of the English Language."

The Greek Relief Society was organized in New York by Mrs. Sarah Platt (Haines) Doremus to aid the movement for autonomy in Greece.

The Musical Fund Society, New York, performed Beethoven's Third Symphony ("Eroica") as a septet.

The National Academy of Design was founded in New York by 30 artists with Samuel Morse, later the inventor of the telegraph, as president.

Niblo's Garden, a theatre in New York which was identified for more than half a century with every artist of significance, was opened (July 4) as the Sans Souci by the restaurateur William Niblo. (The theatre was twice destroyed by fire, in 1846 and in 1848.)

A group of Winnebago Indians visited President Adams at the White House.

ᢓᢁ 1829

From Greenland's Icy Mountains. Hymn. Tune: "Missionary Hymn"; also "Heber." w., Reginald Heber. m., Lowell Mason (in: "The Boston Handel and Haydn Society Collection of Sacred Music," 7th ed. p. 235). Boston: Richardson and Lord, 1829.

Love's Ritornella (The Brigand). w., J[ames] R[obinson] Planché. m., T[homas Simpson] Cooke. London: Chappell & Co. [1829.] ("The Brigand" was a musical play, produced at Covent Garden Theatre, London, 1829. The above song, also known as "Gentle Zitella," was reviewed in the musical journal "The Harmonicon," London, 1830, p. 90. Planché was an English playwright and author of French descent, and the librettist of Weber's famous opera "Oberon," produced in London, 1826. The song immediately became popular in England, and was reprinted in America.)

Serenade—*original German title:* Ständchen (No. 4 in: Schwanengesang). German words, Ludwig Rellstab. m., Franz Schubert. Vienna: Tobias Haslinger [1829].

There's Nothing True but Heaven. w., Thomas Moore. m., Oliver Shaw. Providence, R. I.: the author [Olive Shaw], cop. 1829.

General Andrew Jackson, Democrat, of South Carolina, was inaugurated 7th President. He was popularly known as "Old Hickory."

Canals opened everywhere in the industrial East as aids to shipping and trade—among them the Delaware & Chesapeake, the Delaware & Hudson, and the Oswego in New York, the Farmington in Connecticut, and the Cumberland & Oxford in Maine.

Ironmaster Peter Cooper built the first practical American steam locomotive—the "Tom Thumb," so-called because of its size, which made (in Sept.) a 13-mile trial run in Baltimore on the Baltimore & Ohio tracks in 1 hour, 12 minutes.

William Cullen Bryant was appointed editor of the New York "Evening Post," a post which he held for nearly 50 years (until 1878).

Kit (Christopher) Carson, Kentucky frontiersman, was coming into prominence as a Santa Fe guide for the first overland expeditions to California.

Francis Lieber, German-born political writer and educator, began the publication of the "Encyclopedia Americana." (Completed in 13 volumes in 1833.)

A musical convention was held in Concord N. H., by the local Central Musical Society.

W. A. Burt patented a typewriter.

The fabulous adventures of Mike Fink, a boatman on the Ohio and Mississippi rivers, began appearing in print.

James Fenimore Cooper brought out his Connecticut Indian romance, "The Wept of Wish-ton-Wish." (An anonymous theatrical version, produced in 1834, held the boards for many years.)

Edwin Forrest offered a prize of $500 and the usual half of the third night's proceeds for the "best Tragedy, in five acts, of which the hero, or principal character shall be an aboriginal of this country." The prize-winning play was John Augustus Stone's "Metamora, or, The Last of the Wampanoags," which was produced (Dec. 15) in New York at the Park Theatre, and long remained a popular melodrama on the American stage. (It was parodied in 1847 by John Brougham's highly amusing burlesque, "Metamora, or, The Last of the Pollywogs.")

Richard Penn Smith was a prolific Philadelphia playwright this year, producing "William Penn, or, The Elm Tree," "The Eighth of January," "The Disowned," and "The Sentinels, or, The Two Sergeants."

Sidney Smith, eccentric Episcopalian clergyman and maker of famous witticisms, wrote in the "Edinburgh Review," Jan., 1820: "In the four quarters of the globe, who reads an American book? or goes to an American play? or looks at an American picture or statue?" Now, nine years later, two industrious Massachusetts writers showed what the young country had to offer in literature. Samuel Kettell edited a three-volume anthology "Specimens of American Poetry" from Cotton Mather to Whittier, and Samuel Lorenzo Knapp brought out his diffuse and padded "Lectures on American Literature," an early attempt, nonetheless, to present the subject.

1830

I Know a Bank Where the Wild Thyme Blows. Duet for soprano and alto with piano acc. w., William Shakespeare. m., Charles Edward Horn. E. Riley [1830 or 1831]. (The words are taken from "A Midsummer Night's Dream.")

Jim Crow. w., m., anon. Atwill's Music Saloon [ca. 1829]; Baltimore: Geo. Willig, Jr. [ca. 1829-30]. (The words and music have been ascribed to Thomas Dartmouth (Daddy) Rice, the famous Negro minstrel, who introduced the piece as a song and dance around 1830.)

My Heart and Lute. w., Thomas Moore (sometimes incorrectly attributed to J. P. Kemble). m., Sir Henry Rowley Bishop. (Composed in 1830.)

The Pilgrim Fathers—*better known as:* The Landing of the Pilgrims; *also as:* The Breaking Waves Dashed High. w., Felicia Dorothea Hemans. m., Augusta Browne (Garrett). DuBois & Stodart [ca. 1830]. (An English edition, publisher unnamed, was listed in "The Harmonicon," London, 1831, p. 78, under "New Musical Works" published in March.)

Sparkling and Bright. w. [Charles Fenno Hoffman], publised anonymously—poetry from the "New York American." m., James B. Taylor. T. Birch [183-?].

The U. S. Naval Observatory was established (Dec. 6).

A 21-year-old Harvard graduate named Oliver Wendell Holmes was suddenly catapulted into national prominence. His poem "Old Ironsides" aroused public sentiment to a point which prevented the dismantling of the old, unseaworthy frigate "Constitution" that had been launched in 1797 in Boston and had been a heroic campaigner in the War of 1812.

At the Jefferson Day Dinner, President Jackson in reply to Calhoun's speech that placed liberty above the Union reaffirmed national solidarity with the words: "Our Federal Union; it must be preserved!"

The Mormon Church, known officially as "The Church of Jesus Christ of Latter-Day Saints," was organized (Apr. 6) by the Vermont-born prophet Joseph Smith in Fayette, Seneca County, N. Y., and published its scriptures, the "Book of Mormon," in Palmyra, N. Y.

The "Tom Thumb" (1829) steam locomotive ran (Aug. 25) its famous race with a horse-drawn car. The horse won; the engine, which was ahead for a while, broke down.

March 16 was the dullest day in New York Stock Exchange history; only 31 shares changed hands.

Cincinnati was called "Porkopolis" because it was the nation's greatest meat-packing center.

Louis Antoine Godey brought out the first issue of his monthly "Godey's Lady's Book," the forerunner of women's magazines, incorporating fiction, etiquette, articles on sewing, etc. (It was transferred to New York in 1892 and ceased publication in 1898.)

The word Hoosier was added to the American vocabulary, when John Finley used it for probably the first time in print in his poem "The Hoosier Nest."

The "Boston Daily Evening Transcript" was founded. (Ceased publication in 1941.)

Sarah Josepha Hale published her lines "Mary Had a Little Lamb" in "Poems for Our Children."

Sheba Smith, editor of the "Portland Courier," Me., created the character of Major Jack Downing, a Down East Yankee, who was a prototype of Hosea Biglow of Lowell's "Biglow Papers" (1846-67), David

Harum of Edward Noyes Westcott (1898), Mr. Dooley of Finley Peter Dunne (1898-1919) and, in real life, of Will Rogers.

James Hall, circuit judge, banker, and frontier Illinois editor, brought out "The Illinois Monthly Magazine," the first literary journal to be published west of Ohio.

"To inspire genius and encourage talent" in the native American composer, in consequence of the recent success of foreign language opera, the New York musical journal "The Euterpiad" offered (in July) "a premium of $500 for the best opera; the music as well as the words to be original, and the opera to contain three acts, an overture, and a variety of songs, duets, trios, choruses, etc., with instrumental accompaniments." The competition was scheduled to close on Jan. 1, 1831. (Nothing seems to have come of the noble effort.)

The play "Rip Van Winkle" was running in New York at the Park Theatre.

The banjo is reputed to have been "invented" about this time by the Negro minstrel Joel W. Sweeny.

As a sample of early theatrical production magnitude, an elephant and her calf were introduced on the stage during the performance of "The Forty Thieves" at the Walnut Street Theatre in Philadelphia. At the Arch Street Theatre in the same city, a living rhinoceros was part of the cast of "The Lover's Test."

The national population was 12,866,020.

₰ 1831

Abolitionist movements, directed against Negro slavery, were dividing the nation. In the Virginia legislature, a hotly debated bill providing for the colonization of freed slaves and recommending private emancipation was defeated by only one vote. In Boston, the presently powerful New England Anti-Slavery Society was founded by William Lloyd Garrison. He began at the same time the publication of a widely circulated weekly, "The Liberator," which continued to appear for 34 years (1831-65) in spite of violent opposition.

Some sixty Negro slaves, headed by Nat Turner, who believed himself divinely appointed to lead his people to freedom, terrorized Southampton County, Va. He and other leaders were finally captured and hanged after 61 white persons had lost their lives during the insurrection.

The Sac and Fox Indians resisted the government's attempt to transfer them west of the Mississippi in accordance with a treaty of 1804. Under their chief Black Hawk they involved the United States in hostilities in which the future President of the Union, Abraham Lincoln, and the future president of the Confederacy, Jefferson Davis, served together under Zachary Taylor, another future President of the United States.

The Mormons began to move westward; some established themselves
in Kirtland, O., while others continued into Missouri.

The first known transportation of mail by railroad occurred (in Nov.)
on the South Carolina (now the Southern) Railroad.

Train service by steam locomotive was established (Aug. 9) in New
York State between Albany and Schenectady by the Mohawk & Hudson
Railroad; the "De Witt Clinton" was the first steam locomotive in the
State.

The first streetcars in the United States made their appearance in New
York; they were horse-drawn.

New York University, for men, was founded. (It is now coeducational.)

The "Spirit of the Times" came out in New York as a journal devoted to
"the Turf, Agriculture, Field Sports, Literature, and the Stage." (Ceased
publication in 1858.)

Delaware dramatist Robert Montgomery Bird wrote his most popular
play "The Gladiator" for Edwin Forrest, who acted the role of Spartacus
more than 1,000 times. The jealous actor, whose partisans precipitated
the Astor Place riots in New York in 1849, guarded against the publication
of the play all his life lest it be performed by a rival. The play was first
published in 1919.

Ex-President James Monroe, aged 72, died in New York City. He was
the third former President to die on the Fourth of July.

⅔➤ 1832

America. w., Samuel Francis Smith. m., tune: "God Save the King,"
attributed to Henry Carey. Boston: Carter, Hendee & Co. [cop. 1832]
(in: Lowell Mason, "The Choir, or, Union Collection of Church Music,"
p. 273). (The words were written in February, 1831, and first sung at a
children's Fourth of July celebration in Park Street Church, Boston.)

The Bloom Is on the Rye—*better known as:* My Pretty Jane. w., Edward Fitzball. m., Sir Henry Rowley Bishop. (Composed in 1832.)

Boylston. Hymn tune. m., Lowell Mason. Boston: Carter, Hendee &
Co. [cop. 1832] (in: Lowell Mason, "The Choir, or, Union Collection of
Church Music," p. 165).

My Faith Looks Up to Thee. Hymn; tune: "Olivet." w., Ray Palmer.
m., Lowell Mason. Utica, N. Y.: Hastings & Tracy & W. Williams, 1832
(in: Thomas Hastings and Lowell Mason, "Spiritual Songs for Social
Worship," p. 94).

Rock of Ages. Hymn; tune: "Toplady." w., Augustus Montague Top-lady. m., Thomas Hastings. Utica, N. Y.: Hastings & Tracy & W. Williams, 1832 (in: Thomas Hastings and Lowell Mason, "Spiritual Songs for Social Worship," p. 84).

President Jackson vetoed the bill for rechartering the second Bank of the United States (1816), which came to an end with the expiration of its charter in 1836.

Congress enacted a new tariff bill that repealed the law of 1828 ("Tariff of Abominations") but left the rates substantially unchanged.

In retaliation, the South Carolina Legislature at the instigation of former Vice-President Calhoun passed (in Nov.) an Ordnance of Nullification and threatened to secede from the Union if President Jackson, who had been so authorized by Congress, took military measures to enforce the law.

The Black Hawk War (1831-32) ended.

The first national convention for the nomination of a presidential candidate was held. It replaced the Congressional caucus. In the national election President Jackson was re-elected.

"Ann McKim," the first clipper ship, was built for the China trade, and a new era in shipbuilding was launched.

The first steam locomotive in the Mississippi Valley was placed (Sept. 17) in operation on the Pontchartrain Railroad that ran from Elysian Fields Street, New Orleans, to Lake Pontchartrain, Milneburg. The engine was the "Pontchartrain," built in England.

Bassford, a table maker, opened in New York a billiard parlor with 20 tables, and it was here that pinpool and 15-ball pool were introduced. These superseded the old two-ball pool of early days.

Two fraternal societies of European origin appeared on the American scene—the Ancient Order of Hibernians (from Ireland), and the Ancient Order of Foresters (from England).

American readers of Mrs. Frances Trollope's new book, "Domestic Manners of the Americans," published in London, were incensed by her opinions of American culture and business methods, as well as by her anti-slavery sentiments. The press of the country was flooded with bitter rejoinders. Her observations were based on a three years' (1827-30) residence in Cincinnati, where she had operated a fancy-goods shop.

William Dunlap published his indispensable "History of the American Theatre," derived largely from personal associations with the stage as a playwright, manager, and actor.

The handsome, athletic, English actor Charles Kemble and his highly talented daughter, Fanny, played to great applause on American stages. Since the days of Malibran (1825-26), no actress had made so profound an impression. The illustrious pair made their debuts in New York at the

Park Theatre—the 57-year-old father in "Hamlet" (Sept. 17) and his 23-year-old daughter in "Fazio" (Sept. 18). They appeared (Sept. 20) together in "Romeo and Juliet," in which the father replaced at the last minute an inadequate actor in the part of Romeo.

The second American season of Italian opera opened (Oct. 6) in New York at the Richmond Hill Theater at Varick and Charlton Streets, formerly the residence of Aaron Burr. The company later went to Philadelphia and played at the Chestnut Street Theatre, renamed "Italian Opera House."

The Ravel family (Antoine, Dominique, Gabriel, Jean, Jerome, and Julie) from "the principal theatres of France, Germany, Italy, Prussia, Holland, and lastly before the King of Sardinia" came to America and were long identified with "Rope Dancing, Herculean Feats, and Pantomime Ballets."

Cholera broke out in the East and closed the theatres during the summer months.

In the fall Illinois State elections, young Abraham Lincoln (then 23 years old) ran for his first public office and was defeated.

₰ 1833

Ching A Ring Chaw. w., m., anon. Baltimore: Geo. Willig, Jr. [ca. 1833.] (Also published under the title "Sambo's Address to His Bred'ren," by T. Birch, New York.)

Long Time Ago [or, **Shinbone Alley**]. w., m., anon. (Popularized by Thomas (Daddy) Rice in his "Ethiopian Opera," 1833; published and copyrighted 1835 by George Endicott, New York, with piano accompaniment by William Clifton.)

Rise, Gentle Moon. w., James Robinson Planché. m., John Braham. (The song was composed for the performance of Planché's play "Charles the Twelfth," produced at Drury Lane Theatre, London, 1833. See "Love's Ritornella" under 1829.)

President Andrew Jackson began his second term.

Congress passed (in Feb.) a compromise tariff bill to appease the South Carolina Legislature, which then repealed its Ordinance of Nullification (1832).

Secretary of the Treasury Roger Brooke Taney withdrew the government's deposits from the Bank of the United States, after President Jackson vetoed (1832) the bill for rechartering it.

The American Anti-Slavery Society was established in Philadelphia by the New England Anti-Slavery Society and other sympathetic groups (1831).

Fort Dearborn, Ill., became the incorporated village of Chicago.

"The Sun" was founded in New York as a penny daily. (After other mergers, it became the "New York World-Telegram and Sun" in 1950.)

The Academy of Music, Boston, an educational organization that enrolled 2,200 pupils during its first year, was founded by Lowell Mason.

The Improved Order of Red Men was established (Oct. 14) in Baltimore.

"The Knickerbocker Magazine" was founded in New York as a monthly literary journal. (It ceased publication in 1865. Its contributors included many prominent American writers and poets.)

Tyrone Power, celebrated Irish comedian, made (Aug. 28) his American debut in "The Irish Ambassador" in New York at the Park Theatre. (In 1841 he sailed from New York on the steamer "President," which was lost at sea. He was the grandfather of the American actor of the same name and the great-grandfather of the current film actor.)

In Lowell, Mass., a group of players from Boston opened a theatre and were promptly thrown into jail for not "pursuing an honorable and lawful profession."

೮ಹ 1834

By the Margin of Fair Zurich's Waters (Beulah Spa). w., anon. m., James Gaspard Maeder. ("Beulah Spa" was a play by Charles Dance, produced at the Bowery Theatre, New York, Sept. 18, 1834. The song was later interpolated by Maeder in his opera "The Peri"—see 1852. The words and the tune are reprinted in Grenville Vernon, "Yankee Doodle-Doo," New York, 1927, p. 137-38.)

Jesus, Lover of My Soul. Hymn. Tune: "Martyn." w., Charles Wesley. m., Simeon Butler Marsh. (Composed in 1834.)

Zip Coon—*also known as:* **Turkey in the Straw.** w., m., anon. [claimed by (1) Bob Farrell; (2) George Washington Dixon.] Atwill's Music Saloon, cop, 1834 by Thos. Birch.

Cyrus Hall McCormick, Virginia-born inventor, patented a practical reaper, which he had perfected in 1831.

Stephen Fuller Austin, founder of American settlements in Texas which was then under Mexican rule, went to Mexico City to negotiate for their political independence. He was there imprisoned for a year by Mexican President Santa Anna.

A new kind of cigar, called the locofoco and invented by John Marck of New York, came on the market. It was a self-lighting cigar which had at one end a substance that was ignited by friction.

Brooklyn, N. Y., was chartered as a city. (It became in 1898 a borough of Greater New York.)

The Church of St. Louis of France (Roman Catholic) in St. Louis, Mo., was dedicated. (The edifice was the Roman Catholic cathedral until 1914 when it was replaced by a new church.)

A music school was opened in the village of Chicago by a Miss Wyeth.

Two literary journals that published contributions from Poe, Longfellow, and others were founded—"The Ladies' Companion" in New York and the "Southern Literary Messenger" in Richmond, Va. (They ceased publication in 1844 and in 1864, respectively.)

The "New Yorker Staats Zeitung" was founded in New York as a German language weekly. (It became a daily in 1849 and is still published —the oldest continuous German newspaper in the United States.)

The first of the 28 Rollo stories for children by Jacob Abbott, Massachusetts Congregational clergyman, made its appearance.

George Bancroft, Massachusetts statesman and scholar, began the publication of his monumental "History of the United States" (completed in 10 vols. in 1876).

An attempt to establish Italian grand opera permanently in the United States was made in New York by building a sumptuous theatre—the Italian Opera House, which opened (Nov. 18) with the first American performance of Rossini's "La Gazza Ladra." After eight months, the venture was abandoned as a fiasco. The total expenses were $81,054.98; the receipts amounted to $51,780.89.

ࣷ 1835

Clare de Kitchen [or, De Kentucky Screamer]. w., m., anon. Boston: C. Bradlee [ca. 1835]. (Frequently printed in songsters after 1836; based upon a song of the same title published and copyrighted 1832 by George Willig, Jr., Baltimore.)

Long Time Ago [or, Shinbone Alley]. See 1833.

Old Rosin the Beau. w., m., anon. (The song has enjoyed a consistent popularity since the 1830s, and is still to be found in collections of old-time songs. An edition, arr. by J. C. Beckell, was published by Osbourn's Music Saloon, Philadelphia, 1838; and versions were printed by George Willig, Jr., Baltimore, and other publishers. The title is also spelled "Old Rosin the Bow.")

See, Gentle Patience Smiles on Pain. Hymn; tune: "Federal Street." w., Anne Steele. m., Henry Kemble Oliver. Boston: Carter, Hendee & Co., 1835 (in: Lowell Mason, "The Boston Academy's Collection of Church Music," p. 275).

Roger Brooke Taney of Maryland succeeded John Marshall as Chief Justice of the Supreme Court. (Taney was a brother-in-law of Francis Scott Key, author of "The Star-Spangled Banner.")

Samuel Colt, American inventor, patented the revolver, the "six-shooter" of desperado legends.

The government's attempt to transfer the Seminole Indians of Florida west of the Mississippi started a seven-year conflict, known as the second Seminole War. (The first occurred in 1817-18.)

A mob in South Carolina broke into the United States mails and burned copies of the abolitionist weekly "The Liberator," along with effigies of its editor, William Lloyd Garrison.

The Liberty Bell in Philadelphia cracked (July 8) as it tolled for the funeral of Chief Justice John Marshall.

Texas proclaimed officially (Nov. 13) its independence from Mexico, and called itself the Lone Star Republic, after its flag, until its admission to the Union in 1845.

Antimonopolistic New York City Democrats were called Locofocos, after the recently (1834) invented self-lighting cigars, when they persisted in conducting one of their meetings by the light of candles and locofoco cigars after the lights in the hall had been extinguished by the regular, or Tammany, Democrats.

A fire in New York destroyed property estimated to be worth $20,000,-000. Beginning in a store at Pearl and Merchant (Hanover) Streets, it lasted two days (Dec. 16-17), ravaged 17 blocks (52 acres), and destroyed 674 buildings including the Stock Exchange, Merchants' Exchange, Post Office, and the South Dutch Church.

The public was agog over an article in the New York "Sun" (Aug.), written by Richard Adams Locke, a reporter, which alleged that the astronomer Sir John Herschel had discovered the existence of men and animals on the moon. It was a publicity stunt, but the hoax brought a group of Yale scientists into the investigation and caused Poe to abandon the writing of his story "Hans Pfahl."

Oberlin College, Ohio, became the first institution of higher learning to admit Negro students.

Phineas Taylor Barnum made his first appearance on the stage as assistant to the magician Signor Vivalla. A few months later Barnum leased for $1,000 the services of an old Negress named Joice Heith, whom he billed as "Washington's Nurse," and started his career as an impresario at Niblo's Garden.

Poe's story "Berenice" was published in the newly (1834) founded

"Southern Literary Messenger" at Richmond, Va.; in December he was appointed editor of the magazine at a salary of $15 per week. (He was forced to resign in 1837 because of his objectionable drinking habits, but in that short time his literary contributions and provocative criticisms raised the magazine's subscriptions from 500 to more than 3,500.)

James Gordon Bennett launched the "New York Herald." Among other things, he was largely responsible for society pages in United States newspapers. (The "Herald" merged with the "New-York Tribune" in 1924, becoming the "Herald Tribune.")

Nathaniel Currier, American printer and lithographer, established in New York a firm for making "colored engravings for the people." (He took as a partner in 1850 the artist J. Merritt Ives, but continued to label his prints "N. Currier." After 1857 the firm was called Currier and Ives.)

Henry Charles Carey published his "Essay on the Rate of Wages," a significant study in which he disputed the theories of Ricardo and of Malthus. (He subsequently pursued the subject in other publications.)

The German Männerchor of Philadelphia was founded—now the oldest of its kind in the United States.

The American public was going wild over tall stories about colorful frontiersmen like Daniel Boone, Kit Carson, Mike Fink, Simon Kenton, David (Davy) Crockett, and others.

The 19-year-old Boston-born opera singer Charlotte Cushman made her first stage appearance (Apr. 8) in "The Marriage of Figaro" in Boston. Her debut (Sept. 12) as an actress was made as Lady Macbeth in New York at the Bowery Theatre. She was one of the earliest American actresses to reach stardom.

₹~ 1836

The Carrier Dove. w., anon. m., D[aniel] Johnson. J. F. Atwill, cop. 1836. (The publisher brought out a new edition, cop. 1841, with "Additional words by the Rev. J. N. Maffit." The song provoked an "Answer to Carrier Dove," w., "A Lady," m., J[ames] G[aspard] Maeder, Henry Prentiss, Boston, cop. 1841.)

Corn Cobs Twist Your Hair. w., anon. m., tune: "Yankee Doodle." George Endicott, cop. 1836.

The Light of Other Days (The Maid of Artois). w., Alfred Bunn. m., Michael William Balfe. (Balfe's opera "The Maid of Artois" was produced at the Drury Lane Theatre, London, May 27, 1836. The song was made famous by the celebrated Mme. Malibran who, with her father Manuel Garcia, introduced Italian opera in New York in 1825. The opera was first given in the United States eleven years later, in New York at the Park Theatre, Nov. 5, 1847, and in Philadelphia at the Walnut Street Theatre, Dec. 29, 1847. Bunn later wrote the libretto of Balfe's opera "The Bohemian Girl.")

Rory O'More. w., Samuel Lover. m., "arranged" by Samuel Lover; also attributed to Robert Owenson. (Written before Lover published his novel "Rory O'More" which appeared in 1837 in London and was produced in dramatic form at the Adelphi Theatre in the same year. Lover included the poem in his "Songs and Ballads," Chapman and Hall, London, 1839, p. 7-8.)

The Whig Party, political rival of the Democratic Party, was formally organized by Henry Clay and Daniel Webster.

By this time the erstwhile "Republican" Party had pretty well changed its name to "Democratic." (The present-day "Republican" Party evolved from Federalists, through Whigs, into its current form in the early 1850s.)

Arkansas was admitted (June 15) as the 25th State.

Congress passed the "Gag Resolutions" prohibiting petitions against slavery.

Mexican President Santa Anna led 4,000 troops into Texas (then Mexican territory) to subdue American secessionists and sympathizers, and met with stubborn resistance at a Franciscan mission converted into a fort. This fort is now the Alamo in present-day San Antonio. After 11 days' siege, he massacred its 150 defenders in a desperate battle (Mar. 6) and burned their bodies. Six Americans, among them "Davy" Crockett, survived the carnage and surrendered, but were shot down by Santa Anna's orders. (Crockett once uttered the oft-quoted remark: "Be sure you are right, then go ahead.")

Texas adopted (Mar. 17) a constitution. Samuel (Sam) Houston, Virginia-born soldier, congressman, and former governor of Tennessee, was elected president. A month later (Apr. 21), with a force of 800 men, he defeated at San Jacinto a Mexican army of 3,000. Santa Anna now recognized by treaty Texan independence and the boundary of Texas along the Rio Grande River.

Mount Holyoke College, for women, South Hadley, Mass., was founded. It is the oldest women's college in the United States.

Union Theological Seminary, New York, was established.

Henry Wadsworth Longfellow was appointed professor of modern languages and literature at Harvard. (He occupied the chair for nearly 18 years.)

The first of William Holmes McGuffey's famed "Eclectic Readers" appeared. (Six readers were published between 1836-57. They reached their peak sales from the Civil War period to the end of the century, selling millions of copies; the last copyright on them was taken out in 1900 by the American Book Company.)

The "Philadelphia Public Ledger" was founded as the first penny daily in that city. In Toledo, O., the "Blade" appeared as a daily newspaper. In Cincinnati, the "Volksblatt" became the first German language daily in the United States.

Richard Hildreth, Massachusetts-born jurist, published what is believed to be the earliest antislavery novel, "The Slave, or, Memoirs of Archy Moore." (Immensely popular, it was reprinted under the titles "The White Slave" and "Archy Moore," and did much to further the abolitionist movement.)

John Humphrey Noyes, disbarred Vermont preacher, established his socialized community of Bible Communists at Putney, Vt. (It dissolved in 1846 when charges of adultery, arising from its unorthodox system of marriage, were brought against it.)

Ralph Waldo Emerson and his friends were meeting informally at his home in Concord, Mass., to discuss philosophy, theology, religion, and literature, calling themselves the Symposium. Outsiders called it the Transcendental Club. The meetings were continued for seven or eight years.

Louis Napoleon, later Emperor Napoleon III of France, visited New York.

ᘓᕄ 1837

The Brave Old Oak. [w., Henry Fothergill Chorley.] m. [Edward James Loder], arr. by Henry Russell. James L. Hewitt, cop. 1837.

The Friar of the Olden Time—*better known as:* **I Am a Friar of Orders Grey.** w. [John] O'Keefe. m., "from an old manuscript book," arr. by Henry Russell. J. L. Hewitt & Co., cop. 1837. (Described in the title as "a ballad, supposed to have been written in the 12th century." The words are from O'Keefe's musical play "Merry Sherwood.")

Hark, Brothers, Hark. w., J. H. Willis. m., John Hill Hewitt. Cincinnati: W. C. Peters, cop. 1837; Philadelphia: Geo. W. Hewitt & Co., cop. 1837.

On Wings of Song—*original German title:* **Auf Flügeln des Gesanges** (no. 2 in: Sechs Gesänge, op. 34). German words, Heinrich Heine. m., Felix Mendelssohn. Leipzig: Breitkopf & Härtel [1837].

'Tis Dawn, the Lark Is Singing. w., anon. m., George James Webb. Boston: J. H. Wilkins & R. B. Carter [cop. 1837] (in: George James Webb and Lowell Mason, "The Odeon," p. 8). (The music is now generally sung to the words of George Duffield, Jr., "Stand Up, Stand Up for Jesus" and is called "Webb," or "Goodwin," in present-day hymnbooks. The hymn, "The Morning Light Is Breaking," by Samuel Francis Smith, the author of "America," was set to the music in Moses L. Scudder, "The Wesleyan Psalmist, or, Songs of Canaan," D. S. King, Boston, cop. 1842.)

Woodman! Spare That Tree! w., George Pope Morris. m., Henry Russell. Firth & Hall, cop. 1837.

A Yankee Ship and a Yankee Crew. w., J. S. Jones, Esq. m., C. M. King, Esq. Boston: Parker & Ditson, cop. 1873.

Martin Van Buren, Democrat, of New York, was inaugurated 8th President. Since Van Buren had been a widower since 1818, his son's wife, née Angelica Singleton and a cousin of Dolly Madison, was White House hostess. (Van Buren was the first President to be born an American citizen.)

Congress stabilized (Jan. 18) the American silver dollar at 412½ grains. (Its previous weight, 416 grains, had been fixed by the Act of 1792.)

Michigan was admitted (Jan. 26) as the 26th State.

During the Canadian Rebellion, loyalists crossed the St. Lawrence to the United States and burned the American vessel "Caroline," which carried supplies to the insurgents. War between the United States and Great Britain was narrowly averted.

Samuel Morse demonstrated to Congress his electric telegraph. (Morse, a painter of portraits and historical scenes and a sculptor, abandoned the arts for science when he became interested in telegraphy during a voyage from Havre to New York in 1832.)

In a collision on the Mississippi the steamer "Monmouth" sank with a loss of 234 lives.

The town of Chicago, with an area of 10 square miles and a population of 3,297, was incorporated as a city.

The Annapolis, Md., State Library was founded.

Hiram and John Pitts of Maine patented an improved reaper that separated grain from straw and chaff and also cleaned it.

The "Baltimore Sun" and the "New Orleans Picayune" were founded as dailies. The latter took its name from an old Spanish coin then in use, worth 6¼ cents—the price of the paper. The "Connecticut Courant," the oldest newspaper in the United States, which had been published as a weekly since 1764, became the "Hartford Daily Courant."

The American reading public was becoming increasingly indignant over the opinions of visiting British authors. Mrs. Trollope had offended in 1832. Now Harriet Martineau aroused displeasure with her latest London publication, "Society in America," a recording of the impressions she had gathered during an extended tour of the United States in 1834-36.

Not only were her observations and antislavery sentiments made subjects of attack, but her character was assailed by William Gilmore Simms, a Charleston, S. C., author, who also so lost his temper that he ridiculed her deafness. Another British author who incurred violent resentment was Captain Frederick Marryat of the Royal Navy, author of popular sea stories. After certain tactless remarks and alleged improprieties, he was accused in the American press of assaulting women, insulting Henry Clay, and being a spy, and he was burned in effigy on a pile of his books in Detroit.

The piano-manufacturing firm of William Knabe in partnership with Henry Gaehle began in Baltimore.

࿓ 1838

All Things Love Thee, So Do I. w., anon. m., Charles E[dward] Horn. C. E. Horn, cop. 1838.

Annie Laurie. w., anon. m., "arranged by Finlay Dun." Edinburgh: Paterson & Roy, Music Saloon [1838] (in: Finlay Dun and John Thomson, "The Vocal Melodies of Scotland," vol. 3, p. 89-92). (The words are believed to have been written about 1688 by William Douglas of Fingland, Kirkcudbright, Scotland. The music, or the tune, was composed by Lady John Scott, née Alicia Ann Spottiswoode, wife of Lord John Montague-Douglas Scott, whom she married in 1836. She was born in 1810 at Spottiswoode, Berwickshire, Scotland, and died there on Mar. 12, 1900. For a brief biographical sketch, consult Grove's "Dictionary of Music and Musicians.")

Flow Gently, Sweet Afton—*also known as:* **Afton Water.** w., Robert Burns. m., J[ames] E. Spilman. Philadelphia: George Willig, cop. 1838. (The music of this setting is not the tune to which Burns wrote his words. Spilman's song is found in nearly all collections of old-time songs, at least in the United States.)

A Life on the Ocean Wave. w., Epes Sargent. m., Henry Russell. Hewitt & Jacques, cop. 1838.

Mary of Argyle. w., Ch[arles] Jeffreys. m., S[idney] Nelson. Philadelphia: Fiot, Meignen & Co. [ca. 1838.] (Published earlier in London.)

'Tis Home Where'er the Heart Is (Pocahontas). w., Robert Dale Owens. m., traditional air. ("Pocahontas" was a tragedy, produced at Wallack's National Theatre, New York, Feb. 8, 1838. The words and tune are reproduced in Grenville Vernon, "Yankee Doodle-Doo," New York, 1927, p. 128-29.)

When Stars Are in the Quiet Skies. w., E. L. Bulwer [Edward George Earle Lytton Bulwer-Lytton]. m., Alexander Ball. Philadelphia: W. R. Bayley, cop. 1838.

Antislavery supporters were combining their efforts about this time in a movement known as the Underground Railroad, using their homes as "stations" by means of which fugitive slaves were secretly enabled to reach freedom in the Northern States or in Canada.

Fire devastated (Apr. 27) Charleston, S. C., destroying 1,158 buildings.

The Medical College of Virginia, Richmond, Va., was founded. (Still in existence.)

Music was introduced in the Boston public schools by Lowell Mason.

The steamer "Moselle" exploded on the Ohio River in Cincinnati. One hundred and forty persons were killed.

Ralph Waldo Emerson began to attract attention as a public speaker in Boston in consequence of his Phi Beta Kappa oration (1837) and Divinity School address (1838). His opinions in the latter were received with sharply mixed feelings.

Joseph Clay Neal published the first of his "Charcoal Sketches, or, Scenes in a Metropolis," satires on Philadelphians which became popular not only in the United States, but also in England where they were reprinted by Dickens.

Donizetti's still popular opera "L'Elisir d'Amore" was performed (June 18) for the first time in the United States in New York at the Park Theatre in English.

The Sacred Music Society, New York, sang Mendelssohn's oratorio "St. Paul" (two years after its première in Düsseldorf).

Edward Bulwer-Lytton's current play, "The Lady of Lyons," was put on the boards with an all-star cast: Edwin Forrest as Claude, Mrs. Richardson as Pauline, and Charlotte Cushman as the Widow Melnotte.

J. A. Neafie and E. L. Davenport, two great figures of the theatre, made their debuts.

The first recorded theatrical performance in Chicago was given by the Mackenzie & Jefferson Company.

⁀ 1839

[**Joy to the World.**] Antioch. Hymn. [w., Isaac Watts.] m., "from Handel" [arr. by Lowell Mason]. Boston: J. H. Wilkins and R. B. Carter, 1839 (in: Lowell Mason, "The Modern Psalmist," p. 14). (The music is dated 1836 in hymnbooks—the year of its arrangement. Mr. Henry Lowell Mason, great-great grandson of Lowell Mason, replying to the present compiler's letter of inquiry, wrote: "Lowell Mason's hymn-tune arrangement, 'Antioch,' was written by him in 1836, insofar as I have been able to ascertain the date. Unfortunately Lowell Mason did not affix a date to many of his productions, but research has led me to conclude that the exact date of 'Antioch' was 1836. And the first publication in book form of the tune . . . was in his 'The Modern Psalmist' "—as noted above. The opening strain is derived from the chorus "Glory to God" in Handel's oratorio "Messiah.")

President Van Buren was empowered by Congress to resist British "invasion" when a boundary dispute along the Aroostook River between Maine and New Brunswick, Canada, nearly precipitated a war between the United States and Great Britain. It was averted by Gen. Winfield Scott.

Henry Clay is reputed to have said, when informed that his political utterances would injure his public career, "I had rather be right than be President." (He was, in fact, for many years a regular candidate for the presidential nomination. Never elected, he was defeated for the last time in 1844 by Polk.)

The Liberty Party, the first political anti-slavery organization in the United States, was formed in the Northern States to oppose William Lloyd Garrison's policy of non-political action. (The party merged in 1848 with the Free Soil Party.)

A German-Swiss military officer, Capt. John Augustus [really Johann August] Sutter was stranded (in July) in California on his way from Sitka, Alaska. He established (in Aug.) a settlement called New Helvetia on the present site of Sacramento. (He built there in 1841 a historic fort, now preserved as a museum. It was on his property that gold was discovered in 1848.)

Twelve thousand Mormons, driven from Missouri in the winter, took refuge in Hancock County, Ill., where they founded the city of Nauvoo on the banks of the Mississippi.

The British government awarded James Bogardus, American inventor, a prize for a machine for engraving postage stamps. (England issued its first official postage stamps in Jan., 1840—the first country to do so.)

The Baltimore College of Dental Surgery was established—the first institution of its kind in the world.

Abner Doubleday (later Civil War officer and colonel of the 35th Infantry, United States Army) devised at Cooperstown, N. Y., a game with bases and positions for players, thus founding modern baseball. His fixture of bases and the distances between them has never been changed.

Henry Wadsworth Longfellow brought out his first book of verse, "Voices of the Night," which at once established his reputation and popularity as a poet. A slender volume, it contained such favorites as "Hymn to the Night," "A Psalm of Life," "The Reaper and the Flowers," "Footsteps of Angels," and others.

Theodore Dwight Weld, Massachusetts abolitionist and reformer, published a tract "American Slavery as It Is," which did much to advance the antislavery cause. (It is claimed to have inspired Harriet Beecher Stowe's novel "Uncle Tom's Cabin.")

In Captain Frederick Marryat's unflattering "Diary in America" was recorded the famous joke by John Van Buren (son of the President) anent American prudery. Said Van Buren, Jr., "people even put pantalettes on piano legs."

Beethoven's opera "Fidelio" was performed (Sept. 9) for the first time in the United States in New York at the Park Theatre. The performance was in English. Later the opera was frequently played by stock companies! (One can only wonder how they managed it.)

Edwin Forrest played (Sept. 4) Edward Bulwer-Lytton's "Richelieu" at the National Theatre, New York.

ఆ 1840

Consider the Lilies. w., "selected from the Holy Scriptures." m., R[obert] Topliff. Hewitt & Jacques [ca. 1840].

Cracovienne. (A fast-moving, syncopated Polish dance of peasant origin associated with the country around Cracow, the cracovienne, or according to its native name krakoviak, enjoyed for a time a great vogue in Europe and in America. The dance was introduced to the Parisian stage during 1834-39 by the celebrated Austrian dancer Fanny Elssler, who, after appearances in London, visited the United States in 1840-43. Chopin used the traditional melody in his "Krakoviak," op. 14, for piano and orchestra, and other composers wrote variations on the tune. It is reproduced in Grove's "Dictionary of Music and Musicians" under the heading Krakoviak. Many American editions of the music were issued during Fanny Elssler's stay in the United States—by A. Fiot, Philadelphia; Hewitt & Jacques, New York; Millet's Music Saloon, New York; Geo. P. Reed, Boston, and others. The dancer also popularized the Spanish cachucha. She was the daughter of Haydn's music copyist at Esterhazy.)

The Ingle Side. [w., Hew Ainslie.] m., T. V. Wiesenthal. Philadelphia: Fiot, Meignen & Co. [ca. 1840.] (Hew Ainslie was a Scottish poet who had emigrated to the United States in 1825.)

Jim Along, Josey. w. (and m. ?), Edward Harper. Firth & Hall, cop. 1840. (Sung by the author in his play "The Free Nigger of New York" about 1838.)

Kathleen Mavourneen. w., Annie Crawford [née Barry]. m., Frederick William Nichols Crouch (in his: "Echoes of the Lake"). London [1840].

The Old Arm Chair. w., Eliza Cook. m., Henry Russell. Boston: Geo. P. Reed, cop. 1840.

Ole Tare River. w., m., anon. Boston: Henry Prentiss [ca. 1840]. (Popularized by the Negro minstrel Joel W. Sweeny, the reputed inventor of the banjo about 1830.)

The Pesky Sarpent—*also known as:* (1) **Springfield Mountain;** and (2) **On Springfield Mountain.** w., m., anon. Boston: Geo. P. Reed, cop. 1840.

Rocked in the Cradle of the Deep. w., Mrs. Willard. m., Joseph Philip Knight. Boston: C. F. Chickering, cop. 1840; New York: C. E. Horn, cop. 1840.

Tippecanoe and Tyler Too. w., Alexander C. Ross. m., tune: "Little Pigs." (Song of the Whig Party during the presidential campaign of General William Henry Harrison. John Tyler was his running mate for the vice-presidency. See 1811: "The Battle of the Wabash.")

The Two Grenadiers—*original German title:* **Die beiden Grenadiere** (No. 1 in: "Romanzen und Balladen," op. 49). German words, Heinrich Heine. m., Robert Schumann. Leipzig: Gust. Heinze [1840].

Whar Did You Cum from? w., m., anon. Firth & Hall, cop. 1840. (Popularized by Joel W. Sweeny—see above: "Ole Tare River.")

The Subtreasury was established.

Commander Charles Wilkes of the first United States Antarctic exploring expedition discovered (in Jan.-Feb.) the region named Wilkes Land.

A widespread slang phrase was "Wake me up when Kirby dies" (from the current theatrical hit "The Carpenter of Rouen").

Showmanship got into politics when the conservative Whigs shouted "Tippecanoe and Tyler too" (see above), erected log cabins to typify their "grass-roots" candidate, Harrison, and served cider to the populace.

John W. Draper is believed to have been the first American to take a photograph.

Ladies had special post-office windows and even special bowling alleys (to avoid the tobacco-chewing male).

The "National Anti-Slavery Standard" was founded in New York by the American Anti-Slavery Society as a magazine strongly Union in sympathies that advocated immediate abolition and Negro education. (Ceased publication in 1872.)

The Memphis, Tenn., "Commercial Appeal" was founded as a daily newspaper.

Books of the year included "The Pathfinder" (James Fenimore Cooper) and "Two Years Before the Mast" (Richard Henry Dana; published anonymously).

The picturesque Rainer Family, a quartet of Swiss singers (two men and two women), were entertaining American audiences throughout the United States with the mountain songs of their native land sung in costume.

John Braham, noted English tenor, and his son Charles sang on tour in the United States, but they met with meager success.

Football was played at this time as a crude game among freshmen and sophomores.

A five-year depression (the eleventh since 1790) got under way. It reached its height in 1843.

The national population was 17,069,453.

8~ 1841

Molly Bawn (Il Paddy Whack in Italia). w., m., Samuel Lover. ("Il Paddy Whack in Italia" was an English burlesque of Italian opera performed at the Lyceum Theatre, London, 1841.)

My Mother's Bible. w., George Pope Morris. m., Henry Russell. Firth & Hall, cop. 1841.

Niagara Falls. w., m., Mr. Winchell. Boston: Henry Prentiss, cop. 1841.

Gen. William Henry Harrison, Whig, of Virginia, nicknamed "Tippecanoe," was inaugurated 9th President. He served only 31 days. He contracted pneumonia at the rainy inaugural ceremonies and died, aged 68, on April 4. He was succeeded by Vice-President John Tyler, Whig, of Virginia, as 10th President.

President Tyler vetoed the bill for rechartering the Bank of the United States and all members of his cabinet, except Daniel Webster, resigned in protest.

A cargo of Negro slaves, en route from Richmond, Va., to New Orleans aboard the American vessel "Creole," mutinied, seized the ship, and took it to the British port of New Providence in the West Indies where the local authorities assisted them to escape.

A rival to the paddle wheel was found in the screw propeller, which was used probably for the first time on the U.S.S. "Princeton."

Inability to cope with the conflagration of 1835 led New York to install a fire engine which was built after a recent British model.

The co-operative Brook Farm Institute of Agriculture and Education was established by George Ripley and his wife with the purchase of 200 acres near West Roxbury, Mass., nine miles from Boston. (The undertaking, which enlisted many noted American literary figures, came to an end in 1847 after a fire destroyed the unfinished central phalanstery.)

Coke ovens were a familiar sight in Connellsville, Fayette County, Pa.

The "New-York Tribune" was founded as a daily newspaper by Horace Greeley, who remained its editor until his death in 1872. (The paper merged with the "New York Herald" in 1924, becoming the "Herald Tribune.")

Across the East River, the "Brooklyn Daily Eagle" was established. (Still published. Walt Whitman was editor of the paper from Jan. 1846 to 1848.)

Thomas Cole completed his four allegorical pictures "Voyage of Life" (The Child; The Youth; The Man; The Old Man) which adorned American homes for a long time in engravings.

"The Ladies' Repository" was founded in Cincinnati as a monthly literary magazine. (Called the "National Repository" after 1876; ceased publication in 1880.)

Dion Boucicault scored (Oct. 11) another popular theatrical success with his often-revived comedy "London Assurance" at the Park Theatre, New York.

Longfellow published his second book of verse, "Ballads and Other Poems." It contained the now well-known pieces, "The Skeleton in Armor," "The Wreck of the Hesperus," "The Village Blacksmith," "It Is Not Always May," "The Rainy Day," and "Excelsior."

Other literary publications of the year included James Fenimore Cooper's novel "The Deerslayer," Poe's story "The Murders in the Rue Morgue"—one of the earliest examples of detective fiction—and Ralph Waldo Emerson's first series of "Essays." In the racy, popular magazine "Spirit of the Times" appeared the famous tall story of the Southwest, "The Big Bear of Arkansas," by Thomas Bangs Thorpe, Massachusetts-born humorist.

George Catlin, self-taught painter of Indian scenes, brought out "Manners and Customs of the North American Indians" in two volumes with 300 handsome engravings and text, the result of an eight-year sojourn among various tribes from Yellowstone River to Florida. (He published in 1861 and in 1868 two similar books. He also exhibited Indian troupes in the East and in Europe before P. T. Barnum and Buffalo Bill.)

Donizetti's still popular vehicle for operatic coloratura sopranos, "Lucia di Lammermoor," was performed (Dec. 28) for the first time in the United States at the Théâtre d'Orléans in New Orleans in French. (It was first performed in the United States in the original Italian at Niblo's Garden, New York, Sept. 15, 1843.)

Feminine fashions now prescribed high combs.

⟨⟩ 1842

The Blind Boy. w., anon. m., William R[ichardson] Dempster. Boston: Oliver Ditson, cop. 1842.

Come, O Come with Me, the Moon Is Beaming. w., B. S. Barclay. m., "Italian air." Philadelphia: A. Fiot, cop. 1842.

Glenmary Waltzes. Piano solo. m., Richard Storrs Willis. Boston: Oliver Ditson, cop. 1842.

The Pope He Leads a Happy Life. w., m., anon. Philadelphia: Osbourn's Music Saloon [before 1842]. (Copy in Grosvenor Library, Buffalo. According to the title of this edition, the music was "composed by M. N. Esqr." The publisher was at the given address 30 S. 4th St., Philadelphia, until 1842 or 1843.)

Widow Machree. w., m., Samuel Lover. London: Duff and Hodgson [ca. 1842]. (Reprinted in the United States by A. Fiot, Philadelphia; William Hall & Son, New York, and others.)

The Webster-Ashburton Treaty between the United States and Great Britain settled the dispute of 1839 over the boundary between Maine and New Brunswick.

Gen. Zachary Taylor subdued the Seminole Indians of Florida, when their chief Osceola was killed, and effected the removal of most of the tribe west of the Mississippi. American deaths totalled 1,500; the war cost $20,000,000.

Ether was administered (in March) for the first time in a surgical operation performed at Jefferson, Ga., by Dr. Crawford Williamson Long.

Martial law was invoked (May 18) in Providence, R. I., by newly elected Governor Samuel W. King of the "Landholders" party when Thomas Wilson Dorr, elected to the same office by the opposing "Suffragists" party, attempted to seize the local arsenal. (Dorr fled, but on his return he was arrested, convicted of high treason, and in June 1844 sentenced to life imprisonment. He was, however, released in 1845.)

A Massachusetts Court ruled that Labor unions were Legal organizations and denied that an attempt to establish a "closed shop" was unlawful or evidence of unlawful intent.

Utopian schemes occupied much attention. Socialized and co-operative communities had already been founded in Pennsylvania (1804; 1825), Indiana (1814), Ohio (1819), Tennessee (1825), Vermont (1836), Massachusetts (1841). The movement was further influenced by the theories of the French socialist Charles Fourier (1772-1837). During the next fifteen years many attempts were undertaken in the United States to put the utopian ideas into practice. Notable among such communities were the Amana near Buffalo, N. Y.; Fruitlands at Harvard, Mass.; Hopedale at Milford, Mass. (all 1842); North American Phalanx at Red Bank, N. J. (1843); Bethel in Missouri (1844); Oneida in New York State (1848); at San Antonio, Tex. (1852; 1854); the second Amana near Davenport, Ia. (1855); Aurora in Oregon (1856).

John Charles Frémont and Kit Carson made expeditions to California.

Charles Dickens paid the first of two visits to the United States (Jan.-May), giving lectures in which he advocated international copyright and the abolition of slavery. (He published his unfavorable impressions in "American Notes for General Circulation" on his return to London, and incorporated other American material in his novel "Martin Chuzzlewit," 1843-44.)

P. T. Barnum opened his show place, the "American Museum," in New York at Broadway and Ann Street, paying $12,000 for the setup. His main feature was a four-year-old dwarf, two feet tall, billed as "General Tom Thumb," whose real name was Charles Sherwood Stratton. (At maturity he reached 40 inches in height, and died at the age of 45 in 1883.)

Excitement was running high in Boston over the imprisonment in Leverett Street jail under the Fugitive Slave Bill (1793) of a mulatto named George Latimer, one of the first fugitive slaves to be apprehended in Massachusetts. A grim abolitionist meeting was held (Nov. 17) in Marlboro Chapel; $400 was collected to buy his freedom, and plans to storm the jail were prepared as an alternative to secure his release. However, E. Austin of the Council of Slave-Hunters accepted the money, which was paid to Latimer's master, and the Negro was freed.

The Philharmonic Society was organized (Apr. 2) in New York as a symphonic orchestra by Ureli Corelli Hill. Hill was an American musician who had been a pupil of the celebrated Ludwig Spohr in Cassel, Germany. (The orchestra gave its first concert on Dec. 7, 1842, and has been in continuous existence since then.)

Longfellow contributed to the antislavery cause eight "Poems on Slavery," seven of which were written during a boisterous crossing of the Atlantic from Bristol to New York. It is said that he was inspired by the chapter on slavery in "American Notes" by Dickens whom he met in London. Meanwhile his poetic three-act play "The Spanish Student," which contains many pretty lyrics that repeatedly have been set to music, was appearing serially in "Graham's Magazine."

President John Tyler's invalid wife, Letitia Christian Tyler, died in the White House.

New feminine vogues included mantillas, black varnished leather shoes, lace mitts, small parasols, and large muffs.

⧼≈ 1843

De Boatman's Dance. w., m., Old Dan D. Emmit [Daniel Decatur Emmett]. Boston: C. H. Keith, cop. 1843.

Cape Ann. w., m., anon. Firth & Hall, cop. 1843. (Sung by J. J. Hutchinson of the Hutchinson Family of singers.)

Columbia, the Gem of the Ocean. w., m., Thomas à Becket. (Written in 1843 for a theatrical benefit at the request of David T. Shaw, to whom the words have often been incorrectly attributed.)

Excelsior. Part song for SATB with piano acc. w., Henry Wadsworth Longfellow. m., Hutchinson Family. Firth & Hall, cop. 1843. (Perhaps the earliest setting of Longfellow's poem, published in 1841.)

Go Call the Doctor, or, Anti-Calomel. w., m., Judson Hutchinson. William Hall & Son [ca. 1843]. (Sung by the Hutchinson Family of singers.)

The Grave of Bonaparte. w., Henry S. Washburne. m., Lyman Heath. Boston: Oliver Ditson [ca. 1843].

The Heart Bow'd Down (The Bohemian Girl). w., Alfred Bunn. m., Michael William Balfe. (Balfe's opera "The Bohemian Girl" was produced at the Drury Lane Theatre, London, Nov. 27, 1843, and given at the Park Theatre, New York, Nov. 25, 1844.)

I Dreamt I Dwelt in Marble Halls (The Bohemian Girl). w., Alfred Bunn. m., Michael William Balfe. (See preceding entry.)

The Lament of the Irish Emigrant. w., Mrs. Price Blackwood. m., William Richardson Dempster. Boston: Geo. P. Reed, cop. 1843.

The Long Ago—*better known as:* Long, Long Ago. w., m., Thomas Haynes Bayly. London [1843?].

My Old Aunt Sally. w., m., Old Dan D. Emmit [Daniel Decatur Emmett]. Boston: C. H. Keith, cop. 1843.

Old Dan Tucker. [w., m., Daniel Decatur Emmett?] Millet's Music Saloon, cop. 1843.

The Old Granite State. w., Jesse Hutchinson. [m., revivalist tune: "The Old Church Yard."] Firth & Hall, cop. 1843 by John Hutchinson. (Sung by the Hutchinson Family in 1843 in New York at a temperance meeting at the Broadway Temple.)

Stop Dat Knocking at My Door. w., m., A. F. Winnemore. Boston: Geo. P. Reed [cop. 1843?]

Then You'll Remember Me (The Bohemian Girl). w., Alfred Bunn. m., Michael William Balfe. (See above "The Heart Bow'd Down.")

The Department of the Interior was established (Mar. 3).

The end of the world was at hand! The cosmic cataclysm was to take place between Mar. 21, 1843, and Mar. 21, 1844. The pronouncement was uttered by William Miller, Pittsfield, Mass., preacher. Great ado prevailed among the thousands of his followers, the Millerites, who disposed of property, settled accounts, etc., in preparation for Doomsday.

On the death of Pierre Lorillard, wealthy snuff and cigar manufacturer and pioneer of the current Old Gold cigarette interests, newspapers coined the word "millionaire."

The Bunker Hill Monument, near Boston, was dedicated on the 68th anniversary (June 17) of the battle which it commemorates. Daniel Webster delivered the dedicatory address.

Before adjourning at midnight, Congress hurriedly granted to Samuel Morse an appropriation of $30,000 for the erection of an experimental electric wire between Washington, D. C., and Baltimore, with which to demonstrate his magnetic telegraph.

Samuel Colt, inventor of the revolver (1835), laid the first submarine cable in New York Harbor.

The B'nai Brith was founded in New York as a Jewish fraternal organization.

The steady rise in immigration caused the formation of the secret political Native American Party by antagonistic citizens. (Of no great importance, the party dissolved soon after its national convention in 1845, but it gave impetus to the Know-Nothing movement around 1850.)

The University of Notre Dame for men, near South Bend, Ind., was founded.

Longfellow married (July 13) his second wife, Frances Elizabeth Appleton, daughter of a wealthy cotton-mill proprietor who presented the couple with Craigie House, Cambridge, Mass., as a wedding gift.

The Hutchinson Family, a popular New England quartet of a sister and three brothers (Abby, Judson, John, and Asa) were singing to crowded houses of antislavery and temperance enthusiasts in New York and Philadelphia. They nicknamed themselves "the Tribe of Jesse," after their father.

Beethoven's great 3rd ("Eroica") Symphony received (Feb. 18) its first complete orchestral performance in the United States by the New York Philharmonic Society, in the Apollo Rooms, at the second concert of its first season.

Ole Bull, noted Norwegian violinist, made (Nov. 25) his American debut at the Park Theatre in New York. He toured the Eastern States and visited Havana, Cuba, giving over 200 concerts. His receipts were said to have totalled $400,000.

The Virginia Minstrels, the first regularly organized band of Negro minstrels, gave their initial public performance in New York at the Chatham Square Theatre. The company was composed of Dan (Daniel Decatur) Emmett, Frank Brower, Billy Whitlock, and Dick Pelham. (The troupe visited England in 1844 and returned in 1846. Pelham remained in England.)

Edgar Allan Poe won the $100 prize of the "Dollar Magazine" with his story "The Gold Bug"—largely, according to stories reputedly given out by the judges, because of the author's neat handwriting. Meanwhile, his bizarre murder story "The Black Cat" was appearing in "The Saturday Evening Post" and his tale of the Spanish Inquisition, "The Pit and the Pendulum," in "The Gift."

William Hickling Prescott published his three-volume "History of the Conquest of Mexico." (It was followed in 1847 by his two-volume "History of the Conquest of Peru.")

Deaths of the year included Francis Scott Key, aged 64 (Jan. 11), poet of "The Star-Spangled Banner," in Baltimore, and Noah Webster, aged 85 (May 28), lexicographer, in New Haven, Conn.

Influenza was rampant and called "Tyler grip," all evils being imputed to the unpopular President.

₴ 1844

The Blue Juniata. Words and melody by M[arion] D[ix] Sullivan. Arranged for the pianoforte by E. L. White. Boston: Oliver Ditson, cop. 1844. (The Juniata is a river in Pennsylvania.)

God Bless Our Native Land. Hymn. w., Rev. Charles Timothy Brooks. m., tune: "America." (The words were adapted about 1833, from the German of Siegfried August Mahlmann, written about 1815, and revised by John Sullivan Dwight.)

Miss Lucy Neale. w., m., James Sanford. Philadelphia: A. Fiot [ca. 1844]. (Described as a "favorite Ethiopian song" on the sheet music, the song enjoyed immediate popularity. The tune was used for a number of patriotic songs during the Mexican War, 1846-47.)

The Ole Grey Goose. w., m., anon. Philadelphia: A. Fiot, cop. 1844.

Open Thy Lattice, Love. w., m., Stephen Collins Foster. Philadelphia: George Willig, cop. 1844.

Polka. (The polka, a Bohemian dance of peasant origin, came into existence around 1830 and, after invading Vienna about 1839 and Paris in 1841, swept through Europe and the American continents with a furor that created a veritable "polkamania"—which was actually the title of a theatrical skit performed in New York. The dance was introduced in the United States in May, 1844, at the Chatham Theatre, New York, by Mary Ann Gannon, a 15-year-old dancer, and L. de G. Brockes, who later wrote a book on "Modern Dancing," New York, 1867. Everybody who could devise a tune, from the amateur to Johann Strauss, composed polkas. The traditional tune as danced in London, 1844, is reproduced in Grove's "Dictionary of Music and Musicians."`

Spring Song (No. 6 in: "Sechs Lieder ohne Worte," Book 5, op. 62). Piano solo. m., Felix Mendelssohn. Bonn: N. Simrock [1844].

Vive la Compagnie. w., m., anon. Baltimore: F. D. Benteen, cop. 1844. (Copy in Grosvenor Library, Buffalo.)

Moses Yale Beach, owner of the New York "Sun," published his "Wealth and Biography of Wealthy Citizens of the City of New York." He listed about 850 persons worth $100,000 or more, among them John Jacob Astor ($44,000,000), Stephen Van Rensselaer ($10,000,000), William B. Astor ($5,000,000), Peter Stuyvesant ($4,000,000), and Cornelius Vanderbilt ($1,200,000).

Samuel Morse successfully demonstrated (May 24) before Congress his electric telegraph by sending the first message from the United States Supreme Court room in the Capitol to Baltimore by wire. The message which was tapped out read: "What hath God wrought!" (Mrs. Dolly Madison, widow of the 4th President, despatched the first personal message.)

Charles Goodyear patented (June 15) his process for vulcanizing rubber, which he invented in 1839.

Joseph Smith, founder of the Mormon Church, and his brother, Hyrum, were killed (Apr. 6) by a mob in Carthage, Ill.

Dr. Horace Wells, Hartford, Conn., dentist, used "laughing gas" (nitrous oxide) as an anesthetic to extract one of his own teeth. (Continuing his experimentation with the gas in Boston, he made public in 1847 a statement concerning its use in dental work. He had also experimented with ether as early as 1840, before Long, 1842, and Morton, 1846.)

The U.S.S. "Princeton" (1841) fired one of its guns, called the "Peacemaker," during a pleasure trip on the Potomac. The gun exploded, injuring many persons and killing several. Among those killed were Secretary of State Abel P. Upshur, Secretary of the Navy Thomas W. Gilmer, and David Gardiner of Gardiners Island, New York. President Tyler was aboard the ship and narrowly escaped death. He married soon afterward (June 26) as his second wife Gardiner's daughter, Julia. He composed for her a song, "Sweet Lady, Awake." The Hutchinson Family of singers also were excursionists on the ship.

In New York, the ranks of the Democratic Party were again split for a time into opposing factions, adding two new words to political jargon—Hunker and Barnburner. The Hunkers represented the conservative element that wanted to keep the local "hunk" of the party in the hands of established patronage. Those who were antagonistic to this policy and were against corporations and the extension of slavery were regarded as radicals and called Barnburners, after the man in the fable who burned his barn to destroy the rats. (Many of the latter group joined the Free-Soil Party in 1848.)

"Littell's Living Age" was founded in Boston as a weekly magazine. (Published as a monthly after 1925.)

Edgar Allan Poe joined the staff of the "New-York Mirror" and began his literary attacks, among others, on Longfellow whom he accused of plagiarism.

Michael William Balfe's famous opera "The Bohemian Girl" was introduced (Nov. 25) to American audiences at the Park Theatre in New York.

The popular French play "Don Caesar de Bazan" by Philippe François Dumanoir and Adolphe D'Ennery was introduced (Dec. 9) in English by Charles Walcot at the Olympic Theatre in New York. The play had many revivals and adaptations.

The Hasty Pudding Club, a student body dramatic organization formed in 1770 at Harvard, gave (Dec. 13) its first theatrical production.

For the national campaign, President John Tyler accepted renomination but withdrew before election. Martin Van Buren ran in Tyler's place on the Democratic ticket but was defeated because of his opposition to the annexation of Texas. His opponent was James Knox Polk, the first "dark horse" nominee, whose platform favored not only the annexation of Texas but, in defiance of Great Britain, the whole of the Oregon Territory, as expressed in the slogan "Fifty-four forty or fight!"

ৡৡ 1845

Crambambuli, Bright Source of Pleasure. w., m., anon. Philadelphia: Klemm & Bro., cop. 1845. (Copy in Grosvenor Library, Buffalo.)

Dennis. Hymn tune. m., Hans Georg Nägeli [arr. by Lowell Mason]. Boston: Wilkins, Carter, and Co. [cop. 1845] (in: Lowell Mason and George James Webb, "The Psaltry; a New Collection of Church Music," p. 168). (The hymn was set to the words "How Gently God Commands!" The music now generally sung to the words of John Fawcett, "Blest Be the Tie That Binds.")

Scenes That Are Brightest (Maritana). w., Edward Fitzball. m., Vincent Wallace. ("Maritana" was a four-act English opera, produced at Drury Lane Theatre, London, Nov. 15, 1845; given at the Bowery Theatre, New York, May 4, 1848, and long popular on American professional and amateur stages.)

Yes! Let Me Like a Soldier Fall (Maritana). w., Edward Fitzball. m., Vincent Wallace. (See preceding entry.)

James Knox Polk, Democrat, of North Carolina, was inaugurated 11th President. His wife, Sarah Childress Polk, a Methodist educated by the Moravians, prohibited liquor and dancing in the White House.

Retiring President Tyler signed (Mar. 1) the bill for the annexation of Texas. The territory, comprising the present State of Texas and part of New Mexico, Colorado, and Wyoming, was admitted (Dec. 29) as a State, with the proviso that the area (389,166 square miles) should be divided into no more than five States "of convenient size."

But the Texan question was not thereby resolved. Although Mexico recognized in 1836 the boundary along the Rio Grande, border disputes continued between Americans and Mexicans. To thwart a suspected attempt by the latter to regain the lost territory, President Polk dispatched into the region an armed force under Zachary Taylor—a step that was presently to lead to the Mexican War.

Congress designated (Jan. 23) the national election day as the first Tuesday after the first Monday in November.

Two more States were admitted to the Union—Florida (Mar. 3) as the 27th and Texas (Dec. 29) as the 28th.

The U. S. Naval Academy was founded (Oct. 10) at Annapolis, Md.

The iron age was beginning to hit full stride. The American steamer

"Massachusetts" crossed the Atlantic to Liverpool by means of a screw propeller.

"Manifest destiny" was a new phrase added to the popular vocabulary when New York editor John L. O'Sullivan coined the words in an article published in his July "United States Magazine and Democratic Review."

"The Scientific American" was founded in New York as a weekly "illustrated journal of art, science, and mechanics." (Still published.)

The weekly "National Police Gazette" in its subsequently famous pink covers made its first appearance in New York.

Poe's poem "The Raven" was printed in "The American Review" and republished in his volume "The Raven and Other Poems."

Longfellow's fourth book of verse, "The Belfry of Bruges and Other Poems" contained "The Arsenal at Springfield," "The Bridge," "The Arrow and the Song," "The Day Is Done."

Dorothy Lynde Dix, who spent her life in the relief of paupers, criminals, and the insane, published "Prisons and Prison Discipline."

Equally significant was Sarah Margaret Fuller's study "Woman in the Nineteenth Century."

The first grand opera by a native American composer was produced (June 4) in Philadelphia at the Chestnut Street Theatre—"Leonora" by William Henry Fry, of Philadelphia. The libretto, in four acts, was written by the composer's brother, Joseph Reese Fry, and based on Edward Bulwer-Lytton's successful play "The Lady of Lyons." (The opera was performed 16 times, and given in New York at the Academy of Music, Mar. 29, 1858, in Italian.)

Five members of the famous Hutchinson Family of singers appeared in concerts of their songs in Dublin, Liverpool, Manchester, and London (Feb., 1846). They were entertained by Dickens at his Devonshire Terrace home.

In London, bitter rivalry developed between the American actor Edwin Forrest and the British star William Macready. (The circumstances led to the Astor Place riot in New York in 1849.)

Mrs. Anna Cora Mowatt's popular five-act play "Fashion, or, Life in New York" opened (Mar. 24) in New York at the Park Theatre and ran for 20 nights.

German actors began putting on plays in New York beer halls.

The first set of baseball rules was formulated by the Knickerbocker Club of New York.

Tenpins superseded billiards as a common pastime.

1846

The Bridge of Sighs. w., Thomas Hood. m., arr. by E[dward] L. White. Boston: Oliver Ditson, cop. 1846.

The Low-Back'd Car. w., Samuel Lover. [m., adapted from the Irish tune: "The Jolly Ploughman."] William Hall & Son, cop. 1846. (The tune was printed in Edward Bunting, "The Ancient Music of Ireland," Hodges and Smith, Dublin, 1840, p. 20.)

Miss Lucy Neale. See 1844.

The Rose of Alabama—*also known as:* The Rose ob Alabama. w., S. S. Steele. m., anon. Boston: Geo. P. Reed, cop. 1846.

Well-a-Day. Duet for soprano and alto with piano acc. w., anon. m., George Linley. London: Chappell [1846].

For some songs of the Mexican War (1846-48) consult—

Dolph, Edward Arthur
"Sound Off!" New York: Farrar & Rinehart, Inc. [cop. 1942.]

The successful demonstration of Morse's telegraph before Congress in 1844 led to the establishment of a telegraph line from New York to Washington, D. C. Connections were established between New York and Philadelphia (Jan. 20) and between Philadelphia and Baltimore (June 5). The line of Morse's experiment from Baltimore to Washington completed the circuit.

In consequence of Texan border disputes, Congress debated a bill for the settlement of differences either by a boundary treaty or by purchase. During the discussions, David Wilmot introduced a Proviso for the exclusion of slavery from the area, which was passed by the House but rejected by the Senate. It had repercussions in 1849.

The belligerent atmosphere of "Fifty-four forty or fight," which was created by the Oregon boundary dispute between the United States and Great Britain, was amicably dispelled by the Webster-Ashburton Treaty compromise. It gave Vancouver to Great Britain and settled the northern limits of the Oregon Territory as constituted by the present boundary.

Clashes between American forces under Zachary Taylor and Mexicans in Texas at Palo Alto (May 8) and Resaca de la Palma (May 9) resulted (May 13) in a declaration of war by the United States on Mexico, thus starting the Mexican War (1846-48).

Capt. John Charles Frémont, United States Engineers, took possession of the Mexican province of California and proclaimed (June 14) at Sonoma the Bear Flag Republic.

Monterey was captured by the United States Pacific fleet under Commodore John Drake Sloat (July 7), and Santa Barbara and San Pedro by his successor Commodore Robert Field Stockton (in Aug.). On land, American victories were won at Santa Fe by Stephen Watts Kearney and at El Paso and Chihuahua by Alexander William Doniphan.

In the midst of hostilities, Capt. Frémont, acting as civil governor of California, rashly resisted the superior authority of General Kearney, who had been appointed to organize the local government. Frémont was court-martialed and found guilty of mutiny. His life was saved by order of President Polk.

Iowa was admitted (Dec. 28) as the 29th State.

Ether was administered (Oct. 16) in public at the Massachusetts General Hospital in Boston by Dr. William Thomas Green Morton during an operation performed by Dr. John Collins Warren.

Dr. Morrison of St. Louis devised the "dental engine" or drilling machine.

Congress enacted a law requiring the deposit of one copy of each copyrighted book in the Library of Congress. (Since 1870, the deposit of two copies is required.)

Maine adopted prohibition—the first state to do so—and has remained "dry" ever since.

The American Missionary Association was formed for the propagation of the Christian religion among the Negroes of the Southern States, Jamaica, and West Africa.

The Smithsonian Institution, Washington, D. C., was founded by an act of Congress in accordance with the terms of a bequest made by an Englishman, James Smithson (1765-1829), Oxford graduate and Fellow of the Royal Society, London. Smithson left the sum of 100,000 pounds for "an establishment for the increase and diffusion of knowledge among men."

A wagon train of emigrants en route to California was caught in the Sierra Nevada by severe snowstorms and encamped amid utmost privations on a site now called Donner Lake. Survivors were rescued after being reduced to a state of cannibalism.

Two important inventions signalized the year—the sewing machine of Elias Howe of Spencer, Mass., and the cylinder rotary press by Richard March Hoe. The latter was installed by the "Philadelphia Public Ledger." The sewing machine of Howe was later greatly improved by Isaac Merritt Singer.

The "Boston Herald" was founded as a daily newspaper.

In Hoboken, N. J., the first real game of baseball was played between the Knickerbocker Club of New York and a picked team then calling itself the New York Club.

Edwin T. Christy's "original and far-famed band of Ethiopian Minstrels" opened (Apr. 24) at Palmo's Opera House in New York.

The first American performance of the famous ballet "Giselle," scenario by Théophile Gautier and music by Adolphe Adam, was given (Feb. 2) at the Park Theatre in New York. (Still in the repertory of ballet companies.)

Elijah Kellogg's blank verse classic of schoolboy declamation, "Spartacus to His Gladiators," appeared in Epes Sargent's "School Reader."

English journalists and visitors deplored the American male's habit of chewing tobacco.

The potato famine in Ireland was rapidly increasing American immigration.

Ladies' parasols now could be folded up.

₷ 1847

Be Kind to the Loved Ones at Home. w., m., I[saac] B[aker] Woodbury. Boston: E. H. Wade, cop. 1847.

De Floating Scow—*also known as:* **Carry Me Back to Ole Virginny.** w., m., Charles T. White. Philadelphia: Lee & Walker, cop. 1847.

Footsteps of Angels. w., Henry Wadsworth Longfellow. m., William R[ichardson] Dempster. Boston: Oliver Ditson & Co., cop. 1847.

The Rainy Day. w., Henry Wadsworth Longfellow. m., I[saac] B[aker] Woodbury. Boston: Oliver Ditson & Co., cop. 1847.

Roll On, Silver Moon—*also known as:* **The Silver Moon.** w., m., anon. (The song was of English origin. Two American editions were published and copyrighted in 1847; (1) arr. by Joseph W. Turner, Oliver Ditson & Co., Boston; and (2) arr. by N. Barker, Firth, Pond & Co., New York. The latter edition credited the melody to one Sloman [R. Sloman?]. The Turner arrangement is found in most song collections.)

Row Thy Boat Lightly. w., Miss H. F. Woodman. m., I[saac] B[aker] Woodbury. Boston: Oliver Ditson & Co., cop. 1847.

The Mexican War continued. Notable American victories were won at Buena Vista (Feb. 22-23) by Zachary Taylor, and at Vera Cruz (Mar. 27) and Chapultepec (Sept. 13) by Winfield Scott. Hostilities ended (Sept. 17) with Scott's capture of Mexico City and the capitulation of the Mexican dictator Santa Anna.

Congress authorized (Mar. 3) the issuance of the first United States adhesive postage stamps in 5 and 10 cent values with portraits of Franklin and Washington, light-brown and black in color, respectively. The stamps were placed on sale July 1. Diagonal, vertical, or horizontal halves of the 10-cent stamp were often used as a 5-cent value. The stamps were imperforate. (Previously, mail had been merely marked "Paid" by postmasters by means of pen and ink or by hand stamp impressions. Until 1894 United States postage stamps were printed by private manufacturers for the government.)

New Hampshire became the first state to legalize the ten-hour working day.

The political Free-Soil Party was organized to oppose the extension of slavery in the territories soon to be acquired from Mexico. (It merged with the Republican Party in 1854.)

Following violent clashes over polygamy in Nauvoo, Ill., a band of Mormons (143 men, 3 women, and 2 children) moved westward into Utah under their leader, Brigham Young, and established (July 24) Salt Lake City.

Telephone connection was completed (June 27) between New York and Boston.

The immigrant ship "Phoenix" burned on Lake Michigan with a loss of 240 lives.

The American Association for the Advancement of Science was founded.

Maria Mitchell, American astronomer, discovered (Oct. 1) a comet and was elected the same day to the American Academy of Arts—the first woman to be so honored. The King of Denmark awarded her a gold medal for her discovery.

Henry Ward Beecher, 34-year-old Congregational minister, was called from Indiana to Brooklyn, N. Y., to take charge of the new Plymouth Church and its congregation of nine families. (He served the church for nearly 40 years, and his zeal and brilliant oratory ultimately built an edifice seating about 3,000 persons.)

A frame building erected by John B. Rice was Chicago's first real theatre.

Members of Colonel J. D. Stevenson's Seventh Regiment of New York Volunteers staged minstrel shows in San Francisco at Leidesdorff's City Hotel.

Samuel Lover, Irish poet, novelist, painter, composer, and entertainer, gave "evenings" (the first on Oct. 6) of song and story in New York and Brooklyn. (Victor Herbert was a grandson of Lover.)

Italian opera was in the ascendant. The Havana Opera Company from the Teatro Tacon began giving operatic seasons in New York, Philadelphia, and Boston under the direction of Luigi Arditi, later the composer of "The Kiss Waltz." The company introduced Italian opera to Boston at the Howard Athenaeum with a performance (Apr. 23) of Verdi's "Ernani." In New York, the Astor Place Opera House, the city's first real operatic theatre, was opened (Nov. 22) under the management of Sanquirico and Salvatore Patti (father of the subsequently famous Adelina Patti) with Verdi's "Ernani." In fact, the first Verdi operas were being heard in the United States—"I Lombardi" at Palmo's Opera House in New York (Mar. 3), "Ernani" at the Park Theatre (Apr. 15), and "I Due Foscari" in Boston (in May).

The German male chorus Deutscher Liederkranz was formed (Jan. 9) with 25 members in New York.

The "Chicago Tribune" was founded as a daily newspaper. (Still published.)

Longfellow brought out his narrative poem in hexameters, "Evangeline," a story of French-Canadian lovers and exiles.

The "National Era" was founded as an antislavery magazine in Washington, D. C. (It published Hawthorne's allegorical tale "The Great Stone Face," Harriet Beecher Stowe's "Uncle Tom's Cabin" in serialization before its appearance in book form, and many of Whittier's writings. Ceased publication in 1860.)

Benjamin Penhallow Shillaber, Boston humorist and printer, created the character of Mrs. Parkington, a Yankee Mrs. Malaprop noted for her amusing misuse of words. (He developed the character in "Life and Sayings of Mrs. Parkington," 1854, "Mrs. Parkington's Knitting Work," 1859, "Parkingtonian Patchwork," 1873, and the posthumous "Mrs. Parkington's Grab Bag," 1893. The author died in 1890.)

Dr. Collyer exhibited (Sept. 23) in New York at the Apollo Rooms a tableau of living male and female models "from the Royal Academies of London and Paris." This started such a craze for posturing and scantily clad "artists" viewed rapturously through "prodigious opera glasses and pocket telescopes" by several hundred fashionable old rakes and ineffable scoundrels about town—some of them bankers and brokers in Wall Street, over sixty years of age," that the police were finally forced to take a hand (in Mar., 1848). A group of drunken devotees climbed on the stage during a performance at the Temple of the Muses and chased the female models into the wings.

John Chapman, aged about 72, Swedenborgian planter of apple trees from Pennsylvania to Illinois and better known as "Johnny Appleseed," died (Mar. 11) of pneumonia in Fort Wayne, Ind.

₹⃕ 1848

Ben Bolt, or, Oh! Don't You Remember. w., Thomas Dunn English. m., Nelson Kneass. Louisville, Ky.: W. C. Peters, cop. 1848.

The Cottage of My Mother. w., Jesse Hutchinson. m., Judson Hutchinson. Boston: Oliver Ditson, cop. 1848.

The Folks Are All Waiting to See the Fast Steamer (A Glance at New York). w., Benjamin A. Baker. m., tune: "Jolly Young Waterman." ("A

Glance at New York" was a popular play—see below. The words and the tune are reproduced in Grenville Vernon, "Yankee Doodle-Doo," New York, 1927, p. 132.)

Oh! Susanna. w., m., Stephen C[ollins] Foster. Louisville, Ky., W. C. Peters & Co., cop. 1848.

Old Uncle Ned. w., m., Stephen C[ollins] Foster. W. E. Millet, cop. 1848.

'Twas Off the Blue Canaries, or, My Last Cigar. w., m., James M. Hubbard. New Haven, Conn.: William Skinner, cop. 1848 by Jas. M. Hubbard.

The Mexican War was terminated by a treaty of peace signed at Guadalupe Hidalgo (Feb. 2; ratified by Congress May 19). Mexico relinquished its claims to Texas and ceded to the United States an area comprising California, Nevada, Utah, Arizona, New Mexico, and part of Colorado, or two-fifths of its territory. The United States paid Mexico an indemnity of $15,000,000 and assumed American claims amounting to $3,000,000. The war caused the death of 13,237 enlisted American men. Among the officers serving in the war were Colonel Jefferson Davis, Captain Robert E. Lee, Captain George B. McClellan, and Lieutenant U. S. Grant.

Wisconsin was admitted to the Union (May 29) as the 30th state.

Gold was discovered (Jan. 24) by James Wilson Marshall at his partner Johann August Sutter's sawmill on the South Fork of the American River, near Coloma, Cal. President Polk incorporated the news in his message (Dec. 5) to Congress, which set off the gold rush next year.

Pennsylvania became the first state to pass a child labor law fixing the minimum age in commercial pursuits at twelve years (raised to thirteen in 1849).

Women clamoring for the right to vote met in convention (July 19-20) in Seneca Falls, N. Y., and drafted a "Declaration of Sentiments." Among the leaders in the movement were Lucretia Mott and Elizabeth Cady Stanton.

Congress authorized the erection of the Washington National Monument, Washington, D. C., from funds to be raised by public subscription. The cornerstone was laid on July 4. (The monument was completed in 1884.)

The village of Saint Anthony, Minn., now part of Minneapolis, was established. Maine woodsmen and others were attracted to the place because of the plentiful pine forests in the region.

The China clipper "Sea Witch," built in 1846, became the fastest ship afloat when it made a record trip from Canton to New York in 77 days.

Mrs. Amelia Jenks Bloomer began publishing her magazine "The Lily," devoted to temperance and woman suffrage. She became better known, however, as the creator of the "bloomer," a pantaloon or loose-fitting trouser-like dress gathered about the ankles, for women. ("The Lily" ceased publication in 1854.)

Samuel M. Kier, Pittsburgh druggist, sold petroleum as "a wonderful medical virtue" behind an advertising campaign using imitation bank notes as bait. At this time peddlers generally hawked petroleum as "Seneca oil," with reputed medicinal qualities.

The University of Wisconsin, Madison, Wis., for men and women, and the College of the City of New York, for men, were founded.

Andrew Carnegie, a poor 13-year-old Scottish lad, began work as a "bobbin boy" in a cotton factory in Allegheny, Pa.

John Quincy Adams, 6th President (1825-29) and for 17 years thereafter Massachusetts Representative in Congress, was stricken in the House and died (Feb. 23), aged 81, in the Speaker's room.

Giuseppe Garibaldi, Italian patriot, came to the United States as a refugee and worked in Antoni Meucci's candle factory on Staten Island, New York. He remained about two years.

The first locomotive steamed (Oct. 25) out of Chicago—the "Pioneer" of the Galena & Chicago (now Chicago & North Western) Railroad.

Spiritualism began when certain "rappings" were heard in the home of J. D. Fox in Hydesville, Wayne County, N. Y. (They ultimately led to the formation of the National Spiritualists' Association, incorporated in 1893 in Washington, D. C.)

A band of 69 French Utopians called Icarians attempted to establish a social community on a 400,000-acre tract of land along the Red River, Tex. (The scheme collapsed under the rigors of frontier conditions and involved its leader, Etienne Cabet, who arrived in 1849, in bitter litigation. Cabet became an American citizen in 1854.)

Wilhelm Weitling, educated refugee tailor from Magdeburg, started in New York a German socialist newspaper, "Die Republik der Arbeiter."

"The Independent" was founded in New York as a weekly religious magazine. (It became a secular periodical under later editors. Ceased publication in 1928.)

William Frederick Poole, Massachusetts librarian, began the publication of his "Alphabetical Index to Subjects Treated in . . . Periodicals," the forerunner of the present "Reader's Guide to Periodical Literature."

James Russell Lowell published his parable in verse, "The Vision of Sir Launfal."

Fanny Kemble, celebrated English actress, gave in Boston successful Shakespearean readings, which she repeated elsewhere until her return to England (1851).

Fire destroyed (Dec. 16) the historic Park Theatre, New York, opened in 1798.

"Monte Cristo," a play by Alexandre Dumas, Sr., was introduced

(Dec. 25) at the Broadway Theatre, New York, by J. Lester, stage-name of J. Lester Wallack.

Benjamin A. Baker's melodrama "A Glance at New York" introduced a new Yankee type—Mose, the volunteer fireman, described as "one of the B'hoys" and played by the inimitable Frank S. Chanfrau. The play was produced (Feb. 15) at Mitchell's Olympic Theatre, New York. (Mose figured in Baker's later plays, "New York as It Is," 1848; "Mose in California," 1849; "Mose in China," 1850; "Mose in France," 1851.)

Eduard Reményi, Hungarian violin virtuoso, concertized in the United States.

Palmo's Opera House in New York reopened (July 10), remodelled and improved, as Burton's Theatre, long to remain an important playhouse.

Lovers of light music were being entertained by orchestras made up of German refugee musicians, notably by Joseph Gungl's well-known Berlin orchestra of 25 players. It toured the country (1848-49), playing salon and dance music, mostly composed by Gungl who enjoyed a considerable reputation in the field.

The first Stephen Collins Foster songs were appearing in print (see above).

John Jacob Astor, aged 85, died (Mar. 29) in New York, leaving a fortune of $40,000,000.

₴ 1849

Just as I Am Without One Plea. Hymn. [w., Charlotte Elliot.] m., William B[atchelder] Bradbury. Mark H. Newman & Co. [cop. 1849] (in: Thomas Hastings and William Batchelder Bradbury, "The Mendelssohn Collection, or, Hastings' and Bradbury's Third Book of Psalmody"). (The words were printed anonymously with another tune on p. 255. The tune "Woodworth," to which the hymn is now sung, was printed with other words on p. 60.)

Nelly Bly. w., m., Stephen C[ollins] Foster. Firth, Pond & Co., cop. 1849.

Nelly Was a Lady. w., m., Stephen C[ollins] Foster. Firth, Pond & Co., cop. 1849.

Santa Lucia. w. m., Teodoro Cottrau (1827-79). [Naples: T. Cottrau, 1849.] (Date from A. della Corte and G. M. Gatti, "Dizionario di Musica," Torino, 1925. An early American edition of the song, with an English translation by Thomas Oliphant, was published by M. McCaffrey, Baltimore, n.d.)

For some songs of the Gold Rush period, consult—

Black, Eleanore, and Sidney Robertson

The Gold Rush Song Book, comprising a group of twenty-five authentic ballads as they were sung by the men who dug gold in California during the period of the Gold Rush of 1849. San Francisco: The Colt Press [cop. 1940]. ix, 55 p. 8°.

Sherwin, Sterling, and Louis Katzman

Songs of the Gold Miners. A golden collection of songs as sung by and about the forty-niners. New York: Carl Fischer, Inc. [cop. 1932.] 48 p. 4°.

Gen. Zachary Taylor, Whig, of Virginia, nicknamed "Old Rough and Ready," was inaugurated 12th President.

Gold! The thing was on everybody's mind. Even Congress authorized (Mar. 3) the coinage of gold dollars. More gold was discovered in the Mother Lode, stretching 110 miles along the western foothills of the Sierra Nevada. The "New-York Tribune" sent into the region the adventurous Pennsylvania Quaker writer, Bayard Taylor, who fired the imagination of readers with two volumes of descriptions under the fanciful title "El Dorado" (1850). Poe used the title for a poem in which he referred to the gold rush. The days of the gold-seeking Spanish conquistadores had returned. In fact, so many prospectors hurried to California (1,200 sailed from the East in three months), and so many perished en route, that wiseacres told departing hopefuls to take tombstones with them. By the end of 1850 there were in San Francisco 34,776 inhabitants against 500 in 1840. Stay-at-homes in the East had to content themselves with a then popular type of theatrical presentation, a "Panorama of the Gold Mines of California."

Meantime, California embraced the entertainment business at once with the $80,000 Eagle Theatre in Sacramento, while Stephen C. Massett from the East gave a series of songs and recitations in San Francisco, using the only piano in that section of the country. Henri Herz, celebrated French pianist on tour, also played in Sacramento, performing before an audience of gold miners on a dilapidated piano hauled in from some nearby place. The instrument had only six octaves, with half of the keys out of order. The miners paid their admission at the box office with gold dust which the cashier weighed on a pair of scales. (The story is told in Herz's book "Mes Voyages en Amérique," Paris, 1866.) Before the year ended there occurred in San Francisco an event often repeated in its history—fire destroyed (Dec. 24) more than a million dollars' worth of property.

In New York, a mob invaded (May 10) the Astor Place Opera House, creating a riot against the English actor William Macready, in which 22 persons were killed and 36 wounded. The magnificent interior of the building was reduced almost to a wreck. The outbreak was in retaliation for the treatment accorded Edwin Forrest, American actor, in London in 1845. The demonstration, said to have been instigated by Forrest himself, was led by the notorious Edward Zane Carroll Judson (see 1853; 1869), who was arrested and sentenced to a year in the penitentiary.

Further unrest was stirred in national political circles when William Lowndes Yancey of Georgia, smarting under the concept put forth in the Wilmot Proviso (1846), formulated the Alabama Platform. This asserted that Congress had no constitutional power to abolish slavery and that no territory before it was admitted as a State possessed the right of choice in the question.

Walter Hunt invented the safety pin.

The Mendelssohn Quintette Club was formed in Boston. (It was the first real artistic chamber music group in the United States. It played also on tour throughout the country and did much to acquaint music-lovers with the masterpieces composed for its flexible combination of violin, viola, violoncello, flute, and clarinet, the latter two also playing string instruments. The organization disbanded in 1895.)

A "Sängerfest" of German male choruses was held in Cincinnati.

The recently invented saxophone of Adolphe Sax was introduced (in April) to American audiences at the New York concerts of the English Distin family (father and four sons). The players created quite a sensation and were much in demand.

While Longfellow was going through a less inspired period, publishing a novel "Kavanagh" and a collection of verse "The Seaside and the Fireside" with "The Building of the Ship" as the leading piece, Poe was producing in this last year of his life "The Bells," "Annabel Lee," and "Eldorado."

With feminism stirring the country, Rufus Wilmot Griswold brought out "The Female Poets of America."

Edgar Allan Poe, aged 40, died (Oct. 7) a tragic death in Baltimore. Never able to overcome his drinking habits, he was found in a delirious condition outside a saloon that was used as a voting place.

Death also claimed at the same age "Yankee Hill" (George Handel Hill), Boston-born comedian.

Ladies now puffed their hair over a cushion atop the head.

Gas light was installed (Dec. 29) in the White House

ᣠ 1850

Angelina Baker. w., m., Stephen C[ollins] Foster. Baltimore: F. D. Benteen, cop. 1850.

The Bridge. w., Henry Wadsworth Longfellow. m., Miss M. Lindsay
[Mrs. J. Worthington Bliss]. London: Robert Cocks & Co. [185-?];
Boston: Oliver Ditson & Co. [1861].

By the Sad Sea Waves (The Brides of Venice). w., Alfred Bunn. m.,
Julius Benedict. Firth, Pond & Co. [ca. 1850.] (Published earlier in
London. "The Brides of Venice" was an English opera produced at Drury
Lane Theatre, London, Apr. 22, 1844. The song was sung by Jenny Lind
during her concert tour in the United States, 1850-52.)

[De Camptown Races.] Gwine to Run All Night. w., m., Stephen
C[ollins] Foster. Baltimore: F. D. Benteen, cop. 1850.

Cheer, Boys, Cheer! w., Charles Mackay. m., Henry Russell. London:
Musical Bouquet [1850?]; New York: Wm. Hall & Son [185-]. (London
data from British Museum Catalogue of Printed Books.)

Crusader's Hymn [Fairest Lord Jesus!] Hymn. w., anon. [translated
from the German "Schönster Herr Jesu"]. [m., Silesian folk song.] Clark,
Austin & Smith [cop. 1850] (in: Robert Storrs Willis, "Church Chorals
and Choir Studies," p. 193). (The hymn is erroneously believed to date
from the time of the Crusades. The German words were first printed in
the "Münster Gesangbuch," 1677, and published with the above music
in August Heinrich Hoffmann von Fallersleben's "Schlesische Volkslieder," Leipzig, 1842, p. 339. Another English translation, by the Rev.
Joseph Augustus Seiss, D.D., LL.D., published in the Lutheran "Sunday-
School Book," The United Lutheran Publication House, Philadelphia,
1873, begins "Beautiful Savior! King of Creation!")

I've Left the Snow-Clad Hills. w., m., George Linley. Boston: Oliver
Ditson [ca. 1850]; Boston: Stephen W. Marsh [ca. 1850]; Philadelphia:
E. Ferrett & Co. [ca. 1850.] (Published earlier in London; sung by Jenny
Lind.)

It Came upon the Midnight Clear. Hymn. w., Rev. Edmund Hamilton
Sears. m., Richard Storrs Willis. (Although the words and the above
music of this carol are now inseparably associated with each other, neither
was written to complement the other. The words were published in the
Unitarian periodical The "Christian Register," Boston, Dec. 29, 1849.
According to an account in the "Boston Sunday Herald," Dec. 24, 1933,
the hymn was first sung to another tune, accompanied on a borrowed
spinet, in the author's home at Wayland, Mass. Prior to publication, the
words were read at a Christmas celebration in Quincy, Mass. The manuscript is preserved in the Sears Memorial Chapel, First Parish Church,
Weston, Mass., where the Rev. Sears was minister from 1865, after leaving the Wayland Parish, until his death in 1876. The music, as now sung,

is a lengthened adaptation of a choral exercise, Study No. 23, set to the words "See Israel's gentle shepherd stand," in Willis's "Church Chorals and Choir Studies," p. 93—see above: "Crusader's Hymn." The present compiler has been unable to locate the first appearance in print of the carol in its present form. Sears, in 1834, while an undergraduate at Union College, Schenectady, N. Y., contributed to the student literary magazine the words of another well-known Christmas hymn, "Calm on the Listening Ear of Night.")

The Spacious Firmament on High. Hymn. Tune: "Creation." w., Joseph Addison. m., arr. from Franz Joseph Haydn. F. Huntington [cop. 1850] (in: Isaac Baker Woodbury, "The Dulcimer; or, The New York Collection of Sacred Music," p. 72). (The words are a paraphrase of Psalm XIX, 1-6. The music was adapted from the chorus "The heavens are telling" in Haydn's oratorio "The Creation.")

What Are the Wild Waves Saying? Duet. w., Joseph Edwards Carpenter. m., Stephen Glover. (The words were suggested by the deathbed scene of little Paul, haunted by memories of the sea, in Dickens's novel "Dombey and Son" which was published in London during 1847-48. Glover brought out the song in 1850. It was reprinted by Wm. A. Pond & Co., New York, during the late 1860s or 70s.)

Widow Machree. See 1842.

President Zachary Taylor, aged 66, died (July 9) of typhus. He had served only one year and four months and was succeeded (July 10) by Vice-President Millard Fillmore, Whig, of New York, as 13th President. Fillmore's daughter, Mary Abigail, was the White House hostess in place of her mother who suffered from poor health.

Congress passed (Jan. 29) Henry Clay's Omnibus Bill, the Compromise of 1850. Its provisions were attacked by John Calhoun in his "Fourth of March Speech" ("Speech on the Slavery Question") and defended by Daniel Webster in his "Seventh of March Speech" ("For the Union and Constitution"). In supporting the legislation Webster lost prestige in the Northern States, as reflected in Whittier's poem "Ichabod."

The Clayton-Bulwer Treaty was negotiated by John Middleton Clayton (United States) and Sir Henry Lytton Bulwer (Great Britain) to regulate the interests of both countries in Central America, particularly in regard to the proposed canal across Nicaragua. (The bill was annulled in 1902.)

California was admitted (Sept. 9) as the 31st State.

The woman suffrage movement was spreading rapidly. A convention took place (in April) in Salem, O. In Worcester, Mass., was held the first national convention, at which the movement assumed definite political character and allied itself with the abolitionist cause. Among the leaders were Susan Brownell Anthony, Carrie Chapman Catt, Abbey Kelly Foster, the Grimké sisters (Angelina and Sarah Moore), Elizabeth Cady Stanton, and Lucy Stone. The first tangible results of the movement were achieved when Indiana presently adopted a revised state constitution with liberal provisions for women.

Cincinnati organized the first steam fire department when a native son, A. B. Latta, constructed a practical fire engine.

The first building in the United States to be constructed of cast-iron framework was erected in New York by James Bogardus, inventor of a postage stamp engraving machine (1839).

New York merchant Henry Grinnell outfitted at the expense of $30,000 two ships, the "Advance," 140 tons, and the "Rescue," 90 tons. These ships sailed (May 23) from New York for the Arctic to join in the search for the "lost" English explorer Sir John Franklin who had led an expedition of 219 men into the region in 1845. (The rescue party found no trace of Franklin, who had perished in 1847, but discovered the area now called Grinnell Land.)

The American Express Company was organized (Mar. 18) in Buffalo, N. Y.

Scottish-born Allan Pinkerton, a cooper by trade, was appointed Chicago's first police detective. After uncovering a counterfeiting gang, he opened a detective bureau of his own.

George H. Fox invented an elevator that operated by means of a vertical screw.

Fire damaged San Francisco three times (May 4, June 14, Sept. 17) and destroyed (June 17) the steamer "Griffith" on Lake Erie with a loss of 300 lives.

George Phillips Bond, Harvard astronomer, made (July 17) the first photograph of a star by means of the 15-inch refractor of the Harvard Observatory telescope—a daguerreotype of the star Vega.

James Gordon Bennett, publisher of the daily "New York Herald," was horsewhipped on Broadway by a defeated candidate for the office of district attorney.

After the unsuccessful venture in Texas, Etienne Cabet's dwindling band of Icarians (1848) established for a time their Utopian community in Nauvoo, Ill.

A German socialist Turnverein was started in New York.

The Christadelphians, an American Christian sect with no ordained clergy, was founded about this time by English-born Dr. John Thomas (1805-71); hence the sect was also called Thomasites.

Returning from Italy, Margaret Fuller, the Marquis Angelo Ossoli her husband, and their child lost their lives in a shipwreck during a storm off Fire Island, near New York. Of the victims, only the body of the child was ever recovered.

Mathew B. Brady became famous as a photographer with his pictorial "Gallery of Illustrious Americans."

Harper's "New Monthly Magazine" appeared.

Nathaniel Hawthorne published his novel "The Scarlet Letter."

Fourteen-year-old Jay Gould, later the fabulously rich financier, wrote an essay in Beechwood Seminary entitled "Honesty Is the Best Policy."

Whist and faro were popular gambling games.

Men wore cutaway coats for morning and evening occasions. The coats had ample pockets in the tails.

The sensation of the year was the appearance in New York of extravagantly publicized Jenny Lind, the Swedish nightingale, under the management of Phineas Taylor Barnum. She was met on the arrival of her boat at the dock by a band and escorted by a parade to her hotel. Her first concert took place (Sept. 11) at Castle Garden. Her first selection was the aria "Casta Diva"—what a pun!—from Bellini's opera "Norma," and the concert grossed $17,864.05. The second concert brought in $14,203.03. She gave $10,000 to charity, and when the Widow and Orphans' Fund of the Fire Department got $3,000 the firemen gave her a gold box and a boxed edition of Audubon's "Birds and Quadrupeds of America." (For the record, she sang the "Messiah" in Tripler Hall, Nov. 1, 1850. During the next two years she toured the United States, earning $130,000, of which she donated $100,000 to charitable institutions in Sweden and the United States.)

Theatre-going San Franciscans witnessed (Jan. 16) at the Eagle Theatre (later Washington Hall) their first real play, "The Wife," by the English playwright James Sheridan Knowles, and an afterpiece "Charles the Second." (The play had been given previously in Sacramento.)

Italian opera came to Chicago when Bellini's "La Sonnambula" was performed (July 29) at Rice's Theatre.

Tom Maguire, onetime New York cab driver and saloon-keeper, started his California career as a theatrical manager by opening (Oct. 30) the Jenny Lind Theatre in San Francisco. (He was quick to capitalize on a name; Jenny Lind had just arrived—see above.)

On the New York stage, Mose the volunteer fireman (1848) was followed (in July) by a socially more successful fire-eater in "The New York Fireman and the Bond Street Heiress," which played at the National Theatre.

According to immigration statistics, 379,466 aliens entered the United States, making a total of 1,173,251 for the decade. Fearing the potential voting power of the foreign-born, alarmed nativists revived the prejudices of the Native American Party (1843) and formed the quasi-secret Know-Nothing movement or party, at first not actually an organized political party. "I don't know" was their usual reply to any question concerning their affairs.

The national population was 23,191,876.

₰ 1851

The Arkansas Traveller. Instrumental. Firth, Pond & Co., cop. 1851. (This early edition is recorded in Harry Dichter and Elliott Shapiro, "Early American Sheet Music," New York, 1941. An obituary notice in "The American Art Journal," New York, Jan. 15, 1887, p. 199, of one Joseph Tosso, a violinist, contained this bit of startling information: "His musical war horse was 'The Arkansas Traveller,' which is popularly, though erroneously, considered to be his composition." According to the notice, Tosso was born in Mexico—place unspecified—on Aug. 3, 1802, the son of an Italian father and a French mother; studied the violin with DeBeriot in Paris, and died at Covington, presumably in Kentucky, on Jan. 6, 1887. This astonishing information was, more astonishingly, reprinted in the Belgian musical magazine "Le Guide Musical," Brussels, Feb. 3, 1887, vol. 33, no. 5, p. 39.)

Home Again. w., m., M[arshall] S. Pike; arr. by J. P. Ordway. A. & J. P. Ordway, cop. 1851.

How Can I Leave Thee!—*original German title:* **Ach wie ist's möglich.** w., m., anon. [Baltimore:] F. D. Benteen, cop. 1851.

Hungarian Rhapsody No. 2. Piano solo. m., Franz Liszt. Leipzig: Bartholf Senff [1851]. (Arr. for orch. by Karl Müller-Berghaus and published by B. Senff, Leipzig [1878].)

Nancy Till. w., m., anon. Firth, Pond & Co., cop. 1851. (Sometimes erroneously ascribed to Stephen Collins Foster.)

Oh Boys Carry Me 'Long. w., m., Stephen C[ollins] Foster. Firth, Pond & Co., cop. 1851.

Old Folks at Home. w., m., Stephen C[ollins] Foster. Firth, Pond & Co., cop. 1851.

Poor Old Slave. Negro song. m., arr. by E. M. F. Boston: G. P. Reed & Co., cop. 1851.

Wait for the Wagon. w., anon. m., George P. Knauff. Baltimore: F. D. Benteen, cop. 1851.

The United States was 75 years old.

International difficulties arising from an insurrection in Cuba (1850-51) almost brought the United States into war with Spain but for the intervention of France and Great Britain. At the same time, the United States paid $25,000 to Spain for the damage done to its consulate in New Orleans by riotous Cuban sympathizers and agents.

"Go West, young man" wrote Horace Greeley editorially in his "New-York Tribune." The phrase, however, is incorrectly attributed to him; it was made earlier this year by John Babsone Lane Soule in the Terre Haute, Ind., newspaper "Express."

The United States reduced (July 1) letter postage from 5 and 10 cents to 1, 3, 5, and 12 cents. (Other values were added in 1855, 1856, 1860. The stamps of 1847 and 1851-60 were demonetized at the outbreak of the Civil War.)

In California, vigilance committees were being organized by citizens to counteract the lawlessness of the gold rush adventurers.

The United States purchased (July 23) territory in western Minnesota from the Sioux Indians.

San Francisco suffered (June 22) its sixth fire.

The new, trim clipper "Flying Cloud" made a record trip from New York to San Francisco via Cape Horn in 89 days, 8 hours.

Important railroad developments took place in New York State. The New York & Lake Erie opened (May 14) service between Piedmont on the Hudson and Dunkirk on Lake Erie with gala ceremonies conducted by President Fillmore. The New York & Hudson River (now N. Y. Central) made (Oct. 8) its first run from New York City to Albany. The caboose, or observatory cabin atop the freight car, originated about this time with the New York & Erie Railroad near Suffern, N. Y.

The Wabash-Erie canal, connecting the Ohio River with Lake Erie, was completed.

Sewing machine patents were granted to Isaac Merritt Singer and to A. B. Wilson.

Lorenzo Lorraine Langstroth, American apiarist, designed the modern box beehive (Langstroth hive).

Cyrus Hall McCormick was awarded a gold medal for his reaper (1834) at the first International Exposition in the Crystal Palace, London.

Fire damaged (Dec. 24) the Library of Congress, reducing its collection of books to 20,000 volumes.

"Gleason's Pictorial Drawing-Room Companion" was founded in Boston as the first illustrated weekly magazine in the United States. (Ceased publication in 1859.)

Northwestern University, Evanston, Ill., for men and women, was founded (Jan. 28) by the Illinois Legislature.

Louis Kossuth, Hungarian patriot exiled in Turkey, came to the United States aboard an American naval vessel to thank the nation for its inter-

vention in securing his release. President Fillmore had signed (Mar. 3)
an act of Congress authorizing the procedure. Kossuth was welcomed
(Dec. 5) in New York with a parade and dinner, and was formally received (Dec. 30) in Washington. Daniel Webster delivered the official
address.

William Marcy Tweed was elected alderman to the New York City
Common Council (its 40 members received no pay and were popularly
called The Forty Thieves). During the next twenty years he was a
notorious figure in the city's corrupt politics and gained so much power
that he was nicknamed "The Boss."

International yacht racing was instituted when the American schooner
"America" defeated (Aug. 12) the chief British contender "Aurora" of
the Royal Yacht Squadron in the race around the Isle of Wight for the
Cup, of All Nations. This gave the United States the first victory in what
was to evolve into the America's Cup races, which England has never won.
(The next race was in 1870.)

Emanuel Leutze, German-born American painter, finished his painting "Washington Crossing the Delaware" at Düsseldorf.

The dailies, "New York Times" and Sacramento, Cal., "Union" were
founded. (Both newspapers are still published.)

Harriet Beecher Stowe's novel "Uncle Tom's Cabin," which lifted her
into nation-wide prominence, appeared serially (1851-52) in the "National Era," an antislavery magazine published in Washington, D. C.

Herman Melville published his whaling classic "Moby Dick"; Hawthorne brought out his novel "The House of the Seven Gables."

The "Carpet-Bag" appeared in Boston as a humorous weekly magazine.
The issue for May 1 contained a piece, "The Dandy Frightening the
Squatter," by the 16-year-old Samuel Langhorne Clemens, later better
known as Mark Twain, and an essay by the 17-year-old Artemus Ward.
(The magazine ceased publication in 1853.)

In the theatre, Negro minstrelsy was all the rage. Some groups called
themselves "minstrels"; others were "serenaders." Competing with them
were female "bloomer" troupes. Amelia Bloomer's fad in women's dress
also became the butt of a comedy, "The Bloomers, or, Pets in Pants," and
was the subject of a song, "The Gal with the Bloomers on."

San Francisco had its first glimpse of Italian opera at a performance
(in Feb.) of Bellini's "La Sonnambula." (Bellini's "Norma" and Verdi's
"Ernani" followed.)

The abdication of Ludwig I of Bavaria sent his mistress, the Countess
of Landsfeld, to America. She is better known to history as Lola Montez,
Irish-born actress whose real name was Maria Dolores Eliza Rosanna
Gilbert. She made (Dec. 29) her American debut in "Betley" in New
York at the Broadway Theatre. She failed to impress her audience, composed mainly of male spectators, but played, nevertheless, a two weeks'
engagement.

Irish-born Matilda Heron started her career as a popular American actress in "Fazio" in Philadelphia.

In the shadow of Jenny Lind, who was appearing in New York in opera, an "infant prima donna" was growing up in the city and singing operatic arias in concerts—Adelina Patti, born eight years previously in Madrid.

Eben Tourjée, self-taught 17-year-old Boston musician, introduced class instruction in piano playing at Fall River, Mass.

The first Y.M.C.A. (Young Men's Christian Association) was established (Dec. 29) in Boston.

Deaths of the year included John James Audubon, aged 76 (Jan. 26), in New York, and James Fenimore Cooper, aged 62 (Sept. 14), in Cooperstown, N. Y. (home of baseball's Hall of Fame).

₷ 1852

By the Margin of Fair Zurich's Waters. See below "Home of My Youth," and also 1834.

Do They Miss Me at Home? w., m., S. M. Grannis. Boston: Oliver Ditson & Co., cop. 1852; renewed 1880 by S. M. Grannis.

Ever of Thee. w., George Linley. m., Foley Hall. London: J. A. Turner [1852].

Home of My Youth. (The Peri). w., S. J. Burr. m., James Gaspard Maeder. ("The Peri" was an American "fairy-opera," in 3 acts, the libretto by S. J. Burr and the music by James Gaspard Maeder, produced at the Broadway Theatre, New York, Dec. 13, 1852—one of the characters was Ponce de Leon. Vocal selections were published by Wm. Hall, New York, cop. 1852. The words and music of four songs are reproduced in Grenville Vernon, "Yankee Doodle-Doo," New York, 1927, p. 134-38. They are "Home of My Youth," "Thoughts That Have for Years Been Sleeping," "You'll Meet Me—Won't You?" and "By the Margin of Fair Zurich's Waters.")

Lily Dale. w., m., H. S. Thompson. Boston: Oliver Ditson & Co., cop. 1852.

Massa's in de Cold Ground. w., m., Stephen C[ollins] Foster. Firth, Pond & Co., cop. 1852.

The Rock Beside the Sea. w., anon. m., Charles C[rozat] Converse. Philadelphia: Lee & Walker, cop. 1852.

Swiss Song. w., anon. m., Carl Eckert. Wm. Hall & Son [1852]. (Also known as the "Swiss Echo Song"; published earlier in Germany. The German words are "Er liebt nur mich allein." The above edition was reviewed in "The Musical World and New York Musical Times," Dec. 25, 1852, p. 261.)

Thou Art Gone from My Gaze. w., m., George Linley. W. E. Millet [1852]. (Published earlier in London. The above edition was printed as a musical supplement in "The Musical World and Journal of the Fine Arts," New York, Mar. 1, 1852 [p. 179].)

Thoughts That Have for Years Been Sleeping. See above: "Home of My Youth" (The Peri).

You'll Meet Me—Won't You? See above: "Home of My Youth" (The Peri).

The Young Folks at Home. w., Frank Spencer. m., Miss Hattie Livingston. T. S. Berry & Co., cop. 1852. (Composed for Wood's Minstrels.)

Vermont became the second state to adopt prohibition. (The first was Maine in 1846; Connecticut followed in 1854, and New Hampshire and New York in 1855. All but Maine repealed the law.)

Direct railroad service was established (Dec. 31) between New York and Chicago.

Harriet Beecher Stowe's novel "Uncle Tom's Cabin" appeared in book form; 300,000 copies were reported to have been sold during the first year.

William Walker, lawyer and newspaper editor in California, attempted with a small force to establish (in Nov.) a republic of his own in the Mexican states of Sonora and Lower California on the pretext of defending the natives from the Apache Indians. (He was arrested and tried in May, 1854, for a violation of the neutrality laws, but was acquitted. This episode was the first of his filibustering ventures.)

Ole Bull, renowned Norwegian violin virtuoso, bought a tract of 125,000 acres in Pennsylvania, which he called Oleana. This was to be a colony of his countrymen, "consecrated to freedom, baptized in independence, and protected by the mighty flag of the Union." (The scheme failed, and Ole Bull lost an immense sum of money in the subsequent litigation and through a swindle. To recoup his losses, he concertized during the next five years in the United States, reaching California via Panama.)

Ohio became the first state to limit the working hours of women to ten hours a day.

The United States established its second mint in San Francisco. (The first was established in 1792 in Philadelphia.)

The Boston Public Library was established.

The American Geographical Society was founded in New York.

Catherine Sinclair won a bitterly contested divorce from the actor Edwin Forrest in a suit that gained nationwide publicity. (Miss Sinclair went to San Francisco in the following year and became a notable actress and theatrical manageress there. Forrest unsuccessfully appealed the divorce case until 1868.)

William Makepeace Thackeray, famous English novelist, made (in Nov.) the first of two visits to the United States, lecturing on English literature. (He remained until April, 1853. His second visit was in 1855-56.)

Fire destroyed (July 27) the steamer "Henry Clay" on the Hudson River, N. Y., with a loss of 70 lives. Andrew Jackson Downing, pioneer American landscape gardener, lost his life while rescuing fellow passengers. (He designed the gardens surrounding the Smithsonian Institution, the Capitol, and the White House.) On Lake Erie, the steamer "Atlantic" sank (Aug. 20) in a collision with a loss of 250 lives.

Jenny Lind married (Feb. 5) her pianist and conductor, Otto Goldschmidt, in Boston.

"The Golden Era" in San Francisco and "Globe-Democrat" in St. Louis were founded as daily newspapers. (The former ceased publication in 1893; the latter still is published.)

Nathaniel Hawthorne published his tales for children, "A Wonder Book," based on Greek myths. (Its sequel, "Tanglewood Tales," appeared in 1853.)

The Music Hall in Boston was dedicated (Nov. 20) with a concert by the combined Handel and Haydn and the Musical Fund choral societies.

Two of the world's greatest opera singers made their American debuts in New York—the Italian contralto Marietta Alboni and the German soprano Henriette Sontag. Both appeared first in concert at the Metropolitan Hall (Alboni, June 23; Sontag, Sept. 27). Mme. Sontag, who was the Countess Rossi, was greeted on her arrival in Jenny Lind style with a brass band parade and a reception.

Friedrich von Flotow's opera "Martha" received (Nov. 1) its American première in New York at Niblo's Garden. It was sung in English.

Without the author's consent, George L. Aiken, American actor and playwright, produced (Sept. 27) in Troy, N. Y., for a run of 100 performances, his popular dramatization of Harriet Beecher Stowe's novel "Uncle Tom's Cabin."

Dion Boucicault's much-heralded London play "The Corsican Brothers," a dramatization of Alexandre Dumas's "Les Frères Corses" (1845), was performed (Apr. 21) with spectacular scenic effects at the Bowery Theatre in New York.

James William Wallack opened (Sept. 8) the theatre Wallack's Lyceum in New York. (It was rebuilt in 1861 as Wallack's Theatre.)

Tragedian Junius Brutus Booth and his 19-year-old son Edwin acted in San Francisco and Sacramento. The elder Booth made (July 30) his California debut in San Francisco at the Jenny Lind Theatre in "The Iron Chest," his London success (1818). In Sacramento, the gold miners were not friendly to his style of acting. (The elder Booth died while on his way to Cincinnati.)

At the Democratic convention, Franklin Pierce was nominated on the 49th ballot over Henry Clay, Stephen Douglas, and James Buchanan. In the national election, Pierce defeated the Whig candidate, General Winfield Scott. This ended the Whig party.

John Howard Payne, aged 61, luckless poet of "Home, Sweet Home!" died (Apr. 10) as American consul in Tunis, Africa.

Other deaths of the year included Henry Clay, aged 75 (June 29), in Washington, D. C., and Daniel Webster, aged 70 (Oct. 24), in Marshfield, Mass.

ह≫ 1853

Haydn's Ox Minuet. Piano piece. [m., erroneously ascribed to Franz Joseph Haydn.] Wm. Hall & Son [1853]. (Published earlier in Germany or in Austria. This once popular piano piece was reprinted in "The Musical World," New York, May 28, 1853, p. 56-57, as "just published," preceded by the familiar tale regarding its supposed origin. The composition is an excerpt from a musical play or Singspiel, "Die Ochsenmenuette," produced in Vienna, 1823, and compiled from Haydn's works by Ignaz Xavier Seyfried, a pupil of Mozart and a friend of Beethoven. The burlesque minuet was not composed by Haydn.)

The Hazel Dell. w., m., Wurzel [pseud. of George Frederick Root]. William Hall & Son, cop. 1853.

My Old Kentucky Home, Good Night. w., m., Stephen C[ollins] Foster. Firth, Pond & Co., cop. 1853.

Old Dog Tray. w., m., Stephen C[ollins] Foster. Firth, Pond & Co., cop. 1853.

Franklin Pierce, Democrat, of New Hampshire, was inaugurated 14th President.

Boundary disputes again arose between the United States and Mexico— this time over the lands acquired by the Guadalupe Hidalgo Treaty (1848) affecting present southern Arizona and southwestern New Mexico. James Gadsden, United States minister to Mexico, negotiated for $10,000,000 the purchase of an additional 45,000 square miles to settle the question permanently.

Commodore Matthew Calbraith Perry, U.S.N., brother of Oliver Hazard Perry, hero of the Battle of Lake Erie (1813), arrived with a squadron in Yokohama harbor, Japan. He had been commissioned by (former) President Fillmore to establish trade relations with the country, then closed to all outside contacts. He was formally received (July 14) by the Lord of Toda on Kurikama Beach. The deliberations resulted in a treaty (ratified by Congress Mar. 8, 1854) that opened Japanese ports to American commercial interests.

Stamped envelopes were placed (in June) on sale by the Government.

The Know-Nothing movement in New York (1850) was steadily gaining in momentum and causing riots. It was mainly directed against Irish and German Roman Catholics. To check "the power of the Pope," it started to put Bibles in public schools.

The New York Clearing House was established (Oct. 11).

The Crystal Palace, New York, on the present site of the New York Public Library and Bryant Park, was opened (July 14) with elaborate ceremonies by President Pierce. The structure, built in imitation of its London namesake (1851), was "composed of glass, supported by iron," with a dome 148 feet high and "covered five acres." It housed a world's fair exhibit.

The steamer "San Francisco," bound for California and carrying 700 passengers who included 500 members of the Third Regular U. S. Artillery, foundered (Dec. 24) at sea with a loss of 240 lives.

A. J. Watt of Utica, N. Y., introduced an improved method of filling teeth with gold.

A large 1,413-ton packet was launched at Newburyport, Mass. It was called "Dreadnaught," a name that was to be applied years hence to a powerful type of warship.

Some 50 librarians gathered (Sept. 15-17) in New York at their first convention.

Heinrich Engelhard Steinweg [sic] from Germany established (Mar. 5) the present firm of Steinway & Sons in New York for the manufacture of improved square pianos.

Frank Parmelee started (May 9) the first regular omnibus line in Chicago.

The "New York Clipper" was founded in New York as a weekly theatrical journal. (Ceased publication in 1924.)

A gelding named "Conqueror" ran 100 miles in 8 hours, 55 minutes, 53 seconds, thus winning a $3,000 to $1,000 wager that the stretch couldn't be traversed in nine hours, over the Union Course, Long Island, N. Y.

Commodore Vanderbilt, Hudson River shipping magnate and later railroad king, built the yacht "North Star," which cost him $1,500 a day to operate.

In answer to the attacks on the plausibility of the story in her novel, Harriet Beecher Stowe published "A Key to Uncle Tom's Cabin."

The eccentric French conductor and composer Louis Antoine Jullien came to the United States with his own orchestra. He made (Sept. 16) his American debut in New York and toured the country (1853-54).

Louis Moreau Gottschalk, American piano virtuoso born in New Orleans, returned to the United States after creating a sensation in Europe and toured this country with equal success. (He was to become the composer of the once famous piano piece "The Dying Poet," 1864.)

Luther Whiting Mason, Maine-born school music reformer, went to Louisville, Ky., to become musical superintendent of the local public schools. He soon began publishing with George Augustus Veazie the well-known "National System" of music books and charts, which long remained in vogue in United States schools.

Clark Mills, self-taught sculptor, created what is believed to be the first equestrian statue in the United States—General Jackson on a rearing horse. His original payment was $12,000, but Congress voted an additional $20,000 in appreciation. The statue was cast from captured British cannon and unveiled in Washington, D. C. (He erected there in 1860 a similar statue of Washington. He cast the statue of Freedom, 1863, which adorns the Capitol.)

Dion Boucicault, Irish playwright and actor, came (in Sept.) to the United States, followed on another boat by his secret wife, Agnes Robertson, who became a popular actress in America.

Henri Franconi's newly erected Hippodrome in New York, seating 4,000, opened (May 2) with a new type of amusement. It presented chariot races, clowns, ponies ridden by monkeys in jockey costumes, ostrich races, aerial equilibrists thirty feet in the air, stag hunts, etc.—all at a price scale of 25 cents to one dollar. A competitor was the Washington Circus that opened (June 15) opposite the Crystal Palace.

"Pauline," a romantic and long-popular play imported from London and produced (Mar. 7) in New York at Wallack's Lyceum, brought to the stage a new character—the gentleman "crook."

After a mild reception in New York (1851), Lola Montez became "hot stuff" to the California miners and added another chapter to her strange career. She acted (May 26) Lady Teazle in "The School for Scandal" at the American Theatre in San Francisco, electrified her audience the next night with her naughty Spider Dance, married a local newspaperman, Patrick Purdy Hall, moved on to Sacramento, challenged there the editor of the "Daily Californian" to a duel either with pistols or with pills (one to be poison—"Pistols or pizen" becoming a catchword of the time) and retired for two idyllic years to a remote cottage in the mountains of Grass Valley. She had been particularly effective in a dramatic sketch of her life, "Lola Montez in Bavaria."

The world of feminine fashion avidly copied Empress Eugénie styles. (Eugénie that year became Louis Napoleon's wife and empress.)

ℰ⊷ 1854

Ellen Bayne. w., m., Stephen C[ollins] Foster. Firth, Pond & Co., cop. 1854.

Hard Times Come Again No More. w., m., Stephen C[ollins] Foster. Firth, Pond & Co., cop. 1854.

Jeannie with the Light Brown Hair. w., m., Stephen C[ollins] Foster. Firth, Pond & Co., cop. 1854.

The Monastery Bells—*original French title:* Les Cloches du Monastère. Piano solo. m., Louis Alfred Lefébure-Wély, op. 54, No. 1. Berlin: Schlesinger [1854]; New York: F. Schuberth & Co. [1854]; Munich: Jos. Aibl [1855]. (Published earlier in Paris.)

Poet and Peasant Overture—*original German title:* Dichter und Bauer. Orch. composition. m., Franz von Suppé. Munich: Jos. Aibl [1854].

There's Music in the Air. Hymn for SATB with piano acc. w., Frances Jane Crosby (Mrs. Alexander Van Alstyne). m., George Frederick Root. Wm. Hall & Son [1854].

What Is Home Without a Mother? w., m., Alice Hawthorne [pseud. of Septimus Winner]. Philadelphia: Lee & Walker, cop. 1854.

Willie, We Have Missed You. w., m., Stephen C[ollins] Foster. Firth, Pond & Co., cop. 1854.

Congress passed the Kansas-Nebraska Bill, which opened the territories to slavery on the principle of "squatter sovereignty," i.e., local choice of government. The bill was championed by Stephen Douglas, Vermont-born Democrat of Illinois.

As a result of the Kansas-Nebraska Bill, the appointment of a proslavery governor for "bleeding Kansas," and the proslavery tendencies of President Pierce who was influenced by his proslavery Secretary of State Jefferson Davis of Kentucky, the present Republican Party was organized (July 6) in Ripon, Wis. It evolved as an antislavery party from the dwindling Whig Party and several minor groups. In the national election its first candidate, John Charles Frémont, was defeated (1845) in a stormy campaign.

Three American foreign ministers (Great Britain, France, and Spain) created a political sensation when they drew up at Ostend, Belgium, a Manifesto advocating the purchase or seizure of Cuba from Spain—which, of course, the United States promptly disavowed.

The United States signed trade agreements with Japan (Mar. 8) and with Great Britain (June 27), the latter regulating commercial relations with Canada.

The Emigrant Aid Society was formed to settle antislavery New Englanders in Kansas. (Some 2,000 went into the territory.)

In less than six years about $300,000 had been raised by public subscriptions toward the erection of the Washington National Monument in Washington, D. C. The contributions now suddenly ceased when a marble block from the Temple of Concord in Rome, presented by Pope Pius IX, disappeared. For nearly a quarter of a century (until 1878) work on the shaft, which had reached a height of 154 feet, was interrupted.

Walter Hunt, who had invented the safety pin, now invented the paper collar.

John Mercer Langston, American Negro emancipated from slavery in 1833, became one of the first members of his race to achieve position and distinction when he was admitted to the Ohio bar.

American marine disasters on the Atlantic took a huge toll of lives: 311 were lost on the "Powhatan," grounded (Apr. 16) off Long Beach, N. Y.; 300 on the "New Era," wrecked (Nov. 13) below Sandy Hook, N. J.; the United States war sloop "Albany," sailing (Sept. 29) from Panama disappeared completely. Smaller fatalities occurred elsewhere in United States waters.

P. T. Barnum took his circus troupe on a tour of Europe.

The hoopskirt, a creation supported by steel wires and tape, was the latest feminine wardrobe addition.

The "Chicago Times" was founded as a daily newspaper.

Henry David Thoreau, Concord-born writer of Scottish, Quaker, and Puritan descent, published "Walden," an account of his experiences while living from July 4, 1845 to Sept. 6, 1847 in a hut at Walden Pond near Concord.

Massachusetts author Maria Susanna Cummins won national fame with her novel, "The Lamplighter," a moralistic romance of a Boston orphan girl befriended by a lamplighter.

Timothy Shay Arthur published his melodramatic temperance novel "Ten Nights in a Barroom and What I Saw There." (The book was dramatized by William W. Pratt in 1858.)

The popular Harrison-Pyne Troupe of English singers gave opera in English in New York and elsewhere for the next three years. Their repertory included "La Sonnambula," "Maritana," "Fra Diavolo," "The Crown Diamonds," "The Bohemian Girl," "Cinderella," and others.

The Academy of Music in New York, the city's temple of opera for the next 30 years, succeeding the Astor Place Opera House (1847), opened (Oct. 2) with Bellini's "Norma" sung by the famous singers Giulia Grisi and Giuseppe Mario and conducted by the eminent Luigi Arditi. The building cost $335,000.

Robert Kemp, a Boston shoe dealer, started his famous "Old Folks' Concerts" as a revival of old-fashioned "psalmody" and became known as "Father" Kemp.

The German male chorus Männergesangverein Arion was founded (in Jan.) in New York as a rival to the Deutscher Liederkranz (1847) by 14 dissident members of the latter.

After an inauspicious start in "Camille, or, The Fate of a Coquette" (Broadway Theatre, New York, Dec. 9, 1853), because of the questionable morality of its story, actress Jean Margaret Davenport returned (Aug. 28) to the same theatre in the play and scored a hit with her superb portrayal of Dumas's heroine—the first in a long line of famous Camilles.

Shakespeare's comedy "A Midsummer Night's Dream" was played with Mendelssohn's music at two New York theatres, opening almost simultaneously—at Burton's (Feb. 3) and at the Broadway (Feb. 6).

The old Bowery Amphitheatre in New York reopened (in Aug.) as a German-language playhouse, the Stadt Theater. For the next ten years the theatre harbored opera, operetta, drama, comedy, farce, etc., either imported from the Vaterland or of local origin.

₷➤ 1855

Come, Where My Love Lies Dreaming. Part song for SATB. w., m., Stephen C[ollins] Foster. Firth, Pond & Co., cop. 1855.

Hark! the Herald Angels Sing. Hymn. Tune: "Mendelssohn." w., Charles Wesley. m., Felix Mendelssohn. (The music was adapted by William Hayman Cummings in London about 1855 from Mendelssohn's "Festgesang" for two male choirs and brass instruments. It was written for the 400th anniversary of Gutenberg and the invention of printing, and was performed in the public square at Leipzig, June 24, 1840. The hymn tune is an adaptation of the second movement of the cantata, "Vaterland, in deinen Gauen brach der gold'ne Tag einst an," for unison male chorus and brass instruments.)

Kamennoi Ostrow (No. 22 in: "Kamennoi Ostrow, Album de 24 Portraits, Op. 10"). Piano solo. m., Anton Rubinstein. Mayence: B. Schott's Söhne [1855].

Listen to the Mocking Bird. w., m., Alice Hawthorne [pseud. of Septimus Winner]. Winner & Shuster, cop. 1855.

Melody in F (No. 1 in: "Deux Melodies, Op. 3"). Piano solo. m.,
Anton Rubinstein. Berlin: Schlesinger [1855?].

Rosalie, the Prairie Flower. w., m., Wurzel [pseud. of George Frederick
Root]. Boston: Russell & Richardson, cop. 1855.

Star of the Evening. Words and melody by James M. Sayles; arr. by
Henry Tucker. J. H. Hidley, cop. 1855.

The Sword of Bunker Hill. w., William Ross Wallace. m., Bernard
Covert. Boston: G. P. Reed & Co., cop. 1855.

Twinkling Stars Are Laughing, Love. w., m., John P. Ordway. Cop.
1855 by J. P. Ordway.

Washington Irving coined the expression "the Almighty Dollar" in his
book of stories and sketches "Wolfert's Roost and Miscellanies," originally published in "The Knickerbocker Magazine."

The first section of the Atlantic cable was laid between Cape Breton,
N. S., and Newfoundland by the New York, Newfoundland and London
Telegraph Company, which was organized (May 8, 1854) by Cyrus West
Field and Peter Cooper.

The Western Union Telegraph Company was founded. One of its directors was Ezra Cornell, later founder of Cornell University (1865).

The Know-Nothing political party claimed 1,500,000 voters.

The Knights of the Golden Circle was founded as a secret organization
in the Southern States to aid the cause of slavery. (It was also known as
the Order of American Knights; and its membership included "copper-
heads" or Northern sympathizers with the South.)

James Oliver of Indiana invented the iron plow.

Henry Bessemer, British engineer, patented (Oct. 17) his steel-making
process—a great boon to the industry.

Dentistry made new strides when the American, Charles Goodyear, Jr.,
patented in England the process of making dental plates of hard rubber.

The locomotive "Hamilton Davis," coupled to six cars, made 14 miles in
11 minutes on the New York & Hudson River (now New York Central)
tracks.

Steinway & Sons (1853) won first prize at the New York Industrial
Exhibition for their square pianos.

The suspension bridge at Niagara Falls, connecting the United States
and Canada, was completed.

The first bridge to span the Mississippi was built from Rock Island, Ill.,
to Davenport, Iowa. Two weeks after its completion, a 250-foot span collapsed when the steamer "Effie Afton" collided with one of the piers of

the bridge. In the ensuing litigation Abraham Lincoln was among the counsel representing the Rock Island railroad. The opposing counsel was the eloquent river-lawyer, Judge Wead, whose final address to the jury occupied nearly two hours. Lincoln's summation took little more than a minute. He won the case.

William Makepeace Thackeray made (in Oct.) the second of his two visits to the United States as a lecturer. (The first was in 1852-53; on his second, he remained until April, 1856. He incorporated his observations and studies in a two-volume novel "The Virginians," London, 1858-59.)

Lucy Stone married Dr. Henry B. Blackwell and kept her maiden name after marriage (hence "Lucy Stoners," a synonym for feminine independence as well as social reform).

"Frank Leslie's Illustrated Newspaper" appeared as a weekly journal. It later changed its name to "Leslie's Weekly." An edition in German also was issued. (The periodical was absorbed in 1922 by "Judge.")

The San Francisco "Call-Bulletin" was founded as a daily newspaper.

Henry Wadsworth Longfellow published his narrative poem "The Song of Hiawatha."

Walt Whitman issued the first edition of his "Leaves of Grass," containing 12 poems.

The brothers Evert Augustus and George Long Duychinck published the "Cyclopedia of American Literature" (completed in 1866). Other books of the year included the two standard reference books: "Age of Fable" (Thomas Bulfinch) and "Famous Quotations" (John Bartlett).

The American-minded Norwegian violinist, Ole Bull, took over the operatic management of the Academy of Music in New York. He opened (Feb. 19) with "Rigoletto" (see following entry), and announced a prize of $1,000 for "a grand opera by an American composer on an American subject." The undertaking was a fiasco after two weeks, the singers attacking the impresario in the newspapers.

Verdi's famous repertory operas "Rigoletto" and "Il Trovatore" received their United States premières in New York at the Academy of Music (Feb. 19 and May 2, respectively).

Whether or not Ole Bull's prize, mentioned above, was an incentive is not known, but an American opera by a native composer was forthcoming. It was George Frederick Bristow's "Rip Van Winkle." The opera was produced (Sept. 27) in New York at Niblo's Garden, and it fared better than Fry's "Leonora" (1845).

The New York Philharmonic Orchestra played (Apr. 21) the first American performance of the great overture to Wagner's opera "Tannhäuser." Said the critic in the "Albion" (Apr. 28): " . . . it bears the imprint of great, very great talent, united to but little genius."

Henri Vieuxtemps, Belgian violin virtuoso and composer, and Sigismund Thalberg, piano virtuoso and the rival of Chopin and Liszt, toured the United States in joint recitals.

Rachel, famous French actress, made (Sept. 3) her American debut as Camille in Corneille's tragedy "Les Horaces," under the management of her brother Raphael Félix, at the Metropolitan Theatre in New York.

Wallack's Theatre in New York produced (Dec. 24) John Brougham's hilarious burlesque "Po-co-han-tas, or, Ye Gentle Savage, which amused audiences for the next few years.

English actress Laura Keene became the first theatrical manageress in the United States when she reopened (Dec. 27) the Metropolitan Theatre in New York as Laura Keene's Varieties.

₿⇒ 1856

The Arrow and the Song. w., Henry Wadsworth Longfellow. m., Michael William Balfe. London: Boosey & Sons [1856].

The Cottage by the Sea. w., m., John Rogers Thomas. Firth, Pond & Co., cop. 1856.

Darling Nelly Gray. w., m., Benjamin Russell Hanby. Boston: Oliver Ditson & Co., cop. 1856.

Gentle Annie. w., m., Stephen C[ollins] Foster. Firth, Pond & Co., cop. 1856.

Hark! I Hear an Angel Sing. w., W. C. B. m., R. G. Shrival. Augusta, Ga.: G. A. Oates, cop. 1856.

Kattie Avourneen. w., m., Frederick Nicholls Crouch. S. T. Gordon, cop. 1856.

The Last Hope. Piano solo. m., Louis Moreau Gottschalk, Op. 16. Boston: Oliver Ditson & Co., cop. 1856.

Old Friends and Old Times. w., Charles Swain. m., John Rogers Thomas. Cleveland: S. Brainard's Sons, cop. 1856 by Henry Tolman, Boston.

Root, Hog, or Die. w., m., Richard J. McGowan (?). Boston: Oliver Ditson & Co., cop. 1856.

Stars of the Summer Night. Part song for TTBB. w., Henry Wadsworth Longfellow. m., Isaac Baker Woodbury (usually published anonymously). J. F. Huntington, cop. 1856.

John Brown, abolitionist leader, massacred five proslavery adherents in Osawatomie, Kan., thus becoming a national figure as "Brown of Osawatomie." In Kansas, proslavery supporters sacked the town of Lawrence.

Henry Ward Beecher, minister of Plymouth (Congregational) Church, Brooklyn, New York City, and an ardent supporter of the antislavery cause, held (June 1) a public "auction" of a young mulatto named Sarah to dramatize the evils of slavery. The mock auction raised sufficient funds to purchase her freedom and buy her a modest house in Peekskill, N. Y.

Cyrus Roberts of Illinois so improved the Hiram and John Pitts reaper (1837) that it became a forerunner of the modern machine.

William Walker (1853) carried out his second filibustering expedition. With about 50 followers, he landed (1855) in Nicaragua, proclaimed (1856) himself president, and attempted to establish a slaveholding state. He was recognized by President Pierce. (The scheme collapsed in 1857 when he opposed Cornelius Vanderbilt's mercantile interests there. Walker renewed the attempt in 1860, but was captured and executed by the Honduran government.)

So popular was Longfellow's new poem "Hiawatha" that public readings were given in eastern cities. It was ridiculed in a funny burlesque by Charles Melton Walcot, entitled "Hiawatha, or, Ardent Spirits and Laughing Waters," which was produced (Dec. 15) in New York at Wallack's Theatre.

"Dred, A Tale of the Great Dismal Swamp" was Harriet Beecher Stowe's second antislavery novel. Three dramatizations immediately appeared in New York theatres: by C. W. Taylor at the National (Sept. 22), by John Brougham at the Bowery (Sept. 29), and by H. J. Conway at Barnum's American Museum (Oct. 16) with the midget General Tom Thumb playing a character not in Mrs. Stowe's book.

John Greenleaf Whittier brought out his classic of New England childhood, "The Barefoot Boy," in his collection of verse "The Panorama and Other Poems." Other books of the year included "The Rise of the Dutch Republic" (John Lothrop Motley; 3 vols.) and the fiction, "Prue and I" (George William Curtis; sketches) and "The Quadroon" (Thomas Mayne Reid; the book furnished Dion Boucicault with material for his successful play "The Octoroon," 1859).

Verdi's famous opera "La Traviata" received (Dec. 3) its American première in New York at the Academy of Music with the French coloratura Mme. Anna de La Grange and Luigi Brignoli.

Tom Maguire, former New York cabdriver and saloonkeeper, who had entered the theatrical business in San Francisco in 1850, remodeled the San Francisco Hall. It opened (in November) as Maguire's Opera House.

At the Republican state convention in Illinois, a political personality of national significance became evident—Abraham Lincoln.

In the national elections, the newly organized Republican Party ran its first presidential candidate—John Charles Frémont. His opponents were

Millard Fillmore, Whig, supported by the American (or Know-Nothing) party, and James Buchanan, Democrat, a former Federalist. The Republican nominee polled 1,391,555 votes. Buchanan won the election by 536,440 votes.

₿⮞ 1857

Come into the Garden, Maud. w., Alfred Lord Tennyson. m., Michael William Balfe. London: Boosey & Sons [1857?].

Flee As a Bird. .w., Mrs. Mary S. B. Dana. m., arr. by George Frederick Root. Boston: Oliver Ditson & Co., cop. 1857.

Jingle Bells; or, The One Horse Open Sleigh. w., m., J. S. Pierpont. Boston: Oliver Ditson & Co., cop. 1857.

Little White Cottage. w., M[arshall] S. Pike. Melody by G. S. P.; arr. by J. S. Pierpont. Boston: Oliver Ditson & Co., cop. 1857.

Lorena. w., Rev. H. D. L. Webster. m., J[oseph] P[hilbrick] Webster. Chicago: Higgins Bros., cop. 1857.

Mrs. Lofty and I. w., Mrs. Gildersleeve Longstreet. m., Judson Hutchinson. (Composed about 1857 and sung by the Hutchinson Family.)

My Grandma's Advice. w., m., arr. by Edward Kanski. E. A. Daggett, cop. 1857.

The Village Blacksmith. w., Henry Wadsworth Longfellow. m., Willoughby Hunter Weiss. Boston: Oliver Ditson & Co. [1857].

James Buchanan, Democrat, of Pennsylvania, was inaugurated 15th President. He was a bachelor; his niece Harriet Lane, daughter of his sister Jane, was the White House hostess.

Chief Justice of the U. S. Supreme Court Roger Brooke Taney delivered (Mar. 6) the momentous Dred Scott decision, 5 to 3, which stated that Negroes were not citizens, even when removed into free States, and could not claim any constitutional rights. The case concerned the Negro slave Dred Scott who had been taken to Illinois and Wisconsin territory and who claimed freedom under the Missouri Compromise (1820). The court had five Southern judges.

With the newly organized Atlantic Telegraph Company (formed in

1856), Cyrus West Field began (Aug. 5) the laying of the Atlantic cable between Europe and North America from Ireland. The cable broke 400 miles from the Irish coast.

A wagon train of 120 emigrants was massacred (Sept. 16) in Mountain Meadows, Utah, by a band of Indians alleged to have been abetted by Mormons.

Mardi Gras was first observed in New Orleans.

Philadelphia installed horse-drawn street cars. (They already were in operation in New York since 1831.)

A hand-operated fire-extinguishing apparatus, built by Abel Shawk in Cincinnati, played a 272-foot stream of water.

Elisha Mitchell, state surveyor of North Carolina, was killed (June 27) by a fall from a precipice during a storm while he was making observations on the highest mountain east of the Rockies. This mountain was since named after him, Mt. Mitchell. He was buried on its summit.

"The Atlantic Monthly" was founded in Boston under the editorship of James Russell Lowell and named by Oliver Wendell Holmes.

New England novelist Delia Salter Bacon aroused Shakespeareans with her book "Philosophy of the Plays of Shakespeare Unfolded." In it she sought to prove that the Bard's plays were written by Bacon, Raleigh, and Spenser, and that they concealed a system of philosophy in cipher code.

Charles Farrar Browne began the publication of "Artemus Ward's Sayings" in the "Cleveland Plain Dealer."

Republicans and abolitionists distributed "The Impending Crisis of the South: How to Meet It" by Hinton Rowan Helper. The book, which was unpopular in the South, emphasized free labor from the economic viewpoint and not in the interests of the Negro. The author was a native of North Carolina.

"Flora M'Flimsey, of Madison Square," New York, spent six weeks shopping in Paris and despite her many purchases had "nothing to wear." The story of her adventures was told anonymously in "Harper's Weekly" in a satirical poem that was copied, imitated, and parodied in both the United States and England. There were several claimants to its authorship. The author was a New York lawyer, William Allen Butler; the title of the poem is "Nothing to Wear."

Philadelphia's opera house, the Academy of Music, was opened (Feb. 25) with Verdi's "Il Trovatore."

John V. McVicker, a popular actor, built at a cost of $85,000 Chicago's third theatre and named it after himself.

John Edward McCullough, Irish-born American tragedian, made his American debut in a minor part in Philadelphia at the Arch Street Theatre. (He subsequently became a noted Shakespearean actor throughout the United States, often playing opposite Edwin Forrest.)

Dion Boucicault's production of "The Poor of New York" began (Dec. 9) a long run in New York at Wallack's Theatre.

Paul Morphy, American chess player, won in New York the first chess tournament held in the United States. To make one move, his opponent Louis Paulsen took 14 hours, 28 minutes.

Baseball was raised to the status of a national sport at a convention of delegates from 25 clubs held in New York.

After 12 years of prosperity, largely due to California gold, the United States entered its twelfth depression since 1790. It was particularly felt in the industrial North. The condition was reflected in the box office receipts at the theatres. According to the "New York Herald" (Nov. 3), fourteen of the city's places of amusement, capable of seating a total of 16,747 persons, took in only $5,910 for the previous night's business. The receipts at the six largest theatres (seating capacity in parenthesis) were Bowery (2,580), $480; Christy and Woods (2,000), $500; Broadway (2,000), $800; Niblo's Garden (1,800), $650; Burton's (1,700), $800; the Academy of Music, seating 1,500, fared best with $1,200 (Rossini's opera "Semiramide" was sung, Mme. Elena D'Angri making her American debut).

₿₷ 1858

Bonny Eloise—The Belle of Mohawk Vale. w., George W. Elliott. m., John Rogers Thomas. Wm. Hall & Son, cop. 1858.

Christmas Song—_original French title:_ **Cantique de Noël.** French words, (?) English words, John Sullivan Dwight. m., Adolphe Adam. Albany, N. Y.: J. H. Hidley [1858]. (Published earlier in Paris; first sung at midnight mass, Christmas Eve, 1847.)

La Prière d'une Vierge—_English title:_ **A Maiden's Prayer.** Piano solo. m., Thecla Badarczewska. Paris: G. Brandus et S. Dufour [1858]; London: Boosey & Sons' Music Library [1859]; London: Duncan Davidson & Co. [1859.]

Thou Art So Near and Yet So Far—_original German title:_ **Du Bist Mir Nah und Doch So Fern.** w., m., Alexander Reichardt. London: Duncan Davidson & Co. [1858?]; Cleveland: S. Brainard Co. [1861.]

Warblings at Eve. Piano solo. m., Henry Brinley Richards. London: Robert Cocks & Co. [1858?]

Wedding March. m., Felix Mendelssohn. See 1843. (According to Percy A. Scholes, "The Oxford Companion to Music," London, 1938, p. 1015, the popularity of the march at weddings dates, in England, from 1858. Scholes reports: "The first organist to play the . . . piece was probably Samuel Reay . . . then organist of the parish church of Tiverton, Devon, who in 1847 made an organ arrangement of his own from the pianoforte duet arrangement just published by Novello, Ewer & Co., and introduced it at a wedding in that church. But this use of the music seems first to have become fashionable from the occasion of the wedding of the Princess Royal in 1858." (See also 1874.)

Minnesota was admitted (May 11) as the 32nd State.

Cyrus West Field laid the Atlantic cable with the help of the British and United States governments. The "Niagara," U. S. N., and the "Agamemnon," R. N., met (in June) in midocean and, after splicing the cable, sailed with the cable ends in opposite directions, the former to Newfoundland and the latter to Valentia Harbor, Ireland. Although the cable broke three times, communication was established. It was Field's second attempt (the first was in 1857). President Buchanan and Queen Victoria exchanged (Aug. 5, anniversary of the first attempt) feebly heard messages. The cable went "dead" soon afterward as a result of high voltage.

The first overland mail began (Sept. 16) between St. Louis, Mo., and San Francisco.

Gold was discovered in Colorado.

New York Senator William Henry Seward, former Whig governor (1839-42) and later Secretary of State under Lincoln, delivered (in Oct.) a demagogic speech in which he declared that the slavery question was an "irrepressible conflict between North and South."

"A house divided against itself cannot stand" was the keynote of a convention speech which pitted Republican nominee Abraham Lincoln in the senatorial race in Illinois against a mighty Democratic opponent—Stephen Arnold Douglas, known as the "Little Giant" because of his small stature and powerful personality. He was twice a candidate for the presidency. In seven famous debates during the campaign, Douglas upheld the principle of "popular sovereignty." Less oratorical and more realistic, Lincoln analyzed the political issues with his already characteristic terseness and insight. In the election, however, Douglas defeated Lincoln.

Fire destroyed (Oct. 5) the Crystal Palace (1853) in New York.

The remains of 5th President James Monroe were removed from their resting place in New York, where he had died in 1831, and interred in Richmond, Va.

The cornerstone of the new St. Patrick's Cathedral (Roman Catholic) in New York was laid (Aug. 5); the ground was bought in 1852 for $59,-500.

At the suggestion of Napoleon III of France, an international gift of $80,000 was presented to Samuel Morse for his invention of the telegraph.

Boston became the "Hub of the Universe" when Oliver Wendell Holmes published a volume of imaginary boarding-house table-talk under the title "The Autocrat of the Breakfast-Table." In it occurs the line: "Boston

State-House is the hub of the solar system." The book also contained the poem "The Chambered Nautilus."

Henry Wadsworth Longfellow was the nation's leading poet and best seller. "The Courtship of Miles Standish" followed "Hiawatha" and sold 15,000 copies on the day of its simultaneous appearance in Boston and London.

Chicago had its first season of French opera when the French Opera Company from New Orleans played there while a new opera house was being built in its own city.

At the Academy of Music, New York, the great Italian soprano Maria Piccolomini made (Oct. 20) her American debut in the opera composed expressly for her—Verdi's "La Traviata." The public "literally botanized [her] with bouquets." The critics praised her acting, but found much fault with her singing.

American theatre audiences were introduced to the play which came to be associated with Lincoln's assassination in 1865—Tom Taylor's London hit "Our American Cousin." The comedy was staged (Oct. 18) in New York at Laura Keene's Theatre with the inimitable comedian Joseph Jefferson. The play ran for 149 performances.

Timothy Shay Arthur's melodramatic temperance story "Ten Nights in a Barroom" (1854) was dramatized by William W. Pratt and began (Aug. 23) in New York at the National Theatre its long career on the American stage.

ࢍ᪲ 1859

Ave Maria. w., traditional. m., Charles Gounod, adapted from the First Prelude in J. S. Bach's "The Well-Tempered Clavichord." Paris: Heugel [1859]. (First sung in Paris, May 24, 1859, by the eminent Mme. Caroline Miolan-Carvalho, who created the soprano roles in Gounod's operas "Faust" and "Roméo et Juliette." Gounod's music was originally set to words by Alphonse de Lamartine and published by L. Mayaud et Cie. [1852.] Gounod wrote a second "Ave Maria," based on the Second Prelude in Bach's collection, which was published by Choudens Fils, Paris [1892].)

Il Bacio—*known as:* The Kiss Waltz. Italian words, Aldighieri. m., Luigi Arditi, op. 97 (composed for Maria Piccolomini, famous Italian operatic soprano singer). [London: Cramer, Beale & Co., 1859 or 60?]; Milan: Tito di G. Ricordi [186-?]; Philadelphia: W. R. Smith, cop. 1864, as a piano solo, arr. by R. Wittig.

In the Louisiana Lowlands. w., m., anonymous. Boston: Oliver Ditson & Co., cop. 1859.

Nearer, My God, to Thee. Hymn. Tune: "Bethany." w., Sarah Adams (née Flower). m., Lowell Mason. Mason Bros., cop. 1859 (in: Lowell Mason, A. Edwards and Austin Phelps, "The Sabbath Hymn and Tune Book," p. 244).

Viva l'America: Home of the Free. w., m., Harrison Millard. Firth, Pond & Co., cop. 1859.

Oregon was admitted (Feb. 14) as the 33rd State; gold also was discovered there.

The Territory of Jefferson was established by local vote in what is now the State of Colorado.

With the intention of inciting a slave insurrection in Virginia, abolitionist John Brown of Osawatomie (1855) led (Oct. 16) a raid on the United States arsenal at Harpers Ferry at the junction of the Shenandoah and Potomac rivers in the northwestern part of the State. Five men were killed. Brown and 21 followers were captured by Col. Robert E. Lee. Brown was tried and hanged (Dec. 2). His dignified bearing during the trial won him admiration as a martyr. In his defense, Henry David Thoreau, who met Brown in 1857 at Emerson's home in Concord, delivered three lectures, "A Plea for Captain John Brown," "The Last Days of John Brown," and "After the Death of John Brown." Brown was also the subject of a popular contemporary song, "John Brown's Body" (1861).

The first oil well in the United States was opened (Aug. 28) in Titusville, Pa., by Col. Edward L. Drake.

The celebrated gold and silver lode on the present site of Virginia City, Nev., was discovered (June 11) by H. T. P. Comstock; it came to be known as the Comstock Lode.

Chicago introduced (Apr. 25) its first horse-drawn streetcars.

Cooper Institute was founded in New York City by Peter Cooper, New York inventor, financier, economist, and philanthropist, for the purpose of "giving instruction in branches of knowledge by which men and women earn their daily bread." (The Institute now is called Cooper Union.)

Under the stage name of "the little Florinda," 16-year-old Adelina Patti made (Nov. 24) her world debut in opera in the title role of "Lucia di Lammermoor" at the Academy of Music in New York. (She had been appearing in New York concerts as early as 1852.)

Dion Boucicault appeared (Dec. 5) in New York at the Winter Garden with sensational success in his play "The Octoroon, or, Life in Louisiana," based on Mayne Reid's popular novel "The Quadroon" (1856).

Charles Blondin, a 55-year-old French acrobat, known as "The Little Wonder," whose real name was Jean François Gravelet, performed daredevil feats over Niagara Falls. He crossed (June 30) on a tightrope in five minutes, repeated (July 4) the stunt blindfolded, pushing a wheel-

barrow, and carried (Aug. 19) a man on his back. (On Sept. 14, 1860, he walked a tightrope on stilts in the presence of the Prince of Wales.)
Patrick Sarsfield Gilmore organized his famous band in Boston.
In New Orleans, the new French Opera House was completed in five months. Construction was carried on day and night by special permission. The house opened (Dec. 1) with Rossini's "William Tell."
Young ladies went about with beaver hats trimmed with ostrich feathers.
The potato beetle was recognized as a new agricultural pest.
Washington Irving, aged 76, died (Nov. 28) in Tarrytown, N. Y.

₴⇒ 1860

Annie Lisle. w., m., H. S. Thompson. Boston: Oliver Ditson & Co., cop. 1860. (The tune is now the melody of the Cornell University song "Far above Cayuga's Waters.")

[Dixie's Land.] I Wish I Was in Dixie's Land. w., m., Dan[iel] D[ecatur] Emmett; arr. by W. L. Hobbs. Firth, Pond & Co., cop. 1860.

The Glendy Burk. w., m., Stephen C[ollins] Foster. Firth, Pond & Co., cop. 1860.

Janet's Choice. w., m., Claribel [pseud. of Mrs. Charles C. Barnard, née Charlotte Arlington]. London: Boosey & Sons [1860]; Philadelphia: Lee & Walker [1871].

My Trundle Bed, or, Recollections of Childhood. w., anon. m., John C. Baker. Chicago: H. M. Higgins, cop. 1860.

Old Black Joe. w., m., Stephens C[ollins] Foster. Firth, Pond & Co., cop. 1860.

Rock Me to Sleep, Mother. w., Florence Percy. m., Ernest Leslie. Boston: Russell & Pate, cop. 1860.

Simon the Cellarer. w., anon. m., J[ohn] L[iptrot] Hatton. Wm. Hall & Son [1860?]. (Published earlier in London.)

Sweet Spirit, Hear My Prayer (Lurline). w., Edward Fitzball. m., William Vincent Wallace. Wm. Hall & Son, cop. 1860. ("Lurline" was an English opera by William Vincent Wallace, produced at Covent Garden Theatre, Feb. 23, 1860.)

'Tis But a Little Faded Flower. w., Frederick Enoch. m., John Rogers
Thomas. Wm. A. Pond & Co., cop. 1860.

When the Corn Is Waving, Annie Dear. w., m., Charles Blamphin.
Boston: G. D. Russell & Co.; Cincinnati: John Church Co.; Cleveland:
S. Brainard & Sons; New York: Wm. A. Pond & Co.; Robert M. DeWitt,
cop. 1870; De Marsan's . . . "Singer's Journal" [1871], p. 308; Philadelphia: Lee & Walker; and others. (Published by Metzler & Co., London,
1874-75.)

The first pony express was established (Apr. 3) between St. Joseph,
Mo., and Sacramento, Cal., a distance of 1,980 miles. There were 80
riders and 420 horses who were changed every 10 miles at 190 relay stations. (The service was discontinued in 1861.)

The Prince of Wales (later Edward VII) visited the United States.

Elizabeth Palmer Peabody, sister-in-law of Hawthorne and Horace
Mann, established the first kindergarten in her home in Boston.

The cabinet organ, long popular in American homes and rural churches,
was perfected about this time by the Boston firm Mason & Hamlin.

Longfellow's popular poem "The Children's Hour" appeared in his collection of verse "Birds of Passage."

Ann Sophia Stephen's paper-covered thriller "Malaeska, the Indian Wife
of a White Hunter" started the vogue of the dime novel. It was advertised
as "a dollar book for a dime," and started Erastus Beadle on his 30-odd-
year career as a publisher of sensational fiction about frontiersmen, Indians, train robbers, desperados, and detectives.

Hawthorne published the romance "The Marble Faun."

Kate Josephine Bateman, already known as a juvenile actress, began
(Mar. 19) her adult career in New York at the Winter Garden in her
mother's dramatization of "Evangeline." She was supported by a cast that
included the popular Joseph Jefferson. Jefferson began (Dec. 24) at the
same theatre his lifelong impersonation of the role of "Rip Van Winkle,"
as arranged by himself.

Dion Boucicault's London Adelphi Theatre success, "The Colleen Bawn,
or, The Brides of Garryowen," was a hit at its New York première (Mar.
29) in Laura Keene's Theatre. (The company, which took the play on
tour with John Drew, was among the earliest, if not the first, to perform
on the road a single show instead of repertory.)

J. Fitzpatrick and James O'Neil fought the longest bare-knuckle prizefight in American ring annals—4 hours, 20 minutes, in Berwick, Me.

The hoopskirt, or crinoline, grew so expansive in perimeter that newspapers were full of accidents caused by the skirts catching fire.

Men started to wear knickers for sports.

The waterfall hairdress—made over a frame of horsehair—was a vogue
that lasted until about 1870.

In the national election, the problem of slavery was an acute issue. The antislavery Republican Party nominated for its candidate Abraham Lincoln. The Democratic Party split over the question: the antislavery North chose Stephen Arnold Douglas; the proslavery South selected John C. Breckinridge. The Constitutional Union Party (Whig and Know-Nothing) ran John Bell. Lincoln and Douglas emphasized the preservation of the Union; Breckinridge and Bell supported secession. The Civil War was in the making. At the polls, Lincoln received only 40 per cent of the popular vote, but he won the electoral vote, 180 to 123.

The South girded itself for secession. A last-minute effort to prevent secession was made (in Dec.) in Congress by John Jordan Crittenden, Kentucky senator and former attorney-general, who proposed five Resolutions that were in effect a modified Missouri Compromise. They were disapproved in a Senate committee. Whereupon South Carolina, a powerful slaveholding State, seceded (Dec. 20) from the Union—the first direct step toward the Civil War.

The national population had grown to 31,443,321, of which about 4,000,000 were slaves (Virginia had the most slaves, with 491,000).

℘ 1861

Abide with Me; Fast Falls the Eventide. Hymn. Tune: "Eventide." [w., Henry Francis Lyte. m., William Henry Monk.] London: Novello and Co. [1861] (in: "Hymns Ancient and Modern . . . with Accompanying Tunes," No. 14).

Alice, Where Art Thou? w., Wellington Guernsey. m., Joseph Ascher. London: Duncan, Davidson & Co. [1861.]

Aura Lee. w., W. W. Fosdick. m., Geo[rge] R. Poulton. Cincinnati: John Church, Jr., cop. 1861.

Balm of Gilead. Arr. by H. T. Bryant. Boston: Oliver Ditson & Co., cop. 1861.

The Bridge. See 1850.

Cavatina (No. 3 in: "Six Morceaux, op. 85"). Composition for violin and piano. m., Joachim Raff. Leipzig: Fr. Kistner [1861].

Gideon's Band. Arr. by Charles R. Dodward. Cop. 1861 by C. R. Dodward.

Holy, Holy, Holy! Lord God Almighty. Hymn. Tune: "Nicaea." [w., Reginald Heber. m., John Bacchus Dykes.] London: Novello and Co.

[1861] (in: "Hymns Ancient and Modern . . . with Accompanying Tunes," No. 135).

Jerusalem the Golden. Hymn. Tune: "Ewing." [w., John Mason Neale. m., Alexander Ewing.] London: Novello and Co. [1861] (in: "Hymns Ancient and Modern . . . with Accompanying Tunes," No. 142, Part III).

John Brown's Body. w., anon.; attributed to (1) Charles S. Hall; (2) Henry Howard Brownell; (3) Thomas Brigham Bishop. m., tune: "Glory, Glory, Hallelujah," attributed to William Steffe (see "Battle Hymn of the Republic," 1862). (The words were suggested by the hanging of the abolitionist John Brown, Dec. 2, 1859, and were reported to have been sung by the Boston Light Infantry at Fort Marion, 1861. An early uncopyrighted edition of the song was published in "Root and Cady's Collection of Popular Songs . . . by Various Authors," Chicago, 1861.)

Maryland! My Maryland! w., James Ryder Randall. m., German folksong: "O Tannenbaum, O Tannenbaum!" arr. by C. E. Baltimore: Miller & Beacham, cop. 1861.

Ole Shady; the Song of the Contraband. w., m., Benjamin Russell Hanby. Boston: O. Ditson & Co., cop. 1861.

The Vacant Chair, or, We Shall Meet but We Shall Miss Him. w., H. S. Washburn. m., George Frederick Root. Chicago: Root & Cady, cop. 1861.

For some songs of the Civil War (1861-65), consult—

Dolph, Edward Arthur
"Sound Off!" New York: Farrar & Rinehart, Inc. [cop. 1842.]

Humphreys, Henry S.
Songs of the Confederacy. Cincinnati: The Willis Music Co., cop. 1961
Songs of the Union Cincinnati: The Willis Music Co., cop. 1961.

Songs of Dixie. A collection of camp songs, home songs, marching songs, plantation songs by favorite authors. Chicago: The S. Brainard's Sons Co., cop. 1890.

Abraham Lincoln, Republican, of Kentucky, was inaugurated 16th President. A plot to assassinate Lincoln as he passed on his way through Baltimore to his inaugural was uncovered by Pinkerton detectives.

Kansas was admitted (Jan. 29) as the 34th State.

Meanwhile, following the lead of South Carolina, six other Southern States seceded from the Union in rapid succession—Mississippi (Jan. 9), Florida (Jan. 10), Alabama (Jan. 11), Georgia (Jan. 19), and Texas (Feb. 1). Representatives of the seven States met (Feb. 4-9) in Montgomery, Ala., and formed the "Confederate States of America." Jefferson ("Jeff") Davis, former United States Senator from Mississippi and Secretary of War under 14th President Franklin Pierce, was chosen (Feb. 8) and inducted (Feb. 18) as provisional president of the Confederate States.

Confederate General Peter Beauregard attacked (Apr. 12) Fort Sumter in the harbor of Charleston, S. C., starting the Civil War. The fort surrendered two days later (Apr. 14). President Lincoln issued the next day (Apr. 15) a call for 75,000 volunteers and offered the Union command to Robert Edward Lee of Virginia. Lee declined. When his State seceded (Apr. 17), he resigned (Apr. 20) his commission in the U. S. Army and became commander of the Virginia troops in the Confederate army. The eight Confederate States now were joined by Arkansas (May 6), North Carolina (May 21), and Tennessee (June 8). The invading Union army was routed (July 21) at Bull Run, 30 miles southwest of Washington, D. C., by Confederate General Thomas Jonathan Jackson who checked the Northern forces like a "stone wall," and earned the nickname "Stonewall" Jackson. In the October Confederate elections, Jefferson Davis was elected President of the Confederate States by popular vote. (He was inaugurated Feb. 22, 1862, at Richmond, Va., which became the capital of the Confederate States.)

Great Britain recognized the Confederate States as belligerents.

In consequence of the war, the United States issued (Aug. 17) new postage stamps to replace the series of 1847 and 1851-60 which were demonetized. (They remained in use until Feb. 27, 1869.)

The Confederate States also issued stamps for letter postage—a 5-cent green and a 10-cent blue.

Diplomatic relations between Great Britain and the United States became seriously strained when Union Captain Charles Wilkes seized (Nov. 8) two Confederate commissioners on the British ship "Trent." Britain's entrance in the war was narrowly averted by Secretary of State William Henry Seward who disavowed the act and ordered the release of the prisoners.

Richard Jordan Gatling, American inventor, perfected a rapid-firing gun called the Gatling gun, a forerunner of the machine gun. The new weapon discharged 350 rounds per minute.

The Colorado Territory was established by Congress in what is now the State of Colorado, thus dissolving the Territory of Jefferson (1859).

Transcontinental telegraph service was established (Oct. 24).

There were now 31,799 miles of railroad in the United States, and the Erie and the New York Central began to rival the Erie Canal in freight tonnage.

Vassar College for women, Poughkeepsie, N. Y., was founded.

Longfellow's second wife was burned to death (July 9) in her home at Cambridge, Mass., when her light summer dress caught fire from a wax taper while she was sealing a letter.

John LaFarge, New York painter, began to attract attention in the art world with a painting of St. John.

Longfellow's narrative poem "Paul Revere's Ride" was printed. (It was incorporated in 1863 in the first part of his "Tales of a Wayside Inn.")

Paul Belloni Du Chaillu, American explorer of Africa, published an account of nearly four years' sojourn there in his "Explorations and Adventures in Equatorial Africa." In spite of the author's firsthand knowledge, the book met with a storm of undeserved ridicule.

In New Orleans at the French Opera House, Adelina Patti sang (Feb. 6) the role of Gilda in "Rigoletto" for the first time in her career. In New York at the Academy of Music, Clara Louise Kellogg, a 19-year-old South Carolina soprano who became one of the outstanding singers of her time, made (Feb. 28) her operatic debut in the same role.

The notorious and spectacular actress Lola Montez, aged 43, died (Jan. 17) obscurely in New York and was buried in a Brooklyn cemetery under the name Mrs. Eliza Gilbert.

The thirteenth United States depression since 1790 now set in. It lasted a year, until war prosperity evaporated it.

⟨≈ 1862

Battle Hymn of the Republic. w., Julia Ward Howe (written in 1861). m., tune: "Glory, Glory, Hallelujah"; ascribed to William Steffe, but published anonymously. Boston: Oliver Ditson & Co. [1862.]

The Bonnie Blue Flag. Song of the Confederate States during the American Civil War. w., Mrs. Annie Chambers-Ketchum. m., Henry (Harry) Macarthy.

Evangeline. w., m., William Shakespeare Hays. Cleveland: S. Brainard Co., cop. 1862.

Excelsior. w., Henry Wadsworth Longfellow. m., John Blockley. Boston: Oliver Ditson & Co. [1862.] (Advertised among "Latest Music" in "Dwight's Journal of Music," Boston, Feb. 22, 1862, p. 376.)

Grafted into the Army. w., m., Henry Clay Work. Chicago: Root & Cady, cop. 1862.

Killarney. w., Edmund Falconer. m., Michael William Balfe. London: Duncan Davison & Co. [1862.]

Kingdom Coming. w., m., Henry Clay Work. Chicago: Root & Cady, cop. 1862.

Nazareth—*original French title:* Jésus de Nazareth. French words, A. Porte. English words, Henry Fothergill Chorley. m., Charles Gounod. [London, 1862.] (Originally published by A. LeBeau, Paris [1856]. Data from J. G. Prod'homme and A. Dandelot, "Gounod," Paris, 1911, vol. 2, p. 264.)

We Are Coming, Father Abraham, 300,000 More. w., m., Stephen C[ollins] Foster. S. T. Gordon, cop. 1862.

We've a Million in the Field. w., m., Stephen C[ollins] Foster. S. T. Gordon, cop. 1862.

The Civil War continued. The first congress of the Confederate States convened (Feb. 18) in Richmond, Va. Ulysses Simpson Grant won the first encouraging Union victories when he captured Fort Henry (Feb. 6) on the Tennessee River and Fort Donelson (Feb. 16) on the Cumberland River, held the enemy at Shiloh (Apr. 6-7), and defeated the Confederate army at Corinth (Oct. 4) in northern Mississippi. (After the fall of Fort Donelson, he was nicknamed "Unconditional Surrender" Grant because of his terms of surrender to the fort.) A "cheese box on a raft," constructed by Swedish engineer John Ericsson, and a reconditioned frigate made history in a naval engagement (Mar. 9) at Hampton Roads, Chesapeake Bay, Va. They were the ironclads "Monitor" (Union) and "Merrimac" (Confederate, renamed "Virginia"). Congress abolished (Apr. 16) slavery in the District of Columbia. Admiral David Glasgow Farragut captured (Apr. 25) New Orleans with the Union fleet. President Lincoln read (July 22) to his Cabinet the first draft of the Emancipation Proclamation (1863). Robert Edward Lee began (Sept. 5) an invasion of Maryland with the Confederate army and met (Sept. 17) the Union forces at Antietam Creek in a bitter and indecisive battle, which caused President Lincoln to issue (Sept. 22) a preliminary announcement that all the slaves in the States in rebellion would be declared free on Jan. 1, 1863.

President Lincoln placed Clara Barton, later founder of the American Red Cross, in charge of the search for missing soldiers and the identification of unknown soldiers' graves.

Congress passed the Homestead Act, giving public lands in the West in parcels of 160 acres free to all adult citizens and all aliens filing declaratory papers.

John M. Bozeman and James Bridger mapped out during the winter (1862-63) the so-called Bozeman Trail from Montana through Wyoming to Colorado. (Bozeman was killed by Indians in 1867 while he was guiding an emigrant party over the route.)

Chicago surpassed Cincinnati as the nation's meat center.

John D[avison] Rockefeller, aged 23, became a partner in an oil refinery in Cleveland.

George Peabody, wealthy American dry-goods merchant, improved London's housing conditions by the erection of model tenements for the working class. He contributed to the project $750,000, later increased to $2,500,000. (Queen Victoria offered Peabody a baronetcy, which he declined. London honored him with the freedom of the city in 1866.)

Treasury notes, or "greenbacks" (so-called because they were printed with green ink), were issued as a war measure for legal tender.

Congress chartered the building of the Union Pacific Railroad.

The Wheeling Bridge, W. Va., spanning the Ohio River, was completed.

Mysterious and much-publicized American actress Adah Isaacs Menken (real name: Dolores Adios Fuertos) reappeared (June 16) in New York at the New Bowery Theatre in a daring performance, half-nude and strapped to a dashing steed—"a feat never before attempted by any woman"—in a melodrama "Mazeppa." This started a craze throughout the country for that sort of exhibitionism, duplicated by Kate Fisher, Kate Vance, Kate Raymond, Mlle. Sanyeah, and others. The part also was played by men.

Maggie Mitchell acquired lasting fame as an actress in "Fanchon, the Cricket," an English adaptation of Charlotte Birch-Pfeiffer's German play "Die Grille," produced (June 9) in New York at Laura Keene's Theatre. (The German original had been played at the Stadt Theater, Aug. 28, 1857. "Fanchon" was so popular in New York that three English versions were done simultaneously in 1864.)

Teresa Carreño, aged 9, later world-famous Venezuelan pianist, made her debut (Nov. 25) in New York at Irving Hall.

Attendance at Barnum's American Museum in New York was always stimulated by new attractions. Along with the showing of a living whale and a hippopotamus, he offered such specialties as the Connecticut Giantess, "the Handsomest Fat Girl and the largest mountain of human flesh ever seen," 18 years old and weighing 618 pounds, and one Lizzie Harris, 676 pounds. By way of contrast, he featured a Canadian dwarf man and the tiny midgets General Tom Thumb, Commodore Nutt (even smaller than the "General" and to whom he allegedly paid $30,000), and the sisters Lavinia and Minnie Warren. Lavinia was first exhibited, "undoubtedly the smallest woman alive," and was said to be 21 years old, 32 inches in height, and 30 pounds in weight. When Minnie joined the cast, she was found to be even smaller than her sister, being 25 inches in height, and 30 pounds in weight. Truly, superlatives in everything were Barnum's forte! Lavinia married Tom in Grace Church on Feb. 10 with Minnie and the "Commodore" as bridesmaid and best man.

And, of course, there were always "wild men" at Barnum's—dour-looking, impassive Sioux and Winnebago Indians and squaws.

Boston witnessed (Apr. 7) at the Museum (a theatre, not the art gallery) the production of a comic opera that enjoyed a long popularity, was performed in Europe, and finally passed into the repertory of amateur troupes—"The Doctor of Alcantara" by Julius Eichberg.

Twelve-year-old Fanny Lily Gipsy Davenport, London-born American actress, made her "adult" debut as the King of Spain in "Faint Heart Never Won Fair Lady" in New York at Niblo's Garden.

A Russian naval training ship on a world cruise (1862-65) stopped in New York Harbor. Among the cadets was an 18-year-old lad, the future great composer Nicolai Rimsky-Korsakov. He visited Niagara Falls with his fellow students.

ࣿ 1863

Babylon Is Fallen! w., m., Henry Clay Work. Chicago: Root & Cady, cop. 1863.

The Battle Cry of Freedom. w., m., George Frederick Root. Chicago: Root & Cady, cop. 1863.

Cousin Jedediah. w., m., H. S. Thompson. Boston: Oliver Ditson & Co., cop. 1863.

Daisy Deane. w., T. F. Winthrop. m., James R[amsey] Murray. Chicago: Root & Cady, cop. 1863.

Folks That Put On Airs. w., m., W. H. Coulston. Philadelphia: Lee & Walker, cop. 1863.

Johnny Schmoker. w., m., anon., arr. by B. F. Rix. Chicago: Root & Cady, cop. 1863. (Published under the title "Jemmy Boker" in Charles Butler, "The Silver Bell," Henry Tolman & Co., Boston, cop. 1866, p. 80-81. In this edition, the caption states the "Words by N. Demus" and the music "Arranged by C. Butler." However, except for the substitution of the name Jemmy Boker, both the text and the music are identical with "Johnny Schmoker." The song is a forerunner of "Schnitzelbank"—see 1906.)

Just Before the Battle, Mother. w., m., George Frederick Root. Chicago: Root & Cady, cop. 1863.

Three Kings of Orient—*better known as:* **We Three Kings of Orient Are.** w., m., John Henry Hopkins. Church Book Repository [1863] (in:

John Henry Hopkins, "Carols, Hymns, and Songs," p. 12-13). (According to a notation in ink on the verso of the flyleaf of the copy of the book in the library of Union Theological Seminary, New York, and an autographed letter inserted in a later edition, the little volume appeared "in Dec., 1863." At the end of the hymn is printed the date 1857. This now famous Christmas carol of American origin is the second hymn in the collection. Hopkins also wrote and composed the children's hymn "Gather Around the Christmas Tree.")

Weeping, Sad and Lonely, or, When This Cruel War Is Over. w., Charles Carroll Sawyer. m., Henry Tucker. Brooklyn: Sawyer & Thompson, cop. 1863.

When Johnny Comes Marching Home. w., m., Louis Lambert [supposed pseudonym of Patrick Sarsfield Gilmore]. Boston: H. Tolman & Co., cop. 1863.

The Civil War continued into its third year with important battles at Chancellorsville, Va. (May 2-4), Gettysburg, Pa. (July 1-3), Vicksburg, Miss. (July 4), Chickamauga, Tenn. (Sept. 19-20), and Chattanooga, Tenn. (Nov. 23-25).

On New Year's Day, as announced in the previous September, President Lincoln issued the Emancipation Proclamation, in which he declared "free forever" the slaves in Alabama, Arkansas, Florida, Georgia, Louisiana (certain parts excepted), Mississippi, North Carolina, South Carolina, Texas, and Virginia. It freed about 3,120,000 slaves.

During the battle at Chancellorsville, "Stonewall" Jackson was accidentally shot by his own soldiers. He died May 10.

West Virginia was admitted (June 20) as the 35th State.

President Lincoln ordered conscription. Opposition to the measure in New York City, abetted by corrupt local politics, broke out (July 13-16) in violent "draft riots," in which about 1,000 persons were killed, including several Negroes killed by lynching. Some 50 buildings were burned, and shops were looted. Troops from Pennsylvania and West Point finally quelled the mobsters.

The number of U. S. Supreme Court judges was raised from six to nine.

The United States issued (July 6) its first two-cent postage stamp—a black adhesive with a portrait of Andrew Jackson.

At the dedication (Nov. 19) of a national cemetery at Gettysburg, Pa., President Lincoln followed a two-hour speech by the principal orator, Edward Everett, with an address of three short paragraphs. It was largely impromptu, read from some hastily scribbled notes, and the majority of the audience was not impressed. Everett, however, realized its sublime sentiments when he later briefly congratulated Lincoln.

Two Russian fleets made friendly visits to the United States—one in New York Harbor, the other in San Francisco Bay. In honor of the occasion, a Grand Ball was held in New York at the Academy of Music, the orchestra seats being covered with a flooring.

President Lincoln revived the observance of Thanksgiving Day (first proclaimed by Washington in 1789).

The steel age came into being when Lyman Holley and William Kelley, working independently, devised methods for converting iron into steel.

A hand-propelled semi-submarine, designed by McClintock and Howgate for attack on Union ships, sank four times, each time drowning its crew of eight.

In Philadelphia, the American Wood Paper Company began to make paper of wood pulp. Previously it was made of rags, linen, etc., of which there never was enough.

The Brotherhood of Locomotive Engineers was organized (May 5) in Detroit as the Brotherhood of the Footboard. (The footboard was the narrow platform along the sides of the locomotive.)

Francis Lieber, German-born American political writer and educator, published "A Code for the Government of Armies." It was reissued by the War Department as "General Order No. 100," and is regarded as a standard work on military law.

Edward Everett Hale's classic novelette "The Man Without a Country" appeared in "The Atlantic Monthly."

"East Lynne," a recent (1861) popular novel by the English authoress Mrs. Henry Wood, won even greater success as a play. The story, which concerns a married woman who is turned out by her husband "never to darken the door again," supplied the theatre with probably its first example of "the woman pays" theme, and provided the stage with one of the most popular melodramas ever written. No less than three dramatic versions were seen simultaneously in New York. Those who wanted to weep over the unjustly suspected wife went to see Matilda Heron in "Edith, or, The Earl's Daughter," adapted by Benjamin E. Woolff, at Niblo's Garden (Dec. 9, 1862), or Lucille Western in "East Lynne," adapted by Clifton W. Tayleure, at the Winter Garden (Mar. 23, 1863); on the other hand, those who wanted to witness the heroics of the mistakenly injured husband attended the performance of Edward Eddy, in an adaptation by J. F. Poole, at the New Bowery Theatre (Mar. 6, 1863). Lucille Western's version was first seen (Jan. 6, 1863) at the Brooklyn Academy of Music and brought nationwide fame over the years.

Edwin Booth played (Oct. 12) Victor Hugo's "Ruy Blas" at the Winter Garden, New York.

Augustin Daly, dramatic critic of the "New York Sunday Courier," made a timid beginning as a playwright with "Leah, the Forsaken," an English adaptation for Kate Bateman of Salomon Hermann Mosenthal's German drama "Deborah," then playing in Germany and already familiar to German audiences in New York. The version was tried out in Boston and given (Jan. 19) anonymously in New York at the Winter Garden. The secret of authorship leaked out and the adapter was "panned" by fellow reviewers for bad writing, crudity, and other alleged defects. However, the play about a Jewish maiden's love for a faithless Christian endeared itself to theatre goers, and provided Kate Bateman with a sympathetic role for many years.

Gounod's French opera "Faust" was introduced (Nov. 18) to American opera lovers in Philadelphia at the Academy of Music. New York performances followed in the same year at the Academy of Music, first (Nov. 25) in Italian and then (Dec. 18) in German. (The first French rendition was heard in New Orleans, Nov. 20, 1866.)

The bronze statue of Freedom, surmounting the dome of the Capitol, was placed (Dec. 2) in position. (The statue weighs 14,985 pounds and was cast from a plaster model made in Rome by Thomas Crawford, father of the novelist Francis Marion Crawford.)

⧸⧹ 1864

All Quiet Along the Potomac Tonight. w., Lamar Fontaine. m., John Hill Hewitt. Richmond, Va.: G. Dunn & Co., cop. 1864.

Beautiful Dreamer. w., m., Stephen Collins Foster. Wm. A. Pond & Co., cop. 1864.

Come Home, Father! w., m., Henry Clay Work. Chicago: Root & Cady, cop. 1864. (This celebrated temperance song was introduced in the famous melodramatic play "Ten Nights in a Barroom" by Timothy Shay Arthur.)

Der Deitcher's Dog—*better known as:* **Where, O Where Has My Little Dog Gone?** w., m., Sep[timus] Winner. Philadelphia: Sep. Winner & Co., cop. 1864. (Of course, Sep. Winner didn't compose the music. The tune is the German folk song "Zu Lauterbach hab' i mein Strumpf verlor'n.")

The Dying Poet. Piano solo. m., Seven Octaves [pseud. of Louis Moreau Gottschalk]. Boston: Oliver Ditson & Co., cop. 1864.

Take Back the Heart You Gave. w., m., Claribel [pseud. of Mrs. Charles C. Barnard, née Charlotte Alington]. London: Boosey & Co. [1864.]

Tenting On the Old Camp Ground. w., m., Walter Kittredge. Boston: Oliver Ditson & Co., cop. 1864.

Tramp! Tramp! Tramp! w., m., George Frederick Root. Chicago: Root & Cady, cop. 1864.

Wake Nicodemus! w., m., Henry Clay Work. Chicago: Root & Cady, cop. 1864.

When the War Is Over, Mary. w., George Cooper. m., John Rogers Thomas. Wm. A. Pond & Co., cop. 1864.

Work for the Night Is Coming. Hymn. w., Annie L. Walker. m., Lowell Mason. Mason Bros., cop. 1864 (in: Lowell Mason, "The Song Garden," Second Book, p. 81).

The Civil War went into its fourth year.

Ulysses Simpson Grant was appointed (Mar. 12) commander of the Union armies.

William Tecumseh Sherman captured (Nov. 15) Atlanta, Ga., with the Union forces, burned the city after removing the civilian population, and started on his destructive "march to the sea" through Georgia, which ended (Dec. 21) with the fall of Savannah.

Nevada was admitted (Oct. 31) as the 36th State.

Secretary of the Treasury Salmon Portland Chase introduced the motto "In God We Trust" which has been inscribed on most United States coins since then. The strong religious sentiment during the Civil War inspired the motto, which was suggested by the Rev. M. R. Watkinson to Secretary Chase in 1861. It appeared for the first time on the new bronze two-cent piece, coined in accordance with the Act of Apr. 22, 1864. Another change in the currency was the substitution of the bronze Indian-head one-cent piece for the similarly designed copper and nickel penny of 1859. The coin remained in use until it was superseded by the Lincoln-head piece of 1909.

To speed up mail delivery, the postal car system on railroads was originated in Chicago.

George Mortimer Pullman began the construction of his railroad sleeping cars.

Arlington National Cemetery, Fort Myer, Va., opposite Washington, D. C., was established (June 15) on land that originally belonged to George Washington Parke Curtis, adopted son of George Washington, and that was owned before the Civil War by Confederate General Robert Edward Lee.

The Knights of Pythias was founded in Washington, D. C., as a secret fraternal society.

Winslow Homer, Civil War staff artist of "Harper's Weekly," attracted attention with his first important painting, "Prisoner from the Front," exhibited in New York.

John Greenleaf Whittier published the poem "Barbara Frietchie" in his collection of verse "In War Time and Other Poems."

Humorist Artemus Ward was entertaining New Yorkers at Dodworth's Hall for consecutive weeks (Oct.-Dec.) with his lecture "Artemus Ward among the Mormons, a pictorial tour from Pier 3, North River, to Sait Lake City."

Patrick Sarsfield Gilmore conducted a great Band Festival in New Orleans.

Deaths of the year included Stephen Collins Foster, aged 38 (Jan. 13), in New York, and Nathaniel Hawthorne, aged 60 (May 19), in Plymouth, N. H.

The Austrian Archduke Ferdinand Maximilian Joseph was crowned (Dec. 6) Emperor of Mexico.

₰ 1865

Beautiful Isle of the Sea. w., George Cooper. m., J[ohn] R[ogers] Thomas. Wm. A. Pond & Co., cop. 1865.

Beware. w., Henry Wadsworth Longfellow. m., Charles Moulton. Beer & Schirmer, cop. 1865.

Ellie Rhee; or, Carry Me Back to Tennessee. w., m., Septimus Winner. Philadelphia: Sep. Winner, cop. 1865.

The Little Brown Church. w., m., William S. Pitts. J. L. Peters, cop. 1865.

Marching Through Georgia. w., m., Henry Clay Work. Chicago: Root & Cady, cop. 1865.

Nicodemus Johnson. w., anon. m., J. B. Murphy. Boston: Oliver Ditson & Co., cop. 1865.

President Abraham Lincoln began his second term.

The last shot of the Civil War (1861-65) was fired. Lee surrendered (Apr. 9) to Grant in Appomattox, Va. The death toll of the war amounted to 524,509 (359,528 Union and 164,981 Confederate soldiers).

Almost concurrently with the end of the war, President Lincoln was assassinated (Apr. 14) by actor John Wilkes Booth in Washington, D. C., at Ford's Theatre during a performance of the comedy "Our American

Cousin" (1858). The President died the next day, and the nation went into mourning for the first martyred President.

The same day, crowds of people eager to avenge Lincoln's death stormed the lobby of Burnet House in Cincinnati to seize the tragedian Junius Brutus Booth, a brother of the assassin. The actor was forced to remain hidden for several days until he could be smuggled out of town. Mass meetings were held for the purpose of closing the theatres. In Boston, Cleveland, and Columbus, actors were hissed off the stage; in New York a band of street boys pinned an actress against the fence of Trinity churchyard until she was rescued by a policeman and a naval officer.

The President's murderer, John Wilkes Booth, was shot (Apr. 26) in a burning barn near Port Royal, Va. He was buried under the floor of a prison in Washington, D. C.; the remains were later returned to relatives and interred in Baltimore. Others involved in the plot were hanged or sentenced to prison.

Vice-President Andrew Johnson, of Tennessee, Democrat elected with Lincoln on the National Union ticket, was inaugurated (Apr. 15) as the 17th President. His daughter, Martha, wife of Judge D. T. Patterson, acted as White House hostess in place of her invalid mother.

President Johnson proclaimed (May 26) an amnesty to all Confederate States, conditional to their acceptance of the 13th Amendment then before Congress.

The Freedmen's Bureau was established (in Mar.) by the War Department to handle the problems of refugees and freedmen. (It functioned until 1870.)

The steamboat "Sultana," carrying exchanged Union prisoners of war, exploded (Apr. 27) on the Mississippi near Memphis, with a loss of 1,450 lives.

Jefferson Davis, President of the Confederate States, was captured (May 10) in flight at Irwinville, Ga., a month after Lee's surrender. (Davis was confined for two years at Fort Monroe, Va., awaiting trial for treason. He was released on bail in May, 1867, and proceedings against him were dropped in February, 1869.)

The white-robed and hooded Ku Klux Klan was organized in the Southern States to uphold white supremacy, directed specifically against Negro voters and "carpetbaggers" arrived from the North. (Nominally disbanded in 1869, night raids by the Klan continued for several years. The movement was revived in 1920 for a while.)

The 13th Amendment (abolition of slavery in the United States) was ratified (Dec. 18).

The shield-bearing nickel five-cent piece came into circulation. (The coin remained in use until it was superseded by the Liberty-head design of 1883.)

Cyrus West Field attempted (in July) on the S. S. "Great Eastern" to repair the Atlantic cable which had been damaged in 1858 by high voltage. He was not successful and the cable was lost.

Thanksgiving Day, proclaimed by Lincoln in 1864, was observed on Dec. 7—a week late; President Johnson had neglected to proclaim the day!

Prof. T. S. C. Lowe, famed for his aeronautical exploits in the Civil War, discovered a process of drawing water from coal.

Cornell University for men and women, Ithaca, N. Y., was founded by Ezra Cornell, capitalist and a founder of the Western Union Telegraph Company.

New York City now had a paid fire department to replace the volunteers.

The "Molly Maguires," an Irish secret organization, began terrorizing the coal regions of Pennsylvania. (Their activities ceased in 1876-77 after eleven of their ringleaders were convicted and executed.)

About 295,000 Indians still remained in the United States, whereas in 1492 there had been an estimated 850,000.

Mark Twain gained sudden fame with his retelling of an old Californian folk tale, "The Celebrated Jumping Frog of Calaveras County," which appeared in the "New York Saturday Press."

Mary Mapes Dodge, New York-born authoress of juvenile fiction, published her children's classic "Hans Brinker, or, The Silver Skates."

The $600,000 Crosby Opera House in Chicago opened (Apr. 20).

Fire destroyed (July 13) Barnum's American Museum in New York, with a loss of almost all the live animals and its collection of curios.

The Harvard Musical Association gave (Dec. 28) its first concert in Boston.

Vaudeville, called variety at this time, was attracting chiefly male audiences. In Paterson, N. J., Tony (Antonio) Pastor tried "legitimate" vaudeville and opened (Aug. 14) in New York the grandly named Opera House where that sort of entertainment was offered for family enjoyment.

Dion Boucicault's Irish play "Arrah-na-Poque, or, The Wicklow Wedding" was (July 12) a hit in New York at Niblo's Garden.

P. T. Barnum and Max Maretzek, opera director of New York's Academy of Music, corralled fellow managers to withdraw their advertisements from James Gordon Bennett's newspaper, the "Herald," mainly because of its adverse criticisms.

The baseball championship contest between the Brooklyn Atlantics and the Philadelphia Athletics attracted 30,000 spectators and so clogged the infield that the game was postponed after one inning. It was re-played three weeks later with $1 admission, drew 2,000 customers and 6,000 non-payees, and was called in the seventh inning on account of rain. The Athletics led, 31 to 12.

Postwar gayety marked the social season. It is estimated that in New York alone 600 balls took place.

Mascara and the pork-pie hat had come into vogue.
A postwar depression, lasting scarcely a year, broke out (No. 14 since 1790).

ᚦᚼ 1866

We Parted by the River. w., m., Will[iam] S[hakespeare] Hays. J. L. Peters, cop. 1866; renewed 1893 by W. S. Hays.

When You and I Were Young, Maggie. w., George W. Johnson. m., J. A. Butterfield. Chicago: J. A. Butterfield, cop. 1866.

Congress passed (Apr. 9) a Civil Rights act.

Armed bands of Fenians and Irish sympathizers, numbering from 500 to some 1,500, began (in Apr.) a movement to invade Canada and New Brunswick from Maine, Vermont, and New York. They seized Fort Erie (June 1) and St. Armand (June 7). United States troops under George Gordon Meade of Gettysburg fame put an end to the fantastic undertaking.

After 30 attempts Cyrus West Field, on the S. S. "Great Eastern," succeeded in repairing the Atlantic cable, which had been damaged by high voltage in 1858 and which was lost in 1865. Communication was re-established between Ireland and Newfoundland.

George Armstrong Custer, lieutenant-colonel of the 7th U. S. Cavalry, was sent to quell western Indian uprisings under Sitting Bull and Crazy Horse, Sioux chiefs.

Union leaders formed the National Labor Union, which lasted six years and was one of the first attempts at federating labor.

Civil War veterans of the Union army and navy formed the Grand Army of the Republic ("G.A.R.") to perpetuate the memory of fallen comrades and to aid their widows and dependents.

The "New York World" was founded as a penny daily religious newspaper. However, it soon abandoned its character in favor of a more worldly policy. (The paper was bought by Joseph Pulitzer in 1883 and merged in 1891 with the "New York Telegram," becoming the "New York World-Telegram.")

Christian Science was originated by Mary Baker Eddy.

The Young Women's Christian Association ("Y.W.C.A.") was founded in Boston.

The American Society for the Prevention of Cruelty to Animals ("A.S.P.C.A.") was organized in New York.

Fisk University, Nashville, Tenn., for Negro men and women, was founded.

John Greenleaf Whittier published his poem "Snow-Bound, A Winter Idyl," the story of a New England family isolated by a sudden snowstorm.

Alexander Wheelock Thayer, American consul at Trieste appointed by Lincoln, published the first volume of his monumental and standard biography of Beethoven in a German translation by Dr. Hermann Deiters, entitled "Ludwig van Beethovens Leben" (completed posthumously in five volumes, 1908).

Great excitement preceded the New York world première of the most spectacular, epoch-making melodrama yet seen on an American stage. It was "The Black Crook" by Charles M. Barras, its plot a veritable hodge-podge of German romanticism derived from Weber's opera "Der Frei-schütz," Goethe's "Faust," and other kindred productions. The show opened (Sept. 12) at Niblo's Garden on a stage remodelled at the cost of $25,000 (according to the "New-York Times"), "played by easy stages, from 7¾ o'clock until 1¼," involved the expenditure of $35,000 to $55,000, and ran until 1868 (Jan. 4)—474 performances in 16 months, the longest run up to that time of any play. While the public rhapsodized over its endless revelations, members of the clergy and a certain section of the press railed against the "immoral" production and its spirited ballet of 100 lightly clad legs devised by David Costa and danced in the leading roles by the 15-year-old ballerinas Marie Bonfanti, Rita Sangalli, and Betty Rigl, long afterwards famous. ("The Black Crook" was revived in 1868, 1871, 1873, 1879, 1881, 1884, 1889, 1892, and as lately as 1929 with Agnes de Mille.)

The Mendelssohn Glee Club of male voices was organized (May 21) in New York with Joseph Mosenthal as conductor (1867-96). (Still in existence.)

Fire destroyed (Dec. 7) the historic Théâtre d'Orléans in New Orleans.

The New York-New Orleans steamer "Evening Star" foundered (Oct. 3), with a loss of 250 lives. Aboard were 155 members of a French opera troupe recruited in Paris, en route to the French Opera House in New Orleans. Only 34 passengers on the ship were saved.

French-language drama and operetta found (May 26) a home of their own in New York at the newly built Théâtre Français.

Adelaide Ristori, great Italian tragedienne, made (Sept. 20) her American debut in New York at the above-mentioned new Théâtre Français in an Italian version of Ernest Legouvé's "Medea."

Howard Paul, at the Arch Street Theatre in Philadelphia, first danced the can-can in a piece called "Ripples on the Lake."

Croquet was now such a popular game that the "Nation" printed a lengthy set of rules.

₿✍ 1867

Angel's Serenade—*original Italian title:* La Serenata. Italian words, Marco Marcelliano Marcello; English words, H[arrison] Millard. m., Gaetano Braga. G. Schirmer, cop. 1867. (Published earlier in Italy.)

Beautiful Bird, Sing On. w., m., T. H. Howe. Boston: Oliver Ditson & Co., cop. 1867.

The Blue Danube—*original German title:* An der Schönen Blauen Donau. Waltz. m., Johann Strauss, op. 314, Vienna: C. A. Spina, n.d. (First performed in Vienna, February 13, 1867.)

The Bridge. w., Henry Wadsworth Longfellow. m., Lady Carew. Boston: Oliver Ditson & Co. [1867.]

Champagne Charley Was His Name. w., H. J. Whymark. m., Alfred Lee. Boston: Oliver Ditson & Co., cop. 1867.

Croquet. w., C. H. Webb. m., J[ohn] R[ogers] Thomas. Wm. A. Pond & Co., cop. 1867.

Slave Songs of the United States. S. Simpson & Co., 1867. xliv p., 3 1., 115 p. 8°. (The book is probably the first published collection of Negro spirituals. According to the preface, "The greater part of the music . . . has been taken down by the editors from the lips of the colored people themselves." The editors were William Francis Allen, Charles Pickard Ware, and Lucy McKim Garrison. The latter was particularly active in the field of Negro folk song. Her article "Songs of the Port Royal 'Contrabands' " in "Dwight's Journal of Music," Boston, 1862, p. 254-55, was perhaps the earliest printed reference to the subject. Although most of the material recorded in the above book is now unfamiliar, the songs included "Roll, Jordan, Roll" and "Nobody Knows the Trouble I've Had" [sic].)

Waiting. w., E. H. Flagg. m., Harrison Millard. Wm. A. Pond & Co., cop. 1867.

Were Marching to Zion. Hymn. w., Isaac Watts. m., Rev. Robert Lowry. Cop. 1867 by Robert Lowry.

"Seward's Folly," "Seward's Ice Box," "Icebergia," "Walrussia" were some of the epithets which ridiculed the purchase of Alaska from Russia by Secretary of State William H. Seward and Senator Charles Sumner. The purchase price was $7,200,000 and it added 586,400 square miles (at two cents per acre) to United States territory. President Johnson signed the deal Mar. 30; it was ratified by Congress June 20; payment was made Aug. 1, and the transfer took place in New Archangel on the island of Sitka, Oct. 18. This date is now observed as a holiday in Alaska.

Congress passed (Mar. 2 and Mar. 23), over the President's veto, the Reconstruction Act "to provide for a more efficient government of the rebel States" under military governors until the States were readmitted to Congress. In carrying out the laws, President Johnson came into conflict with Secretary of War Edwin McMasters Stanton, who opposed the President's conciliatory attitude toward the South. Johnson called for Stanton's resignation, which was refused, and thereupon (Aug. 12) suspended him. General Ulysses S. Grant was appointed as Acting Secretary and performed the functions of the office until the next January. There was agitation in the House of Representatives to impeach the President, but the move failed of support.

In spite of the opposition of the Cabinet, President Johnson extended (Sept. 7) amnesty to all but a few Southern leaders and officials.

Nebraska was admitted (Mar. 1) as the 37th State.

The Pullman Palace Car Company was organized by George Mortimer Pullman and Ben Field for the construction of railroad sleeping cars (1864).

The Ohio River Bridge at Cincinnati was completed.

The first elevated railway opened (July 2) in New York, extending from the Battery to 30th Street; it was operated by a cable.

The New York State Legislature declared (Oct. 1) all public schools free within its area.

Three Milwaukee men, Carlos Glidden, Samuel Soulé, and Christopher Sholes (the first a mechanic, the other two printers) devised the first practical typewriting machine. It could write only capital letters on tissue paper. (The invention was patented in June, 1868, and placed on the market in 1873—which see.)

The National Grange of Patrons of Husbandry was formed (in Dec.) as a secret organization to further the interests of farmers and to procure protective legislation, thus starting the Granger movement. (Among the results obtained were the Interstate Commerce Act, 1887, and the establishment of the Department of Agriculture, 1889.)

Stock tickers were installed, greatly facilitating speculation.

Charles Dickens made the second of his two visits to the United States (Nov. 1867-Apr. 1868), giving well-attended public readings from his works. (The first was in 1842.)

The Benevolent and Protective Order of Elks (B.P.O.E.) was founded for actors and literary men. (It is now a social and charitable organization.)

Howard University for men and women, Washington, D. C., was founded by act of Congress. Primarily for Negro students, it was named in honor of General Oliver Otis Howard, head of the Freedman's Bureau (1865).

Just ten years after Hinton Rowan Helper wrote "The Impending Crisis of the South" (1857), he came out with a hysterical satire "Nojoque: A Question for a Continent," in which he advocated the extinction of "all the swarthy and inferior races of men" as a prelude to a "golden age."

"Harper's Bazar" was founded as a women's weekly magazine. (Became a monthly in 1901; now published under the name "Harper's Bazaar.")

"You are my first and my last and my only love," said an orphan girl to a dissipated, atheistic son of a Georgia planter, and the success of the latest novel was assured—Augusta Jane Evans' "St. Elmo."

The popular poem "Curfew Must Not Ring To-Night" by Rose Hartwick Thorpe was printed in a Detroit newspaper.

The first moralistic Horatio Alger stories for boys and the pious Elsie books for girls appeared as complements of each other. Horatio Alger, Jr., chaplain of the Newsboys' Lodging House in New York, began the Ragged Dick series of success stories, while Martha Farquharson (Finley) brought out the first of the 28 tales (1867-1905) about Elsie Dinsmore. (Alger followed the Ragged Dick stories with the Luck and Pluck, 1869, and Tattered Tom, 1871, series.)

Notable conservatories of music were founded in Boston, Cincinnati, and Chicago.

Fanny Janauschek, eminent Bohemian-German tragedienne, made (Oct. 9) her American debut in Franz Grillparzer's German drama "Medea" in New York at the Academy of Music.

Augustin Daly's 5-act melodrama "Under the Gaslight" was produced (Aug. 13) in New York at the Worrel Sisters' Theatre (New York Theatre). It introduced the episode of a man tied to railroad tracks before an onrushing express train. The fact that the machinery failed on the opening night added to the audience's excitement and assured the play's immediate popularity. (The play ran until Oct. 5, reached San Francisco Nov. 23 at the Metropolitan Theatre where the box-office receipts for the first week amounted to $7,622.25, was burlesqued by the San Francisco Minstrels, and revived in 1868 and through the years.)

The American debut of the petite French soprano Lucille Tostée and the United States première (Sept. 24) of Offenbach's recent Paris success "La Grande Duchesse de Gérolstein" in New York at the Théâtre Français combined to start a craze for opéra bouffe, whether sung in French or in English, that swept the country and lasted until the Gilbert and Sullivan operettas challenged its supremacy.

A tragic and disgraceful incident marred the New York Christmas theatrical season. Four well-known actor-managers, Sam Sharpley, his brother Thomas Sharpe, Leon, and Kelly, quarrelled (on the afternoon of Dec. 11) in front of the Fifth Avenue Theatre. During the altercation, Kelly shot and killed Sharpe, and was himself severely wounded by Sharpley. Kelly was tried, but escaped penalty on a legal technicality. Although none of the wranglers was connected with the Fifth Avenue Theatre, the brawl closed the famous house for more than a year.

Baseball was rapidly becoming the national game. In 1867 the greatest contribution to that sport was made by William Arthur Cummings, Brooklyn pitcher, who invented the "curve" ball. Meanwhile, the National baseball club of Washington made a tour, beating the Columbus Capitols 90 to 10, the Cincinnati Red Stockings 53 to 10, the Cincinnati Buckeyes 88 to 12, the Louisville Kentuckians 82 to 21, the Indianapolis Western Club 106 to 21, and the St. Louis Union Club 113 to 26.

Yellow fever raged during the summer and autumn in Louisiana and Texas, and in towns along the Mississippi. About 2,500 died from the disease in New Orleans and a larger number in Galveston.

The Emperor Maximilian (1864) was executed (June 19) in Mexico. Canada was raised (July 1) to the status of a Dominion.

₰ 1868

Addio, Mia Bella Napoli. w., m., Teodoro Cottrau (1827-79). [Naples, 1868.] (Date from A. della Corte and G. M. Gatti, "Dizionario di Musica," Torino, 1925.)

Captain Jinks of the Horse Marines. w., William Horace Lingard. m., T. Maclagan. C. H. Ditson & Co., cop. 1868; J. L. Peters, cop. 1868; Rob't DeWitt, cop. 1868 (in: "The Mabel Waltz Songster"); Cincinnati: J. J. Dobmeyer & Co., cop. 1868; Philadelphia: R. Wittig & Co., cop. 1868; and many others without copyright imprint. (The song was introduced in America at the Theatre Comique [sic], New York, in April, 1868, by The Lingard Comedy Company from London, where it had been sung by them.)

Chant Sans Paroles (No. 3 in: "Souvenir de Hapsal," op. 2). Piano solo. m., Peter Ilyich Tchaikovsky. Moscow: P. Jurgenson [1868].

The Flying Trapeze. w., m., anon. C. M. Tremaine, cop. 1868.

Her Bright Smile Haunts Me Still. w., J. E. Carpenter. m., W. T. Wrighton. Boston: Oliver Ditson & Co., cop. 1868.

Lead, Kindly Light. Hymn. Tune: "Lux Benigna." [w., John Henry Newman. m., John Bacchus Dykes.] London: William Clowes and Sons [1868] (in: "Hymns Ancient and Modern . . . with Appendix," No. 342).

Little Footsteps. w., M[ichael] B[ennett] Leavitt. m., J[ames] A. Barney. Boston: White, Smith & Perry, cop. 1868.

The Long Day Closes. Part-song for ATTB. w., Henry F[othergill] Chorley. m., Arthur Sullivan. London: Novello, Ewer and Co. [1868.]

Lullaby—*original German title:* Wiegenlied (No. 4 in: "Fünf Lieder, op. 49"). German words from "Des Knaben Wunderhorn"; 2nd verse by George Scherer; English words, Mrs. Natalia Macfarren. m., Johannes Brahms. Berlin: N. Simrock [1868].

O Little Town of Bethlehem. Hymn. Tune: "St. Louis." w., Phillips Brooks. m., Lewis H. Redner. (The words and music were written in 1868 for the children's Christmas celebration at Holy Trinity Episcopal Church in Philadelphia, of which the Rev. Phillips Brooks, D.D., was the rector. Lewis H. Redner (1831-1908) was the organist and Sunday-school superintendent of the church. An early appearance of the words and music in print was in William Reed Huntington, "The Church Porch; a service book and hymnal for Sunday schools." New York: E. P. Dutton & Co., [cop. 1874], No. 43.)

Sweet By and By. w., S. Fillmore. m., Joseph P. Webster. Chicago: Lyon & Healy, cop. 1868.

Tales From the Vienna Woods—*original German title:* Geschichten aus dem Wienerwald. Waltz. m., Johann Strauss, op. 325. Vienna: C. A. Spina, n.d. (First performed in Vienna, June 9, 1868.)

Whispering Hope. Duet for soprano and alto. w., m., Alice Hawthorne [pseud. of Septimus Winner]. Boston: Oliver Ditson & Co., cop. 1868 by Sep. Winner.

Yield Not to Temptation. Hymn. w., m., Horatio Richmond Palmer. Cop. 1868 by H. R. Palmer.

·Disagreement over Reconstruction policies in the South widened the breach between President Andrew Johnson and Congress, the radical elements of which favored the reduction of the former Confederate States to a "territorial condition" (words of abolitionist Thaddeus Stevens).

Congress refused (Jan. 13) to concur in the President's suspension of Secretary of War Edwin McMasters Stanton (1867), and Acting Secretary General Ulysses S. Grant resigned. Johnson ordered (Feb. 21) Stanton's removal, appointing in his stead as Secretary ad interim Adjutant-General Thomas who was placed (Feb. 22) under temporary arrest by Stanton. The President's actions were construed a violation of the Tenure of Office Act; and Congress voted his impeachment. The case occupied 32 days of actual trial (Mar. 23-May26) before the Senate, and resulted in a verdict, 35 for conviction and 19 for acquittal. Conviction was lost for lack of a constitutional two-thirds majority; the Chief Justice therefore entered a verdict of acquittal.

Alabama, Arkansas, Florida, Georgia, Louisiana, North Carolina, and South Carolina were the first of the former Confederate States to be readmitted (in June) to Congress. (The remaining four States were readmitted in 1870.)

The 14th Amendment (citizenship and pensions) was ratified (July 28). The bells which were rung at its adoption inspired Whittier to write the poem "Laus Deo!"

President Johnson declared (Dec. 25) amnesty to all, without exception, who had taken a part in the late rebellion.

Congress authorized the formation of the Territories of Wyoming and Alaska, and prohibited the killing of fur seals "within the limit of Alaska territory or the waters thereof."

Through the efforts of Anson Burlingame, United States Minister to China since 1861, that country signed treaties with the United States and other foreign countries acknowledging international law.

Major John Wesley Powell began surveys of the Grand Canyon and Colorado River.

Jay Gould and James ("Jim") Fisk were at the height of their financial power as dealers in railway securities.

Albert James Myer, American signal officer with the Union army during the Civil War, who had arranged an effective system of signaling messages by flags during the day and by torches at night, published "A Manual of Signals for the United States Army and Navy."

George Westinghouse invented the air brake. A. M. Hills invented the lawn mower.

The University of California at Berkeley, for men and women, was established.

Hampton Normal and Agricultural Institute for Negro men and women was founded at Hampton, Va. (Called Hampton Institute since 1930.)

The Ancient Order of United Workmen (A.O.U.W.) was founded in Meadville, Pa., as a fraternal and benevolent society.

San Francisco suffered (Oct. 21) another severe earthquake. Other regions in California were also affected.

The "Atlanta Constitution" was founded as a daily newspaper.

George L. Fox's pantomime "Humpty Dumpty," produced (Mar. 10) in New York at the Olympic Theatre, was the dramatic hit of the year, running 483 performances—nine more than "The Black Crook" (1866) —and later going through periodic revivals (Fox played his role 1,128 times). Public interest in pantomimes, however, began to decline because of the advent of "blondes" on the stage.

Blondes were the latest stage attraction in New York; in less than two years they bedazzled the country. The first troupe came from England— the Lydia Thompson burlesque company. Its pulchritudinous charms were displayed (Sept. 28) at Wood's Theatre in Francis Cowley Burnand's mythical Greek extravaganza "Ixion, or, The Man at the Wheel." Lydia herself was described in the press as "a blonde of the purest type, saucy, blue-eyed, golden-haired and of elegant figure." Their appearance marked the beginning of what later was really American "burlesque."

A three-year-old girl made her stage debut as the child in a revival of "East Lynne" (1863). Later she was the famous American actress Fay Templeton.

When American actress Adah Isaacs Menken failed to appear at a rehearsal in Paris, the management went to court. The officers of the law found that she had been dead for several days in her apartment. She was 33 years old.

ૐ 1869

Birds in the Night. w., Lionel H. Lewin. m., Arthur Sullivan. London: Boosey & Co. [1869.]

Hungarian Dances. Twenty-one pieces for piano, 4 hands. m., Johannes Brahms. Berlin: N. Simrock (Book 1-2, 1869; Book 3-4, 1880). (An arrangement by the composer for piano solo of Book 1-2—ten numbers—was published in 1872. Orchestrations of the dances were published by N. Simrock, Berlin: Nos. 1, 3, 10, arr. by Brahms, 1874; Nos. 11-16, arr. by Albert Parlow, 1881; Nos. 17-21, arr. by Anton Dvorák, 1881; Nos. 2 and 7, arr. by Andreas Hallen, 1894.)

Light Cavalry Overture—*original German title:* **Leichte Cavallerie.** Orch. composition. m., Franz von Suppé. Leipzig: C. F. W. Siegel [1869]. (This composition is the overture to an operetta "Leichte Cavallerie," first produced in Germany, 1866, and performed in New York at the Stadt Theater, Oct. 1, 1868.)

The Little Brown Jug. w., m., R. A. Eastburn [pseud. of J. E. Winner]. J. E. Winner, cop. 1869.

Near the Cross [Jesus, Keep Me Near the Cross]. Hymn. w., Frances Jane Crosby [Mrs. Alexander Van Alstyne]. m., William Howard Doane. The Biglow & Main Co., cop. 1869.

Now the Day Is Over. Hymn. w., Sabine Baring-Gould. m., Joseph Barnby. London: Novello, Ewer and Co. [1869] (in: Joseph Barnby, "Original Tunes to Popular Hymns," p. 67).

Shew! Fly, Don't Bother Me. w., Billy Reeves. m., Frank Campbell, arr. by Rollin Howard. Boston: White, Smith & Perry, cop. 1869.

Sweet Genevieve. w., George Cooper. m., Henry Tucker. Wm. A. Pond & Co., cop. 1869.

Wine, Women and Song—original German title: Wein, Weib und Gesang. Waltz. m., Johann Strauss, op. 333. Vienna: C. A. Spina, n.d. (First performed in Vienna, Feb. 2, 1869.)

Ulysses Simpson Grant, Republican, of Ohio, was inaugurated 18th President.

The first transcontinental railway, the Union Pacific and Central Pacific, was completed and a golden spike was driven (May 10) by Gov. Leland Stanford of California (according to legend, he missed the first stroke) at Ogden, Utah, where the two joined. Regular service began five days later (May 15). (Construction of the road was begun in 1863.)

Cornelius Vanderbilt consolidated the New York Central and the Lake Shore and Michigan Southern railroads, thus connecting New York and Chicago by a direct route.

An Atlantic cable was laid between the United States and France. It extended from Duxbury, Mass., via the island of St. Pierre, south of Newfoundland, to Brest. The undertaking was chartered by Louis Napoleon.

In Chicago, the Washington street railway tunnel under the Chicago River was completed at a cost of $517,000. (Construction began in 1867.)

Christopher Latham Sholes patented the typewriter. (It was placed on the market in 1873.)

Memorial Day (May 30) was first observed.

Sept. 24 became known as "Black Friday" when a clique of speculators cornered virtually all the gold in New York, pushed the price up 6 points (after already having raised it up 13 points previously), and sent the entire financial world into panic. The Subtreasury finally terminated the spectacle by releasing enough gold to break the corner and ease the price down 15 points.

The Noble Order of Knights of Labor, the strongest labor union in United States history until that time, was formed by Uriah Smith Stephens, a tailor. (It was at first a secret order, but public sentiment around 1881 caused it to abandon the policy. Its influence waned with the growth of the American Federation of Labor. The organization disbanded in 1917.)

The National Prohibition Party was organized (in Sept.) in Oswego, N. Y., as a political adjunct to the temperance movement. (The party held its first presidential convention in 1872.)

The National Woman Suffrage Association was formed to bring pressure on the Federal government. Elsewhere woman suffrage was making progress. Women were admitted to the practice of law in Kansas by an act of legislature, and voting privileges were granted by the legislatures of the Territories of Wyoming (Dec. 10) and Utah. At the First Presbyterian Church in Philadelphia women were ordained as deacons.

The construction of the Brooklyn Bridge in New York was begun. (The bridge was completed in 1883.)

Charles William Eliot was elected president of Harvard University, in which office he served for 40 years until his retirement in 1909.

Phillips Brooks was appointed rector of Trinity Protestant Episcopal Church in Boston. (He had previously written the words of the Christmas hymn "O Little Town of Bethlehem.")

Public interest induced James Gordon Bennett, wealthy newspaper owner of the "New York Herald," to finance an expedition to Africa under Sir Henry Morton Stanley to find the "lost" explorer and missionary David Livingstone, who had set out in 1865 to discover the sources of the Nile. (Stanley found Livingstone, in a dying condition, Nov. 10, 1871, at Ujiji, Tanganyika, Central Africa. The rescued Livingstone survived until 1873.)

Fire destroyed (Oct. 27) the steamer "Stonewall" near Cairo, Ill., with a loss of 200 lives.

Everyone's curiosity was aroused when a crude statue of a man, 10½ feet high, was "unearthed" near Cardiff, N. Y. It was found to have been carved from gypsum. The monstrosity was exhibited (in Dec.) in New York at Apollo Hall. The Cardiff Giant, as it was called, turned out later to be a hoax.

The American Museum of Natural History was founded in New York.

Mathew B. Brady added to his reputation as a photographer with his famous "National Photographic Collection of War Views," actual camera pictures of Civil War scenes.

"Appleton's Journal" was founded as a weekly magazine. (Became a monthly in 1876; ceased publication in 1881.)

William Frederick Cody became "Buffalo Bill" and a fictional hero—all because he was so named by Colonel Edward Zane Carroll Judson, who met him at this time. Judson was a founder of the Know-Nothing

Party, a leader in the New York Astor Place riots, an accused murderer, and an author. He began writing under the pseudonym of Ned Buntline some 400 dime novels dealing with imaginary exploits by the colorful pony express rider and frontiersman.

Mark Twain published his humorous, quasi-autobiographical narrative of foreign travel, "The Innocents Abroad, or, The New Pilgrim's Progress."

American bandmaster Patrick Sarsfield Gilmore inaugurated (June 15) in Boston his first colossal Peace Jubilee or music festival. He assembled an orchestra of 1,000 players and a chorus of 10,000 singers, and heightened the performances with many sensational features. The purpose of the festival was to celebrate the return of peace after the Civil War. (Similar "jubilees" were held in 1872 in Boston and in 1873 in Chicago.)

The long-fashionable California Theatre in San Francisco was opened (Jan. 18) with Bulwer-Lytton's play "Money," starring Marie Gordon of the Haymarket Theatre, London, and John McCullough, who also recited the dedicatory address written by Bret Harte. (Among those attending the performance was an unknown, 10-year-old, San Francisco-born lad named David Belasco.)

Clara Morris, Canadian-American actress, became the leading lady of Wood's Theatre in Cincinnati.

Edwin Thomas Booth, brother of Lincoln's assassin, built Booth's Theatre in New York (which he managed until 1874). It opened (Feb. 3) with a superb revival of "Romeo and Juliet," which ran for 10 weeks. Seats for the opening performance were sold at auction, the prices scaling from $125 down. Governor Hoffman and Mayor A. Oakley Hall occupied boxes at the performance.

Augustin Daly renovated and opened (Aug. 16) under his management the Fifth Avenue Theatre in New York, like Booth's above mentioned one of the leading playhouses in America for many years. (Fire destroyed the building in 1873, and Daly built a successor.)

The bicycle (a wooden affair) was put on the American market by the Six Hanlon Brothers. They opened (in Jan.) a shop in New York, which they called Velocipede Hall. The new vehicle was nicknamed a "bone shaker," and was taken up by other stuntists, some of whom performed perilous aerial feats. One of these daring cyclists was August Siegrist. He rode (Aug. 14, 1870) at the Empire City Rink "on a wire half an inch thick in mid-air, the whole length of the rink."

Offenbach's "La Grande Duchesse de Gérolstein" was the first opera to be performed (June 1) in Salt Lake City.

New York heard (Dec. 15) the first Russian opera to be given in the United States at the Théâtre Français—Alexie Nikolaievich Verstovsky's 4-act "Askold's Tomb." The performance was in Russian.

The Cincinnati baseball team became the first outright professional club in America, and made a tour without losing a single game.

At Chicago, the victorious Western tour of the Washington baseball team was stopped by the Rockford, Ill., nine, whose pitcher was a 17-year-old named Albert G. Spalding, later one of the influential figures of baseball.

Princeton and Rutgers played (Nov. 6) the first intercollegiate football game.

The hoopskirt finally gave way to the bustle.

George Peabody, aged 74, Massachusetts-born dry goods merchant and philanthropist, died (Nov. 4) in London. His body was conveyed to the United States on a British warship. Peabody's benefactions to educational institutions, libraries, museums, and other worthy objects, totalled between eight and nine million dollars.

The last surviving soldier of the Revolutionary War died—Daniel F. Bakeman, aged 109 years (Apr. 5), in Freedom, Cattaraugus County, N. Y.

The first patent for chewing gum was issued (Dec. 28).

?⤳ 1870

Looking Back. w., Louisa Gray. m., Arthur Sullivan. London: Boosey & Co. [1870.]

Pass Me Not, O Gentle Saviour. Hymn. w., Fanny J. [Frances Jane] Crosby [Mrs. Alexander Van Alstyne]. m., W[illiam] H[oward] Doane. Biglow & Main [cop. 1870] (in: William Howard Doane, "Songs of Devotion," p. 39).

Rescue the Perishing. Hymn. w., Fanny J. [Frances Jane] Crosby [Mrs. Alexander Van Alstyne]. m., W[illiam] H[oward] Doane. Biglow & Main [cop. 1870] (in: William Howard Doane, "Songs of Devotion," p. 258).

Safe in the Arms of Jesus. Hymn. w., Fanny J. [Frances Jane] Crosby [Mrs. Alexander Van Alstyne]. m., W[illiam] H[oward] Doane. Biglow & Main [cop. 1870] (in: William Howard Doane, "Songs of Devotion," p. 222).

Reconstruction in the South was completed when the four remaining former Confederate States of Georgia, Mississippi, Texas, and Virginia were readmitted to Congress. (Seven other States had been readmitted in 1868.)

Congress chartered (in May) the Northern Pacific Railroad Company. The Kansas Pacific Railroad from Kansas City, Mo., to Denver, Colo., was completed (Aug. 15). Following the boom in railroads, there were 49,168 miles of railway in the country.

Celluloid was patented by John Wesley Hyatt.

The development of Asbury Park, N. J., as a summer resort was begun by James A. Bradley, a New York businessman.

The brothers John D[avison] and William Rockefeller founded the Standard Oil Company with a capitalization of $1,000,000.

Evangelist Dwight Lyman Moody and singer Ira David Sankey combined their talents to spread the Gospel by word and song.

Alfred Ely Beach designed for New York the first American subway. It was 312 feet long, passing under Broadway from Warren to Murray streets. Passengers paid a 25-cent fare and sat in a cylindrical car propelled by a compressed-air apparatus called Root's Patent Force Blast Rotary Blower. The car ran on an irregular schedule; at other times the tunnel was used by pedestrians. The subway operated for about three years.

The Metropolitan Museum of Art in New York was incorporated. (It moved to its present quarters in 1880.)

Through the political machinations of "Boss" William Marcy Tweed, the New York State government passed into the control of the Democrats for the first time in 17 years. In New York City, fraudulent expenditures raised the cost of the new County Court House to $8,000,000. The city's expenses in salaries for the year reached $24,000,000, or nearly as much as the whole civil expenditure of the national government.

The steamboat "Robert E. Lee" paddled from New Orleans to St. Louis in 3 days, 18 hours, 14 minutes, for a record.

Roman Catholic Bishop Fitzgerald of Little Rock, Ark., cast one of the dissenting votes at the Ecumenical Council in Rome which endorsed, 547 to 2, the adoption of the doctrine of papal infallibility.

Bret Harte's story "The Luck of Roaring Camp" appeared in his San Francisco "Overland Monthly."

Augustin Daly achieved another New York success when he staged (Feb. 15) at his Fifth Avenue Theatre for a run of 103 performances his adaptation of Meilhac and Halévy's "Frou Frou" with the charming actress Agnes Ethel. In the fall, he presented (Oct. 10) Fanny Janauschek, Bohemian-German tragedienne, in "Deborah," in English, at the Academy of Music. (Thereafter the famous actress continued to appear on the English-speaking stage.)

Actor and singer Joseph Kline Emmet found a lifelong vehicle for his talents in Charles Gaylor's comedy "Fritz, Our Cousin German," first seen (July 11) in New York at Wallack's Theatre. (Emmet took the play to London for a run and, after his return, put on in 1878 "The New Fritz, Our Cousin German," still singing the long-remembered "Lullaby.")

Actress Clara Morris, forsaking Cincinnati (1869), took New York by storm at her local debut (Sept. 13) in "Man and Wife," a dramatization of Wilkie Collins's popular novel by Augustin Daly, at his Fifth Avenue Theatre. She was paid $35 per week. The play ran 10 weeks.

Pert, saucy, and long popular, French soubrette Marie Aimée made (Dec. 21) her American debut in New York at the Grand Opera House in Offenbach's opéra bouffe "Barbe Bleue."

Bronson Howard, destined to be one of America's foremost playwrights, produced (Dec. 21) his initial effort, a farce comedy entitled "Saratoga," in New York at Daly's Fifth Avenue Theatre. (The play was splendidly staged and ran until Mar. 27, 1871, for 101 performances.)

In the second competition for the American Cup, the American yacht "Magic" defeated (Aug. 8) the British contender "Cambria."

General Robert Edward Lee, aged 63, died (Oct. 12) in Lexington, Va. At the time of his death, he was president of Washington College (now Washington and Lee University), Lexington, Va.

The national population was 38,558,371.

₿❧ 1871

Beware. Part song for ATTB (also for SATB). w., Henry Wadsworth Longfellow. m., John Liptrot Hatton. London: Novello, Ewer & Co. [1871].

Good-bye, Liza Jane. Arr. by Eddie Fox. Philadelphia: Lee & Walker, cop. 1871.

The Little Old Log Cabin in the Lane. w., m., Will[iam] S[hakespeare] Hays. J. L. Peters, cop. 1871.

Mollie Darling. w., m., William Shakespeare Hays. J. L. Peters, cop. 1871.

Onward, Christian Soldiers. w., Sabine Baring-Gould. m., Sir Arthur Sullivan. London: Novello & Co. [1871]. (Published as a supplement to the "Musical Times," London, December, 1871.)

Reuben and Rachel. w., Harry Birch. m., William Gooch. Boston: White, Smith & Perry, cop. 1871.

Romeo and Juliet. Symphonic poem. m., Peter Ilyich Tchaikovsky. Berlin: Bote & Bock [1871].

The Sea Hath Its Pearls. w., Henry Wadsworth Longfellow, translated from the German of Heinrich Heine. m., Charles Gounod. London: Duff and Stewart [1871].

[Silent Night! Holy Night!] Stille Nacht, heilige Nacht! German words, Joseph Mohr. m., Franz Gruber. (See under the caption: 1818. The carol was popularized in Germany by Tyrolean singers, notably by the Strasser Sisters, three sisters and a brother, of Zillerthal, during the early

1830s, and found its way into print in variants during the early 1840s. The earliest printed English translation is probably that of Jane Montgomery Campbell, beginning "Holy Night! Peaceful Night! All is dark, save the light," which was published in London, 1863, and introduced in the United States during the early 1870s by the Rev. Charles Lewis Hutchins, an Episcopal clergyman and an indefatigable compiler of hymn collections. An anonymous American version, "Silent Night! Hallowed Night! Land and deep," was printed in the "Christian Hymn Book," Cincinnati, 1865, No. 131. The more familiar and standardized translation, "Silent Night! Holy Night! All is calm, all is bright," is likewise anonymous and appeared in the Lutheran "Sunday-School Book," Philadelphia: The United Lutheran Publication House, cop. 1871, No. 65, and in the revised edition, cop. 1896, No. 66. The translation was reprinted in William Reed Huntington, "The Church Porch; a Service Book and Hymnal for Sunday Schools," E. P. Dutton & Co., cop. 1874, No. 42.)

Something for Jesus. Hymn. w., S. D. Phelps. m., Rev. Robert Lowry. The Biglow & Main Co., cop. 1871.

Susan Jane. w., m., Will[iam] S[hakespeare] Hays. J. L. Peters, cop. 1871.

There Is a Green Hill Far Away. [w., Mrs. Cecil Frances Alexander (née Humphreys).] m., Charles Gounod. London: Novello, Ewer & Co. [1871.] (The words were wrongly attributed to Henry Wadsworth Longfellow.)

Congress passed an Appropriation Bill (in Mar.) to regulate the admission of persons into the civil service of the United States government, and the Enforcement Act (popularly known as the Ku Klux Act or Force Bill) to suppress the Ku Klux Klan and its activities (1865).

Mrs. O'Leary's cow, according to legend, kicked over a lighted lantern in a barn at 137 DeKoven Street in Chicago on Sunday evening, Oct. 8, and started a fire which, fanned by heavy winds, devastated for two days an area of 2,000 acres, destroyed about 17,500 buildings including the newly renovated Crosby Opera House, rendered some 98,500 persons shelterless, caused the death of about 250 persons, and inflicted a property loss estimated close to $200,000,000.

On the same day (Oct. 8), one of the greatest forest fires in history occurred in Wisconsin. Starting in the town of Peshtigo in Marinette County, the conflagration spread through six counties and across Green Bay to Williamsville. More than 1,000 lives were lost and 3,000 made destitute.

After years of dispute, the United States was awarded $15,500,000 damages in gold against Great Britain by a Court of Arbitration, comprising five commissioners from Italy, Brazil, Switzerland, the United

States, and England. The suit arose from United States claims for the depredations inflicted upon American shipping by the Confederate raiders "Alabama," "Florida," and "Shenandoah," built and equipped in British ports in violation of treaties. The "Alabama" destroyed between 57 and 65 United States vessels before it was sunk (June 19, 1864) by the U. S. S. "Kearsarge" off Cherbourg, France.

Sharp national resentment followed the signing of the Treaty of Washington by which the United States paid Great Britain the sum of $5,500,-000 to mitigate its harsh restrictions against American fishing interests in Canadian waters and ports.

Captain Charles Francis Hall, commanding an Arctic polar expedition on the government ship "Polaris," became (Aug. 29) the first American explorer to reach the farthest North Latitude (82° 11'), near Thank God Harbor, Greenland.

The hydraulic elevator came into use.

A feud in New York between Irish Protestants, or Orangemen, and Irish Roman Catholics broke out (July 12) in a riot during a parade of the former in celebration of the Battle of the Boyne. In spite of precautionary measures by the police and several regiments detailed to protect the line of marchers, over 100 persons were killed or wounded.

Brigham Young, Mormon leader, was arrested (Oct. 2) for polygamy.

A boiler explosion wrecked (July 30) the New York and Staten Island ferryboat "Westfield," with a loss of 100 lives.

Smith College, Northampton, Mass., for women, was founded by the bequest of Sophia Smith.

The tall and handsome Duke Alexis, third son of Czar Alexander II of Russia, made an extended tour (1871-72) of the United States. President Grant's wife shook His Imperial Highness's hand; he was accorded public receptions in Philadelphia at the Navy Yard, and in Chicago; grand balls were held in his honor in New York, Brooklyn, Boston, and San Francisco; he viewed Niagara Falls in the winter and was photographed seated with an immense icicle on his lap, and he shot buffaloes with General Custer on the prairies.

Books of the year included the fiction, "The Hoosier Schoolmaster" (Edward Eggleston) and "The Passionate Pilgrim" (Henry James); the poetry, "Pike County Ballads" (John Hay), "Songs of the Sierras" (Joaquin Miller), William Cullen Bryant's translation of "The Odyssey" (1871-72), and the first volumes of the "New Variorum Edition" of Shakespeare's plays by Horace Howard Furness (completed posthumously in 1913), and that classic of cooking, "Common Sense in the Household: A Manual of Practical Housewifery" (Marion Harland, pseudonym of Mary Virginia Terhune).

The Jubilee Singers, a choral group of 12 Negro students from Fisk University, Nashville, Tenn., undertook (in Oct.), for the purpose of raising funds for the school, a concert tour of the Eastern States, singing "spirituals" and other songs. (They went to Europe in 1873, which see.)

New York witnessed the United States premières of two famous operas —Wagner's "Lohengrin" at the Stadt Theatre (Apr. 3) and Ambroise Thomas's French masterpiece "Mignon" sung in Italian at the Academy of Music (Nov. 22).

Prince George Nicholas Galitzi conducted in New York at Steinway Hall two concerts (Nov. 14 and 21) of Russian music, featuring scenes from Glinka's important opera "A Life for the Czar." These were sung by Italian choristers who had difficulty with the unfamiliar style.

P. T. Barnum organized his circus, the "Greatest Show on Earth." (It merged in 1881 with J. A. Bailey's company to become Barnum & Bailey's Circus.)

Baseball left its former amateur and semi-professional status for an entirely professional plane, when the National Association of Professional Ball Players was organized in New York. It included the Philadelphia Athletics, the Bostons, the Chicago White Stockings, the Brooklyn Eck-fords, the Cleveland Forest Citys, the Rockford (Ill.) Forest Citys, the Troy (N. Y.) Haymakers, the Fort Wayne Kekiongas, and the New York Mutuals.

The New York Canoe Club was organized at St. George, Staten Island, N. Y., and this led to the formation of similar clubs in the East.

₴ 1872

The Angel and the Child. w., Henry Wadsworth Longfellow. m., Virginia Gabriel. London: Duff & Stewart [1872].

Come, Ye Faithful, Raise the Strain. Hymn. Tune: "St. Kevin." w., John Mason Neale, translated from the Greek of St. John of Damascus, 8th century. m., Arthur Sullivan. London: Novello & Co. [1872.]

I Need Thee Every Hour. Hymn. w., Annie S. Hawks. m., Rev. Robert Lowry. Cop. 1872 by Robert Lowry.

Oh! Sam. w., m., Will[iam] S[hakespeare] Hays. J. L. Peters, cop. 1872.

Polish Dance—*original German title:* Polnischer Nationaltanz. Piano solo. m., Xaver Scharwenka, op. 3, no. 1. Leipzig: Breitkopf & Härtel [1872?].

Les Rameaux—The Palm Trees; *better known as:* The Palms. French words, ? m., Jean Baptiste Faure. Arr. by Harrison Millard. G. Schirmer, cop. 1872. (The composer was a famous French operatic baritone; he should not be confused with the composer Gabriel Fauré. The song was published earlier in Paris. It was translated by Theodore T. Barker under the title "Palm-Branches" and published by Oliver Ditson Co., Boston, cop. 1875, in "Gems of English Song," p. 103-05.)

The Son of God Goes Forth to War. Hymn. Tune: "All Saints New." w., Reginald Heber. m., Henry Stephen Cutler. F. J. Huntington and Co. [cop. 1872] (in: John Ireland Tucker, "Hymnal with Tunes Old and New," No. 176).

The "Congressional Record" was founded by Congress to publish the proceedings of the Senate and the House of Representatives.

Congress abolished the tariff on tea and coffee.

National bonds in the amount of $200,000,000 at 6 per cent interest were reduced to 5 per cent. Subsequently, greater saving was effected by conversion into 4 and 4½ per cent bonds.

Yellowstone National Park in Montana and Wyoming Territories was established by act of Congress.

To test the interpretation of the 14th and 15th Amendments in their application to woman suffrage, Susan Brownell Anthony created a sensation by casting a ballot in the New York State and Congressional election at Rochester. She was indicted for illegal voting and sentenced to pay a fine (which was never collected).

New York erected the first elevated railroad (the "el").

A fire in Boston wiped out (Nov. 9) about 60 acres of the wholesale trade district, causing nearly $70,000,000 property damage.

Pago Pago harbor, Tutuila, Samoan Islands, was ceded by the native king to the United States as a naval base.

The brig "Marie Celeste" sailed (Nov. 7) from New York for Genoa with a cargo of alcohol. Five weeks later the boat was found adrift, under full sail, unmanned and undamaged, in the Atlantic some 600 miles west of Gibraltar. Even as in 1872, there is still speculation about the fate of the crew.

Arbor Day (Apr. 10) was first observed in Nebraska, when a million trees were planted in the State on that day. The idea was conceived by J. Sterling Morton, a native of Nebraska City, Nebr.

James Abbott McNeill Whistler, American painter, completed in London his "Portrait of My Mother" (now in the Luxembourg Gallery in Paris). (Whistler had settled permanently in London in 1863.)

Luther Burbank developed the Burbank potato in Worcester, Mass.

To settle the old argument as to whether or not all the legs of a running horse are ever off the ground, Senator Leland Stanford of California engaged Eadweard Muybridge, Scottish-American photographer, to set up a row of 24 cameras, before which a horse was run. The results showed that at one moment all four legs of a running horse are off the ground.

Francis Samuel Drake published the "Dictionary of American Biography," containing 10,000 biographies. Mark Twain brought out "Roughing It."

William Frederick Cody, known as "Buffalo Bill" since 1869, turned actor in Chicago and played the lead in "Scouts of the Plains," written by his friend Colonel Edward Zane Carroll Judson.

The beautiful 22-year-old English actress Rose Coghlan made (Sept. 2) her American debut in New York at Wallack's Theatre as a member of Lydia Thompson's celebrated troupe of blondes (1868). She played in a curtain raiser "A Happy Pair" and appeared as Jupiter in a revival of "Ixion." In after years she gained great fame as a leading actress under Wallack's direction.

The noted James Anthony Froude, publicized here as "the greatest living English historian," lectured (Oct.-Dec.) in New York and in Brooklyn.

Bandmaster Patrick Sarsfield Gilmore conducted in Boston his second monster Peace Jubilee, dedicated to "world peace." The undertaking was even larger than the first (1869) and was still more unwieldy, featuring an orchestra of 2,000, a chorus of 20,000, the discharge of distant cannon by electricity, marching brigades of local uniformed firemen down the aisles of the auditorium, the clanging of anvils, and other spectacular additions. The Fisk University Jubilee Singers and Johann Strauss, "The Waltz King," just arrived from Austria, participated in the performances. Gilmore conducted his huge force with a six-foot baton.

Herr Johann Strauss, celebrated composer of waltzes "The Blue Danube," "Wine, Women and Song," "Tales from the Vienna Woods," and other equally famous works, including the operetta "Die Fledermaus," made (July 8) his debut as a conductor in New York at the Academy of Music. He conducted four concerts in New York and 14 in Boston.

Anton Rubinstein, renowned Russian piano virtuoso and composer, and Henri Wieniawski, distinguished Polish violinist, concertized in joint recitals in the United States. They made (Sept. 23) their first appearance in New York at Steinway Hall. Wieniawski extended his tour alone to California. Rubinstein's leonine style of playing was humorously described in Virginia journalist George William Bagby's sketch "Jud Browning's Account of Rubenstein's [sic] Playing."

Henri Lefèbre, noted French clarinetist and saxophonist, and Edward Böhm, bass clarinetist, played solos on their respective instruments in New York.

The current aspirations of United States society were exemplified by Ward McAllister, social leader, who organized the "Patriarchs," 25 names deemed by him as fit to "create and lead society."

In the national election, President Grant was re-elected by a 760,000 majority, the largest ever polled by a presidential candidate up to that time. He won all but seven States.

❧ 1873

Eilleen Allanna. w., E. S. Marble. m., J[ohn] R[ogers] Thomas. Boston: Oliver Ditson & Co., cop. 1873 by J. R. Thomas.

Good Night! Good Night, Beloved! Part song for SATB. w., Henry Wadsworth Longfellow. m., Ciro Pinsuti. London: Novello, Ewer & Co. [1873].

Good Sweet Ham. Words and melody by Henry Hart; arr. by James E. Stewart. J. L. Peters, cop. 1873.

Jennie, the Flower of Kildare. w., Frank Dumont. m., James E. Stewart. J. L. Peters, cop. 1873.

The Mulligan Guard. w., Edward Harrigan. m., David Braham. Wm. A. Pond & Co., cop. 1873.

Seven-fold Amen. Setting for SATB. m., John Stainer. London: Novello, Ewer & Co. [1873] (in: John Stainer, "Choir-Book for the Office of Holy Communion").

Silver Threads Among the Gold. w., Eben E. Rexford. m., Hart Pease Danks. C. W. Harris, cop. 1873.

Wiener Blut. Waltz. m., Johann Strauss, op. 354. Vienna: C. A. Spina, n.d. (Composed in 1873.)

President Ulysses Simpson Grant began his second term.

The Crédit Mobilier scandal was aired in Congress. The mischief began in 1867 when certain stockholders of the Union Pacific railroad, which had accumulated an excess profit of $20,000,000 through financial jugglery and the exploitation of government land grants during the construction of the road (1863-69), reorganized a quiescent joint-stock called the Crédit Mobilier (formed in 1863, after the pattern of its French namesake, under the laws of Pennsylvania). In the winter of 1867-68, stock valued at $380 or $400 per $100 share was sold in private and never reached the open market. Shares were offered to congressmen and senators as gifts or at the low price of $100 per share. Disclosures that two congressmen, Oakes Ames of Massachusetts and James Brooks of New York, also a government director of the railroad, had made overtures to fellow legislators, including Vice-President Schuyler Colfax, brought charges of bribery of members, and in Dec., 1872, James G. Blaine, Speaker of the House of Representatives, had ordered an inquiry. The investigating House committee now (in Feb., 1873) made its report, recommending the expulsion of Oakes Ames and James Brooks, the censuring of other guilty congressmen, and the impeachment of Vice-President Colfax. However, the two congressmen were only subjected to a rebuke; the others cited for censure; and the impeachment of the Vice-President was withdrawn because the offense had been committed prior to the term of office which was finishing at this time. In the national election (1872), Colfax had been replaced by Henry Wilson as Grant's running mate.

Supreme Court Judge Stephen Johnson Field, in the Slaughterhouse case against the New Orleans butchers, held a dissenting opinion that the 14th Amendment gave the legislature no right of interference in business. The interpretation guided later decisions.

A "trade dollar" was authorized by Congress to facilitate trade with China and Japan. (Its use was discontinued in 1885.)

Bank failures throughout the country resulted in a panic, the effects of which continued to be felt for several years. The crisis was reached when the New York Clearing House suspended (Sept. 20) for 10 days.

One-cent postal cards were placed (May 1) on sale by the Post Office. By act of Congress, free postage to congressmen was rescinded except for public documents.

What was regarded as an insult to the national flag nearly involved the United States in a war with Spain. A sailing vessel, the "Virginius," flying the American colors, was seized (Oct. 31) by the Spanish war steamer "Tornado," on the suspicion that it was conveying munitions to Cuban insurrectionists. After sharp diplomatic exchanges, the "Virginius" was surrendered (Dec. 15) to the United States. The demand that Spain should salute the American flag was waived when that country established the fact that the ship was not entitled to sail under the American flag.

Military difficulties in the removal (1872-73) from northern California to the Klamath, Ore., reservation of some 200 Modoc Indians led by Captain Jack and Scar-faced Charlie resulted (Apr. 11) in the death of General Canby and Commissioner Thomas, and injury to General Meacham, the third commissioner. The Indians entrenched themselves in the lava beds and resisted the government troops for several months. The Indians were finally subdued; three of their ringleaders were hanged (Oct. 3).

Mrs. Belva Ann Lockwood of Washington, D. C., became (Mar. 3) the first woman lawyer admitted to practice before the Supreme Court.

Brigham Young, Mormon leader, renounced (Apr. 10) temporal power over his followers in Utah.

The discovery of silver in Nevada started another "rush."

The first typewriter to be placed on the market was the Sholes and Glidden (patented in 1868). It printed only capital letters.

A railway tunnel, 4¾ miles long, through Hoosac Mountain in Berkshire County, Mass., was completed (Nov. 27). (The construction took about 15 years. The first train passed through the tunnel on Feb. 9, 1875.)

The first cable-car system in the United States was introduced in San Francisco by Andrew S. Hallidie when he equipped the Clay Street Railway with a cable that ran in a slot between the rails.

The New York Society for the Suppression of Vice was founded by Anthony Comstock (1844-1915), social reformer. Its influence was reflected in the enactment by Congress of the so-called "Comstock" law, prohibiting the sending of obscene literature and pictures through the mails.

Henry Clay Frick began consolidating his vast coke-manufacturing business. (In 1889 he became manager of the Carnegie properties, and in 1900 the Frick and Carnegie firms merged into the Carnegie Co.)

After an erratic and romantic career in Europe, Russian-born Helena Petrovna Blavatsky came to the United States and founded in New York the Theosophical Society, a religious cult based on Buddhistic and East Indian mysticism. (The Society's textbook, "Isis Unveiled," was published in 1877.)

Bret Harte published his novel "M'liss: An Idyll of Red Mountain." Thomas Bailey Aldrich brought out his short story "Marjorie Daw" ("Oh, dear Jack . . . there isn't any Marjorie Daw") in "Every Saturday," a Boston magazine of which he was the editor.

Among the periodicals founded were "The Delineator," a monthly magazine for women, by Ebenezer Buttrick in New York; the semimonthly "Home Companion," in Cleveland; and the children's monthly "St. Nicholas," edited by Mary Mapes Dodge. (The "Delineator" merged in 1937 with the "Pictorial Review." The "Home Companion" became in 1886 the "Ladies' Home Companion" and in 1897, as a monthly, the "Woman's Home Companion.")

The first Cincinnati music festival was held. Twenty-nine singing societies, aggregating 1,000 voices, and an orchestra of 108 players participated under the direction of Theodore Thomas. Five concerts (May 6-10) were given; Beethoven's 9th Symphony, Handel's "Dettington Te Deum," and excerpts from Gluck's opera "Orpheus," among other works, were performed.

Verdi's, spectacular Egyptian opera, "Aïda," received (Nov. 26) its United States première in New York at the Academy of Music. The opera was sung by Ostava Torriani (Aïda), Annie Louise Cary (Amneris), Italo Campanini (Rhadames), and Victor Maurel (The King).

The Negro Jubilee Singers (1871) gave concerts of their songs in England, Scotland, and Ireland. (Their campaign to raise funds for Fisk University, Nashville, Tenn., lasted three years, 1871-74, and brought them $90,000.)

The Oratorio Society, a choral organization of mixed voices, was formed in New York by Dr. Leopold Damrosch. (It made its first public appearance on Dec. 3 at Knabe Hall, singing a miscellaneous program, and concluded its season of three concerts on May 12, 1874 at Steinway Hall with Handel's oratorio "Samson," its first major offering.)

Bandmaster Patrick Sarsfield Gilmore conducted in Chicago his third and last Peace Jubilee in celebration of the rebuilding of the city after the great fire of 1871.

"St. Peter" was the first full-scale oratorio composed by an American, John Knowles Paine. It was performed (June 3) in Portland, Me.

Tommaso Salvini, noted Italian actor, made (Sept. 16) his American debut in a fiery and passionate impersonation of Othello. The performance was given in Italian at the Academy of Music in New York.

Augustin Daly opened (Dec. 3) his own Broadway house, retaining for it the name Fifth Avenue Theatre. His first play, "Fortune," by James Albery, was a failure, and it inaugurated a season during which no production caught the public's interest. Meanwhile Booth's Theatre, now under the management of Junius Brutus Booth, was drawing the public largely because of the manager's accomplished wife, Agnes Perry. She had been playing in Boston for some years and now returned to New York to rise to stardom.

Gilbert S. Densmore, dramatic critic of "The Golden Era" in San Francisco, dramatized Mark Twain's just-published novel "The Golden Age" without the author's consent, produced the play at the California Theatre (Apr. 22), was sued for infringement, started John T. Raymond on his career as a famous comic actor, and provided Broadway with one of its brightest successes, under the title "Colonel Sellers" (1874). (Raymond played his role more than a thousand times.)

Barnum built and opened (Oct. 20) in New York a "Hippodrome" to house his circus, the "Greatest Show on Earth" (1872). It was a large wooden amphitheatre, constructed on the site that had been the depot of the New York Central Railroad until 1871 when the railroad moved to its present Grand Central Station. On this site the first Madison Square Garden was erected.

The old Congress Hall Theatre in San Francisco was rebuilt and transformed at the cost of $30,000 into Shiel's Opera House. It presently passed into the hands of Tom Maguire.

Indoor marathon walking exhibitions were the latest attractions for the sport-minded. In New York at the Empire City Rink, Edward Payson Weston, the "great American walker" and a familiar figure to subsequent generations, was advertised to walk (May 15) "one hundred miles inside of twenty-two consecutive hours, for a purse of $1,500" and to do (June 2) 50 miles in 10½ hours. A rival, James Smith, was scheduled (June 4) to reduce the distance of 100 miles to 21½ hours.

ᨀ 1874

The Alabama Blossoms. Words and melody by Frank Dumont; arr. by James E. Stewart. J. L. Peters, cop. 1874.

I Love to Tell the Story. Hymn. w., Catherine Hankey. m., W[illiam] G. Fischer. Cincinnati: John Church & Co. [cop. 1874] (in: Philip Paul Bliss, "Gospel Songs," p. 42).

Patrick's Day Parade. w., Edward Harrigan. m., David Braham. Wm. A. Pond & Co., cop. 1874.

The Skidmore Guard. w., Edward Harrigan. m., David Braham. Wm. A. Pond & Co., cop. 1874.

Trabling Back to Georgia. w., Arthur W. French. m., Charles D. Blake. Boston: G. D. Russell & Co., cop. 1874.

President Grant's daughter Nellie was married (May 21) to Captain Algernon Sartoris in the White House. Mendelssohn's "Wedding March" was played.

Congress feted (Dec. 18) the first royal visitor to the United States— David Kalakaua, King of the Sandwich Islands (now Hawaii).

William Marcy Tweed, political "Boss" of New York, was convicted (Nov. 19) of fraud in the amount of about $6,000,000 and sentenced to 12 years in prison on Blackwells (now Welfare) Island. (He was released in 1875 on a legal technicality, was then convicted in a civil suit, but escaped from jail to Cuba and Spain. He was extradited in 1876, and died in Ludlow Street jail, New York, Apr. 12, 1878.)

Agitation against the evils of alcohol brought into existence the Women's Christian Temperance Union.

A movement to increase the issuance of Treasury notes or "greenbacks" (1862), issued as an emergency during the Civil War and "worthless," but now advocated as a peace-time measure, succeeded in passing through Congress an inflation bill. It was vetoed (in Apr.) by President Grant. The dissatisfied supporters of the bill organized the Independent, or Greenback, party (it held its first convention on Nov. 25).

By this time, as a result of the crusade against "Boss" Tweed, the tiger and the donkey were familiar symbols of Tammany and the Democratic Party. The figures were drawn by cartoonist Thomas Nast and appeared in "Harper's Weekly." He now added (Nov. 7) a third caricature, the elephant, to represent the Republican Party.

The Social Democratic Workingmen's Party was formed, mainly by German socialists. (It changed its name to the Socialist Labor party in 1877 and merged with the Socialist Party in 1899-1900.)

A kidnaping made front page news when a four-year-old infant, Charlie Ross, was stolen (July 1) from his home in Germantown, Pa. (A Superior Court in Phoenix, Ariz., decided May 8, 1939, that Gustav Blair, a carpenter of that place, is, in reality, Charlie Ross, and is entitled to use the name. He testified that the Ross family had refused to recognize him. The kidnaping was introduced as an episode in the play "Pique" in 1875.)

The Independent Order of Foresters (I.O.O.F.) was founded in Newark, N. J., as a fraternal and benevolent society.

Methodist Bishop John H. Vincent and Lewis Miller established Chautauqua, a system of popular education for Bible study and the training of Sunday-school teachers, at a camp meeting at Chautauqua Lake, N. Y. Eventually it grew to be an educational-platform idea, mixed with entertainment.

Charles T. ("Pastor") Russell preached that the millennium or the period of the second coming of Christ had begun invisibly this year and would terminate in 1914. His followers were known as Russellites and as Millennial Dawnists (after his book "Millennial Dawn") and constituted a society called the Internal Bible Students' Association.

The Lambs, a club for actors, was organized in New York.

"Die Fledermaus," Johann Strauss's merry operetta, began (Nov. 21) its varied career in America quite mildly in New York at the Thalia Theatre, sung in German. (Its initial English production in America took place Mar. 16, 1885, at the Casino, New York.)

A Colosseum, modeled after its London namesake, opened (Jan. 10) in New York, presenting cycloramas of London and Paris. From the tower of the building, bells pealed the St. Paul and the Westminster chimes. The house was closed (in Nov.) for arrears in rent, amounting to $18,-000, although shows continued to occupy the place into the next year.

Fourteen-year-old Irish-American actress Ada Rehan made her stage debut in Newark, N. J. (Her New York appearance followed, Apr. 26, 1875, in Frank Rogers's "Thoroughbred" at Wood's Museum and under Augustin Daly's management. She was his stellar feature from 1879, when Wood's Museum became Daly's Theatre, until her retirement in 1899. She was also a notable Shakespearean actress.)

Albert M. Palmer became manager of the Union Square Theatre in New York and proved himself one of the ablest American producers during the next 10 years.

Fred Marsden's melodrama "Zip" played (Mar. 30) in New York at Booth's Theatre for three weeks with the lively Lotta in the name part. In the play, the heroine swings on a rope from the shore to a lighthouse to illuminate the night, and when her vicissitudes end in her ancestral home in England she plays a banjo to relieve her Victorian boredom.

Niblo's Garden in New York produced (July 27) a travesty on a Longfellow poem by two Bostonians, the author a young Harvard graduate
and a reporter on the "Traveler," and the composer a self-taught musician
and a clerk in the Cunard steamship office. Although the piece ran only
two weeks, it became one of the most successful shows for family entertainment—"Evangeline, or, The Belle of Acadie," by J. Cheever Goodwin,
with music by Edward E. Rice.

Three great New York stage successes were "Colonel Sellers," Mark
Twain's comedy (already seen in San Francisco, 1873), at the Park
Theatre (Sept. 16); "The Shaugraun," Dion Boucicault's Irish comedy,
at Wallack's Theatre (Nov. 14), and "The Two Orphans," Hart Jackson's
adaptation from the French, at the Union Square Theatre (Dec. 21).

Tennis was becoming a popular sport.

The American game of baseball was taken to England and Ireland by
the Boston and Philadelphia National Association (predecessor of today's
National League) ball clubs. The teams played 14 baseball games and
seven cricket matches.

Five years of secondary postwar depression began (the 15th since
1790).

ᢒᢀ 1875

All the Way My Saviour Leads Me. Hymn. w., Fanny J. [Frances
Jane] Crosby [Mrs. Alexander Van Alstyne]. m., Rev. R[obert] Lowry.
The Biglow & Main Co., cop. 1875.

Angel Gabriel. w., anon. m., James E. Stewart. J. L. Peters, cop. 1875.

Angels Meet Me at the Cross Roads. w., m., Will[iam] S[hakespeare]
Hays. J. L. Peters, cop. 1875.

The Blue Alsatian Mountains. w., Claribel [pseud. of Mrs. Charles C.
Barnard, née Charlotte Arlington]. w., Stephen Adams [pseud. of Michael
Maybrick]. See below: "Gems of English Song."

Fully Persuaded. Hymn. w., Rev. J. B. Atchinson. m., William F.
Sherwin. The Biglow & Main Co., cop. 1875.

Gems of English Song; a collection of very choice songs, duets and
quartets. With an accompaniment for the pianoforte. Boston: Oliver
Ditson Co., cop. 1875. 232 p. 4°. (The significance of this collection for
our purpose lies in the fact that its year of copyright, in the absence of
other sources, establishes an approximate date for certain contemporary

popular songs, which are included under the caption for this year although published earlier in London.)

It Was a Dream. w., R[obert] E[dward] Francillon. m., F[rederick] H[ymen] Cowen. See above: "Gems of English Song."

The Kerry Dance. w., m., J[ames] L[yman] Molloy. See above: "Gems of English Song."

Let Me Dream Again. w., B. C. Stevenson. m., Arthur Sullivan. London: Boosey & Co. [1875.]

The Midshipmite. w., Fred[erick] E[dward] Weatherly. m., Stephen Adams [pseud. of Michael Maybrick]. See above: "Gems of English Song."

Nancy Lee. w., Fred[erick] E[dward] Weatherly. m., Stephen Adams [pseud. of Michael Maybrick]. See above: "Gems of English Song."

[Non è Ver.] 'Tis Not True. Italian words, anon. English words, Theodore T. Barker. m., Titto Mattei, op. 20, no. 1. See above: "Gems of English Song."

O Fair Dove, O Fond Dove. w., Jane Ingelow. m., Alfred Scott-Gatty. See above: "Gems of English Song."

Twickenham Ferry. w., m., Theo[phile] Marzials. See above: "Gems of English Song." (The song was originally published at the composer's expense by Weekes and Co., London.)

A Warrior Bold. w., Edwin Thomas. m., Stephen Adams [pseud. of Michael Maybrick]. See above: "Gems of English Song."

Within the Cellar's Depth I Sit—*original German title:* **Der Rheinweinzecher;** *also known as:* (1) "Im kühlen Keller"; (2) "Im tiefen Keller sitz' ich hier"; (3) "Ewiger Durst." German words, ? English words, L[ouis] C[harles] Elson. m., [Karl Ludwig] Fischer. Boston: Oliver Ditson & Co., cop. 1875. (The song is also known in English as "Drinking" and "In Cellar Cool.")

The Yeoman's Wedding Song. w., Maria X. Hayes. m., Prince [Josef Michel Xavier Franciszek Jan] Poniatowski. See above: "Gems of English Song."

Congress passed (Jan. 14) the Resumption Act, as a return to specie or "hard money," requiring the coinage of silver to replace other forms of currency and the issuance for every $100 of $80 in "greenbacks," which were to be redeemed in coin by Jan. 1, 1879. The measure was unpopular.

Another unpopular Congressional enactment (Mar. 1) was a third Civil Rights Bill meant to remedy discrimination in the Southern States, particularly discrimination against freedmen in travelling and in places of entertainment. (Certain sections of the Bill were declared unconstitutional in 1883. Other civil rights bills had been passed in 1866 and in 1870.)

A new Atlantic cable between the United States and Great Britain, called the United States Direct Cable, was laid to compete with that of Cyrus West Field (1866). In consequence, the rate fell first to 50 cents and then to 25 cents per word. The two Anglo-American lines were later united.

The dynamo was invented by Charles G. Brush of Cleveland, O.

John McCloskey, Roman Catholic Archbishop of New York since 1864, became the first American cardinal when he was elevated to that rank by Pope Pius IX.

Luther Burbank established his scientific plant and fruit nursery in Santa Rosa, Cal.

A statue of "Stonewall" Jackson was unveiled (Oct. 26) in Richmond, Va.

Mary Baker Eddy published "Science and Health with Key to the Scriptures," only authorized textbook of Christian Science which she founded (1866).

The Chicago "Daily News" was founded; also in the same city the Czech language daily "Svornost."

Josiah Gilbert Holland, Massachusetts author and editor, published "Sevenoaks," a novel about an unscrupulous financier and industrial and social conditions in a New England town.

Hans von Bülow, celebrated German piano virtuoso and conductor, who had been the first husband of Cosima (Liszt) Wagner, concertized in piano recitals in the United States (1875-76). He introduced (Oct. 25) Tchaikovsky's Piano Concerto in B flat minor in America at the Music Hall in Boston.

Brahms's "Deutsches Requiem" was sung (Jan. 24) for the first time in America by the Liederkranz singing society at their hall in New York.

The Cincinnati Biennial Musical Festival Association held (in May) its second festival of concerts. (The first was in 1873. With the exception of 1878, festivals have been given regularly every two years in May.)

Denman Thompson modestly started (in Feb.) his lifelong impersonation of "Joshua Whitcomb" in Pittsburgh at Harry Martin's Varieties Theatre. (At first a skit, it became "The Old Homestead" in 1878. Thompson died in 1911.)

New York was enjoying one of its greatest theatrical years. To "Colonel Sellers," "The Shaugraun," and "The Two Orphans" of the previous year's fall season were added "The Big Bonanza" (Feb. 17) "Our Boys" (Sept. 18), and "Pique" (Dec. 14) at Daly's Fifth Avenue Theatre, "The Mighty Dollar" (Sept. 6) and "Rose Michel" (Nov. 23) at the Union Square. "Henry V" was revived (Feb. 8) with the heroic George Rignold; Edwin Booth played (Sept. 13) a poetic "Hamlet" to enraptured audiences; "Julius Caesar" featured (Dec. 27) a brilliant cast. Even A. Oakey Hall, former Mayor of New York and puppet of "Boss" Tweed, tried the stage as an actor-playwright at the Park with "The Crucible" (Dec. 18) which ran for three weeks, much to the embarrassment of its public. The play dealt with a court action in which an innocent victim (played by Hall!) was led off to jail.

The amusing Vokes Family (5 members) from England was appearing in New York in "Belles of the Kitchen" (Fifth Avenue Theatre, Aug. 2) and other farces.

In spectacular style, the Kiralfy Brothers (Imre, Bolossy, and Arnold), Hungarian dancers and pantomimists, who came to the United States in 1868, put on (Aug. 28) in New York at the Academy of Music a stage version (there were others) of Jules Verne's popular novel, "Around the World in Eighty Days," which outrivalled "The Black Crook" (1866).

"Trial by Jury" (N. Y., Eagle Theatre, Nov. 15) introduced to America the eminent British composer who was turning from sacred music ("The Lost Chord," 1871, etc.) to comic opera—Arthur Sullivan.

German singing actress Mathilde Cottrelly, from the Wallner-Theater, Berlin, made (Oct. 5) her initial American bow in a popular musical play "Ehrliche Arbeit" in New York at the Germania Theater. After busily playing a few seasons for her compatriots, she became a prominent figure on the American English-speaking stage.

A children's troupe from below the Rio Grande, called the Mexican Juvenile Opera Company, performed "The Grand Duchess of Gérolstein" (Aug. 30) and "Robinson Crusoe," both by Offenbach, in New York at the Fifth Avenue Theatre. The former was repeated at other playhouses. The company included Señorita Niña Carmen y Moron, 8 years old; Señorita Guadaloupe, 6 years old; Niño Estevan, and twenty-seven others. The prima donna, Carmen Moron, carried off the honors, according to the press.

The first Kentucky Derby was run at Churchill Downs, Louisville, Ky. It was won by the horse Aristides.

Over 2,000 baseball organizations, still nine-tenths amateur, were in existence, while Yale boasted the best college team.

The National Association of Professional Baseball Players disbanded because of a public scandal created by the dishonesty of players.

Republicans proposed President Grant for a third term, but public sentiment was against breaking the two-term precedent. (He was again considered in 1880.)

Scandal besmirched the national elections. To all appearances, the Democratic nominee Samuel J. Tilden, who polled a 250,000 majority, had defeated the Republican opponent, Rutherford B. Hayes, 184 electoral votes to 163. Not included in either tally were the 12 votes of Florida, Louisiana, Oregon, and South Carolina, which were contested with increasing bitterness. Rash Democrats even threatened to march an army of volunteers to Washington to install Tilden. The dispute was submitted to Congress (in Dec.), which established an Electoral Commission to meet with the Supreme Court (in Feb., 1876). The Commission consisted of five Senators appointed by the Vice-President (three Republicans and two Democrats), five Representatives appointed by the Speaker (three Democrats and two Republicans), and five Judges of the Supreme Court. The tribunal of eight Republicans and seven Democrats concluded its business two days before the inaugural date. The members adhered to party politics and ruled the 22 contested votes in favor of the Republican candidate. Hayes was therefore elected by one electoral vote, 185 to 184, and the cry of "Fraud" went up in the land.

⧽ 1876

Grandfather's Clock. w., m., Henry Clay Work. C. M. Cady, cop. 1876.

I'll Take You Home Again, Kathleen. w., m., Thomas P. Westendorf. Cincinnati: John Church & Co., cop. 1876. (For an exhaustive investigation into the history of the song and its composer, consult: Richard S. Hill, "Getting Kathleen Home Again," in "Notes," Washington, D. C., June 1948, p. 338-353.)

It Is Well with My Soul. Hymn. w., H. C. Spafford. m., Paul P. Bliss. Cincinnati: John Church & Co., cop. 1876.

My Dearest Heart. w., ? m., Arthur Sullivan. London: Boosey & Co. [1876].

The Ninety and Nine. Hymn. w., E. C. Clephane. m., Ira D[avid] Sankey. The Biglow & Main Co., cop. 1876; renewed 1904 by Ira D. Sankey.

Rose of Killarney. w., George Cooper. m., John Rogers Thomas. J. L. Peters, cop. 1876.

Trusting Jesus, That Is All. Hymn. w., E. P. Stites. m., Ira David Sankey. The Biglow & Main Co., cop. 1876.

What a Friend We Have in Jesus. Hymn. w., Horatius Bonar. m., Charles Crozat Converse. Biglow & Main, cop. 1876 (in: Philip Paul Bliss and Ira David Sankey, "Gospel Hymns No. 2," p. 59).

The United States was 100 years old. The event was commemorated by the Centennial Exposition held (May-Nov.) in Philadelphia. It was planned on a grand scale, larger than any previous European or American exhibition, and covered 236 acres. The main structure cost $4,500,000; an electric railway made a circuit of the building for the convenience of the visitors. Congress appropriated $2,000,000, the city of Philadelphia $1,500,000, the State of Pennsylvania $1,000,000. Stocks were issued in the amount of $10,000,000. The general music director was the noted Theodore Thomas, who assumed the musical expenses and lost a personal fortune in the undertaking. It took him 12 years to pay the deficits ("twelve years of sheriffs and scoundrels," he said) and his large orchestral library was sold at auction to meet his obligations. For the occasion —and $5,000—the great German composer Richard Wagner composed a mediocre "Fest Marsch" ("dem Festfeier-Frauenverein gewidmet"), played on the opening day (May 10) on the arrival of President Grant. Thomas was so disappointed with the piece that he never forgave the master whose works he helped to popularize in this country (Wagner himself wrote: "The best thing about that composition was the money I got for it.") On the same program figured Whittier's "Centennial Hymn," with music by John Knowles Paine, sung by a chorus of 150. The celebrated French opéra-bouffe composer Jacques Offenbach conducted popular concerts, mostly of his own works. John Philip Sousa was a member of Offenbach's orchestra. Bandmaster Patrick Sarsfield Gilmore of the monster "Peace Jubilee" concerts was also there. The President failed to attend the elaborate July 4th celebration, preferring, as one writer (James D. McCabe) said, "his selfish ease to a little patriotic exertion." The Exposition attracted 9,789,392 visitors; the receipts were $3,813,750. The number of exhibits was exceeded only by those of the Paris and Vienna Expositions. Dom Pedro II, Emperor of Brazil, and Prince Oscar of Sweden took part in the functions.

Elisha Graves Otis again exhibited his passenger elevator at the Exposition.

A mechanical Orchestrion, or Electro-Magnetic Orchestra, invented by William F. and H. Schmoele of Philadelphia, was displayed at the Exposition in Horticultural Hall. Paper rolls, similar to those of the later player piano, provided the music.

Amid Centennial gayety, 103 American and Canadian librarians met (Oct. 4-7) and formed the American Library Association. One of the leaders was Melvil Dewey, originator of the Dewey decimal system of classifying and shelving books.

Twenty-nine-year-old Scottish-American inventor Alexander Graham

Bell and Prof. Elisha Gray patented independently (by coincidence on the same day, Feb. 14) the American telephone (a German telephone had been devised by Philipp Reis of Friedrichsdorf in 1861). The first intelligible words were sent (Mar. 10) by Bell from the top floor of a boarding house in Boston over a two-mile line to Cambridgeport, Mass. (Litigation between Bell and Gray followed, but Bell's priority—his patent was granted Mar. 7, 1876—was sustained by the U. S. Supreme Court. The first commercial use of the telephone in the United States occurred in 1878—which see. Bell described his invention in his application for the patent as an "improvement in telegraphy.")

About 3,000 Sioux Indians, under Sitting Bull, who had been resisting since 1874 the government's attempt to transfer them from the Black Hills, S. D., to a reservation, killed (June 25) General George Armstrong Custer and 261 men of the Seventh Cavalry and wounded 51 at Little Big Horn, Mont. The episode is known as "Custer's Last Stand." (Sitting Bull fled to Canada and was killed near Fort Yates, N. D., during his flight to escape arrest.)

Colorado was admitted (Aug. 1) as the 38th State.

Secretary of War William B. Belknap was impeached on charges of accepting bribes. He was acquitted. The trial began Mar. 3 and ended Aug. 1. (It was the seventh impeachment in United States history.)

Senator William Henry Blair of New Hampshire introduced (Dec. 12) in Congress a bill proposing federal prohibition of liquor traffic. (New Hampshire was a dry state.)

The St. Louis-San Francisco Railway Company was formed (Sept. 10).

Johns Hopkins University, Baltimore, Md., for men, named after its benefactor, was opened; also, the University of Oregon, at Eugene and Portland, for men and women (Oct. 18).

Colonel Robert Green Ingersoll attracted national attention as an orator at the Republican national convention when he delivered a speech nominating James G. Blaine as a presidential candidate. He called Blaine "the plumed knight." (Blaine was later withdrawn in favor of Rutherford B. Hayes.) Ingersoll was long a hated figure in religious circles, being regarded as an atheist, for his Biblical lectures ("The Gods," 1872, "The Mistakes of Moses," 1879, and others).

"Frank Leslie's Popular Monthly" was founded. (Merged in 1906 with "The American.")

The "Svenska Amerikanaen Tribunen" appeared in Chicago as a Swedish-language weekly.

A modest book that had been rejected by publishers, printed at the author's expense, and finally vended by a Chicago book firm, was t he "Pocket Manual of Rules of Order for Deliberative Assemblies" by Henry M. Robert, a South Carolina major in the U. S. Army. The volume met with immediate response; the 4,000 copies of the first edition—price 75 cents per copy—were sold within six weeks. (Periodically revised,

Robert's "Rules of Order" is today the standard guide for parliamentary procedure.)

Mark Twain published his novel "The Adventures of Tom Sawyer." Equally characteristic of American life were the comic poems by Charles Follen Adams, which appeared under the title "Leedle Yawcob Strauss," written in the "scrapple English" dialect of the Pennsylvania Dutch. (The poems were collected and printed in 1878 in Boston.)

Abreast of the times, Walt Whitman brought out in two volumes the Author's or Centennial edition of his "Leaves of Grass." (It was the 6th edition of the collection.)

Henry James, New York-born novelist, settled in London.

The famous Parisian composer Jacques Offenbach came to the United States. He gave (beginning May 11) a series of 20 concerts of popular music with an orchestra of 100 players in New York at Gilmore's Garden. There Dwight Moody and his musical assistant, Ira David Sankey, had conducted revival meetings during the preceding winter; now the Garden was refurbished with tropical plants and cascades. From New York, Offenbach went to the Centennial Exposition in Philadelphia (see above). And, of course, he visited Niagara Falls.

After several appearances in local concerts, the great German soprano Therese Tietjens made (Jan. 24) her American debut in "Norma" at the Academy of Music in New York. Thereafter she sang in Baltimore and in Boston.

Teresa Carreño, famous pianist, essayed a brief operatic career as a soprano and made (Feb. 15) her debut as Zerlina in Mozart's "Don Giovanni" at the Academy of Music in New York.

The Philharmonic Society of New York, under Carl Bergmann, introduced (Apr. 22) Tchaikovsky's overture "Romeo and Juliet" in America.

The saxophone, before it became a jazz instrument, intrigued women players. Etta Morgan, a member of the Berger Family's Ladies' Orchestra, began (Jan. 17) a two weeks' engagement in New York at the Olympic Theatre with her saxophone.

Oscar Hammerstein, erstwhile East Side cigarmaker from Germany, entered show business as manager of the German-language Stadt Theater in New York.

Fire destroyed (Dec. 5) the Brooklyn Theatre, Brooklyn, N. Y., with a loss of 285 lives (197 victims were identified; 98 remained unidentified), during a performance of the popular melodrama "The Two Orphans" by the New York Union Square Theatre Company. Many persons were trampled to death in the stampede for the doors. Claude Burroughs and Harry S. Murdoch of the cast perished in the flames. The fire was discovered by Kate Claxton, who was playing her famous role. The tragedy —the second largest of its kind in America—was headlined in the newspapers of the country, and affected theatre attendance everywhere for nearly a year. (The previous catastrophe occurred in Richmond, Va.,

1811; a third, similar disaster was the Iroquois Theatre fire in Chicago, 1903.)

Victorien Sardou's exciting French drama "Ferreol" was staged (Mar. 21) in an English version at the Union Square Theatre in New York with C. R. Thorne, Jr., and Kate Claxton. In this production, Ida Jeffreys made her first appearance on any stage. The great play, however, ran only 50 nights.

In keeping with the Centennial spirit, Augustin Daly gave change in gold at the box office of his Fifth Avenue Theatre in New York on the night of the hundredth performance (Mar. 13) of the play "Pique."

The present National League of Professional Baseball Clubs was organized to replace the National Association of Professional Baseball Players (1871) which had disbanded (1875) because of a public scandal created by dishonesty of players, contract-jumping, and gambling accusations.

Representatives from Columbia, Harvard, Princeton, and Yale universities met (Nov. 26) in convention at Springfield, Mass., and formed the American Intercollegiate Football Association which developed modern football. The touchdown became the deciding factor in the game. The new rule read: "A match shall be decided by a majority of touchdowns; a goal shall be equal to four touchdowns; but in case of a tie, a goal kicked from a touchdown shall take precedence over four touchdowns."

Returning from England where the new game of polo was being played (it was introduced there from India by the 10th Hussars), James Gordon Bennett, multi-millionaire owner of the "New York Herald," arranged an indoor match—the first ever so held—in New York at Dick's Riding Academy.

౿֍ 1877

The Better Land. w., Mrs. Felicia Dorothea Hemans (née Browne). m., Frederic H[ymen] Cowen. London: Boosey & Co. [1877.]

Early in de Mornin'. w., m., Will[iam] S[hakespeare] Hays. J. L. Peters, cop. 1877.

Hiding in Thee. Hymn. w., William O. Cushing. m., Ira D[avid] Sankey. The Biglow & Main Co., cop. 1877.

I'll Sing Thee Songs of Araby (Lalla Rookh). w., W[illiam] G[orman] Wills. m., Frederic Clay. London: Chappell & Co., Ltd. [1877.] ("Lalla Rookh" was a popular cantata first produced at the Brighton Festival, England, Feb., 1877.)

In the Gloaming. w., m., Annie Fortesque Harrison. London: Hutchings & Romer [1877]. (The composer became Lady Hill, wife of Lord Alfred Hill, comptroller of Queen Victoria's household; Lady Hill died at Berkshire, England, Feb. 12, 1944, aged 93.)

The Lost Chord. w., Adelaide Procter. m., Arthur Sullivan. London: Boosey & Co. [1877.] (The song was introduced at a Boosey Ballad Concert in London, Jan. 31, 1877, by the American contralto Antoinette Sterling.)

[La Paloma.] La Colombe—The Dove. Spanish words, anon. English words, anon. m., Sebastian Yradier. G. Schirmer, cop. 1877. (Published earlier in Paris by Au Ménestrel [Henri Heugel].)

Roll Out! Heave Dat Cotton. w., m., Will[iam] S[hakespeare] Hays. Boston: Oliver Ditson & Co., cop. 1877.

Where Is My [Wand'ring] Boy To-night? Hymn. w., m., Rev. Robert Lowry. The Biglow & Main Co., cop. 1877.

Rutherford Birchard Hayes, Republican, of Ohio, was inaugurated 19th President. The President and his wife were observers of temperance; no alcoholic beverages were served in the White House. They celebrated their silver wedding anniversary in the executive mansion during the year.

With the election of President Hayes, Reconstruction in the South was considered accomplished. Federal troops were withdrawn from the former Confederate States.

Chief Joseph of the Nez Percé Indian tribes refused to recognize a fraudulent treaty into which his father had been tricked, and he headed an uprising to win back the gold fields which Americans had secured thereby. To avoid capture he led his followers on a remarkable 1,000-mile trek to Canada, which ended after a five-day siege when he was caught near the Canadian border.

Railroad strikes paralyzed the nation, with virtually every major line in a labor battle after 10-per-cent wage cuts. The difficulties began on the Baltimore & Ohio, spread to the Pennsylvania, Erie, New York Central, and Missouri Pacific, and involved their Western and Southern affiliates. Outrageous riots occurred in Martinsburg, W. Va., Baltimore, Pittsburgh, Reading, Buffalo, Columbus, Chicago, and elsewhere. Federal troops and cavalry aided the local police and firemen to quell the disturbances. At least 50 persons were killed and more than 100 wounded. In Pittsburgh, rioters set oil cars afire, burned and pillaged some 2,000 freight cars, and looted the machine shops. Property damage was estimated upward of ten million dollars. (The strikes began July 14 and abated around July 27; nearly all railroads were in operation again by July 30.)

Eleven leaders of the Molly Maguires (1865), labor agitators in the Pennsylvania coal-mining regions, were hanged for murder.

Dennis Kearney, Irish-born San Francisco drayman, was haranguing local workingmen, "The Chinese must go," denouncing the importation and employment of coolies by the Central Pacific Railroad.

Alexander Graham Bell went to England to introduce his newly (1876) invented telephone. Although its demonstration before Queen Victoria met with Her Majesty's approbation, Bell was unable to make headway after a year's effort because of British patent difficulties. Meanwhile, in the United States, telephone service developed over private lines so rapidly that by November some 3,000 telephones were in operation.

Thomas Alva Edison invented the talking machine. He used a cylindrical record that was made of tin foil, and reproduced his own recitation of "Mary Had a Little Lamb." (The talking machine was later called the phonograph when it began transmitting music.)

Astronomer Asaph Hall discovered (in Aug.) the two moons of the planet Mars, which he named Deimos and Phobos.

The University of Colorado, Boulder, Colo., for men and women, opened.

The Royal Arcanum (V.M.C.) was founded in Boston as a fraternal and benevolent society.

"Puck" was issued in New York as a weekly magazine of humor and satire. (Ceased publication in 1918.)

New things were happening on the New York stage because Alexander Graham Bell invented the telephone. At the Academy of Music, manager Maurice Strakosch announced (sometime in March) a concert "in which numerous melodies performed in Philadelphia will be heard (by means of telephonic connection) in New York." Whether the advertised event took place is uncertain. At any rate, the brother-in-law of Adelina Patti actually tried the experiment twice in a much smaller auditorium—at Steinway Hall. At the first concert (Apr. 2), rain made transmission impractical. He then included the doubtful feature in a Brooklyn Academy of Music concert (Apr. 3). But at the second New York concert (Apr. 4), a piano solo played by Frederic Boskovitz in Philadelphia was heard by the New York audience. The world-famous pianist Teresa Carreño, and other notable artists, performed on the stage in these programs. Strakosch immediately repeated the successful experiment (Apr. 6 and 7). Later in the year, Harrigan and Hart played a week's engagement (Nov. 19-24) at the Théâtre Comique in a skit of their own, "The Telephone" (in it, Charles Diamond sang, danced, and played the harp simultaneously).

Wagner's great music drama "Die Walküre," the second of the four "Ring" operas, was heard (Apr. 2) for the first time in the United States at the Academy of Music in New York, and was given fourteen days later (Apr. 16) in Boston. The work was promised as part of a local Wagner "festival," but the other operas had to be postponed for more rehearsals until after the season. The Brünhilde was Mme. Eugenie Pappenheim;

Felix Preusser sang Wotan, and Pauline Canissa and Alexander Bischoff were respectively Sieglinde and Sigmund.

The celebrated English actress Adelaide Neilson made (May 7) her American debut as Viola in a revival of "Twelfth Night" in New York at Daly's Fifth Avenue Theatre.

Two actors who were to appear together twelve years later made their debuts 3,000 miles apart: Otis Skinner at the Museum Theatre in Philadelphia, and Helena Modjeska, Polish actress, in San Francisco (Dec. 22). Modjeska played the title role of "Adrienne Lecouvreur" in English after a brief study of the language. She had gone to San Francisco with a Polish group that planned a colony there. Another subsequently noted actor, Francis Wilson, made his stage bow in Philadelphia at the Chestnut Street Theatre in comedy.

M. Newski's drama "The Danicheffs" (Les Danicheff) duplicated its Paris Odéon success in the United States. Seen (Feb. 5) in New York at the Union Square Theatre, it starred Charles R. Thorne, Jr., Fanny Morant, Sara Jewett, Katherine Rogers, and James O'Neill (father of the playwright Eugene O'Neill). It afterwards played across the country.

The itinerant Hess English Opera Company brought out (Oct. 22) in New York Robert Plaquette's newest and most popular operetta "Les Cloches de Corneville" under the title "The Chimes of Normandy." It played for a week at the Fifth Avenue Theatre.

"Dime" entertainments in New York at Cooper Institute and at the Y.M.C.A. were a new means of attracting the public.

Greco-Roman wrestling was a rage in New York.

Brigham Young, aged 76, Mormon leader, died (Aug. 29) in Salt Lake City, Utah, which he had helped to found (1847). He had at various times 19 to 27 wives and was the father of 56 children.

ᘐ 1878

Baby Mine. w., Charles Mackay. m., Archibald Johnston. [ca. 1878.] (The song was sung by Belle Cole, a popular singer in the late '70s. The composer was a musical conductor in New York.)

Carry Me Back to Old Virginny. w., m., James A. Bland. Boston: John F. Perry & Co., cop. 1878.

[Emmet's] Lullaby (Fritz, Our Cousin German). w., m., Joseph K[line] Emmet. Cincinnati: The John Church Co., cop. 1878 by J. K. Emmet.

A Flower from Mother's Grave. w., m., Harry Kennedy. Boston: Oliver Ditson & Co., cop. 1878 by William H. Kennedy, Brooklyn, N. Y.

Saviour, Breathe an Evening Blessing. Hymn. w., J. Edmeston. m., George Coles Stebbins. Cop. 1878 by George C. Stebbins.

The Skidmore Fancy Ball (The Skidmore Fancy Ball). w., Edward Harrigan. m., Dave [David] Braham. Wm. A. Pond & Co., cop. 1878.

Sweet Mary Ann, or Such an Education Has My Mary Ann (Malone's Night Off, or the German Turnverein). w., Edward Harrigan. m., Dave [David] Braham. Wm. A. Pond & Co., cop. 1878.

Tell Me the Old, Old Story. Hymn. w., Catherine Hankey. m., William H[oward] Doane. London: Morgan and Scott [1878?] (in: Ira David Sankey, "Sacred Songs and Solos," p. 18-19).

Where Was Moses When the Light Went Out? w., anon. m., arr. by Max Vernor. Chicago: S. Brainard's Sons, cop. 1878.

Over President Hayes's veto, Congress passed (Feb. 28) the Bland-Allison silver bill, authorizing the coinage of 2,000,000 silver dollars per month. (The Act was repealed in 1890 by the Sherman Law.)

The newly invented (1876) telephone became a public necessity. The first commercial telephone exchange opened (Jan. 28) in New Haven, Conn. In Massachusetts, a wire was strung (in Apr.) from the home of Charles Williams in Somerville to his business office in Boston, three miles away.

Thomas Alva Edison announced (in Oct.) the invention of an incandescent platinum lamp. As a result, gas prices fell from twelve to twenty per cent. (The lamp was patented in 1880.)

Dissatisfied with the Resumption Act (1875), the Greenback Party (1874), the National Grange (1867), and other political and labor elements formed the Greenback-Labor Party. (It waned around 1884 and was absorbed in 1891 by the Populist Party.)

Work on the erection of the Washington National Monument (begun 1848 and discontinued 1854) was resumed at government expense.

For the first time in 17 years gold and paper money were (Dec. 18) of equal value.

The Military Service Institution was founded on Governors Island, New York, by officers of the U. S. Army for the promotion of military knowledge.

Tidewater Oil began pumping oil over the Alleghenies in pipes instead of shipping it by barrels.

The American painter James Abbott McNeill Whistler sued in a London court the famous art critic John Ruskin for libel. The latter had written of Whistler's impressionistic painting "Black and Gold—The Falling Rocket," exhibited in 1877: "I have seen and heard much cockney impudence before now, but never expected to hear a coxcomb ask 200 guineas for flinging a pot of paint in the public's face." The trial was replete with repartee. Whistler was vindicated and was awarded one farthing damages and no costs. As a result of the heavy expenses incurred in the prosecution, Whistler was forced into bankruptcy.

Anna Katherine Green set the formula of the modern detective story with her novel "The Leavenworth Case."

"Daisy Miller: A Study" established Henry James's reputation as a novelist.

Gilbert and Sullivan's comic opera "H.M.S. Pinafore" reached the United States six months after its London première (May 25). It was first heard (Nov. 25) at the Boston Museum (a theatre, not the present fine arts institution) and was given in San Francisco at the Bush Street Theatre (Dec. 23, with Alice Oates in the male role of the hero, Ralph Rackstraw) and in Philadelphia at the South Broad Street Theatre (Jan. 6, 1879) before the work came (Jan. 15) to New York at the Standard Theatre. Due to the absence of copyright protection, garbled and unauthorized versions followed at the Lyceum (Jan. 23), at Niblo's Garden, and at the Fifth Avenue Theatre (simultaneously, Feb. 10), by a Negro troupe at the Globe (Apr. 28), and elsewhere; in fact, the country was overrun with productions by professional and amateur, adult and juvenile companies and church choirs.

The Bohemian Club of San Francisco gave its first program of open-air "Midsummer High Jinks" in the redwood forest of Sonoma County. (The initial effort, followed by others, led in 1902 to the annual presentation of a "Grove Play." The performances were suspended after 1920.)

San Francisco's Tivoli Opera House, seating a thousand persons, was opened (Dec. 23) with Gilbert and Sullivan's "H.M.S. Pinafore." (The theatre was enlarged in 1880 to accommodate 2,000.)

The German Stadt Theater in New York reopened in the fall as the Windsor Theatre, advertised as "the largest theatre in America." The orchestra played in a visible room over the proscenium arch, as in an Elizabethan playhouse.

Bizet's great French opera "Carmen" had (Oct. 23) its initial United States rendition in New York at the Academy of Music, with Minnie Hauk. It was sung in Italian, and was given two days later (Oct. 25) in Philadelphia at its Academy of Music, also sung in Italian.

Col. James Henry Mapleson, English impresario, gave operatic performances (Oct., 1878-Apr., 1879) in New York, Boston, Philadelphia, Baltimore, Washington, D. C., Cincinnati, Chicago, and St. Louis.

An epidemic of yellow fever took an enormous number of lives despite such home-advised remedies as cigars and whiskey.

₷ 1879

The Babies on Our Block (The Skidmore Fancy Ball). w., Edward Harrigan. m., Dave [David] Braham. Wm. A. Pond & Co., cop. 1879.

Crucifix. Duet. m., Jean Baptiste Faure. Boston: Oliver Ditson Co., cop. 1879, English words by Theodore T. Barker; G. Schirmer, cop. 1879, English words by F. W. Rosier. (Published earlier in Paris.)

Dankgebet (No. 6 in: Sechs Altniederländische Volkslieder aus der Sammlung des "Adrianus Valerius"). Male chorus with piano acc. German words translated from the Dutch by Joseph Weyl. m., arr. by Edward Kremser. Leipzig: F. E. C. Leuckart [1879]. (The music was originally published in Valerius's "Nederlandtsche Gedenkclanck," Haarlem, 1626, which was reprinted in part in 1871. The "Dankgebet" was in the repertory of every German male singing society in the United States. An arrangement for SATB with English words by Theodore Baker, beginning "We gather together to ask the Lord's blessing," was published under the title "Prayer of Thanksgiving" by G. Schirmer, cop. 1894; renewed 1923.)

Oh! dem Golden Slippers. w., m., James Bland. Boston: John F. Perry & Co., 1879.

In the Morning by the Bright Light. w., m., James A. Bland. Boston: John F. Perry & Co., cop. 1879.

Congress passed an army appropriation bill, which was vetoed by President Hayes because a clause provided that no Federal troops should be employed in police duty in the South. The President deemed this a violation of the executive prerogative. At a special session, Congress enacted a new bill retaining the clause. Such Republican legislation helped to create the Democratic "Solid South." An Arrears of Pensions bill was also passed to settle rejected claims. It involved the disbursement of about $300,000,000.

The United States issued its first "postage due" stamps.

William Tecumseh Sherman, Civil War commander, uttered his famous dictum, "War is hell," in an address to the Michigan Military Academy.

Frank Winfield Woolworth opened (Feb. 22) a five-and-ten-cent store in Utica, N. Y.—the first of his subsequent nation-wide chain—thus founding one of America's most fabulous fortunes. (The United States issued its first postage stamps in 1847 in five and 10 cent values.)

Ex-President Ulysses S. Grant was received (Sept. 20) in San Francisco with great éclat on his return from a two-year tour of the world.

St. Patrick's Cathedral (Roman Catholic) in New York was dedicated (in May). The edifice cost $4,000,000 and replaced an older structure of the same name, still used as a place of worship.

The Church of Christ, Scientist (known since 1892 as the Mother Church) was founded in Boston.

The San Francisco Public Library was opened.

The first cash register was devised by James Ritty.

George B. Selden applied for a patent on a vehicle powered with an internal-combustion engine—a forerunner of the automobile. (The patent was granted in 1895.)

The Art Institute of Chicago was founded (May 24) for the "founding and maintenance of schools of art and design, the formation and exhibitions of collections of objects of art, and the cultivation and extension of the arts of design by any appropriate means."

The Luxembourg Art Gallery in Paris bought its first painting by an American artist—"Le Retour" by the New-York-born Henry Mosler.

Henry George, Philadelphia-born economist and New York social reformer, embodied his theory of a "single tax" based on land values in the significant treatise "Progress and Poverty," which made a great sensation both here and abroad.

Frank R. (Francis Richard) Stockton published his humorous and fantastic novel "Rudder Grange," the name of an old, anchored canal boat in which a newly married couple decided to live. (Sequels to the book were "The Rudder Grangers Abroad," 1891, and "Pomona's Travels," 1894.)

The "New York Mirror" was founded as a theatrical weekly. (Called the "New York Dramatic Mirror" in 1889; ceased publication in 1922.)

The Philharmonic Society of New York performed (Feb. 8) the first Tchaikovsky symphony heard in America—Symphony No. 3 in D.

Luther Whiting Mason, school music reformer in Louisville, Ky. (1853), Cincinnati, and Boston (1864), was invited by the Japanese government to introduce in Japan's schools the American system of musical instruction. (He spent three years in Japan with notable results.)

The Central Music Hall in Chicago was dedicated (Dec. 8) with Carlotta Patti.

Gilmore's Band featured (Nov. 9) in a Sunday-night concert at the Grand Opera House, N. Y., a Saxophone Quartet (Lefebre, Walrabe, Steckelberg, and Schultz).

In San Francisco, the indefatigable manager Tom Maguire once more ventured into the field of opera. He produced at the Baldwin the West Coast première of "Carmen" with Marie Rose and Annie Louise Carey, and lost $20,000 in the production.

The unprecedented craze in America for Gilbert and Sullivan's operetta "H.M.S. Pinafore," which started at the end of 1878, brought to New York the famous author and illustrious composer with a company from London under the management of R. D'Oyly Carte in an attempt to protect their masterpiece against unauthorized performances and mutilations. It was a great night (Dec. 1) when Sullivan—he was not yet knighted—entered the orchestra pit of Daly's Fifth Avenue Theatre to conduct the true version of the work. Gilbert is said to have appeared on the stage as a member of the sailors' chorus on that occasion. Their visit added further lustre to American theatrical annals when on the last day of the year (Dec. 31) their new operetta "The Pirates of Penzance" had its world première at the same theatre. (A copyright performance was given in Paignton, England, at the Bijou Theatre, Dec. 30.)

Twenty-year-old playwriting David Belasco of San Francisco gained public attention with "Hearts of Oak," produced in Chicago. (At the San Francisco production in 1880, the author's identity was concealed. After the Chicago success, he set out to try his fortunes in the New York theatrical world.)

Lecocq's delightful operetta "Le Petit Duc" came out as "The Little Duke" at Booth's Theatre in New York, in English (Mar. 17) and in French (Apr. 12), and was sung in other American cities for years to come by travelling opera companies.

In New York, the Broadway Theatre (formerly Wood's Museum) was remodelled by Augustin Daly and opened (Sept. 17) as Daly's Theatre. Another renovated playhouse was the Bowery Theatre which reopened (Sept. 11) as the German-language Thalia Theater, with Heinrich Conried, later impresario of the Metropolitan Opera House, as stage manager.

P. T. Barnum's New York Hippodrome (1873, and soon known as Gilmore's Garden) became Madison Square Garden under Barnum's management. It started (May 31) with a series of summer-night concerts by the famous H. B. Dodworth's Band. (A new structure was built on the site in 1889-90. It was demolished in 1925 when a new "Madison Square Garden" was erected farther uptown.)

The Richmond and Cleveland baseball clubs played the first no-hit game on record.

⧙⧙ 1880

Cradle's Empty, Baby's Gone. w., m., Harry Kennedy. Boston: Oliver Ditson & Co., cop. 1880 by William H. Kennedy, Brooklyn, N. Y.

Daddy. w., Mary Mark Lemon. w., Arthur Henry Behrend. Boston: Oliver Ditson Co. [ca. 1880.] (Published earlier in London.)

Don Juan. Symphonic poem. m., Richard Strauss, op. 20. Munich: Jos. Aibl [1880].

The Five-Cent Shave. w., m., Thomas Cannon. E. H. Harding, cop. 1880.

The Full Moon Union (The Mulligan Guards' Surprise). w., Edward Harrigan. m., Dave [David] Braham. Wm. A. Pond & Co., cop. 1880.

Funiculi-Funicula. Song in Neopolitan dialect. m., Luigi Denza. Milan: G. Ricordi & C. [1880].

De Golden Wedding. w., m., James A. Bland. Boston: John F. Perry & Co., cop. 1880.

Hide Thou Me. Hymn. w., Fanny J. [Frances Jane] Crosby [Mrs. Alexander Van Alstyne]. m., Rev. Robert Lowry. The Biglow & Main Co., cop. 1880.

Locked Out After Nine (The Mulligan Guards' Picnic). w., Edward Harrigan. m., Dave [David] Braham. Wm. A. Pond & Co., cop. 1880.

The Mulligan Braves (The Mulligan Guards' Nominee). w., Edward Harrigan. m., Dave [David] Braham. Wm. A. Pond & Co., cop. 1880.

Never Take the Horse Shoe From the Door (The Mulligan Guards' Surprise). w., Edward Harrigan. m., Dave [David] Braham. Wm. A. Pond & Co., cop. 1880.

The Skidmore Masquerade (The Mulligan Guards' Nominee). w., Edward Harrigan. m., Dave [David] Braham. Wm. A. Pond & Co., cop. 1880.

Songs My Mother Taught Me—*German title:* **Als die Alte Mutter** (No. 4 in: Zigeunermelodien, Op. 55). German words, Adolph Heyduk; English words, Mrs. Natalia Macfarren. m., Anton Dvorák. Berlin: N. Simrock [1880].

When the Mists Have Cleared Away. [w., Annie Herbert.] m., Arthur Henshaw. Boston: G. D. Russell, cop. 1880.

Why Did They Dig Ma's Grave So Deep? w., m., Joseph P. Skelly. Richard A. Saalfield, cop. 1880.

The discovery of gold on the Gastineau Channel, Alaska, developed a "gold rush" to the region.

Kansas adopted a liquor prohibition law—the first Midwestern State to do so.

Thomas Alva Edison patented (Jan. 27) the incandescent lamp, the invention of which was announced in 1878.

John F. Appleby of Wisconsin invented the automatic twine-binding harvester.

Dr. Leslie E. Keeley, Civil War physician, founded in Dwight, Ill., the Keeley Institute for the treatment of alcoholics and drug addicts. His treatment became known as the Keeley cure.

The Salvation Army, first organized in England, established American headquarters in New York. At the Battery, Commissioner George Scott Railton and seven women launched the first Salvation Army drive in the United States.

John Pierpont Morgan reorganized the banking firm of Drexel, Morgan & Co. as J. P. Morgan & Co.

Bryn Mawr College for women, near Philadelphia, was founded by the Society of Friends (Quakers).

Public school teachers now numbered 57.2 per cent women.

"The Dial" was founded as a monthly magazine of literary criticism. (Ceased publication in 1929.)

"The Musical Courier" was founded in New York as a weekly journal of musical events here and abroad.

"Il Progresso" was issued in New York as an Italian-language daily. (The name was later changed to "Il Progresso Italo-Americano." Still published.)

"Ben-Hur, a Tale of the Christ" by Indiana author Lew Wallace was the novel of the year.

John Philip Sousa was appointed leader of the U. S. Marine Band— a post he held until 1892 when he resigned to form his own band of 100 players. (Sousa had been a marine from 1867 until about 1875.)

An unknown "prima donna contralto," later to be the glamorous Lillian Russell, made (Nov. 22) what was probably her stage debut in vaudeville at Tony Pastor's Theatre in New York.

When the Park Theatre, New York, staged (Jan. 31) the farcial comedy "The Wedding March" by Sullivan's librettist William Schwenck Gilbert, the management announced that seats could be procured by telephone!

David Belasco left San Francisco with a play "La Belle Russe," and no doubt others, in his portfolio, and came to New York eager to enter its theatrical world.

The great French actress, the "divine" Sarah Bernhardt, made (Nov. 8) her American debut in "Adrienne Lecouvreur" in New York at Booth's Theatre. Seven days later (Nov. 15) she appeared in her famous role of "La Dame aux Caméllias," which was then (1880-81) being played in English by Clara Morris and Helen Modjeska, in German by Marie

Geistinger, and in French by Mlle. Rhea and Eugénie Legrand. (Bernhardt revisited the United States in 1887, 1891, 1896, 1900, 1911, 1913.)
The Madison Square Theatre, New York, opened (Feb. 4) with Steele
Mackaye's "Hazel Kirke." A fire destroyed (Feb. 26) the drop curtain
while the audience was assembling. Thanks to the latest fire-fighting de-
vices the performance followed on schedule. "Hazel Kirke" was the play
of the year. (It closed late in May, 1881, after an unprecedented run of
486 performances.)

Vying in American popularity were Franz von Suppé's Viennese Karl-
theater operetta "Boccaccio" (Philadelphia, Chestnut Street Theatre, Apr.
15, in English; New York, Thalia Theatre, Apr. 23, in German) and
Edmond Audran's Bouffes-Parisiens success "Les Noces d'Olivette" in
English as "Olivette" (New York, Bijou Theatre, Dec. 25).

Hebe, an elephant in the Cooper & Bailey Circus, gave birth to the
first elephant born in captivity in this country.

At 116th Street and Sixth Avenue, New York, a bullfight was staged,
but the venture was later dropped for lack of customers.

At the Republican national convention, some 306 delegates through 36
ballots persistently supported former President Grant for a third term. To
break the deadlock, his rivals James G. Blaine of Maine, "the plumed
knight" of Robert G. Ingersoll (1876), and John Sherman of Ohio combined to nominate James A. Garfield.

Scandal once more sullied the national elections. A forged letter,
alleged to have been written by the Republican nominee James A. Garfield and favoring the importation of Chinese cheap labor, was circulated
in the Democratic press. Garfield repudiated the authorship of the letter.
An attempt to connect him with the Crédit Mobilier affair (1873) also
failed. Nevertheless, Garfield defeated his Democratic opponent, Gen.
Winfield Scott Hancock, 214 electoral votes to 155.

The national population soared above the fifty million mark—50,155,-
783.

₷ 1881

All on Account of Eliza (Billie Taylor). w., Henry P. Stephens. m.,
Edward Solomon. (See below.)

Good-Bye. w., G. T. Whyte-Melville. m., F[rancesco] Paolo Tosti.
London: G. Ricordi & Co. [1881.]

I Am Coming. Hymn. w., Helen R. Young. m., Ira D[avid] Sankey.
Biglow and Main [cop. 1881 by Biglow and Main, and John Church &
Co.] (in: "Gospel Hymns No. 4" by Ira David Sankey, James McGrana-
han and George C. Stebbins, p. 45).

Paddy Duffy's Cart (Squatter Sovereignty). w., Edward Harrigan. m., Dave [David] Braham. Wm. A. Pond & Co., cop. 1881.

Tell It Out Among the Nations [Heathen] That the Lord is King. Hymn. w., Frances R[idley] Havergal. m., "arranged by Ira D[avid] Sankey." Biglow and Main [cop. 1881 by Biglow and Main, and John Church & Co.] (in: "Gospel Hymns No. 4" by Ira David Sankey, James McGranahan and George C. Stebbins, p. 4).

The Torpedo and the Whale (Olivette). SATB with piano acc. w., H[enry] B[rougham] Farnie. m., [Edmond] Audran. Boston: Oliver Ditson Co., cop. 1881 (in the vocal score). (For "Olivette," see 1880.)

Wait Till the Clouds Roll By. w., J. T. Wood. m., H. T. Fulmer. T. B. Harms & Co., cop. 1881.

James Abram Garfield, Republican, of Ohio, was inaugurated 20th President.

President Garfield was in office only 3 months and 2 days when he was shot (July 2) in the back when entering the Baltimore & Ohio railroad station in Washington, D. C. He was on his way to his home in Elberon, N. J., to visit his invalid wife. The assassin was a mentally unbalanced, disappointed office-seeker named Charles J. Guiteau, who claimed to have been inspired by God, as he later testified at his trial, to "remove Garfield" for the peace of the country. The President was transferred (Sept. 6) with great care from the White House to Francklyn Cottage, his home in Elberon, where he died (Sept. 19). The body was returned to Washington to lie in state and removed to Cleveland, O., for burial. The demonstration of grief was nationwide, even greater than at Lincoln's assassination, for the South was friendly to Garfield. Mrs. Garfield was the recipient of a $364,000 fund raised by her husband's admirers, and Congress voted her his salary for the remainder of the year.

Vice-President Chester Alan Arthur, Republican, of Vermont, was inaugurated (Sept. 19) upon Garfield's death, as 21st President. He was a recent widower (his wife died in 1880), and his sister Mary, wife of John E. McElroy of Albany, N. Y., was the White House hostess.

The U. S. Naval vessel "Jeannette," which had sailed from San Francisco in 1879 (June 2) in search of the North Pole, was crushed (June 12) by ice 500 miles from the Siberian coast. It had been outfitted for the United States Exploring Expedition by James Gordon Bennett, owner of the "New York Herald." The 33 members of the crew dragged three boats across the ice region and discovered (July 29) new land— Bennett Island, named after their sponsor. They reached Simoutki Island

and sailed (Sept. 10) together, but were separated by gales. Capt. George Washington DeLong, U.S.N., and all but two of his crew died of starvation and exposure. Lieutenant Chipp and his associates disappeared entirely. Engineer G. W. Melville and 11 surviving members were rescued.

The American Red Cross was organized (May 21) by Clara Barton of Civil War fame, its first president, as a branch of the Red Cross of the Geneva, Switzerland, Convention (founded in 1864).

Following the successful attempt (1872) to photograph the movements of a racing horse, Eadweard Muybridge invented the zoopraxiscope, an early form of the motion-picture projector, by means of which animals in motion were reproduced on a screen.

Adolph Strasser and Samuel Gompers, cigar makers, united the dissatisfied elements of the old Knights of Labor (1869) and other workingmen's groups into the American Federation of Labor ("A.F. of L."), now an organization of trade unions of the United States, Canada, Puerto Rico, and Panama. (Gompers was its president from the start until his death in 1924.)

The Knights of the Maccabees, a secret fraternal and benevolent society founded in 1878 in Ontario, Can., and based on ancient Maccabean rites, was introduced into the United States.

The interdenominational Christian Endeavor Society was organized in Portland, Me., by the Rev. Francis E. Clark, Congregational minister, for the promotion of the spiritual welfare of young people.

Negro education received further impetus by the founding of Tuskegee Normal and Industrial Institute for men and women, in Alabama. The founder, Booker Taliaferro Washington, was the 25-year-old son of a Negro slave and a white father.

Augustus Saint-Gaudens, Irish-born American sculptor, unveiled his first public statue—the Farragut Monument in Madison Square, New York.

The Boston Symphony Orchestra was established by Major Henry Lee Higginson. (The first concert was given Oct. 22, 1881.)

One Justus Schwab started a short-lived newspaper called the "Anarchist."

Jefferson Davis, former President of the Confederate States, who believed until his death (1889) that he had fought for justice and the right, published his two-volume history "The Rise and Fall of the Confederacy."

Edgar Watson ("Bill") Nye, Wyoming frontiersman and lawyer, became internationally known as a humorist with the publication of "Bill Nye and Boomerang," a collection of his newspaper ("Laramie Boomerang") writings.

Harriet Mulford Stone Lothrop published under the pseudonym Margaret Sidney the famous children's story "Five Little Peppers and How They Grew."

Joel Chandler Harris brought out in book form his first collection of

"Uncle Remus" verses and stories based on Negro folklore, which had previously appeared separately in periodicals.

New periodicals included "The Critic," a weekly literary review; "The Century Illustrated Monthly Magazine"; and "Judge," a weekly comic and rival of "Puck" (1877). (They ceased publication in 1906, 1930, and 1939, respectively.)

"Barnum & Bailey's Circus" was organized by a merger of enterprises.

"Our German Senator," which played (week of Jan. 5) in Brooklyn, N. Y., at the Park Theatre, boasted a double distinction: it starred the comedian Gus Williams, late "variety" actor, and advertised the "debut of the telephone on the stage" (see, however, 1877). The piece was described on the bill as "in three acts and a telephone."

At the Standard Theatre, New York, R. D'Oyly Carte brought out (Feb. 19) to instantaneous acclaim his London success—"Billie Taylor, or, The Reward of Virtue," with music by Edward Solomon, first husband of Lillian Russell. The lady herself at this time took a further step in her stage career when she ventured into light opera—an English version of Edmond Audran's first major success, "The Great Mogol, or, The Snake Charmer," which was produced (Oct. 29) at the Bijou Opera House.

Audran was, indeed, usurping musical honors with his comic operas. "La Mascotte" (The Mascot), his most popular operetta—it reached its 1,000th Paris performance in five years—had its initial American production in English in Boston at the Gaiety Theatre (Apr. 11), moved on to the Chestnut Street Theatre, Philadelphia (in May), was heard in New York at the Bijou (May 5), at Abbey's Park Theatre (Nov. 30) in French, at the Thalia Theater (Dec. 5) in German, and travelled across the country.

Gilbert and Sullivan's latest product "Patience, or, Bunthorne's Bride" had (July 28) its American première in St. Louis and came two months later (Sept. 22) to New York at the Standard Theatre.

Six-day walking matches were staged in New York at Madison Square Garden (Mar. 7) for the Daniel O'Leary belt between Dan himself and Henry Vaughn of England and between Charles Rowell, "champion of the world," and James Albert, and at the American Institute (May 9) with John Sullivan, the walker, and with others (May 23).

ϩ☛ 1882

The Holy City. Cantata. w., selected. m., Alfred R[obert] Gaul, op. 36. London: Novello, Ewer and Co. [1882.] (First performed at the Birmingham Festival, England, in Aug., 1882.)

I Never Drank Behind the Bar (The McSorleys). w., Edward Harrigan. m., Dave [David] Braham. Wm. A. Pond & Co., cop. 1882.

I'll Be Ready When the Great Day Comes. w., m., James S. Putman. Chicago: S. Brainard's Sons, cop. 1882.

The Market on Saturday Night. w., Edward Harrigan. m., Dave [David] Braham. Wm. A. Pond & Co., cop. 1882.

McNally's Row of Flats. w., Edward Harrigan. m., Dave [David] Braham. Wm. A. Pond & Co., cop. 1882.

When the Clock in the Tower Strikes Twelve. w., Edward Harrigan. m., Dave [David] Braham. Wm. A. Pond & Co., cop. 1882.

A report by special inspectors disclosed (in Jan.) extensive frauds on what were known as Star routes of the postal service. No fewer than 296 illegal contracts had been issued, involving a sum in excess of $8,000,000. The Star Route trials occupied the courts for more than six months. Several contractors were arrested for perjury, but ultimately, after 18 months of prosecution, the trials came to naught.

To curb the influx of coolies, Congress prohibited immigration to Chinese laborers and required those leaving the United States to obtain certificates of identification for use on re-entry.

Another enactment by Congress disfranchised and declared ineligible to office all polygamists.

Charles J. Guiteau, assassin of President Garfield, was hanged (June 30). He had been arraigned in Washington, D. C. His trial lasted about 10 weeks, with conflicting testimony by experts concerning his mental condition. His flippant and freakish behavior added to the annoyance of the court. The jury, however, convicted him (Jan. 25).

The first Labor Day parade was held (Sept. 5) in New York.

On Pearl Street, New York, the first Edison electric lighting station opened.

Prince Heinrich Albert Wilhelm of Prussia, brother of Kaiser Wilhelm II, made a protracted visit (1882-84) to the United States and was received favorably everywhere. (He made a second visit in 1903.)

Jesse James, notorious Western robber and murderer after the Civil War, was killed while in hiding by one of his accomplices.

The Roman Catholic benevolent organization Knights of Columbus ("K. C.," or "K. of C.") was organized in New Haven, Conn., by the Rev. J. C. McGinley.

The Clan-na-Gael was founded in Chicago about this time as a society of Irish-American Fenians agitating for Home Rule in Ireland.

Harvard University opened a school of higher education called the Society for the Collegiate Instruction of Women. It was renamed Radcliffe College in 1894 after Ann Radcliffe, Lady Mowlson (died about 1661), wife of the first donor of a scholarship to the University.

Oscar Wilde, English author and esthete, lectured in the United States on art and literature.

Fiction readers were buying the November issue of the new "Century Illustrated Monthly Magazine" for the short story, "The Lady or the Tiger," by Frank Stockton, which became immensely popular. (It was published as a book in 1884 and was turned into an operetta in 1888.)

Mark Twain published his novel "The Prince and the Pauper," a story of Tudor England under Edward VI.

Francis Marion Crawford, nephew of Julia Ward Howe and later a popular American novelist and playwright, produced his first novel, "Mr. Isaacs, A Tale of Modern India."

Ignatius Donnelly, Philadelphia-born politician, journalist, and essayist, printed his account of "Atlantis" in which he endeavored to prove that the fabulous island mentioned in Plato's "Timaeus" had actually existed as the seat of civilization.

Mrs. Edward ("Lillie") Langtry, British actress known as the "Jersey Lily" (she was born on the island of Jersey in the English Channel and had posed for a painting by Sir John Everett Millais named "The Jersey Lily"—hence the sobriquet), made (Nov. 6) her American debut with her own company in Tom Taylor's old play "An Unequal Match" at Wallack's Theatre in New York. Thereafter she toured the country in "As You Like It," "The Lady of Lyons," "Lady Windermere's Fan," which Oscar Wilde wrote for her, and other plays.

Lester Wallack opened (Jan. 4) his third New York theatre, built at the cost of $247,782.47, with a revival of Sheridan's famous comedy "The School for Scandal" (1777).

The 2,500th performance of "The Mighty Dollar" took place in New York at the Grand Opera House.

"Esmeralda" was the play of the year, a sweet and charming dramatization of a story by Frances Hodgson Burnett by herself and William H. Gillette. Staged at the Madison Square Theatre, New York, in the previous year (Oct. 29, 1881), it ran until the autumn of the present year, rivalled "Hazel Kirke" in popular appeal, and raised Annie Russell to stardom.

"La Belle Russe" introduced (May 8) David Belasco, lately arrived from San Francisco, as a playwright to New York audiences at Wallack's Theatre. He sold the play for $1,500, a return railroad ticket to the West Coast, and $100 expenses to his friend Tom Maguire's nephew, Frank L. Goodwin, by arrangement with whom was produced this "new and powerful drama by David Belasco, Esq."

At Haverly's Fourteenth Street Theatre, New York, Bartley Campbell's melodrama "The White Slave" thrilled (Apr. 3) play-goers with such grandiloquent lines as "Rags are royal raiment, when worn for virtue's sake." Later (June 18), at the same theatre, comedian Gus Williams was gaining popularity as John Mishler, the policeman, in "One of the Finest."

New York and London shared the world première of Gilbert and Sullivan's operetta "Iolanthe, or, The Peer and the Peri," given (Nov. 25) simultaneously at the Standard Theatre here and at the Savoy overseas.

Silas Gamaliel Pratt's American opera "Zenobia, Queen of Palmyra" was sung (June 15 and 16) in concert form in Chicago at the Central Music Hall. (It was produced scenically in Chicago at McVicker's Theatre, Mar. 26, 1883, and in New York at the Twenty-Third Street Theatre, Aug. 21, 1883.)

John L. Sullivan was adjudged the loser in a prizefight bout (July 17) at New York's Madison Square Garden when he failed to knock out Joseph Collins (Tug Wilson), the English champion. It seems, however, that Sullivan outslugged Collins.

Jumbo, the elephant, arrived from England and was promptly exhibited (Apr. 10) by Barnum.

Deaths of the year included Henry Wadsworth Longfellow, aged 75 (Mar. 24), in Cambridge, Mass., and Ralph Waldo Emerson, aged 79 (Apr. 27), in Concord, Mass.

ॐ 1883

Forget-Me-Not. Intermezzo for orch. m., Allan Macbeth. (Performed 1883 at the Glasgow Choral Union Concerts, of which the composer was the conductor; date from James Duff Brown, "Biographical Dictionary of Musicians," Paisley, 1886. The piece was long a favorite in American café concerts.)

God Be with You [Till We Meet Again]. Hymn. w., J[eremiah] E[ames] Rankin. m., W[illiam] G[ould] Tomer. Chicago: Henry A. Sumner & Co. [cop. 1883] (in: "Gospel Bells: a choice collection of new and popular songs" by Prof. J. W. Bischoff, Otis F. Presbrey and Rev. J. E. Rankin, p. 51).

Marguerite. w., m., C. A. White. Boston: White-Smith & Co., cop., 1883.

My Dad's Dinner Pail (Cordelia's Aspirations). w., Edward Harrigan. m., Dave [David] Braham. Wm. A. Pond & Co., cop. 1883.

Strolling on the Brooklyn Bridge. w., George Cooper. m., Joseph P. Skelly. Richard A. Saalfield, cop. 1883.

When the Mists Have Rolled Away. Hymn. w., Annie Herbert. m., Ira D[avid] Sankey. Cop. 1883, by Ira D. Sankey.

There's a Tavern in the Town. w., m., anon. Cambridge, Mass.: Moses King, cop. 1883 (in: "Students' Songs, comprising the newest and most popular college songs as now sung at Harvard, Yale, Columbia, etc., etc., compiled and edited by William H. Hills"). (This is apparently the first appearance of the song in print, according to Miss Margaret M. Mott ("A Bibliography of Song Sheets" in "Notes," Washington, D. C., 1949, vol. 6, p. 385). Miss Mott states: "Hill printed a separate copyright notice underneath the song, giving himself as claimant, but he didn't print his name as author, arranger, or composer in the customary spots above the music." The editions of the song, published by Shapiro, Bernstein & Co., cop. 1911 and 1934, ascribe the music to William H. Hills.)

When the Robins Nest Again. w., m., Frank Howard. T. B. Harms & Co., cop. 1883 by J. F. Martindale.

To curb political corruption and favoritism in the appointment of government employees, Congress passed (Jan. 16) Ohio Senator Pendleton's bill, creating the Civil Service Commission. Later in the year, Congress lowered letter postage to 2 cents, introduced (in Sept.) the postal money-order, and removed the internal revenue tax on nearly all commodities except tobacco and spirits.

American railroads adopted at the International Conference in Washington, D. C., four standards of time, namely, Eastern, Central, Mountain, and Pacific.

The East River or Brooklyn Bridge, New York, was opened (May 24). Six days later (May 30), twelve persons were trampled to death in a panic on the bridge. (The work was begun Jan. 3, 1870, and on completion had cost $16,000,000. Twenty workingmen lost their lives during its construction. The structure was designed by John Augustus Roebling, builder of similar suspension bridges at Niagara Falls, 1855, and at Cincinnati, 1867. After his death in 1869, his son Washington Augustus Roebling carried on the work.)

The Northern Pacific railroad was completed (Aug. 22). (Train service began on Sept. 8.)

The Liberty-head five-cent piece went into circulation and remained in use until the appearance of the Indian-head or buffalo nickel in 1913.

Hiram Stevens Maxim, American inventor living in England, changed warfare with his invention of a machine gun which bears his name. It fired 11 shots per second—an improvement over the Gatling gun (1861).

Joseph Pulitzer, Hungarian-born German newspaper editor and owner from St. Louis, Mo., bought the English "New York World" from Jay Gould. Pulitzer immediately began to campaign against prevailing plutocracy. His newspaper's flamboyant editorials and style of reporting helped to develop what those who disagreed with him called "yellow" journalism, a term which originated about 1896 (which see).

The Modern Woodmen of America ("M.W.A.") was founded in Lyons, Iowa, as a fraternal and benevolent society.

Matthew Arnold, English poet and writer, proved an unsatisfactory lecturer on the first (1883-84) of his two visits to the United States. His platform demeanor was awkward; his voice was not sufficiently audible; and his affected manner offended here as it did in London. (His second visit was in 1886.)

The year saw the publication of George Wilbur Peck's book "Peck's Bad Boy and His Pa" (first of the series); John Hay's anonymous novel "The Bread-Winners"; the first of Kate Greenaway's "Almanacks," illustrated in color (issued until 1897); Ella Wheeler Wilcox's "Poems of Passion" (containing "Solitude," with its famous opening line: "Laugh and the world laughs with you") which were called "immoral" because of their eroticism; and the first installment of Francis James Child's "English and Scottish Popular Ballads" (completed in 1898 in 5 volumes).

Among periodicals founded were the "Ladies' Home Journal," in Philadelphia; "The Etude," a musical educational monthly, in Lynchburg, Va. (removed in 1884 to Philadelphia), and "Life," in New York, a comic weekly, as a rival to "Puck" (1877) and "Judge" (1881). ("Life" became a monthly in 1933. The title was bought by Time, Inc., for a new weekly pictorial magazine with complementary text.)

The Metropolitan Opera House in New York was opened (Oct. 22) with a performance of Gounod's French opera "Faust," sung in Italian by Christine Nilsson (Marguerite), Sofia Scalchi (Siebel), Italo Campanini (Faust), Franco Novaro (Mephistopheles), and Giuseppe Del Puente (Valentine). The house seated 3,045 and cost $1,732,978.71. After a few weeks, the seating capacity was increased by the removal of the third-tier boxes and the substitution of the present dress circle. No opera was performed on the following night (Tuesday), thus establishing a custom that still prevails. At the second evening performance (Oct. 24), the management presented its first new star, the incomparable Polish lyric soprano Marcella Sembrich, in "Lucia di Lammermoor." The first novelty was the American première (Dec. 20) of Ponchielli's "La Gioconda." There were two American singers in the company—Franco Novaro, whose real name was Frank Nash, and Baltimore-born soprano Alwina Valleria.

Maine-born soprano Lillian Norton, who was soloist with Gilmore's Band in 1877 and had sung opera in Europe, changed her name to Lillian Nordica and made (Nov. 26) her American operatic debut in "Faust" under Col. Mapleson's management. Mapleson was putting on opera at the Academy of Music in rivalry with the new Metropolitan Opera House, where Nordica was later to sing.

Vaudeville, as distinct from the variety show, began in Boston. Benjamin Franklin Keith, who started his managerial career in the theatre by exhibiting a midget called "Baby Alice," opened Keith's Theatre in partnership with Colonel Williams Austin. They revolutionized the existing entertainment business by introducing the all-day performance of variety acts, or "continuous vaudeville."

Buffalo Bill (William Frederick Cody) launched his "Wild West" shows in partnership with Major John M. Burke and Dr. W. F. Carver.

The Hungarian Kiralfy Brothers (1875) made a bid to outdo the splendor of "The Black Crook" (1866) with a lavish spectacle—"Excelsior," originally conceived by Luigi Manzotti and set to music by Romualdo Marenco for the Milan La Scala Opera House (Jan. 11, 1881). The Brothers succeeded. The production came (Aug. 21) to performance in New York at Niblo's Garden at the alleged cost of $75,000, and was highlighted with "novel electric effects by the Edison Electric Light Company, under the personal direction of Mr. Edison." Other scenic effects were obtained by gas and electric-gas lighting. The show had nothing to do with Longfellow's poem.

The great Henry Irving and Ellen Terry, his leading lady, came from the Lyceum Theatre, London, to New York, and opened at the Star (late Wallack's) Theatre. Irving presented himself (Oct. 29) in his famous impersonation in "The Bells," adapted from Erckmann-Chatrian's "Le Juif Polonais"; Miss Terry came out (Oct. 30) in W. G. Wills's "Charles I."

Helen Modjeska introduced in America Ibsen's tragic play "A Doll's House" under the title "Thora," with a happy ending, in Louisville, Ky.

American actress Fanny Davenport had spent part of a year in Europe and acquired the American rights to Victorien Sardou's drama "Fedora," in which Sarah Bernhardt had won a great triumph in Paris. Miss Davenport invested her savings in the production and with much fear staged (Oct. 1) the play in New York at the Fourteenth Street Theatre with Robert Mantell in the cast. In spite of the fact that the famed Henry Irving and Ellen Terry were the sensation of the season at the Star, Fanny Davenport, advertised as "America's Daughter of Genius," achieved an outstanding success for herself and Sardou's play.

"Ned" Harrigan and Tony Hart scored (Nov. 5) another stage hit, probably their greatest success, with "Cordelia's Aspirations" in New York at the Théâtre Comique. The scene in which Cordelia drank from a bottle marked "poison," but which contained whiskey, lifted Annie Yeamans to stardom as a comedienne.

Chauncey Olcott of later actor-singer fame was appearing at this time as a minstrel.

Karl Millöcker's famous operetta "Der Bettelstudent" (The Beggar Student) was first heard in New York at the Thalia Theatre (Oct. 19) in German and at the Casino Theatre (Oct. 29) in English.

Still performed in New York and around the country were "Hazel Kirke," "East Lynne," "The Mighty Dollar," "The Ticket of Leave Man," "The Two Orphans," and "Esmeralda."

"General Tom Thumb," stage name of Charles Sherwood Stratton, Barnum's famous dwarf, aged 45, died (July 15) in Middleborough, Mass.

He was 40 inches tall. Queen Victoria added the "General" to his name in 1854.

The remains of John Howard Payne, writer of "Home, Sweet Home," who died at Tunis, Africa, in 1852, were removed to Washington, D. C.

ϑ≫ 1884

Always Take Mother's Advice. w., m., Jennie Lindsay. Willis Woodward & Co., cop. 1884.

My Ideal—*original Italian title:* Ideale. Italian words, Carmelo Errica. English words, H[arrison] Millard. m., F[rancesco] Paolo Tosti. G. Schirmer, cop. 1884. (Published earlier in Italy or England.)

Plum Pudding. w., Edward Harrigan. m., Dave [David] Braham. Wm. A. Pond & Co., cop. 1884.

The Sea Hath Its Pearls. Part song for SATB. w., Henry Wadsworth Longfellow [translated from the German of Heinrich Heine]. m., Ciro Pinsuti. London: Novello, Ewer & Co. [1884.]

Voices of the Woods—*also known as:* Welcome, Sweet Springtime! w., anon. m., "adapted to Rubinstein's Melody in F" by M[ichael] Watson. G. Schirmer [1884].

White Wings. w., m., Banks Winter. Willis Woodward & Co., cop. 1884.

Through the efforts of President Arthur, the United States was represented at the Congo Conference (1884-85) in Berlin.

The nation became alarmed about the safety of the Greely Arctic expedition, which had left in the summer of 1881 to make scientific observations at circumpolar stations under the auspices of the U. S. Signal Service in conjunction with other countries. A relief expedition sent out in May, 1883, under Lieutenant E. A. Garlington of the Cavalry Service, had been unsuccessful and had returned with great difficulty after having lost one of its two ships in the ice. A second relief expedition was now equipped under Commander Winfield Scott Schley. It sailed (in May of the present year) from the Brooklyn Navy Yard, New York, and succeeded (June 28) in locating Lieutenant Adolphus Washington Greely and six survivors beyond Brevoort Island. Two of the latter died soon after Schley's arrival. Eighteen other members of the Greely party had perished from starvation shortly before aid arrived. (Greely died in 1935.)

A financial panic developed in New York, causing the failure of former President Grant's banking firm, Grant & Ward, among others.

The Washington National Monument (1848), Washington, D. C., was completed at the cost of $1,300,000 when the capstone, weighing 3,300 pounds, was set (Dec. 6) in place. (The monument was dedicated on Feb. 21, 1885.)

Richmond, Va., became the first city in the world to boast a practical electric streetcar system when Frank J. Prague built 13 miles of electric railway.

Lewis Edson Waterman in this year, and Paul E. Wirt in 1885, evolved the fountain pen.

Samuel Sidney McClure, Irish-born New York publisher, formed the first newspaper syndicate in the United States.

A World's Fair was opened (Dec. 16) in New Orleans by President Arthur pressing an electric button in Washington, D. C. European countries, as well as Mexico and other Central and South American republics, were represented. (The Fair continued until June, 1885, was re-opened in the winter of that year, and closed in May, 1886.)

The American Historical Society was founded in Saratoga, N. Y. (Incorporated in 1889 with headquarters in Washington, D. C.)

Tornadoes caused much property damage and took many lives. Marine disasters added to the number of deaths.

Mark Twain published "The Adventures of Huckleberry Finn."

Gilbert and Sullivan's new operetta "Princess Ida, or, Castle Adamant" was performed (Feb. 11) simultaneously in New York at the Fifth Avenue Theatre and in Boston at the Museum Theatre. The piece was not a success; it ran only a month in New York.

The theatrical sensation of the year was "Adonis," an extravaganza by William Gill with music by Edward E. Rice, starring Henry E. Dixey. Tried out (in July) in Chicago at Hooley's Opera House, the show was staged (Sept. 4) in New York at the Bijou Opera House. The elaborate production enjoyed a record-breaking run of 603 consecutive performances and proved a perfect vehicle for Dixey as a comedian, dancer, and singer. The piece was taken to London, returned to New York in 1887, and reached (June 11) its "eleven hundredth" performance.

Popular operettas were Franz von Suppé's "A Trip to Africa" in Boston at the Bijou Theatre (Feb. 21), and Francis Chassaigne's "Falka" in New York at the Casino Theatre (Apr. 14).

A Bostonian, Russell Montague, and three Scots, George Grant, and Alexander and Roderick McLeod, built in the West Virginia Mountains near Green Brier a nine-hole golf course which they called the Oakhurst Golf Club.

The Equal Rights Party was formed after the Democratic and Republican parties refused to support woman suffrage in the national elections of the year. The party nominated (Aug. 23) in San Francisco the first women candidates for the highest executive offices in the nation—Mrs.

Belva Ann Lockwood (1879) of Washington, D. C., for President, and Mrs. Marietta L. B. Stow of San Francisco for Vice-President. They polled only a small vote.

Nasty and ugly words were bandied about in the Republican national elections and hurt the candidacy of its nominee, James G. Blaine. A violent phrase, "Rum, Romanism, and Rebellion," hurled at the Democratic Party by a New York clergyman, S. D. Burchard, in an interdenominational meeting favoring Blaine, alienated the party's Irish Catholic vote. Equally offensive was a new epithet, "mugwump," of Algonquin Indian origin, applied to a bolter from the ranks. Dissatisfaction with Republican politics had caused prominent independent Republicans such as George W. Curtis, Carl Schurz, and others, to bolt the party and lost the support of influential Republican newspapers, such as the "New York Times," "Boston Herald," and "Springfield (Mass.) Republican." The abusive language greatly aided in winning the election for the Democratic candidate, New York Governor Grover Cleveland, 219 electoral votes to 182— the first of his party to succeed to the presidential office since the 15th President, Buchanan (1857-61), twenty-four years before. Cleveland carried every southern State, besides New York, New Jersey, Connecticut, Delaware, Maryland, and Indiana. The popular vote was over 10,000,000 —the largest ever cast—Cleveland polling 4,911,000 votes, a plurality of 62,000 over Blaine.

ৈ 1885

At the Cross. Hymn. w., Isaac Watts. m., R. E. Hudson. Cop. 1885 by R. E. Hudson.

The Gum Tree Canoe. w., S. S. Steele. m., A. F. Winnemore. Cleveland: S. Brainard's Sons, cop. 1885 ("new edition").

Poverty's Tears Ebb and Flow (Old Lavender). w., Edward Harrigan. m., Dave [David] Braham. Wm. A. Pond & Co., cop. 1885.

Remember, Boy, You're Irish (Shane na Lawn). w., m., William J. Scanlan. T. B. Harms & Co., cop. 1885.

Sleep, Baby, Sleep—also known as: Irene's Lullaby. w., m., John J. Handley. Chicago: National Music Co., cop. 1885; cop. 1912; assigned 1912 to Frank Earl Hathaway, Music Publisher, Chicago; cop. 1912 by F. E. Hathaway.

Still as the Night—original German title: Still wie die Nacht (No. 27 in: Lieder, op. 326). German words, anon. English words, Mrs. John P.

Morgan. m., Karl Bohm. Berlin: N. Simrock [1885?]. (Published in the
United States by Oliver Ditson Co., Boston, cop. 1890, and G. Schirmer,
New York, cop. 1890.)

Grover Cleveland, Democrat, of New Jersey, was inaugurated 22nd
President.

The Washington National Monument (1848), Washington, D. C., was
dedicated (Feb. 21).

The U. S. Post Office issued by act of Congress (Mar. 3) for the first
time a "special postal delivery stamp," a blue 10-cent adhesive with the
picture of a running mail carrier.

By special legislation Congress restored Ulysses Simpson Grant to the
rank of general, a post he resigned when he became 18th President.

Following the lead of Richmond, Va. (1884), Baltimore replaced
(Aug. 10) its horse-drawn streetcars with an electric streetcar railway.

There were now 128,967 miles of railroad in the country.

The American Telephone and Telegraph Company ("A. T. & T.") was
organized.

Ottmar Mergenthaler, German-American inventor, patented the lino-
type machine, the type-casting mechanism that eliminated hand-setting
and gave a powerful stimulus to mass publications.

Dr. Chichester A. Bell and Charles S. Tainter invented the wax cylinder
graphophone (phonograph).

Stanford University, Palo Alto, Cal., for men and women, was founded
by Leland Stanford. Stanford, a founder of the Union Pacific railroad
and a governor of California, established the university in memory of his
son who died in boyhood.

William Dean Howells published his novel of Vermont *nouveau riche,*
"The Rise of Silas Lapham."

The first volume of former President Grant's two-volume "Personal
Memoirs" came off the presses of Mark Twain's publishing firm, Charles
L. Webster and Company, Hartford, Conn. (The second volume was
issued in 1886. The memoirs, completed four days before Grant's death,
realized over $450,000.)

Lilli Lehmann, famous German dramatic soprano, made (Nov. 25) her
American debut as Carmen at the Metropolitan Opera House, New York.
At the same theatre, Massenet's French opera "Manon" received (Dec.
23) its first American performance. It was sung in Italian.

Benjamin Franklin Keith and E. F. Albee combined their vaudeville
enterprises into a nationwide chain of theatres.

Gilbert and Sullivan's newest operetta "The Mikado, or, The Town of
Titipu" achieved even greater popularity in the United States than their
"H. M. S. Pinafore," again due in part to the lack of copyright protection,
and swept the country as perhaps no similar piece has ever done. Curi-
ously, the important work was first heard in the United States in a garbled

version put on (June 29) by a small company in Chicago at the Museum Theatre. The first real performance took place (July 6) in the same city at the Grand Opera House, and the production was brought (July 20) to the Union Square Theatre, New York, for one performance. This was given in violation of an injunction, issued by Judge Wheeler, and landed the producer Sydney Rosenfeld in jail. The D'Oyly Carte Company from London then staged (Aug. 19) the famous operetta at the Fifth Avenue Theatre for a run of 250 performances.

Richard Genée's Viennese comic opera "Nanon, the Hostess of the Golden Lamb" was a long-run success in New York (Thalia Theatre, Jan. 2, in German; Casino Theatre, June 29, in English).

Arthur Wing Pinero and Henry Arthur Jones, craftsmen of the well-made play, were in New York to superintend the rehearsals of their latest stage pieces—respectively, "The Magistrate" (Daly's Theatre, Oct. 7) and "Saints and Sinners" (Madison Square Theatre, Nov. 7).

Travelling comic opera companies were visiting almost every city that had a theatre or opera house. Among the troupes were the Alice Oates Opera Co., Boston Ideal Opera Co., Emma Abbott Opera Co., Clara Louise Kellogg English Opera Co., The Emelie Melville Co., Hess Acme (or English) Opera Co., Norcross Fifth Avenue Opera Co., W. T. Carleton Opera Co., Wm. Lyster's English Opera and Opera Bouffe Troupe, Braham and Scanlan's New Miniature Opera Co., and many others.

Shadowgraphs were popular features in the "variety" theatres and were probably helping to develop the idea of the motion picture in the minds of inventors.

Skiing became an American sport at a tournament held among the Norwegian settlers of Wisconsin and Minnesota.

Death claimed two Civil War commanders—Gen. Ulysses Simpson Grant, aged 63 (July 23), in Mt. McGregor, N. Y., and Major-General George Brinton McClellan, aged 59 (Oct. 29), in Orange, N. J.

Multimillionaire William Henry Vanderbilt, aged 64, who had nearly doubled his father's fortune, died (Dec. 8) in New York. He uttered the famous sentiment: "The public be damned."

ࣹ 1886

At Midnight on My Pillow Lying (Erminie). w., Claxson Bellamy and Harry Paulton. m., Edward Jakobowski.

Darkest the Hour (Erminie). w., Claxson Bellamy and Harry Paulton. m., Edward Jakobowski.

Dear Mother, in Dreams I See Her (Erminie). w., Claxson Bellamy and Harry Paulton. m., Edward Jakobowski.

Forever with the Lord. w., James Montgomery. m., Charles Gounod. London: Phillipps and Page [1886].

The Gladiator March. m., John Philip Sousa. Philadelphia: Harry Coleman, cop. 1886.

The Letter That Never Came. w., m., Paul Dresser. T. B. Harms & Co., cop. 1886.

Maggie, the Cows Are in the Clover. w., m., Al. W. Filson. T. B. Harms & Co., cop. 1886.

Never Take No for an Answer. w., m., J. F. Mitchell. Willis Woodward & Co., cop. 1886.

A Soldier's Life (Erminie). w., Claxson Bellamy and Harry Paulton. m. Edward Jakobowski.

What the Dicky-Birds Say (Erminie). w., Claxson Bellamy and Harry Paulton. m., Edward Jakobowski.

President Cleveland married (June 2) at the White House Miss Frances Folsom, daughter of his law partner in Buffalo, N. Y.

Congress passed (in Jan.) Senator Hoar's bill regulating the succession of the members of the cabinet to the presidency in the historical order of the establishment of their departments in the event of the death, resignation, removal, or disability of the President and the Vice-President. The measure grew out of the situation that seemed likely to develop between the time of death of President Garfield in September, 1881, and the meeting of the first session of the next Congress in December, during which period his successor, President Arthur, was in imminent danger of death. It was felt that the previous statutes naming in order the President of the Senate and the Speaker of the House, either of whom might represent an opposite party to the President's, was contrary to the people's choice at election.

Vice-President Thomas A. Hendricks died (Nov. 25).

Alcatraz, an island fortress in San Francisco Bay, became a military prison. (It was converted in 1934 to a federal penitentiary.)

Geronimo, savage leader of the Apache Indians against the whites of the Southwest, was subdued by Gen. George Crook but escaped. (Geronimo surrendered later, was removed to a reservation in Oklahoma, and died in 1909.)

On the evening of May 4 in Chicago's Haymarket Square, a bomb exploded during a mass meeting that was agitating for the eight-hour work day and protesting the suppression of strikes by the police. A riot started which increased in violence when the police fired into the crowd. Seven policemen were killed and 66 persons were wounded. Eight anarchist Internationalists were arrested and convicted; four were hanged, one committed suicide, and three were sent to jail. (Their trials, however, failed to adduce evidence that the accused were implicated. Seven years later Governor John Peter Altgeld pardoned the prisoners. The event is the subject of a novel, "The Bomb," by Frank Harris, 1908.)

The American Federation of Labor ("A. F. of L."), a consolidation of trade and industrial unions, was organized with Samuel Gompers as the first president.

The United Mine Workers formed their organization.

The United Labor Party was organized to advocate the single-tax theory of Henry George (1879).

Charles Martin Hall invented contemporaneously with Paul Héroult of France a process for making aluminum.

Robert Edwin Peary started his first polar expedition to the Arctic.

New York saloon keeper Steve Brodie gained instantaneous notoriety when he claimed he jumped (July 23), as a stunt, from the Brooklyn Bridge into the East River. He became immortalized in American English by such everyday phrases as to "do a brodie," or "pull a brodie." (Brodie went on the stage in 1891, which see.)

Charleston, S. C., suffered a disastrous earthquake with a loss of 40 lives.

Sultan Abul Hamid II of Turkey presented a collection of native literature to the Library of Congress.

Matthew Arnold made the second of his two visits to the United States as a lecturer. (The first was in 1883-84.)

The first issue of "The World Almanac and Book of Facts" went on sale. (Published annually ever since.)

"Little Lord Fauntleroy," a novel by Frances Hodgson Burnett, and "Triumphant Democracy" by Andrew Carnegie were published.

The "Cosmopolitan" and "The Forum" were founded as monthly magazines. (The former started in Rochester, N. Y., and moved in 1887 to New York City.)

The Madison Square Theatre, New York, presented (Nov. 1) one of the outstanding successes of the stage—Sir Charles Young's social drama "Jim, the Penman" with Frederic Robinson and (Mrs.) Agnes Booth.

Richard Mansfield achieved a great personal triumph in Boston at the Museum Theatre in Archibald C. Gunter's light-hearted comedy "Prince Karl." Mansfield revealed himself not only as a consummate actor but also as a pianist and singer in the role of Karl von Arhmien, a prince turned guide. (The play reached the Madison Square Theatre, May 3.)

Denman Thompson presented in Boston a second version of his old play "The Old Homestead" (1878), based on his "Joshua Whitcomb" (1875). (The famous play had an outstanding New York run of nearly

21 weeks on its first showing, Jan. 10-June 4, 1887, at the 14th Street Theatre. The play still has an occasional revival.)

McIntyre and Heath's Minstrels were doing black-face comedy in New York.

Leila von Koerber, Canadian-born actress, appeared on the American stage. She became better known later as Marie Dressler.

Loie Fuller, who years hence was to become an internationally renowned dancer, acted (June 30) in a play called "Humbug" at the Bijou Opera House, New York.

The song hits of the year came from a two-act comic opera "Erminie," book by Claxson Bellamy and Harry Paulton and music by Edward Jakobowski (see above), which was brought out (May 10) in New York at the Casino Theatre with immense success, starring Pauline Hall and Francis Wilson. At the same theatre, the Waltz King Johann Strauss's newest Viennese operetta "Der Zigeunerbaron" had (Feb. 15) its first American performance as "The Gypsy Baron." It was played (Apr. 1) in German at the Thalia Theater.

Lillian Russell was attracting attention by her singing as much as by her beauty in her husband Edward Solomon's operetta "Pepita, or, The Girl with the Glass Eye" in New York at the Union Square Theatre (Mar. 16-May 22).

Played thereafter by professional and amateur companies, Willard Spenser's operetta "The Little Tycoon" started (Jan. 4) in Philadelphia at the Temple Theatre its long career with a run of 500 performances. (The work was given at the Standard Theatre, New York, Mar. 29, and at the Park Theatre, Boston, Sept. 6.)

Another widely popular operetta was Edmond Audran's "Le Serment d'Amour," performed under various titles—"The Crowing Hen" (New York, Wallack's Theatre, May 29), "The Bridal Trap" (New York, Bijou Opera House, May 31; Boston, Boston Theatre, June 28), "Love's Vow" (Boston, Museum Theatre, July 5), and "Rosetta, or, The Pledge of Love" (St. Louis).

Victor Herbert, grandson of Samuel Lover, Irish novelist, settled in New York as first violoncellist in the Metropolitan Opera House Orchestra.

The Norfolk, Litchfield County, Conn., music festivals were started.

The Metropolitan Opera House, New York, produced the American première of Wagner's two mighty music dramas, "Die Meistersinger von Nürnberg" (Jan. 4) and "Tristan und Isolde" (Dec. 1). Delibes's very French Hindu opera, "Lakmé," was staged (Mar. 1) in English by the rival Academy of Music, with Pauline L'Allemand in the title role singing "The Bell Song."

The Oratorio Society of New York rented the Metropolitan Opera House and sang (Mar. 3 and 4), in concert form under the 24-year-old Walter Damrosch, the first American performance of Wagner's opera "Parsifal."

Franz Kneisel, German violinist, formed the famous "Kneisel Quartet" of string instruments. (The organization disbanded in 1917 after 31 years of successful concert-giving in the United States and in Europe.)

ϑ⇒ 1887

Away in a Manger (or, Luther's Cradle Hymn). w., m., erroneously attributed to Martin Luther. w., anon. m., J. R. M. [James Ramsey Murray]. Cincinnati: The John Church Co., cop. 1887 (in: James Ramsey Murray, "Dainty Songs for Little Lads and Lasses," p. 110); renewed 1915 by Mrs. J. R. Murray. (For an exhaustive investigation into the history of this carol consult Richard S. Hill, "Not So Far Away in a Manger," in "Notes," Washington, D. C., Dec., 1945, p. 12-36.)

Calvary. w., Henry Vaughan. m., Paul Rodney. G. Schirmer [1887?]. (Published earlier in London. An arrangement of the song as an anthem for SATB by William Rees was published by G. Schirmer, cop. 1888.)

Come [Come, Oh, Come to Me]. Hymn. w., Mrs. James G. Johnson. m., James McGranahan. Cop. 1887 by James McGranahan.

The Crucifixion. Cantata. w., selected and written by the Rev. W. J. Sparrow-Simpson. m., John Stainer. London: Novello, Ewer and Co. [1887.] (Reviewed in "The Musical Times," London, Mar., 1887, p. 174-75).

Happy Birds. w., C. T. Steele. m., Edward Holst. Boston: Oliver Ditson Co., cop. 1887.

I Will Sing the Wond'rous Story. Hymn. w., F. H. Rawley. m., Peter Bilhorn. Cop. 1887 by Ira D. Sankey.

If the Waters Could Speak as They Flow. w., m., C. Graham. Willis Woodward & Co., cop. 1887.

If You Love Me, Darling, Tell Me with Your Eyes. w., Samuel Minturn Peck. m., Hubbard T. Smith. Washington, D. C.: John F. Ellis & Co., cop. 1887.

Jerusalem. w., Nella. m., Henry Parker. G. Schirmer [1887]; Boston: Oliver Ditson Co., cop. 1889 (in: "Choice Sacred Solos for Low Voice," p. 102-13). (Published earlier in London. An arrangement of the song as an anthem for SATB by William Rees was published by G. Schirmer, cop. 1887.)

[March of the Tin Soldiers.] Marche des Petits Soldats de Plomb. Orch. piece. m., Gabriel Pierné, op. 14, no. 6. (Originally a piano solo in the composer's "Album pour mes petits Amis.")

The Outcast Unknown. w., m., Paul Dresser. Willis Woodward & Co., cop. 1887.

Petersbourgh Sleighride. Orch. composition. m., Richard Eilenberg, op. 57. Carl Fischer, cop. 1887. (Published earlier in Germany.)

Rock-a-bye Baby. w., m., Effie I. Canning. Boston: C. D. Blake & Co., cop. 1887.

Slavonic Dances. 16 orch. dances. m., Anton Dvorák. Berlin: N. Simrock, 1887. (Originally published for piano, four hands, in sets of two books, each containing four numbers.)

The Song That Reached My Heart. w., m., Julian Jordan. Willis Woodward & Co., cop. 1887.

The Swan—*original French title:* Le Cygne. Duet for violoncello and piano. m., Camille Saint-Saëns. Paris: A. Durand et Fils [1887].

Though Your Sins Be as Scarlet. Hymn. w., F[rances] J[ane] Crosby (Mrs. Alexander Van Alstyne). m., W[illiam] H[oward] Doane. Cop. 1887 by W. H. Doane.

Wait Till the Tide Comes In. w., George Propheter. m., Gussie L. Davis. George Propheter, cop. 1887.

Congress passed (Feb. 4) the Inter-State Railway Law, creating the Inter-State Commerce Commission.

Continued difficulties with Canada over the fishing trade roused Congress to enact (in May) a belligerent bill that empowered the President to "deny vessels, their masters and crews, of the British dominions of North America, any entrance into the waters, ports, or places of or within the United States." President Cleveland, however, moved more cautiously and arranged a joint meeting in Washington, D. C., between Great Britain and the United States to reconsider the problems. (The deliberations were concluded Feb. 16, 1888, but, after long debate in the Senate, were refused ratification, Aug. 21. Fortunately no serious collision of interests occurred at sea.)

The Dawes Act bestowed United States citizenship on American Indians and allotted them land in individual holdings.

The Progressive Labor Party was organized to oppose the United Labor Party (1886) and the single-tax theory of Henry George (1879).

A hundred years had elapsed since the signing of the Constitution of the United States, and the event was duly observed with a Centenary Celebration (Sept. 15-17).

The world's highest statue, "Liberty Enlightening the World" (the Statue of Liberty, 305 feet, 6 inches, in bronze), by the Alsatian sculptor Frédéric Auguste Bartholdi, had been presented to the United States by France in 1876 and erected on Bedloe Island in New York harbor. It was dedicated (Oct. 28) by President Cleveland in the presence of the sculptor and 1,000,000 spectators.

Elizabeth Cochrane Seaman, journalist on the "New York World" writing under the pseudonym Nelly Bly about abuses in social employment, politics, and penal institutions, had herself committed to Blackwells (now Welfare) Island, New York, by feigning insanity, and exposed the horrible conditions there in "Ten Days in a Mad House."

Emil Berliner, German-American inventor, patented the disk phonograph. (It was first publicly demonstrated in 1888 in Philadelphia.)

The Columbia Phonograph Company was founded in Bridgeport, Conn., by a group that acquired the patents of Dr. Chichester A. Bell and Sumner Tainter (1885).

West Street, New York, boasted a line of 90-foot telephone poles each with 25 crossarms.

The Newberry Library, Chicago, Ill., was founded.

George William Childs, American newspaper publisher and philanthropist, presented (Oct. 17) the Shakespeare Memorial fountain to the Bard's native city, Stratford-on-Avon, England.

Augustus Saint-Gaudens' statue of Lincoln was unveiled in Chicago.

Louis Keller began publishing the "Social Register," the blue book of American society.

Fire destroyed (May 26) the stables of the Belt Line Car Company in New York, with a loss of 1,600 horses.

A railroad wreck at Chatsworth, near Piper City, Ill., caused (Aug. 11) the death of 81 persons.

The American yachts "Coronet" and "Dauntless" started (Mar. 12) a race across the Atlantic. For the eighth consecutive time, the United States won the America's Cup in international yacht racing when the "Volunteer" defeated the British "Thistle" in two races (Sept. 27 and 30).

"Scribner's Magazine" was founded in New York as a monthly. (Ceased publication in 1939.)

The Metropolitan Opera House, New York, produced (Nov. 9) the third of Wagner's four "Ring" operas, "Siegfried," for the first time in America.

Master Josef Hofmann, aged 11, Polish pianist, made (Nov. 29) his American debut in New York at a concert in the Metropolitan Opera House and toured (1887-88) in the United States.

The long-famous light opera company The Bostonians was organized.

A month after production in London at the Savoy Theatre, Gilbert and Sullivan's comic opera "Ruddigore, or, The Witch's Curse" reached (Feb. 21) the Fifth Avenue Theatre, New York. Alfred Cellier's popular London Gaiety Theatre success, "Dorothy," came (Nov. 5) to the Standard Theatre, New York.

The touring McCaull Opera Company produced Reginald DeKoven's first light opera, "The Begum," in Philadelphia at the Chestnut Street Theatre (Nov. 17), in New York at the Fifth Avenue Theatre (Nov. 21), in Chicago at the Grand Opera House (Dec. 26), and in other cities. In spite of the presence of De Wolf Hopper, Digby Bell, and Jefferson de Angelis in the cast, the work did not prove a success.

Richard Mansfield played T. R. Sullivan's dramatization of Robert Louis Stevenson's "Dr. Jekyll and Mr. Hyde" in Boston, and created such a sensation by his changes from one character to another that he achieved stardom at its initial performance. He was seen (Mar. 12) in New York at the Madison Square Theatre in his gruesome and unforgettable impersonation.

In New York, the rising young actor Edward Hugh Sothern won further acclaim in a long-popular comedy "The Highest Bidder" (Lyceum Theatre, May 3). Harry Lacy was fireman Jim Manley in "The Still Alarm" (14th Street Theatre, Aug. 30). William Mack played "A Hole in the Ground" (at the same theatre, Sept. 12). David Belasco and H. C. DeMille scored another success with their play "The Wife" (Lyceum, Nov. 1). With Mrs. G. H. Gilbert and John Drew, Ada Rehan won more laurels, including the praise of Ellen Terry, in "The Railroad of Love" (Daly's Nov. 1).

₰ 1888

Anchored! w., Samuel K. Cowan. m., Michael Watson. Boston: Oliver Ditson Co., cop. 1888 (in: "Classic Baritone and Bass Songs"); G. Schirmer, cop. 1889 (in: "Album of Bass Songs," vol. 2). (Published earlier in London and reprinted in the United States before its inclusion in the above collections.)

Bedouin Love Song. w., B[ayard] Taylor. m., Ciro Pinsuti. Boston: Oliver Ditson Co., cop. 1888 (in: "Classic Baritone and Bass Songs"); G. Schirmer, cop. 1889 (in: "Album of Bass Songs," vol. 2). (Published earlier in London and reprinted in the United States before its inclusion in the above collections.)

Berceuse (Jocelyn), or, Cachés dans cet asile. French words, Paul Armand Silvestre and Victor Capoul. m., Benjamin Godard. (The so-called "Berceuse," or Lullaby, is a tenor aria in the opera "Jocelyn," produced in Brussels, 1888. A young seminarist named Jocelyn and a nobleman's daughter, unknown to each other and both fleeing from the terrors of the French Revolution, take refuge in a cave on a mountain and inevitably fall in love. Jocelyn sings the berceuse at the opening of Act II while the girl is asleep. The song is more often performed as a violin solo.)

The Convict and the Bird. w., m., Paul Dresser. Willis Woodward & Co., cop. 1888.

Drill, Ye Tarriers, Drill. w., m., anon. Frank Harding, cop. 1888.

L'Internationale. Original French words, Eugene Pottier, m., Pierre de Geyter. (Composed in 1888.)

Menuet (No. 1 in: Humoresques de Concert, op. 14, Book 1). Piano solo. m., Ignace Paderewski. Berlin: Ed. Bote & C. Bock [1888].

The Mottoes Framed upon the Wall. w., William Devere. m., W. S. Mullaly. Willis Woodward & Co., cop. 1888.

Oh! That We Two Were Maying (No. 8 in: Sketch Book, op. 2). w., Charles Kingsley. m., Ethelbert Nevin. Boston: The Boston Music Co., cop. 1888 by G. Schirmer, Jr.

Peer Gynt Suite No. 1—(1) Morning; (2) Ase's Death; (3) Anitra's Dance; (4) In the Hall of the Mountain King. Orch. excerpts from the incidental music to Ibsen's play "Peer Gynt." m., Edvard Hagerup Grieg, op. 46. Leipzig: C. F. Peters [1888].

Se Saran Rose. Italian words, Pietro Mazzini. m., Luigi Arditi. Leipzig: Wilhelm Hansen [1888]; G. Schirmer, cop. 1890. (This song is popularly known as the "Melba Waltz.")

Semper Fidelis. March. m., John Philip Sousa. Philadelphia: Harry Coleman, cop. 1888.

Where Did You Get That Hat? w., m., Joseph J. Sullivan. Frank Harding, cop. 1888.

The Whistling Coon. w., m., Sam Devere. Wm. A. Pond & Co., cop. 1888.

With All Her Faults I Love Her Still. w., m., Monroe H. Rosenfeld. B. W. Hitchcock, cop. 1888.

The formation of monopolies, called "trusts," was a new subject of debate in Congress, which appointed a Committee on Manufactures to investigate the methods of "big business."

Congress created (June 13) a Department of Labor, and passed (in Aug.) a Chinese Prohibition Bill (Chinese Exclusion Act) stopping immigration from China. Congress also signed its largest Pension Appropriation Bill up to that time—$80,280,000.

The Senate rejected (Aug. 21) the treaty (signed Feb. 15) of the Fisheries Commission, negotiated with Canada to resolve the disputed fishing rights in Alaskan waters. President Cleveland's firm stand, expressed (Aug. 23) in a vigorous Message to Congress, amazed the nation. The House of Representatives thereupon passed (Sept. 19) a drastic Retaliation Bill.

Rebellion in Haiti brought intervention by United States naval forces stationed there. Diplomatic exchanges followed the seizure by the Haitian warship "Dessalines" of the steamship "Haytian Republic," privately chartered and conveying munitions from New York to the national party in south Haiti, which had embarked (Oct. 20) at Cap-Haïtien 250 troops for St. Marc. The vessel was taken to Port-au-Prince and only released on the peremptory demand of the United States.

To embarrass President Cleveland in the coming national elections, Republicans sent from Pomona, Cal., to Lord Sackville, British minister at Washington, D. C., a fictitious letter purporting to be written by a British naturalized citizen and soliciting advice in voting. Lord Sackville replied, enclosing a clipping from the "New York Times" of Aug. 22 that touched on the relations between Great Britain and the United States. In consequence, President Cleveland handed Lord Sackville his passport.

Mrs. Belva Ann Lockwood (1879, 1884) was again the presidential candidate of the Equal Rights Party.

The adoption of formal European dress by the ladies of the Imperial Japanese Court drew a letter of remonstrance from a group of American women headed by Mrs. Grover Cleveland and Mrs. James A. Garfield.

Anthracite miners in the Schuylkill, Pa., region of the Philadelphia and Reading Railway returned (Feb. 17) to work after a protracted strike. This was presently followed by a strike on the Chicago, Burlington and Quincy Railroad, which affected 10,000 employees and completely paralyzed the Midwest.

A pageant celebrating the 100th anniversary of the ceding of the Northwest Territory to the Federal government was held in Marietta, O.

The 25th anniversary of the battle of Gettysburg was observed (July 4) with patriotic ceremonies on the historic spot by 20,000 survivors. Many Confederate soldiers participated.

The Washington National Monument (1848) was opened (Oct. 9) to the public.

The International Council of Women met (Mar. 26) in convention in Washington, D. C.

The Loyal Order of Moose ("L. O. O. M.") was founded in Louisville, Ky., as a secret fraternal and benevolent society.

Steam and hydraulic passenger elevators were being replaced by the electric elevator.

Severe blizzards raged (beginning Jan. 12) through the Northwest and abated only with the coming of spring. In the East, the Atlantic coast, basking in warm early-spring weather, was suddenly chilled by a 60-mile gale which swept in (Mar. 11-14) a blizzard that is still one of New York's most vivid memories. Telegraphic communications along the Eastern seaboard were disrupted, business halted, and food prices soared. More than 200 persons perished from cold and exposure. New York was buried (Mar. 12) in a snowfall that piled up as high as the first stories of apartment houses.

Yellow fever broke out (Aug. 8) in Florida, particularly around Jacksonville. The eminent English astronomer Richard Anthony Proctor was a victim of the epidemic.

The cornerstone of the Catholic University, Washington, D. C., was laid (May 24).

To American cultural organizations were added the National Geographic Society, Washington, D. C., and the American Folk-Lore Society, Boston.

"Casey at the Bat," a mock-heroic ballad about baseball, by Ernest Lawrence Thayer, was printed (June 3) in the San Francisco "Examiner." Actor De Wolf Hopper, a baseball "fan," is said to have recited the poem for the first time in Wallack's Theatre, New York, and so started its enormous popularity.

"Collier's" was founded in New York as a weekly magazine.

"Looking Backward, 2000-1887," a Utopian romance by Massachusetts journalist and novelist Edward Bellamy, and "The American Common-wealth," a two-volume study of "the nation of the future," by James Bryce, were published.

Having proved (1882) to his satisfaction that the island of Atlantis did once exist, Ignatius Donnelly now contributed to the Shakespeare-Bacon controversy (1857) his interpretation of the alleged Shakespearean ciphers by publishing "The Great Cryptogram." (He continued the subject in "The Cipher in the Plays and on the Tombstone," 1899.)

The Metropolitan Opera House, New York, staged (Jan. 25) the fourth and last of Wagner's mighty "Ring" operas, "Götterdämmerung," for the first time in America. Also heard (Apr. 16) for the first time was Verdi's opera "Otello" at the Academy of Music.

Master Fritz Kreisler, aged 13, Viennese violinist, made (Nov. 10) his American debut in New York at Steinway Hall.

The Princeton Dramatic Association was founded by theatrically minded students of the university. (Renamed the Triangle Club in 1893.)

David Warfield made his debut as an actor in "The Ticket-of-Leave Man" in San Francisco.

Edward Hugh Sothern became a popular idol in New York under Daniel

Frohman's management in a Belasco-DeMille comedy called "Lord Chumley" (Lyceum Theatre, Aug. 20). Petite Elsie Leslie turned "Little Lord Fauntleroy" into a reality in the dramatization of the novel (Broadway Theatre, Dec. 3). The operetta of the year was Francis Chassaigne's "Nadjy" (Casino, May 14).

ৡ৵ 1889

Down Went McGinty. w., m., Joseph Flynn. Spaulding & Kornder, cop. 1889.

Fear Not Ye, O Israel! w., Biblical. m., Dudley Buck. G. Schirmer, cop. 1889.

Oh Promise Me (*afterwards introduced in:* **Robin Hood**). w., Clement Scott. m., Reginald DeKoven, op. 50. G. Schirmer, cop. 1889.

Playmates. w., m., Harry Dacre. George M. Klenk & Co., cop. 1889.

Salut d'Amour. Instrumental piece. m., Edward Elgar, op. 12. Mainz: B. Schott's Söhne [1889].

"They Kissed, I Saw Them Do It!" TTBB. w., m., C[harles] B[each] Hawley. G. Schirmer, cop. 1889.

The Thunderer. March. m., John Philip Sousa. Philadelphia: Harry Coleman, cop. 1889.

Thy Sentinel Am I! w., Edward Oxenford. m., Michael Watson. G. Schirmer, cop. 1889 (in: "Album of Bass Songs," vol. 2). (Published earlier in London and reprinted in the United States before its inclusion in the above volume.)

The Washington Post. March. m., John Philip Sousa. Philadelphia: Harry Coleman, cop. 1889.

Benjamin Harrison, Republican, of Ohio, was inaugurated 23rd President. He was the great grandson of Benjamin Harrison, a signer of the Declaration of Independence, and the grandson of 9th President William Henry Harrison.

Outgoing President Cleveland had vetoed during his term of office 312 bills—175 more than the combined total of his twenty-one predecessors. The period marked the beginning of the struggle between organized labor and capital.

Four stars were added to the national flag by the admission of North and South Dakota (Nov. 2), Montana (Nov. 8), and Washington (Nov. 11), respectively, as the 39th 40th, 41st, and 42nd State.

An outcome of the Granger movement (1867) was the establishment (Feb. 9) of the Department of Agriculture by Congress.

The proposed construction, at an estimated cost of $50,000,000, of a canal across Nicaragua that would reduce travel from ocean to ocean to twenty-eight hours found support in Congress which enacted (Feb. 7) the Maritime Canal Company.

The Territory of Oklahoma was opened (Apr. 22) to homesteaders. So great was the rush of waiting settlers that towns of two or three thousand inhabitants at once came into existence. Oklahoma was represented that year at the Republican National Convention by a delegate who was a full-blooded Indian.

The United States purchased 11,000,000 acres from the Sioux Indians in Dakota Territory for $14,000,000.

Financial difficulties in the building of the Panama Canal by France (begun in 1882 by Viscount Ferdinand Marie de Lesseps, promotor of the Suez Canal) caused uneasiness in Congress. A Sundry Civil Bill appropriating $250,000 to the President for the protection of American interests on the Isthmus and a resolution protesting against French control of the canal were passed.

Secretary of Navy Benjamin Franklin Tracy outlined a program of naval activity that included the construction and completion by the close of 1903 of 92 war vessels, aggregating 488,450 tons, at an estimated cost of $268,500,000.

To prevent fraudulent voting at elections, Connecticut, Indiana, Massachusetts, Michigan, Minnesota, Missouri, Montana, Rhode Island, Tennessee, and Wisconsin adopted the Australian secret ballot system.

A tidal wave in the Samoan Islands damaged (Mar. 16) the anchored German and American warships; the U. S. flagship "Trenton," the "Vandalla," and the "Nipsic" were washed ashore.

The U. S. revenue cutter "Rush" seized (July 11) the British sealing schooner "Black Diamond" and, subsequently, the ships "Minnie" and "Pathfinder" in Bering Sea for alleged illegal sealery in United States waters. The vessels were ordered to Sitka, Alaska, but, changing their course, took refuge in their home port at Victoria, British Columbia.

Free mail delivery to the home was introduced (Nov. 9) in cities of 5,000 or more inhabitants.

Steady rains in Pennsylvania burst (on the afternoon of May 31) the reservoir dams above Johnstown, sending down the Conemaugh Valley a flood in which 2,209 persons perished and many towns were wiped out. The fury subsided about 18 miles below the city. The flood had its Paul Revere in Daniel Periton, son of a local merchant, who lost his life while alerting the inhabitants of the region when a railroad bridge collapsed under him and his bay horse. His cry during the unequal race was: "Run for your lives to the hills! Run to the hills! The dam is bursting!"

An elaborate Washington Centenary was celebrated (Apr. 30-May 2) in New York, commemorating the inauguration of George Washington as the first President of the United States. A colorful water pageant in New York Harbor and a parade, including governors of 29 States, foreign consuls, judges, and countless other notables, re-enacted with President Harrison and his official family the scene of the arrival of Washington. The surpliced choir of Trinity Church sang the hymn "Before the Lord We Bow" and the Doxology on the stairway of the Equitable Building when the President reached the place of reception. The Centennial Banquet and Ball at the festooned and metamorphosed Metropolitan Opera House that night was a brilliant social affair. Former Presidents Hays and Cleveland were present. The fact that President Harrison was a descendant of a signer of the Declaration of Independence gave the ceremonies an historical connection with the original event. Thanksgiving services were conducted in St. Paul's Chapel by Episcopal Bishop Potter, the choir singing the hymn "Rise, Crowned with Light, Imperial Salem, Rise." It was said that all the known relics of Washington, including his flute, were on display in New York.

The first Pan American Conference opened (Oct. 2) in Washington, D. C. (It adjourned Apr. 29, 1890. Sixteen Latin American countries were represented. The conference created in 1890 the International Bureau of American Republics, afterwards renamed Pan American Union in 1910.)

The Pilgrim Fathers' Monument in Plymouth, Mass., was dedicated (Aug. 1).

The Sons of the American Revolution was organized in New York.

There were now in the United States over 200 electric street railways, with 2,400 cars, operating on the Thomson-Houston and the Sprague systems.

Hull House was established as a social agency in Chicago on South Halsted Street by Jane Addams and Ellen Starr. It was named after Charles J. Hull, donor of the building.

The Epworth League was organized (May 15) in Cleveland, O., by the Methodist Episcopal Church for the religious instruction of young people.

The "kodak" or hand camera was advertised in "Scribner's Magazine" by the Eastman Kodak Company, Rochester, N. Y., as a simple, snap-shooting device. Thus began the great and profitable vogue of amateur photography.

The first practical electric elevators were installed in the Demarest Building, New York, by Otis Brothers and Company.

The great cantilever railroad bridge spanning the Hudson River at Poughkeepsie, N. Y., was completed.

"Munsey's" was founded in New York as a weekly magazine. (Became a monthly in 1891; ceased publication in 1929.)

Books of the year included Mark Twain's novel "The Connecticut Yankee," William Henry Herndon's three-volume biography "Herndon's Lincoln: The True Story of a Great Life," Theodore Roosevelt's history "The Winning of the West" (completed in 4 volumes in 1896), "Three Men in a Boat" (Jerome K. Jerome).

The Auditorium in Chicago was dedicated.

Andrew Carnegie instituted music recitals, "free to the people," at the Public Library in Allegheny (now North Side, Pittsburgh), Pa.

The Metropolitan Opera House, New York, staged (Mar. 4, 5, 8, 11) the first complete American performance of Wagner's four-opera cycle "Der Ring des Nibelungen."

Maud Powell, American violinist, introduced (Jan. 19) Tchaikovsky's Violin Concerto in New York. Theodore Thomas conducted (Mar. 5) the first American performance of the composer's Fifth Symphony at Chickering Hall.

Eugen d'Albert, renowned German composer and piano virtuoso, made (Nov. 18) his American debut in New York at a concert in the Metropolitan Opera House.

Artur Nikisch, famous Hungarian-German musical conductor, was appointed director of the Boston Symphony Orchestra.

Charles Frohman, new in the theatrical managerial business, turned Bronson Howard's Boston Museum failure "Shenandoah" into a New York Star Theatre success (Sept. 9) with Wilton Lackaye in a Civil War role. Frohman tried (Dec. 26) the interesting experiment of exchanging the New York and Philadelphia casts for a number of performances.

Maude Adams, a young actress of sixteen in Edward H. Sothern's company in New York and Brooklyn, came into prominence as the school-girl in Charles H. Hoyt's long-run rural comedy "A Midnight Bell" (Bijou Theatre, Mar. 5).

English comedienne Marie Tempest arrived in New York with an operetta "The Red Hussar" (Palmer's Theatre, Aug. 5) by Lillian Russell's husband, Edward Solomon, and was "a revelation," said the "New York Herald" the next day.

Baldwin Brothers advertised "double balloon ascensions with parachute descents."

The last heavyweight boxing championship bout fought with bare knuckles took place (July 8) in Richburg, Miss., between John L. Sullivan and Jack Kilrain. Kilrain was defeated in 75 rounds.

Jefferson Davis, aged 80, president of the former Confederate States, died (Dec. 11) in New Orleans.

ॐ 1890

Annie Rooney. w., m., Michael Nolan. (The song, a London music-hall favorite but non-copyright in the United States, was reprinted by local publishers.)

The Birthday of a King. Sacred song. w., anon. m., W[illiam] H[arold] Neidlinger. G. Schirmer, cop. 1890; renewed 1918 by W. H. Neidlinger.

I've Come Here to Stay. w., Edward Harrigan. m., Dave [David] Braham. Wm. A. Pond & Co., cop. 1890.

The Irish Jubilee. w., James Thornton. m., Charles Lawler. M. Witmark & Sons, cop. 1890.

Jolly Commodore. w., Edward Harrigan. m., Dave [David] Braham. Wm. A. Pond & Co., cop. 1890.

Love Will Find a Way. w., J. Cheever Goodwin. m., Woolson Morse. T. B. Harms & Co., cop. 1890.

Maggie Murphy's Home (Reilly and the 400). w., Edward Harrigan. m., Dave [David] Braham. Wm. A. Pond & Co., cop. 1890.

Passing By. w., Robert Herrick (1591-1674). m., Edward C. Purcell [pseud. of Edward Purcell Cockram]. London: Edwin Ashdown, Ltd. [ca. 1890.] (The song was "printed by permission" in the 3rd edition of "The Scottish Students' Song Book," Bayley & Ferguson, Glasgow, preface dated 1892. An American imprint appeared in "Encore Songs," Oliver Ditson Co., Boston, 1910. The music is usually ascribed to the 17th century Henry Purcell and is mistakenly featured by singers as an old English song. The composer was an English organist, who died Oct. 15, 1932, at Clifton, Bristol. His obituary was printed in the "Monthly Musical Record," London, 1932, p. 186.)

Scheherazade. Symphonic poem. m., Nicolai Rimsky-Korsakoff. Leipzig: M. P. Belaieff [1890].

Skirt Dance (Faust Up-to-Date). m., Meyer W. Lutz [pseud. of Wilhelm Meyer-Lutz]. Carl Fischer, cop. 1890.

Still as the Night. See 1885.

Taking in the Town. w., Edward Harrigan. m., Dave [David] Braham. Wm. A. Pond & Co., cop. 1890.

Tell Mother I'll Be There. Hymn. w., m., Charles M. Fillmore. Cincinnati: Fillmore Bros., cop. 1890; renewed 1918 by Charles M. Alexander.

Tenderly Calling. Hymn. w., F[rances] J[ane] Crosby (Mrs. Alexander. Van Alstyne). m., Ira D[avid] Sankey. Cop. 1890 by Ira D. Sankey.

Throw Him Down, McCloskey. w., m., J. W. Kelly. Frank Harding, cop. 1890.

Thy Beaming Eyes (No. 4 in: Six Love Songs, op. 40). w., W[illiam] H[enry] Gardner. m., Edward MacDowell. Boston: Arthur P. Schmidt, cop. 1890.

True-Hearted, Whole-Hearted—*also known as:* Peal Out the Watchword! Hymn. w., Frances R[idley] Havergal. m., Geo[rge] C[oles] Stebbins. Cop. 1890 by Ira D. Sankey.

The 43rd and 44th stars were added to the national flag by the admission, respectively, of Idaho (July 3) and Wyoming (July 10) as States.

Congress had a busy year. It passed (Feb. 13) the Oklahoma bill, opening the territory to settlers who rushed thither by the thousands in endless wagon trains. Guthrie, the capital, was laid out in a day and during the first week a bank and a newspaper were established. Congress enacted (July 2) the Sherman Anti-Trust Act, as a result of the investigations of the Committee on Manufactures (1888); established (Oct. 1) the Weather Bureau, and passed (the same day) Ohio Representative William McKinley's high tariff bill "to protect infant industries." This bill placed sugar among other articles on the free list and safeguarded the woolen industry by a heavy duty on imported wool.

The Bering Sea fishing dispute took another turn when Lord Salisbury of Great Britain offered (Aug. 2) a new basis for arbitration. Secretary of State James G. Blaine, however, rejected (Dec. 17) its legal premises. Rumors that Great Britain had sent a powerful squadron into northern Pacific waters were proven false when the official correspondence was made public.

Failures in business were widespread. The government closed (Feb. 30) the First National, the Lenox Hill, and the Equitable banks in New York, suspended the Bank of America in Philadelphia, and arrested the president of the Sixth National Bank. Three Wall Street failures amounted to $10,000,000.

The State prison at Auburn, N. Y., was (Aug. 6) the scene of the first execution of a criminal in the United States by electricity. So inadequately was the electrocution managed at the first attempt, that a second charge of current was required to accomplish its purpose. The victim was William Kemmler, convicted of the murder of Tillie Ziegler at Buffalo. Public sentiment urged the repeal of the law, but it was upheld by the Court of Appeals.

Telegraphic communication with Europe was now possible by means of seven Atlantic cables.

The business of the country was seriously affected for several days when a million-dollar fire damaged (July 18) the building of the Western Union Telegraph Company in New York.

The construction of the Niagara Falls power plant was begun (Oct. 4).

Ellis Island in New York Harbor replaced (Dec. 31) Castle Garden as a port of entry for immigrants.

The Mormons in Utah renounced (Oct. 6) polygamy.

"Nelly Bly" (New York "World" journalist Elizabeth Cochrane Seaman) completed a tour of the world, sponsored by the newspaper, in 72 days, 6 hours, 10 minutes, 58 seconds (Nov. 14, 1889-Jan. 25, 1890), bettering Jules Verne's imaginary trip of 80 days. She published an account of the journey, entitled "Nelly Bly's Book: Around the World in Seventy-Two Days." Her time was reduced in the current year by George Francis Train, who made the trip in 67 days, 12 hours, 3 minutes.

The Daughters of the American Revolution ("D.A.R.") was founded in Washington, D. C., by women descendants of persons who gave "material aid to the cause of independence."

The Woodmen of the World ("W.O.W.") was established in Omaha, Neb., as a fraternal and benevolent society.

The General Federation of Women's Clubs was formed.

The Blue and the Gray, former Confederate soldiers, assembled (May 26) at a reunion in Vicksburg, Miss., the scene of a Civil War battle in 1863.

Tornadoes swept through the western and central States. Three hundred buildings were demolished (Mar. 27) in Louisville, Ky., and the adjacent town of Bowling Green was wiped out with a loss of 200 lives. The excursion steamer "Sea Wing" capsized (July 13) on Lake Pepin, Minn., drowning 147 persons. Floods devastated (in Mar. and Apr.) the Mississippi Valley.

An influenza epidemic started (in Jan.) in the East and spread westward and into Canada and Mexico, taking a large toll of lives.

The "Literary Digest" was founded in New York as a weekly magazine. (Ceased publication in 1938.)

Captain Alfred Thayer Mahan, U. S. N., published his epoch-making Newport War College lectures on "The Influence of Sea Power upon History, 1660-1783," which was followed two years later by his no less significant two-volume study of "The Influence of Sea Power upon the

French Revolution and Empire, 1793-1812." Both books largely determined the subsequent naval policies of the United States, Great Britain, Germany, and Japan.

"Lippincott's Monthly Magazine" published (in July) simultaneously with its London edition Oscar Wilde's novel "The Picture of Dorian Gray."

Worthington Chauncey Ford brought out "Winnowings in American History" in 15 volumes (1890-91).

Lafcadio Hearn, American writer of Irish-Greek parentage, born in the Ionian Islands, settled permanently in Japan.

A new and magnificent Madison Square Garden with a reproduction of the Giralda Tower of Seville, soon to be crowned by Augustus Saint-Gaudens's statue of Diana, and financed by some of Wall Street's most noted tycoons, was erected in New York to replace the older structure of the same name that was demolished in 1889 (operations began Aug. 7). The auditorium was opened (June 16) with a series of orchestral concerts, including two ballets, conducted by Eduard Strauss, brother of Johann Strauss the "Waltz King." The architect was Stanford White.

The French Opera House, New Orleans, offered the American premières of Lalo's "Le Roi d'Ys" (Jan. 23) and Massenet's "Le Cid" (Feb. 23).

Walter Damrosch conducted (Feb. 1) with his Symphony Society the first American performance of Tchaikovsky's Fourth Symphony in New York.

Exactly a month after its production at the Savoy Theatre, London, Gilbert and Sullivan's new comic opera "The Gondoliers, or, The King of Barataria" was heard (Jan 7) in New York at the Park Theatre.

Play-minded Clyde Fitch, a recent graduate of Amherst College, and actor-manager Richard Mansfield combined their youthful talents to produce (May 17) the stage success "Beau Brummel" at the Madison Square Theatre, New York.

Reginald DeKoven's still-popular light opera "Robin Hood" was premièred (June 9) in Chicago at the Grand Opera House, and given (Sept. 20) in London at Camden Town Park Hall. The work was performed in Boston (Music Hall, Sept. 22), in New York (Standard Theatre, Sept. 28), and elsewhere on tour. Jessie Bartlett Davis, playing Allan-a-Dale, sang the hit song "O Promise Me." Since "Erminie" (1886), no operetta achieved comparable popularity.

Mrs. Leslie (Louise) Carter of Chicago, her marital troubles and divorce now over, achieved the ambition of her life. She made (Nov. 10) her stage debut as an actress, after careful training by David Belasco, in Paul M. Potter's play "The Ugly Duckling" in New York at the Broadway Theatre.

Jefferson de Angelis established not only his reputation as a comedian but the American popularity of Karl Millöcker's comic opera "Der arme Jonathan." The piece was undoubtedly exotic fare to the Viennese public, with one scene of the Bowery and another of Negroes picking cotton along the Battery! Imported by Heinrich Conried, the locale was transferred to West Point!! So it was produced (Oct. 10) as "Poor Jonathan" in New York at the Casino Theatre with Lillian Russell in the soprano lead.

Joseph Arthur's rural melodrama "Blue Jeans" (New York, 14th Street Theatre, Oct. 6) drew capacity audiences because of its thrilling scene with the hero strapped to a threatening buzzsaw.

Bostonians flocked to their spacious Boston Theatre (Sept. 16, 1890-Jan. 10, 1891) to see the spectacular London Drury Lane melodrama "The Soudan." (Revived there Apr. 20, 1891, the spectacle came to New York's large Academy of Music and played from Sept. 3, 1891, to Nov. 21).

Feminine fashions came back to the hour-glass figure, leg-of-mutton sleeves, and the gored skirt.

The old high type of bicycle gave way to the "drop frame" model, equipped with pneumatic tires. Thereupon bicycling reached its heyday. The new bicycles were safe for women, and they, too, took up the sport.

The national population was 62,979,766. The Bureau of Statistics of the Treasury Department reported (June 30, 1891) that the total number of immigrants from 1820 to 1890 was 15,641,688, of whom 5,246,613 had entered during the past ten years. The largest numbers during the 70-year period came from Germany (4,551,719), Ireland (3,501,683), and England (2,460,034).

1891

Actions Speak Louder than Words. w., George Horncastle. m., Felix McGlennon. Frank Tousey, cop. 1891.

American Patrol. March. m., F. W. Meacham. Carl Fischer, cop. 1891; renewed 1912 by Cora Meacham.

Armorer's Song (Robin Hood). w., Harry B[ache] Smith. m., Reginald DeKoven. G. Schirmer, cop. 1891.

Ask the Man in the Moon (Wang). w., J. Cheever Goodwin. m., Woolson Morse. T. B. Harms & Co., cop. 1891.

Brown October Ale (Robin Hood). w., Harry B[ache] Smith. m., Reginald DeKoven. G. Schirmer, cop. 1891.

Death and Transfiguration—*original German title:* **Tod und Verklärung.** Symphonic poem. m., Richard Strauss, op. 24. Munich: Jos. Aibl [1891].

For All Eternity—*Italian title:* Eternamente; *French title:* A Jamais; *German title:* In alle Ewigkeit. Italian words, Pietro Mazzoni. French words, Gabriel Leprevost. German words, A. L. Mackechnie. English words, S. A. Herbert. m., Angelo Mascheroni. London: Gould & Bolttler, cop. 1891 by Martyn Van Lennep; renewed 1919 by Giovanni Mascheroni.

Happy Day. Hymn. w., P[hilip] Doddridge. m., "from E. F. Rimbault." The Biglow & Main Co. [cop. 1891 by the Biglow & Main Co. and The John Church Co.] (in: "Gospel Hymns No. 6 . . . edited by Ira D. Sankey, James McGranahan and George Coles Stebbins," p. 133). (To this tune are sung the words "How dry I am.")

Hats Off to Me. w., Edward Harrigan. m., Dave [David] Braham. Wm. A. Pond & Co., cop. 1891.

Hey, Rube! w., J. Sherrie Matthews. m., Harry Bulger. M. Witmark & Sons, cop. 1891.

Hosanna. Original French words, Julien Didée. English words, N[athan] H[askell] Dole. m., Jules Granier. G. Schirmer, cop. 1891. (Published earlier in France and reprinted in the United States in numerous vocal arrangements. The Schirmer publication was rubber-stamped, in facsimile, "Authorized Edition, Jules Granier.")

Kiss and Let's Make Up. w., m., Charles K. Harris. Chas. K. Harris, cop. 1891.

Knights of the Mystic Star. w., Edward Harrigan. m., Dave [David] Braham. Wm. A. Pond & Co., cop. 1891.

The Last of the Hogans. w., Edward Harrigan. m., Dave [David] Braham. Wm. A. Pond & Co., cop. 1891.

Life's Railway to Heaven. Hymn. w., M. E. Abbey. m., Charles D. Tillman. Cop. 1891 by Charles D. Tillman.

Little Boy Blue. w., Eugene Field. m., Ethelbert Nevin. Boston: G. Schirmer, Jr. (The Boston Music Co.), cop. 1891.

Molly O! (Mavourneen). w., m., William J. Scanlan. T. B. Harms & Co., cop. 1891.

Narcissus (No. 4 in: Water Scenes, op. 13). Piano solo. m., Ethelbert Nevin. Boston: G. Schirmer, Jr. (The Boston Music Co.), cop. 1891.

The Pardon Came Too Late. w., m., Paul Dresser. Willis Woodward & Co., cop. 1891.

The Picture That's Turned Toward the Wall. w., m., Charles Graham. M. Witmark & Sons, cop. 1891.

A Pretty Girl (Wang). w., J. Cheever Goodwin. m., Woolson Morse. T. B. Harms & Co., cop. 1891.

De Rainbow Road. w., Edward Harrigan. m., Dave [David] Braham. Wm. A. Pond & Co., cop. 1891.

Scarf Dance—*original French title:* **Pas des Echarpes.** Piano solo. m., Cécile Chaminade, op. 73. G. Schirmer, cop. 1891; edited by William Scharfenberg. (The dance was a movement in the ballet "Callirhoë," produced at Marseilles, 1888, and at Lyons, 1891. An orchestral suite from the ballet was published by Enoch & Cie., Paris [1890]; and a piano arrangement of the "Scarf Dance" by the composer was issued by the same firm about that time.)

Sometime We'll Understand. Hymn. w., Maxwell N. Cornelius, D.D. m., James McGranahan. Cop. 1891 by James McGranahan.

Take a Day Off, Mary Ann. w., Edward Harrigan. m., Dave [David] Braham. Wm. A. Pond & Co., cop. 1891.

Ta-ra-ra-bom-der-e. w., m., Henry J. Sayers. Willis Woodward & Co., cop. 1891.

Whosoever Will May Come. Hymn. w., A. Montieth. m., Ira D[avid] Sankey. The Biglow & Main Co., cop. 1891.

After several decades of agitation, Congress passed (Mar. 4) the International Copyright Act. Another public-spirited bill that was enacted was the Forest Reserve Act for the protection of forest lands.

The United States and Spain signed a reciprocity treaty (proclaimed July 31) by which Cuban sugar was exempted from duty in the United States.

A war with Chile was a much-discussed topic in the press when that country failed to make proper amends for the killing in the streets of Valparaiso of two sailors from the U. S. cruiser "Baltimore," the wounding of other bluejackets, and the imprisonment of 35 members of the crew. (Chile apologized belatedly in Jan., 1892, and later paid an indemnity of $75,000 to the wounded sailors and to the families of the two who lost their lives.)

The Washington home of Benjamin Franklin Tracy, Secretary of the Navy, was destroyed (Feb. 3) by fire, resulting in the death of Mrs.

Tracy, her daughter, and a woman servant, and in injury to other members of the family. The Secretary himself was unconscious when removed from the building and was revived only with difficulty.

The Populist or People's Party was organized (in May) in Cincinnati as a political rival of the Republican and Democratic parties by farmers', labor, and reform organizations. In the fall elections, the party elected governors in Georgia, South Carolina, Tennessee, and Texas, and sent a senator from Kansas to Congress. (The party came to an end about 1904.)

A violent miners' strike occurred (Feb. 19) in Connellsville, Pa. It affected 18,000 men and lasted four months (subsiding toward the end of June).

The employment of convict labor in the mines of Tennessee brought (July 14) the local miners and the State government into conflict. The miners opposed the practice, and in spite of the surveillance of the State militia evicted the leased convicts that were employed by the Tennessee Coal Mining Company at Briceville and by the Knoxville Iron Company. Fortunately, no blood was shed. The State, however, failed to pass, according to its promise, either a modification or a repeal of the convict lease system.

Two men wrecked (Dec. 4) the Wall Street, New York, office of financier Russell Sage with a dynamite bomb after demanding $1,200,000. Sage was unharmed, but the bomb blew both men to pieces, killed three persons, and injured several others.

New Orleans citizens rose (Mar. 14) in arms when a local jury acquitted six of nineteen Italians suspected of the murder (Oct. 15, 1890) of Chief of Police David C. Hennessy. The Italians were believed to be members of a Sicilian secret society called the Mafia, which had been terrorizing the city for years. It was thought that they had feared the consequences of an investigation conducted by Hennessy with the help of the Italian government, and that they had him shot down in a public street. An immense armed mob stormed the city jail, dragged forth eleven of the Italian prisoners, and either shot or hanged them from lampposts. The Italian government protested to Secretary of State James G. Blaine, who asked the Governor of Louisiana to bring the lynchers to justice. The request was ignored; and a Grand Jury in New Orleans whitewashed the perpetrators, among whom were many prominent citizens.

Thomas Alva Edison patented the forerunner of the motion-picture camera—the kinetograph, or kinetoscope, a lantern for projecting moving pictures on a screen. (The invention was first publicly exhibited Apr. 15, 1892, in New York.)

Edward Goodrich Acheson discovered carborundum.

James Northrop invented the power (or "Draper") cotton loom which, with subsequent improvements, has made it possible for one operator to run 30 looms whereas formerly three operators were required for a single loom.

The Free Library of Philadelphia was established.

The Drexel Institute of Art, Science, and Industry was founded in Philadelphia by the banker Anthony Joseph Drexel.

Isaac Kauffman Funk, clergyman, publisher, and lexicographer, began the publication of "A Standard Dictionary of the English Language" (1891-93, 1903, 1910-12).

The "Review of Reviews" was founded as a monthly magazine. (Ceased publication in 1937.)

Teresa Carreño, Venezuelan pianist, introduced the Piano Concerto, op. 23, by Edward MacDowell, American composer, in Leipzig at a Gewandhaus concert.

The great Russian composer Peter Ilich Tchaikovsky arrived (Apr. 27) in New York for a month's visit. He conducted four concerts in New York (in connection with the dedication of Carnegie Music Hall, see below), one in Philadelphia (May 18), and one in Baltimore.

Elaborate ceremonies dedicated (May 5) the Carnegie Music Hall in New York, built by Andrew Carnegie for the Oratorio Society of which he was president (1888-1918). Tchaikovsky (see above) shared conducting honors with Walter Damrosch, director of the Oratorio Society.

Ignace Jan Paderewski, Polish piano virtuoso, made (Nov. 17) his American debut in New York at the new Carnegie Music Hall.

Mascagni's famous Sonzogno-prize (1888) opera "Cavalleria Rusticana" was heard (Sept. 29) for the first time in the United States in Philadelphia at the Grand Opera House, in English. It was introduced (Oct. 1) in New York in rival performances at the Casino Theatre (matinée) and the Lenox Lyceum (evening). At the Casino performance, the opera was preceded by the first American production of Carl Zeller's popular comic opera "The Tyrolean" (Der Vogelhändler) in English, starring Marie Tempest.

Theodore Thomas established the Chicago Symphony Orchestra.

The DeReszke brothers, Jean (tenor) and Edouard (bass), made (Dec. 14) their American debuts in Gounod's opera "Roméo et Juliette" in New York at the Metropolitan Opera House.

New York saloon keeper Steve Brodie, famed jumper from the Brooklyn Bridge (1886), now lengthened his biography by turning actor and repeated his stunt from a stage bridge in Steele MacKaye's melodrama "Mad Money" (Niblo's Garden, Feb. 22). (There is more to be said about Steve. He went on the road with MacKaye's play, was exhibited as a wax figure at Huber's Palace Museum, New York, Aug. 21-26, 1893, and played in a show entitled "On the Bowery," which reached the California Theatre, San Francisco, in 1896.)

Comedy topped all serious effort in the New York theatre. Edward Harrigan was playing his "Reilly and the Four Hundred" at his new 35th Street Theatre since the last days of the previous year (Dec. 29, 1890) with Ada Lewis of later "tough girl" fame in the cast. DeWolf Hopper, now a star via last year's comic opera "Castles in the Air," came out (May 4) with the petite soubrette Della Fox in an operatic burletta

"Wang," which was a smash hit at the Broadway Theatre—"Wang goes with a bang!" was the advertising slogan. (After a run, the piece went on a successful tour of the country, reaching the Baldwin Theatre, San Francisco, 1895, which was described in an illustrated pamphlet entitled "DeWolf Hopper's Wagner Tour." The reference had nothing to do with the German composer of that name but denoted the elegant George Wagner Palace Cars in which the company travelled.) After playing the Harlem and Brooklyn circuit for nearly a year with varying success, Charles H. Hoyt established (Nov. 9) his pseudo-oriental nonsense "A Trip to Chinatown"—San Francisco's, not New York's—at the Madison Square Theatre for a run of 650 performances (Aug. 7, 1893), the largest tally scored by any theatrical work in New York up to that time.

Sarah Bernhardt introduced (Feb. 5) Victorien Sardou's powerful five-act drama "La Tosca" to America at the Garden Theatre in New York. (The play furnished the subject for Puccini's Italian opera of the same name in 1900.)

Mrs. Leslie Carter made (Nov. 3) in New York at the Star Theatre her only appearance in a musical work—"Miss Helyett," a comic opera by the Bouffes-Parisiens composer Edmond Audran, rewritten by David Belasco.

The melodious singing actor William J. Scanlan opened (Sept. 28) at the 14th Street Theatre, New York, in "Mavourneen" and carried on bravely until its 102nd performance (Dec. 25) when he was removed from the company to his manager's home "for his own safety and that of others." (Scanlan had shown signs of increasing insanity during the run of the play and, becoming violently insane, was transferred Jan. 7, 1892, to Bloomingdale Asylum. He died Feb., 1898, at the asylum in White Plains, New York.)

James Naismith, an instructor in the Y. M. C. A. Training School at Springfield, Mass., devised the game of basketball.

The first international continuous 6-day bicycle race was won by the American "Plugger Bill" Martin in New York at Madison Square Garden.

One Zoe Gayton arrived in New York, claiming to have walked all the way from San Francisco, or 3,395 miles.

Deaths of the year included Phineas Taylor Barnum, aged 81 (Apr. 7), in Bridgeport, Conn., and Herman Melville, aged 72 (Sept. 28), author of "Moby Dick" and other stories, in New York.

‿ 1892

After the Ball. w., m., Charles K. Harris. Chas. K. Harris, cop. 1892.

The Bowery (A Trip to Chinatown). w., Charles H. Hoyt. m., Percy Gaunt. T. B. Harms & Co., cop. 1892.

Daddy Wouldn't Buy Me a Bow-Wow. w., m., Joseph Tabrar. T. B. Harms & Co., cop. 1892 by Francis, Day & Hunter.

Daisy Bell. w., m., Harry Dacre. T. B. Harms & Co., cop. 1892.

The Holy City. w., F[rederick] E[dward] Weatherly. m., Stephen Adams [pseud. of Michael Maybrick]. London: Boosey & Co., cop. 1892.

The Man That Broke the Bank at Monte Carlo. w., m., Fred Gilbert. T. B. Harms & Co., cop. 1892 by Francis, Day & Hunter.

My Sweetheart's the Man in the Moon. w., m., James Thornton. Frank Harding, cop. 1892.

The Nut-Cracker Suite—(1) Miniature Overture; (2) March; (3) Dance of the Sugar-Plum Fairy; (4) Trepak; (5) Arabian Dance; (6) Chinese Dance; (7) Dance of the Mirlitons; (8) Waltz of the Flowers. Orch. excerpts from the ballet "Casse-Noisette." m., Peter Ilich Tchaikovsky, op. 71. Moscow: P. Jurgenson [1892].

Push Dem Clouds Away (A Trip to Chinatown). w., m., Percy Gaunt. T. B. Harms & Co., cop. 1892.

Social leader Samuel Ward McAllister is reported to have declared in New York's exclusive Union League Club that there were "only about four hundred people in New York society." He named society's elite on the occasion of a great ball tendered (Feb. 1) by Mrs. William Astor when no more than that number of guests could be accommodated in her ballroom. (The phrase seems already to have been current in 1890; it figured in the title of a popular comedy, "Reilly and the Four Hundred," which Edward Harrigan wrote and introduced Dec. 29 of that year at his new 35th Street Theatre.)

The United States launched its first armored battleship—the "Texas."

The Louisiana Lottery Company, doing a profitable illegal business by authority of the State, was suppressed by the United States government.

In Homestead, near Pittsburgh, a steel mill strike incited by anarchists broke out (July 1), developed (July 6) into a battle between the miners and 300 Pinkerton guards in which 11 of the latter and eight strikers and spectators were killed, and was put down (July 12) by martial law under the National Guard (but not before a Russian anarchist had attempted to assassinate Henry Clay Frick, of the Carnegie group, and wounded him).

The empty buildings of the Columbian Exposition in Chicago were dedicated (Oct. 21) on the 400th anniversary of the discovery of America. The formal opening took place in the next year.

Lieutenant Robert Edwin Peary explored the Greenland coast.

The Anti-Saloon League was organized (Mar. 26).

The cornerstone of the Cathedral of St. John the Divine (Protestant Episcopal) in New York was laid on St. John's Day (Dec. 27).

Thomas Alva Edison exhibited (Apr. 15) publicly in New York his motion-picture camera, the kinetograph (1891).

The horseless buggy or self-propelled carriage, which is called the automobile today, was becoming a mechanical reality in America. (In Germany, engineer Karl Benz had already exhibited an automobile in 1885, but tinkering American inventors hadn't heard of it.) William Morrison of Des Moines, Ia., built an electric automobile, while the brothers Charles E. and J. Frank Duryea, bicycle makers, displayed a gasoline-driven car on the streets of Springfield, Mass.

Direct telephone service between New York and Chicago was established (Oct. 18).

Steam-powered elevated trains began (June 29) running in Chicago.

Rudyard Kipling, English poet and writer, settled for several years in Brattleboro, Vt. (Here he wrote, with his brother-in-law Wolcott Balestier, "The Naulahka," 1892, a novel about a California speculator in India. "Captains Courageous," 1897, is Kipling's only novel dealing with America.)

The notorious Dalton Boys, who for five years had been the nation's top-ranking public enemies, were wiped out by the citizens of Coffeyville, Kans., while attempting to rob a couple of banks.

Lizzie Borden became a sensational figure when she was accused on circumstantial evidence of the murder of her step-parents who were hacked to death (Aug. 4) in their home in Fall River, Mass. (She was acquitted at her trial the next year, and became the subject of popular ballads and fiction.)

Nature wreaked frightful havoc throughout the country, bringing death to thousands of persons and animals and causing enormous damage to property. There were blizzards, cyclones, and floods in the usual areas, an earthquake in California (the first since 1868), a "hot wave" (in July) in the Atlantic States, a cloudburst in the Pennsylvania oil regions during which lightning ignited the oil, and other disasters.

Fire destroyed (Aug. 27) the interior of the Metropolitan Opera House in New York.

John Philip Sousa, leader of the U. S. Marine Corps band, resigned (Aug. 1) his post to organize his own famous band of 100 players, which concertized for many years in the United States and Canada. (The band undertook European tours in 1900, 1901, 1903, 1905, and made a world tour in 1910-11.)

Frank Damrosch organized the People's Choral Union in New York.

Theodore Thomas conducted (Jan. 9) the first American performance of Richard Strauss's symphonic poem "Tod und Verklärung" (Death and Transfiguration) with the Philharmonic Society Orchestra in New York.

The Negro soprano Mme. Sisseretta Jones, called the Black Patti, was a busy concert singer in New York and its environs. (She first appeared Apr. 30 at the Academy of Music.)

England's Poet Laureate, Lord Tennyson, wrote a play about Robin Hood but because of the vogue of DeKoven's light opera of the same name was compelled to call it "The Foresters." The poetical play was acted and sung (Mar. 17) with Sir Arthur Sullivan's music in New York at Daly's Theatre.

If Chicago's Columbian Exposition was a year late in opening its commemoration of the 400th anniversary of Columbus's discovery, Boston was able to greet the historic event at the Globe Theatre with a timely extravaganza, "1492," book by Robert Ayres Barnet and music by Carl Pflueger, that proved extremely popular.

Sir Arthur Wing Pinero's London play of the new school of dramatic writing, "The Second Mrs. Tanqueray," shocked New York (Star Theatre, Oct. 9) as it had scandalized the British capital.

Other New York plays were "Captain Lettarblair" (Lyceum, Aug. 16), "The Masked Ball" (Palmer's, Oct. 3), "Diplomacy" (Star, Oct. 24), "Americans Abroad" (Lyceum, Dec. 5).

James J. ("Gentleman Jim") Corbett became the first heavyweight boxing champion according to the Marquis of Queensberry rules when he defeated John L. Sullivan in 21 rounds at New Orleans.

Deaths of the year included Walt Whitman, aged 73 (Mar. 27), in Camden, N. J., and John Greenleaf Whittier, aged 85 (Sept. 7), in Hampton Falls, N. H.

₰ 1893

The Cat Came Back. w., m., Henry S. Miller. Chicago: Will Rossiter, cop. 1893.

December and May (or, **"Mollie Newell Don't Be Cruel"**). w., Edward B. Marks. m., William Lorraine. Frank Harding, cop. 1893.

Do, Do, My Huckleberry, Do. w., Harry Dillon. m., John Dillon. M. Witmark & Sons, cop. 1893.

The Fatal Wedding. w., W. H. Windom. m., Gussie L. Davis. Spaulding & Kornder, cop. 1893 by Gussie L. Davis.

From the New World—*original German title:* **Aus der neuen Welt.** Symphony. m., Anton Dvorák, op. 95. Berlin: N. Simrock, cop. 1894 [sic]. (See below. For the adaptation "Goin' Home," see 1922.)

Good-Morning to All (*also adapted to the words:* Happy Birthday to You, cop. 1962 by Summy-Birchard Company). w., Patty S[mith] Hill. m., Mildred J. Hill (in: "Song Stories for the Kindergarten," p. 3), Chicago: Clayton F. Summy, cop. 1893.

I Long to See the Girl I Left Behind. w., m., John T. Kelly. M. Witmark & Sons, cop. 1893.

Little Alabama Coon. w., m., Hattie Starr. Willis Woodward & Co., cop. 1893.

Love Me Little, Love Me Long. w., m., Percy Gaunt. T. B. Harms & Co., cop. 1893.

Mamie! Come Kiss Your Honey (*introduced in:* A Country Sport). w., m., May Irwin. Boston: White-Smith Music Pub. Co., cop. 1893.

My Mother's Bible. Hymn. w., M. B. Williams. m., Charles D. Tillman. Cop. 1893 by Charles D. Tillman; renewed 1921.

Say "Au Revoir," but Not "Good-bye." w., m., Harry Kennedy. Brooklyn: Kennedy Publishing House, cop. 1893 by Will H. Kennedy.

See, Saw, Margery Daw. w., m., Arthur West. M. Witmark & Sons, cop. 1893.

Sweet Marie. w., Cy Warman. m., Raymon Moore. Manhattan Music Pub. Co., cop. 1893.

They Never Tell All What They Know. w., Edward Harrigan. m. Dave [David] Braham. Wm. A. Pond & Co., cop. 1893.

Two Little Girls in Blue. w., m., Charles Graham. Spaulding & Kornder, cop. 1893.

The Volunteer Organist. w., William B. Glenroy, m., Henry Lamb. Spaulding & Kornder, cop. 1893.

When the Roll Is Called Up Yonder. Hymn. w., m., James M. Black. Cop. 1893 by Chas. H. Gabriel.

Won't You Be My Sweetheart? w., J. G. Judson. m., H. C. Verner. Chicago: The S. Brainard's Sons Co., cop. 1893.

Grover Cleveland, Democrat, of New Jersey, was inaugurated for a second term as 24th President—the only President with two serial numbers (22 and 24).

Departing from Executive custom, President Cleveland closed the White House against office seekers.

Congress enacted a law requiring American consuls at foreign ports to register intending immigrants and to deny entry to the United States of persons who were insane, destitute, illiterate, criminal, or physically unfit. Another enactment was the repeal of the Sherman Silver Purchase Act.

The Secretary of the Interior Hoke Smith suspended more than 2,000 pensioners whose names had been fraudulently placed on the pension list (it numbered almost a million names and drained the national treasury of about one-third of its disbursements).

Thomas Francis Bayard, Wilmington, Del., lawyer and senator, was appointed the first United States Ambassador to Great Britain (1893-97). Hitherto the American representative there held the rank of Minister Plenipotentiary.

A revolt in Hawaii (in Jan.), instigated by its foreign-born and English-speaking inhabitants, deposed the ruling Queen Liliuokalani and set up a provisional government which made overtures to the United States for annexation. Outgoing President Harrison recommended the annexation to the Senate, but his successor, President Cleveland, withdrew the proposal and recalled the United States minister. (Hawaii carried on under a Republican government until its annexation in 1898 on a more proper basis.)

William Jennings Bryan, Representative from Nebraska, became a significant national figure after his eloquent three-hour speech (Aug. 16) in Congress in defense of silver coinage.

The Columbian Exposition, celebrating the 400th anniversary of Columbus's discovery of America, was formally opened (May 1) in Chicago. The buildings had been dedicated the preceding year. In connection with the celebration, the U. S. Post Office placed (Jan. 2) on sale its first commemorative postage stamps. As in 1876, Theodore Thomas again conducted the concerts. A feature of the Exposition was a brilliant naval display in New York City, reviewed by President Cleveland, of war vessels representing the United States, Great Britain, Russia, France, Italy, Spain, Germany, Holland, Brazil, and the Argentine Republic. Out of courtesy, no foreign power sent any vessel, as one writer said (Nugent Robinson, "A History of the World," v. 2, p. 1586), "which would by comparison put to shame our own little navy, which then was without battleships." Norway's unique contribution, a Viking ship propelled by oars and a single sail and traditionally adorned with war shields along its sides, arrived too late and was exhibited in Chicago. The festivities were saddened (Oct. 28) by the assassination of the Mayor of Chicago, Carter H. Harrison, Sr., at his residence by a man who fired five shots from a revolver. The trial court refused to entertain the plea of insanity.

Eugene Victor Debs, Indiana-born railway worker and secretary of the Locomotive Firemen organization, formed the American Railway Union.

Twenty-five government employees were killed and many others were seriously injured in the collapse of Ford's Theatre, Washington, D. C., the building in which Lincoln was assassinated in 1865. The old structure was occupied by the Records Division of the War Department.

New York Central locomotive Engine No. 999, pulling four heavy cars (as the "Empire Express"), made 112½ miles per hour between Critten-den and Wende, N. Y., with Engineer C. Hogan at the throttle. New speeds were also developed by the U. S. Navy with the gunboat "Detroit," the commerce destroyer "Columbia," and the protected cruiser "New York"—all new vessels.

The Great Northern Railroad, connecting St. Paul, Minn., and the Northwest, was completed.

There were at this time 170,607 miles of railroad in the country.

The Lincoln Memorial House was formally opened (Oct. 17).

Various types of automobiles were being tested, among them Henry Ford's. The automobile of this period was usually a one-cylinder gasoline-driven wagon, resting on high wheels, with the engine placed under a seat for two persons. The vehicle was then called a motorcycle, and was capable of travelling seven or eight miles per hour.

Thomas Alva Edison built in West Orange, N. J., the first movie studio in America, "The Kinetographic Theatre." It was a weird, black structure, costing $637.37, and was popularly called "The Black Maria." At this studio, comedian Fred Ott, generally regarded as the first movie actor, recorded on film a man in the act of sneezing—"Fred Ott's Sneeze" be-came a classic phrase.

A cyclone swept (in Aug.) the Atlantic coast from Florida to New England, damaging coastwise shipping, destroying millions of dollars' worth of crops, and causing the loss of about a thousand lives. The greatest damage occurred in Savannah, Ga., where hundreds of buildings were wrecked.

Among new literary periodicals were "McClure's Magazine," a monthly (ceased publication in 1929), and "The Outlook," a weekly (ceased publi-cation in 1935), in New York.

Henry Blake Fuller published "The Cliff-Dwellers," a realistic novel about Chicago.

New operas heard for the first time in the United States were Camille Saint-Saëns's "Samson et Dalila" (New Orleans, French Opera House, Jan. 4; already sung in concert form by the New York Oratorio Society, Carnegie Hall, Mar. 25, 1892); Leoncavallo's "Pagliacci" (Philadelphia, Grand Opera House, June 15; New York, Metropolitan Opera House, Dec. 11, in Italian); Bizet's "Les Pêcheurs des Perles" (The Pearl Fishers) (Philadelphia, Grand Opera House, Aug. 25).

The Metropolitan Opera House, New York, damaged by fire (1892), reopened (Nov. 27) with a French performance of "Faust"—the same opera that had inaugurated the famous house ten years earlier (Oct. 23, 1883), when the work was sung in Italian. In fact, the opera was so frequently performed by the "Met" that the opera house was popularly called the "Faustspielhaus." Among notable debuts there this year were those of the world-famous French mezzo-soprano Emma Calvé in "Cavalleria Rusticana" (Nov. 29) and the Australian soprano Nellie Melba in "Lucia di Lammermoor" (Dec. 4). It was in this season that the Siamese twins of opera, "Pagliacci" and "Cavalleria Rusticana," were paired (Dec. 22— in that order) for the first time; Melba sang in the former, Calvé in the latter. Previously "Pagliacci" was performed with Gluck's "Orphée et Euridice" and "Cavalleria Rusticana" with Gounod's "Philémon et Baucis."

Alexandre Guilmant, noted French organist, concertized in the United States. (He made a second tour in 1897-98).

Horatio Parker's oratorio "Hora Novissima" had (May 3) its première in New York at the Church of Zion and St. Timothy by the Church Choral Society.

Anton Dvořák's Fifth Symphony, called "From the New World," received (Dec. 15) its world première in New York at Carnegie Hall. Anton Seidl conducted the Philharmonic Society in the presence of the composer. Dvořák was at this time artistic director of the National Conservatory in New York.

James A. Herne's Maine woods play "Shore Acres" established itself as one of the outstanding dramas of the American stage. Tried out for four weeks in Chicago (McVicker's Theatre, May-June, 1892), the revised version ran 113 performances in Boston (Boston Museum, beginning Feb., 1893) and made a modest start in New York (Fifth Avenue Theatre, Oct. 30). The great success of the play dates from its transference (Dec. 25) to Daly's Theatre. Herne himself played the principal role, an uncouth, ill-tempered, and domineering farmer. A real turkey dinner was eaten in the kitchen scene at each performance and aroused much comment.

Lionel Barrymore made his stage debut in Richard Brinsley Sheridan's (1775) comedy "The Rivals" in Philadelphia.

Eleonora Duse, great Italian tragedienne, made (Jan. 23) her American debut in "Camille" at Miner's Fifth Avenue Theatre in New York.

Charles Frohman, always importing London successes, produced (Oct. 2) the uproarious farce "Charley's Aunt" at the Standard Theatre, New York. Etienne Girardot, especially brought over for the part, played the disguised aunt from Brazil, "where the nuts come from." The comedy retained its fun through the years in many revivals and enjoyed even greater popularity in a musical version (1948) with Ray Bolger.

Oscar Hammerstein tried his hand at a one-act comic opera, writing both the book and the music, entitled "Koh-I-Noor"; it was put on (Oct. 30) in New York at Koster and Bial's Theatre.

Sandow, the strong man who permitted the ladies to feel his muscles, was a theatrical attraction at the Columbian Exposition. He was managed by a young man, the later famous "Flo" (Florenz) Ziegfeld, Jr.

The international yacht race for the America Cup was run for the first time in American waters off New York Harbor. The American "Vigilant" defeated the British "Valkyrie II" in all three races (Oct. 7, 9, 13), thus winning the coveted trophy for the ninth consecutive time since 1851.

T. Bowen and J. Burke, at New Orleans, fought the longest prize-fight in which gloves were used, on record—7 hours, 18 minutes, 10 seconds. It went 110 rounds and ended in a draw.

A panic and a two-year depression marked the seventeenth United States financial calamity since 1790.

૨જ 1894

Airy, Fairy Lillian. w., Tony Raymond. m., Maurice Levi. M. Witmark & Sons, cop. 1894.

And Her Golden Hair Was Hanging Down Her Back. w., Monroe H. Rosenfeld. m., Felix McGlennon. Leo Feist, Inc., cop. 1894.

La Cinquantaine. Air dans le style ancien. Instrumental piece. m., Gabriel Marie. G. Schirmer, cop. 1894 (arr. for violoncello and piano by Philip Mittell). (Published earlier, in various arrangements, in Paris.)

Comrades. w. m., Felix McGlennon. [Before 1894.] (This song of English origin was already widely popular in America by this date. It was reprinted in a collection, among others, entitled "Musical Gems, Vocal and Instrumental, compiled by Joseph E. Winner," p. 222-25, which was published by Monroe Book Co., Chicago, and copyrighted in 1895 by J. R. Jones.)

Forgotten. w., Flora Wulschner. m., Eugene Cowles. Boston: Oliver Ditson Co., cop. 1894.

Her Eyes Don't Shine Like Diamonds. w., m., Dave Marion. M. Witmark and Sons, cop. 1894.

His Last Thoughts Were of You. w., Edward B. Marks. m., Joseph W. Stern. Jos. W. Stern & Co., cop. 1894.

The Honeymoon March. w., George Rosey [pseud. of George M. Rosenberg]. Jos. W. Stern & Co., cop. 1894; renewed 1922 by G. M. Rosenberg; assigned 1923 to Edward B. Marks Music Co.

Humoresque (No. 7 in: Humoresken, op. 101). Piano solo. m., Anton Dvorák. Berlin: N. Simrock [1894].

I Don't Want to Play in Your Yard. w., Philip Wingate. m., H. W. Petrie. Chicago: Petrie Music Co., cop. 1894.

Kathleen. w., m., Helene Mora. Cop. 1894 by Helene Mora; assigned 1920 to Edward B. Marks Music Co.

The Little Lost Child. w., Edward B. Marks. m., Joseph W. Stern. Jos. W. Stern & Co., cop. 1894.

Lo, How a Rose E'er Blooming—*original German title:* Es ist ein' Ros' (Reis) entsprungen. Christmas carol for SATB. German words, anon. English words, Theodore Baker. m., traditional, arr. by Michael Praetorius (1571-1621). G. Schirmer, cop. 1894; renewed 1923; assigned 1923 to G. Schirmer, Inc. (The German words first appeared in "Alte Katholische Geistliche Kirchengesang," Cologne, 1599. The harmonization by Praetorius was published in the section of his "Musae Sionae" printed in 1609. Probably the earliest English translation is that of Catherine Winkworth, "A spotless rose is blooming," 1869. It was followed by those of Mrs. Harriett Reynolds Spaeth, née Krauth, "Behold a branch is growing," 1875, and of G. R. Woodward "The noble stem of Jesse," 1897. Novello & Co., London, published a translation, "From Jesse's stock upspringing," by M. E. Butler. The carol made its way slowly into English-language hymnals.)

Long Ago in Alcala (Mirette). w., F[rederick] E[dward] Weatherly and Adrian Ross. m., André Meassager. London: Chappell & Co. [1894.] ("Mirette" was a comic opera, produced at the Savoy Theatre, London, 1894. The song was afterwards introduced in the English version of the composer's comic opera "The Little Michus," performed in London, 1897.)

My Friend, the Major. w., m., E. W. Rogers. T. B. Harms & Co., cop. 1894.

My Pearl's a Bowery Girl! w., William Jerome. m., Andrew Mack. T. B. Harms & Co., cop. 1894.

Once Ev'ry Year. w., m., Paul Dresser. Howley, Haviland & Co., cop. 1894.

Only a Bowery Boy. w., Charles B. Ward. m., Gussie L. Davis. The New York Music Co., cop. 1894.

Only Me. w., Walter H. Ford. m., John W. Bratton. M. Witmark & Sons, cop. 1894.

Prayer of Thanksgiving. See 1879; "Dankgebet."

Saved by Grace. Hymn. w., Frances Jane Crosby [Mrs. Alexander Van Alstyne]. m., George C[oles] Stebbins. The Biglow & Main Co., cop. 1894.

She May Have Seen Better Days. w., m., James Thornton. T. B. Harms & Co., cop. 1894.

The Sidewalks of New York. w., m., Charles B. Lawlor and James W. Blake. Howley, Haviland & Co., cop. 1894.

Sweet Bunch of Daisies. w., m., Anita Owen. Jerome H. Remick & Co., cop. 1894 by Anita Owen.

Take a Seat, Old Lady. w., m., Paul Dresser. Howley, Haviland & Co., cop. 1894.

Would God I Were a Tender Apple Blossom. w., Katherine Hinkson (née Tyman). m., traditional Irish air. London: T. F. Unwin [1894] (in: Alfred Perceval Graves, "The Irish Song Book," p. 141).

You Can't Play in Our Yard Any More. w., Philip Wingate. m., H. W. Petrie. St. Louis: Thiebes Stierlin Music Co., cop. 1894 by Bollman-Drumheller Music Co.

The United States recognized the newly established Republic of Hawaii (1893).

Congress designated the first Monday in September as Labor Day.

The Bureau of Engraving and Printing of the Treasury Department took over (July 1) from private manufacturers the printing of United States postage stamps.

During the insurrection in Brazil, Admiral Andrew Ellicott Kennedy Benham, U.S.N., fired in Rio de Janeiro harbor on a rebel war vessel which attempted to prevent American cargo ships from entering the port. The act hastened the end of the rebellion.

Admiral Henry Erben and Captain Alfred Thayer Mahan (1890) of the U. S. European fleet were tendered an elaborate banquet in London.

The last of the noted war vessels of the Civil War, the "Kearsarge," foundered on a reef in the Caribbean Sea and was wrecked by pounding breakers after thirty years of service.

The United States government was compelled twice this year to borrow money, each time $50,000,000 in gold—an indication of the political and labor unrest in the country.

The financial depression that started in 1893 created so much unemployment throughout the United States that one Jacob Sechler Coxey, a Massillon, O., owner of sand quarries and a racing stable, organized an "army"—without weapons—of some 500-odd laborers, one of several "Industrial Armies," and marched with his followers to Washington to present "a petition in boots" to Congress for relief legislation. The marchers were supplied with sustenance along the route by hospitable persons and communities, often to get rid of them. Coxey himself rode in a buggy drawn by his $40,000 pacer "Acolyte," while his second-in-command, Carl Browne, sat astride Coxey's $7,500 stallion. The famous march at first alarmed the country, but it soon became an object of ridicule. In Washington, a mild demonstration took place (Apr. 29) on the steps of the Capitol. Coxey and other leaders were arrested by the police for walking on the grass and spent 20 days in jail for the offense. Coxey at the time had been nominated for Congress by an Ohio district, but he was defeated in the fall elections. (Coxey led a second "army" to Washington in 1944. He died May 18, 1951, at the age of 97, in Massillon, O.)

More serious than Coxey's demonstration were the numerous strikes and lockouts in the country. Particularly widespread was the strike for higher wages of 150,000 coal miners in Pennsylvania, Ohio, Indiana, Illinois, and Michigan.

Of national scope was the strike which originated (in the last week of June) in the workshops of the Pullman Car Company, near Chicago, and involved nearly every railroad between the Mississippi and the Pacific. When the movement of the mails was hindered, government troops were ordered (July 2) by President Cleveland into the disrupted areas, particularly in Chicago and Sacramento, after the Federal courts had enjoined the strikers. Illinois Governor John Peter Altgeld (1886) called out the state militia. Eugene Victor Debs, president of the American Railway Union (1893) who had declared the strike, and his associates were arrested on writs of indictment by the United States courts. They were released on bail, and Debs found himself a national figure. Federal troops were withdrawn (July 19), and peace was restored (Aug. 5) when the union called off the strike. The Illinois militia was recalled two days later (Aug. 7). Much property damage resulted from the conflict, partly due to uncontrollable strikers and partly to lawless elements outside the labor ranks. Debs and other union members were fined for interfering with the transit of the mails.

At Cramps Docks was launched (Nov. 12) for the American Line one of the fastest transatlantic steamships—the two-funnelled "St. Louis," 554 feet long, 11,000 tons, and 20,000 horsepower. The boat sailed between New York and Liverpool, England.

The American Academy in Rome was founded. (Chartered in 1905 by Congress.)

The Field Museum of Natural History was established in Chicago by a gift of $1,000,000 from Marshall Field. (On his death in 1906, he bequeathed the institution $4,000,000 for the erection of a permanent building and $4,000,000 for endowment.)

The world's largest meteorite, weighing 37½ tons and called the Ahnighito (The Tent), was found by Lieutenant Robert Edwin Peary, later discoverer of the North Pole, near Melville Bay in northern Greenland. (It was placed on permanent exhibition under the arch to the entrance of the Museum of Natural History, New York.)

Thomas Alva Edison publicly exhibited (Apr. 14) in New York on Broadway his motion-picture machine, the kinetoscope.

The California Mid-Winter Exposition was held (Jan. 1-July 4) in San Francisco.

An unprofitable investment of $200,000 brought Mark Twain's publishing firm Charles L. Webster and Company, Hartford, Conn., into bankruptcy. To recoup his losses, Mark Twain went on a lecture tour of the world. (He published his experiences in "Following the Equator," 1897.)

Books of the year included Mark Twain's stories "The Tragedy of Pudd'nhead Wilson" and "Tom Sawyer Abroad, by Huck Finn, edited by Mark Twain," the novels "The Honorable Peter Sterling" (Paul Leicester Ford; a story about a "practical idealist," supposedly Grover Cleveland) and "Katherine Lauderdale" (Francis Marion Crawford; its sequel "The Ralstons" followed in 1895), and Henry Demarest Lloyd's trenchant study "Wealth against Commonwealth."

The "New York World" began the publication of the first colored comic serial—"Hogan's Alley," by R. F. Outcault, which picturized the exploits of the "bad boy" hero, the Yellow Kid.

"The Billboard" was founded in Cincinnati as a theatrical weekly journal.

Walter Damrosch conducted (Mar. 16) the first American performance of Tchaikovsky's Sixth Symphony in New York with his Symphony Society. At the same concert, Victor Herbert played his own Second Violoncello Concerto.

Eugène Ysaye, world-renowned Belgian violin virtuoso, made (Nov. 16) his American debut in a remarkable performance of Beethoven's Violin Concerto with the New York Philharmonic Society.

Massenet's opera "Werther" was performed in Chicago at the Auditorium (Mar. 29), in New York at the Metropolitan Opera House (Apr. 19), and in New Orleans at the French Opera House (Nov. 3).

Forsaking serious music for light opera, Victor Herbert produced his first venture in that field—"Prince Ananias," performed (Nov. 20) in New York at the Broadway Theatre by The Bostonians and starring Henry Clay Barnabee. It was not successful.

The enterprising Kinetoscope Exhibition Company in Nassau Street, New York, found a new way of making money with the latest (screenless) moving-picture mechanism by showing in separate machines each of the six rounds of a prize fight between Michael Leonard, "Beau Brummell of the prize ring," and Jack Cushing. The so-called fight was staged and photographed in Edison's "Black Maria" studio (1893) in West Orange, N. J. Only six of the ten photographed rounds were exhibited. Public interest in this early form of movies led in the same year to the photographing of a similar boxing match between the heavyweight champion James J. ("Gentleman Jim") Corbett and Pete Courtney of Trenton, N. J.

"Arms and the Man" was the first George Bernard Shaw play to be performed in the United States. The play, which was later turned into the operetta "The Chocolate Soldier" (1909), was produced and acted (Sept. 17) by Richard Mansfield at the Herald Square Theatre, New York.

Fifteen-year-old Ethel Barrymore made her stage debut in Montreal, Can., in Richard Brinsley Sheridan's (1775) comedy "The Rivals," the same play in which her brother Lionel had made his first bow the preceding year. Subsequently she appeared in New York at the Empire Theatre.

"Streamlining" the chorus was a theatrical innovation when George Edwardes transferred (Sept. 18) from the Gaiety Theatre, London, to Daly's Theatre, New York, his bevy of chorines in "A Gaiety Girl," replacing the statuesque, padded Lydia Thompson blondes of 1868 with more slender types of beauty. Soon there were to be the Florodora Girls, the Follies Girls, the Nell Brinkley Bathing Beauties, and others, leading ultimately to the "tall-stemmed roses" of Billy Rose.

Another New York theatrical innovation was the beginning of a type of show that developed into the American revue—"The Passing Show," staged (May 12) with an abundance of talent at the Casino Theatre. "Jeff" (Jefferson) de Angelis headed the cast.

Willard Spenser's new operetta "The Princess Bonnie" started (Mar. 26) its long career in Philadelphia at the Chestnut Street Theatre. Through the years it was performed more than 3,000 times.

ɞ⤳ 1895

The Afternoon of a Faun—*original French title:* Prélude à "L'Après-midi d'un Faune." Symphonic poem. m., Claude Debussy. Paris: Eugène Fromont [1895].

"Algy," the Piccadilly Johnny with the Little Glass Eye. w., m., Harry B. Morris. T. B. Harms & Co., cop. 1895 by Francis, Day & Hunter.

America, the Beautiful. w., Katherine Lee Bates. m., tune: "Materna,"
by Samuel Augustus Ward. (The words were first published in the weekly
periodical "The Congregationalist," Boston, July 4, 1895. The tune
"Materna," set to the words "O Mother Dear, Jerusalem," appeared in
"The Parish Choir," Boston, July 12, 1888.)

The Band Played On. w., John E. Palmer. m., Charles B. Ward. The
New York Music Co., cop. 1895.

The Belle of Avenoo A. w., m., Safford Waters. Howley, Haviland &
Co., cop. 1895.

By the Sad Sea Waves. w., Lester Barrett. m., Lester Thomas. T. B.
Harms & Co., cop. 1895 by Francis, Day & Hunter.

Don't Go Out To-night, Boy. w., George Cooper. m., Charles E.
Pratt. M. Witmark & Sons, cop. 1895.

Down in Poverty Row. w., Gussie L. Davis. m., Arthur Trevelyan.
Jos. W. Stern & Co., cop. 1895.

A Dream. w., Charles B. Cory. m., J. C. Bartlett. Boston: Oliver Ditson Co., cop. 1895.

The Hand That Rocks the Cradle. w., Charles W. Berkeley. m.,
William H. Holmes. Willis Woodward & Co., cop. 1895.

The Handicap. March. m., George Rosey [pseud. of George M. Rosen-
berg]. Jos. W. Stern & Co., cop. 1895; assigned 1920 to Edward B. Marks
Music Co.; assigned 1932 to Edward B. Marks Music Corp. (Published
as a song with words by Dave Reed Jr., cop. 1923.)

I Was Looking for My Boy, She Said; or, Decoration Day. w., m., Paul
Dresser. Howley, Haviland & Co., cop. 1895.

Jean. w., m., Paul Dresser. Howley, Haviland & Co., cop. 1895.

Just Tell Them That You Saw Me. w., m., Paul Dresser. Howley,
Haviland & Co., cop. 1895.

King Cotton. March. m., John Philip Sousa. Cincinnati: The John
Church Co., cop. 1895.

My Angeline (The Wizard of the Nile). w., Harry B. Smith. m., Victor
Herbert. Edward Schuberth & Co., cop. 1895.

My Best Girl's a New-Yorker [Corker]. w., m., John Stromberg. Jos. W. Stern & Co., cop. 1895.

Only One Girl in the World for Me. w., m., Dave Marion. M. Witmark & Sons, cop. 1895.

Put Me Off at Buffalo. w., Harry Dillon. m., John Dillon. M. Witmark & Sons, cop. 1895.

Rastus on Parade. Two step march. m., Kerry Mills. F. A. Mills, cop. 1895.

The Same Sweet Girl To-day. w., m., Dan W. Quinn. Howley, Haviland & Co., cop. 1895.

The Singer in the Gallery. w., m., Harry A. Mayo. M. Witmark & Sons, cop. 1895.

The Streets of Cairo. w., m., James Thornton. Frank Harding, cop. 1895. (The music of the verse is the hootchy-kootchy tune.)

The Sunshine of Paradise Alley. w., Walter H. Ford. m., John W. Bratton. M. Witmark & Sons, cop. 1895.

There'll Come a Time. w., m., Charles K. Harris. Chas. K. Harris, cop. 1895.

Till Eulenspiegel—*original German title:* Till Eulenspiegels lustige Streiche. Symphonic poem. m., Richard Strauss, op. 28. Munich: Jos. Aibl, cop. 1895.

We Were Sweethearts for Many Years. w., m., Paul Dresser. Howley, Haviland & Co., cop. 1895.

When Your Love Grows Cold. w., m., Charles Miller. Howley, Haviland & Co., cop. 1895.

Zenda Waltzes. Piano solo. m., Frank M. Witmark. M. Witmark & Sons, cop. 1895.

Congress passed an income tax law, which was declared unconstitutional by the U. S. Supreme Court.

A territorial dispute between Venezuela and Great Britain over the former's boundary with British Guiana involved the United States on the basis of the Monroe Doctrine (1823). President Cleveland's firm stand won him the support of Congress and the American press, but it alarmed those who realized the inadequacy of the U. S. army and navy and the defenseless character of the country's coast and those who feared a war with Great Britain, a subject given much prominence in the European press. (A Commission was appointed Jan. 1, 1896, and a satisfactory treaty was signed Feb. 2, 1897.)

The U. S. Post Office established rural free delivery.

The manufacture of automobiles became a regular industry in the United States. George Baldwin Seldon patented a gasoline-driven automobile. So keen was the interest in the speeds developed by the various types of automobiles that Herman Kohlsaat, a Chicago newspaper owner, sponsored an endurance contest. Six contestants participated in the event over a 53½-mile course. The Duryea Wagon Motor Company won the race in 10 hours, 23 minutes.

A serious trolley car strike inconvenienced Brooklynites for four weeks. The militia was brought out to maintain order. Other labor strikes occurred elsewhere throughout the year.

Amateur pianists became parlor virtuosi when the automatic player-piano came upon the market. (Among the earliest forms of the mechanism were the angelus, autopiano, pianolo, ampico, and others.)

The Cotton States and Industrial Exposition was held (Sept. 15-Dec. 31) in Atlanta, Ga.

Chiropractic was put into practice by D. D. Palmer.

The Carnegie Institute was founded in Pittsburgh.

William Randolph Hearst, already owner of the "San Francisco Journal," now acquired the "New York Journal," thereby establishing his newspaper chain.

William Allen White purchased the "Emporia, Kan., Gazette" and quickly became one of the nation's leading independent editors.

Elbert Hubbard began issuing from his Roycroft Press in East Aurora, near Buffalo, N. Y., his small-sized, oddly printed inspirational magazine "The Philistine." (Ceased publication in 1915.)

Gelett Burgess's famous quatrain "The Purple Cow" appeared in his magazine "The Lark." (He also invented the Goops, circle-faced children who did naughty and ill-mannered things, and words such as "bromide," a person who utters platitudes and "blurb.")

Among new periodicals in New York were "The Bookman" (ceased publication in 1933), a monthly devoted to literature and criticism, and "The Musical Courier," as a weekly journal of the musical profession.

The New York Metropolitan Opera House produced (Feb. 4) the American première of Verdi's "Falstaff."

The Castle Square Opera Company was organized in Boston by Henry Wilson Savage, taking its name from the theatre which he owned. (Its success led in 1900 to the formation of the more ambitious Henry W. Savage Opera Company.)

Humperdinck's fairy-tale opera "Hänsel und Gretel" was produced (Oct. 8) for the first time in the United States in New York at Daly's Theatre in English.

Theodore Thomas conducted (Nov. 15) with his Chicago Orchestra the first American rendition of Richard Strauss's symphonic poem "Till Eulenspiegel's Merry Pranks."

Actor-manager Richard Mansfield acquired Harrigan's 35th Street Theatre, New York, which he renamed the Garrick, and introduced an innovation by furnishing it with a basement lounge and a Pompeiian Room where coffee, tea, and ices were served.

Mrs. Leslie Carter was the star of David Belasco's hit play "The Heart of Maryland," performed (Oct. 22) in New York at the Herald Square Theatre. The Civil War melodrama established Mrs. Carter as a leading actress and Belasco as a playwright.

The famous French actress Mme. Réjane (Gabrielle Réju) made (Feb. 27) her American debut in "Mme. Sans Gene," written for her by Victorien Sardou and Emile Moreau, in New York at Abbey's Theatre.

Dramatizations of two recent (1894) English novels, "Trilby" and "The Prisoner of Zenda," were successes on the New York stage. "Trilby," adapted from George DuMaurier and staged (Apr. 15) at the Garden Theatre with Wilton Lackaye (Svengali) and Virginia Harned (Trilby), started a wild craze across the country. As the reminiscing Amelia Ransome Neville wrote ("The Fantastic City," Boston, 1932, p. 254): "The Trilby craze was terrific. We wore Trilby hats, Trilby coats, Trilby slippers, and what not; ate Trilby chocolates, played Trilby waltzes, and developed a 'Trilby type' in beauty." "The Prisoner of Zenda," derived from Anthony Hope (Hawkins) and produced (Sept. 4) at the Lyceum Theatre, provided Edward Hugh Sothern with a new romantic role.

Victor Herbert's first collaboration with librettist Harry Bache Smith produced the successful comic opera "The Wizard of the Nile" with Frank Daniels in the cast (Detroit, Opera House, Oct. 14; New York, Casino Theatre, Oct. 20, and elsewhere on tour; given in Vienna, Carl Theater, Sept. 26, 1896, and in London, Shaftesbury Theatre, Sept. 1897).

Olga Nethersole acted (Dec. 24) the American première of Prosper Mérimée's own dramatization of "Carmen" in New York at the Empire Theatre in English.

A prize fight between Young Griffo and Battling Barnett on the roof of Madison Square Garden, New York, was filmed and publicly exhibited (May 20) on a screen by a projecting machine invented in the preceding year by Woodville Latham.

In Newport, R. I., the first open golf championship match ever held in the United States took place and was won by Horace Rawlins, with a card showing 173 strokes for 36 holes. At the same time, the first championship for women was held at Meadowbrook, L. I., the victor being Mrs. C. S. Brown, who carded 132 strokes for 18 holes. During this year the number of United States golf clubs increased from about 40 to 100.

⧽⋍ 1896

All Coons Look Alike to Me. w., m., Ernest Hogan. M. Witmark & Sons, cop. 1896.

The Amorous Goldfish (The Geisha). w., Harry Greenbank. m., Sidney Jones. London: Ascherberg, Hopwood & Crew, Ltd., cop. 1898 by Hopwood & Crew.

Beloved, It Is Morn. w., Emily Hickey. m., Florence Aylward. London: Chappell & Co., Ltd., cop. 1896.

El Capitan. March. m., John Philip Sousa. Cincinnati: The John Church Co., cop. 1896.

Chin, Chin, Chinaman (The Geisha). w., Harry Greenbank. m., Sidney Jones. London: Ascherberg, Hopwood & Crew, Ltd., cop. 1896 by Hopwood & Crew.

Chon Kina (The Geisha). w., Harry Greenbank. m., Sidney Jones. London: Ascherberg, Hopwood & Crew, Ltd., cop. 1896 by Hopwood & Crew.

Don't Give Up the Old Love for the New. w., m., James Thornton. Jos. W. Stern & Co., cop. 1896.

Don't Tell Her That You Love Her. w., m., Paul Dresser. Howley, Haviland & Co., cop. 1896.

A Dream of My Boyhood Days. w., m., Paul Dresser. Howley, Haviland & Co., cop. 1896.

Elsie from Chelsea. w., m., Harry Dacre. Jos. W. Stern & Co., cop. 1896 by Frank Dean & Co., London.

Going for a Pardon. w., James Thornton and Clara Hauenschild. m., James Thornton. Jos. W. Stern & Co., cop. 1896.

Happy Days in Dixie. Two step march. m., Kerry Mills. F. A. Mills, cop. 1896.

He Brought Home Another. w., m., Paul Dresser. Howley, Haviland & Co., cop. 1896.

He Fought for a Cause He Thought Was Right. w., m., Paul Dresser. Howley, Haviland & Co., cop. 1896.

A Hot Time in the Old Town. w., Joe Hayden. m., Theodore M. Metz. Willis Woodward & Co., cop. 1896; renewed 1924 by Theo. A. Metz; assigned 1924 to Edward B. Marks Music Co.; assigned 1932 to Edward B. Marks Music Corp.

I Can't Think ob Nuthin' Else but You. w., m., Harry Dacre. Jos W. Stern & Co., cop. 1896 by Frank Dean & Co., London.

I Love You in the Same Old Way—Darling Sue. w., Walter H. Ford. m., John W. Bratton. M. Witmark & Sons, cop. 1896.

I Wish That You Were Here To-night. w., m., Paul Dresser. Howley, Haviland & Co., cop. 1896.

I Wonder if She'll Ever Come Back to Me. w., m., Paul Dresser. Howley, Haviland & Co., cop. 1896.

In a Persian Garden. Song cycle for four solo mixed voices with piano acc. w., Edward Fitzgerald, translated from the "Rubáiyát" of Omar Khayyám. m., Liza Lehmann. London: Metzler & Co., Ltd., cop. 1896. (First performed in private, at the residence of Mrs. E. L. Goetz, in London, 1896, by Mme. Albani, Miss Hilda Wilson, and Messrs. Ben Davies and David Bispham; in public, at the Monday Popular Concerts, St. James's Hall, Dec. 14, 1896.)

In the Baggage Coach Ahead. w., m., Gussie L. Davis. Howley, Haviland & Co., cop. 1896.

I'se Your Nigger if You Wants Me, Liza Jane. w., m., Paul Dresser. Howley, Haviland & Co., cop. 1896.

The Jewel of Asia (The Geisha). w., Harry Greenbank. m., James Philp. London: Ascherberg, Hopwood & Crew, Ltd., cop. 1896 by Hopwood & Crew by arrangement with Willcocks & Co., Ltd., London.

Kentucky Babe. w., Richard Buck. m., Adam Geibel. Boston: White-Smith Music Pub. Co., cop. 1896.

Laugh and the World Laughs with You. w., Ella Wheeler Wilcox. m., L[ouis] F. Gottschalk. M. Witmark & Sons, cop. 1896.

Love Makes the World Go 'Round (*introduced in:* Bohemia). w., Clyde Fitch. m., arr. by William Furst. Howley, Haviland & Co., cop. 1896.

Lucky Jim. w., Charles Horwitz. m., Frederick V. Bowers. M. Witmark & Sons, cop. 1896.

Mister Johnson, Turn Me Loose. w., m., Ben R. Harney. M. Witmark & Sons, cop. 1896 by Frank Harding; cop. 1896 by M. Witmark & Sons.

Mother Was a Lady, or, If Jack Were Only Here. w., Edward B. Marks. m., Joseph W. Stern. Jos. W. Stern & Co., cop. 1896.

My Gal Is a High Born Lady. w., m., Barney Fagan. Arr. by Gustave Luders. M. Witmark & Sons, cop. 1896.

No One Ever Loved You More Than I. w., Edward B. Marks. m., Joseph W. Stern. Jos. W. Stern & Co., cop. 1896.

On the Benches in the Park. w., m., James Thornton. Jos. W. Stern & Co., cop. 1896.

Rustle of Spring—*original German title:* Frühlingsrauschen (No. 3 in: Sechs Stücke, op. 32). Piano solo. m., Christian Sinding. Leipzig: C. F. Peters, cop. 1896.

Show Me the Way. Sacred Song. w., m., Paul Dresser. Howley, Haviland & Co., cop. 1896.

Sweet Rosie O'Grady. w., m., Maud Nugent. Jos. W. Stern & Co., cop. 1896.

The Toy Monkey (The Geisha). w., Harry Greenbank. m., Lionel Monckton. London: Ascherberg, Hopwood & Crew, cop. 1896 by Hopwood & Crew.

Whisper Your Mother's Name. w., Harry Braisted. m., Stanley Carter. Jos. W. Stern & Co., cop. 1896.

Won't You Be My Little Girl. w., Isaac G. Reynolds. m., Homer Tourjee. Jos. W. Stern & Co., cop. 1896 by The Homer Tourjee Pub. Co.

Woodland Sketches—(1) **To a Wild Rose;** (2) **Will o' the Wisp;** (3) **At an Old Trysting Place;** (4) **In Autumn;** (5) **From an Indian Lodge;** (6) **To a Water Lily;** (7) **From Uncle Remus;** (8) **A Deserted Farm;** (9) **By a Meadow Brook;** (10) **Told at Sunset.** Piano solo. m., Edward MacDowell, op. 51. P. L. Jung, cop. 1896.

You're de Apple of My Eye. w., George H. Emerick. m., Herbert Dillea. Jos. W. Stern & Co., cop. 1896.

You're Not the Only Pebble on the Beach. w., Harry Braisted. m., Stanley Carter. Jos. W. Stern & Co., cop. 1896.

Utah was admitted (Jan. 4) as the 32nd State.

The discovery of gold in Alaska and the Yukon territory of northwestern Canada started the Klondike gold rush (1897-99).

The first American subway was built in Boston.

Emile Berliner, German-American inventor, patented the disk phonograph and record.

The first commercial automobile in Detroit appeared (Mar. 6) on its streets.

Man's attempts to fly, dating from the mythical times of Daedalus and Icarus, were being slowly realized scientifically. Otto Lilienthal, a German engineer, had been experimenting for five years (since 1891) in flights with a glider plane near Berlin. In the United States this year, Octave Chanute, assisted by Herring and Avery, carried out (in June) several successful flights in a glider over the sand dunes of northern Indiana.

The Volunteers of America was founded (Nov. 6) in New York as a religious and philanthropic organization.

The College of New Jersey, founded in 1746, was renamed Princeton University after the town of its location.

William Ashley ("Billy") Sunday, professional baseball player (1883-90) and assistant secretary at the Y.M.C.A. in Chicago (1891-95), embarked on his career as an earnest but theatrical evangelist.

R. F. Outcault, whose newspaper series of comic pictures "Hogan's Alley" had been appearing in the "New York World" since 1894, joined the staff of William Randolph Hearst's "Journal" and both papers printed "Yellow Kid" serials which originated the term "yellow press."

Books of the year included Mark Twain's "Personal Recollections of Joan of Arc" (a fictional biography purportedly written by "The Sieur Louis de Conte"), Negro poet Paul Lawrence Dunbar's "Lyrics of Lowly Life," John Kendrick Bangs's farcical stories "The Houseboat on the Styx," and the fiction "The Damnation of Theron Ware" (Harold Frederic), "In His Steps" (Charles Monroe Shelden; translated into 23 languages), "The Little Regiment" (Stephen Crane), and "The Story of the Other Wise Man" (Henry Van Dyck). William Gilbert Patten began the publication of the first of his 200-odd "Frank Merriwell" tales.

"The Musician" was founded in Philadelphia as a monthly magazine. (It was bought in 1904 by Ditson Company, of Boston.)

The American Guild of Organists ("A.G.O.") was formed in New York.

New York's Academy of Music produced (Nov. 13) the American première of Giordano's opera "Andrea Chénier."

Walter Damrosch's first American opera "The Scarlet Letter," with a libretto based on Hawthorne's story by Damrosch's son-in-law, George Parsons Lathrop, was performed (Feb. 10) in Boston at the Boston Theatre and repeated (Mar. 6) in New York at the Academy of Music.

Bandmaster John Philip Sousa scored his first real success as a composer of operettas with "El Capitan" (Boston, Tremont Theatre, Apr. 13; New York, Broadway Theatre, Apr. 20, and elsewhere in the United States; performed in London, Lyric Theatre, July 10, 1899, and in Paris).

Augustin Daly opened Daly's Theatre in London and achieved (Apr. 25) a brilliant success with Sidney Jones's operetta "The Geisha." During its run of 760 performances there with Marie Tempest, he brought out (Sept. 9) the tuneful work in New York at his Fifth Avenue Theatre with equal acclaim. One of the dancers during the latter part of the New York run was the still-unknown Isadora Duncan, who had not yet discovered interpretative Greek dancing.

Anna Held made (Sept. 21) her American debut in "A Parlor Match" in New York at the Herald Square Theatre.

Comedians "short" Joe Weber and "long" Lew Fields opened (Sept. 5) Weber and Fields Music Hall in New York.

"The Village Postmaster," which enjoyed revivals in later years, was seen (Apr. 13) in New York at the 14th Street Theatre.

Vaudeville theatres now began to show motion pictures, but the whole thing was still more novelty than reality.

Peep-shows, penny arcades, and nickelodeons were showing a film version of the latest stage success, "The Widow Jones," both of which starred a matronly-looking May Irwin and a fatherly-looking John C. Rice. In the film, they indulged in a protracted kiss. It was assailed as "a lyric of the stockyards" by a section of the clergy. Needless to say, the film drew capacity crowds. Another shocker was the action short of "The Empire State Express," which rushed full speed toward the audience. So realistic was the effect that it is said spectators in the front rows jumped up to get out of its way. And to placate patrons who shied at the darkness in motion-picture houses, T. L. Tally erected in the lighted area of his new Phonograph and Vitascope Parlor in Los Angeles a partition through which to view the screen.

William Jennings Bryan delivered his "cross-of-gold" speech, outlining his silver money policy, at the Democratic national convention in Chicago, and was nominated the party's presidential candidate although he was only 36 years old. In the national elections, which were bitterly fought, he was defeated by the Republican opponent William McKinley, who favored the gold standard and high protective tariff. (Bryan ran unsuccessfully in 1900 and in 1908.)

Agitation for free coinage of silver created a depression which lasted a year—the eighteenth since 1790.

Frederick Nicholls Crouch, aged 88, London-born composer of "Kathleen Mavourneen," died (Aug. 18) in Portland, Me.

8~ 1897

Asleep in the Deep. w., Arthur J. Lamb. m., H. W. Petri. F. A. Mills, cop. 1897 by Julie C. Petri.

At a Georgia Camp Meeting. Two-step march. m., Kerry Mills. F. A. Mills, cop. 1897. (Published as a song: F. A. Mills, cop. 1899.)

Badinage. Orch. composition, arr. by Otto Langey. m., Victor Herbert. Edward Schuberth & Co., cop. 1897 (arr. for piano solo by Alexandre Rihm, do., cop. 1895).

Beautiful Isle of Somewhere. w., Mrs. Jessie Brown Pounds. m., John S. Fearis. Chicago: E. O. Excell, cop. 1897.

Break the News to Mother. w., m., Charles K. Harris. Chas. K. Harris, cop., 1897.

Cupid and I (The Serenade). w., Harry B. Smith. m., Victor Herbert. Edward Schuberth & Co., cop. 1897.

Danny Deever. w., Rudyard Kipling. m., Walter Damrosch, op. 2, No. 7. Cincinnati: The John Church Co., cop. 1897.

Face to Face. w., m., Herbert Johnson. Boston: the Waldo Music Co., cop. 1897 by Herbert Johnson; assigned to The Waldo Music Co.

If You See My Sweetheart. w., m., Paul Dresser. Howley, Haviland & Co., cop. 1897.

I've Just Come Back to Say Good-bye. w., m., Charles K. Harris. Chas. K. Harris, cop. 1897.

Just for the Sake of Our Daughter. w., m., Monroe H. Rosenfeld. Jos. W. Stern & Co., cop. 1897; assigned to Edward B. Marks Music Co.

The Lord Is My Light. w., Biblical. m., Frances Allitsen. London: Boosey & Co., cop. 1897.

Let Bygones Be Bygones. w., Charles Shackford. m., Kerry Mills. F. A. Mills, cop. 1897.

Mammy's Little Pumpkin Colored Coons (*introduced in:* The Good Mr. Best). w., m., Hillman and Perrin. M. Witmark & Sons, cop. 1897. (See below.)

On the Banks of the Wabash Far Away. w., m., Paul Dresser. Howley, Haviland & Co., cop. 1897; renewed 1925.

The Sorcerer's Apprentice—*original French title:* L'Apprenti Sorcier. Symphonic poem. m., Paul Dukas. Paris: Durand et Fils [1897].

The Stars and Stripes Forever. March. m., John Philip Sousa. Cincinnati: The John Church Co., cop. 1897.

Take Back Your Gold. w., Louis W. Pritzkow. m., Monroe H. Rosenfeld. Jos. W. Stern & Co., cop. 1897.

There's a Little Star Shining for You. w., m., James Thornton. Jos. W. Stern & Co., cop. 1897.

Wedding of the Winds. Waltz. m., John T. Hall. John T. Hall Pub. Co., cop. 1897.

You're Goin Far Away, Lad; or, I'm Still Your Mother, Dear. w., m., Paul Dresser, Howley, Haviland & Co., cop. 1897.

William McKinley, Republican, of Ohio, was inaugurated 25th President.

The Klondike gold rush began (July 1).

Steam-powered elevated railway trains started running (Oct. 19; electric power was substituted July 27, 1898) in a circuit around the business center of Chicago; thereafter that part of the city was called "The Loop."

The Library of Congress was transferred from the Capitol to a building of its own that was erected at a cost of $6,347,000.

The remains of Gen. Ulysses Simpson Grant, 18th President of the United States, were removed from a temporary vault on Riverside Drive, New York, on the bank of the Hudson River, and interred (Apr. 27) with an impressive all-day ceremony in a large vault erected on the site. The Tomb was built by popular subscription; 90,000 citizens contributed $600,000 of the cost, no person being permitted to subscribe more than $5,000.

Books of the year included Mark Twain's travel account "Following the Equator," John Luther Long's story "Madame Butterfly," and the novels, "The Choir Invisible" (James Lane Allen; published in 1893 under the title "John Gray"), "Hugh Wynne, Free Quaker" (Silas Weir Mitchell), "Soldiers of Fortune" (Richard Harding Davis), "What Maisie Knew" (Henry James), and "Wolfville" (Alfred Henry Lewis; the first of his six "Old Cattleman's" tales, published under the pseudonym Dan Quin).

"The Jewish Daily Forward" was founded in New York as a Yiddish newspaper.

"There is a Santa Claus," declared the "New York Sun" in its editoria. (Sept. 21), "Is There a Santa Claus," in response to a letter from eight-year-old Virginia, daughter of Dr. and Mrs. Philip F. O'Hanlon of New York. The famous editorial was written by associate editor Francis Pharcellus Church.

Los Angeles, Cal., heard (Oct. 14) the American première of Puccini's opera "La Bohème." It was performed at the Los Angeles Theatre by the Del Conti Company. The performances were unauthorized.

Theodore Thomas conducted (Feb. 5) his Chicago Orchestra in the first American performance of Richard Strauss's great tone poem "Also sprach Zarathustra."

The Boston Symphony Orchestra played (Apr. 17) the first American rendition of Rimsky-Korsakoff's symphonic suite "Scheherazade."

Walter Damrosch organized the Damrosch-Ellis Opera Company which gave (1897-98) performances on tour in many cities. The company included the sopranos Melba, Nordica, and Gadski.

John J. McNally's musical farce "The Good Mr. Best" featured (Aug. 3) in its third act the new "cinematograph" in New York at the Garrick Theatre.

Maude Kiskadden Adams made (Sept. 27) her stellar debut as Lady Babbie in James Matthew Barrie's play "The Little Minister" in New York at the Empire Theatre.

Richard Mansfield produced and acted (Oct. 4) George Bernard Shaw's play "The Devil's Disciple" at the Fifth Avenue Theatre in New York.

Importations from the Gaiety Theatre, London, introduced the musical comedies of Ivan Caryll and Lionel Monckton, which enjoyed popularity on the American stage until the outbreak of World War I. "The Circus Girl" was their first joint production seen here (New York, Daly's Theatre, Apr. 26).

Gustave Kerker's musical comedy "The Belle of New York" was (Sept. 18) the hit of the Casino Theatre. The show proved an even greater success in London. The New York production made a star of an unknown chorus girl, 17-year-old Edna May, as the Salvation Army lassie, Violet Gray.

Anna Held starred in Edmond Audran's most popular operetta "La Poupée" (New York, Lyric Theatre, Oct. 21).

Bob Fitzsimmons defeated (Mar. 17) James J. ("Gentleman Jim") Corbett in 14 rounds at Carson City, Nev., for the heavyweight boxing championship. The bout was filmed for the motion-picture theatres, but the screen version was marred by a continuous copyright notice.

In Belleville, Ill., Jacob Wainwright added a new thrill to the bicycle era when he pedaled backward 440 yards in 37⅞ seconds, and 880 yards (also backward) in 51⅗ seconds.

1898

Baby's Prayer. w., R. A. Mullen. m., R. L. Halle. Mullen Music Co., cop. 1898.

Because. w., Charles Horwitz. m., Frederick V. Bowers. M. Witmark & Sons, cop. 1898.

The Boy Guessed Right (A Runaway Girl). w., m., Lionel Monckton. London: Chappell & Co., Ltd., cop. 1898.

Come Tell Me What's Your Answer, Yes or No. w., m., Paul Dresser. Howley, Haviland & Co., cop. 1898.

Don't Leave Me, Dolly! w., William H. Gardner. m., Harry Weill. Jos. W. Stern & Co., cop. 1898.

Every Night There's a Light. w., m., Paul Dresser. Howley, Haviland & Co., cop. 1898.

Gold Will Buy Most Anything but a True Girl's Heart. w., Charles E. Foreman. m., Monroe H. Rosenfeld. Howley, Haviland & Co., cop. 1898.

Good Night, Little Girl, Good Night. w., Julia M. Hays. m., J. C. Macy. Boston: Oliver Ditson Co., cop. 1898.

Gypsy Love Song (The Fortune Teller). w., Harry B. Smith. m., Victor Herbert. M. Witmark & Sons, cop. 1898.

I Guess I'll Have to Telegraph My Baby. w., m., George M[ichael] Cohan. George L. Spaulding, cop. 1898.

Just As the Sun Went Down. w., m., Lyn Udall. M. Witmark & Sons, cop. 1898.

Just One Girl. w., Karl Kennett. m., Lyn Udall. M. Witmark & Sons, cop. 1898.

Kiss Me, Honey, Do. w., Edgar Smith. m., John Stromberg. Weber, Fields & Stromberg, cop. 1898; assigned to M. Witmark & Sons.

Little Birdies Learning How to Fly (The Telephone Girl). w., Hugh Morton. m., Gustave Kerker. T. B. Harms & Co., cop. 1898.

'Mid the Green Fields of Virginia. w., m., Charles K. Harris. Chas. K Harris, cop. 1898.

Mister Johnson Don't Get Gay. w., m., Dave Reed, Jr. George L. Spaulding, cop. 1898.

The Moth and the Flame. w., George Taggart. m., Max S. Witt. Jos. W. Stern & Co., cop. 1898.

My Creole Sue. w., m., Gussie L. Davis. Hamilton S. Gordon, cop. 1898; renewed 1926.

My Old New Hampshire Home. w., Andrew B. Sterling. m., Harry Von Tilzer. Wm. C. Dunn & Co., cop. 1898.

The Old Flame Flickers, and I Wonder Why. w., m., Paul Dresser. Howley, Haviland & Co., cop. 1898.

Our Country, May She Always Be Right. w., m., Paul Dresser. Howley, Haviland & Co., cop. 1898.

The Path That Leads the Other Way. w., m., Paul Dresser. Howley, Haviland & Co., cop. 1898.

Prelude [in C Sharp Minor] (No. 1 in a collection of 5 piano pieces: Morceaux de Fantaisie; first published in Russia.) m., Sergei Rachmaninoff. G. Schirmer, cop. 1898; Edward Schuberth & Co., cop. 1898 by C. F. Tretbar and others.

Recessional. w., Rudyard Kipling. m., Reginald DeKoven. Cincinnati: The John Church Co., cop. 1898; renewed 1926 by Anna DeKoven. (The words are said to have been inspired by Queen Victoria's Diamond Jubilee, and were published in the same year in "The Times," London, July 17, 1897.)

The Rosary. w., Robert Cameron Rogers. m., Ethelbert Nevin. Boston: The Boston Music Co., cop. 1898 by G. Schirmer, Jr.

Salome. Piano solo. m., William Loraine. F. A. Mills, cop. 1898.

She Is the Belle of New York (The Belle of New York). w., Hugh Morton. m., Gustave Kerker. Harms, Inc., cop. 1898.

She Was Bred In Old Kentucky. w., Harry Braisted. m., Stanley Carter. Jos. W. Stern & Co., cop. 1898.

Society [Oh! I Love Society] (A Runaway Girl). w., Aubrey Hopwood and Harry Greenbank. m., Lionel Monckton. London: Chappell & Co., Ltd., cop. 1898.

Soldiers In the Park (A Runaway Girl). w., Aubrey Hopwood and Harry Greenbank. m., Lionel Monckton. London: Chappell & Co., Ltd., cop. 1898.

A Stein Song. Part song for TTBB. w., Richard Hovey. m., Frederic Field Bullard. Boston: Oliver Ditson Co., cop. 1898.

Sweet Savannah. w., m., Paul Dresser. Howley, Haviland & Co., cop. 1898.

We Fight Tomorrow, Mother. w., m., Paul Dresser. Howley, Haviland & Co., cop. 1898.

When a Fellah Has Turned Sixteen. w., m., E. W. Rogers. T. B. Harms & Co., cop. 1898 by Francis, Day & Hunter.

When You Ain't Got No More Money, Well, You Needn't Come 'Round. w., Clarence S. Brewster. m., A. Baldwin Sloane. M. Witmark & Sons, cop. 1898.

When You Were Sweet Sixteen. w., m., James Thornton. M. Witmark & Sons, cop. 1898.

Who Dat Say Chicken in Dis Crowd. w., Paul Lawrence Dunbar. m., Will Marion. M. Witmark & Sons, cop. 1898.

You'se Just a Little Nigger, Still You'se Mine, All Mine. w., m., Paul Dresser. Howley, Haviland & Co., cop. 1898.

Your God Comes First, Your Country Next, Then Mother Dear. w., m., Paul Dresser. Howley, Haviland & Co., cop. 1898.

Zizzy, Ze Zum, Zum! w., Karl Kennett. m., Lyn Udall. M. Witmark & Sons, cop. 1898.

A revolt in Cuba against Spain, which had begun in 1895, became of increasing concern to the United States. For the protection of American interests, the United States despatched (in Jan. 1898) the battleship "Maine" to the harbor at Havana. An explosion of undetermined origin wrecked (Feb. 15) the ship with a loss of 260 lives. The pro-war press was greatly aroused and Congress appropriated (Mar. 9) the sum of $50,000,000 for eventualities. In spite of President McKinley's humanitarian efforts to avert hostilities, Spain, which was long dissatisfied with American sympathy with the Cuban insurgents, declared war (Apr. 24) against the United States. The defeat of the Spanish fleets at Manila in the Philippines (May 1) by Admiral George Dewey and at Santiago, in Cuba (July 3), by Rear-Admiral William Thomas Sampson and Commodore Winfield Scott Schley, along with American victories on the island, brought about (Aug. 12) an armistice. "Rough Riders," recruited by Lieutenant Colonel Theodore Roosevelt, aided in the battle at El Caney (July 1) and in the highly publicized assault on San Juan Hill (July 3). A spectacular feat was accomplished when the U. S. battleship "Oregon" made a 16,000-mile journey from the Pacific Coast via Cape Horn to join (May 26) the Atlantic fleet of Admiral Sampson. The treaty of peace was signed (Dec. 10) in Paris and the United States acquired all Spanish claims on Puerto Rico and Guam, paid $20,000,000 for the Philippine Islands, and undertook the supervision of Cuba (until 1934). 6,472 American soldiers and sailors lost their lives in the war.

The United States annexed (July 7) the Hawaiian Islands. (The twenty islands, nine of which are inhabited, became the Territory of Hawaii by act of Congress June 14, 1900.)

A New York legislative act (signed May 11, 1896, and effective Jan. 1, 1898) created the city of "Greater New York," combining the five boroughs of Manhattan, Brooklyn, Bronx, Richmond, and Queens.

The Western Labor Union was founded. (It adopted the name American Labor Union after its Denver convention in 1902.)

The Trans-Mississippi-Omaha Exposition was held (June 1-Nov. 1) in Omaha, Neb. For the occasion the U. S. Post Office issued (June 10) a series of nine commemorative postage stamps.

The National Institute of Arts and Letters was founded as an American equivalent to the Académie Française with 250 members representing art, literature, and music.

Popular novels of the year were "David Harum, A Story of American Life" (Edward Noyes Westcott, published posthumously) and "When Knighthood Was in Flower" (Charles Major; an historical romance). "David Harum" contained such familiar bits of homespun philosophy as "The's as much human nature in some folks as th'is in others, if not more"; and "A reasonable amount of fleas is good for a dog—they keep him f'm broodin' on bein' a dog." The novel was dramatized in 1900.

Victor Herbert was appointed musical conductor of the Pittsburgh Symphony Orchestra.

Mme. Ernestine Schumann-Heink, famous German operatic contralto, made (Nov. 7) her American debut as Ortrud in "Lohengrin" in Chicago.

The music of César Franck was becoming known in the United States. Theodore Thomas conducted (Jan. 29) the symphonic poem "Le Chasseur Maudit" (The Wild Huntsman) in Cincinnati. Raoul Pugno, French piano virtuoso, played (Mar. 7) the "Variations Symphoniques" for piano and orchestra in New York with the Chicago Symphony Orchestra. (The symphonic poem "Les Éolides" had been played by the Chicago Orchestra in Chicago. The Liederkranz singing society of New York produced, Mar. 25, 1899, the oratorio "Les Béatitudes," and the Boston Symphony Orchestra performed, Aug. 14, 1899, the Symphony in D minor.)

Victor Herbert scored his first major comic opera success with "The Fortune Teller" (Buffalo, Star Theatre, Sept. 19; New York, Wallack's, Sept. 26, and elsewhere on tour). The cast included Alice Nielsen, Marguerite Sylva, Eugene Cowles, Joseph Cawthorn, and Joseph Herbert. (The London performance of the operetta in 1901 started Alice Nielsen on her operatic career. She made her grand opera debut in 1903 in Naples.)

"Way Down East," a play by Lottie Blair Parker, started (Feb. 7) its run of popularity with Phoebe Davis and Howard Kyle at the Manhattan Theatre, New York.

Another popular play of the year was "The Moth and the Flame" with Herbert Kelcey and Effie Shannon, first put on in Philadelphia (Chestnut Street Theatre, Feb. 14) and afterwards seen in New York (Lyceum Theatre, Apr. 11).

Edmond Rostand's play "Cyrano de Bergerac" was seen (Oct. 3) in English versions simultaneously in New York (Garden Theatre) with Richard Mansfield, Margaret Anglin, and William Courtney, and in Philadelphia with Ada Rehan and Charles Richman.

ಶ್ಘ 1899

Absent. w., Catherine Young Glen. m., John W. Metcalf. Boston: The Arthur P. Schmidt Co., cop. 1899.

Always. w., Charles Horwitz. m., Frederick V. Bowers. M. Witmark & Sons, cop. 1899.

Ben Hur Chariot Race. March. m., E. T. Paull. E. T. Paull Music Co., cop. 1899.

Come Home, Dewey, We Won't Do a Thing to You. w., m., Paul Dresser. Howley, Haviland & Co., cop. 1899.

The Curse of the Dreamer. w., m., Paul Dresser. Howley, Haviland & Co., cop. 1899.

Doan Ye Cry, Mah Honey. w., m., Albert W. Noll. Boston: Oliver Ditson Co., cop. 1899.

Face to Face. Hymn. w., Mrs. Frank A. Breck. m., Grant Colfax Tullar. Tullar-Meredith Co., cop. 1899.

Hands Across the Sea. March. m., John Philip Sousa. Cincinnati: The John Church Co., cop. 1899.

Hearts and Flowers. w., Mary D. Brine. m., Theodore Moses Tobani. Carl Fischer, cop. 1899.

Hello! Ma Baby. w., m., Joseph E. Howard and Ida Emerson. T. B. Harms & Co., cop. 1899.

I've Waited, Honey, Waited Long for You. w., m., George A. Nichols. Hugo V. Schlam, cop. 1899.

I Wonder If She's Waiting. w., Andrew B. Sterling. m., Harry Von Tilzer. T. B. Harms & Co., cop. 1899.

I Wonder Where She Is Tonight. w., m., Paul Dresser. Howley, Haviland & Co., cop. 1899.

I'd Leave My Happy Home for You. w., Will A. Heelan. m., Harry Von Tilzer. Wm. C. Dunn & Co., cop. 1899.

If Only You Were Mine (The Singing Girl). w., Harry B. Smith. m., Victor Herbert. M. Witmark & Sons, cop. 1899.

In Good Old New York Town. w., m., Paul Dresser. Howley, Haviland & Co., cop. 1899.

Mandy Lee. w., m., Thurland Chattaway. Howley, Haviland & Co., cop. 1899.

Maple Leaf Rag. Piano piece. m., Scott Joplin. Sedalia, Mo.: John Stark & Son, cop. 1899.

The Mosquitos' Parade. Orch. piece. m., Howard Whitney. Arr. by Theodore Bendix. M. Witmark & Sons, cop. 1899. (Published as a piano piece, do., cop. 1900.)

My Little Georgia Rose. w., Robert F. Roden. m., Max S. Witt. Jos. W. Stern & Co., cop. 1899.

My Wild Irish Rose (A Romance of Athlone). w., m., Chauncey Olcott. M. Witmark & Sons, cop. 1899.

One Night in June. w., m., Charles K. Harris. Chas. K. Harris, cop. 1899; renewed 1926.

Pavane for a Dead Infanta—*original French title:* Pavane pour une Infante Défunte. Piano solo. m., Maurice Ravel. Paris: E. Demets [1899]. (Arr. for orch. by the composer and published by E. Demets, cop. 1910.)

A Picture No Artist Can Paint. w., m., J. Fred Helf. Hylands, Spencer & Yaeger, cop. 1899.

She Was Happy Till She Met You. w., Charles Graham. m., Monroe H. Rosenfeld. Howley, Haviland & Co., cop. 1899.

The Singer and the Song. w., Will D. Cobb. m., Gus Edwards. Howley, Haviland & Co., cop. 1899.

Six Little Wives (San Toy). w., Harry Greenbank and Adrian Ross. m., Sidney Jones. London: Keith Prowse & Co., Ltd., cop. 1899 by Sidney Jones.

Smoky Mokes. Cake walk. m., Abe Holzmann. Feist & Frankenthaler, cop. 1899.

Stay in Your Own Back Yard. w., Karl Kennett, m., Lyn Udall. M. Witmark & Sons, cop. 1899.

The Story of the Rose. w., "Alice." m., Andrew Mack. Howley, Haviland & Co., cop. 1899; cop. 1926 by Edward B. Marks Music Co.; assigned 1932 to Edward B. Marks Music Corp.

There's Where My Heart Is Tonight. w., m., Paul Dresser. Howley, Haviland & Co., cop. 1899.

We Came from the Same Old State. w., m., Paul Dresser. Howley, Haviland & Co., cop. 1899.

Where the Sweet Magnolias Grow. w., Andrew B. Sterling. m., Harry Von Tilzer. Wm. C. Dunn & Co., cop. 1899.

Whistling Rufus. Two step. m., Kerry Mills. F. A. Mills, cop. 1899 (arr. as song with words by W. Murdock Lind, do., cop. 1899).

Released from the imperialist yoke of Spain (1898), the Philippine Islands now clamored for independence from the military government of the United States and commenced (Feb. 4) guerrilla warfare (1899-1901). (The leader of the insurgents, Emilio Aquinaldo, was captured Mar. 23, 1901, by Brigadier General Frederick Funston. The rebellion ended officially Apr. 30, 1902; military governorship was terminated July 4 of that year.)

Under a tripartite treaty with Great Britain and Germany, the United States acquired (in November) the Samoan island Tutuila, its four adjacent islets (Aunu'm, Ofu, Olosega, and Ta'u) and the Manua Islands including the atoll Rose Island.

The "open-door policy," advocating equal commercial opportunities for all nations in China, was announced (in September) by Secretary of State John Milton Hay in a note to the foreign powers.

The United States was represented at the Universal Peace Conference, called by Czar Nicholas II of Russia, which met (May 18-July 29) in The Hague, Holland, and prepared the way for the first International Arbitration Court (1902).

Admiral George Dewey, hero of the battle of Manila (May 1, 1898), received (Sept. 30) a tremendous reception in New York.

The automobile now was such a nuisance that it was barred from Central Park, New York.

Edward Henry Harriman, financier and director of the Union Pacific Railroad, organized the scientifically important Harriman Alaska Expedition. (The results were published in the "Harrison Alaska Series," in 14 volumes, 1902-14.)

Medicine Lodge, Kan., was startled by an irate woman who began smashing up the local saloons with a hatchet in a spectacular fashion. She was Carry (or Carrie) Amelia Nation, formerly the wife of an intemperate clergyman named Gloyd and remarried since 1877.

Mount Rainier National Park, Wash., was established (Mar. 2) by act of Congress.

Martha Place was the first woman to be put to death in the electric chair, at Sing Sing, N. Y.

"Everybody's" magazine began publication as a house organ of Wanamaker's Department Store. (Became an independent magazine in 1903 and merged with "Romance" in 1928.)

Books of the year included Thorstein Veblen's savage analysis of the commercialism of the wealthy, entitled "The Theory of the Leisure Class"; Edwin Markham's collection of verse "The Man with the Hoe and Other Poems"; George Ade's sketches "Fables in Slang," and the novels "The Awkward Age" (Henry James), "The Gentleman from Indiana" (Booth Tarkington), "McTeague" (Frank Norris), "Janice Meredith" (Paul Leicester Ford), "The Man That Corrupted Hadleyburg" (Mark Twain), and "Richard Carvel" (Winston Churchill). Elbert Hubbard published "A Message to Garcia," an inspirational essay on an episode in the Spanish-American War, which so appealed to business executives that they distributed copies of the booklet among their employees to promote greater efficiency. Arthur M. Winfield (Edward Stratemeyer) brought out the first of his long "Rover Boys" series.

Richard Strauss's tone poem "Don Quixote" received (Jan. 7) its first American rendition by the Chicago Symphony Orchestra under Theodore Thomas.

César Franck's Symphony in D minor was played (Apr. 14) for the first time in the United States by the Boston Symphony Orchestra.

"The Roger Brothers in Wall Street" began a series of Roger Brothers comedies which ran for many years.

Chauncey Olcott starred (Jan. 9) in "A Romance of Athlone" at the 14th Street Theatre, New York.

"The Four Cohans" (papa Jerry J., mother Helen F., 21-year-old George Michael, and his sister Josephine) were appearing modestly in New York on Broadway in vaudeville comedy sketches such as "Money to Burn," "The Professor's Wife," and "Running for Office."

New York plays included "Zaza" with Mrs. Leslie Carter (Garrick, Jan. 9); "The Man in the Moon" with Sam Bernard, Marie Dressler, and Christie MacDonald (New York Theatre, Apr. 24); "Becky Sharpe" with Minnie Maddern Fiske (Fifth Avenue Theatre, Sept. 12); "Barbara Frietchie" with Julia Marlowe (Criterion, Oct. 23); "Sherlock Holmes" with William Gillette (Garrick, Nov. 6); "Ben Hur" with Edward Morgan in the name part and William S. Hart as Messala (Broadway Theatre, Nov. 29). Alice Nielsen appeared in Victor Herbert's comic opera "The Singing Girl" (Casino, Oct. 23). Anna Held sang Reginald DeKoven's "Papa's Wife" (Manhattan Theatre, Nov. 13). Ex-heavyweight boxing champion James J. ("Gentleman Jim") Corbett did a prizefight scene in a revue "Around New York in Eighty Minutes."

Sir Thomas Lipton made his first attempt to take the America's yacht trophy back to England, which had never won it, with his boat "Shamrock," but the American "Columbia" defeated the Lipton entry thrice in a row (Oct. 16, 17, 20).

James J. Jeffries won (June 9) the heavyweight boxing championship from Robert ("Bob") Fitzsimmons in 11 rounds at Coney Island, New York. In the same arena Jeffries defended (Nov. 3) his newly won title against Tom Sharkey in 25 rounds, and William A. Brady filmed the first indoor fight pictures for the movies.

ᚎᢌ 1900

Absence Makes the Heart Grow Fonder. w., Arthur Gillespie. m., Herbert Dillea. M. Witmark & Sons, cop. 1900.

A Bird in a Gilded Cage. w., Arthur J. Lamb. m., Harry Von Tilzer. Shapiro, Bernstein & Von Tilzer, cop. 1900.

The Blue and the Gray; or, A Mother's Gift to Her Country. w., m., Paul Dresser. Howley, Haviland & Co., cop. 1900.

The Bridge of Sighs. w., m., James Thornton. M. Witmark & Sons, cop. 1900.

Calling to Her Boy Just Once Again. w., m., Paul Dresser. Howley, Haviland & Co., cop. 1900.

Creole Belle. w., George Sidney. m., J. Bodewalt Lampe. Jerome H. Remick & Co., cop. 1900 by The Lampe Music Co.

Every Race Has a Flag But the Coon. w., m., Will A. Heelan and J. Fred Helf. Jos. W. Stern & Co., cop. 1900.

The Fatal Rose of Red. w., m., J. Fred Helf and Ed. Gardenier. F. A. Mills, cop. 1900.

For Old Times' Sake. w., m., Charles K. Harris. Chas. K. Harris, cop. 1900.

Good-bye, Dolly Gray. w., m., Barnes and Cobb. The Morse Music Co., cop. 1900; recop. 1900 by Howley, Haviland & Co.

I Can't Tell Why I Love You, But I Do. w., Will D. Cobb. m., Gus Edwards. Howley, Haviland & Co., cop. 1900.

I'd Still Believe You True. w., m., Paul Dresser. Howley, Haviland & Co., cop. 1900.

I've a Longing in My Heart for You, Louise. w., m., Charles K. Harris. Charles K. Harris, cop. 1900.

In the House of Too Much Trouble. w., m., Will A. Heelan and J. Fred Helf. Jos. W. Stern & Co., cop. 1900.

Just Because She Made Dem Goo-Goo Eyes. w., m., John Queen and Hughie Cannon. Howley, Haviland & Co., cop. 1900.

Ma Blushin' Rosie. w., Edgar Smith. m., John Stromberg. M. Witmark & Sons, cop. 1900.

Midnight Fire-Alarm. March. m., Harry J. Lincoln; arranged by E. T. Paull. E. T. Paull Music Co., cop. 1900.

O That Will Be Glory for Me; or, The Glory Song. Hymn. w., m., Charles H. Gabriel. Chicago: E. O. Excell, cop. 1900; renewed 1920 by Homer A. Rodeheaver.

Quiller Has the Brains (Foxy Quiller). w., Harry Bache Smith. m., Reginald DeKoven. Edward Schuberth & Co., cop. 1900.

The Shade of the Palm (Florodora). w., Owen Hall. m., Leslie Stuart [pseud. of Thomas A. Barrett]. T. B. Harms and Francis, Day & Hunter, cop. 1900 by Francis, Day & Hunter.

Strike Up the Band—Here Comes a Sailor. w., Andrew B. Sterling. m., Charles B. Ward. Harry Von Tilzer Music Pub. Co., cop. 1900.

The Tale of the Kangaroo (The Burgomaster). w., Frank Pixley. m., Gustav Luders. M. Witmark & Sons, cop. 1900.

Tell Me Pretty Maiden (Florodora). Sextet. w., Owen Hall. m., Leslie Stuart [pseud. of Thomas A. Barrett]. T. B. Harms and Francis, Day & Hunter, cop. 1900 by Francis, Day & Hunter.

Violets. w., Julian Fane. m., Ellen Wright. G. Ricordi & Co., cop. 1900.

When de Moon Comes Up Behind de Hill. w., m., Paul Dresser. Howley, Haviland & Co., cop. 1900.

When the Harvest Days Are Over, Jessie Dear. w., Howard Graham. m., Harry Von Tilzer. Shapiro, Bernstein & Von Tilzer Co., cop. 1900.

The Year's at the Spring. w., Robert Browning. m., Mrs. H. H. A. Beach. Op. 44, no. 1. Boston: Arthur P. Schmidt, cop. 1900.

You Can't Keep a Good Man Down. w., m., M. F. Carey. Jos. W. Stern & Co., cop. 1900; assigned 1920 to Edward B. Marks Music Co.

Congress standardized (Mar. 14) the gold dollar as the unit of monetary value in the United States, and raised (June 14) the status of the Hawaiian Islands to that of a Territory.

Two thousand U. S. Marines aided in the capture (Aug. 14) of Peking, China, terminating the Boxer uprising.

William Goebel, Governor of Kentucky, was assassinated (Jan. 30).

The Socialist Party of the United States was formed by a merger of the Socialist Labor Party of the United States (1876) and the Social Democratic Party of Eugene Victor Debs.

Booklets of postage stamps were placed (Apr. 16) on sale by the U. S. Post Office.

Drs. Walter Reed, Aristides Agramonte, Jesse Lazear, and James Carroll began an intensive study at Camp Lazear, Cuba, to eradicate yellow fever ("yellow jack").

Fire destroyed (June 30) the docks of the North German Lloyd and Hamburg American steamship companies, and the ocean liners, the "Main," "Bremen," "Saale," and other ships, in Hoboken, N. J., with a loss of 145 lives. The property damage amounted to $10,000,000.

The Associated Press news service was founded (May 23) in New York.

The Carnegie Institute of Technology was established in Pittsburgh, Pa., by a fund of $1,000,000 (later increased to four millions for equipment and seven millions for endowment) from Andrew Carnegie.

The Hall of Fame, New York City, was originated by New York University as a memorial to famous Americans with places for 150 commemorative tablets and busts. Five great names are chosen every five years for inclusion in the memorial.

A tornado and tidal wave wreaked havoc (Sept. 8) in Galveston, Tex., killing 6,000 persons and causing untold property damage. Victor Herbert conducted a monster concert with 420 players in Madison Square Garden, New York, for the benefit of the sufferers.

The first issue of "Who's Who in America" made its appearance.

"World's Work" was founded as a monthly magazine. (It merged in 1932 with the "Review of Reviews.")

Cartoonist Frederick Burr Opper began the comic strip, Happy Hooligan and his mule named Maud, which appeared regularly in American newspapers for more than 30 years.

Books of the year included Theodore Roosevelt's essays "The Strenuous Life," the first volume of Josiah Royce's University of Aberdeen lectures "The World and the Individual" (2 vols., 1900-01), Jack London's Yukon stories "The Son of the Wolf," and the novels "Alice of Old Vincennes" (Maurice Thompson), "Eben Holden" (Irving Bacheller), "Monsieur Beaucaire" (Booth Tarkington), "Sister Carrie" (Theodore Dreiser), "To Have and To Hold" (Mary Johnson), "Unleavened Bread" (Robert Grant), "The Wonderful Wizard of Oz" (Lyman Frank Baum).

The Bethlehem (Pa.) Bach Choir was founded by John Frederick Wolle, organist of the local Moravian Church.

John Philip Sousa's band of 100 players (1892) made the first of five concert tours in Europe.

Bach's B minor Mass was performed by the newly organized Bach Choir in Bethlehem, Pa., and by the Oratorio Society in New York.

Nicola Spinelli's opera "A Basso Porto" (At the Lower Harbor) received (Jan. 8) its American première in St. Louis at the Exposition Music Hall, in English, and was performed (Jan. 22) in New York at the American Theatre.

The New York Metropolitan Opera House staged (Nov. 19) its first opera in the English language—"Esmeralda" by Arthur Goring Thomas, English composer.

Theodore Thomas's Chicago Orchestra gave (Mar. 10) the first American rendition of Richard Strauss's gigantic symphonic poem "Ein Heldenleben."

During the preliminary tour of the New York Metropolitan Opera Company, Louise Homer, Pittsburgh-born contralto, and Fritzi Scheff, Viennese soprano, made (Nov. 14 and Nov. 19, respectively) their American debuts in San Francisco. (Both sang at the "Met" in December.)

Eduard Strauss made a second tour of the United States with his father's famous orchestra. (The first was in 1890.)

Clyde Fitch's adaptation of Alphonse Daudet's novel "Sapho" opened (Feb. 5) in New York at Wallack's Theatre with Olga Nethersole. The play was condemned as immoral; the theatre was closed (Mar. 5) by order of the police, and Miss Nethersole was arrested. Released on bail, the actress revived (Mar. 6) Arthur Wing Pinero's once scandalous play "The Second Mrs. Tanqueray." Meanwhile Miss Nethersole's cause was taken up by the women suffragists and the ladies of the "smart world," as well as by writers like Arthur Brisbane, Samuel Untermyer, and Harriet Hubbard Ayer. A petition was sent to the Mayor of the city. The front pages of the newspapers had good "copy." Through all the hubbub, the creator of the "Nethersole kiss" retained the dignity she imparted to her "courtesan" roles on the stage. The "Sapho" trial lasted three days (Apr. 3-6). Miss Nethersole was duly cleared and resumed the play, which ran for 86 performances. It was revived (Nov. 12) at the same theatre for 28 additional performances.

David Belasco turned John Luther Long's story of "Madame Butterfly" (1897) into a successful one-act play (New York, Herald Square Theatre, Mar. 5) with Blanche Bates, as an afterpiece to his farce "Naughty Anthony." "Madame Butterfly" had 24 performances.

Edward Hugh Sothern played (Mar. 26) an English version of Gerhart Hauptmann's famous German play "The Sunken Bell" in New York at the Knickerbocker Theatre, and made (Sept. 7) his first local appearance in "Hamlet" at the Garden Theatre with Virginia Harned as Ophelia.

Two dramatizations of Henryk Sienkiewicz's novel "Quo Vadis" opened (Apr. 9) simultaneously in New York at the New York Theatre and at the Herald Square Theatre.

Maude Adams played (Oct. 23) Sarah Bernhardt's famous role in Edmond Rostand's play "L'Aiglon" when it was first produced in New York at the Knickerbocker Theatre in Louis N. Parker's English version. The "divine Sarah" herself performed the play in French a month later.

Outstanding New York successes included Augustus Thomas's "Arizona" (Herald Square Theatre, Sept. 10), "Richard Carvel" (Empire, Sept. 11), "David Harum" (Garrick, Oct. 1), and the musical productions "The Casino Girl" (Casino, Mar. 19), "Fiddle-dee-dee" (Weber and Fields Music Hall, Sept. 6), and "San Toy" (Daly's, Oct. 1). By all odds—and the production ran 505 performances—the New York theatrical hit was Owen Hall and Leslie Stuart's musical comedy "Florodora" (Casino Theatre, Nov. 10, 1900, New York Theatre, Jan. 25, 1902) with its still famous sextette of girls. In the show, they were "typewriter girls," as typists then were called.

The Western League of baseball clubs assumed the name American League.

Dwight Filley Davis, American diplomat, donated the Davis Cup tennis trophy, awarded annually since then to the winning men's team in international matches.

William Jennings Bryan made his second bid for the presidency in the national elections on the Democratic ticket, and was again defeated by William McKinley. (He ran unsuccessfully in 1896 and in 1908.)

The national population was 76,303,387.

ᘒᜄ 1901

Any Old Place I Can Hang My Hat Is Home Sweet Home to Me. w., William Jerome. m., Jean Schwartz. Shapiro, Bernstein & Von Tilzer, cop. 1901.

The Billboard. March. m., John N. Klohr. Cincinnati: The John Church Co., cop. 1901.

Blaze Away! March. m., Abe Holzmann. Feist & Frankenthaler, cop. 1901.

Coon! Coon! Coon! w., m., Leo Friedman. Sol Bloom, cop. 1901.

Davy Jones' Locker. w., m., H. W. Petrie. Jos. W. Stern & Co., cop. 1901.

Don't Put Me Off at Buffalo Any More. w., William Jerome. m., Jean Schwartz. Shapiro, Bernstein & Von Tilzer, cop. 1901.

Down Where the Cotton Blossoms Grow. w., Andrew B. Sterling. m., Harry Von Tilzer. Shapiro, Bernstein & Von Tilzer, cop. 1901.

Eyes of Blue, Eyes of Brown. w., m., Costen and Sterling. T. B. Harms & Co., cop. 1901.

Finlandia. Symphonic poem. m., Jan Sibelius, op. 26, no. 7. Leipzig: Breitkopf & Härtel [1901].

Go Way Back and Sit Down. w., Elmer Bowman. m., Al Johns. F. A. Mills, cop. 1901.

Hello, Central, Give Me Heaven. w., m., Charles K. Harris. Milwaukee: Chas. K. Harris, cop. 1901.

Hiawatha. Piano solo. m., Neil Moret, op. 6. Detroit: The Whitney-Warner Pub. Co., cop. 1901 by Daniels & Russell: assigned 1902 to The Whitney-Warner Pub. Co. (Published as a song, with words by James O'Dea; The Whitney-Warner Pub. Co., cop. 1903.)

I've Grown So Used to You. w., m., Thurland Chattaway. Howley, Haviland & Dresser, cop. 1901.

I Just Want to Go Back and Start the Whole Thing Over. w., m., Paul Dresser. Howley, Haviland & Co., cop. 1901.

I'll Be with You When the Roses Bloom Again. w., Will D. Cobb. m., Gus Edwards. F. A. Mills, cop. 1901; assigned 1928 to Paull-Pioneer Music Co.

In a Cozy Corner. Piano piece. m., John W. Bratton. M. Witmark & Sons, cop. 1901.

In the Great Somewhere. w., m., Paul Dresser. Howley, Haviland & Dresser, cop. 1901.

Josephine, My Jo. w., R. C. McPherson. m., James T. Brymn. Shapiro, Bernstein & Von Tilzer, cop. 1901.

Just A-Wearyin' for You. w., Frank Stanton. m., Carrie Jacobs-Bond. Chicago: Carrie Jacobs-Bond & Son, cop. 1901 by Carrie Jacobs-Bond.

Mighty Lak' a Rose. w., Frank L. Stanton. m., Ethelbert Nevin. Cincinnati: The John Church Co., cop. 1901.

Mr. Volunteer; or, You Don't Belong to the Regulars, You're Just a Volunteer. w., m., Paul Dresser. Howley, Haviland & Dresser, cop. 1901.

My Castle on the Nile. w., J. W. Johnson and Bob Cole. m., Rosamond Johnson. Jos. W. Stern & Co., cop. 1901.

My Heart Still Clings to the Old First Love. w., m., Paul Dresser. Howley, Haviland & Dresser, cop. 1901.

O Dry Those Tears! w., m., Teresa Del Riego. London: Chappell & Co., Ltd., cop. 1901.

Panamericana. Orch. composition. m., Victor Herbert. M. Witmark & Sons, cop. 1901.

Rip Van Winkle Was a Lucky Man. w., William Jerome. m., Jean Schwartz. Shapiro, Bernstein & Von Tilzer, cop. 1901.

Serenade (Les Millions d'Arlequin). Composition for violin and piano. m., Riccardo Drigo (1846-1930). St. Petersburg: Jul. Heinr. Zimmermann, cop. 1901. (The piece is an excerpt from Drigo's ballet "Les Millions d'Arlequin," produced at St. Petersburg, 1900, under the choreographic direction of the famous ballet master Marius Petipa.)

The Swan of Tuonela. Symphonic poem. m., Jan Sibelius, op. 22, no. 3. Leipzig: Breitkopf & Härtel, cop. 1901.

Sweet Annie Moore (The Casino Girl). w., m., John H. Flynn. Howley, Haviland & Dresser, cop. 1901.

The Tale of a Bumble Bee (King Dodo). Frank Pixley. m., Gustav Luders. M. Witmark & Sons, cop. 1901.

There's No North or South Today. w., m., Paul Dresser. Howley, Haviland & Dresser, cop. 1901.

Tobermory. w., m., Harry Lauder. Francis, Day & Hunter, cop. 1901.

Way Down in Old Indiana. w., m., Paul Dresser. Howley, Haviland & Dresser, cop. 1901.

When the Birds Have Sung Themselves to Sleep. w., m., Paul Dresser. Howley, Haviland & Dresser, cop. 1901.

When the Blue Sky Turns to Gold. w., m., Thurland Chattaway. Howley, Haviland & Dresser, cop. 1901.

Where the Silv'ry Colorado Wends Its Way. w., C. H. Scoggins. m., Charles Avril. Chicago: Will Rossiter, cop. 1901 by C. H. Scoggins and Charles Avril.

You're as Welcome as the Flowers in May. w., m., Dan J. Sullivan. Broadway Music Pub. Co., cop. 1901; renewed 1929 by Dan J. Sullivan; assigned 1932 to Paull-Pioneer Music Corp.

The United States was 125 years old.

President William McKinley began his second term.

The Pan-American Exposition was held (May 1-Nov. 2) in Buffalo, N. Y. President McKinley, returning from a tour of the West, visited the celebration. While receiving callers, he was shot (Sept. 6) and fatally wounded by an anarchist, Leon Czolgosz, who concealed a pistol in his right hand which was covered by a handkerchief. The President lingered for eight days. His last words were: "It is God's way; His will, not ours, be done." The assassin was executed.

Following President McKinley's death (Sept. 14), Vice-President Theodore Roosevelt, Republican, of New York, was inaugurated 26th President. He was 43 years of age—the youngest man ever to hold the office.

The Hay-Pauncefote Treaty between the United States and Great Britain, so named after Secretary of State John Milton Hay and Baron Julian Pauncefote, virtually established American supremacy in the Caribbean by removing the restrictions of the Clayton-Bulwer Treaty (1850) against the construction of a canal through the Isthmus of Panama.

In the campaign to eradicate yellow fever, Dr. Henry Rose Carter discovered that the disease was transmitted by mosquitoes.

Wireless telegraphy (radio) became (Dec. 12) a reality when Guglielmo Marconi, Italian electrician and inventor, had so developed an apparatus that he could hear at St. Johns, Newfoundland, the three dots of the letter S transmitted without wires across the Atlantic from Wales. (The first radio message was sent in the following year.)

The South Carolina Interstate and West Indian Exposition was held (Dec. 1, 1901-June 1, 1902) in Charleston, S. C.

Andrew Carnegie retired (in Jan.) from business, selling his steel interests to the U. S. Steel Corporation for $250,000,000, to carry out the principle set forth in his book "The Gospel of Wealth" (1900) that rich men should be "trustees" of wealth for public benefit.

A panic occurred (May 9) in Northern Pacific Railway stock.

The steamer "Islander," carrying $3,000,000 in gold, struck (Aug. 14) an iceberg in Steven's Passage, Alaska, and sank, with a loss of 70 lives.

The Junior League of the City of New York was founded. (The national organization came into being exactly 20 years later.)

Chicagoan Charles Fitzmorris, later Chief of Police, travelled around the world in a new record time of 60 days, 13 hours, 29 minutes.

William Sydney Porter, Texan journalist, came to New York after having served two and one half years in the Ohio State Penitentiary for alleged embezzlement in a carelessly conducted bank in Austin, Tex., and started his career as a short-story writer under the pseudonym O. Henry.

Books of the year included the autobiographies "The Making of an American" by Jacob Riis and "Up from Slavery" by Booker T. Washington, the first volume of "The Jewish Encyclopedia" (completed in 12 volumes in 1909), and the novels "The Crisis" (Winston Churchill), "Graustark" (George Barr McCutcheon), "The Octopus" (Frank Norris), and "Mrs. Wiggs of the Cabbage Patch" (Alice Hegan Rice).

The Metropolitan Opera House, New York, gave (Feb. 4) the American première of Puccini's "Tosca," produced a year earlier in Rome.

Jan Kubelik, Bohemian violin virtuoso, began (Dec. 2) at Carnegie Hall, New York, his first American concert tour.

Theodore Thomas introduced (Dec. 7) in America the music of the Finnish composer Jan Sibelius with a performance by his Chicago Orchestra of two excerpts from the "Kalevala" suite.

David Warfield started his great reputation as an actor and his long career under David Belasco in the latter's play "The Auctioneer," which opened (Sept. 23) in New York at the Bijou Theatre. Warfield played the role 1,400 times during his life.

"The Governor's Son" presented (Feb. 25) in New York at the Savoy Theatre "The Four Cohans" (Jerry J., Helen F., and their children George Michael and Josephine) in their first musical comedy appearance. The production was written and composed by George M. Cohan.

"Hoity Toity," an extravaganza produced (Sept. 5) by Weber and Fields at their Music Hall in New York, featured a stellar cast including, besides the comedians themselves, De Wolff Hopper, Sam Bernard, John T. Kelly, Lillian Russell, Fay Templeton, and others. The show ran 225 performances.

The diamond horseshoe Metropolitan Opera House, New York, admitted musical comedy to its precincts for the first time. Ivan Caryll's London show "The Ladies' Paradise" opened (Sept. 16) there with a ballet of 250.

Interest in the half-legendary 15th century French poet François Villon was revived by Justin Huntly M'Carthy's romantic four-act drama "If I Were King," known today in its musical and film versions as "The Vagabond King." Edward Hugh Sothern played the roisterous hero; Cecilia ("Cissie") Loftus, who had married McCarthy in 1894 and divorced him in 1899, was Katherine de Vaucelles. A pert newcomer, Suzanne Sheldon, delighted her audiences as the tavern light-o'-love Huguette, disguised in boys' attire which displayed her shapely limbs to advantage in tights. The play was produced (Oct. 14) in New York at the Garden Theatre.

Popular New York plays included "When Knighthood Was in Flower" with Julia Marlowe (Criterion, Jan. 14), "Captain Jinks of the Horse Marines" (Garrick, Feb. 4), "Under Two Flags" (Lyceum, Feb. 4), "On the Quiet" (Madison Square, Feb. 11), "A Message from Mars" (Garrick, Oct. 7), "Quality Street" with Maude Adams (Knickerbocker, Nov. 11), "Monsieur Beaucaire" (Herald Square, Dec. 2), "Du Barry" with Mrs. Leslie Carter (Criterion, Dec. 25). Popular musical productions included "The Girl from Up There" with Edna May (New York Theatre, Jan. 7), "The Strollers" with Francis Wilson (Knickerbocker, June 24), "The Messenger Boy" (Daly's, Sept. 16), "The Liberty Belles" (Madison Square, Sept. 30), "The Little Duchess" with Anna Held (Casino, Oct. 14), "The Sleeping Beauty and the Beast" (Broadway, Nov. 4).

Connie Mack (Cornelius McGillicuddy) became manager of the Philadelphia American League ("Athletics") baseball club—a post he held until 1950.

The Three-I League class B baseball clubs, Bloomington and Decatur, played (May 31) the longest game on record—26 innings. Decatur won by a score of 2 to 1. (The record was equalled May 1, 1920, in the National League when Boston and Brooklyn battled to a 1-1 tie score in a game that was stopped by darkness after 3 hours, 50 minutes of play.)

ৡ৵ 1902

Because. w., Edward Teschemacher. m., Guy d'Hardelot [pseud. of Mrs. W. I. Rhodes, née Helen Guy]. London: Chappell & Co., Ltd., cop. 1902.

Bill Bailey, Won't You Please Come Home? w., m., Hughie Cannon. Howley, Haviland & Dresser, cop. 1902.

Come Down Ma Evenin' Star (Twirly Whirly). w., Robert B. Smith. m., John Stromberg. M. Witmark & Sons, cop. 1902.

Down on the Farm. w., Raymond A. Browne. m., Harry Von Tilzer. Harry Von Tilzer Music Pub. Co., cop. 1902.

Down Where the Wurzburger Flows. w., Vincent P. Bryan. m., Harry Von Tilzer. Harry Von Tilzer Music Pub. Co., cop. 1902.

Heidelberg-Stein Song (The Prince of Pilsen). w., Frank Pixley. m., Gustav Luders. M. Witmark & Sons, cop. 1902.

I'm Unlucky (introduced in: The Wild Rose). w., William Jerome. m., Jean Schwartz. Shapiro, Bernstein & Co., cop. 1902.

If Money Talks, It Ain't on Speaking Terms with Me. w., m., J. Fred Helf. Sol Bloom, cop. 1902.

In Dear Old Illinois. w., m., Paul Dresser. Howley, Haviland & Dresser, cop. 1902.

In the Good Old Summer Time. w., Ren Shields. m., George Evans. Howley, Haviland & Dresser, cop. 1902.

In the Sweet Bye and Bye. w., Vincent P. Bryan. m., Harry Von Tilzer. Harry Von Tilzer Music Pub. Co., cop. 1902.

Jennie Lee. w., Arthur J. Lamb. m., Harry Von Tilzer. Shapiro, Bernstein & Von Tilzer, cop. 1902.

The Land of Hope and Glory. w., Arthur C. Benson. m., Edward Elgar. London: Boosey & Co., cop. 1902.

The Mansion of Aching Hearts. w., Arthur J. Lamb. m., Harry Von Tilzer. Harry Von Tilzer Music Pub. Co., cop. 1902.

The Message of the Violet (The Prince of Pilsen). w., Frank Pixley. m., Gustav Luders. M. Witmark & Sons, cop. 1902.

Mister Dooley (*introduced in:* The Chinese Honeymoon). w., William Jerome. m., Jean Schwartz. Shapiro, Bernstein & Von Tilzer, cop. 1902.

Oh, Didn't He Ramble. w., m., Will Handy [pseud. of Bob Cole and J. Rosamond Johnson]. Jos. W. Stern, cop. 1902.

On a Sunday Afternoon. w., Andrew B. Sterling. m., Harry Von Tilzer. Harry Von Tilzer Music Pub. Co., cop. 1902.

Pardon Me, My Dear Alphonse, After You, My Dear Gaston. w., Vincent P. Bryan. m., Harry Von Tilzer. Harry Von Tilzer Music Pub. Co., cop. 1902.

Please Go 'Way and Let Me Sleep. w., m., Harry Von Tilzer. Harry Von Tilzer Music Pub. Co., cop. 1902.

Pomp and Circumstance. March. m., Edward Elgar, op. 39, No. 1. London: Boosey & Co., cop. 1902.

Since Sister Nell Heard Paderewski Play. w., Wm. Jerome. m., Jean Schwartz. Shapiro, Bernstein & Co., cop. 1902 by Shapiro, Bernstein & Von Tilzer.

The Tale of the Seashell (The Prince of Pilsen). w., Frank Pixley. m., Gustav Luders. M. Witmark & Sons, cop. 1902.

Tessie, You Are the Only, Only, Only (*introduced in:* The Silver Slipper). w., m., Will R. Anderson. M. Witmark & Sons, cop. 1902.

Three Dances from the Music to Shakespeare's Henry VIII: (1) Morris dance; (2) Shepherds' dance; (3) Torch dance. For orch. m., Edward German. London: Novello & Co., Ltd., cop. 1901. (According to the title page, the music was "composed for the production of the play at the Lyceum Theatre [London], January, 1902.")

Under the Bamboo Tree (Sally In Our Alley). w., m., Bob Cole. Jos. W. Stern & Co., cop. 1902.

When It's All Goin' Out, and Nothin' Comin' In. w., m., [Bert] Williams and [George] Walker. Jos. W. Stern & Co., cop. 1902; renewed 1929 by James W. Johnson and Lottie Williams; assigned to Edward B. Marks Music Corp.

When Kate and I Were Comin' Thro' the Rye. w., Andrew B. Sterling. m., Harry Von Tilzer. Harry Von Tilzer Music Pub. Co., cop. 1902.

When You Come Back They'll Wonder Who the —— You Are. w., m., Paul Dresser. Howley, Haviland & Dresser, cop. 1902.

Where the Sunset Turns the Ocean's Blue to Gold. w., Eva Fern Buckner. m., Henry W. Petrie. Jos. W. Stern & Co., cop. 1902 by H. W. Petrie Music Co.

The United States established civil government in the Philippines.

The American occupation of Cuba ended (May 20) with the establishment of the Republic of Cuba.

Congress passed the Reclamation Act creating the Reclamation Service, a bureau of the Department of the Interior, for the purpose of improving American desert areas by irrigation and other means.

Oregon became the first State to adopt the "initiative and referendum."

Maryland passed the first workingmen's state compensation law.

The first International Arbitration Court opened (in Oct.) in The Hague, Holland, to discuss plans for universal peace and for the limitation of military and naval armaments.

The first radio message was transmitted (Dec. 17) across the Atlantic.

Admiral Robert Edwin Peary discovered Ellesmere Island in the Arctic.

One hundred and eighty-four miners lost their lives in the Frayterville Mine, Coal Creek, Tenn.

A general strike occurred (May 12) among 145,000 anthracite miners in Pennsylvania. A Commission established by President Theodore Roosevelt restored peace by its negotiations (Oct. 15-23).

The Carnegie Institution, Washington, D. C., was established (Jan. 28) by a gift of $10,000,000 from Andrew Carnegie "to encourage in the broadest and most liberal manner investigation, research, and discovery, and the application of knowledge to the improvement of mankind." (The Institution was incorporated Apr. 28, 1904, by act of Congress, and received further gifts from Carnegie of 2 millions in 1907 and 10 millions in 1911.)

The "South Atlantic Quarterly" was founded in Durham, N. C., as a medium to acquaint the North on questions pertaining to the South.

Books of the year included "A History of the American People" (5 vols.) by Woodrow Wilson, Admiral Robert Edwin Peary's "Northward over the 'Great Ice' " (2 vols.; an account of his Arctic polar expeditions), James Gibbons Huneker's satirical sketches "Melomaniacs," and the novels "Brewster's Millions" (George Barr McCutcheon), "The Leopard's Spots" (Thomas Dixon), "The Little Shepherd of Kingdom Come" (John Fox), "The Valley of Decision" (Edith Wharton; her first major work of fiction), and "The Virginian, A Horseman of the Plains" (Owen Wister).

Arnold Dolmetsch, French-English musician, concertized in the United States with his wife and a pupil Kathleen Salmon. Their performances on obsolete musical instruments started in Europe and America the vogue for "old" music and its rendition on contemporary instruments. (He settled from 1902-09 in Boston, working on the construction of such instruments in the Chickering factory.)

The famous Italian opera composer Pietro Mascagni toured (1902-03) the United States with a company of his own, giving his operas "Cavalleria Rusticana," "L'Amico Fritz," "Zanetto," and "Iris" (which had its American première in Philadelphia at the Academy of Music, Oct. 14, 1902). The tour, which extended from New York to San Francisco, was a financial failure because of mismanagement, and it cost him his position as director of the conservatory at Pesaro which had refused him permission for the undertaking.

Claude Debussy's orchestral piece "Prélude à l'Après-midi d'un Faune" was performed (Apr. 1) for the first time in America by the Orchestral Club of Boston.

In Los Angeles, a theatre was opened by Thomas J. Talley exclusively for the showing of motion pictures.

David Belasco opened (Sept. 29) his first New York playhouse, the Belasco Theatre (formerly the Republic), with a revival of his play "Du Barry" (1901). Mrs. Leslie Carter again played the role of "La Du Barry."

George Bernard Shaw's play "Mrs. Warren's Profession" was played (Oct. 27) in New Haven, Conn., for the first time in America. The play was given its first New York performance in 1905.)

Mrs. Patrick Campbell opened (Jan 13) her first American season in New York at the Republic Theatre in repertory with Hermann Sudermann's "Magda." George Arliss was a member of the company.

Maurice Maeterlinck's poetic French drama "Pelléas et Mélisande" was performed (Jan. 28) for the first time in the United States in New York at the Victoria Theatre. It was given in English with Mrs. Patrick Campbell (Mélisande), Herbert Waring (Pélleas), G. S. Titheradge (Golaud), and George Arliss (Old Servant). The play had two performances.

By arrangement with The Elizabethan Society of London, Ben Greet staged (Oct. 12) the 15th century morality play "Everyman" in New York at Mendelssohn Hall. In the cast were Edith Wynne Matthison and Charles Rann Kennedy.

Musical comedy ruled the New York stage. At least ten productions ran over 100 performances; "Twirly Whirly" (Weber and Fields Music Hall, Sept. 11) went to 244; "A Chinese Honeymoon" (Casino, June 2) reached 376. Notable plays included "The Ninety and Nine" based on Ira D. Sankey's hymn (Academy of Music, Oct. 7), "Mary of Magdala" with Minnie Maddern Fiske (Manhattan, Nov. 12), Hall Caine's dramatization of his novel "The Eternal City" with Viola Allen (Victoria, Nov. 17), "The Darling of the Gods" with Blanche Bates (Belasco, Dec. 3), "The Girl with the Green Eyes" (Savoy, Dec. 25).

John J. McGraw became manager of the New York National League ("Giants") baseball club. (He managed the team until 1932, and won 10 National League pennants and 3 world series championships, 1905, 1921, 1922. He was nicknamed "Little Napoleon.")

ट⋙ 1903

Ain't It Funny What a Difference Just a Few Hours Make? (The Yankee Consul). w., Henry M. Blossom, Jr. m., Alfred G. Bobyn. M. Witmark & Sons, cop. 1903.

Always in the Way. w., m., Charles K. Harris. Chas. K. Harris, cop. 1903.

Always Leave Them Laughing When You Say Good-bye (Mother Goose). w., m., George M[ichael] Cohan. F. A. Mills, cop. 1903.

Bedelia. w., William Jerome. m., Jean Schwartz. Shapiro, Bernstein & Co., cop. 1903.

The Boys Are Coming Home To-day. w., m., Paul Dresser. Howley, Haviland & Dresser, cop. 1903.

The Burning of Rome. March. m., E. T. Paull. E. T. Paull Music Co., cop. 1903.

Dear Old Girl. w., Richard Henry Buck. m., Theodore F. Morse. Howley, Haviland & Dresser, cop. 1903.

Four Indian Love Lyrics—(1) The Temple Bells; (2) Less Than the Dust; (3) Kashmiri Song; (4) Till I Wake. w., Laurence Hope. m., Amy Woodeforde-Finden. London: Boosey & Co., Ltd., cop. 1902 by Mrs. Woodeforde-Finden; new edition, cop. 1903 by Boosey & Co.

Good-bye, Eliza Jane. w., Andrew B. Sterling. m., Harry Von Tilzer. Harry Von Tilzer Music Pub. Co., cop. 1903.

Hannah! w., Joseph C. Farrell. m., Henry Frantzen. Howley, Haviland & Dresser, cop. 1903.

I'm on the Water Wagon Now. w., Paul West. m., John W. Bratton. M. Witmark & Sons, cop. 1903.

I Can't Do the Sum (Babes in Toyland). w., Glen MacDonough. m., Victor Herbert. M. Witmark & Sons, cop. 1903.

Ida! Sweet As Apple Cider! w., m., Eddie Leonard. Jos. W. Stern & Co., cop. 1903.

In the Merry Month of June. w., m., George Evans and Ren Shields. Whitney Warner Pub. Co., cop. 1903.

Laughing Water (Mother Goose). w., George Totten Smith. m., Frederick W. Hager. Sol Bloom, cop. 1903.

Lazy Moon. w., Bob Cole. m., Rosamond Johnson. Jos. W. Stern & Co., cop. 1903.

Lincoln, Grant or Lee. w., m., Paul Dresser. Howley, Haviland & Dresser, cop. 1903.

The March of the Toys (Babes in Toyland). Victor Herbert. M. Witmark & Sons, cop. 1903.

Mother o' Mine! w., Rudyard Kipling. m., Frank E. Tours. Chappell & Co., cop. 1903.

My San Domingo Maid (The Yankee Consul). w., Henry Blossom. m., Alfred G[eorge] Robyn. M. Witmark & Sons, cop. 1903.

My Task. Sacred song. w., Maude Louise Ray. m., Emma L. Ashford [Mrs. John Ashford, née Hindle]. Dayton, Ohio: Lorenz Pub. Co., cop. 1903.

Navajo. w., Harry H. Williams. m., Egbert Van Alstyne. Shapiro, Bernstein & Co., cop. 1903.

Oh, Isn't It Singular! w., J. P. Harrington. m., George LeBrunn. T. B. Harms & Co., cop. 1903 by Francis, Day & Hunter.

Open the Gates of the Temple. Sacred song. w., Fanny Crosby [Mrs. Alexander Van Alstyne]. m., Mrs. Joseph F. Knapp [née Phoebe Palmer]. Wm. A. Pond & Co., cop. 1903 by Mrs. Joseph F. Knapp.

Show the White of Yo' Eye. w., m., Stanley Crawford. Shapiro, Bernstein & Co., cop. 1903.

Spring, Beautiful Spring—*original German title:* O Frühling, Wie Bist Du So Schön. Waltz. m., Paul Lincke. Berlin: Apollo Verlag, cop. 1903; assigned 1920 to Edward B. Marks Music Co., New York. (Published as a song: "Chimes of Spring," w., L. Wolfe Gilbert, Edward B. Marks Music Co., cop. 1930.)

[Sweet Adeline] You're the Flower of My Heart, Sweet Adeline. w., Richard H. Gerard [pseud. of Richard Gerard Husch]. m., Harry Armstrong. M. Witmark & Sons, cop. 1903.

That's What the Daisy Said. w., m., Albert Von Tilzer. Harry Von Tilzer Music Pub. Co., cop. 1903.

Toyland (Babes in Toyland). w., Glen MacDonough. m., Victor Herbert. M. Witmark & Sons, cop. 1903.

The Voice of the Hudson. w., m., Paul Dresser. Howley, Haviland & Dresser, cop. 1903.

Where Are the Friends of Other Days? w., m., Paul Dresser. Howley, Haviland & Dresser, cop. 1903.

Your Dad Gave His Life for His Country. w., Harry J. Breen. m., T. Mayo Geary. The American Advance Music Co., cop. 1903.

Congress established (Feb. 14) the Department of Commerce and Labor.

The United States signed (May 22) a Treaty of Relations with Cuba and leased (July 2) for an annual rental of $2,000 the Cuban coastal city of Guantánamo as a naval base.

The United States extended (Nov. 8) recognition to the newly created Republic of Panama, which established (Nov. 3) its independence from Colombia, and negotiated (Nov. 18) with the former country a treaty for the construction of a canal through the Isthmus from Cristobál on the Atlantic to Balboa on the Pacific. The Canal Zone was created, a strip of land five miles on each side of the proposed canal and about fifty miles in length. For the privilege of using this zone the United States paid $10,-000,000 and agreed to an annual rental of $250,000 in gold (changed in 1936, because of the devaluation of the dollar, to 430,000 balboas in Panamanian currency). (In 1904 the United States purchased the uncompleted canal that was begun in 1882 by the French De Lesseps Company for $40,000,000, and in 1933 paid $25,000,000 for all claims of Colombia. The first ship passed through the United States constructed canal eleven years later, Aug. 3, 1914.)

Wisconsin became the first State to introduce the direct primary.

Direct wireless communication between Europe and America was established near Wellfleet, Cape Cod, Mass.; President Roosevelt sent the first message to King Edward VII.

Women's agitation for union rights resulted in the formation of the National Women's Trade Union League.

The laying of a Pacific cable between San Francisco and Manila was begun.

The popular Prince Heinrich Albert Wilhelm of Prussia, brother of the Kaiser, made the second of his two visits to the United States. (The first was in 1882-84.)

Two Americans set records for 'round-the-world travel—J. W. Willis Sayre of Seattle, Wash., in 54 days, 9 hours, 42 minutes, and Henry Frederick in 54 days, 7 hours, 2 minutes.

Fire destroyed (Dec. 30) the Iroquois Theatre in Chicago, and 602 persons perished in the holocaust—the third major catastrophe in the annals of the American theatre (the previous disasters had occurred in Richmond, Va., 1811, and in Brooklyn, New York, 1876). Most of the victims were trampled to death in the stampede for the exits.

Denis Dougherty was consecrated in Rome by Pope Pius X as the first American Roman Catholic Bishop of the Philippines.

Dr. H. Nelson Jackson and Sewell K. Crocker made the first transcontinental automobile trip from San Francisco to New York in 70 days (May 23-Aug. 1).

Henry Ford withdrew from the Detroit Automobile Company and organized the Ford Motor Company in that city.

Emma Lazarus's poem "The New Colossus," cast in a tablet, was set in place (in May) on the inside of the base of the Statue of Liberty in New York Harbor.

The Williamsburg Bridge, New York, spanning the East River from Manhattan Island to Long Island, was completed.

American aviation added an epoch-making event to its history. Wilbur and Orville Wright, who had been experimenting with glider planes, installed a light motor in their equipment and launched (Dec. 17) from Kill Devil Hill, near Kittyhawk, N. C., the first successful mechanical airplane. In its first flight, Orville Wright travelled 120 feet in 12 seconds. On the fourth attempt that day Wilbur Wright covered 852 feet in 59 seconds.

William Butler Yeats, Irish poet, toured (1903-04) in the United States as a lecturer.

Books of the year included Jack London's graphic picture of London slum life "The People of the Abyss," William DuBois's study "The Souls of Black Folk," and the novels "The Ambassadors" (Henry James), "The Bar Sinister" (Richard Harding Davis), "The Call of the Wild" (Jack London), "The Pit, A Story of Chicago" (Frank Norris; published posthumously), "Rebecca of Sunnybrook Farm" (Kate Douglas Wiggin). Charles Evans began the publication of his monumental chronological catalogue (1639-1799) "American Bibliography" (completed in 12 volumes in 1934).

Phonograph recordings of operatic arias, sung by celebrated artists to piano accompaniment, began to be issued by the Columbia Company, a pioneer in the industry.

Heinrich Conried became impresario of the Metropolitan Opera House, New York. He had been an actor in Vienna and the manager of the Stadttheater in Bremen, had come to the United States as an actor, and managed successively the Germania, Thalia, and Irving Place theatres in New York. His first bold undertaking in his new capacity was the staging (Dec. 24) of the first scenic performance outside Bayreuth, for his benefit, of Wagner's sacred festival music drama "Parsifal." It was given over the protests of the composer's heirs and the denunciations on the part of certain American clergymen, notably Dr. Charles Henry Parkhurst, of the theatrical enactment of the Eucharist. The performance was carefully prepared by no less an authority than the Bayreuth conductor Felix Mottl, who relinquished the baton at the performance to Alfred Hertz to escape the censure of the Wagner family, and by Anton Fuchs, the stage manager of Wagner's own opera house. Orchestra seats sold for $10 and speculators asked as high as $75 for the historic occasion. The cast included Alois Burgstaller (Parsifal), Milka Ternina (Kundry), Robert Blass (Gurnemanz), Otto Goritz (Klingsor), Anton Van Rooy (Amfortas), and Marcel Journet (Titurel). The opera was performed eleven times during the season (1903-04). Conried's other novelty was Ethel Smyth's one-act opera "Der Wald" (Mar. 11)—the first and only operatic work by a woman composer ever performed at the "Met."

Enrico Caruso, famous Italian tenor, made (Nov. 23) his American debut as the Duke in "Rigoletto" in New York at the Metropolitan Opera House.

New York heard (in June) its first Polish opera, "Halka" (1854) by Stanislaw Moniuszko, at the People's Theatre; the opera had a single performance and was sung in Russian.

Fritzi Scheff forsook grand opera at the Metropolitan Opera House for musical comedy at another Broadway house. She made (Nov. 16) her first appearance in this medium in Victor Herbert's "Babette" at the Broadway Theatre.

John Barrymore, younger son of Maurice Barrymore and Georgiana Drew Barrymore, made his stage debut in Herman Sudermann's play "Magda" in Chicago at the Cleveland Theatre.

George M. Cohan made (Apr. 27) his stellar debut in a production of his own, a musical comedy entitled "Running for Office," in New York at the 14th Street Theatre. The cast included his father Jerry J., his mother helen F., his sister Josephine, and his wife Ethel Levey.

New York plays included "Mice and Men" (Garrick, Jan. 19), "The Earl of Pawtucket" (Manhattan, Mar. 23), "Under Cover" (Murray Hill, Sept. 14), "Her Own Way" (Garrick, Sept. 28), "Raffles" (Princess, Oct. 27), "The Admirable Crichton" (Lyceum, Nov. 17), "The County Chairman" (Wallack's, Nov. 24), "Candida" (Princess, Dec. 9), "Sweet Kitty Bellairs" (Belasco, Dec. 9), "Merely Mary Ann" (Garden, Dec. 28), "The Other Girl" (Criterion, Dec. 29). Musical productions included the successes "The Wizard of Oz" with Fred Stone and Dave Montgomery (Majestic, Jan. 21), "Mr. Bluebeard" (Knickerbocker, Jan. 21), "Nancy Brown" with Marie Cahill (New York, Feb. 16), "The Prince of Pilsen" (Broadway, Mar. 17), "The Runaways" (Casino, May 11), "Whoop-Dee-Doo" (Weber and Fields, Sept. 24), "Babes in Toyland" (Majestic, Oct. 13), "The Girl from Kay's" (Herald Square, Nov. 2), "Mother Goose" (New Amsterdam, Dec. 2).

Progress was made in the motion-picture field with the filming of the silent movie "The Great Train Robbery," featuring G. M. Anderson of later "Broncho Billy" fame. Pictures were shown in nickelodeons.

In baseball, the "world series," as it is known in modern times, was launched. Boston (American League) beat Pittsburgh (National League) five games to three.

What the well-dressed woman should wear for bicycling, outings, and such, included: a shirtwaist, a skirt, a straw sailor hat, and a stiff collar with a bow tie.

"Calamity Jane" died. The name was the sobriquet of Martha Jane Burke (born about 1852), a noted frontier character, who frequented mining camps in South Dakota, dressed in man's attire, and since she was a crack shot threatened "calamity" on anyone who attempted to molest her.

ࣷ෴ 1904

Absinthe Frappé (It Happened in Nordland). w., Glen MacDonough. m., Victor Herbert. M. Witmark & Sons, cop. 1904.

Al Fresco. Orch. composition. m., Victor Herbert. M. Witmark & Sons, cop. 1904.

Alexander, Don't You Love Your Baby No More. w., Andrew B. Sterling. m., Harry Von Tilzer. Harry Von Tilzer Music Pub. Co., cop. 1904.

Back, Back, Back to Baltimore. w., Harry H. Williams. m., Egbert Van Alstyne. Shapiro, Remick & Co., cop. 1904.

Blue Bell. w., Edward Madden. m., Theodore F. Morse, F. B. Haviland Pub. Co., Inc., cop. 1904.

Come, Take a Trip in My Airship. w., Ren Shields. m., George Evans. Chas. K. Harris, cop. 1904.

Czardas. Piece for violin and piano. m., V[ittorio] Monti. Milano: G. Ricordi & Co., cop. 1904.

Down on the Brandywine. w., Vincent P. Bryan. m., J. B. Mullen. Shapiro, Remick & Co., cop. 1904.

Fascination. "Valse tzigane" [for café orchestra]. m., F. D. Marchetti. Paris: F. D. Marchetti, cop. 1904.

Give My Regards to Broadway (Little Johnny Jones). w., m., George M[ichael] Cohan. F. A. Mills, cop. 1904.

Gold and Silver—*original German title:* Gold und Silber. Waltz. m., Franz Lehár [op. 75]. London: Hawkes & Son, cop. 1904; assigned 1932 to Edward B. Marks Music Corp.; Carl Fischer, cop. 1911, arr. for orch. by S. K. Wright.

Good-bye, Flo (Little Johnny Jones). w., m., George M[ichael] Cohan. F. A. Mills, cop. 1904.

Good-bye, Little Girl, Good-bye. w., Will D. Cobb. m., Gus Edwards. M. Witmark & Sons, cop. 1904 by Cobb & Edwards; assigned 1904 to M. Witmark & Sons.

Good Bye, My Lady Love. w., m., Jos. E. Howard. Chas. K. Harris, cop. 1904.

Hannah, Won't You Open That Door? w., Andrew B. Sterling. m., Harry Von Tilzer. Harry Von Tilzer Music Pub. Co., cop. 1904.

I've Got a Feelin' for You; or, Way Down in My Heart. w., Edward Madden. m., Theodore F. Morse. F. B. Haviland Pub. Co., Inc., cop. 1904.

I May Be Crazy, But I Ain't No Fool. w., m., Alex. Rogers. The Attucks Music Pub. Co., cop. 1904.

In Zanzibar—My Little Chimpanzee (The Medal and the Maid). w., Will D. Cobb. m., Gus Edwards. Shapiro, Remick & Co., cop. 1904.

Life's a Funny Proposition After All (Little Johnny Jones). w., m., George M[ichael] Cohan. F. A. Mills, cop. 1904.

A Little Boy Called "Taps." w., Edward Madden. m., Theodore F. Morse. F. B. Haviland Pub. Co., cop. 1904.

The Man with the Ladder and the Hose. w., m., T. Mayo Geary. The Paul Dresser Pub. Co., cop. 1904 by The American Advance Music Co.

Mattinata—'Tis the Day. Italian words and music, Ruggiero Leoncavallo. English words, Ed[ward] Teschemacher. G. Ricordi & Co., Inc., cop. 1904.

Meet Me in St. Louis, Louis. w., Andrew B. Sterling. m., Kerry Mills. F. A. Mills, cop. 1904; renewed 1931 by Kerry Mills; assigned 1935 to Jerry Vogel Music Co., Inc.

My Ain Folk. w., Wilfrid Mills. m., Laura G. Lemon. London: Boosey & Co., cop. 1904.

My Honey Lou. w., m., Thurland Chattaway. F. B. Haviland Pub. Co., Inc., cop. 1904.

Nan! Nan! Nan! w., Edward Madden. m., Theodore F. Morse. F. B. Haviland Pub. Co., Inc., cop. 1904.

Now Sleeps the Crimson Petal. w., Alfred Lord Tennyson. m., Roger Quilter. London: Boosey & Co., cop. 1904.

Please Come and Play in My Yard. w., Edward Madden. m., Theodore F. Morse. F. B. Haviland Pub. Co., Inc., cop. 1904.

The Preacher and the Bear. w., m., Joe Arzonia. Philadelphia: Eclipse Publishing Co., cop. 1904 by Longbrake and Arzonia; assigned 1905 to Jos. Morris Co., Philadelphia.

She Went to the City. w., m., Paul Dresser. James H. Curtin, cop. 1904.

Stop Yer Tickling, Jock! w., Harry Lauder and Frank Folley. m., Harry Lauder. Harms, Inc., cop. 1904 by Francis, Day & Hunter.

Sweet Thoughts of Home (Love's Lottery). w., Stanislaus Stange. m., Julian Edwards. M. Witmark & Sons, cop. 1904.

The Tale of the Turtle Dove (Woodland). w., Frank Pixley. m., Gustav Luders. M. Witmark & Sons, cop. 1904.

Teasing. w., Cecil Mack. m., Albert Von Tilzer. The York Music Co., cop. 1904.

There Once Was an Owl (Babette). w., Harry B. Smith. m., Victor Herbert. M. Witmark & Sons, cop. 1904.

Three for Jack. w., Fred[erick] E[dward] Weatherly. m., W. H. Squire. London: Chappell & Co., Ltd., cop. 1904.

The Trumpeter. w., J. Francis Barron. m., J. Airlie Dix. London: Boosey Co., Ltd., cop. 1904.

When I'm Away from You, Dear. w., m., Paul Dresser. Howley-Dresser Co., cop. 1904.

When the Bees Are in the Hive. w., Alfred Bryan. m., Kerry Mills. F. A. Mills, cop. 1904; assigned 1928 to Paull-Pioneer Music Co.

Where the Southern Roses Grow. w., Richard H. Buck. m., Theodore F. Morse. F. B. Haviland Pub. Co., cop. 1904.

The Yankee Doodle Boy (Little Johnny Jones). w., m., George M[ichael] Cohan. F. A. Mills, cop. 1904.

American occupation of the Canal Zone, Panama, began (May 4); and the construction of the Panama Canal was undertaken under Colonel George Washington Goethals. The maintenance of sanitary conditions was entrusted to Surgeon-General Dr. William Crawford Gorgas.

The United States established its third mint, in Denver, Col. (The first was established in 1792 in Philadelphia; the second in 1852 in San Francisco.)

The St. Louis Exposition, celebrating the 100th anniversary of the Louisiana Purchase, opened (May 1).

The 22-floor, 280-foot high Fuller office building (known as the Flat Iron Building because of its triangular shape) was completed in New York —at that time the tallest building in the world. (Its construction was begun in 1902.)

The New York subway opened (Oct. 27).

The Williamsburg Bridge, New York, spanning the East River, was completed.

The steamer "General Slocum," carrying (June 15) up the East River, New York, about 1,400 persons, mostly women and children, on an excursion sponsored by St. Mark's Lutheran Church, caught fire and collapsed in mid-stream. The disaster took the lives of 1,021 aboard the vessel.

In Baltimore, fire destroyed (Feb. 7) 2,500 buildings.

One hundred and seventy-eight miners lost their lives in the Harwick Mine at Cheswick, Pa.

A strike occurred among the Chicago meat packers.

The Ziegler Polar Expedition, under Major Anthony Fiala, explored Franz Josef Land in the Arctic.

The Carnegie Hero Fund was established by a gift of $5,000,000 from Andrew Carnegie to honor "heroes of civilization" instead of "heroes of barbarism."

The American Academy of Arts and Letters was founded as an honorary group of 50 members within the National Institute of Arts and Letters (1898).

The Hispanic Society of America was founded in New York to promote American cultural appreciation of Spanish- and Portuguese-speaking peoples.

The United Spanish War Veterans organization was formed.

The Camp-Fire Club of America was incorporated in New York as a social organization for the preservation of forests and wild life.

Helen Adams Keller, who lost her sight, hearing, and speech in infancy, was graduated from Radcliffe College. She became in after years a noted American writer and lecturer.

The "Massachusetts Spy," a newspaper founded in 1770, came to an end after 134 years of publication.

"Musical America" was founded in New York as a weekly journal devoted to musical activities.

Books of the year included: "The History of the Standard Oil Company" (Ida Tarbell; an exposé, 2 vols.) and the fiction, "Cabbages and Kings" (William Sydney Porter), "The Crossing" (Winston Churchill), "Freckles" (Gene Stratton-Porter), "The Law of the Land" (Emerson Hough), "The Sea-Wolf" (Jack London).

The highly publicized American première (Dec. 24, 1903) of Wagner's "Parsifal" and its subsequent ten performances at the Metropolitan Opera House led to other productions of the opera in America in forms which the composer had never imagined, the masterpiece being uncopyrighted in the United States. A dramatic version by Edward Locke with the original music arranged by Oscar Radin was played (Mar. 14) in Pittsburgh at the Grand Opera House. A stock company of actors in Philadelphia gave performances of the opera as a play for a week (in May) at Forepaugh's Theatre. A dramatization by Marie Doran was performed (May 23) in New York at the West End Theatre. Henry Wilson Savage, Boston theatrical manager, staged the local première (Oct. 17) in English and toured the United States for a year with the Savage English Opera Company, giving the work in all major cities (New York, Philadelphia, New Orleans, Los Angeles, etc.) and in Montreal, Can.

Richard Strauss, famed German composer of symphonic works and operas, visited the United States for the first time, conducting (Mar. 21) the world première of his "Symphonia Domestica" in New York at Carnegie Hall with the Hermann Wetzler Symphony Orchestra, organized for the composer's benefit. (Strauss made a second visit in 1922.)

Samuel Coleridge-Taylor, eminent British composer of African Negro descent, made the first of three visits to America to conduct concerts of his own music. (The other visits occurred in 1906 and 1910.)

Orchestra Hall, erected in Chicago by subscriptions from more than 8,000 persons, was dedicated (Dec. 14) by Theodore Thomas and his Chicago Orchestra.

Luisa Tetrazzini, Italian operatic coloratura soprano, made her American debut in San Francisco at the Tivoli Opera House. (She began her sensational career in the United States when she appeared as Violetta in "La Traviata" at the Manhattan Opera House, New York, Jan. 15, 1908).

Edward Hugh Sothern and Julia Marlowe began their joint appearances in Shakespearean plays. (They married in 1911.)

Johnston Forbes-Robertson made (Mar. 8) his first New York appearance in "Hamlet" at the Knickerbocker Theatre.

Following the example of Fritzi Scheff (1903), the great operatic contralto Mme. Ernestine Schumann-Heink essayed light opera in "Love's Lottery," produced (Oct. 3) in New York at the Broadway Theatre. It was her only venture in this field; the operetta ran for 50 performances.

New York plays included "The Virginian" with Dustin Farnum (Manhattan, Jan. 5), "The Secret of Polichinelle" (Madison Square, Jan. 19), "The Dictator" (Criterion, Apr. 4), "Mrs. Wiggs of the Cabbage Patch"

(Savoy, Sept. 3), "The Duke of Killicrankie" (Empire, Sept. 5), "The College Widow" (Garden, Sept. 20), "The Music Master" with David Warfield (Belasco, Sept. 26), "Leah Kleschna" (Manhattan, Dec. 12). Long-run musical productions included "The Yankee Consul" (Broadway, Feb. 22), "Piff! Paff!! Pouf!!!" with Eddie Foy (Casino, Apr. 2), "The School Girl" (Daly's, Sept. 1), "The Sho-gun" (Wallack's, Oct. 10), "Higgledy-Piggledy" (Weber Music Hall, Oct. 20), "Humpty Dumpty" (New Amsterdam, Nov. 14), "Woodland" (New York, Nov. 21), "It Happened in Nordland" (Lew Fields', Dec. 5).

The Olympic games were held for the first time in the United States in St. Louis, Mo. The marathon honors went for the first time to an American runner, T. J. Hicks, who ran the distance in 3 hours, 28 minutes, 53 seconds.

The New York National League baseball champions ("Giants") refused to play the Boston American League champions in the second World's Series.

The "rich man's" depression of 1904 was the nineteenth financial setback since 1790; it lasted one year.

In the national elections, President Theodore Roosevelt was reëlected by a majority of nearly 2,000,000 votes, the largest number yet received by any candidate.

Daniel Decatur Emmett, aged 89, composer of "Dixie," "Old Dan Tucker," and other minstrel songs, died (June 28) in Mt. Vernon, O.

࿐ 1905

Bandana Land (It Happened in Nordland). w., Glen MacDonough. m., Victor Herbert. M. Witmark & Sons, cop. 1905.

A Bowl of Roses. w., W. E. Henley. m., Robert Coningby Clarke. London: Chappell & Co., Ltd., cop. 1905.

Carissima. w., m., Arthur Penn. Chicago: Sol Bloom, cop. 1905; assigned 1907 to M. Witmark & Sons.

Claire de Lune (in: Suite Bergamasque). Piano solo. m., Achille Claude Debussy. Paris: E. Fronont, cop. 1905; renewed 1932.

Daddy's Little Girl. w., Edward Madden. m., Theodore F. Morse. F. B. Haviland Pub. Co., Inc., cop. 1905.

The Day That You Grew Colder. w., m., Paul Dresser. The Paul Dresser Pub. Co., cop. 1905.

Dearie. w., m., Clare Kummer. Jos. W. Stern & Co., cop. 1905.

Down Where the Silv'ry Mohawk Flows. w., Monroe H. Rosenfeld. m., John and Otto Heinzman. Jos. W. Stern & Co., cop. 1905.

Everybody Works but Father. w., m., Jean Havez. Helf & Hager Co., Inc., cop. 1905.

Forty-five Minutes from Broadway (Forty-five Minutes from Broadway). w., m., George M[ichael] Cohan. F. A. Mills, cop. 1905.

Fou the Noo; or, Something in the Bottle for the Morning. w., Harry Lauder and Gerald Grafton. m., Harry Lauder. T. B. Harms & Francis, Day & Hunter, cop. 1905 by Francis, Day & Hunter, London.

He's Me Pal. w., Vincent P. Bryan. m., Gus Edwards. M. Witmark & Sons, cop. 1905.

I Don't Care. w., Jean Lenox. m., Harry O. Sutton. Shapiro, Jerome H. Remick & Co., cop. 1905.

I Want What I Want When I Want It (Mlle. Modiste). w., Henry Blossom. m., Victor Herbert. M. Witmark & Sons, cop. 1905.

If a Girl Like You, Loved a Boy Like Me. w., m., [Will D.] Cobb and [Gus] Edwards. M. Witmark & Sons, cop. 1905.

In My Merry Oldsmobile. w., Vincent P. Bryan. m., Gus Edwards. M. Witmark & Sons, cop. 1905.

In the Shade of the Old Apple Tree. w., Harry H. Williams. m., Egbert Van Alstyne. Shapiro, Jerome H. Remick & Co., cop. 1905.

Jim Judson—from the Town of Hackensack. w., m., Paul Dresser. The Paul Dresser Pub. Co., cop. 1905.

Just a Little Rocking Chair and You. w., Bert Fitzgibbon and Jack Drislane. m., Theodore F. Morse. F. B. Haviland Pub. Co., cop. 1905.

Keep a Little Cozy Corner in Your Heart for Me. w., Jack Drislane. m., Theodore F. Morse. F. B. Haviland Pub. Co., cop. 1905.

Kiss Me Again [If I Were on the Stage] (Mlle. Modiste). w., Henry Blossom. m., Victor Herbert. M. Witmark & Sons, cop. 1905.

A Knot of Blue (It Happened in Nordland). w., Glen MacDonough. m., Victor Herbert. M. Witmark & Sons, cop. 1905.

The Leader of the German Band. w., Edward Madden. m., Theodore F. Morse. F. B. Haviland Pub. Co., cop. 1905.

Longing for You. w., Jack Drislane. m., Theodore F. Morse. F. B. Haviland Pub. Co., cop. 1905.

Mary's a Grand Old Name (Forty-five Minutes From Broadway). w., m., George M[ichael] Cohan. F. A. Mills, cop. 1905.

The Moon Has His Eyes on You. w., Billy Johnson. m., Albert Von Tilzer. The York Music Co., cop. 1905.

La Musica Proibita [Forbidden Music]. w., N. Malpadi. m., Stanislao Gastoldon, op. 5. (Published in Italy probably during the mid-1880s. The song swept Europe as a vocal composition and in countless instrumental versions. An English orch. arrangement by Adolf Schmid was published by Hawkes & Son, London, cop. 1905; an American arrangement by Alfred Roth was published by Carl Fischer, New York, cop. 1905.)

My Gal Sal; or, They Called Her Frivolous Sal. w., m., Paul Dresser. The Paul Dresser Pub. Co., cop. 1905.

My Guiding Star. w., m., Thurland Chattaway. m., Jean Schwartz. Jerome H. Remick & Co., cop. 1905.

My Irish Molly O. w., William Jerome. m., Jean Schwartz. Jerome H. Remick & Co., cop. 1905.

Nobody. w., Alex Rogers. m., Bert A. Williams. The Attucks Music Pub. Co., cop. 1905.

One Called "Mother" and the Other "Home Sweet Home." w., William Cahill. m., Theodore F. Morse. F. B. Haviland Pub. Co., cop. 1905.

A Picnic for Two. w., Arthur J. Lamb. m., Albert Von Tilzer. The York Music Co., cop. 1905.

"Razzazza Mazzazza." Composition for band. m., Arthur Pryor. Carl Fischer, cop. 1905; renewed 1933.

Rufus Rastus Johnson Brown. See below: "What You Goin' to Do When the Rent Comes 'Round?"

She Is Ma Daisy. w., Harry Lauder and J. D. Harper. m., Harry Lauder. Francis, Day & Hunter, cop. 1905.

She Waits by the Deep Blue Sea. w., Edward Madden. m., Theodore F. Morse. F. B. Haviland Pub. Co., cop. 1905.

So Long Mary (Forty-five Minutes from Broadway). w., m., George M[ichael] Cohan. F. A. Mills, cop. 1905.

Stand Up and Fight Like H—— (Forty-five Minutes from Broadway). w., m., George M[ichael] Cohan. F. A. Mills, cop. 1905.

Starlight. w., Edward Madden. m., Theodore F. Morse. F. B. Haviland Pub. Co., cop. 1905.

Take Me Back to Your Heart Again. w., Collin Davis. m., Frank J. Richmond. M. Witmark & Sons, cop. 1905.

Tammany. w., Vincent P. Bryan. m., Gus Edwards. M. Witmark & Sons, cop. 1905.

The Town Where I Was Born. w., m., Paul Dresser. Jerome H. Remick & Co., cop. 1905 by Paul Dresser.

Wait 'Til the Sun Shines, Nellie. w., Andrew B. Sterling. m., Harry Von Tilzer. Harry Von Tilzer Music Co., cop. 1905.

We've Been Chums for Fifty Years. w., m., Thurland Chattaway. New York Music Pub. House, cop. 1905.

What You Goin' to Do When the Rent Comes 'Round?—Rufus Rastus Johnson Brown. w., Andrew B. Sterling. m., Harry Von Tilzer. Harry Von Tilzer Music Pub. Co., cop. 1905.

When the Bell in the Lighthouse Rings Ding Dong. w., Arthur J. Lamb. m., Alfred Solman. Jos. W. Stern & Co., cop. 1905.

When the Mocking Birds Are Singing in the Wildwood. w., Arthur J. Lamb. m., H. B. Blake. Jerome H. Remick & Co., cop. 1905.

Where the Morning Glories Twine Around the Door. w., Andrew B. Sterling. m., Harry Von Tilzer. Harry Von Tilzer Music Pub. Co., cop. 1905.

Where the River Shannon Flows. w., m., James J. Russell. M. Witmark & Sons, cop. 1905.

The Whistler and His Dog. Orch. composition. m., Arthur Pryor. Carl Fischer, cop. 1905.

Will You Love Me in December As You Do in May? w., James J. Walker. m., Ernest R. Ball. M. Witmark & Sons, cop. 1905.

A Woman Is Only a Woman but a Good Cigar Is a Smoke (Miss Dolly Dollars). w., Harry B. Smith. m., Victor Herbert. M. Witmark & Sons, cop. 1905.

Would You Care? w., m., Charles K. Harris. Chas. K. Harris, cop. 1905.

_____

President Theodore Roosevelt began his second term.

Congress discontinued the coinage of gold dollars (minted since 1849).

President Roosevelt mediated (Sept. 5) at Portsmouth, N. H., the treaty of peace terminating the Russo-Japanese War (1904-05).

The Lewis and Clark Centennial American Pacific Exposition and Oriental Fair was held (June 1-Oct. 15) in Portland, Ore.

Frank Steunenberg, former Governor of Idaho, was assassinated (Dec. 30). Clarence Seward Darrow defended William D. Haywood, accused of instigating the murder.

The remains of John Paul Jones (his real name was John Paul), Scottish seaman and naval hero in the American Revolutionary War who died in 1792 in Paris, were removed to Annapolis, Md.

The Staten Island ferry, New York, opened (Oct. 25).

Orville Wright accomplished (Sept. 26) the first officially recorded airplane flight at Dayton, O. He flew 11.12 miles in 18 minutes, 9 seconds. Orville Wright and his brother Wilbur again demonstrated (Oct. 5) their airplane in a flight of about 25 miles, covering the distance in 38 minutes.

The first of the Rotary International businessmen's luncheon clubs was founded in Chicago.

The Carnegie Foundation for the Advancement of Teaching was established (Apr. 16) with an endowment of $10,000,000 by Andrew Carnegie, for the purpose of encouraging higher education in the United States, Canada, and Newfoundland by providing pensions for university and college teachers and their widows.

The last surviving soldier of the War of 1812 died—Hiram Crouk, aged 105 (May 13), in Ava, N. Y.

"Variety" was founded in New York as a weekly journal of the theatre, developing a unique literary style of its own. The periodical included in its scope movies, radio, and television, as these came along.

Books of the year included: "The Life of Reason" (George Santayana; a philosophical treatise, 5 vols., 1905-06), "Iconoclasts, A Book of Dramatists" (James Gibbons Huneker), "The War of the Classes" (Jack London; a socialistic study) and the fiction, "The Clansman" (Thomas Dixon), "The Game" (Jack London; a story about a prize fight), "The House of Mirth" (Edith Wharton).

Prof. George Pierce Baker founded at Harvard University his "47 Workshop," a student theatre for the writing and production of plays. (He transferred his activities in 1925 to Yale. Among his students were George Abbott, Philip Barry, Samuel Nathaniel Behrman, John Dos Passos, Sidney Howard, Eugene O'Neill, Edward Sheldon, John V. A. Weaver, Thomas Wolfe, and others.)

Abandoning piano accompaniments for operatic arias on phonograph records, companies now issued recordings with specially adapted orchestral backgrounds. (The use of the composer's original orchestration was a later development.)

Vincent d'Indy, eminent French composer, visited the United States and conducted (Dec. 1 and 2) two concerts of the Boston Symphony Orchestra.

At the Metropolitan Opera House, New York, the stage bridge in Act I of "Carmen" collapsed (Jan. 7) during the public performance of the opera. The curtain was lowered, and after eight injured members of the chorus were removed to a hospital the performance continued.

"Zenobia" by the Newark-born composer Louis Adolphe Coerne was probably the first opera by an American to be performed in Germany; it was given (Dec. 1) in Bremen.

Will Rogers began his stage career at Hammerstein's Roof Garden theatre in New York.

R. F. Outcault's "New York Herald" comic cartoons of Buster Brown were transferred to the stage (New York, Majestic Theatre, Jan. 24; 95 performances) in a two-act comedy with Master Gabriel as Buster Brown and George Ali as the dog Tige.

Richard Mansfield played (Apr. 10) in New York at the New Amsterdam Theatre seven English performances of Molière's (1666) French comedy "Le Misanthrope."

A new Hippodrome, built at the cost of $1,750,000, opened (Apr. 12) in New York with a musical extravaganza "A Yankee Circus on Mars"— a type of spectacular production that was to be an annual event for many years.

George Bernard Shaw's play "Man and Superman" was produced (Sept. 5) in New York at the Hudson Theatre.

Fritzi Scheff, lyric queen of light opera since 1903, displayed her versatility in a series of revivals in New York at the Broadway Theatre ("Fatinitza," Dec. 26, 1904; "Giroflé-Girofla," Jan. 30, 1905; "Boccaccio," Feb. 27). She reappeared later in Victor Herbert's "Mlle. Modiste" (Knickerbocker Theatre, Dec. 25) to score one of her greatest triumphs, which carried the now famous operetta into the next year to 224 performances with return engagements in 1907.

Arnold Daly presented (Sept. 11-Nov. 11) in New York at the Garrick Theatre a cycle of George Bernard Shaw's plays—"Candida," "The Man of Destiny," "How He Lied to Her Husband," "You Never Can Tell," "John Bull's Other Island," and "Mrs. Warren's Profession." The police

stopped the latter as an immoral play after the first night (Oct. 23) and
arrested Daly and Mary Shaw (the Mrs. Warren of the production) on a
technical charge of disorderly conduct. The actors were released on bail,
resumed their season, and were acquitted eight months later.

New York plays included "Adrea" (Belasco, Jan. 11; Mrs. Leslie Carter's last appearances under Belasco's management), "Mrs. Leffingwell's
Boots" (Savoy, Jan. 11), "Zira" (Princess, Sept. 21), "The Walls of Jericho" (New York, Sept. 25), "The Man on the Box" (Madison Square,
Oct. 3), "The Squaw Man" (Wallack's, Oct. 23), "Peter Pan" with Maude
Adams (Empire, Nov. 6), "The Girl of the Golden West" (Belasco, Nov.
14), and a new long-run play "The Lion and the Mouse" (Lyceum, Nov.
20; 686 performances). Musical productions included "Fantana" (Lyric,
Jan. 14), "The Duchess of Dantzic" (Daly's, Jan. 16), "Sergeant Brue"
(Knickerbocker, Apr. 24), "The Rollicking Girl" (Herald Square, May
1), "The Catch of the Season" (Daly's, Aug. 28), "The Earl and the Girl"
(Casino, Nov. 4).

Tyrus Raymond ("Ty") Cobb joined the Detroit American League
("Tigers") baseball club as an outfielder. Although he hit only .240 the
first year, his batting average thereafter never fell below .320. He always
was a terror to the opposing pitcher and established a record of having hit
safely in 40 consecutive games.

Christopher ("Christy") Mathewson, baseball pitcher of the New York
National League ("Giants") club, achieved the greatest single feat in the
history of the game when he pitched three shut-outs against the Philadelphia American League club in the World's Series.

Undefeated heavyweight boxing champion James J. Jeffries retired from
the ring. (He returned in 1910 and was kayoed by Jack Johnson.)

ᘒᕉ 1906

All In Down and Out. w., R. C. McPherson (Cecil Mack). m., Smith,
Johnson and Elmer Bowman. The Gotham-Attucks Music Co., cop.
1906.

Anchors Aweigh. w., A. H. Miles and R. Lovell. m., Charles A. Zimmerman. Cop. 1906 by Ida M. Zimmerman; assigned 1929 to Robbins
Music Corp.

Arrah Wanna. w., Jack Drislane. m., Theodore F. Morse. F. B. Haviland Pub. Co., cop. 1906.

At Dawning. w., Nelle Richmond Eberhart. m., Charles Wakefield
Cadman, op. 29, no. 1. Boston: Oliver Ditson Co., cop. 1906.

Bake Dat Chicken Pie. w., m., Frank Dumont. M. Witmark & Sons, cop. 1906.

Because You're You (The Red Mill). w., Henry Blossom. m., Victor Herbert. M. Witmark & Sons, cop. 1906.

The Bird on Nellie's Hat. w., Arthur J. Lamb. m., Alfred Solman. Jos. W. Stern & Co., cop. 1906.

Blow the Smoke Away (The Time, the Place and the Girl). w., Will M. Hough and Frank R. Adams. m., Joseph E. Howard. Chas. K. Harris, cop. 1906.

Cheyenne. w., Harry H. Williams. m., Egbert Van Alstyne. Jerome H. Remick & Co., cop. 1906.

Chinatown My Chinatown. w., William Jerome. m., Jean Schwartz. Jerome H. Remick & Co., cop. 1906.

College Life. w., Porter Emerson Browne. m., Henry Frantzen. F. B. Haviland Pub. Co., Inc., cop. 1906.

Dreaming. w., L. W. Heiser. m., J. Anton Dailey. Jerome H. Remick & Co., cop. 1906.

Ethel Levey's Virginia Song—I Was Born in Virginia (George Washington, Jr.). w., m., George M[ichael] Cohan. F. A. Mills, cop. 1906.

Every Day Is Ladies' Day to Me (The Red Mill). w., Henry Blossom. m., Victor Herbert. M. Witmark & Sons, cop. 1906.

The Good Old U. S. A. w., Jack Drislane. m., Theodore F. Morse. F. B. Haviland Pub. Co., cop. 1906.

He's a Cousin of Mine (Marrying Mary). w., Cecil Mack. m., Chris. Smith and Silvio Hein. Gotham-Attucks Music Co., Inc., cop. 1906.

He Walked Right In, Turned Around and Walked Right Out Again. w., Ed. Rose. m., Maxwell Silver. F. A. Mills, cop. 1906.

I Just Can't Make My Eyes Behave (A Parisian Model). w., m., Will D. Cobb and Gus Edwards. Gus Edwards Music Pub. Co., cop. 1906.

I Love a Lassie, or, Ma Scotch Bluebell. w., m., Harry Lauder and Gerald Grafton. Harmes, Inc., cop. 1906, by Francis, Day & Hunter, London.

I Love You Truly. w., m., Carrie Jacobs-Bond, Chicago: Carrie Jacobs-Bond & Son, cop. 1906 by Carrie Jacobs-Bond.

If Washington Should Come to Life (George Washington, Jr.). w., m., George M[ichael] Cohan. F. A. Mills, cop. 1906.

In Old New York. "The Streets of New York."

The Isle of Our Dreams (The Red Mill). w., Henry Blossom. m., Victor Herbert. M. Witmark & Sons, cop. 1906.

Keep on the Sunny Side. w., Jack Drislane. m., Theodore F. Morse. F. B. Haviland Pub. Co., cop. 1906.

A Lemon in the Garden of Love (The Spring Chicken). w., M. E. Rourke. m., Richard Carle. M. Witmark & Sons, cop. 1906.

Let It Alone. w., Alex Rogers. m., Bert A. Williams. The Gotham-Attucks Music Co., cop. 1906.

Love Me and the World Is Mine. w., Dave Reed, Jr. m., Ernest R. Ball. M. Witmark & Sons, cop. 1906.

Moonbeams (The Red Mill). w., Henry Blossom. m., Victor Herbert. M. Witmark & Sons, cop. 1906.

My Laddie. w., Princess Troubetzkoy. m., William Armour Thayer. G. Schirmer, Inc., cop. 1906.

My Mariuccia Take a Steamboat. w., George Ronklyn. m., Al Piantadosi. Shapiro, Bernstein & Co., cop. 1906.

National Emblem. March. m., E. E. Bagley. Boston: Walter Jacobs, Inc., cop. 1906 by Ernest S. Williams; renewed 1933 by Clare Ester Dodge; assigned 1934 to Walter Jacobs, Inc.

No Wedding Bells for Me. w., E. P. Moran and Will A. Heelan. m., Seymour Furth. Shapiro Music Publisher, cop. 1906 by Maurice Shapiro.

Nothing New Beneath the Sun (The Governor's Son). w., m., George M[ichael] Cohan. F. A. Mills, cop. 1906.

Poor John! w., Fred W. Leigh. m., Henry E. Pether. Francis, Day & Hunter, cop. 1906.

Since Father Went to Work. w., m., William Cahill. Jos. Stern & Co., cop. 1906.

Schnitzelbank. w., m., anon. Buffalo: Broadway Pub. Co. [cop. 1906 by Henry Schwabl.] (See 1863—"Johnny Schmoker.")

The Streets of New York (The Red Mill). w., Henry Blossom. m., Victor Herbert. M. Witmark & Sons, cop. 1906.

Sunbonnet Sue. w., Will D. Cobb. m., Gus Edwards. Gus Edwards Music Pub. Co., cop. 1906; renewed 1934 by Gus Edwards and Kate A. Cobb; assigned 1936 to Mills Music, Inc.

That's the Reason Noo I Wear a Kilt. w., Harry Lauder and A. B. Kendal. m., Harry Lauder. T. B. Harms & Francis, Day & Hunter, cop. 1906 by Francis, Day & Hunter, London.

Waiting at the Church; or, My Wife Won't Let Me. w., Fred W. Leigh. m., Henry E. Pether. T. B. Harms & Co., cop. 1906 by Francis, Day & Hunter.

Waltz Me Around Again Willie—'Round, 'Round, 'Round. w., Will D. Cobb. m., Ren Shields. F. A. Mills, cop. 1906.

What's the Use of Loving If You Can't Love All the Time? w., Joseph Mittenthal. m., Harry Armstrong. Shapiro Music Publisher, cop. 1906 by Maurice Shapiro.

When You Know You're Not Forgotten by the Girl You Can't Forget. w., Ed. Gardenier. m., J. Fred Helf. Helf & Hager Co., Inc., cop. 1906.

Won't You Come Over to My House? w., Harry H. Williams. m., Egbert Van Alstyne. Jerome H. Remick & Co., cop. 1906.

You're a Grand Old Flag (George Washington, Jr.). w., m., George M[ichael] Cohan. F. A. Mills, cop. 1906.

You Can Have Broadway (George Washington, Jr.). w., m., George M[ichael] Cohan. F. A. Mills, cop. 1906.

President Theodore Roosevelt was awarded the Nobel prize of $40,000 for efforts in terminating the Russo-Japanese War (1904-05)—the first American to receive a Nobel prize. He contributed a sizable part of the money to the endowment of the Foundation for the Promotion of Industrial Peace.

Upton Sinclair's exposure in his novel "The Jungle" of conditions in the Chicago meat-packing industry led President Roosevelt to institute a Congressional investigation, which culminated (June 30) in the passage of the Federal Food and Drug Act by Congress.

Theodore Roosevelt was the first United States President to set foot on foreign soil when he visited Panama.

Congress passed (June 8) "An Act for the preservation of American antiquities," empowering the President to set aside historic landmarks and phenomena of nature, within the jurisdiction of the United States, as national monuments. During the same session, Congress passed (June 29) the Hepburn Act, supplementing the Interstate Commerce Act (1887) for the regulation of rates and transportation of certain products (chiefly coal).

The Cherokee, Chickasaw, Choctaw, Creek, and Seminole Indians of Oklahoma, known as the Five Civilized Nations or Tribes, were admitted to citizenship.

Admiral Robert Edwin Peary on his dash to the North Pole reached (Apr. 21) the farthest north latitude—87° 6′.

Alice Lee Roosevelt, daughter of President Theodore Roosevelt, married Congressman Nicholas Longworth in the White House—a long-remembered social event. The bride started the vogue for Alice Blue.

Already familiar with earthquakes for nearly half a century, San Francisco experienced (Apr. 18 at 5:15 A.M.) its worst catastrophe in that form. The violent tremors tumbled down houses, hotels, office buildings, churches, theatres, and structures of every kind, and split pavements asunder. The ensuing fire added to the devastation. The lives of 452 persons were lost in the disaster, 1,500 were injured, 265,000 made homeless, 60,000 buildings were destroyed, 453 city blocks were burned, and property damage amounted to $350,000,000. Insurance companies paid $132,-823,067.21.

Victor Herbert's new comic opera "Babes in Toyland" was playing at the Columbia Theatre in San Francisco. The New York Metropolitan Opera Company was in the city on tour and had performed "Carmen" the preceding night with Caruso in the cast. In New York, Victor Herbert conducted a monster concert at the Hippodrome for the benefit of the sufferers.

Pace Institute, New York, was founded as one of the earliest schools of accountancy and business administration. (Chartered as Pace College in Dec., 1948.)

Reginald Aubrey Fessenden, American physicist and inventor, experimenting in wireless telephony (radio), succeeded in transmitting (Dec. 24) a musical program from Brant Rock, Mass., to Plymouth, 11 miles away. A steamer about 12 to 15 miles at sea also heard the broadcast.

One Roy Knabenshue upset the schedule of both Houses of Congress when he sailed a dirigible around the dome of the Capitol.

Stanford White, noted architect and designer of Madison Square Garden, New York, was shot (June 25) by Harry K. Thaw, heir to a Pittsburgh fortune, at the opening of its roof garden theatre during a professional performance of a former Columbia University revue, "Mamzelle Champagne." At the trial the defense counsel coined a term when he said that Thaw had "a brainstorm."

Upton Sinclair, who was much in the limelight at this time, and 40 associates, mostly literary people, established the communal Helicon Home Colony in Englewood, N. J. The enterprise was ridiculed in the press, and was abandoned the next year when a fire destroyed the main building.

"The American Magazine" was founded as a continuation of "Frank Leslie's Popular Monthly" (1876).

Books of the year included: "With Walt Whitman at Camden," vol. 1 (Horace Traubel, one of the poet's executors; a diary, completed in 3 volumes in 1914), "The Cynic's Word Book" (Ambrose Bierce; a collection of witty newspaper squibs and odd definitions, retitled "The Devil's Dictionary," 1911), and the fiction, "The Awakening of Helena Ritchie" (Margaret Deland), "Coniston" (Winston Churchill), "The Jungle" (Upton Sinclair; see above), "White Fang" (Jack London), "The Spoilers" (Rex Beach).

The famous Italian opera composer Ruggiero Leoncavallo came to America from Milan with an opera troupe called "La Scala." He made (Oct. 8) his American debut as a conductor at Carnegie Hall, New York, and toured the United States and Canada, giving performances of his operas "Pagliacci" and a new work "La Jeunesse de Figaro." The latter proved unsuccessful and was never produced in Europe.

Returning from triumphs at the Royal Opera in Berlin, Massachusetts-born lyric soprano Geraldine Farrar made (Nov. 26) her American debut in Gounod's opera "Roméo et Juliette" in New York at the Metropolitan Opera House.

Forsaking show business on Broadway, Oscar Hammerstein invaded the field of grand opera and opened (Dec. 3) his Manhattan Opera House in New York with Bellini's "I Puritani." The celebrated Italian tenor Alessandro Bonci made his American debut on this occasion.

Camille Saint-Saëns, French pianist and composer of "Samson et Dalila" and other works, made the first of two visits to the United States. He appeared (Nov. 3) in New York with the Symphony Society, playing his fantasia "Africa" for piano and orchestra. (His second visit was in 1915.)

Dr. Karl Muck, famous German orchestra conductor, became musical director of the Boston Symphony Orchestra.

Alexander Scriabin, important Russian composer and pianist, concertized (Dec. 1906-1907) in the United States, giving recitals of his own works.

Henry Wilson Savage, who had successfully toured (1904-05) the country giving English performances of Wagner's "Parsifal," staged in English (Oct. 15) at the Columbia Theatre in Washington, D. C., the American première of Puccini's "Madame Butterfly" and went on tour (1906-07) with the production (New York, Garden Theatre, Nov. 12, 1906; New Orleans, French Opera House, Jan. 9, 1907; San Francisco, Van Ness Theatre, Mar. 11, 1907, one of the first gala occasions in the city after the earthquake, and elsewhere).

Harry MacLennan Lauder, Scottish singer and London music-hall comedian, made the first of 40 visits to the United States.

B. F. Keith and F. F. Proctor formed the Keith and Proctor Amusement Company, which controlled for many years a chain of vaudeville theatres across the country. (At the time of Keith's death in 1914, the company supervised over 400 houses. It later was incorporated in the Radio-Keith-Orpheum circuit.)

George M. Cohan produced in New York with Fay Templeton his "Forty-five Minutes from Broadway" (New Amsterdam Theatre, Jan. 1) and with his family the flag-waving "George Washington, Jr." (Herald Square Theatre, Feb. 12).

George Bernard Shaw's play "Caesar and Cleopatra" with Johnston Forbes-Robertson and Gertrude Elliott was produced (Oct. 30) at the New Amsterdam Theatre, New York.

Anna Held, toast of Broadway blades, was singing "I Just Can't Make My Eyes Behave" in the musical comedy "The Parisian Model" (New York, Broadway Theatre, Nov. 27) for 179 performances.

The New York Hippodrome staged (Nov. 28) another of its gigantic shows—"Pioneer Days," with "Little Hip, the Smallest Elephant in the World," a group of full-grown elephants and performing stallions, and other features. The spectacle included an operatic extravaganza, "Neptune's Daughter," in which for the first time the Hippodrome girls disappeared amid water effects devised by H. L. Bowdoin.

Ruth St. Denis, who had appeared in 1904 as an actress under the name of Ruth Denis in David Belasco's "Du Barry," featuring Mrs. Leslie Carter, now introduced herself as an exotic dancer in a choreographic composition of her own entitled "Egypta," with which she had toured Europe the preceding year.

The New York stage carried over many of its previous year's successes and offered a rich choice of musical comedies. Among new long-run plays were "The Hypocrites" with Richard Bennett and Doris Keane (Hudson, Aug. 30), "The Chorus Lady" with Rose Stahl (Savoy, Sept. 1), "His House in Order" with John Drew and Margaret Illington (Empire, Sept. 3), "The Great Divide" (Princess, Oct. 3), "The Rose of the Rancho" with Frances Starr and Charles Richman (Belasco, Nov. 27), "The Man of the Hour" (Savoy, Dec. 4). Of the numerous popular musical comedies none equalled the success or longevity of Victor Herbert's operetta "The Red Mill" (Knickerbocker, Sept. 24) with Fred A. Stone

and David Montgomery; the first New York run totalled 274 performances.

The name "George Spelvin" appeared for the first time on a New York
playbill, heading the cast of Winchell Smith and Byron Ongley's dramatization of George Barr McCutcheon's novel "Brewster's Millions" (New
Amsterdam Theatre, Dec. 31). He was a creation of Winchell Smith, entirely fictitious, and figured in nearly all of Smith's subsequent productions
("Via Wireless," 1908, "The Fortune Hunter," 1909, "Love among the
Lions," 1910, "The Only Son," 1911, "Turn to the Right," 1916, "Lightnin'," 1918, "Thank You," 1921, etc.). The part was "doubled" by another actor in the cast. It was Smith's superstition that the presence of
"George Spelvin" in a play ensured its success.

Picture hats with ostrich plumes were the latest feminine headgear.

In Athens, Greece, the United States won the Olympic Games with 75
points. England trailed in second place with 41.

The American balloon "America" won a 402-mile race to win the James
Gordon Bennett cup.

The Philadelphia and Boston American League baseball clubs battled
(Sept. 1) twenty-four innings at Boston in a major league record game
that ended, after 4 hours, 47 minutes of play, in favor of Philadelphia 4
to 1. (The record was broken in the National League in 1920, which see.)

ठ़ 1907

Amina. Instrumental composition. m., Paul Lincke. Jos. W. Stern &
Co., cop. 1907 by Apollo Verlag, Berlin; assigned 1920 to Edward B.
Marks Music Co.

As Long as the World Rolls On. w., George Graff, Jr. m., Ernest R.
Ball. M. Witmark & Sons, cop. 1907.

Because I'm Married Now. w., m., Herbert Ingraham. Shapiro, Bernstein & Co., cop. 1907.

The Best I Get Is Much Obliged to You. w., m., Benjamin Hapgood
Burt. Jerome H. Remick & Co., cop. 1907.

Bon Bon Buddy. w., Alex Rogers. m., Will Marion Cook. The
Gotham-Attucks Music Co., cop. 1907.

Budweiser's a Friend of Mine. w., Vincent P. Bryan. m., Seymour
Furth. Shapiro, Bernstein & Co., cop. 1907.

Come Along My Mandy! (The Jolly Bachelors). w., m., Tom Mellor, Alfred J. Lawrence and Harry Gifford. American version by Nora Bayes and Jack Norworth. T. B. Harms & Francis, Day & Hunter, cop. 1907 by Francis, Day & Hunter.

Come to the Land of Bohemia. w., m., Ren Shields and George Evans. F. A. Mills, cop. 1907.

Every Little Bit Added to What You've Got Makes Just a Little Bit More. w., m., Dillon Bros. [i.e., William A. and Lawrence M. Dillon.] Helf & Hager Co., cop. 1907.

The Glow-Worm—*original German title:* Glühwürmchen. English words, Lilla Cayley Robinson. German words and music, Paul Lincke. Jos. W. Stern & Co., cop. 1902 by Apollo Verlag, Berlin; cop. 1907 by Jos. W. Stern & Co.

Harrigan (Fifty Miles from Boston). w., m., George M[ichael] Cohan. F. A. Mills, cop. 1907.

He Goes to Church on Sunday (*introduced in:* The Orchid). w., Vincent Bryan. m., E. Ray Goetz. Shapiro Music Publisher, cop. 1907 by Maurice Shapiro.

Honey Boy. w., Jack Norworth. m., Albert Von Tilzer. Broadway Music Corp., cop. 1907.

I'm a Popular Man (The Honeymooners). w., m., George M[ichael] Cohan. F. A. Mills, cop. 1907.

I'm Afraid to Come Home in the Dark. w., Harry H. Williams. m., Egbert Van Alstyne. Jerome H. Remick & Co., cop. 1907.

I Love You So [Merry Widow Waltz] (The Merry Widow). w., Adrian Ross. m., Franz Lehár. London: Chappell & Co., Ltd., cop. 1907.

I Want You (The Talk of New York). w., m., George M[ichael] Cohan. Leo Feist, Inc., cop. 1907.

I Wish I Had a Girl. w., Gus Kahn. m., Grace Le Boy. Thompson Music Co., cop. 1907; assigned 1909 to Jerome H. Remick & Co.

I'd Rather Be a Lobster Than a Wise Guy. w., Edward Madden. m., Theodore F. Morse. F. B. Haviland Pub. Co., Inc., cop. 1907.

If I'm Going to Die I'm Going to Have Some Fun (The Honeymooners). w., m., George M[ichael] Cohan. F. A. Mills, cop. 1907.

In the Wildwood Where the Bluebells Grew. w., m., Herbert H. Taylor. New York Music Pub. House, cop. 1907.

It's Delightful to Be Married (The Parisian Model). w., Anna Held. m., V. Scotto. Jos. W. Stern & Co., cop. 1907.

It's Great to Be a Soldier Man. w., Jack Drislane. m., Theodore F. Morse. F. B. Haviland Pub. Co., cop. 1907.

Maxim's (The Merry Widow). w., Adrian Ross. m., Franz Lehár. London: Chappell & Co., Ltd., cop. 1907.

The Merry Widow Waltz. See above: "I Love You So."

Nobody's Little Girl. w., Jack Drislane. m., Theodore F. Morse. F. B. Haviland Pub. Co., Inc., cop. 1907.

On the Road to Mandalay. w., Rudyard Kipling. m., Oley Speaks. Cincinnati: The John Church Co., cop. 1907.

La Partida—The Farewell. w., E. Blasco. m., F. M. Alvarez. G. Schirmer, Inc., cop. 1907.

Red Wing. w., Thurland Chattaway. m., Kerry Mills. F. A. Mills, cop. 1907.

San Antonio. w., Harry H. Williams. m., Egbert Van Alstyne. Jerome H. Remick & Co., cop. 1907.

School Days. w., Will D. Cobb. m., Gus Edwards. Gus Edwards Pub. Co., cop. 1907.

She's the Fairest Little Flower Dear Old Dixie Ever Grew. w., Ashley S. Johnson. m., Theodore F. Morse. F. B. Haviland Pub. Co., cop. 1907.

The Sweetest Flower the Garden Grew. w., m., Thurland Chattaway. F. B. Haviland Pub. Co., cop. 1907.

Take Me Around Again. w., Ed. Rose. m., Kerry Mills. F. A. Mills, cop. 1907.

Take Me Back to New York Town. w., Andrew B. Sterling. m., Harry Von Tilzer. Harry Von Tilzer Music Pub. Co., cop. 1907.

That Lovin' Rag. w., Victor H. Smalley. m., Bernie Adler. F. B. Haviland Pub. Co., Inc., cop. 1907.

There's a Girl in This World for Every Boy, and a Boy for Every Girl. w., Will D. Cobb. m., Ted Snyder. F. A. Mills, cop. 1907.

There Never Was a Girl Like You. w., Harry H. Williams. m., Egbert Van Alstyne. Jerome H. Remick & Co., cop. 1907.

Tommy, Lad! w., Edward Teschemacher. m., E. J. Margetson. London: Boosey & Co., Ltd., cop. 1907.

Two Blue Eyes. w., Edward Madden. m., Theodore F. Morse. F. B. Haviland Pub. Co., Inc., cop. 1907.

Two Little Baby Shoes. w., Edward Madden. m., Theodore F. Morse. F. B. Haviland Pub. Co., Inc., cop. 1907.

Under Any Old Flag at All (The Talk of New York). w., m., George M[ichael] Cohan. F. A. Mills, cop. 1907.

Vilia (The Merry Widow). w., Adrian Ross. m., Franz Lehár. London: Chappell & Co., Ltd., cop. 1907.

Wal, I Swan! or, Ebenezer Frye. w., m., Benjamin Hapgood Burt. M. Witmark & Sons, cop. 1907.

When a Fellow's on the Level with a Girl That's on the Square (The Talk of New York). w., m., George M[ichael] Cohan. F. A. Mills, cop. 1907.

When Sweet Marie Was Sweet Sixteen. w., Raymond Moore. m., Ernest R. Ball. M. Witmark & Sons, cop. 1907.

When the Birds in Georgia Sing of Tennessee. w., Arthur J. Lamb. m., Ernest R. Ball. M. Witmark & Sons, cop. 1907.

When We Are M-a-double-r-i-e-d (Fifty Miles from Boston). w., m., George M[ichael] Cohan. F. A. Mills, cop. 1907.

Won't You Be My Honey? w., Jack Drislane. m., Theodore F. Morse. F. B. Haviland Pub. Co., Inc., cop. 1907.

Won't You Waltz "Home Sweet Home" with Me? w., m., Herbert Ingraham. Shapiro, Bernstein & Co., cop. 1907.

You Splash Me and I'll Splash You. w., Arthur J. Lamb. m., Alfred Solman. Jos. W. Stern & Co., cop. 1907.

Oklahoma was admitted (Nov. 16) as the 46th State.

Alabama and Georgia adopted liquor prohibition.

The first 'round-the-world cruise was made by the United States battle fleet, 16 ships under the command of Admiral Robley Dunglison ("Bob") Evans. (The flotilla left Hampton Roads, Va., Dec. 16, 1907, and returned Feb. 22, 1909.)

In a scandal over the Honduras Lottery that resulted in fines and court sentences of various kinds, lotteries in the United States came to an end.

The Jamestown Tercentennial Exposition, celebrating the founding of the first permanent English settlement in the New World by Capt. John Smith, was held (Apr. 26-Nov. 30) in Hampton Roads, Va.

The second Hague Peace Conference convened at the suggestion of President Theodore Roosevelt.

Judge Kenesaw Mountain Landis, later "czar" of baseball, became a national figure when he sentenced the Standard Oil corporation to a fine of $29,240,000. (The decision was reversed subsequently by higher courts.)

Mine disasters took the lives of 361 laborers at the Monongah Mines, West Va. (Dec. 6), and of 230 at the Darr Mine, Pa.

The United Press news service was established in New York.

The Sage Foundation was founded (Mar. 12) in New York by Mrs. Russell Sage with an endowment of $10,000,000 for "the improvement of social and living conditions in the United States" by means of "research, publication, education, the establishment and maintenance of charitable and beneficial activities, agencies, and institutions" and of such already established.

Lee De Forest demonstrated (Mar. 5) in New York an experimental radio broadcast from Tellharmonic Hall, playing the "William Tell" overture from a phonograph record. During the summer he used phonograph records of celebrated opera singers in testing the wireless telephone transmitters to be installed on Admiral "Bob" Evans world-touring fleet (above).

Books of the year included: "The Education of Henry Adams, A Study of Twentieth Century Multiplicity" (Henry Adams; an autobiography, published privately), "The American Scene" (Henry James), "Christian Science" (Mark Twain; a controversial treatment of the subject), "Pragmatism: A New Name for Some Old Ways of Thinking" (William James), and the fiction, "The Iron Heel" (Jack London), "The Shepherd of the Hills" (Harold Bell Wright), "Three Weeks" (Elinor Glyn), "The Traitor"

(Thomas Dixon), "The Trimmed Lamp" (O. Henry). The first two volumes of "The Catholic Encyclopedia" were issued (completed in 15 volumes in 1914).

Richard Strauss's one-hour German opera "Salome," based on Oscar Wilde's French play of the same name, created a vast scandal in New York when its American première was staged (Jan. 22) by Heinrich Conried at the Metropolitan Opera House with Olive Fremstad in the title role. The board of directors immediately forbade its repetition on moral grounds. Mlle. Bianca Froelich of the Corps de Ballet performed the "Dance of the Seven Veils." A program of vocal music preceded the opera. Not long afterwards vaudeville was overrun by Salome dancers. (When Mme. Fremstad sang the Paris première May 8, 1907, she was decorated by the French government. Oscar Hammerstein revived the opera Jan. 28, 1909, in French, at his Manhattan Opera House, New York. Performances followed in Chicago and Milwaukee in 1910 and in St. Louis in 1911. The opera later was reinstated at the Metropolitan and has proven always a well-attended attraction.)

Sir Edward Elgar, foremost British composer, visited the United States and made (Mar. 19) his debut in New York at Carnegie Hall with the Oratorio Society as conductor of a performance of his oratorio "The Apostles." The Society sang (Mar. 26) the American première of his oratorio "The Kingdom."

Feodor Chaliapin, famed Russian basso, made (Nov. 20) his American debut in the title role of Boito's opera "Mefistofele" at the Metropolitan Opera House, New York. His realistic art failed at the time to impress American audiences.

Mary Garden, Scottish-born American soprano already acclaimed in Paris, made (Nov. 25) her American debut in Massenet's opera "Thaïs" in New York at the Manhattan Opera House. (Emma Trentini of later "Naughty Marietta" fame, 1910, was in the cast.)

Ellen Terry produced (Jan. 28) at the Empire Theatre, New York, the American première of George Bernard Shaw's comedy "Captain Brassbound's Conversion," and married (Mar. 22) her leading man James Carew.

Ibsen's "Peer Gynt" with Edvard Grieg's incidental music was performed (Feb. 25) in New York at the New Amsterdam Theatre for 22 performances with actor-producer Richard Mansfield (Peer Gynt), Emma Dunn (Ase), Adelaide Nowak (Solveig), and Irene Prahar (Anitra).

Ermete Novelli, noted Italian actor, made (Mar. 18) his American debut at the Lyric Theatre, New York, with his own company. The repertory was mostly Shakespearean.

Walter Hampden, returning from England, made (Sept. 2) his American bow opposite Alla Nazimova in "The Comtesse Coquette" at the Bijou Theatre, New York.

Mme. Hanako, Japanese tragedienne, and her company appeared in a series of native one-act plays in New York under Arnold Daly's management.

An enterprising young manager and French theatre enthusiast named Florenz Ziegfeld, the son of a Chicago music conservatory director, staged (July 8) on the roof of the New York Theatre, renamed by him Jardin de Paris, a modest revue patterned after the Folies Bergère of Paris. This production, which cost only $13,000, inaugurated the Ziegfeld Follies that developed in subsequent years into lavish spectacles of feminine beauty— "the most beautiful girls in the world."

New York plays included: "Brewster's Millions" (New Amsterdam, Dec. 31, 1906), "Caught in the Rain" (Garrick, Dec. 31, 1906), "The Road to Yesterday" (Herald Square, Dec. 31, 1906), "My Wife" with John Drew and Billie Burke (Empire, Aug. 31, 1907), "A Grand Army Man" with David Warfield (Stuyvesant, Oct. 16), "The Warrens of Virginia" (Belasco, Dec. 3; the youthful Mary Pickford made her New York debut in the cast), and "Polly of the Circus" (Liberty, Dec. 23). The outstanding long-run play was "The Thief" with Kyrle Bellew and Margaret Illington (Lyceum, Sept. 9). But musical comedy dominated the stage although none, with the exception of "The Girl Behind the Counter" (Herald Square, Oct. 1; 260 performances), could vie in popularity with "The Merry Widow" (New Amsterdam, Oct. 21), which amassed a total of 416 performances. The romantic Donald Brian and a previously unknown soprano, Ethel Jackson, sang and danced the operetta to its American success. Lehár's music captured the public inside and outside the theatre; some of the music was uncopyrighted and was reprinted in cheap editions; and the famous waltz swept off the musical comedy stage the regimented convolutions that had hitherto passed for dancing and introduced a more intimate and appealing type of dance.

There were more than 400 nickelodeons in business, and David Wark Griffith became a motion-picture director. Song slides were popular as a screen feature and a way of "plugging" the latest songs. Meanwhile William N. Selig transferred a company of movie actors from Chicago to Los Angeles, and thus started off the West Coast city as a motion-picture center. (In 1911, Al Christie and Dave Horsley arrived independently at the same spot opposite the Blondeau Tavern. Horsley built there for the Nestor Company the first permanent studio.)

The latest craze was the game of "diabolo"—a piece of wood tossed around by a cord attached to two sticks.

Fashion finally did something to the shirtwaist—perforations, embroidered at the edges, were put into it, and it was now called the "peek-a-boo" shirtwaist. It was very daring. Ladies also considered feather boas very stylish.

The United States went through its twentieth depression since 1790.

Deaths of the year included Augustus Saint-Gaudens, America's greatest sculptor, aged 59 (Aug. 3), in Cornish, N. H., and Richard Mansfield, noted actor-manager, aged 50 (Aug. 30), in New London, Conn. (Mansfield made his last stage appearance Mar. 23, 1907, in New York at the New Amsterdam Theatre in "A Parisian Romance.")

ൠ 1908

All for Love of You. w., Dave Reed. m., Ernest R. Ball. M. Witmark & Sons, cop. 1908.

Any Old Port in a Storm. w., Arthur J. Lamb. m., Kerry Mills. M. Witmark & Sons, cop. 1908. (Formerly published by Maurice Richmond, Inc., cop. 1908.)

Ask Her While the Band Is Playing (The Rose of Algeria). w., Glen MacDonough. m., Victor Herbert. Chas. K. Harris, cop. 1908.

Bl—nd and P—g Spells Blind Pig. w., Junie McCree. m., Albert Von Tilzer. The York Music Co., cop. 1908.

Come on Down Town (The Yankee Prince). w., m., George M. Cohan. Cohan and Harris, cop. 1908.

Consolation. w., Edward Madden. m., Theodore F. Morse. F. B. Haviland Pub. Co., cop. 1908.

Cuddle Up a Little Closer (The Three Twins). w., Otto Harbach. m., Karl Hoschna. M. Witmark & Sons, cop. 1908.

Daisies Won't Tell. w., m., Anita Owen. Jerome H. Remick & Co., cop. 1908.

Danse Nègre. Piano solo. m., Cyril Scott, op. 58, No. 5. London; Elkin & Co., cop. 1908.

Don't Take Me Home. w., Vincent Bryan. m., Harry Von Tilzer. Harry Von Tilzer Music Pub. Co., cop. 1908.

Down Among the Sugar Cane. w., Avery and Hart. m., Cecil Mack and Chris Smith. The Gotham-Attucks Music Co., cop. 1908.

Down in Jungle Town. w., Edward Madden, m., Theodore F. Morse. F. B. Haviland Music Pub. Co., cop. 1908.

Golliwog's Cake Walk (*in:* The Children's Corner). Piano solo. m., Achille Claude Debussy. Paris: Durand & Cie., cop. 1908.

Good Evening, Caroline. w., Jack Norworth. m., Albert Von Tilzer. The York Music Co., cop. 1908.

Good Night, Dear (Love Watches). w., m., Will R. Anderson. M. Witmark & Sons, cop. 1908.

Hoo-oo—Ain't You Coming Out To-night? w., m., Herbert Ingraham. "Shapiro," Music Publisher, cop. 1908 by Maurice Shapiro.

How Lovely Are Thy Dwellings. w., Biblical. m., Samuel Liddle. London: Boosey & Co., cop. 1908.

I Don't Want Another Sister. w., Leroi Scarlett. m., Edna Williams. Jos. W. Stern & Co., cop. 1908.

I've Taken Quite a Fancy to You. w., Edward Madden. m., Theodore F. Morse. F. B. Haviland Pub. Co., cop. 1908.

If I Had a Thousand Lives to Live. w., Sylvester Maguire. m., Alfred Solman. Jos. W. Stern & Co., cop. 1908; assigned 1920 to Edward B. Marks Music Co.; assigned 1932 to Edward B. Marks Music Corp.; renewed 1935.

If You Cared for Me. w., Ed. Rose. m., Ted Snyder. Ted Snyder Co., Inc., cop. 1908 by Rose & Snyder Co.: assigned 1908 to H. Waterson

If You Were I and I Were You (Prima Donna). w., Henry Blossom. m., Victor Herbert. M. Witmark & Sons, cop. 1908.

In the Garden of My Heart. w., Caro Roma. m., Ernest R. Ball. M. Witmark & Sons, cop. 1908.

It Looks Like a Big Night To-night. w., Harry Williams. m., Egbert Van Alstyne. Jerome H. Remick & Co., cop. 1908.

The Lanky Yankee Boys in Blue. w., Edward Madden. m., Theodore F. Morse. F. B. Haviland Pub. Co., cop. 1908.

The Longest Way 'Round Is the Sweetest Way Home. w., Ren Shields. m., Kerry Mills. F. A. Mills, cop. 1908.

Love Is Like a Cigarette (The Rose of Algeria). w., Glen MacDonough. m., Victor Herbert. Chas. K. Harris, cop. 1908.

Love's Roundelay (The Waltz Dream). w., Joseph Herbert. m., Oscar Straus. Jos. W. Stern & Co., cop. 1908.

Rose of the World (The Rose of Algeria). w., Glen MacDonough. m., Victor Herbert. Chas. K. Harris, cop. 1908.

Roses Bring Dreams of You. w., m., Herbert Ingraham. Maurice Shapiro, cop. 1908.

She Sells Sea-Shells (The Beauty Shop). w., Terry Sullivan. m., Harry Gifford. T. B. Harms, cop. 1908 by Francis, Day & Hunter.

Shine On, Harvest Moon (The Follies of 1908.) w., Jack Norworth. m., Nora Bayes and Jack Norworth. Jerome H. Remick & Co., cop. 1908.

Smarty. w., Jack Norworth. m., Albert Von Tilzer. The York Music Co., cop. 1908.

S. R. Henry's Barn Dance. Instrumental. m., S. R. Henry [pseud. of Henry R. Stern]. Jos. W. Stern & Co., cop. 1908; assigned 1920 to Edw. B. Marks Music Co. (Published as a song, "Down at the Huskin' Bee," words by Monroe H. Rosenfeld, cop. 1909.)

Sweet Violets. Intermezzo two step. m., W. C. Powell. Jerome H. Remick & Co., cop. 1908.

Sweetest Maid of All (The Waltz Dream). w., Joseph Herbert. m., Oscar Straus. Jos. W. Stern & Co., cop. 1908.

Take Me Out to the Ball Game. w., Jack Norworth. m., Albert Von Tilzer. The York Music Co., cop. 1908.

There's Something About a Uniform (The Man Who Owns Broadway). w., m., George M. Cohan. Cohan and Harris, cop. 1908.

Up in a Balloon. w., Ren Shields. m., Percy Wenrich. E. B. Marks, cop. 1908.

A Vision of Salome. Orchestral piece. m., J. Bodewalt Lampe. Jerome H. Remick & Co., cop. 1908.

When You First Kissed the Last Girl You Loved (A Stubborn Cinderella). w., Will M. Hough and Frank R. Adams. m., Joseph E. Howard. Chas. K. Harris, cop. 1908.

When You Wore a Pinafore. w., Edward Madden. m., Theodore F. Morse. F. B. Haviland Pub. Co., Inc., cop. 1908.

The Yama-Yama Man (The Three Twins). w., [George] Collin Davis. m., Karl Hoschna. M. Witmark & Sons, cop. 1908.

You're in the Right Church, but the Wrong Pew. w., Cecil Mack. m., Chris Smith. The Gotham-Attucks Music Co., cop. 1908. by R. C. McPherson.

The Federal Bureau of Investigation (F.B.I.) was established.

Immigration from Japan was restricted by "gentleman's agreement."

Admiral Robert Edwin Peary sailed for the Arctic in a specially constructed 184-foot, 600-ton steamer, the "Roosevelt," on his sixth and, as it proved, last expedition to find the North Pole. He established (in September) his winter camp at Cape Sheridan, Ellesmere Island. His expedition comprised 66 members. In the Arctic 49 Eskimos and 246 dogs were added to the party.

Movements against drinking of liquor and smoking began in earnest. The Henry C. Frick Co., U. S. Steel subsidiary, ordered its employees to be total abstainers both on and off the premises. Likewise, the Baltimore & Ohio Railway (as regards all those running or directing trains). Pressure was afoot everywhere to stop the incipient vogue of feminine smoking. Alabama and Georgia had already adopted (1907) liquor prohibition.

Orville Wright made another successful flight in his flying machine, remaining in the air 1 hour, 14 minutes.

Charles D. Herrold, a San Jose, Cal., wireless experimenter, opened (Jan. 16) a local radio station—a pioneer in the field. (The call letters KQW were assigned to the station Dec. 9, 1921.)

The U. S. Post Office placed (Feb. 18) coils of postage stamps on sale.

The manufacture of automobiles passed the 50,000 mark. The limousine, a motorcar with a glass-enclosed body, was a new type.

Six automobiles undertook a 'round-the-world race from New York to Paris, travelling westward. From Seattle, Wash., the cars were shipped to Kobe, Japan. Only one, the American E. R. Thomas "Speedway Flier," completed (July 30) the journey.

Fires caused much property damage and the loss of many lives—169 died (Jan. 13) in a theatre fire at Boyertown, Pa.; 174 children and two teachers were killed (Mar. 4) in a fire and panic at the Lake View

School in Collinwood, near Cleveland; and more than $6,000,000 worth of property was destroyed (Apr. 12) in Chelsea, Mass.

Books of the year included: "The Philosophy of Loyalty" (Josiah Royce), "The Scarecrow" (Percy MacKaye; a drama) and the fiction, "The Bomb" (Frank Harris; a story about the Chicago Haymarket riot, 1886), "The Circular Staircase" (Mary Roberts Rinehart), "Mr. Crewe's Career" (Winston Churchill), "The Trail of the Lonesome Pine" (John Fox).

"The Gibson Girl," so-called from Charles Dana Gibson drawings, was the acme of American womanhood.

Another prominent illustrator at this time was Howard Chandler Christy, who was said to be getting $1,000 a week.

George MacManus, creator of "Maggie and Jiggs," was cartooning "The Newlyweds" and appearing in vaudeville.

Women were wearing sheath gowns that were slit to the knee, large "Merry Widow" hats that were bedecked with bird wings, artificial flowers, etc., dotted veils, and high buttoned or laced shoes.

Gustav Mahler, famous German conductor and symphonic composer, made (Jan. 1) his American debut conducting "Tristan und Isolde" at the Metropolitan Opera House, New York.

Giulio Gatti-Casazza, impresario of the La Scala opera house in Milan, Italy, succeeded Heinrich Conried as general manager of the Metropolitan Opera House in New York after the close of the season of 1907-08.

Arturo Toscanini, renowned Italian opera conductor, made (Nov. 16) his American debut conducting "Aïda" at the Metropolitan Opera House, New York.

Mary Garden was the bright star in the galaxy of singers at Hammerstein's Manhattan Opera House, New York. For her, he staged the American premières of Charpentier's "Louise" (Jan. 3), Debussy's then controversial "Pelléas et Mélisande" (Feb. 19) with Jean Perier, who sang with her in the original (1902) Paris production, and Massenet's "Le Jongleur de Nôtre Dame" (Nov. 27).

The ambitious Oscar Hammerstein built his second operatic theatre— the Philadelphia Opera House, which he opened (Nov. 17) with Bizet's "Carmen."

Mischa Elman, 16-year-old Russian violin virtuoso, made (Dec. 10) his American debut in New York playing the Tchaikovsky Violin Concerto with the Russian Symphony Orchestra.

Isadora Duncan now was an accomplished terpsichorean, doing interpretative dances in barefoot Greek style and flowing draperies. After displaying her art in Budapest (1903), Berlin (1904), and in London, she came back to America.

The Dixieland Jazz Band was organized in New Orleans.

Mme. Vera F. Komisarzhevsky, Russian actress, appeared (Mar. 2) for three weeks in Russian repertory at Daly's Theatre, New York.

The New York stage was crowded with successes. Conspicuous among the plays were "The Honor of the Family" with Otis Skinner (Hudson, Feb. 17), "Paid in Full" (Astor, Feb. 25), "The Servant in the House" with Walter Hampden (Savoy, Mar. 23), "The Traveling Salesman" (Liberty, Aug. 10; 280 performances), "The Man from Home" (Astor, Aug. 27; 496 performances, after a long run in Chicago, 1907), "Jack Straw" (Empire, Sept. 14), "A Gentleman from Mississippi" with Thomas A. Wise and Douglas Fairbanks (Bijou, Sept. 29; 407 performances), "The Blue Mouse" (Lyric, Nov. 30), "The Battle" with Wilton Lackaye (Savoy, Dec. 21), "What Every Woman Knows" with Richard Bennett and Maude Adams (Empire, Dec. 23). Ferenc Molnar's uncopyrighted Hungarian play, "The Devil," opened (Aug. 18) simultaneously at the Belasco with George Arliss and at the Garden with Edwin Stevens.

Outstanding among New York musical comedies were "A Waltz Dream" (Broadway, Jan. 27), "The Soul Kiss" (New York, Jan. 28), "Nearly a Hero" (Casino, Feb. 24), "Three Twins" with Bessie McCoy (Herald Square, June 15), "The Girls of Gottenburg" (Knickerbocker, Sept. 2), "Little Nemo" by Victor Herbert (New Amsterdam, Oct. 20), "The Boys and Betty" (Wallack's, Nov. 2), "Miss Innocence" with Anna Held (New York, Nov. 30), "The Queen of the Moulin Rouge" with Frank X. Bushman, later the movie idol Francis X. Bushman, in the cast (Circle, Dec. 7).

Vaudeville headliners included: Eva Tanguay, Irene Franklin, Bert Leslie, Cecilia Loftus (as a mimic), James J. Corbett (ex-heavyweight champ, who tried his hand at legit), Louise Dresser, Ed. Wynn, Leon Errol, and Annette Kellerman (said to have a perfect figure).

Motion pictures, still tail-enders for vaudeville shows, were becoming longer, such as "Bobby's Kodak" (518 feet), "Dr. Skinum" (592 feet), "The Snow Man" (717 feet). "The Lonely Villa" featured an unknown, sweet, little actress, known only as Little Mary since screen actors were anonymous at this time. To later generations she was Mary Pickford. (She had made her New York stage debut in the preceding year in "The Warrens of Virginia.") As an experiment in higher drama, the movies offered Shakespeare's "Romeo and Juliet." The pictures, of course, were silent films.

At the Polo Grounds, New York, Fred Merkle committed the historic baseball play involving the question of whether or not he touched second base. The game was a crucial battle between the New York "Giants" and the Chicago "Cubs." When the game was declared a tie, it nearly provoked a major riot. After this "bonehead" and "boner" were baseball (and general) slang.

In Sydney, Australia, Negro boxer Jack Johnson defeated (Dec. 26) Tommy Burns in 14 rounds to annex the heavyweight championship title. The police stopped the bout.

In the national elections, President Theodore Roosevelt declined to run for a third term and favored William Howard Taft, Republican, who was elected over William Jennings Bryan, Democrat, making his third and last bid for the presidency.

Financial panic again prevailed in the nation.

Edward MacDowell, aged 47, America's foremost musical composer, died (Jan. 23), in New York.

₰ 1909

Beautiful Eyes (Mr. Hamlet of Broadway). w., George Whiting and Carter De Haven. m., Ted Snyder. Ted Snyder Co., cop. 1909.

A Birthday. w., Christina Rossetti. m., Raymond Huntington Woodman. G. Schirmer, Inc., cop. 1909.

Bring Me a Rose (The Arcadians). w., Lionel Monckton and Arthur Wimperis. m., Lionel Monckton. London: Chappell & Co., Ltd., cop. 1909.

By the Light of the Silvery Moon. w., Edward Madden. m., Gus Edwards. Jerome H. Remick & Co., cop. 1909 by Gus Edwards Music Pub. Co.; assigned 1909 to Jerome H. Remick & Co.

Carrie; or, Carrie Marry Harry. w., Junie McCree. m., Albert Von Tilzer. The York Music Co., cop. 1909.

Casey Jones. w., T. Lawrence Seibert. m., Eddie Newton. Los Angeles: Southern California Music Co., cop. 1909 by Newton & Seibert.

Clavelitos—Carnations. Spanish words and music, Estic and Joaquin Valverde. English words, Mrs. M. T. E. Sandwith. G. Schirmer, cop. 1909; cop. 1911.

Come After Breakfast, Bring 'Long Your Lunch and Leave 'Fore Supper Time. w., m., Brym[a]n, Smith and Burris. Jos. W. Stern & Co., cop. 1909; assigned 1920 to Edward B. Marks Music Co.; renewed 1936 by James T. Bryman and Chris Smith; assigned 1937 to Edward B. Marks Music Corp.

The Cubanola Glide. w., Vincent P. Bryan. m., Harry Von Tilzer. Harry Von Tilzer Music Pub. Co., cop. 1909.

For You Alone. w., P. J. O'Reilly. m., Henry E. Geehl. Ed. Schuberth & Co., cop. 1909 by Gould & Co., London.

Four American Indian Songs: (1) From the Land of the Sky-Blue Water; (2) The White Dawn Is Stealing; (3) Far Off I Hear a Lover's Flute; (4) The Moon Drops Low. w., Nelle Richmond Eberhart. m., Charles Wakefield Cadman, op. 45. Boston: White-Smith Music Pub. Co., cop. 1909.

The Garden of Roses. w., J. E. Dempsey. m., Johann C. Schmid. Jerome H. Remick & Co., cop. 1909.

The Girl with a Brogue (The Arcadians). w., Arthur Wimperis. m., Lionel Monckton. London: Chappell & Co., Ltd., cop. 1909.

Has Anybody Here Seen Kelly! (The Jolly Bachelors). w., m., C. W. Murphy and Will Letters. American version by William C. McKenna. T. B. Harms & Francis, Day & Hunter, cop. 1909 by Francis, Day & Hunter.

Heaven Will Protect the Working Girl. (Tillie's Nightmare). w., Edgar Smith. m., A. Baldwin Sloane. Chas. K. Harris, cop. 1909.

I'm Awfully Glad I Met You. w., Jack Drislane. m., George W. Meyer. F. B. Haviland Pub. Co., Inc., cop. 1909.

I've Got a Pain in My Sawdust. w., Henry Edward Warner. m., Herman Avery Wade. Jos. W. Stern Co., cop. 1909.

I've Got Rings on My Fingers; or, Mumbo Jumbo Jijjiboo J. O'Shea (The Midnight Sons; and The Yankee Girl). w., Weston and Barnes. m., Maurice Scott. T. B. Harms & Francis, Day & Hunter, cop. 1909 by Francis, Day & Hunter.

I Love, I Love, I Love My Wife, but Oh, You Kid. w., Jimmy Lucas. m., Harry Von Tilzer. Harry Von Tilzer Music Pub. Co., cop. 1909.

I Love My Wife, but Oh, You Kid! w., m., Harry Armstrong and Billy Clark. Chicago: Harold Rossiter Music Co., cop., 1909 by Armstrong & Clark; assigned 1909 to Victor Kremer Co., Chicago.

I Wish I Had My Old Girl Back Again. w., Ballard MacDonald. m., Paul Wallace. Jos. W. Stern Co., cop. 1909.

I Was a Very Good Baby (Listen Lester). w., Harry L. Cort and George E. Stoddard. m., Harold Orlob. Shapiro, Bernstein & Co., Inc., cop. 1909.

I Wonder Who's Kissing Her Now (The Prince of Tonight). w., Will M. Hough and Frank R. Adams, m., Joseph E. Howard [and Harold

Orlob]. Chas. K. Harris, cop. 1909. (Introduced in the film "I Wonder Who's Kissing Her Now"; published by (1) Chas. K. Harris Music Pub. Co., cop. 1936; (2) Jerry Vogel Music Co., Inc.; renewed 1936 by Will M. Hough and Frank R. Adams; assigned to Jerry Vogel Music Co., Inc.; (3) Edward B. Marks Music Corp., renewed 1936 by Joseph E. Howard; assigned 1936 to Edward B. Marks Music Corp.)

The Letter Song (The Chocolate Soldier). w., Stanislaus Stange. m., Oscar Straus. Jerome H. Remick & Co., cop. 1908 by Ludwig Doblinger, Leipzig; cop. 1909 by Jerome H. Remick & Co.

Meet Me Tonight in Dreamland. w., Beth Slater Whitson. m., Leo Friedman. Chicago; Will Rossiter, cop. 1909.

Monkey Doodle Dandy. w., Jack Drislane. m., Henry Frantzen. F. B. Haviland Pub. Co., cop. 1909.

Moving Day in Jungle Town. w., A. Seymour Brown. m., Nat D. Ayer. Jerome H. Remick & Co., cop. 1909.

My Hero (The Chocolate Soldier). w., Stanislaus Stange. m., Oscar Straus. Jerome H. Remick & Co., cop. 1908 by Ludwig Doblinger, Leipzig; cop. 1909 by Jerome H. Remick & Co.

My Own United States (When Johnny Comes Marching Home). w., Stanislaus Stange. m., Julian Edwards. M. Witmark & Sons, cop. 1909.

My Pony Boy (Miss Innocence). w., Bobby Heath. m., Charley O'Donnell. Jerome H. Remick & Co., cop. 1909 by Up to Date Music Pub. Co.; assigned 1909 to Thos. J. Kennedy; assigned 1909 to Jerome H. Remick & Co.

My Southern Rose. w., m., Earl Taylor. Harry Von Tilzer Music Pub. Co., 1909.

Next to Your Mother, Who Do You Love? w., Irving Berlin. m., Ted Snyder. Ted Snyder Co., cop. 1909.

Nobody Knows, Nobody Cares. w., m., Charles K. Harris. Chas. K. Harris, cop. 1909.

On Wisconsin! March song and two step. m., W. T. Purdy. Milwaukee. Flanner-Hafsoos Music House, cop. 1909 by W. T. Purdy; assigned 1910 to Joseph H. Flanner.

Put On Your Old Gray Bonnet. w., Stanley Murphy. m., Percy Wenrich. Jerome H. Remick & Co., cop. 1909.

"Ship Ahoy!"—All the Nice Girls Love a Sailor. w., A. J. Mills. m., Bennett Scott. The Star Music Pub. Co., cop. 1909.

Song of the Soul (The Climax). w., Edward Locke. m., Joseph Carl Breil. London: Chappell & Co., Ltd., cop. 1909; new edition cop. 1929.

Take Me Up with You, Dearie. w., Junie McCree. m., Albert Von Tilzer. The York Music Co., cop. 1909.

That's A Plenty. w., Henry Creamer. m., Bert A. Williams. Chicago: Will Rossiter, cop. 1909; renewed 1937 by Henry S. Creamer; assigned 1908 to Jerry Vogel Music Co., Inc.

That Mesmerizing Mendelssohn Tune. w., m., Irving Berlin. Ted Snyder Co., cop. 1909.

Waiting (Listen Lester). w., Harry L. Cort and George E. Stoddard. m., Harold Orlob. Shapiro, Bernstein & Co., Inc., cop. 1909.

When I Dream in the Gloaming of You. w., m., Herbert Ingraham. Shapiro, Bernstein & Co., cop. 1909.

Where My Caravan Has Rested. w., Edward Teschemacher. m., Herman Loehr. London: Chappell & Co., Ltd., cop. 1909.

The Wiffenpoof Song. See 1936.

Yip-I-Addy-I-Ay! w., Will D. Cobb. m., J[oh]n H. Flynn. Maurice Shapiro, cop. 1908 by Will D. Cobb; assigned 1909 to Maurice Shapiro.

You Taught Me How to Love You, Now Teach Me to Forget. w., Jack Drislane and Alfred Bryan. m., George W. Meyer. F. B. Haviland Pub. Co., Inc., cop. 1909.

William Howard Taft, Republican, of Ohio, was inaugurated 27th President.

Former President Theodore Roosevelt undertook with his son Kermit an extensive hunting trip (1909-10) in East Africa. (The party left the United States Apr. 23, 1909, and concluded its expedition in Feb., 1910. Roosevelt then went on a lecture tour of Europe of several months' duration. He returned June 18, 1910.)

A world still skeptical of the utility of the radio learned suddenly to believe in its effectiveness when the S.O.S. (then C.Q.D.) brought the S. S. "Baltic," and other vessels to the rescue of the White Star liner "Republic." The "Republic" was rammed (Jan. 23) by the "Florida" in a fog off Nantucket Lightship in the Atlantic, but 1,500 people were transferred to safety. Only six persons lost their lives in the disaster.

The Stars and Stripes were planted (Apr. 6) in the cold sunlight of the Arctic on the northernmost point of the earth. "The Pole at last . . . Mine at last" wrote Admiral Robert Edwin Peary in his diary several days after the historic event. On this, his sixth attempt, after 20 years of effort, Peary achieved the goal of his ambition. He claimed the discovery of the North Pole. He was accompanied on the last dangerous leg of the journey by only his Negro attendant ("Matt," Matthew Henson), four Eskimos (Egingwah, Ooqueah, Ootah, and Seegloo), and 40 dogs (two had to be killed on the way for food). Peary stayed 30 hours at the Pole. The news of the discovery reached the world exactly five months later (Sept. 6). Five days earlier Frederick Albert Cook, a physician who had accompanied Peary on a previous expedition, startled the world with the announcement that he had discovered the North Pole in 1908 (Apr. 21). Cook was royally entertained in Europe and America on his return. When Peary got back to civilization and heard of Dr. Cook's claim, he said: "He has simply handed the public a gold brick." (Peary's claim was established by the National Geographic Society in 1910 when he published his book "The North Pole." Dr. Cook's tale was exposed as a fraud, as was his claim of having climbed Mt. McKinley. Subsequently Cook was convicted of a mail fraud and spent seven years in a federal penitentiary. In 1911 Peary received the congratulations of Congress and the rank of rear-admiral for his achievement.)

The United States and Canada signed (Jan. 12) an Arbitration treaty.

Events in American history provided occasions for two civic functions. In Seattle, Washington, was held (June 1-Oct. 15) the Alaska-Yukon-Pacific Exposition celebrating the development of the territory. In New York was observed (Sept.-Nov.) the Hudson-Fulton Celebration commemorating the tercentenary of the discovery of the Hudson River and the centennial of its first navigation by steam. Replicas of Henry Hudson's ship "Half Moon" and Robert Fulton's steamboat "Clermont" were features of the display. In keeping with these events and with the 100th anniversary of Abraham Lincoln's birth, the U. S. Post Office issued three separate commemorative postage stamps and a two-cent red adhesive. At the same time the Lincoln-head penny came into circulation, replacing the Indian girl head one-cent piece after half a century of use (1859). The coin was designed by Victor D. Brenner and was the first one-cent piece to bear the motto "In God We Trust."

The National Kindergarten Association was founded in New York for the educational advancement of children.

The Queensborough and Manhattan bridges, each spanning the East River, New York, were opened (Mar. 30 and Dec. 31, respectively).

Mass production of automobiles began with Henry Ford's Model T, thus inaugurating the gasoline era. (15,000,000 cars of this design were built by 1928 when a new type was adopted.)

Three hundred and ninety-three miners lost their lives in the St. Paul Mine at Cherry, Ill.

Books of the year included: "The Wine of the Puritans" (Van Wyck Brooks; a critical study, developing the thesis that the barren esthetic tradition established by the early New England settlers was the cause of the American emphasis on material values), "Egoists: A Book of Supermen" (James Gibbons Huneker), "Personae" and "Exultations" (Ezra Pound; collections of verse), and the fiction, "A Girl of the Limberlost" (Gene Stratton-Porter), "54-40 or Fight!" (Emerson Hough), "Martin Eden" (Jack London), "Three Lives" (Gertrude Stein; her first book of fiction), "The White Sister" (Francis Marion Crawford).

Sergei Rachmaninoff, Russian piano virtuoso and composer of the popular "Prelude in C sharp minor," concertized (1900-10) for the first time in the United States.

The Boston Opera House opened (Nov. 8) with a performance of Ponchielli's Italian opera "La Gioconda."

John McCormack, celebrated Irish opera tenor, made (Nov. 10) his American debut as Alfredo in Verdi's "La Traviata" at Hammerstein's Manhattan Opera House in New York.

The New York stage presented a succession of successful plays: "The Easiest Way" (Stuyvesant, Jan. 19), "The Girl from Rector's" (Weber's, Feb. 1), "The Third Degree" (Hudson, Feb. 1), "The Climax" (Weber's Apr. 12), "Is Matrimony a Failure?" (Belasco, Aug. 24), "Arsene Lupin" (Lyceum, Aug. 26), "The Fortune Hunter" (Gaiety, Sept. 4; 345 performances), "The Melting Pot" (Comedy, Sept. 6), "The Passing of the Third Floor Back" (Maxine Elliott, Oct. 4), "The Lottery Man" (Bijou, Dec. 6). Among musical productions that ran over 250 performances were "Havana" (Casino, Feb. 11), "The Midnight Sons" (Broadway, May 22), "The Dollar Princess" (Knickerbocker, Sept. 6), "The Chocolate Soldier" (Lyric, Sept. 13). The Hippodrome staged (Sept. 4) two presentations daily of a spectacle "A Trip to Japan" and achieved thereby 447 performances. The "Ziegfeld Follies of 1909" (Jardin de Paris, June 14) burlesqued former President Theodore Roosevelt, teeth and all, and his historic African hunting trip (above) and introduced the Nell Brinkley Bathing Girls.

In the (still) silent movies things were happening. Ten thousand drawings made possible the first animated cartoon—"Gertie the Dinosaur" by artist Winsor McKay of the daily newspaper "New York American." When a William N. Selig cameraman was unable to accompany the Roosevelt African expedition, the company simply relied on its imagination and filmed indoors with the aid of tropical scenery the travelogue "Hunting Big Game in Africa." Audiences believed their eyes. A film version of Dumas's novel "The Count of Monte Cristo" also was being shown. The first colored motion pictures (scenes and short subjects) were exhibited (Dec. 11) in New York.

Edward Payson Weston walked from New York to San Francisco in 105 days.

The latest creation in feminine fashions was the hobble skirt.

ࢿ~ 1910

Ah! Sweet Mystery of Life (Naughty Marietta). w., Rida Johnson Young. m., Victor Herbert. M. Witmark & Sons, cop. 1910.

All Aboard for Blanket Bay. w., Andrew B. Sterling. m., Harry Von Tilzer. Harry Von Tilzer Music Pub. Co., 1910.

All That I Ask of You Is Love. w., Edgar Selden. m., Herbert Ingraham. Maurice Shapiro, cop. 1910.

Alma Where Do You Live? (Alma Where Do You Live). w., George V. Hobart. m., Adolph Philipp. Jerome H. Remick & Co., cop. 1910.

Any Little Girl, That's a Nice Little Girl, Is the Right Little Girl for Me. w., Thomas J. Gray. m., Fred Fisher. Shapiro Music Publisher, Cop. 1910 by Maurice Shapiro.

As Deep As the Deep Blue Sea. w., René Bronner. m., H. W. Petrie. F. B. Haviland Pub. Co., Inc., cop. 1910.

A Banjo Song. w., Howard Weeden. m., Sidney Homer, op. 22, no. 4. G. Schirmer, cop. 1910.

The Big Bass Viol. w., m., M. T. Bohannon. Waterson, Berlin, Snyder Co., cop. 1910 by Ted Snyder Co.

The Birth of Passion (Madame Sherry). w., Otto A. Hauerbach. m., Karl Hoschna. M. Witmark & Sons, cop. 1910.

Bunch of Roses—*original Spanish title:* El puñoa de rosas. March. m., Ruperto Chapi y Lorente. Jos. W. Stern & Co., cop. 1907 by Hawkes & Son, London; assigned 1910 to Jos. W. Stern & Co.; assigned 1921 to Edward B. Marks Music Co. (Originally composed for band and published in Madrid.)

By the Saskatchewan (The Pink Lady). w., C. M. S. McLellan. m., Ivan Caryll. London: Chappell & Co., Ltd., cop. 1910.

Call Me Up Some Rainy Afternoon. w., m., Irving Berlin. Ted Snyder Co., cop. 1910.

Caprice Viennois. Composition for violin and piano. m., Fritz Kreisler. Carl Fischer, Inc., cop. 1910.

The Chanticleer Rag. w., Edward Madden. m., Albert Gumble. Jerome H. Remick & Co., cop. 1910.

Chicken Reel. Two step. m., Joseph M. Daly. Boston: Jos. M. Daly, cop. 1910.

Come, Josephine, in My Flying Machine. w., Alfred Bryan. m., Fred Fisher. Shapiro, Bernstein & Co., cop. 1910.

Constantly. w., [Chris] Smith and [James Henry] Burris. m., Bert Williams. Jerome H. Remick & Co., cop. 1910.

Day Dreams (The Spring Maid). w., Robert B. Smith. m., Heinrich Reinhardt. Jos. W. Stern & Co., cop. 1909 by Breitkopf & Härtel, Leipzig; assigned 1910 to Jos. W. Stern & Co.; cop. 1910 by Jos. W. Stern & Co.

Doctor Tinkle Tinker (The Girl of My Dreams). w., Otto Harbach. m., Karl Hoschna. M. Witmark & Sons, cop. 1910.

Don't Wake Me Up, I'm Dreaming. w., Beth Slater Whitson. m., Herbert Ingraham. Shapiro, Bernstein & Co., cop. 1910.

Down By the Old Mill Stream. w., m., Tell Taylor. Chicago: Tell Taylor, Music Publisher, cop. 1910.

Every Girl Loves Me But the Girl I Love (The Girl of My Dreams). w., Otto Harbach. m., Karl Hoschna. M. Witmark & Sons, cop. 1910.

Every Little Movement (Madame Sherry). w., Otto A. Harbach. m., Karl Hoschna. M. Witmark & Sons, cop. 1910.

Fountain Fay (The Spring Maid). w., Robert B. Smith. m., Heinrich Reinhardt. Jos. W. Stern & Co., cop. 1909 by Breitkopf & Härtel, Leipzig; assigned 1910 to Jos. W. Stern & Co.; cop. 1910 by Joseph W. Stern & Co.

Gee, But It's Great to Meet a Friend from Your Home Town. w., William Tracey. m., James McGavisk. J. Fred Helf Co., cop. 1910 by the NYBO Music Pub. Co.; assigned to J. Fred Helf Co.

The Girl with the Flaxen Hair—*original French title:* La Fille aux Cheveux de Lin (*in:* Douze Préludes). Piano solo. m., Achille Claude Debussy. Paris; Durand & Cie., cop. 1910.

Good-bye, Rose. w., Addison Burkhart. m., Herbert Ingraham. Shapiro, Bernstein & Co., cop. 1910.

How Beautiful upon the Mountains. w., Biblical. m., F. Flaxington Harker, cop. 41, no. 3. G. Schirmer, Inc., cop. 1910.

I'm Falling in Love with Someone (Naughty Marietta). w., Rida Johnson Young. m., Victor Herbert. M. Witmark & Sons, cop. 1910.

I'm Looking for a Nice Young Fellow Who Is Looking for a Nice Young Girl. w., Jeff T. Branen. m., S. R. Henry. Jos. W. Stern & Co., cop. 1910.

I've Got the Time—I've Got the Place, But It's Hard to Find the Girl. w., Ballard MacDonald. m., S. R. Henry. Jos. W. Stern & Co., cop. 1910.

If He Comes In, I'm Going Out. w., Cecil Mack. m., Chris Smith. The Gotham-Attucks Music Co., cop. 1910.

If I Was a Millionaire. w., Will D. Cobb. m., Gus Edwards. Jerome H. Remick & Co., cop. 1910.

In the Shadows. Dance for orch. m., Herman Finck. Jos. W. Stern & Co., cop. 1910 by Hawkes & Sons, London; assigned 1910 to Jos. W. Stern & Co.; assigned 1912 to Edw. B. Marks Music Co. (Published as a song, with words by E. Ray Goetz, 1911.)

Italian Street Song (Naughty Marietta). w., Rida Johnson Young. m., Victor Herbert. M. Witmark & Sons, cop. 1910.

Kiss Me, My Honey, Kiss Me. w., Irving Berlin. m., Ted Snyder. Ted Snyder Co., Inc., cop. 1910.

Let Me Call You Sweetheart. w., m., Beth Slater Whitson and Leo Friedman. Chicago: Harold Rossiter Music Co., cop. 1910 by Leo Friedman, Chicago; assigned 1910 to Harold Rossiter Music Co.

Liebesfreud. Composition for violin and piano. m., Fritz Kreisler. Carl Fischer, Inc., cop. 1910.

Life Is Only What You Make It After All (Tillie's Nightmare). w., Edgar Smith. m., A. Baldwin Sloane. Chicago: Chas. K. Harris, cop. 1910.

Macushla. w., Josephine V. Rowe. m., Dermot Macmurrough. London: Boosey & Co., cop. 1910.

Morning. w., Frank L. Stanton. m., Oley Speaks. G. Schirmer, Inc., cop. 1910.

The Morning After the Night Before. w., Ed Moran. m., J. Fred Helf. J. Fred Helf Co., cop. 1910.

Mother Machree (Barry of Ballymore). w., Rida Johnson Young. m., Chauncey Olcott and Ernest R. Ball. M. Witmark & Sons, cop. 1910.

My Heart Has Learned to Love You, Now Do Not Say Good-Bye. w., Dave Reed. m., Ernest R. Ball. M. Witmark & Sons, cop. 1910.

Oh, That Beautiful Rag (Up and Down Broadway). w., Irving Berlin. m., Ted Snyder. Ted Snyder Co., cop. 1910.

On Mobile Bay. w., Earle C. Jones. m., Charles N. Daniels. Jerome H. Remick & Co., cop. 1910.

Passing By. See 1890.

A Perfect Day. w., m., Carrie Jacobs-Bond. Chicago: Carrie Jacobs-Bond & Son, cop. 1910 by Carrie Jacobs-Bond.

Plant a Watermelon on My Grave and Let the Juice Soak Through. w., m., Frank Dumont and R. P. Lilly. M. Witmark & Sons, cop. 1910.

Play That Barber Shop Chord. w., William Tracey. m., Lewis F. Muir. J. Fred Helf Co., cop. 1910; renewed 1937; assigned 1937 to Alfred Music Co.

Put Your Arms Around Me, Honey. w., Junie McCree, m., Albert Von Tilzer. The York Music Co., cop. 1910.

Schön Rosmarin—Fair Rosmarin. Composition for violin and piano. m., Fritz Kreisler. Carl Fischer, Inc., cop. 1910.

She Took Mother's Advice. w., Stanley Murphy. m., Percy Wenrich. Jerome H. Remick & Co., cop. 1910.

Silver Bell. w., Edward Madden. m., Percy Wenrich, Jerome H. Remick & Co., cop. 1910.

Some of These Days. w. m., Shelton Brooks. Chicago: Will Rossiter, cop. 1910.

Somebody Else, It's Always Somebody Else. w., Jack Drislane. m., George W. Meyer. F. B. Haviland Pub. Co., Inc., cop. 1910.

Steamboat Bill. w., Ren Shields. m., Leighton Bros. F. A. Mills, cop. 1910.

Stein Song. w., Lincoln Colcord. m., E. A. Fenstad. Carl Fischer, cop. 1910.

Tambourin Chinois. Composition for violin and piano. m., Fritz Kreisler, op. 3. Carl Fischer, Inc., cop. 1910.

That Minor Strain. w., Cecil Mack. m., Ford Dabney. The Gotham-Attucks Music Co., cop. 1910 by R. C. McPherson and Ford Dabney.

That's Why They Call Me "Shine." w., Cecil Mack. m., Ford Dabney, Shapiro, Bernstein & Co., cop. 1910.

That's Yiddish Love. w., m., James Brockman. M. Witmark & Sons, cop. 1910.

Two Little Love Bees (The Spring Maid). w., Robert B. Smith. m., Heinrich Reinhardt. Jos. W. Stern & Co., cop. 1909 by Breitkopf & Härtel, Leipzig; assigned 1910 to Jos. W. Stern & Co., cop. 1910 by Jos. W. Stern & Co.

Under the Yum, Yum Tree. w., Andrew B. Sterling. m., Harry Von Tilzer. Harry Von Tilzer Pub Co., cop. 1910.

Washington and Lee Swing. w., C. A. Robbins. m., Thornton W. Allen and M. W. Sheafe. Thornton W. Allen, cop. 1910 and 1920 by Thornton W. Allen and R. G. Thach; cop. 1930 by Thornton W. Allen.

What's the Matter with Father? w., Harry H. Williams. m., Egbert Van Alstyne. Jerome H. Remick & Co., cop. 1910.

The Wild Rose (When Sweet Sixteen). w., George V. Hobart. m. Victor Herbert. M. Witmark & Sons, cop. 1910.

Winter. w., Alfred Bryan. m., Albert Gumble. Jerome H. Remick & Co., cop. 1910.

You Are the Ideal of My Dreams. w., m., Herbert Ingraham. Shapiro, Bernstein & Co., cop. 1910.

You Remind Me of the Girl That Used to Go to School with Me! w., Jack Drislane. m., Charles Miller. F. B. Haviland Pub. Co., Inc., cop. 1910.

Congress passed the White Slave Act (June 25), known also as the Mann Act after Illinois Representative James Robert Mann, which prohibited interstate transportation of women and girls for immoral purposes; also the Mann-Elkins Act (June 18), so-named after James R. Mann and West Virginia Senator Stephen B. Elkins, which placed telephone, telegraph, and cable companies under the control of the Interstate Commerce Commission.

Former President Theodore Roosevelt returned (June 18) from his hunting trip (1909-10) in East Africa and his subsequent triumphal lecture tour of Europe.

New York Governor Charles Evans Hughes was appointed (Apr. 25) an associate justice of the U. S. Supreme Court by President Taft.

Woodrow Wilson, president of Princeton University, resigned (Oct. 20) to enter upon a political career.

Victor Berger of Milwaukee was the first socialist to be elected to Congress.

New York Mayor William Jay Gaynor was shot (Aug. 9) by a discharged Dock Department employee while he was boarding a steamer for Europe. The Mayor recovered but suffered thereafter from the effects of the wound.

During a labor dispute between building contractors and iron workers in Los Angeles, a dynamite explosion occurred (Oct. 1) in the local "Times" newspaper building killing 21 persons and causing a fire. Bitter attacks on labor by Harrison Gray Otis, owner of the paper, were in part responsible for the outrage. The brothers J. B. and J. J. McNamara, who were apprehended by detective William J. Burns, pleaded guilty through their attorney Clarence Seward Darrow and were sentenced to San Quentin prison. The sensational trial was further highlighted by the arrest of the defense lawyer who was accused of suborning a juror. Darrow was tried twice for the offense; in each case the jury disagreed.

Halley's comet, discovered in 240 B.C., reappeared in 1910 and caused considerable consternation. (It had previously appeared in 1835 and will be visible again in 1985.) Earlier in the year a new comet, 1910A, was discovered.

St. Patrick's Cathedral (Roman Catholic), New York, was consecrated (Oct. 5).

The building of the Pan-American Union (1899), Washington, D. C., which was erected from funds provided by Andrew Carnegie, was dedicated (Apr. 26).

The Camp Fire Girls of America was founded by Dr. and Mrs. Luther Halsey Gulick. (Incorporated in Washington, D. C., in Mar. 1912. Dr. Gulick was director of physical education in the New York public schools and social engineer in the Russell Sage Foundation.)

The Boy Scouts of America was organized (incorporated Feb. 8) by the union of Dan C. Beard's Sons of Daniel Boone and Ernest Seton-Thompson's Woodcraft Indians, thus becoming the American equivalent of the English organization founded in 1908 by Sir (now Baron) Robert Stephenson Smyth Baden-Powell.

The Carnegie Endowment for International Peace was established (Dec. 14) by a gift of $10,000,000 from Andrew Carnegie.

Glenn Hammond Curtis won (May 29) the $10,000 prize of the New York newspaper "The World" for the first continuous airplane flight from Albany to New York, travelling 137 miles in 2 hours, 32 minutes. Shortly thereafter (in June) he accomplished a successful airplane landing on water at Hammondsport, Steuben County, N. Y. Later in the year (Sept. 12) Ralph Johnston flew a distance of 101 miles in 3 hours, 14 minutes.

Walter Wellman made (Oct. 15-18) an unsuccessful attempt to fly the Atlantic in a dirigible. He travelled about 1,000 miles.

Robert Henri, American painter, and seven colleagues formed a group calling itself "The Eight."

The Russian language newspaper "Novoye Russkoye Slovo" was founded in New York.

Nearly every woman carried a sunshade, and the right length for sweaters was to the knees.

Books of the year included: "Twenty Years at Hull House" (Jane Addams), "The Growth of Socialism" (Eugene Victor Debs), "The North Pole" (Adm. Robert Edwin Peary), "Shakespeare and His London Associates As Revealed in Recently Discovered Documents" (Charles William Wallace, who had unearthed the papers in the Public Office, London) and the fiction, "Franklin Winslow Kane" (Anne Douglas

Sedgwick), "Hopalong Cassidy" (Clarence Mulford), "A Modern Chronicle" (Winston Churchill). Charles William Eliot, former president of Harvard University, brought out "The Harvard Classics," a series of 50 volumes with selections from the literature of the world popularly known as "Dr. Eliot's Five-Foot Shelf of Books."

The Russian ballerina Anna Pavlova and her dancing partner Mikhail Mordkin made (Feb. 28) their American debuts in a performance of Act I of Delibes's ballet "Coppelia" at the Metropolitan Opera House, New York. Although the performance followed Massenet's four-act opera "Werther" at a late hour, Pavlova at once established herself as the foremost dancer of the time. (Her exquisite choreographic interpretation of "The Swan," designed for her in 1905 by Michel Fokine to Camille Saint-Saëns's music, justly earned her world-wide recognition.)

Maud Allen, an American girl who had gone to Europe to study the piano, returned as a classic dancer with her own version of the Salome dance.

The first experimental radio broadcast from the stage of the New York Metropolitan Opera House took place. Lee De Forest had erected antennae on the roof of the building and, by means of radiophones, broadcast (Jan. 13) portions of the night's twin bill, "Cavalleria Rusticana" and "Pagliacci." Emmy Destinn, Riccardo Martin, Dinh Gilly, Jeanne Maubourg, and Marie Mattfeld sang in the former; Enrico Caruso, Bella Alten, and Pasquale Amato in the latter. The broadcast was reported to have been tuned in by amateurs at Bridgeport, Conn., and picked up at sea by the S. S. "Avon."

Oscar Hammerstein's lavish expenditures at his Manhattan Opera House, New York, forced him to sell (in April) his interests to the rival Metropolitan Opera House for $2,000,000.

The Metropolitan Opera House, New York, produced (Mar. 18) for the first time an opera by an American composer—"The Pipe of Desire" by Frederick Shepherd Converse (it had been previously heard in Boston at Jordan Hall, Jan. 31, 1906). The opera had two performances. In the presence of the composers, the famous house gave the world premières of Giacomo Puccini's "La Fanciulla del West" (The Girl of the Golden West) with Caruso, Emmy Destinn, and Pasquale Amato (Dec. 10) and Engelbert Humperdinck's "Die Königskinder" with Geraldine Farrar (Dec. 28). At Hammerstein's Manhattan Opera House, Richard Strauss's German one-act opera "Elektra" received (Feb. 1) in French its first American performance with Marietta Mazarin.

John Philip Sousa's band of 100 players (1892) made a 14-months' concert tour (1910-11) of the world.

The Berlin Royal Opera House produced (Apr. 23) for the first time in its history an opera by an American composer—Arthur Finley Nevin's "Poia."

The Philadelphia-Chicago Opera Company was formed with the former Metropolitan Opera House tenor Andreas Dippel as manager.

The MacDowell Festivals began (in Sept.) at Peterboro, N. H., under the auspices of the MacDowell Memorial Association.

The Russian Symphony Orchestra, New York, under Modest Altschuler played (Dec. 1) Igor Stravinsky's "Feuerwerk," the first orchestral work by the Russian composer to be heard in America.

Victor Herbert's newest operetta "Naughty Marietta" featured (Nov. 7) at the New York Theatre two recruits from the operatic stage—the soprano Emma Trentini of the Manhattan Opera House and the tenor Orville Harrold of the Metropolitan Opera House. The familiar song "Ah, Sweet Mystery of Life" was originally an instrumental entr'acte in the work and was converted into a vocal number for the tenor at the suggestion of Orville Harrold. The operetta ran 136 performances.

Fanny Brice, a burlesque house singer, started on her road to success in the "Ziegfeld Follies of 1910" (Jardin de Paris, June 20) at an initial salary of $18 a week, singing a character song "Good-bye, Becky Cohen." In the same show, Bert Williams, who had been playing in Negro musical comedies, made the first of his many Follies appearances.

Marie Dressler (she had long since abandoned her real name, Leila von Koerber) convulsed her New York audiences for 77 performances in a musical play "Tillie's Nightmare" that opened (Sept. 10) at the Herald Square Theatre.

New York plays included: "Alias Jimmy Valentine" (Wallack's, Jan. 21), "Madame X" (New Amsterdam, Feb. 2), "The Commuters" (Criterion, Aug. 15), "The Country Boy" (Liberty, Aug. 30), "Get-Rich-Quick Wallingford" (Gaiety, Sept. 19; 424 performances), "The Blue Bird" by Maurice Maeterlinck (New Theatre, Oct. 1), "Rebecca of Sunnybrook Farm" (New York, Oct. 3; 216 performances), "The Concert" with Leo Ditrichstein (Belasco, Oct. 4; 264 performances), "The Gamblers" (Maxine Elliott, Oct. 31), "Nobody's Widow" (Hudson, Nov. 15; 215 performances), "Pomander Walk" (Wallack's, Dec. 20). Musical productions included: "The Arcadians" (Liberty, Jan. 17), "The Summer Widowers" (Broadway, June 4), "Madame Sherry" with Lina Abarbanell (New Amsterdam, Aug. 30; 231 performances), "Hans, the Flute Player" (Manhattan Opera House, Sept. 20), "He Came from Milwaukee" (Casino, Sept. 21), "Alma, Where Do You Live" (Weber, Sept. 26; 232 performances), "The Spring Maid" with Christie MacDonald (Liberty, Dec. 26).

Censorship of films was going on everywhere. In San Francisco, the board of censors clamped down on 32 releases as "unfit for public exhibition." They included "Saved by a Sailor," "In Hot Pursuit," "The Black Viper," and "Maggie, the Dock Rat."

Undefeated heavyweight boxing champion James J. ("Jim") Jeffries returned to the ring after five years of retirement (1905) and lost his title when he was knocked out (July 4) in 15 rounds at Reno, Nev., by Negro challenger Jack Johnson. Jeffries was impressive physically at 227 pounds, but slow of movement; Johnson was perfectly trained at 208 pounds, tall, sleek, and agile. The sun, which poured down on the open arena, was so hot that Jeffries's second held a huge parasol over him between rounds. The bout was filmed. The gate drew $270,775. Jeffries received $66,666 and Johnson, $50,000. Their total receipts from all sources was $192,066 and $145,000, respectively. The fight was originally scheduled for San Francisco but was transferred to Reno after official objections were made by Governor Gillet. The fight had an unfortunate aftermath of racial feeling and riots.

The American balloon "America II" won a 1,171 mile race to capture the James Gordon Bennett cup. (The balloon had won a 695 mile race for the cup in 1909.)

The United States suffered its twenty-first depression since 1790. It lasted one year.

Deaths of the year included Mark Twain (real name: Samuel Langhorne Clemens), aged 75 (Apr. 21), in Redding, Conn., and Julia Ward Howe, author of "The Battle Hymn of the Republic" and other works, aged 91 (Oct. 17), in Middletown, R. I.

The national population was 93,402,151.

₿ℯ 1911

Alexander's Ragtime Band. w., m., Irving Berlin. Ted Snyder Co., Inc., cop. 1911.

All Alone. w., Will Dillon. m., Harry Von Tilzer. Harry Von Tilzer Music Pub. Co., cop. 1911.

Baby Rose. w., Louis Weslyn. m., George Christie. M. Witmark & Sons, cop. 1911.

Barnum Had the Right Idea (The Little Millionaire). w., m., George M. Cohan. Cohan and Harris, cop. 1911.

Bring Back My Golden Dreams. w., Alfred Bryan. m., George W. Meyer. F. B. Haviland Pub. Co., Inc., cop. 1911.

Can't You Take It Back, and Change It for a Boy? w., m., Thurland Chattaway. F. B. Haviland Pub. Co., Inc., cop. 1911.

Child Love. w., Dave Oppenheim. m., Joe Cooper. Jos. W. Stern & Co., cop. 1911.

Daly's Reel. Two step. m., Joseph M. Daly. Boston: Jos. M. Daly, cop. 1911.

Daphnis et Chloé. [Suite 1-2.] m., Maurice Ravel. Paris: Durand & Fils, cop. 1911[-13].

Down the Field. March and two step. w., C. W. O'Connor. m., Stanleigh P. Freedman. Leo Feist, Inc., cop. 1911.

Everybody's Doing It Now. w., m., Irving Berlin. Ted Snyder Co., cop. 1911.

The Gaby Glide (Vera Violetta). w., Harry Pilcer. m., Louis A. Hirsch. Shapiro, Bernstein & Co., cop. 1911.

A Girlie Was Made to Love. w., Joe Goodwin. m., George W. Meyer. F. B. Haviland Pub. Co., Inc., cop. 1911.

Good-Night Ladies. w., Harry Williams. m., Egbert Van Alstyne. Jerome H. Remick & Co., cop. 1911.

The Harbor of Love. w., Earle C. Jones. m., Charlotte Blake. Jerome H. Remick & Co., cop. 1911.

Honey-Love. w., Jack Drislane. m., George W. Meyer. F. B. Haviland Pub. Co., Inc., cop. 1911.

I Love Love (The Red Widow). w., Channing Pollock and Rennold Wolf. m., Charles J. Gebest. M. Witmark & Sons, cop. 1911.

I Want a Girl—Just Like the Girl That Married Dear Old Dad. w., William Dillon. m., Harry Von Tilzer. Harry Von Tilzer Music Pub. Co., cop. 1911.

If You Talk in Your Sleep, Don't Mention My Name. w., A. Seymour Brown. m., Nat D. Ayer. Jerome M. Remick & Co., cop. 1911; assigned to Remick Music Corp.

In the Land of Harmony. w., Bert Kalmar. m., Ted Snyder. Ted Snyder Co., Inc., cop. 1911.

Jimmy Valentine. w., Edward Madden. m., Gus Edwards. Gus Edwards, Inc., cop. 1911; assigned 1912 to Jerome H. Remick & Co.

Little Grey Home in the West. w., D. Eardley-Wilmot. m., Herman Lohr. London: Chappell & Co., Ltd., cop. 1911.

Molly on the Shore. Instrumental piece. m., arr. by Percy Aldridge Grainger. London: Schott & Co., cop. 1911.

My Beautiful Lady (The Pink Lady). w., C. M. S. McLellan. m., Ivan Caryll. London: Chappell & Co., Ltd., cop. 1911.

My Rosary of Dreams. w., m., E. F. Dusenberry and C. M. Denison. F. B. Haviland Pub. Co., cop. 1911.

Oh You Beautiful Doll. w., A. Seymour Brown. m., Nat D. Ayer. Jerome H. Remick & Co., cop. 1911.

Oh! You Circus Day (Hanky Panky). w., m., Edith Maida Lessing and Jimmie V. Monaco. Chicago: Will Rossiter, cop. 1911.

The Oceana Roll. w., Roger Lewis. m., Lucien Denni. Remick Music Corp., cop. 1911 by Roger Lewis; assigned 1911 to Aubrey Stauffer & Co.; assigned 1911 to Jerome H. Remick & Co.

Parade of the Wooden Soldiers. See 1922.

Ragtime Violin. w., m., Irving Berlin. Ted Snyder Co., cop. 1911.

A Ring on the Finger Is Worth Two on the 'Phone. w., Jack Mahoney. m., George W. Meyer. F. B. Haviland Pub. Co., Inc., cop. 1911.

Roamin' in the Gloamin'. w., m., Harry Lauder. T. B. Harms & Francis, Day & Hunter, cop. 1911 by Francis, Day & Hunter.

Say Not Love Is a Dream (The Count of Luxembourg). w., Basil Hood. m., Franz Lehár. London: Chappell & Co., Ltd., cop. 1911.

Somewhere a Voice Is Calling. w., Eileen Newton. m., Arthur F. Tate. T. B. Harms and Francis, Day & Hunter, Inc., cop. 1911 by J. H. Larway, London.

The Spaniard That Blighted My Life. w., m., Billy Merson. Francis, Day & Hunter, cop. 1911.

Take Me Back to the Garden of Love. w., E. Ray Goetz. m., Nat Osborne. Ted Snyder Co., cop. 1911.

That Mysterious Rag. w., m., Irving Berlin and Ted Snyder. Ted Snyder Co., cop. 1911.

That Was Before I Met You. w., Alfred Bryan. m., George W. Meyer. F. B. Haviland Pub. Co., cop. 1911.

There's a Dixie Girl Who's Longing for a Yankee Doodle Boy. w., Robert F. Roden. m., George W. Meyer. F. B. Haviland Pub. Co., Inc., cop. 1911.

There'll Come a Time. w., m., Shelton Brooks. Chicago: Harold Rossiter Music Co., cop. 1911.

They Always Pick on Me. w., Stanley Murphy. m., Harry Von Tilzer. Harry Von Tilzer Music Pub. Co., cop. 1911.

Till the Sands of the Desert Grow Cold. w., George Graff, Jr., m., Ernest R. Ball. M. Witmark & Sons, cop. 1911.

To the Land of My Own Romance (The Enchantress). w., Harry B. Smith. m., Victor Herbert. M. Witmark & Sons, cop. 1911.

Très Moutarde—Too Much Mustard. One step. m., Cecil Macklin, London: Cary & Co., cop. 1911.

A Wee Deoch-an-Doris. w., m., Gerald Grafton and Harry Lauder. T. B. Harms & Francis, Day & Hunter, cop. 1911 by B. Feldman; cop. 1911 by T. B. Harms & Francis, Day & Hunter.

When I Was Twenty-one and You Were Sweet Sixteen. w., Harry H. Williams. m., Egbert Van Alstyne. Jerome H. Remick & Co., cop. 1911.

When You're Away. w., A. Seymour Brown and Joe Young. m., Bert Grant. Jerome H. Remick & Co., cop. 1911.

Woodman, Woodman, Spare That Tree! w., m., Irving Berlin. Waterson, Berlin & Snyder Co., cop. 1911 by Ted Snyder Co.

The United States Supreme Court dissolved the Standard Oil and the American Tobacco companies as monopolies (May 15 and May 30, respectively).

The postal bank system was introduced (Aug. 1) in New York, Chicago, St. Louis, and Boston.

The New York Court of Appeals declared the Workmen's Compensation Law unconstitutional.

Admiral Robert Edwin Peary received (Mar. 3) the congratulations of

Congress and promotion to the rank of Rear Admiral for his discovery of the North Pole (1909).

Charles Franklin Kettering invented the automobile self-starter in Dayton, O.

Maurice Maeterlinck, Belgian playwright and author, made the first of two visits to the United States. (The second was in 1921.)

John Murphy Farley, Roman Catholic Archbishop of New York, was made (Nov. 27) cardinal by Pope Pius X—the fourth American to be so honored.

The Carnegie Corporation of New York was established (June 9) with an endowment of $125,000,000 by Andrew Carnegie for "the advancement and diffusion of knowledge and understanding among the people of the United States."

The New York Public Library, New York City, was dedicated (May 23) by President Taft.

The Great Lakes Naval Training Station, North Chicago, Ill., opened (July 1).

One hundred and twenty-eight miners lost their lives in the Banner Mine in Alabama.

Fire destroyed (Mar. 25) the Triangle shirtwaist factory in New York, with a loss of 145 lives. Many victims jumped from the windows and were impaled on the iron spike fence in front of the building.

Aviation made further strides in the United States. Glenn Hammond Curtis invented the hydro-airplane. Aviator McCurdy flew (Jan. 29) from Key West, Fla., to a landing near Havana, Cuba, a distance of 100 miles in two hours. Earl Ovington transported airmail on Long Island, New York, from the Nassau Boulevard Airdrome to Mineola. C. P. Rodgers made (Sept. 17-Nov. 4) the first transcontinental flight from New York, reaching Pasadena, Cal., after several forced landings in 84 hours, 2 minutes flying time.

"The Masses" was founded in New York as a weekly Socialist magazine. (It suspended in 1924 and resumed in 1926 as "The New Masses.")

Books of the year included: "The Children of the Poor" (Victor Eugene Debs) and the fiction, "Ethan Frome" (Edith Wharton), "The Iron Woman" (Margaret Deland), "Jennie Gerhardt" (Theodore Dreiser), "The Long Roll" (Mary Johnston; its sequel "Cease Firing" followed in 1912), "The Ne'er-Do-Well" (Rex Beach), "Queed" (Henry Sydnor Harrison), "Stover at Yale" (Owen Johnson), "Tante" (Anne Douglas Sedgwick), "The Winning of Barbara Worth" (Harold Bell Wright; a best seller).

Pianos in the United States were thumping out ragtime. This brought great revenue to the music publishing business, especially after the five-and-ten-cent stores put the publishers' wares on their counters and engaged piano players to stimulate sales. Ragtime produced a batch of new dance steps. Most popular was the turkey trot (which actually had originated in Denver vaudeville circles in 1883). Variations on the turkey trot included the crab step, kangaroo dip, fish walk, the Texas Tommy, the snake, and the grizzly bear. Still popular dances, however, were the waltz and the two step.

Oscar Hammerstein, who had sold his New York operatic interests to the Metropolitan Opera House in the preceding year, transferred his activities to London and erected in Kingsway an opera house for French opera. It opened (Nov. 13) with Nouguès's "Quo Vadis?" (The venture was unsuccessful, and Hammerstein sold the house. It became the Stoll Picture Theatre.)

Henry Wilson Savage toured (1911-12) the United States with his opera company, giving performances of Puccini's latest opera "The Girl of the Golden West" in English as he had done with "Parsifal" (1904-05) and "Mme. Butterfly" (1906-07).

Paul Hastings Allen, Massachusetts-born composer, produced in Florence, Italy, an opera in Neapolitan dialect, "O Munasterio." A second performance followed shortly afterward in the Teatro Verdi. (The opera was performed in Naples, 1913, and in Palermo, Sicily. It was heard in the United States in a radio rendition from New York in 1948.)

Actor Edward Hugh Sothern married his leading lady Julia Marlowe. Together they won tremendous popularity, notably in Shakespearean plays. (It was Miss Marlowe's second marriage. Her real name was Sarah Frances Frost. She was born in 1866 near Keswick, Cumberland, England. Sothern was born in 1859 in London.)

Edmond Rostand's gallinaceous play "Chantecler" with Maude Adams was staged (Jan. 23) in New York at the Knickerbocker Theatre. It had 96 performances.

Mme. Simone, noted French actress, started her first American tour (Oct. 16) at Daly's Theatre, New York, in an English version of Henri Bernstein's play "The Thief."

The Irish Players from the Abbey Theatre, Dublin, made the first of several visits to the United States. They opened (in October) in Boston, played en route to Washington, D. C., appeared (Nov. 20) in New York, and went on to Philadelphia and Chicago. The company met in America the same turbulent reception from partisan Irishmen as it had experienced in Ireland. John Millington Synge's play, "The Playboy of the Western World," aroused animosity everywhere and caused disturbances in the theatres.

Gaby Deslys made her first American appearances at the Winter Garden, New York, in "The Revue of Revues" (Sept. 27) and in "Vera Violetta" (Nov. 20). In the last named, Annette Kellermann danced a ballet "Undine" instead of swimming in a stage tank. Al Jolson also was in the cast.

New York plays included: "The Deep Purple" (Lyric, Jan. 9), "The Piper" (New Theatre, Jan. 30), "Excuse Me" (Gaiety, Feb. 13), "Everywoman" (Herald Square, Feb. 27), "As a Man Thinks" (39th Street

Theatre, Mar. 13), "Maggie Pepper" (Harris, Aug. 31), "Disraeli" with George Arliss (Wallack's, Sept. 18; 280 performances), "The Woman" (Republic, Sept. 19), "Bought and Paid For" (Playhouse, Sept. 26; 431 performances), "Bunty Pulls the Strings" (Comedy, Oct. 10; 391 performances), "The Return of Peter Grimm" with David Warfield (Belasco, Oct. 17; 231 performances), "The Garden of Allah" (Century, Oct. 21; 241 performances), "Kismet" with Otis Skinner (Knickerbocker, Dec. 25). Musical productions included: "The Slim Princess" (Globe, Jan. 2), "The Hen-Pecks" with dancing specialist Vernon Castle (Broadway, Feb. 4), "The Balkan Princess" (Herald Square, Feb. 9), "The Pink Lady" (New Amsterdam, Mar. 13; 312 performances—and pink became a fashionable color), "The Siren" (Knickerbocker, Aug. 28), "The Little Millionaire" (Cohan, Sept. 25), "The Quaker Girl" (Park, Oct. 23; 240 performances), "The Red Widow" (Astor, Nov. 6), "Little Boy Blue" (Lyric, Nov. 27), "Jumping Jupiter" (New York Theatre, Mar. 6) presented Edna Wallace Hopper, Jeanne Eagles of later (1922) "Rain" fame, Helen Broderick, and Ina Claire, late of vaudeville. The stately Valeska Suratt displayed herself in innumerable gorgeous costumes of her own designing, the envy of every woman, in "The Red Robe" (Globe, June 22), and beheld herself imitated by that exquisite impersonator of feminine charms Julian Eltinge in "The Fascinating Widow" (Liberty, Sept. 11).

To film a screen version of the Gospel story with an authentic background, American motion-picture cameras were taken to the Holy Land to photograph "From the Manger to the Cross." It cost $35,000 to make and grossed nearly a million dollars' profit. R. Henderson Bland portrayed the white-robed Christ.

Ty Cobb wound up the baseball season with a batting average of .385, bettering his previous year's average of .377. (Between 1910 and 1919 there was only one year in which he wasn't American League batting champion—1916, when Tris Speaker topped the league with .386.)

There was grave concern in the United States when Porfirio Diaz, president of Mexico since 1877, was deposed (Mar. 25) in a revolution by Francisco Indalecio Madero. Madero was elected (Oct. 1) to the presidency.

৪৯ 1912

After All That I've Been to You. w., Jack Drislane. m., Chris Smith. F. B. Haviland Pub. Co., cop. 1912.

And the Green Grass Grew All Around. w., William Jerome. m., Harry Von Tilzer. Harry Von Tilzer Music Pub. Co., cop. 1912.

As Long as the Shamrock Grows Green. w., James Brockman. m., Nat Osborne. Waterson, Berlin & Snyder Co., cop. 1912.

At the Devil's Ball. w., m., Irving Berlin. Waterson, Berlin & Snyder Co., cop. 1912.

Bagdad (The Lady of the Slipper). w., Anne Caldwell. m., Victor Herbert. M. Witmark & Sons, cop. 1912.

Be My Little Baby Bumble Bee. w., Stanley Murphy. m., Henry I. Marshall. Jerome H. Remick & Co., cop. 1912.

Beans! Beans!! Beans!!! w., Elmer Bowman. m., Chris Smith. F. B. Haviland Pub. Co., Inc., cop. 1912.

Daddy Has a Sweetheart and Mother Is Her Name. w., Gene Buck. m., Dave Stamper. The Penn Music Co., Inc., cop. 1912 by William H. Penn, Gene Buck and Dave Stamper.

Dear Old Rose. w., Jack Drislane. m., George W. Meyer. F. B. Haviland Pub. Co., cop. 1912.

Do It Again. w., m., Irving Berlin. Waterson, Berlin & Snyder Co., cop. 1912.

Down In Dear Old New Orleans (The Ziegfeld Follies of 1912). w., Joe Young. m., Conrad and Whidden. Jerome H. Remick & Co., cop. 1912.

Down South. Orch. piece. m., W. H. Myddleton, op. 10. Jos. W. Stern & Co., cop. 1901 by Hawkes & Son, London; assigned 1912 to Jos. W. Stern & Co.; assigned 1920 to Edward B. Marks Music Co.

Dreams of Long Ago—*Italian title:* Sogni d'altra Età. English words, Earl Carroll; Italian words, John Focacci. m., Enrico Caruso. Leo Feist, Inc., cop. 1912.

Everybody Two-Step. w., Earl C. Jones. m., Wallie Herzer. Jerome H. Remick & Co., cop. 1912.

The Ghost of the Violin. w., Bert Kalmar. m., Ted Snyder. Waterson, Berlin & Snyder Co., cop. 1912.

Giannina Mia (The Firefly). w., Otto Hauerbach. m., Rudolf Friml. G. Schirmer, Inc., cop. 1912.

Good Night Nurse. w., Thomas J. Gray. m., W. Raymond Walker. Jerome H. Remick & Co., cop. 1912.

Here Comes My Daddy Now—Oh Pop-Oh Pop-Oh Pop. w., L. Wolfe Gilbert. m., Lewis F. Muir. F. A. Mills, cop. 1912.

Hitchy Koo. w., L. Wolfe Gilbert. m., Lewis F. Muir and Maurice Abrahams. F. A. Mills, cop. 1912.

I'm the Lonesomest Gal in Town. w., Lew Brown. m., Albert Von Tilzer. The York Music Co., cop. 1912.

In the Evening By the Moonlight, Dear Louise. w., Andrew B. Sterling. m., Harry Von Tilzer. Harry Von Tilzer Music Pub. Co., cop. 1912.

In the Garden. Hymn. w., m., C. Austin Miles. Philadelphia: Hall-Mack Co., cop. 1912.

In Twilight Town. w., C. M. Denison. m., E. F. Dusenberry. F. B. Haviland Pub. Co., cop. 1912.

Isle o' Dreams (The Isle o' Dreams). w., George Graff, Jr., and Chauncey Olcott. m., Ernest R. Ball. M. Witmark & Sons, cop. 1912.

It's a Long, Long Way to Tipperary. w., m., Jack Judge and Harry H. Williams. London: Chappell & Co., Ltd., cop. 1912 by B. Feldman & Co., London.

Jimmy Valentine. w., Edward Madden. m., Gus Edwards. Jerome H. Remick & Co. [cop. 1910 by Gus Edwards; cop. 1912 by Song Review Co.], assigned 1912 to Jerome H. Remick & Co.; assigned 1928 to Remick Music Corp.

Kentucky Sue. w., Lew Brown. m., Albert Von Tilzer. The York Music Co., cop. 1912.

The Land of Golden Dreams. w., C. M. Denison. m., E. F. Dusenberry. F. B. Haviland Pub. Co., Inc., cop. 1912.

Last Night Was the End of the World. w., Andrew B. Sterling. m., Harry Von Tilzer. Harry Von Tilzer Pub. Co., cop. 1912.

A Little Love a Little Kiss—Un Peu d'Amour. Original French w., Nilson Fysher; English w., Adrian Ross. m., Lao Silesu. London: Chappell

& Co., Ltd., cop. 1912 by L. Digoude-Diodet, Paris; assigned 1912 to Chappell & Co., Ltd.

Love Is Like a Firefly (The Firefly). w., Otto Hauerbach. m., Rudolf Friml. G. Schirmer, Inc., cop. 1912.

Malinda. w., Stanley Murphy. m., Henry I. Marshall. Jerome H. Remick & Co., cop. 1912.

Maria Wiegenlied (No. 52 in: Schlichte Weisen, op. 76). w., Martin Boelitz. m., Max Reger. Berlin: Ed. Bote & G. Bock, cop. 1912. (An American edition under the title "The Virgin's Slumber Song," English words by Edward Teschemacher, was published by Oliver Ditson Co., Boston, cop. 1912 by Ed. Bote & G. Bock.)

Melody. Instrumental. m., Charles G[ates] Dawes. Chicago: Gamble Hinged Music Corp., cop. 1912. (Published as a song in 1951; see 1958: "It's All In the Game." The composer was Vice-President of the United States 1925-29.)

The Memphis Blues. piano solo. m., W[illiam] C[hristopher] Handy. Memphis, Tenn.: Handy Music Co., cop. 1912 by W. C. Handy; assigned 1912 to Theron C. Bennett Co.; assigned 1916 to Joe Morris Music Co.; renewed 1940 by W. C. Handy; published by Handy Bros. Music Co., Inc. (Published as a song, words by George A. Norton, Theron C. Bennett Co., New York, cop. 1913; assigned to Joe Morris Music Co.; arr. with new lyrics and melody interpolations by Charlie Tobias and Peter DeRose, Joe Morris Music Co., cop. 1931. On the subject of the "blues" and the history of the above song, consult—W. C. Handy, "Blues; an Anthology," A. & C. Boni, New York, cop. 1926; and his: "A Treasury of the Blues," Charles Boni, New York, cop. 1949. For much of the preceding information, the compiler is indebted to Mr. Edward Abbe Niles, the writer of the historical texts to Handy's two books.)

Moonlight Bay. w., Edward Madden. m., Percy Wenrich. Jerome H. Remick & Co., cop. 1912.

My Melancholy Baby. w., George A. Norton. m., Ernie Burnett. Joe Morris Music Co., cop. 1911 by Ernest M. Burnett; assigned 1912 to Theron C. Bennett; assigned 1912 to Joe Morris Music Co.

Oh, You Cutie—You Ever, Ever Loving Child. w., Harry H. Williams. m., Nat D. Ayer. Jerome H. Remick & Co., cop. 1912.

Oh, You Million Dollar Baby. w., Eddie Doerr. m., Lou S. Lashley. Royal Music Pub. Co., cop. 1912 by Jeff T. Branen; assigned 1912 to Royal Music Pub. Co.

On the Mississippi. w., Ballard MacDonald. m., Harry Carroll and Fields. Shapiro, Bernstein & Co., cop. 1912.

Please Don't Take My Lovin' Man Away. w., Lew Brown. m., Albert Von Tilzer. The York Music Co., cop. 1912.

Pucker Up Your Lips, Miss Lindy. w., Eli Dawson. m., Albert Von Tilzer. The York Music Co., cop. 1912.

Row, Row, Row. w., William Jerome. m., Jimmie V. Monaco. Harry Von Tilzer Music Pub. Co., cop. 1912; renewed 1939.

Siamese Patrol—*original German title:* **Siamesische Wachtparade.** m., Paul Lincke. Jos. W. Stern & Co., cop. 1912 by Apollo Verlag, Berlin; assigned 1921 to Edward B. Marks Music Co.; assigned 1932 to Edward B. Marks Music Corp.

Spirit of Independence. Military march-two step. m., Abe Holzmann. Jerome H. Remick & Co., cop. 1912.

The Star. w., Charles F. Lummis. m., James H. Rogers. G. Schirmer, Inc., cop. 1912.

The Sweetheart of Sigma Chi. w., Byron D. Stokes. m., F. Dudleigh Vernor. Chicago: Melrose Bros. Music Co., Inc., cop. 1912 by Richard E. Vernor Pub. Co.; assigned 1927 to Melrose Bros. Music Co., Inc.

Sympathy (The Firefly). w., Otto Hauerbach. m., Rudolf Friml. G. Schirmer, Inc., cop. 1912.

Take a Little Tip from Father. w., m., Irving Berlin and Ted Snyder. Ted Snyder Co., cop. 1912.

That Daffydill Rag. w., m., Bill and Frank Mueller. The Joe Morris Co., cop. 1912.

That's How I Need You. w., Joe McCarthy and Joe Goodwin. m., Al Piantadosi. Leo Feist, Inc., cop. 1912.

That Mellow Melody. w., Sam M. Lewis. m., George W. Meyer. Geo. W. Meyer Music Co., cop. 1912.

That Old Girl of Mine. w., Earle C. Jones. m., Egbert Van Alstyne. Jerome H. Remick & Co., cop. 1912.

They Gotta Quit Kickin' My Dawg Aroun'. w., Webb M. Oungst. m., Cy Perkins. M. Witmark & Sons, cop. 1912 by Stark Music Ptg. & Pub. Co.; assigned 1912 to M. Witmark & Sons. (The song was used by Senator Champ Clark, Missouri Democrat, in an unsuccessful campaign for the presidency.)

Wait Until Your Daddy Comes Home. w., m., Irving Berlin. Waterson, Berlin & Snyder Co., cop. 1912.

Waiting for the Robert E. Lee. w., L. Wolfe Gilbert. m., Lewis F. Muir. F. A. Mills, cop. 1912.

When a Maid Comes Knocking at Your Heart (The Firefly). w., Otto Hauerbach. m., Rudolf Friml. G. Schirmer, Inc., cop. 1912.

When I Lost You. w., m., Irving Berlin. Waterson, Berlin & Snyder Co., cop. 1912.

When Irish Eyes Are Smiling (The Isle o' Dreams). w., Chauncey Olcott and George Graff, Jr. m., Ernest R. Ball. M. Witmark & Sons, cop. 1912.

When It's Apple Blossom Time in Normandy. w., m., Mellor Gifford and Trevor. Jerome H. Remick & Co., cop. 1912 by Francis, Day & Hunter.

When the Midnight Choo-Choo Leaves for Alabam'. w., m., Irving Berlin. Waterson, Berlin & Snyder Co., cop. 1912.

Where the Twilight Comes to Kiss the Rose "Good Night!" w., Robert F. Roden. m., Henry W. Petrie. F. B. Haviland Pub. Co., cop. 1912.

When You've Had a Little Love You Want a Little More. w., Arthur Lamb. m., John T. Hall. Chas. K. Harris, cop. 1912.

You Can't Stop Me from Loving You. w., Gerber and Murphy. m., Henry I. Marshall. Jerome H. Remick & Co., cop. 1912.

You're My Baby. w., A. Seymour Brown. m., Nat D. Ayer. Jerome H. Remick & Co., cop. 1912.

Two more stars were added to the national flag with the admission of New Mexico (Jan. 6) and of Arizona (Feb. 14), as the 47th and the 48th State, respectively, thus completing the roster of States to date.

Massachusetts was the first State to establish a minimum wage for women and children.

The palatial $7,500,000 White Star liner "Titanic" on its maiden voyage from Southampton, England, to New York struck (Apr. 14-15) an iceberg off Cape Race, Newfoundland, and sank. The ship carried 2,223 persons. The catastrophe took the lives of 1,517, of whom 103 were women and children. Seven hundred and six persons were rescued. Among the prominent Americans who were drowned were John Jacob Astor, Isidor Straus, and Francis D. Millet, the painter.

New York Governor William Sulzer was impeached (Oct. 16) and removed (Oct. 18) from office.

The Girl Scouts of the United States of America was founded (Mar. 12) in Savannah, Ga., by Juliette Low, a friend of Lieutenant General Robert Stephenson Smyth Baden-Powell, as an American equivalent of the latter's Boy Scouts (1908) and his sister Agnes's "Girl Guides" (1910). The name of the organization originally was "Girl Guides" but was changed the next year to "Girl Scouts."

Hadassah, the Women's Zionist Organization of America, was founded in New York.

Nobel prizes were awarded to Elihu Root for peace and to Dr. Alexis Carrel for medicine and physiology.

"September Morn," a painting of a nude woman bathing at sunrise by the French artist Paul Emile Chabas, was the talk and scandal of the time. (The next year came the wonderful, shocking, Armory exhibition of "modern" art.)

The memorial for the Oscar Wilde tomb in Père Lachaise Cemetery, Paris, sculptured by New York-born Jacob Epstein, created such a furor over its alleged indecency that the monument was kept covered for months by tarpaulins.

Books of the year included: "The Autobiography of an Ex-Colored Man" (James Weldon Johnson) and the fiction, "Daddy Long Legs" (Jean Webster; sequel, "Dear Enemy," 1914), "The Financier" (Theodore Dreiser), "Riders of the Purple Sage" (Zane Grey), "Smoke Bellew" (Jack London). James Loeb, New York banker, began the publication of the Loeb Classical Library, a series of Greek and Latin texts with English translations.

Dr. Horatio William Parker of Yale University won the $10,000 prize offered by the Metropolitan Opera House, New York, for an English-language opera by a native American composer with his three-act "Mona" (première, Mar. 14). The opera had four performances.

Ermanno Wolf-Ferrari's Italian opera "I Gioielli della Madonna" (The Jewels of the Madonna) received (Jan. 16) its American première in the Auditorium, Chicago. This was the first performance of the work in its original language. (Its world première in Berlin, 1911, was sung in German.)

Leopold Stokowski was appointed musical director of the Philadelphia Symphony Orchestra. (He held the post until 1926.)

The vast growth of the entertainment business in the past generation was exemplified in an estimate by "Variety" of the wealth of various theatrical personalities: George M. Cohan, $1,500,000; David Belasco, $1,-000,000; Daniel Frohman, $1,000,000; Chauncy Olcott, $750,000; Maxine Elliott, $400,000; David Warfield, $350,000; William Gillette, $300,000; Maude Adams, $225,000; Fred Stone, $175,000; Eddie Foy, $100,000.

New York plays that ran 175 or more performances included: "The Butterfly on the Wheel" (39th Street Theatre, Jan. 9), "Officer 666'" (Gaiety, Jan. 29), "Within the Law" (Eltinge, Sept. 11; 541 performances), "Fanny's First Play" (Comedy, Sept. 16; 256 performances), "Milestones" (Liberty, Sept. 17; 215 performances), "Broadway Jones" (Cohan, Sept. 23), "Little Women" (Playhouse, Oct. 14), "Peg o' My Heart" (Cort, Dec. 20; 603 performances), "The Argyle Case" (Criterion, Dec. 24), "Years of Discretion" (Belasco, Dec. 25). Max Reinhardt and his company from the Deutsches Theater, Berlin, brought "Sumurun," a wordless play in 9 tableaux, to America. (Casino, Jan. 16) for 62 performances. For realism, Belasco staged an exact duplicate of a Childs restaurant in "The Governor's Lady" (Republic, Sept. 10). "The Yellow Jacket" (Fulton, Nov. 4) ran for 82 performances. "Julius Caesar," with William Faversham (Lyric, Nov. 14) had 32 performances. "Hamlet," as played by John E. Kellerd (Garden, Nov. 18), achieved a record-breaking run of 102 consecutive presentations. Musical productions included: "Whirl of Society" (Winter Garden, Mar. 5), "A Winsome Widow" (Moulin Rouge, Apr. 11), "The Rose Maid" (Globe, Apr. 22), "The Count of Luxembourg" (New Amsterdam, Sept. 16), "Oh! Oh! Delphine" (Knickerbocker, Sept. 30; 249 performances), "The Lady of the Slipper" by Victor Herbert (Globe, Oct. 28; 232 performances), "The Firefly" with Emma Trentini (Lyric, Dec. 2). The first "Passing Show" revue opened (July 22) at the Winter Garden. These shows were for many years summer rivals of the "Ziegfeld Follies." The Minsky brothers took over the National Winter Garden theatre and became notorious for their bawdy burlesque productions.

The motion-picture industry began to flourish and in consequence made great strides in production techniques. Like the legitimate stage, the picture companies were adopting the star system. "This is my one chance of immortality," said the "divine" Sarah Bernhardt, and she acted the elaborate and silently screened "Queen Elizabeth" before the cameras of Louis Mercanton in France. The film was first shown publicly (July 12) in America in New York at Daniel Frohman's Lyceum Theatre, and established Adolph Zukor in the motion-picture industry. The picture was artistically ahead of the times, and it was also one of the first long films —a "four-reeler." In San Diego, Cal., a high-school girl named Anita

Loos got $15 for a story that was made into a movie called "The New York Hat." It starred Mary Pickford, previously known as "Little Mary," and a young American actor, an erstwhile student of painting in Paris, Lionel Barrymore. Mary Pickford, a 19-year-old actress, had left the legitimate stage to join the Biograph Motion Picture Company which had just featured her in the first full-length film, "Her First Biscuit." Meanwhile, Mary's future husband, Douglas Fairbanks, was starting his movie career. Two other early screen stars were William Faversham and Julia Opp, who appeared in a film version of "Julius Caesar." And Mack Sennett, via the Keystone Company, put bathing beauties on the screen.

James ("Jim") Thorpe, American part-Indian athlete, won the pentathlon and the decathlon at the Olympic games in Stockholm, Sweden, thereby gaining acclaim as the world's greatest all-around athlete. Two months after his return to the United States he was shorn of his honors by the Amateur Athletic Union of the United States when it was discovered that he had played professional baseball in 1909, an act which eliminated him from amateur standing. The A.A.U. apologized to the International Olympic Committee, and Thorpe was compelled to relinquish his trophies.

Mountain climbers reached new altitudes. Dr. Hudson Stuck and H. P. Karstens ascended Mt. McKinley (20,300 feet), Alaska; Miss Dora Keen, traveller and social worker, made the ascent of Mt. Blackburn (16,140 feet), Alaska.

Regarding the conservative tendencies of President Taft as inimical to liberal policies, former President Theodore Roosevelt and former Indiana Senator Albert Jeremiah Beveridge organized (June 22) the Progressive Party and adopted the Bull Moose as its symbol—hence, popularly called the Bull Moose Party. The name is said to have originated in a remark made by Roosevelt who declared on a certain occasion, "I feel as fit as a bull moose." The result of the Republican split won the national election for Woodrow Wilson, Democrat, former president of Princeton University.

1913

The Angelus (Sweethearts). w., Robert B. Smith. m., Victor Herbert. G. Schirmer, Inc., cop. 1913.

Asia (All Aboard). w., E. Ray Goetz. m., John Lindsay. Waterson, Berlin & Snyder Co., cop. 1912 by Richard Birnbach; assigned 1913 to Waterson, Berlin & Snyder Co.

Ballin' the Jack. w., Jim [James Henry] Burris. m., Chris Smith. Jos. W. Stern & Co., cop. 1913.

The Blind Ploughman. w., Marguerite Radclyffe-Hall. m., Robert Coningsby Clarke. London: Chappell & Co., Ltd., cop. 1913.

Brighten the Corner Where You Are. Hymn. w., Ina Duley Ogdon. m., Charles H. Gabriel. Philadelphia: The Rodeheaver Co., cop. 1913 by Chas. H. Gabriel.

The Bubble (High Jinks). w., Otto Hauerbach. m., Rudolf Friml. G. Schirmer, Inc., cop. 1913.

El Choclo. Argentine tango. m., A. G. Villoldo; arr. for orch. by G.J.S.W. G. Schirmer, Inc., cop. 1913.

The Cricket on the Hearth (Sweethearts). w., Robert B. Smith. m., Victor Herbert. G. Schirmer, Inc., cop. 1913.

The Curse of an Aching Heart. w., Henry Fink. m., Al Piantadosi. Leo Feist, Inc., cop. 1913.

Danny Boy. w., Fred[erick] E[dward] Weatherly. m., "adapted from an old Irish air by Fred E. Weatherly." London: Boosey & Co., cop. 1913; renewed 1941 by Mrs. Miriam Weatherly; assigned 1941 to Boosey & Hawkes, Inc.

Don't Blame It All on Broadway. w., Joe Young and Harry Williams. m., Bert Grant. Harry Williams Music Co., cop. 1913.

Do You Take This Woman for Your Lawful Wife? (The Passing Show of 1913). w., Andrew B. Sterling. m., Harry Von Tilzer. Harry Von Tilzer Music Pub. Co., cop. 1913.

Down by the Silvery Rio Grande. w., Dave Weisberg and Robert F. Roden. m., Charles Speidel. The Joe Morris Music Co., cop. 1913.

Down on the Farm in Harvest Time. w., Andrew K. Allison. m., Dick Richards. F. B. Haviland Pub. Co., Inc., cop. 1913.

Fifteen Cents. w., m., Chris Smith. F. B. Haviland Pub. Co., Inc., cop. 1913.

Friend o' Mine. w., Frederick E[dward] Weatherly. m., Wilfrid Sanderson. London: Boosey & Co., Ltd., cop. 1913.

Good-Bye Boys. w., Andrew B. Sterling and William Dillon. m., Harry Von Tilzer. Harry Von Tilzer Music Pub. Co., cop. 1913.

Goodbye, Little Girl of My Dreams. w., Richard Howard. m., A. Fred Philips. F. B. Haviland Pub. Co., cop. 1913.

He'd Have to Get Under—Get Out and Get Under to Fix Up His Automobile. w., Grant Clarke and Edgar Leslie. m., Maurice Abrahams. Maurice Abrahams Music Co., Inc., cop. 1913.

I Hear a Thrush at Eve. w., Nelle Richmond Eberhardt. m., Charles Wakefield Cadman. White-Smith Music Pub. Co., cop. 1913.

If I Had My Way. w., Lou Klein. m., James Kendis. James Kendis Music Corp., cop. 1913.

In My Harem. w., m., Irving Berlin. Waterson, Berlin & Snyder Co., cop. 1913.

Isle d'Amour (*introduced in:* Ziegfeld Follies of 1913). w., Earl Carroll. m., Leo Edwards. Leo Feist, Inc., cop. 1913.

It Takes a Little Rain with the Sunshine to Make the World Go Round. w., Ballard MacDonald. m., Harry Carroll. Shapiro, Bernstein & Co., Inc., cop. 1913.

Juba Dance (*in the suite:* In the Bottoms). Piano solo. m., R. Nathaniel Dett. Chicago: Clayton F. Summy Co., cop. 1913.

A Little Bunch of Shamrocks. w., William Jerome and Andrew B. Sterling. m., Harry Von Tilzer. Harry Von Tilzer Music Pub. Co., cop. 1913.

Love Has Wings (Sari). w., C. C. S. Cushing and E. P. Heath. m., Emmerich Kalman. Jos. W. Stern & Co., cop. 1912 by Josef Weinberger; cop. 1913 by Jos. W. Stern & Co.

Low Bridge!—Everybody Down; or, Fifteen Years on the Erie Canal. w., m., Thomas S. Allen. F. B. Haviland Pub. Co., Inc., cop. 1913.

Mammy Jinny's Jubilee. w., L. Wolfe Gilbert. m., Lewis F. Muir. F. A. Mills, cop. 1913.

Marcheta. w., m., Victor Schertzinger. The John Franklin Music Co., cop. 1913.

My Faithful Stradivari (Sari). w., C. C. S. Cushing and E. P. Heath. m., Emmerich Kalman. Jos. W. Stern & Co., cop. 1912 by Josef Weinberger, cop. 1913 by Jos. W. Stern & Co.

My Wife's Gone to the Country. w., George Whiting and Irving Berlin. m., Ted Snyder. Waterson, Berlin & Snyder Co., cop. 1913.

My Wonderful Dream Girl. w., Oliver Morosco. m., Victor Schertzinger. The John Franklin Music Co., cop. 1913.

Oh, You Million Dollar Doll. w., Grant Clarke and Edgar Leslie. m., Maurice Abrahams. Maurice Abrahams Music Co., cop. 1913.

The Old Rugged Cross. Hymn. w., m., Rev. George Bennard. Chicago: The Rodeheaver Co., cop. 1913 by George Bennard. Homer A. Rodeheaver, owner.

On the Old Fall River Line. w., William Jerome and Andrew B. Sterling. m., Harry Von Tilzer. Harry Von Tilzer Music Pub. Co., cop. 1913.

Peg o' My Heart. w., Alfred Bryan. m., Fred Fisher. Leo Feist, Inc., cop. 1913; renewed 1941; cop. 1947.

The Pullman Porters on Parade. w., Ren. G. May [i.e., Germany, pseud. of Irving Berlin]. m., Maurice Abrahams. Maurice Abrahams Music Co., cop. 1913.

Sailing Down the Chesapeake Bay. w., Jean C. Havez. m., George Botsford. Jerome H. Remick & Co., cop. 1913.

Snooky Ookums. w., m., Irving Berlin. Waterson, Berlin & Snyder Co., cop. 1913.

Softly Thro' the Summer Night (Sari). w., C. C. S. Cushing and E. P. Heath. m., Emmerich Kalman. Jos. W. Stern & Co., cop. 1912 by Josef Weinberger; cop. 1913 by Jos. W. Stern & Co.

Somebody's Coming to My House. w., m., Irving Berlin. Waterson, Berlin & Snyder Co., cop. 1913.

Something Seems Tingle-Ingleing (High Jinks). w., Otto Hauerbach. m., Rudolf Friml. G. Schirmer, Inc., cop. 1913.

Such a Li'l' Fellow. w., Frances Lowell. m., William Dichmont. Boston: Oliver Ditson Co., cop. 1913.

Sweethearts (Sweethearts). w., Robert B. Smith. m., Victor Herbert. G. Schirmer, Inc., cop. 1913.

That International Rag. w., m., Irving Berlin. Waterson, Berlin & Snyder Co., cop. 1913.

There's a Girl in the Heart of Maryland—with a Heart That Belongs to Me. w., Ballard MacDonald. m., Harry Carroll. Shapiro, Bernstein & Co., cop. 1913.

There's a Long, Long Trail. w., Stoddard King. m., Zo Elliott. M. Witmark & Sons, cop. 1913 by West & Co., London; assigned 1914 to M. Witmark & Sons.

To Have, to Hold, to Love. w., Darl MacBoyle. m., Ernest R. Ball. M. Witmark & Sons, cop. 1913.

The Trail of the Lonesome Pine. w., Ballard MacDonald. m., Harry Carroll. Shapiro, Bernstein & Co., cop. 1913.

What's the Good of Being Good—When No One's Good to Me. w., Stanley Murphy. m., Harry Von Tilzer. Harry Von Tilzer Music Pub. Co., cop. 1913.

When You're All Dressed Up and No Place to Go (The Beauty Shop). w., Benjamin Hapgood Burt. m., Silvio Hein. T. B. Harms & Francis, Day & Hunter, cop. 1913.

When You Play in the Game of Love. w., Joe Goodwin. m., Al Piantadosi. Leo Feist, Inc., cop. 1913.

Where Did You Get That Girl? w., Bert Kalmar. m., Harry Puck. Kalmar & Puck Music Co., cop. 1913.

You're a Great Big Blue Eyed Baby. w., m., A. Seymour Brown. Jerome H. Remick & Co., cop. 1913.

You Can't Play Every Instrument in the Band (*introduced in:* **The Sunshine Girl**). w., Joseph Cawthorn. m., John L. Golden. Harms, Inc., cop. 1912 by T. B. Harms & Francis, Day & Hunter. (See below.)

You've Got Your Mother's Big Blue Eyes. w., m., Irving Berlin. Waterson, Berlin & Snyder Co., cop. 1913.

You Made Me Love You—I Didn't Want to Do It. w., Joe McCarthy. m., James V. Monaco. Broadway Music Corp., cop. 1913.

Woodrow Wilson, Democrat, of Virginia, was inaugurated 28th President.

Outgoing President Taft vetoed (Feb. 14) an immigration bill which would impose a literacy test for the admission of aliens.

Added to the Constitution were two amendments—the 16th (Feb. 25) establishing income taxes, and the 17th (May 13) regulating the election of senators by popular vote.

Congress passed the Webb-Kenyon Act (Mar. 1), so-named after North Carolina Representative Edwin Y. Webb and Iowa Senator William S. Kenyon, prohibiting the interstate shipment of liquor, and the Owen-Glass Federal Reserve Act (Dec. 23), named after Oklahoma Senator Robert Latham Owen and Virginia Senator Carter Glass, establishing the Federal Reserve Bank System.

The presidential cabinet was strengthened by the addition of a Secretary of Labor, the first being William B. Wilson, ex-officer of the United Mine Workers' Union and since 1907 congressman from Pennsylvania.

The United States Post Office established (Jan. 1) parcel post service.

President Wilson created the Teapot Dome, Natrona County, Wyo., government naval oil reserve, which was to figure in 1924 in a national scandal.

Former President William Howard Taft was appointed professor of constitutional law at Yale (1913-21).

The Indian head or buffalo nickel came into circulation—the first five-cent piece since the Liberty head of 1883. The new coin was designed by James E. Fraser who used as models for the head three different Indians and for the animal the bison "Black Diamond" in the New York Zoological Gardens.

President Wilson refused to recognize Mexican dictator General Victoriano Huerta's "government by assassination," set up after the midnight shooting (Feb. 23-24) of President Francisco Indalecio Madero and Vice-President José Piño Suárez, and sent (Nov. 2) a note requesting Huerta's resignation from office.

The Gatun locks on the Panama Canal were completed (June 14).

Floods in Ohio, Indiana, and Texas took more than 1,200 lives; the property damage was enormous.

The Rockefeller Foundation was established by John D. Rockefeller, Sr., with an endowment of $165,281,624 for the study of medical sciences.

The Actors' Equity Association was founded in New York.

The 60-floor Woolworth office building, New York, was completed—then the tallest building in the world.

John Henry Mears travelled around the world in a new record time of 35 days, 21 hours, 36 minutes.

Harry Kendall Thaw, who had fatally shot (June 25, 1906) the architect Stanford White in the Madison Square Garden Roof Theatre, New York, and had been adjudged insane at his second trial (Jan. 6-Feb. 1, 1908), escaped (Aug. 17) from Matteawan Asylum. He was taken into custody (Aug. 19) in Coaticook, Que., deported (Sept. 10) to Vermont, and arrested in Colebrook, N. H.

A mine disaster at Dawson, N. M., took the lives of 258 miners. (In 1923, another disaster there killed 120 miners.)

"Reedy's Mirror" was founded in St. Louis by Missouri journalist William Marion Reedy as a liberal magazine. During the seven years of its existence, it brought before the public many new writers and published Edgar Lee Masters's free-verse poems "Spoon River Anthology."

A vogue for turbans was started by Queen Mary and copied in America.

Modern art in the guise of cubism, expressionism, fauvism, futurism, etc., hit New York and the country at large with a bang at an international exhibition held in the Armory of the 69th Regiment and sponsored by the Association of American Painters and Sculptors. In the popular mind, Marcel Duchamp's representation of a "Nude Descending a Staircase" was the main attraction. The "new" art was, of course, widely written up in the press.

Books of the year included: "A Boy's Will" (Robert Frost; his first book of verse), "General Booth Enters into Heaven and Other Poems" (Vachel Lindsay), "Mr. Faust" (Arthur Davison Ficke; a poem), "Old Fogy" (James Gibbons Huneker; sketches about an old musician), and the fiction, "His Great Adventure" (Robert Herrick), "The Inside of the Cup" (Winston Churchill), "The Iron Trail" (Rex Beach), "John Barleycorn" and "The Valley of the Moon" (Jack London), "O Pioneers!" (Willa Cather), "Rolling Stones" (O. Henry; published posthumously), "Virginia" (Ellen Glasgow).

The first American-made orchestral phonograph records were manufactured by the Columbia Company, Bridgeport, Conn., with the famous Felix Weingartner conducting a shortened version of the "Liebestod" from "Tristan und Isolde" and his own arrangement of Weber's "Invitation to the Dance."

Arturo Toscanini made (Apr. 13) his first American appearance as a symphonic conductor at the Metropolitan Opera House, New York, in Beethoven's Ninth Symphony.

The Century Opera Company was organized in New York under the auspices of the City Club of New York.

The Chicago-Philadelphia Opera Company produced on tour Victor Herbert's grand opera "Natoma" (première, Philadelphia, Metropolitan Opera House, Feb. 25; New York, Metropolitan Opera House, Feb. 28; Baltimore, Lyric Theatre, Mar. 9; Chicago, Auditorium, Dec. 13). The cast comprised such able singers as Mary Garden (in the title role), Lillian Grenville (Barbara), John McCormack (Lieutenant Merrill), Gustave Huberdau (Don Francesco), Hector Dufranne (Father Peralta), and Mario Sammarco (Alvorado); Cleofonte Campanini conducted. Before its production, the opera had gone the rounds of New York's two opera houses. It was announced for performance in 1907 by Oscar Hammerstein at his Manhattan Opera House, and was then submitted to Gatti-Casazza at the Metropolitan Opera where it was partially rehearsed and abandoned. ("Natoma" was revived by the Chicago company in 1913 and given in Los Angeles and San Francisco by them. It was also given by the Aborn company Mar. 13, 1914 in New York at the Century Theatre for eight performances.)

Dr. Horatio William Parker of Yale University for the second time won a $10,000 operatic prize. His "Fairyland" gained the award of the National Federation of Music Clubs. (The opera was produced in Los Angeles, July 1, 1915, at the Federation Biennial. The composer's "Mona" had won the New York Metropolitan Opera prize in the preceding year.)

Novelties at the Metropolitan Opera House, New York, included, among other American first performances, Damrosch's "Cyrano" (world première, Feb. 27, in English), Moussorgsky's "Boris Godounoff" (Mar. 19, in Italian), and "Der Rosenkavalier" by Richard Strauss (Dec. 9).

Exotic dancer Roshanara (her real name was Olive Craddock) organized her own troupe and toured the United States performing Eastern dances.

"Class" dancers had their advent in hotels, Mr. and Mrs. Vernon Castle's salary being reported at $1,000. Meantime "thé dansants"—i.e., matinee dances at public places—were bitterly condemned because of "male idlers" and were fading out.

New York plays included: "A Good Little Devil" (Republic, Jan. 8), "Joseph and His Brethren" (Century, Jan. 11), "The Poor Little Rich Girl" (Hudson, Jan. 21), "Romance" with Doris Keane (Maxine Elliott, Feb. 10), "The Lure" (Maxine Elliott, Aug. 14), "Potash and Perlmutter" (Cohan, Aug. 16; 441 performances), "The Temperamental Journey" (Belasco, Sept. 4), "Nearly Married" (Gaiety, Sept. 5), "Madame President" with Fannie Ward (Garrick, Sept. 15), "Seven Keys to Baldpate" (Astor, Sept. 22; 320 performances), "Today" (48th Street Theatre, Oct. 6; 280 performances), "Grumpy" (Wallack's, Nov. 19), "The Misleading Lady" (Fulton, Nov. 25), "The Secret" (Belasco, Dec. 23), "The Philanderer" (Little Theatre, Dec. 30). Much comment followed a matinee performance (Fulton Theatre, Mar. 14), staged by Edward L. Bernays, co-editor of the "Medical Review of Reviews," of Eugene Brieux's sociological drama "Damaged Goods" with Richard Bennett, Wilton Lackaye, and Margaret Wycherly. To overcome the prejudice against the play, Bernays organized the Medical Review of Reviews Sociological Fund with John D. Rockefeller, Jr., Abraham Flexner, and others, and admission to subsequent performances was limited originally only to members. The Princess Players, organized by Holbrook Blinn, played their first New York season of one-act plays. Musical productions included: "The Honeymoon Express" (Winter Garden, Feb. 6), "The Purple Road" (Liberty, Apr. 7), "All Aboard" (44th Street Roof Garden, June 5), "Sweethearts" by Victor Herbert (New Amsterdam, Sept. 8), "The Little Café" (New Amsterdam, Nov. 10), "High Jinks" by Rudolph Friml (Lyric, Dec. 10;

213 performances). Paul Rubens's musical comedy "The Sunshine Girl" (Knickerbocker Theatre, Feb. 3) brought forth a new singing star, Julia Sanderson, and introduced the husband-and-wife dancing team, Vernon and Irene Castle. Their dancing of the turkey trot and Vernon's tango with Julia Sanderson eliminated the waltz from the musical comedy stage and substituted a vogue for dances of Western origin. Joseph Cawthorn's song "You Can't Play Every Instrument in the Band" (see above) always stopped the show. All this gave "The Sunshine Girl" a run of 160 performances—in spite of the fact that its story was about soap!

The motion-picture serial began about this time; one of the earliest was "What Happened to Mary." The "Vamp" also made her appearance on the screen in a silent film entitled "The Vampire," starring Alice Hollister as the first of the type which later included Lucille Younge, Theodosia Goodman (better known as Theda Bara), and others. David Wark Griffith produced a four reeler, "Judith of Bethulia," photographed in California. Charlie (Charles Spencer) Chaplin entered the movies. Minnie Maddern Fiske acted a screen version of her stage success "Tess of the D'Urbervilles" for Zukor's Famous Players film company. Other noted screen stars were William Faversham, Mabel Taliafero, and Florence Nash. The present Paramount Pictures, Inc., was founded in Hollywood, Cal., by Jesse Lasky under the name Jesse L. Lasky Feature Play Company. Their first picture was "The Squaw Man," followed by "Brewster's Millions," both of which proved gold mines. (Lasky's group merged in 1916 with Zukor's Famous Players Company.) A highly impressive film was "Cabiria," a spectacular Italian production.

Ping-pong was a new indoor game.

ᘔᕽ 1914

The Aba Daba Honeymoon. w., m., Arthur Fields and Walter Donovan. Leo Feist, Inc., cop. 1914.

After the Roses Have Faded Away. w., Bessie Buchanan. m., Ernest R. Ball. M. Witmark & Sons, cop. 1914.

"By Heck." Instrumental. m., S. R. Henry [pseud. of Henry R. Stern]. Jos. W. Stern & Co., cop. 1914; renewed 1942 and assigned to Edward B. Marks Music Corp. (Published as a song, words by L. Wolfe Gilbert, copy. 1915.)

By the Beautiful Sea. w., Harold R. Atteridge. m., Harry Carroll. Shapiro, Bernstein & Co., Inc., 1914.

By the Watermelon Vine, Lindy Lou. w., m., Thomas S. Allen. Boston: Walter Jacobs, cop. 1914; renewed 1931 by Arthur J. Allen; assigned 1935 to Mills Music, Inc.

By the Waters of Minnetonka. w., J. M. Cavanass. m., Thurlow Lieurance. Phila.: Theo. Presser Co., cop. 1914.

Can't Yo' Heah Me Callin', Caroline. w., William H. Gardner. m., Caro Roma. M. Witmark & Sons, cop. 1914.

Cecile Waltz. m., Frank W. McKee. G. Ricordi & Co., cop. 1914.

Duna. w., Marjorie Pickhall. m., Josephine McGill. London: Boosey & Co., Ltd., cop. 1914.

Face to Face with the Girl of My Dreams. w., m., Richard Howard. F. B. Haviland Pub. Co., Inc., cop. 1914.

Fido Is a Hot Dog Now. w., Charles McCarron and Thomas J. Gray. m., Raymond Walker. Leo Feist, Inc., cop. 1914.

The Garden of Your Heart. w., Edward Teschemacher. m., Francis Dorel. London: Boosey & Co., Ltd., cop. 1914.

Goodbye, Girls, I'm Through (Chin-Chin). w., John Golden. m., Ivan Caryll. London: Chappell & Co., Ltd., cop. 1914.

He's a Devil in His Own Home Town. w., Grant Clarke and Irving Berlin. m., Irving Berlin. Waterson, Berlin & Snyder Co., cop. 1914.

He's a Rag Picker. w., m., Irving Berlin. Waterson, Berlin & Snyder Co., cop. 1914.

I Love the Ladies. w., Grant Clarke. m., Jean Schwartz. Waterson, Berlin & Snyder Co., cop. 1914.

I Want to Go Back to Michigan—Down on the Farm. w., m., Irving Berlin. Waterson, Berlin & Snyder Co., cop. 1914.

I Wonder Where My Lovin' Man Has Gone. w., Earle C. Jones. m., Richard Whiting and Charles L. Cooke. Jerome H. Remick & Co., cop. 1914.

In the Town Where I Was Born. w., Dick Howard and Billy Tracey. m., Al Harriman. F. B. Haviland Pub. Co., cop. 1914.

The Land of My Best Girl. w., Ballard MacDonald. m., Harry Carroll. Shapiro, Bernstein & Co., Inc., cop. 1914.

A Little Bit of Heaven, Sure They Call It Ireland. w., J. Keirn Brennan. m., Ernest R. Ball. M. Witmark & Sons, cop. 1914.

Love's Own Sweet Song (Sari). w., C. C. S. Cushing and E. P. Heath. m., Emmerich Kalman. Jos. W. Stern & Co., cop. 1912 by Jos. Weinberger, Leipzig; cop. 1914 by Jos. W. Stern & Co.; assigned 1920 to Edward B. Marks Music Co.

Mary, You're a Little Bit Old Fashioned. w., Marion Sunshine. m., Henry I. Marshall. Jerome H. Remick & Co., cop. 1914.

Missouri Waltz. w., J. R. Shannon [pseud. of James Royce]. m., Frederick Knight Logan "from an original melody procured by John Valentine Eppell." Chicago: Forster Music Publisher, Inc., cop. 1914 by Frederick Knight Logan; assigned 1915 to F. A. Forster.

Moonlight on the Rhine (One Girl in a Million). w., Bert Kalmar and Edgar Leslie. m., Ted Snyder. Waterson, Berlin & Snyder Co., cop. 1914.

On the 5:15. w., Stanley Murphy. m., Henry I. Marshall. Jerome H. Remick & Co., cop. 1914.

On the Good Ship Mary Ann. w., Gus Kahn. m., Grace LeBoy. Jerome H. Remick & Co., cop. 1914.

Pigeon Walk. m., James V. Monaco. Broadway Music Corp., cop. 1914.

Play a Simple Melody. w., m., Irving Berlin. Irving Berlin, cop. 1914.

Poor Pauline. w., Charles McCarron. m., Raymond Walker. Broadway Music Corp., cop. 1914.

Rebecca of Sunny-Brook Farm. w., Seymour Brown. m., Albert Gumble. Jerome H. Remick & Co., cop. 1914.

Roll Them Cotton Bales. w., James W. Johnson. m., J. Rosamond Johnson. Jos. W. Stern & Co., cop. 1914.

St. Louis Blues. w., m., W[illiam] C[hristopher] Handy. Memphis, Tenn.: Pace & Handy Music Co., cop. 1914 by W. C. Handy; renewed 1942 by W. C. Handy; published by Handy Bros. Music Co., Inc.

Shadowland. Piano solo. m., Lawrence B. Gilbert. Leo Feist, Inc., cop. 1914 by Charles W. Homeyer & Co., Boston; assigned 1915 to Leo Feist, Inc.

Sister Susie's Sewing Shirts for Soldiers. w., R. P. Weston. m., Hermann E. Darewski. T. B. Harms, and Francis, Day & Hunter, cop. 1914 by Francis, Day & Hunter.

The Song of Songs—Chanson du Coeur Brisé. English words, Clarence Lucas; French words, Maurice Vancaire. m., Moya [pseud. of Harold Vicars]. London: Chappell & Co., Ltd., cop. 1914.

The Springtime of Life (The Debutante). w., Robert B. Smith. m., Victor Herbert. G. Schirmer, Inc., cop. 1914.

Sweet Kentucky Lady. w., William Jerome. m., Louis A. Hirsch. M. Witmark & Sons, cop. 1914.

Sylvia. w., Clinton Scollard. m., Oley Speaks. G. Schirmer, Inc., cop. 1914.

Tell It All Over Again (The Only Girl). w., Henry Blossom. m., Victor Herbert. M. Witmark & Sons, cop. 1914.

There's a Little Spark of Love Still Burning. w., Joe McCarthy. m., Fred Fisher. Leo Feist, Inc., cop. 1914.

They Didn't Believe Me (The Girl from Utah). w., Herbert Reynolds. m., Jerome Kern. Remick Music Corp., cop. 1914 by T. B. Harms & Francis, Day & Hunter; assigned 1916 to Jerome H. Remick & Co.

This Is the Life. w., m., Irving Berlin. Waterson, Berlin & Snyder Co., cop. 1914.

Tip-Top Tipperary Mary. w., Ballard MacDonald. m., Harry Carroll. Shapiro, Bernstein & Co., cop. 1914.

Too-ra-loo-ra-loo-ral, That's an Irish Lullaby (Shameen Dhu). w., m., J. R. Shannon. M. Witmark & Sons, cop. 1914.

Twelfth Street Rag. See 1916.

Way Out Yonder in the Golden West. w., m., Percy Wenrich. Leo Feist, Inc., cop. 1914.

When It's Night Time Down in Burgundy. w., Alfred Bryan. m., Herman Paley. Jerome H. Remick & Co., cop. 1914.

When It's Night Time in Dixie Land. w., m., Irving Berlin. Waterson, Berlin & Snyder Co., cop. 1914.

When the Angelus Is Ringing. w., Joe Young. m., Bert Grant. Waterson, Berlin & Snyder Co., cop. 1914.

When You're a Long, Long Way from Home. w., Sam M. Lewis. m., George M. Meyer. Broadway Music Corp., cop. 1914.

When You're Away (The Only Girl). w., Henry Blossom. m., Victor Herbert. M. Witmark & Sons, cop. 1914.

When You're Wearing the Ball and Chain (The Only Girl). w., Harry B. Smith. m., Victor Herbert. M. Witmark & Sons, cop. 1914.

When You Wore a Tulip and I Wore a Big Red Rose. w., Jack Mahoney. m., Percy Wenrich. Leo Feist, Inc., cop. 1914.

Wien, Du Stadt meiner Träume. See 1937: "Vienna Dreams."

You're More Than the World to Me. w., Jeff Branen. m., Alfred Solman. Joe Morris Music Co., cop. 1914.

You Planted a Rose in the Garden of Love. w., J. Will Callahan. m., Ernest R. Ball. M. Witmark & Sons, cop. 1914.

The Mexican political situation, which had grown yearly since 1910 more chaotic and violent, had become by now a serious menace to American life and property. President Wilson removed (Feb. 3) the embargo on munitions to Mexico and continued his "watchful waiting" policy. This policy was severely criticized (Mar. 9) in the Senate by New Mexico Senator Albert Bacon Fall who cited between seventy and eighty outrages against Americans in Mexico. The arrest by Tampico soldiers of seven sailors from the U. S. gunboat "Dolphin," while they were loading (Apr. 9) gasoline into a whaleboat, brought the United States almost to the verge of war. Admiral Henry Thomas Mayo demanded an apology, punishment of the officer in charge of the arrest, and a 21-gun salute to the American flag. The conditions were reported (Apr. 10) to have been carried out but the salute was withheld and, after a United States note (Apr. 18), was refused (Apr. 19) by the Mexican President General Victoriano

Huerta. The United States Atlantic fleet under Admiral Frank Friday Fletcher thereupon was ordered into Mexican waters and, under the fire of Mexican snipers, landed (Apr. 21) at Vera Cruz marines and sailors who seized the custom house and part of the city. Nineteen Americans were killed. In an effort to prevent further bloodshed, Argentina, Brazil, and Chile undertook (Apr. 25) to mediate a peace. Meanwhile, the 5th Brigade, U.S.A., under General Frederick Funston arrived (Apr. 28) to occupy Vera Cruz. In the United States, public funeral services for the dead were held (May 11) in New York, President Wilson speaking at the occasion. Honors also were paid (May 13) to them in Philadelphia, Chicago, Cambridge, Mass., and elsewhere. While the peace conference was meeting (May 20-July 1) in Niagara Falls, Ont., the political situation in Mexico changed. General Alvaro Obregón captured (July 9) Guadalajara; Provisional President Huerta resigned (July 15) and escaped to Jamaica on the German cruiser "Dresden"; Venustiano Carranza succeeded to the presidency; the rebel General Francisco ("Pancho") Villa, Chihuahua bandit, loomed as a new threat, and sharp fighting developed between Carranzistas and Villistas. American troops were withdrawn (Nov. 23) from Vera Cruz.

Congress passed Alabama Representative Henry D. Clayton's Anti-Trust Act (Oct. 14), supplementing the Sherman Anti-Trust Act (1890) and the Harrison Anti-Narcotic Act (Dec. 31).

For the first time citizens had to pay income tax, following the 16th Amendment to the Constitution which 42 of the 48 States had ratified. (Three States—Connecticut, Rhode Island, and Utah—rejected it.) Individual payments amounted to $28,263,535.

President Wilson established national observance of Mother's Day by the designation of the second Sunday in May. (The day was originated by Anna Jarvis of Philadelphia and was first celebrated May 10, 1908, in the churches of that city.)

The Panama Canal was opened (Aug. 15) to commercial traffic. The "Cristobal" was the first steamship to pass through the waterway. Frequent landslides and war conditions interferred for several years with its operation. (The canal was declared officially opened July 12, 1920.)

The Cape Cod, Mass., canal was completed.

U. S. Marines were landed (Dec. 13) in Haiti.

Former President Theodore Roosevelt again was on an exploring expedition—this time in the jungles of Brazil where he discovered with Col. Candido Rondon, Brazilian explorer, an uncharted 940-mile tributary of the Amazon. The discovery occasioned much ridicule, and was popularly called the "river of doubt." Named the Rio da Duvida, it was renamed Rio Roosevelt in his honor by the Brazilian government. (The expedition left the United States in Oct., 1913, and returned in May, 1914.)

Secretary of the Treasury William Gibbs McAdoo married (in May) as his second wife Eleanor B. Wilson, second daughter of President Wilson. (They later were divorced.)

President Wilson's first wife, Mrs. Ellen Louise Axson Wilson, died (Aug. 6) in the White House.

For the second time (the famous first was in 1894) Jacob Sechler Coxey of Ohio led an "army" of unemployed to Washington, D. C.

Theodore William Richards was awarded the Nobel prize for chemistry —the first American to be so honored in that field.

The erection of the Lincoln Memorial in Potomac Park, Washington, D. C., at a cost of $2,594,000, was begun on his birthday (Feb. 12).

The new Roman Catholic Cathedral in St. Louis, Mo., was dedicated. (The building was begun in 1907 and replaced the edifice of 1834.)

William Ashley ("Billy") Sunday, former baseball player, was touring the country as a sawdust trail evangelist.

Detroit manufacturer Henry Ford set a new standard for labor wages when he fixed a five-dollar minimum for an eight-hour day.

A sweeping fire devastated (June 25) a large section of Salem, Mass., making many thousands homeless and destroying property to the extent of $12,000,000.

An Atlantic tidal wave again inundated (Aug. 17) the coastal city of Galveston, Tex., brought death to 275 persons and caused great property damage.

A coal miners' strike against the Rockefeller-controlled Colorado Fuel and Iron Company had broken out in the preceding year (Sept., 1913) and had grown to such violence, after the company had imported strikebreakers and summoned the State militia, that President Wilson despatched Federal troops to the region. Many lives were lost in the armed conflicts. The final belligerent stand of the miners came to be known as the "Battle of Ludlow" (Apr. 1914). The strike ended (in December) after months of unsatisfactory negotiations. The Federal troops were not recalled until the next year.

The American Society of Composers, Authors and Publishers ("A.S. C.A.P.") was formed by five composers (Silvio Hein, Victor Herbert, Louis A. Hirsch, Raymond Hubbell, Gustave Kerker), one librettist (Glen MacDonough), and three publishers' representatives (Nathan Burkan, George Maxwell, Jay Witmark) to protect and license public performances of musical compositions.

"The New Republic" was founded in New York as a weekly magazine, "less to inform or entertain its readers than to start little insurrections in the realm of their convictions."

"The Little Review" appeared in Chicago as a monthly devoted to "extreme" tendencies in art and aesthetics. (It later was published in San Francisco and in New York, and was issued as a quarterly in Paris, 1924-29. Ceased publication in 1929.)

The newspaper column "The Conning Tower" by "F. P. A." (Franklin Pierce Adams) began to appear in the "New York Tribune."

Books of the year included: "Other People's Money" (Louis Dembitz Brandeis; the book earned the author his appointment to the U. S. Supreme Court in 1916), "Progressive Democracy" (Herbert Croly), and the fiction, "The Auction Block" (Rex Beach), "Clark's Field" (Robert Herrick), "Penrod" (Booth Tarkington; sequels "Penrod and Sam," 1916, and "Penrod Jashber," 1929), "The Rise of Jennie Cushing" (Mary Watts), "Vandover and the Brute" (Frank Norris). American poetry showed signs of rebirth with the publication of "The Congo and Other Poems" (Vachel Lindsay), "North of Boston" (Robert Frost), "The Single Hound" (Emily Dickinson; printed posthumously by her niece Martha Dickinson Bianchi), "Songs of the New Age" (James Oppenheim), "Sword Blades and Other Poems" (Amy Lowell), "Trees and Other Poems" (Joyce Kilmer).

Oscar Hammerstein, having sold his unsuccessful London opera house, in violation of his 1910 Metropolitan Opera House contract erected his second New York operatic theatre—the American Opera House. (It was his fourth venture in the field.) The Metropolitan secured an injunction that prevented the opening of the Opera House and compelled him to adhere to the agreement. The building became the Lexington Theatre. (It is now a motion-picture house.)

Jan Sibelius, Finland's greatest composer, visited the United States to conduct the world première of his symphonic poem "Oceanides" and other of his works at the Norwalk, Conn., music festival (June 4). Yale University conferred (June 19) on him the honorary doctor's degree.

In the sacred symphonic precincts of Carnegie Hall, New York, Negro dance band leader Jim Reese Europe gave (Mar. 11) a concert of his type of music, thus anticipating jazz and Paul Whiteman (1924).

"The Sun Dance," a five-act American Indian opera by William F. Hanson of Brigham Young University, Provo, Utah, received (May 25) its first professional performance in the Salt Lake Theatre, Salt Lake City. (The opera was first given Feb. 20, 1913, at Orpheus Hall, Vernal, Utah, by the music department of Uinta Academy and was then performed in other cities of the State. A half-hour version was broadcast June 29, 1932 from radio station KSL. The opera was heard Apr. 27 and 28, 1938, in New York at the Broadway Theatre.)

Alice Brown's play "Children of the Earth," selected from 2,640 manuscripts, won the $10,000 prize offered by New York theatrical manager Winthrop Ames for the best play by a native writer on a local subject. (The play was staged Jan. 12, 1915, at the Booth Theatre, and ran 39 performances.)

New York enjoyed an unprecedented season of long-run plays; among those that played 200 or more performances were: "Kitty Mackay" (Comedy, Jan. 7; 278 perf.), "Too Many Cooks" (39th Street, Feb. 24; 223 perf.), "A Pair of Sixes" (Longacre, Mar. 17; 207 perf.), "The Dummy" (Hudson, Apr. 13; 200 perf.), "Twin Beds" (Fulton, Aug. 14; 411 perf.), "On Trial" (Candler, Aug. 19; 365 perf.), "Under Cover" (Cort, Aug.

26; 349 perf.), "It Pays to Advertise" (Cohan, Sept. 8, 399 perf.), "Daddy Long-Legs" (Gaiety, Sept. 28; 264 perf.), "The Law of the Land" (48th Street, Sept. 30; 221 perf.), "A Pair of Silk Stockings" (Little Theatre, Oct. 20; 233 perf.), "Experience" (Booth, Oct. 27; 255 perf.). Musical productions included: "The Whirl of the World" (Winter Garden, Jan. 10), "Sari" (Liberty, Jan. 13), "The Girl from Utah" (Knickerbocker, Aug. 24), "Wars of the World" (Hippodrome, Sept. 7), "Dancing Around" (Winter Garden, Oct. 10), "Chin-Chin" (Globe, Oct. 20), "The Lilac Domino" (44th Street, Oct. 28), "The Only Girl" by Victor Herbert (39th Street, Nov. 2; 240 performances), "Watch Your Step" (New Amsterdam, Dec. 8), "Hello Broadway" (Astor, Dec. 25). "H. M. S. Pinafore" was revived (Hippodrome, Apr. 9) for 89 performances with two complete casts, the operetta being given twice daily. New as the movies were at this time, they already supplied the theatre with material for musical comedies —"The Girl on the Film" (44th Street Music Hall, Dec. 29, 1913), imported from George Edwardes's London Gaiety Theatre, and "The Queen of the Movies" (Globe, Jan. 12, 1914), adapted from the German "Die Kino-Königin."

Motion-picture houses sprang up everywhere, just as music halls had been the rage 30 years before. Samuel Rothafel ("Roxy") took charge of the Strand Theatre, New York, and an era of de luxe houses began. Meantime, Theda Bara (Theodosia Goodman of The Bronx, New York) was "vamping" not only her fellow players on the screen but also her audiences in films with such lurid titles as "Destruction" and "A Fool There Was."

The New York National League ("Giants") baseball club defeated (July 17) the Pittsburgh club ("Pirates"), 3 to 1, in the first 21-inning game in their league.

The assassination (June 28) of the Archduke Franz Ferdinand, heir to the Austrian throne, and his wife, Duchess of Hohenberg, by a Serbian terrorist in Sarajevo, Bosnia, started what became World War I in which the United States was involved three years later (1917). As an ally of Austria, Germany declared (Aug. 1) war on Russia, ally of Serbia; Great Britain, as an ally of Russia, issued (Aug. 4) a declaration of war against Germany. President Wilson immediately proclaimed (Aug. 4) the United States' neutrality.

₰ 1915

All for You (The Princess Pat). w., Henry Blossom. m., Victor Herbert. M. Witmark & Sons, cop. 1915.

Along the Rocky Road to Dublin. w., Joe Young. m., Bert Grant. Waterson, Berlin & Snyder Co., cop. 1915.

America I Love You. w., Edgar Leslie. m., Archie Gottler. Kalmar & Puck Music Co., Inc., cop. 1915.

Araby. w., m., Irving Berlin. Waterson, Berlin & Snyder Co., cop. 1915.

Auf Wiedersehn (The Blue Paradise). w., Herbert Reynolds. m., Sigmund Romberg. G. Schirmer, Inc., cop. 1915.

Babes in the Wood (Very Good Eddie). w., Jerome Kern and Schuyler Greene. m., Jerome Kern. T. B. Harms & Francis, Day & Hunter, cop. 1915.

Back Home in Tennessee. w., William Jerome. m., Walter Donaldson. Waterson, Berlin & Snyder Co., cop. 1915.

By Heck. w., L. Wolfe Gilbert. m., S. R. Henry. Jos. W. Stern & Co., cop. 1915.

Canadian Capers. w., m., Gus Chandler, Bert White and Henry Cohen. Jerome H. Remick & Co., cop. 1915 by Roger Graham, Chicago; assigned 1921 to Jerome H. Remick Co.

Close to My Heart. w., Andrew B. Sterling. m., Harry Von Tilzer. Harry Von Tilzer Music Pub. Co., cop. 1915.

Don't Bite the Hand That's Feeding You. w., Thomas Hoier. m., James Morgan. Leo Feist, Inc., cop. 1915.

Down Among the Sheltering Palms. w., James Brockman. m., Abe Olman. Leo Feist, Inc., cop. 1915.

Down Home in Tennessee. See above: "Back Home in Tennessee."

Down in Bom-Bombay. w., Ballard MacDonald. m., Harry Carroll. Shapiro, Bernstein & Co., cop. 1915.

The Girl on the Magazine Cover (Stop! Look! Listen!). w., m., Irving Berlin. Waterson, Berlin & Snyder Co., cop. 1915.

Hello, Frisco! w., Gene Buck. m., Louis A. Hirsch. M. Witmark & Sons, cop. 1915.

Hello, Hawaii, How Are You? w., Bert Kalmar and Edgar Leslie. m., Jean Schwartz. Waterson, Berlin & Snyder Co., cop. 1915.

How'd You Like to Spoon with Me? (The Earl and the Girl). w., Edward Laska. m., Jerome D. Kern. T. B. Harms Co., cop. 1915.

I Didn't Raise My Boy to Be a Soldier. w., Alfred Bryan. m., Al Piantadosi. Leo Feist, Inc., cop. 1915.

I've Been Floating Down the Old Green River (Maid in America). w., Bert Kalmar. m., Joe Cooper. Waterson, Berlin & Snyder Co., cop. 1915.

In a Monastery Garden. Orch. composition. m., Albert William Ketelbey. London: J. H. Larway, cop. 1915.

In the Gold Fields of Nevada. w., Edgar Leslie. m., Archie Gottler. Maurice Abrahams Music Co., cop. 1915.

Ireland Is Ireland to Me. w., Fiske O'Hara and J. Keirn Brennan. m., Ernest R. Ball. M. Witmark & Sons, cop. 1915.

It's Tulip Time in Holland. w., Dave Radford. m., Richard A. Whiting. Jerome H. Remick & Co., cop. 1915.

Keep the Home-Fires Burning. w., Lena Guilbert Ford. m., Ivor Novello. Chappell & Co., Ltd., cop. 1914 by Ascherberg, Hopwood & Crew, Ltd., London; new edition cop. 1915 by Ascherberg, Hopwood & Crew, Ltd.

The Ladder of Roses (Hip, Hip, Hooray). w., R. H. Burnside. m., Raymond Hubbell. T. B. Harms & Francis, Day & Hunter, cop. 1915.

The Little House upon the Hill. w., Ballard MacDonald and Joe Goodwin. m., Harry Puck. Shapiro, Bernstein & Co., cop. 1915.

Love, Here Is My Heart!—Mon coeur est pour toi. English w., Adrian Ross. m., Lao Silesu. Leo Feist, Inc., cop. 1915 by Ascherberg, Hopwood & Crew, Ltd., London.

Love Is the Best of All (The Princess Pat). w., Henry Blossom. m., Victor Herbert. M. Witmark & Sons, cop. 1915.

Memories. w., Gustave Kahn. m., Egbert Van Alstyne. Jerome H. Remick & Co., cop. 1915.

M-O-T-H-E-R, a Word That Means the World to Me. w., Howard Johnson. m., Theodore F. Morse. Leo Feist, Inc., cop. 1915.

My Little Girl. w., Sam M. Lewis and William Dillon. m., Albert Von Tilzer. Broadway Music Corp., cop. 1915.

My Mother's Rosary. w., Sam M. Lewis. m., George W. Meyer. Waterson, Berlin & Snyder Co., cop. 1915.

My Sweet Adair. w., m., L. Wolfe Gilbert and Anatol Friedland. Jos. W. Stern & Co., cop. 1915.

Neapolitan Love Song (The Princess Pat). w., Henry Blossom. m., Victor Herbert. M. Witmark & Sons, cop. 1915.

Norway. w., Joe McCarthy. m., Fred Fisher. Leo Feist, Inc., cop. 1915.

The Old Refrain. A Viennese popular song transcribed for violin and piano by Fritz Kreisler. Carl Fischer, Inc., cop. 1915. (The melody is derived from the song "Du alter Stefanturm" in the operetta "Der liebe Augustin," libretto by Hugo Klein and music by Joseph Brandl, produced in Vienna Jan. 15, 1887.)

The Old Grey Mare. m., Frank Panella. Pittsburgh: Panella Music Co., cop. 1915; assigned 1917 to Joe Morris Music Co.; cop. 1917 by Joe Morris Music Co.; assigned to Edwin H. Morris & Co., Inc.

On the Beach at Waikiki. w., G. H. Stover. m., Henry Kailimai. Honolulu: Bergstrom Music Co., Ltd., cop. 1915.

Pack Up Your Troubles in Your Old Kitbag and Smile, Smile, Smile. w., George Asaf. m., Felix Powell. London: Chappell & Co., Ltd., cop. 1915 by Francis, Day & Hunter.

The Perfect Song. w., Clarence Lucas. m., Joseph Carl Breil. London: Chappell & Co., Ltd., cop. 1915; new edition, cop. 1929 by Chappell & Co., Ltd.

Piney Ridge. w., Ballard MacDonald. m., Halsey K. Mohr. Shapiro, Bernstein & Co., Inc., cop. 1915.

Pretty Edelweiss (Alone at Last). w., Matthew Woodward and Joseph Herbert. m., Franz Lehár. Karczag Pub. Co., cop. 1915.

Put Me to Sleep With an Old Fashioned Melody. w., Sam M. Lewis and Dick Howard. m., Harry Jentes. Broadway Music Corp., cop. 1915.

Ragging the Scale. Piano solo. m., Edward B. Claypoole. Artmusic, Inc., cop. 1915 by Broadway Music Corp.; assigned to Artmusic, Inc.

Railroad Jim. w., m., Nat H. Vincent. F. B. Haviland Pub. Co., Inc., cop. 1915.

She's the Daughter of Mother Machree. w., Jeff T. Nenarb. m., Ernest R. Ball. M. Witmark & Sons, cop. 1915.

Siam. w., Howard Johnson. m., Fred Fisher. Leo Feist, Inc., cop. 1915.

So Long Letty (So Long Letty). w., m., Earl Carroll. M. Witmark & Sons, cop. 1915.

Some Little Bug Is Going to Find You (*introduced in:* **Alone at Last**). w., Benjamin Hapgood Burt and Roy Atwell. m., Silvio Hein. T. B. Harms & Francis, Day & Hunter, cop. 1915.

Song of the Islands. w., m., Charles E. King. Honolulu: Bergstrom Music Co., Ltd., cop. 1915; assigned 1917 to Charles E. King.

The Sunshine of Your Smile. w., Leonard Cooke. m., Lillian Ray. T. B. Harms & Francis, Day & Hunter, cop. 1915 by Francis, Day & Hunter.

Take Me to the Midnight Cake Walk Ball. w., m., Eddie Cox, Arthur Jackson and Maurice Abrahams. Maurice Abrahams Music Co., cop. 1915.

There's a Broken Heart for Every Light on Broadway. w., Howard Johnson. m., Fred Fisher. Leo Feist, Inc., cop. 1915.

There's a Little Lane Without a Turning on the Way to Home, Sweet Home. w., Sam M. Lewis. m., George W. Meyer. Broadway Music Corp., cop. 1915.

Throw Me a Rose (Miss Springtime). w., P. G. Wodehouse and Herbert Reynolds. m., Emmerich Kalman. T. B. Harms & Francis, Day & Hunter, cop. 1915.

Two Laughing Irish Eyes (The Princess Pat). w., Henry Blossom. m., Victor Herbert. M. Witmark & Sons, cop. 1915.

Underneath the Stars. w., Fleta Jan Brown. m., Herbert Spencer. Jerome H. Remick & Co., cop. 1915.

We'll Have a Jubilee in My Old Kentucky Home. w., Coleman Goetz. m., Walter Donaldson. Waterson, Berlin & Snyder Co., cop. 1915.

What a Wonderful Mother You'd Be. w., Joe Goodwin. m., Al Piantadosi. Shapiro, Bernstein & Co., Inc., cop. 1915.

When I Leave the World Behind. w., m., Irving Berlin. Waterson, Berlin & Snyder Co., cop. 1915.

You Know and I Know (Nobody Home). w., Schuyler Greene. m., Jerome Kern. T. B. Harms & Francis, Day & Hunter, cop. 1915.

You'd Never Know the Old Home-Town of Mine. w., Howard Johnson. m., Walter Donaldson. Leo Feist, Inc., cop. 1915.

You'll Always Be the Same Sweet Girl. w., Andrew B. Sterling. m., Harry Von Tilzer. Harry Von Tilzer Music Pub. Co., cop. 1915.

World War I between the Central Powers and the Allies continued. The Central Powers comprised Germany, Austria-Hungary, Turkey, and Bulgaria; the Allies comprised Russia, Great Britain, France, Belgium, Serbia, Montenegro, Japan, and Italy. American sentiment began turning against the Central Powers when the German armies introduced (Apr. 23-28) "poison gas" at Ypres; German "atrocities" in Belgium were reported; German U-boats (submarines) attacked and sank American vessels; the Cunard Line steamer "Lusitania," bound from New York to England, was torpedoed (May 7) by U-20 and sank off Old Head of Kinsale, Ireland, with a loss of 1,198 lives (including 124 Americans, among them Alfred Gwynne Vanderbilt, Mr. and Mrs. Elbert Hubbard, the playwright Charles Klein, and the theatrical producer Charles Frohman), and the British Red Cross nurse Edith Cavell was shot (Oct. 12) as a spy. Meanwhile more than 40 large German and Austrian steamships, including the 54,282-ton "Vaterland," were interned in American ports. Numerous acts of alien sabotage were perpetrated, such as the attempt to dynamite the international bridge between Vanceboro, Me., and New Brunswick (Feb. 2) and the incendiary fires at the John A. Roebling plant, Trenton, N. J. (Jan. 18; loss, $1,500,000) and at the Bethlehem Steel machine shop, South Bethlehem, Pa. (Nov. 10; loss, $5,000,000).

Secretary of State William Jennings Bryan resigned (June 8) in protest against President Wilson's aggressive notes to Germany over the sinking of the "Lusitania." Robert Lansing was appointed (June 23) to succeed Bryan.

In New York, 25,000 women marched (Oct. 23) in a suffrage parade. One hundred years of Anglo-American peace were celebrated (Jan. 8) in New Orleans on the centennial of General Andrew Jackson's victory over the British in the battle at nearby Chalmette where, as part of the commemoration, a statue of Jackson was unveiled amid the formal exchange of greetings between British and American representatives.

Two fairs in California commemorated historical events—the Panama-California Exposition (opened Jan. 1) in San Diego, and the Panama-Pacific International Exposition (Feb. 20-Dec. 4) in San Francisco, celebrating the opening of the Panama Canal and the 400th anniversary of the discovery of the Pacific. The 80-year-old French composer Camille Saint-Saëns represented his government at the latter exposition, and conducted (June 19) a choral work with orchestra, "Hail California" that had been composed for the occasion.

Fires, storms, floods, mine explosions, and marine disasters caused millions of dollars' worth of damage and loss of life in the United States and Alaska. The U. S. submarine F-4 sank (Mar. 25) in Honolulu Harbor, Hawaii, with the loss of its commanding officer and a crew of twenty. In the Chicago River, the steamer "Eastland" capsized (July 24) and 812 excursionists were drowned. A mine explosion at Layland, W. Va., took the lives of 111 miners.

The legislatures of Wisconsin and Minnesota attempted to abolish by state law the giving or receiving of "tips" or gratuities in public places. In Wisconsin the bill was vetoed by Gov. Philipp as interfering with personal liberty, was then passed over his veto, but was disapproved by the State senate. In Minnesota a similar measure failed to secure the approval of the senate committee on general legislation.

The first New-York-to-San-Francisco telephone line was opened. Alexander Graham Bell, inventor of the telephone (1876), took part in the inaugural ceremonies.

Progress also was being made in wireless telephony (radio). Speech was transmitted experimentally from Arlington, Va., to Honolulu and to Paris (Sept. 30) and across the Atlantic (Oct. 22).

President Wilson married (Dec. 18) as his second wife Mrs. Edith Bolling Galt, widow of a Washington jeweler. (The President's first wife had died in 1914 at the White House.)

Some 80 American women, headed by Jane Addams of Hull House, Chicago, attended the Women's Peace Conference (Apr. 27-May 1) at The Hague, Holland, to protest against war and attempted to restore peace in the conflict now in progress in Europe. Certain representatives from the wronged nations voiced sentiments that were more national than universal.

Former Republican New York State committeeman William Barnes, Jr., sued former President Theodore Roosevelt in Syracuse, N. Y., for $50,000 in a libel suit charging that the latter was party to the corrupt politics of which he accused Barnes. After 40 ballots by the jury the trial (Apr. 19-May 22) ended in Roosevelt's acquittal.

The first businessmen's Kiwanis Club, a forerunner of others of the same name throughout the United States and Canada, was formed in Detroit.

"The Musical Quarterly" was founded in New York as the first American periodical to be devoted to musicological studies.

Books of the year included: "America's Coming-of-Age" (Van Wyck Brooks), "Ivory, Apes and Peacocks" (James Gibbons Huneker; a book of essays), the fiction, "The Bent Twig" (Dorothy Canfield), "The 'Genius'" (Theodore Dreiser), "The Gray Dawn" (Stewart Edward White), "The Harbor" (Ernest Poole), "Old Judge Priest" (Irvin Cobb), "Ruggles of Red Gap" (Harry Leon Wilson), "The Song of the Lark" (Willa Cather), and the poetry, "Rivers to the Sea" (Sara Teasdale), "The Song of Hugh Glass" (John Neihardt), "Spoon River Anthology" (Edgar Lee Masters).

The Victor phonograph company, Camden, N. J., introduced in American public schools its record-playing machine known commercially as the Victrola.

Alexander Scriabin's symphony "Prometheus," which combined music and color and utilized a "color keyboard" to project color on a screen, was performed (Mar. 20) for the first time in the United States at Carnegie Hall in New York by the Russian Symphony Orchestra under Modest Altschuler.

Paul Whiteman left the symphonic field and organized an orchestra of his own to play what he called "syncopation" but what was most commonly referred to as "jazz."

New York plays that ran more than 175 performances included: "The Boomerang" (Belasco, Aug. 10; 522 perf.), "Common Clay" (Republic, Aug. 26; 316 perf.), "The House of Glass" (Candler, Sept. 1), "Hit-the-Trail Holiday" (Astor, Sept. 13; 336 perf.), "The Unchastened Woman" (39th Street, Oct. 9), "Potash and Perlmutter in Society" (Lyric, Oct. 21), "The Great Lover" with Leo Ditrichstein (Fulton, Nov. 10), "Treasure Island" (Punch and Judy, Dec. 1). The Washington Square Players gave their first season of one-act plays. Musical productions included: "The Blue Paradise" (Casino, Aug. 5; 356 perf.), "The Princess Pat" (Cort, Sept. 29), "Alone at Last" (Schubert, Oct. 14), "Katinka" (44th Street, Dec. 23; 220 perf.), "Very Good, Eddie" (Princess, Dec. 23; 341 perf.), "Stop! Look! Listen!" (Globe, Dec. 25). The spectacle at the Hippodrome (Sept. 30) was called "Hip-Hip-Hooray." In it was Sousa's band, as well as a kaleidoscope of performers. It grossed $37,600 in one week and ran 425 performances.

David Wark Griffith produced the silent movie classic "The Birth of a Nation," starring Lillian Gish and Henry B. Walthall, with specially composed music by Joseph Carl Breil. The film was based on Thomas Dixon's Ku Klux Klan novel "The Clansman" (1905) and was first shown publicly (Feb. 8) in Los Angeles at Clune's Auditorium. From a box-office standpoint the picture ranks among the first 10 movies of all time.

The St. Louis National League baseball club ("Cardinals") bought second baseman Rogers Hornsby for $400. He became one of the great figures in the game and was seven times National League batting champion.

Jess Willard knocked out (Apr. 5) the Negro heavyweight boxing champion Jack Johnson after 26 rounds in Havana, Cuba, thus winning the title.

The United States loaned (Oct. 15) $500,000,000 to Great Britain and France.

Congress created the U. S. Coast Guard (Jan. 28) and the U. S. Naval Reserve (Mar. 3), and re-established the ranks of Admiral and Vice-Admiral.

President Wilson vetoed (Jan. 28) an immigration bill which again (as in 1913) imposed a literacy test for the admission of aliens.

In accordance with a Congressional act (Mar. 12, 1914), President Wilson announced (Apr. 10) the establishment of a railroad route in Alaska.

The United States Supreme Court voided (June 21) the Oklahoma and Maryland "grandfather" clause (barring from voting any persons not qualified by Jan. 1, 1866, or any whose ancestors were not so qualified) as a violation of the 15th Amendment.

The United States extended (Oct. 19) recognition to the government of Venustiano Carranza in Mexico, and placed an embargo on arms to other revolutionary leaders including Francisco ("Pancho") Villa.

₴◟ 1916

Allah's Holiday (Katinka). w., Otto Hauerbach. m., Rudolf Friml. G. Schirmer, Inc., cop. 1916.

Any Time Is Kissing Time (Chu Chin Chow). w., m., Frederic Norton. London: Keith, Prowse & Co., Ltd., cop. 1916.

Arrah Go On, I'm Gonna Go Back to Oregon. w., Sam M. Lewis and Joe Young. m., Bert Grant. Waterson, Berlin & Snyder Co., cop. 1916.

At the End of a Beautiful Day. w., m., William H. Perkins. F. B. Haviland Pub. Co., cop. 1916.

Baby Shoes. w., Joe Goodwin and Ed. Rose. m., Al Piantadosi. Shapiro, Bernstein & Co., cop. 1916.

Beale Street—*later called:* Beale Street Blues. w., m., W[illiam] C[hristopher] Handy. Memphis, Tenn.: Pace & Handy, cop. 1916; cop. 1917; renewed 1944 by W. C. Handy; published by Handy Bros. Music Co., Inc.

Bugle Call Rag. Piano piece. m., J. Hubert Blake and Carey Morgan. Jos. W. Stern & Co., cop. 1916.

Colonel Bogey. March. m., Kenneth J. Alford [pseud. of Major F. J. Ricketts]. London: Hawkes & Son, cop. 1916. (The composer was the bandmaster of the British 2nd Battalion, Argyll and Sutherland Highlanders.)

The Cobbler's Song (Chu Chin Chow). w., Oscar Asche. m., Frederic Norton. London; Keith, Prowse & Co., Ltd., cop. 1916.

Down Where the Swanee River Flows. w., Charles McCarron and Charles S. Alberte. m., Albert Von Tilzer. Broadway Music Corp., cop. 1916.

"Forever" Is a Long, Long Time. w., Darl MacBoyle. m., Albert Von Tilzer. Artmusic, Inc., cop. 1916.

Give a Little Credit to Your Dad. w., William Tracey. m., Nat Vincent. Broadway Music Corp., cop. 1916.

Good-bye, Good-Luck, God Bless You. w., J. Keirn Brennan. m., Ernest R. Ball. M. Witmark & Sons, cop. 1916.

Have a Heart (Have a Heart). w., P[elham] G[renville] Wodehouse. m., Jerome Kern. T. B. Harms & Francis, Day & Hunter, cop. 1916.

He May Be Old, but He's Got Young Ideas. w., m., Howard Johnson, Alex Gerber and Harry Jentes. Leo Feist, Inc., cop. 1916.

How's Ev'ry Little Thing in Dixie. w., Jack Yellen. m., Albert Gumble. Jerome H. Remick & Co., cop. 1916.

I Ain't Got Nobody. w., Roger Graham. m., Spencer Williams and Dave Peyton. Chicago: Craig & Co., cop. 1916 (cop. 1915 in manuscript by Spencer Williams and Dave Peyton); assigned 1916 to Frank K. Root and Co.; assigned 1928 to Triangle Music Pub. Co.; assigned 1931 to Joe Davis, Inc.

I Can Dance with Everyone but My Wife (*introduced in:* Sybil). w., Joseph Cawthorn and John L. Golden. m., John L. Golden. T. B. Harms & Francis, Day & Hunter, cop. 1916.

I've a Shooting Box in Scotland (*introduced in:* See America First). w., m., T. Lawrason Riggs and Cole Porter. G. Schirmer, cop. 1916.

I Know I Got More Than My Share. w., m., Grant Clarke and Howard Tohnson. Leo Feist, Inc., cop. 1916.

I Want to Marry a Male Quartette (Katinka). w., Otto Hauerbach. m., Rudolf Friml. G. Schirmer, Inc., cop. 1916.

If I Knock the "L" Out of Kelly. w., Sam M. Lewis and Joe Young. m., Bert Grant. Waterson, Berlin & Snyder Co., cop. 1916.

Ireland Must Be Heaven, for My Mother Came from There. w., m., Joe McCarthy, Howard Johnson and Fred Fisher. Leo Feist, Inc., cop. 1916.

It's the Irish in Your Eye, It's the Irish in Your Smile. w., William Dillon. m., Albert Von Tilzer. Broadway Music Corp., cop. 1916.

Katinka (Katinka). w., Otto Hauerbach, m., Rudolf Friml. G. Schirmer, Inc., cop. 1916.

Li'l Liza Jane. w., m., Countess Ada De Lachau. San Francisco: Sherman, Clay & Co., cop. 1916.

Mammy's Little Coal Black Rose. w., Raymond Egan. m., Richard A. Whiting. Jerome H. Remick & Co., cop. 1916.

M-i-s-s-i-s-s-i-p-p-i. w., Bert Hanlon, Benny Ryan. m., Harry Tierney. Wm. Jerome Pub. Corp., cop. 1916; assigned 1918 to Leo Feist, Inc.

Mother (Her Soldier Boy). w., Rida Johnson Young. m., Sigmund Romberg. G. Schirmer, Inc., cop. 1916.

My Own Iona. w., L. Wolfe Gilbert. m., Anatol Friedland and Carey Morgan. Jos. W. Stern & Co., cop. 1916.

Nat'an—for What Are You Waitin', Nat'an. w., m., James Kendis. Kendis Music Pub. Co., Inc., cop. 1916.

Nodding Roses (Very Good Eddie). w., Schuyler Greene and Herbert Reynolds. m., Jerome Kern. T. B. Harms & Francis, Day & Hunter, cop. 1916.

Since Maggie Dooley Learned the Hooley Hooley. w., Bert Kalmar and Edgar Leslie. m., George W. Meyer. Waterson, Berlin & Snyder, cop. 1916; assigned 1932 to Mills Music, Inc.

Nola. Piano solo. m., Felix Arndt. Cleveland; Sam Fox Pub. Co., cop. 1915, by Felix Arndt; assigned 1916 to Sam Fox Pub. Co.

Oh! How She Could Yacki, Hacki, Wicki, Wacki, Woo. w., Stanley Murphy and Charles McCarron. m., Albert Von Tilzer. Broadway Music Corp., cop. 1916.

Poor Butterfly (The Big Show). w., John L. Golden. m., Raymond Hubbell. T. B. Harms & Francis, Day & Hunter, cop. 1916.

Pretty Baby. w., Gus Kahn. m., Tony Jackson and Egbert Van Alstyne. Jerome H. Remick & Co., cop. 1916.

Put on Your Slippers and Fill Up Your Pipe. w., Ed. P. Moran and Will A. Heelan. m., Albert Von Tilzer. Broadway Music Corp., cop. 1916.

Rackety Coo! (Katinka). w., Otto Hauerbach. m., Rudolf Friml. G. Schirmer, Inc., cop. 1916.

Robbers' March (Chu Chin Chow). m., Frederic Norton. London: Keith, Prowse & Co., Ltd., cop. 1916.

Rolling Stones—All Come Rolling Home Again. w., Edgar Leslie. m., Archie Gottler. Kalmar, Puck & Abrahams Consolidated, Inc., cop. 1916.

Roses of Picardy. w., Frederick E[dward] Weatherly. m., Haydn Wood. London: Chappell & Co., Ltd., cop. 1916.

She Is the Sunshine of Virginia. w., Ballard MacDonald. m., Harry Carroll. Shapiro, Bernstein & Co., cop. 1916.

There's a Garden in Old Italy. w., Joe McCarthy. m., Jack Glogau. Leo Feist, Inc., cop. 1916.

There's a Little Bit of Bad in Every Good Little Girl. w., Grant Clarke. m., Fred Fisher. Leo Feist, Inc., cop. 1916.

There's a Quaker Down in Quaker Town. w., David Berg. m., Alfred Solman. Joe Morris Music Co., cop. 1916.

They're Wearing 'Em Higher in Hawaii. w., Joe Goodwin. m., Halsey K. Mohr. Shapiro, Bernstein & Co., cop. 1916.

Turn Back the Universe and Give Me Yesterday. w., J. Keirn Brennan. m., Ernest R. Ball. M. Witmark & Sons, cop. 1916.

Twelfth Street Rag. Piano solo. m., Euday L. Bowman. Kansas City, Mo.: Jenkins Music Co., cop. 1914 by Euday L. Bowman; assigned 1916 to Jenkins Music Co.; cop. 1919 as a song, with words by James S. Summer; renewed 1941 by Euday L. Bowman; assigned 1941 to Shapiro, Bernstein & Co., Inc.; cop. 1942 as a song, with words by Andy Razaf, by Shapiro, Bernstein & Co., Inc.

Way Down in Iowa I'm Going to Hide Away. w., Sam M. Lewis and Joe Young. m., George W. Meyer. Waterson, Berlin & Snyder Co., cop. 1916.

What Do You Want to Make Those Eyes at Me For? w., m., Joe McCarthy, Howard Johnson and James V. Monaco. Leo Feist, Inc., cop. 1916.

When the Black Sheep Returns to the Fold. w., m., Irving Berlin. Waterson, Berlin & Snyder Co., cop. 1916.

Where Did Robinson Crusoe Go with Friday on Saturday Night? w., Sam M. Lewis and Joe Young. m., Geo. W. Meyer. Waterson, Berlin & Snyder Co., cop. 1916.

Yacka Hula Hickey Dula (Robinson Crusoe, Jr). w., m., E. Ray Goetz, Joe Young and Pete Wendling. Waterson, Berlin & Snyder Co., cop. 1916.

You're in Love (You're in Love). w., Otto Hauerbach and Edward Clark. m., Rudolf Friml. G. Schirmer, Inc., cop. 1916.

You Belong to Me (The Century Girl). w., Harry B. Smith. m., Victor Herbert. T. B. Harms & Francis, Day & Hunter, cop. 1916.

You Can't Get Along with 'Em or Without 'Em. w., Grant Clarke. m., Fred Fisher. Leo Feist, Inc., cop. 1916.

World War I continued. The German submarine U-53 "Deutschland" crossed the Atlantic twice to the United States for medical supplies (July 9, to Norfolk, Va., and Nov. 1, to New London, Conn.) and each time eluded British naval vigilance and returned safely to its European base. American tension was increased further when the liner "Sussex" was torpedoed (Mar. 24) in the English Channel (the famous Spanish composer Enrique Granados, whose opera "Goyescas" had just been performed at the Metropolitan Opera House, New York, being a victim) and when alleged German saboteurs caused (July 30) the "Black Tom" explosion at the docks of Jersey City, N. J., killing two persons and creating a property damage of $22,000,000. Nevertheless, President Wilson made efforts to bring about a cessation of hostilities, suggesting (Dec. 18) in a note to the warring powers "peace without victory." The offer was scorned.

A near panic of stock selling developed in New York following Secretary of State Robert Lansing's warning that the United States was being drawn into the European conflict.

In retaliation against American recognition (1915) of the Carranza government in Mexico, the Chihuahua revolutionary leader Francisco ("Pancho") Villa shot (Jan. 10) eighteen Americans in Santa Isabel, Mex., and raided (Mar. 9) the city of Columbus, Luna County, N. M., where he killed 17 persons. The United States sent (Mar. 15) General John Joseph Pershing with 12,000 troops into Mexico in pursuit of Villa. Fighting took place (Apr. 12) at Parral, Durango. Villa, whose real name was Doroteo Arango, eluded capture. After 11 months of fruitless search (Mar. 1916-Feb. 1917), the American armed forces were withdrawn.

Congress passed the Federal Farm Loan Act (July 17), known also as the Rural Credits Act, which established the Federal Land Bank of twelve regional banks for the financial assistance of farmers, and Virginia Representative William A. Jones's bill (Aug. 29) promising independence to the Philippines on the establishment of a stable government there.

American marines were landed in Nicaragua and in Santo Domingo (Dominican Republic).

The Liberty-winged head or "Mercury" dime and the Liberty-standing half dollar went into circulation. Both coins were designed by A. A. Weinman.

The U. S. cruiser "Memphis" was wrecked (Aug. 29) at Trujillo City (then Santo Domingo), Dominican Republic, with a loss of 33 lives.

In San Francisco the explosion of a bomb disrupted the Preparedness Day (July 12) parade organized by labor leader "Tom" (Thomas J.) Mooney, killed 10 persons, and wounded 40 others. Mooney, his wife, and several associates were arrested for murder. The long trial of the accused resulted in sentences of death to Mooney and of life imprisonment to a colleague. The other members of the group were released. The case aroused nationwide interest. Many organizations and influential people believed in Mooney's innocence, and in 1918 President Wilson had the death sentence commuted to life imprisonment in San Quentin. (Mooney and his associate, Billings, were pardoned in 1939 by Governor C. L. Olson of California.)

Dr. Roy Chapman Andrews conducted explorations in the Gobi Desert and elsewhere in Mongolia.

The National Research Council was established by the National Academy of Sciences, Washington, D. C., at the suggestion of President Wilson, to co-ordinate for national defense all branches of scientific study.

Books of the year included the fiction, "Cappy Ricks" (Peter Bernard Kyne), "Casuals of the Sea" (William McFee), "The Dwelling Place of Light" (Winston Churchill), "The Leatherwood God" (William Dean Howells; his last novel), "Seventeen" (Booth Tarkington), "Xingu" (Edith Wharton), "You Know Me, Al; A Busher's Letters" (Ring Lardner; baseball stories), and the poetry, "Chicago Poems" (Carl Sandburg), "Heap o' Livin'" (Edgar Guest), "The Man Against the Sky" (Edwin Arlington Robinson), "Men, Women, and Ghosts" (Amy Lowell), "Spectra" (Witter Bynner and Arthur Davison Ficke; a literary hoax, a satirical parody of contemporary "modern" poetry, published under the pseudonyms Emmanuel Morgan and Anne Knish).

The luxatone, a keyboard instrument projecting color on a satin screen in conjunction with music, was demonstrated by its inventor, Dr. H. Spencer Lewis, in San Jose, Cal.

Serge Diaghilev brought to the Metropolitan Opera House, New York, from Paris his dazzling, epoch-making Ballet Russe for its first American season (Jan.-May). The great Russian male dancer Vaslav Nijinsky, arrived three months later (debut Apr. 12) after his release from Austria as an enemy alien. The company returned in the fall (Oct. 1916-Feb., 1917) to make an extended tour of the United States.

American classical dancer Maud Allen toured the United States with the eminent Swiss composer Ernest Bloch as her musical director. The Russian ballerina Anna Pavlova was dancing two daily performances at the Hippodrome, New York, in "The Big Show" at a reputed salary of $8,500 per week. Albertina Rasch was in vaudeville.

New York plays that ran for more than 150 performances included: "Erstwhile Susan" (Gaiety, Jan. 18), "Cheating Cheaters" with Marjorie Rambeau (Eltinge, Aug. 9), "Turn to the Right!" (Gaiety, Aug. 18; 453 perf.), "The Man Who Came Back" (Playhouse, Sept. 2; 457 perf.), "Upstairs and Down" (Cort, Sept. 25; 320 perf.), "Come Out of the Kitchen" (Cohan, Oct. 23), "Keeping Up Appearances" (Bramhall, Nov. 8), "The Yellow Jacket" with Mr. and Mrs. Charles Coburn (Cort, Nov. 9), "The Thirteenth Chair" (48th Street, Nov. 20; 328 perf.), "A Kiss for Cinderella" with Maude Adams (Empire, Dec. 25). Notable also were John Galsworthy's "Justice" (Candler, Apr. 3; 104 perf.) and "Good Gracious Annabelle" (Republic, Oct. 31; 111 perf.). Stuart Walker's Portmanteau Theatre (opening Nov. 27 at the 39th Street) presented its first New York season of short plays. At the Lewisohn Stadium of City College was put on (May 24) with elaborate scenery and with music by Arthur Farwell a dramatic spectacle, "Caliban of the Yellow Sands" by Percy MacKaye. Top Broadway stars were featured and a colorful array of national folk groups was introduced. Musical productions included: "Sybil" (Liberty, Jan. 10), "Robinson Crusoe, Jr." (Winter Garden, Feb. 17), "Pom-Pom" (Cohan, Feb. 28), "The Big Show" (Hippodrome, Aug. 31; 425 perf.), "Flora Bella" (Casino, Sept. 11), "Miss Springtime" (New Amsterdam, Sept. 25), "The Century Girl" by Victor Herbert and Irving Berlin (Century, Nov. 6), "Her Soldier Boy" (Astor, Dec. 6).

The Metropolitan Opera House, New York, produced (Jan. 28) the world première of Enrique Granados's "Goyescas"—the first and so far only opera to be sung there in the Spanish language.

Amelita Galli-Curci, Italian coloratura soprano, made (Nov. 18) her American debut in Chicago as Gilda in "Rigoletto."

"Cavalleria Rusticana" and "Pagliacci" were presented (Sept. 21) in a double-bill open-air performance at the Lewisohn Stadium of the City College, New York.

The movies, still silent, were in their heyday, showing "The Daughter of the Gods" (with swimming champion Annette Kellerman), "The Dumb Girl of Portici" (with ballerina Anna Pavlova), "The Fall of a Nation" (with original music by Victor Herbert), "The Foolish Virgin" (Clara Kimball Young), "The Good Bad Man" (Douglas Fairbanks), "Intolerance" (produced by David Wark Griffith), "Less Than the Dust" (Mary Pickford), "Pearl of the Army" (Pearl White), "Rose of the South" (Peggy Hyland and Antonio Moreno), "The Vixen" (Theda Bara), "War Brides" (Alla Nazimova, introducing a later star, Richard Barthelmess), "Wharf Rat" (Mae Marsh), "The Witching Hour" (C. Aubrey Smith). Other film names were Richard Bennett, Billie Burke (Mrs. Florenz Ziegfeld, who later went back to the stage), Francis X. Bushman, Marie Empress, Harry Fox, Anita Stewart, and Norma and Constance Talmadge. A significant merger of movie interests was the consolidation of Zukor's Famous Players and the Jesse L. Lasky Feature Play companies.

Charles Evans Hughes resigned from the U. S. Supreme Court to run as Republican presidential candidate against Democratic President Wilson in the national elections. The voters retired to bed after an exciting day at the polls believing that Hughes had captured the election, only to wake up the next morning and learn that President Wilson had won re-election by a bare 600,000 votes on the slogan "He kept us out of war."

Hetty Green, aged 82, the world's wealthiest woman, often called "The Witch of Wall Street," died (July 3) in New York and left a fortune of one hundred million dollars.

ᢒᔌ 1917

All the World Will Be Jealous of Me. w., Al Dubin. m., Ernest R. Ball. M. Witmark & Sons, cop. 1917.

Au Revoir, but Not Good-Bye, Soldier Boy. w., Lew Brown. m., Albert Von Tilzer. Broadway Music Corp., cop. 1917.

The Bells of St. Mary's. w., Douglas Furber. m., A. Emmett Adams. London: Chappell & Co., Ltd., cop. 1917 by Ascherberg, Hopwood & Crew, Ltd., London.

The Bombo-shay. w., m., Henry Creamer, Henry Lewis, and Turner Layton. Jerome H. Remick & Co., cop. 1917.

Bring Back My Daddy to Me. w., William Tracey and Howard Johnson. m., George M. Meyer. Leo Feist, Inc., cop. 1917.

Come and Have a Swing with Me (Jack o' Lantern). w., Anne Caldwell. m., Ivan Caryll. London: Chappell & Co., Ltd., cop. 1917.

Come, Ye Blessed. w., Biblical. m., John Prindle Scott. G. Schirmer, cop. 1917.

The Darktown Strutters' Ball. w., m., Shelton Brooks. Leo Feist, Inc., cop. 1917 by Will Rossiter; assigned to Leo Feist, Inc.

Deep River. Negro spiritual arr. for voice and piano by H[enry] T[hacker] Burleigh. G. Ricordi & Co., Inc., cop. 1917.

Eileen Alanna Asthore (Eileen). w., Henry Blossom. m., Victor Herbert. M. Witmark & Sons, cop. 1917.

For Me and My Gal. w., Edgar Leslie and E. Ray Goetz. m., George W. Meyer. Waterson, Berlin & Snyder Co., cop. 1917.

Gesù Bambino. English words, Frederick H[erman] Martens. Italian words and music, Pietro A. Yon. J. Fischer & Bro., cop. 1917.

Give a Man a Horse He Can Ride. w., James Thomson. m., Geoffrey O'Hara. Huntzinger & Dilworth, cop. 1917.

Give Me the Moonlight, Give Me the Girl. w., Lew Brown. m., Albert Von Tilzer. Broadway Music Corp., cop. 1917.

Go Down, Moses. Negro spiritual arr. for voice and piano by H[enry] T[hacker] Burleigh. G. Ricordi & Co., Inc., cop. 1917.

Going Up (Going Up). w., Otto Harbach. m., Louis A. Hirsch. M. Witmark & Sons, cop. 1917.

Good-Bye, Broadway, Hello France! (Passing Show of 1917). w., C. Francis Reisner and Benny Davis. m., Billy Baskette. Leo Feist, Inc., cop. 1917.

Good-Bye, Ma! Good-Bye, Pa! Good-Bye, Mule. w., William Herschell. m., Barclay Walker. Shapiro, Bernstein & Co., cop. 1917 by William Herschell and Barclay Walker; assigned to Shapiro, Bernstein & Co., Inc.

Hail, Hail, the Gang's All Here. w., D. A. Esrom [Morse!]. m., Theodore Morse and Arthur Sullivan. Leo Feist, Inc., cop. 1917. (The melody is derived from the tenor strain, "Come, friends, who plough the sea," of the song and chorus "With catlike tread" in Act II of Sir Arthur Sullivan's operetta "The Pirates of Penzance.")

Hawaiian Butterfly. w., George A. Little. m., Billy Baskette and Joseph P. Santly. Leo Feist, Inc., cop. 1917.

Homing. w., Arthur L. Salmon. m., Teresa del Riego. London: Chappell & Co., Ltd., cop. 1917.

Huckleberry Finn. w., m., Cliff Hess, Sam M. Lewis and Joe Young. Waterson, Berlin & Snyder Co., cop. 1917.

I'm All Bound 'Round with the Mason Dixon Line. w., Sam M. Lewis and Joe Young. m., Jean Schwartz. Waterson, Berlin & Snyder Co., cop. 1917.

I Don't Know Where I'm Going, but I'm On My Way. w., m., George Fairman. Harry Von Tilzer Music Pub. Co., cop. 1917.

I Don't Want to Get Well. w., Howard Johnson and Harry Pease. m., Harry Jentes. Leo Feist, Inc., cop. 1917.

I May Be Gone for a Long, Long Time (Hitchy-Koo). w., Lew Brown. m., Albert Von Tilzer. Broadway Music Corp., cop. 1917.

I'd Love to Be a Monkey in the Zoo. w., Bert Hanlon. m., Willie White. M. Witmark & Sons, cop. 1917.

Indiana. w., Ballard MacDonald. m., James F. Hanley. Shapiro, Bernstein & Co., cop. 1917.

Indianola. Piano solo. m., S. R. Henry and D. Onivas [pseud. of Domenico Savino]. Jos. W. Stern & Co., cop. 1917.

It's a Long Lane That Has No Turning. w., Arthur A. Penn. m., Manuel Klein. M. Witmark & Sons, cop. 1917.

Joan of Arc, They Are Calling You. w., Alfred Bryan and Willie Weston. m., Jack Wells. Waterson, Berlin & Snyder Co., cop. 1917.

Jump Jim Crow (Maytime). w., Rida Johnson Young. m., Sigmund Romberg. G. Schirmer, Inc., cop. 1917.

Leave It to Jane (Leave It to Jane). w., P. G. Wodehouse. m., Jerome Kern. T. B. Harms Co., cop. 1917.

Liberty Bell—It's Time to Ring Again. w., Joe Goodwin. m., Halsey K. Mohr. Shapiro, Bernstein & Co., cop. 1917.

Lily of the Valley. w., L. Wolfe Gilbert. m., Anatole Friedland. Jos. W. Stern & Co., cop. 1917.

Little Mother of Mine. w., Walter H. Brown. m., H[enry] T[hacker] Burleigh. G. Ricordi & Co., Inc., cop. 1917.

Lorraine—My Beautiful Alsace Lorraine. w., Alfred Bryan. m., Fred Fisher. McCarthy & Fisher, Inc., cop. 1917.

Love Will Find a Way (The Maid of the Mountains). w., Harry Graham. m., Harold Fraser-Simson. Leo Feist, Inc., cop. 1917 by Ascherberg, Hopwood & Crew, Ltd., London.

Macnamara's Band. w., John J. Stamford. m., Shamus O'Connor. London: J. H. Larway, cop. 1917.

The Magic of Your Eyes. w., m., Arthur A. Penn. M. Witmark & Sons, cop. 1917.

Meet Me at the Station, Dear. w., Sam M. Lewis and Joe Young. m., Ted Snyder. Waterson, Berlin & Snyder Co., cop. 1917.

My Mother's Lullaby. w., Charles Louis Ruddy. m., Harold Brown Freeman. Providence, R. I.: Harold Freeman Co., cop. 1917.

My Sunshine Jane. w., J. Keirn Brennan. m., Ernest R. Ball. M. Witmark & Sons, cop. 1917.

Nobody Knows de Trouble I've Seen. Negro spiritual arr. for voice and piano by Henry Thacker Burleigh. G. Ricordi & Co., Inc., cop. 1917.

Oh Johnny, Oh Johnny, Oh! w., Ed. Rose. m., Abe Olman. Chicago: Forster Music Publisher, Inc., cop. 1917.

Out Where the West Begins. w., Arthur Chapman. m., Estelle Philleo. Forster Music Pub. Co., Inc., cop. 1917 by Estelle Philleo.

Over There. w., m., George M[ichael] Cohan. Leo Feist, Inc., cop. 1917.

The Regiment of Sambre and Meuse—*original title:* Le Regiment de Sambre et Meuse. French words, Paul Cezano; English words, George Harris, Jr. m., Robert Planquette. Boston: Oliver Ditson Co., cop. 1917.

Repent Ye. w., Biblical. m., John Prindle Scott. G. Schirmer, Inc., cop. 1917.

The Road to Paradise (Maytime). w., Rida Johnson Young. m., Sigmund Romberg. G. Schirmer, Inc., cop. 1917.

Roadways. w., John Masefield. m., John Hopkins Densmore. Boston: Oliver Ditson Co., cop. 1917.

Rockaway. w., m., Howard Johnson, Alex Rogers and C. Luckeyth Roberts. Leo Feist, Inc., cop. 1917.

Sailin' Away on the Henry Clay. w., Gus Kahn. m., Egbert Van Alstyne. Jerome H. Remick & Co., cop. 1917.

Send Me Away with a Smile. w., m., Louis Weslyn and Al Piantadosi. Al Piantadosi & Co., Inc., cop. 1917.

Shim-Me-Sha-Wabble. m., Spencer Williams. Jos. W. Stern & Co., cop. 1916 by Roger Graham; cop. 1917 by Roger Graham; assigned 1917 to Jos. W. Stern & Co.; assigned 1921 to Edward B. Marks Music Co.; assigned 1932 to Edward B. Marks Music Corp.

The Siren's Song (Leave It to Jane). w., P. G. Wodehouse. m., Jerome Kern. T. B. Harms Co., cop. 1917.

Smiles. w., J. Will Callahan. m., Lee G. Roberts. Jerome H. Remick & Co., cop. 1917 by Lee G. Roberts; assigned 1918 to Jerome H. Remick & Co.

Some Sunday Morning. w., Gus Kahn and Raymond Egan. m., Richard A. Whiting. Jerome H. Remick & Co., cop. 1917.

Sweet Emalina, My Gal. w., m., Creamer and Layton. Broadway Music Corp., cop. 1917.

Sweet Little Buttercup. w., Alfred Bryan. m., Herman Paley. Jerome H. Remick & Co., cop. 1917.

Swing Low, Sweet Chariot. Negro spiritual arr. for voice and piano by H[enry] T[hacker] Burleigh. G. Ricordi & Co., Inc., cop. 1917.

There's Egypt in Your Dreamy Eyes. w., Fleta Jan Brown. m., Herbert Spencer. Jerome H. Remick & Co., cop. 1917.

They Go Wild Simply Wild Over Me. w., Joe McCarthy. m., Fred Fisher. McCarthy & Fisher, Inc., cop. 1917.

Thine Alone (Eileen). w., Henry Blosson. m., Victor Herbert. M. Witmark & Sons, cop. 1917.

Tiger Rag. Fox-trot. m., Original Dixieland Jazz Band. Leo Feist, Inc., cop. 1917.

Tiger Rose. w., m., Gene Buck. T. B. Harms & Francis, Day & Hunter, cop. 1917.

'Til the Clouds Roll By (Oh Boy). w., Jerome Kern, P. G. Wodehouse and Guy Bolton. m., Jerome Kern. T. B. Harms & Francis Day & Hunter, cop. 1917.

Wait Till the Cows Come Home (Jack o' Lantern). w., Anne Caldwell. m., Ivan Caryll. London: Chappell & Co., Ltd., cop. 1917.

We're Going Over. w., m., Andrew B. Sterling, Bernie Grossman and Arthur Lange. The Joe Morris Music Co., cop. 1917.

We'll Knock the Heligo-Into Heligo-Out of Heligoland! w., John O'Brien. m., Theodore F. Morse. Leo Feist, Inc., cop. 1917.

When Shall I Again See Ireland (Eileen). w., Henry Blossom. m., Victor Herbert. M. Witmark & Sons, cop. 1917.

When the Boys Come Home. w., John Hay. m., Oley Speaks. G. Schirmer, Inc., cop. 1917.

When Yankee Doodle Learns to Parlez Vous Français. w., William Hart. m., Ed. Nelson. A. J. Stasny Music Co., cop. 1917.

Where Do We Go from Here? w., m., Howard Johnson and Percy Wenrich. Leo Feist, Inc., cop. 1917.

Where the Black-Eyed Susans Grow (Robinson Crusoe, Jr). w., Dave Radford. m., Richard A. Whiting. Jerome H. Remick & Co., cop. 1917.

Where the Morning Glories Grow. w., Gus Kahn and Raymond Egan. m., Richard A. Whiting. Jerome H. Remick & Co., cop. 1917.

The White Peacock. Piano solo. m., Charles Tomlinson Griffes. G. Schirmer, cop. 1917.

Whose Little Heart Are You Breaking Now? w., m., Irving Berlin. Waterson, Berlin & Snyder Co., cop. 1917.

Will You Remember [Sweetheart] (Maytime). w., Rida Johnson Young. m., Sigmund Romberg. G. Schirmer, Inc., cop. 1917.

For some songs of World War I, consult—

Dolph, Edward Arthur

"Sound Off!" New York: Farrar & Rinehart, Inc. [cop. 1942].

Niles, John J.

"Singing Soldiers." New York: Charles Scribner's Sons [cop. 1927].

Niles, John J., Douglas S. Moore and A. A. Wallgren.

"The Songs My Mother Never Taught Me." New York: The Macaulay Co. [cop. 1929].

Peat, Frank E.

"Legion Airs." Edited by Lee Orean Smith. New York: Leo Feist, Inc., cop. 1932; cop. 1949.

President Woodrow Wilson began his second term.

After 11 months (Mar., 1916-Feb., 1917) of fruitless search in northern Mexico for the revolutionary leader Francisco ("Pancho") Villa, the American punitive army under Gen. John Joseph Pershing was withdrawn.

World War I continued. When Germany instituted (Feb. 1) unrestricted submarine warfare, the United States recalled (Feb. 2) its ambassador to the German Empire, James Watson Gerard, and began (Mar. 12) to arm merchant ships. The declaration of war on Germany followed (Apr. 6, Good Friday). Congress enacted (May 18) the Selective Military Conscription Bill (draft), passed (June 15) the Espionage Act (amended May 16, 1918 by a Sedition Act), and created the War Industries Board. The government took over the control of all American railroads. American troops ("A.E.F.," American Expeditionary Force) arrived (June 26) in France and entered (Oct. 27) into the conflict. The United States declared (Dec. 7) war on Germany's ally, Austria-Hungary. The teaching of the German language in the New York public schools was abolished and the Metropolitan Opera House, New York, banned German opera.

With America's entry into the world war, mothers and sweethearts knitted for the "boys over there" and windows displayed flags starred with the number of men from each family serving in the army and navy. Churches, colleges, and business firms erected tablets bearing the names of their soldiers. "Meatless," "wheatless," "fuel-less" days were observed everywhere to conserve food and fuel for the armed forces.

To meet the expenditures of the war, Congress authorized (Apr. 24) the first Liberty Loan and War Savings Certificates. Nationwide drives swung into action.

Engineers in the U. S. War Department designed the 12-cylinder automotive "Liberty motor," capable of developing up to 400 horsepower.

The Liberty-standing 25-cent piece went into circulation. The coin was designed by Herman A. MacNeil.

President Wilson rejected former President Theodore Roosevelt's offer to organize a volunteer division to help the Allies against Germany.

The Browning machine gun (tested in May) was adopted by the U. S. Army.

The United States purchased (Jan. 25) from Denmark for $25,000,000 the Danish West Indies (now Virgin Islands), a group of about 25 rocky islands east of Puerto Rico.

The Lansing-Ishii Agreement, so named after Secretary of State Robert Lansing and the Japanese Viscount K. Ishii, was signed (Nov. 2), recognizing Japan's special interest in China and reaffirming the open-door policy (1899). (The Agreement was annulled Apr. 14, 1932.)

Mt. McKinley National Park, Alaska, was established.

The Lake Washington Ship Canal, eight miles long, connecting Seattle, Wash., with the Pacific, was opened.

The Hell Gate Bridge, New York, spanning the East River, was completed.

A mine disaster at Hastings, Colo., took the lives of 121 miners.

The Rosenwald Fund was established for the furtherance of the philanthropies in Negro education of Julius Rosenwald, president of the mercantile firm Sears, Roebuck Company, Chicago, Ill.

The American Anthropological Society was founded.

The International Association of Lions Clubs was formed to promote national and international welfare.

The first of the Civitan Clubs ("Builders of Good Citizenship") was organized in Birmingham, Ala.; the movement spread in the United States and into Canada.

The Russian daily newspaper "Russky Golos" was founded in New York.

The first Pulitzer prizes in Journalism and Letters were awarded. The awards went to the "New York Tribune" (editorial writing), Herbert Bayard Swope of the "New York World" (reporting), Jean Jules Jusserand ("With Americans of Past and Present Days"; history), Laura E. Richards and Maude House Elliott, assisted by Florence Howe Hall ("Julia Ward Howe"; biography).

Books of the year included: "A Book of Prefaces" (Henry Mencken), "The Cambridge History of American Literature" (4 vols., 1917-21), "Love Songs" (Sara Teasdale; poems), "The Unpublished Memoirs" (Abraham Rosenbach; a satire on bibliomania), and the fiction, "The Cream of the Jest" (James Branch Cabell), "The Dwelling Place of Light" (Winston Churchill), "Fanny Herself" (Edna Ferber), "Gullible's Travels" (Ring Lardner), "His Family" (Ernest Poole; Pulitzer prize 1918), "Parnassus on Wheels" (Christopher Morley), "Susan Lenox: Her Fall and Rise" (David Graham Phillips), "The Three Black Pennys" (Joseph Hergesheimer).

Phonograph recordings of the Chicago, Cincinnati, and New York Philharmonic orchestras under their respective conductors, Frederick Stock, Dr. Ernst Kunwald, and Josef Stransky, were issued by the Columbia Company, Bridgeport, Conn.

The New York Philharmonic Orchestra celebrated the 75th year of its existence.

Arnold Volpe established the Lewisohn Stadium Summer Concerts in New York at the College of the City of New York.

Paul Whiteman conducted (1917-18) a 40-piece band in the U. S. Navy.

Jascha Heifetz, 16-year-old Russian violin virtuoso, made (Oct. 27) his American debut in New York in a recital at Carnegie Hall.

Dr. Ernst Kunwald of Frankfort, Germany, conductor of the Cincinnati Symphony Orchestra, was arrested (Dec. 8) and interned as an enemy alien.

Two major operas by American composers received their world premières—"The Canterbury Pilgrims" by Reginald DeKoven (New York, Metropolitan Opera House, Mar. 8) and "Azora" by Henry Kimball Hadley (Chicago, Auditorium, Dec. 26). Hadley also won with his "Bianca" the $1,000 William Wade Hinshaw prize of the Society of American Singers, New York, for a one-act opera by an American composer. (The work was produced Oct. 18, 1918 at the Park Theatre.)

Rope-twirling "cowboy philosopher" Will Rogers joined the "Ziegfeld Follies of 1917" (New York, New Amsterdam Theatre, June 12). (Reference books invariably give the date as 1907; obviously a misprint.)

New York plays that ran for 200 or more performances included: "Business before Pleasure" (Eltinge, Aug. 15; 357 perf.), "A Tailor Made Man" (Cohan and Harris, Aug. 27; 398 perf.), "Polly with a Past" (Belasco, Sept. 6; 315 perf.), "Lombardi, Ltd." (Morosco, Sept. 24; 296 perf.), "Tiger Rose" (Lyceum, Oct. 3; 384 perf.), "Parlor, Bedroom and Bath" (Republic, Dec. 24; 232 perf.). Jesse Lynch Williams's social comedy "Why Marry?" was the first play to be awarded a Pulitzer prize (1918). Musical productions included: "Canary Cottage" (Morosco, Feb. 5), "You're in Love" (Casino, Feb. 6), "Oh, Boy" (Princess, Feb. 20; 463 perf.), "Hitchy-Koo" with Raymond Hitchcock and Irene Bordoni (Cohan and Harris, June 7), "Maytime" with Peggy Wood (Shubert, Aug. 16; 492 perf.), "Chu Chin Chow" with Tyrone Power (Manhattan Opera House, Oct. 22), "Flo-Flo" (Cort, Dec. 20), "Going Up" (Liberty, Dec. 25; 351 perf.).

In vaudeville Lou Holtz appeared with a blackface act. Blossom Seeley, Benny Fields, and Benny Davis had an act called "Seeley's Syncopated Studio." Another vaudeville performer was Barbara LaMarr (later in films).

The motion-picture business continued to grow. Douglas Fairbanks was starred in "A Modern Musketeer." Bespectacled comedian Harold Lloyd and 15-year-old Bebe Daniels started their movie careers together in a comedy "Just Nuts." Operatic soprano Mary Garden took time out from grand opera to do a silent film version of her favorite opera "Thaïs." Ince Productions now had a roster including William S. Hart, Dorothy Dalton, Charles Ray, and Enid Bennett. Other film names of the year included William Desmond, Polly Moran (in Mack Sennett comedies), Fatty Arbuckle, Mae Murray, and Harry Carey.

"Diamond Jim" Brady, aged 61, symbol of New York's "Gay 90s," died (Apr. 13). His real name was James Buchanan Brady.

୧୬ 1918

After You've Gone. w., m., Henry Creamer and Turner Layton. Broadway Music Corp., cop. 1918.

Bagdad (Sinbad). w., Harold Atteridge. m., Al Jolson. G. Schirmer, Inc., cop. 1918.

Beautiful Ohio. w., Ballard MacDonald. m., Mary Earl [pseud. of Robert A. King]. Shapiro, Bernstein & Co., Inc., cop. 1918.

Bing! Bang! Bing 'Em on the Rhine. w., m., Jack Mahoney and Allan Flynn. Jerome H. Remick & Co., cop. 1918.

Come on, Papa. w., m., Edgar Leslie and Harry Ruby. Waterson, Berlin & Snyder Co., cop. 1918.

The Daughter of Rosie O'Grady. w., Monty C. Brice. m., Walter Donaldson. M. Witmark & Sons, cop. 1918.

Dear Little Boy of Mine. w., J. Keirn Brennan. m., Ernest R. Ball. M. Witmark & Sons, cop. 1918.

Dear Old Pal of Mine. w., Harold Robe. m., Lieut. Gitz Rice. G. Ricordi & Co., cop. 1918.

Every Day Will Be Sunday When the Town Goes Dry. w., m., William Jerome and Jack Mahoney. Leo Feist, Inc., cop. 1918.

Ev'rybody Ought to Know How to Do the Tickle Toe (Going Up). w., Otto Harbach. m., Louis A. Hirsch. M. Witmark & Sons, cop. 1918.

Everything Is Peaches Down in Georgia. w., Grant Clarke. m. Milton Ager and George W. Meyer. Leo Feist, Inc., cop. 1918.

Good Morning, Mr. Zip-Zip-Zip! w., m., Robert Lloyd. Leo Feist, Inc., cop. 1918.

Hello, Central! Give Me No Man's Land (*introduced in:* Sinbad). w., Sam M. Lewis and Joe Young. m., Jean Schwartz. Waterson, Berlin & Snyder Co., cop. 1918.

Hinky-Dinky Parlez-vous—*also known as:* Mad'moiselle from Armentières. World War I song. w., m., anon.

Hindustan. w., m., Oliver G. Wallace and Harold Weeks. Chicago: Forster Music Publisher, Inc., cop. 1918 by Melody Shop; assigned 1918 to Forster Music Publisher, Inc.

How Can You Tell? (Demi-Tasse Revue). w., Ned Wayburn. m., Harold Orlob. Leo Feist, Inc., cop. 1918.

How'd You Like to Be My Daddy? (Sinbad). w., Sam M. Lewis and Joe Young. m., Ted Snyder. Waterson, Berlin & Snyder Co., cop. 1918.

I'm Always Chasing Rainbows (Oh Look!). w., Joseph McCarthy. m., Harry Carroll. McCarthy & Fisher Inc., cop. 1918.

I'm Gonna Pin My Medal On the Girl I Left Behind. w., m., Irving Berlin. Waterson, Berlin & Snyder Co., cop. 1918.

I'm Sorry I Made You Cry. w., m., N. J. Clesi. Leo Feist, Inc., cop. 1918.

I Found the End of the Rainbow. w., m., John Mears, Harry Tierney, and Joseph McCarthy. McCarthy & Fisher, Inc., cop. 1918.

I Hate to Lose You. w., Grant Clarke. m., Archie Gottler. Waterson, Berlin & Snyder Co., cop. 1918.

I'll Say She Does (Sinbad). w., m., Bud DeSylva, Gus Kahn and Al Jolson. Jerome H. Remick & Co., cop. 1918.

I'd Like to See the Kaiser with a Lily in His Hand (Doing Our Bit). w., m., Henry Leslie, Howard Johnson, and Billy Frisch. Leo Feist, Inc., cop. 1918.

If He Can Fight Like He Can Love, Good Night Germany! w., Grant Clarke and Howard E. Rogers. m., George W. Meyer. Leo Feist, Inc., cop. 1918.

If You Look in Her Eyes (Going Up). w., Otto Harbach. m., Louis A. Hirsch. M. Witmark & Sons, cop. 1918.

Ja-Da. w., m., Bob Carleton. Leo Feist, Inc., cop. 1918.

Just a Baby's Prayer at Twilight. w., Sam M. Lewis and Joe Young. m., M. K. Jerome. Waterson, Berlin & Snyder Co., cop. 1918.

Just Like Washington Crossed the Delaware, General Pershing Will Cross the Rhine. w., Howard Johnson. m., George W. Meyer. Leo Feist, Inc., cop. 1918.

K-K-K-Katy. w., m., Geoffrey O'Hara. Leo Feist, Inc., cop. 1918.

Keep Your Head Down, "Fritzie Boy." w., m., Gitz Rice. Leo Feist, Inc., cop. 1918.

Kisses—the Sweetest Kisses of All. w., Alex Sullivan. m., Lynn Cowan. McCarthy & Fisher, Inc., cop. 1918.

Lafayette—We Hear You Calling. w., m., Mary Earl [pseud. of Robert A. King]. Shapiro, Bernstein & Co., Inc., cop. 1918.

Madelon. French words, Louis Bousquet. English words, Alfred Bryan. m., Camille Robert. Jerome H. Remick & Co., cop. 1918.

Mammy's Chocolate Soldier. w., Sidney Mitchell. m., Archie Gottler. Waterson, Berlin & Snyder Co., cop. 1918.

Mickey (film: Mickey). w., Harry H. Williams. m., Neil Moret. Waterson, Berlin & Snyder Co., cop. 1918 by Daniels & Wilson, Inc., San Francisco; assigned 1919 to Waterson, Berlin & Snyder Co.

My Belgian Rose. w., m., George Benoit, Robert Levenson, and Ted Garton. Leo Feist, Inc., cop. 1918.

Oh! Frenchy. w., Sam Ehrlich. m., Con Conrad. Broadway Music Corp., cop. 1918.

Oh! How I Hate to Get Up in the Morning. w., m., Irving Berlin. Waterson, Berlin & Snyder Co., cop. 1918.

Oh! How I Wish I Could Sleep Until My Daddy Comes Home. w., Sam M. Lewis and Joe Young. m., Pete Wendling. Waterson, Berlin & Snyder Co., cop. 1918.

Oh Peter Go Ring Dem Bells. Negro spiritual arr. for voice and piano by Henry Thacker Burleigh. G. Ricordi & Co., Inc., cop. 1918.

Oui, Oui, Marie. w., Alfred Bryan and Joe McCarthy. m., Fred Fisher. McCarthy & Fisher, Inc., cop. 1918.

Ride On! Ride On! [w., Henry Hart Milman.] m., John Prindle Scott. Harold Flammer, Inc., cop. 1918.

Rock-a-Bye Your Baby With a Dixie Melody. w., Sam M. Lewis and Joe Young. m., Jean Schwartz. Waterson, Berlin & Snyder Co., cop. 1918.

The Rose of No Man's Land. w., Jack Caddingan. m., Joseph A. Brennan. Leo Feist, Inc., cop. 1918.

Sometime (Sometime). w., Rida Johnson Young. m., Rudolf Friml. G. Schirmer, Inc., cop. 1918.

Sometimes I Feel Like a Motherless Child. Negro spiritual arr. for voice and piano by H[enry] T[hacker] Burleigh. G. Ricordi & Co., Inc., cop. 1918.

Spooky Ookum (The Velvet Lady). w., Henry Blossom. m. Victor Herbert. M. Witmark & Sons, cop. 1918.

Sunrise and You. w., m., Arthur A. Penn. M. Witmark & Sons, cop. 1918.

That Tumble-Down Shack in Athlone. w., Richard W. Pascoe. m., Monte Carlo and Alma M. Sanders. Waterson, Berlin & Snyder Co., cop. 1918 by Oxford Music Pub. Co., London; assigned 1918 to Waterson, Berlin & Snyder Co.

That Wonderful Mother of Mine. w., Clyde Hager. m., Walter Goodwin. M. Witmark & Sons, cop. 1918.

There's a Light in Your Eyes (The Girl Behind the Gun). w., P. G. Wodehouse. m., Ivan Caryll. London: Chappell & Co., Ltd., cop. 1918.

There's Life in the Old Dog Yet (The Girl Behind the Gun). w., P. G. Wodehouse. m., Ivan Caryll. London: Chappell & Co., Ltd., cop. 1918.

They Were All Out of Step but Jim. w., m., Irving Berlin. Waterson, Berlin & Snyder Co., cop. 1918.

Three Wonderful Letters from Home. w., Joe Goodwin and Ballard MacDonald. m., James F. Hanley. Shapiro, Bernstein & Co., Inc., cop. 1918.

Till We Meet Again. w., Raymond B. Egan. m., Richard A. Whiting. Jerome H. Remick & Co., 1918.

'Tis Me, O Lord—Standin' in the Need of Pray'r. Negro spiritual arr. for voice and piano by H[enry] T[hacker] Burleigh. G. Ricordi & Co., Inc., cop. 1918.

Until. w., Edward Teschemacher. m., Wilfred Sanderson. London: Boosey & Co., Ltd., cop. 1918.

The U. S. Field Artillery March. m., John Philip Sousa. Carl Fischer, Inc., cop. 1918.

Waters of Venice—Floating Down the Sleepy Lagoon. w., Neville Fleeson. Melody by Albert Von Tilzer. Artmusic, Inc., cop. 1918.

We Don't Want the Bacon—What We Want Is a Piece of the Rhine. w., m., Howard Carr, Harry Russell, and Jimmie Havens. Shapiro, Bernstein & Co., cop. 1918.

When Alexander Takes His Ragtime Band to France. w., m., Alfred Bryan, Cliff Hess and Edgar Leslie. Waterson, Berlin & Snyder Co., cop. 1918.

When You Come Back. w., m., George M[ichael] Cohan. M. Witmark & Sons, cop. 1918.

When You Look into the Heart of a Rose. w., Marian Gillespie. m., Florence Methven. Leo Feist, Inc., cop. 1918.

Why Do They All Take the Night Boat to Albany. w., Joe Young and Sam M. Lewis. m., Jean Schwartz. Waterson, Berlin & Snyder Co., cop. 1918.

Would You Rather Be a Colonel with an Eagle on Your Shoulder, or a Private with a Chicken on Your Knee? (introduced in: Ziegfeld Follies). w., Sidney D. Mitchell. m., Archie Gottler. Leo Feist, Inc., cop. 1918.

World War I entered its last year. President Wilson delivered (Jan. 8) before Congress his "Fourteen Points of Peace" speech. Russia moved (Mar. 9) its capital from Petrograd to Moscow. The collapse of the German armies along a battle-line extending across Europe led (Oct. 20) to the country's acceptance of defeat. A revolution in Kiel and Hamburg

(Nov. 7) and the establishment of a republic in Bavaria (Nov. 8) resulted in the abdication of the German emperor Wilhelm II (Nov. 9). The armistice was signed (Nov. 11, at 11 A.M.) in a railway car, near Compiègne, France. The United States had mobilized 4,355,000 men; the casualties amounted to 126,000 killed in action, 234,000 wounded, 4,500 prisoners or missing.

A wild and noisy public demonstration in the United States greeted the premature and the real announcement of the armistice. In New York alone, 150 tons of paper and ticker tape were swept off the streets. Signs on shop doors read: "Closed for the Kaiser's funeral" and "Too happy to work; come back tomorrow." And of course "hooch" was everywhere available.

An episode of the war's last days was the heroism of the "Lost Battalion." This fighting unit comprised the First Battalion of the 308th Infantry and parts of the 306th and 307th Infantry Machine Gun Battalion of the 77th (New York) Division, under the command of Major C. W. Whittlesey. The force was completely surrounded (Oct. 3-7) in a ravine near Binarville, France, by the Germans during the Meuse-Argonne battle. The isolated battalion was believed "lost," but it withstood the enemy until relieved by the 154th Brigade.

The United States adopted daylight saving time, first used as an economy measure by England and Germany during the war. (Though the congressional act was repealed in 1919, the practice has been continued in many States and usually is observed from the last Sunday in April to the last Sunday in September.)

The 19,300-ton U.S.S. "Cyclops" sailed (Mar. 4) from Barbados, W. I., and disappeared without a trace.

Commercial aviation began in the United States when air mail was established (May 15) between New York, Philadelphia, and Washington, D. C. The postage rate was fixed at 24 cents per ounce or fraction thereof; the Post Office Department accordingly had issued (May 13) a distinctive postage stamp. The rate, however, was reduced twice soon thereafter—to 16 cents (July 15) and to 6 cents (Dec. 15).

A subway wreck in Brooklyn, New York, in the Malbone Street tunnel of the Brighton Beach line brought (Nov. 2) death to 97 persons and injury to 100 others.

The St. Louis Municipal Outdoor Theatre, seating 10,000, was built.

The bellboy hat—a towering affair turned down over one eye—commanded feminine attention.

Books of the year included: "Cornhuskers" (Carl Sandburg; poems, special Pulitzer prize 1919), "The Education of Henry Adams" (Henry Adams, published posthumously; Pulitzer prize 1919), and the fiction, "Biltmore Oswald" (Thorne Smith), "Birth" (Zona Gale), "Dere Mable: Love Letters of a Rookie" (Edward Streeter), "Java Head" (Joseph Hergesheimer), "The Magnificent Ambersons" (Booth Tarkington; Pulitzer prize 1919), "My Antonia" (Willa Cather), "The Passing of the Frontier" (Emerson Hough), "The Restless Sex" (Robert Chambers), "Treat 'Em Rough" (Ring Lardner; short stories).

The Victor Company, Camden, N. J., began to issue phonograph recordings of the Boston Symphony Orchestra. (The Philadelphia Symphony Orchestra was added in 1919.)

The Metropolitan Opera House, New York, produced among other new operas, Rimsky-Korsakoff's "Le Coq d'Or" (Mar. 6, in French), Charles Wakefield Cadman's American work "Shanewis" (Mar. 23, world première, with Henry Franklin Belknap Gilbert's ballet "The Dance in Place Congo"), and Puccini's operatic triptych "Il Tabarro," "Suor Angelica," and "Gianni Schicchi" (Dec. 14, world première). A feature of the production of "Le Coq d'Or" was the use of a ballet to mime the action while the singers sang from positions on both sides of the stage as part of the décor.

Dr. Karl Muck, famous German conductor of the Boston Symphony Orchestra, was interned as an enemy alien.

The Paris Conservatory orchestra, Société des Concerts du Conservatoire, conducted by André Messager gave concerts (Oct.-Dec.) in 50 American cities under the auspices of the French government.

Rosa Ponselle, Connecticut-born opera soprano, made (Nov. 14) her American debut as Leonora in Verdi's "La Forza del Destino" with Caruso in New York at the Metropolitan Opera House.

Sergei Prokofieff, Russian pianist and composer, concertized in the United States. He played his First Piano Concerto and conducted his violent Scythian Suite "Ala et Lolly" at a concert (Dec. 6) with the Chicago Symphony Orchestra.

The Society of American Singers, composed of notable former grand and light opera artists, presented in New York a season of operatic revivals (Park Theatre, Sept. 30, 1918 through Apr. 12, 1919).

The Berkshire, Mass., festivals of chamber music began.

The New York theatrical season was high-lighted by the production of "Lightnin' " (Gaiety Theatre, Aug. 25)—a dramatization of the novel by its author and Frank Bacon. With the latter heading the cast, the play achieved the unprecedented run of 1,291 New York performances—the first play in American stage history to pass the one thousand mark. When Bacon died in 1922, he had acted the leading role more than 2,000 times. Other long-run plays included: "Seventeen" (Booth, Jan. 22), "Friendly Enemies" with Louis Mann and Sam Bernard (Hudson, July 22; 440 performances), "Three Faces East" (Cohan and Harris, Aug. 13; 335 perf.), "Daddies" (Belasco, Sept. 5; 340 perf.), "Forever After" (Central, Sept. 9; 312 perf.), "Tea for Three" (Maxine Elliott, Sept. 19; 300 perf.), "Redemption" by Tolstoy (Plymouth, Oct. 3), "Three Wise Fools" (Criterion, Oct. 31; 316 perf.), "East Is West" with Fay Bainter (Astor, Dec. 25; 680 perf.), "A Little Journey" (Little Theatre, Dec. 26). Musical productions included: "Oh, Lady, Lady" (Princess, Feb. 1; 219 perf.),

"Sinbad" (Winter Garden, Feb. 14), "The Rainbow Girl" (New Amsterdam, Apr. 1), "Fancy Free" (Shubert, Apr. 11), "The Girl Behind the Gun" (New Amsterdam, Sept. 16), "Sometime" with Mae West (Shubert, Oct. 4; 283 perf.), "Oh, My Dear!" (Princess, Nov. 27), "Listen Lester" (Knickerbocker, Dec. 23; 272 perf.), "Somebody's Sweetheart" (Central, Dec. 23). At the Century Theatre was produced (Aug. 19) for 32 performances "Yip Yip Yaphank," a "musical mess cooked up for the boys of Camp Upton by Sergeant Irving Berlin."

Motion-picture patrons saw David Wark Griffith's "Hearts of the World," with Mary Miles Minter, Tom Mix, Anna Q. Nilsson, and Wallace Reid.

Knute Kenneth Rockne was appointed head football coach at the University of Notre Dame, near South Bend, Ind. (During his 13 years there, Notre Dame teams won 105 games, lost 12, and tied 5. Rockne was born in Norway. He died Mar. 31, 1931, in an airplane accident over Kansas.)

Charles Pores, long-distance runner, won (Sept. 21) at Great Lakes, Ill., the Amateur Athletic Union five-mile outdoor foot race in 24 minutes, 36.8 seconds, setting for the distance a world's record which is still (1951) unbeaten.

ᘓᕍ 1919

Alice Blue Gown. See below: "In My Sweet Little Alice Blue Gown" (Irene).

All the Quakers Are Shoulder Shakers—Down in Quaker Town. w., Bert Kalmar and Edgar Leslie. m., Pete Wendling. Waterson, Berlin & Snyder Co., cop. 1919.

And He'd Say Oo-la La! Wee-Wee. w., m., Harry Ruby and George Jessel. Waterson, Berlin & Snyder Co., cop. 1919.

Ask the Stars (Nothing but Love). w., Frank Stammers. m., Harold Orlob. T. B. Harms & Francis, Day & Hunter, cop. 1919.

Baby, Won't You Please Come Home. w., m., Charles Warfield and Clarence Williams. Clarence Williams Music Publishing Co., Inc., cop. 1919 by Williams and Piron; assigned to Clarence Williams Music Publishing Co., Inc.

The Big Brown Bear. w., H. A. Weydt. m., Mana-Zucca, op. 52, no. 1. G. Schirmer, Inc., cop. 1919.

Boats of Mine. w., Robert Louis Stevenson. m., Anne Stratton Miller. Harold Flammer, Inc., cop. 1919.

Carolina Sunshine. w., Walter Hirsch. m., Erwin R. Schmidt. Harry von Tilzer Music Pub. Co., cop. 1919.

Castle of Dreams (Irene). w., Joseph McCarthy. m., Harry Tierney. Leo Feist, Inc., cop. 1919.

Chinese Lullaby (East Is West). w., m., Robert Hood Bowers. G. Schirmer, Inc., cop. 1919.

Chong—He Come from Hong Kong. w., m., Harold Weeks. Leo Feist, Inc., cop. 1919.

Daddy Long Legs. w., Sam M. Lewis and Joe Young. m., Harry Ruby. Waterson, Berlin & Snyder Co., cop. 1919.

Dardanella. w., Fred Fisher. m., Felix Bernard and Johnny S. Black. McCarthy & Fisher, Inc., cop. 1919.

Don't Cry, Frenchy, Don't Cry. w., Sam M. Lewis and Joe Young. m., Walter Donaldson. Waterson, Berlin & Snyder Co., cop. 1919.

Dreamy Alabama. w., m., Mary Earl [pseud. of Robert A. King]. Shapiro, Bernstein & Co., Inc., cop. 1919.

How Ya Gonna Keep 'Em Down on the Farm? w., Sam M. Lewis and Joe Young. m., Walter Donaldson. Waterson, Berlin & Snyder Co., cop. 1919.

I'm Forever Blowing Bubbles (The Passing Show of 1918). w., m., Jean Kenbrovin and John William Kellette. Jerome H. Remick & Co., cop. 1919 by Kendis-Brockman Music Co.; assigned to Jerome H. Remick & Co.

I'm in Love (Apple Blossoms). w., William Le Baron. m., Fritz Kreisler. T. B. Harms & Francis, Day & Hunter, cop. 1919.

I Might Be Your "Once-in-a-While" (Angel Face). w., Robert Bache Smith. m., Victor Herbert. T. B. Harms & Francis, Day & Hunter, cop. 1919.

I'll Be Happy When the Preacher Makes You Mine. w., Sam M. Lewis and Joe Young. m., Walter Donaldson. Waterson, Berlin & Snyder Co., cop. 1919.

I'll Remember You (Nothing but Love). w., Frank Stammers. m., Harold Orlob. T. B. Harms & Francis, Day & Hunter, cop. 1919.

In My Sweet Little Alice Blue Gown (Irene). w., Joseph McCarthy. m., Harry Tierney. Leo Feist, Inc., cop. 1919.

Indian Summer. Piano solo. m., Victor Herbert. T. B. Harms & Francis, Day & Hunter, cop. 1919. (Arr. for orch. by Harold Sanford, cop. 1919; arr. as a song, with words by Al Dubin, cop. 1939.)

Just Like a Gypsy (Ladies First). w., m., Seymour B. Simons and Nora Bayes. Jerome H. Remick & Co., cop. 1919.

Kid Days. w., Jesse G. M. Glick. m., Irving M. Wilson. Waterson, Berlin & Snyder Co., cop. 1919.

The Lamplit Hour. w., Thomas Burke. m., Arthur A. Penn. M. Witmark & Sons, cop. 1919.

Let the Rest of the World Go By. w., J. Keirn Brennan. m., Ernest R. Ball. M. Witmark & Sons, cop. 1919.

Letter Song (Apple Blossoms). w., William Le Baron. m., Fritz Kreisler. T. B. Harms & Francis, Day & Hunter, cop. 1919.

The Little Church Around the Corner (The Magic Melody). w., Alexander Gerber. m., Sigmund Romberg. M. Witmark & Sons, cop. 1919.

Little Girls, Good Bye! (Apple Blossoms). w., William Le Baron. m., Victor Jacobi. T. B. Harms & Francis, Day & Hunter, cop. 1919.

Love Sends a Little Gift of Roses. w., Leslie Cooke. m., John Openshaw. T. B. Harms & Francis, Day & Hunter, cop. 1919 by Francis, Day & Hunter.

Mammy o' Mine. w., William Tracey. m., Maceo Pinkard. Shapiro, Bernstein & Co., Inc., cop. 1919.

Mandy (Ziegfeld Follies of 1919; *afterwards introduced in the film:* Kid Millions). w., m., Irving Berlin. Irving Berlin, Inc., cop. 1919.

Meet Me in Bubble Land. w., Casper Nathan and Joe Manne. m., Isham Jones. Waterson, Berlin & Snyder Co., cop. 1919.

My Barney Lies Over the Ocean—Just the Way He Lied to Me. w., Sam H. Lewis and Joe Young. m., Bert Grant. Waterson, Berlin & Snyder Co., cop. 1919.

My Buddies (Buddies). w., m., B. C. Hilliam. M. Witmark & Sons, cop. 1919.

My Isle of Golden Dreams. w., Gus Kahn. m., Walter Blaufuss. Jerome H. Remick & Co., cop. 1919.

Nobody Knows—and Nobody Seems to Care. w., m., Irving Berlin. Irving Berlin, Inc., cop. 1919.

Oh! How I Laugh When I Think How I Cried About You. w., Roy Turk and George Jessel. m., Willy White. Waterson, Berlin & Snyder Co., cop. 1919.

Oh! What a Pal Was Mary. w., Edgar Leslie and Bert Kalmar. m., Pete Wendling. Waterson, Berlin & Snyder Co., cop. 1919.

On Miami Shore. w., William Le Baron. m., Victor Jacobi. London: Chappell & Co., Ltd., cop. 1919.

Peggy. w., Harry Williams. m., Neil Moret. Leo Feist, Inc., cop. 1919.

A Pretty Girl Is Like a Melody (Ziegfeld Follies of 1919). w., m., Irving Berlin. Irving Berlin, Inc., cop. 1919.

Sipping Cider Thru' a Straw. w., m., Carey Morgan and Lee David. Jos. W. Stern & Co., cop. 1919.

Smilin' Through (*afterwards introduced in the film:* Smilin' Through). w., m., Arthur A. Penn. M. Witmark & Sons, cop. 1919.

Someone Like You (Angel Face). w., Robert B. Smith. m., Victor Herbert. Harms, Inc., cop. 1919.

Swanee (Sinbad). w., Irving Caesar. m., George Gershwin. T. B. Harms & Francis, Day & Hunter, cop. 1919.

Sweet Sixteen (Ziegfeld Follies of 1919). w., Gene Buck. m., Dave Stamper. T. B. Harms & Francis, Day & Hunter, cop. 1919.

Tell Me. w., J. Will Callahan. m., Max Kortlander. Jerome H. Remick & Co., cop. 1919 by Lee S. Roberts; assigned 1919 to Jerome H. Remick & Co.

That Naughty Waltz. w., Edwin Stanley. m., Sol P. Levy. Belwin, Inc., cop. 1919.

There Is No Death! w., Gordon Johnstone. m., Geoffrey O'Hara. London: Chappell & Co., Ltd., cop. 1919.

They're All Sweeties. w., Andrew B. Sterling. m., Harry Von Tilzer. Harry Von Tilzer Music Pub. Co., cop. 1919.

Tulip Time (Ziegfeld Follies of 1919). w., Gene Buck. m., Dave Stamper. T. B. Harms & Francis, Day & Hunter, cop. 1919.

Wait Till You Get Them Up in the Air, Boys. w., Lew Brown. m., Albert Von Tilzer. Broadway Music Corp., cop. 1919.

What'll We Do on a Saturday Night—When the Town Goes Dry. w., m., Harry Ruby. Waterson, Berlin & Snyder Co., cop. 1919.

When the Cherry Blossoms Fall (The Royal Vagabond). w., Stephen Ivor Szinnyey and William Cary Duncan. m., Anselm Goetzel. M. Witmark & Sons, cop. 1919.

Who Can Tell (Apple Blossoms). w., William Le Baron. m., Fritz Kreisler. T. B. Harms & Francis, Day & Hunter, cop. 1919. (Afterwards introduced in the film: "The King Steps Out," with words by Dorothy Fields. Chappell & Co., Inc., cop. 1936.)

The World Is Waiting for the Sunrise. w., Eugene Lockhart. m., Ernest Seitz. Chappell & Co., Ltd., cop. 1919.

You Ain't Heard Nothing Yet. w., m., Al Jolson, Gus Kahn, and Bud De Sylva. Jerome H. Remick & Co., cop. 1919.

You're a Million Miles From Nowhere. w., Sam M. Lewis and Joe Young. m., Walter Donaldson. Waterson, Berlin & Snyder Co., cop. 1919.

You Are Free (Apple Blossoms). w., William Le Baron. m., Victor Jacobi. T. B. Harms & Francis, Day & Hunter, cop. 1919.

You Said It. w., Bert Kalmar and Eddie Cox. m., Henry W. Santley. Waterson, Berlin & Snyder Co., cop. 1919.

Your Eyes Have Told Me So. w., Gustave Kahn. m., Egbert Van Alstyne. m., Walter Blaufuss. Jerome H. Remick & Co., cop. 1919.

The 18th Amendment (liquor prohibition) was ratified (Jan. 16) and proclaimed (Jan. 29; effective Jan. 16, 1920). As an instrument for its enforcement, Congress passed (Oct. 8, by the Senate; Oct. 10, by the House) Minnesota Representative Andrew Joseph Volstead's National Prohibition Act, known also as the Prohibition Enforcement Act and, more commonly, as the Volstead Act. President Wilson vetoed the bill; it was passed (Oct. 28) over the veto. (The Amendment, called the "noble experiment," was repealed Dec. 5, 1933, by the 21st Amendment.)

The World War Peace Conference opened (Jan. 18) in Paris; the peace treaty was signed (June 28) in Versailles. President Wilson attended— the first American President to set foot on European soil—and returned to the United States in disappointment at the results of the conference, his idealism crushed by the national prejudices of the European representatives. Wilson presented the treaty (July 10) to the Senate, which rejected it (Nov. 19). President Wilson, however, was awarded the Nobel prize for peace.

The United States Post Office issued (Mar. 3) a three-cent purple Victory postage stamp to commemorate the successful conclusion of the World War.

Following a preliminary meeting (Feb. 15-16) in Paris, the American Legion was formed (Mar. 15-17) as a national organization of men and women war veterans. The first caucus in the United States was held (May 8-10) at St. Louis, Mo. The organization was chartered (Sept. 16) by Congress and met (Nov. 10-12) in Minneapolis, Minn., at its first national convention.

Every city and community held parades for returning soldiers.

President Wilson collapsed (Sept. 25) in Pueblo, Colo., while on a strenuous speaking tour, and several days later suffered a stroke that made him an invalid.

A race riot broke out (July 27) in Chicago, causing the death of 31 persons and injury to about 500 others.

Haiti revolted against occupation by the United States (1914). More than 1,800 Haitians lost their lives in the conflict with American marines.

Strikes were nationwide phenomena. Some 4,100,00 employees during this year went on strike, walked out, or were locked out, in a series of troubles that affected all major industries. Among them was the entertainment business, which had an actors' strike that at once shut down 12 legitimate shows and caused a precarious season for the managers.

Massachusetts Republican Governor Calvin Coolidge came into national prominence when he suppressed (Sept. 9) a strike of the Boston police. He wired Samuel Gompers, president of the American Federation of Labor: "There is no right to strike against the public safety by anybody, anywhere, anytime." (The next year Coolidge was nominated by 674¼ votes at the Republican convention as vice-presidential running mate to Warren G. Harding.)

Leftist elements of the Socialist Party formed the Communist Labor Party or the Communist Party of America. (They merged in 1920 to form the United Communist Party, renamed in 1921 the Workers' Party.)

Eight cigars per minute, or 4,000 per day, were turned out by the first cigar-making machine operated in Newark, N. J.

Henry Ford sued the "Chicago Tribune" for $1,000,000 libel, charging that the newspaper had in an editorial made him out to be an anarchist. The trial ran four months, resulted in several million words of testimony, and terminated when the jury, after nine ballots, awarded Ford six cents' damages and costs.

The Carnegie Corporation of New York presented an endowment of $5,000,000 to the National Academy of Sciences, Washington, D. C.

Aviation was prominent in newspaper headlines. Captain E. F. White made (Apr. 19) a nonstop flight from Chicago to New York. Three U. S. Navy seaplanes under Lieutenant Commander Albert C. Read attempted (May 16) the first transatlantic flight from Trepassy, Newfoundland, to the Azores. Only the N-C 4 of Read reached (May 17) its destination; the plane flew (May 27) to Lisbon, Portugal, and arrived (May 31) in Plymouth, England. Lieutenants W. B. Maynard and Alexander Pearson completed (Oct. 8-18) the first transcontinental round-trip flight from New York to San Francisco and back.

The gigolo and bobbed hair timidly made their social beginnings.

Skirts, now six inches off the ground, were a sensation. Women's hats were adorned with very large brims and fussy, fragile decorations.

Eamon de Valera, New York-born Irish Republican leader of Spanish descent, was proclaimed "President of the Irish Republic" by the illegal Sinn Fein ("We Ourselves") in Dublin. (He resigned in 1926 and became in 1938 premier of the Irish Free State, which adopted the name "Eire.")

Books of the year included: "The American Language" (Henry Mencken), "The Life of John Marshall" (Albert Jeremiah Beveridge; Pulitzer prize 1920), "Ten Days That Shook the World" (John Reed; an account of the Russian Revolution), "Twelve Men" (Theodore Dreiser), "The War with Mexico" (Justin H. Smith; Pulitzer prize 1920), and the fiction, "The Builders" (Ellen Glasgow), "Dr. Jonathan" (Winston Churchill), "Humoresque" (Fannie Hurst; short stories), "Jurgen" (James Branch Cabell), "Lad: A Dog" (Albert Payson Terhune; a story about a collie), "Linda Condon" (Joseph Hergesheimer), "The Sagebrusher" (Emerson Hough), "Winesburg, Ohio" (Sherwood Anderson; 23 short stories). No Pulitzer prize was awarded for this year's fiction.

Fire destroyed the New Orleans Opera House.

Respighi's symphonic poem "Fontane di Roma" (Fountains of Rome) received (Feb. 13) its American première by the New York Philharmonic Society.

Deems Taylor's suite of five musical pictures, "Through the Looking Glass," after Lewis Carroll, was played (Feb. 18) by the New York Chamber Music Society for the first time.

The Metropolitan Opera House, New York, produced (Mar. 12) two one-act American operas—"The Legend" by Joseph Carl Breil and "The Temple Dancer" by John Adam Hugo. The operas had three performances.

Summer open-air opera was attempted in New York; Verdi's "Aïda" was given (Aug. 16) at Sheepshead Bay Speedway.

The Washington Square Players, New York (1915), reorganized as The Theatre Guild and produced (Apr. 19) at the Garrick Theatre as their first play "The Bonds of Interest." (The Guild opened its own theatre in 1925.)

The Yiddish Art Theatre was founded in New York by the Russian-American actor Maurice Schwartz. The first production was Hershbein's play "An Abandoned Nook" at the Irving Place Theatre.

New York plays that ran more than 200 performances included: "Up in Mabel's Room" (Eltinge, Jan. 15), "Scandal" with Francine Larrimore (39th Street, Sept. 12; 318 perf.), "Adam and Eve" (Longacre, Sept. 13; 312 perf.), "Clarence" with Alfred Lunt (Hudson, Sept 20; 300 perf.), "The Gold Diggers" with Ina Claire (Lyceum, Sept. 30; 282 perf.), "The Storm" (48th Street, Oct. 2), "Déclassée" (Empire, Oct. 6), "His Honor, Abe Potash" (Bijou, Oct. 14), "The Son-Daughter" with Lenore Ulric (Belasco, Nov. 19), "My Lady Friends" (Comedy, Dec. 3). John and Lionel Barrymore played an English adaptation of Sem Benelli's "La Cena delle Beffe" as "The Jest" (Plymouth, Apr. 9; 77 perf.). John Drinkwater's "Abraham Lincoln" (Cort, Dec. 15) with Frank McGlynn ran 193 performances. Musical productions included: "The Velvet Lady" by Victor Herbert (New Amsterdam, Feb. 3), "Good Morning, Judge" (Schubert, Feb. 6), "Tumble In" (Selwyn, Mar. 24), "La, La Lucille" (Henry Miller, May 26), "Happy Days" (Hippodrome, Aug. 23; 425 perf.), "Apple Blossoms" by Fritz Kreisler and Victor Jacobi (Globe, Oct. 7; 256 perf.), "The Little Whopper" (Casino, Oct. 13), "Buddies" (Selwyn, Oct. 27; 259 perf.), "Irene" (Vanderbilt, Nov. 18; 670 perf.), "Monsieur Beaucaire" (New Amsterdam, Dec. 11). The Winter Garden show "Whirl of Society" (Mar. 5) provided Blossom Seeley an opportunity for 136 performances to run up and down the aisles of the theatre from the stage over a runway across the pit, which also afforded a closer —a very much closer—view of the chorus girls when they came forward. The first of George White's "Scandals" was staged (Liberty, June 2). Henri Fevrier's French opera "Aphrodite" (Century, Nov. 24; 148 perf.) was a spectacular perversion of the original with additional Broadway music. Elsie Janis and Her Gang (George M. Cohan Theatre, Dec. 1) played 55 performances "in a bombproof revue" of acts selected from the entertainments which she gave for the soldiers in France.

Motion-picture actors Mary Pickford and Douglas Fairbanks, Charles ("Charlie") Chaplin, and producer David Wark Griffith formed the United Artists Company. Griffith's film this year was "Broken Blossoms." Prominent movie actors and actresses were Lillian and Dorothy Gish, Elaine Hammerstein, Hope Hampton, Lila Lee, Tully Marshall, Alma Rubens, Pauline Stark. "The Miracle Man" made stars of Lon Chaney, Betty Compson, and Thomas Meighan.

Jack Dempsey, "the Manassa Mauler," became (July 4) the heavyweight boxing champion when title holder Jess Willard failed to answer the bell in the 4th round of their title bout at Toledo, O.

Charles Pores, long-distance runner and holder of the world's five-mile outdoor record (1918), won (June 1) at Great Lakes, Ill., the Amateur Athletic Union 15-mile foot race in 1 hour, 23 minutes, 45.3 seconds, setting a time for the distance which has not yet (1951) been equalled.

Deaths of the year included Theodore Roosevelt, aged 61 (Jan. 6), at Sagamore Hill, N. Y., and Andrew Carnegie, aged 82 (Aug. 11), in Lenox, Mass.

ॐ 1920

All She'd Say Was "Umh Hum" (Ziegfeld Follies of 1920). w., m., King Zany, MacEmery, Van, and Schenck. Harry Von Tilzer Music Pub. Co., cop. 1920.

Alt Wien. Piano solo. m., Leopold Godowsky. G. Schirmer, Inc., cop. 1920.

Avalon. w., m., Al Jolson and Vincent Rose. Jerome H. Remick & Co., cop. 1920.

Bright Eyes. w., Harry B. Smith. m., Otto Motzan and M. K. Jerome. Waterson, Berlin and Snyder Co., cop. 1920.

Broadway Rose. w., Eugene West. m., Martin Fried and Otis Spencer. Fred Fisher, Inc., cop. 1920.

Chili Bean. w., Lew Brown. m., Albert Von Tilzer. Broadway Music Corp., cop. 1920.

Daddy, You've Been a Mother to Me. w., m., Fred Fisher. McCarthy & Fisher, Inc., cop. 1920.

Deep in Your Eyes (The Half Moon). w., William Le Baron. m., Victor Jacobi. T. B. Harms & Francis, Day & Hunter, cop. 1920.

Feather Your Nest. w., m., James Kendis, James Brockman, and Howard Johnson. Leo Feist, Inc., cop. 1920.

Hiawatha's Melody of Love. w., Alfred Bryan and Artie Mehlinger. m., George W. Meyer. Jerome H. Remick & Co., cop. 1920.

Hold Me (Ziegfeld Follies of 1920). w., m., Art Hickman and Ben Black. Jerome H. Remick & Co., cop. 1920 by Sherman, Clay & Co., San Francisco; assigned to Jerome H. Remick & Co.

I Lost the Best Pal That I Had. w., m., Dick Thomas. Harry Von Tilzer Music Pub. Co., cop. 1920.

I Never Knew—I Could Love Anyone Like I'm Loving You. w., m., Tom Pitts, Ray Egan, and Roy Marsh. Leo Feist, cop. 1920.

I Used to Love You but It's All Over Now. w., Lew Brown. m., Albert Von Tilzer, Broadway Music Corp., cop. 1920.

I'll Be with You in Apple Blossom Time. w., Neville Fleeson. m., Albert Von Tilzer. Broadway Music Corp., cop. 1920.

The Japanese Sandman. w., Raymond B. Egan. m., Richard A. Whiting. Jerome H. Remick & Co., cop. 1920.

Jazz Babies' Ball (Shubert Gaieties of 1919). w., Charles Bayha. m., Maceo Pinkard. Shapiro, Bernstein & Co., Inc., cop. 1920.

Left All Alone Again Blues (The Night Boat). w., Anne Caldwell. m., Jerome Kern. T. B. Harms Co., cop. 1920.

The Lilac Tree—Perspicacity. w., m., George H. Gartlan. Hinds, Hayden & Eldredge, Inc., cop. 1920; assigned 1940 to Broadcast Music, Inc.; renewed 1948 by G. H. Gartlan; assigned to Witmark & Sons.

Look for the Silver Lining (Good Morning, Dearie; *afterwards introduced in:* Sally). w., Bud De Sylva. m., Jerome Kern. T. B. Harms Co., cop. 1920.

The Love Boat (Ziegfeld Follies of 1920). w., Gene Buck. m., Victor Herbert. T. B. Harms & Francis, Day & Hunter, cop. 1920.

The Love Nest (Mary). w., Otto Harbach. m., Louis A. Hirsch. Victoria Pub. Corp., cop. 1920.

Mah Lindy Lou. w., m., Lily Strickland. G. Schirmer, Inc., cop. 1920.

Margie. w., Benny Davis. m., Con Conrad and J. Russel Robinson. Waterson, Berlin & Snyder Co., cop. 1920.

Mary (Mary). w., Otto Harbach. m., Louis A. Hirsch. Victoria Pub. Corp., cop. 1920.

The Moon Shines on the Moonshine (Broadway Brevities). w., Francis DeWitt. m., Robert Hood Bowers. Shapiro, Bernstein & Co., cop. 1920.

My Home Town Is a One-Horse Town—but It's Big Enough for Me. w., Alex Gerber. m., Abner Silver. M. Witmark & Sons, cop. 1920.

My Mammy (Sinbad). w., Joe Young and Sam Lewis. m., Walter Donaldson. Irving Berlin, Inc., cop. 1920.

O Little Town of Bethlehem. [w., Phillips Brooks.] m., John Prindle Scott. Harold Flammer, Inc., cop. 1920.

Old Pal, Why Don't You Answer Me? w., Sam M. Lewis and Joe Young. m., M. K. Jerome. Waterson, Berlin & Snyder Co., cop. 1920.

Pale Moon. w., Jesse G. M. Glick. m., Frederick Knight Logan. Chicago: Forster Music Pub. Co., cop. 1920.

Palesteena. w., m., Con Conrad and J. Russel Robinson. Shapiro, Bernstein & Co., Inc., cop. 1920.

Pretty Kitty Kelly. w., Harry Pease. m., Ed. Nelson. A. J. Stasny Music Co., Inc., cop. 1920.

Rose of Washington Square (Ziegfeld Midnight Frolic). w., Ballard MacDonald. m., James F. Hanley. Shapiro, Bernstein & Co., Inc., cop. 1920.

San. w., m., Lindsay McPhail and Walter Michels. Van Alstyne & Curtis, cop. 1920.

So Long! oo-Long. w., m., Bert Kalmar and Harry Ruby. Waterson, Berlin & Snyder Co., cop. 1920.

Tell Me, Little Gypsy. w., m., Irving Berlin. Irving Berlin, Inc., cop. 1920.

That Naughty Waltz. w., Edwin Stanley. m., Sol P. Levy. Belwin, Inc., cop. 1919; cop. 1920 by Forster Music Publisher, Inc., Chicago.

That Old Irish Mother of Mine. w., William Jerome. m., Harry Von Tilzer. Harry Von Tilzer Music Pub. Co., cop. 1920.

Timbuctoo. w., m., Bert Kalmar and Harry Ruby. Waterson, Berlin & Snyder Co., cop. 1920.

Tripoli—On the Shores of Tripoli. w., Paul Cunningham and Al Dubin. m., Irving Weill. M. Witmark & Sons, cop. 1920.

La Veeda. w., Nat Vincent. m., John Alden. Maurice Richmond Co., cop. 1920.

When I'm Gone I Won't Forget. w., Ivan Reid. m., Peter DeRose. F. B. Haviland Pub. Co., Inc., cop. 1920.

When I'm Gone You'll Soon Forget. w., m., E. Austin Keith. F. B. Haviland Pub. Co., Inc., cop. 1911 by E. Austin Keith; assigned 1920 to F. B. Haviland Pub. Co., Inc.

When My Baby Smiles at Me. w., Andrew B. Sterling and Ted Lewis. m., Bill Munro. Harry Von Tilzer Music Co., cop. 1920.

Where Do They Go When They Row, Row, Row? w., Bert Kalmar and George Jessel. m., Harry Ruby. Waterson, Berlin & Snyder Co., cop. 1920.

Whispering. w., Malvin Schonberger. m., John Schonberger. San Francisco: Sherman, Clay & Co., cop. 1920.

Who Ate Napoleons with Josephine When Bonaparte Was Away? (As You Were). w., Alfred Bryan. m., E. Ray Goetz. Jerome H. Remick & Co., cop. 1920.

Whose Baby Are You? (The Night Boat). w., Anne Caldwell. m., Jerome Kern. T. B. Harms Co., cop. 1920.

Wild Rose (Sally). w., Clifford Grey. m., Jerome Kern. T. B. Harms Co., cop. 1920.

The Wooing of the Violin (Some Colonel). w., Robert B. Smith. m., Victor Herbert. T. B. Harms & Francis, Day & Hunter, cop. 1920.

The Wreck of the "Julie Plante." w., William Henry Drummond. m., Geoffrey O'Hara. Boston: Oliver Ditson Co., cop. 1920.

You Oughta See My Baby. w., Roy Turk. m., Fred E. Ahlert. Waterson, Berlin & Snyder Co., cop. 1920.

A Young Man's Fancy. w., John Murray Anderson and Jack Yellen. m., Milton Ager. Leo Feist, Inc., cop. 1920.

The United States went "dry" and began (Jan. 16) "the noble experiment" of national prohibition of liquor. Prohibition—the 18th Amendment, ratified by 46 States but not by Connecticut or Rhode Island—became effective with the Volstead Act, defined what constituted prohibited beverages.

Likewise the 19th Amendment—giving women the right to vote—became (Aug. 26) the law of the land after nearly 75 years of agitation.

Congress abolished (May 29) the Subtreasury (1836). Its functions were assumed by Federal Reserve Banks.

The government distributed (as of Jan. 16) about 4,265,000 bronze "Victory" medals to soldiers, sailors, nurses, and others who participated in military service during World War I.

The League of Nations held (Feb. 11) its first meeting, in London.

The telephone dial system was introduced.

Food prices by now were sky-high and the term "high cost of living" was on everyone's lips.

Following the wave of strikes, and various other post-war disturbances, the country developed a great "red scare" out of which the Ku Klux Klan, officially defunct since 1869, re-emerged for a time.

Transcontinental air mail service was established between New York and San Francisco.

The Panama Canal was officially opened (July 12). (It had been opened to traffic Aug. 15, 1914. The canal cost $366,650,000.)

The Arlington Memorial Amphitheatre, opposite Washington, D. C., was dedicated (May 15).

The Farmer-Labor political party was organized.

John Llewellyn Lewis was elected president of the United Mine Workers' Union.

A bomb explosion (Sept. 16) in Wall Street, New York, killed 30 persons, wounded 100, and caused a $2,000,000 property damage.

Four U. S. Army aviators, under Lieutenant Street, flew (July 15-Aug. 24) from New York to Nome, Alaska.

The radio compass was used (July 27) for the first time to direct the navigation of aircraft.

Radio was passing out of the hands of amateurs with their homemade sets into the control of commercial organizations and manufacturers. Lee De Forest installed (in Mar.) a transmitter on the roof of the California Theatre in San Francisco. The "Detroit News" began (Aug. 20) the operation of station WWJ. The Westinghouse Company launched in Pittsburgh its station KDKA, which reported (Nov. 2) to listeners the returns of the Harding-Cox presidential election, and opened (later in November) its station WJZ in Newark, N. J.

Mah-jongg, a Chinese game of 136 ivory tiles, and the ouija board were popular pastimes.

Books of the year included: "The Americanization of Edward Bok" (Edward William Bok; a biography; Pulitzer prize 1921), "Smoke and Steel" (Carl Sandburg; poems), "Steeplejack" (James Gibbons Huneker; an autobiography), "The Tiger in the House" (Carl Van Vechten; a book about cats), "The Victory at Sea" (William Sowden Sims and Burton J. Hendrick; a history; Pulitzer prize in 1921), and the fiction, "The Age of Innocence" (Edith Wharton; Pulitzer prize 1921), "Main Street" (Sinclair Lewis), "Miss Lulu Bett" (Zona Gale), "Moon-Calf" (Floyd Dell; sequel "The Briary-Bush," 1921), "Painted Veils" (James Gibbons Huneker), "Poor White" (Sherwood Anderson), "The Third Woman" (Anne Douglas Sedgwick), "This Side of Paradise" (Francis Scott Fitzgerald).

Enrico Caruso made (Dec. 24) the last appearance of his career in New York at the Metropolitan Opera House in Halévy's "La Juive." (He died in Naples, Italy, Aug. 2, 1921.)

Beniamino Gigli, Italian operatic tenor, made (Nov. 17) his American debut as Faust in Boito's "Mefistofele" at the Metropolitan Opera House in New York.

Albert Coates, English conductor, made (Dec. 30) his American debut in New York at Aeolian Hall with the New York Symphony Society giving the first American performance of Ralph Vaughan Williams's "A London Symphony." On the same day, Arturo Toscanini began at Carnegie Hall the American tour (1920-21) of his "La Scala," Milan, orchestra.

The New York Symphony Society under Walter Damrosch concertized in Europe, playing in France, the Low Countries, and England.

At the Auditorium, Chicago, Reginald DeKoven's opera "Rip van Winkle" was produced (Jan. 2; New York, Lexington Theatre, Jan. 30); at the Metropolitan Opera House, New York, Henry Kimball Hadley's "Cleopatra's Night" was performed (Jan. 31). A Bohemian opera, "V Studni," by Wilhelm Blodek, was sung (Mar. 6) in its native language at the Jan Huss Neighborhood House, New York.

Music lovers heard the first American performances of Elgar's "Enigma" Variations (Philadelphia Symphony, Feb. 13), Sibelius's symphonic poem "Finlandia" (Metropolitan Opera House orchestra, Dec. 24, conducted by Arturo Vigna), and Holst's symphony "The Planets" (Chicago Symphony, Dec. 31).

New York plays that ran 200 or more performances included: "Ladies' Night" (Eltinge, Aug. 9), "Enter Madame" (Garrick, Aug. 16; 350 perf.), "Spanish Love" (Maxine Elliott, Aug. 17; 308 perf.), "The Bat" (Morosco, Aug. 23; 867 perf.), "The Bad Man" (Comedy, Aug. 30; 342 perf.), "The Woman of Bronze" (Frazee, Sept. 7), "Little Old New York" (Plymouth, Sept. 8; 308 perf.), "Welcome Stranger" (Cohan and Harris, Sept. 13; 308 perf.), "The Tavern" with Arnold Daly (Cohan, Sept. 27), "Three Live Ghosts" (Greenwich Village Theatre, Sept. 29), "The Meanest Man in the World" (Hudson, Oct. 12), "The First Year" (Little Theatre, Oct. 20; 760 perf.), "The Emperor Jones" (Neighborhood Playhouse, Nov. 1), "Rollo's Wild Oat" (Punch and Judy, Nov. 23), "Miss Lulu Bett" (Belmont, Dec. 27; Pulitzer prize 1921). Eugene O'Neill's "Beyond the Horizon" (Morosco, Feb. 2; 111 perf.) was the Pulitzer prize play of 1920. Musical production included: "As You Were" (Central, Jan. 27), "The Night Boat" (Liberty, Feb. 2), "My Golden Girl" by Victor Herbert (Nora Bayes, Feb. 2), "Cinderella on Broadway" (Winter Garden, June 24), "Poor Little Ritz Girl" (Central, July 27), "Good Times" (Hippodrome, Aug. 9; 456 perf.), "Tickle Me" (Selwyn, Aug. 17), "Honeydew" (Casino, Sept. 6), "Mecca" (Century, Oct. 4), "Tip Top" (Globe, Oct. 5), "Mary" (Knickerbocker, Oct. 18), "Afgar" (Central, Nov. 8), "Lady Bill" (Liberty, Dec. 14), "Sally" (New Amsterdam, Dec. 21; 570 perf.).

The motion pictures presented Will Rogers in "Jes' Call Me Jim," Mary Pickford in "Pollyanna," Charlie Chaplin with the child star Jackie Coogan in "The Kid."

The world of sports, particularly baseball, was in an uproar when a Chicago grand jury brought indictments against eight members of the 1919 Chicago American League "White Sox" club, on the grounds that they had allegedly "thrown" the world series to the Cincinnati National League "Reds." Although the jury eventually voted acquittal, baseball put its house in order by appointing (1921) Judge Kenesaw Mountain Landis as "czar" or supreme arbiter.

New York State legalized (in Sept.) public prize fighting by the adoption of the Walker Law, sponsored by James J. Walker then Speaker of the State senate and later (1926) Mayor of New York City.

Tex Rickard, Alaskan gold prospector, became a promoter in the prize fighting business and rose to international prominence. (He staged his first fight at the old Madison Square Garden, New York, Sept. 1, 1920.)

Rogers Hornsby, second baseman of the St. Louis National League club ("Cardinals"), began his six-year reign as batting champion.

The Brooklyn and Boston National League baseball clubs battled (May 1) 26 innings at Boston in the longest major league game on record only to end in a tie score 1-1. The game occupied 3 hours, 50 minutes and was terminated on account of darkness. (A 26-inning minor league record was established in 1906—which see.)

The race horse "Man o' War" was clocked at 2 minutes, 14⅕ seconds at Belmont Park, New York, for a 1⅜-mile stretch. The great horse in this year won stakes totalling $166,140.

The United States complained of the twenty-third depression since 1790. It lasted two years and was severe.

The national population soared to 105,710,620.

࿋ 1921

Ain't We Got Fun? w., m., Richard A. Whiting. Jerome H. Remick & Co., cop. 1921.

The Answer. w., m., Robert Huntington Terry. G. Schirmer, Inc., cop. 1921.

April Showers (Bombo). w., Bud G. DeSylva. m., Louis Silvers. Sunshine Music Co., Inc. [Harms, Inc.], cop. 1921.

Bandana Days (Shuffle Along). w., m., Noble Sissle and Eubie Blake. M. Witmark & Sons, cop. 1921.

Coal-black Mammy. w., Laddie Cliff. m., Ivy St. Helier. Leo Feist, Inc., cop. 1921 by Francis, Day & Hunter, London.

Dapper Dan. w., Lew Brown. m., Albert Von Tilzer. Broadway Music Corp., cop. 1921.

Dear Old Southland. w., Henry Creamer. m., Turner Layton. Jack Mills, Inc., cop. 1921.

Eve Cost Adam Just One Bone. w., m., Charles Bayha. Skidmore Music Co., cop. 1921.

De Gospel Train. Negro spiritual arr. for voice and piano by H[enry] T[hacker] Burleigh. G. Ricordi & Co., Inc., cop. 1921.

Heav'n, Heav'n. Negro spiritual arr. for voice and piano by H[enry] T[hacker] Burleigh. G. Ricordi & Co., Inc., cop. 1921.

I Ain't Nobody's Darling. w., Elmer Hughes. m., Robert A. King. Skidmore Music Co., cop. 1921.

I'm Just Wild About Harry (Shuffle Along). w., m., Noble Sissle and Eubie Blake. M. Witmark & Sons, cop. 1921.

I'm Missin' Mammy's Kissin'—and I Know She's Missin' Mine. w., Sidney Clare. m., Lew Pollack. Waterson, Berlin & Snyder Co., cop. 1921.

I'm Nobody's Baby. w., m., Benny Davis, Milton Ager and Lester Santly. Leo Feist, Inc., cop. 1921.

I Found a Rose in the Devil's Garden. w., m., Fred Fisher and Willie Raskin. Fred Fisher, Inc., cop. 1921.

I Wonder if You Still Care for Me? w., Harry B. Smith and Francis Wheeler. m., Ted Snyder. Waterson, Berlin & Snyder Co., cop. 1921.

Ka-lu-a (Good Morning, Dearie). w., Anne Caldwell. m., Jerome Kern. T. B. Harms Co., cop. 1921.

Kitten on the Keys. Piano solo. m., Zez Confrey. Jack Mills, Inc., cop. 1921.

Learn to Smile (The O'Brien Girl). Otto Harbach. m., Louis A. Hirsch. Harms, Inc., cop. 1921.

Leave Me with a Smile. w., m., Charles Koehler and Earl Burtnett. Waterson, Berlin & Snyder Co., cop. 1921.

Little David, Play on Your Harp. Negro spiritual arr. for voice and piano by H[enry] T[hacker] Burleigh. G. Ricordi & Co., Inc., cop. 1921.

Love Will Find a Way (Shuffle Along). w., m., Noble Sissle and Eubie Blake. M. Witmark & Sons, cop. 1921.

Ma—He's Making Eyes at Me (The Midnight Rounders). w., Sidney Clare. m., Con Conrad. Fred Fisher, Inc., cop. 1921.

Ma Li'l Batteau (*in the cycle:* Bayou Songs). w., Michael de Longpré [pseud. of Lily Strickland]. m., Lily Strickland. J. Fisher & Bro., cop. 1921.

Make Believe. w., Benny Davis. m., Jack Shilkret. Waterson, Berlin & Snyder Co., cop. 1921 by Benny Davis Music Pub. Co.; assigned 1921 to Waterson, Berlin & Snyder Co.

Mandy 'n' Me. w., Bert Kalmar. m., Con Conrad and Otto Motzan. Shapiro, Bernstein & Co., Inc., cop. 1921.

My Man [Mon Homme] (Ziegfeld Follies of 1921). French words, Albert Willemetz and Jacques Charles. English words, Channing Pollock. m., Maurice Yvain. Leo Feist, Inc., cop. 1920 by Francis Salabert, Paris; American version cop. 1921 by Leo Feist, Inc.

My Sunny Tennessee (The Midnight Rounders). w., m., Bert Kalmar, Harry Ruby, and Herman Ruby. Waterson, Berlin & Snyder Co., cop. 1921.

Nichavo! w., Helene Jerome. m., Mana-Zucca, op. 66. Cincinnati: The John Church Co., cop. 1921.

Peggy O'Neil. w., m., Harry Pease, Ed. G. Nelson, and Gilbert Dodge. Leo Feist, Inc., cop. 1921.

Sally (Sally). w., Clifford Grey. m., Jerome Kern. T. B. Harms Co., cop. 1921.

Say It with Music (Music Box Revue). w., m., Irving Berlin. Irving Berlin, Inc., cop. 1921.

Second Hand Rose (Ziegfeld Follies of 1921). w., Grant Clarke. m., James F. Hanley. Shapiro, Bernstein & Co., cop. 1921.

She's Mine, All Mine! w., m., Bert Kalmar and Harry Ruby. Waterson, Berlin & Snyder Co., cop. 1921.

The Sheik of Araby (Make It Snappy). w., Harry B. Smith and Francis Wheeler. m., Ted Snyder. Waterson, Berlin & Snyder Co., cop. 1921.

Shuffle Along (Shuffle Along). w., m., Noble Sissle and Eubie Blake. M. Witmark & Sons, cop. 1921.

Some Day I'll Find You (Kiki). w., Schuyler Greene. m., Zoel Parenteau. Harms, Inc., cop. 1921.

Song of Love (Blossom Time). w., Dorothy Donnelly. m., Sigmund Romberg. Leo Feist, Inc., cop. 1921 by Karczag Pub. Co.

Steal Away. Negro spiritual arr. for voice and piano by H[enry] T[hacker] Burleigh. G. Ricordi & Co., Inc., cop. 1921.

Swanee River Moon. w., m., H. Pitman Clarke. Leo Feist, Inc., cop. 1921.

Sweet Lady (Tangerine). w., Howard Johnson. m., Frank Crumit and Dave Zoob. Leo Feist, Inc., cop. 1921.

Ten Little Fingers and Ten Little Toes—Down in Tennessee. w., Harry Pease and Johnny White. m., Ira Schuster and Ed. G. Nelson. Leo Feist, Inc., cop. 1921.

There's a Million Girlies Lonesome Tonight—and Still I'm All Alone. w., William Tracy, Alfred Jentes, and Murray Roth. m., James F. Hanley. Shapiro, Bernstein & Co., cop. 1921.

Tuck Me to Sleep in My Old 'Tucky Home. w., Sam H. Lewis and Joe Young. m., George W. Meyer. Irving Berlin, Inc., cop. 1921.

Wabash Blues. w., Dave Ringle. m., Fred Meinken. Leo Feist, Inc., cop. 1921.

The Wang, Wang Blues. w., m., Gus Mueller, "Buster" Johnson, and Henry Busse. Leo Feist, Inc., cop. 1921.

When Big Profundo Sang Low "C." w., Marion T. Bohannon. m., George Botsford. Jerome H. Remick & Co., cop. 1921.

When Buddha Smiles. w., Arthur Freed. m., Nacio Herb Brown. Harms Inc., cop. 1921.

When Francis Dances with Me. w., Benny Ryan. m., Violinsky. Leo Feist, Inc., cop. 1921.

When Shall We Meet Again. w., Raymond B. Egan. m., Richard A. Whiting. Jerome H. Remick & Co., cop. 1921.

When the Honeymoon Was Over. w., m., Fred Fisher. Fred Fisher, Inc., cop. 1921.

Whip-poor-will (Sally). w., Bud De Sylva. m., Jerome Kern. T. B. Harms Co., cop. 1921.

Yoo-hoo. w., B. G. De Sylva. Melody by Al Jolson. Richmond-Robbins, Inc., cop. 1921 by Maurice Richmond, Inc.

Warren Gamaliel Harding, Republican, of Ohio, was inaugurated 29th President. (He did not live to complete his term; he died Aug. 2, 1923, having served only two years and seven months.)

The United States officially ended World War I by concluding separate peace agreements with Germany and Austria-Hungary. (The treaty was passed by the House, June 30, and by the Senate, July 1, and signed by President Harding, July 2.)

The Tomb of the Unknown Soldier (World War I) in Arlington National Cemetery was dedicated on Armistice Day (Nov. 11) by President Harding, whose speech was broadcast to the nation by radio.

The tercentenary of the landing of the Pilgrims was celebrated with pageantry at Plymouth, Mass. The U. S. Post Office issued (Dec. 18) three commemorative postage stamps for the occasion.

For the centennial (1919) of Alabama's admission to the Union, a commemorative silver half-dollar was minted. It bore the busts of W. W. Bibb, first governor of the State, and T. E. Kilby, incumbent at the time of the celebration—the first instance of a living person's portrait on a United States coin. The piece was designed by Laura Gardin Fraser.

A trial (May-June) of two alleged murderers in Dedham, Mass., engaged widespread public attention. The proceedings developed opposing opinions and furnished the subject matter for Maxwell Anderson's plays "Gods of the Lightning" (1928) and "Winterset" (1935), Upton Sinclair's novel "Boston" (1928), poems, and documentary surveys by Felix Frankfurter (1927) the future United States Supreme Court judge, by Eugene Lyons (1927), and others. A paymaster and his guard who were carrying the payroll of a Massachusetts shoe company in two boxes were shot (Apr. 15) in Braintree, Mass., by two men. Nicola Sacco, 29, fish peddler, and Bartolomeo Vanzetti, 32, shoe factory employee, were arrested as perpetrators of the crime. Both men were found to be armed with concealed pistols and owned the automobile said by the police to have been connected with the commission of the murders. Vanzetti had a previous conviction for a holdup. A Sacco-Vanzetti Defense Committee raised $50,000 for the accused. The men were convicted and sentenced to death by Judge Webster Thayer. (There was a general public feeling that the conduct of the trial was unfair, the presiding judge prejudiced—he had previously convicted Vanzetti—and the evidence inadequate. Legal maneuvers to set aside the verdict failed. During the course of the case, a jailed murderer testified to the commission of the crime and exonerated Sacco and Vanzetti. At the request of prominent citizens, Massachusetts Governor Alvan T. Fuller appointed a committee of eminent persons to review the case. They concurred in the conviction of Sacco and Vanzetti, who were executed, Aug. 22, 1927, in Charlestown, Mass. In 1931 a bomb wrecked Judge Thayer's home at Worcester.)

The 18th Amendment—national prohibition of liquor—had been in force now one year and had inaugurated an era of bootlegging and gangsterism. Outside the three-mile limit along the Atlantic seaboard stretched a row of speedy boats with contraband liquor ready for smuggling. It came to be known as "Rum Row." Luxury liners also made brief excursions to sea to appease patrons' cravings.

The Limitation of Armaments Conference met (Nov. 11-Feb. 6, 1922) in Washington, D. C.

The collapse and explosion of the dirigible balloon ZR-2 over Hull, England, caused (Aug. 24) the death of 62 persons, of whom 17 were U. S. Naval representatives.

Former President William Howard Taft was appointed Chief Justice of the United States Supreme Court. (He resigned in 1930, on account of ill health and died Mar. 8 of that year.)

Denis Dougherty, Roman Catholic Archbishop of Philadelphia, was made (Mar. 7) cardinal by Pope Benedict XV—the fifth American to be so honored.

Maurice Maeterlinck, Belgian playwright and author, made the second of his two visits to the United States. (The first was in 1911.)

The Cleveland Clinic Foundation was established by Dr. George Washington Crile.

Atlantic City, N. J., held its first "Miss America" bathing beauty contest as part of a pageant organized by local hotelmen to promote business after Labor Day. As a result, the form-fitting one-piece bathing suit was adopted by feminine bathers.

The New Orleans Industrial Canal was completed.

Radio broadcasting stations had mushroomed so rapidly in America that conflicts of all sorts, technical, personal, and otherwise, arose among broadcasters and threatened to bring about a chaotic condition on the air. The United States Government, as far as it was able without congressional legislation in the matter, sought to regulate the affairs in the new industry and began (in September) the practice of licensing broadcasting stations.

The American Birth Control League was organized by Margaret Sanger, leader of the movement in the United States.

Plastic surgeons were advertising heavily in trade journals about the wonders they could work on actors' faces.

Books of the year included: "The American Novel" (Carl Van Doren), "Collected Poems" (Edwin Arlington Robinson; Pulitzer prize 1922), "A Daughter of the Middle Border" (Hamlin Garland; a biography; Pulitzer prize 1922), "The Founding of New England" (James Truslow Adams; Pulitzer prize 1922), and the fiction, "Alice Adams" (Booth Tarkington; Pulitzer prize 1922—his second award), "The Big Town" (Ring Lardner), "Eric Dorn" (Ben Hecht), "The Grey Room" (Eden Phillpotts) "Messer Marco Polo" (Brian Oswald Donn-Byrne), "The Old Soak" (Don Marquis), "Scaramouche" (Rafael Sabatini), "Three Soldiers" (John Dos Passos), "The Triumph of the Egg" (Sherwood Anderson).

The American Orchestral Society was founded in New York by Mrs. E. H. Harriman.

Maria Jeritza made (Nov. 19) her American debut in the United States première of Korngold's opera "Die tote Stadt" at the Metropolitan Opera House, New York.

New York plays that ran 175 or more performances included: "The Champion" (Longacre, Jan. 3), "The Green Goddess" with George Arliss (Booth, Jan 18), "Dulcy" with Lynn Fontanne (Frazee, Aug. 13), "Six-Cylinder Love" (Sam H. Harris, Aug. 25), "The Circle" with Mrs. Leslie Carter returning after an absence of seven years' retirement in France (Selwyn, Sept. 12; 175 perf.), "Thank You" (Longacre, Oct. 3), "The Demi-Virgin" with Hazel Dawn (Times Square, Oct. 18), "Anna Christie" by Eugene O'Neill (Vanderbilt, Nov. 2; Pulitzer prize 1922—his second award in three years), "Kiki" with Lenore Ulric (Belasco, Nov. 29; 600 perf.), "The Dover Road" (Bijou, Dec. 23), "Captain Applejack" (Cort, Dec. 30). Musical productions included: "Shuffle Along" (63rd Street Music Hall, May 23; 504 perf.), "Tangerine" with Julia Sanderson (Casino, Aug. 9; 337 perf.), "Blossom Time" with Bertram Peacock (Ambassador, Sept. 29; 592 perf.), "Bombo" with Al Jolson (Jolson's 59th Street Theatre, Oct. 6), "Good Morning, Dearie" (Globe, Nov. 1), "The Perfect Fool" with Ed Wynn (George M. Cohan, Nov. 7). John Charles Thomas and Fred Astaire appeared in the brief run of "The Love Letter" (Globe, Oct. 4).

Will Rogers, after two and a half years in motion pictures, went into vaudeville. He wisecracked that he was the only movie actor who so far had come out of Hollywood with the same wife.

Motion-picture patrons saw Mary Pickford in "Little Lord Fauntleroy," shuddered at the cubistic horrors of "The Cabinet of Dr. Calagari," enjoyed "Bunty Pulls the Strings," and went into raptures over a new romantic star—Rudolph Valentino in "The Sheik" and "The Four Horsemen of the Apocalypse." Other films were "Cappy Ricks," "Cup of Life," "East Lynne," "The Golem," "Heart of the North," "Jim the Penman," "Tol'able David" (Richard Barthelmess).

Following the Chicago disclosures in the "White Sox" baseball scandal of 1919, Judge Kenesaw Mountain Landis was appointed "czar" of baseball to formulate rules, regulate the conduct of players, and handle other questions pertaining to the game.

Newspaper ballyhoo helped to stimulate the first million-dollar gate in prize fighting when heavyweight champion Jack Dempsey fought (July 2) the French challenger Georges Carpentier at Boyle's Thirty Acres, Jersey City, N. J. The bout went 4 rounds before Dempsey kayoed the Frenchman. It was the first major prize fight to be broadcast by radio.

ᘖ᛫ 1922

Aggravatin' Papa. w., m., Roy Turk, J. Russel Robinson and Addy Britt. Waterson, Berlin & Snyder Co., cop. 1922.

Ain't It a Shame. w., m., W. A. Hann, Joseph Simms and Al W. Brown. M. Witmark & Sons, cop. 1922.

All Over Nothing at All. w., J. Keirn Brennan and Paul Cunningham. m., James Rule. M. Witmark & Sons, cop. 1922.

L'Amour-Toujours-L'Amour—Love Everlasting. w., Catherine Chisholm Cushing. m., Rudolf Friml. Harms, Inc., cop. 1922 by Harms-Friml Corp.

Angel Child. w., m., George Price, Abner Silver, and Benny Davis. M. Witmark & Sons, cop. 1922.

Baby Blue Eyes. w., m., Walter Hirsch, George Jessel, and Jesse Greer. Richmond-Robbins, Inc., cop. 1922.

A Brown Bird Singing. w., Royden Barrie. m., Haydn Wood. London: Chappell & Co., Ltd., cop. 1922.

Carolina in the Morning (Passing Show of 1922). w., Gus Kahn. m., Walter Donaldson. Jerome H. Remick & Co., cop. 1922.

"Chicago," That Toddling Town. w., m., Fred Fisher. Fred Fisher, Inc., cop. 1922.

China Boy. w., m., Dick Winfree and Phil Boutelje. Leo Feist, Inc., cop. 1922.

Couldn't Hear Nobody Pray. Negro spiritual arr. for voice and piano by Henry Thacker Burleigh. G. Ricordi & Co., Inc., cop. 1922.

Crinoline Days (Music Box Revue). w., m., Irving Berlin. Irving Berlin, Inc., cop. 1922.

Dancing Fool. w., Harry B. Smith and Francis Wheeler. m., Ted Snyder. Waterson, Berlin & Snyder Co., cop. 1922.

Dearest, You're the Nearest to My Heart. w., Benny Davis. m., Harry Akst. Irving Berlin, Inc., cop. 1922.

Do It Again. (The French Doll). w., B. G. De Sylva. m., George Gershwin. Harms Inc., cop. 1922.

Down the Winding Road of Dreams. w., Margaret Cantrell. m., Ernest R. Ball. M. Witmark & Sons, cop. 1922.

Dreamy Melody. w., m., Ted Koehler, Frank Magine, and C. Naset. Jerome H. Remick & Co., cop. 1922.

Georgette (Greenwich Village Follies). w., Lew Brown. m., Ray Henderson. Shapiro, Bernstein & Co., Inc., cop. 1922.

Georgia. w., Howard Johnson. m., Walter Donaldson. Leo Feist, Inc., cop. 1922.

Goin' Home. w., m., William Arms Fisher, adapted from the Largo of the symphony, "From the New World," by Anton Dvorák, op. 95. Boston: Oliver Ditson Co., cop. 1922.

Hot Lips. w., m., Henry Busse, Henry Lange, and Lou Davis. Leo Feist, Inc., cop. 1922.

I Gave You Up Just Before You Threw Me Down. w., m., Bert Kalmar, Harry Ruby, and Fred E. Ahlert. Waterson, Berlin & Snyder Co., cop. 1922.

I Wish I Could Shimmy Like My Sister Kate. w., m., A[rmand] J. Piron. Clarence Williams Music Pub. Co., cop. 1919 by A. J. Piron; assigned 1922 to Clarence Williams Music Pub. Co., Inc.

In the Little Red School-House. w., m., Al Wilson and James Brennan. Edw. B. Marks Pub. Co., cop. 1922.

A Kiss in the Dark (Orange Blossoms). w., Bud G. DeSylva. m., Victor Herbert. Harms, Inc., cop. 1922.

The Lady in Ermine (The Lady in Ermine). w., Cyrus Wood. m., Alfred Goodman. Harms, Inc., cop. 1922.

Lady of the Evening (Music Box Revue). w., m., Irving Berlin. Irving Berlin, Inc., cop. 1922.

The Little White Donkey—original French title: Le petit âne blanc (in: Histoires). Piano solo. m., Jacques Ibert. Paris: A. Leduc & Cie., cop. 1922.

Lovin' Sam, the Sheik of Alabam'. w., Jack Yellen. m., Milton Ager. Ager, Yellen & Bornstein, Inc., cop. 1922.

Mary, Dear. w., m., Harry DeCosta and M. K. Jerome. Waterson, Berlin & Snyder Co., cop. 1922.

Mister Gallagher and Mister Shean (Ziegfeld Follies of 1922). w., m., Ed. Gallagher and Al Shean. Jack Mills, Inc., cop. 1922 by Ed. Gallagher and Al Shean.

My Buddy. w., Gus Kahn. m., Walter Donaldson. Jerome H. Remick & Co., cop. 1922.

My Lover Is a Fisherman. w., m., Lily Strickland. Boston: Oliver Ditson Co., cop. 1922.

My Rambler Rose (Ziegfeld Follies of 1922). w., Gene Buck. m., Louis A. Hirsch and Dave Stamper. Harms, Inc., cop. 1922.

'Neath the South Sea Moon (Ziegfeld Follies of 1922). w., m., Gene Buck, Louis A. Hirsch, and Dave Stamper. Harms, Inc., cop. 1922.

Nellie Kelly, I Love You (Little Nellie Kelly). w., m., George M. Cohan. M. Witmark & Sons, cop. 1922.

[O-hi-o] Round on the End and High in the Middle O-hi-o. w., m., Alfred Bryan and Bert Hanlon. Jerome H. Remick & Co., cop. 1922.

On the Alamo. w., Gus Kahn. m., Isham Jones. Chicago: Foster Music Pub. Co., cop. 1922.

On the 'Gin, 'Gin, 'Ginny Shore. w., Edgar Leslie. m., Walter Donaldson. Shapiro, Bernstein & Co., Inc., cop. 1922.

Ooo Ernest—Are You Earnest with Me. w., Sidney Clare and Harry Tobias. m., Cliff Friend. Arr. by J. Dell Lampe. Jerome H. Remick & Co., cop. 1922.

Parade of the Wooden Soldiers (*introduced in:* La Chauve Souris)— *original German title:* Die Parade der Holzsoldaten. m., Leon Jessel, op. 123. Jos. W. Stern & Co., cop. 1911 by Heinrichshofen's Verlag, Magdeburg; assigned 1911 to Jos. W. Stern & Co.; assigned 1920 to Edward B. Marks Music; renewed 1932 by Leon Jessel; assigned 1933 to Edward B. Marks Music Corp. (Featured in Nikita Balieff's unique and colorful Russian revue, "La Chauve Souris," which opened a long run on Broadway in 1922. For some details, consult Edward B. Marks, "They all Sang," The Viking Press, New York, cop. 1934, p. 203.)

Rose of the Rio Grande. w., Edgar Leslie. m., Harry Warren and Ross Gorman. Stark & Cowan, cop. 1922.

Runnin' Wild! w., Joe Grey and Leo Wood. m., A. Harrington Gibbs. Leo Feist, Inc., cop. 1922.

Say It While Dancing. w., Benny Davis. m., Abner Silver. M. Witmark & Sons, cop. 1922.

Sister Kate. See above: "I Wish I Could Shimmy Like My Sister Kate!"

Sixty Seconds Every Minute, I Think of You (Greenwich Village Follies). w., Irving Caesar and John Murray Anderson. m., Louis A. Hirsch. Victoria Pub. Co., cop. 1922.

Somebody Stole My Gal. w., m., Leo Wood. Denton & Haskins Music Co., cop. 1918 by Meyer Cohen Music Pub. Co.; cop. 1922 by Denton & Haskins.

Some Sunny Day. w., m., Irving Berlin. Irving Berlin, Inc., cop. 1922.

Stumbling. w., m., Zez Confrey. Leo Feist, Inc., cop. 1922.

Three O'clock in the Morning. w., Dorothy Terris. m., Julian Robeldo. Leo Feist, Inc., cop. 1922 by West's, Ltd., London.

Throw Me a Kiss (Ziegfeld Follies of 1922). w., m., Louis A. Hirsch, Gene Buck, Dave Stamper, and Maurice Yvain. Harms, Inc., cop. 1922.

Toot, Toot, Tootsie! (Bombo). w., m., Gus Kahn, Ernie Erdman, and Dan Russo. Leo Feist, Inc., cop. 1922.

Trees. w., Joyce Kilmer. m., Oscar Rasbach. G. Schirmer, Inc., cop. 1922.

Water Boy. A Negro convict song. m., "arranged by Avery Robinson." London: Winthrop Rogers, Ltd., cop. 1922. (Actually an original composition by Avery Robinson.)

'Way Down Yonder in New Orleans. w., m., Henry Creamer and J. Turner Layton. Shapiro, Bernstein & Co., cop. 1922.

When Hearts Are Young (The Lady in Ermine). w., Cyrus Wood. m., Sigmund Romberg and Alfred Goodman. Harms, Inc., cop. 1922.

When the Leaves Come Tumbling Down. w., m., Richard Howard. Leo Feist, Inc., cop. 1922.

Who Cares (Bombo). w., Jack Yellen. m., Milton Ager. Ager, Yellen & Bornstein, Inc., cop. 1922.

Wonderful One. w., Dorothy Terris. m., Paul Whiteman and Ferde Grofe, adapted from a theme by Marshall Nielan. Leo Feist, Inc., cop. 1922.

You Remind Me of My Mother (Little Nellie Kelly). w., m., George M[ichael] Cohan. M. Witmark & Sons, cop. 1922.

You Tell Her, I S-t-u-t-t-e-r. w., m., Billy Rose and Cliff Friend. Irving Berlin, Inc., cop. 1922.

The United States, Great Britain, France, Italy, and Japan signed (Feb. 6) at the Washington Conference the Five-Power Treaty limiting naval armament (Great Britain 22 capital ships, the United States 18, France, Italy, and Japan 10 each).

The Lincoln Memorial, Potomac Park, Washington, D. C., costing $2,940,000, was dedicated (May 30).

Coal miners and sympathizers clashed (June 22-23) with non-union workers in Herrin, Ill., causing the death of 26 persons. Most of the slain were "scabs."

Lieutenant James H. Doolittle flew (Sept. 5-6) an airplane from Jacksonville, Fla., to San Diego, Cal., in 21 hours, 18 minutes, in two hops. At Hampton, Va., the dirigible balloon "Roma," built for the United States in Italy, exploded, with a loss of 34 lives. In San Antonio, Tex., the blimp C-2 blew up, but no one was killed.

Mrs. Rebecca L. Felton of Georgia became (Oct. 3) the first woman to be appointed to the U. S. Senate.

William Duane, Philadelphia-born physicist, was awarded the John Scott Medal and a gift of $800, and the Comstock Prize of $1,000 by the National Academy of Science for his researches in radioactivity.

Protestant Episcopal bishops voted to eliminate the word "obey" from the marriage ceremony.

An American, Howard Carter, was with Lord Carnarvon as assistant when the latter opened the tomb of King Tutankhamen (B.C. about 1358) of the XVIIIth dynasty in Egypt.

The construction of the Holland tunnel, connecting New York and Jersey City under the Hudson River, was begun (Oct. 26).

The roof of the Knickerbocker Theatre, a movie theatre, in Washington, D. C., collapsed (Jan. 28), killing 98 persons.

"Pike's Peak or Bust" was a new expression. It was the title of a book by Lewis Bennett Miller, published this year.

Frederick William MacMonnies's fountain statue "Civic Virtue" was unveiled (Apr. 21) in City Hall Park, New York, and thoroughly offended the citizenry, especially its womenfolk, for its alleged obscenity. The statue represented a nude, robust, club-carrying male (Virtue) standing with one foot on the neck of a prostrate female (Vice). (The monument was removed Oct. 7, 1941, to the lawn of Queens Borough Hall, L. I.)

Books of the year included: "American Songs and Ballads" (Louise Pound), "The Life and Letters of Walter H. Page" (Burton J. Hendrick; Pulitzer prize 1923), "The Supreme Court in United States History" (Charles Warren; Pulitzer prize 1923), "The Waste Land" (Thomas Stearns Eliot; poems) and the fiction, "Babbitt" (Sinclair Lewis), "The Beautiful and the Damned" (Francis Scott Fitzgerald), "Birthright" (Thomas Stribling), "The Covered Wagon" (Emerson Hough), "The Enormous Room" (Edward Estlin Cummings), "One of Ours" (Willa Cather; Pulitzer prize 1923), "Peter Whiffle" (Carl Van Vechten), "Vandemark's Folly" (Herbert Quick; sequels, "Hawkeye," 1923, and "The Invisible Woman," 1924), "Where the Blue Begins" (Christopher Morley).

Radio station KGU, Honolulu, Hawaii, was opened (May 11). In New York, the American Telephone and Telegraph Company established (in July) its radio station WEAF and radio turned commercial when the station broadcast the first etherized advertisement—a program sponsored by a real estate firm, the Queensborough Corporation. At the same time, the A.T. & T. utilized its telephone facilities to broadcast programs and reports of events from places of origin outside its studios. Among the earliest such long-distance relays was the football game played by the universities of Chicago and Princeton at Chicago, the description of the game being telephoned from the scene of the contest to New York, nearly 1,000 miles away, and broadcast. In a similar manner, the program of the Bond Club of Chicago was conveyed to twenty stations forming a circuit that extended via New York to Havana, Cuba, and San Francisco, Cal. A feature of the broadcast was that twelve stations of the circuit contributed parts to the program.

The International Composers' Guild was organized in New York for the performance of "modern" music in smaller forms. (Disbanded in 1927.)

A season of Russian opera entertained New York at the New Amsterdam Theatre with performances of "Russalka" (May 8), "The Czar's Bride" (May 9), "The Demon" (May 13), and "Christmas Eve" (May 26)—all new to New York.

The New York stage produced (Fulton Theatre, May 23) a play which not only exceeded the run of 1,291 performances of "Lightnin' " (1918) but established a new record with 2,532 performances—"Abie's Irish Rose," a comedy by Anne Nichols of Jewish and Irish life on New York's East Side. Other plays that ran 175 or more performances included: "Lawful Larceny" (Republic, Jan. 2), "The Cat and the Canary" (National, Feb. 7), "Whispering Wires" (48th Street, Aug. 7; 352 perf.), "The Old Soak" (Plymouth, Aug. 22; 423 perf.), "So This Is London" (Hudson, Aug. 30), "Loyalties" (Gaiety, Sept. 27), "The Fool" (Times Square, Oct. 23), "The Last Warning" (Klaw, Oct. 24), "Seventh Heaven" (Booth, Oct. 30; 704 perf.), "Rain" (Maxine Elliott, Nov. 7; 648 perf.), "Merton of the Movies" (Cort, Nov. 13). Other plays were George Bernard Shaw's philosophical fantasy "Back to Methuselah" (Garrick, Feb. 28, Mar. 6 and 22, in three sections), Eugene O'Neill's "The Hairy Ape" (Provincetown, Mar. 9), Čapek's melodrama "R.U.R." (Garrick, Oct. 9), Pirandello's "Six Characters in Search of an Author" (Princess, Oct. 30), Claudel's mystery "The Tidings Brought to Mary" (Garrick, Dec. 25). David Warfield played Shylock in "The Merchant of Venice" (Lyceum, Dec. 21; 92 perf.) and Fritz Lieber appeared in "Macbeth," "Julius Caesar," and "Romeo and Juliet." Musical productions included: "The Blue Kitten" (Selwyn, Jan. 13), "The Blushing Bride" (Astor, Feb. 6), "The Gingham Girl" (Earl Carroll, Aug. 28; 422 perf.), "Better Times" (Hippodrome, Sept. 2; 409 perf.), "Sally, Irene and Mary" (Casino, Sept. 4; 312 perf.), "The Lady in Ermine" (Ambassador, Oct. 2), "Music Box Revue" (Music Box, Oct. 23), "Up She Goes" (Playhouse, Nov. 6), "Little Nellie Kelly" (Liberty, Nov. 13). Nikita Balieff brought his "Chauve Souris" revue of Russian folksongs, dances, and burlesque skits to New York (49th Street Theatre, Feb. 4) from London and Paris; the show went through many "editions," amusing audiences who enjoyed its fun and artistry in spite of a language handicap for 520 performances over the years.

In consequence of a sensational series of manslaughter trials involving Roscoe C. ("Fatty") Arbuckle, the Motion Picture Producers and Distributors of America, Inc., was organized (in Mar.) in New York, with branches in Hollywood, Washington, D. C., and Paris. Its president was Will H. Hayes, former Postmaster General of the United States under President Harding, and its purpose was to improve and regulate standards of production. (The name of the group was changed in 1945 to the Motion Picture Association of America, Inc.)

Motion pictures (still silent) included: "Blood and Sand" (Rudolph Valentino, Lila Lee, Nita Naldi), "Grandma's Boy" (Harold Lloyd, Mildred Davis), "Nanook of the North," "Oliver Twist" (Jackie Coogan), "Orphans of the Storm" (Lillian and Dorothy Gish; produced by David Wark Griffith), "Prisoner of Zenda," "Robin Hood" (Douglas Fairbanks), "Smilin' Through" (Norma Talmadge), "When Knighthood Was in Flower" (Marion Davies).

George Herman ("Babe") Ruth, who began his baseball career as a pitcher and was bought in 1919 from the Boston American League ("Red Sox") club by the New York American League ("Yankees") club for a reputed price of $125,000, became an outfielder for his club, and displayed such phenomenal hitting ability that he soon was called "Sultan of Swat."

Alexander Graham Bell, aged 75, inventor of the telephone, died (Aug. 2) on his estate near Boddeck, Nova Scotia.

ৡ৸ 1923

Annabelle. w., Lew Brown. m., Ray Henderson. Shapiro, Bernstein & Co., Inc., cop. 1923.

Bambalina (The Wildflower). w., Otto Harbach and Oscar Hammerstein, 2nd. m., Vincent Youmans and Herbert Stothart. Harms, Inc., cop. 1923.

Barney Google. w., m., Billy Rose and Con Conrad. Jerome H. Remick & Co., cop. 1923.

Beside a Babbling Brook. w., Gus Kahn. m., Walter Donaldson. Jerome H. Remick & Co., cop. 1923.

Bugle Call Rag. Instrumental. m., Jack Pettis, Billy Meyers, and Elmer Schoebel. Mills Music, Inc., cop. 1923.

The Builder. w., James W. Foley. m., Charles Wakefield Cadman, op. 78, no. 1. Harold Flammer, Inc., cop. 1923.

Charleston (Runnin' Wild). w., m., Cecil Mack and Jimmy Johnson. Harms, Inc., cop. 1923.

Come On, Spark Plug! w., m., Billy Rose and Con Conrad. Waterson, Berlin & Snyder Co., cop. 1923.

Covered Wagon Days (film: The Covered Wagon). w., m., Will Morrissey and Joe Burrows. Waterson, Berlin & Snyder Co., cop. 1923.

Dizzy-Fingers. Piano solo. m., Zez Confrey. Jack Mills, Inc., cop. 1923.

Estrellita. See below: "Little Star."

First Last and Always. w., Benny Davis. m., Harry Akst. Jerome H. Remick & Co., cop. 1923.

I'm Goin' South (Bombo; and Kid Boots). w., m., Abner Silver and Harry Woods. M. Witmark & Sons, cop. 1923.

I Cried for You. w., m., Arthur Freed, Gus Arnheim and Abe Lyman. Miller Music, Inc., cop. 1923.

I Love Life. w., Irwin M. Cassel. m., Mana-Zucca, op. 83. Cincinnati: The John Church Co., cop. 1923.

I Love You (Little Jessie James). w., Harlan Thompson. m., Harry Archer. Leo Feist, Inc., cop. 1923.

I Won't Say I Will but I Won't Say I Won't (Little Miss Bluebeard). w., Buddy G. De Sylva and Arthur Francis. m., George Gershwin. Harms, Inc., cop. 1923.

Indiana Moon. w., Benny Davis. m., Isham Jones. Irving Berlin, Inc., cop. 1923.

It Ain't Gonna Rain No Mo'. w., m., Wendell Hall. Chicago: Forster Music Publisher, Inc., cop. 1923 by Wendell Hall; assigned 1923 to Forster Music Publisher, Inc.

Last Night On the Back Porch—I Loved Her Best of All. w., m., Lew Brown and Carl Schraubstader. Skidmore Music Co., cop. 1923.

Little Star—Estrellita. m., Manuel M. Ponce. Arranged and translated by Frank LaForge. G. Ricordi & Co., Inc., cop. 1923. (First published and copyright 1914 by Friedrich Hofmeister, Leipzig; assigned 1929 to Associated Music Publishers, Inc., owners of the copyright.)

Louisville Lou, the Vampin' Lady. w., Jack Yellen. m., Milton Ager, Yellen & Bornstein, Inc., cop. 1923.

Mexicali Rose. w., Helen Stone. m., Jack B. Tenny. Chicago: W. A. Quincke, cop. 1923; assigned 1935 to M. M. Cole Pub. Co., Chicago.

My Little Nest of Heavenly Blue—Hab' ein Blaues Himmelbett [Frasquita Serenade] (Frasquita). Original German words, Dr. A. M. Willner and Heinz Reichert; English words, Sigmund Spaeth. m., Franz Lehár. Edw. B. Marks Music Co., cop. 1922 by Joseph Weinberger; assigned 1923 to Edw. B. Marks Music Co.

No, No, Nora. w., Gus Kahn. m., Ted Fiorito, and Ernie Erdman. Leo Feist, Inc., cop. 1923.

Oh! Didn't It Rain. w., m., Eddie Leonard. Edward B. Marks Music Co., cop. 1923.

√ **Oh! Gee, Oh! Gosh, Oh! Golly, I'm in Love.** w., Olson and Johnson. m., Ernest Breuer. Waterson, Berlin & Snyder Co., cop. 1923.

On the Mall. March. m., Edwin Franko Goldman. Carl Fischer, Inc., cop. 1923.

Out There in the Sunshine with You. w., J. Keirn Brennan. m., Ernest R. Ball. M. Witmark & Sons, cop. 1923.

Raggedy Ann (The Stepping Stones). w., Anne Caldwell. m., Jerome Kern. T. B. Harms Co., cop. 1923.

Rememb'ring (Topsy and Eva). w., m., Duncan Sisters. Irving Berlin, Inc., cop. 1923.

La Rosita. w., Allan Stuart. m., Paul Dupont. Cleveland: Sam Fox Pub. Co., cop. 1923.

Serenade—Rimpianto. Italian words, Alfred Silvestri; English translation, Sigmund Spaeth. m., Enrico Toselli. Boston: The Boston Music Co., cop. 1923.

Seven or Eleven—My Dixie Pair o' Dice. w., Lew Brown. m., Walter Donaldson. Shapiro, Bernstein & Co., Inc., cop. 1923.

She Wouldn't Do—What I Asked Her To. Words revised by Sidney D. Mitchell. m., Sam Gottlieb, Philip Boutelje, and Al Burt. Richmond-Robbins, Inc., cop. 1923.

Sittin' In a Corner. w., Gus Kahn. m., George W. Meyer. Irving Berlin, Inc, cop. 1923.

Sleep. w., m., Earl Lebieg. San Francisco: Sherman, Clay & Co., cop. 1923.

A Smile Will Go a Long, Long Way. w., m., Benny Davis and Harry Akst. Waterson, Berlin & Snyder Co., cop. 1923.

Some Sweet Day (Ziegfeld Follies of 1922). w., Gene Buck. m., Dave Stamper and Louis A. Hirsch. Harms, Inc., cop. 1923.

Stella. w., m., Al Jolson, Benny Davis, and Harry Akst. Waterson, Berlin & Snyder Co., cop. 1923.

Sugar Blues. w., Lucy Fletcher. m., Clarence Williams. Clarence Williams Music Pub. Co., Inc., cop. 1923.

Swingin' Down the Lane. w., Gus Kahn. m., Isham Jones. Leo Feist, Inc., cop. 1923.

Ten Thousand Years from Now. w., J. Keirn Brennan. m., Ernest R. Ball. M. Witmark & Sons, cop. 1923.

That Old Gang of Mine. w., Billy Rose and Mort Dixon. m., Ray Henderson. Irving Berlin, Inc., cop. 1923.

Thumb Marks. w., from "Ballads of Immorality." m., John Barnes Wells. Boston: The Boston Music Co., cop. 1923.

Two Little Magpies. w., anon. m., John Barnes Wells. Boston: The Boston Music Co., cop. 1923.

Westward Ho!—The Covered Wagon March. w., R. A. Barnet. m., Hugo Riesenfeld. Jerome H. Remick & Co., cop. 1923.

When It's Night-time in Italy, It's Wednesday Over Here. w., m., James Kendis and Lew Brown. Shapiro, Bernstein & Co., Inc., cop. 1923.

When You Walked Out Someone Else Walked Right In. w., m., Irving Berlin. Irving Berlin, Inc., cop. 1923.

Who's Sorry Now? w., Bert Kalmar and Harry Ruby. m., Ted Snyder. Waterson, Berlin & Snyder Co., 1923.

Who'll Buy My Violets?—*original Spanish title:* **La Violetera** (*introduced in:* Little Miss Bluebeard). English words by E. Ray Goetz. m., José Padilla. Harms, Inc., cop. 1923.

Wild Flower (The Wildflower). w., Otto Harbach and Oscar Hammerstein, 2nd. m., Vincent Youmans and Herbert Stothart. Harms, Inc., cop. 1923.

Yes! We Have No Bananas. w., m., Frank Silver and Irving Cohn. Shapiro, Bernstein & Co., cop. 1923 by Skidmore Music Co.

You've Got to See Mamma Ev'ry Night—or You Can't See Mamma at All. w., m., Billy Rose and Con Conrad. Leo Feist, Inc., cop. 1923.

President Harding visited Alaska late in June. On his return he became seriously ill and died (Aug. 2) in San Francisco. Vice-President Calvin Coolidge, Republican, of Vermont, was sworn into office the next day as 30th President at his home in Plymouth, Vt., by his father, a justice of the peace, and again (Aug. 17) before Justice A. A. Hoehling of the Supreme Court of the District of Columbia.

The U. S. Post Office issued (Sept. 1) a two-cent black commemorative postage stamp bearing the portrait of the late President as a tribute to his memory.

Congress passed (Mar. 14) the Agricultural Credits Act creating the Federal Intermediate Credit Bank (12 regional banks to loan money to farmers).

As a result of national liquor prohibition, some 5,000 speakeasies—a new word—operated in New York City alone. Champagne was $25 a quart, and Scotch of questionable merit went for $20 a quart. Bathtub gin and needle beer sold for whatever the market would bear in any particular community.

"Day by day in every way I'm getting better and better" was on the tip of everybody's tongue. The rage was initiated by Emile Coué who claimed that his system of "auto-suggestion" would cure mental and physical ailments.

Seven United States destroyers, the "Chauncey," "Delphy," "Fuller," "S. P. Lee," "Nicholas," "Woodbury," and "Young," went aground (Sept. 3) in a fog off Honda Point, Cal.; 22 lives were lost.

Dr. Frederick Albert Cook, who claimed to have discovered the North Pole before Admiral Robert Edwin Peary (1909), was convicted of a mail fraud in Texas, fined $12,000 and costs, and sentenced to 14 years, 9 months in a Federal prison. (He was released on parole in 1930, discharged from parole in 1935, and pardoned and restored to civil rights by President Franklin Delano Roosevelt in 1940.)

Robert Andrews Millikan, president of the California Institute of Technology, was awarded the Nobel prize for physics—the first American to be so honored in that field.

Lieutenants Kelly and Macready made (May 2-3) the first nonstop transcontinental airplane flight from New York to San Diego, Cal., 2,516 miles, in 26 hours, 50 minutes. Lieutenant Al Williams set (Nov. 4) an American speed record by flying 266 miles in an hour.

Fire destroyed (May 17) the Cleveland Rural Graded School, Camden, S. C. Seventy-six persons, including 41 children, were burned or crushed to death.

Trinity College, Durham, N. C., chartered in 1841, was renamed Duke

University after its benefactor James Buchanan Duke, tobacco manufacturer.

The Charleston, a new, fast fox-trot introduced by Cecil Mack and
Jimmy Johnston in a Negro revue, captured the fancy of ballroom dancers.

Radio station KDKA, Pittsburgh, Pa., successfully sent (Dec. 31) a
"short-wave" program to England. (A similar program was sent to England Feb. 5, 1924, and rebroadcast there.)

Women now preferred the cape-line hat—a wide-brimmed affair curving
down on either side of the face.

"Time" was founded in New York as a weekly news magazine.

Books of the year included: "Damaged Souls" (Gamaliel Bradford;
studies of famous Americans), "From Immigrant to Inventor" (Michael
Pupin; an autobiography; Pulitzer prize 1924), "New Hampshire" (Robert
Frost; poems; Pulitzer prize 1924), "The Story of the Bible" (Hendrik
Willem van Loon), and the fiction, "The Able McLaughlins" (Margaret
Wilson; Pulitzer prize 1924), "Black Oxen" (Gertrude Atherton), "The
Hi-Jackers" (Robert Chambers), "Impromptu" (Elliot Paul), "A Lost
Lady" (Willa Cather), "Streets of Night" (John Dos Passos).

Gustav Holst, eminent English composer, toured the United States as a
lecturer and conductor of his own works.

Siegfried Wagner, conductor and composer, son of the great Richard
Wagner, visited (1923-24) the United States to raise funds for the reopen-
ing of the famous Festspielhaus at Bayreuth, Bavaria, which was closed in
consequence of World War I.

The League of Composers was organized in New York for the performance of "modern" music.

Eleanora Duse made her last visit to America, and the 64-year-old
Italian actress broke every box office record in existence. She opened
(Nov. 29) her farewell with a gala performance at the Metropolitan Opera
House, New York, and, because of the opera season, continued at the
Century Theatre for nine appearances. At each performance the capacity
audience rose and cheered in ovation. (She was seized with an acute chill
on her way to Pittsburgh and died there April 21, 1924.)

New York plays that ran 175 or more performances included: "Little
Miss Bluebeard" (Lyceum, Aug. 28), "Tarnish" (Belmont, Oct. 1), "The
Nervous Wreck" (Sam H. Harris, Oct. 9), "For All of Us" (49th Street,
Oct. 15), "The Shame Woman" (Greenwich Village, Oct. 16), "The
Swan" (Cort, Oct. 23), "Cyrano de Bergerac" with Walter Hampden
(National, Nov. 1), "White Cargo" (Greenwich Village, Nov. 5; 686
perf.), "Spring Cleaning" (Eltinge, Nov. 9), "Meet the Wife" (Klaw,
Nov. 26), "The Potters" (Plymouth, Dec. 8), "Saint Joan" by George
Bernard Shaw (Garrick, Dec. 28). The Moscow Art Theatre visited New
York (59th Street Theatre, Jan.-Feb.) and gave 96 performances in Rus-
sian of plays by Tolstoy, Tchekov, Turgeniev, Gorky, and Dostoievsky.
The Company toured as far west as Chicago. Their visit inspired produc-

tions in English of Andreyeff's "Anathema" (48th Street Theatre, Apr. 10) and Gogol's "The Inspector General" (Apr. 30). "Icebound" (Sam H. Harris Theatre, Feb. 10) won the Pulitzer prize in 1924. Twenty Little Theatre groups in and around New York held their first tournament (Bayes Theatre, week of May 7) for three $100 prizes and a David Belasco trophy. The Grand Guignol players of Paris came to New York (Frolic Theatre, Oct. 15) and were joined by Alla Nazimova after the Keith Vaudeville circuit banned her sketch "The Unknown." Musical productions included: "Wildflower" (Casino, Feb. 7), "Go-Go" (Daly's, Mar. 12), "Helen of Troy, New York" (Selwyn, June 19), "Little Jessie James" (Longacre, Aug. 15), "Artists and Models" (Shubert, Aug. 20), "Poppy" (Apollo, Sept. 3), "Music Box Revue" (Music Box, Sept. 22), "Battling Butler" (Selwyn, Oct. 8), "Ziegfeld Follies" (New Amsterdam, Oct. 20; 333 perf.), "Runnin' Wild" (Colonial, Oct. 29), "Stepping Stones" (Globe, Nov. 6), "Kid Boots" (Earl Carroll, Dec. 31).

Night clubs were evolving out of the old-style cabarets.

In vaudeville theatres, patrons now saw as part of the program an organ console rising out of the orchestra pit on which Jesse Crawford, or some local contemporary, played a solo.

Motion pictures (still silent) included: "The Covered Wagon" (Lois Wilson, Ernest Torrence, J. Warren Kerrigan), "Down to the Sea in Ships," "The Green Goddess" (George Arliss), "The Hunchback of Notre Dame" (Lon Chaney), "Little Old New York" (Marion Davies), "The Merry-Go-Round," "Rosita" (Mary Pickford), "Safety Last" (Harold Lloyd, Mildred Davis), "Scaramouche," "The Ten Commandments."

Mrs. F. I. Mallory lost the National Women's Tennis championship to Helen Wills, who retained it through 1929 with the exception of one year—1926.

Robert T. Jones, Jr., won the National Open golf championship (and again in 1926, 1929, and 1930).

Charles Proteus Steinmetz, aged 58, famed experimenter in electricity and electrical apparatus, died (Oct. 26) in Schenectady, N. Y.

ह~ 1924

All Alone (Music Box Revue). w., m., Irving Berlin. Irving Berlin, Inc., cop. 1924.

Amapola—Pretty Little Poppy. Spanish and English words and music, Joseph M. Lacalle. J. M. Lacalle, cop. 1924; assigned 1933 to Edward B. Marks Music Corp.; cop. 1940, with new English words by Albert Gamse, by Edward B. Marks Music Corp.

Bagdad. w., Jack Yellen. m., Milton Ager. Ager, Yellen & Bornstein, Inc., cop. 1924.

California, Here I Come (Bombo). w., m., Al Jolson, Bud De Sylva, and Joseph Meyer. M. Witmark & Sons, cop. 1924.

Charley, My Boy. w., m., Gus Kahn and Ted Fiorito. Irving Berlin, Inc., cop. 1924.

Copenhagen. Fox-trot. m., Charlie Davis. Chicago: Melrose Bros. Music Co., cop. 1924.

Deep in My Heart, Dear (The Student Prince). w., Dorothy Donnelly. m., Sigmund Romberg. Harms, Inc., cop. 1924.

Does the Spearmint Lose Its Flavor on the Bedpost Over Night? w., Billy Rose and Marty Bloom. m., Ernest Breuer. Waterson, Berlin & Snyder Co., cop. 1924; assigned 1932 to Mills Music, Inc.

Drinking Song (The Student Prince). w., Dorothy Donnelly. m., Sigmund Romberg. Harms, Inc., cop. 1924.

Everybody Loves My Baby, but My Baby Don't Love Nobody but Me. w., m., Jack Palmer and Spencer Williams. Clarence Williams Music Co., Inc., cop. 1924.

Fascinating Rhythm (Lady, Be Good!). w., Ira Gershwin, m., George Gershwin. Harms, Inc., cop. 1924.

Follow the Swallow. w., Billy Rose and Mort Dixon. m., Ray Henderson. Jerome H. Remick & Co., cop. 1924.

Hinky Dinky Parlay Voo. w., m., Al Dubin, Irving Mills, Jimmy McHugh, and Irwin Dash. Jack Mills, Inc., cop. 1924.

How Come You Do Me Like You Do? w., m., Gene Austin and Roy Bergere. Stark & Cowan, Inc., cop. 1924.

I Want to Be Happy (No, No, Nanette). w., Irving Caesar. m., Vincent Youmans. Harms, Inc., cop. 1924.

I'll See You in My Dreams. w., Gus Kahn. m., Isham Jones. Leo Feist, Inc., cop. 1924.

I Wonder What's Become of Sally? w., Jack Yellen. m., Milton Ager. Ager, Yellen & Bornstein, Inc., cop. 1924.

I Wonder Who's Dancing with You Tonight. w., Mort Dixon and Billy Rose. m., Ray Henderson. Jerome H. Remick & Co., cop. 1924.

In Shadowland. w., Sam M. Lewis and Joe Young. m., Ruth Brooks and Fred E. Ahlert. Henry Waterson, Inc., cop. 1924.

In the Garden of Tomorrow. w., George Graff, Jr. m., Jessie L. Deppen. London: Chappell & Co., Ltd., cop. 1924.

Indian Love Call (Rose Marie). w., Otto Harbach and Oscar Hammerstein, 2nd. m., Rudolf Friml. Harms, Inc., cop. 1924.

A Japanese Sunset. w., Archie Bell. m., Jessie L. Deppen. Cleveland: Sam Fox Pub. Co., cop. 1924.

Jealous. w., Tommie Malie and Dick Finch. m., Jack Little. Henry Waterson, Inc., cop. 1924.

June Brought the Roses. w., Ralph Stanley. m., John Openshaw. Harms, Inc., cop. 1924.

June Night. w., Cliff Friend. m., Abel Baer. Leo Feist, Inc., cop. 1924.

Keep Smiling at Trouble (Big Boy). w., Al Jolson and B. G. De Sylva. m., Lewis Gensler. Harms, Inc., cop. 1924.

King Porter Stomp. m., Ferd[inand] "Jelly Roll" Morton. Melrose Bros., cop. 1924.

Let Me Linger Longer in Your Arms. w., Cliff Friend. m., Abel Baer. Leo Feist, Inc., cop. 1924.

Limehouse Blues (Charlot's Revue of 1924). w., Douglas Furber. m., Philip Braham. Harms, Inc., cop. 1922 by Ascherberg, Hopwood & Crew, Ltd., London.

The Man I Love (Strike Up the Band; *originally in:* **Lady, Be Good!).** w., Ira Gershwin. m., George Gershwin. Harms, Inc., cop. 1924.

Mandalay. w., m., Earl Burtnett, Abe Lyman, and Gus Arnheim. Jerome H. Remick & Co., cop. 1924.

Memory Lane. w., Buddy G. De Sylva. m., Larry Spier and Con Conrad. Harms, Inc., cop. 1924.

My Best Girl. w., m., Walter Donaldson. Jerome H. Remick & Co., cop. 1924.

My Dream Girl (The Dream Girl). w., Rida Johnson Young. m., Victor Herbert. Harms, Inc., cop. 1924.

O, Katharina! (Chauve Souris). w., L. Wolfe Gilbert. m., Richard Fall. Leo Feist, Inc., cop. 1924 by Wiener Boheme Verlag, Vienna.

Oh, Miss Hannah! w., Thekla Hollingsworth. m.,. Jessie L. Deppen. Harms, Inc., cop. 1924.

The Prisoner's Song. w., m., Guy Massey. Shapiro, Bernstein & Co., Inc., cop. 1924.

Put Away a Little Ray of Golden Sunshine for a Rainy Day. w., Sam M. Lewis and Joe Young. m., Fred E. Ahlert. Henry Waterson, Inc., cop. 1924.

Ritual Fire Dance—*original Spanish title:* **Danza Ritual del Fuego (El Amor Brujo).** Orch. composition. m., Manuel De Falla. London: J. & W. Chester, Ltd. [cop. 1924.]

Rose Marie (Rose Marie). w., Otto Harbach and Oscar Hammerstein, 2nd. m., Rudolf Friml. Harms, Inc., cop. 1924.

Serenade (The Student Prince). w., Dorothy Donnelly. m., Sigmund Romberg. Harms, Inc., cop. 1924.

S-h-i-n-e. w., Cecil Mack and Lew Brown. m., Ford Dabney. Shapiro, Bernstein & Co., cop. 1924.

Somebody Loves Me (George White's Scandals). w., Ballard MacDonald and B. G. De Sylva. m., George Gershwin. Harms, Inc., cop. 1924.

Sometime You'll Wish Me Back Again. w., m., E. Austin Keith. F. B. Haviland Pub. Co., Inc., cop. 1924.

Spain. w., Gus Kahn. m., Isham Jones. Chicago: Milton Weil Music Co., cop. 1924.

Tea for Two (No, No, Nanette). w., Irving Caesar. m., Vincent Youmans. Harms, Inc., cop. 1924.

West of the Great Divide. w., George Whiting. m., Ernest R. Ball. M. Witmark & Sons, cop. 1924.

What'll I Do (Music Box Revue). w., m., Irving Berlin. Irving Berlin, Inc., cop. 1924.

When You and I Were Seventeen. w., Gus Kahn. m., Charles Rosoff. Irving Berlin, Inc., cop. 1924.

Where the Lazy Daisies Grow. w., m., Cliff Friend. Jerome H. Remick & Co., cop. 1924.

Congress passed the Soldiers' Bonus Bill over President Coolidge's veto.

A Congressional investigating committee uncovered questionable practices in the granting and obtaining of leases at the Elks Hills, Cal., and the Teapot Dome, Wyo. (1913) government oil reserves. The disclosures created a national scandal and involved Secretary of the Navy Edwin Denby, Secretary of the Interior Albert Bacon Fall, Attorney-General Harry M. Daugherty, Edward Doheny of the Doheny Oil Company, and Harry F. Sinclair of the Mammoth Oil Company. Denby, Fall, and Daugherty resigned under the pressure of public opinion. (Fall was sentenced in 1929 to a $100,000 fine and a prison term of one year.)

The Dawes Reparation plan, drafted by General Charles Gates Dawes, Vice-President of the United States and chairman of the Reparation Committee, to stabilize German currency and insure the payment. of 2,500 million marks (about $595,000,000) by Germany to the Allies as reparation for World War I (1914-18), was accepted (Aug. 16) by both sides. Owen D. Young was appointed Agent General of Reparation Payments.

J. Edgar Hoover became head of the Federal Bureau of Investigation ("F.B.I.") (1908).

In Chicago, the disappearance (May 22) of 13-year-old Robert ("Bobby") Franks led to kidnaping and murder charges against N. F. Leopold, Jr., and Richard Loeb, both 19, who pleaded (July 19) guilty at their trial. The noted Clarence Darrow, their attorney, saved them from the gallows and the sentence was life imprisonment plus 99 years. (Loeb was killed in 1936 by a fellow convict.)

Pope Pius XI elevated (Mar. 24) two American Roman Catholic Archbishops to the cardinalate—Patrick Joseph Hayes of New York and George William Mundelein of Chicago.

The Bear Mountain and the Castleton bridges, N. Y., spanning the Hudson River, were completed.

Four U. S. Army transport airplanes set out on a round-the-world flight from Seattle, Wash., travelling westward. Two completed the journey, a distance of 27,553 miles, in 371 hours, 11minutes' flying time (14 days, 15 hours) over a period of 175 days (Apr. 6-Sept. 28). Lieutenant Russell Maughan carried out (June 23) a transcontinental "dawn-to-dusk" flight from New York to San Francisco. A successful aeronautical experiment was conducted (Oct. 3) over Dayton, O., where an airplane was launched from a dirigible and continued on its course under its own power. Hugo Eckner's Zeppelin R-3 flew (Oct. 12-15) from Friedrichshafen, Germany, to Lakehurst, N. J., where the U. S. Navy took it over under the name "Los Angeles." The dirigible covered the distance of 5,066 miles in 81 hours, 17 minutes.

Mine disasters took the lives of 171 miners at Castle Gate, Utah, and of 119 at Benwood, W. Va.

The crossword puzzle appeared and took the nation by storm. Recognizing the crossword puzzle's popular dimensions, the Baltimore & Ohio Railroad put dictionaries in its mainline trains.

New York's municipal radio station WNYC went (July 8) on the air.

Twenty-seven radio stations combined (Nov. 3) in a coast-to-coast network to broadcast a speech by President Coolidge.

"The American Mercury" was founded in New York as a monthly magazine "to attempt a realistic presentation of the whole gaudy, gorgeous American scene."

"The Daily Worker" appeared as a continuation of the New York weekly "The Worker."

Books of the year included: "Autobiography" (Mark Twain; published 14 years after his death), "Black Cameos" (R. Emmet Kennedy), "The Man Who Died Twice" (Edwin Arlington Robinson; a narrative poem, Pulitzer prize 1925), "Seven Lively Arts" (Gilbert Seldes), "A Story Teller's Story" (Sherwood Anderson), and the fiction, "The Avalanche" (Ernest Poole), "Cowboys, North and South" (Will James), "The Green Bay Tree" (Louis Bromfield), "Hopalong Cassidy Returns" (Clarence Mulford), "In Our Time" (Ernest Hemingway), "The Little French Doll" (Anne Douglas Sedgwick), "Mother of Gold" (Emerson Hough), "Old New York" (Edith Wharton), "So Big" (Edna Ferber; Pulitzer prize 1925), "Waste" (Robert Herrick).

Sergei Koussevitzky, Russian double bass virtuoso and conductor, was appointed musical director of the Boston Symphony Orchestra.

Ernest Schelling, American pianist, conductor, and composer, inaugurated (1924-25) the unique children's concerts of the New York Philharmonic Society.

Paul Whiteman, conductor of "symphonic jazz," invaded the field of serious music by giving (Feb. 12) a concert of his type of music in

Aeolian Hall, New York. At this concert he performed for the first time George Gershwin's "Rhapsody in Blue," with the composer playing the piano part. Later in the year Whiteman took his orchestra on a tour of Europe.

Ernest Carter's opera "The White Bird" received (Mar. 6) its world première in Chicago at the Studebaker Theatre. (A reading rehearsal with orchestra was given in New York at the Carnegie Chamber Music Hall, May 23, 1922. The opera was performed in Osnabrück, Germany, Stadttheater, Nov. 15, 1927; in New York, Hudson Theatre, Feb. 7, 1937; in Riverside, Cal., Mar. 2, 1939.)

Firmin Gemier, noted French actor, and a company from the Théâtre National de l'Odéon, Paris, played repertory in New York (Jolson Theatre, No. 10; 24 performances).

New York plays that ran 175 or more performances included: "The Show-Off" (Playhouse, Feb. 5; 571 perf.), "Dancing Mothers" (Booth, Aug. 11; 312 perf.), "Pigs" (Little, Sept. 1; 312 perf.), "What Price Glory?" (Plymouth, Sept. 3; 299 perf.), "My Son" (Princess, Sept. 17), "The Guardsman" (Garrick, Oct. 13), "The Firebrand" (Morosco, Oct. 15), "Desire under the Elms" (Greenwich Village, Nov. 11), "Silence" (National, Nov. 12), "They Knew What They Wanted" (Garrick, Nov. 24; Pulitzer prize 1925), "The Harem" (Belasco, Dec. 2), "Old English" (Ritz, Dec. 23). "Hell-Bent fer Heaven" (Klaw, Jan. 4; 122 perf.) by Hatcher Hughes won the 1924 Pulitzer prize. Musical productions included: "Ziegfeld Follies" (New Amsterdam, June 24; 401 perf.), "Rose Marie" (Imperial, Sept. 2; 557 perf.), "The Grab Bag" with Ed Wynn (Globe, Oct. 6), "Artists and Models" (Astor, Oct. 15), "My Girl" (Vanderbilt, Nov. 24), "Music Box Revue" (Music Box, Dec. 1), "Lady, Be Good" (Liberty, Dec. 1), "The Student Prince" (Jolson, Dec. 2; 608 perf.), "Topsy and Eva," a jazz version of "Uncle Tom's Cabin" (Sam H. Harris, Dec. 23).

Motion pictures (still silent) included: "Abraham Lincoln" (George Billings, Louise Fazenda), "America" (Carol Dempster, Lionel Barrymore), "Beau Brummel" (John Barrymore), "Girl Shy" (Harold Lloyd), "Monsieur Beaucaire" (Rudolph Valentino), "The Sea Hawk" (Milton Sills, Enid Bennett, Wallace Beery), "Secrets" (Norma Talmadge), "The Thief of Bagdad" (Douglas Fairbanks). The handsome German shepherd dog Rin-Tin-Tin was appearing in pictures.

Sports continued to occupy national attention. Bobby Jones now annexed the National Amateur golf championship, and repeated the feat in 1925, 1927, 1928, and 1929. Babe Ruth of the New York "Yankees" topped all American League baseball batting averages of the year with .378. At Notre Dame University the "Four Horsemen" made their alma mater and their coach, Knute Rockne, the giants of football.

A new Progressive Party was organized by the forceful Wisconsin Senator Robert Marion LaFollette, who ran as its presidential candidate in the fall elections. He polled 4,822,319 votes. His opponents were

President Coolidge, Republican, and John W. Davis, Democrat. The nation, however, re-elected President Coolidge by a landslide of 15,718,789 votes. Radio announcers, political commentators, and analysts noisily kept the people informed of the election trend.

In the State elections of the year (Nov. 9), women were elected for the first time in American history to the gubernatorial office: they were Nellie Tayloe Ross of Wyoming and Miriam ("Ma") Ferguson of Texas.

A short-lived, but sharp, depression was the 24th since 1790.

৯৶ 1925

Alabamy Bound. w., Bud De Sylva and Bud Green. m., Ray Henderson. Shapiro, Bernstein & Co., cop. 1925.

Always. w., m., Irving Berlin. Irving Berlin, Inc., cop. 1925.

Bam, Bam, Bamy Shore. w., Mort Dixon. m., Ray Henderson. Jerome H. Remick & Co., cop. 1925.

Brown Eyes—Why Are You Blue? w., Alfred Bryan. m., George W. Meyer. Henry Waterson, Inc., cop. 1925.

Bye and Bye (Dearest Enemy). w., Lorenz Hart. m., Richard Rodgers. Harms, Inc., cop. 1925.

Cecilia—_full title:_ **Does Your Mother Know You're Out, Cecilia?** w., Herman Ruby. m., Dave Dreyer. A B C Music Corp., cop. 1925.

Collegiate. w., m., Moe Jaffe and Nat Bonx. Shapiro, Bernstein & Co., Inc., cop. 1925.

A Cup of Coffee, a Sandwich and You (Charlot's Revue of 1926). w., Billy Rose and Al Dubin. m., Joseph Meyer. Harms, Inc., cop. 1925.

Dinah. w., Sam M. Lewis and Joe Young. m., Harry Akst. Henry Waterson, Inc., cop. 1925.

Do I Love You (Naughty Cinderella). w., E. Ray Goetz. m., H. Christine and E. Ray Goetz. Francis Salabert, Inc., cop. 1923 by Francis Salabert; cop. 1925 by Francis Salabert, Inc.

Don't Bring Lulu. w., Billy Rose and Lew Brown. m., Ray Henderson. Jerome H. Remick & Co., cop. 1925.

Don't Wake Me Up. w., L. Wolfe Gilbert. m., Mabel Wayne and Abel Baer. Leo Feist, Inc., cop. 1925.

Down by the Winegar Woiks. w., m., Don Bestor, Roger Lewis, and Walter Donovan. Shapiro, Bernstein & Co., Inc., cop. 1925.

Drifting and Dreaming. w., Haven Gillespie. m., Egbert Van Alstyne, Erwin R. Schmidt and Loyal Curtis. L. B. Curtis, cop. 1925.

D'Ye Love Me (Sunny). w., Otto Harbach and Oscar Hammerstein, 2nd. Jerome Kern. T. B. Harms Co., cop. 1925.

Five Foot Two, Eyes of Blue. w., Sam M. Lewis and Joe Young. m., Ray Henderson. Leo Feist, Inc., cop. 1925.

Freshie. w., Jesse Greer and Harold Berg. m., Jesse Greer. Robbins-Engel, Inc., cop. 1925.

Headin' for Louisville. w., Bud G. De Sylva. m., Joseph Meyer. Shapiro, Bernstein & Co., cop. 1925.

Here in My Arms (Dearest Enemy). w., Lorenz Hart. m., Richard Rodgers. Harms, Inc., cop. 1925.

The Hills of Home. w., Floride Calhoun. m., Oscar J. Fox. Carl Fischer, Inc., cop. 1925.

I'm Gonna Charleston Back to Charleston. w., m., Roy Turk and Lou Handman. Jerome H. Remick & Co., cop. 1925.

I'm Sitting on Top of the World. w., Sam M. Lewis and Joe Young. m., Ray Henderson. Leo Feist, Inc., cop. 1925.

I Love My Baby—My Baby Loves Me. w., Bud Green. m., Harry Warren. Shapiro, Bernstein & Co., Inc., cop. 1925.

I Miss My Swiss (Chauve Souris). w., L. Wolfe Gilbert. m., Abel Baer. Leo Feist, Inc., cop. 1925.

I Never Knew That Roses Grew. w., Gus Kahn. m., Ted Fiorito. Irving Berlin, Inc., cop. 1925.

If I Had a Girl Like You. w., m., Billy Rose, Mort Dixon, and Ray Henderson. Jerome H. Remick & Co., cop. 1925.

If You Knew Susie—Like I Know Susie. w., m., Bud G. De Sylva. Shapiro, Bernstein & Co., cop. 1925.

If You Were the Only Girl (*afterward introduced in film:* The Vagabond Lover, 1929). w., Clifford Grey. m., Nat D. Ayer. Chappell-Harms, Inc., cop. 1925 by B. Feldman & Co., London.

In the Luxembourg Gardens. w., m., Kathleen Lockhart Manning. G. Schirmer, Inc., cop. 1925.

In the Middle of the Night. w., Billy Rose. m., Walter Donaldson. Irving Berlin, Inc., cop. 1925.

Isn't She the Sweetest Thing. w., Gus Kahn. m., Walter Donaldson. Jerome H. Remick & Co., cop. 1925.

Just a Cottage Small—By a Waterfall. w., Bud G. DeSylva. m., James F. Hanley. Harms, Inc., cop. 1925.

Keep Your Skirts Down, Mary Ann. w., Andrew B. Sterling. m., Robert A. King and Ray Henderson. Shapiro, Bernstein & Co., Inc., cop. 1925.

Let It Rain! Let It Pour!—I'll Be in Virginia in the Morning. w., Cliff Friend. m., Walter Donaldson. Leo Feist, Inc., cop. 1925.

Looking for a Boy (Tip-Toes). w., Ira Gershwin. m., George Gershwin. Harms, Inc. cop. 1925.

Manhattan (Garrick Gaieties). w., Lorenz Hart. m., Richard Rodgers. Edward B. Marks Music Co., cop. 1925.

Milenberg Joys. Fox-trot. m., Leon Rappolo, Paul Mares, and "Jelly Roll" Morton. Chicago: Melrose Bros. Music Co., Inc., cop. 1925.

Moonlight and Roses. w., m., Edwin H. Lemare, Ben Black, and Neil Moret. San Francisco: Villa Moret, Inc., cop. 1925.

My Sweetie Turned Me Down. w., Gus Kahn. m., Walter Donaldson. Irving Berlin, Inc., cop. 1925.

Neapolitan Nights. w., Harry D. Kerr. m., J. S. Zamecnik. Cleveland: Sam Fox Pub. Co., cop. 1925.

Oh! Boy, What a Girl (Gay Paree). w., Bud Green. m., Wright and Bessinger. Shapiro, Bernstein & Co., Inc., cop. 1925.

Only a Rose (The Vagabond King). w., Brian Hooker. m., Rudolf Friml. Henry Waterson, Inc., cop. 1925.

Remember. w., m., Irving Berlin. Irving Berlin, Inc., cop. 1925.

Rhapsody in Blue. Orch. composition. m., George Gershwin. Harms, Inc., cop. 1925.

Riverboat Shuffle. m., Hoagy Carmichael. Mills Music, Inc., cop. 1925; new edition, words by Dick Voynow, Irving Mills, and Mitchell Parish, cop. 1939.

Save Your Sorrow—for To-morrow. w., Bud G. De Sylva. m., Al Sherman. Shapiro, Bernstein & Co., Inc., cop. 1925.

Sentimental Me (Garrick Gaieties). w., Lorenz Hart. m., Richard Rodgers. Edward B. Marks Music Co., cop. 1925.

Show Me the Way to Go Home. w., m., Irving King. Harms, Inc., cop. 1925 by Campbell Connelly & Co.

Sleepy Time Gal. w., Joseph R. Alden and Raymond B. Egan. m., Ange Lorenzo and Richard A. Whiting. Leo Feist, Inc., cop. 1925.

Some Day (The Vagabond King). w., Brian Hooker. m., Rudolf Friml. Henry Waterson, Inc., cop. 1925.

Sometime. w., Gus Kahn. m., Ted Fiorito. Jerome H. Remick & Co., cop. 1925.

Song of the Flame (Song of the Flame). w., Otto Harbach and Oscar Hammerstein, 2nd. m., George Gershwin and Herbert Stothart. Harms, Inc., cop. 1925.

Song of the Vagabonds (The Vagabond King). w., Brian Hooker. m., Rudolf Friml. Henry Waterson, Inc., cop. 1925.

Sunny (Sunny). w., Otto Harbach and Oscar Hammerstein, 2nd. m., Jerome Kern. T. B. Harms Co., cop. 1925.

Sweet and Low-Down (Tip-Toes). w., Ira Gershwin. m., George Gershwin. Harms, Inc., cop. 1925.

Sweet Georgia Brown. w., m., Ben Bernie, Maceo Pinkard, and Kenneth Casey. Jerome H. Remick & Co., cop. 1925.

That Certain Feeling (Tip-Toes). w., Ira Gershwin. m., George Gershwin. Harms, Inc., cop. 1925.

That Certain Party. w., Gus Kahn. m., Walter Donaldson. Irving Berlin, Inc., cop. 1925.

Then I'll Be Happy. w., Sidney Clare and Lew Brown. m., Cliff Friend. Irving Berlin, Inc., cop. 1925.

Two Guitars. Orch. composition. m., arranged by Harry Horlick. Carl Fischer, Inc., cop. 1925.

Ukulele Lady. w., Gus Kahn. m., Richard A. Whiting. Irving Berlin, Inc., cop. 1925.

Waltz Huguette (The Vagabond King). w., Brian Hooker. m., Rudolf Friml. Henry Waterson, Inc., cop. 1925.

Waters of Perkiomen. w., Al Dubin. m., F. Henri Klickmann. Jack Mills, Inc., cop. 1925.

Who (Sunny). w., Otto Harbach and Oscar Hammerstein, 2nd. m., Jerome Kern. T. B. Harms Co., cop. 1925.

Who Takes Care of the Caretaker's Daughter While the Caretaker's Busy Taking Care? w., m., Chick Endor. Shapiro, Bernstein & Co., Inc., cop. 1925.

Why Do I Love You (My Fair Lady). w., Bud G. De Sylva and Ira Gershwin. m., George Gershwin. Harms, Inc., cop. 1925.

Yearning—Just for You. w., m., Benny Davis and Joe Burke. Irving Berlin, Inc., cop. 1925.

Yes Sir, That's My Baby. w., Gus Kahn. m., Walter Donaldson. Irving Berlin, Inc., cop. 1925.

President Calvin Coolidge began his second term.

Nellie Tayloe Ross was installed (Jan. 5) as Governor of Wyoming— the first woman to hold such an office. Miriam ("Ma") Ferguson, who was elected Governor of Texas in the previous year's election, was installed fifteen days later (Jan. 20).

The United States, along with Belgium, China, France, Great Britain, Holland, Italy, Japan, and Portugal, ratified (Aug. 5) the two Nine-

Power treaties of the Limitation of Armaments Conference. The pacts were signed at the Washington Conference (Feb. 6, 1922), and the signing nations agreed to respect China's sovereignty, territorial integrity, and equality in commerce.

The United States annexed Swain's Island in the Samoan group as a naval base.

United States Marines were withdrawn from Nicaragua. (They returned there in 1927.)

The government Bureau of Engraving and Printing brought delight this year to philatelists with new issues of postage stamps. Congress passed (Feb. 28) the Postal Service Act raising the rates of postage. To meet the increase, the Post Office issued a 1½-cent and a ½-cent stamp (Mar. 19 and Apr. 4, respectively), a 25-cent "special handling" stamp (Apr. 11) for fourth-class mail matter, two 15- and 20-cent "special delivery" stamps (Apr. 11 and 25), and a ½-cent "postage-due" stamp (Apr. 13). Events in American history were also commemorated with adhesives— the 150th anniversary of the Battle of Lexington and Concord, with three stamps (Apr. 4) and the 100th anniversary of the arrival Oct. 9, 1825, of the sloop "Restaurationen," which transported the first group of Norwegian immigrants to the United States, with two stamps (May 18). Lastly, a black 17-cent ordinary postage stamp bearing the portrait of former President Woodrow Wilson, completed (Dec. 28) the year's new issues.

Commander J. Rogers, U. S. N., accomplished (Aug. 31) a nonstop flight in a seaplane from San Francisco to Honolulu, Hawaii.

A severe thunderstorm over Ava, O., tore (Sept. 3, 5 A.M.) to pieces the U. S. N. dirigible "Shenandoah" which was on its way from Lakehurst, N. J., to St. Paul, Minn. Lieutenant Commander Zachary Lansdowne and 13 members of the crew lost their lives in the destruction.

The trial of a high school teacher in Dayton, Tenn., attracted so much attention that part of it had to be held outdoors. The point at issue was the teaching of the theory of evolution in contradiction of the church doctrine of fundamentalism. The case provoked much discussion among people throughout the country and much ridicule in certain sections of the press. The liberal Clarence Darrow was counsel for the defendent John Thomas Scopes; the fundamentalist William Jennings Bryan represented the prosecution. Scopes was found guilty (July 24) and fined $100 and costs.

The National Headquarters Building of the American Legion was dedicated (in June) in Indianapolis, Ind.

Vice-President Charles Gates Dawes was awarded the Nobel prize for peace.

The annual Guggenheim Fellowships were established by the John Simon Guggenheim Memorial Foundation, New York, to foster creative talent and research in various fields.

A violent storm swept (Mar. 18) through Missouri, southern Illinois, and Indiana, causing the death of more than 830 persons.

An earthquake partly destroyed (June 29) Santa Barbara, Cal.

Florida was enjoying a land boom that sent real estate prices skyrocketing. Coral Gables and Miami now were important places.

In Washington, D. C., the last fire engine drawn by a span of three horses made its final appearance.

Women's skirts flapped around their knees, disclosing legs encased in flesh-colored silk stockings. Hats were close-fitting.

The police dog now was a household pet; one, Rin-Tin-Tin, was in the movies.

The Louisville, Ky., newspaper "Courier-Journal" organized the first National Spelling Bee.

Telephotography was introduced by the American Telephone and Telegraph Company.

The latest development in radio sets for the home was the all-electric mechanism that eliminated cabinets full of batteries or the earlier crystal sets equipped with earphones.

Radio station WEAF, New York, began weekly broadcasts of standard operas. The operas were sung in their original languages by experienced singers and performed by a medium-size orchestra under the direction of Cesare Sodero. The broadcasts continued regularly for a number of years.

The New York radio station WJZ broadcast (Sept. 7) a stage performance of the opera "Aïda" by the Boston Civic Opera Company from the Manhattan Opera House, New York.

"The New Yorker" was founded in New York as a humorous weekly magazine for "caviar sophisticates."

Books of the year included: "History of the United States" (Edward Channing; Pulitzer prize 1926), "The Life of Sir William Osler" (Dr. Harvey Cushing; Pulitzer prize 1926), "Seventy Years of Life and Labor" (Samuel Gompers; a biography); the poetry, "Roan Stallion" (Robinson Jeffers; a pantheistic allegory), "What's O'Clock?" (Amy Lowell; Pulitzer prize 1926), and the fiction, "An American Tragedy" (Theodore Dreiser), "Arrowsmith" (Sinclair Lewis; Pulitzer prize 1926, but declined by the author), "Barren Ground" (Ellen Glasgow), "Dark Laughter" (Sherwood Anderson), "Drums" (James Boyd), "Gentlemen Prefer Blondes" (Anita Loos), "The Great Gatsby" (Francis Scott Fitzgerald), "The Making of Americans" (Gertrude Stein), "Manhattan Transfer" (John Dos Passos), "Porgy" (DuBose Heyward), "The Professor's House" (Willa Cather), "Pluck and Luck" (Robert Benchley), "Thunder on the Left" (Christopher Morley).

Elizabeth Sprague Coolidge (Mrs. Frederick Shurtleff Coolidge) established the Elizabeth Sprague Coolidge Foundation of the Library of Congress, Washington, D. C., for the cultivation of music.

Igor Stravinsky, Russian "modernist" composer, toured in the United

States as pianist and conductor. He played (Jan. 23) the world première of his Concerto for Piano and Wind Instruments with the Boston Symphony Orchestra.

Wilhelm Furtwängler, great German conductor, directed (1925-26) the New York Philharmonic-Symphony Orchestra.

Open-air performances of opera were given in the baseball park Ebbets Field, Brooklyn, New York. The operas given were "Aïda" (Aug. 1), "Cavalleria Rusticana" and "Pagliacci" (Aug. 5), and "Faust" (Aug. 8). The performances were broadcast by the municipal radio station WNYC.

New York heard (Sept. 27) a Greek opera, "Perouze" by Theodore Sakellarides, at Terrace Garden. The opera had a single performance.

New York plays that ran 200 or more performances included: "Is Zat So?" (39th Street, Jan. 5; 618 perf.), "Cradle Snatchers" (Music Box, Sept. 7; 478 perf.), "The Jazz Singer" (Fulton, Sept. 14; 303 perf.), "The Green Hat" (Broadhurst, Sept. 15), "The Butter and Egg Man" (Longacre, Sept. 23), "Craig's Wife" (Morosco, Oct. 12; 360 perf.; Pulitzer prize 1926), "The Enemy" (Times Square, Oct. 20), "Young Woodley" (Belmont, Nov. 2), "Laff That Off" (Wallack's, Nov. 2; 390 perf.), "The Last of Mrs. Cheyney" (Fulton, Nov. 9; 385 perf.), "Alias the Deacon" (Sam H. Harris, Nov. 24), "One of the Family" (49th Street, Dec. 21), "The Patsy" (Booth, Dec. 22). Max Reinhardt transformed the stage of the Century Theatre into a cathedral and staged (Jan. 16) his elaborate production of "The Miracle" with a large cast headed by Lady Diana Manners and Rosamond Pinchot, and a symphony orchestra. Musical productions included: "George White's Scandals" (Apollo, June 22; 424 perf.), "Artists and Models" (Winter Garden, June 24; 411 perf.), "Earl Carroll Vanities" (Earl Carroll, July 6; 390 perf.), "No! No! Nanette" (Globe, Sept. 16; 321 perf.), "Dearest Enemy" (Knickerbocker, Sept. 18), "The Vagabond King" with Dennis King (Casino, Sept. 21; 511 perf.), "Sunny" (New Amsterdam, Sept. 22; 517 perf.), "The Cocoanuts" (Lyric, Dec. 8; 377 perf.), "Song of the Flame" (44th Street, Dec. 30; 219 perf.).

Motion pictures (still silent) included: "The Big Parade" (John Gilbert, Renée Adorée), "Don Q, Son of Zorro" (Douglas Fairbanks), "The Freshman" (Harold Lloyd), "The Gold Rush" (Charlie Chaplin; generally regarded as his best picture), "Kiss Me Again" (Marie Prevost, Monte Blue), "The Last Laugh" (Emil Jannings), "The Lost World" (Bessie Love, Lewis Stone), "The Merry Widow" (Mae Murray, John Gilbert), "The Phantom of the Opera" (Lon Chaney), "The Son of the Sheik" (Rudoph Valentino; his last picture).

In New York, a new Madison Square Garden sports arena, about two and one-half miles north of its historic predecessor, opened (Dec. 15).

"Red" Grange (Harold Edward Grange) was the football star of the University of Illinois. (During his three years he scored 31 touchdowns in 20 games.) In the fall of this year he became a professional player and joined the Chicago Bears football club—a move that created much heated controversy.

⚬⤞ 1926

After I Say I'm Sorry. w., m., Walter Donaldson and Abe Lyman. Leo Feist, Inc., cop. 1926.

All Alone Monday (The Ramblers). w., Bert Kalmar. m., Harry Ruby. Harms, Inc., cop. 1926.

Am I Wasting My Time over You? w., m., Howard Johnson and Irving Bibo. Bibo, Bloedon, and Lang, cop. 1926; assigned to Stasny Music Corp.

Animal Crackers. See below: "I'm Just Wild about Animal Crackers."

Are You Lonesome Tonight? w., m., Roy Turk and Lou Handman. Irving Berlin, Inc., cop. 1926.

Baby Face. w., m., Benny Davis and Harry Akst. Jerome H. Remick & Co., cop. 1926.

Because I Love You. w., m., Irving Berlin. Irving Berlin, Inc., cop. 1926.

The Birth of the Blues (George White's Scandals). w., B. G. De Sylva and Lew Brown. m., Ray Henderson. Harms, Inc., cop. 1926.

Black Bottom (George White's Scandals). w., B. G. De Sylva and Lew Brown. m., Ray Henderson. Harms, Inc., cop. 1926.

Black Eyes [Dark Eyes]. Orch. composition. m., arranged by Harry Horlick and Gregory Stone. Carl Fischer, Inc., cop. 1926.

The Blue Room (The Girl Friend). w., Lorenz Hart. m., Richard Rodgers. Harms, Inc., cop. 1926.

Breezin' Along with the Breeze. w., m., Haven Gillespie, Seymour Simons, and Richard A. Whiting. Jerome H. Remick & Co., cop. 1926.

Bring Back Those Minstrel Days. w., Ballard MacDonald. m., Martin Broones. Shapiro, Bernstein & Co., Inc., cop. 1926.

Bye Bye Blackbird. w., Mort Dixon. m., Ray Henderson. Jerome H. Remick & Co., cop. 1926.

Charmaine. w., m., Erno Rapee and Lew Pollack. San Francisco: Sherman, Clay & Co., cop. 1926 by Belwin, Inc.

Cherie, I Love You. w., m., Lillian Rosedale Goodman. Harms, Inc., cop. 1926.

Clap Yo' Hands (Oh, Kay!). w., Ira Gershwin. m., George Gershwin. Harms, Inc., cop. 1926.

Climbing Up the Ladder of Love (Earl Carroll's "Vanities," 5th Edition). w., Raymond Klages. m., Jesse Greer. Robbins-Engel, Inc., cop. 1926.

Cossack Love Song (Song of the Flame). w., Otto Harbach and Oscar Hammerstein, 2nd. m., Herbert Stothart and George Gershwin. Harms, Inc., cop. 1926.

Cross Your Heart (Queen High). w., B. G. DeSylva. m., Lewis E. Gensler. Harms, Inc., cop. 1926.

La Cumparsita. m., G. H. Matos Rodriquez; arr. for orch. by Vincenzo Billi. Milan: G. Ricordi & Co., cop. 1926. (Published as a song, with words by Carol Raven, Edward B. Marks Music Corp., cop. 1932; as an orch. piece, arr. (1) by Edgar Carver, Alfred Music Co., Inc., cop. 1932; (2) by George F. Briegel, Edward B. Marks Music Corp., cop. 1932; (3) by George H. Sanders, Emil Ascher, Inc., cop. 1937; (4) by Harry Horlick, Broadcast Music, Inc., cop. 1940.)

The Desert Song (The Desert Song). w., Otto Harbach and Oscar Hammerstein, 2nd. m., Sigmund Romberg. Harms, Inc., cop. 1926.

Do-Do-Do (Oh, Kay!). w., Ira Gershwin. m., George Gershwin. Harms, Inc., cop. 1926.

Everything's Gonna Be All Right. w., m., Benny Davis and Harry Akst. Henry Waterson, Inc., cop. 1926.

Flapperette. Piano solo. m., Jesse Greer. Jack Mills, Inc., cop. 1926.

Florida, the Moon and You (Ziegfeld's American Revue of 1926). w., Gene Buck. m., Rudolf Friml. Harms, Inc., cop. 1926.

You Do Something to Me (Fifty Million Frenchmen). w., m., Cole Porter. Harms, Inc., cop. 1929.

You Don't Know Paree (Fifty Million Frenchmen). w., m., Cole Porter. Harms, Inc., cop. 1929.

Yours Sincerely (Spring Is Here). w., Lorenz Hart. m., Richard Rodgers. Harms, Inc., cop. 1929.

Zigeuner (Bitter Sweet). w., m., Noel Coward. London: Chappell & Co., Ltd., cop. 1929.

Herbert Clark Hoover, Republican, of Iowa, was inaugurated 31st President.

The United States signed (Feb. 11) a treaty with the Holy See and with Italy recognizing the former as a sovereignty.

Congress passed (Mar. 2) Washington Senator Wesley L. Jones's bill, providing severe penalties for conviction under the Volstead Act (1919).

"Coolidge prosperity" suddenly collapsed with dire effects. The worst stock market crash since "Black Friday" (Sept. 24, 1869) occurred (Oct. 29) when 16,400,000 shares in declining values exchanged hands in a single day's selling rush. The ticker barely caught up with transactions by nightfall, and some stocks plunged over 35 points in a day. The New York Stock Exchange closed for three days. By the end of the year, $15,-000,000,000 had vanished "into thin air." It was testified before the Senate investigating committee that 25,000,000 persons had been affected by this financial catastrophe—the twenty-fifth in U. S. history since 1790, and by all odds the most disastrous, far-reaching, and protracted.

The Young Plan, framed by a committee under the chairmanship of Owen D. Young as a method for the German payment of World War I reparations to the Allies, went into effect (Sept. 1). The plan fixed the total amount at $7,826,868,000 and provided for an annual payment of 59 years. (To provide a machinery for the administration of the funds, the Bank of International Settlements was organized in January (1930) at The Hague, Holland, and established at Geneva, Switzerland.)

Commodore Richard Evelyn Byrd conducted explorations in the Antarctic. He reported (Feb. 20) the finding of new regions, and discovered (Nov. 29) the South Pole while flying in the tri-motored airplane "Floyd Bennett" accompanied by Bernt Balchen (pilot), Harold I. June (radio operator), and Capt. Ashley C. McKinley (photographer). For this feat, Commodore Byrd was raised to the rank of Rear Admiral. (Byrd made a second crossing of the South Pole in 1947.)

Charles Augustus Lindbergh married Anne Spencer Morrow, daughter of Dwight Morrow, U. S. Ambassador to Mexico.

Former Secretary of the Interior Albert Bacon Fall, implicated in the Teapot Dome scandal (1934), was found guilty of accepting a bribe of $100,000 from Edward Doheny in the leasing of the Elk Hills, Cal., naval oil reserve. Fall was sentenced to a year in jail and a fine of $100,-000.

The German dirigible balloon "Graf Zeppelin," commanded by Dr. Hugo Eckener, made (July 31-Aug. 10) its second trip (the first was in 1928) from Friedrichshafen, Germany, to Lakehurst, N. J., and back. The airship then proceeded eastward with 20 passengers on a journey (Aug. 14-Sept. 4) around the world, stopping (Aug. 29-Sept. 1) en route at Lakehurst.

A strike of textile workers in Gastonia, N. C., caused the death of several persons. A number of strikers were arrested and convicted of homicide. (The episode furnished the material of Mary Vorse's "Strike— A Novel of Gastonia," 1930, and Grace Lumpkin's novel "To Make My Bread," 1932, dramatized by Albert Bein as "Let Freedom Ring," 1936.)

Bridges that were completed this year included the Ambassador, connecting Detroit, Mich., and Canada; the Bristol-Portsmouth, R. I., spanning Mt. Hope Bay, and the Cooper River, Charleston, S. C.

A nitrogen-dioxide explosion and fire in the Cleveland Clinic Hospital of Dr. George Washington Crile caused (May 15) the death of 124 persons.

Mrs. T. W. Evans of Miami, Fla., became (Oct. 26) the mother of the first child to be born on an airplane.

In Chicago, gangsterism reached its height when seven of the O'Banion gang were mowed down by machine-gun fire (St. Valentine's Day massacre).

The Museum of Modern Art, New York, was founded.

Television in color was demonstrated (in June) in the Bell laboratories.

Books of the year included: "Are We Civilized?" (Robert Heinrich Lowie), "The Modern Temper" (Joseph Wood Krutch), "A Preface to Morals" (Walter Lippmann), "The Raven" (Marquis James; a biography of Sam Houston; Pulitzer prize 1930), "Selected Poems" (Conrad Aiken; Pulitzer prize 1930), "Sound Off!" (Edward Arthur Dolph; soldier songs), "The War of Independence" (Claude H. Van Tyne; Pulitzer prize 1930), and the fiction, "Dodsworth" (Sinclair Lewis), "A Farewell to Arms" (Ernest Hemingway), "The Fugitive's Return" (Susan Glaspell), "Is Sex Necessary?" (James Thurber and E. B. White), "Laughing Boy" (Oliver LaFarge; Pulitzer prize 1930), "Look Homeward, Angel" (Thomas Wolfe), "Magnificent Obsession" (Lloyd Douglas), "Mamba's Daughters" (DuBose Heyward), "Peder Victorious" (Ole Rölvaag), "The Roman Hat Mystery" ("Ellery Queen," pseudonym of Frederick Danny and Manfred B. Lee; first of their detective stories), "She Stooped to Folly" (Ellen Glasgow), "The Sound and the Fury" (William Faulkner). Erich Maria Remarque's German war novel "Im Westen nichts

Neues" was popular in its English translation "All Quiet on the Western Front." (It was made into a movie the next year.)

"Amos 'n' Andy" started (Aug. 19) their radio career. The two amusing Negro characters were impersonated by Freeman Gosden (Amos) and Charles Correll (Andy).

The Civic Opera Building, Chicago, was opened.

Cesare Sodero's Italian opera "Ombre Russe" received its world première in a radio performance by the National Broadcasting Company, New York, in two broadcasts (Act. I-II, May 27; Act III, June 3).

A novel one-hour radio version of the opera "Aïda" with speaking actors, singing principals, and a chorus was broadcast (Dec. 26) over a network of 45 stations from New York by the National Broadcasting Company under the auspices of the R.C.A. Victor Company. The singers were Elizabeth Rethberg (Aïda), Marion Telva (Amneris), and Giacomo Lauri-Volpi (Rhadames); the speaking parts were delivered by Virginia Gardiner (Aïda), Rosaline Greene (Amneris), Allyn Joselyn (Rhadames), Fred Forrester (King), and Charles Webster (High Priest). There was no Amonasro in the version.

New York plays that ran 175 or more performances included: "Street Scene" by Elmer Rice (Playhouse, Jan. 16; 601 perf.; Pulitzer prize 1929), "My Girl Friday" (Republic, Feb. 12), "Journey's End" (Henry Miller, Mar. 22; 485 perf.), "Bird in Hand" (Booth, Apr. 4; 500 perf.), "Camel Through the Needle's Eye" (Martin Beck, Apr. 15), "It's a Wise Child" (Belasco, Aug. 6; 378 perf.), "Houseparty" (Knickerbocker, Sept. 9), "Strictly Dishonorable" (Avon, Sept. 18; 557 perf.), "Subway Express" (Liberty, Sept. 24), "The Criminal Code" (National, Oct. 2; 173 perf.), "June Moon" (Broadhurst, Oct. 9; 273 perf.), "Berkeley Square" (Lyceum, Nov. 4), "Broken Dishes" (Ritz, Nov. 5), "Mendel, Inc." (Sam H. Harris, Nov. 25), "Young Sinners" (Morosco, Nov. 28; 289 perf.), "Michael and Mary" (Charles Hopkins, Dec. 13; 246 perf.), "Death Takes a Holiday" (Ethel Barrymore, Dec. 26), "The First Mrs. Fraser" (Playhouse, Dec. 28; 352 perf.). Musical productions included: "Follow Thru" (46th Street, Jan. 9; 403 perf.), "The Little Show" (Music Box, Apr. 30; 321 perf.), "A Night in Venice" (Shubert, May 21), "Hot Chocolates" (Hudson, June 20; 219 perf.), "Earl Carroll's Sketch Book" (Earl Carroll, July 1; 400 perf.), "Sweet Adeline" (Hammerstein's, Sept. 3; 243 perf.), "Street Singer" (Shubert, Sept. 17), "Bitter Sweet" (Ziegfeld, Nov. 5; 159 perf.), "Heads Up" (Alvin, Nov. 11), "Sons o' Guns" (Imperial, Nov. 26; 295 perf.), "Fifty Million Frenchmen" (Lyric, Nov. 27; 254 perf.).

Motion pictures included: "The Broadway Melody," "Bulldog Drummond" (Ronald Coleman), "The Cock-Eyed World," "Coquette" (Mary Pickford), "Disraeli" (George Arliss), "Gold Diggers of Broadway," "Hallelujah," "In Old Arizona" (Warner Baxter), "The Innocents of Paris" (Maurice Chevalier, Jeanette MacDonald), "The Last of Mrs. Cheyney" (Norma Shearer), "Madame X" (Ruth Chatterton; directed by

Lionel Barrymore), "Rio Rita" (John Boles, Bebe Daniels), "Sunny Side Up."

Connie Mack (Cornelius McGillicuddy), manager of the Philadelphia American League ("Athletics") baseball club, was awarded the $10,000 Edward W. Bok prize for distinguished service to the city—an honor previously bestowed only on scientists, educators, artists, and philanthropists.

֍ 1930

All the King's Horses (Three's a Crowd). w., m., Alex Wilder, Edward Brandt, and Howard Dietz. Harms, Inc., cop. 1930.

Andalucia (in the suite: Andalucia). Piano solo. m., Ernesto Lecuona. Edward B. Marks Music Co., cop. 1928 by Ernesto Lecuona; assigned 1930 to Edward B. Marks Music Co.; assigned 1932 to Edward B. Marks Music Corp.

The Battle of Jericho. Negro spiritual for TTBB, arr. by Marshall Bartholomew. G. Schirmer, Inc., cop. 1930.

A Bench in the Park (film: King of Jazz). w., Jack Yellen. m., Milton Ager. Ager, Yellen & Bornstein, Inc., cop. 1930.

Betty Co-ed. w., m., J. Paul Fogarty and Rudy Vallee. Carl Fischer, Inc., cop. 1930.

Beyond the Blue Horizon (film: Monte Carlo). w., Leo Robin. m., Richard Whiting and W. Franke Harling. Famous Music Corp., cop. 1930.

Bidin' My Time (Girl Crazy). w., Ira Gershwin. m., George Gershwin. New World Music Corp., cop. 1930.

Blue Again. w., Dorothy Fields. m., Jimmy McHugh. Robbins Music Corp., cop. 1930 by Metro-Goldwyn-Mayer Corp.

Blue Is the Night (film: Their Own Desire). w., m., Fred Fisher. Robbins Music Corp., cop. 1930 by Metro-Goldwyn-Mayer Music Corp.; assigned 1930 to Robbins Music Corp.

Body and Soul (Three's a Crowd). w., Edward Heyman, Robert Sour, and Frank Eyton. m., John W. Green. Harms, Inc., cop. 1930.

Can This Be Love? (Fine and Dandy). w., Paul James. m., Kay Swift. Harms, Inc., cop. 1930.

Cheerful Little Earful (Sweet and Low). w., Ira Gershwin and Billy Rose. m., Harry Warren. Remick Music Corp., cop. 1930.

Chimes of Spring. See 1903: "Spring, Beautiful Spring."

Come Out of the Kitchen, Mary Ann. w., m., James Kendis and Charles Bayha. Kendis Music Corp., cop. 1930.

Cryin' for the Carolines (film: Spring Is Here). w., Sam M. Lewis and Joe Young. m., Harry Warren. Remick Music Corp., cop. 1930.

Dancing on the Ceiling. w., Lorenz Hart. m., Richard Rodgers. Harms, Inc., cop. 1930; cop. 1931 by Rodart Music Corp.

Dancing with Tears in My Eyes. w., Al Dubin. m., Joe Burke. M. Witmark & Sons, cop. 1930.

Embraceable You (Girl Crazy). w., Ira Gershwin. m., George Gershwin. New World Music Corp., cop. 1930.

Exactly Like You (Lew Leslie's International Revue). w., Dorothy Fields. m., Jimmy McHugh. Shapiro, Bernstein & Co., Inc., cop. 1930.

Fine and Dandy (Fine and Dandy). w., Paul Jones. m., Kay Swift. Harms, Inc., cop. 1930.

The "Free and Easy" (film: Free and Easy). w., Roy Turk. m., Fred E. Ahlert. Robbins Music Corp., cop. 1930 by Metro-Goldwyn-Mayer Corp.

Georgia on My Mind. w., Stuart Gorrell. m., Hoagy Carmichael. Southern Music Pub. Co., Inc., cop. 1930.

Get Happy. w., Ted Koehler. m., Harold Arlen. Remick Music Corp., cop. 1930.

Give Me a Moment Please (film: Monte Carlo). w., Leo Robin. m., Richard A. Whiting and W. Franke Harling. Famous Music Corp., cop. 1930.

Go Home and Tell Your Mother (film: Love in the Rough). w., Dorothy Fields. m., Jimmy McHugh. Robbins Music Corp., cop. 1930 by Metro-Goldwyn-Mayer Corp.

Hangin' on the Garden Gate. w., Gus Kahn. m., Ted Fiorito. M. Witmark & Sons, cop. 1930.

Happy Feet (film: King of Jazz). w., Jack Yellen. m., Milton Ager. Ager, Yellen & Bornstein, Inc., cop. 1930.

Hora Staccato. Composition for violin and piano. m., Dinicu-[Jascha] Heifetz. Carl Fischer, Inc., cop. 1930.

Hospodi Pomiloi. Anthem. w., liturgical (Greek Orthodox Church). m., S. V. Lvovsky; arr. for TTBB by Paul John Weaver. Boston: Oliver Ditson Co., .cop. 1930.

I'm Confessin'—That I Love You. w., m., Doc Dougherty and Ellis Reynolds. Irving Berlin, Inc., cop. 1930 by General Music Publications; assigned 1930 to Irving Berlin, Inc.

I'm Yours (film: Leave It to Lester). w., E. Y. Harburg. m., John W. Green. Famous Music Corp., cop. 1930.

I Got Rhythm (Girl Crazy). w., Ira Gershwin. m. George Gershwin. New World Music Corp., cop. 1930.

If I Were King (film: If I Were King). w., Leo Dubin. m., Newell Chase and Sam Coslow. Spier & Coslow, Inc., cop. 1930 by Famous Music Corp.

It Happened in Monterey (film: King of Jazz). w., William Rose. m., Mabel Wayne. Leo Feist, Inc., cop. 1930.

Just a Gigolo—*original German title:* Schöner Gigolo. German words, Julius Brammer. English words, Irving Caesar. m., Leonello Casucci. DeSylva, Brown & Henderson, Inc., cop. 1929 by Wiener Boheme Verlag, Vienna; cop. 1930 by DeSylva, Brown & Henderson, Inc.

The Kiss Waltz. w., Al Dubin. m., Joe Burke. M. Witmark & Sons, cop. 1930.

Lady Play Your Mandolin. w., Irving Caesar. m., Oscar Levant. Harms, Inc., cop. 1930.

Lazy Lou'siana Moon. w., m., Walter Donaldson. Donaldson, Douglas & Gumble, Inc., cop. 1930.

Little White Lies. w., m., Walter Donaldson. Donaldson, Douglas & Gumble, Inc., cop. 1930.

Love for Sale (The New Yorkers). w., m., Cole Porter. Harms, Inc., cop. 1930.

Lucky Seven (The Second Little Show). w., Howard Dietz. m., Arthur Schwartz. Harms, Inc., cop. 1930.

Malaguena (in the suite: Andalucia). Piano solo. m., Ernesto Lecuona. Edward B. Marks Music Co., cop. 1929 by Ernesto Lecuona; assigned 1932 to Edward B. Marks Music Co.; assigned 1932 to Edward B. Marks Music Corp.

The March of Time (Earl Carroll Vanities). w., Ted Koehler. m., Harold Arlen. Remick Music Corp., cop. 1930.

Moonlight on the Colorado. w., Billy Moll. m., Robert A. King. Shapiro, Bernstein & Co., Inc., cop. 1930.

My Future Just Passed (film: Safety in Numbers). w., George Marion, Jr. m., Richard A. Whiting. Famous Music Corp., cop. 1930.

My Ideal (film: Playboy of Paris). w., Leo Robin. m., Richard A. Whiting and Newell Chase. Famous Music Corp., cop. 1930.

Mysterious Mose. w., m., Walter Doyle. M. Witmark & Sons, cop. 1930.

On the Sunny Side of the Street (Lew Leslie's International Revue). w., Dorothy Fields. m., Jimmy McHugh. Shapiro, Bernstein & Co., Inc., cop. 1930.

Overnight (Sweet and Low). w., Billy Rose and Charlotte Kent. m., Louis Alter. Robbins Music Corp., cop. 1930 by William Rose, Inc.

Rockin' Chair. w., m., Hoagy Carmichael. Southern Music Pub. Co., Inc., cop. 1930.

Roses Are Forget-Me-Nots. w., m., Al Hoffman, Charles O'Flynn, and Will Osborne. M. Witmark & Sons, cop. 1930.

St. James Infirmary. m., Joe Primrose. Gotham Music Service, Inc., cop. 1930.

Sleepy Lagoon. w., Jack Lawrence. m., Eric Coates. Chappell & Co., Inc., cop. 1930 by Chappell & Co., Ltd.; cop. 1940 by Chappell & Co., Ltd.

Sing Something Simple (The Second Little Show). w., m., Herman Hupfeld. Harms, Inc., cop. 1930.

So Beats My Heart for You. w., m., Pat Ballard, Charles Henderson, and Tom Waring. DeSylva, Brown & Henderson, cop. 1930.

Something to Remember You By (Three's a Crowd). w., Howard Dietz. m., Arthur Schwartz. Harms, Inc., cop. 1930.

Sweet and Hot (You Said It). w., Jack Yellen. m., Harold Arlen. Ager, Yellen & Bornstein, Inc., cop. 1930.

Swingin' in a Hammock. w., Tot Seymour and Charles O'Flynn. m., Pete Wendling. Irving Berlin, Inc., cop. 1930.

Ten Cents a Dance (film: Ten Cents a Dance). w., Lorenz Hart. m., Richard Rodgers. Harms, Inc., cop. 1930.

Them There Eyes. w., m., Maceo Pinkard, William Tracey, and Doris Tauber. Irving Berlin, Inc., cop. 1930.

Three Little Words (film: Amos 'n' Andy). w., Bert Kalmar. m., Harry Ruby. Harms, Inc., cop. 1930.

Time on My Hands. w., Harold Adamson and Mack Gordon. m., Vincent Youmans. Vincent Youmans, Inc., cop. 1930.

Two Hearts [in ¾ Time] (film: Zwei Herzen Im Dreivierteltakt). w., W. Reisch and A. Robinson. American version by Joe Young. m., Robert Stolz. Harms, Inc., cop. 1930 by Abrobi Musikverlag, Berlin; cop. 1930 by Harms, Inc.

Walkin' My Baby Back Home. w., m., Roy Turk, Fred E. Ahlert, and Harry Richman. DeSylva, Brown & Henderson, Inc., cop. 1930.

The Waltz You Saved for Me. w., Gus Kahn. m., Wayne King and Emil Flindt. Leo Feist, Inc., cop. 1930.

What Is This Thing Called Love? (Wake Up and Dream). w., m., Cole Porter. Harms, Inc., cop. 1930.

Where Have You Been? (The New Yorkers). w., m., Cole Porter. Harms, Inc., cop. 1930.

The White Dove (film: The Rogue Song). w., Clifford Grey. m., Franz Lehár. London: Chappell & Co., Ltd., cop. 1930.

Would You Like to Take a Walk? (Sweet and Low). w., Mort Dixon and Billy Rose. m., Harry Warren. Remick Music Corp., cop. 1930.

You're Driving Me Crazy!—What Did I Do? w., m., Walter Donaldson. Donaldson, Douglas & Gumble, Inc., cop. 1930.

You Brought a New Kind of Love to Me (film: The Big Pond). w., m., Sammy Fain, Irving Kahal, and Pierre Norman. Famous Music Corp., cop. 1930.

Financial gloom, resulting from the stock market crash of the preceding year, kept spreading. An indication of the prevailing economic condition was the appearance of apple vendors on the street corners in New York and elsewhere.

Bootleg liquor prices were high. American Bourbon sold for $100 per case; Canadian Bourbon, $150; gin, $35 and $50; champagne, $110; Scotch, $110, and cordials, $120.

Charles Evans Hughes was reappointed Justice of the United States Supreme Court. He had resigned in 1916 to run in the unsuccessful Republican presidential campaign against Woodrow Wilson.

Joseph F. Crater, Justice of the State Supreme Court in New York City, mysteriously disappeared (Aug. 6); nothing has ever been heard of him.

Captain Frank W. Hawkes successfully carried out (Mar. 30-Apr. 6) an aeronautical experiment by flying from San Diego, Cal., to New York in a glider towed by an airplane. Later (Aug. 3) he flew from Los Angeles to New York and reduced his previous (1929) New-York-to-Los-Angeles record from 19 hours, 10 minutes, to 12 hours, 25 minutes. Lieutenant A. Soucek, U.S.N., achieved (June 4) a world altitude record when his plane rose to a height of 43,166 feet over Anacostia, D. C. Dale Jackson and Forrest O'Brine increased (July 21-Aug. 7) their previous year's endurance record from 420 hours, 21 minutes, to 647 hours, 28 minutes.

A meteor, visible in several States, fell (Feb. 17) near Paragould, Ark. It split into fragments, one of which weighed 820 pounds.

A fire broke out (Apr. 21) in the Ohio State Penitentiary at Columbus and caused the death of 320 convicts.

The Mid-Hudson Bridge at Poughkeepsie, N. Y., was completed.

Lynchings suddenly increased throughout the United States; 30 occurred during the year.

Sinclair Lewis was awarded the Nobel prize for literature—the first American to be so honored in that field.

Radio was reaching out over oceans, continents, and hemispheres. A Five-Power naval conference opened (Jan. 21) in London. The inaugural address by His Majesty George V, spoken into a gold microphone, was broadcast by more than twenty-five European radio stations and rebroadcast in the United States, Japan, Australia via Manila, and India. It was estimated that 100,000,000 people listened to the speeches of the King and the delegates. Premier Ramsay MacDonald said: "Truly, we are living in times of great miracles."

To a nation in mourning, radio brought (Mar. 11) the funeral services of William Howard Taft from Washington, D. C.; it carried into millions of homes the prayers, the music, and descriptions of the solemn cortege as it passed from the Capitol to Arlington Cemetery; at midnight it brought from London a tribute to the late former President and Chief Justice by one of England's notable statesmen, Viscount Cecil.

On the same day, partial success attended a round-the-world broadcast. Two speakers, 10,000 miles apart, addressed each other over the air and the radio public was privileged to eavesdrop on a conversation between Rear Admiral Richard Evelyn Byrd, speaking from Dunedin, New Zealand, on his return from the Antarctic, and Adolph Ochs, owner of the "New York Times" newspaper, facing a microphone at Schenectady, New York. It was 1 A.M., March. 12 when Rear Admiral Byrd spoke to America, and 7:30 A.M., Mar. 11, in New York when Mr. Ochs greeted the explorer. Communication between the two points was maintained for forty-five minutes. Unfortunately the voice of Byrd was distorted by static and at times unintelligible.

Another attempt of a different kind was (Mar. 16) an American rebroadcast of a performance of Beethoven's opera "Fidelio" from the State Opera House, Dresden, Germany. The broadcast, sent across the Atlantic by the Reichs-Rundfunk Gesellschaft via its station at Königswusterhausen, Berlin, lasted one hour and although only a portion of the opera was put on the air it was the first European direct-from-the-stage pick-up sent over an American network.

Although television still was in its experimental stages, radio station WEEI, Boston, televised daily programs for local receivers.

Books of the year included: "Charles W. Eliot" (Henry James; a biography; Pulitzer prize 1931), "Collected Poems" (Robert Frost; Pulitzer prize 1931), "The Coming of the War, 1914" (Bernadotte E. Schmitt; Pulitzer prize 1931), "The Strange Death of President Harding" (Gaston Bullock Means), and the fiction, "The Adventures of Ephraim Tutt" (Arthur Train), "Alison's House" (Susan Glaspell; Pulitzer prize 1931), "Arundel" (Kenneth Roberts), "Cimarron" (Edna Ferber), "The

42nd Parallel" (John Dos Passos; sequels, "1919," 1932, and "The Big Money," 1936), "Flowering Judas" (Katherine Anne Porter), "The Great Meadow" (Elizabeth Madox Roberts), "Jews without Money" (Michael Gold), "North of Suez" (William McFee), "Tiger! Tiger!" (Honoré Willsie Morrow). The first volume of the "Encyclopedia of Social Sciences" appeared (completed in 1935).

Arturo Toscanini made a triumphal tour of Europe with the New York Philharmonic-Symphony Society orchestra.

"Transatlantic," an opera by the American composer, George Antheil, had (May 25) its world première in Frankfurt, Germany.

The National Broadcasting Company, New York, produced (Apr. 17) the première of Charles Sanford Skilton's one-act Indian opera "The Sun-Bride."

The Columbia Broadcasting System, New York, began (Oct. 5) its Sunday broadcasts of the concerts of the New York Philharmonic-Symphony Society. The first broadcast concert was conducted by Erich Kleiber.

For the 50th anniversary of the Boston Symphony Orchestra, Igor Stravinsky composed his "Symphony of Psalms" for chorus and orchestra. Owing to a change of dates, the Boston performance (Dec. 19) followed the Brussels première (Dec. 13).

New York plays that ran 200 or more performances included: "The Last Mile" (Sam H. Harris, Feb. 13), "Apron Strings" (Bijou, Feb. 17), "The Green Pastures" by Marc Connelly (Mansfield, Feb. 26; 640 perf.; Pulitzer prize 1930), "Stepping Sisters" (Belmont, Apr. 22; 333 perf.), "Lysistrata" (44th Street, June 5), "Once in a Lifetime" (Music Box, Sept., 24; 406 perf.), "The Greeks Had a Word for It" (Sam H. Harris, Sept. 25), "Mrs. Moonlight" (Charles Hopkins, Sept. 29; 321 perf.), "Grand Hotel" (National, Nov. 13; 459 perf.), "Tonight or Never" (Belasco, Nov. 18), "The Vinegar Tree" (Playhouse, Nov. 19). Mei Lan-Fang, China's greatest actor, appeared in a program of five traditional one-act plays (49th Street, Feb. 17; 41 perf.). The 1931 Pulitzer prize was awarded to "Alison's House" by Susan Glaspell (Civic Repertory Theatre, Dec. 1; 41 perf.). Musical productions included: "Strike Up the Band" (Times Square, Jan. 14), "Flying High" (Apollo, Mar. 3; 357 perf.), "Earl Carroll's Vanities" (New Amsterdam, July 1), "Nina Rosa" (Majestic, Sept. 20), "Fine and Dandy" (Erlanger's, Sept. 23; 255 perf.), "Girl Crazy" (Alvin, Oct. 14; 272 perf.), "Three's a Crowd" (Selwyn, Oct. 15; 272 perf.), "Sweet and Low" (46th Street, Nov. 17), "The New Yorkers" (Broadway, Dec. 8), "Meet My Sister" (Shubert, Dec. 30).

Motion pictures of the year included: "Abraham Lincoln" (Griffith production), "All Quiet on the Western Front," "Anna Christie" (Greta Garbo), "The Big House," "Blushing Brides" (Joan Crawford), "Caught Short" (Marie Dressler, Polly Moran), "Common Clay" (Constance

Bennett), "Divorce" (Norma Shearer), "Hell's Angels" (Jean Harlow; the emphasis was on platinum blonde hair), "Holiday" (Ann Harding), "Journey's End" (Colin Clive), "King of Jazz," "Love Parade" (Maurice Chevalier), "Morocco" (Marlene Dietrich; her first American picture), "The New Moon" (Grace Moore), "Old English" (George Arliss), "The Rogue Song" (Lawrence Tibbett), "The Vagabond King" (Dennis King, Jeanette MacDonald; technicolor), "With Byrd at the South Pole."

Max Schmeling of Germany claimed the heavyweight boxing title (vacated in 1928 by Gene Tunney) when he was fouled (June 12) by Jack Sharkey in the fourth round of their bout at Boston.

The national population was 122,775,046. There still remained 332,-000 Indians.

෫~ 1931

All of Me. w. m., Seymour Simons and Gerald Marks. Irving Berlin, Inc., cop. 1931.

Barnacle Bill the Sailor. w., m., Carson Robison and Frank Luther. Southern Music Pub. Co., Inc., cop. 1931.

Bend Down, Sister (film: **Palmy Days**). w., Ballard MacDonald and Dave Silverstein. m., Con Conrad. Harms, Inc., cop. 1931 by Con Conrad Music Publisher, Ltd., London.

Between the Devil and the Deep Blue Sea (**Rhythmania**). w., Ted Koehler. m., Harold Arlen. Mills Music, Inc., cop. 1931.

By the River Sainte Marie. w., Edgar Leslie. m., Harry Warren. Robbins Music Corp., cop. 1931 by Metro-Goldwyn-Mayer Corp.

By the Sycamore Tree. w., Haven Gillespie. m., Pete Wendling. Irving Berlin, Inc., cop. 1931.

Call Me Darling—*original German title:* **Sag' mir Darling.** German words and music, Bert Reisfeld, Mart Fryberg, and Rolf Marbet. English words, Dorothy Dick. Santly Bros., cop. 1931 by Musikverlag "City," Leipzig; assigned 1931 to Santly Bros.

Come to Me. w., m., Bud G. DeSylva, Lew Brown, and Ray Henderson. DeSylva, Brown & Henderson, Inc., cop. 1931.

Cuban Love Song (film: **The Cuban Love Song**). w., m., Herbert Stothart, Jimmy McHugh, and Dorothy Fields. Robbins Music Corp., cop. 1931 by Metro-Goldwyn-Mayer Corp.

Dancing in the Dark (The Band Wagon). w., Howard Dietz. m., Arthur Schwartz. Harms, Inc., cop. 1931.

Delishious (film: Delicious). w., Ira Gershwin. m., George Gershwin. New World Music Corp., cop. 1931.

Do the New York (Ziegfeld Follies of 1931). w., m., J. P. Murray, Barry Trivers, and Ben Oakland. Miller Music, Inc., cop. 1931.

Dream a Little Dream of Me. w., Gus Kahn. m., W. Schwandt and F. Andree. Davis, Coots & Engel, Inc., cop. 1931; assigned 1936 to Words and Music, Inc.

Drums in My Heart (Through the Years). w., Edward Heyman. m., Vincent Youmans. Miller Music, Inc., cop. 1931 by Miller Music, Inc., and Vincent Youmans, Inc.

Elizabeth (Wonder Bar). w., Irving Caesar. m., Robert Katscher. Harms, Inc., cop. 1930 by Ludwig Doblinger (Bernard Hermansky), Vienna; cop. 1931 by Harms, Inc.

Goodnight, Sweetheart (*introduced in:* Earl Carroll's Vanities). w., m., Ray Noble, James Campbell, and Reg. Connelly. American version by Rudy Vallee. Robbins Music Corp. cop. 1931 by Campbell, Connelly & Co., London; assigned to Robbins Music Corp.

Got the Bench, Got the Park. w., m., Al Lewis, Al Sherman, and Fred Phillips. Irving Berlin, Inc., cop. 1931.

Heartaches. w., John Klenner. m., Al Hoffman. Olman Music Corp., cop. 1931.

Home. w., m., Peter Van Steedan, Harry and Jeff Clarkson. Marlo Music Corp., cop. 1931; assigned 1943 to American Academy of Music, Inc.

I Apologize. w., m., Al Hoffman, Al Goodhart and Ed Nelson. De Sylva, Brown and Henderson, Inc., cop. 1931.

I Found a Million Dollar Baby—In a Five and Ten Cent Store (Billy Rose's Crazy Quilt). w., Billy Rose and Mort Dixon. m., Harry Warren. Remick Music Corp., cop. 1931.

I've Got Five Dollars (America's Sweetheart). w., Lorenz Hart. m., Richard Rodgers. Harms, Inc., cop. 1931.

I Love a Parade. w., Ted Koehler. m., Harold Arlen. Harms, Inc., cop. 1931.

I Love Louisa (The Band Wagon). w., Howard Dietz. m., Arthur Schwartz. Harms, Inc., cop. 1931.

It's the Darndest Thing (film: Singing the Blues). w., Dorothy Fields. m., Jimmy McHugh. Robbins Music Corp., cop. 1931 by Metro-Goldwyn-Mayer Corp.

Jazz Nocturne. Piano solo. m., Dana Suesse. Famous Music Corp., cop. 1931.

Lady of Spain. w., Erell Reaves. m., Tolchard Evans. Cleveland: Sam Fox Pub. Co., cop. 1931 by Cecil Lennox, Ltd., London.

Lies. w., George E. Springer. Melody, Harry Barris. Shapiro, Bernstein & Co., cop. 1931.

Life Is Just a Bowl of Cherries (George White's Scandals, 11th Edition). w., m., Lew Brown and Ray Henderson. DeSylva, Brown & Henderson, Inc., cop. 1931.

Love Is Sweeping the Country (Of Thee I Sing). w., Ira Gershwin. m., George Gershwin. New World Music Corp., cop. 1931.

Love Letters in the Sand. w., Nick Kenny and Charles Kenny. m., J. Fred Coots. Irving Berlin, Inc., cop. 1931.

Mama Inez. w., L. Wolfe Gilbert. m., Eliseo Grenet. Edw. B. Marks Music Co., cop. 1931.

Maria, My Own—*original Spanish title:* Maria-la-o. English words, L. Wolfe Gilbert. m., Ernesto Lecuona. Edward B. Marks Music Co., cop. 1931; assigned 1932 to Edward B. Marks Music Corp.

Marta. English words, L. Wolfe Gilbert. m., Moises Simon. Edward B. Marks Music Co., cop. 1931.

Minnie, the Moocher—The Ho De 'Ho Song. w., m., Cab Calloway and Irving Mills. Gotham Music Service, Inc., cop. 1931.

Mood Indigo. w., m., Duke Ellington, Irving Mills, and Albany Bigard. Gotham Music Service, Inc., cop. 1931.

My Song (George White's Scandals, 11th Edition). w., m., Lew Brown and Ray Henderson. DeSylva, Brown & Henderson, Inc., cop. 1931.

Nevertheless. w., m., Bert Kalmar and Harry Ruby. DeSylva, Brown & Henderson, Inc., cop. 1931.

New Sun in the Sky (The Band Wagon). w., Howard Dietz. m., Arthur Schwartz. Harms, Inc., cop. 1931.

The Night Was Made for Love (The Cat and the Fiddle). w., Otto Harbach. m., Jerome Kern. T. B. Harms Co., cop. 1931 by Jerome Kern.

Of Thee I Sing (Of Thee I Sing). w., Ira Gershwin. m., George Gershwin. New World Music Corp., cop. 1931.

Ooh That Kiss (The Laugh Parade). w., Mort Dixon and Joe Young. m., Harry Warren. Harms, Inc., cop. 1931.

Out of Nowhere. w., Edward Heyman. m., John W. Green. Famous Music Corp., cop. 1931.

The Peacock—*original Spanish title:* **Pavo real.** Spanish words and music, Ernesto Lecuona. English words, Carol Raven. Edward B. Marks Music Co., cop. 1931; assigned 1932 to Edward B. Marks Music Corp.

The Peanut Vendor—*original Spanish title:* **El Manisero.** w., Marion Sunshine and L. Wolfe Gilbert. m., Moises Simons. Edw. B. Marks Music Co., cop. 1931.

Penthouse Serenade (When We're Alone). w., m., Will Jason and Val Burton. Famous Music Corp., cop. 1931.

Prisoner of Love. w., Leo Robin. m., Russ Columbo and Clarence Gaskill. Con Conrad, Music Publishers, Ltd., cop. 1931.

River, Stay 'Way from My Door. w., Mort Dixon. m., Harry Woods. Shapiro, Bernstein & Co., Inc., cop. 1931.

Running Between the Rain-drops. w., James Dyrenforth. m., Carroll Gibbons. Santly Bros., Inc., cop. 1931.

Shadrack. w., m., Robert MacGimsey. Carl Fischer, Inc., cop. 1931.

She Didn't Say "Yes" (The Cat and the Fiddle). w., Otto Harbach. m., Jerome Kern. T. B. Harms Co., cop. 1931 by Jerome Kern.

Singin' the Blues (film: Singin' the Blues). w., Dorothy Fields. m., Jimmy McHugh. Robbins Music Corp., cop. 1931 by Metro-Goldwyn-Mayer Corp.

Smile, Darnya, Smile. w., Charles O'Flynn and Jack Meskill. m., Max Reese. DeSylva, Brown & Henderson, Inc., cop. 1931.

Someday I'll Find You (Private Lives). w., m., Noel Coward. London: Chappell & Co., Ltd., cop. 1931.

Sweet and Lovely. w., m., Gus Arnheim, Harry Tobias, and Jules Lemare. Robbins Music Corp., cop. 1931 by Metro-Goldwyn-Mayer Corp.

That's Why Darkies Were Born (George White's Scandals, 11th Edition). w., m., Lew Brown and Ray Henderson. DeSylva, Brown & Henderson, cop. 1931.

This Is the Mrs. (George White's Scandals, 11th Edition). w., m., Lew Brown and Ray Henderson. DeSylva, Brown & Henderson, Inc., cop. 1931.

The Thrill Is Gone (George White's Scandals, 11th Edition). w., m., Lew Brown and Ray Henderson. DeSylva, Brown & Henderson, Inc., cop. 1931.

Through the Years (Through the Years). w., Edward Heyman. m., Vincent Youmans. Miller Music, Inc., and Vincent Youmans, Inc., cop. 1931.

Till the Real Thing Comes Along (Rhapsody in Black). w., Mann Holiner. m., Alberta Nichols. Shapiro, Bernstein & Co., Inc., cop. 1931.

The Torch Song (The Laugh Parade). w., Mort Dixon and Joe Young. m., Harry Warren. Harms, Inc., cop. 1931.

Try to Forget (The Cat and the Fiddle). w., Otto Harbach. m., Jerome Kern. T. B. Harms Co., cop. 1931 by Jerome Kern.

Under a Roof in Paree (film: Sous les Toits de Paris). French words, René Nazelles. English words, Irving Caesar. m., Raoul Moretti. Harms, Inc., cop. 1930 by Francis Salabert; cop. 1931 by Harms, Inc.

Wabash Moon. w., m., Dave Dreyer and Morton Downey. Irving Berlin, Inc., cop. 1931.

When I Take My Sugar to Tea. w., m., Sammy Fain, Irving Kahal, and Pierre Norman. Famous Music Corp., cop. 1931.

When the Moon Comes Over the Mountain. w., m., Kate Smith, Harry Woods, and Howard Johnson. Robbins Music Corp., cop. 1931 by Metro-Goldwyn-Mayer, Corp.

When Yuba Plays the Rumba on the Tuba (The Third Little Show). w., m., Herman Hupfeld. Harms, Inc., cop. 1931.

Where the Blue of the Night Meets the Gold of the Day. w., m., Roy Turk, Bing Crosby, and Fred E. Ahlert. DeSylva, Brown & Henderson, Inc., cop. 1931.

While Hearts Are Singing (film: Smiling Lieutenant). w., Clifford Grey. m., Oscar Straus. Famous Music Corp., cop. 1931.

Why Dance? w., Roy Turk. m., Fred E. Ahlert. Irving Berlin, Inc., cop. 1931.

You're My Everything (The Laugh Parade). w., Mort Dixon and Joe Young. m., Harry Warren. Harms, Inc., cop. 1931.

You Didn't Have to Tell Me—I Knew It All the Time. w., m., Walter Donaldson. Donaldson, Douglas & Gumble, Inc., cop. 1931.

You Forgot Your Gloves (The Third Little Show). w., Edward Eliscu. m., Ned Lehak. Robbins Music Corp., cop. 1931 by Metro-Goldwyn-Mayer Corp.

You Try Somebody Else. w., m., B. G. DeSylva, Lew Brown, and Ray Henderson. DeSylva, Brown & Henderson, Inc., cop. 1931.

Yours—original Spanish title: Quiérme mucho. English words, Jack Sherr. Spanish words, Agustin Rodriquez. m., Gonzalo Roig. Edward B. Marks Music Co., cop. 1931; assigned 1932 to Edward B. Marks Music Corp.

Yours Is My Heart Alone—original German title: Dein Ist Mein Ganzes Herz. German words, Ludwig Herzer and Fritz Lohner. English words, Harry Bache Smith. m., Franz Lehár. Harms, Inc., cop. 1931 by Shubert Theatre Corp.

"The Star-Spangled Banner" was declared (Mar. 3) the national anthem of the United States by act of Congress. Those who opposed the adoption of the anthem favored "America, the Beautiful."

The United States purchased from Denmark for $25,000,000 the Danish West Indies, known now as the Virgin Islands. They comprise some 50 small islands, the largest of which are St. Croix, St. Thomas, and St. John.

In the wake of the stock market crash of 1929, some 2,300 banks failed. Even bootleg liquor sales fell off, and prices went down with the depression now in force.

President Hoover signed (Jan. 15) the Stobbs bill, so named after Massachusetts Representative George Russell Stobbs, reducing the penalties imposed by the Jones Act (1929) for convictions under the Volstead Act.

Massachusetts Congressmen presented (Mar. 13) the first resolution to repeal or amend the 18th Amendment (liquor prohibition).

The United States State Department apologized (Jan. 29) to Premier Benito Mussolini of Italy for a statement uttered (Jan. 19) in an address at Philadelphia by Major General Smedley Darlington Butler of the Marine Corps that the Premier had run over and killed a child while motoring in Italy. Mussolini denied the act in a cablegram to the Italian Embassy in Washington. Butler was cited for court-martial, but he escaped trial by apologizing to Secretary of the Navy Charles F. Adams, who reprimanded the officer.

President Hoover rededicated (June 17) the remodeled tomb of Abraham Lincoln in Oak Ridge Cemetery, Springfield, Ill.

Prince Takamatsu, younger brother of Emperor Hirohito of Japan, and his bride, Princess Kikuko, visited the United States on their honeymoon trip. (They arrived in New York, Apr. 11.)

The King of Siam, Prajadhipok, came to the United States to undergo an eye operation. He was accompanied by his Queen, Rambai Barni. They were received in Washington (Apr. 28) and in New York (May 4). The King was operated on (May 10) at Ophir Hall, Westchester County, N. Y., his official United States residence. (The royal party departed July 28, after witnessing a New York "Yankees" and Detroit baseball game.)

Other notable foreign visitors to the United States included Edwin Thompson, Lord Mayor of Liverpool, Eng. (May 4), Premier Pierre Laval of France (Oct. 22), and Italian Minister of Foreign Affairs Dino Grandi (Nov. 16). In Philadelphia, an Italian jumped on Grandi's automobile and shouted "Down with Mussolini."

Radio telephone service was established between the Pacific Coast and the Far East.

Infantile paralysis was a prevalent disease in many states.

Dr. Nicholas Murray Butler and Jane Addams were awarded the Nobel prize for peace.

Rockefeller Center, New York, started rising from the ground when work was begun (in September) on the erection of the RKO building. The project ultimately embraced 15 structures, including Radio City.

The Tennessee House of Representatives upheld (June 10), 58 to 14, its statute that prohibited the teaching of the theory of evolution in schools maintained wholly or in part by State funds. The verdict of the Scopes evolution case (1925) was thereby reaffirmed.

In New York City, a committee under the chairmanship of Senator S. H. Hofstadter and headed by Samuel Seabury as counsel, got under way (Apr. 22) to investigate the city's government. This investigation led to the resignation of Mayor James J. ("Jimmy") Walker the next year (Sept. 1, 1932). Meanwhile, Mayor Walker visited Europe. He was elevated (Sept. 4) by the French government to the rank of Commander of the Legion of Honor without passing through the preliminary ranks of knight and officer.

The Pulitzer heirs sold (Feb. 24) the daily newspapers "The World" and "The Evening World," along with "The Sunday World," to the Scripps-Howard newspaper organization.

A naturalized Bronx, New York, banana dealer named Michele Schirru attempted (May 28) to assassinate Italian Premier Benito Mussolini in Rome and was shot to death.

The remains of Myles Standish, military leader of the "Mayflower" Pilgrims who died in 1656, were removed (Apr. 25) from their wooden coffin, transferred to a metal casket, and interred in the cemetery in Duxbury, Mass. Traces of his iron-gray hair were said to have been still visible.

The tomb of former President Warren Gamaliel Harding was dedicated (June 16) in Marion, O., by President Hoover.

Newly completed bridges included the Bayonne, N. Y., over the Kill van Kull; the George Washington, N. Y., over the Hudson, from New York to New Jersey; the Maysville, Ky., over the Ohio; the Willamette, Portland, Ore.

The Ford Motor Company, Detroit, Mich., turned out (Apr. 14) its 20,000,000th automobile. Henry Ford and his son, Edsel, drove the car to his museum in Dearborn and parked it alongside car No. 1, which was constructed in 1893.

The waters of Niagara Falls tore away (Jan. 17-18) about 1,000,000 cubic feet of rock on the American side.

The $4,000,000 Riverside Church (Baptist), New York, was dedicated (Feb. 8) by its pastor Dr. Harry Emerson Fosdick.

Theodore Dreiser twice slapped Sinclair Lewis across the face at a dinner (Mar. 19) of American writers in honor of the Russian novelist Boris Pilnyak at the Metropolitan Club, New York.

The Empire State office building, New York, tallest in the world—102 floors, 1,449 feet—was opened (May 1). The structure cost $54,000,000.

An armada of 597 airplanes of the First Air Division, United States Army Air Corps, dedicated in New York (May 23) the Municipal Airport at North Beach (which eventually became LaGuardia Airport) and Rentschler Field in Hartford, Conn. (May 24), flew over New England in army maneuvers, and repulsed (May 27) a mythical enemy over the New Jersey coast. The planes then circled (May 30) over Arlington National Cemetery, Va.

The new 47-floor Waldorf Astoria Hotel, New York, replacing the old structure of the same name farther downtown which formerly occupied the land that is now the site of the Empire State Building (above), was completed.

Jack ("Legs") Diamond, gangster boss, was shot (Dec. 18) to death in a boarding house in Albany, N. Y., after having been acquitted of a kidnaping charge.

Iowa, Nebraska, and South Dakota were overrun (in July) by hordes of grasshoppers.

Nine Negro boys were accused by two white girls of rape on a freight train in Alabama and brought to a trial in Scottsboro, Ala., that resulted in death sentences to eight of the boys. The conduct and verdict of the trial aroused nationwide criticism; an appeal was taken to the United States Supreme Court, which ordered (1932) a new trial. (At the second trial, one of the girls recanted her testimony. This time only one of the boys was sentenced to death. Again appealed to the Supreme Court, the verdict was set aside because of the exclusion of Negroes from the jury. At the retrial, four defendants were sentenced to life imprisonment and the rape charges against the five others were dropped. The case had its echo in literature, notably in the plays "Scottsboro Limited" by Langston Hughes, 1932, and "They Shall Not Die" by John Wexley, 1934.)

New records were established in aviation. United States pilot Wiley Post and Australian navigator Harold Gatty circled (June 23-July 1) the Globe in their monoplane "Winnie Mae" in 8 days, 15 hours, 51 minutes, flying 15,474 miles. Russell N. Boardman and John Polando flew (July 28-30) from Brooklyn, New York, to Istanbul, covering 5,011 miles in 49 hours, 20 minutes. Major James H. Doolittle crossed (Sept. 4) the continent from Burbank, Cal., to Newark, N. J., setting a record of 11 hours, 16 minutes. Hugh Herndon, Jr., and Clyde Pangborn accomplished (Oct. 4-5) the first nonstop flight across the Pacific from Tokyo, Japan, to Wenatchee, Wash., in 41 hours, 13 minutes. The U.S.S. "Akron," the world's largest dirigible, made (Nov. 3) a 10-hour flight with 207 persons aboard, the largest number carried up to that time.

The nation played bridge and more bridge. Culbertson and Lenz were the focal points for argument and tournaments.

Women wore stockings of transparent mesh, and the Empress Eugénie hat was the latest rage.

"Ballyhoo," a magazine, mocked advertising and built an enormous circulation over night.

Books of the year included: "Autobiography" (Lincoln Steffens),

"Classic Americans" (Henry Seidel Canby), "The Flowering Stone" (George Dillon; poems; Pulitzer prize 1932), "How to Write" (Gertrude Stein), "My Experiences in the World War" (Gen. John Joseph Pershing; Pulitzer prize 1932), "Theodore Roosevelt" (Henry P. Pringle; Pulitzer prize 1932) and the fiction, "Ambrose Holt and Family" (Susan Glaspell), "Back Street" (Fannie Hurst), "Black Daniel" (Honoré Willsie Morrow; a story about Daniel Webster), "The Forge" (Thomas S. Stribling), "The Good Earth" (Pearl Buck; Pulitzer prize 1932), "The Limestone Tree" (Ernest Hemingway), "The Night Life of the Gods" (Thorne Smith), "Sanctuary" (William Faulkner), "Shadows on the Rock" (Willa Cather), "Their Father's God" (Ole Rölvaag).

American radio stations broadcast (Feb. 12) the Latin speech of Pope Pius XI dedicating the Vatican radio station HVJ on the ninth anniversary of his coronation. In some sections of the world, the papal address was marred by signals sent out by the Russian Soviet station. Later, on the same day, in celebration of Lincoln's Birthday, President Hoover delivered a radio speech from the room in which the Emancipator had signed the Emancipation Proclamation.

The long-popular radio program, "Lady Esther Serenade," began (Sept. 27).

The first radio broadcast of a complete stage performance of an opera from the Metropolitan Opera House, New York, took place (Dec. 25) when Humperdinck's "Hänsel und Gretel" was transmitted by the National Broadcasting Company.

Experimental television was being pursued with improved results. In New York, the Columbia Broadcasting System established a television station W2XAB which was the first to maintain in its area a daily schedule of aural and visual transmission. Vocalists and performers such as Kate Smith, the Boswell Sisters, and others of radio fame were featured. Meanwhile John Logie Baird, internationally known British television engineer, came (in October) to New York to negotiate with radio station WMCA for the use of the telecasting machinery of his company, Baird Television Corp., Ltd., London. However, the Federal Radio Commission denied the application of WMCA for a license as "in violation of the section of the Radio Law prohibiting alien ownership or directorates of Companies holding wavelength privileges in the United States."

Lily Pons, French opera coloratura soprano, made (Jan. 31) her American debut in the title role of Donizetti's "Lucia di Lammermoor" in New York at the Metropolitan Opera House.

Alban Berg's modernist Austrian opera "Wozzeck" had two sensational performances in the United States under Leopold Stokowski—in Philadelphia at the Academy of Music (American première, Mar. 19) and in New York at the Metropolitan Opera House (Nov. 19). The opera was sung in the original German.

The Metropolitan Opera House, New York, produced (Feb. 7) the world première of Deems Taylor's second opera, "Peter Ibbetson," and gave (Nov. 7) the first American performance of Jaromir Weinberger's Czech opera "Schwanda, der Dudelsackpfeiffer" in German. The Polka and Fugue from the opera enjoyed for a time considerable popularity in orchestral concerts.

Martha Graham became known to devotees of the dance with her appearance in "Primitive Mysteries," a choreographic composition of her own. (She later gained a wider public when she was the mysterious "Miss Hush" of radio whose voice was to be identified in a guessing contest.)

Maude Adams returned (Nov. 3) to the stage, after an absence of 13 years, in "The Merchant of Venice" in Cleveland, O., at the Ohio Theatre.

New York plays that ran 175 or more performances included: "Tomorrow and Tomorrow" (Henry Miller, Jan. 13), "Private Lives" (Times Square, Jan. 27; 256 perf.), "The Barretts of Wimpole Street" (Empire, Feb. 9; 370 perf.), "Cynara" (Morosco, Nov. 2), "Counsellor at Law" (Plymouth, Nov. 6; 292 perf.), "Reunion in Vienna" (Martin Beck, Nov. 16; 264 perf.), "Springtime for Henry" (Bijou, Dec. 9). Eugene O'Neill's "Mourning Becomes Electra" was staged (Guild, Oct. 26; 150 perf.). Musical productions included: "You Said It" (46th Street, Jan. 19), "America's Sweetheart" (Broadhurst, Feb. 10), "The Band Wagon" (New Amsterdam, June 3; 260 perf.), "Ziegfeld Follies, 1931" (Ziegfeld, July 1), "Earl Carroll's Vanities" (Earl Carroll, Aug. 27; 278 perf.), "George White's Scandals" (Apollo, Sept. 14; 202 perf.), "Everybody's Welcome" (Shubert, Oct. 13), "The Cat and the Fiddle" (Globe, Oct. 15; 395 perf.), "The Laugh Parade" (Imperial, Nov. 2; 231 perf.), "Of Thee I Sing," book by George S. Kaufman and Morrie Ryskind, lyrics by Ira Gershwin, music by George Gershwin (Music Box, Dec. 26; 441 perf.; Pulitzer prize 1932—the first musical production to receive such an award).

Motion pictures of the year included: "Bad Girl" (James Dunn, Sally Eilers), "Charlie Chan Carries On" (Warner Oland; one of his first Charlie Chan impersonations), "Cimarron" (Irene Dunne, Richard Dix), "City Lights" (Charlie Chaplin), "Daddy Long Legs" (Janet Gaynor, Warner Baxter), "Five Star Final," "Flowers and Trees" (Walt Disney's first technicolor film), "A Free Soul" (Norma Shearer), "Front Page" "Min and Bill" (Marie Dressler, Wallace Beery), "The Sin of Madelon Claudet," "Skippy" (Jackie Cooper), "The Smiling Lieutenant" (Maurice Chevalier), "Street Scene," "Trader Horn."

Knute Rockne, noted football coach of Notre Dame University, South Bend, Ind., was killed (Mar. 31) in an airplane crash near Bazaar, Kan.

Rogers ("Rajah") Hornsby, star second baseman of the St. Louis National League ("Cardinals") baseball club, set a record when he hit three home runs in one game.

Thomas Alva Edison, aged 84, died (Oct. 18) in West Orange, N. J.

ᢒᢐ 1932

Alone Together (Flying Colors). w., Howard Dietz. m., Arthur Schwartz. Harms, Inc., cop. 1932.

April in Paris (Walk a Little ·Faster). w., E. Y. Harburg. m., Vernon Duke [pseud. of Vladimir Dukelsky]. Harms, Inc., cop. 1932.

Brother, Can You Spare a Dime (Americana). w., E. Y. Harburg. m., Jay Gorney. Harms Inc., cop. 1932.

Cabin in the Cotton. w., Mitchell Parish. m., Frank Perkins. Mills Music, Inc., cop. 1932.

La Cumparsita. See 1926.

Eadie Was a Lady (Take a Chance). w., B. G. DeSylva. m., Richard Whiting and Nacio Herb Brown. Harms, Inc., cop. 1932 by George G. DeSylva.

Eres Tu. w., m., Miguel Sandoval. Southern Music Pub. Co., cop. 1932.

Forty-Second Street (film: Forty-Second Street). w., Al Dubin. m., Harry Warren. M. Witmark & Sons, cop. 1932.

Granada. w., m., Augustin Lara. Peer International Corp., cop. 1932.

How Deep Is the Ocean? w., m., Irving Berlin. Irving Berlin, Inc., cop. 1932.

I'm Gettin' Sentimental over You. w., Ned Washington. m., George Bassman. Lawrence Music Publishers, Inc., cop. 1932; assigned 1934 to Mills Music, Inc.

I Gotta Right to Sing the Blues (Earl Carroll Vanities). w., Ted Koehler. m., Harold Arlen. Harms, Inc., cop. 1932.

I've Told Ev'ry Little Star (Music in the Air). w., Oscar Hammerstein, 2nd. m., Jerome Kern. T. B. Harms Co., cop. 1932.

I Surrender, Dear. w., Gordon Clifford. m., Harry Barris. Mills Music, Inc., cop. 1931 by Freed & Powers, Ltd., Hollywood; assigned 1932 to Mills Music, Inc.

If I Love Again (Hold Your Horses). w., J. P. Murray. m., Ben Oakland. Harms, Inc., cop. 1932.

In a Shanty in Old Shanty Town. w., Joe Young. m., Little Jack Little and John Siras. M. Witmark & Sons, cop. 1932.

Is I in Love? I Is. w., Mercer Cook. m., J. Russell Robinson. De-Sylva, Brown & Henderson, Inc., cop. 1932.

It Don't Mean a Thing. w., Irving Mills. m., Duke Ellington. Gotham Music Service, Inc., cop. 1932.

Just Because You're You. w., m., Cliff Friend. Olman Music Corp., cop. 1932.

Let's All Sing Like the Birdies Sing. w., Robert Hargreaves and Stanley J. Damerell. m., Tolchard Evans. Mills Music, Inc., cop. 1932 by Cecil Lennox, Ltd., London.

Let's Call It a Day (Strike Me Pink). w., m., Lew Brown and Ray Henderson. Elar Music Corp. (Harms, Inc., selling agents), cop. 1932.

Let's Have Another Cup o' Coffee (Face the Music). w., m., Irving Berlin. Irving Berlin, Inc., cop. 1932.

Let's Put Out the Lights. w., m., Herman Hupfeld. Harms, Inc., cop. 1932.

Louisiana Hayride (Flying Colors). w., Howard Dietz. m., Arthur Schwartz. Harms, Inc., cop. 1932.

Lullaby of the Leaves. w., Joe Young. m., Bernice Petkere. Irving Berlin, Inc., cop. 1932.

Mimi (film: Love Me Tonight). w., Lorenz Hart. m., Richard Rodgers. Famous Music Corp., cop. 1932.

Night and Day (Gay Divorce; film: The Gay Divorcée). w., m., Cole Porter. Harms, Inc., cop. 1932.

On a Roof in Manhattan (Face the Music). w., m., Irving Berlin. Irving Berlin, Inc., cop. 1932.

The Organ Grinder. w., Herb Magidson. m., Sam H. Stept. M. Witmark & Sons, cop. 1932.

Play, Fiddle, Play. w., Jack Lawrence. m., Emery Deutsch and Arthur Altman. Edw. B. Marks Music Corp., cop. 1932.

Rise 'n Shine (Take a Chance). w., Bud G. DeSylva. m., Vincent Youmans. Harms, Inc., cop 1932 by George G. DeSylva.

Sentimental Gentleman from Georgia. w., Mitchell Parish. m., Frank Perkins. Mills Music, Inc., cop. 1932.

A Shine on Your Shoes (Flying Colors). w., Howard Dietz. m., Arthur Schwartz. Harms, Inc., cop. 1932.

Shuffle Off to Buffalo (film: Forty-Second Street). w., Al Dubin. m., Harry Warren. M. Witmark & Sons, cop. 1932.

So Do I (Take a Chance). w., Bud G. DeSylva. m., Vincent Youmans. Harms, Inc., cop. 1932 by George G. DeSylva.

Soft Lights and Sweet Music (Face the Music). w., m., Irving Berlin. Irving Berlin, Inc., cop. 1932.

The Song Is You (Music in the Air). w., Oscar Hammerstein, 2nd. m., Jerome Kern. T. B. Harms Co., cop. 1932 by Jerome Kern.

Speak to Me of Love—*original French title:* Parlez-Moi d'Amour. French words and music, Jean Lenoir. American version, Bruce Siever. Harms, Inc., cop. 1930 by Editions Smyth, Paris; cop. 1932 by Harms, Inc.

Strange Interlude. w., Ben Bernie and Walter Hirsch. m., Phil Baker. Miller Music, Inc., cop. 1932.

Tell Me Why You Smile, Mona Lisa?—*original German title:* Warum lächelst du, Mona Lisa? German words, Walter Reisch. English words, Raymond B. Egan. m., Robert Stolz. Leo Feist, Inc., cop. 1931 by Alrobi Musikverlag, Berlin; cop. 1932 by Leo Feist, Inc.

Three's a Crowd (film: The Crooner). w., Al Dubin and Irving Kahal. m., Harry Warren. M. Witmark & Sons, cop. 1932.

Turn Out the Light (Take a Chance). w., m., Bud G. DeSylva, Richard A. Whiting, and Nacio Herb Brown. Harms, Inc., cop. 1932.

Underneath the Harlem Moon. w., Mack Gordon. m., Harry Revel. DeSylva, Brown & Henderson, Inc., cop. 1932.

Willow Weep for Me. w., m., Ann Ronell. Irving Berlin, Inc., cop. 1932.

Wintergreen for President (Of Thee I Sing). w., Ira Gershwin. m., George Gershwin. New World Music Corp., cop. 1932.

You're an Old Smoothie (Take a Chance). w., m., Bud G. DeSylva, Richard A. Whiting, and Nacio Herb Brown. Harms, Inc., cop. 1932.

You're Getting to Be a Habit with Me (film: Forty-Second Street). w., Al Dubin. m., Harry Warren. M. Witmark & Sons, cop. 1932.

Young and Healthy (film: Forty-Second Street). w., Al Dubin. m., Harry Warren. M. Witmark & Sons, cop. 1932.

In commemoration of the 200th anniversary of George Washington's birth, the U. S. Post Office issued (Jan. 1) a special series of twelve postage stamps, each displaying a portrait of Washington at a different age. Also, a Washington-head 25-cent piece went (Aug. 1) into circulation; the coin was designed by New York sculptor John Flanagan after the bust modeled by Jean Antoine Houdon who visited Washington at Mount Vernon in 1785.

The financial repression, dating from 1929, still afflicted the country. In an effort to stimulate business, Congress established (Jan. 22) the Reconstruction Finance Corporation ("R.F.C.") to make federal loans available to banks and insurance, mortgage, loan, and credit companies. In line with economy measures, President Hoover declared (June 20) a Moratorium on reparations and war debt payments. Meanwhile in Minnesota began a movement instituting a moratorium on mortgage foreclosures that rapidly spread to other states. As in the time of Coxey (1894), an "army" converged on Washington, D. C.—the Bonus Army, which camped in the mud flats near the city.

Organized labor in the United States won an important legislative victory when President Hoover signed (Mar. 23) the anti-injunction Norris-LaGuardia Act, so named after Nebraska Senator George William Norris and New York Representative Fiorello Henry LaGuardia.

The Lansing-Ishii Agreement (1917) between the United States and Japan was annulled (Apr. 14).

The United States and Canada negotiated a treaty for the development of a waterway for ocean-going ships between the Great Lakes and the Atlantic.

The Federal Bureau of Investigation ("F.B.I.") established a laboratory for the scientific examination of evidence in criminal cases.

Radio telephone service was established between New York and Mexico City.

The term "forgotten man" passed into popular usage when Franklin Delano Roosevelt used (Apr. 7) the words in a presidential campaign speech. The expression had already been coined by William Graham Sumner, a former Yale professor of political science, as the title of a book "The Forgotten Man and Other Essays" (1919).

Nineteen-month-old Charles Augustus Lindbergh, Jr., son of Col. Charles A. Lindbergh and Anne Morrow Lindbergh, disappeared (Mar. 1) from his crib in his parents' home at Hopewell, N. J., near Princeton. While a wide search for the infant and its abductor was in progress, John F. Condon, a Bronx, New York, public school principal, obtained $50,-000 ransom money from Lindbergh to contact an alleged agent of the kidnaping. Meanwhile, wealthy Mrs. Evalyn Walsh McLean was swindled out of $100,000 by Gaston Bullock Means on his promise to restore the child. Later Means went to prison for the fraud. The lifeless body of the baby, reduced almost to a skeleton, was located (May 12) in a bush on the roadway between Hopewell and Princeton, less than five miles from the Lindbergh house. A marked ransom banknote was presented at a gasoline filling station in the Bronx, New York City, and the police took into custody the passer of the note, one Bruno Richard Hauptmann, a paroled German convict who had entered the country illegally in 1923. In the garage at Hauptmann's Bronx home was discovered more than $14,000 of the ransom money. The excessive publicity given to the tragic case drove the Lindberghs to seek peace of mind in England (1935-38) and in France (1939). (In consequence of the case, Congress passed the Patterson Act, known generally as the Lindbergh Act, making the transportation of a kidnaped person across State boundaries punishable with life imprisonment. The act was amended in 1934 to include the death penalty for failure to return the victim unharmed unless the jury recommends clemency.)

Aviatrix Amelia Earhart (now Mrs. George Palmer Putnam), who had made in 1928 a transatlantic crossing in an airplane with Wilmer Stultz and Louis Gordon, became the first woman to make a solo flight across the Atlantic when she flew (May 20-21) from Harbor Grace, Newfoundland, to Londonderry, Ireland, a distance of 2,026½ miles in 14 hours, 50 minutes. James Mattern and Bennett Griffin made (July 5) a plane trip from Harbor Grace to Berlin in 18 hours, 41 minutes. James G. Haislip set (Aug. 29) a new transcontinental record from Los Angeles, Cal., to Brooklyn, New York City, of 10 hours, 19 minutes.

The air mail rate was changed (July 6) to eight cents and the U. S.

Post Office accordingly issued (Sept. 26) an olive-green postage stamp of that denomination.

The Tomb of the Unknown Soldier in the National Cemetery, Arlington, Va., was dedicated on Armistice Day (Nov. 11).

Gerhart Hauptmann, Germany's great dramatist, poet, and novelist, came to the United States on the invitation of the Carnegie Endowment for International Peace on the occasion of his 70th birthday to deliver a memorial address in celebration of the 100th anniversary of Goethe's death. Columbia University conferred upon him an honorary doctor's degree and he was made a member of the American Academy of Arts and Letters.

The Radio City Music Hall, New York, opened (Dec. 27) as the largest indoor theatre in the world with a seating capacity of 6,200.

In a suit for plagiarism brought before the United States District Court, presiding Judge Woolsey ruled (Dec. 28) that the 1932 Pulitzer prize play "Of Thee I Sing" was not an infringement on the revue "U. S. A. with Music."

The Folger Shakespeare Memorial Library, Washington, D. C., was dedicated. It was the gift of Henry Clay Folger, former president of the Standard Oil Company of New York, and his wife. The library contains the largest collection of Shakespeariana in the United States.

Books of the year included: "Conquistador" (Archibald MacLeish; an epic poem; Pulitzer prize 1933), "Earth Horizon" (Mary Austin; an autobiography), "Grover Cleveland" (Allan Nevins; a biography; Pulitzer prize 1933), "The Liberation of American Literature" (Victor Francis Calverton), "Life Begins at Forty" (Walter Boughton Pitkin), "Mark Twain's America" (John Dos Passos), "The Significance of Sectionalism in American History" (Frederick Jackson Turner, published posthumously; Pulitzer prize 1933) and the fiction, "Beyond Desire" (Sherwood Anderson), "The Bishop's Jaegers" (Thorne Smith), "Bright Skin" (Julia Peterkin), "The End of Desire" (Robert Herrick), "The Harbourmaster" (William McFee), "In Tragic Life" (Vardis Fisher), "Mutiny on the Bounty" (Charles Bernard Nordhoff and James Norman Hall), "The Sheltered Life" (Ellen Glasgow), "State Fair" (Philip Duffield Stong), "The Store" (Thomas S. Stribling; Pulitzer prize 1933), "The Thin Man" (Dashiell Hammett), "Tobacco Road" (Erskine Caldwell), "Young Lonigan" (James Farrell; sequels, "The Young Manhood of Studs Lonigan," 1934, and "Judgement Day," 1935).

Florent Schmitt, eminent French composer, visited the United States, appearing as piano soloist in performances of his own works.

Bruno Walter, famous German orchestra director, was guest conductor of the New York Philharmonic-Symphony Society.

The Scottish singing comedian Harry MacLennan Lauder—since 1919, Sir Harry Lauder—made his 25th tour of America.

New York columnist Walter Winchell started (Dec. 4) his radio program.

New York plays that ran 175 or more performances included: "The Animal Kingdom" (Broadhurst, Jan. 12), "That's Gratitude" (Waldorf, June 16; 204 perf.), "When Ladies Meet" (Royale, Oct. 6), "Dinner at Eight" (Music Box, Oct. 22; 232 perf.), "Dangerous Corner" (Empire, Oct. 27; 206 perf.), "The Late Christopher Bean" (Henry Miller, Oct. 31; 224 perf.), "Autumn Crocus" (Morosco, Nov. 19; 210 perf.), "Biography" (Guild, Dec. 12; 283 perf.), "Goodbye Again" (Masque, Dec. 28; 216 perf.). La Compania Dramatica Española from Madrid played Spanish repertory (New Yorker, Apr. 1; 40 perf.). Shakespeare's "Troilus and Cressida" had its first professional presentation in America (Broadway, June 8; 8 perf.—the only other known production was by the Yale Dramatic Society). Musical productions included: "Through the Years" (Manhattan, Jan. 28; 20 perf.), "Face the Music" (New Amsterdam, Feb. 17), "Hot-Cha!" (Ziegfeld, Mar. 8), "Flying Colors" (Imperial, Sept. 15; 188 perf.), "Music in the Air" (Alvin, Nov. 8; 342 perf.), "Take a Chance" (Apollo, Nov. 26; 243 perf.), "Gay Divorce" (Ethel Barrymore, Nov. 29; 248 perf.), "Walk a Little Faster" (St. James, Dec. 7; 119 perf.). "Show Boat" was revived (Casino, May 19; 180 perf.).

Puppet shows enjoyed a sudden and unprecedented revival in New York in the productions of Tony Sarg, Sue Hastings, the Yale Puppeteers, the Marionette Guild, and Vittorio Podrecca's Teatro dei Piccoli from Italy, which travelled across the country to San Francisco and arrived in Hollywood to take part in the film "I Am Suzanne."

The double bill became a feature in the motion-picture theatres. Films of the year included: "Arrowsmith" (Ronald Coleman, Helen Hayes), "Back Street" (Irene Dunne, John Boles), "Bill of Divorcement" (John Barrymore, Katharine Hepburn), "The Champ" (Wallace Beery, Jackie Cooper), "Dr. Jekyll and Mr. Hyde" (Fredric March), "Emma" (Marie Dressler), "Forty-Second Street" (the later well-known Ginger Rogers appearing in a minor part), "Grand Hotel" (Greta Garbo, John and Lionel Barrymore, Joan Crawford, Wallace Beery), "The Guardsman" (Alfred Lunt, Lynn Fontanne), "Scarface" (Paul Muni).

Jack Sharkey brought back to America the heavyweight boxing championship when he defeated (June 21) in New York the German title holder Max Schmeling in 15 rounds on a decision. (Sharkey lost to Schmeling on a foul in 1930.)

For the second time (the first was in 1904), the Olympic games were held in the United States; they took place (July 30-Aug. 14) in Los Angeles, Cal.

૱ 1933

After All You're All I'm After (She Loves Me Not). w., Edward Heyman. m., Arthur Schwartz. Harms, Inc., cop. 1933.

Ah, but Is It Love? (film: Moonlight and Pretzels). w., E. Y. Harburg. m., Jay Gorney. Harms, Inc., cop. 1933.

Annie Doesn't Live Here Anymore. w., Joe Young and Johnny Burke. m., Harold Spina. Irving Berlin, Inc., cop. 1933.

The Boulevard of Broken Dreams (film: Moulin Rouge). w., Al Dubin. m., Harry Warren. Remick Music Corp., cop. 1933.

By a Waterfall (film: Footlight Parade). w., Irving Kahal. m., Sammy Fain. M. Witmark & Sons, cop. 1933.

Carioca (film: Flying Down to Rio). w., Gus Kahn and Edward Eliscu. m., Vincent Youmans. T. B. Harms Co., cop. 1933 by Max Dreyfus and Vincent Youmans.

Did You Ever See a Dream Walking (film: Sitting Pretty). w., Mack Gordon. m., Harry Revel. DeSylva, Brown & Henderson, Inc., cop. 1933 by Paramount Productions, Inc.; assigned 1933 to DeSylva, Brown & Henderson, Inc.

Dinner at Eight (film: Dinner at Eight). w., Dorothy Fields. m., Jimmy McHugh. Robbins Music Corp., cop. 1933 by Metro-Goldwyn-Mayer Corp.; assigned 1933 to Robbins Music Corp.

Doin' the Uptown Lowdown (film: Broadway Thru a Keyhole). w., Mack Gordon. m., Harry Revel. DeSylva, Brown & Henderson, Inc., cop. 1933.

Don't Blame Me. w., Dorothy Fields. m., Jimmy McHugh. Robbins Music Corp., cop. 1933 by Metro-Goldwyn-Mayer Corp.; assigned 1933 to Robbins Music Corp.

Easter Parade (As Thousands Cheer). w., m., Irving Berlin. Irving Berlin, Inc., cop. 1933.

Everything I Have Is Yours (film: Dancing Lady). w., Harold Adamson. m., Burton Lane. Robbins Music Corp., cop. 1933 by Metro-Goldwyn-Mayer Corp.; assigned 1933 to Robbins Music Corp.

Flying Down to Rio (film: Flying Down to Rio). w., Gus Kahn and Edward Eliscu. m., Vincent Youmans. T. B. Harms Co., cop. 1933.

The Gold Diggers' Song—We're in the Money (Gold Diggers of 1933). w., Al Dubin. m., Harry Warren. Remick Music Corp., cop. 1933 by M. Witmark & Sons.

Heat Wave (As Thousands Cheer). w., m., Irving Berlin. Irving Berlin, Inc., cop. 1933.

Hey! Young Fella (Radio City's Music Hall First New York Production). w., Dorothy Fields. m., Jimmy McHugh. Robbins Music Corp., cop. 1933 by Metro-Goldwyn-Mayer Corp.

I Cover the Waterfront. w., Edward Heyman. m., John W. Green. Harms, Inc., cop. 1933.

I Like Mountain Music. w., James Cavanaugh. m., Frank Weldon. M. Witmark & Sons, cop. 1933.

I Wanna Be Loved. w., Billy Rose and Edward Heyman. m., Johnny Green. Famous Music Corp., cop. 1933.

In the Valley of the Moon. w., m., Charlie Tobias and Joe Burke. Joe Morris Music Co., cop. 1933.

Inka Dinka Doo (film: Palooka). w., m., Jimmie Durante, Ben Ryan, and Harry Donnelly. Irving Berlin, Inc., cop. 1933.

It Isn't Fair. w., Richard Himber. m., Richard Himber, Frank Warshauer and Sylvester Sprigato. Words and Music, Inc., cop. 1933.

It's Only a Paper Moon. w., Billy Rose and E. Y. Harburg. m., Harold Arlen. Harms, Inc., cop. 1933.

It's the Talk of the Town. w., Marty Symes and Al. J. Neiburg. m., Jerry Livingston. Santly Bros., Inc., cop. 1933; assigned 1938 to Santly-Joy-Select, Inc.; assigned 1942 to Santly-Joy, Inc.

Keep on Doin' What You're Doin' (film: Hips Hips Hooray). w., m., Bert Kalmar and Harry Ruby. Irving Berlin, Inc., cop. 1933.

Keep Young and Beautiful (film: Roman Scandals). w., Al Dubin. m., Harry Warren. M. Witmark & Sons, cop. 1933.

The Last Round-Up. w., m., Billy Hill. Shapiro, Bernstein & Co., cop. 1933.

Lazybones. w., m., Johnny Mercer and Hoagy Carmichael. Southern Music Pub. Co., cop. 1933.

Let 'Em Eat Cake (Let 'Em Eat Cake). w., Ira Gershwin. m. George Gershwin. New World Music Corp., cop. 1933.

Let's Fall in Love (film: Let's Fall in Love). w., Ted Koehler. m., Harold Arlen. Irving Berlin, Inc., cop. 1933.

Love Is the Sweetest Thing. w., m., Ray Noble. Harms, Inc., cop. 1932 by Francis, Day & Hunter, Ltd., London; cop. 1933 by Harms, Inc.

Love Locked Out. w., Max Kester. m., Ray Noble. Harms, Inc., cop. 1933 by The Victoria Music Pub. Co., Ltd.

Love Songs of the Nile (film: The Barbarian). w., Arthur Freed. m., Nacio Herb Brown. Robbins Music Corp., cop. 1933 by Metro-Goldwyn-Mayer Corp.; assigned 1933 to Robbins Music Corp.

Lovely. w., Edgar Leslie. m., Fred E. Ahlert. T. B. Harms Co., cop. 1933.

Lover (film: Love Me Tonight). Lorenz Hart. m., Richard Rodgers. Famous Music Corp., cop. 1933.

Maria Elena. Spanish words and music, Lorenzo Barcelata. English words, S. K. Russell. Southern Music Publishing Co., Ltd., cop. 1933; assigned 1941 to Peer International Corp.

Mine (Let 'Em Eat Cake). w., Ira Gershwin. m., George Gershwin. New World Music Corp., cop. 1933.

Moonlight and Pretzels (Moonlight and Pretzels). w., E. Y. Harburg. m., Jay Gorney. Harms, Inc., cop. 1933.

Music Makes Me (film: Flying Down to Rio). w., Gus Kahn and Edward Eliscu. m., Vincent Youmans. T. B. Harms Co., cop. 1933 by Dreyfus and Vincent Youmans.

My Hat's on the Side of My Head (film: Jack Ahoy). w., m., Harry Woods and Claude Hurlbert. Shapiro, Bernstein & Co., Inc., cop. 1933 by The Cinephonic Music Co., Ltd., London.

My Moonlight Madonna. w., Paul Francis Webster. m., adapted from Zdenko Fibich's "Poem" by William Scotti. Carl Fischer, Inc., cop. 1933.

Not for All the Rice in China (As Thousands Cheer). w., m., Irving Berlin. Irving Berlin, Inc., cop. 1933.

The Old Spinning Wheel. w., m., Billy Hill. Shapiro, Bernstein & Co., Inc., cop. 1933.

On the Trail (*in:* Grand Canyon Suite). Orch. composition. m., Ferdie Grofé. Robbins Music Corp., cop. 1933.

Once in a Blue Moon (The Stepping Stones). w., Anne Caldwell. m., Jerome Kern. T. B. Harms Co., cop. 1933.

Orchids in the Moonlight (film: Flying Down to Rio). w., Gus Kahn and Edward Eliscu. m., Vincent Youmans. T. B. Harms Co., cop. 1933 by Max Dreyfus and Vincent Youmans.

Shadow Waltz (film: Gold Diggers of 1933). w., Al Dubin. m., Harry Warren. Remick Music Corp., cop. 1933 by M. Witmark & Sons.

Shanghai Lil (film: Footlight Parade). w., Al Dubin. m., Harry Warren. M. Witmark & Sons, cop. 1933.

Smoke Gets in Your Eyes (Roberta). w., Otto Harbach. m., Jerome Kern. T. B. Harms Co., cop. 1933 by Jerome Kern.

Sophisticated Lady. Instrumental. m., Duke Ellington. Gotham Music Service, Inc., cop. 1933.

Stormy Weather—Keeps Rainin' All the Time. w., Ted Koehler. m., Harold Arlen. Mills Music, Inc., cop. 1933.

Sweet Madness (Murder at the Vanities). w., Ned Washington. m., Victor Young. Harms, Inc., cop. 1933.

Temptation (film: Going Hollywood). w., Arthur Freed. m., Nacio Herb Brown. Robbins Music Corp., cop. 1933 by Metro-Goldwyn-Mayer Corp.; assigned 1933 to Robbins Music Corp.

Tony's Wife. w., Harold Adamson. m., Burton Lane. Irving Berlin, Inc., cop. 1933.

The Touch of Your Hand (Roberta). w., Otto Harbach. m., Jerome Kern. T. B. Harms Co., cop. 1933 by Jerome Kern.

Two Tickets to Georgia. w., m., Joe Young, Charles Tobias, and J. Fred Coots. Irving Berlin, Inc., cop. 1933.

Under a Blanket of Blue. w., Marty Symes and Al. J. Neiburg. m., Jerry Levinson. Santly Bros., Inc., cop. 1933.

Underneath the Arches. w., m., Bud Flanagan. Additional American lyric, Joseph McCarthy. Robbins Music Corp., cop. 1932 by Campbell, Connelly & Co., Ltd., London, assigned 1933 to Robbins Music Corp.

We'll Make Hay While the Sun Shines (film: Going Hollywood). w., Arthur Freed. m., Nacio Herb Brown. Robbins Music Corp., cop. 1933 by Metro-Goldwyn-Mayer Corp.; assigned 1933 to Robbins Music Corp.

Who's Afraid of the Big Bad Wolf? (film: The Three Little Pigs). w., m., Frank E. Churchill; additional lyrics, Ann Ronell, Irving Berlin, Inc., cop. 1933.

Without That Certain Thing. w., m., Max and Harry Nesbitt. T. B. Harms Co., cop. 1933 by Irwin Dash Music Co., Ltd., London.

Yesterday (Roberta). w., Otto Harbach. m., Jerome Kern. T. B. Harms Co., cop. 1933 by Jerome Kern.

You're Devastating (Roberta). w., Otto Harbach. m., Jerome Kern. T. B. Harms Co., cop. 1933 by Jerome Kern.

You're My Past, Present and Future (film: Broadway Thru a Keyhole). w., Mack Gordon. m., Harry Revel. DeSylva, Brown & Henderson, Inc., cop. 1933.

You Have Taken My Heart. w., John Mercer. m., Gordon Jenkins. Santly Bros., Inc., cop. 1933.

Franklin Delano Roosevelt, Democrat, of New York, was inaugurated 32nd President.

The 20th Amendment was proclaimed (Feb. 6) as ratified. Known as the "lame duck" amendment, it set the date of the beginning of the terms of the President and the Vice-President as Jan. 20 and those of the Senators and Representatives as Jan. 3. It also regulated the meeting of Congress and the succession to the Presidency.

Beer—3.2 per cent—became legal (passed by Congress Mar. 14, signed by President Roosevelt Mar. 22, effective Apr. 7), and prohibition in the United States came to an end when Utah, as the necessary 36th State, ratified (Dec. 5) the 21st Amendment that repealed the 18th Amendment.

Drastic steps were taken to break the nation's economic depression now in its fourth year. A local "bank holiday" of eight days (Feb. 14-22) was instituted by Minnesota Governor W. A. Comstock. Following this President Roosevelt proclaimed a national "bank holiday" of ten days (Mar. 4-14). A movement to ferret out "hoarded gold" in private possession began. Gold exports were banned (Apr. 19) by the President. The United States went off the gold standard and started (in Oct.) to buy domestic and foreign gold above the market price. Meanwhile Congress passed the Agricultural Adjustment Act (signed May 12) and the National Industrial Recovery Act (signed June 16), commonly known as the N.R.A. Its operations were directed by Gen. Hugh Johnson. (Both enactments were voided by the U. S. Supreme Court—the N.R.A. in 1935; the A.A.A. in 1936.)

To focus public attention on the N.R.A., the U. S. Post Office issued (Aug. 15) a special three-cent purple postage stamp, picturing a forward-going farmer, an office worker, a laborer, and a woman "in common determination."

President Roosevelt decided to take the nation into his confidence—he began (Mar. 12) his "fireside chats" over the radio.

"New Deal" and "brain trust" were words which now were added to the vocabulary. The first referred to the policies of the Roosevelt administration; the second, to its body of advisers comprised mostly of college professors (hence, "brain trusters").

Federal relief (dole) went into effect (in May).

Congress created the Tennessee Valley Authority (May 18) to develop the water power of the Tennessee River and to prevent floods in its area. Also, the Civilian Conservation Corps was established as a government agency to recruit unemployed youth for service on public works (it was liquidated June 30, 1943).

The Century of Progress Exposition was held (May 27-Nov. 12) in Chicago. (The Exposition reopened May, 26, 1934, and closed Oct. 31.) In honor of the occasion, the U. S. Post Office issued (May 25) two commemorative postage stamps, one picturing Fort Dearborn (the pioneer site of Chicago) and the other the massive three-tower Federal building on the Exposition grounds. Also, a special 50-cent green air mail adhesive was issued (Oct. 2) for mail to be carried on the flight of the German dirigible balloon "Graf Zeppelin" to the Exposition.

The United States extended (Nov. 18) official recognition to Russia (Union of Socialist Soviet Republics).

U. S. Marines, sent to Nicaragua in 1927, were withdrawn.

Headline sensation for a few weeks was Howard Scott and "technocracy."

Lynchings again engaged public attention. Maryland Governor Richie called out (in October) the National Guard to protect Negro prisoners. California Governor Rolph shocked people when he condoned (in Nov.)

a lynching in San Jose. In Missouri, a Negro was the victim of a lynching in spite of the presence of troops.

The United States established a post office in Little America at the camp of the Byrd Antarctic Expedition and the Post Office Department issued (Oct. 9) a special three-cent navy blue postage stamp. The mail was transported through the facilities of the Expedition because the government had no other means of conveyance.

Thomas H. Morgan was awarded the Nobel prize for medicine and physiology—the first native American to be so honored.

The colorful and dynamic Fiorello Henry LaGuardia, popularly called "the Little Flower," was elected (Nov. 7) mayor of New York City on the Fusion (anti-Tammany) ticket. (He was re-elected repeatedly until 1945 when ill health forced his withdrawal.)

Radio City, a towering 70-floor office building in Rockefeller Center, New York, was opened (in Nov.) with an exhibition showing the first thirteen years of radio progress.

Albert Einstein, internationally known German-Swiss physicist and discoverer of relativity, settled in Princeton, N. J., as professor of mathematics at the Institute for Advanced Study.

Arnold Schönberg, Viennese "modernist" composer, came (in Oct.) to America as a teacher at the Malkin Conservatory in Boston. (He settled in 1935 in California and became an American citizen in 1940.)

Aviation was featured again in newspaper headlines. The world's largest dirigible balloon "Macon" was launched (Mar. 11). Less than a month later (Apr. 4), a storm off Barnegat, N. J., destroyed the U. S. Navy dirigible balloon "Akron"; 73 of the personnel, including Aviation Chief Rear Admiral W. A. Moffett, were drowned. With great national pride, Italy sent to the Chicago Century of Progress Exposition an armada of 24 seaplanes in formation carrying 96 men under the command of General Italo Balbo. (The planes left Orbetello, Italy, July 2, arrived by seven hops in Chicago July 15, and afterwards returned to Italy.) In a second flight around the world (July 15-22), Wiley Post covered 15,596 miles in 7 days, 18 hours, 49½ minutes. (On his first world flight in 1931 he flew 15,128 miles in 8 days, 15 hours, 51 minutes.) Six Navy flying boats made (Sept. 7-8) a nonstop flight of 2,059 miles from Norfolk, Va., to Coco Solo, Canal Zone. Flying for the Pan-American Airways Company, Col. and Mrs. Charles Augustus Lindbergh completed a 29,081-mile survey of transoceanic air routes over Greenland, Iceland, Russia, the Azores, West Africa, and South America.

Books of the year included: "Autobiography of Alice B. Toklas" (Gertrude Stein; her own autobiography), "Collected Verse" (Robert Hillyer; Pulitzer prize 1934), "Every Man a King" (Huey Long; an autobiography), "John Hay" (Tyler Dennett; a biography; Pulitzer prize 1934), "The People's Choice" (Herbert Agar; a history; Pulitzer prize 1934) and the fiction, "Anthony Adverse" (Hervey Allen), "God's Little Acre" (Erskine Caldwell), "Lamb in His Bosom" (Caroline Miller;

Pulitzer prize 1934), "No Castle in Spain" (William McFee), "One More Spring" (Robert Herrick), "Stranger's Return" (Philip Stong), "Winner Take Nothing" (Ernest Hemingway).

The Metropolitan Opera House, New York, produced (Jan. 7) the world première of Louis Gruenberg's American opera "Emperor Jones," based on Eugene O'Neill's play (1920). The opera had seven performances.

Charles Wakefield Cadman's opera "The Willow Tree," composed expressly for radio, received (Oct. 3) its première by the National Broadcasting Company, New York.

An interesting season of ballet and dance succeeded the puppet shows of the preceding year in New York. Col. W. de Basil's Ballet Russe de Monte Carlo, in part made up of former members of the historic Diaghileff Company, presented revivals and an American ballet drama by Archibald MacLeish, with music by Nicolas Nabokoff, entitled "Union Pacific" (première, Philadelphia, Forrest Theatre, Apr. 6). The troupe toured the country to the delight of audiences everywhere. Uday Shan-Kar and 14 Hindu dancers were seen in native art (Carnegie Hall, Oct. 21). The Jooss Ballet, a German company of 20 members, came on (Forrest Theatre, Oct. 31; 48 performances) and went on tour of the country. Most significant in its repertory was a satire "The Green Room." The internationally famous dancer Serge Lifar came over from Paris with a troupe of eight colleagues (Forrest Theatre, Nov. 5).

This year saw the productions of "Tobacco Road" (New York, Masque Theatre, Dec. 4), a play by John Kirkland based on the novel of the same name by Erskine Caldwell. The play ran over the years to 3,182 performances—855 more than the 2,327 of its runner-up "Abie's Irish Rose" (1922), and was topped only by "Life with Father" (1939). Maxwell Anderson's "Both Your Houses" (Royale, Mar. 6, 104 perf.) won the 1933 Pulitzer prize. New York plays that ran over 200 performances included: "One Sunday Afternoon" (Little, Feb. 15; 322 perf.), "Another Language" (Waldorf, May 8; 433 perf.), "Men in White" by Sidney Kingsley (Broadhurst, Sept. 26; 351 perf.; Pulitzer prize 1934), "Sailor, Beware!" (Lyceum, Sept. 28; 500 perf.), "Ah, Wilderness!" (Guild, Oct. 2; 289 perf.), "The Pursuit of Happiness" (Avon, Oct. 9; 252 perf.), "Her Master's Voice" (Plymouth, Oct. 23; 224 perf.), "She Loves Me Not" (46th Street, Nov. 20; 360 perf.), "Mary of Scotland" (Alvin, Nov. 27; 248 perf.). Musical productions included: "Murder at the Vanities" (New Amsterdam, Sept. 8), "As Thousands Cheer" (Music Box, Sept. 30; 400 perf.), "Champagne Sec" (Morosco, Oct. 14; 113 perf.; an adaptation of "Die Fledermaus" by Johann Strauss), "Let 'Em Eat Cake" (Imperial, Oct. 21; 90 perf.), "Roberta" (New Amsterdam, Nov. 18; 295 perf.).

Among popular radio programs that began were "Romance of Helen Trent" (July 24), "The Woman in White" (Sept. 11), "Lone Ranger" (in Nov.).

Motion pictures of the year included: "Cavalcade," "A Farewell to Arms," "Flying Down to Rio" (Fred Astaire with Ginger Rogers as his singing and dancing partner), "Forty-Second Street" (Warner Baxter, Bebe Daniels, George Brent, Ruby Keeler), "Gold Diggers of 1933" (Dick Powell, Ruby Keeler, Joan Blondell, Warren Williams), "I Am a Fugitive from a Chain Gang," "King Kong" (a thriller about a giant gorilla), "Lady for a Day," "Mädchen in Uniform" (foreign), "Morning Glory" (Katharine Hepburn), "Private Life of Henry VIII" (Charles Laughton), "Rasputin and the Empress" (John, Ethel, and Lionel Barrymore), "She Done Him Wrong" (Mae West; she appeared earlier this year in her first picture, "Night after Night"), "State Fair" (Janet Gaynor, Will Rogers, Lew Ayres), "Three Little Pigs" (Walt Disney cartoon), "Tugboat Annie" (Marie Dressler, Wallace Beery).

In baseball, the All-Star game was originated; it was played (July 6) in Chicago, the American League defeating the National League 4 to 2.

Adolf Hitler came (Jan. 30) to power in Germany as Chancellor of the Third Reich. (The next year he became "Der Führer.")

ᔄᕁ 1934

All I Do Is Dream of You (film: Sadie McKee). w., Arthur Freed. m., Nacio Herb Brown. Robbins Music Corp., cop. 1934 by Metro-Goldwyn-Mayer; assigned 1934 to Robbins Music Corp.

All Through the Night (Anything Goes). w., m., Cole Porter. Harms, Inc., cop. 1934.

Alla en el Rancho Grande—My Ranch. w., Bartley Costello. m., Emilio D. Uranga. Edward B. Marks Music Corp., cop. 1934.

Anything Goes (Anything Goes). w., m., Cole Porter. Harms, Inc., cop. 1934.

Baby, Take a Bow (film: Stand Up and Cheer!) w., m., Lew Brown and Jay Gorney. Cleveland: Sam Fox Pub. Co., cop. 1934 by Movietone Music Corp.

Be Still My Heart. w., m., Allan Flynn and Jack Egan. Broadway Music Corp., cop. 1934.

The Beat of My Heart. w., Johnny Burke. m., Harold Spina. Irving Berlin, Inc., cop. 1934.

Blow, Gabriel, Blow (Anything Goes). w., m., Cole Porter. Harms, Inc., cop. 1934.

Blue Moon. w., Lorenz Hart. m., Richard Rodgers. Robbins Music Corp., cop. 1934 by Metro-Goldwyn-Mayer; assigned 1934 to Robbins Music Corp.

Carry Me Back to the Lone Prairie. w., m., Carson Robison. Mills Music, Inc., cop. 1934.

The Champagne Waltz. w., m., Con Conrad, Ben Oakland, and Milton Drake. Famous Music Corp., cop. 1934.

The Continental (film: Gay Divorcee). w., Herb Magidson. m., Con Conrad. Harms, Inc., cop. 1934. (Academy Award Winner, 1934)

Cocktails for Two (film: Murder at the Vanities). w., m., Arthur Johnston and Sam Coslow. Famous Music Corp., cop. 1934 by Paramount Productions Music Corp.; assigned 1934 to Famous Music Corp.

La Cucaracha. Mexican folk song. w., m., traditional. Arranged (1) as a fox-trot by Hawley Ades, American adaptation by Juan Y. D'Lorah, and introduced in the film "La Cucaracha," Irving Berlin, Inc., cop. 1934; (2) as a song, words by Stanley Adams, Edward B. Marks Music Corp., cop. 1934; words by Carl Field, M. M. Cole Pub. Co., Chicago, cop. 1935; etc.

Deep Purple. Piano solo. m., Peter DeRose. Robbins Music Corp., cop. 1934. (Arr. for orch. by Domenico Savino, Robbins Music Corp., cop. 1935; arr. as a song, words by Mitchell Parish, Robbins Music Corp., cop. 1939.)

Don't Let It Bother You (film: Gay Divorcee). w., Mack Gordon. m., Harry Revel. DeSylva, Brown & Henderson, Inc., cop. 1934.

Easy Come, Easy Go. w., Edward Heyman. m., John W. Green. Harms, Inc., cop. 1934.

Emaline. w., Mitchell Parish. m., Frank Perkins. Mills Music, Inc., cop. 1934.

Fair and Warmer (film: Twenty Million Sweethearts). w., Al Dubin. m., Harry Warren. M. Witmark & Sons, cop. 1934.

Fare Thee Well, Annabelle (film: Sweet Music). w., Mort Dixon. m., Allie Wrubel. Remick Music Corp., cop. 1934.

For All We Know. w., Sam M. Lewis. m., J. Fred Coots. Leo Feist, Inc., cop. 1934.

Fun to Be Fooled (Life Begins at 8:40). w., Ira Gershwin and E. Y. Harburg. m., Harold Arlen. Harms, Inc., cop. 1934.

Good-Night, My Love (film: We're Not Dressing). w., Mack Gordon. m., Harry Revel. DeSylva, Brown & Henderson, Inc., cop. 1934 by Paramount Productions Music Corp.; assigned 1934 to DeSylva, Brown & Henderson, Inc.

Got the Jitters. w., Billy Rose and Paul Francis Webster. m., John Jacob Loeb. Keit-Engel, Inc., cop. 1934.

Hands Across the Table. w., Mitchell Parish. m., Jean Delettre. Mills Music, Inc., cop. 1934.

Haunting Me. w., Eddie DeLange. m., Joe Myrow. Mills Music, Inc., cop. 1934.

Here Come the British. w., John Mercer. m., Bernard Hanighan. Irving Berlin, Inc., cop. 1934.

I Get a Kick Out of You (Anything Goes). w., m., Cole Porter. Harms, Inc., cop. 1934.

I Only Have Eyes for You (film: Dames). w., Al Dubin. m., Harry Warren. Remick Music Corp., cop. 1934.

I'll Follow My Secret Heart (Conversation Piece). w., m., Noel Coward. London: Chappell & Co., Ltd., cop. 1934.

I'll String Along with You. (film: Twenty Million Sweethearts). w., Al Dubin. m., Harry Warren. M. Witmark & Sons, cop. 1934.

If There Is Someone Lovelier Than You (Revenge with Music). w., Howard Dietz. m., Arthur Schwartz. Harms, Inc., cop. 1934.

Isle of Capri. w., Jimmy Kennedy. m., Will Grosz. T. B. Harms Co., cop. 1934 by The Peter Maurice Music Co., Ltd., London.

June in January (film: Here Is My Heart). w., m., Leo Robin and Ralph Rainger. Famous Music Corp., cop. 1934 by Paramount Productions Music Corp.; assigned 1934 to Famous Music Corp.

Let's Take a Walk Around the Block (Life Begins at 8:40). w., Ira Gershwin and E. Y. Harburg. m., Harold Arlen. Harms, Inc., cop. 1934.

Little Man, You've Had a Busy Day. w., Maurice Sigler and Al Hoffman. m., Mabel Wayne. T. B. Harms Co., cop. 1934.

Lost in a Fog. w., Dorothy Fields. m., Jimmy McHugh. Robbins Music Corp., cop. 1934 by Metro-Goldwyn-Mayer Corp.; assigned 1934 to Robbins Music Corp.

Love in Bloom (film: She Loves Me Not). w., m., Leo Robin and Ralph Rainger. Famous Music Corp., cop. 1934 by Paramount Productions Music Corp.; assigned 1934 to Famous Music Corp.

Love Thy Neighbor (film: We're Not Dressing). w., Mack Gordon. m., Harry Revel. DeSylva, Brown & Henderson, Inc., cop. 1934 by Paramount Productions Music Corp.; assigned 1934 to DeSylva, Brown & Henderson, Inc.

Mr. and Mrs. Is the Name (film: Flirtation Walk). w., Morton Dixon. m., Allie Wrubel. M. Witmark & Sons, cop. 1934.

The Moon Was Yellow. w., Edgar Leslie. m., Fred E. Ahlert. Donaldson, Douglas & Gumble, Inc., cop. 1934.

Moonglow. w., m., Will Hudson, Eddie DeLange, and Irving Mills. Exclusive Publications, Inc., cop. 1934.

A Needle in a Hay Stack (film: The Gay Divorcee). w., Herb Magidson. m., Con Conrad. Harms, Inc., cop. 1934.

No! No! a Thousand Times No!! w., m., Al Sherman, Al Lewis, and Abner Silver. Leo Feist, Inc., cop. 1934.

The Object of My Affection. w., m., Pinky Tomlin, Coy Poe, and Jimmie Grier. Irving Berlin, Inc., cop. 1934.

An Old Water Mill. w., m., Charles Tobias, Jack Scholl, and Murray Mencher. Leo Feist, Inc., cop. 1934.

On the Good Ship Lollipop. w., m., Sidney Clare and Richard A. Whiting. Movietone Music Corp., cop. 1934.

One Night of Love (film: One Night of Love). w., Gus Kahn. m., Victor Schertzinger. Irving Berlin, Inc., cop. 1934.

Pardon My Southern Accent. w., Johnny Mercer. m., Matt Malneck. Irving Berlin, Inc., cop. 1934.

Play to Me, Gypsy. Original words, Beda. English words, Jimmy Kennedy. m., Karel Vacek. Irving Berlin, Inc., cop. 1932 by Wiener Operetten Verlag; English version cop. 1934 by B. Feldman & Co., London; American version cop. 1934 by Irving Berlin, Inc.

P. S. I Love You. w., Johnny Mercer. m., Gordon Jenkins. La Salle Music Publishers, Inc., cop. 1934.

Solitude. w., Eddie DeLange and Irving Mills. m., Duke Ellington. Milson's Music Pub. Corp., cop. 1934.

Song of the Blacksmith. w., m., Peter DeRose and Al Stillman. Famous Music Corp., cop. 1934.

Stand Up and Cheer! (film: Stand Up and Cheer!). w., m., Lew Brown and Harry Akst. Cleveland: Sam Fox Pub. Co., cop. 1934 by Movietone Music Corp.

Stars Fell on Alabama. w., Mitchell Parish. m., Frank Perkins. Mills Music, Inc., cop. 1934.

Stay As Sweet As You Are (film: College Rhythm). w., Mack Gordon. m., Harry Revel. DeSylva, Brown & Henderson, Inc., cop. 1934.

Thank You for a Lovely Evening. w., Dorothy Fields. m., Jimmy McHugh. Robbins Music Corp., cop. 1934 by Metro-Goldwyn-Mayer Corp.; assigned 1934 to Robbins Music Corp.

There Goes My Heart. w., Benny Davis. m., Abner Silver. Leo Feist, Inc., cop. 1934.

True. w., m., Walter G. Samuels and Leonard Whitcup. Santly Bros., Inc., cop. 1934.

Tumbling Tumbleweeds. w., m., Bob Nolan. Williamson Music, Inc., cop. 1934.

Two Cigarettes in the Dark (film: Kill That Story). w., Paul Francis Webster. m., Lew Pollack. DeSylva, Brown & Henderson, Inc., cop. 1934.

The Very Thought of You. w., m., Ray Noble. M. Witmark & Sons, cop. 1934 by Campbell, Connelly & Co., Ltd.

Wagon Wheels (*introduced in:* The New Ziegfeld Follies). w., Billy Hill. m., Peter DeRose. Shapiro, Bernstein & Co., Inc., cop. 1934.

What a Diff'rence a Day Made—*original Spanish title:* Cuando vuelva a tu lado. English words, Stanley Adams. Spanish words and music, Maria Grever. Edward B. Marks Music Corp., cop. 1934.

When I Have Sung My Songs. w., m., Ernest Charles. G. Schirmer, Inc., cop. 1934.

Winter Wonderland. w., Dick Smith. m., Felix Bernard. Donaldson, Douglas & Gumble, Inc., cop. 1934.

With My Eyes Wide Open I'm Dreaming (film: Shoot the Works). w., m., Mack Gordon and Harry Revel. DeSylva, Brown & Henderson, Inc., cop. 1934 by Paramount Productions Music Corp., assigned 1934 to DeSylva, Brown & Henderson, Inc.

Wonder Bar (film: Wonder Bar). w., Al Dubin. m., Harry Warren. M. Witmark & Sons, cop. 1934.

You and the Night and the Music (Revenge with Music). w., Howard Dietz. m., Arthur Schwartz. Harms, Inc., cop. 1934.

You're a Builder Upper (Life Begins at 8:40). w., Ira Gershwin and E. Y. Harburg. m., Harold Arlen. Harms, Inc., cop. 1934.

You're the Top (Anything Goes). w., m., Cole Porter. Harms, Inc., cop. 1934.

You Oughta Be in Pictures. w., Edward Heyman. m., Dana Suesse. Harms, Inc., cop. 1934.

Congress devalued (Jan. 31) the dollar by reducing its gold content 40.94 per cent, passed (Mar. 22) the Tydings-McDuffie Act providing for Philippine independence (voted in 1916) in 1946, established (in

June) the Federal Housing Administration under the Federal Housing Act, prohibited (June 28) the exportation of silver, created (July 9) the National Labor Relations Board, and set up the Federal Communications Commission ("F.C.C.") of seven commissioners appointed by the President to replace the Federal Radio Commission of five members.

The United States signed along with 18 Latin-American Republics an anti-war agreement (Apr. 27) in Buenos Aires, and with Cuba signed a Treaty of Relations (May 29) abrogating the treaty of 1903.

From Long Beach, Cal., came an idea for a national pension plan of $200 per month for every United States citizen 60 years of age or older. It was proposed by Francis Townsend and was known as the Townsend Plan. The proposal gained a nationwide following for a number of years and was discussed in the 74th Congress. Subsequent legislation nullified the scheme.

To fight infantile paralysis (polio) President Roosevelt launched for the Warm Springs, Georgia, Foundation a fund-raising campaign that developed (Jan. 3, 1938) into the March of Dimes. (The President himself suffered from the effects of the dreaded disease.)

Alcatraz, an island fortress in San Francisco Bay, became a Federal penitentiary. (It had been a military prison since 1886.)

John Dillinger, leader of a notorious band of bank robbers, was shot (July 22) to death in front of a motion-picture theatre in Chicago by Department of Justice agents after he had escaped twice from prison. Others of his gang were shot in the round-up.

As a tribute to the mothers of America, a special three-cent purple postage stamp was issued (May 2), reproducing James Abbott McNeill Whistler's famous painting "Portrait of My Mother."

Air mail was reduced (July 1) to six cents and a new orange postage stamp of that denomination appeared.

"National Parks Year" was observed and the Post Office Department issued (July 16-Oct. 8) for the first time a series of all-scenic postage stamps (in ten denominations).

Adm. Richard Evelyn Byrd established a solitary base in the Antarctic 120 miles from his headquarters at Little America to record daily meteorological observations.

The Ford Motor Company began the growing and cultivation of soy beans.

Fire destroyed (Sept. 8) the American cruise liner "Morro Castle" off Asbury Park, N. J., with a loss of 134 lives. It was returning from Havana, Cuba, to New York and carried 318 passengers and a crew of 231.

Four Americans were awarded Nobel prizes—H. C. Urey for chemistry, and G. R. Minot, W. P. Murphy, and G. H. Whipple for medicine and physiology.

Six U. S. Navy seaplanes flew (Jan. 10-11) a distance of 2,400 miles from San Francisco to Pearl Harbor, Hawaii, in 25 hours. Jack Frye carried (May 13) air mail from Los Angeles, Cal., to Newark, N. J., in 11 hours, 31 minutes. Colonel Roscoe Turner reduced (Sept. 1) transcontinental flying time from Burbank, Cal., to Bennett Field, New York, to 10 hours, 2 minutes, 57 seconds.

Major W. E. Kepner, Captain O. A. Anderson, and Captain A. W. Stevens ascended (July 28) in a balloon at Rapid City, S. D. They reached a height of 60,613 feet before a tear in the bag forced them down at Loomis, Neb.

Dust storms and drought ruined crops in the Midwest.

The Mutual Broadcasting System became the third American broadcasting chain.

Books of the year included: "American Ballads and Folk Songs" (John Lomax), "Bright Ambush" (Audrey Wurdemann; poems; Pulitzer prize 1935), "The Colonial Period of American History" (Charles McL. Andrews; vol. 1; Pulitzer prize 1935), "Robert E. Lee" (Douglas Southall Freeman; 4 vols., 1934-35), "Wine from These Grapes" (Edna St. Vincent Millay), "Stars Fell on Alabama" (Carl Carmer), and the fiction, "The Daring Young Man on the Flying Trapeze" (William Saroyan), "The Folks" (Ruth Suckow), "The Land of Plenty" (Robert Cantwell), "The Native's Return" (Louis Adamic), "Now in November" (Josephine Johnson; Pulitzer prize 1935), "So Red the Rose" (Stark Young).

Virgil Thomson's surrealistic opera "Four Saints in Three Acts," to a libretto by Gertrude Stein, received (Feb. 7) its first stage performance in Hartford, Conn., at the opening of the Avery Memorial Theatre of the Wadsworth Athenaeum. It was presented with an all-Negro cast by the Society of Friends and Enemies of Modern Music. (The opera was first heard in concert form in Ann Arbor, Mich., May 20, 1933, and was given in New York at the 44th Street Theatre, Feb. 20, 1934, for 48 performances. A complete radio performance was broadcast from New York by the Columbia Broadcasting System May 25, 1947, under the direction of the composer.)

The Metropolitan Opera House, New York, gave (Feb. 10) the world première of another American opera—"Merry Mount" by Dr. Howard Hanson, director of the Eastman School of Music, Rochester, N. Y. The opera had six performances.

More than a mile and a half away from New York's glittering center of theatrical production (May 7) in an obscure hall on 23rd Street, a Negro group calling itself the Unity Theatre Study staged a unique African "dance-opera" entitled "Kykunkor, the Witch" by Asadata Dafora Horton. The composer was a native of Sierra Leone. The production aroused sufficient interest to warrant more than 100 performances in various auditoriums and on Broadway (Little Theatre, June 10; 65 perf.).

New York heard (Nov. 25) at Mecca Auditorium the première of an opera in the Hebrew language—"Hechalutz" (The Pioneers) by Jacob Weinberg.

The Berkshire Music Festivals were inaugurated by Henry Kimball Hadley.

André Kostelanetz and his orchestra began (Oct. 1) the long-popular Chesterfield radio program with its distinctive orchestral arrangements.

New York plays included: "No More Ladies" (Booth, Jan. 23), "Dodsworth" (Shubert, Feb. 24; 315 perf.), "The Distaff Side" (Booth, Sept. 25), "Personal Appearance" (Henry Miller, Oct. 17; 501 perf.), "The Children's Hour" (Maxine Elliott, Nov. 20; 691 perf.), "Post Road" (Masque, Dec. 4; 212 perf.), "Accent on Youth" (Plymouth, Dec. 25; 229 perf.). Musical productions included: "Ziegfeld Follies" (Winter Garden, Jan. 4), "Life Begins at 8:40" (Winter Garden, Aug. 27; 237 perf.), "The Great Waltz" (Center, Sept 22; 347 perf.), "Anything Goes" (Alvin, Nov. 21; 420 perf.), "Revenge with Music" (New Amsterdam, Nov. 28), "Thumbs Up" (St. James, Dec. 27).

Motion pictures of the year included: "The Barretts of Wimpole Street" (Norma Shearer, Fredric March, Charles Laughton), "Berkeley Square" (Leslie Howard), "The Bowery" (Wallace Beery, George Raft, Jackie Cooper), "The Count of Monte Cristo" (Robert Donat, Elissa Landi), "Dinner at Eight" (Marie Dressler, John Barrymore, Wallace Beery, Jean Harlow, Lionel Barrymore), "The House of Rothschild" (George Arliss), "I'm No Angel" (Mae West), "It Happened One Night" (Claudette Colbert, Clark Gable), "Judge Priest" (Will Rogers), "Little Women" (Katharine Hepburn), "One Night of Love" (Grace Moore), "The Orphans' Benefit" (Walt Disney cartoon, introducing "Donald Duck" in an inconspicuous part), "The Thin Man" (William Powell, Myrna Loy), "Viva, Villa!" (Wallace Beery). Government morals experts were mulling over (as they still did in 1951) the admission to the American screen of the Czechoslovakian film "Ecstasy."

Adolf Hitler, German Chancellor, became (Aug. 19) "Der Führer" of Germany following the death (Aug. 2) of President von Hindenburg.

ৡ৵ 1935

About a Quarter to Nine (film: Go into Your Dance). w., Al Dubin. m., Harry Warren. M. Witmark & Sons, cop. 1935.

Accent on Youth (film: Accent on Youth). w., Tot Seymour. m., Vee Lawnhurst. Famous Music Corp., cop. 1935.

Alone (film: A Night at the Opera). w., Arthur Freed. m., Nacio Herb Brown. Robbins Music Corp., cop. 1935.

Beautiful Lady in Blue. w., Sam H. Lewis. m., J. Fred Coots. Chappell & Co., Inc., cop. 1935.

Begin the Beguine (Jubilee). w., m., Cole Porter. Harms, Inc., cop. 1935.

Bess, You Is My Woman (Porgy and Bess). w., DuBose Heyward and Ira Gershwin. m., George Gershwin. Gershwin Pub. Corp., cop. 1935 by George Gershwin.

Broadway Rhythm (film: Broadway Melody of 1936). w., Arthur Freed. m., Nacio Herb Brown. Robbins Music Corp., cop. 1935.

The Broken Record. w., m., Cliff Friend, Charlie Tobias, and Boyd Bunch. Chappell & Co., Inc., Cop. 1935.

Cheek to Cheek (film: Top Hat). w., m., Irving Berlin. Irving Berlin, Inc., cop. 1935.

Cosi Cosa (film: A Night at the Opera). w., Ned Washington. m., Bronislaw Kaper and Walter Jurmann. Robbins Music Corp., cop. 1935.

Dance, My Darlings (May Wine). w., Oscar Hammerstein, 2nd. m., Sigmund Romberg. Chappell & Co., Inc., cop. 1935.

Dodging a Divorcee. Piano solo. m., Reginald Foresythe. Robbins Music Corp., cop. 1935 by Irwin Dash Music Co., Ltd., London.

East of the Sun—and West of the Moon (Stags at Bay). w., m., Brooks Bowman. Santly Bros., Inc., cop. 1935 by Princeton University Triangle Club; assigned 1935 to Santly Joy, Inc.

Eeny Meeny Miney Mo (film: To Beat the Band). w., m., Johnny Mercer and Matt Malneck. Irving Berlin, Inc., cop. 1935.

From the Top of Your Head to the Tip of Your Toes (film: Two for Tonight). w., Mack Gordon. m., Harry Revel. Crawford Music Corp., cop. 1935 by Paramount Productions Music Corp.; assigned 1935 to Crawford Music Corp.

Fugato on a Well Known Theme. Orch. piece. m., Robert McBride. (Composed in 1935 and first performed, in its original form, by the University of Arizona Student Orchestra; published in Karl D. Van Hoesen, Music of Our Time, Carl Fischer, Inc., cop. 1943.)

Here's to Romance (film: Here's to Romance). w., Herb Magidson. m., Con Conrad. Cleveland: Sam Fox Pub. Co., cop. 1935 by Movietone Music Corp.

I'm Building Up to an Awful Let-Down. w., Johnny Mercer. m., Fred Astaire. Irving Berlin, Inc., cop. 1935.

I'm Gonna Sit Right Down and Write Myself a Letter. w., Joe Young. m., Fred E. Ahlert. Crawford Music Corp., cop. 1935.

I'm in the Mood for Love (film: Every Night at Eight). w., Dorothy Fields. m., Jimmy McHugh. Robbins Music Corp., cop. 1935.

I'm Shooting High (film: King of Burlesque). w., Ted Koehler. m., Jimmy McHugh. Robbins Music Corp., cop. 1935.

I Dream Too Much (film: I Dream Too Much). w., Dorothy Fields. m., Jerome Kern. T. B. Harms Co., cop. 1935 by Jerome Kern.

I Feel a Song Comin' on (film: Every Night at Eight). w., m., Jimmy McHugh, Dorothy Fields, and George Oppenheim. Robbins Music Corp., cop. 1935.

I Got Plenty o' Nuttin' (Porgy and Bess). w., Ira Gershwin and Du-Bose Heyward. m., George Gershwin. Gershwin Pub. Corp., cop. 1935 by George Gershwin.

In a Gypsy Tea Room. w., Edgar Leslie. m., Joe Burke. Joe Morris Co., cop. 1935.

In a Sentimental Mood. w., m., Duke Ellington. Milsons Music Pub., cop. 1935.

Isn't Love the Grandest Thing? (film: The Rain Makers). w., Jack Scholl. m., Louis Alter. Leo Feist, Inc., cop. 1935.

Isn't This a Lovely Day—to Be Caught in the Rain? (film: Top Hat). w., m., Irving Berlin. Irving Berlin, Inc., cop. 1935.

It Ain't Necessarily So (Porgy and Bess). w., Ira Gershwin. m., George Gershwin. Gershwin Pub. Corp., cop. 1935 by George Gershwin.

The Jockey on the Carousel (film: I Dream Too Much). w., Dorothy Fields. m., Jerome Kern. T. B. Harms Co., cop. 1935 by Jerome Kern.

Just One of Those Things (Jubilee). w., m., Cole Porter. Harms, Inc., cop. 1935.

Lights Out. w., m., Billy Hill. Shapiro, Bernstein & Co., Inc., cop. 1935.

The Little Things You Used to Do (film: Go Into Your Dance). w., Al Dubin. m., Harry Warren. M. Witmark & Sons, cop. 1935.

The Lord's Prayer. w., Biblical. m., Albert Hay Malotte. G. Schirmer, Inc., cop. 1935.

Love and a Dime (Stags at Bay). w., m., Brooks Bowman. Santly Bros., cop. 1935 by Princeton University Triangle Club; assigned 1935 to Santly-Joy, Inc.

Love Is a Dancing Thing (At Home Abroad). w., Howard Dietz. m., Arthur Schwartz. Chappell & Co., Inc., cop. 1935.

Love Me Forever. w., Gus Kahn. m., Victor Schertzinger. Irving Berlin, Inc., cop. 1935.

The Loveliness of You (film: Love in Bloom). w., Mack Gordon. m., Harry Revel. Crawford Music Corp., cop. 1935 by Paramount Productions Music Corp.; assigned 1935 to Crawford Music Corp.

Lovely Lady (film: King of Burlesque). w., Ted Koehler. m., Jimmy McHugh. Robbins Music Corp., cop. 1935.

Lovely to Look At (film: Roberta). w., Dorothy Fields and Jimmy McHugh. m., Jerome Kern. T. B. Harms Co., cop. 1935 by Jerome Kern.

Lullaby of Broadway (film: Gold Diggers of 1935). w., Al Dubin. m., Harry Warren. M. Witmark & Sons, cop. 1935. (Academy Award Winner, 1935)

Lulu's Back in Town (film: Broadway Gondolier). w., Al Dubin. m., Harry Warren. M. Witmark & Sons, cop. 1935.

Mad About the Boy (Words and Music). w., m., Noel Coward. London: Chappell & Co., Ltd., cop. 1935.

Maybe. w., m., Allan Flynn and Frank Madden. Robbins Music Corp., cop. 1935.

Midnight in Paris (film: Here's to Romance). w., m., Con Conrad and Herb Magidson. Cleveland: Sam Fox Pub. Co., cop. 1935 by Movietone Music Corp.

Moon Over Miami. w., Edgar Leslie. m., Joe Burke. Irving Berlin, Inc., cop. 1935.

The Music Goes 'Round and Around. w., "Red" Hodgson. m., Edward Farley and Michael Riley. Select Music Publications, Inc., cop. 1935.

My Romance (Jumbo). w., Lorenz Hart. m., Richard Rodgers. T. B. Harms Co., and Max Dreyfus, cop. 1935.

The Piccolino (film: Top Hat). w., m., Irving Berlin. Irving Berlin, Inc., cop. 1935.

Please Believe Me. w., Larry Yoell. m., Al Jacobs. San Francisco: Sherman, Clay & Co., cop. 1935.

Red Sails in the Sunset. w., Jimmy Kennedy. m., Hugh Williams (Will Grosz). Shapiro, Bernstein & Co., Inc., cop. 1935 by The Peter Maurice Music Co., Ltd., London; assigned to Shapiro, Bernstein & Co., Inc.

Roll Along, Covered Wagon. w., m., Jimmy Kennedy. Irving Berlin, Inc., cop. 1934 by Peter Maurice Music Co., Ltd.; cop. 1935 by Irving Berlin, Inc.

She's a Latin from Manhattan (film: Go into Your Dance). w., Al Dubin. m., Harry Warren. M. Witmark & Sons, cop. 1935.

She Shall Have Music (film: She Shall Have Music). w., m., Maurice Sigler, Al Goodhart, and Al Hoffman. Chappell & Co., Inc., cop. 1935 by The Cinephonic Music Co., Ltd., London.

Sing an Old Fashioned Song to a Young Sophisticated Lady. w., Joe Young. m., Fred E. Ahlert. Crawford Music Corp., cop. 1935.

Song of the Open Road (film: Hi Gaucho). w., m., Albert Hay Malotte. A B C Standard Music Publications, Inc., cop. 1935 by Irving Berlin, Inc.; assigned 1936 to A B C Standard Music Publications, Inc.

Stairway to the Stars. w., Mitchell Parish. m., Matt Malneck and Frank Signorelli. Robbins Music Corp., cop. 1935; cop. 1939.

Summertime (Porgy and Bess). w., DuBose Heyward. m., George Gershwin. Gershwin Pub. Corp., cop. 1935 by George Gershwin.

Tell Me That You Love Me. w., Al Silverman. m., C. A. Bixio. T. B. Harms Co., cop. 1933 by Italian Book Co., New York; cop. 1935 by T. B. Harms Co. (An American version of the Italian song "Parlami d'amore, Mariù!" words by Ennio Neri, published by Casa Editrice Musicale C. A. Bixio, Milan, cop. 1933 by Italian Book Co., New York.)

Thanks a Million (film: Thanks a Million). w., Gus Kahn. m., Arthur Johnston. Robbins Music Corp., cop. 1935.

These Foolish Things Remind Me of You (Spread It Abroad). w., Holt Marvell. m., Jack Strachey and Harry Link. Irving Berlin, Inc., cop. 1935 by Boosey & Co., Ltd., London.

This Time It's Love. w., Sam M. Lewis. m., J. Fred Coots. Leo Feist, Inc., cop. 1935.

Top Hat, White Tie and Tails (film: Top Hat). w., m., Irving Berlin. Irving Berlin, Inc., cop. 1935.

Truckin' (Cotton Club Parade, 26th Edition). w., Ted Koehler. m., Rube Bloom. Mills Music Inc., cop. 1935.

When I Grow Too Old to Dream (film: The Night Is Young). w., Oscar Hammerstein, 2nd. m., Sigmund Romberg. Robbins Music Corp., cop. 1935 by Metro-Goldwyn-Mayer Corp.; assigned 1935 to Robbins Music Corp.

Where Am I? (film: Stars Over Broadway). w., Al Dubin. m., Harry Warren. Harms, Inc., cop. 1935.

Why Shouldn't I? (Jubilee). w., m., Cole Porter. Harms, Inc., cop. 1935.

With All My Heart (film: Her Master's Voice). w., Gus Kahn. m., Jimmy McHugh. Leo Feist, Inc., cop. 1935.

Without a Word of Warning (film: Two for Tonight). w., m., Mack Gordon and Harry Revel. Crawford Music Corp., cop. 1935 by Paramount Productions Music Corp.; assigned 1935 to Crawford Music Corp.

A Woman Is a Sometime Thing (Porgy and Bess). w., DuBose Heyward. m., George Gershwin. Gershwin Pub. Corp., cop. 1935 by George Gershwin.

The Words Are in My Heart (film: Gold Diggers of 1935). w., Al Dubin. m., Harry Warren. M. Witmark & Sons, cop. 1935.

You Are My Lucky Star (film: Broadway Melody of 1936). w., Arthur Freed. m., Nacio Herb Brown. Robbins Music Corp., cop. 1935 by Metro-Goldwyn-Mayer Corp.; assigned 1935 to Robbins Music Corp.

You Let Me Down (film: Stars Over Broadway). w., Al Dubin. m., Harry Warren. Harms, Inc., cop. 1935.

You're An Angel (film: Hooray for Love). w., m., Jimmy McHugh and Dorothy Fields. Irving Berlin, Inc., cop. 1935.

Zing! Went the Strings of My Heart (Thumbs Up). w., m., James F. Hanley. Harms, Inc., cop. 1935.

Congress voted (Apr. 5) an economic relief program involving $4,880,000,000, which established (May 6) the Works Progress Administration ("W.P.A.") and passed (Aug. 14) the Social Security Act. The public debt stood at $28,700,000,000, or $225.71 per capita. Under the W.P.A., various literary, musical, theatrical, and artistic projects were sponsored.

In consequence of the above relief legislation, the federal dole (1933) was discontinued (Nov. 29); $3,694,000,000 had been expended in this form since May, 1933.

A revolt in the Philippines, instigated by the Sakdalista political party against the presence of the United States (which had granted the islands in the preceding year the right to organize self-government), was suppressed. In the Philippine elections (Sept. 17), Manuel Quezon became president of the new republic.

The United States Supreme Court voided the Railroad Pension Act (May 6) and the National Recovery Act, or N.R.A., of 1933 (May 27).

Congress authorized (Aug. 30) the construction of the Bonneville Dam, Ore.

Louisiana Senator Huey P. Long was assassinated (Sept. 8) in Baton Rouge, La. His assailant was shot on the spot by Long's bodyguards.

The California Pacific International Exposition opened (May 29) in San Diego in celebration of the 400th anniversary of the city.

The Committee for Industrial Organization ("C.I.O.") was formed by officials of the American Federation of Labor under the chairmanship of John Llewellyn Lewis.

The Huey P. Long Bridge, spanning the Mississippi River at New Orleans, was completed.

The Hayden Planetarium, New York, named in honor of its donor Charles Hayden, was opened (Oct. 3).

Mrs. Fletcher M. Johnson of Gainesville, Ga., became the first American Mother of the Year to be selected by the Golden Rule Foundation Mothers' Committee, New York.

The $4,000,000 U. S. Navy dirigible balloon "Macon" suffered disaster over the Pacific and sank (Feb. 13) off Point Sur, Cal.; 83 out of 85 persons aboard were rescued.

Humorist Will Rogers and aviator Wiley Post were killed (Aug. 15) near Point Barrow, Alaska, when Post's rebuilt airplane crashed in a fog.

Lincoln Ellsworth explored (Nov. 23-Dec. 15) the Antarctic regions by airplane.

Aviation again made news. Amelia Earhart (Mrs. George Palmer Putnam) became the first woman to make a solo flight in the Pacific. She flew (Mar. 23) from Pearl Harbor, Hawaii, to San Francisco. D. W. Tomlinson, Jack Frye, Harold Snead, and Peter Redpath set (Apr. 30) a new transcontinental record of 11 hours, 5 minutes in a transport plane guided by an automatic or gyro-pilot. In an endurance test over Meridian, Miss., the brothers Fred and Al Kay stayed in the air 27 days, 5 hours, 34 minutes (June 4-July 1)—a new record for the feat. Major Alexander P. de Seversky broke speed records at Detroit when he piloted (Sept. 15) an amphibian plane 230 miles per hour. Lieutenant Commander Knefler McGinnis and a crew of five accomplished (Oct. 15) the longest nonstop flight in a seaplane in 34 hours, 45 minutes from Panama to Alameda, Cal. The Pan American Airways company began (in Nov.) regular passenger service across the Pacific from San Francisco to Manila, P. I., with the super-plane "China Clipper," making landings at Honolulu, Midway Island, Wake Island, and Guam. Accordingly, the U. S. Post Office issued (Nov. 22) a 25-cent postage stamp for trans-Pacific air mail. (The rate was revised the next year to 20 and 50 cents to include delivery to China.)

Books of the year included: "Constitutional History of the United States" (Andrew C. McLaughlin; Pulitzer prize 1936), "Strange Holiness" (Robert Coffin; poems, Pulitzer prize 1936), "The Thought and Character of William James" (Ralph B. Perry; 2 vols.; Pulitzer prize 1936), "War Is a Racket" (Major General Smedley Darlington Butler), and the fiction, "Absalom, Absalom!" (William Faulkner), "Honey in the Horn" (H. L. Davis; Pulitzer prize 1936), "It Can't Happen Here" (Sinclair Lewis), "Life with Father" (Clarence Day), "Of Time and the River" (Thomas Wolfe), "Tortilla Flat" (John Steinbeck), "The Vein of Iron" (Susan Glaspell).

The Metropolitan Opera House, New York, produced (Jan. 24) the première of John Laurence Seymour's one-act opera "In a Pasha's Garden." The opera was performed three times.

The Canadian-born American opera tenor, Edward Johnson, became (season of 1935-36) manager of the Metropolitan Opera House, New York.

Dmitri Shostakovich's Soviet opera "Lady Macbeth of Mtsensk" had three sensational performances in the United States under Artur Rodzinski—in Cleveland at Severance Hall (Jan. 31; American première), in New York at the Metropolitan Opera House (Feb. 5), and in Philadelphia at the Academy of Music (Apr. 5). The opera was sung in the original Russian.

Boston heard (Sept. 30) at the Colonial Theatre the first performance of George Gershwin's opera "Porgy and Bess." (The opera was given in New York at the Alvin Theatre, Oct. 10, 1935, and had 124 performances.)

New York plays that ran 175 or more performances included: "The Petrified Forest" (Broadhurst, Jan. 7), "The Old Maid" by Zoë Akins (Empire, Jan. 7; 305 perf.; Pulitzer prize 1935), "Fly Away Home" (48th Street, Jan. 15), "Three Men on a Horse" (Playhouse, Jan. 30; 837 perf.), "Awake and Sing" (Belasco, Feb. 19), "Night of January 16" (Ambassador, Sept. 16), "Winterset" (Martin Beck, Sept. 25), "Mulatto" (Vanderbilt, Oct. 24; 373 perf.), "Dead End" (Belasco, Oct. 28; 687 perf.), "Pride and Prejudice" (Music Box, Nov. 5), "First Lady" (Music Box, Nov. 26), "Boy Meets Girl" (Cort, Nov. 27; 669 perf.), "One Good Year" (Lyceum, Nov. 27), "Victoria Regina" (Broadhurst, Dec. 26; 517 perf.). Lynn Fontanne and Alfred Lunt revived "The Taming of the Shrew" (Guild, Sept. 30; 129 perf.). Musical productions included: "Earl Carroll Sketch Book" (Winter Gardens, June 4), "At Home Abroad" (Winter Garden, Sept. 19), "Jubilee" (Imperial, Oct. 12), "Jumbo" (Hippodrome, Nov. 16; 233 perf.), "May Wine" (St. James, Dec. 5; 213 perf.).

Motion pictures of the year included: "Anna Karenina" (Greta Garbo), "Broadway Melody of 1936" (Jack Benny, Eleanor Powell), "China Seas" (Clark Gable, Jean Harlow, Wallace Beery), "Curly Top" (Shirley Temple), "Dangerous" (Bette Davis), "David Copperfield" (Freddie Bartholomew, W. C. Fields, Lionel Barrymore), "G Men" (James Cagney, Margaret Lindsay, Ann Dvorak, Robert Armstrong), "The Informer" (Victor McLaglen), "Lives of a Bengal Lancer" (Gary Cooper), "Les Misérables" (Fredric March, Charles Laughton, Cedric Hardwicke), "Mutiny on the Bounty" (Clark Gable, Charles Laughton, Franchot Tone), "Ruggles of Red Gap" (Charles Laughton, Mary Boland, Charles Ruggles), "Top Hat" (Fred Astaire, Ginger Rogers).

Radio station KINY, Juneau, Alaska, opened (June 1).

Popular radio programs that began this year included "Vox Pop" (Feb. 7), "One Man's Family" (Apr. 3), "Fibber McGee and Molly" (Apr. 16), "Your Hit Parade" (Apr. 20), "Lum and Abner" (Sept. 19), Phil Baker (Sept. 29), "Metropolitan Opera Auditions of the Air" (Oct. 18).

The first night game in major league baseball was played (May 23) between the Cincinnati and Philadelphia National League clubs.

⟨⟩ 1936

All My Life (film: Laughing Irish Eyes). w., Sidney Mitchell. m., Sam H. Stept. Cleveland: Sam Fox Pub. Co., cop. 1936.

Bojangles of Harlem (film: Swing Time). w., Dorothy Fields. m., Jerome Kern. Chappell & Co., Inc., cop. 1936 by Jerome Kern.

Bye Bye Baby. w., Walter Hirsch. m., Lou Handman. Irving Berlin, Inc., cop. 1936.

Carol of the Bells. Ukrainian carol for SATB. English words, Peter J. Wilhousky. m., M. Leontovich; arr. by Peter J. Wilhousky. Carl Fischer, Inc., cop. 1936.

Did I Remember (film: Suzy). w., Harold Adamson. m., Walter Donaldson. Leo Feist, Inc., cop. 1936.

Gloomy Sunday. Original Hungarian words, Laszlo Javor. English words, Sam M. Lewis. m., Rezso Seress. Chappell & Co., Inc., cop. 1933 by "Csardas," Budapest; cop. 1936 by Chappell & Co., Inc.

A Hawaiian War Chant. English words, Ralph Freed. m., Johnny Noble and Leleiohaku. San Francisco; Sherman, Clay & Co., cop. 1936; cop. 1938 by Miller Music Corp.

I'm an Old Cowhand (film: Rhythm on the Range). w., m., Johnny Mercer. Leo Feist, Inc., cop. 1936.

I'm Putting All My Eggs in One Basket (film: Follow the Fleet). w., m., Irving Berlin. Irving Berlin, Inc., cop. 1936.

I Can't Get Started with You (Ziegfeld Follies of 1936). w., Ira Gershwin. m., Vernon Duke [pseud. of Vladimir Dukelsky]. Chappell & Co., Inc., cop. 1936.

I've Got You Under My Skin (film: Born to Dance). w., m., Cole Porter. Chappell & Co., Inc., cop. 1936.

Is It True What They Say About Dixie? w., m., Irving Caesar, Sammy Lerner, and Gerald Marks. Irving Caesar, Inc., cop. 1936.

It's a Sin to Tell a Lie. w., m., Billy Mayhew. Donaldson, Douglas & Gumble, Inc., cop. 1936.

It's D'lovely (Red, Hot and Blue). w., m., Cole Porter. Chappell & Co., Inc., cop. 1936.

Let My Song Fill Your Heart. w., m., Ernest Charles. G. Schirmer, Inc., cop. 1936.

Let's Face the Music and Dance (film: Follow the Fleet). w., m., Irving Berlin. Irving Berlin, Inc., cop. 1936.

Let Yourself Go (film: Follow the Fleet). w., m., Irving Berlin. Irving Berlin, Inc., cop. 1936.

May I Have the Next Romance With You (film: Head Over Heels in Love). w., Mack Gordon. m., Harry Revel. Leo Feist, Inc., cop. 1936 by The Cinephonic Music Co., Ltd., London.

Me and the Moon. w., Walter Hirsch. m., Lou Handman. Santly Bros.-Joy, Inc., cop. 1936.

A Melody From the Sky (film: The Trail of the Lonesome Pine). w., Sidney D. Mitchell. m., Louis Alter. Famous Music Corp., cop. 1936.

Moonlight and Shadows (film: Jungle Princess). w., m., Leo Robin and Frederick Hollander. Popular Melodies, Inc., cop. 1936.

The Night Is Young and You're So Beautiful. w., Billy Rose and Irving Kahal. m., Dana Suesse. Words and Music, Inc., cop. 1936.

No Greater Love. See: "There Is No Greater Love."

No Regrets. w., Harry Tobias. m., Roy Ingraham. San Francisco: Sherman, Clay & Co., cop. 1936.

On Your Toes (On Your Toes). w., Lorenz Hart. m., Richard Rodgers. Chappell & Co., Inc., cop. 1936.

The One Rose. w., m., Del Lyon and Lani McIntire. Shapiro, Bernstein & Co., Inc., cop. 1936.

One, Two, Button Your Shoe (film: Pennies from Heaven). w., John Burke. m., Arthur Johnston. Select Music Publications, Inc., cop. 1936.

The Organ Grinder's Swing. w., Mitchell Parish and Irving Mills. m., Will Hudson. Exclusive Publications, Inc., cop. 1936.

Pennies from Heaven (film: Pennies from Heaven). w., John Burke. m., Arthur Johnston. Select Music Publications, Inc., cop. 1936.

Picture Me Without You (film: Dimples). w., Ted Koehler. m., Jimmy McHugh. Leo Feist, Inc., cop. 1936.

Rainbow on the River (film: Rainbow on the River). w., Paul Francis Webster. m., Louis Alter. Leo Feist, Inc., cop. 1936.

Seal It with a Kiss (film: That Girl from Paris). w., Edward Heyman. m., Arthur Schwartz. Chappell & Co., Inc., cop. 1936.

Shoe Shine Boy. w., Sammy Cahn. m., Saul Chaplin. Mills Music, Inc., cop. 1936.

Sing, Baby, Sing (film: Sing, Baby, Sing). w., Jack Yellen. m., Lew Pollack. Cleveland: Sam Fox Pub. Co., cop. 1936 by Movietone Music Corp.

So Do I (film: Pennies from Heaven). w., John Burke. m., Arthur Johnston. Select Music Pub., Inc., cop. 1936.

A Star Fell Out of Heaven. w., Mack Gordon. m., Harry Revel. Crawford Music Corp., cop. 1936.

Stars in My Eyes (film: The King Steps Out). w., Dorothy Fields. m., Fritz Kreisler. Chappell & Co., Inc., cop. 1936 by Chappell & Co., Inc., and Carl Fischer, Inc. (An adaptation of "Who Can Tell," words by William LeBaron, from Kreisler and Jacobi's operetta "Apple Blossoms"; T. B. Harms & Francis Day & Hunter, cop. 1919).

Stompin' at the Savoy. Piano solo. m., Benny Goodman, Chick Webb and Edgar Sampson. Robbins Music Corp., cop. 1936.

Summer Night (film: Sing Me a Love Song). w., Al Dubin. m., Harry Warren. M. Witmark & Sons, cop. 1936.

Take My Heart. w., Joe Young. m., Fred E. Ahlert. Crawford Music Corp., cop., 1936.

There's a Small Hotel (On Your Toes). w., Lorenz Hart. m., Richard Rodgers. Chappell & Co., Inc., cop. 1936.

There Is No Greater Love. w., Marty Symes. m., Isham Jones. Isham Jones Music Corp., cop. 1936; assigned 1944 to World Music, Inc.

The Touch of Your Lips. w., m., Ray Noble. Santly-Joy, Inc., cop. 1936.

Twilight on the Trail. w., Sidney D. Mitchell. m., Louis Alter. Famous Music Corp., cop. 1936.

Twinkle, Twinkle, Little Star (film: Hats Off). w., Herb Magidson. m., Ben Oakland. Popular Melodies, Inc., cop. 1936.

Until the Real Thing Comes Along. w., m., Sammy Cahn, Saul Chaplin, and L. E. Freeman. Chappell & Co., Inc., cop. 1936.

Wah-hoo! w., m., Cliff Friend. Crawford Music Corp., cop. 1936.

The Way You Look To-night (film: Swing Time). w., Dorothy Fields. m., Jerome Kern. Chappell & Co., Inc., cop. 1936 by Jerome Kern. (Academy Award Winner, 1936)

When Did You Leave Heaven? (film: Sing, Baby, Sing). w., Walter Bullock. m., Richard A. Whiting. Robbins Music Corp., cop. 1936.

When I'm With You (film: The Poor Little Rich Girl). w., Mack Gordon. m., Harry Revel. Robbins Music Corp., cop. 1936.

When My Dream Boat Comes Home. w., m., Cliff Friend and Dave Franklin. M. Witmark & Sons, cop. 1936.

Where Are You (film: Top of the Town). w., Harold Adamson. m., Jimmy McHugh. Leo Feist, Inc., cop. 1936.

The Whiffenpoof Song. w., Meade Minnigerode and George S. Pomeroy. m., Tod B. Galloway. Revision by Rudy Vallee. Miller Music, Inc., cop. 1936. (Adopted as a theme song by the newly formed Whiffenpoof Society, an organization within the Yale Glee Club, early in 1909. The writers of the words, freely adapting some lines from Kipling's poem "Gentlemen-Rankers," were members of the Yale Class of '10; the composer was an Amherst graduate, '85. Rudy Vallee was a Yale man, '27. The name Whiffenpoof was derived from that of an imaginary creature mentioned in Victor Herbert's operetta "Little Nemo," which began a run in New York on Oct. 20, 1908. Further information on the origin of the song was contributed to the "Yale Alumni Magazine," Oct., 1950, p. 4, in a letter by Carl B. Spitzer, '99. Mr. Spitzer writes that a Harvard student, Guy H. Scull, later a war correspondent in the Boer

War and elsewhere, "composed the melody of 'The Whiffenpoof Song' before entering college, about 1893 or 1894, and during [his] college career he was accustomed to play the tune with one finger, improvising some chords for the bass. [His roommate] and some of their friends sang this song often, using the words of Kipling's poem 'Gentlemen-Rankers' . . . Another Harvard friend, Eliot Spalding, retired businessman from New York City, knew Mr. Scull well in college and for many years afterwards, and vouches for the above story.")

You (film: **The Great Ziegfeld**). w., Harold Adamson. m., Walter Donaldson. Leo Feist, Inc., cop. 1936.

You Can't Pull the Wool Over My Eyes. w., m., Milton Ager, Charles Newman, and Murray Mencher. Ager, Yellen & Bornstein, Inc., cop. 1936.

You Do the Darn'dest Things, Baby (film: **Pigskin Parade**). w., Sidney D. Mitchell. m., Lew Pollack. Cleveland: Sam Fox Pub. Co., cop. 1936 by Movietone Music Corp.

You Dropped Me Like a Red Hot Penny. w., Joe Young. m., Fred E. Ahlert. Crawford Music Corp., cop. 1936.

You Turned the Tables on Me (film: **Sing, Baby, Sing**). w., Sidney D. Mitchell. m., Louis Alter. Cleveland: Sam Fox Pub. Co., cop. 1936 by Movietone Music Corp.

Social security or job insurance (established by Congress the preceding year) went into effect (Jan. 1).

The United States Supreme Court voided (Jan. 6) the Agricultural Adjustment Act (1933).

The United States withdrew (Mar. 2) its guarantee of the independence of Panama, and signed (Mar. 25) with Great Britain and France a treaty limiting naval armaments for a period of six years (Jan. 1, 1937-Dec. 31, 1942).

Congress authorized (May 15) a commemorative half-dollar with the head of Phineas Taylor Barnum for the 150th anniversary of the incorporation of the city of Bridgeport, Conn. (Barnum was born there.) The coin was designed by Henry Kreiss.

The head of Stephen Collins Foster, "America's troubadour," composer of "My Old Kentucky Home," " 'Way Down upon the Swanee River" (Old Folks at Home), and other favorites, also appeared on a commemorative half-dollar to celebrate the 50th anniversary of Cincinnati as a center of music. The coin was designed by Constance Ortmayer of Washington, D. C.

The city of Cleveland, O., celebrated the centennial of its founding with the Great Lakes Exposition. For the occasion, another commemorative half-dollar was struck. The coin was designed by Brenda Putnam and bore the head of Moses Cleveland, founder of the city.

Woman suffrage had fought a long battle from 1848 to recognition in 1920 and now, sixteen years later, the United States commemorated one of the pioneer leaders in the movement, Susan Brownell Anthony (1820-1906), by placing her portrait on a three-cent purple postage stamp. (In 1948, the Post Office similarly honored three of her co-workers—Elizabeth Stanton, Carrie Chapman Catt, and Lucretia Mott.)

At the invitation of Nazi Field Marshal Hermann Göring, Colonel Charles Augustus Lindbergh made a tour of inspection of Germany's aviation centers. On his return, he warned the world of that country's growing air power. The message was discountenanced.

German pro-Nazi "Bund" societies made their appearance in the United States under the name "Amerika-deutscher Volksbund," ostensibly devoted to social and athletic pursuits.

The Boulder (now Hoover) Dam, situated about 25 miles southeast of Las Vegas, Nev., on the Colorado River, was completed by the Bureau of Reclamation. The dam, authorized (Dec. 21, 1928) by Congress, is the largest in the world, being 726 feet high, 1,244 feet long, 45 feet wide at the top, and 650 feet wide at the bottom. The U. S. Post Office issued (Sept. 30) a special three-cent purple commemorative postage stamp at Boulder City, Nev., for the event.

The $60,000,000 Triborough Bridge, spanning the East River, New York, was opened (July 11).

Submarine builder Simon Lake attempted to raise the British frigate "Hussar" which sank in 1780 at "Pot Rock" or Hell Gate in the East River, New York. Lost with the ship was a consignment of gold and silver, estimated at $4,000,000, to be used as pay for the British troops then engaged in the American Revolution. Lake was unable to locate the ship because of the changed shore line. Similar attempts were made in 1794 and in 1856.

Newspaper reporter H. R. Elkins of the "New York World-Telegram" made, using six airplane routes, a trip around the world of approximately 25,654 miles in 18 days, 11 hours, 14 minutes, 33 seconds (Sept. 30-Oct. 19).

In an effort to unionize the automobile industry, the United Workers of America went (Dec. 30) on strike in Flint, Mich.

Bruno Richard Hauptmann, kidnaper of the Lindbergh baby (1932), was put to death (Apr. 3) in the electric chair in the prison at Trenton, N. J.

Nobel prizes were awarded to Carl D. Anderson for physics and to Eugene O'Neill for literature.

"Life" was founded in New York as a weekly pictorial magazine, using the name of an older but totally dissimilar publication (1883).

Books of the year included: "Enjoyment of Laughter" (Max Eastman), "The Flowering of New England" (Van Wyck Brooks; Pulitzer
prize 1937), "Green Laurels: The Lives and Achievements of the Great
Naturalists" (Donald Culross Peattie), "Hamilton Fish" (Allan Nevins;
a biography; Pulitzer prize 1937), "How to Win Friends and Influence
People" (Dale Carnegie), "Inside Europe" (John Gunther), "Listen for
the Lonesome Drum" (Carl Carmer), "Works" (George Santayana; 14
vols., 1936-37); the poetry, "A Further Range" (Robert Frost; Pulitzer
prize 1937), "Not So Deep as a Well" (Dorothy Parker), "The People,
Yes" (Carl Sandburg), and the fiction, "The Big Money" (John Dos
Passos), "Drums Along the Mohawk" (Walter Dumaux Edmonds),
"Gone with the Wind" (Margaret Mitchell; sold a million copies in the
first six months; Pulitzer prize 1937), "In Dubious Battle" (John Steinbeck), "The Last Pilgrim" (George Santayana).

The Federal Theatre Project of the Works Progress Administration
relief program (1935) was organized under Mrs. Hallie Flanagan of
Vassar College in the interests of the theatrical profession. Producing
centers were established in Atlanta, Boston, Chicago, Denver, Los
Angeles, New Orleans, New York, Philadelphia, San Francisco, and
Seattle. (The project ended July 31, 1939. For a history of the movement, consult Mrs. Hallie Flanagan, "Arena," 1940.)

New York plays included: "Call It a Day" (Morosco, Jan. 28), "Idiot's
Delight" by Robert E. Sherwood (Shubert, Mar. 24; 300 perf.; Pulitzer
prize 1936), "Pre-Honeymoon" (Lyceum, Apr. 30), "Tovarich" (Plymouth, Oct. 15; 356 perf.), "Stage Door" (Music Box, Oct. 22), "You
Can't Take It with You" by Moss Hart and George S. Kaufman (Booth,
Dec. 14; 837 perf.; Pulitzer prize 1937), "Brother Rat" (Biltmore, Dec.
16; 577 perf.), "The Women" (Ethel Barrymore, Dec. 26; 657 perf.).
"Hamlet" was revived by John Gielgud (Empire, Oct. 8; 132 perf.)
and by Leslie Howard (Imperial, Nov. 10; 39 perf.). Musical productions included: "On Your Toes" (Imperial, Apr. 11; 315 perf.), "White
Horse Inn" (Center, Oct. 1; 223 perf.), "Red, Hot and Blue" (Alvin, Oct.
29), "The Show Is On" (Winter Garden, Dec. 25; 237 perf.).

Motion pictures of the year included: "Anthony Adverse" (Fredric
March), "Dodsworth" (Walter Huston, Ruth Chatterton, David Niven),
"The Garden of Allah" (technicolor), "The Great Ziegfeld" (Luise
Rainer, William Powell, Myrna Loy), "The Green Pastures," "A Mid-
summer Night's Dream" (James Cagney, Joe E. Brown, Dick Powell),
"Mr. Deeds Goes to Town" (Gary Cooper), "Modern Times" (Charlie
Chaplin; after an absence of five years), "One Hundred Men and a Girl"
(Deanna Durbin, Leopold Stokowski and a huge symphony orchestra),
"Romeo and Juliet" (Leslie Howard, Norma Shearer, Basil Rathbone,
John Barrymore, Edna May Oliver), "San Francisco" (Clark Gable,
Jeanette MacDonald), "The Story of Louis Pasteur" (Paul Muni), "A
Tale of Two Cities" (Ronald Colman).

With television still in the laboratory, radio enjoyed a profitable year.

Kate Smith, Easy Aces, newscaster Boake Carter were top personalities. New programs were Gang Busters (Jan. 15) and Major Bowes' Amateur Hour (Sept. 17). The Columbia Broadcasting System inaugurated (July 18) the Columbia Workshop, a radio theatre for the production of experimental forms of broadcast drama.

The "candid" camera craze hit the country. The amateurs loved it; so did the manufacturers, for, by the following year, production in the industry had jumped 157 per cent over 1935.

The presidential campaign this year was one of the most dramatic in United States history. Not since 1896 had feeling run so high, and both parties were equally confident. The Democrats ran President Franklin Delano Roosevelt for a second term. Passing over Hoover, Borah, Frank Knox, and Senator Vandenberg, the Republicans nominated an unknown—Kansas Governor Alfred Landon. Sunflower political campaign buttons (the sunflower was the floral emblem of Kansas) blossomed on the lapels of voters out to kill the Rooseveltian New Deal, while the blustering Roman Catholic priest of Detroit, Father Charles E. Coughlin, harangued over the radio about "Roosevelt and Ruin," even calling the President a "liar" and a "scab." Predictions on the outcome of the election flattered the Republicans. "The Literary Digest," which for years had been conducting straw votes on a huge scale, proclaimed an overwhelming victory for Landon. Jim Farley, Roosevelt's campaign manager, declared the President would carry every State but Maine and Vermont. Farley was right, and the old political adage "As Maine goes, so goes the Nation" became "As Maine goes, so goes Vermont." Roosevelt polled 27,476,673 votes; Landon, 16,679,583.

Meanwhile, America watched with increasing concern as Hitler's armies marched unopposed into the demilitarized Rhineland in violation of the Locarno Pact, as Mussolini completed his Ethiopian campaign with the seizure of Addis Ababa, as Germany signed pacts with Italy and with Japan, and as civil war flared in Spain and established General Francisco Franco in power. In Great Britain, Edward VIII succeeded to the throne and abdicated less than eleven months later, while millions of radio listeners the world over eagerly heard for the first time the farewell speech of a king. (Edward was proclaimed king, but never crowned. After his abdication, he was created His Royal Highness, Duke of Windsor, and married June 3, 1937, Mrs. Wallis Simpson, an American divorcée of Baltimore, Md., for whom he renounced the throne.)

࿐ 1937

Am I In Love? (film: Mr. Dodd Takes the Air). w., Al Dubin. m., Harry Warren. M. Witmark & Sons, cop. 1937.

Bei Mir Bist du Schön—Means That You're Grand. Original words, Jacob Jacobs. English words, Sammy Cahn and Saul Chaplin. m., Sholom Secunda. Harms, Inc., cop. 1937 by arrangement with J. & J. Kammen Music Co.

Blue Hawaii (film: Waikiki). w., m., Leo Robin and Ralph Rainger. Famous Music Corp., cop. 1937.

Bob White—Whatcha Gonna Swing Tonight? w., Johnny Mercer. m., Bernie Hanighen. Remick Music Corp., cop. 1937.

Dancing Under the Stars. w., m., Harry Owens. Select Music Publications, Inc., cop. 1937.

The Dipsy Doodle. w., m., Larry Clinton. Lincoln Music Corp., cop. 1937.

The Donkey Serenade (film: The Firefly). w., Bob White and Chet Forrest. m., Rudolf Friml and Herbert Stothart. G. Schirmer, Inc., cop. 1937.

A Foggy Day (film: Damsel in Distress). w., Ira Gershwin. m., George Gershwin. Gershwin Publishing Corp., cop. 1937.

Harbor Lights. w., Jimmy Kennedy. m., Hugh Williams (Will Grosz). Marlo Music Corp., cop. 1937 by The Peter Maurice Music Co., Ltd., London.

Have You Got Any Castles, Baby? (film: Varsity Show). w., Johnny Mercer. m., Richard A. Whiting. Harms, Inc., cop. 1937.

I Can Dream, Can't I? (Right This Way). w., Irving Kahal. m., Sammy Fain. Marlo Music Corp., cop. 1937.

I've Got My Love to Keep Me Warm (film: On the Avenue). w., m., Irving Berlin. Irving Berlin, Inc., cop. 1937.

I Hit a New High (film: Hitting a New High). w., Harold Adamson. m., Jimmy McHugh. Robbins Music Corp., cop. 1937.

I Know Now (film: The Singing Marine). w., Al Dubin. m., Harry Warren. Remick Music Corp., cop. 1937.

I See Your Face Before Me (Between the Devil). w., Howard Dietz. m., Arthur Schwartz. Crawford Music Corp., cop. 1937.

In the Still of the Night (film: Rosalie). w., m., Cole Porter. Chappell & Co., Inc., cop. 1937.

Johnny One Note (Babes in Arms). w., Lorenz Hart. m., Richard Rodgers. Chappell & Co., Inc., cop. 1937.

The Lady Is a Tramp (Babes in Arms). w., Lorenz Hart. m., Richard Rodgers. Chappell & Co., Inc., cop. 1937.

Lambeth Walk (Me and My Girl). w., m., Noel Gay and Douglas Furber. Mills Music, Inc., cop. 1937 by Cinephonic Music Co., Ltd., London. (On the subject of this song and dance, consult—Percy, A. Scholes, "The Oxford Companion to Music," Oxford University Press, 1942, 2nd American edition, p. 1114.)

Let's Call the Whole Thing Off (film: Shall We Dance). w., Ira Gershwin. m., George Gershwin. Chappell & Co., Inc., cop. 1937 by George Gershwin; assigned to Gershwin Publishing Corp.

The Merry-Go-Round Broke Down. w., m., Cliff Friend and Dave Franklin. Harms, Inc., cop. 1937.

The Moon Got in My Eyes (film: Double Or Nothing). w., John Burke. m., Arthur Johnston. Select Music Publications, Inc., cop. 1937.

The Moon of Manakoora (film: The Hurricane). w., Frank Loesser. m., Alfred Newman. Hollywood, Cal.: Kalmar & Ruby Corp., cop. 1937.

My Funny Valentine (Babes in Arms). w., Lorenz Hart. m., Richard Rodgers. Chappell & Co., Inc., cop. 1937.

My Little Buckaroo (film: Cherokee Strip). w., Jack Scholl. m., M. K. Jerome. M. Witmark & Sons, cop. 1937.

Never in a Million Years (film: Wake Up and Live). w., Mack Gordon. m., Harry Revel. Robbins Music Corp., cop. 1937.

Nice Work if You Can Get It (film: Damsel in Distress). w., Ira Gershwin. m., George Gershwin. Gershwin Publishing Co., cop. 1937.

One Song (film: Snow White and the Seven Dwarfs). w., Larry Morey. m., Frank Churchill. Irving Berlin, Inc., cop. 1937.

Peter and the Wolf. Symphonic fable for narrator and orch. m., Serge Prokofieff, op. 67. (Piano score.) Moscow: State Edition, 1937. (First performed in Moscow, 1936.)

Remember Me? (film: Mr. Dodd Takes the Air). w., Al Dubin. m., Harry Warren. M. Witmark & Sons, cop. 1937.

Rosalie (film: Rosalie). w., m., Cole Porter. Chappell & Co., Inc., cop. 1937.

September in the Rain (film: Melody for Two). w., Al Dubin. m., Harry Warren. Remick Music Corp., cop. 1937.

Seventh Heaven (film: Seventh Heaven). w., Sidney D. Mitchell. m., Lew Pollack. Hollywood Songs, Inc., cop. 1937 by Movietone Music Corp.

Slumming on Park Avenue (film: On the Avenue). w., m., Irving Berlin. Irving Berlin, Inc., cop. 1937.

So Rare. w., Jack Sharpe. m., Jerry Herst. San Francisco: Sherman, Clay & Co., cop. 1937.

Somebody Else Is Taking My Place. w., m., Dick Howard, Bob Ellsworth, and Russ Morgan. Shapiro, Bernstein & Co., Inc., cop. 1937 by The Back Bay Music Co.; assigned 1941 to Shapiro, Bernstein & Co., Inc.

Stop! You're Breaking My Heart (film: Artists and Models). w., Ted Koehler. m., Burton Lane. Famous Music Corp., cop. 1937.

Sweet Is the Word for You (film: Waikiki Wedding). w., Leo Rubin. m., Ralph Rainger. Famous Music Corp., cop. 1937.

Sweet Leilani (film: Waikiki Wedding). w., m., Harry Owens. Select Music Publications, Inc., cop. 1937. (Academy Award Winner, 1937)

Swing High, Swing Low (film: Swing High, Swing Low). w., Ralph Freed. m., Burton Lane. Famous Music Corp., cop. 1937.

Thanks for the Memory (film: Big Broadcast of 1938). w., m., Leo Robin and Ralph Rainger. Paramount Music Corp., cop. 1937. (Academy Award Winner, 1938)

That Old Feeling (film: Vogues of 1938). w., m., Lew Brown and Sammy Fain. Leo Feist, Inc., cop. 1937.

There's a Gold Mine in the Sky. w., m., Charles and Nick Kenny. Irving Berlin, Inc., cop. 1937.

There's a Lull in My Life (film: Wake Up and Live). w., Mack Gordon. m., Harry Revel. Robbins Music Corp., cop. 1937.

This Year's Kisses (film: On the Avenue). w., m., Irving Berlin. Irving Berlin, Inc., cop. 1937.

To a Sweet Pretty Thing. w., Joe Young. m., Fred E. Ahlert. Shapiro, Bernstein & Co., Inc., cop. 1937.

Too Marvelous for Words (film: Ready, Willing and Able). w., Johnny Mercer. m., Richard A. Whiting. Harms, Inc., cop. 1937.

Toy Trumpet. Instrumental piece. m., Raymond Scott [pseud. of Harry Warnow]. Circle Music Pub., Inc., cop. 1937.

True Confession (film: True Confession). w., m., Sam Coslow and Frederick Hollander. Famous Music Corp., cop. 1937.

Twilight in Turkey. Piano solo. m., Raymond Scott [pseud. of Harry Warnow]. Circle Music Publications, Inc., cop. 1937.

Vieni, Vieni. w., George Koger and H. Varna. English version, Rudy Vallee. m., Vincent Scotto. M. Witmark & Sons, cop. 1934; new arrangement cop. 1937.

Vienna Dreams—*original German title:* Wien, du Stadt meiner Träume. English words, Irving Caesar. m., Rudolf Sieczynski. Harms, Inc., cop. 1937. (German edition: w., m., Rudolf Sieczynski, op. 1; Adolph Robitschek, Vienna, cop. 1914.)

Wake Up and Live (film: Wake Up and Live). w., Mack Gordon. m., Harry Revel. Robbins Music Corp., cop. 1937.

Was It Rain? (film: The Hit Parade). w., Walter Hirsch. m., Lou Handman. Santly Bros., Joy, Inc., cop. 1937 by Republic Pictures Corp.; assigned 1937 to Santly-Joy, Inc.

Where or When (Babes in Arms). w., Lorenz Hart. m., Richard Rodgers. Chappell & Co., Inc., cop. 1937.

Whispers in the Dark (film: Artists and Models). w., m., Leo Robin and Frederick Hollander. Famous Music Corp., cop. 1937.

Whistle While You Work (film: Snow White and the Seven Dwarfs). w., Larry Morey. m., Frank Churchill. Irving Berlin, Inc., cop. 1937.

You're a Sweetheart (film: You're a Sweetheart). w., Harold Adamson. m., Jimmy McHugh. Universal Music Corp., cop. 1937.

You Can't Stop Me from Dreaming. w., m., Cliff Friend and Dave Franklin. Remick Music Corp., cop. 1937.

President Franklin Delano Roosevelt began his second term.

The U. S. gunboat "Panay," stationed on the Yangtze River near Nanking, China, and several American oil carriers were sunk by Japanese gunfire. A number of lives were lost. The United States issued a vigorous protest; Japan apologized for the "accidental" destruction and made financial restitution.

The United States Supreme Court ruled (Dec. 20) that "tapped" telephone conversations could not he made public.

Nylon was patented by Wallace Hume Carothers, chemist of the DuPont Company, Wilmington, Del. (The patents were granted posthumously in 1938; Carothers died in 1937.)

A new transcontinental airplane speed record was established (Jan. 19) when Howard Hughes flew from Los Angeles to New York in 7 hours, 28 minutes.

Amelia Earhart (Mrs. George Palmer Putnam) and Fred Noonan undertook an airplane flight around the world and were lost (their last message was radioed July 2) in the mid-Pacific between New Guinea and Howland Island. No trace of either the aviators or their plane was ever found in spite of an intensive two-week search by the U. S. Navy. (During a stopover at Hawaii by the two aviators, a plaque was dedicated to Miss Earhart. When originally set in place, the stone bearing the plaque broke from the foundation and fell face downward, arousing an old superstition among Hawaiians that the flier would never return to the islands.)

The "Hindenburg," the world's largest dirigible balloon and the pride of Germany, exploded and burst into flames while approaching (May 6) its mooring mast at the U. S. Naval Air Station in Lakehurst, N. J., after a successful Atlantic crossing. Thirty-six of 97 persons aboard, including its commander Captain Ernst Lehmann, died in the disaster that was witnessed by a horrified throng who had gathered to welcome the historic arrival. The tragedy occurred at night; the flames were seen miles away. Radiocasters thrillingly reported the approach of the majestic airship and presently found themselves compelled to change the paean to a dirge in broadcasting the details of the catastrophe.

"Sitdown" strikes were a new C.I.O. weapon in the glass and automobile industries. The strike of the United Automobile Workers of America, backed by the C.I.O., against the General Motors Corp. at Flint, Mich., which began in the preceding year (Dec. 30), won (Feb. 11) a wage increase of five cents an hour. The Little Steel Strike, at the

Republic Steel Plant, flared into violence in the "South Chicago Riot" on Memorial Day (May 30); ten were killed, 90 wounded.

The Golden Gate Bridge, spanning the entrance to San Francisco Bay, Cal., was completed.

The south tube of the Lincoln Vehicular Tunnel, connecting New York City and Weehawken, N. J., under the Hudson River, was opened (Dec. 21). (The north tube was opened Feb. 1, 1945.)

An explosion of natural gas wrecked (Mar. 18) the Consolidated Public School, New London, Tex., and caused the death of 294 persons.

Floods inundated the Allegheny, Mississippi, and Ohio River regions. About 300 persons were drowned in Arkansas, Illinois, Kentucky, Missouri, and Tennessee.

Public libraries became over-busy as contestants all over the nation spent every spare moment on the Old Gold Contest.

Paul Hindemith, German composer, settled in the United States.

Dance-conscious Carolina students worked out the steps of The Big Apple, a modified square dance, which was taken up avidly by the younger generation.

Books of the year included: "Andrew Jackson" (Marquis James; Pulitzer prize 1938), "Cold Morning Sky" (Marya Zaturenska; poems; Pulitzer prize 1938), "Damien the Leper" (John Farrow), "The Fall of the City" (Archibald MacLeish; a radio drama produced by the Columbia Broadcasting System, New York, Apr. 11, 1937, with incidental music by Bernard Herrmann), "The Life and Death of a Spanish Town" (Elliot Paul), "Pedlar's Progress" (Odell Shephard; a biography of Bronson Alcott; Pulitzer prize 1938), "The Road to Reunion: 1865-1900" (Paul H. Buck; Pulitzer prize 1938), and the fiction, "The Citadel" (Archibald Joseph Cronin), "The Late George Apley" (John Philip Marquand; Pulitzer prize 1938), "Northwest Passage" (Kenneth Lewis Roberts), "Of Mice and Men" (John Steinbeck), "The Rains Came" (Louis Bromfield), "Slogum House" (Mari Sandoz), "To Have and Have Not" (Ernest Hemingway).

New American operas were "Amelia Goes to the Ball" by Gian-Carlo Menotti (Philadelphia, Academy of Music, Apr. 1) and "The Man without a Country" by Walter Damrosch (New York, Metropolitan Opera House, May 12).

The London Intimate Opera Company visited (in Dec.) the United States and presented (1937-38) revivals of early English operas by Arne, Carey, Dibdin, and Purcell, and works by Pergolesi and Bach.

The Salzburg International Opera Guild from Austria toured (1937-38) the United States and Canada, performing unfamiliar operas by Ibert, Milhaud, Monteverdi, Mozart, and Rossini.

The Columbia Broadcasting System, New York, performed six commissioned orchestral works by American composers. The compositions were "Lenox Avenue" by William Grant Still (May 23), "Concertino for Piano and Orchestra" by Walter Piston (June 20), "Music for Radio" by Aaron Copland (July 25), "Time Suite" by Roy Harris (Aug. 8), "Third Symphony" by Howard Hanson (Sept. 19; three movements; the fourth was added later), "Green Mansions," a radio opera, by Louis Gruenberg (Oct. 17).

Arturo Toscanini was appointed musical director of the reorganized NBC Symphony Orchestra. He conducted his first program on Christmas Day (Dec. 25). On this memorable occasion, the audience of about 1,000 were supplied with satin programs so that the great maestro would not be distracted by the rustling of paper.

New York plays included: "High Tor" (Martin Beck, Jan. 9), "Behind Red Lights" (Mansfield, Jan. 13), "Yes, My Darling Daughter" (Playhouse, Feb. 9; 405 perf.), "Having a Wonderful Time" (Lyceum, Feb. 20; 372 perf.), "Room Service" (Cort, May 19; 500 perf.), "The Star-Wagon" (Empire, Sept. 29), "Susan and God" (Plymouth, Oct. 7; 288 perf.), "Amphitryon 38" (Shubert, Nov. 1), "Golden Boy" (Belasco, Nov. 4). Revivals of classics included Orson Welles in Marlowe's "Dr. Faustus" (Maxine Elliott, Jan. 8; 128 perf.), Maurice Evans in "Richard II" (St. James, Feb. 5; 133 perf.) and a modern-dress version of a Fascist "Julius Caesar" (Mercury, Nov. 11; 157 perf.). The Bulgarian National Theatre Company of Sofia toured the country in native dramas before being heard in New York (Heckscher Theatre, Aug. 14, 15, 16). Musical productions included: "The Eternal Road" (Manhattan Opera House, Jan. 7), "Naughty Naught '00" (American Music Hall, Jan. 23), "Babes in Arms" (Shubert, Apr. 14; 289 perf.), "I'd Rather Be Right" (Alvin, Nov. 2; 290 perf.), "Hooray for What!" (Winter Garden, Dec. 1; 200 perf.), "Three Waltzes" (Majestic, Dec. 25; 122 perf.). "Pins and Needles" was produced (Labor Stage, Nov. 27) by the International Ladies' Garment Workers' Union Players, none of whom was paid more than $55 a week. A plea for the cause of unions, the show startled Broadway by surviving until 1939 and breaking all previous musical show endurance records with 1,108 performances. Equally proletarian in character was Marc Blitzstein's so-called opera about steel unionization, entitled "The Cradle Will Rock" and performed without scenery and with piano accompaniment to overcome certain union restrictions (Venice Theatre, June 16; after three performances, the work was banned by the W.P.A. Federal Theatre on an order from Washington, D. C., moved to the Mercury Theatre, Dec. 5, and finally staged at the Windsor Theatre, Jan. 3, 1938, for 108 performances).

Popular radio programs which began this year were "Myrt and Marge" (Jan. 4), "The Goldbergs" (Sept. 13), "Voice of Experience" (Sept. 13), "Tony Wons and His Scrapbook" (Sept. 27), "Kate Smith's Bandwagon" (Sept. 30), "March of Time" (Oct. 14), "The Voice of Niagara" (Carborundum Hour, Oct. 16). Ventriloquist Edgar Bergen and his dummy Charlie McCarthy leaped (May 9) into national publicity as features of the Chase and Sanborn coffee program.

Motion pictures of the year included: "The Awful Truth" (Irene Dunn,

Cary Grant), "Captains Courageous" (Freddie Bartholomew, Spencer Tracy, Lionel Barrymore), "Dead End" (Sylvia Sidney, Joel McCrea), "The Firefly" (Jeanette MacDonald, Allan Jones), "The Good Earth" (Luise Rainer), "The Life of Emile Zola" (Paul Muni), "Lost Horizon" (Ronald Colman), "Maytime," "Saratoga," "Stage Door" (Katharine Hepburn, Ginger Rogers, Adolphe Menjou), "A Star Is Born" (Janet Gaynor, Fredric March), "Waikiki Wedding," "Wake Up and Live," "Winterset" (Burgess Meredith, Margo).

Benny Goodman, King of Swing, opened at the Paramount Theatre in New York. By 6 A.M., 3,000 were assembled, most of them high school students. By 7:30, the crowd was so large that 10 mounted policemen were assigned to control the eager patrons. There was frenzied dancing in the aisles of the theatre by these teen-age "jitterbugs" or "alligators," who were adding to the American vocabulary such expressions as "in the groove," "spank the skin," "schmaltz," "boogie woogie," "jam session," and "killer-diller."

In baseball, center fielder Joe DiMaggio of the New York American ("Yankees") club, became the batting hero of his league for the first but not the last time, and continued to be an increasingly popular idol for more than a decade, even as late as the present writing (1962), thus earning the nickname "The Yankee Clipper."

Skiing, once the pastime of Scandinavian settlers of Minnesota and Wisconsin and later the sport of the privileged few, was taken up by the masses. Snow trains and buses came on the American scene, operating out of New York, Chicago, Pittsburgh, Portland, San Francisco, and other cities.

Joe Louis, the "Brown Bomber," kayoed (June 22) the heavyweight boxing champion James J. Braddock in eight rounds in Chicago to win the title that he held until his retirement in 1949.

John Davison Rockefeller, aged 98, regarded as the world's richest man, died (May 23) at Ormond Beach, Fla. His fortune was estimated at $1,000,000,000 and was believed to have been exceeded only by that of the Aga Khan, leader of the Ismailian Mohammedans.

The cauldron of war again was beginning to seethe. Hitler repudiated (Jan. 30) the Versailles Treaty of World War I, released the Reichsbank from the payment of reparations, and prohibited Germans from receiving Nobel prizes, substituting similar awards for Germans only. In Spain, the armies of General Francisco Franco besieged Madrid, and the "non-intervention" policy of the United States smoothed the road for Mussolini to help the Spanish dictator. In midsummer, the Japanese began systematic attacks upon China, thus adding a new major invasion to the lengthening list of international aggressions.

George VI and his wife Elizabeth were crowned (May 12) as King and Queen of Great Britain in succession to Edward VIII who had abdicated in the preceding year (Dec. 11, 1936).

The Irish Free State became (Dec. 28) the State of Eire.

ᏸᏮ 1938

A-Tisket A-Tasket. w., m., Ella Fitzgerald and Al Feldman. Robbins Music Corp., cop. 1938.

Bach Goes to Town. Prelude and fugue in modern style. m., Alec Templeton. Sprague-Coleman, cop. 1938.

Camel Hop. Instrumental. m., Mary Lou Williams. Robbins Music Corp., cop. 1938.

Cathedral in the Pines. w., m., Charles and Nick Kenny. Irving Berlin, Inc., cop. 1938.

Change Partners (film: Carefree). w., m., Irving Berlin. Irving Berlin, Inc., cop. 1938.

Chiapanecas—While There's Music There's Romance. Spanish words, Emilio de Torre. English words, Albert Gamse. m., M. V. de Campo; arr. by Ricardo Romero. Edward B. Marks Music Corp., cop. 1938.

Chiquita Banana. w., m., Len Mackenzie, Garth Montgomery, and William Wirges. Maxwell-Wirges Publications, Inc., cop. 1938.

Falling in Love With Love (The Boys from Syracuse). w., Lorenz Hart. m., Richard Rodgers. Chappell & Co., Inc., cop. 1938.

F.D.R. Jones (Sing Out the News). w., m., Harold J. Rome. Chappell & Co., Inc., cop. 1938.

Ferdinand the Bull (film: Ferdinand the Bull). w., Larry Morey. m., Albert Hay Malotte. ABC Music Corp., cop. 1938.

The Flat Foot Floogie. w., m., Slim Gaillard, Slam Stewart, and Bud Green. Green Bros. & Knight, cop. 1938.

Get Out of Town (Leave It to Me). w., m., Cole Porter. Chappell & Co., Inc., cop. 1938.

Heigh-Ho (film: Snow White and the Seven Dwarfs). w., Larry Morey. m., Frank Churchill. Irving Berlin, Inc., cop. 1938.

I Hadn't Anyone 'Til You. w., m., Ray Noble. ABC Music Corp., cop. 1938.

I Married an Angel (I Married an Angel). w., Lorenz Hart. m., Richard Rodgers. Robbins Music Corp., cop. 1938.

I'll Be Seeing You. w., Irving Kahal. m., Sammy Fain. Williamson Music, Inc., cop. 1938. (Popularized in 1943.)

Jeepers Creepers (film: Going Places). w., Johnny Mercer. m., Harry Warren. M. Witmark & Sons, cop. 1938.

Love Walked In (film: The Goldwyn Follies). w., Ira Gershwin. m., George Gershwin. Chappell & Co., Inc., cop. 1938.

Music, Maestro, Please! w., Herb Magidson. m., Allie Wrubel. Irving Berlin, Inc., cop. 1938.

My Heart Belongs to Daddy (Leave It to Me). w., m., Cole Porter. Chappell & Co., Inc., cop. 1938.

My Reverie. w., m., Larry Clinton, based on Debussy's "Reverie." Robbins Music Corp., cop. 1938.

The Night Is Filled With Music (film: Carefree). w., m., Irving Berlin. Irving Berlin, Inc., cop. 1938.

Ol' Man Mose. w., m., Louis Armstrong and Zilner Trenton Randolph. Santly-Joy, Inc., cop. 1938.

Pavanne (*in:* **American Symphonette No. 2).** Piano piece. m., Morton Gould. Mills Music, Inc., cop. 1938. (Published for orchestra, Mills Music, Inc., cop. 1939.)

Semper Paratus. Official U. S. Coast Guard March Song. w., m., Francis Saltus Van Boskerck, U.S.C.G. Cleveland: Sam Fox Pub. Co., cop. 1928 by U. S. Coast Guard Magazine; assigned 1938 to Sam Fox Pub. Co.

September Song (Knickerbocker Holiday). w., Maxwell Anderson. m., Kurt Weill. Crawford Music Corp., cop. 1938.

Sing for Your Supper (The Boys from Syracuse). w., Lorenz Hart. m., Richard Rodgers. Chappell & Co., Inc., cop. 1938.

Small Fry. w., Frank Loesser. m., Hoagy Carmichael. Famous Music Corp., cop. 1938.

So Help Me. w., Eddie DeLange. m., Jimmy Van Heusen. Remick Music Corp., cop. 1938.

They Say. w., Edward Heyman. m., Paul Mann and Stephen Weiss. M. Witmark & Son, cop. 1938.

This Can't Be Love (The Boys from Syracuse). w., Lorenz Hart. m., Richard Rodgers. Chappell & Co., Inc., cóp. 1938.

Ti-Pi-Tin. Spanish words and music, Maria Grever. English words, Raymond Leveen. Leo Feist, Inc., cop. 1938.

Two Sleepy People. w., Frank Loesser. m., Hoagy Carmichael. Famous Music Corp., cop. 1938.

You're a Sweet Little Headache (film: Paris Honeymoon). w., m., Leo Robin and Ralph Rainger. Paramount Music Corp., cop. 1938.

You Go to My Head. w., Haven Gillespie. m., J. Fred Coots. Remick Music Corp., cop. 1938.

You Must Have Been a Beautiful Baby (film: Hard to Get). w., Johnny Mercer. m., Harry Warren. Remick Music Corp., cop. 1938.

The House Committee Investigating un-American Activities was formed (in May) under the chairmanship of Texas Democratic Representative Martin Dies.

The Jefferson-head nickel five-cent piece, designed by Felix Schlag, went into circulation. The design won a $1,000 prize in a competition among some 390 artists.

The March of Dimes was organized (Jan. 3) as a fund-raising institution to fight infantile paralysis (1934).

A container made of indestructible metal and containing phonograph records and other examples of contemporary culture was buried (Sept. 23) in the New York World's Fair grounds, to be opened five thousand years hence—A.D. 6938.

Howard Hughes and four technical assistants made (July 10) a remarkable airplane flight around the world, flying eastward from New York, in 91 hours (3 days, 19 hours, 8 minutes, 10 seconds). Douglas G. Corrigan left Floyd Bennett Field, Brooklyn, New York, in his nine-year-old plane without permit or passport, and landed 28 hours, 13 minutes later at Baldonnel Airfield, Dublin (July 17-18).

Pearl Buck was awarded the Nobel prize for literature.

Thomas Mann, noted German novelist and essayist, settled in the United States.

Bingo became the new rage and easily the popular money game in the United States, and one which generally met with the approval of churches.

Books of the year included: "Alone" (Admiral Richard Evelyn Byrd), "Benjamin Franklin" (Carl Van Doren; Pulitzer prize 1939), "The Fifth Column and the First Forty-Nine Stories" (Ernest Hemingway; a play and short stories), "A History of American Magazines" (Frank L. Mott; Pulitzer prize 1939), "Listen! the Wind" (Anne Morrow Lindbergh), "A Prairie Grove" (Donald Culross Peattie), "Selected Poems" (John Gould Fletcher, Pulitzer prize 1939), and the fiction, "Action at Aquilla" (Hervey Allen), "All This, and Heaven Too" (Rachel Lyman Field), "And Tell of Time" (Laura Lettie Kay), "Concert Pitch" (Elliot Paul), "Dynasty of Death" (Janet Taylor Caldwell), "The Long Valley" (John Steinbeck; short stories), "My Son, My Son" (Howard Spring), "The Yearling" (Marjorie K. Rawlings; Pulitzer prize 1939).

"The Scarlet Letter," an American opera by Philadelphia-born composer Vittorio Giannini, had (June 2) its world première at the State Opera House in Hamburg, Germany. The composer's sister Dusolina sang the principal role.

The Society for the Preservation and Encouragement of Barber Shop Quartet Singing in America was founded.

Jazz orchestras took to making "swing" arrangements of Johann Sebastian Bach's works.

The Carnival of Swing, at Randall's Island, New York—featuring 25 bands—drew more than 23,000 "jitterbugs" who listened for five and three-quarter hours with such unrestrained enthusiasm that police and park officers had all they could do, according to a report in the "New York Times" the following morning, to protect the players from "destruction by admiration."

In Chicago at the Great Northern Theatre an all-Negro jazz version of Gilbert and Sullivan's operetta "The Mikado" was staged (in Sept.) with smashing success by the local W.P.A. Federal Theatre unit. (The show was taken to New York the next year.)

New York plays included: "Bachelor Born" (Morosco, Jan. 25; 400 perf.), "Shadow and Substance" (Golden, Jan. 26; 274 perf.), "On Borrowed Time" (Longacre, Feb. 3; 321 perf.), "Our Town" by Thornton Wilder (Henry Miller, Feb. 4; 336 perf.; Pulitzer prize 1938), "What a Life" (Biltmore, Apr. 13; 538 perf.), "Kiss the Boys Good-Bye" (Henry Miller, Sept. 28; 286 perf.), "Oscar Wilde" (Fulton, Oct. 10; 247 perf.), "Abe Lincoln in Illinois" by Robert Emmet Sherwood (Plymouth, Oct. 15; 472 perf.; Pulitzer prize 1939, declined by the author), "Outward Bound" (Playhouse, Dec. 22; 255 perf.; revival, first produced in 1924).

Musical productions included: "I Married an Angel" (Shubert, May 11; 338 perf.), "The Fireman's Flame" (American Music Hall, Oct. 9; 204 perf.), "Hellzapoppin" (46th Street, Sept. 22; 1,404 perf.), "Knickerbocker Holiday" (Ethel Barrymore, Oct. 19; 168 perf.), "Leave It to Me" (Imperial, Nov. 9; 307 perf.), "The Boys from Syracuse" (Alvin, Nov. 23; 235 perf.).

Motion pictures of the year included: "The Adventures of Robin Hood" (Errol Flynn), "Alexander's Ragtime Band" (Tyrone Power, Alice Faye, Don Ameche), "Angels Have Dirty Faces," "Boys Town" (Spencer Tracy, Mickey Rooney), "The Citadel" (Robert Donat, Rosalind Russell), "The Hurricane" (Dorothy Lamour, Jon Hall, Mary Astor), "In Old Chicago" (Tyrone Power, Alice Faye, Don Ameche), "Jezebel" (Bette Davis, Fay Bainter), "Kentucky," "The Lady Vanishes," "Love Finds Andy Hardy" (Mickey Rooney, Lewis Stone, Judy Garland, Cecilia Parker), "Marie Antoinette" (Norma Shearer, Tyrone Power), "Pygmalion" (Leslie Howard, Wendy Hiller), "Snow White and the Seven Dwarfs" (Walt Disney's first full-length color cartoon), "Three Comrades" (Margaret Sullavan), "You Can't Take It with You" (Jean Arthur, Lionel Barrymore, James Stewart, Edward Arnold). Walt Disney's "Snow White" was "the happiest thing that has happened in the world since the Armistice," said columnist Westbrook Pegler. The charming fantasy set the whole country humming "Heigh Ho—Heigh Ho" and "Whistle While You Work." Incidentally, the picture was a boon to toy manufacturers in the bleak first third of '38, when economic recession was at its worst. More than 3,000,000 Disney toys were sold, and the Sieberling-Latex factory near Akron, O., couldn't keep up with the demand for rubber reproductions of the seven dwarfs, even by working 24 hours a day.

Radio station WOR, New York, of the Mutual Broadcasting System began (in the fall) weekly broadcasts of Johann Sebastian Bach's cantatas. (The station gave in 1940 the complete piano concertos of Mozart.)

A new radio feature was a quiz program of mature stature: "Information Please," with John Kieran, Franklin P. Adams, and guests; Clifton Fadiman was quizmaster. Other popular new programs were "Dick Tracy" (Jan. 3) and "True or False" (Jan. 3).

"War of the Worlds," a radio drama, was so realistically enacted (Oct. 30) by Orson Welles and his cast over the Columbia Broadcasting System network from New York that a public uproar, quite unknown to the actors, occurred during the presentation. The script dealt with a supposed invasion of the earth by the inhabitants of Mars. When the fictitious Martians attacked the 15-mile Pulaski Skyway bridge in New Jersey near New York, people in the surrounding areas became panic-stricken; a section of the listening public excitedly telephoned from all parts of the country to the radio station for information, and the police had to be summoned to calm an anxious crowd that had gathered in front of the broadcasting building. (A similar "Martian" broadcast in Quito,

Ecuador, Feb. 13, 1949, resulted in a riot in which 21 persons were killed.)

Twenty-year-old Bobby (Robert) Feller, pitcher of the Cleveland American League ("Indians") baseball club, "struck out" (Oct. 2) 18 batsmen in a game with the Detroit "Tigers."

ᘒᕀ 1939

All the Things You Are (Very Warm for May). w., Oscar Hammerstein, 2nd. m., Jerome Kern. Chappell & Co., Inc., cop. 1939.

Beer Barrel Polka. w., m., Lew Brown, Wladimir A. Timm, and Jaromir Vejvoda. Shapiro, Bernstein & Co., Inc., cop. 1934 by Jana Hoffmanna; assigned and copyrighted 1939 by Shapiro, Bernstein & Co., Inc.

Brazil—Aquarela do Brasil. Brazilian samba. English words, Bob Russell. m., Ary Barroso. Southern Music Publishing Co., Inc., cop. 1939 by Irmaos Vitale, Rio de Janeiro, Brazil, and Southern Music Publishing Co., Inc.; assigned and copyrighted 1942 by Peer International Corporation.

Careless. w., m., Lew Quadling, Eddy Howard, and Dick Jurgens. Irving Berlin, Inc., cop. 1939.

Cavalry of the Steppes. Soviet Army song. Russian words, Victor Gussev; English words, M. L. Korr. m., Lev Knipper. Workers Library Publishers, cop. 1939 (in: "Songs of America," p. 36-370). Also published as (1) "Meadowlands," English words by Olga Paul, Edward B. Marks Music Corp., cop. 1942; (2) "Meadowland," English words by Harold J. Rome, Leeds Music Corp., cop. 1943.

Darn That Dream (Swingin' the Dream). w., Eddie De Lange. m., Jimmy Van Heusen. Bregman, Vocco & Conn, Inc., cop. 1939.

Do I Love You? (DuBarry Was a Lady). w., m., Cole Porter. Chappell & Co., Inc., cop. 1939.

Frenesi. Spanish words and music, Albert Dominguez. English words, Ray Charles and S. K. Russell. Southern Music Publishing Co., Inc., cop. 1939; assigned and copyrighted 1941 by Peer International Corporation.

God Bless America. w., m., Irving Berlin. Irving Berlin, Inc., cop. 1939.

I Concentrate on You (film: Broadway Melody of 1940). w., m., Cole Porter. Crawford Music Corp., cop. 1939.

I Didn't Know What Time It Was (Too Many Girls). w., Lorenz Hart. m., Richard Rodgers. Chappell & Co., Inc., cop. 1939.

I've Got My Eyes on You (film: Broadway Melody of 1940). w., m., Cole Porter. Crawford Music Corp., cop. 1939.

I Poured My Heart Into a Song (film: Second Fiddle). w., m., Irving Berlin. Irving Berlin, Inc., cop. 1939.

I'll Never Smile Again. w., m., Ruth Lowe. Sun Music Co., Inc., cop. 1939.

If I Didn't Care. w., m., Jack Lawrence. Chappell & Co., Inc., cop. 1939.

In an Eighteenth Century Drawing Room. Instrumental piece. m., Raymond Scott [pseud. of Harry Warnow]. Circle Music Publications, Inc., cop. 1939.

The Incredible Flutist. Orch. suite from the ballet "The Incredible Flutist." m., Walter Piston. Arrow Music Press, Inc., cop. 1938 by Walter Piston; assigned 1939 to Arrow Music Press, Inc.

The Lamp Is Low. w., Mitchell Parish. m., Peter DeRose and Bert Shefter, adapted from Ravel's "Pavane for a Dead Infanta." Robbins Music Corp., cop. 1939.

Lilacs in the Rain. w., Mitchell Parish. m., Peter DeRose. Robbins Music Corp., cop. 1939.

Meadowland; Meadowlands. See above: "Cavalry of the Steppes."

Moon Love. w., m., Mack David, Mack Davis, and André Kostelanetz, adapted from the second movement of Tchaikovsky's Symphony No. 5. Famous Music Corp., cop. 1939.

My Last Goodbye. w., m., Eddy Howard. Irving Berlin, Inc., cop. 1939.

My Prayer. w., Jimmy Kennedy. m., Georges Boulanger. Skidmore Music Co., Inc., cop. 1939.

Old Mill Wheel. w., m., Benny Davis, Milton Ager, and Jesse Greer. Ager, Yellen & Bornstein, Inc., cop. 1939.

Our Love. w., m., Larry Clinton, Buddy Bernier, and Bob Emmerich, adapted from Tchaikovsky's symphonic poem "Romeo and Juliet." Chappell & Co., Inc., cop. 1939.

Over the Rainbow (film: The Wizard of Oz). w., E. Y. Harburg. m., Harold Arlen. Leo Feist, Inc., cop. 1939. (Academy Award Winner, 1939).

South of the Border. w., m., Jimmy Kennedy and Michael Carr. Shapiro, Bernstein & Co., Inc., cop. 1939.

There'll Always Be an England. w., m., Ross Parker and Hughie Charles. London: The Irwin Dash Music Co., cop. 1939.

Three Little Fishies. w., m., Saxie Dowell. Santly-Joy, Inc., cop. 1939.

Wishing (film: Love Affair). w., m., Bud G. DeSylva. Crawford Music Corp., cop. 1939.

Yours for a Song (Billy Rose's Aquacade at the New York World's Fair, 1939). w., Billy Rose and Ted Fetter. m., Dana Suesse. Robbins Music Corp., cop. 1939.

The year marked the beginning of World War II. Adolf Hitler, "Führer" of Germany, had marched (Mar. 13, 1938) into Austria after the collapse of its government and proclaimed (Sept. 1, 1939) war on Poland. Great Britain and France, as allies of the latter, declared (Sept. 3) war on Germany—the start of seven years' hostilities that were to engage the world (Sept. 3, 1939-Sept. 2, 1945). By the end of the year Germany had begun to bomb British towns from the air.

Congress passed the Hatch Act, named after New Mexico Senator Carl Atwood Hatch, prohibiting the participation of government employees in political activity.

The Townsend Pension Plan (1934) was defeated (June 1) in the House.

Two great expositions, a continent apart, were held—the Golden Gate International Exposition in San Francisco (Feb. 18-Oct. 29) and the New York World's Fair (Apr. 30-Oct. 31; May 11-Oct. 21, 1940). The latter was a stupendous, colorful affair, in which sixty nations took part. Germany was not represented. The National Broadcasting Company, New York, telecast the opening ceremonies.

King George VI and Queen Elizabeth of Great Britain visited (June 7-11) the United States, via Canada. They were received (June 8-9) at the White House, made (June 10) a triumphal tour of New York City amid great jubilation, visiting the World's Fair, and were entertained by President Roosevelt at his home in Hyde Park, N. Y., in American style by being treated to "hot dogs."

The $18,000,000 Bronx-Whitestone Bridge, New York, spanning the East River, was completed.

Mrs. Clara Adams of New York became the first woman to make a trip around the world by airplane. The journey was accomplished in 16 days, 19 hours, 4 minutes (June 28-July 15).

Captain James W. Chapman, Jr., U. S. Army Air Corps, made a round-trip flight by plane from Washington, D. C., to Moscow and back in 5 days, 1 hour, 55 minutes' flying time.

E. O. Lawrence was awarded the Nobel prize for physics.

Erich Maria Remarque, German author of "All Quiet on the Western Front" and other novels, came to the United States.

Alexander Gretchaninov, Russian composer, settled in the United States.

Books of the year included: "Abraham Lincoln: The War Years" (Carl Sandburg; Pulitzer prize), "America in Midpassage" (Charles and Mary Beard; a history), "Collected Poems" (Mark Van Doren; Pulitzer prize 1940), "Hardly a Man Is Now Alive" (Daniel Carter Beard; a history), "I'm a Stranger Here Myself" (Ogden Nash), "Woodrow Wilson" (Ray Stannard Baker; vols. 7-8; Pulitzer prize 1940), and the fiction, "Adventures of a Young Man" (John Dos Passos), "The Bridegroom Cometh" (Waldo Frank), "Children of God" (Vardis Fisher; a novel about the Mormons), "Claudia" (Rose Franken; sequels, "Claudia and David," 1940, and "The Book of Claudia," 1941), "Disputed Passage" (Lloyd Cassel Douglas), "The Grapes of Wrath" (John Steinbeck: Pulitzer prize 1940), "Kitty Foyle" (Christopher Morley), "The March of the Hundred" (Manuel Komroff), "The Nazarene" (Sholem Asch), "Peace, It's Wonderful" (William Saroyan), "Song of Years" (Bess Streeter Aldrich), "Tommy Gallagher's Crusade" (James Farrell), "The Web and the Rock" (Thomas Wolfe, published posthumously), "Wickford Point" (John Phillips Marquand).

Marian Anderson, noted Negro contralto, was barred by the Washington, D. C., chapter of the Daughters of the American Revolution from giving a concert in Constitution Hall, which was owned by them. She then gave (Apr. 9) in Lincoln Memorial Park to an audience of 75,000 people an open-air concert that was sponsored by many eminent political leaders, among them Secretary of State Harold Leclaire Ickes and Mrs. Franklin Delano Roosevelt.

Gian-Carlo Menotti's opera "The Old Maid and the Thief" received (Apr. 22) its world première in a radio broadcast from New York by the National Broadcasting Company. (The opera had its first stage performance in Philadelphia, Feb. 11, 1941.)

Unfavorable testimony before the House Committee Investigating Un-

American Activities (during June) led (July 31) to the disbandment of the Federal Theatre Project of the Works Progress Administration relief program. The Project had given employment to more than 13,000 actors and other workers in the theatrical profession, and had produced about 1,200 plays. Mrs. Hallie Flanagan of Vassar College was the director of the undertaking and published (1940) its history under the title "Arena."

The New York stage again produced a play that broke all existing box office records, topping both "Tobacco Road" (1933; 3,182 performances) and "Abie's Irish Rose" (1922; 2,327 performances). The play was "Life with Father," adapted from Clarence Day's novel by Howard Lindsay and Russel Crouse. When the show closed nearly eight years later (July 12, 1947), it had run up a total of 3,224 performances. Other plays that ran 175 or more performances included: "The American Way" (Center, Jan. 21; 244 perf.), "I Must Love Someone" (Longacre, Feb. 7), "The Little Foxes" (National, Feb. 15; 410 perf.), "The Philadelphia Story" (Shubert, Mar. 28; 417 perf.), "No Time for Comedy" (Ethel Barrymore, Apr. 17), "See My Lawyer" (Biltmore, Sept. 27; 224 perf.), "Skylark" (Morosco, Oct. 11; 256 perf.), "The Man Who Came to Dinner" (Music Box, Oct. 16; 739 perf.), "The Time of Your Life" by William Saroyan (Booth, Oct. 25; Pulitzer prize 1940), "Margin for Error" (Plymouth, Nov. 3; 264 perf.). Musical productions included: "Stars in Your Eyes" (Majestic, Feb. 9), "Street of Paris" (Broadhurst, June 19; 274 perf.), "Yokel Boy" (Majestic, July 6; 208 perf.), "Too Many Girls" (Imperial, Oct. 18; 249 perf.), "DuBarry Was a Lady" (46th Street, Dec. 6; 408 perf.). Jazz versions of Gilbert and Sullivan's operetta "The Mikado" were heard as "The Swing Mikado" (New Yorker, Mar. 1; 62 perf.; originally produced in Chicago in Sept. 1938 by the Chicago W.P.A. Federal Theatre) and as "The Hot Mikado" (Broadhurst, Mar. 23; 85 perf.). A similar treatment of Shakespeare's "A Midsummer Night's Dream" was unsuccessful as "Swingin' the Dream" (Center, Nov. 29; 13 perf.).

Motion pictures of the year included: "Broadway Melody of 1940," "Dark Victory" (Bette Davis), "Goodbye, Mr. Chips" (Robert Donat, Greer Garson), "Juarez" (Paul Muni), "Mr. Smith Goes to Washington" (Jean Arthur, James Stewart), "The Old Maid" (Bette Davis), "Stanley and Livingstone," (Spencer Tracy, Nancy Kelly, Richard Greene), "The Ugly Duckling" (Walt Disney cartoon), "The Wizard of Oz" (Judy Garland, Frank Morgan, Ray Bolger, Bert Lahr, Jack Haley), "The Women" (Norma Shearer, Joan Crawford, Rosalind Russell), "Wuthering Heights" (Merle Oberon, Laurence Olivier).

Baseball was 100 years old, according to the reckoning of Cooperstown, N. Y., which claims the origin of the game. The U. S. Post Office honored the centennial by issuing (June 12) a three-cent commemorative postage stamp.

1940

Accidently on Purpose. w., m., Don McCray and Ernest Gold. Broadcast Music, Inc., cop. 1940.

All or Nothing at All. w., m., Jack Lawrence and Arthur Altman. Leeds Music Corp., cop. 1940.

Ballad for Americans. Cantata. w., John Latouche. m., Earl Robinson; arr. by Domenico Savino. Robbins Music Corp., cop. 1940.

The Breeze and I. w., Al Stillman. m., Ernesto Lecuona, adapted from his "Andalucia." Edward B. Marks Music Co., cop. 1929; cop. 1940.

Cabin in the Sky (film: Cabin in the Sky). w., John Latouche. m., Vernon Duke [pseud. of Vladimir Dukelsky]. Leo Feist, Inc., cop. 1940.

Fools Rush in. w., Johnny Mercer. m., Rube Bloom. Bregman, Vocco & Conn, Inc., cop. 1940.

How High the Moon (Two for the Show). w., Nancy Hamilton. m., Morgan Lewis. Chappell & Co., Inc., cop. 1940.

I'm Stepping Out with a Memory To-night. w., Herb Magidson. m., Allie Wrubel. Robbins Music Corp., cop. 1940.

I Hear a Rhapsody. w., m., George Fragos and Jack Baker. Broadcast Music, Inc., cop. 1940.

Imagination. w., Johnny Burke. m., Jimmy Van Heusen. ABC Music Corp., cop. 1940.

It's a Big, Wonderful World (All in Fun). w., m., John Rox. Broadcast Music, Inc., cop. 1940.

It's a Lovely Day Tomorrow (Louisiana Purchase). w., m., Irving Berlin. Irving Berlin, Inc., cop. 1940.

The Last Time I Saw Paris. w., Oscar Hammerstein, 2nd. m., Jerome Kern. Chappell & Co., Inc., cop. 1940. (Academy Award Winner, 1941)

Louisiana Purchase (Louisiana Purchase). w., m., Irving Berlin. Irving Berlin, Inc., cop. 1940.

A Love Story—Intermezzo (film: Intermezzo). w., Robert Henning. m., Heinz Provost. Edward Schuberth & Co., Inc., cop. 1940 by arrangement with Carl Gehrman's Musikforlag, Stockholm (cop. 1936).

The Nearness of You. w., Ned Washington. m., Hoagy Carmichael. Famous Music Corp., cop. 1940.

Only Forever (film: Rhythm on the River). w., Johnny Burke. m., James V. Monaco. Santly-Joy-Select, Inc., cop. 1940; assigned 1942 to Santly-Joy, Inc.

Rhumboogie (film: Argentine Nights). w., m., Don Raye and Hughie Prince. Leeds Music Corp., cop. 1940.

San Antonio Rose. w., m., Bob Wills. Irving Berlin, Inc., cop. 1940.

The Sky Fell Down. w., Edward Heyman. m., Louis Alter. M. Witmark & Sons, cop. 1940.

Taking a Chance on Love (Cabin in the Sky). w., John Latouche and Ted Fetter. m., Vernon Duke [pseud. of Vladimir Dukelsky]. Leo Feist, Inc., cop. 1940.

There I Go. w., Hy Zaret. m., Irving Weiser. Broadcast Music, Inc., cop. 1940.

This Is My Country. w., Don Raye. m., Al Jacobs. Words and Music, Inc., cop. 1940.

We Could Make Such Beautiful Music. w., Robert Sour. m., Henry Manners. Broadcast Music, Inc., cop. 1940.

When You Wish upon a Star (film: Pinocchio). w., Ned Washington. m., Leigh Harline. Irving Berlin, Inc., cop. 1940. (Academy Award Winner, 1940)

You Are My Sunshine. w., m., Jimmie Davis and Charles Mitchell. Southern Music Pub., Inc., cop. 1940.

You Stepped Out of a Dream (film: Ziegfeld Girl). w., Gus Kahn. m., Nacio Herb Brown. Leo Feist, Inc., cop. 1940.

World War II continued. The year saw German troops invade Denmark and Norway (there was no resistance in the former country; the latter was paralyzed by treachery), the violation of the neutrality of Belgium, Luxembourg, and the Netherlands, with the subsequent surrender of the Dutch and Belgian armies after enormous casualties. The British were driven from the Continent, and some 300,000 British and French soldiers were taken from the beaches of Dunkirk in the most heroic rescue of the war. Most of the armament was lost in the retreat, and Britain faced the future nearly helpless to ward off invasion. The Germans almost reached Paris, Italy declared war on Great Britain and France, and the latter sued (June 17) for an armistice. Italy extended the war to the Balkans by attacking Greece, Germany came to Italy's assistance, overran Greece and Yugoslavia, and brought Hungary, Bulgaria, and Rumania under German control.

Hitler's conquests, unequalled since the days of Napoleon, shocked America out of its isolationist stand. Congress enacted (Aug. 27) a law requiring alien residents to register and passed the Selective Service and Training Act (signed by President Roosevelt Sept. 16), inaugurating the first peace-time military draft in United States history. October 16 was the appointed day for the registration of all male citizens up to the age of thirty-five inclusive—16,313,240 received registration cards. Secretary of War Henry Lewis Stimson set the draft in motion by drawing, blind-folded, the card of the first selectee from a glass bowl in the War Department Auditorium in Washington, D. C. To impress further upon the public the necessity of adequate national defense, the Post Office Department issued on that fateful day (Oct. 16) three special postage stamps to replace temporarily the regular issues. The new adhesives pictured the Statue of Liberty (one cent), an anti-aircraft gun (two cents), and an uplifted torch (three cents), each bearing the words "For Defense."

In exchange for 50 old destroyers, the United States obtained from Great Britain naval and air bases in American waters.

I Am an American Day (third Sunday in May) was proclaimed (May 3) by Act of Congress.

During the year, the Post Office issued, among other commemorative postage stamps, a special series of 35 stamps in groups of five each, with portraits celebrating famous Americans (artists, authors, educators, inventors, musical composers, poets, and scientists).

The Pan American Airways "Yankee Clipper" flew (Apr. 1-2) from New York to Lisbon, Portugal, in a record time of 18 hours, 35 minutes, and made the return trip in 25 hours, 1 minute—the round trip occupying 43 hours, 36 minutes.

John Llewellyn Lewis, boss of the United Mine Workers Union, who had been noted chiefly for his dictatorial and obstructive ways and who had become unpopular with many of the mine workers themselves, resigned (Nov. 18) as president of the Congress of Industrial Organizations ("C.I.O.") which he had founded in 1935.

The $58,000,000 Manhattan-Queens vehicular tunnel under the East River, New York, was opened (Nov. 15).

Books of the year included: "Arena" (Hallie Flanagan; a history of the Federal Theatre project), "The Atlantic Migration" (Marcus Lee Hansen; a history; Pulitzer prize 1941, awarded posthumously), "Dictionary of American History" (James Truslow Adams; 6 vols.), "Jonathan Edwards" (Ola Elizabeth Winslow; Pulitzer prize 1941), "New England: Indian Summer" (Van Wyck Brooks), "Sunderland Capture" (Leonard Bacon; poetry; Pulitzer prize 1941), "Trojan Horses in America" (Martin Dies), and the fiction, "For Whom the Bell Tolls" (Ernest Hemingway), "How Green Was My Valley" (Richard Llewellyn), "My Name Is Aram" (William Saroyan), "Native Son" (Richard Wright), "Pal Joey" (John O'Hara), "Sapphira and the Slave Girl" (Willa Cather), "World's End" (Upton Sinclair; sequel, "Between Two Worlds," 1941), "You Can't Go Home Again" (Thomas Wolfe). No Pulitzer prize was awarded for this year's fiction.

Darius Milhaud, French composer, settled in the United States.

Arturo Toscanini made a triumphal tour of South America with the NBC Symphony Orchestra.

Leopold Stokowski organized his All-American Youth Orchestra from 15,000 auditioned aspirants.

New York plays included: "The Male Animal" (Cort, Jan. 9; 243 perf.), "Separate Rooms" (Maxine Elliott, Mar. 23; 613 perf.), "There Shall Be No Night" by Robert Emmet Sherwood (Alvin, Apr. 29; 181 perf.; Pulitzer prize 1941, his second award), "Johnny Belinda" (Belasco, Sept. 18; 321 perf.), "Charley's Aunt" (Cort. Oct. 17; 233 perf., revival), "George Washington Slept Here" (Lyceum, Oct. 18; 173 perf.), "The Corn Is Green" (National, Nov. 26; 477 perf.), "My Sister Eileen" (Biltmore, Dec. 26; 865 perf.). Helen Hayes revived "Twelfth Night" (St. James, Nov. 19; 129 perf.). Musical productions included: "Louisiana Purchase" (Imperial, May 28; 444 perf.), "Boys and Girls Together" (Broadhurst, Oct. 1; 191 perf.), "It Happens on Ice" (Center, Oct. 10; 662 perf.), "Panama Hattie" (46th Street, Oct. 30; 501 perf.), "Pal Joey" (Ethel Barrymore, Dec. 25; 374 perf.).

Motion pictures of the year included: "Abraham Lincoln in Illinois" (Raymond Massey), "All This, and Heaven Too" (Bette Davis, Charles Boyer), "Boom Town" (Clark Gable, Spencer Tracy, Claudette Colbert), "Fantasia" (spectacular Walt Disney cartoon with musical accompaniments by Leopold Stokowski and a large symphony orchestra; first shown in New York, Broadway Theatre, Nov. 13), "Foreign Correspondent" (Joel McCrea, Laraine Day), "Gone with the Wind" (Vivien Leigh, Clark Gable, Thomas Mitchell, Olivia de Haviland, Leslie Howard, "The Grapes of Wrath" (Henry Fonda, Jane Darwell), "The Great Dictator" (Charlie Chaplin), "Kitty Foyle" (Ginger Rogers), "The Mortal Storm" (Margaret Sullavan, James Stewart), "Ninotchka" (Greta Garbo), "Northwest Passage" (Spencer Tracy, Robert Young), "Our Town" (William Holden), "The Philadelphia Story" (Katharine Hepburn, Cary Grant, James Stewart), "Pinocchio," "The Westerner."

The Columbia Broadcasting System, New York, gave (Sept. 4) a public demonstration of television in color over its station W2XAB.

An event in American television was (Mar. 10) the first telecast of an opera in the New York area by the National Broadcasting Company. The opera was a tabloid version of "Pagliacci," sung at Radio City by Metropolitan Opera singers. (The British Broadcasting Company had telecast opera and ballet in London in 1937-38.)

"Staticless" radio (F.M. or Frequency Modulation) was demonstrated (Jan. 5) by Major Edwin H. Armstrong from station WIXOJ, Worcester, Mass.

Harry James, trumpeter, left the Benny Goodman orchestra to form his own band, and took on a young, unknown vocalist—Frank Sinatra —who created no stir at first!

The national population was 131,669,275.

₰ 1941

The Anniversary Waltz. w., m., Al Dubin and Dave Franklin. Mayfair Music Corp., cop. 1941 by Saunders Music Co., Hollywood.

Bewitched (Pal Joey). w., Lorenz Hart. m., Richard Rodgers. Chappell & Co., Inc., cop. 1941.

Blues in the Night (film: Blues in the Night). w., Johnny Mercer. m., Harold Arlen. Remick Music Corp., cop. 1941.

Chattanooga Choo Choo (film: Sun Valley Serenade). w., Mack Gordon. m., Harry Warren. Leo Feist, Inc., cop. 1941 by Twentieth Century Music Corp.

Concerto for Two. w., m., Jack Lawrence and P. I. Tchaikovsky, arranged by Robert C. Haring; based on the first movement of Tchaikovsky's First Piano Concerto. Shapiro, Bernstein & Co., Inc., cop. 1941.

Day Dreaming. w., Gus Kahn. m., Jerome Kern. T. B. Harms Co., cop. 1941.

Deep in the Heart of Texas. w., June Hershey. m., Don Swander. Melody Lane Publications, Inc., cop. 1941

Dolores. w., Frank Loesser. m., Louis Alter. Famous Music Corp., cop. 1941 by Paramount Music Corp.

Don't Take Your Love from Me. w., m., Henry Nemo. M. Witmark & Sons, cop. 1941.

Flamingo. w., Ed Anderson. m., Ted Grouya. Tempo Music, Inc., cop. 1941.

Hi, Neighbor! (film: San Antonio Rose). w., m., Jack Owens. Broadcast Music Inc., cop. 1941.

How About You? (film: Babes on Broadway). w., Ralph Freed. m., Burton Lane. Leo Feist, Inc., cop. 1941.

I Don't Want to Walk without You (film: Sweater Girl). w., Frank Loesser. m., Julie Styne. Paramount Music Corp., cop. 1941.

I Don't Want to Set the World on Fire. w., m., Eddie Seiler, Sol Marcus, Bennie Benjemen, and Eddie Durham. Cherio Music Publishers, Inc., cop. 1941.

I Got It Bad and That Ain't Good. w., Paul Webster. m., Duke Ellington. Robbins Music Corp., cop. 1941.

I'll Remember April. w., m., Don Raye, Gene de Paul and Pat Johnston. Leeds Music Corp., cop. 1941.

It's Always You. w., Johnny Burke. m., Jimmy Van Heusen. Famous Music Corp., cop. 1941.

Jersey Bounce. Instrumental piece. m., Bobby Plater, Tiny Bradshaw, Edward Johnson, and Robert B. Wright. Lewis Music Pub. Co., Inc., cop. 1941. (Published as a song, words by Buddy Feyne and Robert B. Wright, cop. 1946.)

Jim. w., Nelson Shawn. m., Caesar Petrillo and Edward Ross. Kaycee Music Co., Inc., cop. 1941.

I Think of You. w., m., Jack Elliot and Don Marcotte, based on the first movement of Rachmaninov's Second Piano Concerto. Embassy Music Corp., cop. 1941.

Music Makers. w., Don Raye. m., Harry James. Paramount Music Corp., cop. 1941.

My Adobe Hacienda. w., m., Louise Massey and Lee Penny. Southern Music Pub. Co., Inc., cop. 1941.

There! I've Said It Again. w., m., Redd Evans and Dave Mann. Radio Tunes Inc., cop. 1941; assigned to Valiant Music Co. (Popularized in 1947.)

This Is New (Lady in the Dark). w., Ira Gershwin. m., Kurt Weill. Chappell & Co., Inc., cop. 1941.

This Love of Mine. w., Frank Sinatra. m., Sol Parker and Henry Sanicola. Embassy Music Corp., cop. 1941.

Tonight We Love. w., Bobby Worth. m., Ray Austin and Freddy Martin, based on the first movement of Tchaikovsky's First Piano Concerto. Maestro Music Co., cop. 1941.

Two Hearts That Pass in the Night. w., Forman Brown. m., Ernesto Lecuona. Edward B. Marks Music Corp., cop. 1941.

Waltzing Matilda. Australian song. w., A. B. Paterson. m., Marie Cowan, arr. by Orrie Lee. Carl Fischer, Inc., cop. 1936 by Allan & Co., Melbourne; cop. 1941 by Carl Fischer, Inc.

The White Cliffs of Dover. w., Nat Burton. m., Walter Kent. Shapiro, Bernstein & Co., cop. 1941.

World War II continued.

President Franklin Delano Roosevelt began his third term—the first American President to be so elected, breaking the tradition against a third term that was established by George Washington. (Roosevelt also was the first President to be inaugurated on Jan. 20 in accordance with the 20th Amendment.)

As safeguards of American democracy against the spreading menace of Hitlerism, the United States instituted various government agencies and policies. Of far-reaching effect abroad was the seven-billion-dollar Lend-Lease Act (signed by President Roosevelt Mar. 10) of aid to Great Britain. To prevent profiteering at home, the Office of Price Administration ("O.P.A.") was set up (Apr. 11); to protect the country against the hazards of war, the Office of Civilian Defense was created (May 20). President Roosevelt declared (May 21) "an unlimited state of national emergency," pledged (May 27) assistance to all nations engaged in resisting Nazi aggression, and ordered (June 14) the "freezing" of the assets of Germany and Italy in the United States, the seizure of their vessels in American ports, and the closing of the German consulates. The President enunciated (July 6) four principles of human liberty, known collectively as the "four freedoms," namely, freedom of speech and expression, freedom of worship, freedom from want, and freedom from fear.

Meanwhile, U. S. Marines were landed (July 7) in Iceland at the request of its government; and President Roosevelt and Prime Minister Winston Churchill of Great Britain met (Aug. 12-14) at an undisclosed spot in the North Atlantic and drafted the eight principles of a document called the Atlantic Charter. By executive order, the Office of Lend-Lease Administration was established (Oct. 28) and the sum of $1,000,000,000 was made (Nov. 6) available to Russia under the plan. In Washington, a conference on the situation in the Far East was held (Nov. 17) with Japanese envoys concerning their country's invasion of Thailand (Siam), the Malay Peninsula, and the Burma Road. In Havana, Cuba, representatives of Latin-American republics and the United States met in a Pan American conference to consolidate economic and military co-operation for the defense of the Western hemisphere.

Without warning, after President Roosevelt had addressed (Dec. 6) a personal appeal to Emperor Hirohito of Japan to avoid further conflict in the Pacific, Japanese warplanes blasted (Dec. 7) the port of Pearl Harbor, near Honolulu, Hawaii, the Philippines, and Wake and Guam islands. The country was stunned by the terrible losses at Pearl Harbor; five battleships sunk or beached, three more badly damaged, 10 smaller warships destroyed or heavily hurt, and the destruction of the bomber command at Clark Field in the Philippines. War on Japan was declared (Dec. 8) by the United States. As allies of Japan, Germany and Italy declared (Dec. 11) war on the United States. The Office of Defense Transportaton was established (Dec. 18) to co-ordinate every inland and coastal means of transport. To supply the labor demands of wartime production the U. S. Employment Service was organized (during the month; transferred to the War Manpower Commission Sept. 17, 1942). Premier Churchill again visited the United States and began (Dec. 23) in Washington a second conference with President Roosevelt.

In defiance of President Roosevelt's "national emergency" proclamation, the United Mine Workers President John Llewellyn Lewis called (Oct. 25) a strike in the coal mines of seven large steel companies that would involve more than 50,000 miners. President Roosevelt succeeded in delaying the strike (until Nov. 5), pending negotiation, but irreconcilable union officials were determined on the strike (set for Nov. 16). It was called off (Nov. 22) by Lewis when President Roosevelt again intervened with a proposal of arbitration.

The old U. S. submarine O-9 sank (June 13) with a loss of 33 men during a deep-sea diving test in the Atlantic about 24 miles east of Portsmouth, N. H.

The National Gallery of Art, Washington, D. C., was opened. It is housed in a marble building erected at a cost of $15,000,000 from funds that were provided by Andrew William Mellon, Pittsburgh capitalist and Secretary of the Treasury under Presidents Harding, Coolidge, and

Hoover. The museum contains, as gifts to the nation, Mellon's valuable collection of 126 paintings and 26 pieces of sculpture, and the remarkable Samuel H. Kress Collection of Italian art consisting of 551 paintings and 54 pieces of sculpture, the largest collection assembled by a single person.

Books of the year included: "Berlin Diary" (William Lawrence Shirer), "Crusader in Crinoline" (Forrest Wilson; Pulitzer prize 1942), "The Dust Which Is God" (William Rose Benét; poetry; Pulitzer prize 1942), "James Madison" (Irving Newton Brant; Vol. 1), "The Oxford Companion to American Literature" (James D. Hart), "Reveille in Washington" (Margaret Leach; a history; Pulitzer prize 1942) and the fiction, "H. M. Pulham, Esq." (John Phillips Marquand), "In This Our Life" (Ellen Glasgow; Pulitzer prize 1942), "The Keys of the Kingdom" (Archibald Joseph Cronin), "The Strange Woman" (Ben Ames Williams).

Ignace Jan Paderewski, world-renowned Polish piano virtuoso, composer, and former Premier of Poland, aged 81, died (June 29) in New York. His body lay in state at St. Patrick's Cathedral and was viewed by throngs of reverent people. By President Roosevelt's order, Paderewski's body was laid to rest under the mast of the battleship "Maine" in Arlington National Cemetery to await proper burial in the musician's native land.

New York plays included: "Arsenic and Old Lace" (Fulton, Jan. 10; 1,444 perf.), "Mr. and Mrs. North" (Belasco, Jan. 12), "Claudia" (Booth, Feb. 12; 722 perf.), "Watch on the Rhine" (Martin Beck, Apr. 1, 378 perf.), "Blithe Spirit" (Morosco, Nov. 5; 657 perf.), "Spring Again" (Henry Miller, Nov. 1); 241 perf.), "Junior Miss" (Lyceum, Nov. 18; 710 perf.), "Angel Street" (Golden, Dec. 5; 1,295 perf.). Maurice Evans revived "Macbeth" (National, Nov. 11; 131 perf.). Musical productions included: "Lady in the Dark" (Alvin, Jan. 23; 467 perf.), "Best Foot Forward" (Ethel Barrymore, Oct. 1; 326 perf.), "Let's Face It" (Imperial, Oct. 29; 547 perf.), "High Kickers" (Broadhurst, Oct. 31), "Sons o' Fun" (Winter Garden, Dec. 1; 742 perf.).

Motion pictures of the year included: "Blossoms in the Dust" (Greer Garson), "Citizen Kane" (Orson Welles), "Here Comes Mr. Jordan" (Robert Montgomery), "How Green Was My Valley" (Walter Pidgeon, Maureen O'Hara), "Kings Row" (Ann Sheridan, Robert Cummings, Ronald Regan, Betty Field), "The Little Foxes" (Bette Davis), "The Man Who Came to Dinner" (Monty Woolley, Bette Davis, Ann Sheridan), "Meet John Doe" (Gary Cooper, Barbara Stanwyck), "Sergeant York" (Gary Cooper), "Suspicion" (Cary Grant, Joan Fontaine).

Joe DiMaggio, center fielder of the New York American League ("Yankees") baseball club, set a record when he hit safely in 56 games.

ક્રે 1942

Back to Donegal. w., m., Steve Graham. Leeds Music Corp., cop. 1942.

Be Careful! It's My Heart (film: Holiday Inn). w., m., Irving Berlin. Irving Berlin, Inc., cop. 1942.

Dearly Beloved (film: You Were Never Lovelier). w., Johnny Mercer. m., Jerome Kern. Chappell & Co., Inc., cop. 1942.

Don't Get Around Much Anymore. w., Bob Russell. m., Duke Ellington. Robbins Music Corp., cop. 1942.

I'm Old Fashioned (film: You Were Never Lovelier). w., Johnny Mercer. m., Jerome Kern. Chappell & Co., Inc., cop. 1942.

I Had the Craziest Dream (film: Springtime in the Rockies). w., Mack Gordon. m., Harry Warren. Bregman, Vocco & Conn, Inc., cop. 1942 by Twentieth Century Music Corp.

I Left My Heart at the Stage Door Canteen (This Is the Army). w., m., Irving Berlin. This Is The Army, Inc., cop. 1942.

I Threw a Kiss in the Ocean. w., m., Irving Berlin. Irving Berlin, Inc., cop. 1942.

Idaho. w., m., Jesse Stone. American Academy of Music, Inc., cop. 1942.

In the Blue of Evening. w., Tom Adair. m., Alfred A. D'Artega. Shapiro, Bernstein & Co., Inc., cop. 1942.

It Can't Be Wrong (film: Now, Voyager). w., Kim Gannon. m., Max Steiner. Harms, Inc., cop. 1942.

Jingle, Jangle, Jingle (film: The Forest Rangers). w., Frank Loesser. m., Joseph J. Lilley. Paramount Music Corp., cop. 1942.

The Lamplighter's Serenade. w., Paul Francis Webster. m., Hoagy Carmichael. Robbins Music Corp., cop. 1942.

My Devotion. w., m., Roc Hillman and Johnny Napton. Santly-Joy, Inc., cop. 1942.

One Dozen Roses. w., Roger Lewis and Country Washburn. m., Dick Jergens and Walter Donovan. Famous Music Corp., cop. 1942.

Paper Doll. w., m., Johnny S. Black. Edward B. Marks Music Corp., cop. 1942.

Praise the Lord and Pass the Ammunition! w., m., Frank Loesser. Famous Music Corp., cop. 1942.

Serenade in Blue (film: Orchestra Wives). w., Mack Gordon. m., Harry Warren. Bregman, Vocco & Conn, Inc., cop. 1942 by Twentieth Century Music Corp.

That Old Black Magic (film: Star Spangled Rhythm). w., Johnny Mercer. m., Harold Arlen. Famous Music Corp., cop. 1942.

This Is the Army, Mr. Jones (This Is the Army). w., m., Irving Berlin. This Is the Army, Inc., cop. 1942.

Warsaw Concerto. Orch. piece. m., Richard Addinsell. Chappell & Co., cop. 1942 by Keith, Prowse & Co., Ltd., London.

When the Lights Go on Again. w., m., Eddie Seiler, Sol Marcus, and Bennie Benjemen. Campbell, Loft & Porgie, Inc., cop. 1942.

White Christmas (film: Holiday Inn). w., m., Irving Berlin. Irving Berlin, Inc., cop. 1942. (Academy Award Winner, 1942)

You Were Never Lovelier (film: You Were Never Lovelier). w., Johnny Mercer. m., Jerome Kern. T. B. Harms, cop. 1942.

You'd Be So Nice to Come Home To (film: Something to Shout About). w., m., Cole Porter. Chappell & Co., Inc., cop. 1942.

World War II continued—with the United States now in it. The Japanese effected (Jan. 2) a landing in Manila, Philippine Islands, forced (Apr. 9) the surrender of the American-Filipino forces at Batan, and, after overcoming stout resistance, captured Corregidor Fortress in Manila Bay. American troops arrived (Jan. 26) in northern Ireland. The United States began (Mar. 23) the removal of Japanese-American resi-

dents of the western coastal States to inland areas. Lieutenant Colonel
James H. Doolittle and 79 airmen with a large squadron of Army B-25
bombers raided (Apr. 18) the Japanese coastal cities of Tokyo, Yokohama, Kobe, Nagoya, and Osaka. They started from an undesignated
place called Shangri-La, a name derived from James Hilton's novel "Lost
Horizon." Japan occupied (June 7-8) several of the Aleutian Islands.
American troops landed (July 7) in Iceland at the request of that government. American army and naval forces began (Aug. 7) the attack on
Guadalcanal in the Solomon Islands and finally defeated (Nov. 12-15)
the Japanese in a great naval battle. Allied and American forces under
General Dwight David Eisenhower, Commander in Chief of the Allied
armies, invaded (in Nov.) northern Africa. The U. S. Air Forces commenced (Dec. 5) at Naples the bombardment of Italian cities.

Rationing of food, clothing, and other articles went into effect under
the Office of Price Administration ("O.P.A.") (1941). Gasoline was
placed on ration in the Eastern States (May 15) and later in the
West (Dec. 1).

Air raid sirens were installed and periodic blackout drills were introduced.

President Roosevelt called for—and got—60,000 planes, 45,000 tanks,
20,000 anti-aircraft guns, and 8,000,000 deadweight tons of merchant
shipping. Americans old enough to remember World War I were skeptical about the possibilities of American workers filling this order, because
they recalled that during the first war the United States had produced
only 80 tanks and had failed completely to produce the airplanes, artillery,
and ships needed by the armed forces.

New government agencies were set up—the War Production Board
(Jan. 16), the War Manpower Commission (Apr. 18) which absorbed
the Selective Service System (1940), and the U. S. Employment Service
(1941), and the Office of War Information ("O.W.I.") (June 13).

Congress empowered (Oct. 2) the President to stabilize prices and
wages, and voted (Nov. 14) the conscription of boys of eighteen years
of age and over for military service.

The U. S. Post Office issued (July 4) a three-cent purple "Win the
War" postage stamp.

Wendell Lewis Willkie, "The Barefoot Boy of Wall Street" and unsuccessful Republican presidential candidate in 1940, made (Sept. 2-
Oct. 25) a tour of inspection of England, the Near East, the Soviet Union,
and China as emissary for President Roosevelt.

The Works Progress Administration ("W.P.A.") (1935) was terminated (Dec. 4).

The United States Supreme Court voided (Jan. 12) the 40-year-old
Georgia Contract Labor Law as violation of the anti-slavery Amendments, and upheld (Dec. 21) the validity of Nevada's six-weeks-residence
divorce decrees in that State.

Capt. Edward ("Eddie") Vernon Rickenbacker, American aviator and

World War I ace, and seven Army men were found (Nov. 13) in the Southern Pacific after drifting 23 days on a life raft. Their plane had been forced down while on a special government mission. The discovery climaxed one of the greatest rescue hunts in history.

Representatives of 26 nations at war with the Axis powers formed (Jan. 1) in Washington, D. C., the nucleus of the UN, or United Nations (1945).

Joseph E. Widener presented the priceless Widener Collection of paintings and sculpture to the National Gallery of Art, Washington, D. C., which had been opened in the preceding year.

The National Geographic-Palomar Observatory Sky Survey, a project to photograph 500,000,000 stars, was begun (July 1) at Mt. Palomar, Cal., under the joint auspices of the National Geographic Society and the California Institute of Technology.

Brigadier General William Lendrum ("Billy") Mitchell, who had caused the government much embarrassment by his outspoken criticisms during the 1920s and was in consequence court-martialed (1926), was posthumously restored to the rank of major general. He had died in 1936.

The French luxury liner "Normandie" burned (Feb. 9) at her pier in New York and sank. (The ship later was raised with difficulty and scrapped on account of its damaged condition.)

Boston's Cocoanut Grove fire horrified the entire nation. The place was a night club which was jammed (Nov. 28) with 800 people after the Holy Cross College football game. A busboy lit a match and the unfireproofed artificial palm trees went up in flames; 491 persons perished and scores were injured.

Books of the year included: "Admiral of the Ocean Sea" (Samuel Eliot Morison; a biography of Columbus; Pulitzer prize 1943), "Lee's Lieutenants" (Douglas Southall Freeman; 3 vols. 1942-44), "Paul Revere and the World He Lived In" (Esther Forbes; Pulitzer prize 1943), "A Witness Tree" (Robert Frost; poetry; Pulitzer prize 1943), and the fiction, "Dragon's Teeth" (Upton Sinclair; Pulitzer prize 1943), "The Robe" (Lloyd Cassel Douglas), "See Here, Private Hargrove" (Marion Hargrove).

Francisco Mignone, Brazilian composer, toured the United States and conducted performances of his works.

An all-Negro performance of "Aïda" was given (Oct. 10) in Chicago at the Civic Opera House by the Chicago Negro Opera Guild.

New York plays included: "Guest in the House" (Plymouth, Feb. 24), "Uncle Harry" (Broadhurst, May 20; 430 perf.), "Janie" (Henry Miller, Sept. 10; 642 perf.), "The Eve of St. Mark" (Cort, Oct. 7; 307 perf.), "The Skin of Your Teeth" by Thornton Wilder (Plymouth, Nov. 18; 359 perf.; Pulitzer prize 1943), "Counsellor-at-Law" (Royale, Nov. 24; 258 perf.; revival), "The Pirate" (Martin Beck, Nov. 25), "The Doughgirls" (Lyceum, Dec. 30; 671 perf.). Musical productions included: "Porgy and Bess" (Majestic, Jan. 23; 286 perf.; revival), "Priorities of 1942" (46th Street, Mar. 12; 353 perf.), "By Jupiter" (Shubert, June 3; 427 perf.), "Star and Garter" (Music Box, June 24; 609 perf.), "Stars on Ice" (Center, July 2; 830 perf.), "This Is the Army" (Broadway, July 4; 113 perf.), "Show Time" (Broadhurst, Sept. 16; 342 perf.), "Rosalinda" (44th Street, Oct. 28; 521 perf.; a new adaptation of "Die Fledermaus").

Motion pictures of the year included: "In Which We Serve" (Noel Coward), "Mrs. Miniver" (Greer Garson, Walter Pidgeon), "One Foot in Heaven" (Fredric March, Martha Scott), "The Pied Piper" (Monty Woolley, Roddy McDowall), "The Pride of the Yankees" (Gary Cooper, Teresa Wright), "Random Harvest" (Ronald Colman, Greer Garson), "Wake Island" (Brian Donlevy, Robert Preston, Macdonald Carey), "Woman of the Year" (Katharine Hepburn, Spencer Tracy), "Yankee Doodle Dandy" (James Cagney).

ৡৣ৶ 1943

Amor. Spanish words, Ricardo Lopez Mendez. English words, Sunny Skylar. m., Gabriel Ruiz. Peer International Corp., cop. 1941 and 1943 by Promotora Hispano Americana de Musica, Mexico City.

Besame Mucho—Kiss Me Much. Spanish words and music, Consuelo Velazquez. English words, Sunny Skylar. Southern Music Publishing Co., cop. 1941 and 1943 by Promotora Hispano Americana de Musica, Mexico City.

Comin' in on a Wing and a Prayer. w., Harold Adamson. m., Jimmy McHugh. Robbins Music Corp., cop. 1943.

Don't Sweetheart Me. w., m., Cliff Friend and Charlie Tobias. Advanced Music Corp., cop. 1943.

Do Nothin' Till You Hear from Me. w., Bob Russell. m., Duke Ellington. Robbins Music Corp., cop. 1943.

Gertie from Bizerte. w., m., James Cavanaugh, Walter Kent, and Bob Cutter. Shapiro, Bernstein & Co., Inc., cop. 1943.

Goodbye Sue. w., m., Jimmy Rule, Lou Ricca, and Jules Loman. Jewel Music Pub. Co., Inc., cop. 1943.

Holiday for Strings. Instrumental piece. m., David Rose. Bregman, Vocco & Conn, Inc., cop. 1943.

How Many Hearts Have You Broken? w., Marty Symes. m., Al Kaufman. Advanced Music Corp., cop. 1943.

How Sweet You Are (film: Thank Your Lucky Stars). w., Frank Loesser. m., Arthur Schwartz. Remick Music Corp., cop. 1943.

I Couldn't Sleep a Wink Last Night (film: Higher and Higher). w., Harold Adamson. m., Jimmy McHugh. T. B. Harms Co., cop. 1943.

I've Heard That Song Before. w., m., Jule Styne and Sammy Cahn. Edwin H. Morris & Co., cop. 1943.

I'll Be Seeing You. See 1938.

If You Please (film: Dixie). w., Johnny Burke. m., Jimmy Van Heusen. Famous Music Corp., cop. 1943.

In My Arms (film: See Here, Private Hargrove). w., m., Frank Loesser and Ted Grouya. Hollywood, Cal.: Saunders Publications, cop. 1943.

It's Love, Love, Love. w., m., Mack David, Joan Whitney, and Alex Kramer. Santly-Joy, Inc., cop. 1943.

A Lovely Way to Spend an Evening. w., Harold Adamson. m., Jimmy McHugh. Crawford Music Corp., cop. 1943.

Mairzy Doats. w., m., Milton Drake, Al Hoffman, and Jerry Livingston. Miller Music Corp., cop. 1943.

My Heart Tells Me (film: Sweet Rosie O'Grady). w., Mack Gordon. m., Harry Warren. Bregman, Vocco & Conn, Inc., cop. 1943 by Twentieth Century Music corp.

Oh What a Beautiful Mornin' (Oklahoma). w., Oscar Hammerstein 2nd. m., Richard Rodgers. Marlo Music Corp., cop. 1943.

Oklahoma (Oklahoma). w., Oscar Hammerstein 2nd. m., Richard Rodgers. Marlo Music Corp., cop. 1943.

People Will Say We're in Love (Oklahoma). w., Oscar Hammerstein 2nd. m., Richard Rodgers. Marlo Music Corp., cop. 1943.

Pistol Packin' Mama. w., m., Al Dexter. Edwin H. Morris & Co., Inc., cop. 1943.

Shoo-Shoo Baby (film: Three Cheers for the Boys). w., m., Phil Moore. Leeds Music Corp., cop. 1943.

Speak Low (One Touch of Venus). w., Ogden Nash. m., Kurt Weill. Chappell & Co., Inc., cop. 1943.

Star Eyes (film: I Dood It). w., m., Don Raye and Gene DePaul. Leo Feist, Inc., cop. 1943.

Sunday, Monday, or Always (film: Dixie). w., Johnny Mercer. m., Jimmy Van Heusen. Mayfair Music Corp., cop. 1943.

The Surrey with the Fringe on Top (Oklahoma). w., Oscar Hammerstein 2nd. m., Richard Rodgers. Marlo Music Corp., cop. 1943.

Take It Easy. w., m., Albert DeBru, Irving Taylor, and Vic Mizzy. Santly-Joy, Inc., cop. 1943.

They're Either Too Young or Too Old (film: Thank Your Lucky Stars). w., Frank Loesser. m., Arthur Schwartz. M. Witmark & Sons, cop. 1943.

Tico-Tico. English words, Ervin Drake. Portuguese words, Aloysio Oliveira. m., Zequinha Abreu. Peer International Corp., cop. 1943.

What Do You Do in the Infantry? w., m., Frank Loesser. Hollywood, Cal.: Saunders Publications, cop. 1943.

You Keep Coming Back Like a´ Song (film: Blue Skies). w., m., Irving Berlin. Irving Berlin Music Corp., cop. 1943.

You'll Never Know (film: Hello, Frisco, Hello). w., Mack Gordon. m., Harry Warren. Bregman, Vocco & Conn, Inc., cop. 1943 by Twentieth Century Music Corp. (Academy Award Winner, 1943)

World War II continued. President Roosevelt and Prime Minister Churchill of Great Britain conferred (Jan. 14-20) at Casablanca, Morocco, on the "unconditional surrender of Germany, Italy, and Japan." (The President on his return to the United States visited Liberia, Jan. 27, Natal, Jan. 28, and Trinidad, Jan. 30.) He also attended conferences in Quebec, Canada (in Aug.) and in Teheran, Iran (in Nov.-Dec.). The British and American armies captured (Mar. 13) the German-held cities of Tunis and Bizerte. Premier Benito Mussolini of Italy resigned (July 25), Italy ended (Sept. 8) hostilities with the United States, severed relations with Germany, and declared (Oct. 13) war on its former ally.

General Dwight David Eisenhower was appointed (Dec. 24) Supreme Commander of the Anglo-American forces for the invasion of Europe. The American war effort was really under way on a scale hitherto unknown. As a British observer, D. W. Brogan, remarked, "To the Americans, war is a business, not an art."

The cost of the war staggered everyone's imagination. World War I, which lasted less than two years, cost about $35,000,000,000. By mid year of '43, World War II was costing $8,000,000,000 per month.

To impress upon the public mind the need to uphold the ideals of American liberty, the U. S. Post Office issued a one-cent green "Four Freedoms" postage stamp (Feb. 12) and a series of 13 stamps (June 22-Nov. 2, 1944) in tribute to the countries invaded by the Axis powers, with the flag of each nation pictured on a stamp.

As never before in American history, women found a place in military service. The "Wacs" came into existence when the Women's Army Corps of the U. S. Army was established (July 1). Soon there were "Waves" (Women Appointed for Volunteer Emergency Service), "Spars" (Women's Reserve of the U. S. Coast Guard Reserve), and "Wasps" (Women's Air Force Service Pilots of the U. S. Army Air Forces).

After the middle of the year (July 1), all wage earners and salaried employees received their pay minus 20 per cent in compliance with the pay-as-you-go income tax law (signed by President Roosevelt June 10).

The F.B.I. captured eight Nazi spies and saboteurs who landed at Amagansett, L. I., N. Y., and Jacksonville, Fla. All were tried and died in the electric chair.

A War Bond rally auction was held in the basement of Gimbel's department store in New York with 750 persons on hand to bid for such precious items as Jefferson's Bible and George Washington's letters. Orchestra leader Jack Benny's violin, a $75 imitation Amati nicknamed "Old Love in Bloom," was put on the block and the nation fell flat on its collective face when one Julius Klorfein bought it for $1,000,000. Mr. Klorfein turned out to be the president of the Garcia Grande Cigar Company.

When more than half a million coal miners of the United Mine Workers persisted in their strike (1941), Secretary of the Interior Harold L. Ickes assumed (Nov. 1) control of the mines by order of President Roosevelt.

The United Nations Relief and Rehabilitation Administration ("U.N.R.R.A.") was organized (Nov. 9) by 44 nations to supply food, clothing, medicine, and other necessities to the liberated peoples of the world.

Anti-Communist and anti-Fascist newspaper editor Carlo Tresca was assassinated (Jan. 11) in New York by Soviet O.G.P.U. agent Carlos Contreras.

Race riots broke out in Detroit (June 21) and in New York (Aug. 1). In Detroit, 34 persons were killed, 700 were injured, and more than

1,000 arrested. In the New York 125th Street Harlem section, an unfounded rumor incited Negroes to wreck about $1,000,000 worth of property and caused the death of 6 Negroes.

Chicagoans rode (Oct. 16) in a subway for the first time.

The Pentagon, the world's largest office building covering 34 acres outside Washington, D. C., was completed (Jan. 25) at a cost of about $64,000,000.

The Thomas Jefferson Memorial, East Potomac Park, Washington, D. C., was dedicated (Apr. 13) by President Roosevelt on the 200th anniversary of Jefferson's birth.

The Pan American Airways plane "Yankee Clipper," whose passenger list included famous stars of the entertainment world who were going abroad to perform for GI's, crashed (Feb. 22) in the Tagus River near Lisbon, Portugal. Twenty-four persons were drowned. Among the survivors were radio singer Jane Froman and night club accordionist Gypsy Markoff; among the dead, Tamara ("Smoke Gets in Your Eyes"), and foreign correspondent Ben Robertson.

Lessing J. Rosenwald presented his rare collection of prints and drawings to the National Gallery of Art, Washington, D. C.

Books of the year included: "The American Leonardo: The Life of Samuel F. B. Morse" (Carlton Mabee; Pulitzer prize 1944), "The Growth of American Thought" (Merle Curti; Pulitzer prize 1944), "One World" (Wendell Lewis Willkie), "Western Star" (Stephen Vincent Benét; poetry; Pulitzer prize 1944), and the fiction, "The Apostle" (Sholem Asch), "The Fountainhead" (Ayn Rand), "The Human Comedy" (William Saroyan), "Journey in the Dark" (Martin Flavin; Pulitzer prize 1944), "A Tree Grows in Brooklyn" (Betty Smith).

William Schuman was awarded the Pulitzer music prize for his "Secular Cantata No. 2, A Free Song"—the first award in that field.

The non-profit Shoestring Opera Company in New York was something new in opera production "to demonstrate that artistic, dramatic music can be presented without the prohibitive cost of present-day grand opera." The first production was "The Tales of Hoffmann" (Jan. 19) at Hunter College.

New York plays included: "Dark Eyes" (Belasco, Jan. 14; 230 perf.), "The Patriots" (National, Jan. 29), "Harriet" (Henry Miller, Mar. 3; 377 perf.), "Kiss and Tell" (Biltmore, Mar. 17; 956 perf.), "The Two Mrs. Carrolls" (Booth, Aug. 3; 585 perf.), "Tomorrow the World" (Ethel Barrymore, Apr. 14; 500 perf.), "Lovers and Friends" (Plymouth, Nov. 29), "The Voice of the Turtle" (Morosco, Dec. 8; 1,557 perf.). "Othello" was revived by the Negro actor Paul Robeson (Shubert, Oct. 19; 296 perf.). Musical productions included: "Something for the Boys" (Alvin, Jan. 7; 422 perf.), "Oklahoma!" (St. James, Mar. 31; 2,248 perf.—longest run of any musical comedy), "Ziegfeld Follies" (Winter Garden, Apr. 1; 553 perf.), "Early to Bed" (Broadhurst, June 17; 382 perf.), "The Merry Widow" (Majestic, Aug. 4; 322 perf.; revival), "One

Touch of Venus" (Imperial, Oct. 7; 567 perf.), "Winged Victory" (44th Street, Nov. 20; 212 perf.), "Carmen Jones" (Broadhurst, Dec. 2; 503 perf.).

Motion pictures of the year included: "Casablanca" (Humphrey Bogart, Ingrid Bergman), "For Whom the Bell Tolls" (Gary Cooper, Ingrid Bergman), "A Guy Named Joe" (Spencer Tracy, Irene Dunne, Van Johnson), "The Human Comedy" (Mickey Rooney, Frank Morgan), "So Proudly We Hail!" (Claudette Colbert, Paulette Goddard, Veronica Lake), "Stage Door Canteen," "This Gun for Hire" (Alan Ladd), "This Is the Army," "Watch on the Rhine" (Paul Lukas, Bette Davis).

Radio Station WRGB of the General Electric Company, Schenectady, N. Y., televised Offenbach's operetta "The Marriage by the Lantern" (in May) and a full-length opera, Humperdinck's "Hänsel und Gretel" (Dec. 20). (The performances were given scenically with piano accompaniment and sung in English by the Hartt Opera Workshops of The Julius Hartt Musical Foundation, Hartford, Conn. Other productions by the school were telecast by the Schenectady station—"Le Médecin malgré lui," June, 1944; "The Secret of Suzanne," Feb., 1945; Reznicek's "Fact and Fiction," May, 1945; Paisiello's "The Barber of Seville," Feb., 1947; Gounod's "Romeo and Juliet," Feb., 1948.)

A skinny, thin-voiced crooner, Frank Sinatra, so captivated bobbysoxers of both sexes that the popular radio and screen singer Bing Crosby was his only rival. Thirty thousand of Sinatra's fans reacted so violently during his appearance at the Paramount Theatre in New York that a riot call was sent out, and 421 policemen, 20 policewomen, and 20 patrol cars responded. No less vocally appealing was a dark-haired beauty who arrived on the entertainment scene—Dinah Shore, charming audiences with her rendition of "One Dozen Roses."

There was much chuckling over the true story of a lady hoarder who filled her cellar with canned goods. A rainstorm flooded the cellar and washed all the labels off the cans!

₰ 1944

Ac-cent-tchu-ate the Positive (film: Here Come the Waves). w., Johnny Mercer. m., Harold Arlen. Edwin H. Morris & Co., Inc., cop. 1944.

Candy. w., m., Mack Davis, Joan Whitney, and Alex Kramer. Leo Feist, Inc., cop. 1944.

Close as Pages in a Book (Central Park). w., Dorothy Fields. m., Sigmund Romberg. Williamson Music, Inc., cop. 1944.

Don't Fence Me in (film: Hollywood Canteen). w., m., Cole Porter. Harms, Inc., cop. 1944.

Dream. w., m., Johnny Mercer. Capitol Songs, Inc., cop. 1944.

Ev'rytime We Say Goodbye (Seven Lively Arts). w., m., Cole Porter. Chappell & Co., Inc., cop. 1944.

Going My Way (film: Going My Way). w., Johnny Burke. m., Jimmy Van Heusen. Burke and Van Heusen, Inc., cop. 1944.

How Blue the Night (film: Four Jills in a Jeep). w., Harold Adamson. m., Jimmy McHugh. Robbins Music Corp., cop. 1944 by Twentieth Century Music Corp.

I'm Making Believe (film: Sweet and Low-Down). w., Mack Gordon. m., James V. Monaco. Bregman, Vocco & Conn, Inc., cop. 1944 by Twentieth Century Music Corp.

I Dream of You. w., m., Marjorie Goetschius and Edna Osser. Embassy Music Corp., cop. 1944.

I Should Care (film: Thrill of a Romance). w., m., Sammy Cahn, Axel Stordahl, and Paul Weston. Dorsey Brothers' Music Inc., cop. 1944.

I'll Walk Alone. w., Sammy Cahn. m., Jule Styne. Mayfair Music Corp., cop. 1944.

Irresistible You (film: Broadway Rhythm). w., m., Don Raye and Gene DePaul. Leo Feist, Inc., cop. 1944.

It Could Happen to You (film: And the Angels Sing). w., Johnny Burke. m., Jimmy Van Heusen. Famous Music Corp., cop. 1944

Jealous Heart. w., m., Jenny Lou Carson. Nashville, Tenn.: Acuff-Rose Publications, cop. 1944. (Popularized in 1949.)

Lilli Marlene. w., m., Hans Leip, Norbert Schultze, and Tommie Connor. Edward B. Marks Music Corp., cop. 1941 by Apollo Music Co.; words cop. 1944 by Peter Maurice Music Co., Ltd.; published by permission by Edward B. Marks Music Corp.

A Little on the Lonely Side. w., m., Dick Robertson, James Cavanaugh, and Frank Weldon. Advanced Music Corp., cop. 1944.

Long Ago and Far Away (film: Cover Girl). w., Ira Gershwin. m., Jerome Kern. Crawford Music Corp., cop. 1944 by Jerome Kern.

Magic Is the Moonlight—*Spanish title:* Te quiero dijiste (film: Bathing Beauty). Spanish words and music, Maria Grever. English words, Charles Pasquale. Melody Lane Publications, Inc., cop. 1930; cop. 1944. (The song was published by Southern Music Pub. Co., Inc., cop. 1932, as a Spanish canción.)

More and More (film: Can't Help Singing). w., E. Y. Harburg. m., Jerome Kern. T. B. Harms Co., cop. 1944.

Right as the Rain (Bloomer Girl). w., E. Y. Harburg. m., Harold Arlen. Crawford Music Corp., cop. 1944.

Rum and Coca-Cola. w., Morey Amsterdam. w., Jeri Sullavan and Paul Baron. Leo Feist, Inc., cop. 1944.

Sentimental Journey. w., m., Bud Green, Les Brown, and Ben Homer. Edwin H. Morris & Co., Inc., cop. 1944.

Spring Will Be a Little Late This Year (film: Christmas Holiday). w., m., Frank Loesser. Hollywood, Cal.: Saunders Publications, cop. 1944.

Strange Music (Song of Norway). w., m., Robert Wright and George Forrest, based on Edvard Grieg's piano piece "Wedding Day at Trold-hauger.." Chappell & Co., Inc., cop. 1944.

Swinging on a Star (film: Going My Way). w., Johnny Burke. m., Jimmy Van Heusen. Burke and Van Heusen, Inc., cop. 1944. (Academy Award Winner, 1944)

Twilight Time. w., m., Buck Ram, Morty Nevins, and Artie Dunn. Campbell-Porgie, Inc., cop. 1944.

World War II continued—and D-Day (June 6) arrived. The carefully planned invasion of German-held western Europe was successfully carried out in Normandy (in June) and in southern France (in August), and broke (Nov. 25) the supposedly impregnable Siegfried Line of the German defense west of the Rhine.

Congress approved (Dec. 15) the appointment of the first five-star generals (Arnold, Eisenhower, MacArthur, Marshall) and the first five-star admirals (King, Leahy, Nimitz).

The United States Supreme Court upheld in two decisions (Apr. 3 and May 8) the right of Negroes to vote in State primaries.

The national debt was $260,000,000,000 when President Roosevelt affixed (June 10) his signature to the bill setting that limit.

Representatives of 44 Allied nations met (July 1-22) at Mount Washington Hotel, Bretton Woods, N. H., and set up the International Bank for Reconstruction and Development, known as the World Bank. (Its operation began June 25, 1946, with a capital of $10,000,000.)

The United Nations ("U.N.") was established (Aug. 21-Oct. 7) in a conference at Dumbarton Oaks, on the outskirts of Washington, D. C., by delegates from the United States, Great Britain, Soviet Russia, and China.

Ninety-year-old "General" Jacob Sechler Coxey of Ohio finally achieved the ambition of his life—he delivered (May 1) from the steps of the Capitol the speech which was denied him as the leader of his famous "army" of unemployed in 1894.

The "Flying Ace," a 30-ton American Export Airlines plane, made a nonstop flight from Foynes, Ireland, to New York, a distance of 3,329 miles, in 15 hours, 30 minutes. It arrived May 1.

A tornado passed (June 23) through western Pennsylvania, West Virginia, and Maryland, causing the death of 153 persons.

The worst circus fire in history occurred (July 6) at Hartford, Conn., when the big top tent of the Ringling Brothers and Barnum & Bailey Circus caught fire during a performance. The conflagration and panic claimed 107 lives and injured 412 persons.

Explosions took the lives of 322 persons at Port Chicago, Cal. (July 17), and of 135 in Cleveland, O.

Nobel prizes were awarded to Isador Isaac Rabi for physics, and to James Erlanger and Herbert S. Gasser for medicine and physiology.

Books of the year included: "George Bancroft: Brahmin Rebel" (Russell Baline Nye; Pulitzer prize 1945), "Unfinished Business" (Stephen Bonsal; Pulitzer prize 1945), "V-Letter and Other Poems" (Karl Shapiro; Pulitzer prize 1945) and the fiction, "A Bell for Adano" (John Hersey; Pulitzer prize 1945), "Forever Amber" (Kathleen Winsor), "Leave Her to Heaven" (Ben Ames Williams).

Howard Hanson was awarded the Pulitzer music prize for his Symphony No. 2, op. 34—the second such award.

The National Negro Opera Company presented performances of "La Traviata" in Chicago, Pittsburgh, New York, and Washington, D. C.

New York plays included: "Over 21" (Music Box, Jan. 3), "Ramshackle Inn" (Royale, Jan. 5), "Wallflower" (Cort, Jan. 26), "Jacobowsky and the Colonel" (Martin Beck, Mar. 14; 417 perf.), "Chicken Every Sunday" (Henry Miller, Apr. 5; 318 perf.), "The Searching Wind" (Fulton, Apr. 12; 318 perf.), "Pick-Up Girl" (48th Street, May 3), "Ten Little Indians" (Broadhurst, June 27; 426 perf.), "School for Brides" (Royale, Aug. 1; 375 perf.), "Catherine Was Great" (Shubert, Aug. 2), "Anna Lucasta" (Mansfield, Aug. 30; 957 perf.), "Soldier's Wife" (Golden, Oct. 4), "I Remember Mama" (Music Box, Oct. 19; 714 perf.), "Harvey" by Mary Coyle Chase (48th Street, Nov. 1; 1,775 perf.; Pulitzer prize 1945), "The Late George Apley" (Lyceum, Nov. 23; 385 perf.), "A Bell for Adano" (Cort, Dec. 6; 304 perf.), "Dear

Ruth" (Henry Miller, Dec. 13; 683 perf.). Musical productions included: "Mexican Hayride" (Winter Garden, Jan. 28; 481 perf.), "Follow the Girls" (Century, Apr. 8; 882 perf.), "Hats Off to Ice" (Center, June 22; 889 perf.), "Song of Norway" (Imperial, Aug. 21; 860 perf.), "Bloomer Girl" (Shubert, Oct. 5; 654 perf.), "Seven Lively Arts" (Ziegfeld, Dec. 7), "Laffing Room Only" (Winter Garden, Dec. 23; 233 perf.), "On the Town" (Adelphi, Dec. 28; 463 perf.).

To commemorate the 50th anniversary of motion pictures, the U. S. Post Office issued (Oct. 31) a three-cent purple postage stamp.

Motion pictures of the year included: "Dragon Seed" (Katharine Hepburn, Walter Houston), "Gaslight" (Ingrid Bergman), "Going My Way" (Bing Crosby), "Jane Eyre" (Joan Fontaine, Orson Welles), "Lifeboat" (Tallulah Bankhead, William Bendix), "Madame Curie" (Greer Garson, Walter Pidgeon), "None but the Lonely Heart," "See Here, Private Hargrove," "Since You Went Away," "The Song of Bernadette" (Jennifer Jones), "The Story of Dr. Wassell" (Gary Cooper, Laraine Day), "The White Cliffs of Dover" (Irene Dunne, Alan Marshall).

Horse racing in the U. S. was banned (Dec. 21) on account of the war.

ᘐᕲ 1945

Aren't You Glad You're You (film: The Bells of St. Mary's). w., Johnny Burke. m., Jimmy Van Heusen. Burke & Van Heusen, Inc., cop. 1945.

Autumn Serenade. w., Sammy Gallop. m., Peter DeRose. Robbins Music Corp., cop. 1945.

Cruising Down the River. w., m., Eily Beadell and Nell Tollerton. Henry Spitzer Music Pub. Co., Inc., cop. 1945 by Cinephonic Music Co., Ltd.

Dig You Later—A Hubba-Hubba-Hubba (film: Doll Face). w., Harold Adamson. m., Jimmy McHugh. Robbins Music Corp., cop. 1945 by Twentieth Century Music Corp.

Doctor, Lawyer, Indian Chief (film: Stork Club). w., Paul Francis Webster. m., Hoagy Carmichael. Melrose Music Corp., cop. 1945; assigned 1945 to Burke and Van Heusen, Inc.; re-assigned 1947 to Melrose Music Corp.; assigned 1950 to Edwin H. Morris & Co., Inc.

For Sentimental Reasons. w., Deke Watson. m., William Best. Duchess Music Corp., cop. 1945.

Give Me the Simple Life (film: Give Me the Simple Life). w., Harry Ruby. m., Rube Bloom. Triangle Music Corp., cop. 1945 by Twentieth Century Music Corp.

I Can't Begin to Tell You (film: The Dolly Sisters). w., Mack Gordon. m., James V. Monaco. Bregman, Vocco & Conn, Inc., cop. 1945 by Twentieth Century Music Corp.

I'll Be Yours—*original French title:* J'attendrai. English words, Anna Sosenko. French words, Louis Poterat. m., Dino Olivieri. Southern Music Pub. Co., Inc., cop. 1938 by P. Leonardi, Milan; cop. 1945 by Southern Music Pub. Co.

I'll Close My Eyes. w., Buddy Kaye. m., Billy Reid. Peter Maurice Music Co., Ltd., cop. 1945 by World Wide Music Co., Ltd., London; cop. 1945 by Peter Maurice Co., Ltd.; cop. 1946 by Peter Maurice Music Co., Ltd.

If I Loved You (Carousel). w., Oscar Hammerstein, 2nd. m., Richard Rodgers. Williamson Music Inc., cop. 1945.

It's a Grand Night for Singing (film: State Fair). w., Oscar Hammerstein, 2nd. m., Richard Rodgers. Williamson Music Inc., cop. 1945.

It's Been a Long, Long Time. w., Sammy Cahn. m., Jule Styne. Edwin H. Morris & Co., Inc., cop. 1945.

It Might as Well Be Spring (film: State Fair). w., Oscar Hammerstein, 2nd. m., Richard Rodgers. Williamson Music Inc., cop. 1945. (Academy Award Winner, 1945)

June Is Bustin' Out All Over (Carousel). w., Oscar Hammerstein, 2nd. m., Richard Rodgers. Williamson Music Inc., cop. 1945.

Laura (film: Laura). w., Johnny Mercer. m., David Raksin. Robbins Music Corp., cop. 1945.

Let It Snow! Let It Snow! Let It Snow! w., Sammy Cahn. m., Jule Styne. Edwin H. Morris & Co., cop. 1945.

Love Is So Terrific. w., m., Sunny Skylar and Artie Shaftel. Merlin Music, Inc., cop. 1945.

The More I See of You (film: Diamond Horseshoe. w., Mack Gordon. m., Harry Warren. Bregman, Vocco & Conn, Inc., cop. 1945 by Twentieth Century Music Corp.

No Can Do. w., Charlie Tobias. m., Nat Simon. Robbins Music Corp., cop. 1945.

Oh! What It Seemed to Be. w., m., Bennie Benjamin. George Weiss and Frankie Carle. Santly-Joy, Inc., cop. 1945.

On the Atchison, Topeka and the Santa Fe (film: The Harvey Girls). w., Johnny Mercer. m., Harry Warren. Leo Feist, Inc., cop. 1945. (Academy Award Winner, 1946)

Rodger Young. w., m., Frank Loesser. Bob Miller Inc., cop. 1945.

Some Sunday Morning (film: San Antonio). w., Ted Koehler. m., M. K. Jerome and Ray Heindorf. Harms, Inc., cop. 1945.

Symphony. w., Jack Lawrence. m., Alstone. Chappell & Co., cop. 1945 by Editions Salabert, Paris; assigned 1945 to Chappell & Co.

That's For Me (film: State Fair). w., Oscar Hammerstein, 2nd. m., Richard Rodgers. Williamson Music Inc., cop. 1945.

There Must Be a Way. w., m., Sammy Gallop, David Saxon and Robert Cook. Stevens Music Corp., cop. 1945.

Till the End of Time. w., m., Buddy Kaye and Ted Mossman, based on Chopin's Polonaise in A flat, op. 53. Santly-Joy, Inc., cop. 1945.

Waitin' for the Train to Come in. w., m., Sunny Skylar and Martin Block. Martin Block Music, cop. 1945.

You Came Along—Out of Nowhere (film: You Came Along). w., Edward Heyman. m., John W. Green. Famous Music Corp., cop. 1931; cop. 1945.

You Won't Be Satisfied. w., m., Freddy James and Larry Stock. Mutual Music Society, Inc., cop. 1945.

President Franklin Delano Roosevelt began (Jan. 20) his fourth term. He served only 96 days. A tremendous worker who carried on in spite of physical handicaps—he was stricken in 1921 with poliomyelitis which paralyzed his legs—and in failing health, he succumbed (Apr. 12) to a cerebral hemorrhage in Warm Springs, Ga. Vice-President Harry S. Truman, Democrat, of Missouri, was inaugurated 33rd President.

World War II entered its last year. The American invasion of the Philippines began (Jan. 9), leading to the recapture (Mar. 2) of the islands. Gen. George S. Patton's American Third Army invaded Germany (Jan. 27) and crossed the Rhine (Mar. 7). U. S. Marines landed (Feb. 10) in Iwo Jima and suffered heavy losses in the capture (Mar. 16) of this important air base. (In 34 days of fighting there were 20,196 casualties, of which 4,305 were killed.) President Roosevelt, Prime Minister Churchill, and Premier Stalin conferred (Feb. 3-11) at Yalta in Crimea on the Black Sea. American planes—more than 1,000 of them— began (Feb. 3) nightly bombings of Berlin and Allied planes dropped (Mar. 18) 12,400 explosives and 650,000 fire bombs on the city. Deposed Premier Mussolini of Italy was captured (Apr. 28) in flight by Italian Partisans in the village of Dongo on Lake Como and was shot by a firing squad. Russian forces advancing from the East captured (Apr. 30) the Reichstag building of the German government in Berlin. That same day Hitler committed suicide in a bunker of the ruined structure. Totally defeated, Germany capitulated (May 6) and its representatives signed (May 8, V-E Day) the articles of surrender in Berlin.

Meanwhile, in the Far East, ready to begin the actual invasion of the Japanese homeland, waited the largest armed fleet ever assembled in any waters. Its power of destruction was never unleashed—a greater weapon had been discovered. A long and costly research project by American and British scientists to solve the secret of atomic fission achieved its aim when an experimental atomic bomb was successfully exploded (July 16) in a test at Alamogordo, N. M. The U.S.S. "Indianapolis" carried (July 26) to Saipan the terrible new missiles. With President Roosevelt's successor, Harry S. Truman (see below), rested the momentous decision to use the A, or atom, bomb. On his order, one bomb was dropped (Aug. 6) on Hiroshima, Japan, completely wiping out the city; five days later (Aug. 11) a second destroyed Nagasaki. Japan sued (Aug. 10) for peace and surrendered (Sept. 1; Sept. 2, Tokyo time, V-J Day) aboard the U.S.S. "Missouri" in Tokyo Bay. American forces occupied (Sept. 3) Korea and General Douglas MacArthur became (Sept. 9) the military governor of Japan.

A Japanese sniper's bullet killed (Apr. 18) Ernest ("Ernie") Pyle during the battle on the island of Ie in the Pacific, and all Americans— but most especially the GI Joes in all theatres of operations—mourned the loss of the nation's most beloved war correspondent. (He was buried Feb. 14, 1949, in the National Cemetery of the Pacific in Pearl Harbor, Hawaii.)

The F.B.I. reported that it had rounded up 1,500 Axis spies in North and South America during the war.

President Truman attended (July 17-Aug. 2) the Potsdam Conference with Premier Stalin of Soviet Russia and Premier Attlee of Great Britain.

Rationing of meat, butter, and other commodities ended (Nov. 23).

Representatives of 50 nations met (Apr. 25-June 26) in San Francisco and established the United Nations Conference on International Organization ("U.N."). A charter was signed on the last day of the session (effective Oct. 24). The signatories pledged "to save succeeding generations from the scourge of war . . . to maintain international peace and security . . . to employ international machinery for the promotion of the economic and social advancement of all people." The United States was chosen (Dec. 15) as the permanent seat of the "U.N."

The United States Supreme Court, which had upheld (1942) the validity of Nevada's six-weeks-residence divorce law, now affirmed (May 21) the right of each state to recognize or reject a Nevada divorce decree.

New York Governor Thomas E. Dewey abolished (Mar. 12) in his state discrimination in employment on account of race, creed, color, or national origin.

Round-the-world airplane service was inaugurated (Sept. 28) when the "Globester" of the U. S. Army Transport Command left the National Airport, Washington, D. C., and completed (Oct. 4) a global trip of 23,279 miles in 149 hours, 44 minutes. An A-26, piloted by Colonel Joseph R. Holzapple and flying westward, circumnavigated the globe in a flight covering 24,859 miles in 96 hours, 50 minutes' air time (Nov. 26-30).

An Army B-25 bomber airplane, flying from New Bedford, Mass., to Newark, N. J., crashed (July 28) headlong into the tower of the 102-floor Empire State office building in New York, 915 feet above street level (the building is 1,250 feet tall). The tragedy killed three occupants of the plane and 10 persons in the building, and turned the upper structure into a huge torch in the world's highest blaze. The plane was piloted by a war veteran who was unfamiliar with the New York area.

Military aviation carried out some remarkable missions during the last months of the war. Brigadier General Lawrence A. Fritz flew (Aug. 1) in C-69 Army Transport plane from New York to Paris, a distance of 3,600 miles, in 14 hours, 12 minutes. Lieutenant Colonel Charles J. Miller travelled (Sept. 1) in a B-29 from Honolulu, Hawaii, to Washington, D. C., a distance of 4,640 miles, in 17 hours, 21 minutes, averaging 285 miles per hour. Major G. E. Cain flew in an O-54 Air Transport plane from Tokyo, Japan, to Washington, D. C. (arriving Nov. 1), in 31 hours, 25 minutes. A B-29 accomplished a flight of 7,576 miles from Iwo Jima, via a stop-over at Spokane, Wash., to Washington, D. C. (arriving Sept. 4) in 30 hours, 33 minutes. Brigadier General Frank A. Armstrong brought four B-29 planes in a nonstop flight from Japan to Washington, D. C. (arriving Nov. 1), a distance of 6,544 miles, in 27 hours, 29 minutes.

Portal-to-portal pay for coal miners was upheld (May 7) by the United States Supreme Court.

Pennsylvania anthracite miners again went on strike (May 1). By executive order, Secretary of the Interior Harold L. Ickes seized (May 3) the mines and the miners returned (May 21) to work.

Cordell Hull was awarded the Nobel prize for peace.

Ezra Pound, the American poet who was indicted for treason for broadcasting pro-Axis propaganda from Italy during the war, was committed to a mental hospital in Washington, D. C.

Books of the year included: "The Age of Jackson" (Arthur M. Schlesinger, Jr.; Pulitzer prize 1946), "Son of the Wilderness" (Linnie Marsh Wolfe; Pulitzer prize 1946) and the fiction, "The Black Rose" (Thomas Bertram Costain), "Captain from Castile" (Samuel Shellabarger), "Daisy Kenyon" (Elizabeth Janeway), "The Egg and I" (Betty MacDonald). No Pulitzer prizes were awarded for this year's fiction or poetry.

Heitor Villa-Lobos, Brazilian composer, toured the United States, as conductor of his own works. (He again visited the United States in 1947.)

Aaron Copland was awarded the Pulitzer music prize for his ballet "Appalachian Spring." (It was performed for the first time in Washington, D. C., Oct. 30, 1944, by Martha Graham and her dancers.)

The first Annual Festival of Contemporary American Music, sponsored by the Alice M. Ditson Fund, was held (May 12-14) at Columbia University, New York.

New York plays included: "The Hasty Heart" (Hudson, Jan. 3), "The Overtons" (Booth, Feb. 6), "Dark of the Moon" (46th Street, Mar. 14; 320 perf.), "The Glass Menagerie" (Playhouse, Mar. 31; 561 perf.), "Deep Are the Roots" (Fulton, Sept. 26; 477 perf.), "State of the Union" by Howard Lindsay and Russell Crouse (Hudson, Nov. 14; 765 perf.; Pulitzer prize 1946), "Dream Girl" (Coronet, Dec. 14; 348 perf.). "The Tempest" was revived in a streamlined version (Alvin, Jan. 25; 100 perf.). Maurice Evans presented his GI version of "Hamlet" (Columbus Circle, Dec. 13; 131 perf.), which he had played in the South Pacific during World War II. Musical productions included: "Up in Central Park" (Century, Jan. 27; 504 perf.), "Carousel" (Majestic, Apr. 19; 890 perf.), "The Red Mill" (Ziegfeld, Oct. 16; 531 perf.; revival), "Are You with It?" (Century, Nov. 10; 267 perf.), "Billion Dollar Baby" (Alvin, Dec. 21; 220 perf.).

Motion pictures of the year included: "Anchors Aweigh" (Frank Sinatra, Kathryn Grayson, Gene Kelly), "The Bells of St. Mary's" (Bing Crosby, Ingrid Bergman), "The Corn Is Green" (Bette Davis), "The Keys of the Kingdom" (Gregory Peck), "Laura" (Gene Tierney, Dana Andrews, Clifton Webb), "Leave Her to Heaven" (Gene Tierney, Cornel Wilde), "The Lost Weekend" (Ray Milland, Jane Wyman), "Mildred Pierce" (Joan Crawford), "National Velvet" (Mickey Rooney), "Saratoga Trunk" (Gary Cooper, Ingrid Bergman), "A Song to Remember" (Paul Muni, Merle Oberon), "Spellbound" (Ingrid Bergman, Gregory Peck), "State Fair," "The Story of G.I. Joe" (Burgess Meredith), "A Tree Grows in Brooklyn" (Dorothy McGuire, Joan Blondell, James Dunne), "The Valley of Decision" (Greer Garson, Gregory Peck), "Wilson" (Alexander Knox).

ᘐᕁ 1946

All through the Day (film: Centennial Summer). w., Oscar Hammerstein, 2nd. m., Jerome Kern. Williamson Music Inc., cop. 1946.

Along with Me (Call Me Mister). w., m., Harold Rome. M. Witmark & Sons, cop. 1946.

Anniversary Song (film: The Jolson Story). w., m., Al Jolson and Saul Chaplin, based on J. Ivanovici's waltz "Donauwellen" (Danube Waves). Mood Music Co., cop. 1946.

Chiquita Banana. w., m., Len Mackenzie, Garth Montgomery, and William Wirges. Maxwell-Wirges Publications, Inc., cop. 1946.

Colas Breugnon. Overture for orch. m., Dmitri Kabalevsky. Leeds Music Corp., cop. 1946.

Come Rain or Come Shine (St. Louis Woman). w., Johnny Mercer. m., Harold Arlen. A-M Music Corp., cop. 1946.

Do You Love Me? (film: Do You Love Me?). w., m., Harry Ruby. Bergman, Vocco & Conn, Inc., cop. 1946.

Doin' What Comes Natur'lly (Annie Get Your Gun). w., m., Irving Berlin. Irving Berlin Music Co., cop. 1946 by Irving Berlin.

Five Minutes More. w., Sammy Cahn. m., Jule Styne. Melrose Music Corp., cop. 1946.

For You, for Me, for Evermore (film: The Shocking Miss Pilgrim). w., Ira Gershwin. m., George Gershwin. Gershwin Pub. Co., cop. 1946.

Full Moon and Empty Arms. w., m., Buddy Kaye and Ted Mossman, based on Rachmaninoff's Piano Concerto No. 2. Barton Music Corp., cop. 1946.

The Girl That I Marry (Annie Get Your Gun). w., m., Irving Berlin. Irving Berlin Music Co., cop. 1946 by Irving Berlin.

Golden Earrings (film: Golden Earrings). w., Jay Livingston and Ray Evans. m., Victor Young. Paramount Music Corp., cop. 1946.

The Gypsy. w., m., Billy Reid. Leeds Music Co., cop. 1945 by Peter Maurice Music Co., Ltd., London; cop. 1945 by Peter Maurice, Inc., New York; cop. 1946 by Peter Maurice, Inc.

How Are Things in Glocca Morra (Finian's Rainbow). w., E. Y. Harburg. m., Burton Lane. Crawford Music Corp., cop. 1946 by The Players Music Corp.

I Got the Sun in the Morning (Annie Get Your Gun). w., m., Irving Berlin. Irving Berlin Music Co., cop. 1946 by Irving Berlin.

If This Isn't Love (Finian's Rainbow). w., E. Y. Harburg. m., Burton Lane. Crawford Music Corp., cop. 1946 by The Players Music Corp.

In Love in Vain (film: Centennial Summer). w., Leo Robin. m., Jerome Kern. T. B. Harms Co., cop. 1946.

It's a Good Day. w., m., Peggy Lee and Dave Barbour. Capitol Songs, Inc., cop. 1946.

Laughing on the Outside—Crying on the Inside. w., Ben Raleigh. m., Bernie Wayne. Broadcast Music Inc., cop. 1946.

Linda. w., m., Jack Lawrence. Edwin H. Morris & Co., Inc., cop. 1946.

Midnight Masquerade. w., m., Bernard Bierman, Arthur Bierman, and Jack Manus. Shapiro, Bernstein & Co., Inc., cop. 1946; cop. 1947.

Now Is the Hour. w., m., Maewa Kaihan, Clement Scott, and Dorothy Stewart. Leeds Music Corp., cop. 1913 by W. H. Paling & Co., Ltd.; cop. 1946 by Leeds Music Corp.

Old Devil Moon (Finian's Rainbow). w., E. Y. Harburg. m., Burton Lane. Crawford Music Corp., cop. 1946.

The Old Lamp-Lighter. w., Charles Tobias. m., Nat Simon. Shapiro, Bernstein & Co., Inc., cop. 1946.

Ole Buttermilk Sky (film: Canyon Passage). w., m., Hoagy Carmichael and Jack Brooks. Burke and Van Heusen, Inc., cop. 1946.

Rumba Rhapsody. Instrumental piece. m., Rafael Audinot and Alberto de Bru. Remick Music Corp., cop. 1946.

Shoofly Pie and Apple Pan Dowdy. w., Sammy Gallop. m., Guy Woods. Capitol Songs, Inc., cop. 1946.

South America, Take It Away (Call Me Mister). w., m., Harold Rome. M. Witmark & Sons, cop. 1946.

Tenderly. w., Jack Lawrence. m., Walter Gross. Edwin H. Morris & Co., Inc., cop. 1946.

There's No Business Like Show Business (Annie Get Your Gun). w., m., Irving Berlin. Irving Berlin Music Co., cop. 1946 by Irving Berlin.

They Say It's Wonderful (Annie Get Your Gun). w., m., Irving Berlin. Irving Berlin Music Co., cop. 1946 by Irving Berlin.

To Each His Own. w., m., Jay Livingston and Ray Evans. Paramount Music Corp., cop. 1946.

When I'm Not Near the Girl I Love (Finian's Rainbow). w., E. Y. Harburg. m., Burton Lane. Crawford Music Corp., cop. 1946 by The Players Music Corp.

The World Is Singing My Song. w., Mann Curtis. m., Vic Mizzy. Robbins Music Corp., cop. 1946.

Zip-a-Dee-Do-Dah (film: Song of the South). w., Ray Gilbert. m., Allie Wrubel. Santly-Joy, Inc., cop. 1946. (Academy Award Winner, 1947)

Many imaginative people have thought and written about a trip to the moon—the U. S. Signal Corps this year did something about it scientifically; it experimented (Jan. 24) in the sending of a radar beam to the satellite.

The League of Nations (1920) disbanded (Apr. 18) at Geneva, Switzerland, and assigned its assets to the United Nations.

James Caesar Petrillo, president of the American Federation of Musicians, tried to force the radio stations to replace "canned music" with "live music" by employing more instrumentalists. The increasing use of mechanical music during the last two decades was reflected in the corresponding decline in the employment of musicians. Petrillo's efforts were stymied by Congress which passed the Lea "anti-Petrillo" act (signed by President Truman Apr. 16 and later upheld by the United States Supreme Court).

The International Court of Justice of the United Nations, successor to the League of Nations' Permanent Court of International Justice, elected

(Feb. 6) its first judges, fifteen in number. (The first session was held Apr. 18 in The Hague, the permanent seat of the court.)

A loan of $1,400,000,000 to France was negotiated in Washington between Secretary of State James Francis Byrnes and Léon Blum, special French emissary.

Atomic bomb tests were carried out at Bikini Atoll in the Pacific. The fourth bomb ever to be exploded was dropped (June 30) from a super-fortress airplane on an assortment of old battleships and vessels, among them several German warships, with animal life aboard; the fifth was set off (July 25) under water. Radio broadcast the sound of the explosions and the descriptions of the events by eye-witnesses.

Following the United States Supreme Court ruling (1944), Negroes voted (July 2) for the first time in Mississippi Democratic primaries.

Interference with interstate commerce by labor unions was made a felony by Alabama Representative Sam Hobbs's bill (signed by President Truman, July 3).

The Philippine Islands became a self-governing country, independent of the United States, with the establishment (July 4) of the Republic of the Philippines.

The late President Franklin Delano Roosevelt was absolved (July 20) of blame, by a vote of 8 to 2, by a Congressional investigating committee that was probing alleged American unpreparedness in the Japanese assault on Pearl Harbor (Dec. 6, 1941).

Secretary of State James Francis Byrnes assailed (Aug. 15) at the Paris Peace Conference the "repeated abuse and misrepresentation" of. the United States by Soviet Russia.

Two unarmed U. S. Army transport airplanes, flying from Austria to Italy, were shot down as they passed over Yugoslavia. Five American airmen were killed in the attack; others of the crews were arrested. The United States sent (Aug. 21) a 48-hour ultimatum to Belgrade demanding an explanation. No sooner were the surviving Americans released (Aug. 22) than a similar fate befell (Aug. 23) another unarmed United States plane of the same type. The Yugoslav government expressed its regrets over the incidents and promised indemnity for the lost lives and the damage.

Commander Thomas D. Davies flew a Navy P2V patrol bomber plane in a flight of 11,236 miles from Perth, West Australia, to Columbus, O. (arriving Oct. 1), in 55 hours, 15 minutes. Colonel Clarence S. Irvine, pilot, and Lieutenant Colonel Beverly Warren, co-pilot, made a 9,422-mile nonstop flight from Honolulu, Hawaii, via the North Pole, to Cairo, Egypt (arriving Oct. 6), in the B-29 Army plane "Pacusan Dreamboat" in 39 hours, 36 minutes.

Secretary of Commerce Henry Agard Wallace censured (Sept. 12) in a speech at New York the "get tough with Russia" policy; eight days later (Sept. 20) President Truman requested the Secretary's resignation.

(Wallace was endorsed in 1948 as a presidential candidate by the Communist Party of the United States.)

General Pulaski Memorial Day (Oct. 11) was authorized (June 21) by President Truman in honor of the Polish hero who died Oct. 11, 1779, from wounds received in fighting for the American cause during the siege of Savannah, Ga.

The Damon Runyon Memorial Fund for Cancer Research was founded (in Dec.) in New York. (Incorporated Feb. 18, 1947.)

John D. Rockefeller, Jr., offered (Dec. 11) the United Nations a six-block area, valued at $8,500,000, along the East River in New York as a site for the headquarters of its capital. The United Nations committee accepted (Dec. 12) the offer by a vote of 37 to 7.

The end of World War II was officially proclaimed (Dec. 31) by President Truman.

The Franklin-Delano-Roosevelt-head dime went into circulation. The coin was designed by John R. Sinnock. As a critical wartime material, nickel was eliminated from the current Jefferson-head five-cent piece (1938) which was minted now in a composition composed of copper (56 per cent), silver (35 per cent), and manganese (9 per cent).

Commemorative half-dollars were coined in honor of the great Negro educator Booker Taliaferro Washington. The coin bore the inscription "From Slave to Hall of Fame."

Pope Pius XII elevated (Feb. 18) three American Roman Catholic Archbishops to the cardinalate—John Glennon of St. Louis, Francis Joseph Spellman of New York, and Samuel Stritch of Chicago—and canonized (July 17) Frances Xavier Cabrini, American Roman Catholic nun of Italian birth (she died in Chicago, Dec. 22, 1917), noted for her charities. She was the first American citizen to be raised to sainthood.

Telephone service was installed on railroad trains.

Fire destroyed the La Salle Hotel, Chicago (June 25), with a loss of 61 lives, and the 15-floor Winecoff Hotel, Atlanta, Ga. (Dec. 7), with a loss of 121 lives.

An Army C-45 airplane crashed (May 20) into the 58th floor of the Bank of Manhattan building in Wall Street, New York, and killed five persons.

John L. Lewis's United Mine Workers union was readmitted (Jan. 25) to the American Federation of Labor.

President Truman predicted a prosperous year "if workers stay on their jobs," but strikes were plentiful throughout the year. 750,000 miners of John L. Lewis's C.I.O. United Mine Workers' Union went (Jan. 20) on strike, closing plants in 29 States. (The miners returned to work Feb. 15-16.) Because of a soft coal miners' strike (May 2-29), the government ordered a 50 per cent reduction of passenger service on coal-burning railroads and seized the mines. A threatened strike (May 17) of railroad engineers and trainmen ended when President Truman ordered the seizure of the country's railroads. A nine-day strike of anthracite miners won (June 7) an 18½ cents-per-hour increase in wages. Fifteen thousand truck drivers in New York held out in an 18-day strike (Aug. 31-Sept. 17). A demand for higher wages by licensed seamen resulted in a strike on the Atlantic Coast (Oct. 1-26) and on the Pacific (Oct. 1-Nov. 23). 3,000 airplane passengers were stranded between the Pacific Coast and Cairo, Egypt, by a strike (Oct. 21-Nov. 15) of 1,400 pilots and co-pilots of the Transcontinental & Western Line, Inc. John ·L. Lewis defied the government by calling (Nov. 18) a strike of 400,000 United Mine Workers in the government-controlled soft coal mines. When he further ignored (Nov. 20) a Federal court injunction, both he and his union were tried (Nov. 25) for contempt of court, found (Dec. 4) guilty, and fined—Lewis, $10,000, and his organization, $3,500,000 (the United States Supreme Court upheld Mar. 6, 1947, the fine against Lewis, but reduced the union fine to $700,000). In the first eleven months of the year, statistics showed that 14,545,000 workers lost 107,475,000 work days in 4,335 strikes.

The American Mother of the Year, selected by the Golden Rule Foundation Mothers' Committee, was Mrs. Emma Clarissa Clement of Louisville, Ky. She was a Negress and a granddaughter of a slave—the first of her race to be so honored.

Former President Woodrow Wilson's library of 9,000 volumes was presented to the Library of Congress by his widow.

Nobel prizes were awarded to six Americans—Percy W. Bridgman for physics; Dr. James B. Sumner, Dr. Wendell K. Stanley, and John H. Northrop for chemistry; Herman J. Muller for medicine and physiology, and John R. Mott for peace.

Books of the year included: "The Autobiography of William Allen White" (posthumous; Pulitzer prize 1947), "Lord Weary's Castle" (Robert Lowell; poetry; Pulitzer prize 1947), "Peace of Mind" (Joshua Loth Liebman), "Scientists Against Time" (Dr. James Phinney Baxter 3rd; Pulitzer prize 1947) and the fiction, "All the King's Men" (Robert Penn Warren; Pulitzer prize 1947), "The Dark Wood" (Christine Weston), "Foxes of Harrow" (Frank Yerby), "The Miracle of the Bells" (Russell Janney), "The Snake Pit" (Mary Jane Ward).

The RCA Victor recording company pressed its one billionth phonograph record. The record was John Philip Sousa's march "Stars and Stripes Forever."

Leo Sowerby was awarded the Pulitzer music prize for his choral composition "The Canticle of the Sun."

Benjamin Britten's English opera "Peter Grimes" had (Aug. 6) its American première at the Berkshire Music Center, Lenox, Mass., in the presence of the composer.

Igor Stravinsky, famed American composer (he became a citizen in Dec., 1945), who once wrote a piece entitled "Ragtime" (1920), now produced what he called an "Ebony Concerto" for clarinet and swing band which received (Mar. 25) its première by Woody Herman's Band in New York at Carnegie Hall.

New York plays included: "O Mistress Mine" (Empire, Jan. 23; 452 perf.), "Born Yesterday" (Lyceum, Feb. 4; 1,642 perf.), "Call Me Mister" (National, Apr. 18; 734 perf.), "Lady Windermere's Fan" (Cort, Oct. 14; 228 perf.; revival), "Joan of Lorraine" (Alvin, Nov. 18), "Another Part of the Forest" (Fulton, Nov. 20), "Years Ago" (Mansfield, Dec. 3; 206 perf.), "Burlesque" (Belasco, Dec. 25; 439 perf.; revival). Laurence Olivier and the Old Vic Theatre Company of London appeared in repertory ("Henry IV, Parts I-II," etc.). Webster's Elizabethan play "The Duchess of Malfi" was revived (Barrymore, Oct. 15; 38 perf.). There was no 1947 Pulitzer prize for this year's drama. Musical productions included: "Three to Make Ready" (Adelphia, Mar. 7; 327 perf.), "Annie Get Your Gun" (Imperial, May 16; 1,147 perf.), "Icetime" (Center, June 20; 405 perf.), "Happy Birthday" (Broadhurst, Oct. 31; 564 perf.).

Motion pictures of the year included: "Anna and the King of Siam" (Irene Dunne, Rex Harrison), "The Best Years of Our Lives" (Myrna Loy, Fredric March), "Caesar and Cleopatra" (Claude Rains, Vivien Leigh), "The Green Years" (Charles Coburn, Tom Drake), "Henry V" (Laurence Olivier), "The Jolson Story" (Larry Parks, William Demarest), "Notorious" (Cary Grant, Ingrid Bergman, Claude Rains), "The Postman Always Rings Twice" (Lana Turner, John Garfield), "To Each His Own" (Olivia de Havilland, John Lund), "The Yearling" (Gregory Peck, Jane Wyman).

The Cincinnati and Brooklyn National League baseball clubs battled (Sept. 11) 19 innings at Brooklyn, New York, in a scoreless game that was terminated after 4 hours, 40 minutes because of darkness.

ॐ 1947

Almost Like Being in Love (Brigadoon). w., Alan Jay Lerner. m., Frederick Loewe. Sam Fox Pub. Co., cop. 1947 by Alan Jay Lerner and Frederick Loewe.

As Years Go By (film: Song of Love). w., m., Charles Tobias and Peter DeRose, based on Brahms' "Hungarian Dance No. 4." Miller Music Corp., cop. 1947.

Ask Anyone Who Knows. w., m., Eddie Seiler, Sol Marcus, and Al Kaufman. M. Witmark & Sons, cop. 1947.

Ballerina. w., Bob Russell. m., Carl Sigman. Jefferson Music Co., Inc., cop. 1947.

Beyond the Sea. w., Jack Lawrence. m., Charles Trenet. T. B. Harms Co., cop. 1947.

But Beautiful (film: Road to Rio). w., Johnny Burke. m., James Van Heusen. Burke and Van Heusen, Inc., cop. 1947.

Chi-Baba Chi-Baba. w., m., Mack David, Al Hoffman, and Jerry Livingston. Oxford Music Corp., cop. 1947.

Civilization. w., m., Bob Hilliard and Carl Sigman. Edwin H. Morris & Co., cop. 1947.

Come to the Mardi Gras. w., Ervin Drake and Jimmy Shirl. m., Max Bulhoes and Milton de Oliveira. Southern Music Pub. Co., cop. 1937 by Irmaos Vitale, Rio de Janeiro, Brazil; cop. 1937 by Peer International Corp.; cop. 1947 by Peer International Corp.

A Fellow Needs a Girl (Allegro). w., Oscar Hammerstein, 2nd. m., Richard Rodgers. Williamson Music, Inc., cop. 1947.

Feudin' and Fightin'. w., Al Dubin and Burton Lane. m., Burton Lane. Chappell & Co., Inc., cop. 1947.

The Gentleman Is a Dope (Allegro). w., Oscar Hammerstein, 2nd. m., Richard Rodgers. Williamson Music, Inc., cop. 1947.

Heartaches. See 1931.

I'll Dance at Your Wedding. w., Herb Magidson. m., Ben Oakland. George Simon, Inc., cop. 1947.

I Wish I Didn't Love You So (film: The Perils of Pauline). w., m., Frank Loesser. Susan Publications, Inc., cop. 1947.

Ivy. w., m., Hoagy Carmichael. Burke & Van Heusen, Inc., cop. 1947.

Mam'selle (film: The Razor's Edge). w., Mack Gordon. m., Edward Goulding. Leo Feist, Inc., cop. 1947.

Open the Door, Richard. w., "Dusty" Fletcher and John Mason. m., Jack McVea and Dan Howell. Duchess Music Corp., cop. 1947.

Papa, Won't You Dance with Me? (High Button Shoes). w., Sammy Cahn. m., Jule Styne. Edwin H. Morris & Co., Inc., cop. 1947.

So Far (Allegro). w., Oscar Hammerstein, 2nd. m., Richard Rodgers. Williamson Music, Inc., cop. 1947.

The Stanley Steamer (film: Summer Holiday). w., Ralph Blane. m., Harry Warren. Harry Warren Music, Inc., cop. 1947.

There but for You Go I (Brigadoon). w., Alan Jay Lerner. m., Frederick Loewe. Sam Fox Pub. Co., cop. 1947 by Alan Jay Lerner and Frederick Loewe.

There! I've Said It Again. See 1941.

Too Fat Polka. w., m., Ross MacLean and Arthur Richardson. Shapiro, Bernstein & Co., Inc., cop. 1947.

We Three—My Echo, My Shadow and Me. w., m., Dick Robertson, Nelson Cogne and Sammy Mysels. Mercer and Morris, Inc., cop. 1940.

Wedding Samba—*originally called:* The Wedding Rhumba. w., m., Abraham Ellstein, Allan Small, and Joseph Leibowitz. Duchess Music Corp., cop. 1940; cop. 1947. (Popularized in 1950.)

Woody Woodpecker. w., m., George Tibbles and Ramey Idriss. Leeds Music Corp., cop. 1947.

For the first time in 14 years, Republicans controlled Congress (the 80th). The proceedings on the opening day (Jan. 3) were immediately halted by their opposition to the seating of Mississippi Democratic Senator-elect Theodore G. Bilbo on the grounds that he had won his election in a campaign based on "white supremacy." Bilbo died (Aug. 31) in New Orleans and never was seated.

A new member was added (Jan. 6) to the Presidential Cabinet—a Secretary of Defense, unifying the Army and Navy commands. President Truman named (July 26) James Forrestal to the post.

President Truman appointed (Jan. 8) General George Catlett Marshall as Secretary of State in succession to James Francis Byrnes who had resigned.

The Speaker of the House of Representatives was designated (July 18) by Act of Congress in line of succession to the Presidency "if, by reason of death, resignation, removal from office, inability, or failure to qualify, there is neither President nor Vice-President."

Disclosures before the House Investigating Committee on Un-American Activities was creating great concern over the spread of Communist ideology in the United States and led President Truman to order (Mar.

22) an examination into the loyalty of all government employees. Testimony by Hollywood producers Louis B. Mayer, Jack Warner, and by director Sam Wood before the same Committee revealed (Oct. 20) that at least a score of persons, chiefly writers, harbored Communist sympathies, but they had been unable to use the motion-picture screen for subversive purposes.

President Truman visited Mexico (Mar. 3-5); President Aleman of Mexico returned the visit (Apr. 29-May 2). Later, President Truman visited Canada (June 9-12).

The United States leased (Mar. 14) for a 99-year period military and naval bases in the newly (1946) created Republic of the Philippines.

Congress passed (June 20 by the House, June 23 by the Senate) over President Truman's veto (June 20) the Taft-Hartley Labor Act, named after Ohio Senator Robert Alphonso Taft and New Jersey Representative Fred Allan Hartley, Jr.

Secretary of State George Catlett Marshall announced (June 5) in a speech at Harvard University a government plan to aid the economic and military rehabilitation of Europe and China by financial assistance. This plan materialized as the Economic Co-operation Administration (Apr. 3, 1948).

The Freedom Train, symbol of the 160th anniversary of the signing of the Constitution, was dedicated in Philadelphia before starting its 33,000-mile tour of the country. It contained 100 priceless documents relating to the birth of the Republic.

The Friendship Train—200 carloads of food donated by American communities to feed France and Italy—arrived (Nov. 18) in New York for shipment to Europe.

The charred hulk of the old battleship "Oklahoma," bombed first at Pearl Harbor, Hawaii, and later in atomic tests at Bikini Atoll, sank in mid-Pacific while it was being towed to Oakland, Cal., to be scrapped.

The United Nations ("U.N.") adopted (Oct. 20) at Flushing Meadow, New York, a flag—a blue field with a white polar map of the world embraced in twin olive branches. The ensign was first flown (Oct. 21) at the organization's temporary headquarters at Flushing Meadow and Lake Success, N. Y.

The first bodies of the American dead in World War II arrived in the United States—3,028 from the Pacific in San Francisco (Oct. 10); 6,248 from Europe in New York (Oct. 26).

A gubernatorial dilemma existed in Georgia as a result of an election (Jan. 15)—the State had two governors: the incumbent Ellis G. Arnall and Herman Talmadge, son of the late Governor-elect Eugene Talmadge. Arnall resigned (Jan. 19) and the Georgia Supreme Court designated Lieutenant Governor Melvin E. Thompson to the office.

Strikes by public employees and schoolteachers were outlawed in New York State by Governor Thomas E. Dewey (Mar. 27) with the penalty of dismissal for violations.

The last streetcars in Manhattan, New York City, stopped running; they were replaced by Diesel-engine buses.

The annual convention of the American Legion in New York was climaxed by a parade of 52,000 veterans of World War I down Fifth Avenue. The procession, seen by 2,000,000 persons, took 12 hours to pass.

The Superior Court in Atlanta, Ga., revoked (June 13) the national charter of the Ku Klux Klan (revived in 1915).

"Flying saucers" were seen in the sky during the summer in various parts of the United States. They continued to appear during 1948-49.

A strike of 2,400 teachers for higher salaries closed the public schools of Buffalo, N. Y., for seven days (Feb. 24-Mar. 3).

Members of Local 180, United Automobile Workers, C.I.O., voted (Mar. 9) to end their 440-day strike against the J. I. Case Co., of Racine, Wis., thus terminating one of the longest walkouts in American labor history.

More than 300,000 telephone workers in 39 States walked out in the first country-wide strike in the industry's history. Long-distance service was cut 80 per cent, but local service was almost normal on dial phones. The strike lasted 23 days (Apr. 7-30).

"We disaffiliate" wired (Dec. 12) John Llewellyn Lewis of the United Mine Workers to President William Green of the A.F.L. (American Federation of Labor).

Rear-Admiral Richard Evelyn Byrd, while making his second flight over the South Pole, dropped (Feb. 16) the flags of all the United Nations. (His first flight was in 1929.)

Captain William P. Odom made (Apr. 12-16) in a converted twin-engine Army bomber plane a global trip of 20,000 miles from New York, flying via Paris, Cairo, Calcutta, Tokyo, Alaska, and Canada, in 78 hours, 55 minutes, 12 seconds. Captain Odom later completed a solo flight of 19,645 miles around the world in 63 hours, 15 minutes. Captain Hugh Gordon and co-pilot Captain Gordon F. Maxwell flew (June 17-30) the four-engine Pan American World Airways clipper "Constellation" from New York on a round-the-world flight of 22,219 miles, via Newfoundland, London, Istanbul, India, Manila, China, Tokyo, Honolulu, and San Francisco, in 13 days, 3 hours, 10 minutes (flying time, 101 hours, 32 minutes). The plane carried 15 American newspapermen and six other passengers.

Aviation also had its tragic side. Grace Moore, American opera, radio, and screen star, and Prince Gustaf Adolf, second in line to the throne of Sweden, were among 22 killed when a KLM Royal Dutch airliner crashed (Jan. 26) and exploded outside Copenhagen, Denmark. A four-engine DC-4 burst (May 29) into flames at LaGuardia Field airport, New York, bringing death to 43 passengers and crew. Another DC-4 met (May 30) a similar fate at Port Deposit, Md., killing 53 passengers and members of the crew. A third DC-4 en route from Chicago to Washington, D. C., crashed (June 14) in the Blue Ridge Mountains, W. Va.; all persons aboard lost their lives. An Army B-17 dropped (Aug. 17) into the Pacific causing the death of 10 persons, including George Atcheson, Jr., chairman of the Allied Control Commission in Japan and adviser to General Douglas MacArthur. A Los Angeles-New York bound United Air Lines plane plunged (Oct. 24) in flames into Bryce Canyon, Utah; all 52 passengers met their death. A private plane crash deprived (Oct. 29) Oregon of its Governor Earl Snell, its Senate President Marshall Cornett, and its Secretary of State Robert S. Farrell, Jr.

A cyclone that crossed (Apr. 10) the western part of Texas and Oklahoma killed 134 persons and injured 1,300. A severe hurricane swept (Sept. 16-19) over Florida, Louisiana, and Mississippi, and took the lives of 100 persons. The Missouri River again overflowed and inundated nearly a million acres of farmland. A heavy snowfall of 25.8 inches, the worst experienced in New York since the blizzard of 1888, blanketed (Dec. 27) the Eastern States from Maine to Washington, D. C., and halted railroad, airplane, and bus service.

President John L. Lewis of the United Mine Workers union closed (Mar. 29) all soft coal mines for six days in memory of the 111 miners who died (Mar. 25) in a gas-filled chamber as a result of a mine explosion in Centralia, Ill.

The waterfront and surrounding area of Texas City, Tex., was devastated (Apr. 16) when a nitrate-laden French freighter exploded at its wharf. Five hundred and twelve persons were killed, and property damage amounted to $50,000,000.

A sweeping forest fire destroyed (Oct. 23) a large section of Bar Harbor, Me., and the surrounding country and caused an estimated $30,000,-000 property damage.

The signature of President Truman changed the name Boulder Dam to Hoover Dam in honor of 31st President Herbert Hoover.

Colonel Jack W. Durant was sentenced to 15 years at hard labor and cashiered out of the Army by a U. S. Military Court in Frankfurt am Main, Germany, for his part in the theft of the $1,500,000 Hesse crown jewels in 1945.

The trial of a $6,450,000 damage suit by writer Konrad Bercovici against actor Charles ("Charlie") Chaplin for plagiarism charges ended in Federal Court when the latter agreed to pay $95,000.

In the world of feminine fashions, the "new look," consisting of unusually full dresses that reached nearly to the wearer's ankles, was the style—and the source of much heated argument pro and con.

The Nobel prize for peace was awarded jointly to the American Friends Service Committee (Quakers) and the Friends Service Council, London.

Dr. A. S. W. Rosenbach, rare book dealer, paid $151,000 for a copy of the "Bay Psalm Book," the first book printed in the English colonies in America.

The Library of Congress opened (July 26) to the public for the first time the collection of 18,350 letters and documents of Abraham Lincoln bequeathed to the Library by his son Robert Todd Lincoln in 1926.

Additions to the National Gallery of Art, Washington, D. C., included 113 paintings, chiefly American, through the A. W. Mellon Educational and Charitable Trust, and loans and gifts from the Chester Dale Collection.

Books of the year included: "Across the Wide Missouri" (Bernard DeVoto; Pulitzer prize 1948), "The Age of Anxiety" (Wystan Hugh Auden; poetry; Pulitzer prize 1948), "Columbia Dictionary of Modern European Literature" (Horatio Smith), "Forgotten First Citizen: John Bigelow" (Margaret Clapp; Pulitzer prize 1948), "Geoffrey Chaucer of England" (Marchette Chute), "Inside U. S. A." (John Gunther), and the fiction, "The Apple Orchard" (John Kafka), "The Bishop's Mantle" (Agnes Sligh Turnbull), "Came a Cavalier" (Frances Parkinson Keyes), "Drums of Destiny" (Graham Montague Jeffries), "Gentleman's Agreement" (Laura Hobson), "House Divided" (Ben Ames Williams), "Kingsblood Royal" (Sinclair Lewis), "Lydia Bailey" (Kenneth Roberts), "Marry for Money" (Faith Baldwin), "The Moneyman" (Thomas Bertram Costain), "Prince of Foxes" (Samuel Shellabarger), "Tales of the South Pacific" (James A. Michener; Pulitzer prize 1948), "Unconquered" (Neil Harmon Swanson), "The Wayward Bus" (John Steinbeck), "The Vixens" (Frank Yerby), "Yankee Pasha" (Edison Marshall).

The Metropolitan Opera Company, New York, presented (Jan. 11) the première of "The Warrior" by Bernard Rogers, an American opera based on the story of Samson and Delilah. It was performed twice.

Gian-Carlo Menotti's curtain-raiser "The Telephone" and the two-act opera "The Medium" reached Broadway (Barrymore Theatre, May 1) and drew fascinated audiences for 212 performances. ("The Medium" had its first hearing May 8, 1946, in Brander Matthews Hall, Columbia University, New York; "The Telephone" was first given Feb. 18, 1947 in the Heckscher Theatre.)

Charles Ives was awarded the Pulitzer music prize for his Third Symphony. The composer, a unique figure in American music, was 63 years old. (The symphony, which had its first performance Apr. 5, 1946, by the New York Little Symphony under Lou Harrison, was composed around 1911.)

Margaret Truman, daughter of the President, made her professional singing debut with the Detroit Symphony Orchestra.

New York plays included: "All My Sons" (Coronet, Jan. 29; 328 perf.), "John Loves Mary" (Booth, Feb. 4; 423 perf.), "A Young Man's Fancy" (Plymouth, Apr. 29; 335 perf.), "The Heiress" (Biltmore, Sept. 29; 410 perf.), "Command Decision" (Fulton, Oct. 1; 408 perf.), "Man and Superman" (Alvin, Oct. 8; revival), "Medea" by Euripides (National, Oct. 20; 214 perf.), "The Winslow Boy" (Empire, Oct. 29), "For Love or Money" (Henry Miller, Nov. 4), "A Streetcar Named Desire" by Tennessee Williams (Ethel Barrymore, Dec. 3; 855 perf.; Pulitzer Prize

1948). Katharine Cornell revived "Antony and Cleopatra" (Martin Beck, Nov. 26; 126 perf.). Musical productions included: "Finian's Rainbow" (46th Street, Jan. 10; 725 perf.), "Sweethearts" (Shubert, Jan. 21; 288 perf.), "Brigadoon" (Ziegfeld, Mar. 13; 581 perf.), "Inside U. S. A." (Century, Apr. 30; 399 perf.), "High Button Shoes" (Century, Oct. 9; 727 perf.), "Allegro" (Majestic, Oct. 10; 315 perf.), "Angel in the Wings" (Coronet, Dec. 11; 308 perf.).

Motion pictures of the year included: "Boomerang," "Crossfire," "Great Expectations," "Life with Father" (William Powell, Irene Dunne), "Miracle on 34th Street" (Maureen O'Hara), "Odd Man Out."

Mrs. Mildred (Babe) Didrickson Zaharias, famed golfer from Texas, defeated Jacqueline Gordon of London, in Scotland. She thus became the first American ever to win the British women's amateur golf championship.

In New York, more than 58,000 baseball fans roared a tribute to Babe Ruth, retired "Sultan of Swat," at Yankee Stadium in ceremonies attended by Francis Cardinal Spellman and Baseball Commissioner A. B. ("Happy") Chandler.

Rocky Graziano, middleweight prize fighter, told a N. Y. County grand jury that he had been offered $100,000 to "throw" a fight.

The New York National League ("Giants") baseball club set a record of 221 home runs for a season.

Henry Ford, aged 83, died (Apr. 7) in Dearborn, Mich. He left an estate estimated between five and seven hundred million dollars.

ᘛ 1948

"A"—You're Adorable (The Alphabet Song). w., m., Buddy Kaye, Fred Wise, and Sidney Lippman. Laurel Music Co., cop. 1948.

Baby, It's Cold Outside (film: Neptune's Daughter). w., m., Frank Loesser. Edwin H. Morris & Co., Inc., cop. 1948 by Susan Publications, Inc. (Academy Award Winner, 1949)

Buttons and Bows (film: Paleface). w., m., Jay Livingston and Ray Evans. Famous Music Corp., cop. 1948. (Academy Award Winner, [1948])

Candy Kisses. w., m., George Morgan. Hill and Range Songs, Inc., cop. 1948.

Cuanto le Gusta (film: A Date with Judy). w., Ray Gilbert. m., Gabriel Ruiz. Peer International Corp., cop. 1940 by Promotora Hispano Americana de Musica, Mexico City; cop. 1948 by Peer International Corp.

Enjoy Yourself—It's Later Than You Think. w., Herb Magidson. m., Carl Sigman. Edwin H. Morris & Co., cop. 1948. (Popularized in 1950.)

A Fella with an Umbrella (film: Easter Parade). w., m., Irving Berlin. Leo Feist, Inc., cop. 1948 by Irving Berlin.

Hair of Gold, Eyes of Blue. w., m., Sunny Skylar. Robert Music Co., cop. 1948.

Haunted Heart (Inside U. S. A.). w., Howard Dietz. m., Arthur Schwartz. Chappell & Co., Inc., cop. 1948 by Arthur Schwartz and Howard Dietz.

Here I'll Stay (Love Life). w., Alan Jay Lerner. m., Kurt Weill. Chappell & Co., Inc., cop. 1948 by Alan Jay Lerner and Kurt Weill.

I Love You So Much It Hurts. w., m., Floyd Tillmann. Melody Lane Publications, Inc., cop. 1948.

It's a Most Unusual Day (film: A Date with Judy). w., Harold Adamson. m., Jimmy McHugh. Robbins Music Corp., cop. 1948.

It's Magic (film: Romance on the High Seas). w., Sammy Cahn. m., Jule Styne. M. Witmark & Sons, cop. 1948.

A Little Bird Told Me. w., m., Harvey O. Brooks. Bourne, Inc., cop. 1948.

Mañana—Is Soon Enough for Me. w., m., Peggy Lee and Dave Barbour. Barbour-Lee Music Corp., cop. 1948.

Matinee. w., Bob Russell. m., Carl Sigman. Edwin H. Morris & Co., Inc., cop. 1948.

My Darling, My Darling (Where's Charley?). w., m., Frank Loesser. Edwin H. Morris & Co., cop. 1948 by Susan Publications, Inc.

My Happiness. w., Betty Peterson. m., Borney Bergantine. Kansas City, Mo.: Blasco Music, Inc., cop. 1948.

Nature Boy. w., m., Eden Ahbez. Crestview Music Corp., cop. 1948.

The Night Has a Thousand Eyes (film: The Night Has a Thousand Eyes). w., Buddy Bernier. m., Jerry Brainin. Paramount Music Corp., cop. 1948.

On a Slow Boat to China. w., m., Frank Loesser. Melrose Music Corp., cop. 1948 by Susan Publications, Inc.

Once in Love with Amy (Where's Charley?). w., m., Frank Loesser. Edwin H. Morris & Co., Inc., cop. 1948 by Susan Publications, Inc.

Powder Your Face with Sunshine. w., m., Carmen Lombardo and Stanley Rochinski. Lombardo Music, Inc., cop. 1948.

Sabre Dance (from the ballet: Gayne, or Gayanne). Orch. piece. m., Aram Khachaturian. Leeds Music Corp., cop. 1948. (1. Re-arranged for orch.: by Richard Mohaupt, Russian-American Music Publishers, Inc., cop. 1947. 2. Arr. for fox-trot: by Vic Schoen, Leeds Music Corp., cop. 1948; by Paul Weirick, Russian-American Music Publishers, Inc., cop. 1948).

So in Love (Kiss Me, Kate). w., m., Cole Porter. Buxton Hill Music Corp., cop. 1948 by Cole Porter.

Tennessee Waltz. w., m., Redd Stewart and Pee Wee King. Nashville, Tenn.: Acuff-Rose Publications, cop. 1948.

A Tree in the Meadow. w., m., Billy Reid. Campbell-Connelly, Inc., cop. 1947 by Bevan Music Productions, Ltd.; assigned 1948 to Campbell-Connelly.

You're Breaking My Heart. w., m., Pat Genaro and Sunny Skylar. Algonquin Music, Inc., cop. 1948.

You Call Everybody Sweetheart. w., m., Sam Martin, Ben Trace, and Chem Watts. Mayfair Music Corp., cop. 1946-48.

You Can't Be True, Dear. w., Hal Cotton. m., Ken Griffen. The Biltmore Music Corp., cop. 1948. (Based on the German song "Du kannst nicht treu sein," w., Gerhard Ebeler, m., Hans Otten; published by Gerhard Ebeler Verlag, Cologne, cop. 1935.)

You Say the Nicest Things (As the Girls Go). w., Harold Adamson. m., Jimmy McHugh. Sam Fox Pub. Co., cop. 1948 by Jimmy McHugh and Harold Adamson.

Congress passed (Apr. 2) the Foreign Assistance Act, thus setting up the Economic Co-operation Administration (Marshall Plan) for the rehabilitation of Europe and China with a fund of $6,098,000,000. Paul G. Hoffman, president of the Studebaker automobile company, a Republican, was appointed (Apr. 5) Administrator. Within nine hours after the confirmation of the appointee by the Senate, $21,000,000 was authorized for the relief of France, Italy, Greece, Austria, and the Netherlands. At a conference in Paris of the Foreign Ministers of Great Britain, France, and Russia, the latter attacked (July 2) the Marshall Plan as a scheme to gain control over smaller nations.

The military draft came back when Congress passed (June 12) the Selective Service Act.

Congressional legislation (Displaced Persons Act) sanctioned (June 19) the admission of 205,000 homeless persons and refugees from Europe during a two-year period; four months later the first shipload arrived (Oct. 30) in New York.

The Senate unanimously approved the State Department's request for additional funds to enlarge the "Voice of America" radio programs that are beamed abroad to counteract worldwide anti-American propaganda of the Soviet Union.

The House Un-American Activities Committee reported that its agents had found microfilm copies of "documents of tremendous importance," which had been removed from State Department files and given "Russian communist agents." The microfilms were found in a hollowed-out pumpkin on the farm, at Westminster, Md., of Whittaker Chambers, New York magazine editor, who previously had accused Alger Hiss, former State Department official, of passing the documents to him. (Early in 1950, Hiss was convicted of perjury and sentenced to five to 10 years in prison.)

Indictments were brought (July 30) in New York against William Z. Foster, national chairman of the American Communist Party, and 11 party leaders on charges of conspiring to overthrow the U. S. government. (The case of Foster was dropped because of his illness. The eleven others were convicted Oct. 14, 1949, after a nine-months jury trial before Federal Judge Harold R. Medina in New York. They were sentenced Oct. 21—ten to five years in prison and one, a war veteran, to three years. Some 400 police were on duty when the trial began; Communists and their sympathizers carrying placards paraded in front of the courthouse. The defendants were released Nov. 3 on bail pending appeal to the United States Supreme Court.)

The U. S. Post Office issued twenty-nine separate three-cent postage stamps in honor of noted American historical events and national movements. Americans so honored were Dr. George Washington Carver (the first Negro to be pictured on a United States stamp), Elizabeth Stanton, Carrie Chapman Catt, and Lucretia Mott (pioneers in woman suffrage), William Allen White (journalist), Francis Scott Key (author of the "Star-Spangled Banner"), Harlan Fiske Stone (late Chief Justice of the Supreme Court), Clara Barton (founder of the American Red Cross), Juliette Gordon Low (founder of the Girl Scouts), Will Rogers, Moina Michael (founder of the Memorial Poppy movement), and Joel Chandler Harris (author of the Uncle Remus stories). The Gold Star Mothers of America also were honored.

The third anniversary of the death (Apr. 12) of Franklin Delano Roosevelt was observed in London with the unveiling by his widow of a statue in Grosvenor Park. The entire Royal Family and Winston Churchill attended.

A Russian schoolteacher who was sought as a witness by the House Un-American Activities Committee leaped (Aug. 12) from the third-floor window of the Soviet Consulate in New York. The woman accused Soviet Consul General Jacob M. Lomakin of confining her in the building as a prisoner. The State Department demanded (Aug. 20) the recall of the Consul General for violation of his diplomatic privileges.

New York City's traditional five-cent subway fare ("you could ride all day for a nickel") was raised to 10 cents.

President Walter P. Reuther of the United Automobile Workers (C.I.O.) union, was seriously wounded (Apr. 20) by a blast from a shotgun fired through the kitchen window of his house in Detroit. Rewards aggregating $117,000 were offered, but the assailant was not found.

On the same day, President John Llewellyn Lewis of the United Mine Workers and his union were fined for the second time (the first was in 1946) by a Federal court—this time for $20,000 and $1,400,000, respectively—for ignoring an injunction against a strike (Mar. 15-Apr. 22) by 350,000 soft coal miners.

In commemoration of the first New York-to-Washington air mail flight in 1918, which took 194 minutes, two jet-propelled P-80 Shooting Star fighter planes, flying in opposite directions, covered the same route in 27 minutes.

On Kitty Hawk Day, the 45th anniversary of the first flight by the Wright brothers in a heavier-than-air flying machine, Lawrence D. Bell, producer of the rocket plane X-1 which was the first plane to fly faster than sound, predicted that in the near future planes two or three times as fast as the X-1 would be built. The X-1 attained speeds exceeding 700 miles per hour, the speed of sound at sea level.

At a convention in Birmingham, Ala., some 6,000 Southern Democrats organized (July 17) the States Rights Party in opposition to the regular Democratic Party. South Carolina Gov. J. Strom Thurmond was nominated as the party's Presidential candidate.

Henry Agard Wallace, Presidential candidate of the Progressive Party, was subjected (Aug. 29) to heckling and a shower of eggs when he rose to address a political rally in Durham, N. C. President Truman denounced (Aug. 31) the anti-Wallace demonstration as "highly un-American."

A strike of 9,400 truck drivers interfered with New York's business for 18 days (Sept. 1-18). A strike of C.I.O. longshoremen paralyzed shipping on the Pacific Coast (Sept. 2-Nov. 25) and in Atlantic ports (Nov. 12-25).

The world's largest telescope, situated on Mt. Palomar 66 miles north of San Diego, Cal., was dedicated (June 3) and named the Hale Telescope in honor of the astronomer, George Ellery Hale.

The 4,900-acre International Airport at Idlewild, Queens County, N. Y., was dedicated (July 31) by President Truman.

The ban placed by James C. Petrillo, president of the American Federation of Musicians, on the making of commercial master recordings went into effect at midnight, Jan. 1, when the contract with 771 recording companies expired. "We're never going to make records, ever," said Petrillo. (He switched 15 months later.)

Meanwhile, Dr. Peter Goldmark of the Columbia Broadcasting System, Inc., New York, demonstrated (June 21) his "long-playing" (LP) microgroove phonograph record.

Walter Piston was awarded the Pulitzer music prize for his Symphony No. 3.

Books of the year included: "Crusade in Europe" (General Dwight David Eisenhower), "The Disruption of American Democracy" (Roy F. Nichols; Pulitzer prize 1949), "How to Stop Worrying and Start Living" (Dale Carnegie), "Jefferson, the Virginian" (Dumas Malone; Vol. 1), "The Life and Times of the Shmoo" (Al Capp), "Roosevelt and Hopkins" (Robert E. Sherwood; Pulitzer prize 1949), "The Seven Story Mountain" (Thomas Merton; sequel, "The Waters of Siloe," 1949), "Terror and Decorum" (Peter Viereck; poetry; Pulitzer prize 1949), "Wine, Woman and Words" (Billy Rose) and the fiction, "The Big Fisherman" (Lloyd Cassel Douglas), "Dinner at Antoine's" (Frances Parkinson Keyes), "The Golden Hawk" (Frank Yerby), "Guard of Honor" (James Gould Cozzens; Pulitzer prize 1949), "The Naked and the Dead" (Norman Mailer), "Pilgrim's Inn" (Elizabeth Goudge), "Raintree County" (Ross Franklin Lockridge), "Shannon's Way" (Archibald Joseph Cronin), "Tomorrow Will Be Better" (Betty Smith), "The Young Lions" (Irwin Shaw).

New York plays that ran over 200 performances included: "Strange Bedfellows" (Morosco, Jan. 14), "The Respectful Prostitute" (New Stages, Feb. 9; 358 perf.), "Mister Roberts" (Alvin, Feb. 18; 1,157 perf.), "The Play's the Thing" (Booth, Apr. 28), "Edward, My Son" (Martin Beck, Sept. 30), "Private Lives" (Plymouth, Oct. 4; revival), "Life with Mother" (Empire, Oct. 20), "Goodbye, My Fancy" (Morosco, Nov. 17; 466 perf.), "Light Up the Sky" (Royale, Nov. 18), "The Silver Whistle" (Biltmore, Nov. 24), "Anne of the Thousand Days"

(Shubert, Dec. 8; 286 perf.), "The Madwoman of Chaillot" (Belasco, Dec. 27; 368 perf.). Musical productions included: "Make Mine Manhattan" (Broadhurst, Jan. 15; 429 perf.), "Inside U. S. A." (Century, Apr. 30), "Howdy, Mr. Ice!" (Center, June 24; 406 perf.), "Love Life" (46th Street, Oct. 7), "Where's Charley?" (St. James, Oct. 11; 792 perf.), "As the Girls Go" (Winter Garden, Nov. 13; 414 perf.), "Lend an Ear" (National, Dec. 16; 460 perf.), "Kiss Me, Kate" (New Century, Dec. 30; 1,077 perf.).

Motion pictures of the year included: "Apartment for Peggy," "Easter Parade," "A Foreign Affair," "Hamlet" (Laurence Olivier; British film), "I Remember Mama," "Johnny Belinda" (Jane Wyman, Lew Ayres), "Paisan" (Italian film), "Portrait of Jenny," "Red River," "The Snake Pit," "Sorry, Wrong Number," "Treasure of the Sierra Madre" (Humphrey Bogart).

The first telecast of a major American symphony orchestra took place (Mar. 20). By a coincidence, the event brought together two noted orchestras on rival networks at the same time. The Philadelphia Symphony, playing under Eugene Ormandy at the Academy of Music, Philadelphia, was put on the air by cable to New York by the Columbia Broadcasting System through WCBS-TV at 5:30 P.M.; the NBC Symphony in an all-Wagner program under the 81-year-old Arturo Toscanini went on the air in New York through WNBT of the National Broadcasting Company an hour later, at 6:30 P.M.

Opera was televised (Nov. 29) for the first time from the stage of the Metropolitan Opera House, New York, when the National Broadcasting Company transmitted Verdi's "Otello," performed on the opening night of the season.

"Babe" Ruth, famous and beloved baseball player, made (July 26) his last public appearance at the initial showing in New York of the autobiographical motion picture "The Babe Ruth Story." He died (Aug. 16) of cancer in Memorial Hospital, New York.

Citation was the race horse of the year. The animal won 25 of his 27 races, including the Kentucky Derby, the Preakness, and the Belmont Stakes. In the Pimlico Special, he galloped alone around the track; no other horse was regarded his equal.

In the national elections, as in the Roosevelt-Landon campaign (1936), all predictions pointed to the defeat of the Democratic incumbent and the election of the Republican nominee. President Truman opposed New York Governor Thomas E. Dewey. Again the polls reversed expectations. President Truman captured 28 States with 304 electoral votes; Dewey carried 16 States with 189 electoral votes. Dewey ran 36,213 votes behind his 1944 campaign against Roosevelt.

ᘒ 1949

Bali Ha'i (South Pacific). w., Oscar Hammerstein, 2nd. m., Richard Rodgers. Williamson Music, Inc., cop. 1949 by Richard Rodgers and Oscar Hammerstein, 2nd.

Bibbidi-Bobbidi-Boo (film: Cinderella). w., m., Mack David, Al Hoffman, and Jerry Livingston. Burbank, Cal.: Walt Disney Music Co., cop. 1948; cop. 1949.

Bonaparte's Retreat. m., Peewee King. Nashville, Tenn.: Acuff-Rose Publications, cop. 1949.

Careless Hands. w., m., Bob Hilliard and Carl Sigman. Melrose Music Corp., cop. 1949.

Copper Canyon (film: Copper Canyon). w., m., Jay Livingston and Ray Evans. Famous Music Corp., cop. 1949.

The Cry of the Wild Goose. w., m., Terry Gilkyson. Hollywood, Cal.: American Music, Inc., cop. 1949. (Popularized in 1950.)

Daddy's Little Girl. w., m., Bobby Burke and Horace Gerlach. Beacon Music Co., cop. 1949.

Dear Hearts and Gentle People. w., Bob Hilliard. m., Sammy Fain. Edwin H. Morris & Co., Inc., cop. 1949.

Diamonds Are a Girl's Best Friend (Gentlemen Prefer Blondes). w., Leo Robin. m., Jule Styne. J. J. Robbins & Sons, Inc., cop. 1949.

Don't Cry, Joe. w., m., Joe Marsala. Harms, Inc., cop. 1949.

A Dreamer's Holiday. w., m., Kim Gannon and Mabel Wayne. Skidmore Music Co., Inc., cop. 1949.

Hop-Scotch Polka. w., m., Willam Whitlock, Carl Sigman, and Gene Rayburn. Cromwell Music, Inc., cop. 1949.

The Hot Canary. Composition for violin and piano. m., Paul Nero. Leeds Music Corp., cop. 1948; cop. 1949. (A jazz version of a once popular European piece entitled "Le Canari" by F. Poliakin, Edition Cranz, Brussels, n.d.)

How It Lies, How It Lies, How It Lies! w., Paul Francis Webster. m., Sonny Burke. Edwin H. Morris & Co., Inc., cop. 1949. (Popularized in 1950.)

Huckle-Buck. w., Roy Alfred. m., Andy Gibson. United Music Corp., cop. 1949.

I'm Gonna Paper All My Wall with Your Love Letters. w., m., Teddy Powell and Bernie Wayne. Goday Music Corp., cop. 1949.

I Can Dream, Can't I? See 1937.

I've Got a Lovely Bunch of Cocoanuts. w., m., Fred Heatherton. Campbell Music, Inc., cop. 1944 and 1948 by The Irwin Dash Music Co., Ltd., London; cop. 1949 by Cornell Music, Inc.

Jealous Heart. See 1944.

Johnson Rag. w., Jack Lawrence. m., Guy Hall and Henry Kleinauf. Miller Music Corp. (by Arrangement with Robbins Music Corp.), cop. 1917 by Robbins Music Corp.; cop. 1940 by Robbins Music Corp.; renewed 1945 by Robbins Music Corp.; cop. 1949 by Robbins Music Corp.

Let's Take An Old-Fashioned Walk (Miss Liberty). w., m., Irving Berlin. Irving Berlin Music Corp., cop. 1949 by Irving Berlin.

A Lovely Bunch of Cocoanuts. See above: "I've Got a Lovely Bunch of Cocoanuts."

Lovesick Blues. w., m., Hank Williams. Nashville, Tenn.: Acuff-Rose Publications, cop. 1949.

Mona Lisa. w., m., Jay Livingston & Ray Evans. Famous Music Corp., cop. 1949. (Academy Award Winner, 1950)

Monday, Tuesday, Wednesday. w., m., Ross Parker. Leeds Music Corp., cop. 1949 by Irwin Dash Music Co., Ltd., London. (Popularized in 1950.)

Mule Train. w., m., Johnny Lange, Hy Heath, and Fred Glickman. Burbank, Cal.: Walt Disney Music Co., cop. 1949.

My Foolish Heart (film: My Foolish Heart). w., Ned Washington. m., Victor Young. Santly-Joy, Inc., cop. 1949.

Some Enchanted Evening (South Pacific). w., Oscar Hammerstein 2nd. m., Richard Rodgers. Williamson Music, Inc., cop. 1949 by Richard Rodgers and Oscar Hammerstein 2nd.

The Old Master Painter. w., Haven Gillespie. m., Beasley Smith. Robbins Music Corp., cop. 1949.

Room Full of Roses. w., m., Tim Spencer. Beverly Hills, Cal.: Hill and Range Songs, Inc., and Tim Spencer Music, Inc., cop. 1949.

Rudolph the Red-Nosed Reindeer. w., m., Johnny Marks. St. Nicholas Music Pub. Co., cop. 1949.

Sitting by the Window. w., m., Paul Insetta. Shapiro, Bernstein & Co., Inc., cop. 1949.

President Truman began his second term. For the first time the nation was able not only to hear the inaugural address by radio but to see the parade and ceremonies by television.

In appreciation of the gift-laden Friendship Train which was shipped to France in the preceding year by the American people, the French sent a Gratitude Train of 49 provisioned boxcars, one for each State and the District of Columbia. A rousing welcome in New York greeted (Feb. 2) the arrival of the freighter "Magellan" which transported the train.

A temporary period of coffee hoarding began (Oct. 26) when imports of the commodity took a sharp decline because of crop failures in Central and South American countries.

Mildred E. Gillars, "Axis Sally," who had broadcast Nazi propaganda from Germany to the United States and to GIs in Europe and Africa during World War II, was sentenced (Mar. 25) to prison for 10 to 30 years and fined $10,000 for treason.

A referendum (in Nov., 1948) in Kansas resulted (June 6) in the repeal of the State constitution's 69-year-old prohibition amendment.

A December shortage of water in New York made it necessary for inhabitants to observe shaveless and bathless days. The flushing of sidewalks and the washing of automobiles were banned by the city's legislators.

A 16-ton truck that was illegally transporting carbon disulphide exploded (May 13) in the Holland Tunnel under the Hudson River and caused great havoc. Sixty-three persons suffered injuries, and 23 other trucks and vehicles were damaged.

An alleged arsonist caused (Sept. 13) a $250,000 damage to the "Million Dollar Pier" in Atlantic City, N. J.

The 6,905-ton steamer "Noronic" of the Canada Steamship Lines, the largest passenger liner on the Great Lakes, was totally destroyed (Sept. 17) by fire while on an overnight stop at Toronto, Ont. One hundred and thirty-two passengers, chiefly American citizens, lost their lives in the disaster.

Canasta was the newest card game, and 330,000 eager players bought Oswald Jacoby's manual "How to Win at Canasta."

Speed was the keynote in aviation. The latest 92-ton Lockheed U. S. Navy transport plane "Constitution," which cost $30,000,000 to build, flew (Feb. 3) from Moffet,Field, Cal., to Washington National Airport, Washington, D. C., in 9 hours, 31 minutes. Major Russell E. Schleeh and Major Joseph W. Howell piloted (Feb. 8) a small six-jet Boeing B-47 bomber from Moses Lake, Wash., to Andrews Field, Md., a distance of 2,269 miles, in 3 hours, 46 minutes, thus establishing a new transcontinental record. Captain James Gallagher circumnavigated (Feb. 26-Mar. 2) the globe from Caswell Air Force Base, Forth Worth, Tex., in the Air Force Boeing B-50 superfortress "Lucky Lady II," flying eastward a distance of 23,452 miles in 94 hours, 1 minute. The plane averaged 249 miles per hour and was re-fuelled four times in the air by converted B-29 bombers. William P. Odom completed (Mar. 8) a nonstop solo flight in a monoplane from Honolulu, Hawaii, to Teterboro, N. J., covering 5,300 miles in 36 hours. The famous aviator was killed (Sept. 5) when his plane, which had just established a new record of 397.071 miles per hour to win the Thompson Trophy in the National Air Races at Cleveland, O., crashed into a house in Berea, a suburb. The Pan American World Airways four-engine "Constellation Mayflower" set (Apr. 28) a new commercial record of 10 hours, 2 minutes, for a distance of 3,153 miles from New York to London. On the same day, the company's double-decker "Stratocruiser" flew from New York to London on a 3,565-mile route in 9 hours, 16 minutes. The American airlift into Berlin set a new record by flying in 12,940 short tons of supplies on 1,398 flights during a 24-hour period. The previous record was 8,246 tons.

In commemoration of the Wright brothers' first airplane flight (Dec. 17, 1903) at Kittyhawk, N. C., World War II flier Tom Lanphier, Jr., completed (Dec. 7) a 22,180-mile trip around the world in commercial planes in a new record time of 4 days, 23 hours, 47 minutes. The undertaking was sponsored by the Air Force Association.

According to the United States Weather Bureau, the country was hit by 290 tornadoes—the highest number in American history. Severe blizzards isolated 2,000,000 cattle and sheep in snowbound areas in Western States. The U. S. Air Force instituted (Jan. 24) "Operation Haylift" by sending seventeen C-82 "Flying Boxcars" over the territory, each of which dropped five tons of hay to feed the stranded livestock. Large sections of New England, New York, and New Jersey were inundated by floods that were caused by swollen rivers. Damage was estimated at $2,500,000 and several hundred families were made homeless. A record freezing spell with temperatures down to 14 degrees hit Southern California and destroyed one-fifth of the $100,000,000 citrus fruit crop.

William F. Giauque was awarded the Nobel prize for medicine and physiology.

Albert Schweitzer, Alsatian philosopher, theologian, medical missionary, musician, organist, writer, and biographer of Johann Sebastian Bach, made a brief visit from Equatorial Africa to the United States to deliver a lecture on Goethe at Aspen, Colo., at a celebration of the 200th anniversary of the great German poet's death.

Books of the year included: "John Quincy Adams and the Foundations of American Foreign Policy" (Samuel Flagg Bemis; Pulitzer prize 1950), "Annie Allen" (Gwendolyn Brook; poetry; Pulitzer prize 1950), "Art and Life in America" (O. W. Larkin; Pulitzer prize 1950), "Father Flanagan of Boys Town" (Fulton and Will Oursler), "Peace of Soul" (Fulton John Sheen), "Shakespeare of London" (Marchette Chute), "This I Remember" (Anna Eleanor Roosevelt), and the fiction, "The Brave Bulls" (Tom Lea), "The Chain" (Paul Iselin Wellman), "Cutlass Empire" (Van Wyck Mason), "The Egyptian" (Mika Waltari; translated from the Finnish), "Father of the Bride" (Edward Streeter), "The Greatest Story Ever Told" (Fulton Oursler), "High Towers" (Thomas Bertram Costain), "Kinfolk" (Pearl Buck), "Let Love Come Last" (Taylor Caldwell), "Mary" (Sholem Asch), "Point of No Return" (John Phillips Marquand), "Pride's Castle" (Frank Yerby), "A Rage to Live" (John O'Hara), "The Road Between" (James Thomas Farrell), "The Way West" (A. B. Guthrie, Jr.; Pulitzer prize 1950).

Virgil Thomson was awarded the Pulitzer music prize for his orchestral suite from his incidental music to the motion picture "Louisiana Story."

"Troubled Island," an opera by the Negro composer William Grant Still, received (Mar. 31) its première in New York at the City Center of Music and Drama.

"Ouanga," an American opera based on Haitian folklore by Clarence Cameron White, had (June 10) its world première in South Bend, Ind., in the Central High School Auditorium by the H. T. Burleigh Music Association. (The opera was awarded the Bispham Memorial Medal for American opera in 1932, and was performed at the Academy of Music, Philadelphia, Oct. 27, 1950, by the Dra Mu Opera Company.)

New ballet companies that were seen in New York were Roland Petit's Les Ballets de Paris (Winter Garden, Oct. 6; 118 performances), which featured a bold, highly sexed dance version of Bizet's opera "Carmen," and the Sadler's Wells Ballet from the Royal Opera House, London (Metropolitan Opera House, Oct. 9-Nov. 6).

New York plays included: "Diamond Lil" (Coronet, Feb. 5), "Death of a Salesman" by Arthur Miller (Morosco, Feb. 10; 742 perf.; Pulitzer prize 1949), "Detective Story" (Hudson, Mar. 23; 581 perf.), "I Know My Love" (Shubert, Nov. 2; 246 perf.), "Clutterbuck" (Biltmore, Dec. 3; 218 perf.). Musical productions included: "Along Fifth Avenue"

(Broadhurst, Jan. 13), "South Pacific," book by Oscar Hammerstein 2nd and Joshua Logan, lyrics by Oscar Hammerstein 2nd, music by Richard Rodgers (Majestic, Apr. 7; still running in 1952; Pulitzer prize 1950), "Miss Liberty" (Imperial, July 15; 308 perf.), "Touch and Go" (Broadhurst, Oct. 13), "Lost in the Stars" (Music Box, Oct. 30; 281 perf.), "Texas Li'l Darlin' " (Mark Hellinger, Nov. 25; 293 perf.), "Gentlemen Prefer Blondes" (Ziegfeld, Dec. 8; 740 perf.). Daniel Cordoba's "Cabalgata," Spanish revue of folksongs and dances, which had played seven years in Spain, performed in New York (Broadway, July 7; 76 perf.).

Motion pictures of the year included: "All the King's Men" (Broderick Crawford, Mercedes McCambridge), "The Barkleys of Broadway," "The Champion" (Kirk Douglas), "Dancing in the Dark," "Francis" (Donald O'Connor), "The Hasty Heart," "The Heiress" (Olivia de Havilland), "I Was a Male War Bride" (Cary Grant, Rosalind Russell), "Letter to Three Wives" (Linda Darnell, Ann Sothern, Jeanne Crain), "On the Town," "Samson and Delilah" (Victor Mature, Hedy Lamarr), "Sands of Iwo Jima" (John Wayne), "The Stratton Story" (James Stewart), "They Live by Night," "Twelve O'Clock High" (Gregory Peck).

Vaudeville returned (May 19) to the Palace Theatre, New York, after an absence of 14 years.

Ralph Kiner, left fielder of the Pittsburgh National League ("Pirates") baseball club, had his best season as a batsman, hiting 54 home runs. (The National League record is 56, hit in 1930 by Wilson of the Chicago club.)

Joe Louis, undefeated heavyweight boxing champion, retired from the ring. Louis, whose real name is Joseph Barrow, was the victor in 60 bouts, of which he won 51 by knockouts and 9 by decision. (He attempted a comeback the next year and was defeated by Ezzard Charles.)

ৡ 1950

All My Love—*original French title:* **Boléro.** English words. Mitchell Parish. French words, Henri Contet. m., Paul Durand. Mills Music, Inc., cop. 1948 by Editions Continental, Paris; cop. 1950.

American Beauty Rose. w., m., Hal David, Redd Evans, and Arthur Altman. Jefferson Music Co., Inc., cop. 1950.

Autumn Leaves. English words, Johnny Mercer. French words, Jacques Prevert. m., Joseph Kosma. Ardmore Music, cop. 1947; cop. 1950 by Enoch et cie., Paris.

A Bushel and a Peck (Guys and Dolls). w., m., Frank Loesser. Susan Publications, Inc., cop. 1950 by Frank Loesser.

Candy and Cake. w., m., Bob Merrill. Oxford Music Corp., cop. 1950.

C'est Si Bon. w., m., André Hornez and Henri Betti. English words, Jerry Seelen. Leeds Music Corp., cop. 1947, 1949 and 1950 by Arpége Editions Musicales, Paris.

Chattanoogie Shoe Shine Boy. w., m., Harry Stone and Jack Stapp. Nashville, Tenn.: Acuff-Rose Publications, cop. 1950.

Christmas in Killarney. w., m., John Redmond, Jas. Cavanaugh, and Frank Weldon. Remick Music Corp., cop. 1950.

Count Every Star. w., Sammy Gallop. m., Bruno Coquatrix. Paxton Music Inc., cop. 1950.

The Cry of the Wild Goose. See 1949.

Dearie. w., m., Bob Hilliard and Dave Mann. Laurel Music Corp., cop. 1950.

Enjoy Yourself—It's Later Than You Think. See 1948.

Gone Fishin'. w., m., Nick and Charles Kenny. Leo Feist, Inc., cop. 1950.

Goodnight, Irene. w., m., Huddie Ledbetter and John Lomax. Spencer Music Corp., cop. 1936 by Macmillan Co.; assigned 1950 to World Wide Music Pub. Co.; cop. 1950 by World Wide Music Pub. Co.; assigned 1950 to Spencer Music Corp.; cop. 1950 by Spencer Music Corp.

Harbor Lights. See 1937.

Hoop-Dee-Doo. w., Frank Loesser. m., Milton DeLugg. Edwin H. Morris & Co., Inc., cop. 1950 by Susan Publications, Inc.

I Didn't Slip, I Wasn't Pushed, I Fell. w., m., Eddie Pola and George Wyle. Remick Music Corp., cop. 1950.

I Said My Pajamas. w., m., Eddie Pola and George Wyle. Leeds Music Corp., cop. 1949; cop. 1950.

I'd 'Ave Baked a Cake. See below: "If I Knew You Were Comin' I'd 'Ave Baked a Cake."

If. w., Robert Hargreaves and Stanley J. Damerell. m., Tolchard Evans. Shapiro, Bernstein & Co., Inc., cop. 1934 by Cecil Lennox, Ltd., London; assigned 1950 to Shapiro, Bernstein & Co., Inc.

If I Knew You Were Comin' I'd 'Ave Baked a Cake. w., m., Al Hoffman, Bob Merrill, and Clem Watts. Robert Music Corp., in co-operation with Orten Music Co., cop. 1950 by Robert Music Corp.

It's a Lovely Day Today (Call Me Madam). w., m., Irving Berlin. Irving Berlin Music Corp., cop. 1950 by Irving Berlin.

It's So Nice to Have a Man Around the House. w., Jack Elliott. m., Harold Spina. Edwin H. Morris & Co., Inc., cop. 1950.

A Marshmallow World. w., Carl Sigman. m., Peter De Rose. Shapiro, Bernstein & Co., Inc., cop. 1949; cop. 1950.

Monday, Tuesday, Wednesday. See 1949.

Music! Music! Music! w., m., Stephen Weiss and Bernie Baum. Cromwell Music, Inc., cop. 1950.

My Heart Cries for You. w., m., Carl Sigman and Percy Faith. Massey Music Co., Inc., cop. 1950.

The Old Piano Roll Blues. w., m., Cy Coben. Leeds Music Corp., cop. 1949; cop. 1950.

Our Lady of Fatima. w., m., Gladys Gollahon. Robbins Music Corp., cop. 1950.

Play a Simple Melody. See 1914.

Rag Mop. w., m., Johnnie Lee Wills and Deacon Anderson. Beverly Hills, Cal.: Hill and Range Songs, Inc., cop. 1950 by Bob Wills Music, Inc.; assigned 1950 to Hill and Range Songs, Inc.

Sam's Song. w., Jack Elliott. m., Lew Quadling. Sam Weiss Music, Inc., cop. 1950.

Sentimental Me. w., m., Jim Morehead and Jimmy Cassin. Knickerbocker Music Publishers, Inc., cop. 1950.

Sunshine Cake (film: Riding High). w., Johnny Burke. m., James Van Heusen. Burke-Van Heusen & Associates Music Corp., cop. 1950.

Tennessee Waltz. See 1948.

The Thing. w., m., Charles R. Grean. Hollis Music, Inc., cop. 1950.

The Third Man Theme (film: The Third Man). m., Anton Karas. Chappell & Co., Inc., cop. 1949; cop. 1950.

Tzena, Tzena, Tzena. (1) w., Gordon Jenkins, m., arr. by Spencer Ross, Cromwell Music, Inc., cop. 1950; (2) w., Mitchell Parish, m., Issacher Miron (Michrovsky) and Julius Grossman, Mills Music, Inc., cop. 1950.

La Vie en Rose. French words, Edith Piaf. English words, Mack David. m., Louiguy. Harms, Inc., cop. 1947 by Editions Arpége, Paris; cop. 1950 by Harms, Inc.

Wanderin'. w., m., traditional; arr. (1) by Ed. Jackson, Edwards Music Co., Inc., cop. 1950; (2) by Sammy Kaye, Republic Music Corp., cop. 1950. (The tune and two sets of words were published in Carl Sandburg, "The American Songbag," Harcourt, Brace & Co., cop. 1927, p. 188-89.)

Wedding Samba. See 1940.

Wilhelmina (film: Wabash Avenue). w., Mack Gordon. m., Josef Myrow. Leo Feist, Inc., cop. 1950 by Twentieth Century Music Corp.

You Wonderful You (film: Summer Stock). w., Jack Brooks and Saul Chapin. m., Harry Warren. Miller Music Corp., by arrangement with Harry Warren Music, cop. 1950 by Harry Warren Music, Inc.

Armed forces of the People's Republic of Korea (Communist) invaded (June 25, Far Eastern time; June 24, Eastern time) the Republic of Korea. The United Nations Security Council declared the action a breach of the peace and called upon all its members for support. General of the U. S. Army Douglas MacArthur was appointed (July 8) commander of all U. N. forces in Korea. These suffered severe reverses for 83 days until a powerful offensive, supported by American and British warships and flying superfortresses and jet planes, pushed the enemy beyond the 38th Parallel where the latter were joined (in Nov.) by the Communist troops of the People's Republic of China. (General MacArthur was recalled in 1951 by President Truman because of differences in policy and received tremendous ovations everywhere in the United

States on his return. Subsequently, United Nations and Communist negotiators met in Kaesong to discuss terms of a truce.)

President Truman authorized (Jan. 31) the continuation of work by the Atomic Energy Commission on a new bomb—the "H" or hydrogen bomb. Twelve leading United States physicists protested (Feb. 4) in New York against its use as "a weapon of war."

Two Puerto Rican Nationalist fanatics attempted (Nov. 1) to assassinate President Truman by shooting their way into the President's temporary residence at Blair House in Washington, D. C. They were immediately shot down, but not before one of the President's guards was killed and two others were seriously injured.

Diplomatic relations were severed (Feb. 21) with Communist-ruled Bulgaria by the United States over indignities inflicted on members and employees at the American legation in Sofia.

Russians shot down (Apr. 8) an unarmed U. S. Navy "Privateer" airplane in the Baltic while the plane was on a training flight from Wiesbaden, Germany, to Copenhagen, Denmark. The Russian government contended that the plane flew over Latvia "to photograph Soviet defense installations." The United States vigorously denied the allegation and conferred (Apr. 25) the Distinguished Flying Cross posthumously on the 10 lost members of the plane.

After 64 years, the federal tax on oleomargarine was repealed (Jan. 18) by the Senate.

The National Capitol was 150 years old. In honor of the event, the U. S. Post Office issued (Apr. 20, June 12, and Nov. 23) three special commemorative postage stamps.

Congress passed (Sept. 23) over President Truman's veto the Internal Security Act, aimed at Communists and totalitarians, compelling them to register with the Department of Justice, excluding them from Federal and defense employment, and denying them passport privileges.

The Senate, after a closely contested vote (35 to 35, broken by Vice-President Alben W. Barkley), formed (May 3) a five-man committee under the chairmanship of Tennessee Senator Estes Kefauver to investigate organized interstate crime; $150,000 was appropriated for the purpose. When the committee began (Oct. 12) its inquiry into crime in the New York area, sensational disclosures resulted that involved persons in high positions besides police officials, racketeers, and gangsters.

United Nations Day was designated (Oct. 24) by President Truman.

Prime Minister Liaquat Ali Khan of Pakistan and his wife, the Begum Shaiba, visited the United States. They were received (May 3) in Washington by President Truman.

To overcome a water shortage in New York that had existed since the preceding December, the city engaged (Mar. 14) Dr. Wallace E. Howell, director of Mt. Washington Observatory, N. H., at a fee of $100 per day to conduct a six-month experiment in artificial rain-making over the Catskill reservoir area. In the first attempt (Apr. 12), the clouds were "seeded" with 100 pounds of dry ice; in the second attempt (Apr. 13), they were sprayed with silver iodide—a five-hour snowstorm occurred (Apr. 14). Dr. Howell disclaimed credit for this act of nature.

The U. S. Post Office issued (Jan. 27) a special three-cent purple postage stamp with the portrait of the noted labor leader Samuel Gompers.

President Truman seized (Aug. 25) all railroads of the country to forestall a general strike for higher pay by the Brotherhood of Railway Trainmen and the Order of Railway Conductors.

The fastest ocean-going passenger ship ever to be built in the United States, the 26,000-ton liner "Independence," was launched (June 3) at Quincy, Mass.

Books of the year included: "John C. Calhoun: American Portrait" (Margaret Louise Colt; Pulitzer prize 1951), "Complete Poems" (Carl Sandburg; Pulitzer prize 1951), "Kon-Tiki; Across the Pacific by Raft" (Thor Heyerdahl), "Listen for a Lonesome Drum" (Carl Lamson Carmer), "Roosevelt in Retrospect" (John Gunther), and the fiction, "The Cardinal" (Henry Morton Robinson), "The Disenchanted" (Budd Schulberg), "Floodtide" (Frank Yerby), "Joy Street" (Frances Parkinson Keyes), "The Little Princesses" (Marion Crawford), "River of the Sun" (James Ramsey Ullman), "The Town" (Conrad Richter; Pulitzer prize 1951), "Valley Forge" (Van Wyck Mason), "The Wall" (John Richard Hersey).

New York City's worst railroad wreck occurred (Thanksgiving eve, Nov. 22) when an eastbound express train of the Long Island Railroad plowed into a stalled passenger train in Richmond Hill, Queens, L. I. The trains were carrying about 2,000 homeward-bound commuters (it was 6:26 P.M.); 78 persons were killed and hundreds injured. Previously (Feb. 17), a head-on collision on the same railroad near Rockville Center caused the death of 32 persons and injury to 100.

A Pan-American World Airways stratocruiser set (Apr. 28) a new transatlantic record from New York to London, flying 3,565 miles in 9 hours, 16 minutes.

Nobel prizes were awarded to Philip Showalter Hench and Edward Calvin Kendall for medicine and physiology and to Dr. Ralph J. Bunche for peace. Novelist William Faulkner received the 1949 award in literature after the Swedish Academy was criticized for making no award that year.

The Federal Communications Commission, after several years of debate between the Columbia Broadcasting System and the Radio Corporation of America, granted (Oct. 11) the former the right to broadcast its form of color television. The RCA obtained (Nov. 25) a temporary restraining order from the Federal District Court in Chicago.

Gian-Carlo Menotti's latest opera "The Consul" (New York, Ethel

Barrymore Theatre, Mar. 15; 269 performances) proved even more effective than "The Medium" (1947). The opera was awarded the Pulitzer music prize.

Long-run New York plays included: "The Member of the Wedding" (Empire, Jan. 5; 500 perf.), "The Cocktail Party" (Henry Miller, Jan. 21; 409 perf.), "The Happy Time" (Plymouth, Jan. 24; 614 perf.), "Peter Pan" (Imperial, Apr. 24, revival; 321 perf.), "Affairs of State" (Royale, Sept. 25; 610 perf.), "Season in the Sun" (Cort, Sept. 28; 367 perf.). A surprise run was the revival of Shakespeare's "As You Like It" (Cort, Jan. 26; 145 perf.) with Katherine Hepburn of the movies. The newspapers and illustrated magazines revelled in pictures of the actress's legs—the Bard hardly could have imagined such publicity for himself, the play, and its star. The ballroom of the Hotel Edison was converted into a theatre and opened (May 31) as New York's first theatre-in-the-round or arena theatre—a type of production new to the city but already familiar in Texas and the West. Musical productions included: "Tickets, Please" (Coronet, Apr. 27; 245 perf.), "Michael Todd's Peep Show" (Winter Garden, June 28; 278 perf.), "Call Me Madam" (Imperial, Oct. 12), "Guys and Dolls" (46th Street, Nov. 24).

Motion pictures of the year included: "All About Eve" (Bette Davis, Anne Baxter), "The Blue Angel" (Marlene Dietrich), "Born Yesterday" (Judy Holliday, William Holden, Broderick Crawford), "Cyrano de Bergerac" (José Ferrer), "Halls of Montezuma," "Kim" (Errol Flynn, Dean Stockwell), "Kind Hearts and Coronets" (Alec Guinness), "King Solomon's Mines" (Deborah Kerr, Stewart Granger, Richard Carlsen), "Macbeth" (Orson Welles), "Mr. Music" (Bing Crosby), "The Mudlark" (Irene Dunne, Alec Guinness), "Pagan Love Song" (Esther Williams, Howard Keel), "Rio Grande" (John Wayne, Maureen O'Hara), "Stromboli" (Ingrid Bergman), "Vendetta" (Faith Domergue), "Wonderful Adventures of Pinocchio" (Walt Disney cartoon).

Connie Mack (Cornelius McGillicuddy), manager of the Philadelphia American League ("Athletics") baseball club, retired (Oct. 18) after 67 years in the sport, 50 of which he spent with the Philadelphia club. He won 9 American League championships and 5 World Series.

Joe Louis, undefeated heavyweight boxing champion who had retired from the ring in the preceding year, attempted a comeback and was defeated (Sept. 27) by Ezzard Charles in 15 rounds in New York—Louis's first defeat since winning the title.

George Bernard Shaw, aged 94, died (Nov. 2) in Ayot St. Lawrence, England.

The national population was 150,697,361. The five largest cities were New York (7,835,099), Chicago (3,606,436), Philadelphia (2,064,794), Los Angeles (1,957,692), and Detroit (1,838,517).

₰ 1951

And So to Sleep Again. w., m., Joe Marsala and Sunny Skylar. George Paxton, Inc., cop. 1951.

Any Time. w., m., Herbert Happy Lawson. Hill & Range Songs, Inc., cop. 1921 by Herbert Happy Lawson Music Publishing Co.; assigned 1948 to Hill & Range Songs, Inc.; renewed 1949 by Herbert Happy Lawson; assigned to Hill & Range Songs, Inc. (Popularized in 1951.)

Be My Life's Companion. w., m., Bob Hilliard and Milton De Lugg. Edwin H. Morris & Co., Inc., cop. 1951.

Be My Love (*film:* The Toast of New Orleans). w., Sammy Cahn. m., Nicholas Brodszky. Miller Music Corp., cop. 1949, 1950, 1951 by Loew's Inc.

Because of You. w., m., Arthur Hammerstein and Dudley Wilkinson. Broadcast Music, Inc., cop. 1940. (Popularized in 1951; introduced in the film "I Was an American Spy.")

Bonne Nuit—Goodnight (*film:* Here Comes the Groom). w., m., Jay Livingston and Ray Evans. Burke-Van Heusen & Associates, cop. 1951.

Cold, Cold Heart. w., m., Hank Williams. Nashville, Tenn.: Acuff-Rose Publications, cop. 1951.

Come on-a My House. w., m., Ross Bagdasarian and William Saroyan. Duchess Music Corp., cop. 1950; cop. 1951.

Cry. w., m., Churchill Kohlman. Mellow Music Publishing, cop. 1951.

Domino. English words, Don Raye. French words, Jacques Plante. m., Louis Ferrari. Pickwick Music Corp., cop. 1950 by "Arpege" Editions Musicales, Paris; cop. 1951 by "Arpege" Editions Musicales, Paris.

Half as Much. w., m., Curley Williams. Nashville, Tenn.: Acuff-Rose Publications, cop. 1951.

Hello, Young Lovers (The King and I). w., Oscar Hammerstein, 2nd.

m., Richard Rodgers. Williamson Music, Inc., cop. 1951 by Richard Rodgers and Oscar Hammerstein, 2nd.

I'm in Love Again. w., m., Cole Porter. Crawford Music Corp., cop. 1925; cop. 1951 by Harms, Inc.

I Get Ideas. w., Dorcas Cochran. m., Sanders. Hill and Range Songs, Inc., cop. 1951.

I Talk to the Trees (Paint Your Wagon). w., Alan Jay Lerner. m., Frederick Loewe. Chappell & Co., Inc., cop. 1951 by Alan Jay Lerner and Frederick Loewe.

I Whistle a Happy Tune (The King and I). w., Oscar Hammerstein, 2nd. m., Richard Rodgers. Williamson Music, Inc., cop. 1951 by Richard Rodgers and Oscar Hammerstein, 2nd.

If. w., Robert Hargreaves and Stanley J. Damerell. m., Tolchard Evans. Shapiro, Bernstein & Co., Inc., cop. 1934 and 1950 by Cecil Lennox, Ltd., London.

In the Cool, Cool, Cool of the Evening (*film:* Here Comes the Groom). w., Johnny Mercer. m., Hoagy Carmichael. Burke-Van Heusen & Associates, cop. 1951. (Academy Award Winner, 1951)

It Is No Secret. w., m., Stuart Hamblen. Duchess Music Corp., cop. 1950. (Popularized in 1951.)

It's No Sin. *See below:* **Sin.**

Jezebel. w., m., Wayne Shanklin. Broadcast Music, Inc., cop. 1950 by Folk Songs; assigned 1951 to Broadcast Music, Inc.

Kisses Sweeter than Wine. w., Paul Campbell. m., Joel Newman. Folkways Music Publishers, Inc., cop. 1951.

The Little White Cloud That Cried. w., m., Johnnie Ray. Larry Spier, Inc., cop. 1951 by Carlyle Music Publishing Corp.

The Loveliest Night of the Year (*film:* The Great Caruso). w., Paul Francis Webster. m., adapted by Irving Aaronson [from Juventino Rosas's waltz, "Sobre las Olas"]. Robbins Music Corp., cop. 1950 by Loew's, Inc., cop. 1951 by Loew's, Inc.

Make the Man Love Me (A Tree Grows in Brooklyn). w., Dorothy Fields. m., Arthur Schwartz. Putnam Music, Inc. [selling agent, T. B. Harms Co.], cop. 1951 by Arthur Schwartz and Dorothy Fields.

Marshmallow Moon (*film:* Aaron Slick from Punkin Creek). w., m., Jay Livingston and Ray Evans. Famous Music Corp., cop. 1951.

Mister and Mississippi. w., m., Irving Gordon. Shapiro, Bernstein & Co., cop. 1951.

Mixed Emotions. w., m., Stuart F. Loucheim. Roger Music, cop. 1951.

Mockin' Bird Hill. w., m., Vaughn Horton. Southern Music Publishing Co., Inc., cop. 1949. (Popularized in 1951.)

My Truly, Truly Fair. w., m., Bob Merrill. Santly-Joy, Inc., cop. 1951.

On Top of Old Smokey. w., anon. m., arr. by Fred Barovick. Lewis Music Pub. Co., Inc., cop. 1951.

Please, Mr. Sun. w., Sid. Frank. m., Ray Getzov. Weiss and Barry, Inc., cop. 1951.

Rose, Rose, I Love You. w., Wilfred Thomas. m., arr. by Chris Langdon. Chappel & Co., Inc., cop. 1951 by Chappell & Co., Ltd., London.

Shrimp Boats. w., m., Paul Mason Howard and Paul Weston. Walt Disney Music Co., cop. 1951.

Sin. w., Chester R. Shull. m., George Hoven. Algonquin Music, Inc., cop. 1951.

Slowpoke. w., m., Pee Wee King, Redd Stewart and Chilton Price. Hollywood, Cal.: Ridgeway Music, Inc., cop. 1951.

Sound Off. w., m., Willie Lee Duckworth. Shapiro, Bernstein & Co., Inc., cop. 1950 by Bernard Lentz; assigned to and cop. 1951 by Shapiro, Bernstein & Co., Inc. (Originally published in "The Cadence System of Teaching Close Order Drill" by Colonel Bernard Lentz, U. S. Army, retired; The Military Service Publishing Co., Harrisburg, Pa., cop. 1951 by Bernard Lentz.)

Sparrow in the Tree Top. w., m., Bob Merrill. Santly-Joy, Inc., cop. 1951.

Tell Me Why. w., Al Alberts. m., Marty Gold. Signet Music Co., cop. 1951.

Tennessee Waltz. w., m., Redd Stewart and Pee Wee King. Nashville, Tenn.: Acuff-Rose Publications, cop. 1948. (Popularized in 1951.)

Too Young. w., Sylvia Dee. m., Sid Lippman. Jefferson Music Co., Inc., cop. 1951.

Undecided. w., Sid Robin. m., Charles Shavers. Leeds Music Corp., cop. 1939; cop. 1951.

Unforgettable. w., m., Irving Gordon. Bourne, Inc., cop. 1951.

We Kiss in a Shadow (The King and I). w., Oscar Hammerstein, 2nd. m., Richard Rodgers. Williamson Music, Inc., cop. 1951 by Richard Rodgers and Oscar Hammerstein, 2nd.

(When We Are Dancing) I Get Ideas. *See above:* **I Get Ideas.**

Wonder Why *(film:* **Rich, Young and Pretty).** w., Sammy Cahn. m., Nicholas Brodszky. Robbins Music Corp., cop. 1950, 1951, by Loew's, Inc.

The military operations in Korea continued. Divergent views in the conduct of the war caused President Truman to relieve (Apr. 11) the outspoken and critical General Douglas MacArthur of his command there, an act which raised a widespread outcry of disapproval, and to appoint General Matthew B. Ridgway to the post.

Returning to the United States, General MacArthur arrived (Apr. 16) in Honolulu amid wild acclaim, reached (Apr. 18) San Francisco, where a tremendous ovation greeted him, and flew (Apr. 19) to Washington, D. C., to deliver before the Senate and House of Representatives an address, which was carried by television and radio to a nation-wide audience. In the peroration to his speech of retirement, he recalled from his days at West Point "the refrain of one of the most popular barracks ballads of that day, which proclaimed, most proudly, that old soldiers never die; they just fade away," making the words forever memorable.

The Twenty-second Amendment (limiting the presidency to two terms) was added (Feb. 27) to the Constitution.

World War II ended officially for the United States with the signing of peace treaties with Japan (Sept. 8) and Germany (Oct. 19).

Four United States fliers were forced down (Nov. 19) in Hungary and arrested for border violation; they were released (Dec. 28) after the United States paid $120,000 in "fines."

Julius Rosenberg, 35, and his wife Ethel, 37, were sentenced (Apr. 6) to death for treason, as spies, for supplying atom bomb information to Russia. They were executed on June 19, 1953, at Sing Sing Prison, Ossining, New York.

The United States Army ended (Feb. 9) a railroad strike by ordering the trainmen to return to work or lose their jobs; pleading guilty to a "sick" walkout, the trainmen were fined $75,000.

American transcontinental television was inaugurated (Sept. 4) with the telecast of the opening ceremonies of the Japanese Peace Treaty Conference in San Francisco.

The Columbia Broadcasting System televised (June 25) the first full hour commercial program in color; the program was sponsored by sixteen national advertisers. (The telecasts were suspended on Oct. 19 at the request of the Director of Defense Mobilization "to conserve critical materials.")

The first transcontinental demonstration of a major heart operation, the coarctation of the aorta, on a 20-year-old youth, was telecast (Dec. 7) by Columbia Broadcasting System Color Television. The operation, performed sucecssfully in Los Angeles by Dr. John C. Jones, eminent thoracic surgeon, was witnessed by groups of doctors and others in Los Angeles, Chicago, and New York.

The National Broadcasting Company telecast (Dec. 24) the first commissioned opera composed specifically for television—Gian-Carlo Menotti's fifty-minute "Amahl and the Night Visitors."

Popular among books of fiction were: "The Caine Mutiny" (Herman Wouk; Pulitzer prize 1952), "The Catcher in the Rye" (Jerome David Salinger), "The Cruel Sea" (Nicholas Monsarrat), "From Here to Eternity" (James Jones), "God's Men" (Pearl S. Buck), "Joy Street" (Frances Parkinson Keyes), "Melville Goodwin, U. S. A." (John Marquand), "Moses" (Scholem Asch), "Requiem for a Nun" (William Faulkner). Non-fiction best sellers included: "The Man Called Peter" (Catherine Marshall), "The Sea Around Us" (Rachel L. Carson). The first of Walt Kelly's series of "Pogo" books appeared.

Uncle Sam, who is also in the publishing business, turned out this year through the Government Printing Office nearly half a billion copies of publications. The best seller was the 15-cent booklet "Infant Care," which passed the seven million mark. Runner-up was another 15-cent pamphlet, "Prenatal Care," which sold four million copies. In third place was "Your Child—One to Six," price 20 cents. A five-cent publication, "The Sex of Watermelons," was completely sold out.

The New York stage presented the plays: "The Rose Tattoo" (Martin Beck, Feb. 4; 306 perf.), "The Moon Is Blue" (Henry Miller, Mar. 8; 924 perf.), "Stalag 17" (Forty-eighth Street Th., May 8; 472 perf.), "The Fourposter" (Ethel Barrymore, Oct. 24; 632 perf.), "Gigi" (Fulton, Nov. 24; 217 perf.), "I Am a Camera" (Empire, Nov. 28; 262 perf.), "Point of No Return" (Alvin, Dec. 13; 364 perf.). The musicals included: "The King and I" (St. James, Mar. 29; 1,246 perf.), "A Tree Grows in Brooklyn" (Alvin, Apr. 19; 267 perf.), "Two on the Aisle" (Mark Hellinger, July 19; 279 perf.), the Yiddish "Bagels and Yox" (Holiday, Sept. 12; 204 perf.), "Top Banana" (Winter Garden, Nov. 1; 356 perf.), "Paint Your Wagon" (Shubert, Nov. 12; 289 perf.).

Among motion pictures, the top-money grossing film was "David and Bathsheba" (Gregory Peck, Susan Hayward). Other pictures were: "Showboat" (Kathryn Grayson, Howard Keel), "An American in Paris" (Gene Kelly), "The Great Caruso" (Mario Lanza), "A Streetcar Named Desire" (Vivien Leigh, Marlon Brando), "Quo Vadis?" (Deborah Kerr, Robert Taylor).

Thirty-two-year old San Diego, Cal., swimmer Florence Chadwick swam (Sept. 11) the English Channel from England to France—the first woman to swim the waters both ways. (She swam from France to England in 1950.)

In an attempted come-back, former heavyweight boxing champion Joe Louis (he abandoned the title in 1949) engaged in eight bouts, winning seven victories, but was TKO'd (Oct. 26) in New York by the rising Rocky Marciano in the eighth round, ending an outstanding ring career of 71 battles.

⑧ 1952

Am I in Love (*film:* Son of Paleface). w., m., Jack Brooks. Famous Music Corp., cop. 1952.

Anywhere I Wander (*film:* Hans Christian Andersen). w., m., Frank Loesser. Frank Music Corp., cop. 1952.

Auf Wiederseh'n, Sweetheart. w., John Sexton and John Turner. m., Eberhard Storch. Beverly Hills, Cal.: Hill and Range Songs, Inc., cop. 1949 by Editions Corso, G. m. b. H., Berlin; cop. 1951 by Hill and Range Songs, Inc.; cop. 1952 by Peter Maurice Music Co., Ltd., London.

Because You're Mine (*film:* Because You're Mine). w., Sammy Cahn. m., Nicholas Brodszky. Leo Feist, Inc., cop. 1951 by Loew's, Inc.; cop. 1952 by Loew's, Inc.

The Blacksmith Blues. w., m., Jack Holmes. Beverly Hills, Cal.: Hill and Range Songs, Inc., cop. 1950 by Tune Towne Tunes; assigned 1952 to Hill and Range Songs, Inc.; cop. 1952 by Hill and Range Songs, Inc.

Blue Tango. Instrumental. m., Leroy Anderson. Mills Music, Inc., cop. 1951; cop. 1952.

Botch-a-Me. Italian words and music, R. Morbelli and L. Astore. English words and musical adaptation, Eddie Y. Stanley. Hollis Music, Inc., cop. 1941 by Fono Enic S. A., Milan; assigned 1952 to Hollis Music, Inc.; new English words, cop. 1952 by Hollis Music, Inc.

Count Your Blessings Instead of Sheep (*film:* White Christmas). w., m., Irving Berlin. Irving Berlin, cop. 1952.

Delicado. w., Jack Lawrence. m., Waldyr Azevedo. Remick Music Corp., cop. 1951; cop. 1952.

Don't Let the Stars Get in Your Eyes. w., m., Slim Willet. Four Star Sales Co. (selling agent, Meridian Music Corp.), cop. 1952.

Forgive Me. w., Jack Yellen. m., Milton Ager. Advanced Music Corp., cop. 1927; cop. 1952.

The Gandy Dancers' Ball. w., m., Paul Weston and Paul Mason Howard. Walt Disney Music Co., cop. 1952.

Glow-Worm. w., Johnny Mercer. m., Paul Lincke. Edward B. Marks Music Corp., cop. 1902 by Apollo Verlag; renewed 1930 by Edward B. Marks Music Corp.; cop. 1952 by Edward B. Marks Music Corp. (See 1907.)

A Guy Is a Guy. w., m., Oscar Brand. Ludlow Music, Inc., cop. 1952.

Here in My Heart. w., m., Pat Genaro, Lou Levinson and Bill Borrelli. Mellin Music, Inc., cop. 1952.

High Noon—Do Not Forsake Me (*film:* High Noon). w., Ned Washington. m., Dimitri Tiomkin. Leo Feist, Inc., cop. 1952. (Academy Award Winner, 1952.)

How Do You Speak to an Angel? (Hazel Flagg). w., Bob Hilliard. m., Jule Styne. Chappell & Co., Inc., cop. 1952 by Jule Styne and Bob Hilliard.

I'm Yours. w., m., Robert Mellin. Algonquin Music, Inc., cop. 1952.

I Saw Mommy Kissing Santa Claus. w., m., Tommie Connor. Harman Music, Inc., cop. 1952.

I Went to Your Wedding. w., m., Jessie Mae Robinson. St. Louis Music Corp., cop. 1952.

Jambalaya—on the Bayou. w., m., Hank Williams. Nashville, Tenn.: Acuff-Rose Publications, cop. 1952.

Keep It a Secret. w., m., Jessie Mae Robinson. Shapiro, Bernstein & Co., Inc., cop. 1952

Kiss of Fire. w., m., Lester Allen and Robert Hill [music adapted from A. G. Villoldo's "El Choclo"]. Duchess Music Corp., cop. 1952.

Pittsburgh, Pennsylvania. w., m., Bob Merrill. Oxford Music Corp., cop. 1952.

Pretend. w., m., Lew Douglas, Cliff Parman and Frank Lavere. Chicago: Brandon Music Corp., cop. 1952.

Somewhere Along the Way. w., Sammy Gallop. m., Kurt Adams. United Music Corp., cop. 1952.

Takes Two to Tango. w., m., Al Hoffman and Dick Manning. Harman Music, Inc., cop. 1952.

Tell Me You're Mine. w., m., R. Fredianelli and D. Ravasino. Capri Music Corp., cop. 1939; cop. 1952 by Edizioni Suvini-Zerboni, Milan.

Thumbelina (film: Hans Christian Andersen). w., m., Frank Loesser. Frank Music Corp., cop. 1952.

Till I Waltz Again with You. w., m., Sidney Prosen. Village Music Co., cop. 1952.

Trying. w., m., Billy Vaughn. Gallatin, Tenn.: Randy-Smith Music Corp., cop. 1952.

Wheel of Fortune. w., m., Bennie Benjamin and George Weiss. Laurel Music Corp., cop. 1952.

Why Don't You Believe Me. w., m., Lew Douglas, King Laney and Roy Rodde. Chicago: Brandon Music Co., cop. 1952.

Wish You Were Here (Wish You Were Here). w., m., Harold Rome. Chappell & Co., Inc., cop. 1952 by Harold Rome.

You Belong to Me. w., m., Pee Wee King, Redd Stewart and Chilton Price. Hollywood, Cal.: Ridgeway Music, Inc., cop. 1952.

Your Cheatin' Heart. w., m., Hank Williams. Nashville, Tenn.: Acuff-Rose Publications, cop. 1952.

Zing a Little Zong (film: Just for You). w., Leo Robin. m., Harry Warren. Famous Music Corp., cop. 1952 by Burvan Music Corp.

The war in Korea continued.

To prevent a strike by 60,000 C.I.O. steel workers, President Truman ordered (Apr. 8) on his own authority, ignoring the Labor Management Relations Act of 1947 (Taft-Hartley Act), the Government's seizure and operation of the mills. The action was declared (Apr. 30) unconstitutional, in the U. S. District Court, whereupon the workers walked out, but returned two days later when the U. S. Supreme Court accepted jurisdiction and restored the mills to Government control, pending its decision. By a vote of 6 to 3, the Supreme Court ruled (June 2) the seizure illegal and in violation of Article I of the Constitution—the first time that the Supreme Court passed on the inherent constitutional powers of a President. Following the ruling, the workers again walked out. United Mine Workers President John L. Lewis set up (June 18) a $10,000,000 fund for the support of the strikers, repayable "when you have achieved victory and convenience permits." The strike lasted 53 days (until July 25)—the longest and costliest strike in the nation's experience.

The Mississippi and Missouri rivers went (Apr. 14) on the worst rampage in history and ravaged eight Midwestern States, driving more than 65,000 persons from their homes.

The U. S. Supreme Court ruled (May 26) that radio broadcasts to "captive" audiences on public buses are not an invasion of privacy.

A shortage of potatoes prevailed (May-June) throughout the country. Black market prices ranged from $5 to $8 per 100-lb. bag; the ceiling price was $3.55. Spaghetti, rice, and noodles were substituted for the item on most menus.

The country sweltered (late June) under a heat wave which topped local records everywhere, particularly in the East; in New York the thermometer rose to 104 degrees, causing the death of seven persons in one day. The heat wave struck Texas (in August), taking a toll of 18 lives and costing the farmers and rangers at least $68,000,000 in the destruction of crops.

President Truman approved (July 3) the newly framed constitution of Puerto Rico; the territory became (July 25) the first commonwealth of the United States.

Southern California suffered (July 21) its severest earthquake in 46 years (see 1906), the effects of which were felt inland as far as Las Vegas, Nev., and Phoenix, Ariz. The mountain town of Tehachapi, Cal., where 11 persons were killed, was the focal point of the disaster, causing the Southern Pacific Railroad tunnel in the 7,000-foot-high Tehachapi Mountains to cave in.

The United States resumed diplomatic relations with Germany by signing (Aug. 2) a treaty of peace with the new West German Republic (Bundesrepublik Deutschland, proclaimed in 1949).

The nation's most treasured documents, the Declaration of Independence and the United States Constitution, were removed (Dec. 13) in Washington, D. C., amid military pomp and protection, from the Library of Congress to their permanent home in the National Archives Building, in accordance with the Federal Records Act (1950). (The documents were placed with the Bill of Rights, transferred in 1938.)

The Chesapeake Bay Bridge, Md., was opened (in July) as the world's third longest expressway, 4.3 miles in length.

The 53,300 ton, 990-foot long Atlantic superliner S.S. United States, costing $70,000,000, made (July 7) a record crossing on its maiden trip from New York to Le Havre in 3 days, 10 hours and 40 minutes, reducing by 10 hours and 2 minutes the 14-year-old record of the British Cunard liner Queen Elizabeth. (The United States made the return trip on July 11 in the record time of 3 days, 12 hours and 12 minutes.)

The New York Central railroad ran (Sept. 11) its last steam locomotive in passenger service.

American scientists of the Atomic Energy Commission conducted (Nov. 1) a thermonuclear test in the Marshall Islands, exploding a hydrogen bomb which tore a cavity, measuring a mile in diameter and 175 feet in depth at its lowest point, in the floor of the Pacific and completely obliterated the Eniwetok atoll.

In cooperation with the American Medical Association, as part of its sixth annual clinical session held in Denver, the National Broadcasting

Company televised (Dec. 2), for the first time, the Caesarean birth of a baby.

Mars Hill (N. C.) College honored the Negro slave named Joe who was posted in 1856 by his master, a trustee of the newly established school, as collateral for the final $1,000 of its building debt, by removing his remains to a resting place on the campus.

The year marked the quincentenary of the printing of the first Gutenberg Bible. To commemorate the event, the United States Post Office issued (Sept. 30) a special three-cent purple postage stamp; and two new English versions of the Bible appeared in America—the New Testament of the Confraternity Bible for Catholics, and the Old Testament of the National Council of Churches' Revised Standard Version for Protestants (their New Testament was published in 1946).

In books, fiction was represented by "East of Eden" (John Steinbeck), "Giant" (Edna Ferber), "The Gown of Glory" (Agnes Sligh Turnbull), "The Houses in Between" (Howard Spring; London, 1951), "My Cousin Rachel" (Daphne Du Maurier), "The Old Man and the Sea" (Ernest Hemingway; Pulitzer prize 1953), "The Saracen Blade" (Frank Yerby), "The Silver Chalice" (Thomas Costain). Prominent among non-fiction were such diverse publications as "Anne Frank: The Diary of a Young Girl," "The Power of Positive Thinking" (Norman Vincent Peale), "Show Biz" (Abel Green and Joe Laurie, Jr.), "U. S. A. Confidential" (Jack Lait and Lee Mortimer), "Witness" (Whittaker Chambers).

Broadway offered in plays, among others: "The Shrike" (Cort, Jan. 15; 161 perf.; Pulitzer prize 1952), "Mrs. McThing" (ANTA Playhouse, Feb. 20; 239 perf.), "The Male Animal" (City Center, Apr. 30; 213 perf.), "The Time of the Cuckoo" (Empire, Oct. 15; 263 perf.), "Dial 'M' for Murder" (Plymouth, Oct. 29; 552 perf.), "The Seven Year Itch" (Fulton, Nov. 20; 1,141 perf.). Beatrice Lillie entertained in an "Evening with Beatrice Lillie" (Booth, Oct. 2; 276 perf.). Distinguished foreign-language productions were provided by the Madeleine Renaud-Jean Louis Barrault Company of Paris and by Katina Paxinou's National Theatre of Greece. Competing with the long-running musicals "South Pacific," "Guys and Dolls," and "The King and I," were "Pal Joey" (Broadhurst, Jan. 3; 540 perf.) and "Wish You Were Here" (Imperial, June 25; 598 perf.).

Among motion pictures, "The Greatest Show on Earth" (Betty Hutton, Cornel Wilde) proved to be the top money-grossing film. Other pictures were: "Ivanhoe" (Robert Taylor, Elizabeth Taylor), "The Snows of Kilimanjaro" (Gregory Peck, Susan Hayward), "The African Queen" (Humphrey Bogart, Katharine Hepburn), "Hans Christian Andersen" (Danny Kaye), "Come Back, Little Sheba" (Shirley Booth, Burt Lancaster). The British film version of Offenbach's opera "The Tales of

Hoffmann," starring Moira Shearer, was shown in theatres and on television.

Cinerama, a new type of three-dimensional motion picture projection, was exhibited (Sept. 30) by its inventor Fred Waller in New York at the Broadway Theatre. (It was used during World War II for training gunnery students in the Air Corps, and was known as the Waller Flexible Gunnery Trainer.)

Under Government sponsorship, Gershwin's opera "Porgy and Bess" was performed in Europe on a tour which opened (Sept. 7) in Vienna.

Paying viewers in 31 motion picture houses in 27 American cities from coast to coast, situated as far south as Richmond, Va., and as far west as Los Angeles, witnessed (Dec. 21) in a telecast over a "closed circuit" (i.e., not visible on home sets) a full-length stage presentation of Bizet's opera "Carmen" at the Metropolitan Opera House in New York.

President Truman was seen and heard (May 3) on television by an estimated 30,000,000 people in a twenty-minute impromptu piano performance from the East Room of the White House. (He played Mozart's Ninth Sonata. The event, which was an unexpected feature of a television tour of the Executive Mansion, was broadcast by the three major networks. As a musician, our most piano-minded President violated no union regulations—he had been made an honorary member of the American Federation of Musicians by its president James C. Petrillo several years previously.)

The popular radio program "Amos 'n' Andy" (1929) reached (Nov. 16) its 10,000th broadcast.

What is probably the first serious musical composition inspired by atomic energy, an "Overture to the Dedication of a Nuclear Reactor" by Arthur Roberts, Associate Professor of Physics at the University of Rochester and a graduate of the Manhattan School of Music in New York, was played (Mar. 19) by the Oak Ridge, Tenn., Symphony Orchestra under Waldo Cohn, its conductor and a biochemist. (The principal theme, played by clarinets with oboes as Geiger counters, was derived from the atomic number of uranium; plutonium was delineated by scale steps of nine and four, its atomic number 94; the Atomic Energy Commission was represented by the notes of its initials.)

Some 50,000 boxing fans in New York's Yankee Stadium saw (June 25) the superlative "Sugar" Ray Robinson, holder of the middleweight and welterweight titles, so exhausted and dazed by the extreme heat of the night and the ringside temperature that he was unable to respond to the bell in the 14th round of his bout with the lightheavyweight title holder, Joey Maxim, in an attempt to become a triplecrown champion (a distinction held previously only by Robert "Bob" Fitzsimmons and Henry Armstrong). Referee Ruby Goldstein suc-

cumbed to the heat in the 10th round and was replaced by Ray Miller—
the first time such an incident occurred.

In Philadelphia, "Rocky" Marciano defeated (Sept. 23) "Jersey Joe"
Walcott in the 13th round for the heavyweight boxing championship.
(The bout was televised in a closed circuit to 125,000 paying spectators
in 50 motion picture theatres across the country.)

The United States maintained its supremacy in international sports
events at the Fifteenth Olympiad, held in Helsinki, Finland, by collecting
614 points in the face of strong opposition from 69 nations, especially
from Russia. The latter, competing for the first time, achieved second
place with 553½ points. The ritual of the opening day ceremony was
interrupted by the sudden and unexpected appearance on the scene of a
"lady in white," thought by some to have been Soviet-inspired, in a
spectacular attempt to make a plea for peace.

Television brought for the first time into American homes the national
conventions of the two major political parties, held in Chicago (Republican, July 7-12 inclusive; Democratic, July 21-26 inclusive).

In the national elections, the Republicans broke the Democratic
Party's 20-year hold on the White House, with Dwight D. Eisenhower's
smashing victory over Illinois Governor Adlai E. Stevenson. Urged by
the nation's press, industry, and churches, 61,547,861 citizens went to
the polls—the largest in American history—giving Eisenhower a plurality
of 6,616,233 votes. President Truman declined (Mar. 19) to be a
candidate. General Eisenhower, at his own request, was retired (June 3)
from the United States Army, after 37 years of service; he formally
resigned (July 18), and was free to accept the nomination. The Republican slogan was "I Like Ike," as he was popularly called.

In accordance with a campaign promise, President-elect Eisenhower
flew (Nov. 29) to Korea to review the military situation as a preliminary
step to "bring the boys home."

৪ 1953

Allez-Vous-En, Go Away (Can-Can). w., m., Cole Porter. Buxton Hill
Music Corp., cop. 1953 by Cole Porter.

And This Is My Beloved (Kismet). w., m., Robert Wright and George
Forrest [music based on a theme from the third movement, "Nocturne,"
of Alexander Borodin's String Quartet No. 2]. Frank Music Corp., cop.
1953.

April in Portugal. Portuguese words, José Galhardo. English words,

Jimmy Kennedy. m., Raul Ferrão. Chappel & Co., Inc., cop. 1947 and 1949; cop. 1953 by Chappel & Co., Inc.

Baubles, Bangles and Beads (Kismet). w., m., Robert Wright and George Forrest [music "based on themes of A. Borodin"]. Frank Music Corp., cop. 1953.

C'est Magnifique (Can-Can). w., m., Cole Porter. Buxton Hill Music Corp., cop. 1953 by Cole Porter.

Changing Partners. w., Joe Darion. m., Larry Coleman. Porgie Music Corp., cop. 1953.

Crying in the Chapel. w., m., Artie Glenn. Knoxville, Tenn.: Valley Publishers, Inc., cop. 1953.

A Dear John Letter. w., m., Billy Barton, Lewis Talley and Fuzzy Owen. Hollywood, Cal.: American Music, Inc., cop. 1953.

Dragnet. Instrumental. m., Walter Schumann. Alamo Music, Inc., cop. 1953 by Schumann Music Co.

Ebb Tide. w., Carl Sigman. m., Robert Maxwell. Robbins Music Corp., cop. 1953.

Eh, Cumpari! w., m., traditional (Italian), transcribed by Julius La Rosa and Archie Bleyer. Rosarch Publishing Corp., cop. 1953.

Eternally (*film:* Limelight). w., Geoffrey Parsons. m., Charles Chaplin. Bourne, Inc., cop. 1953. (Vocal version of "The Terry Theme"—see below.)

Gambler's Guitar. w., m., Jim Lowe. Chicago: Frederick Music Co., cop. 1953.

Hi-Lili, Hi-Lo (*film:* Lili). w., Helen Deutsch. m., Bronislau Kaper. Robbins Music Corp., cop. 1952 by Loew's Incorporated. (Popularized in 1953 with the showing of the film.)

I Am in Love (Can-Can). w., m., Cole Porter. Buxton Hill Music Corp., cop. 1953 by Cole Porter.

I Believe. w., m., Erwin Drake, Irvin Graham, Jimmy Shirl and Al Stillman. Cromwell Music, Inc., cop. 1952; cop. 1953.

I Love Paris (Can-Can). w., m., Cole Porter. Buxton Hill Music Corp., cop. 1953 by Cole Porter.

Istanbul. w., Jimmy Kennedy. m., Nat Simon. Alamo Music, Inc., cop. 1953.

It's All Right with Me (Can-Can). w., m., Cole Porter. Buxton Hill Music Corp., cop. 1953 by Cole Porter.

Make Love to Me! w., Bill Norvas and Allan Copeland. m., Leon Roppolo, Paul Mares, Benny Pollack, George Brunes, Mel Stitzel and Walter Melrose. Melrose Music Corp., cop. 1953.

My Love, My Love. w., Bob Haymes. m., Nick Acquaviva. Meridan Music Corp., cop. 1952, cop. 1953.

No Other Love (Me and Juliet). w., Oscar Hammerstein, 2nd. m., Richard Rodgers. Williamson Music, Inc., cop. 1953 by Richard Rodgers and Oscar Hammerstein, 2nd.

"O." w., Byron Gay. m., Byron Gay and Arnold Johnson. Leo Feist, Inc., cop. 1919; renewed 1947; cop. 1953.

Oh Happy Day. w., m., Nancy Binns Reed and Don Howard Koplow. Bregmann, Vocco & Conn, Inc., cop. 1953.

Oh! My Pa-pa (*Swiss film:* Fireworks). German words and music, Paul Burkhard. English words, John Turner and Geoffrey Parsons. Shapiro, Bernstein & Co., Inc., cop. 1948 and 1950 by Musikverlag und Bühnenvertrieb Zürich A. G., Zürich, Switzerland; cop. 1953 by Shapiro, Bernstein & Co., Inc.

Rags to Riches. w., m., Richard Adler and Jerry Ross. Saunders Publications, Inc., cop. 1953.

Rock Around the Clock. w., m., Max C. Freedman and Jimmy De Knight. Philadelphia: Myers Music, cop. 1953.

Ruby (*film:* Ruby Gentry). w., Mitchell Parish. m., Heinz Roemheld. Miller Music Corp., cop. 1953.

Say You're Mine Again. w., m., Charles Nathan and Dave Heisler. Blue-River Music Corp., cop. 1952; cop. 1953 (selling agent, Meridan Music Corp.).

Secret Love (*film:* Calamity Jane). w., Paul Francis Webster. m., Sammy Fain. Remick Music Corp., cop. 1953. (Academy Award Winner, 1953.)

The Song from Moulin Rouge—Where Is Your Heart (*film:* Moulin Rouge). w., William Engvick. m., Georges Auric. Broadcast Music, Inc., cop. 1953.

Stranger in Paradise (Kismet). w., m., Robert Wright and George Forrest [music based on a theme from the Polovetzian Dances of Alexander Borodin's opera "Prince Igor"]. Frank Music Corp., cop. 1953.

That Doggie in the Window. w., m., Bob Merrill. Santly-Joy, Inc., cop. 1953.

That's Amoré—That's Love (*film:* The Caddy). w., Jack Brooks. m., Harry Warren. Paramount Music Corp., cop. 1953.

The Terry Theme. Instrumental. m., Charles Chaplin. Bourne, Inc., cop. 1953. (Published as a song, "Eternally"—see above.)

Vaya con Dios. w., m., Larry Russell, Inez James and Buddy Pepper. Ardmore Music Corp., cop. 1953.

With These Hands. w., Benny Davis. m., Abner Silver. Ben Bloom Music Corp., cop. 1950. (Popularized in 1953.)

You Alone—Solo Tu. w., Al Stillman. m., Robert Allen. Roncom Music Co., cop. 1953.

You, You. You. w., Robert Mellin. m., Lotar Olias. Robert Mellin, Inc., cop. 1952; cop. 1953 by Edition Accord; assigned to Zodiac Music Corp.; assigned 1953 to Robert Mellin, Inc.

Dwight David Eisenhower, Republican, of Texas, was inaugurated 34th President. The ceremonies, preceded by segments of the parade televised by the use of portable transmitters in automobiles, were telecast (Jan. 20) to the nation through the facilities of 125 stations.

The war in Korea entered its final stages. After repeated delays and disagreements, an armistice was signed (July 27; July 26, EST). According to the Department of Defense, 5,720,000 Americans were involved in the conflict. The total number of casualties, in the four branches of the armed service, amounted to 157,530 (33,629 killed in action; 20,617 dead from other causes; 103,284 wounded).

Republican Senator Joseph Raymond McCarthy, of Wisconsin, as chairman of the Senate Permanent Investigating Subcommittee loomed before the nation, as a ruthless prober into possible Communist connections of prominent Americans, his methods giving rise to the term "McCarthyism."

To rectify an oversight in 1803, the House Interior Committee voted (May 5) "to admit Ohio to the union."

Czechoslovakia released (May 16) Associated Press correspondent William N. Oatis, imprisoned in July 1951 on spy charges.

A bill, signed (May 20) by the President, granted coastal states title to all submerged lands within their boundaries three miles out to sea, except in the Gulf of Mexico, where the claims of Florida and Texas extend to a 10½-mile limit.

The American people witnessed (June 2) on television film the coronation of Queen Elizabeth II in Westminster Abbey, London.

The House Un-American Activities Committee subpoenaed (Nov. 6) ex-President Truman to answer Attorney General Herbert Brownell's charge that Truman had appointed the late Harry Dexter White, reported by the Federal Bureau of Investigation as spying for the Soviet Union, to the responsible post of executive director of the International Monetary Fund. President Eisenhower opposed (Nov. 11) the subpoena, on the basis that Truman would not knowingly have committed an act detrimental to the United States. Truman rejected (Nov. 12) the subpoena, contending the order was an invasion of Presidential powers by a "trespassing" Congress. Official records showed that the appointment had been confirmed without debate by the Senate in 1946.

An eleven-day strike of some 400 photoengravers in New York caused (Nov. 28-Dec. 9) six major metropolitan newspapers to suspend publication; about 20,000 other newspaper workers refused to cross the picket lines.

The Bureau of the Mint issued a commemorative half-dollar piece in honor of two eminent Negroes, Booker Taliaferro Washington and George Washington Carver.

Sagamore Hill, the summer home of 26th President Theodore Roosevelt, at Oyster Bay, Long Island, N. Y., was dedicated (June 14) as a national shrine by President Eisenhower.

General George C. Marshall received the Nobel prize for peace.

Among books, continuing as best sellers from the previous year, were "The Power of Positive Thinking," "A Man Called Peter," "The Silver Chalice," and the new Revised Standard Version of the Bible. In line with the first named were "Life Is Worth Living" (Fulton J. Sheen), and "The Greatest Faith Ever Known" (Fulton Oursler)—the sales of all three carrying over into the next year. Fiction contributed: "Battle Cry" (Leon M. Uris), "Beyond This Place" (A. J. Cronin), "The Bridges of Toko-Ri" (James Michener), "Come, My Beloved" (Pearl S. Buck), "Desiree" (Annemarie Selinko), "The High and the Mighty" (Ernest K. Gann), "The Robe" ((Lloyd Douglas), "Too Late the Phalarope" (Alan Paton), "Time and Time Again" (James Hilton), "The Unconquered" (Ben Ames Williams).

The New York Metropolitan Opera House produced (Feb. 14) the American première of Igor Stravinsky's English opera "The Rake's Progress."

The Broadway stage produced, among other plays: "The Fifth Season" (Cort, Jan. 23; 653 perf.), "Picnic" (Music Box, Feb. 19; 485 perf.; Pulitzer prize 1953), "My Three Angels" (Morosco, Mar. 11; 344 perf.), "Tea and Sympathy" (Ethel Barrymore, Sept. 30; 712 perf.), "The Teahouse of the August Moon" (Martin Beck, Oct. 15; 1,027 perf.; Pulitzer prize 1954), "The Solid Gold Cadillac" (Belasco, Nov. 5; 532 perf.), "Sabrina Fair" (National, Nov. 11; 302 perf.), "Oh, Men! Oh, Women!" (Henry Miller's, Dec. 17; 390 perf.), "The Remarkable Mr. Pennypacker" (Coronet, Dec. 30; 221 perf.). An off-Broadway production to enjoy a run was "The World of Sholem Aleichem" (Barbizon-Plaza, Sept. 11; 306 perf.). The musicals included: "Hazel Flagg" (Mark Hellinger, Feb. 11; 190 perf.), "Wonderful Town" (Winter Garden, Feb. 25; 556 perf.), "Can-Can" (Shubert, May 7; 892 perf.), "Me and Juliet" (Majestic, May 28; 358 perf.), "Kismet" (Ziegfeld, Dec. 3; 583 perf.), "John Murray Anderson's Almanac" (Imperial, Dec. 10; 227 perf.). Pianist Victor Borge delighted audiences with his one-man show "Comedy in Music" (John Golden, Oct. 2; 849 perf.) until Jan. 21, 1956. A revival of Gershwin's "Porgy and Bess" (Ziegfeld, Mar. 9; 312 perf.) featured the Negro soprano Leontyne Price of future New York Metropolitan Opera fame.

In films, following "Cinerama" (1952), the motion picture industry exhibited other processes of wide-screen projection, in "Bwana Devil" (3-dimension Natural Vision), "The Man in the Dark" (3-D film), "The Robe" (CinemaScope). "The Robe" (Richard Burton, Jean Simmons, Victor Mature), based on the year's best selling novel, rose also to top-money in films. Other pictures were: "The Band Wagon" (Fred Astaire), "Call Me Madam" (Ethel Merman), "From Here to Eternity" (Montgomery Clift, Burt Lancaster, Deborah Kerr, Frank Sinatra), "Gentlemen Prefer Blondes" (Marilyn Monroe, Jane Russell), "How to Marry a Millionaire" (Marilyn Monroe, Betty Grable, Lauren Bacall), "Julius Caesar" (all-star cast), "Lili" (Leslie Caron), "Moulin Rouge" (José Ferrer), "Peter Pan" (Walt Disney animated drawings), "Shane" (Alan Ladd, Van Heflin), "Victory at Sea" (documentary). A controversial film was the Lutheran-sponsored "Martin Luther" (Niall Mac-Ginis).

In television, the controversy over a method for the transmission of color resolved itself in favor of the "compatible" color system of the Radio Corporation of America, when the Columbia Broadcasting System withdrew (in March) its process. (The CBS method required a special mechanism for transforming color into black and white in television sets unequipped to receive color; that of the RCA made reception available either in color or in black and white.)

The game of scrabble, devised about 20 years ago by Alfred Butts, was a popular pastime.

By defeating the Brooklyn (Dodgers) National League baseball club, four games to two, the New York (Yankees) American League team became the first to win five successive world championships.

Deaths of the year included: former heavyweight boxing champion "Jim" (James J.) Jeffries, 77 (Mar. 3), in Burbank, Cal.; actress Maude Adams (the original American "Peter Pan," 1906), 80 (July 17), in Tannersville, N. Y.; America's leading playwright Eugene Gladstone O'Neill, 65 (Nov. 27), in Boston.

Joseph V. Stalin, Premier of the Soviet Union, died (Mar. 5), aged 73, in the Kremlin in Moscow and was buried beside his predecessor Lenin in the latter's tomb in Red Square. Known as the "Man of Steel," he was dictator for 29 years. Present at the funeral was Nikita S. Khrushchev, who was to succeed in 1958 to the premiership.

ঌ 1954

All of You (Silk Stockings). w., m., Cole Porter. Buxton Hill Music Corp., cop. 1954.

Cara Mia. w., m., Tulio Tranpani and Lee Lange. Leo Feist, Inc., cop. 1954.

Cross Over the Bridge. w., m., Bennie Benjamin and George Weiss. Laurel Music Corp., cop. 1954.

Fanny (Fanny). w., m., Harold Rome. Chappell & Co., Inc., cop. 1954.

The Happy Wanderer. w., Antonia Ridge. m., Friedrich W. Möller. Sam Fox Publishing Co., cop. 1954 by Bosworth & Co., Ltd., London.

Here. w., m., Dorcas Cochran and Harold Grant [music based on the soprano aria "Caro Nome" from Verdi's opera "Rigoletto"]. Hill and Range Songs, Inc., cop. 1954.

Hernando's Hideaway (The Pajama Game). w., m., Richard Adler and Jerry Ross. Frank Music Corp., cop. 1954.

Hey There (The Pajama Game). w., m., Richard Adler and Jerry Ross. Frank Music Corp., cop. 1954.

The High and the Mighty (*film:* The High and the Mighty). w., Ned Washington. m., Dimitri Tiomkin. M. Witmark & Sons, cop. 1954.

Home for the Holidays. w., Al Stillman. m., Robert Allen. Roncom Music Co., cop. 1954.

I'm Walking Behind You. w., m., Billy Reid. London: The Peter Maurice Co., Ltd., cop. 1953. (Popularized in the United States in 1954; selling agent, Leeds Music Corp., New York.)

I Get So Lonely. *See below:* **Oh, Baby Mine.**

If I Give My Heart to You. w., m., Jimmie Crane, Al Jacobs and Jimmy Brewster. Miller Music Corp., cop. 1953; cop. 1954.

Joey. w., m., Herb Wiener, James J. Kriegsman and Salmirs-Bernstein. Lowell Music Corp., cop. 1952. (Popularized in 1954.)

Let Me Go, Lover! w., m., Jenny Lou Carson. Special lyrics, Al Hill. Hill & Range Songs, Inc., cop. 1953 as "Let Me Go, Devil!"; new version, cop. 1954.

Little Things Mean a Lot. w., m., Edith Lindeman and Carl Stutz. Leo Feist, Inc., cop. 1954.

Lost in Loveliness (The Girl in Pink Tights). w., Leon Robin. m., Sigmund Romberg. Chappell & Co., Inc., cop. 1954.

Make Yourself Comfortable. w., m., Bob Merrill. Rylan Music Corp., cop. 1954.

Mambo Italiano. w., m., Bob Merrill. Rylan Music Corp., cop. 1954.

The Man That Got Away (*film:* A Star Is Born). w., Ira Gershwin. m., Harold Arlen. Harwin Music Corp., cop. 1954 (selling agent, Edwin H. Morris & Co., Inc.).

Mister Sandman. w., m., Pat Ballard. Edwin H. Morris & Co., Inc., cop. 1954.

The Naughty Lady of Shady Lane. w., m., Sid Tepper and Roy C. Bennett. George Paxton, Inc., cop. 1954.

Oh, Baby Mine—I Get So Lonely. w., m., Pat Ballard. Melrose Music Corp., cop. 1953; cop. 1954.

Papa Loves Mambo. w., m., Al Hoffmann, Dick Manning and Bix Reichner. Shapiro, Bernstein & Co., Inc., cop. 1954.

Shake, Rattle and Roll. w., m., Charles Calhoun. Criterion Music Corp., cop. 1954 by Progressive Music Co., Inc.

Sh-Boom. w., m., James Keyes, Claude Feaster, Carl Feaster, Floyd F. McRae and James Edwards. Hill and Range Songs, Inc., cop. 1954.

Somebody Bad Stole de Wedding Bell. w., Bob Hilliard. m., Dave Mann. Mercedes Music Corp., cop. 1954.

Steam Heat (The Pajama Game). w., m., Richard Adler and Jerry Ross. Frank Music Corp., cop. 1954.

Teach Me Tonight. w., Sammy Cahn. m., Gene DePaul. Leeds Music Corp., cop. 1953; cop. 1954 by The Hub Music Co.

That's All I Want from You. w., m., M. Rotha. Weiss & Barry, Inc., cop. 1954.

This Ole House. w., m., Stuart Hamblen. Arcadia, Cal.: Hamblen Music Co., cop. 1954.

Three Coins in the Fountain (*film:* Three Coins in the Fountain). w., Sammy Cahn. m., Jule Styne. Robbins Music Corp., cop. 1954. (Academy Award Winner, 1954)

Wanted. w., m., Jack Fulton and Lois Steele. M. Witmark & Sons, cop. 1954.

Young and Foolish (Plain and Fancy). w., Arnold B. Horwitt. m., Albert Hague. Chappell & Co., Inc., cop. 1954.

Young at Heart. w., Carolyn Leigh. m., Johnny Richards. Sunbeam Music Corp., cop. 1954.

The United States launched two powerful war craft: the world's first atom-powered submarine (Jan. 21)—the 2,800-ton 300-foot "Nautilus," at Groton, Conn., and the world's largest war vessel (Dec. 11)—the 59,650-ton aircraft carrier "Forrestal," at Newport News, Va.

Four terrorists, three men and a woman, of the Puerto Rican "Nationalist" independence movement, fired (Mar. 1) a volley of bullets from the Ladies Gallery in the House of Representatives in Washington, D.C., during the morning session, wounding five Congressmen.

The Atomic Energy Commission conducted (Mar. 1, Mar. 26, Apr. 6) thermonuclear tests at Pacific Proving Grounds (Bikini Atoll, Marshall Islands). (31 Americans, 236 natives, and 23 Japanese fishermen in the area received injuries from radio-active particles during the first experiment. The United States offered Japan an indemnity of $800,000 for the inflictions on her nationals.)

Rival longshoremen unions tied up (Mar. 5-Apr. 3) the port of New York in the longest strike in the city's history, resulting in a loss of $500,000,000 to industry.

In a unanimous decision, the nine judges of the United States Supreme Court ruled (May 17) racial segregation unconstitutional in public schools.

Haile Selassie, Emperor of Ethiopia, visited (May-June) the United States at the invitation of President Eisenhower.

A spectacular air-raid drill with squadrons of airplanes dropping theoretical bombs involved (June 14) the United States, Hawaii, Alaska, Puerto Rico, the Virgin Islands and ten provinces of Canada in the world's largest demonstration of its kind.

Migratory labor was an acute problem in California and Texas, Mexican farm laborers having illegally entered the United States in quest of the few available jobs. (A roundup in June netted some 55,000 violators in California.)

The Communist Control Act outlawed (Aug. 24) the Communist party in the United States.

Chinese Communist bombing planes, shelling Nationalist-controlled Formosa, killed (Sept. 3) two U. S. Army officers on Quemoy Island.

The United States established (Sept. 9), by agreement, air bases in Libya, Africa.

Queen Mother Elizabeth of England toured (Oct.-Nov.) the United States and Canada on a 24-day visit.

The United States and Canada agreed (Nov. 19) upon the construction of a 3,000-mile radar warning system, extending across arctic Canada from Alaska to Greenland.

The Senate rebuked (Dec. 2), by a vote of 67 to 22, Republican Senator Joseph R. McCarthy of Wisconsin for his tactics and behavior as chairman of the public hearings (Apr. 22-June 27) by the Senate Permanent Investigating subcommittee of U. S. Army Department officials. Thereafter his influence and "McCarthyism" began to wane.

Violent Caribbean hurricanes blazed paths of destruction and death across the Atlantic states; named for women, they were "Carol" (Aug. 30-31), "Edna" (Sept. 11), and "Hazel" (Oct. 15-16).

Juvenile delinquency was becoming a major civic concern everywhere.

A 75-foot statue by sculptor Felix de Weldon, depicting the flag raising on Iwo Island in the Pacific during World War II, was dedicated (Nov. 10) in Arlington National Cemetery, Arlington, Va., in honor of the U. S. Marine Corps.

A controversy over the effects of cigarette-smoking as an alleged cause of lung cancer agitated the public, the tobacco industry, and the medical profession.

Novelist Ernest Hemingway and his wife were injured (Jan. 24) in East Africa, when a rescue plane crashed on takeoff at Butiaba, on Lake Albert, after their own plane had crashed the day before near Murchinson Falls.

Once eminent poet and novelist Maxwell Bodenheim, 63, and his wife Ruth, 35, were murdered (Feb. 8) by a maniac in their $5-a-week furnished room in the Greenwich Village section of New York.

McCall's magazine coined, in the editorial of its May issue, a new word—"togetherness."

Among books, there was a prolific output of fiction: "Benton's Row" (Frank Yerby), "Beyond This Place" (A. J. Cronin), "Blue Hurricane" (F. van Wyck Mason), "The Dollmaker" (Harriet Arnouw), "A Fable" (William Faulkner; Pulitzer prize 1955), "Good Morning, Miss Dove" (Frances Gary Patton), "Hadrian's Memoirs" (Marguerite Yourcenar), "The High and the Mighty" (Ernest Kellogg Gann), "High Water" (Richard Bissell), "The Iron Maiden" (Edwin Lanham), "Katherine" (Anya Seton), "Lord Vanity" (Samuel Shellabarger), "Love Is Eternal" (Irving Stone), "Mary Anne " (Daphne du Maurier), "No Time for Sergeants" (Mac Hyman), "Not as a Stranger" (Morton Thompson), "The Pride of the Peacock" (Ruth Chatterton), "Reunion" (Merle Miller), "The Royal Box" (Frances Parkinson Keyes), "Sweet Thursday" (John Steinbeck), "The View from Pompey's Head" (Hamilton Basso). "The Robe" (1953) continued to head the list as the best seller.

Conspicuous among non-fiction were: "Call to Greatness" (Adlai E. Stevenson), "The Mind Alive" (Harry and Benaro Overstreet), "TNT, the Power Within You" (Charles Myron Bristol), "Second Tree from the Corner" (E. B. White), "I'll Cry Tomorrow" (Lillian Roth).

Arturo Toscanini, 87, retired (Apr. 4) as conductor of the NBC Symphony Orchestra, closing a musical career of over 68 years.

The seventieth gala opening (Nov. 8) of the New York Metropolitan Opera House, comprising acts from four operas, was televised before paying audiences in 32 theatres in more than 25 cities.

Sponsored by the State Department, Gershwin's opera "Porgy and Bess" was performed by a Negro company on an extended goodwill tour (1954-55) of Europe, the Near East, Africa, South and Central America.

On the Broadway stage, two outstanding musicals ended their runs: "South Pacific" (1949) with 1,925 performances (Jan. 16), and "The King and I" (1951) with 1,246 performances (Mar. 20). The plays produced included: "Caine Mutiny Court Martial" (Plymouth, Jan. 20; 405 perf.), "King of Hearts" (Lyceum, Apr. 1; 276 perf.), "Anniversary Waltz" (Broadhurst, Apr. 7; 615 perf.), "Bad Seed" (Forty-Sixth Street, Dec. 8, 326 perf.), "Lunatics and Lovers" (Broadhurst, Dec. 13; 344 perf.), "Witness for the Prosecution" (Henry Miller's, Dec. 16; 646 perf.), "Anastasia" (Lyceum, Dec. 29; 284 perf.). New musicals included: "By the Beautiful Sea" (Majestic, Apr. 8; 270 perf.), "The Pajama Game" (St. James, May 13; 1,061 perf.), "The Boy Friend" (Royale, Sept. 30; 485 perf.), "Fanny" (Majestic, Nov. 4; 887 perf.) "Mrs. Patterson" (National, Dec. 1; 310 perf.). Menotti produced a new opera, "The Saint of Bleecker Street" (Broadway, Dec. 27; 92 perf. Pulitzer prize 1955). Kurt Weill's "The Threepenny Opera" was revived in a small off-Broadway theatre (Theatre de Lys, Mar. 10).

"White Christmas" (Bing Crosby, Danny Kaye) was the top-money film. Other pictures were: "The Caine Mutiny" (Humphrey Bogart) "The Country Girl" (Bing Crosby, Grace Kelly, William Holden), "Desiree" (Marlon Brando, Jean Simmons), "The Glenn Miller Story" (James Stewart, June Allyson), "The High and the Mighty" (John Wayne), "Magnificent Obsession" (Jane Wyman, Rock Hudson), "Rear Window" (James Stewart, Grace Kelly), "Seven Brides for Seven Brothers" (Jane Powell, Howard Keel), "A Star Is Born" (Judy Garland James Mason), "There's No Business Like Show Business" (Ethel Merman, Donald O'Connor, Marilyn Monroe), "Three Coins in the Fountain" (Clifton Webb, Dorothy McGuire). Two notable foreign films were "Ugetsu," from Japan, and a screen version of Verdi's opera "Aida," from Italy.

The Cuban mambo suddenly became a craze with ballroom dancers (The dance, devised by bandleader Perez Prado, had been introduced by him in the United States, by way of Mexico, in 1949.)

The games of bingo and raffles were legalized (Apr. 20) in New Jersey.

✌ 1955

Ain't That a Shame! w., m., Antoine Domino and Dave Bartholomew. Hollywood, Cal.: Commodore Music Corp., cop. 1955.

All at Once You Love Her (Pipe Dream). w., Oscar Hammerstein 2nd. m., Richard Rodgers. Williamson Music, Inc., cop. 1955 by Richard Rodgers and Oscar Hammerstein 2nd.

Ballad of Davy Crockett (*film:* **Davy Crockett**). w., Tom Blackburn. m., George Bruns. Wonderland Music Co., cop. 1954 by Walt Disney Productions; assigned to Wonderland Music Co. (Popularized in 1955.)

The Bible Tells Me So. w., m., Dale Evans. Paramount-Roy Rogers Music Co., Inc., cop. 1955 (selling agent, Famous Music Corp.).

A Blossom Fell. w., m., Howard Barnes, Harold Cornelius and Dominic John. Shapiro, Bernstein & Co., Inc., cop. 1954; cop. 1955 by John Fields Music Co., Ltd., London.

Cherry Pink and Apple Blossom White. English words, Mack David. French words, Jacques Larue. m., Louiquy. Chappell & Co., Inc., cop. 1950 by Hortensia-Music, Paris; assigned 1950 to Chappell & Co., Inc., New York; cop. 1951 by Chappell & Co., Inc. (Popularized in 1955.)

The Crazy Otto Rag. w., Edward R. White. m., Mack Wolfson. George Pincus Music Corp., cop. 1955.

Cry Me a River. w., m., Arthur Hamilton. Saunders Publications, Inc., cop. 1953; cop. 1955.

Dance with Me, Henry. w., m., Etta James. Modern Music Publications, cop. 1955.

Domani—Tomorrow. w., Tony Velona. m., Ulpio Minucci. Montauk Music Co., Inc., cop. 1955 (selling agent, Larry Spier, Inc.).

Don't Be Angry. w., m., Napoleon Brown, Rose Marie McCoy, and Fred Mendelssohn. Republic Music Corp., cop. 1955 by Savoy Music Co.; assigned 1955 to Republic Music Corp.

Dungaree Doll. w., Ben Raleigh. m., Sherman Edwards. Edward B. Marks Music Corp., cop. 1955.

Forgive My Heart. w., Sammy Gallop. m., Chester Conn. Bregman, Vocco & Conn, Inc., cop. 1955.

Hard to Get. w., m., Jack Segal. M. Witmark & Sons, cop. 1955.

He. w., Richard Mullan. m., Jack Richards. Avas Music Publishing Co., Inc., cop. 1954 (selling agent, Key Music). (Popularized in 1955.)

Heart (Damn Yankees). w., m., Richard Adler and Jerry Ross. Frank Music Corp., cop. 1955.

Hey, Mr. Banjo. w., m., Freddy Morgan and Norman Malkin. Mills Music, Inc., cop. 1955.

Honey Babe (*film:* **Battle Cry**). w., Paul Francis Webster. m., Max Steiner. M. Witmark & Sons, cop. 1954; cop. 1955.

How Important Can It Be? w., m., Bennie Benjamin and George Weiss. Aspen Music Corp., cop. 1955.

Hummingbird. w., m., Don Robertson. Ross Jungnickel, Inc., cop. 1955 (selling agent, Hill and Range Songs, Inc.).

I'll Never Stop Loving You (*film:* **Love Me or Leave Me**). w., Sammy Cahn. m., Nicholas Brodszky. Leo Feist, Inc., cop. 1955.

Impatient Years. w., Sammy Cahn. m., James van Heusen. Barton Music Corp., cop. 1955.

It's Almost Tomorrow. w., Wade Buff. m., Gene Adkinson. Northern Music Corp., cop. 1953 by Wade Buff and Gene Adkinson; assigned to Northern Music Corp.; cop. 1955 by Northern Music Corp. (selling agent, Keys Music, Inc.).

Ko Ko Mo—I Love You So. w., m., Forest Wilson, Jake Porter, and Eunice Levy. Meridian Music Corp., cop. 1955.

Learnin' the Blues. w., m., Dolores Vicki Silvers. Barton Music Corp., cop. 1955.

Love and Marriage (*TV production:* **Our Town**). w., Sammy Cahn. m., James Van Heusen. Barton Music Corp., cop. 1955.

Love Is a Many-Splendored Thing (*film:* **Love Is a Many-Splendored Thing**). w., Paul Francis Webster. m., Sammy Fain. Miller Music Corp., cop. 1955 by Twentieth Century Music Corp. (Academy Award Winner, 1955.)

Maybellene. w. m., Chuck Berry, Russ Frato, and Alan Freed. Arc Music Corp., cop. 1955.

Melody of Love. w., Tom Glazer. m., H. Engelmann. Shapiro, Bernstein & Co., Inc., cop. 1903 by Theodore Presser; renewed and assigned 1942 to Shapiro, Bernstein & Co., Inc.; cop. 1954 by Theodore Presser Co. (Popularized in 1955.)

Moments to Remember. w., Al Stillman. m., Robert Allen. Beaver Music Publishing Corp., cop. 1955 (selling agent, Larry Spier, Inc.).

Only You. w., m., Buck Ram and Ande Rand. Wildwood Music, Inc., cop. 1955 (selling agent, Robert Mellin, Inc.).

Open Up Your Heart. w., m., Stuart Hamblen. Hamblen Music Co., cop. 1955 (selling agent, Keys Music, Inc.).

Pete Kelly's Blues (*film:* **Pete Kelly's Blues**). w., Sammy Cahn. m., Ray Heinsdorf. Mark VII Music, cop. 1955 (selling agent, Edwin H. Morris & Co., Inc.).

The Rock and Roll Waltz. w., Dick Ware. m., Shorty Allen. Sheldon Music, Inc., cop. 1955.

Seventeen. w., m., John Young Jr., Chuck Gorman, and Boyd Bennett. Lois Publishing Co., cop. 1955 (selling agent, Hill and Range Songs, Inc.).

Sincerely. w., m., Harvey Fuqua and Alan Freed. Regent Music Corp., cop. 1954 by Arc Music Corp.

Sixteen Tons. w., m., Merle Travis. Hollywood, Cal.: American Music, Inc., cop. 1947. (Popularized in 1955.)

Something's Gotta Give (*film:* **Daddy Long Legs**). w., m., Johnny Mercer. Robbins Music Corp., cop. 1954; cop. 1955.

Sweet and Gentle. w., m., Otillio and George Thorn. Peer International Corp., cop. 1955 (selling agent, Southern Music Publishing Co., Inc.).

A Teen-Age Prayer. w., m., Bix Reichner and Bernie Lowe. La Salle Publishers, Inc., cop. 1955 (selling agent, Southern Music Publishing Co.).

The Tender Trap (*film:* **The Tender Trap**). w., Sammy Cahn. m., James Van Heusen. Barton Music Corp., cop. 1955.

Tweedle Dee. w., m., Winfield Scott. Criterion Music Corp., cop. 1954 by Progressive Music Co., Inc.

Two Lost Souls (**Damn Yankees**). w., m., Richard Adler and Jerry Ross. Frank Music Corp., cop. 1955.

Unchained Melody (*film:* **Unchained**). w., Hy Zaret. m., Alex North. Frank Music Corp., cop. 1955.

Unsuspecting Heart. w., Freddy James. m., Joe Beal, Bob Singer, and Joe Shank. Tee Pee Music Co., cop. 1955.

Wake the Town and Tell the People. w., Sammy Gallop. m., Jerry Livingston. Joy Music, Inc., cop. 1954; cop. 1955.

Whatever Lola Wants (**Damn Yankees**). w., m., Richard Adler and Jerry Ross. Frank Music Corp., cop. 1955.

The Yellow Rose of Texas. w., m. (adapted), Don George. Planetary Music Publishing Corp., cop. 1955.

Dr. Jonas Edward Salk, New York-born physician, perfected the vaccine against paralytic polio, which bears his name.

The Soviet Union expressed (June 25), for the first time, "regret" over the firing by two of its MIG planes on a United States naval patrol plane on a routine flight (June 22) over Bering Strait. (Seven crewmen were injured; Russia paid 50 per cent of the damage, on Mar. 17, 1956.)

The People's Republic of China (Communist) released (Aug. 3) eleven American airmen, shot down in 1953 for "spying" near Antung, Manchuria.

President Eisenhower suffered (Sept. 24) a heart attack in Denver while vacationing in Colorado. (The illness created grave concern throughout the nation. The President left Fitzsimmons Army Hospital in Denver on Nov. 11 for convalescence on his Gettysburg farm.)

A time bomb in an airplane, placed by a 23-year-old son in his mother's luggage with the intent to collect $37,000 insurance money, exploded (Nov. 1) in midair near Longmont, Cal., killing all forty-four persons aboard.

The A. F. L. (American Federation of Labor) and the C.I.O. (Committee for Industrial Organization) ended (Dec. 5) a 20-year separation by a merger.

Besides devastating tornadoes and floods in many sections of the country, two violent hurricanes from the Caribbean swept northward through the Atlantic states: called "Connie" (Aug. 8), and "Diane" (Aug. 19).

The 114-year-old New York newspaper *Brooklyn Eagle* ceased (Mar. 16) publication, following a 45-day strike of employees. (Walt Whitman served as editor 1846-48.)

The year was well represented in top-selling fiction, with "Andersonville" (MacKinlay Kantor; Pulitzer prize 1956), "Auntie Mame" (Patrick Dennis, pseud. of Edward Everett Tanner), "Band of Angels" (Robert Penn Warren), "Bonjour Tristesse" (Françoise Sagan; from the French), "Cash McCall" (Cameron Hawley), "The Man in the Gray Flannel Suit" (Sloan Wilson), "Marjorie Morningstar" (Herman Wouk), "The Prophet" (Sholem Asch), "Sincerely, Willis Wayde" (John Phillips Marquand), "Something of Value" (Robert Ruark), "Ten North Frederick" (John O'Hara), "The Tontine" (Thomas D. Costain). Non-fictional literature produced "The Day Lincoln Was Shot" (James Bishop), "The Dead Sea Scrolls" (Edmund Wilson), "Gift from the Sea" (Anne Morrow Lindbergh), "How to Live 365 Days a Year" (John A. Schindler), "Inside Africa" (John Gunther), "Inspiring Messages for Daily Living" (Norman Vincent Peale), "A Night to Remember" (Walter Lord), "The Secret of Happiness" (evangelist Billy Graham), "Thinking Life Through" (Fulton J. Sheen). From previous years, "The Power of Positive Thinking" (1951) and "A Man Called Peter" (1952) continued to head the list.

Marian Anderson, noted American Negro concert contralto, made (Jan. 7) her operatic debut at the New York Metropolitan Opera House in "Un Ballo in Maschera," thereby becoming the first of her race to be engaged as a permanent member of the company.

Gershwin's opera "Porgy and Bess" was performed (Feb. 22) in Milan at the Teatro alla Scala by an American Negro company on a goodwill tour (see 1954)—the first American opera to be given at the historic opera house and the first American company to appear there.

Carlisle Floyd's opera "Susannah" was premiered (Feb. 24) in Tallahassee, Fla., at Florida State University. (Performed in New York on

Sept. 27, 1956 by a professional company, the opera has been given in other cities.)

Films grossing top money led off with "Cinerama Holiday" (documentary). Other pictures were: "Battle Cry" (Van Heflin, Aldo Ray), "Blackboard Jungle" (Glenn Ford), "East of Eden" (Julie Harris, James Dean), "Guys and Dolls" (Marlon Brando, Jean Simmons, Frank Sinatra), "I Am a Camera" (Julie Harris), "Lady and the Tramp" (Walt Disney cartoon), "A Man Called Peter" (Richard Todd), "Mister Roberts" (Henry Fonda, James Cagney), "Not as a Stranger" (Olivia de Haviland, Robert Mitchum), "Oklahoma!" (Gordon MacRae, Shirley Jones), "Rebel without a Cause" (James Dean), "The Sea Chase" (John Wayne, Lana Turner), "The Seven Year Itch" (Marilyn Monroe), "Strategic Air Command" (James Stewart), "To Hell and Back" (Audie Murphy), "20,000 Leagues under the Sea" (James Mason), "The View from Pompey's Head" (Richard Egan, Dana Wynter).

Television introduced (in June) a new form of entertainment—the quiz show, with fabulous rewards, or "give-aways," as they were called, for the correct answers. (They began with "The $64,000 Question," which continued until November, 1959, when allegedly unethical practices by its imitators came under investigation by the New York district attorney's office.)

The National Broadcasting Company telecast (Mar. 7) in "compatible" color (see 1953), with Mary Martin in the name part, a two-hour version of "Peter Pan"—a major event in color television history.

New to the New York stage were: "Bus Stop" (Music Box, Mar. 2; 478 perf.), "Cat on a Hot Tin Roof" (Morosco, Mar. 24; 694 perf.; Pulitzer prize 1955), "Inherit the Wind" (National, Apr. 21; 805 perf.), "The Diary of Anne Frank" (Cort, Oct. 5; 717 perf.; Pulitzer prize 1955), "Will Success Spoil Rock Hunter" (Belasco, Oct. 13; 452 perf.), "No Time for Sergeants" (Alvin, Oct. 20; 796 perf.), "A Hatful of Rain" (Lyceum, Nov. 9; 391 perf.), "The Matchmaker" (Royale, Dec. 5; 486 perf.). The outstanding musicals were: "Plain and Fancy" (Mark Hellinger, Jan. 27; 460 perf), "Silk Stockings" (Imperial, Feb. 24; 477 perf.), "Damn Yankees" (Forty-Sixth Street, May 5; 1,019 perf.), "Pipe Dream" (Shubert, Nov. 30, with the noted opera singer Helen Traubel; 246 perf.). The company of the Paris Comédie-Française visited (in October) the United States for the first time.

"Davy Crockett" caps were the rage among little boys.

Deaths of the year included Dr. Albert Einstein, 76 (Apr. 18), in Princeton, N. J.

༄ 1956

Allegheny Moon. w., m., Al Hoffman and Dick Manning. Oxford Music Corp., cop. 1956.

Anastasia (*film:* **Anastasia**). w., Paul Francis Webster. m., Alfred Newman. Twentieth Century Music Corp., cop. 1956.

Around the World (*film:* **Around the World in 80 Days**). w., Harold Adamson. m., Victor Young. Beverly Hills, Cal.: Victor Young Publications, cop. 1956.

Band of Gold. w., Bob Musel. m., Jack Taylor. Ludlow Music, Inc., cop. 1956.

Bells Are Ringing (*film:* **Bells Are Ringing**). w., Betty Comden and Adolph Green. m., Jule Styne. Stratford Music Corp., cop. 1956 by Betty Comden, Adolph Green and Jule Styne (selling agents, Chappell & Co., Inc., and G. Schirmer, Inc.).

Blue Suede Shoes. w., m., Carl Lee Perkins. Hi-Lo Music, cop. 1956 (selling agent, Hill and Range Songs, Inc.).

Blueberry Hill. w., m., Al Lewis, Larry Stock and Vincent Rose. Chappell & Co., Inc., cop. 1940. (Popularized in 1956.)

Canadian Sunset. w., Norman Gimbel. m., Eddie Heywood. Meridian Music Corp., cop. 1956.

Cindy, Oh Cindy. w., m., Bob Barron and Burt Long. Edward B. Marks Music Corp., cop. 1956.

Don't Be Cruel. w., m., Otis Blackwell and Elvis Presley. Shalimar-Presley Music Co., cop. 1956 (selling agent, Sheldon Music, Inc.).

Don't Forbid Me. w., m., Charles Singleton. Roosevelt Music Co., Inc., cop. 1956.

Friendly Persuasion (*film:* **Friendly Persuasion**). w., Paul Francis Webster. m., Dimitri Tiomkin. Leo Feist, Inc., cop. 1956.

Glendora. w., m., Ray Stanley. Hollywood, Cal.: American Music, Inc., cop. 1956.

The Great Pretender. w., m., Buck Ram. Panther Music Corp., cop. 1956 (selling agent, Southern Music Publishing Co.).

The Green Door. w., Marvin Moore. m., Bob Davie. Trinity Music, Inc., cop. 1956.

Heartbreak Hotel. w., m., Mae Boren Axton, Tommy Durden and Elvis Presley. Tree Publishing Co., cop. 1956.

Hey, Jealous Lover. w., m., Sammy Cahn, Kay Twoomey and Bee Walker. Barton Music Corp., cop. 1956.

Honky Tonk. w., Henry Glover. m., Bill Doggett, Billy Butler, Shep Sheppard and Clifford Scott. Billace Music Co., cop. 1956 (selling agent Ludlow Music, Inc.).

Hot Diggity. w., m., Al Hoffman and Dick Manning. Roncom Music Co., cop. 1956.

Hound Dog. w., m., Jerry Leiber and Mike Stoller. Elvis Presley Music, Inc., and Lion Publishing Co., Inc., cop. 1956.

I Almost Lost My Mind. w., m., Ivory Joe Hunter. New York: St. Louis Music Corp., cop. 1950 (selling agent, Hill and Range Songs, Inc.). (Popularized in 1956.)

I Could Have Danced All Night (My Fair Lady). w., Alan Jay Lerner. m., Frederick Loewe. Chappell & Co., Inc., cop. 1956 by Alan Jay Lerner and Frederick Loewe.

I Want You, I Need You, I Love You. w., Maurice Mysels. m., Ira Kosloff. Elvis Presley Music, Inc., cop. 1956.

It Only Hurts for a Little While. w., Mack David. m., Fred Spielman. Advanced Music Corp., cop. 1956.

Ivory Tower. w., m., Jack Fulton and Lois Steele. Melrose Music Corp., cop. 1956.

Joey, Joey, Joey (Most Happy Fella). w., m., Frank Loesser. Frank Music Corp., cop. 1956.

Juke Box Baby. w., Noel Sherman. m., Joe Sherman. Winneton Music Corp., cop. 1956 (selling agent, George Paxton, Inc.).

Just in Time (film: Bells Are Ringing). w., Betty Comden and Adolph Green. m., Jule Styne. Stratford Music Corp., cop. 1956 by Betty Comden, Adolph Green and Jule Styne (selling agents, Chappell & Co., Inc., and G. Schirmer, Inc.).

Just Walkin' in the Rain. w., m., Johnny Bragg and Robert S. Riley. Hollywood, Cal.: Golden West Melodies, Inc., cop. 1956.

Lisbon Antigua—In Old Lisbon. Portuguese words, Jose Galhardo and Amadeu do Vale. English words, Harry Dupree. m., Raul Portela. Southern Music Publishing Co., cop. 1937 by Sassetti y Cia., Lisbon; assigned 1949 to Southern Music Publishing Co., Ltd.; cop. 1954 by Southern Music Publishing Co., Inc. (Original title: Lisboa Antigua. Popularized in 1956.)

Long Tall Sally. w., m., Enotris Johnson. Venice Music Corp., cop. 1956 (selling agent, Criterion Music Corp.).

Love Me Tender (film: Love Me Tender). w., m., Elvis Presley and Vera Matson. Elvis Presley Music, Inc., cop. 1956. (Based on George R. Poulton's song "Aura Lee"—see 1861.)

Mack the Knife (The Threepenny Opera). German words, Bertolt Brecht. English words, Marc Blitzstein. m., Kurt Weill. Harms, Inc., cop. 1928 by Universal Edition, Vienna; cop. 1956 by Harms, Inc. (Published for piano solo as "Moritat," cop. 1956.)

The Man with the Golden Arm (film: The Man with the Golden Arm). w., Sammy Cahn. m., James Van Heusen. Barton Music Corp., cop. 1955.

Memories Are Made of This. w., m., Terry Gilkyson, Richard Dehr and Frank Miller. Montclare Music Corp., cop. 1955 (selling agent, Keys Music, Inc.).

Mr. Wonderful (Mr. Wonderful). w., m., Jerry Bock, Larry Holofcener and George Weiss. Laurel Music Corp., cop. 1956.

Moonglow. w., m., Will Hudson, Eddie DeLange and Irving Mills. Mills Music, Inc., cop. 1934. (Revived in 1956 in the film: Picnic.)

More. w., Tom Glazer. m., Alex Alstone. Shapiro, Bernstein & Co., Inc., cop. 1956.

Moritat. *See above:* **Mack the Knife.**

My Prayer. Words and musical adaptation, Jimmy Kennedy. m., George Boulanger. Skidmore Music Co., Inc., cop. 1939 by The World Wide Music Co., London (selling agent Shapiro, Bernstein & Co., Inc.). (Based on Boulanger's melody "Avant de Mourir," op. 17; see 1939. Revived in 1956.)

No, Not Much! w., Al Stillman. m., Robert Allen. Beaven Music Publishing Corp., cop. 1956 (selling agent, Larry Spier, Inc.).

On the Street Where You Live (My Fair Lady). w., Alan Jay Lerner. m., Frederick Loewe. Chappell & Co., Inc., cop. 1956 by Alan Jay Lerner and Frederick Loewe.

The Party's Over (*film:* **Bells Are Ringing**). w., Betty Comden, and Adolph Green. m., Jule Styne. Stratford Music Corp., cop. 1956 by Betty Comden, Adolph Green and Jule Styne (selling agents, Chappell & Co., Inc., and G. Schirmer, Inc.).

Picnic (*film:* **Picnic**). w., Steve Allen. m., George W. Duning. Shapiro, Bernstein & Co., Inc., cop. 1955 and 1956 by Columbia Pictures Music Corp.

The Poor People of Paris. w., Jack Lawrence. m., Marguerite Monnot. Reg Connelly Music, Inc., cop. 1956 by René Rouzaud and Marguerite Monnot (selling agent, Hill and Range Songs, Inc.).

Que Será, Será. *See below:* **Whatever Will Be, Will Be.**

The Rain in Spain (My Fair Lady). w., Alan Jay Lerner. m., Frederick Loewe. Chappell & Co., Inc., cop. 1956 by Alan Jay Lerner and Frederick Loewe.

See You Later, Alligator. w., m., Robert Guidry. Arc Music Corp., cop. 1956.

Singing the Blues. w., m., Melvin Endsley. Nashville, Tenn.: Acuff-Rose Publications, cop. 1954. (Popularized in 1956.)

Soft Summer Breeze. w., Judy Spencer. m., Eddie Heywood. Regent Music Corp., cop. 1955 and 1956.

Somebody Up There Likes Me (*film:* **Somebody Up There Likes Me**). w., Sammy Cahn. m., Bronislau Kaper. Leo Feist, Inc., cop. 1956 by Loew's Incorporated.

Song for a Summer Night. w., m., Robert Allen. Cromwell Music, Inc., cop. 1956.

Standing on the Corner (Most Happy Fella). w., m., Frank Loesser. Frank Music Corp., cop. 1956.

A Sweet Old Fashioned Girl. w., m., Bob Merrill. Valyr Music Corp., cop. 1956.

Teen-Age Crush. w., m., Audrey and Joe Allison. Hollywood, Cal.: Central Songs, Inc., cop. 1956.

Tonight You Belong to Me. w., Billy Rose. m., Lee David. Double-A Music Corp., cop. 1926 and renewed 1953 by Billy Rose and Lee David; assigned to Double-A Music Corp. (Revived in 1956.)

Too Close for Comfort (Mr. Wonderful). w., m., Jerry Bock, Larry Holofcener and George Weiss. Laurel Music Corp., cop. 1956.

True Love (*film:* **High Society**). w., m., Cole Porter. Buxton Hill Music Corp., cop. 1955 and 1956.

Walk Hand in Hand. w., m., Johnny Cowell. Republic Music Corp., cop. 1956.

Whatever Will Be, Will Be (*film:* **The Man Who Knew Too Much**). w., m., Jay Livingston and Ray Evans. Artists Music, cop. 1956. (Academy Award Winner, 1956).

Why Do Fools Fall in Love? w., m., Frank Lymon and George Goldner. Patricia Music Publishing Corp., cop. 1956.

You're Sensational (*film:* **High Society**). w., m., Cole Porter. Buxton Hill Music Corp., cop. 1955 and 1956.

Anti-American demonstrations broke out (in January) in Amman, Hebron, Nablus, and in the Jordanese sector of Jerusalem.

The launching by United States military authorities in West Germany of meteorological balloons, carrying camera equipment, brought protests to Washington from the Soviet Union (Feb. 5) and Hungary (Feb. 8), and to the United Nations by Albania, Bulgaria, and Czechoslovakia, for passage over their territories.

Nikita S. Khrushchev, head of the eight-man Communist party Secretariat, astonished (Feb. 14) the world by condemning, before the 20th Soviet Communist Party Congress in Moscow, the isolationist policies of Stalin and his "cult of personality," as alien to Marxist-Lenin principles, thereby opening the Soviet Union to foreign trade, journalists, and a restricted number of tourists.

A Federal Court order, ending a six-year-old anti-trust suit, dissolved (Feb. 17) the Shubert chain of 12 theatres in six cities and its booking agency.

The Senate rejected (Mar. 27) a five-point proposal to change the electoral system in favor of nationwide popular elections.

The Parliament of Iceland requested (Mar. 28) the removal of United States NATO troops, stationed at Keflavik air base since 1951, in order to take over the defense of the island.

Crusading New York newspaper labor columnist Victor Riesel was blinded (Apr. 5) in both eyes, while leaving a restaurant in the city's theatre district, by an acid-throwing gangster.

The Association of University Professors, at a meeting in St. Louis, censured (Apr. 6-7) six universities, a medical school, and an agricultural college as violating academic freedom for the dismissal or suspension of faculty members who had invoked the 5th Amendment or refused to sign loyalty oaths.

The international social event of the year was the colorful wedding of blonde Hollywood actress Grace Kelly, 26, of Philadelphia, and Prince Rainier III, 32 of Monaco, performed (Apr. 18) in a civil ceremony in the throne room of the Grimaldi palace of the 375-acre principality and consecrated (Apr. 19) at a nuptial mass in the St. Nicholas Cathedral. (The pair met while Prince Rainier was on a two-month visit to the United States.)

The New York Coliseum, costing $35,000,000, opened (Apr. 28) as the world's largest exhibitions building.

Oxford University conferred (June 10) the honorary degree of Doctor of Civil Law on an American cited in Latin as "Harricum" Truman—none other than 33rd President Harry S. Truman.

Two eastbound air liners, leaving Los Angeles within three minutes of each other, collided and crashed (June 30) into the Grand Canyon in northern Arizona, in the worst commercial air disaster in history, killing 117 passengers and 11 crew members.

A strike of 650,000 United Steelworkers of America (AFL-CIO) crippled (July 1-27) 90 per cent of the country's steel output.

Grand scale circus in America played (July 16) its last performance in Pittsburgh, when the Ringling Brothers and Barnum and Bailey Circus folded its tents of "The Greatest Show on Earth" as "a thing of the past," according to John Ringling North, head of the enterprise.

The transatlantic luxury liners, Italian S.S. Andrea Doria and Swedish-American S.S. Stockholm, collided (July 25) at night forty miles off Nantucket; the Italian ship sank in eleven hours, with a loss of fifty lives. (The Andrea Doria was named after the admiral of the French-Genovese fleet of 1524, who aided in the capture of Tunis in 1535; he died in 1560. During the American Revolution, a United States brig was called Andrea Doria.)

An Army helicopter accomplished (Aug. 24) the first non-stop transcontinental flight, from San Diego to Washington, D.C., in 37 hours, with a crew of five.

The non-Communist, or "free," world witnessed the ruthless display of Russian military might when widespread political demonstrations against Communist rule in Hungary led (Nov. 4) to a surprise invasion by Soviet armed forces, reckoned at 200,000 troops and 2,500 war tanks and armored cars, which annihilated an estimated 32,000 persons; subsequently more than 25,000 Hungarians were deported to Siberia.

Patrick Air Force Base, Fla., fired (Dec. 8) the first American test rocket for sending a man-made satellite into orbit. (The missile reached a height of 125 miles, travelling at a speed of 4,000 miles per hour.)

New books of fiction gave readers: "A Certain Smile" (Françoise Sagan; from the French), "Don't Go Near the Water" (William Brinkley), "The Last Hurrah" (Edwin O'Connor), "Peyton Place" (Grace Metalious), "A Single Pebble" (John Hersey). Non-fiction offered: "Deliver Us from Evil" (Thomas A. Dooley), "The Nun's Story" (Kathryn Hulme), "Profiles in Courage" (John Fitzgerald Kennedy, later our 35th President), "The Search for Bridey Murphy" (Morey Bernstein).

Among plays new to Broadway were: "Middle of the Night" (ANTA Playhouse, Feb. 8; 479 perf.), "Separate Tables" (Music Box, Oct. 25; 432 perf.), "Auntie Mame" (Broadhurst, Oct. 31; 639 perf.). "Long Day's Journey into Night" (Helen Hayes, Nov. 7; 389 perf.), "The Happiest Millionaire" (Lyceum, Nov. 20; 271 perf.). Musicals were represented by "My Fair Lady" (Mark Hellinger, Mar. 15; running into 1962), "Mr. Wonderful" (Broadway, Mar. 22; 388 perf.), "The Most Happy Fella" (Imperial, May 3; 687 perf.), "Li'l Abner" (St. James, Nov. 15; 693 perf.), "Bells Are Ringing" (Shubert, Nov. 29; 924 perf.), "Happy Hunting" (Majestic, Dec. 6; 412 perf.).

The Central City Opera House premiered (July 7) Douglas Moore's opera "The Ballad of Baby Doe."

"The Ten Commandments" (Charlton Heston, Anne Baxter) and "Around the World in 80 Days" (all-star) were the top-money films. Other pictures included: "Anastasia" (Ingrid Bergman, Yul Brynner), "The Conqueror" (John Wayne, Susan Hayward), "The Eddy Duchin Story" (Tyrone Power, Kim Novak), "Friendly Persuasion" (Gary Cooper, Dorothy McGuire), "Giant" (Elizabeth Taylor, Rock Hudson), "High Society" (Bing Crosby, Grace Kelly), "I'll Cry Tomorrow" (Susan Hayward), "The King and I" (Deborah Kerr, Yul Brynner), "The Man in the Gray Flannel Suit" (Gregory Peck, Jennifer Jones), "The Man Who Knew Too Much" (James Stewart, Doris Day), "The Man with the Golden Arm" (Frank Sinatra), "The Rainmaker" (Burt Lancaster, Katharine Hepburn), "Seven Wonders of the World" (documentary), "The Teahouse of the August Moon" (Marlon Brando, Glenn Ford), "Trapeze" (Burt Lancaster), "War and Peace" (Audrey Hepburn, Henry Fonda).

In baseball, right-hand pitcher Don Larsen, of the New York American League ("Yankee") club, achieved (Oct. 8) at Yankee Stadium, New York, against the Brooklyn National League ("Dodgers") team the first "perfect game" in Worlds Series history, allowing no hits, no runs, and no man to reach first base.

In boxing, heavyweight world's champion Rocky Marciano (real name, Rocco Marchegiano), 31, known as the "Brockton (Mass.) Blockbuster," undefeated in 49 professional bouts, renounced (Apr. 27), his title: 21-year-old Floyd Patterson and the 39-or-more-year-old Archie Moore fought (Nov. 30) in Chicago for the vacated honor, Patterson scoring a knockout victory in the fifth round and thus becoming the youngest fighter in history to succeed to the title.

The last Union Army veteran, Albert Woolson, a drummer boy at seventeen, died (Aug. 2) at the age of 109 in Duluth, Minn.

In the November presidential elections, Dwight D. Eisenhower, Republican, was reelected to office, defeating the Democratic opponent Adlai E. Stevenson.

1957

All Shook Up! w., m., Otis Blackwell and Elvis Presley. Shalimar Music Corp., cop. 1957 (selling agent, Sheldon Music, Inc.).

An Affair to Remember (*film:* **An Affair to Remember**). w., Harold

Adamson and Leo McCarey. m., Harry Warren. Twentieth Century Music Corp., cop. 1957.

All the Way (*film:* **The Joker Is Wild**). w., Sammy Cahn. m., James Van Heusen. Maravaille Music Corp., cop. 1957. (Academy Award Winner, 1957.)

April Love (*film:* **April Love**). w., Paul Francis Webster. m., Sammy Fain. Leo Feist, Inc., cop. 1957.

Are You Sincere. w., m., Wayne Walker. Nashville, Tenn.: Cedarwood Publishing Co., cop. 1957 (selling agent, Southern Music Publishing Co.).

The Banana Boat Song. w., m., Erik Darling, Bob Carey, and Alan Arkin. Edward B. Marks Music Corp., cop. 1956, by arrangement with Bryden Music, Inc.

Be-Bop Baby. w., m., Pearl Lenghurst. Travis Music, Inc., cop. 1957.

Blue Monday. w., m., Dave Bartholomew and Antoine Domino. Hollywood, Cal.: Commodore Music Corp., cop. 1957.

Butterfly. w., m., Anthony September. New York: Maryland Music Publishing Co., cop. 1957 (selling agent, Aberbach, Inc., New York).

Bye Bye, Love. w., m., Felice Bryant and Boudleaux Bryant. Nashville, Tenn.: Acuff-Rose Publications, cop. 1957.

Ca, C'est l'Amour (*film:* **Les Girls**). w., m., Cole Porter. Buxton Hill Music Corp., cop. 1957.

Calypso Melody. w., m., Larry Clinton. Cromwell Music, Inc., cop. 1957.

Chances Are. w., Al Stillman. m., Robert Allen. Korwin Music, cop. 1957.

Colonel Bogey. *See* 1916. (*Featured in the film:* **The Bridge on the River Kwai.**)

Come to Me (*TV production:* **Come to Me**). w., Peter Lind Hayes. m., Robert Allen. Korwin Music, Inc., cop. 1957.

Dark Moon. w., m., Ned Miller. Malibu, Cal.: Dandelion Music Co., cop. 1957.

The Day the Rains Came. English words, Carl Sigman. French words, Pierre Delanoe. m., Gilbert Becaud. France Music, cop. 1957 (selling agent, Music Dealers Service, Inc.).

Did You Close Your Eyes When We Kissed (New Girl in Town). w., m., Bob Merrill. Chappell & Co., Inc., cop. 1957.

Fascination (*film:* **Love in the Afternoon**). w., Dick Manning. m., F. D. Marchetti. Southern Music Publishing Co., Inc., cop. renewed 1932 by F. D. Marchetti; assigned 1945 to Les Editions Philippo; assigned 1945 to Southern Music Publishing Co., Ltd., London; cop. 1954 by Liber-Southern, Ltd., London. (A vocal version of Marchetti's "Valse Tzigane" of the same name—see 1904.)

The Four Walls. w., m., Marvin Moore and George Campbell. Sheldon Music, cop. 1957.

Gone. w., m., Smokey Rogers. North Hollywood, Cal.: Dallas Music Co., Inc., cop. 1952 (selling agent, Hill and Range Songs, Inc.). (Popularized in 1957.)

Honeycomb. w., m., Bob Merrill. Hawthorne Music Corp., cop. 1954 (selling agent, Joy Music, Inc.). (Popularized in 1957.)

I'm Gonna Sit Right Down and Write Myself a Letter. See 1935. (Revived in 1957.)

I Feel Pretty (West Side Story). w., Stephen Sondheim. m., Leonard Bernstein. G. Schirmer, Inc., and Chappell & Co., Inc., cop. 1957 by Leonard Bernstein and Stephen Sondheim.

In the Middle of an Island. w., m., Nick Acquaviva and Ted Varnick. Mayfair Music Corp., cop. 1957.

It's Not for Me to Say (*film:* **Lizzie**). w., Al Stillman. m., Robert Allen. Korwin Music, Inc., cop. 1956.

Jailhouse Rock (*film:* **Jailhouse Rock**). w., m., Jerry Leiber and Mike Stoller. Elvis Presley Music, Inc., cop. 1957.

Jamaica Farewell. w., m., Herbie Lovell, Roy McIntyre and Lillian Keyser. Top Notch Music Corp., cop. 1957.

Let Me Be Your Teddy Bear. *See below:* **Teddy Bear.**

Liechtensteiner Polka. w., m., Edmund Kötscher and R. Lindt. Burlington Music Corp., cop. 1957 by Minerva Music (M. Bohm), Berlin; assigned to Burlington Music Corp. (selling agent, Keys-Hansen, Inc.).

Little Biscuit (Jamaica). w., E. Y. Harburg. m., Harold Arlen. Edwin H. Morris & Co., Inc., cop. 1957 by Harold Arlen and E. Y. Harburg.

Little Darlin'. w., m., Maurice Williams. Nashville, Tenn.: Excellorec Music, cop. 1957.

Love Is Strange. w., m., Mickey Baker and Ethel Smith. Ben Ghazi Enterprises, cop. 1957.

Love Letters in the Sand. w., Nick and Charles Kenny. m., J. Fred Coots. Bourne, Inc., cop. 1931. (See 1931; revived in 1957.)

Mama Look a Booboo. w., m., Lord Melody (Fitzroy Alexander). Duchess Music Corp., cop. 1957.

Maria (West Side Story). w., Stephen Sondheim. m., Leonard Bernstein. G. Schirmer, Inc., and Chappell & Co., Inc., cop. 1957 by Leonard Bernstein and Stephen Sondheim.

Marianne. w., m., Terry Gilkyson, Frank Miller and Richard Dehr. Hollywood, Cal.: Montclare Music Corp., cop. 1955 (selling agent, Keys Music, Inc.). (Popularized in 1957.)

Melodie d'Amour. w., Leo Johns. m., Henri Salvador. Rayven Music Co., Inc., cop. 1949 by Editions Transatlantiques, Paris; cop. 1957 by Rayven Music Co., Inc.

My Heart Reminds Me. *See below:* **And That Reminds Me.**

Old Cape Cod. w., m., Claire Rothrock, Milt Yakus and Allan Jeffrey. George Pincus & Sons, cop. 1956.

Party Doll. w., m., Jimmy Bowen and Buddy Knox. Jackie Music Corp., cop. 1957.

Rainbow. w., m., Russ Hamilton. Robbins Music Corp., cop. 1957.

Return to Me. w., m., Carmen Lombardo and Danny di Minno. Southern Music Publishing Co., cop. 1957.

A Rose and a Baby Ruth. w., m., John Loudermilk. Chapel Hill, N. C.: Bentley Music Co., cop. 1956.

Round and Round. w., m., Joe Shapiro and Lou Stallman. Rush Music Co., cop. 1956. (Popularized in 1957.)

School Day. w., m., Chuck Berry. Arc Music Corp., cop. 1957.

Send for Me. w., m., Ollie Jones. Winneton Music Corp., cop. 1957 (selling agent, George Paxton, Inc.).

Seventy-Six Trombones (The Music Man). w., m., Meredith Willson. Frank Music Corp., cop. 1957.

Tammy (film: Tammy and the Bachelor). w., m., Jay Livingston and Ray Evans. Northern Music Corp., cop. 1957.

(Let Me Be Your) Teddy Bear. w., m., Kal Mann and Bernie Lowe. Gladys Music, Inc., cop. 1957 (selling agent, Hill and Range Songs, Inc.).

Tonight (West Side Story). w., Stephen Sondheim. m., Leonard Bernstein. G. Schirmer, Inc., and Chappell & Co., Inc., cop. 1957 by Leonard Bernstein and Stephen Sondheim.

Too Much. w., m., Lee Rosenberg and Bernard Weinman. Elvis Presley Music, Inc., New York, and Southern Belle Music, Nashville, Tenn., cop. 1956.

A White Sport Coat—And a Pink Carnation. w., m., Marty Robbins. Nashville, Tenn.: Acuff-Rose Publications, cop. 1957.

Whole Lot-ta Shakin' Goin' On. w., m., Dave Williams and Sunny David. Philadelphia: Marlyn Music Publishers, Inc., cop. 1957.

Why Baby Why. w., m., Luther Dixon and Larry Harrison. Winneton Music Corp., cop. 1957 (selling agent, George Paxton, Inc.).

Wonderful! Wonderful! w., Ben Raleigh. m., Sherman Edwards. Edward B. Marks Music Corp., cop. 1957.

Young Love. w., m., Carole Joyner and Ric Cartey. Atlanta, Ga.: Stars, Inc., cop. 1956 (selling agent, Hill and Range Songs, New York).

President Dwight D. Eisenhower began his second term.

Three American military airplanes, giant B-52 stratofortresses, circled (Jan. 16-18) the globe in a nonstop flight in the record time of 45 hours and 19 minutes.

A 16-year undercover search by the New York police for an unknown person, called the Mad Bomber, who had planted 32 homemade bombs in the city (one at the Public Library), of which 23 exploded and injured 15 people, ended when a mentally deranged electric company ex-employee was arrested (Jan. 22) in his Waterbury (Conn.) home.

A succession of seven earthquakes rocked (Mar. 22) San Francisco—the worst in 51 years (see 1906).

Bandits ambushed and killed (Mar. 24) in a desert region of southeastern Iran three American representatives of the International Cooperation Administration and their two native jeep drivers.

New York's last electric passenger streetcar trolley, a service in operation since 1888, ran (Apr. 7) its final trip, over the Queensboro Bridge.

The U. S. Post Office suspended (Saturday, April 13) for one day regular mail delivery for "lack of funds."

Accompanied by President Eisenhower, famed British Field Marshal Viscount Bernard Law Montgomery of World War II inspected (May 12) the Gettysburg battlefield and roused popular resentment, particularly in the South, by his adverse criticism of the military tactics of Union Gen. George G. Meade and Confederate Gen. Robert E. Lee.

Capacity audiences crowded (May 15-Aug. 30) the nightly revival meetings in New York's Madison Square Garden to hear the Rev. Dr. Billy Graham, 38-year-old Southern Baptist evangelist; during his crusade, he attracted (July 20) to an open-air session in Yankee Stadium at least 92,000 persons with more than 2,000 outside—the largest assemblage ever to gather there—and jammed (Sept. 1) Times Square in a farewell rally.

The 30th anniversary of Charles A. Lindbergh's historic transatlantic solo airplane crossing in 1927 was commemorated (May 21) with a duplication of the flight by an Air Force Super Sabre jet, called "Spirit of St. Louis II," from McGuire Air Force Base, N. J., to Le Bourget Airport, Paris, in the identical time of 33 hours 29 minutes 30 seconds.

Nearly 337 years after the Mayflower sailed from England with its cargo of 102 Pilgrims and crew of 48, an exact replica of the small square rigger, named the Mayflower II and equipped with only one modern device, a wireless radio, crossed the Atlantic from Plymouth, England, over a southern route to Plymouth, Mass., in 53 days (Apr. 20-June 13; fourteen less than the original voyage).

A 20-foot tidal wave swept (June 28) the Louisiana coast in the wake of hurricane "Audrey," leaving ultimately more than 300 persons dead, many hundreds injured and missing, and 40,000 homeless.

Festivities marked (in June) the 350th anniversary of the founding of Jamestown, Va.; a feature of the celebration was (June 12) a 14-mile double column array of 114 warships from eighteen nations, 81 United States vessels and 33 from seventeen foreign countries, staged in Chesapeake Bay—the largest such aggregation ever assembled in United States waters.

The crescent-shaped Harry S. Truman Library in Independence, Mo., erected at the cost of $1,750,000 by public subscription for the preservation of the former President's 3,500,000 official documents, was dedicated (July 6) and presented to the Federal Government.

Forty-one members of the United States delegation to the World Youth Festival in Moscow undertook (Aug. 14), against remonstrance by the U. S. Government, a tour of Communist China at the invitation of the All-China Youth Federation; the State Department confiscated (Sept. 18) their passports.

A balloon, manned by a doctor in the Air Force, set (Aug. 19-20) an altitude record of 102,000 feet, remaining in the stratosphere 32 hours; much valuable scientific data were obtained as a step in space travel.

The movement to desegregate the public schools met with violent segregationist opposition in Little Rock, Ark., where Governor Orval Faubus called out (Sept. 2) the National Guard, which was replaced (Sept. 24) on Presidential order, as rioting increased, by Federal troops, armed with rifles and bayonets; other disorders occurred in Nashville, Tenn., where a new $500,000 elementary school was dynamited (Sept. 9-10), in Montgomery, Ala., Atlanta, New Orleans, and Wichita Falls, Tex.

The U. S. Coast Guard cutter "Spar" circumnavigated North America via the Panama Canal and the Northwest Passage—the first American vessel to accomplish the undertaking and to cross the top of the continent. (The operation ended officially on Sept. 7.)

Soviet Union scientists launched (Oct. 4) into space the first artificial man-made earth-orbiting satellite, called "Sputnik I"; thirty days later, a second, bearing a small female dog named Laika, was fired (Nov. 3).

The last battleship of the U. S. Navy, the $110,000,000, 45,000-ton Wisconsin, commissioned in 1944, was withdrawn (Nov. 6) from service and consigned to the mothball fleet at Bayonne, N. J.

Captured operating a photographic studio in Brooklyn, N. Y., under the name of Emil R. Goldfus, Rudolf Ivanovich Abel, 53, a colonel of the

Soviet counter-intelligence and espionage in the United States, was sentenced (Nov. 15) to 30 years in prison and a fine of $3,000. He was returned to Soviet authorities in exchange for U-2 pilot Francis Gary Powers on February 10, 1962.

Five months of legal controversy, engaging the State Department and the Supreme Court, preceded the trial in Japan of an American soldier who had discharged from a grenade launcher on a United States-Japanese firing range 60 miles north of Tokyo an empty shell case that struck and accidentally killed a native woman, gathering scrap iron; he was convicted (Nov. 19) by a Japanese court and given a suspended sentence.

An eight-day strike of motormen crippled (Dec. 8-16) New York's subway traffic system.

Books about the Civil War showed a marked increase, in anticipation of its centenary. Fiction brought forth: "Below the Salt" (Thomas B. Costain), "A Death in the Family" (James Agee; Pulitzer prize 1958), "Fairoaks" (Frank Yerby), "The Lady" (Conrad Richter), "Letter from Peking" (Pearl Buck), "By Love Possessed" (James Gould Cozzens), "On the Beach" (Nevil Shute), "Rally Round the Flag, Boys" (Max Shulman), "Remember Me to God" (Myron S. Kaufman), "The Scapegoat" (Daphne du Maurier), "Sing Out the Glory" (Gladys Hasty Carroll), "The Town" (William Faulkner). Non-fiction introduced "The Hidden Persuaders" (Vance Packard).

New plays were: "A Visit to a Small Planet" (Booth, Feb. 7; 388 perf.), "The Tunnel of Love" (Royale, Feb. 13; 420 perf.), "Look Back in Anger" (Lyceum, Oct. 1; 496 perf.), "Romanoff and Juliet" (Plymouth, Oct. 11; 388 perf.), "Look Homeward, Angel" (Ethel Barrymore, Nov. 28; 564 perf.; Pulitzer prize 1958), "The Dark at the Top of the Stairs" (Music Box, Dec. 3; 469 perf.), and the musicals: "New Girl in Town" (46th Street, May 14; 432 perf.), "West Side Story" (Winter Garden, Sept. 26; 732 perf.), "Jamaica" (Imperial, Oct. 31; 555 perf.), "The Music Man" (Majestic, Dec. 19; 1,377 perf.).

Heading top-money films was "The Bridge on the River Kwai" (Alec Guinness, William Holden, Jack Hawkins). Other pictures included: "Don't Go Near the Water" (Glenn Ford, Gia Scala), "Les Girls" (Gene Kelly, Mitzi Gaynor), "A Hatful of Rain" (Eva Marie Saint, Don Murray), "Heaven Knows, Mr. Allison" (Deborah Kerr, Robert Mitchum), "Island in the Sun" (James Mason, Joan Fontaine), "Pal Joey" (Rita Hayworth, Frank Sinatra), "The Pride and the Passion" (Cary Grant, Frank Sinatra), "The Prince and the Showgirl" (Sir Laurence Olivier, Marilyn Monroe), "Raintree County" (Montgomery Clift, Elizabeth Taylor), "Sayonara" (Marlon Brando), "The Spirit of St. Louis" (James Stewart). A French documentary, "Albert Schweitzer," with English narration, attracted nationwide interest.

Arturo Toscanini, aged 90, died (Jan. 16) in New York.

The name of Fidel Castro, of Cuba, became known to the American public when he led (Sept. 5) an uprising in Cienfuegos against the government of President Fulgencio Batista.

ᘒᙀ 1958

All I Have to Do Is Dream. w., m., Boudleaux Bryant. Nashville, Tenn.: Acuff-Rose Publications, cop. 1958.

At the End of a Rainbow. *See below:* **The End.**

Big Man. w., m., Glen Larson and Bruce Belland. Beechwood Music Corp., cop. 1958.

Bird Dog. w., m., Boudleaux Bryant. Nashville, Tenn.: Acuff-Rose Publications, cop. 1958.

Catch a Falling Star. w., m., Paul Vance and Lee Pockriss. Marvin Music Co., cop. 1957 (selling agent, Fred Fisher Music Co., Inc.).

A Certain Smile. w., Paul Francis Webster. m., Sammy Fain. Twentieth Century Music Corp., cop. 1958.

Chanson d'Amour. w., m., Wayne Shanklin. Los Angeles: Thunderbird Music, Inc., cop. 1958 (selling agent, Criterion Music Corp., New York).

The Chipmunk Song—Christmas Don't Be Late. w., m., Ross Bagdasarian. Chicago: Monarch Music Co., Inc., cop. 1958.

Come Prima. *See below:* **For the First Time.**

Enchanted Island. w., Al Stillman. m., Robert Allen. Korwin Music, Inc., cop. 1958 (selling agent, Border Music Publishing Corp.).

The End. w., Sid Jacobson. m., Jimmy Krondes. Criterion Music Corp., cop. 1958.

Everybody Loves a Lover. w., Richard Adler. m., Robert Allen. Korwin Music, Inc., cop. 1958 (selling agent, Border Music Publishing Co.).

Firefly. w., Carolyn Leigh. m., Cy Coleman. Edwin H. Morris & Co., Inc., cop. 1958.

For the First Time—Come Prima. English words, Buck Ram. Italian words, M. Panzeri. m., S. Taccani and V. di Paola. A. M. C., Inc., cop. 1957 by Edizioni Musicali La Cicala Casa Editrice, Milan; cop. 1958 by A. M. C., New York.

Gigi (film: Gigi). w., Alan Jay Lerner. m., Frederick Loewe. Mara-Lane Music Corp., cop. 1958 (selling agent, Chappell & Co., Inc.). (Academy Award Winner, 1958)

The Hawaiian Wedding Song. English words, Al Hoffman and Dick Manning. Hawaiian words and music, Charles E. King. Elmhurst, New York: Charles E. King Music Co., cop. 1926 and 1958 (selling agent, Pickwick Music Corp.).

I Enjoy Being a Girl (Flower Drum Song). w., Oscar Hammerstein 2nd. m., Richard Rodgers. Williamson Music, Inc., cop. 1958 by Richard Rodgers and Oscar Hammerstein 2nd.

If Dreams Come True. w., Al Stillman. m., Robert Allen. Korwin Music, Inc., cop. 1958 (selling agent, Border Music Corp.).

It's All in the Game. w., Carl Sigman. m., Gen. Charles G[ates] Dawes. Remick Music Corp., cop. 1912; cop. 1951. (Revived in 1958; see 1912.)

Kewpie Doll. w., m., Sid Tepper and Roy C. Bennett. Leeds Music Corp., cop. 1957 and 1958.

Left Right Out of Your Heart. w., Earl Shuman. m., Mort Garson. Shapiro, Bernstein & Co., Inc., cop. 1958.

Lollipop. w., m., Beverly Ross and Julius Dixon. Edward B. Marks Music Corp., cop. 1958.

Love, Look Away (Flower Drum Song). w., Oscar Hammerstein 2nd. m., Richard Rodgers. Williamson Music, Inc., cop. 1958 by Richard Rodgers and Oscar Hammerstein 2nd.

Mandolins in the Moonlight. w., m., George Weiss and Aaron Schroeder. Roncom Music Co., cop. 1958.

Padre. French words, Jacques Larue. English words, Paul Francis Webster. Charles N. Daniels, Inc., cop. 1957 and 1958.

Pink Shoe Laces. w., m., Mickie Grant. Hollywood, Cal.: Pioneer Music Publishing Co., cop. 1958 (selling agent, Keys-Hansen, Inc., New York).

The Purple People Eater. w., m., Sheb Wooley. Hollywood, Cal.: Cordial Music Co., cop. 1958 (selling agent, Granite Music Co., Hollywood, Cal.).

Sail Along Silvery Moon. w., Harry Tobias. m., Percy Wenrich. Joy Music, Inc., cop. 1937 by Select Music Publications; Inc.; assigned 1942 to Joy Music, Inc. (Revived in 1958.)

Secretly. w., m., Al Hoffman, Dick Manning and Mark Markwell. Planetary Music Publishing Co., cop. 1958.

Stagger Lee. w., m., Lloyd Price and Harold Logan. Sheldon Music, Inc., cop. 1958.

Sugartime. w., m., Charlie Phillips and Odis Echols. Nor Va Jak Music, Inc., cop. 1956 (selling agent, Melody Lane Publications, Inc.). (Popularized in 1958.)

The Swingin' Shepherd Blues. w., Rhoda Roberts and Kenny Jacobson. m., Moe Kossman. Benell Music Co., cop. 1958; assigned to Kahl Music, Inc., and Benell Music Co. (selling agent, Kahl Music, Inc.).

Tears on My Pillow. w., m., Sylvester Bradford and Al Lewis. Vanderbilt-Bonnie Music, cop. 1958.

Tequila. Instrumental. m., Chuck Rio. Hollywood, Cal.: Golden West Melodies, Inc., cop. 1958.

To Know Him Is to Love Him. w., m., Phil Spector. Hollywood, Cal.: Warman Music Co., cop. 1958 (selling agent, Criterion Music Corp., New York).

Tom Dooley. w., m., traditional, arr. by Dave Guard. Beechwood Music Corp., cop. 1958.

Twilight Time. w., Buck Ram. m., Morty Lewis, Al Nevins and

Artie Dunn. Porgie Music Corp., cop. 1944 by Campbell-Porgie, Inc.; assigned 1948 to Porgie Music Corp. (Revived in 1958.)

Volare. Italian words, Domenico Modugno and F. Migliacci. English words, Mitchell Parish. m., Domenico Modugno. Robbins Music Corp., cop. 1958 by Edizioni Curci, Milan.

Who's Sorry Now. w., Bert Kalmar and Harry Ruby. m., Ted Snyder. Mills Music, Inc., cop. 1923 by Waterson, Berlin & Snyder Co.; assigned 1932 to Mills Music, Inc. (Revived in 1958.)

Witch Doctor. w., m., Ross Bagdasarian. Chicago: Monarch Music Co., Inc., cop. 1958.

Yakety Yak. w., m., Jerry Leiber and Mike Stoller. Tiger Music, Inc., cop. 1958 (selling agent, Hill and Range Songs, Inc.).

You Are Beautiful (Flower Drum Song). w., Oscar Hammerstein 2nd. m., Richard Rodgers. Williamson Music, Inc., cop. 1958 by Richard Rodgers and Oscar Hammerstein 2nd.

Young and Warm and Wonderful. w., Hy Zaret. m., Lou Singer. Frank Music Corp., cop. 1958.

Three months after the Soviet Union's launching of the first earth-orbiting man-made planet (Oct. 4, 1957), U. S. scientists spurred by public censure duplicated the Russian accomplishment: the Army released (Jan. 31) the first American satellite, "Explorer I," at Cape Canaveral, Fla.; the Navy followed (Mar. 17) with "Vanguard I;" and the Air Force orbited (Dec. 18) an Atlas missile equipped with a radio which broadcast a Christmas message by President Eisenhower—the world's first talking satellite. In other developments, the Air Force conducted (Feb. 9-16) at Randolph Air Base, Tex., a seven-day simulated flight of an airman in a hermetically sealed steel chamber, and the Army experimented (Dec. 13) with a squirrel monkey as a passenger in a "Jupiter" intermediate range missile at Cape Canaveral. Four attempts to reach or circle the moon failed (Aug. 17, Oct. 11, Nov. 8, Dec. 6).

At sea, American nuclear-powered submarines added notable peacetime achievements to the Navy's history. The "Skate" set (Feb. 24-Mar. 5) a new record for an underwater transatlantic crossing to England in 8 days 11 hours, making the return to Nantucket in 7 days 5 hours. The "Nautilus" crossed (Aug. 3) under the icecap of the North Pole in a trans-polar trip of 1,830 miles from the Pacific to the Atlantic, accomplishing the feat in the Arctic regions that was envisioned 94 years ago by Jules Verne of a similarly named vessel in his story "Twenty Thousand Leagues under the Sea" (1864). The "Skate" duplicated (Aug. 11) the journey in the opposite direction, from the Atlantic to the Pacific. The "Seawolf" conducted (Aug. 7-Oct. 6) undersea operations for 60 days without surfacing, bettering the earlier record (31 days 5½ hours, in May) of the "Skate."

The United States participated in the Brussels World's Fair (Apr.-Oct.); at the American Pavilion, performances were given of Rodgers and Hammerstein's musical comedy "Carousel" (June 14), Carlisle Floyd's opera "Susannah" (June 25), the world première of Gian Carlo Menotti's opera "Maria Golovin" (Aug. 20), Archibald MacLeish's allegory "J.B." (Sept. 10, by Yale University students).

East German police seized nine members of the U.S. Army's Third Armored Division when their helicopter landed (June 9) by error in Zwickau. After fruitless diplomatic exchanges, the International Red Cross obtained the release of the men on July 19 and the United States paid $1,748 for their upkeep while in custody.

The Cuban insurrectionist forces of Fidel Castro kidnapped (June 26-July 1) 29 United States sailors and marines, 18 American civilians and three Canadians near the U.S. Navy base at Guantanamo Bay, apparently to gain world recognition for the rebel cause. (The prisoners were freed by July 18, through the efforts of the American consul.)

Russian jet fighters shot down (June 27) in Soviet Armenia during a storm, for invasion of Soviet air space, an unarmed U. S. Air Force transport plane, which had lost its way, flying from Turkey to Iran with freight; the nine crewmen escaped death.

A five-mile-long suspension bridge, the longest in the world, across the turbulent Straits of Mackinac, between Lake Michigan and Lake Huron, was opened (June 28) after four years of construction (ground was broken on May 7, 1954), at a cost of $80,000,000.

Seeking to allay growing anti-U.S. sentiment in Latin America, Vice President Richard M. Nixon undertook (in April-May) an 18-day goodwill tour of eight South American countries, meeting with mixed receptions and, in some places, with hostile demonstrations. On a similar mission, Dr. Milton S. Eisenhower, president of Johns Hopkins University and brother of President Eisenhower, made (in July) a 20-day trip through six Central American republics.

In response to "an urgent plea" by President Camille Chamoun of Lebanon, following the bloody overthrow (July 14) of the Iraqi government of 23-year-old King Faisal by pro-Nassar rebels in Baghdad, 3,500 United States Marines were landed (July 15-16) at Beirut to protect American lives and property. (Later reinforced by 2,000 British paratroopers, the number of U. S. Marine and Army forces reached a total of 14,300; their gradual withdrawal began on Aug. 17, after the local political situation gained a degree of stability.)

The U. S. Post Office increased (Aug. 1) 3¢ letter postage to 4¢.

More than 250,000 members of the sect of Jehovah's Witnesses gathered (Aug. 3) from all parts of the world in New York's baseball parks, Yankee Stadium and Polo Grounds, and in the surrounding areas to climax an eight-day Divine Will International Assembly—the largest convention assemblage in the city's history.

As part of a cultural exchange agreement, four American composers—Roy Harris, Ulysses Kay, Peter Mennin, and Roger Sessions—went for a month's visit to the Soviet Union (Sept. 18-Oct. 18).

The Nobel prize in literature went to 68-year Russian writer and poet Boris Pasternak, of Moscow. He declined the award under heavy pressure from his Soviet colleagues, creating a worldwide sensation and headlined his novel "Doctor Zhivago," critical of Russian life and conditions (first published in 1957 in Italy and translated during the next year into twelve languages).

Books of fiction were overshadowed by Pasternak's Nobel prize novel "Doctor Zhivago" (above). American fiction was represented by "Anatomy for a Murder" (Robert Traver), "The Enemy Camp" (Jerome Weidman), "Exodus" (Leon M. Uris), "From the Terrace" (John O'Hara), "Home from the Hills" (William Humphrey), "Ice Palace" (Edna Ferber), "Lolita" (Vladimir Nabokov), "North from Rome" (Helen MacInnes), "The Travels of Jamie McPheeters" (Robert Lewis Taylor, Pulitzer Prize, 1959), "The Winthrop Woman" (Anya Seton), "Women and Thomas Harrow" (John P. Marquand). Nonfiction produced: "The Affluent Society" (John Kenneth Galbraith), "The Edge of Tomorrow" (Thomas A. Dooley), "Kids Say the Darndest Things!" (Art Linkletter), "Only in America" (Harry Golden). Books about the Civil War continued on the increase.

New plays on the New York stage included: "Two for the Seesaw" (Booth, Jan. 16; 750 perf.), "Sunrise at Campobello" (Cort, Jan. 30; 558 perf.), "Who Was the Lady I Saw You With" (Martin Beck, Mar. 3; 208 perf.), "Say, Darling" (ANTA Playhouse, Apr. 3; 332 perf.), "A Touch of the Poet" (Helen Hayes, Oct. 3; 284 perf.), "The World of Suzie Wong" (Broadhurst, Oct. 14; 506 perf.), "Once More with Feeling" (National, Oct. 21; 264 perf.), "The Pleasure of His Company" (Longacre, Oct. 22; 454 perf.), "Make a Million" (Playhouse Th., Oct. 23; 309 perf.), "The Marriage-Go-Round" (Plymouth, Oct. 29; 433 perf.), "J. B." (ANTA Playhouse, Dec. 11; 364 perf.; Pulitzer prize 1959—originally produced in New Haven, Apr. 22, by Yale University students), "The Gazebo" (Lyceum, Dec. 12; 219 perf.). Among successful musicals were "La Plume de Ma Tante" (Royale, Nov. 11; 827 perf.) and "Flower Drum Song" (Dec. 1; 601 perf.).

Among films, "South Pacific" (Mitzi Gaynor, Rossano Brazzi) earned top-money. Other pictures were: "Auntie Mame" (Rosalind Russell), "The Big Country" (Gregory Peck, Jean Simmons), "The Brothers Karamazov" (Yul Brynner, Maria Schell), "Cat on a Hot Tin Roof" (Elizabeth Taylor, Paul Newman), "A Farewell to Arms" (Rock Hudson, Jennifer Jones), "Gigi" (Leslie Caron, Maurice Chevalier), "No Time for Sergeants" (Andy Griffith, Myron McCormick), "Peyton Place" (Lana Turner, Hope Lange), "The Vikings" (Kirk Douglas, Tony Curtis), "Windjammer" (documentary), "Young Lions" (Marlon Brando, Montgomery Clift).

A nationwide scandal, resulting from investigations by the district attorney's office in New York, caused the gradual cancellation of almost all quiz shows (1955) on network television, for allegedly unethical practices, particularly the giving of answers beforehand to selected contestants. (Ten of the twenty arraigned contestants pleaded guilty to charges of perjury on Jan. 17, 1962 before the Court of Special Sessions in New York and received suspended sentences in consideration of their "humiliation." The contestants won from $500 to a record $220,500.)

The New York Metropolitan Opera House produced (Jan. 15) the world première of Samuel Barber's "Vanessa," to a book by composer-turned-librettist Gian Carlo Menotti (Pulitzer prize 1958).

Twenty-three-year-old American pianist Van Cliburn, of Kilgore, Tex., but a native of Shreveport, La., figured in front-page news when he won (Apr. 13) at Moscow in the Soviet Union's international competition the coveted Tchaikovsky prize (a gold medal and 25,000 rubles—$6,250 in official exchange).

New York lost its two National League baseball clubs: the New York "Giants" to San Francisco, and the Brooklyn "Dodgers" to Los Angeles.

"Beatnik," "beat generation," "angry young man," were new words in common parlance; beards were the fashion among young males of this type. The "beat" movement has evolved a literature of its own, expressed in America by Jack Kerouac in his novels "On the Road" (1957), "The Subterraneans" (1958), "Maggie Cassidy" (1959), a book of reminiscences "Lonesome Traveler" (1960), and his poems "Mexico City Blues" (1959). Poets of the category include, among others, Allen Ginsberg ("Kaddish," 1961) and Charles Olson ("The Maximus Poems," 1961).

Deaths of the year included Negro composer William Christopher Handy, "father of the blues" (1912), 84 (Mar. 28), in New York.

Nikita S. Khrushchev was elected (Mar. 27) Premier of the Union of Soviet Socialist Republics.

࠵ 1959

Alvin's Harmonica. w., m., Ross Bagdasarian. Chicago: Monarch Music Co., Inc., cop. 1959.

The Battle of New Orleans. w., m., Jimmy Driftwood. Nashville, Tenn.: Warden Music Co., cop. 1959 (selling agent, Keys-Hansen, Inc., New York).

A Big Hunk o' Love. w., m., Aaron Schroeder and Sid Wyche. Elvis Presley Music, cop. 1959.

Bobby Sox to Stockings. w., m., Russell Faith, Clarence Way Kehner and R. di Cicco. Criterion Music Corp., cop. 1959.

Charlie Brown. w., m., Jerry Leiber and Mike Stoller. Tiger Music, Inc., cop. 1959 (selling agent, Hill and Range, Inc.).

The Children's Marching Song (*film:* **The Inn of the Sixth Happiness**). w., m., M. Arnold. Miller Music Corp., cop. 1958 by B. Feldman & Co., Ltd., London.

Climb Ev'ry Mountain (The Sound of Music). w., Oscar Hammerstein 2nd. m., Richard Rodgers. Williamson Music, Inc., cop. 1959 by Richard Rodgers and Oscar Hammerstein 2nd.

Do-Re-Mi (The Sound of Music). w., Oscar Hammerstein 2nd. m., Richard Rodgers. Williamson Music, Inc., cop. 1959 by Richard Rodgers and Oscar Hammerstein 2nd.

Dream Lover. w., m., Bobby Darin. Progressive Music Publishing Co., cop. 1959.

Everything's Coming Up Roses (Gypsy). w., Stephen Sondheim. m., Jule Styne. Williamson Music, Inc., cop. 1959.

A Fool Such as I. w., m., Bill Trader. Leeds Music Corp., cop. 1952. (Popularized in 1959.)

Frankie. w., Howard Greenfield. m., Neil Sedaka. Aldon Music, Inc., cop. 1959.

Goodbye Jimmy, Goodbye. w., m., Jack Vaughn. Criterion Music Corp., cop. 1959.

The Happy Organ. w., m., Ken Wood [pseud. of Walter R. Moody] and David Clowney. Lowell Music Corp., cop. 1959; assigned to Dorothy Music, New York.

High Hopes (film: A Hole in the Head). w., Sammy Cahn. m., James Van Heusen. Maraville Music Corp., cop. 1959. (Academy Award Winner, 1959)

I'm Just a Lonely Boy. w., m., Paul Anka. Spanka Music Corp., cop. 1958.

Just for Once (Redhead). w., Dorothy Fields. m., Albert Hague. Chappell & Co., Inc., cop. 1959 by Dorothy Fields and Albert Hague.

Kansas City. w., Mike Stoller. m., Jerry Leiber. Cincinnati: Armo Music Corp., cop. 1959; assigned to Lois Music Publishing Co., Cincinnati.

Kookie, Kookie (TV production: 77 Sunset Strip). w., m., Irving Taylor. M. Witmark & Sons, cop. 1959.

Lipstick on Your Collar. w., Edna Lewis. m., George Goehring. Joe Music, Inc., cop. 1959.

Lonely Boy. See above: I'm Just a Lonely Boy.

Lonely Street. Instrumental. m., Phil Villipigue. Indigo Music, Inc., cop. 1959.

Morgen—One More Sunrise. English words, Noel Sherman. German words and music, Peter Mösser. Border Music Publishing Co., cop. 1959 by Monopol-Verlag, G.m.b.H., Berlin; cop. 1959 by Skidmore Music, Inc. (selling agent, Skidmore Music, Inc.).

My Heart Is an Open Book. w., Hal David. m., Lee Pockriss. Sequence Music, Inc., cop. 1958.

Never Be Anyone Else But You. w., m., Baker Knight. Hollywood, Cal.: Eric Music, Inc., cop. 1959.

No Other Arms, No Other Lips. w., m., Joan Whitney, Alex Kramer and Hy Zaret. Whitney-Kramer-Zaret Music Co., cop. 1952 and 1959.

On an Evening in Roma—Setter Celo de Roma. English words, Nan Frederics. Italian words, A. Bertini. m., S. Taccani. Zodiac Music Corp., cop. 1957 by Edizioni Musicali Successo, Milan; cop. 1959 by Zodiac Music Corp. (selling agent, Keys-Hansen, Inc., New York).

Once Knew a Fella (Destry Rides Again). w., m., Harold Rome. Chappell & Co., Inc., cop. 1959.

Personality. w., m., Harold Logan and Lloyd Price. Lloyd and Logan, Inc., cop. 1959 (selling agent, Keys-Hansen, Inc.).

Peter Gunn. Instrumental. m., Henry Mancini. Northridge Music, Inc., cop. 1958 and 1959 (selling agent, Chappell & Co., Inc.).

Petite Fleur. Instrumental. m., Sidney Bechet. Hill and Range Songs, Inc., cop. 1952 by Vogue Records, Paris.

La Plume de Ma Tante. w., m., Al Hoffman and Dick Manning. Korwin Music, Inc., cop. 1959 (selling agent, Border Music Publishing Corp.).

Put Your Head on My Shoulder. w., m., Paul Anka. Spanka Music Corp., cop. 1959.

Quiet Village. Instrumental. m., Les Baxter. Hollywood, Cal.: Baxter Wright Music Co., Inc., cop. 1959.

Sixteen Going on Seventeen (The Sound of Music). w., Oscar Hammerstein 2nd. m., Richard Rodgers. Williamson Music, Inc., cop. 1959 by Richard Rodgers and Oscar Hammerstein 2nd.

Sleep Walk. w., Don Wolf. m., Johnny Santo and Ann Farina. Trinity Music, Inc., cop. 1959.

Small World (Gypsy). w., Stephen Sondheim. m., Jule Styne. Williamson Music, Inc., cop. 1959.

Some People (Gypsy). w., Stephen Sondheim. m., Jule Styne. Williamson Music, Inc., cop. 1959.

Sorry—I Ran All the Way Home. w., m., Harry Giosasi and Artie Zwirn. Figure Music, Inc., cop. 1958 (selling agent, Keys-Hansen, Inc.).

The Sound of Music (The Sound of Music). w., Oscar Hammerstein 2nd. m., Richard Rodgers. Williamson Music, Inc., cop. 1959 by Richard Rodgers and Oscar Hammerstein 2nd.

Staying Young (Take Me Along). w., m., Bob Merrill. Valyr Music Corp., cop. 1959 (selling agent, Hansen Publications).

Take Me Along (Take Me Along). w., m., Bob Merrill. Valyr Music Corp., cop. 1959 (selling agent, Hansen Publications).

A Teen-ager in Love. Jerome "Doc" Pomus and Mort Shuman. Rumbalero Music, Inc., cop. 1959 (selling agent, Hill and Range Songs, Inc.).

The Three Bells. *See below under:* **While the Angelus Was Ringing.**

Two Faces in the Dark (Redhead). w., Dorothy Fields. m., Albert Hague. Chappell & Co., Inc., cop. 1958 by Dorothy Fields and Albert Hague.

Waterloo. w., m., John Loudermilk and Marijohn Wilkin. Nashville, Tenn.: Cedarwood Publishing Co., cop. 1959.

While the Angelus Was Ringing—Les Trois Cloches. w., Dick Manning. m., Jean Villard. Chas. K. Harris Music Publishing Co., Inc., cop. 1945 by Les Nouvelles Editions Meridan, Paris; cop. 1948 by Chas. K. Harris Music Publishing Co., Inc. (Revived in 1959 on records. An earlier version, titled "The Three Bells—Les Trois Cloches," or "The Jimmy Brown Song," with English words by Bert Reisfeld and French words and music by Jean Villard, was published by Southern Music Publishing Co., Inc., New York, cop. 1945 by Les Nouvelles Editions Meridian, Paris; cop. 1948 by Southern Music Publishing Co., Inc.).

Two stars were added to the nation's flag: admitted to the Union as the 49th and 50th State, respectively, were Alaska (Jan. 3) and Hawaii (Aug. 21)—the first additions since 1912 (Arizona and New Mexico).

In the nuclear race to outer space between the United States and the Soviet Union, the latter's scientists released four missiles carrying dogs and a rabbit, and rocketted the first missile to hit the moon, 35 hours after launching ("Lunik II," Sept. 18). The United States engaged in an equally intensive schedule, discharging missiles variously numbered and named "Titan," "Discoverer," "Pioneer," "Regulus," "Explorer," "Vanguard," and other types of rockets. The Army's "Pioneer IV," launched (Mar. 3) at Cape Canaveral, Fla., was the first successful U. S. man-made satellite placed in orbit. The Navy, from its air base there, orbited (Feb. 17) the world's first space-weather station, rocketted (May 28) three hundred miles into the air a missile which carried two small monkeys named Able and Baker (recovered alive fifteen minutes later off Antigua), launched (Sept. 18) the twelfth U.S. earth satellite ("Vanguard III"). In an experimental test for the Post Office Department, the first to be conducted for the purpose, a guided missile, fired (June 8) from a submarine off the Florida coast, delivered 3,000 letters in 22 minutes to the naval airport at Jacksonville.

A Navy radar picket ship intercepted (Feb. 26) a Soviet fishing trawler off Newfoundland, where four American transatlantic cables had recently been broken. In reply to the U.S.S.R.'s protest, the United States Government cited, Mar. 25, evidence that the trawler had tampered with the cables.

The nuclear submarine "Skate" set (Mar. 14-26) on its second submerged trip under the North Pole's icepack a new record of 12 days, bettering its own in 1958 by five days; the craft only surfaced (Mar. 17) to scatter the ashes of Sir Hubert Wilkins, British Polar explorer (d. Dec. 1, 1958), at the Pole, in accordance with his last wishes.

Serious prison riots broke out in Massachusetts (in March and April), Montana (in April), Tennessee (in May), and Missouri (in June).

After six attempts, Oklahoma repealed (Apr. 7) state liquor prohibition, which came in with statehood in 1907. (Mississippi is the only remaining state legally "dry.")

Cuban Premier Fidel Castro, whose bearded guerilla forces overthrew (Jan. 1) the government of Fulgencio Batista, came (in April) to the United States on an unofficial eleven-day goodwill tour, visiting Washington, Princeton, New York, Boston, Montreal, Houston: he met ovations everywhere and delivered lengthy speeches.

An unprecedented strike against seven major hospitals in New York by eleven hundred nurses' aides, cooks, orderlies, porters and housekeeping employees, lasted forty-five days (May 8-June 22).

The Navy launched at Groton, Conn., the nation's first ballistic-missile submarine (June 9)—the 380-foot, 5,400-ton, $100,000,000 "George Washington," and at Quincy, Mass., its first nuclear-powered surface vessel (July 14)—the 725-foot, 14,000-ton cruiser "Long Beach."

Two Communist fighter planes of uncertain origin attacked (June 15) a U.S. Navy routine patrol plane over the Sea of Japan, wounding the tail gunner.

The 2,222-mile St. Lawrence Seaway, linking the Great Lakes with the Atlantic, a project in planning for 40 years, was formally dedicated (June 26) by Queen Elizabeth II of England and President Eisenhower of the United States near Montreal aboard the royal yacht "Britannia."

As part of a cultural exchange program, the U.S.S.R. presented in New York's Coliseum the Soviet Exhibition of Science, Technology and Culture (opened June 30) and the United States held in Moscow's Sokolniki Park the American National Exhibition (opened July 24, by Vice President Richard M. Nixon). From a display of 8,000 books at the American exhibit, the Soviet Ministry of Culture ordered the removal of 100 volumes, as objectionable in contents; 70 were later returned under plastic covers.

In another development of the exchange program, reciprocating the previous year's visit of four American composers, six Soviet musicians—composers Dmitri Shostakovich, Dmitri Kabalevsky, General Secretary Tikhon Krennikov of the Composers' Union, Fikret Amirov, Konstantin Dankevich, and musicologist Boris Yarutovsky—paid a month's visit to this country (Oct. 22-Nov. 21).

A nationwide strike of 500,000 members of the United Steelworkers of America crippled industry for 116 days (July 15-Nov. 7), the longest walkout in the nation's steel history.

The world's first atomic-powered merchant ship, the 22,000-ton, 595½-foot N.S. [Nuclear Ship] "Savannah," named for the first trans-atlantic steamship (1819) and costing forty million dollars, was christened (July 21) at Camden, N. J.

A series of earthquakes occurred (Aug. 17-18) at West Yellowstone, Mont., the first to be known there in this century, causing heavy land-slides of rock and earth which trapped and killed many vacationists and damaged the Hebgen Dam on the Madison River.

Soviet Premier Nikita S. Khrushchev came to the United States on a 13-day visit (Sept. 15-27), which extended from Washington, D. C., and New York to Los Angeles and San Francisco. At Hyde Park, N. Y., he placed a wreath on the grave of former President Franklin D. Roosevelt. In Los Angeles, he engaged in a lively debate with the president of 20th Century-Fox film company and witnessed a special can-can performance ("A person's face is more beautiful than his backside," was his comment). In Des Moines, he examined a farm machinery factory and a meat pack-ing house ("We have beaten you to the moon, but you have beaten us in sausage making," he declared). At Coon Rapids, Ia., he inspected the farm of a hybrid corn grower. He threatened twice to leave the country, the first time when he was denied a tour of Disneyland for security reasons and again when he resented remarks in the speech of the Los Angeles mayor. In San Francisco, he faced seven leaders of the AFL-CIO in a stormy labor discussion. He conferred with President Eisenhower at the latter's Camp David retreat in Maryland.

A mob of some 2,000 anti-U. S.-minded Panamanian demonstrators attempted (Nov. 3) to seize the Canal Zone; being repelled, they tore down the American flag at the U.S. Embassy in Panama, burned American citizens' automobiles, and stoned United States buildings and property.

Sixteen days before Thanksgiving, the Government health department alarmed the public by pronouncing certain cranberry crops of 1958 and 1959 to be contaminated by a weed-killer (aminotriazole); the scare subsided as the affected produce was destroyed during the next week.

President Eisenhower attended a Western Summit conference in Paris as part of a 19-day (Dec. 3-22) goodwill mission to nine European, Middle East and African countries—the longest trip yet made by a President in office.

Thin, transparent plastic bags for clothes came into use—bringing, during the first four months of the year, death by suffocation to at least twenty young children while either playing with the flimsy things, or sleeping on them as mattress covers in their cribs.

In American literary history, the year will be remembered for a judicial pronouncement: Federal Judge Frederick van Pelt Bryan ruled (July 21) as unconstitutional the U. S. Post Office ban on the first unexpurgated American edition (declared by the Postmaster General "an obscene and filthy work") of D. H. Lawrence's 1928 English novel "Lady Chatterley's Lover"—a decision which recalls a similar ruling in favor of James Joyce's "Ulysses" (1933). Following the decree, questionable sex stories multiplied in such numbers that outraged religious and civic leaders appealed to Congress for some restrictive legislation while municipal authorities confiscated quantities of undercounter publications deemed pornographic. Other fiction included "Advise and Consent" (Allen Drury; Pulitzer prize 1960), "Dear and Glorious Physician" (Taylor Caldwell), "From the Terrace" (John O'Hara), "Hawaii" (James Michener), "The Ugly American" (William J. Lederer and Eugene Burdick). Non-fiction brought forth: "Act One" (Moss Hart), "Folk Medicine" (Dr. DeForest Clinton Jarvis, 1959; which induced diet faddists to imbibe vinegar sweetened with honey), "The House of Intellect" (Jacques Barzun), "The Papers of Benjamin Franklin," "The Status Seekers" (Vance Packard, the title adding a new phrase to the current vocabulary), "Twixt Twelve and Twenty" (Pat Boone), "The Years with Ross" (James Thurber), "My Brother Was an Only Child" (Jack Douglas), "For 2¢ Plain" (Harry Golden).

On the New York stage were seen, among other plays: "A Majority of One" (Shubert, Feb. 16; 558 perf.), "Sweet Bird of Youth" (Martin Beck, Mar. 10; 378 perf.), "A Raisin in the Sun" (Ethel Barrymore,

Mar. 11; 530 perf.), "At the Drop of a Hat" (John Golden, Oct. 8; 217 perf.), "The Miracle Worker" (Playhouse, Oct. 19; 702 perf.), "The Tenth Man" (Booth, Nov. 5; 624 perf.), "Five Finger Exercise" (Music Box, Dec. 2; 337 perf.). New musicals included: "Redhead" (46th Street, Feb. 5; 453 perf.), "Destry Rides Again" (Imperial, Apr. 23; 472 perf.), "Gypsy" (Broadway, May 21; 704 perf.), "Take Me Along" (Shubert, Oct. 22; 448 perf.), "The Sound of Music" (Lunt-Fontanne, Nov. 16, running into 1962), "Fiorello" (Broadhurst, Nov. 23; 796 perf.; Pulitzer prize 1960), "Once upon a Mattress" (Phoenix, Nov. 25; 458 perf.).

Released late in the year, "Ben Hur" (Charlton Heston, Martha Scott, Stephen Boyd), a new screen version of Lewis Wallace's novel of 1880, became the top box office attraction among films. Other pictures included: "Anatomy of a Murder" (James Stewart, Lee Remick, Ben Gazzara, Joseph N. Welch), "Hercules" (Steve Reeves), "A Hole in the Head" (Frank Sinatra, Edward G. Robinson, Eddie Hodges), "Imitation of Life" (Lana Turner, John Gavin), "North by Northwest" (Cary Grant, Eva Marie Saint), "The Nun's Story" (Audrey Hepburn, Peter Finch, Edith Evans), "On the Beach" (Gregory Peck, Ava Gardner, Anthony Perkins, Fred Astaire in his first non-dancing role), "Operation Petticoat" (Cary Grant, Tony Curtis), "Pillow Talk" (Doris Day, Rock Hudson, Thelma Ritter), "Porgy and Bess" (Sidney Poitier, Dorothy Dandridge, Sammy Davis), "Sleeping Beauty" (Walt Disney cartoon), "Some Like It Hot" (Marilyn Monroe, Joe E. Brown, Jack Lemmon), "They Came to Cordura" (Gary Cooper, Van Heflin, Rita Hayworth).

After 31 years on radio and television, the "Voice of Firestone" concluded (June 1) its Monday night programs of light classic and operatic music. (Howard Barlow was the orchestra conductor since 1943.)

Popular among the current dances was the cha-cha.

The world's heavyweight championship title went to Sweden, when Ingemar Johansson, European champion, of Goteborg defeated (June 26) the American title holder Floyd Patterson, a 5-1 favorite, at Yankee Stadium, New York, by a third round knockout with his much vaunted right hand, having floored Patterson seven times before the referee halted the bout.

For the first time in baseball, a second All-Star game was played (Aug. 3, at Los Angeles Stadium).

Deaths of the year included Ethel Barrymore, 79 (June 18), last of the famous Drew-Barrymore family of actors, in Beverly Hills, Cal., and Walter Williams, 117 (Dec. 19), a soldier in General Hood's Texas Brigade and the last Confederate Army and Civil War veteran, in Houston, Tex.

ঽ৵ 1960

Alley Oop. w., m., Dallas Frazier. Los Angeles: Kavelin Music, Inc., cop. 1960.

The Apartment. *See below:* **Theme from The Apartment.**

Are You Lonesome To-Night? (*answer version:* **Yes, I'm Lonesome To-Night**). w., m., Roy Turk and Lou Handman. Bourne, Inc., and Cromwell Music, Inc., cop. 1926 by Bourne, Inc. [originally, Irving Berlin, Inc.]; cop. 1960 by Bourne, Inc., and Cromwell Music, Inc. (See 1926.)

The Best of Everything (*film:* **The Best of Everything**). w., Sammy Cahn. m., Alfred Newman. Twentieth Century Music Corp., cop. 1960.

Calcutta. w., Lee Pockriss and Paul J. Vance. m., Heino Gaze. George Pincus & Sons Music Corp. and Symphony House Music Publishers Corp., cop. 1958 and 1960 by Edition Takt und Ton, G.m.b.H., Berlin; cop. 1960 by George Pincus & Sons Music Corp. and Symphony House Music Publishers Corp.

Camelot (Camelot). w., Alan Jay Lerner. m., Frederick Loewe. Chappell & Co., Inc., cop. 1960 by Alan Jay Lerner and Frederick Loewe.

Cathy's Clown. w., m., Don Everly and Phil Everly. Nashville, Tenn.: Acuff-Rose Publications, cop. 1960.

Chain Gang. w., m., Sam Cooke. Hollywood, Cal.: Kags Music Corp., cop. 1960.

Dolce Far Niente (The Unsinkable Molly Brown). w., m., Meredith Willson. Frank Music Corp.—Rinimer Corp., cop. 1960 by Rinimer Corp.

Everybody's Somebody's Fool. w., Jack Keller. m., Howard Greenfield. Aldon Music, Inc., cop. 1960.

Footsteps. w., m., Barry Mann and Hank Hunter. Aldon Music, Inc., cop. 1960.

Green Fields. w., m., Terry Gilkyson, Richard Dehr and Frank Miller. Hollywood, Cal.: Montclare Music Corp., cop. 1960.

I Ain't Down Yet (The Unsinkable Molly Brown). Instrumental. m., Meredith Willson. Frank Music Corp.—Rinimer Corp., cop. 1960 by Rinimer Corp.

I'm Sorry. w., m., Ronnie Self and Dub Albritton. Champion Music Corp., cop. 1960.

I Want to Be Wanted—Per Tutta la Vita. English words, Kim Gannon. Italian words, A. Testa. m., Pino Spotti. Leeds Music Corp., cop. 1960 by Casa Editrice Santa Cecilia.

If Ever I Would Leave You (Camelot). w., Alan Jay Lerner. m., Frederick Loewe. Chappell & Co., Inc., cop. 1960 by Alan Jay Lerner and Frederick Loewe.

It's Now or Never. w., m., Aaron Schroeder and Wally Gold. Gladys Music, Inc., cop. 1960.

Itsy Bitsy, Teenie Weenie, Yellow Polka-Dot Bikini. w., m., Paul J. Vance and Lee Pockriss. George Pincus & Sons Music Corp.

Mr. Lucky (*TV production:* **Mr. Lucky**). Instrumental. m., Henry Mancini. Southdale Music Corp., cop. 1960 (selling agent, Chappell & Co., Inc.).

My Heart Has a Mind of Its Own. w., Howard Greenfield. m., Jack Keller. Aldon Music, Inc., cop. 1960.

My Love for You. w., Sid Wayne. m., Abner Silver. Cathryl Music Corp., cop. 1960 (selling agent, Hill and Range Songs, Inc.).

Never on Sunday (*film:* **Never on Sunday**). w., Billy Towne. m., Manos Hadjidakis. Esteem Music Corp., and Sidmore Music, Inc., cop. 1960 by U.A. Cine-Music, Inc.; cop. 1960 by Esteem Music Corp., and Sidmore Music, Inc. (selling agent, Keys-Hansen, Inc.) (Academy Award Winner, 1960)

North to Alaska (*film:* **North to Alaska**). w., m., Mike Phillips. Twentieth Century Music Corp., cop. 1960.

Only the Lonely Know the Way I Feel. w., m., Roy Orbison and Joe Melson. Nashville, Tenn.: Acuff-Rose Publications, cop. 1960.

La Pachanga. Spanish words and music, Eduardo Davidson. English words, Jeanne Pollack. Peer International Corp., cop. 1959 by Peer y Compania, Havana, Cuba; cop. 1960 by Peer International Corp.

Per Tutta La Vita. *See above:* **I Want to Be Wanted.**

Puppy Love. w., Hy [Hyman Robert] Fenster. m., Dick Chaffin. Heigh-Ho Music Co., cop. 1960.

Save the Last Dance for Me. w., m., Jerome "Doc" Pomus and Mort Shuman. Rumbalero Music, Inc., cop. 1960 (selling agent, Hill and Range Songs, Inc.).

Sink the Bismarck. w., m., Johnny Horton and Tillman Franks. Shreveport, La.: Cajun Publishing Co., Inc., cop. 1960.

Starlight. w., m., Lee Pockriss and Paul J. Vance. Cathryl Music Corp., cop. 1959 (selling agent, Hill and Range Songs, Inc.).

Stuck on You. w., m., Aaron Schroeder and J. Leslie McFarland. Gladys Music, Inc., cop. 1960.

Theme from The Apartment (*film:* **The Apartment**). Instrumental. m., Clarence Williams. Mills Music, Inc., cop. 1949 by Lawrence Wright Music Co., Ltd., London.

Tracy's Theme (*TV production:* **The Philadelphia Story**). w., Rozz Gordon. m., Robert Ascher. Devon Music, Inc., cop. 1960.

The Twist. w., m., Hank Ballard. Chicago: Tollie Music, cop. 1959; assigned to Lois Music Publishing Co., Cincinnati. (Originally copyright in 1958 by Gladstone Music, Inc., Chicago. The song, which created a dance craze in 1961, was popularized by Chubby Checker, a 20-year-old vocalist and dancer from South Philadelphia, whose real name is Ernest Evans.)

The Unforgiven—The Need for Love (*film:* **The Unforgiven**). w., Ned Washington. m., Dimitri Tiomkin. Hecht & Buzzell, Inc., cop. 1960 (selling agent, Keys, Hansen, Inc.).

The Village of St. Bernadette. w., m., Eula Parker. Ludlow Music, Inc., cop. 1960.

Walk, Don't Run. w., m., Johnny Smith. Forshay Music, Inc., cop. 1960.

We'll Have to Go. w., Charles Green. m., Joe and Audrey Allison. Hollywood, Cal.: Central Songs, Inc., cop. 1960.

Yes, I'm Lonesome To-Night. *See above:* Are You Lonesome To-Night?

You Talk Too Much. w., m., Joseph Jones and Reginald Hall. Kahl Music, Inc., cop. 1960.

In protest against segregation at lunch counters in variety stores, Negro students in Greensboro, N. C., staged (Feb. 1) a "sit-down" demonstration—a movement which quickly spread to other Southern cities, while similar stores in New York were picketed in sympathy; more than 1,000 participants faced trial for the disturbances.

The training manuals of the U.S. Air Force came (Feb. 3) under criticism for questionable statements, one of which declared that 30 of the 95 persons who revised the English translation of the Bible for the National Council of Churches were members of subversive groups.

President Eisenhower made two two-week goodwill tours: the first (in February) to Latin America (Puerto Rico, Brazil, Argentina, Chile, and Uruguay, where he received a temporary eye irritation from a tear gas bomb during an anti-American outburst in Montevideo); and the second (in June) to the Orient (the Philippine Islands, Formosa, Okinawa, in which place 1,500 Leftists staged a derisive snake-dance, and South Korea—a contemplated visit to Japan being cancelled because of mounting anti-U.S. demonstrations there).

During the President's visit to Brazil, 19 musicians of the U.S. Navy band and 42 other persons lost (Feb. 25) their lives in a collision of a U.S. Navy transport plane and a Brazilian airliner over Sugar Loaf Mountain near Rio de Janeiro—only three of the 64 aboard the planes were saved.

Communist China continued its periodic shelling of the off-shore island of Nationalist-held Quemoy and increased its bombardments during President Eisenhower's visit to Formosa.

The world's largest submarine, the nuclear-powered 7,750-ton U.S.S. Triton, circumnavigated the globe on a submerged voyage of 41,519 miles in 84 days (Feb. 26-May 10), pursuing in general the route of the sixteenth century Portuguese explorer Ferdinand Magellan.

Following a disastrous explosion (Mar. 4) on a French munitions ship in Havana harbor, Cuban Premier Fidel Castro charged the United States with participation in the sabotage.

A Soviet rocket shot down (May 1) a U.S. weather research plane (U-2) which had strayed on a mission in Turkey into Soviet-Afghan territory; the Russians characterized the flight "an aggressive provocation aimed at wrecking the summit conference," scheduled to be that month in Paris by the heads of Great Britain, France, the United States, and Russia. Soviet Premier Nikita S. Khrushchev angrily denounced the United States and President Eisenhower personally, and rescinded his invitation to the latter to visit the U.S.S.R. As a result, the "summit" meeting was disbanded. (Francis Gary Powers, pilot of the ill-fated U-2, was sentenced on Aug. 19, by a Moscow court, to 10 years' imprisonment for espionage. On February 10, 1962 Powers was exchanged for Soviet spy Colonel Rudolf Ivanovich Abel.)

A strike of 12,000 actors in New York caused (June 2-12) a ten-day blackout of the city's 22 Broadway theatres.

A second U.S. plane, an R-B 47, on a routine scientific research flight, was shot down (July 1) over Barents Sea by Russian flyers over allegedly Soviet territorial waters. (The two surviving crewmen were released on Jan. 25, 1961.)

The 15th session of the United Nations General Assembly brought together (Sept. 20-Oct. 13) in New York so large a concentration of foreign governmental representatives that their protection required the vigilance of the city's entire police, the FBI, and other secret service agencies. Conspicuous were Soviet Premier Nikita S. Khrushchev and Cuban Premier Fidel Castro, both of whom fraternized familiarly on the streets and before news and television cameras. Khrushchev also appeared on the balcony of the Russian Embassy and answered questions directed at him by the public. At the UN, during a stormy debate, he twice angrily interrupted a speech by British Prime Minister Harold Macmillan; on another occasion, he signified his disapproval of the remarks by the Philippine delegate by removing his shoe and pounding his desk with the heel.

The white S.S. Hope, a privately financed floating hospital and medical school, sailed (Sept. 22) from San Francisco on a year's mission to carry medical knowledge and treatment to the people of Indonesia and South Vietnam. (The ship returned to its home port on Sept. 14, 1961.)

The Post Office Department established its first automated post office in Providence, R. I., and issued (Oct. 20) a special postage stamp commemorating the event.

At the request of Guatemala and Nicaragua, the United States despatched (Nov. 16) naval vessels to patrol Central American waters during an abortive uprising in these countries, originating in Costa Rica and believed to have been inspired by Cuban Premier Fidel Castro.

A U.S. Air Force transport plane, taking off from Munich Riem Municipal Airport for England, crashed (Dec. 17) in the heart of the German city on a streetcar crowded with Christmas shoppers, killing at least 50 persons.

Among the year's books of popular fiction were: "The Constant Image" (Marcia Davenport), "The Dean's Watch" (Elizabeth Goudge), "The Leopard" (Giuseppe de Lampedusa), "The Lovely Ambition" (Mary Ellen Chase), "To Kill a Mockingbird" (Harper Lee; Pulitzer prize 1961). Readers of non-fiction bought: "Arthritis and Folk Medicine (DeForest Clinton Jarvis), "Born Free" (Joy Adamson), "The Conscience of a Conservative" (Barry Goldwater, Arizona's Republican Senator), "The Night They Burned the Mountain" (Thomas A. Dooley), "Pictorial History of the Civil War" (Bruce Catton), "The Rise and Fall of the Third Reich" (William L. Shirer), "This Is My God" (Herman Wouk), "The Waste Makers" (Vance Packard). Newly discovered diaries and memoirs increased the output of books about the Civil War for the coming centenary.

The Broadway stage presented, among other plays: "Toys in the Attic" (Hudson, Feb. 25; 464 perf.), "A Thurber Carnival" (ANTA Playhouse, Feb. 26; 127 and 86 later perf.); "The Best Man" (Morosco, Mar. 31; 521 perf.), "A Taste of Honey" (Lyceum, Oct. 4; 391 perf.), "Advise and Consent" (Cort, Nov. 17; 212 perf.), "All the Way Home" (Belasco, Nov. 30; 334 perf.; Pulitzer prize 1961). Popular among new musicals were: "Bye Bye Birdie" (Martin Beck, Apr. 14; 608 perf.), "The Fantasticks" (Sullivan Street Playhouse, May 3; running into 1962), "Tenderloin" (46th Street, Oct. 17; 217 perf.), "The Unsinkable Molly Brown" (Winter Garden, Nov. 3; running into 1962), "Camelot" (Majestic, Dec. 3; running into 1962), "Wildcat" (Alvin, Dec. 16; 172 perf.), "Do Re Mi" (St. James, Dec. 26; 400 perf.). "West Side Story" returned for a run (Apr. 27; 241 perf.).

The top picture, money-wise, was "Can-Can" (Frank Sinatra, Shirley MacLaine, Maurice Chevalier, Louis Jourdan). Other films were: "The Apartment" (Jack Lemmon, Shirley MacLaine), "Butterfield 8" (Elizabeth Taylor, Laurence Harvey), "Elmer Gantry" (Burt Lancaster, Jean Simmons), "Exodus" (Paul Newman, Eva Marie Saint), "From the Terrace" (Paul Newman, Joanne Woodward), "G.I. Blues" (Elvis Presley), "Journey to the Center of the Earth" (Pat Boone, Arlene Dahl), "The Man in the Cocked Hat" (Peter Sellers, Terry Thomas), "Please Don't Eat the Daisies" (Doris Day, David Niven), "Psycho" (Janet Leigh, Anthony Perkins), "Solomon and Sheba" (Yul Brynner,

Gina Lollobrigida), "Spartacus" (Laurence Olivier, Kirk Douglas, Charles Laughton), "Suddenly Last Summer" (Elizabeth Taylor, Katharine Hepburn), "The World of Susie Wong" (Nancy Kwan, William Holden). Two films dealt with England's great esthete: "Oscar Wilde" (Robert Morley, Phyllis Calvert) and "The Trials of Oscar Wilde" (Peter Finch, Yvonne Mitchell).

After 27 years on radio, "The Romance of Helen Trent" (1933), a daytime soap opera, came (June 24) to an end with the 7,222th episode.

Floyd Patterson, 25-year-old boxer, became (June 20) the first, and youngest, man in boxing to regain the world's heavyweight championship, at the Polo Grounds, New York, with a fifth round knockout of the defending title holder Ingemar Johansson of Sweden, to whom Patterson lost the title in 1959.

Deaths of the year included: Oscar Hammerstein 2nd, 65 (Aug. 23), in Doylestown, Pa.; Emily Post, 86 (Sept. 25), in New York; Lawrence Tibbett, 63 (July 15), in New York; Clara Kimball Young, 70 (Oct. 15), in Hollywood.

In the November elections, Democratic Senator John Fitzgerald Kennedy of Massachusetts nosed out by a small popular majority his Republican opponent Vice President Richard Milhous Nixon. During the campaign, they engaged in four nationally televised debates—a new political technique.

The national population was 179,323,175 (or 183,300,000 with members of the Armed Forces and other Americans abroad).

Ϩ☞ 1961

Apache. Instrumental. m., Jerry Lordan. Regent Music Corp., cop. 1960 by Francis, Day & Hunter, Ltd., London.

Big Bad John. w., m., Jimmy Dean. Nashville, Tenn.: Cigma Music Co., cop. 1961.

The Bilboa Song (Happy End). English words, Johnny Mercer. German words, Bert[olt] Brecht. m., Kurt Weill. Harms, Inc., cop. 1929 by Universal Editions; cop. renewed and assigned to Harms, Inc.

Dum Dum. w., m., Sharon Sheely and Jackie Deshannon. Hollywood. Cal.: Metric Music, Inc., cop. 1961 (selling agent, Keys-Hansen, Inc., New York).

Ebony Eyes. w., m., John D. Loudermilk. Nashville, Tenn.: Acuff-Rose Publications, cop. 1961.

Exodus. *See below:* (Main Theme from) **Exodus.**

Hey, Look Me Over (Wildcat). w., Carolyn Leigh. m., Cy Coleman. Morley Music Co., Inc., cop. 1960 by Carolyn Leigh and Cy Coleman (selling agent, Edwin H. Morris & Co., Inc.)

A 100 Pounds of Clay. w., m., B. Elgin, L. Dixon and K. Rogers. Gil Music Corp., cop. 1961 (selling agent, George Pincus & Sons Music Corp.).

Hurt. w., m., Jimmy Crane and Al Jacobs. Miller Music Corp., cop. 1953. (Popularized in 1961.)

I Believe in You (How to Succeed in Business without Really Trying). w., m., Frank Loesser. Frank Music Corp., cop. 1961 by Frank Loesser.

The Lion Sleeps Tonight—Wimoweh. New words and revised music, Hugo Peretti, Luigi Creatore, George Weiss and Albert Stanton. "Based on a song by Paul Campbell." Folkways Music Publishers, Inc., cop. 1951 and 1952; cop. 1961 with new matter. (Based on "Wimoweh—Hey Up, Joe! On Your Way!," English words by Roy Ilene, musical adaptation and arrangement by Paul Campbell, Folkways Music Publishers, Inc., cop. 1951; cop. 1952 with new English lyrics.)

Little Devil. w., m., Neil Sedaka and Howard Greenfield. Aldon Music, Inc., cop. 1961.

Little Sister. w., m., Jerome "Doc" Pomus and Mort Shuman. Elvis Presley Music, Inc., cop. 1961.

Love Makes the World Go 'Round (Carnival!) *See below:* **Theme from "Carnival!"**

(Main Theme from) Exodus (*film:* **Exodus**). Instrumental. m., Ernest Gold. Chappell & Co., Inc., cop. 1960 by Carlyle-Alpina S. A. (Published as a song, words by Pat Boone, Chappell & Co., Inc., cop. 1960 and 1961.)

Michael—Row the Boat Ashore. w., m., traditional; arr. by Albert Gamse. Larrabee Publications, cop. 1961.

Moody River. w., m., G. Bruce. Nashville, Tenn.: Keva Music Co., cop. 1961.

Moon River *(film:* **Breakfast at Tiffany's).** w., John Mercer. m., Henry Mancini. Famous Music Corp., cop. 1961.

Pocketful of Miracles *(film:* **Pocketful of Miracles).** w., Sammy Cahn. m., James Van Heusen. Maraville Music Corp., cop. 1961.

Pony Time. w., m., Don Covay and John Berry. Alan K. Music Corp. and Harvard Music., Inc., cop. 1961.

Raindrops. w., m., Dee Clark. Chicago: Conrad Publishing Co., Inc., cop. 1961.

Runaround Sue. w., m., Ernie Maresca and Dion Di Mucci. Schwartz Music Co. and Disal Music Corp., cop. 1961.

Runaway. w., m., Max T. Crook and Charles Westover. Detroit: Vickie Music, Inc., and McLaughlin Publishing Co., cop. 1961.

Running Scared. w., m., Ray Orbison and Joe Melson. Nashville, Tenn.: Acuff-Rose Publications, cop. 1961.

Surrender. w., m., Jerome "Doc" Pomus and Mort Shuman. Elvis Presley Music, Inc., cop. 1960.

Take Good Care of My Baby. w., m., Gerry Goffin and Carole King. Aldon Music, Inc., cop. 1961 (selling agent, Keys-Hansen, Inc.).

Theme from "Carnival!"–Love Makes the World Go 'Round (Car-nival!). w., m., Bob Merrill. Robbins Music Corp., cop. 1961.

Travelin' Man. w., m., Ricky Nelson. Hollywood, Cal.: Four Star Sales Co., Inc., cop. 1961.

Where the Boys Are *(film:* **Where the Boys Are).** w., m., Howard Greenfield and Neil Sedaka. Aldon Music, Inc., cop. 1961.

Wimoweh. *See above:* **The Lion Sleeps Tonight.**

Wonderland by Night. w., Lincoln Chase. m., Klauss Gunter Newman. Roosevelt Music Co., Inc., cop. 1960.

Wooden Heart (*film:* **G.I. Blues**). w., m., Fred Wise, Benjamin Weisman, Kathleen G. Twomey and Kaempfert. Gladys Music, Inc., cop. 1961.

Yellow Bird. w., m., N. Luboff, M. Keith and A. Bergman. Frank Music Corp., cop. 1958.

You Don't Have to be a Tower of Strength. w., Burt F. Bacharach. m., Bob Hilliard. Famous Music Corp., cop. 1961.

John Fitzgerald Kennedy, Democrat, of Massachusetts, was inaugurated 35th President.

The rocking chair became a familiar article of Presidential furniture.

Marking two years of declining relations with Cuba as its Premier Fidel Castro pursued a pro-Soviet line, the outgoing Eisenhower administration severed (Jan. 3) diplomatic relations with the island republic in consequence of Castro's demand that the United States reduce its embassy in Havana to eleven persons.

The Civil War, or "War between the States," reached its 100th anniversary. A five-year centennial celebration opened (Jan. 8) with ceremonies at the tombs of Ulysses S. Grant in New York and Robert E. Lee in Lexington, Va.; they were followed (Jan. 9) by a reenactment by cadets in Charleston, S. C., of the bombardment of the "Star of Hope," a Federal ship sent to reinforce the Union garrison at Fort Sumter located in the harbor.

The great scientific event of the year was the successful orbiting (Apr. 13) by the Soviet Union of the first man-carrying space missile around the earth, with "cosmonaut" Major Yuri Gagarin—a feat duplicated (Aug. 7) by the Soviets with Major Gherman S. Titov. United States scientists tested (May 5) at Cape Canaveral, Fla., their first man-in-space missile, carrying "astronaut" Navy Commander Alan B. Shepard Jr. in a suborbital flight of fifteen minutes—a successful experiment repeated (July 21) with Air Force Captain Virgil I. Grissom.

Forty-two American tourists, along with 565 other nationals and 350 crew members, on a Caribbean cruise, were trapped aboard the Portuguese luxury liner "Santa Maria" when the vessel which sailed from Lisbon for Port Everglades, Fla., was seized (Jan. 22) at sea by native rebels and finally debarked (Feb. 2) at Recife, Brazil, after pursuit and capture by U. S. Navy planes and ships.

President Kennedy authorized (Mar. 1) the formation of the Peace Corps, a group of skilled and dedicated men and women for volunteer service in undeveloped overseas areas in education, agriculture, and hygiene.

An abortive attempt to overthrow the Castro regime in Cuba, launched (Apr. 17) by Cuban exiles on the marshy beaches of Las Villas province with U.S. military equipment, involved the prestige of the United States and brought denunciation from abroad, for alleged participation in the operation by the U.S. Central Intelligence Agency. Premier Castro offered (May 17) to exchange captured invaders for American tractors, but the negotiations were abandoned after a five-week deadlock on terms.

The U.S. Department of Labor created (Apr. 30) an Office of Automation, to study its effects on labor.

Four instances of "hijacking" American airliners occurred (May 1, July 24, Aug. 3, Aug. 9): in three cases the planes were diverted at gunpoint to Havana; in the fourth, the attempt was foiled by a landing in El Paso, Tex.

Anti-segregationists, forming a bi-racial passive resistence group called Congress of Racial Equality (known as CORE), started a movement of so-called Freedom Rides into the Deep South on interstate public busses. The Riders encountered mob violence in Anniston, Ala. (May 14) and in Montgomery, Ala. (May 20). To maintain peace, President Kennedy ordered 400 (later 200 more) U.S. marshals to the areas, until normal conditions were restored.

In commemoration of the 34th anniversary of Lindbergh's solo transatlantic flight (1927), a U.S. Air Force jet bomber flew (May 26) from New York to Paris in 3 hours 19 minutes 41 seconds for the opening of the Paris International Air Show.

Ernest Hemingway, Nobel Prize-winning American author (1953), fatally shot himself (July 2) at his home in Ketchum, Idaho.

By invoking the Taft-Hartley Labor Act (1947), President Kennedy halted (July 3) a crippling 18-day tie-up of the nation's merchant fleet, which resulted from a jurisdictional dispute over American-owned, or so-called "runaway," ships under foreign registry.

The Soviet Union added to the growing international tension over the military occupation of Berlin by imposing (Aug. 12-13) drastic restrictions in travel between East and West Berlin to halt the flow of refugees from East Germany to the "free" world and, to thwart further flights, erected a 25-mile concrete wall, 5 feet high, along the dividing line, across which Western and Communist battle-armed units faced each other only a few yards apart. President Kennedy thereupon reinforced (Aug. 18) the 5,000-man U.S. garrison in West Berlin by the addition of 1,500 men.

The Soviet Union resumed (Sept. 1) nuclear testing, despite a Big Power moratorium, and, overriding protests from non-Communist nations and an appeal from the United States, exploded (Oct. 31) at its Arctic probing ground a bomb estimated from 62 to 90 megatons.

Hurricane "Carla," described as the fiercest storm of the century, lashed (Sept. 10-11) the coastal regions of Louisiana and upper Texas; later, hurricane "Esther" swept (Sept. 19-21) the Atlantic coast from North Carolina to Cape Cod.

On an invitation extended by Vice President Lyndon B. Johnson during his visit to Karachi, a 40-year-old Pakastani camel driver toured (Oct. 15-21) the United States, as a guest of the People-to-People exchange program.

The Metropolitan Museum of Art, New York, acquired (Nov. 15) at a local public auction Rembrandt's painting "Aristotle Contemplating the Bust of Homer" for the highest sum ever paid for any canvas—$2,300,000 (the painter received 500 florins, or about $7,800, in 1653).

To prevent the return to power by the slain Dominican dictator Rafael Trujillo's family, the United States intervened (Nov. 19) by a show of naval strength in the island's waters.

As a further step in the project to orbit a human astronaut, the Air Force at Cape Canaveral, Fla., flew (Nov. 29) a chimpanzee, named Enos, in two complete 17,500-mile-an-hour revolutions around the Earth in 3 hours 21 minutes and safely recovered the capsule and the living animal in the Atlantic 250 miles south of Bermuda.

President Kennedy paid a weekend goodwill visit to Caracas, Venezuela (Dec. 16), and to Bogotá, Colombia (Dec. 17).

The year's books of fiction included: "The Agony and the Ecstasy" (Irving Stone), "The Carpetbaggers" (Harold Robbins), "Clock without Hands" (Carson McCullers), "Daughter of Silence" (Morris L. West), "The Edge of Sadness" (Edwin O'Connor), "Franny and Zooey" (J. D. Salinger), "God Must Be Sad" (Fannie Hurst), "The Incredible Journey" (Sheila Burnford), "The Judas Tree" (A. J. Cronin), "Midcentury" (John Dos Passos), "Mila 18" (Leon M. Uris), "A New Life" (Bernard Malamud), "Pomp and Circumstance" (Noel Coward), "Spirit Lake" (MacKinlay Kantor), "To Kill a Mockingbird" (Harper Lee), "The White Rajah" (Nicholas Monsarrat), "Wilderness" (Robert Penn Warren), "The Winter of Our Discontent" (John Steinbeck). Non-fiction was represented by: "Before I Sleep" (Thomas A. Dooley), "Citizen Hearst" (W. A. Swanberg), "Diary and Autobiography of John Adams" (first four volumes), "Living Free" (Joy Adamson), "The Making of the President 1960" (Theodore H. White), "A Nation of Sheep" (William J. Lederer). "Ring of Bright Water" (Gavin Maxwell).

New to the stage were the plays: "Rhinoceros" (Longacre, Jan. 9; 277 perf.), "Come Blow Your Horn" (Brooks Atkinson, Feb. 22; running into 1962); "Mary, Mary" (Helen Hayes, Mar. 8; running into 1962), "A Far Country" (Apr. 4; 271 perf.), and the musical, "Carnival!" (Imperial, Apr. 13; running into 1962). Opening later in the season and continuing into 1962 were the plays: "Purlie Victorious" (Cort, Sept. 28), "The Caretaker" (Lyceum, Oct. 4), "A Shot in the Dark" (Booth,

Oct. 18), "Write Me a Murder" (Belasco, Oct. 26), "Gideon" (Plymouth, Nov. 9), "Take Her, She's Mine" (Biltmore, Dec. 21), "Ross" (O'Neill, Dec. 26), "The Night of the Iguana" (Royale, Dec. 28); and the musicals: "Sail Away" (Broadhurst, Oct. 3), "Milk and Honey" (Beck, Oct. 10), "How to Succeed in Business without Really Trying" (46th Street, Oct. 14), "The Gay Life" (Shubert, Nov. 18), "Subways Are for Sleeping" (St. James, Dec. 27). "The Threepenny Opera" closed (Dec. 17; 2,611 perf.) a run that began in 1954.

Among films, the top-money picture was "The Guns of Navarone" (Gregory Peck, David Niven, Anthony Quinn). Other motion pictures were: "Butterfield 8" (Elizabeth Taylor, Laurence Harvey), "Come September" (Rock Hudson, Gina Lollobrigida), "La Dolce Vita" (Anita Ekberg, Marcello Mastroianni), "Exodus" (Paul Newman, Eva Marie Saint), "The Flower Drum Song" (Nancy Kwan, James Shigeta), "King of Kings" (Jeffrey Hunter, Siobhan McKenna), "Splendor in the Grass" (Natalie Wood, Warren Beatty), "West Side Story" (Natalie Wood, Richard Beymer), "The World of Suzie Wong" (Nancy Kwan, William Holden). The "shooting" of films outside the United States caused American labor unions to seek restrictive legislation.

A bitter salary dispute between management and musicians threatened to prevent the opening of New York's Metropolitan Opera for its 77th season.

"Nausicaa," an American opera by Australia-born composer Peggy Glanville-Hicks, received (Aug. 19) its world première in Athens, Greece, in the recently restored ancient open-air theatre of Herodes Atticus, below the Acropolis.

The San Francisco Opera produced at the War Memorial Auditorium the world première of Normal Dello Joio's American opera "Blood Moon" (Sept. 18) and the first American performance of Benjamin Britten's new opera "A Midsummer Night's Dream" (Oct. 10).

Intense excitement was generated in baseball by the efforts and rivalry of Mickey Mantle and Roger Maris, both of the American League New York Yankees club, to equal or better Babe Ruth's 1927 record of 60 home runs in a 154-game season. The "M Boys," as they were called, didn't make it: Mantle hit 54 and Maris 59; however, the latter went on to set the new record of 61 for a season of 162 games.

Dancing couples favored, among new dances, "The Twist" and "La Pachanga" (by Cuban composer and dancer Eduardo Davidson). (Less popular were "The Fish," "The Pony," "The Madison," "The Mess Around," and "The Bristol Stomp.")

Deaths of the year included: playwright George S. Kaufman, 71 (June 2), in New York; Dr. Lee de Forest, "the father of radio," inventor of the audion tube and more than 300 other inventions, 87 (June 30), in Hollywood, Cal.; Ernest Hemingway, 61 (*see above*); baseball's great

"Ty" (Tyrus Raymond) Cobb, known as the "Georgia Peach," 74 (July 17), in Atlanta, Ga.; Dag Hammarskjold, Swedish-born Secretary General of the United Nations for 8½ years, killed in a plane crash near Ndola, Northern Rhodesia, on a mission to negotiate a cease-fire between Katangan and UN forces, 56 (Sept. 18); James Thurber, 66 (Nov. 2), in New York; "Grandma Moses" (Mrs. Thomas Salmon Moses, née Anna Mary Robertson), self-taught painter of American scenes, 101 (Dec. 13), in Hoosick Falls, N. Y.; Moss Hart, 57 (Dec. 20), in Palm Spring, Cal.

ᏁᎠ 1962

Addio, Addio. w., Migliacci and Domenico Modugno. m., Modugno. English lyric by Carl Sigman. Edizioni Curci, Milan; Miller Music Corp., cop. 1962. (Winner of 1962 San Remo Song Festival.)

Alley Cat. w., Jack Harlen. m., Frank Bjorn. Original Danish title, "Omkring et Flygel." Eureka Anstalt, Switzerland; Metorion Music Corp., cop. 1961, 1962.

Big Girls Don't Cry. w., m., Bob Crewe and Bob Gaudio. Claridge Music, Inc., cop. 1962.

Breaking Up Is Hard to Do. w., m., Neil Sedaka and Howard Greenfield. Screen Gems-Columbia Music, Inc., cop. 1962.

Can't Help Falling in Love (film: **Blue Hawaii**). w., m., George Weiss, Hugo Peretti and Luigi Creatore. Gladys Music, Inc., cop. 1961.

Cast Your Fate to the Wind. w., Carol Werber. m., Vincent Guaraldi. Atzal Music, Inc., cop. 1960.

Days of Wine and Roses (film: **Days of Wine and Roses**). w., Johnny Mercer. m., Henry Mancini. M. Witmark & Sons., cop. 1962. (Academy Award Winner, 1962.)

Desafinado. English words, Jon Hendricks and Jessie Cavanaugh. Portuguese words, Newton Mendonca. m., Antonio Carlos Jobim. Editora Musical Arapua, Brazil; Hollis Music, Inc.; Bendig Music Corp., cop. 1962.

Do You Love Me? w., m., Berry Gordy, Jr. Jobete Music Co., Inc., cop. 1962.

Don't Break the Heart That Loves You. w., m., Benny Davis and Ted Murry. Francon Music Corp., cop. 1962.

Duke of Earl. w., m., Earl Edwards, Bernie Williams and Eugene Dixon. Conrad Publishing Co., Inc.; Aba, Inc., cop. 1961.

Green Onions. w., m., Steve Cropper, Al Jackson, Jr., Lewis Steinberg and Booker T. Jones. East Publications; Bais Music, cop. 1962.

He's a Rebel. w., m., Gene Pitney. January Music Corp., cop. 1962.

Hey! Baby. w., m., Margaret Cobb and Bruce Channel. Le Bill Music, Inc., cop. 1962.

I Can't Stop Loving You. w., m., Don Gibson, Acuff-Rose Publications, Inc., cop. 1958.

I Know. w., m., Barbara George. Saturn Music, Inc., cop. 1961.

I Left My Heart in San Francisco. w., Douglass Cross. m., George Cory. General Music Publishing Co., Inc., cop. 1954.

If I Had a Hammer. w., m., Lee Hays and Pete Seeger. Ludlow Music, Inc., cop. 1958.

Johnny Angel. w., Lyn Duddy. m., Lee Pockriss. Post Music, Inc., cop. 1962.

Loco-Motion. w., m., Gerry Goffin and Carole King. Screen Gems-Columbia Music, Inc., cop. 1962.

Mashed Potato Time. w., m., Jon Sheldon and Harry Land. Rice Mill Publishing Co., Inc.; Jobete Music Co., Inc., cop. 1962.

Misty. w., Johnny Burke. m., Erroll Garner. Vernon Music Corp.; Octave Music Publishing Corp., cop. 1955.

Monster Mash. w., m., Bobby Pickett and Leonard Capizzi. Garpax Music Publishing Co.; Capizzi Music., cop. 1962.

My Coloring Book. w., Fred Ebb. m., John Kander. Sunbeam Music Corp., cop. 1962.

The One Who Really Loves You. w., m., William Robinson. Jobete Music Co., Inc., cop. 1962.

Palisades Park. w., m., Chuck Barris. Claridge Music, Inc., cop. 1962.

Please Mr. Postman. w., m., Brian Holland and Freddy C. Gorman. Jobete Music Co., Inc., cop. 1962.

Ramblin' Rose. w., m., Noel Sherman and Joe Sherman. Sweco Music Corp., cop. 1962.

Roses Are Red. w., m., Al Byron and Paul Evans. Lyle Music, Inc., cop. 1961.

Run to Him. w., m., Gerry Goffin and Jack Keller. Screen Gems-Columbia Music, Inc., cop. 1961.

Sheila. w., m., Tommy Roe. Eager Music; Low-Twi Music, cop. 1962.

Sherry. w., m., Bob Gaudio. Claridge Music, Inc., cop. 1962.

Soldier Boy. w., m., Florence Green and Luther Dixon. Ludix Publishing Co., cop. 1961.

The Stripper. m., David Rose. David Rose Publishing Co., cop. 1961.

Surfin' Safari. w., m., Mike Love and Brian Wilson. Guild Music Co., cop. 1962.

A Taste of Honey. w., Ric Marlow. m., Bobby Scott. Songfest Music Corp., cop. 1960 and 1962.

Telstar. m., Joe Meek. Ivy Music, Ltd., London; Campbell-Connelly, Inc., cop. 1962.

Town Without Pity (film: **Town Without Pity**). w., Ned Washington. m., Dimitri Tiomkin. United Artists Music Co., Inc., cop. 1961.

Twist and Shout. w., m., Bert Russell and Phil Medley. Robert Mellin, Inc.; Progressive Music Publishing Co., Inc., cop. 1960.

Twistin' the Night Away. w., m., Sam Cooke. Kags Music, cop. 1962.

Walk On By. w., m., Kendall Hayes. Lowery Music Co., Inc., cop. 1961.

The Wanderer. w., m., Ernest Maresca. Marimba Music Corp.; Schwartz Music Co., Inc., cop. 1960.

What Kind of Fool Am I? (Stop the World—I Want To Get Off). w., m., Leslie Bricusse and Anthony Newley. Essex Music. Ltd., London; Ludlow Music, Inc., cop. 1961.

Wolverton Mountain. w., m., Merle Kilgore and Claude King. Painted Desert Music Corp., cop. 1962.

You'll Lose a Good Thing. w., m., Barbara Lynn Ozen. Jamie Music Publishing Co.; Crazy Cajun Music Co., cop. 1962.

Deteriorating relations with Cuba were the prime concern of the United States foreign policy during 1962. The U. S. State Department publicized (Jan. 3) a report that said Cuba represents "a bridgehead of Sino-Soviet imperialism and a base for Communist agitation and subversion within the inner defense of the Western Hemisphere." Late in the year, the United States and the Soviet Union stood eyeball to eyeball in a confrontation over Soviet atomic missile sites that were being built in Cuba. The world was on the brink of war (Oct. 22) as President Kennedy imposed a quarantine, effective Oct. 24, against arms shipments to Cuba. The Soviet Union challenged (Oct. 23) the United States right to quarantine. The U. S. Navy was ordered (Oct. 24) to sink any Soviet ship that refused to obey the quarantine order. A fleet of 24 Soviet ships had been sighted en route to Cuba. The U. S. Navy stopped a Cuban-bound Soviet ship (Oct. 25) but allowed it to proceed since it was not carrying arms. The next day the United States and the Soviets agreed at the United Nations to avoid clashes at sea. Soviet Premier Khrushchev offered (Oct. 27) to withdraw Soviet offensive weapons from Cuba if the United States reciprocated in Turkey. President Kennedy rejected the proposal. The Cuban crisis was resolved (Oct. 28) when the Soviet Union agreed to remove its rocket bases in Cuba in return for an American pledge not to invade Cuba.

Ten money winners on rigged television quiz shows received suspended sentences in New York Special Sessions Court (Jan. 17) after pleading guilty to perjury charges. The defendants had previously testified that they had not been tipped off to answers prior to the shows.

United States involvement in Vietnam was becoming more visible. The U. S. Defense Dept. set up (Feb. 8) a new military command in South Vietnam, to be known as U. S. Military Assistance Command. President Kennedy said (Feb. 14) that United States troops in Vietnam training missions had been instructed only "to fire to protect themselves if fired upon."

In 1962 America leaped forward in its space race with the Soviet Union: Lt. Col. John H. Glenn, Jr., the first American in orbit, circled the Earth three times in Friendship 7 (Feb. 20). Navy Lt. Comdr. M. Scott Carpenter in Aurora 7 also completed a three-orbit flight (May 24). Navy Comdr. Walter M. Schirra completed (Oct. 3) six orbits of the Earth.

President Kennedy's first appointment (Mar. 30) to the U.S. Supreme Court was Deputy Attorney General Bryon R. White; he succeeded Charles Evan Whittaker, who resigned on advice of his doctors.

Century 21 Exposition in Seattle, the first World's Fair to be held in the United States in 22 years, opened Apr. 21 with a "space age" theme.

Prices on the New York Stock Exchange were hit (May 28) by the largest one-day drop since the "Black Tuesday" of Oct. 28, 1929. The Dow-Jones index fell 34.95 points to 576.93. In the next few days, the stock market rebounded and recovered virtually all of that loss.

Adolf Eichmann, 56, former Gestapo officer convicted by an Israeli court of playing a major role in the Nazi extermination of Jews, was hanged (May 31).

Aviation's worst disaster involving a single plane occurred when an Air France Boeing-707 Jet crashed (June 3) on takeoff from Paris, killing 130 persons.

An overwhelming majority of Algerians voted (July 1) for independence from France, officially ending a bitter seven-year struggle.

The 1962 Pulitzer prize for fiction was awarded to William Faulkner for "The Reivers." The Pulitzer committee found no play worthy of the award that year.

Paul Scofield in "A Man for All Seasons" and Margaret Leighton in "The Night of the Iguana" were named for giving the best performances in Broadway drama for the 1961–62 season in the Variety Poll of New York Drama Critics. Cited for outstanding performances in supporting roles were Sandy Dennis in "A Thousand Clowns" and Barbra Streisand in "I Can Get It for You Wholesale." Peter Fonda in "Blood, Sweat and Stanley Poole," and Barbara Harris in "From the Second City," were rated as most promising performers.

The New York Yankees beat the San Francisco Giants in the seventh game (Oct. 16) to win baseball's World Series.

The Academy of Motion Picture Arts and Sciences' Oscars for 1962 were awarded to "Lawrence of Arabia," best picture; Anne Bancroft in "The Miracle Worker," best actress; and Gregory Peck in "To Kill a Mockingbird," best actor.

Other major films of the year included "The Wonderful World of the Brothers Grimm" (Laurence Harvey, Claire Bloom), "What Ever Happened to Baby Jane?" (Bette Davis, Joan Crawford), "Advise and Consent" (Walter Pidgeon, Charles Laughton, Franchot Tone, Don Murray, Henry Fonda, Gene Tierney), "Bird Man of Alcatraz" (Burt Lancaster), "Divorce—Italian Style" (Marcello Mastroianni), "Hatari" (John Wayne), "The Longest Day" (John Wayne, Robert Mitchum, Robert Ryan), "The

Music Man" (Robert Preston, Shirley Jones), "Requiem for a Heavy-weight" (Anthony Quinn, Julie Harris), "Sergeants Three" (Frank Sinatra, Dean Martin, Sammy Davis, Jr.).

Two modestly scaled films, "David and Lisa" and "The Connection," had profound impact on the moviemaking industry. Both were independently made at relatively low cost. They were harbingers of a cycle of films dealing boldly with contemporary themes and made outside the orbit of major studio control.

Telstar, an experimental communications satellite, successfully transmitted (July 10) transatlantic television signals for the first time.

Film star Marilyn Monroe, 36, died (Aug. 5), an apparent suicide from an overdose of pills.

James E. Meridith, 29, an Air Force veteran, became the first Negro to be enrolled at the University of Mississippi (Sept. 30) after a clash between state officials and the U. S. Justice Department. This clash led to a contempt citation against Mississippi Governor Ross Barnett in the Fifth U. S. Circuit Court in New Orleans.

Pope John XXIII opened the 21st Ecumenical Council of the Roman Catholic Church in Rome (Oct. 11).

Serious border clashes erupted (Oct. 20) on the Indian-Chinese border. India declared a national emergency and requested United States assistance. Communist China declared a unilateral cease-fire (Nov. 2) and withdrew its troops (Dec. 1) from the disputed area.

Former Vice President Richard M. Nixon was defeated (Nov. 6) by incumbent Democratic Governor Edmund G. Brown in the race for the California governorship. Nixon bitterly attacked the press for unfair reporting and said, "You won't have Nixon to kick around anymore."

Mrs. Eleanor Roosevelt, 78, widow of President Franklin Delano Roosevelt, died (Nov. 7) in her New York City home. Kirsten Flagstad, 67, the opera singer, died (Dec. 8) in Oslo, Norway.

A heavy fog over London from Dec. 3 to Dec. 10 was blamed for the death of at least 170 people.

६० 1963

Abilene. w., John Loudermilk, Lester Brown, Bob Gibson and Albert Stanton. m., adapted from a traditional song. Acuff-Rose Publications, Inc., cop. 1963.

Be My Baby. w., m., Jeff Barry, Ellie Greenwich and Phil Spector. Trio Music Co., Inc.; Mother Bertha Music, Inc., cop. 1963.

Blame It on the Bossa Nova. w., m., Cynthia Weil and Barry Nann. Screen Gems-Columbia Music, Inc., cop. 1962.

Blowin' in the Wind. w., m., Bob Dylan. M. Witmark & Sons, cop. 1962 and 1963.

Blue Velvet. w., m., Bernie Wayne and Lee Morris. Vogue Music Co., cop. 1951.

Busted. w., m., Harlan Howard. Pamper Music, Inc., cop. 1962 and 1963.

Call Me Irresponsible (film: **Papa's Delicate Condition**). w., Sammy Cahn. m., James Van Heusen. Paramount Music Corp., cop. 1962 and 1963. (Academy Award Winner, 1963.)

Can't Get Used to Losing You. w., m., Doc Pomus and Mort Shuman. Brenner Music, Inc., cop. 1962.

Charade (film: **Charade**). w., Johnny Mercer. m., Henry Mancini. Southdale Music Corp.; Northern Music Corp., cop. 1963.

Danke Schoen. w., Kurt Schwabach and Milt Gabler. m., Bert Kaempfert. Tonika-Verlag Horst Bussow, Hamburg; Roosevelt Music, Inc., cop. 1962 and 1963.

Dominique. w., m., by Soeur Sourire, O.P. English lyric by Noel Regney. Editions Primavera, s.a., Brussels; General Music Publishing Co., Inc., cop. 1962 and 1963.

Don't Think Twice, It's All Right. w., m., Bob Dylan. M. Witmark & Sons, cop. 1963.

Easier Said Than Done. w., m., William Linton and Larry Huff. Nom Music, Inc., cop. 1963.

Et Pourtant. French words, Charles Aznavour. m., Georges Garvarentz. English words for the song, "Yet . . . I Know," Don Raye. Les Editions French Music, Paris; Editions Musicales Charles Aznavour, Paris; Leeds Music Corp., cop. 1963 and 1964.

Fingertips. w., m., Henry Cosby and Clarence Paul. Jobete Music Co., Inc., cop. 1962 and 1963.

For Mama. English words, Don Black. French words, Robert Gall. m., Charles Aznavour. Original French title, "La Mamma." Editions Musicales Charles Aznavour, Paris; Ludlow Music, Inc., cop. 1963 and 1964.

Go Away, Little Girl. w., m., Gerry Goffin and Carole King. Screen Gems-Columbia Music, Inc., cop. 1962.

Heat Wave. w., m., Eddie Holland, Brian Holland and Lamont Dozier. Jobete Music Co., Inc., cop. 1963.

Hello Muddah, Hello Fadduh (A Letter from Camp). w., Allan Sherman. Musical adaptation by Lou Busch from Ponchielli's "Dance of the Hours." Curtain Call Productions, Inc., cop. 1963.

He's So Fine. w., m., Ronnie Mack. Bright-Tunes Music Corp., cop. 1962.

Hey, Paula. w., m., Ray Hildebrand. Le Bill Music, Inc.; Marbill Music., cop. 1962.

How Insensitive. English words, Norman Gimbel. Portuguese words, Vinicius de Moraes. m., Antonio Carlos Jobim. Also known by its Portuguese title, "Insensatez." Antonio Carlos Jobim & Vinicius de Moraes, Brazil; Duchess Music Corp., cop. 1963 and 1964.

I Love You Because. w., m., Leon Payne. Fred Rose Music, Inc., cop. 1949.

I Will Follow Him. English words, Norman Gimbel and Arthur Altman. French words, Jacques Plante. m., J. W. Stole and Del Roma. Also known as "I Will Follow You." Original French title, "Chariot." Les Editions Jacques Plante, Paris; Leeds Music Corp., cop. 1962 and 1963.

If I had a Hammer. w., m., Lee Hays and Pete Seeger. Ludlow Music, Inc., cop. 1958.

If You Wanna Be Happy. w., Carmela Guida, Frank J. Guida and Joseph Royster. m., Frank J. Guida and Joseph Royster. Rock Masters, Inc., cop. 1962.

I'm Leaving It Up to You. w., m., Dewey Terry and Don F. Harris. Venice Music, Inc., cop. 1957.

Insensatez. *See* How Insensitive.

It's My Party. w., m., Herb Wiener, Wally Gold and John Gluck, Jr. Arch Music Co., Inc., cop. 1963.

La Mamma. *See* For Mama.

Limbo Rock. w., m., Jon Sheldon and William E. Strange. Four Star Music Co., Inc.; Twist Music., cop. 1962.

The Lonely Bull. m., Sol Lake. Almo Music Corp., cop. 1962.

Louie Louie. w., m., Richard Berry. Limax Music, Inc., cop. 1963.

Meditation. English words, Norman Gimbel. Portuguese words, Newton Mendonca. m., Antonio Carlos Jobim. Portuguese title, "Meditacao." Antonio Carlos Jobim & Mrs. Newton Mendonca, Brazil; Duchess Music Corp., cop. 1962 and 1963.

Mockingbird. w., m., Inez Foxx and Charlie Foxx. Saturn Music, Inc., cop. 1963.

More (Theme from "Mondo Cane") (film: Mondo Cane). English words, Norman Newell. Italian words, M. Ciociolini. m., Riz Ortolani and N. Oliviero. Ed. C.A.M., Rome; Ardmore & Beechwood, Ltd., London; Edward B. Marks Music Corp., cop. 1962 and 1963.

The Night Has a Thousand Eyes. w., m., Dottie Wayne, Marilyn Garrett and Ben Weisman. Blen Music, Inc.; Mabs Music Co., cop. 1962.

The Nitty Gritty. w., m., Lincoln Chase. Al Gallico Music Corp., cop. 1963.

Our Day Will Come. w., Mort Garson. m., Bob Hilliard. Rosewood Music Corp., cop. 1962.

Puff (The Magic Dragon). w., m., Peter Yarrow and Leonard Lipton. Pepamar Music Corp., cop. 1963.

Return to Sender (film: Girls! Girls! Girls!). w., m., Otis Blackwell and Winfield Scott. Elvis Presley Music, Inc., cop. 1962.

Rhythm of the Rain. w., m., John Gummoe. Sherman-De Vorzon Music Corp., cop. 1962 and 1963.

Ruby Baby. w., m., Jerry Lieber and Mike Stoller. Tiger Music, Inc., cop. 1955 and 1963.

So Much in Love. w., William Jackson and George Williams. m., Roy Straigis. Cameo-Parkway Publishing Co., Inc., cop. 1963.

Sugar Shack. w., m., Keith McCormack and Faye Voss. Dundee Music, cop. 1962.

Sukiyaki (My First Lonely Night). English words, Tom Leslie and Buzz Cason. Japanese words and music, Hachidai Makamura and Rokusuke Ei. Original Japanese title, "Ueo Muite Arukuo." Toshiba Music Publishing Co., Ltd., Tokyo; Beechwood Music Corp., cop. 1961 and 1963.

Surfin' U.S.A. w., Brian Wilson. m., Chuck Berry. Adapted from "Sweet Little Sixteen." Arc Music Corp., cop. 1958 and 1963.

The Times They Are A-Changin'. w., m., Bob Dylan. M. Witmark & Sons, cop. 1963.

Up on the Roof. w., m., Gerry Goffin and Carole King. Screen Gems-Columbia Music, Inc., cop. 1962.

Walk Right In. w., m., Erik Darling, Willard Svanoe, Hosie Woods, Gus Cannon. Peer International Corp.; Ryerson Music Publishers, Inc., cop. 1930 and 1963.

Wipe Out. m., Robert Berryhill, Patrick Connolly, James Fuller and Ron Wilson. Miraleste Music; Robin Hood Music Co., cop. 1963.

Wives and Lovers. w., Hal David. m., Burt Bacharach. Famous Music Corp., cop. 1963. (Inspired by, but not used in the film, "Wives and Lovers.")

Yet . . . I Know. *See* **Et Pourtant.**

You're the Reason I'm Living. w., m., Bobby Darin. Adaris Music, Inc., cop. 1962 and 1963.

John Fitzgerald Kennedy, the 35th President of the United States and the youngest man ever to be elected to that office, was killed (Nov. 22) by an assassin in Dallas, Texas. A few hours later, police arrested Lee Harvey Oswald, 24, on charges of firing the fatal bullet from a building along the President's parade route.

Exactly 99 minutes after President Kennedy was pronounced dead, Lyndon Baines Johnson, the Vice President, was sworn in as President by Federal District Judge Sarah Hughes at the Dallas airport. In Washington, D.C., President Johnson said to the nation: "I will do my best. That is all I can do. I ask for your help and God's."

In full view of a nationwide television audience, Lee Harvey Oswald was fatally shot (Nov. 24) in the basement of the Dallas municipal building by Jack Ruby, a nightclub owner.

President Kennedy was buried at Arlington National Cemetery (Nov. 25) after a solemn ritual attended by an unprecedented number of world dignitaries.

Nature went on a rampage in 1963: An earthquake (Feb. 21–22) at Skopje, Yugoslavia, destroyed most of the town and killed 1,100 persons. Floods in Kentucky, West Virginia, Virginia and Tennessee (Mar. 13) left 18 dead and 30,000 homeless. Hurricanes and tidal waves killed 12,000 persons in East Pakistan (May 29). Hurricane Flora slammed into Haiti and caused 2,500 deaths (Oct. 3–4). A tidal wave (Oct. 9), caused by the collapse of a dam near Belluno, Italy, killed 1,800.

The United States and the Soviet Union announced (Jan. 7) an end to their negotiations on the Cuban crisis and declared the matter closed. Some 17,000 Russian troops remaining in Cuba were to be withdrawn. The two world powers agreed (Apr. 5) to establish a "hot line" between Washington and Moscow to speed communications in a crisis, as in the Cuban confrontation.

The U. S. Navy nuclear submarine *Thresher* was lost (Apr. 10) in the North Atlantic with 129 aboard.

After large demonstrations and mass arrests, Negroes and civic leaders in Birmingham, Ala., reached an agreement (May 6–7) to desegregate public facilities.

Astronaut Maj. L. Gordon Cooper, Jr., orbited the Earth 22 times in Mercury capsule Faith 7.

Pope John XXIII, 81, died (June 3) in Vatican City. The Sacred College of Cardinals elected (June 21) Giovanni Battista Montini as Pope of the Roman Catholic Church. He took the name Paul VI.

Rift in the Communist camp between the U.S.S.R. and Red China deepened after ideological talks ended July 20 without an agreement.

A gang of 8 to 15 bandits halted the Glasgow-to-London train on the outskirts of London (Aug. 15) and got away with a spectacular haul of $7,368,000. (This caper overshadowed the Apr. 14, 1962, mail truck robbery near Plymouth, Mass., which netted $1,551,227 to a gang posing as policemen.) Within a few months, Scotland Yard rounded up 19 persons in connection with the robbery, but only about 10 percent of the loot was recovered.

"March on Washington," a demonstration (Aug. 28) in behalf of civil rights legislation, drew over 250,000 persons in Washington, D.C.

A bomb explosion in a Negro church in Birmingham, Ala., killed four children (Sept. 15).

The 114-day strike against all of New York City's major newspapers ended Apr. 1. The cost of the settlement with the printers and other craft unions resulted in a decision by the Hearst Corporation to close the *Daily Mirror* (Oct. 15).

Konrad Adenauer retired (Oct. 16) as Chancellor of West Germany and was succeeded by Ludwig Erhard. Britain also had a change of command when Prime Minister Harold Macmillan was succeeded (Oct. 19) by Sir Alec Douglas-Home.

South Vietnamese President Ngo Dinh Diem was killed in an Army-led coup (Nov. 1–2).

Best-selling fiction of the year included Mary McCarthy's "The Group," Daphne du Maurier's "The Glass Blowers," Morris West's "Shoes of the Fisherman," J. D. Salinger's "Raise High the Roof Beam, Carpenters." In the non-fiction category, leaders included Charles M. Schulz's "Happiness Is a Warm Puppy," Emmet J. Hughes' "Ordeal of Power," Jessica Mitford's "The American Way of Death," James Baldwin's "The Fire Next Time," Bob Hope's "I Owe Russia $1200." There was a total of 25,784 titles published in 1963, up from 21,904 in 1962.

The Pulitzer Prize committee found no 1963 works meriting awards in the categories of fiction, drama and music.

Motion Picture Academy Oscars for 1963 were awarded to "Tom Jones," best picture; Patricia Neal in "Hud," best actress; Sidney Poitier in "Lilies of the Field," best actor. Poitier's Oscar was the first in a major category to be given to a black actor. (The late Hattie McDaniel had previously won an Oscar for her supporting role in "Gone with the Wind.")

"Cleopatra," starring Elizabeth Taylor, Richard Burton and Rex Harrison, had its world premier (June 12) in New York City. Costing $37,000,000, it was the most expensive film in the history of the cinema. Seats for "Cleopatra" cost as much as $5.50. Other important films of the year included "Dr. No" (Sean Connery), Alfred Hitchcock's "The Birds," "Charade" (Cary Grant, Audrey Hepburn), "America, America," "The Balcony," "Days of Wine and Roses" (Jack Lemmon, Lee Remick, Charles Bickford), Federico Fellini's "8½" (Marcello Mastroianni), "The Great Escape" (Steve McQueen, James Garner), "How the West Was Won" (James Stewart, Debbie Reynolds), "Irma La Douce" (Jack Lemmon, Shirley MacLaine), "It's a Mad, Mad, Mad, Mad World" (Sid Caesar, Buddy Hackett, Jonathan Winters, Jimmy Durante), "Lord of the Flies," "Mondo Cane," "PT 109" (Cliff Robertson), "The Ugly American" (Marlon Brando).

The New York newspaper strike (Dec. 8, 1962, to Apr. 1, 1963) was a devastating blow to the Broadway stage. Theatre attendance dropped sharply as long-running shows and new productions found it difficult to survive without reviews and publicity. Edward Albee's "Who's Afraid of Virginia Woolf?" was the biggest critical and box-office hit of the 1962–1963 season. Plays by several established writers had very brief lives. Among these were Tennessee Williams' "The Milk Train Doesn't Stop Here Anymore," Sidney Kingsley's "Night Life," Lillian Hellman's "My Mother, My Father and Me," Garson Kanin's "Come on Strong" and Irwin Shaw's "Children from Their Games." Two hit musicals, "Oliver!" and "Stop the World—I Want to Get Off," were British imports.

Deaths during the year included Dick Powell, 58 (Jan. 2); Otto Harbach, 89 (Jan. 24); Clifford Odets, 57 (Aug. 15); Edith Piaf, 47 (Oct. 11); Adolphe Menjou, 73 (Oct. 29).

ဢ 1964

All I Really Want to Do. w., m., Bob Dylan. M. Witmark & Sons, cop. 1964.

Amen. w., m., John W. Pate, Sr., and Curtis Mayfield. Pamco Music. Inc., cop. 1964.

And I Love Her (film: A Hard Day's Night). w., m., Paul McCartney and John Lennon. Maclen Music, Inc., Unart Music Corp., cop. 1964.

Baby Love. w., m., Brian Holland, Eddie Holland and Lamont Dozier. Jobete Music Co., Inc., cop. 1964.

Bits and Pieces. w., m., Dave Clark and Mike Smith. Ardmore & Beechwood, Ltd., London; Beechwood Music Corp., cop. 1964.

Can't Buy Me Love (film: A Hard Day's Night). w., m., John Lennon and Paul McCartney. Maclen Music, Inc., cop. 1964.

Chapel of Love. w., m., Phil Spector. Ellie Greenwich and Jeff Barry. Trio Music Co., Inc., cop. 1964.

Chim Chim Cher-ee (film: Mary Poppins). w., m., Richard M. Sherman and Robert B. Sherman. Wonderland Music Co.. Inc., cop. 1963. (Academy Award Winner, 1964.)

Come See About Me. w., m., Brian Holland. Eddie Holland and Lamont Dozier. Jobete Music Co., Inc., cop. 1964.

Dang Me. w., m., Roger Miller. Tree Publishing Co., Inc., cop. 1964.

Dear Heart (film: **Dear Heart**). w., Jay Livingston and Ray Evans. m., Henry Mancini. M. Witmark & Sons., cop. 1964.

Do Wah Diddy Diddy. w., m., Jeff Barry and Ellie Greenwich. Trio Music Co., Inc., cop. 1963.

Don't Let the Rain Come Down (Crooked Little Man). w., m., Ersel Hickey and Ed E. Miller. Serendipity Publishing Corp.; Robert Mellin, Inc., cop. 1964.

Downtown. w., m., Tony Hatch. Welbeck Music, Ltd., London; Leeds Music Corp., cop. 1964.

Everybody Loves Somebody. w., Irving Taylor. m., Ken Lane. Sands Music Corp., cop. 1948.

G.T.O. w., m., John Wilkin. Buckhorn Music Publishers, cop. 1964.

The Girl from Ipanema. English words, Norman Gimbel. Portuguese words, Vinicius De Moraes. m., Antonio Carlos Jobim. Original Portuguese title, "Garota de Ipanema." Antonio Carlos Jobim & Vinicius De Moraes, Brazil; Duchess Music Corp., cop. 1963.

Glad All Over. w., m., Dave Clark and Mike Smith. Ivy Music, Ltd.; Campbell-Connelly, cop. 1963.

Goin' Out of My Head. w., m., Teddy Randazzo and Bobby Weinstein. South Mountain Music Corp., cop. 1964.

Good News. w., m., Sam Cooke. Kags Music, cop. 1964.

A Hard Day's Night (film: **A Hard Day's Night**). w., m., John Lennon and Paul McCartney. Maclen Music, Inc.; Unart Music Corp., cop. 1964.

Hello, Dolly! (**Hello, Dolly!**). w., m., Jerry Herman. Title song of the stage musical and later a film. Edwin H. Morris & Co., Inc., cop. 1963.

Hi-Heel Sneakers. w., m., Robert Higginbotham. Medal Music, Inc., cop. 1964.

The House of the Rising Sun. w., m., Alan Price. Adapted from a traditional American song. Keith Prowse Music Publishing Co., Ltd.,

London; Al Gallico Music Corp., cop. 1964.

I Feel Fine. w., m., John Lennon and Paul McCartney. Maclen Music, Inc., cop. 1964.

I Get Around. w., m., Brian Wilson. Sea of Tunes Publishing Co., cop. 1964.

I Want to Hold Your Hand. w., m., John Lennon and Paul McCartney. Northern Songs, Ltd., London; Duchess Music Corp., cop. 1963.

I Wish You Love. w., Lee Wilson. m., Charles Trenet. Original French title, "Que Reste-t-il De Nos Amours." Leeds Music Corp., cop. 1956.

It Ain't Me, Babe. w., m., Bob Dylan. M. Witmark & Sons, cop. 1964.

It's All Right. w., m., Curtis Mayfield. Curtom Publishing Co., cop. 1963.

Java. w., m., Allen Toussaint, Alvin O. Tyler and Murray Sporn. Tideland Music Publishing Corp., cop. 1958.

The Jerk. w., m., Don Julian. Cash Songs, cop. 1964.

Leader of the Pack. w., m., George Morton, Jeff Barry and Ellie Greenwich. Tender Tunes Music; Elmwin Music, Inc., cop. 1964.

Little Children. w., m., Mort Shuman and J. Leslie McFarland. Rumbalero Music, Inc., cop. 1964.

Love Me Do. w., m., John Lennon and Paul McCartney. Ardmore & Beechwood, Ltd., London; Beechwood Music Corp., cop. 1963.

Love Me with All Your Heart. English words, Michael Vaughn. Spanish words, Mario Rigual. m., Carlos Rigual. Original Mexican title "Cuando Caliente El Sol." Editorial Mexicana De Musica Internacional, S.A., Mexico; Peer International Corp., cop., 1961.

Matchmaker, Matchmaker (Fiddler on the Roof). w., Sheldon Harnick. m., Jerry Bock. Sunbeam Music Corp., cop. 1964.

Memphis. w., m., Chuck Berry. Arc Music Corp., cop. 1959 and 1963.

Mister Lonely. w., m., Bobby Vinton and Gene Allan. Ripley Music Inc., cop. 1962.

My Guy. w., m., William Robinson. Jobete Music Co., Inc., cop. 1964.

My Kind of Town (film: Robin and the Seven Hoods). w., Sammy Cahn. m., James Van Heusen. Sergeant Music Co.; Glorste, Inc.; Van Heusen Music Corp., cop. 1964.

Oh, Pretty Woman. w., m., Roy Orbison and Bill Dees. Acuff-Rose Publications, Inc., cop. 1964.

People (Funny Girl). w., Bob Merrill. m., Jule Styne. From the stage musical, starring Barbra Streisand, who also starred in the film version. Chappell & Co., cop. 1964.

Pink Panther Theme (film: The Pink Panther). w., Johnny Mercer. m., Henry Mancini. Northridge Music, Inc.; United Artists Music Co., Inc., cop. 1963.

Please, Please Me. w., m., John Lennon and Paul McCartney. Dick James Music, Ltd., London; Concertone Songs, Inc., cop. 1962 and 1964.

Rag Doll. w., m., Bob Crewe and Bob Gaudio. Saturday Music, Inc.; Gavadima Music, Inc., cop. 1964.

Ringo. w., Hal Blair and Don Robertson. m., Don Robertson. Don Robertson Music Corp., cop. 1963.

She Loves You. w., m., John Lennon and Paul McCartney. Northern Songs, Ltd., London; Gil Music Corp., cop. 1963.

She's a Fool. w., m., Ben Raliehg and Mark Barkan. Helios Music Corp.; M.R.C. Music, Inc., cop. 1963.

Sunrise, Sunset (Fiddler on the Roof). w., Sheldon Harnick. m., Jerry Bock. Sunbeam Music Corp., cop. 1964.

Suspicion. w., m., Doc Pomus and Mort Shuman. Elvis Presley Music, Inc., cop. 1962.

Twist and Shout. w., m., Bert Russell and Phil Medley. Progressive Music Publishing Co., Inc., cop. 1960.

Under the Boardwalk. w., m., Artie Resnick and Kenny Young. T. M. Music, Inc., cop. 1964.

Walk On By. w., Hal David. m., Burt Bacharach. Blue Seas Music, Inc.; Jac Music Co., Inc., cop. 1963.

We'll Sing in the Sunshine. w., m., Gale Garnett. Lupercalia Music Publishing Co., cop. 1963.

Where Did Our Love Go? w., m., Eddie Holland, Lamont Dozier and Brian Holland. Jobete Music Co., Inc., cop. 1964.

White on White. w., Bernice Ross. m., Lor Crane. Painted Desert Music Corp., cop. 1963 and 1964.

Who Can I Turn To (When Nobody Needs Me) (The Roar of the Greasepaint—The Smell of the Crowd). w., m., Leslie Bricusse and Anthony Newley. Concord Music, Ltd., London; Musical Comedy Productions, Inc., cop. 1964.

A World Without Love. w., m., John Lennon and Paul McCartney. Maclen Music, Inc., cop. 1964.

You Don't Own Me. w., m., John Madara and David White. Merjoda Music, Inc., cop. 1963.

The Beatles, a rock 'n' roll quartet from Liverpool, England, arrived in the United States early in the year and triggered the American outbreak of Beatlemania, a form of hysteria that gripped teen-age audiences wherever the Beatles performed. The Beatles (Paul McCartney, 23; John Lennon, 24; George Harrison, 22; and Ringo Starr, 24) were estimated to have earned $56,000,000 from records, concert appearances and their film, "A Hard Day's Night."

Pope Paul VI visited the Holy Land (Jan. 4–6), the first Roman Catholic pontiff to make the pilgrimage to the birthplace of Christianity.

Twenty-three persons were killed (Jan. 9–12) in the Panama Canal Zone, in riots sparked by the raising of the United States flag by American high school students.

The ninth Winter Olympic Games were held (Jan. 29–Feb. 9) in Innsbruck, Austria. The Russians led the field with 11 gold medals.

The 24th amendment to the U. S. Constitution, banning the poll tax as a condition for voting in federal elections, became part of the Constitution when South Dakota became the 38th state to ratify the amendment (Jan. 23).

Cassius Marcellus Clay knocked out Sonny Liston, the 8-to-1 favorite, in the heavyweight championship fight (Feb. 25). Clay, who later adopted the name Muhammad Ali and revealed his membership in the Black Muslim sect, would ultimately be stripped of the title because of his resistance to the draft.

Jack L. Ruby was condemned (Feb. 14) to die in the electric chair for the murder of Lee Harvey Oswald, the alleged assassin of President Kennedy.

The most violent earthquake in North America in recent times killed some 131 persons in Alaska (Mar. 27).

General of the Army Douglas MacArthur, 84, a dominant American military figure of the 20th century, died (Apr. 5).

The New York World's Fair opened (Apr. 22) at Flushing Meadows in Queens, N. Y.

Northern Dancer won the Kentucky Derby (May 2) in the record time of two minutes.

Jawaharlal Nehru, 75, Prime Minister of India since that country became independent in 1947, died (May 27).

The Civil Rights Act of 1964, designed to give the Federal Government more power to protect the Constitutional rights of Negro citizens, was signed (July 2) by President Johnson. It was the most comprehensive civil rights legislation since Reconstruction.

Riots in Harlem (July 18–23), in Jersey City (July 24–26) and in Philadelphia (Aug. 28–30) punctuated the "long, hot summer."

The Warren Commission report on the assassination of President Kennedy, filed (Sept. 24) with President Johnson, found that Lee Harvey Oswald acted alone in firing the fatal bullet. This conclusion was challenged by supporters of a conspiracy theory.

Fifty-seven people fled East Germany and entered West Berlin through a secret tunnel, the largest such escape since the German Communist regime built the wall in 1961.

The St. Louis Cardinals beat the New York Yankees four games out of seven to win the baseball World Series (Oct. 7–15).

The XVIII Olympiad, the first to be held in Asia, ended Oct. 24 in Tokyo. American athletes dominated in track and field, swimming and basketball.

Nikita S. Khrushchev, Premier of the Soviet Union and Soviet Communist Party chief, suddenly was stripped of his power (Oct. 15) and was replaced by Leonid I. Brezhnev, who became first secretary of the Communist Party, and Aleksei N. Kosygin, who became Premier.

Communist China exploded its first atom bomb (Oct. 16).

Herbert Clark Hoover, 90, the 31st President of the United States, died Oct. 20.

Lyndon B. Johnson was elected (Nov. 3) the 36th President of the United States in a landslide victory over the Republican nominee, Senator Barry Goldwater.

Martin Luther King, Jr., leader of the non-violent movement for Negro rights in the United States, received (Dec. 10) the Nobel Peace Prize.

Motion Picture Academy Oscars for 1964 were awarded to "My Fair Lady," best picture; Julie Andrews in "Mary Poppins," best actress; Rex Harrison in "My Fair Lady," best actor.

The top money-making film of the year was "The Carpetbaggers" (George Peppard, Carroll Baker, Alan Ladd). Other films of the year included "The Americanization of Emily" (Julie Andrews, James Garner), "Becket" (Richard Burton, Peter O'Toole), "Behold a Pale Horse" (Anthony Quinn, Gregory Peck, Omar Sharif), "The Best Man" (Henry Fonda, Cliff Robertson), "Dr. Strangelove" (Peter Sellers, George C. Scott, Sterling Hayden), "From Russia with Love" (Sean Connery), "Goldfinger" (Sean Connery), "Hamlet" (Richard Burton), "A Hard Day's Night" (the Beatles), "Marriage, Italian Style" (Sophia Loren, Marcello Mastroianni), "The Night of the Iguana" (Richard Burton, Deborah Kerr, Ava Gardner), "The Pink Panther" (David Niven, Peter Sellers), "Seven Days in May" (Burt Lancaster, Kirk Douglas, Fredric March, Edmund O'Brien), "Topkapi" (Melina Mercouri, Peter Ustinov, Maximilian Schell), "The Unsinkable Molly Brown" (Debbie Reynolds, Harve Presnell), "What a Way to Go" (Shirley MacLaine, Paul Newman, Robert Mitchum, Dean Martin), "Zorba the Greek" (Anthony Quinn).

The year's fiction included Saul Bellow's "Herzog," Shirley Ann Grau's "The Keeper of the House" (a 1964 Pulitzer prize winner), Louis Auchincloss' "The Rector of Justin," Gore Vidal's "Julian," R. V. Cassill's "The President," Peter de Vries' "Reuben, Reuben," Thomas Berger's "Little Big Man," Wallace Markfield's "To an Early Grave," Borden Deal's "The Loser." Non-fiction books included Ernest Hemingway's "A Moveable Feast," Vance Packard's "The Naked Society," William Shannon's "The American Irish," Luigi Barzini's "The Italians."

The 400th anniversary of William Shakespeare's birth was celebrated with numerous productions of the Bard's plays, including "Hamlet" on Broadway, with Richard Burton starring and John Gielgud directing. Other plays of the season included Frank D. Gilroy's "The Subject Was Roses" (Pulitzer prize winner), Rolf Hochhuth's "The Deputy," Sidney Michaels' "Dylan," Muriel Resnick's "Any Wednesday," Murray Schisgal's "Luv." Hit musical productions were "Hello, Dolly!" based on Thornton Wilder's "The Matchmaker"; "Funny Girl," based on the life of Fanny Brice; and "Fiddler on the Roof," adapted from the stories of Sholom Aleichem.

Deaths during 1964 included Brendan Behan, 41 (Mar. 20), in Dublin; Eddie Cantor, 72 (Oct. 10) in Hollywood; Rachel Carson, 56 (Apr. 14) in Silver Spring, Md.; Ian Fleming, 56 (Aug. 12) in Sandwich, England; Ben Hecht, 70 (Apr. 18) in New York; Alan Ladd, 50 (Jan. 29) in Palm Springs, Calif.; Harpo Marx, 70 (Sept. 28) in Hollywood; Sean O'Casey, 84 (Sept. 18), in Torquay, England; Cole Porter, 71 (Oct. 16) in Santa Monica.

§≈ 1965

Back in My Arms Again. w., m., Eddie and Brian Holland and Lamont Dozier. Jobete Music Co., Inc., cop. 1965.

Crying in the Chapel. w., m., Artie Glenn. Hill & Range Songs, Inc., cop. 1953.

Do You Believe in Magic? w., m., John Sebastian, Jr. Faithful Virtue Music Co., cop. 1965.

Down in the Boondocks. w., m., Joe South. Lowery Music Co., Inc., cop. 1965.

England Swings. w., m., Roger Miller. Tree Publishing Co., Inc., cop. 1965.

Eve of Destruction. w., m., Phil Sloan. Trousdale Music Publishers, Inc., cop. 1965.

The Game of Love. w., m., Clint Ballard. Skidmore Music Co., Inc., cop. 1964.

Get Off My Cloud (also known as **Get Off of My Cloud**). w., m., Keith Richard and Mick Jagger. Gideon Music, Inc., cop. 1965.

Goldfinger (film: Goldfinger). w., Leslie Bricusse and Anthony Newley. m., John Barry. Unart Music Corp., cop. 1964.

Hang on Sloopy. w., m., Bert Russell and Wes Farrell. Picturetone Music Publishing Corp.; Robert Mellin, Inc., cop. 1964.

Help! (film: Help!). w., m., Paul McCartney and John Lennon. Maclen Music, Inc., cop. 1965.

Help Me, Rhonda. w., m., Brian Wilson. Irving Music, Inc., cop. 1965.

I Can't Help Myself. w., m., Eddie and Brian Holland and Lamont Dozier. Jobete Music Co., Inc., cop. 1965.

I Got You Babe. w., m., Sonny Bono. Cotillion Music, Inc.; Chris-Mark Music Co., cop. 1965.

I Hear a Symphony. w., m., Eddie Holland, Brian Holland and Lamont Dozier. Jobete Music Co., Inc., cop. 1965.

I Know a Place. w., m., Tony Hatch. Duchess Music Corp., cop. 1965.

I Will Wait for You (film: The Umbrellas of Cherbourg). w., Norman Gimbel. m., Michel Legrand. French lyric, Jacques Demy. Productions Michel Legrand, Paris; Productions Francis Lemarque, La Verne; Vogue Music, Inc., cop. 1964.

The "In" Crowd. w., m., Billy Page. Elvis Presley Music, Inc.; Rumbalero Music, Inc., cop. 1964.

It Was a Very Good Year. w., m., Ervin Drake. Dolfi Music, Inc., cop. 1961.

It's Not Unusual. w., m., Gordon Mills and Les Reed. Duchess Music Corp., cop. 1965.

Jolly Green Giant. w., m., Don F. Harris, Lynn Easton and Dewey Terry, Jr. Flomar Music Publishing, Inc.; Burdette Music Co.; Venice Music, Inc., cop. 1965.

King of the Road. w., m., Roger Miller. Tree Publishing Co., Inc., cop. 1964.

Like a Rolling Stone. w., m., Bob Dylan. M. Witmark & Sons., cop. 1965.

Look of Love. w., m., Jeff Barry and Ellie Greenwich. Trio Music, Inc., cop. 1964.

Love Potion No. 9. w., m., Mike Stoller and Jerry Lieber. Quintet Music, Inc., cop. 1964.

Make the World Go Away. w., m., Hank Cochran. Pamper Music, Inc., cop. 1963.

Mr. Tambourine Man. w., m., Bob Dylan. M. Witmark & Sons., cop. 1964.

Mrs. Brown, You've Got a Lovely Daughter. w., m., Trevor Peacock. Brackenbury Music, Inc.; Bigtop Records, Inc., cop. 1964.

My Girl. w., m., William Robinson and Ronald White. Jobete Music Co., Inc., cop. 1964 and 1965.

The Name Game. w., m., Shirley Ellison and Lincoln Chase. Al Gallico Music Corp., cop. 1964.

Red Roses for a Blue Lady. w., m., Sid Tepper and Roy Bennett. Belwin-Mills Publishing Corp., cop. 1948.

(I Can't Get No) Satisfaction. w., m., Mick Jagger and Keith Richard. Immediate Music, Inc., cop. 1965.

The Shadow of Your Smile (film: The Sandpiper). w., Paul Francis Webster. m., Johnny Mandel. Miller Music Corp., cop. 1965. (Academy Award Winner, 1965.)

Silhouettes. w., m., Bob Crewe. Regent Music Corp., cop. 1957.

Sounds of Silence. w., m., Paul Simon. Charing Cross Music, cop. 1964.

Stop! In the Name of Love. w., m., Eddie and Brian Holland and Lamont Dozier. Jobete Music Co., Inc., cop. 1965.

This Diamond Ring. w., m., Bob Brass, Irwin Levine and Al Kooper. Sea-Lark Enterprises, Inc., cop. 1964.

Turn! Turn! Turn! (To Everything There Is a Season). w., m., Pete Seeger. Adapted from a passage in Ecclesiastes. Melody Trails, Inc., cop. 1962.

Unchained Melody. w., Hy Zaret. m., Alex North. Frank Music Corp., cop. 1955.

A Walk in the Black Forest. m., Horst Jankowski. Capriccio Music Verlag, Germany; MRC Music, Inc., cop. 1965.

What the World Needs Now Is Love. w., Hal David. m., Burt Bacharach. Blue Seas Music, Inc.; Jac Music Co., cop. 1965.

Wooly Bully. w., m., Domingo Samudio. Beckie Publishing Co., Inc., cop. 1964.

Yesterday. w., m., John Lennon and Paul McCartney. Maclen Music, Inc., cop. 1965.

You Were on My Mind. w., m., Sylvia Fricker. M. Witmark & Sons, cop. 1965.

You've Lost That Lovin' Feelin'. w., m., Phil Spector, Barry Mann and Cynthia Weil. Screen Gems-Columbia Music, Inc., cop. 1964.

President Johnson outlined his program for a "Great Society" in the State of the Union message (Jan. 4) to the 89th Congress.

Sir Winston Churchill, 90, England's great World War II leader, died (Jan. 24) in London.

The United States expanded the war in Vietnam by bombing the northern zone (Feb. 7) after Vietcong attacks in South Vietnam.

Gambia, England's last colonial outpost in Africa, declared its independence (Feb. 18).

Malcolm X, Negro nationalist leader, was slain (Feb. 21) by assassins in New York.

Soviet cosmonaut Lt. Col. Aleksei A. Leonov became the first man to float in space outside of his spacecraft while orbiting the Earth (March 18–19).

President Johnson proposed unconditional peace negotiations on Vietnam in a speech (Apr. 7) at Johns Hopkins University.

The Astrodome, the world's largest air-conditioned room, opened (Apr. 9) in Houston.

Civil war broke out in the Dominican Republic when the ruling junta was overthrown (Apr. 24) by rebels demanding the return of deposed President Juan Bosch. President Johnson ordered (Apr. 28) U. S. Marines to the area to protect American citizens, and in the President's words, "to prevent another Communist state in this hemisphere."

A national "teach-in" debate on the Vietnam war was held (May 15) on 100 college campuses.

The United States resumed air attacks on North Vietnam after a six-day suspension produced no progress toward peace negotiations.

Cyclones in East Pakistan (May 15, June 1–2) killed 30,000 persons.

Adlai Stevenson, 65, collapsed on a London street and died (July 15).

Supreme Court Justice Arthur Goldberg was picked (July 20) to succeed Adlai Stevenson as U. S. Ambassador to the United Nations. Washington lawyer Abe Fortas was named (July 28) by President Johnson to succeed Goldberg on the Supreme Court.

The Medicare Bill to provide medical care for the aged, was signed (July 30) by President Johnson.

The Watts district in Los Angeles, a Negro slum area, was set aflame (Aug. 11–16) by rioting that resulted in 30 persons being killed.

Dr. Albert Schweitzer, 90, died (Sept. 4) in his jungle hospital at Lambaréné, Gabon.

The Indonesian army blocked (Sept. 30) a Communist-backed coup and launched a campaign of retaliation that resulted in the killing of at least 200,000 persons.

Sandy Koufax, Los Angeles Dodgers star hurler, who had four no-hit games to his credit, pitched two shutouts during the World Series to give the Dodgers a 4–3 victory over the Minnesota Twins.

Electric power failure blacked out parts of northeastern United States and Canada for about 16 hours (Nov. 9–10).

Rhodesia declared (Nov. 11) its independence from Great Britain. England called the declaration unconstitutional and instituted economic countermeasures. The dispute grew out of the policy of Rhodesia's 220,000 whites to maintain political domination over the country's 4,000,000 blacks.

Lt. Col. Frank Borman and Comdr. James A. Lovell, Jr., completed (Dec. 18) a record 14-day, 206-orbit flight in their Gemini 7 capsule.

The United States suspended air attacks (Dec. 24) on North Vietnam in a Christmas truce and began a major diplomatic peace offensive.

Motion Picture Academy Oscars for 1965 were awarded to "The Sound of Music," best film; Julie Christie in "Darling," best actress; Lee Marvin in "Cat Ballou," best actor. Other major films released during the year included "What's New Pussycat" (Peter Sellers, Peter O'Toole), "Shenandoah" (James Stewart), "The Sandpiper" (Elizabeth Taylor, Richard Burton), "Dr. Zhivago" (Geraldine Chaplin, Julie Christie, Omar Sharif, Rod Steiger), "Von Ryan's Express" (Frank Sinatra, Trevor Howard), "The Yellow Rolls-Royce" (Rex Harrison, Jeanne Moreau, George C. Scott, Ingrid Bergman, Omar Sharif), "Help!" (the Beatles), "Those Magnificent Men in Their Flying Machines" (Stuart Whitman, Terry Thomas), "The Spy Who Came in from the Cold" (Richard Burton, Claire Bloom, Oskar Werner), "Thunderball" (Sean Connery), "The Agony and the Ecstacy" (Charlton Heston, Rex Harrison), "Lord Jim" (Peter O'Toole, James Mason), "The Cincinnati Kid" (Steve McQueen, Edward G. Robinson).

The world of literature mourned the death of the master storyteller, William Somerset Maugham, who died (Dec. 16) at the age of 91 at St. Jean-Cap-Ferrat, France.

Among the year's books of fiction were Irving Wallace's "The Man," James Michener's "The Source," Bel Kaufman's "Up the Down Staircase," Morris West's "The Ambassador," Arthur Hailey's "Hotel," John Le Carre's "The Looking Glass War," Irving Stone's "Those Who Love," Robin Moore's "The Green Berets." Non-fiction books included Dag Hammarskjöld's "Markings," Theodore White's "The Making of a President—1964," Larry Collins and Dominique Lapierre's "Is Paris Burning?" Theodore Sorenson's "Kennedy," Arthur Schlesinger, Jr.'s "A Thousand Days" (a Pulitzer prize winner), Sammy Davis, Jr.'s "Yes, I Can," Eric Berne's "Games People Play" and Ruth Montgomery's "A Gift of Prophecy."

Most striking play of the season was German playwright Peter Weiss's "The Persecution and Assassination of Marat as Performed by the Inmates of the Asylum of Charenton Under the Direction of the Marquis de Sade." Other productions launched during 1965 included "The Odd Couple," "On a Clear Day You Can See Forever," "The Roar of the Greasepaint—The Smell of the Crowd," "The Royal Hunt of the Sun," "Man of La Mancha," "Half a Sixpence," and one-man shows by Maurice Chevalier (at the age of 77), and Charles Aznavour. The Pulitzer Prize committee skipped the drama award for 1965.

Deaths during the year included Nat "King" Cole, 45 (Feb. 15) in Santa Monica, Calif.; Judy Holliday, 42 (June 7) in New York; H. V. Kaltenborn, 86 (June 14) in New York; Stan Laurel (Arthur Stanley Jefferson), 74 (Feb. 23) in Santa Monica; David O. Selznick, 63 (June 22) in Hollywood.

໑ 1966

The Ballad of the Green Berets. w., m., Barry Sadler and Robin Moore. Music, Music, Music, Inc., cop. 1966.

Bang Bang (My Baby Shot Me Down). w., m., Sonny Bono. Cotillion Music, Inc.; Chris-Mark Music., cop. 1966.

Born Free (film: Born Free). w., Don Black. m., John Barry. Screen Gems-Columbia Music, Inc., cop. 1966. (Academy Award Winner, 1966.)

Bus Stop. w., m., Gratham Gouldman. Man-Ken Music, Ltd.; Bramsdene Music Corp., cop. 1966.

California Dreamin'. w., m., John E. A. Phillips. Honest John Music Publishers, Inc., cop. 1965.

Cherish. w., m., Terry Kirkman. Beechwood Music Corp., cop. 1965.

Cool Jerk. w., m., Donald Storball. McLaughlin Publishing Co., cop. 1966.

Day Tripper. w., m., John Lennon and Paul McCartney. Maclen Music, Inc., cop. 1965.

Daydream. w., m., John Sebastian, Jr. Faithful Virtue Music Co., Inc., cop. 1966.

Elusive Butterfly. w., m., Bob Lind. Metric Music Co., cop. 1965.

Good Lovin'. w., m., Rudy Clark and Arthur Resnick. T. M. Music, Inc., cop. 1965.

Good Vibrations. w., m., Brian Wilson and Mike Love. Irving Music, Inc., cop. 1966.

A Groovy Kind of Love. w., m., Toni Wine and Carole Bayer. Screen Gems-Columbia Music, Inc., cop. 1966.

Guantanamera. w., José Marti. m., Pete Seeger and Hector Angulo. Based on a work by the Cuban poet, José Marti. Fall River Music Co., Inc., cop. 1963.

Hanky Panky. w., m., Jeff Barry and Ellie Greenwich. T. M. Music, Inc., cop. 1962.

Homeward Bound. w., m., Paul Simon. Charing Cross Music, cop. 1966.

I Got You (I Feel Good). w., m., James Brown. Lois Publishing Co.; Try Me Music, Inc., cop. 1966.

If I Were a Carpenter. w., m., Tim Hardin. Faithful Virtue Music Co., Inc., cop. 1966.

I'm a Believer. w., m., Neil Diamond. Screen Gems-Columbia Music, Inc., cop. 1966.

The Impossible Dream (Man of La Mancha). w., Joe Darion. m., Mitch Leigh. Sam Fox Publishing Co., Inc., cop. 1965.

Kicks. w., m., Barry Mann and Cynthia Weil. Screen Gems-Columbia Music, Inc., cop. 1966.

Last Train to Clarksville. w., m., Tommy Boyce and Bobby Hart. Screens Gems-Columbia Music, Inc., cop. 1966.

Lightnin' Strikes. w., m., Lou Christie and Twyla Herbert. Rambed Publishing Co., Inc., cop. 1966.

Li'l Red Riding Hood. w., m., Ronald Blackwell. Fred Rose Music, Inc., cop. 1966.

Monday, Monday. w., m., John E. A. Phillips. Honest John Music; Wingate Music Corp., cop. 1966.

19th Nervous Breakdown. w., m., Mick Jagger and Keith Richard. Gideon Music, Inc., cop. 1966.

96 Tears. w., m., Rudy Martins. Merlin Music, Inc., cop. 1966.

Nowhere Man. w., m., John Lennon and Paul McCartney. Maclen Music, Inc., cop. 1966.

On a Clear Day You Can See Forever (On a Clear Day You Can See Forever). w., Alan Jay Lerner. m., Burton Lane. Chappell & Co., Inc., cop. 1965.

Over and Over. w., m., Robert Byrd. Recordo Music Publishers, cop. 1958.

Paint It Black. w., m., Mick Jagger and Keith Richard. Gideon Music Inc., cop. 1966.

Paperback Writer. w., m., John Lennon and Paul McCartney. Maclen Music, Inc., cop. 1966.

Reach Out, I'll Be There. w., m., Eddie and Brian Holland and Lamont Dozier. Jobete Music Co., Inc., cop. 1966.

Red Rubber Ball. w., m., Paul Simon and Bruce Woodley. Charing Cross Music, cop. 1966.

See You in September. w., Sid Wayne. m., Sherman Edwards. Jack Gold Music Co., cop. 1959.

Somewhere My Love (Lara's Theme from Dr. Zhivago). w., Paul Francis Webster. m., Maurice Jarre. Robbins Music Corp., cop. 1965.

(You're My) Soul and Inspiration. w., m., Barry Mann and Cynthia Weil. Screen Gems-Columbia Music, Inc., cop. 1966.

Strangers in the Night (film: A Man Could Get Killed). w., Eddie Snyder. m., Bert Kaempfert. Champion Music Corp.; Roosevelt Music Co., Inc., cop. 1966.

Summer in the City. w., m., John B. Sebastian, Mark Sebastian and Joe Butler. Faithful Virtue Music Co., Inc., cop. 1966.

Sunny. w., m., Bobby Hebb. Portable Music Co., Inc.; MRC Music, Inc., cop. 1966.

Sunshine Superman. w., m., Donovan Leitch. Peer International Corp., cop. 1966.

These Boots Are Made for Walking. w., m., Lee Hazlewood. Criterion Music Corp., cop. 1966.

Up Tight (Everything's Alright). w., m., Sylvia May, Stevie Judkins and Henry Cosby. Jobete Music Co., Inc., cop. 1965.

What Now, My Love. w., Carl Sigman. m., Gilbert Becaud. French words by P. Delanoe to the original French song, "Et Maintenant." Editions Le Rideau Rouge, Paris; Remick Music Corp., cop. 1962.

When a Man Loves a Woman. w., m., Calvin H. Lewis and Andrew Wright. Pronto Music, Inc.; Quinvy Music Publishing Co., Inc., cop. 1966.

Wild Thing. w., m., Chip Taylor. Blackwood Music, Inc., cop. 1965.

Winchester Cathedral. w., m., Geoff Stephens. Southern Music Publishing Co., cop. 1966.

Yellow Submarine (film: Yellow Submarine). w., m., John Lennon and Paul McCartney. Maclen Music, Inc., cop. 1966.

You Can't Hurry Love. w., m., Eddie and Brian Holland and Lamont Dozier. Jobete Music Co., Inc., cop. 1965.

Charles de Gaulle began (Jan. 8) his second seven-year term as President of France.

Four hydrogen bombs aboard a U. S. B-52 bomber were lost (Jan. 17) over Polomares, Spain, after a mid-air collision with a jet tanker. Three of the four bombs were quickly recovered. The fourth was found intact (Apr. 7) in the Mediterranean Sea.

Mrs. Indira Gandhi, the only child of Jawaharlal Nehru, leader in India's emergence as an independent nation, was sworn in (Jan. 24) as Prime Minister of India. She succeeded Lai Bahadur Shastri, who died Jan. 11.

The United States resumed (Jan. 31) air raids over North Vietnam after a 37-day suspension to explore the possibilities for peace negotiations.

Russia's unmanned Luna IX capsule made the first successful soft landing on the moon.

President de Gaulle declared (Feb. 21) that France would take over jurisdiction of all Allied military forces and bases on its territory on expiration of NATO commitments Apr. 4, 1969.

Kwame Nkrumah, President of Ghana, was deposed (Feb. 24) by military leaders while he was on a mission to the Far East.

Russian spacecraft Venus III reached (Mar. 1) the planet Venus. It had been launched Nov. 16, 1965.

Astronauts Neil A. Armstrong and David R. Scott were forced to make an emergency landing near Okinawa after achieving the first docking in space (Mar. 16).

The British Labor Party won (Mar. 1) a decisive election victory and gained a 97-vote majority in the House of Commons.

New York's old Metropolitan Opera House, a landmark for 83 years, closed (Apr. 16) after a gala program—nostalgic and sentimental. Efforts to preserve the building as a landmark were unsuccessful. The company moved to new quarters in Lincoln Center for the Performing Arts.

Communist China's "cultural revolution," which sparked profound social and political upheaval, was launched early in May.

Unmanned U. S. spacecraft Surveyor I made a perfect soft landing on the moon (June 1) and transmitted 10,388 pictures of the lunar surface over a 12-day period.

In an historic ruling (June 13), in the case of *Miranda* vs. *Arizona,* the U. S. Supreme Court decreed that accused persons under arrest must be informed of their Constitutional rights against self-incrimination before police commence interrogation.

Large-scale rioting in Negro areas broke out (July 14–15) on Chicago's West Side and in Cleveland's Hough district (July 18–23).

Charles J. Whitman went berserk and shot 45 persons, 12 fatally, from the top of a 27-story tower in Austin, Texas (Aug. 1). Earlier he had murdered both his mother and wife. The episode ended when police shot him to death.

An avalanche of coal-mining waste killed 144 children and 28 adults in the Welsh village of Aberfan (Oct. 21).

Baltimore beat the Los Angeles Dodgers four straight games to win the baseball World Series. The New York Yankees finished last in the American League for the first time since 1912.

Historic buildings and priceless art works were damaged in floods that engulfed Florence and Venice in November.

Attorney General Edward W. Brooke of Massachusetts was elected (Nov. 8) U. S. Senator on the Republican ticket. He became the first Negro ever elected to the Senate by popular vote.

Deaths during the year included Montgomery Clift, 45 (July 23) in New York; Walt Disney (Walter Elias), 65 (Dec. 15) in Los Angeles; Minnie Guggenheimer (Mrs. Charles S.), 83 (May 23) in New York; Hedda Hopper, 75 (Feb. 1) in Hollywood; Kathleen Norris, 85 (Jan. 18) in San Francisco; Billy Rose (William Samuel Rosenberg), 66 (Feb. 10) in Montego Bay, Jamaica; Clifton Webb, 72 (Oct. 13), in Beverly Hills, Calif.; Ed Wynn (Isiah Edwin Leopold), 79 (June 19) in Beverly Hills.

The Motion Picture Association of America adopted a new production code in 1966 that distinguished between films suitable for children and those for adults only. The code was designed to permit bolder films to be made for adult audiences, such as the film adaptation of Edward Albee's play, "Who's Afraid of Virginia Woolf?"

Motion Picture Academy Oscars for 1966 went to "A Man for All Seasons," best film; Elizabeth Taylor in "Who's Afraid of Virginia Woolf?"; Paul Scofield in "A Man for All Seasons," best actor. Other major films of the year included "Alfie" (Michael Caine, Shelly Winters), "The Bible . . . In the Beginning" (John Juston, Ava Gardner, Peter O'Toole, Stephen Boyd), "Blow-up" (David Hemmings, Vanessa Redgrave), "Born Free" (Virginia McKenna, Bill Travers), "Fantastic Voyage" (Stephen Boyd, Raquel Welch), "The Fortune Cookie" (Jack Lemmon, Walter Matthau), "A Funny Thing Happened on the Way to the Forum" (Zero Mostel, Phil Silvers), "Georgy Girl" (Lynn Redgrave, James Mason), "Hawaii" (Julie Andrews, Max Von Sydow, Richard Harris), "How to Steal a Million" (Audrey Hepburn, Peter O'Toole), "Is Paris Burning?" (Gert Frobe, Leslie Caron), "Khartoum" (Charlton Heston, Laurence Olivier), "A Man and a Woman" (Anouk Aimee), "A Man for All Seasons" (Paul Scofield), "The Professionals" (Burt Lancaster, Lee Marvin).

Among the year's top novels were Jacqueline Susann's "Valley of the Dolls," Allen Drury's "Capable of Honor," Bernard Malamud's "The Fixer" (a Pulitzer Prize winner), John Barth's "Giles Goat-Boy," Thomas Pynchon's "The Crying of Lot 49," Richard Condon's "Any God Will Do," William Brinkley's "The Ninety and Nine," Walder Perry's "The Last Gentleman," Evan S. Connell, Jr.'s "The Diary of a Rapist," Carter Wilson's "Crazy February," Robert Coover's "The Origin of the Brunists," Edwin O'Connor's "All in the Family," Conrad Richter's "A Country of Strangers," Louis Auchincloss' "The Embezzler." In the non-fiction category were Truman Capote's "In Cold Blood," John Toland's "The Last 100 Days," Cornelius Ryan's "The Last Battle," Pierre Salinger's "With Kennedy," Mark Lane's "Rush to Judgment," Edward Jay Epstein's "Inquest: The Warren Commission and the Establishment of Truth," William Manchester's "Death of a President."

Most successful musical productions of the Broadway season were "Mame," starring Angela Lansbury in a comedy based on the Patrick Dennis novel "Auntie Mame"; "Cabaret," an adaptation of Christopher Isherwood's "Berlin Stories"; and "Sweet Charity," based on Federico Fellini's film, "Nights of Cabiria." Other productions included Edward Albee's "A Delicate Balance," a Pulitzer Prize winner; "I Do, I Do," a musical based on Jan de Hartog's play, "The Fourposter"; "The Killing of Sister George"; "Philadelphia, Here I Come"; "Don't Drink the Water."

ꝰ 1967

All (film: Run for Your Wife). w., Marian Grudeff and Raymond Jessell. m., Nino Oliviero. Italian words, Domenico Colarossi. Edizioni Musicali RCA Italiana, Italy; Edward B. Marks Music Corp., cop. 1966.

All You Need Is Love. w., m., John Lennon and Paul McCartney. Maclen Music, Inc., cop. 1967.

Almost Persuaded. w., m., Glenn Sutton and Billy Sherrill. Al Gallico Music Corp., cop. 1966.

The Beat Goes On. w., m., Sonny Bono. Cotillion Music, Inc.; Chris-Mark Music, cop. 1967.

By the Time I Get to Phoenix. w., m., Jimmy Webb. Rivers Music, cop. 1967.

Cabaret (Cabaret). w., m., Fred Ebb and John Kander. Sunbeam Music Corp., cop. 1966.

Can't Take My Eyes Off You. w., m., Bob Crewe and Bob Gaudio. Saturday Music, Inc.; Seasons Four Music Corp., cop. 1967.

Come Back When You Grow Up. w., m., Martha Sharp. Painted Desert Music Corp., cop. 1966.

Daydream Believer. w., m., John C. Stewart. Screen Gems-Columbia Music, Inc., cop. 1967.

Dedicated to the One I Love. w., m., Lowman Pauling and Ralph Bass. Trousdale Music Publishers, Inc., cop. 1967.

The 59th Street Bridge Song (Feelin' Groovy). w., m., Paul Simon. Charing Cross Music, cop. 1967.

Gentle on My Mind. w., m., John Hartford. Glaser Publications, Inc., cop. 1967.

Georgy Girl (film: Georgy Girl). w., Jim Dale. m., Tom Springfield. Springfield Music, Ltd., cop. 1966.

Green Green Grass of Home. w., m., Curly Putnam. Tree Publishing, Inc., cop. 1965.

Groovin'. w., m., Felix Cavaliere and Eddie Brigati. Slacsar Publishing Co., Ltd., cop. 1967.

The Happening (film: The Happening). w., Eddie and Brian Holland and Lamont Dozier. m., Frank DeVol. Jobete Music Co., Inc., cop. 1967.

Happy Together. w., m., Alan Lee Gordon and Garry Bonner. Chardon Music, Inc., cop. 1966.

I Think We're Alone Now. w., m., Richie Cordell and Richard Rosenblatt. Patricia Music Publishing Corp., cop. 1967.

Incense and Peppermint. w., m., John Carter and Tim Gilbert. Claridge Music, Inc., cop. 1967.

It Must Be Him. w., Mack David. m., Gilbert Becaud. French words by M. Vidalim to original French song, "Seul Sur Son Etoile." Editions Le Rideau Rouge, France; Asa Music Co., cop. 1966.

Kind of a Drag. w., m., James Holvey. Daphne Music Co.; Bag of Tunes, Inc., cop. 1966.

The Letter. w., m., Wayne Carson Thompson. Earl Barton Music, Inc., cop. 1967.

Light My Fire. w., m., Robert Krieger, James Morrison, John Densmore and Raymond Manzarek. Nipper Music Co., Inc., cop. 1967.

A Little Bit Me, a Little Bit You. w., m., Neil Diamond. Screen Gems-Columbia Music, Inc., cop. 1967.

A Man and a Woman (film: A Man and a Woman). w., Jerry Keller. m., Francis Lai. Northern Music Co., cop. 1966.

Mercy, Mercy, Mercy. m., Josef Zawinul, cop. 1967.

Michelle. w., m., John Lennon and Paul McCartney. Maclen Music, Inc., cop. 1965.

Moon over Naples. *See* Spanish Eyes.

Ode to Billy Joe. w., m., Bobbie Gentry. Larry Shayne Music, Inc., cop. 1967.

Penny Lane. w., m., John Lennon and Paul McCartney. Maclen Music, Inc., cop. 1967.

The Rain, the Park and Other Things. w., m., Artie Kornfeld and Steve Duboff. Luvlin Music, Inc.; Akbestal Music, Inc., cop. 1967.

Reflections. w., m., Brian and Eddie Holland and Lamont Dozier. Jobete Music Co., Inc., cop. 1967.

Release Me. w., m., Eddie Miller and W. S. Stevenson. Four Star Music Co., Inc., cop. 1954.

Respect. w., m., Otis Redding, Jr. Redwal Music Co., Inc., cop. 1965.

Ruby Tuesday. w., m., Mick Jagger and Keith Richard. Gideon Music, Inc., cop. 1967.

Snoopy vs. the Red Baron. w., m., Richard Holler and Phil Gernhard. Roznique Music, Inc., cop. 1966.

Somethin' Stupid. w., m., Carson Parks. Greenwood Music Co., cop. 1967.

Spanish Eyes (also known as Moon over Naples). w., Eddie Snyder and Charles Singleton. m., Bert Kaempfert. Roosevelt Music Co., Inc., cop. 1965.

Strangers in the Night (film: A Man Could Get Killed). w., Eddie Snyder and Charles Singleton. m., Bert Kaempfert. Roosevelt Music Co., Inc.; Champion Music Corp., cop. 1966.

Sunrise, Sunset (Fiddler on the Roof). w., Sheldon Harnick. m., Jerry Bock. Sunbeam Music Corp., cop. 1964.

Sweet Soul Music. w., m., Sam Cooke, Otis Redding, Jr., and Arthur Conley. Kags Music Corp.; Redwal Music Co., Inc.; Time Music Co., Inc., cop. 1967.

Talk to the Animals (film: Dr. Dolittle). w., m., Leslie Bricusse. Hastings Music Corp., cop. 1967. (Academy Award Winner, 1967.)

This Is My Song (film: **A Countess from Hong Kong**). w., m., Charles Chaplin. Shamley Music Corp., cop. 1967.

There's a Kind of Hush. w., m., Les Reed. Donna Music, Ltd., cop. 1966.

To Sir, with Love (film: **To Sir, with Love**). w., m., Don Black and Marc London. Screen Gems-Columbia Music, Inc., cop. 1967.

Up, Up and Away. w., m., Jimmy Webb. Rivers Music, cop. 1967.

Windy. w., m., Ruthan Friedman. Irving Music, Inc., cop. 1967.

Yesterday. w., m., John Lennon and Paul McCartney. Maclen Music, Inc., cop. 1965.

Three United States astronauts, Virgil I. Grissom, Edward H. White and Roger B. Chaffee, were killed (Jan. 27) in a flash fire in an Apollo spacecraft during a test at Cape Kennedy, Fla.

A tanker, the *Torray Canyon,* owned by the Union Oil Company of California, ran aground (Mar. 18) at the western channel of the English Channel. The ship broke apart, and its cargo of oil spilled and polluted the beaches of southwest Britain and Normandy in France.

North Vietnam President Ho Chi Minh rejected (Mar. 21) President Johnson's proposal for peace talks.

The first U. S.-U. S. S. R. consular treaty since the Russian Revolution was signed (Mar. 31) by President Johnson.

A military junta assumed control of Greece (Apr. 21).

Svetlana Alliluyeva, only daughter of the late Soviet dictator Joseph Stalin, arrived (Apr. 21) in the United States after having broken her ties with Russia in March while on a trip to India.

Soviet Cosmonaut Vladimir M. Komarov became the first casualty of an actual space mission when his spacecraft crashed to Earth (Apr. 24) during a re-entry maneuver.

The worst crisis in the Middle East since the outbreak of war in 1956 flared up in May when United Arab Republic President Nasser requested the withdrawal of United Nations peace-keeping troops from the Egyptian-Israel border. The U. A. R. closed the Gulf of Aqaba to Israeli shipping (May 22). Full-scale fighting began (June 5) between Israel and Egypt, Syria and Jordan. It was a "six-day war" in which Israel smashed the Arab forces and occupied the Sinai Peninsula, the Gaza Strip, Jordanian territory west of the Jordan River and the Golan Highlands of southeast Syria.

Thurgood Marshall, U. S. Solicitor General, became the first Negro to be appointed to the U. S. Supreme Court (June 13).

Fighting broke out (July 6) between Nigerian federal troops and secessionist forces seeking independence for the region of Biafra.

A total of 69 persons were killed in rioting in Newark (July 12–17) and Detroit (July 23–30).

Nguyen Van Thieu and Nguyen Cao Ky were elected (Sept. 3) President and Vice-president of South Vietnam.

Che Guevara, right-hand man to Fidel Castro during the Cuban revolution, was captured (Oct. 8) and killed (Oct. 10) by the Bolivian army.

Opponents of American participation in the Vietnam war demonstarted (Oct. 21) in Washington, D. C. Marshalls and soldiers were used to block attempts to storm the Pentagon.

The world's first human heart transplant was performed (Dec. 3) by South African surgeon Dr. Christiaan N. Barnard. He replaced the damaged heart of a 53-year-old man with the heart of a 25-year-old woman who had died of brain injuries suffered in an automobile accident. A series of similar transplants by surgeons in various countries followed.

A suspension bridge over the Ohio River between Point Pleasant, W. Va., and Kanauga, Ohio, collapsed (Dec. 15), killing at least 46 persons.

William Styron's novel "The Confessions of Nat Turner" won the Pulitzer award for fiction. His portrait of the leader of slave rebellions in the antebellum South generated a sharp controversy among blacks and literary critics.

Other important novels of the year included Wallace Stegner's "All the Little Live Things," Norman Mailer's "Why Are We in Vietnam?" Leon Uris' "Topaz," Gore Vidal's "Washington, D. C.," Vance Bourjaily's "The Man Who Knew Kennedy," Herbert Gold's "Fathers," Philip Roth's "When She Was Good," Chaim Potok's "The Chosen," Susan Sontag's "Death Kit," John A. Williams' "The Man Who Cried I Am," John Hersey's "Under the Eye of the Storm," Thornton Wilder's "The Eighth Day" and Stanley Elkin's "A Bad Man." Non-fiction books included Oscar Lewis' "La Vida," Piri Thomas' "Down These Mean Streets," Jonathan Kozol's "Death at an Early Age: The Destruction of the Hearts and Minds of Negro Children in the Boston Public Schools," John Kenneth Galbraith's "The New Industrial State" and Marshall McLuhan's "The Medium Is the Massage" (in collaboration with Quentin Fiore).

Motion Picture Academy Oscars for 1967 were awarded to "In the Heat of the Night," best film; Katharine Hepburn in "Guess Who's Coming to Dinner?" best actress; Rod Steiger in "In the Heat of the Night," best actor.

"The Dirty Dozen" (Lee Marvin, Ernest Borgnine, Charles Bronson, Jim Brown, John Cassavetes) was the year's top money-making film.

Other big films at the box office were "You Only Live Twice" (Sean Connery), "Casino Royale" (Peter Sellers, Ursula Andress), "Thoroughly Modern Millie" (Julie Andrews), "Barefoot in the Park" (Robert Redford, Jane Fonda), "To Sir with Love" (Sidney Poitier, Judy Geeson, Suzy Kendall), "Hombre" (Paul Newman, Frederic March, Richard Boone, Cameron Mitchell), "Bonnie and Clyde" (Warren Beatty, Faye Dunaway), "Camelot" (Richard Harris, Vanessa Redgrave), "The Comedians" (Elizabeth Taylor, Richard Burton), "Cool Hand Luke" (Paul Newman), "A Countess from Hong Kong" (Sophia Loren, Marlon Brando), "Doctor Dolittle" (Rex Harrison, Samantha Eggar), "Elvira Madigan" (Pia Degermark, Thommy Berggren), "In the Heat of the Night" (Sidney Poitier, Rod Steiger), "Ulysses" (Milo O'Shea).

British playwrights came to the rescue of the Broadway theatre. Among the top plays of the season were Tom Stoppard's "Rosencrantz and Guildenstern Are Dead," Harold Pinter's "The Homecoming" and John Bowen's "After the Rain," all from England. "Hello, Dolly!" turned up in a black version starring Pearl Bailey and Cab Calloway. A Yiddish musical revue, "Hello, Solly!" ran for six weeks. Other productions of the season included "Black Comedy," "Little Murders," "Spofford," "You Know I Can't Hear You When the Water's Running," "Hallelujah, Baby!" "How Now, Dow Jones," "Ilya, Darling" and "Sherry!"

For the fourth time in six years, there was no drama award made by the Pulitzer Prize committee for 1967.

Deaths during the year included Charles Bickford, 78 (Nov. 9) in Los Angeles; Primo Carnera, 60 (June 29) in Sequals, Italy; Nelson Eddy, 65 (Mar. 6) in Miami Beach; John Nance Garner, 98 (Nov. 7) in Uvalde, Texas; Woody Guthrie, 55 (Oct. 3) in New York; Bert Lahr, 72 (Dec. 4) in New York; Jayne Mansfield, 34 (June 29) near New Orleans in an auto accident; Paul Muni, 71 (Aug. 25) in Santa Barbara; Elmer Rice, 74 (May 8) in Southampton, England; Francis Cardinal Spellman, 78 (Dec. 2) in New York; Spencer Tracy, 67 (June 10) in Beverly Hills, Calif.; Paul Whiteman, 77 (Dec. 29) in Doylestown, Pa.

ᔆᕊ 1968

Abraham, Martin and John. w., m., Dick Holler. Roznique Music, Inc., cop. 1968.

A Beautiful Morning. w., m., Felix Cavaliere and Eddie Brigati. Slacsar Publishing Co., cop. 1968.

The Ballad of Bonnie and Clyde. w., m., Peter Callander and Mitch

Murray. Inspired by, but not used in the film "Bonnie and Clyde." Peer International Corp., cop. 1967.

Bend Me, Shape Me. w., m., Laurence Weiss and Scott English. Helios Music Corp., cop. 1967.

Born to Be Wild. w., m., Mars Bonfire. Duchess Music Corp., cop. 1968.

Classical Gas. w., m., Mason Williams. Irving Music, Inc., cop. 1968.

Cry Like a Baby. w., m., Spooner Oldham and Dan Penn. Press Music, Inc., cop. 1968.

(Sittin on) The Dock of the Bay. w., m., Otis Redding, Jr. and Stephen Cropper. East/Memphis Music Corp.; Redwal Music Co., Inc.; Time Music Co., Inc., cop. 1968.

Eleanor Rigby. w., m., John Lennon and Paul McCartney. Maclen Music, Inc., cop. 1966.

Fire. w., m., Arthur Brown, Vincent Crane, Peter Ker and Michael Finesilver. Track Music, Inc., cop. 1968.

Folsom Prison Blues. w., m., Johnny Cash. Hi-Lo Music, Inc., cop. 1956.

The Good, the Bad and the Ugly (film: The Good, the Bad and the Ugly). m., Ennio Morricone. Unart Music Corp., cop. 1966.

Grazin' in the Grass. w., Harry Elston. m., Philemon Hou. Cherio Corp., cop. 1968.

Green Tambourine. w., m., Shelley Pinz and Paul Leka. Kama Sutra Music, Inc., cop. 1967.

Harper Valley P.T.A. w., m., Tom T. Hall. Newkeys Music, Inc., cop. 1967.

Hello, I Love You. w., m., Robert Krieger, James Morrison, John Densmore and Raymond Manzarek. Nipper Music Co., Inc., cop. 1968.

Hey, Jude. w., m., John Lennon and Paul McCartney. Maclen Music, Inc., cop. 1968.

Honey. w., m., Bobby Russell. Russell-Cason Music, Inc., cop. 1968.

Hurdy Gurdy Man. w., m., Donovan Leitch. Peer International Corp., cop. 1968.

I Wish It Would Rain. w., m., Rodger Penzabene, Barrett Strong and Norman Whitfield. Jobete Music Co., Inc., cop. 1967.

I've Got to Get a Message to You. w., m., Barry, Robin and Maurice Gibb. Casserole Music, Inc., cop. 1968.

Judy in Disguise. w., m., John Fred and Andrew Bernard. Su-Ma Publishing Co., Inc., cop. 1967.

Jumpin' Jack Flash. w., m., Mick Jagger, Keith Richard. Gideon Music, Inc., cop. 1968.

Lady Madonna. w., m., John Lennon and Paul McCartney. Maclen Music, Inc., cop. 1968.

Lady Willpower. w., m., Jerry Fuller. Viva Music, Inc., cop. 1968.

Little Green Apples. w., m., Bobby Russell. Russell-Cason Music, Inc., cop. 1968.

Love Is Blue. w., Bryan Blackburn. m., Andre Popp. French words by Pierre Cour to original French song, "L'Amour Est Bleu." Croma Music Co., Inc., cop. 1968.

MacArthur Park. w., m., Jimmy Webb. Canopy Music, cop. 1968.

Mrs. Robinson (film: The Graduate). w., m., Paul Simon. Charing Cross Music, cop. 1968.

Mony, Mony. w., m., Bobby Bloom, Ritchie Cordell, Bo Gentry and Tommy James. Patricia Music Publishing Corp., cop. 1968.

Music to Watch Girls By. w., Tony Velona. m., Sid Ramin. SCP Music Corp., cop. 1967.

One, Two, Three, Red Light. w., m., Sal and Bobbi Trimachi. Kaskat Music, Inc., cop. 1968.

Over You. w., m., Jerry Fuller. Viva Music, Inc., cop. 1968.

People Got to Be Free. w., Felix Cavaliere. m., Eddie Brigati. Slacsar Publishing Co., Ltd., cop. 1968.

Scarborough Fair-Canticle. w., m., Paul Simon and Art Garfunkel. Charing Cross Music, cop. 1966.

Simon Says. w., m., Elliot Chiprut. Kaskat Music, Inc., cop. 1967.

Son of a Preacher Man. w., m., John Hurley and Ronnie Wilkins. Tree Publishing Co., Inc., cop. 1968.

Stone Soul Picnic. w., m., Laura Nyro. Publication rights are in litigation; clearance through Broadcast Music, Inc., cop. 1967.

Sunshine of Your Love. w., m., Jack Bruce, Peter Brown and Eric Clapton. Casserole Music, cop. 1968.

This Guy's in Love with You. w., Hal David. m., Burt Bacharach. Blue Seas Music, Inc.; Jac Music Co., Inc., cop. 1968.

Those Were the Days. w., m., Gene Raskin. Inspired by a traditional East European melody. Essex Music Co., Inc., cop. 1968.

Tighten Up. w., m., Billy H. Buttier and Archie Bell. Cotillion Music, Inc.; Orellia Publishing, cop. 1968.

The Unicorn. w., m., Shel Silverstein. Hollis Music, Inc., cop. 1962.

Valleri. w., m., Tommy Boyce and Bobby Hart. Screen Gems-Columbia Music, Inc., cop. 1967.

Wichita Lineman. w., m., Jimmy Webb. Canopy Music, cop. 1968.

The Windmills of Your Mind (film: The Thomas Crown Affair). w., Alan and Marilyn Bergman. m., Michel Legrand. United Artists Music Co., Inc., cop. 1968. (Academy Award Winner, 1968.)

Young Girl. w., m., Jerry Fuller. Viva Music, Inc., cop. 1968.

Yummy, Yummy, Yummy. w., m., Arthur Resnick and Joe Levine. T. M. Music, Inc., cop. 1968.

Dr. Christiaan N. Barnard performed the world's third heart transplant operation (Jan. 2). The patient, Dr. Philip Blaiberg, 58, a retired

South African dentist, became the world's longest survivor of this new surgical technique (he lived until Aug. 17, 1969).

A Strategic Air Command B-52 carrying four hydrogen bombs crashed near Thule, Greenland (Jan. 22). Radioactive material spread over a wide area, although there was no nuclear explosion.

A U. S. Navy electronic intelligence vessel, the U. S. S. *Pueblo,* was seized (Jan. 23) by North Korean patrol boats in the Sea of Japan. North Korea claimed that the ship had violated its territorial waters and demanded an apology before releasing the 83-man crew. A formal apology was made, and the crew was released after nearly a year of terror-filled imprisonment.

Communist forces in Vietnam opened devastating strikes (Jan. 30) on Saigon and 30 provincial capitals on the first day of the Tet, or New Year, truce. Fighting in the city of Hué continued until Feb. 24.

Alexander Dubcek was elected (Jan. 25) First Secretary of the Czecho-slovakian Communist Party. He promised to liberalize the regime.

Minnesota Sen. Eugene J. McCarthy, running in the New Hampshire primary (Mar. 12) for the Democratic Presidential nomination, polled 42 percent of the vote against 48 percent for President Johnson. Senator Robert Kennedy's entry into the Presidential race came four days later.

President Johnson surprised the world with a televised statement (Mar. 31) that he would not seek re-election. The announcement climaxed a speech in which he also disclosed America's intention to suspend uni-laterally the bombing of North Vietnam.

The Reverend Dr. Martin Luther King, Jr., 39, leader of the non-violent civil rights movement, was killed (Apr. 4) by a sniper in Mem-phis. President Johnson proclaimed April 7 a day of mourning. Dr. King's burial in Atlanta (Apr. 9) was attended by 100,000 mourners in-cluding a host of political leaders. The assassin, James Earl Ray, an escaped convict, was captured (June 8) at a London airport; he subse-quently was convicted and sentenced to 99 years.

The campus revolution was in full swing around the world. In the United States the problems of student alienation, administrative bureauc-racy, the Vietnam war, the draft and black protests against racism were seen as the prime causes of student unrest. "New Left" groups, headed by the Students for a Democratic Society (S. D. S.), occupied several build-ings at Columbia University in New York late in April. The events at Columbia followed a pattern set at the Berkeley campus of the University of California in 1964. Large-scale student outbreaks also occurred for various reasons in France, West Germany, Poland, Czechoslovakia and Japan.

Vice President Hubert H. Humphrey entered (Apr. 27) the race for the Democratic Presidential nomination.

Senator Robert F. Kennedy, 42, was shot (June 5) by an assassin at the Hotel Ambassador in Los Angeles, where he was celebrating his victory in the California primary election. He died the following day, less than five years after the assassination of his older brother, President John F. Kennedy. Sirhan Bishara Sirhan, a Jordanian Arab, was seized with gun in hand.

The Soviet Union directed more than 200,000 of its own allied troops to invade Czechoslovakia (Aug. 20–21) in an effort to halt the democratization process.

Vice President Humphrey was nominated for President at the Democratic Convention in Chicago (Aug. 26–29). Violence inside the convention hall and on the streets of Chicago plagued the Democratic meeting. Senator Edmund S. Muskie of Maine was chosen as the Vice Presidential nominee.

Mrs. Jacqueline Kennedy, widow of President John F. Kennedy, was married (Oct. 20) to Aristotle Onassis, Greek shipping magnate, on his private island of Skorpios off the coast of Greece.

Richard Milhous Nixon was elected (Nov. 5) 37th President of the United States by a narrow margin. He won 302 of the 538 electoral votes and 43.4 percent of the popular vote against Humphrey's 191 electoral votes and 42.7 percent of the popular vote. George Wallace, running on the American Independent Party ticket, won 9,906,000 popular votes and 45 electoral votes.

Yale University announced (Nov. 14) that it would admit women for the first time in its 267-year history.

"Oliver!" won the Motion Picture Academy award for best film of 1968. Katharine Hepburn, for her role in "The Lion in Winter," and Barbra Streisand, for her role in "Funny Girl," were named best actresses, the first tie in the Oscar competition since 1931. Cliff Robertson was named best actor for his role in "Charly."

"The Graduate" (Anne Bancroft, Dustin Hoffman) was the biggest money-maker of the films released during 1968. Oher major films of the year included "The Odd Couple" (Jack Lemmon, Walter Matthau), "Planet of the Apes" (Charlton Heston), "Rosemary's Baby" (Mia Farrow, John Cassavetes), "Yours, Mine and Ours" (Lucille Ball, Henry Fonda), "The Green Berets" (John Wayne), "2001: A Space Odyssey," (Keir Dullea, Gary Lockwood); "The Fox" (Sandy Dennis, Keir Dullea), "The Thomas Crown Affair" (Steve McQueen), "In Cold Blood" (Robert Blake, Scott Wilson), "Charlie Bubbles" (Albert Finney), "Rachel, Rachel" (Joanne Woodward, Estelle Parsons), "The Valley of the Dolls" (Barbara Parkins, Patty Duke), "The Happiest Millionaire" (Fred MacMurray, Tommy Steele).

Theatre productions of the year included "How to Be a Jewish Mother," "Staircase," "The Prime of Miss Jean Brodie," "The Happy Time," "I Never Sang for My Father," "A Day in the Death of Joe Egg," "Golden Rainbow," "The Price," "Plaza Suite," "George M.," "Hair," "The Man in the Glass Booth" and Howard Sackler's "The Great White Hope."

Bestselling fiction in 1968 included Fletcher Knebel's "Vanished," Gore Vidal's "Myra Breckenridge," Arthur Hailey's "Airport," John Updike's "Couples," M. Scott Momaday's "House Made of Dawn" (a Pulitzer prize winner), Taylor Caldwell's "Testimony of Two Men," Morris L. West's "The Tower of Babel," Charles Portis's "True Grit," John O'Hara's "The Instrument," Helen MacInnes' "The Salzburg Connection," James Baldwin's "Tell Me How Long the Train's Been Gone." Non-fiction of the year included Stephen Birmingham's "Our Crowd," R. K. Massie's "Nicholas and Alexandra," Dr. Haim G. Ginott's "Between Parent and Child," Dwight D. Eisenhower's "At Ease: Stories I Tell to Friends," James A. Michener's "Iberia," James D. Watson's "The Double Helix," Adam Smith's "The Money Game," Ferdinand Lundberg's "The Rich and the Super-Rich," Desmond Morris's "The Naked Ape."

Deaths during the year included Peter Arno, 64 (Feb. 22) in New York; Fay Bainter, 74 (Apr. 16) in Hollywood; Dorothy Baker, 61 (June 17) in Terra Bella, Calif.; Edna Ferber, 82 (Apr. 16) in New York; Dorothy Gish, 70 (June 4) in Italy; Helen Keller, 87 (June 1) in Westport, Conn.; Edwin O'Connor, 49 (Mar. 23) in Boston; Franchot Tone, 63 (Sept. 18) in New York.

ເ► 1969

Aquarius (Hair). w., James Rado and Gerome Ragni. m., Galt MacDermot. United Artists Music Corp., cop. 1968.

Baby, I Love You. w., m., Phil Spector, Ellie Greenwich and Jeff Barry. Bertha Music, cop. 1963.

Bad Moon Rising. w., m., John C. Fogerty. Jondora Music, cop. 1969.

A Boy Named Sue. w., m., Shel Silverstein. Evil Eye Music, Inc., cop. 1969.

Build Me Up Buttercup. w., m., Tony Macaulay and Michael D'Abo. January Music Corp.; Nice Songs, Inc., cop. 1969.

Crimson and Clover. w., m., Tommy James and Peter Lucia. Big Seven Music Corp., cop. 1968.

Crystal Blue Persuasion. w., m., Tommy James, Mike Vale and James Zgorecki. Big Seven Music Corp., cop. 1969.

Dizzy. w., m., Freddy Weller and Tommy Rose. Low-Twi Music, Inc., cop. 1968.

Do Your Own Thing. w., m., Jerry Leiber and Mike Stoller. Trio Music Co., Inc., cop. 1968.

Easy to Be Hard (Hair). w., James Rado and Gerome Ragni. m., Galt MacDermot. United Artists Music Corp., cop. 1968.

Everyday People. w., m., Sylvester Stewart. Daly City Music, cop. 1969.

Galveston. w., m., Jimmy Webb. Ja-Ma Music, cop. 1968.

Games People Play. w., m., Joe South. Lowery Music Co., Inc., cop. 1968.

Get Back. w., m., John Lennon and Paul McCartney. Maclen Music, Inc., cop. 1969.

Get Together. w., m., Chet Powers. Also known as "Let's Get Together". Irving Music Co., Inc., cop. 1963.

Good Morning Sunshine (Hair). w., James Rado and Gerome Ragni. m., Galt MacDermot. United Artists Music Corp., cop. 1968.

Hair (Hair). w., James Rado and Gerome Ragni. m., Galt MacDermot. United Artists Music Corp., cop. 1968.

Honky Tonk Women. w., m., Mick Jagger and Keith Richard. Gideon Music, Inc., cop. 1969.

Hooked on a Feeling. w., m., Francis Zambon. Press Music Co., cop. 1969.

Hot Fun in the Summertime. w., m., Sylvester Stewart. Stone Flower Music, cop. 1969.

Hurt So Bad. w., m., Teddy Randazzo, Bobby Hart and Bobby Wilding. Vogue Music, Inc., cop. 1965.

I Can't Get Next to You. w., m., Barrett Strong and Norman Whitfield. Jobete Music Co., Inc., cop. 1969.

I'll Never Fall in Love Again (Promises, Promises). w., Hal David. m., Burt Bacharach. Blue Seas Music, Inc./Jac Music Co., cop. 1969.

In the Ghetto. w., m., Scott Davis. B-n-B Music, Inc.; Gladys Music, Inc., cop. 1969.

In the Year 2525 (Exordium and Terminus). w., m., Richard S. Evans. Zerlad Music Enterprises, Ltd., cop. 1968.

It's Your Thing. w., m., Rudolph, Ronald and O'Kelley Isley. Jobete Music Co., Inc., cop. 1969.

I've Gotta Be Me (Golden Rainbow). w., m., Walter Marks. Damila Music, Inc., cop. 1967.

Jean (film: The Prime of Miss Jean Brodie). w., m., Rod McKuen. Twentieth Century Music Corp., cop. 1969.

Lay Lady Lay. w., m., Bob Dylan. Big Sky Music, cop. 1969.

Love Theme from "Romeo and Juliet" (film: Romeo and Juliet). m., Nino Rota. Famous Music Corp., cop. 1968.

My Cherie Amour. w., m., Stevie Wonder, Henry Cosby and Sylvia Moy. Jobete Music Co., Inc., cop. 1968.

Oh Happy Day. w., m., Edwin R. Hawkins. Kama Rippa Music, Inc.; Edwin R. Hawkins Music, Inc., cop. 1969.

One. w., m., Harry Nilsson. Dunbar Music, Inc., cop. 1968.

Only the Strong Survive. w., m., Kenny Gamble, Leon Huff and Jerry Butler. Parabut Music Corp.; Downstairs Music Co.; Double Diamond Music Co., cop. 1968.

Proud Mary. w., m., John Fogerty. Jondora Music, cop. 1968.

Spinning Wheel. w., m., David Clayton Thomas. Blackwood Music, Inc.; Bay Music, Ltd., cop. 1968.

Sugar, Sugar. w., m., Jeff Barry, Andy Kin. Don Kirshner Music, Inc., cop. 1969.

Suspicious Minds. w., m., Francis Zambon. Press Music Co., Inc., cop. 1968.

Too Busy Thinking About My Baby. w., m., Norman Whitfield, Janie Bradford and Barrett Strong. Jobete Music Co., Inc., cop. 1966.

Wedding Bell Blues. w., m., Laura Nyro. Celestial Music; Cherry River Music, cop. 1966.

What Does It Take to Win Your Love? w., m., Johnny Bristol, Harvey Fuqua and Vernon Bullock. Jobete Music Co., Inc., cop. 1968.

President Richard M. Nixon was inaugurated Jan. 20.

Tornadoes killed 31 persons and injured hundreds (Jan. 23) in the Mississippi hill country.

General of the Army Dwight David Eisenhower, 34th President of the United States, died (Mar. 28) at the age of 78 in Walter Reed Army Hospital, Washington, D. C., after a long illness.

The world's first total artificial heart transplant on a human was performed (Apr. 4) by Dr. Denton A. Cooley in Houston.

The toll of Americans killed in the Vietnam conflict reached 33,641 in April, 12 more than died in the Korean War.

Clashes between Catholics and Protestants in Northern Ireland forced the British to send in troops (Apr. 20).

Charles de Gaulle resigned (Apr. 28) as president of France after being defeated in a national referendum.

Charles Evers, Negro civil rights leader, was elected (May 13) mayor of Fayette, Miss.

Associate Justice Abe Fortas, under pressure from attacks on his relationship with convicted financier Louis Wolfson, resigned (May 15) from the U. S. Supreme Court. Judge Warren Earl Burger, of the U. S. Court of Appeals, was nominated (May 21) by President Nixon to become Chief Justice of the Supreme Court, succeeding Earl Warren, who had earlier announced his intention to retire.

The U. S. Navy destroyer *Frank E. Evans* was cut in two (June 2) by an Australian aircraft carrier in the South China Sea during practice maneuvers. Seventy-three American seamen were lost.

President Nixon announced (June 8) that 25,000 American soldiers would be withdrawn from Vietnam by the end of August. It was the opening step in his plan to "Vietnamize" the war.

Astronauts Neil Armstrong and Edwin E. Aldrin became (July 20) the first men to walk on the moon, fulfilling a pledge made by the late President Kennedy that Americans would succeed in making a manned lunar landing before the 1960s were over.

Film actress Sharon Tate and four other persons were found (Aug. 9) murdered and mutilated in a Los Angeles home rented by Miss Tate and her husband, Polish film director Roman Polanski. Late in the year, members of a wandering colony of mystical cultists were arrested as the alleged killers.

Over 400,000 persons, most of them youngsters, gathered (Aug. 16) at Bethel, N. Y., for the start of the four-day Woodstock Music and Art

Fair. It was an unprecedented phenomenon made up of monumental traffic jams, minimal food and sanitary facilities, widespread marijuana smoking, nudity and public love-making. Most surprising aspect of all, there were no serious incidents of violence.

A United States jetliner, with 146 persons aboard, was hijacked (Jan. 3) to Cuba. Since Fidel Castro came to power in Cuba in 1959, dozens of American aircraft were diverted to that Caribbean country by persons threatening the lives of hostesses or pilots. Aviation hijacking also became a weapon in the conflict between Israel and Arab guerrilla forces. A spectacular hijacking took place (Oct. 31) when an armed U. S. Marine, Lance Corp. Raffaele Minichiello, commandeered a TWA jetliner between Los Angeles and San Francisco and forced it to fly to Rome after several refueling stops. Minichiello was arrested by Italian police shortly after the plane landed.

Hurricane Camille hit (Aug. 17) with devastating impact along the Gulf Coast, leaving about 300 dead and thousands homeless in Mississippi, Louisiana and Alabama.

Ho Chi Minh, 79, president of North Vietnam, died (Sept. 3) in Hanoi.

The first nationwide Moratorium Day (Oct. 15) in protest against the war in Vietnam was observed by millions of Americans of all political persuasions.

The New York Mets dazzled the sports world by winning the National League pennant and then going on to win the World Series, four games to one, against the Baltimore Orioles (Oct. 16). It was another stunning upset by a New York team. Early in the year (Jan. 12), the New York Jets beat the Baltimore Colts, 16–7, scoring the first victory for the American Football League in the Super Bowl. Jets quarterback "Broadway" Joe Namath completed 17 of 28 passes in that game and emerged as football's most glamorous star. The New York Knickerbockers dominated professional basketball in 1969 by setting a new record of 18 consecutive victories. In hockey, the New York Rangers also led their division at year's end.

Astronauts Charles Conrad, Jr., and Alan L. Bean completed (Nov. 24) the second round-trip flight from the Earth to the moon.

Fiction bestsellers of 1969 included Vladimir Nabokov's "Ada," Michael Crichton's "The Andromeda Strain," John Cheever's "Bullet Park," Jessamyn West's "Except for Me and Thee," Aleksandr L. Solzhenitsyn's "The First Circle," Alistair MacLean's "Force 10 from Navarone," Mario Puzo's "The Godfather," Jacqueline Susann's "The Love Machine," Philip Roth's "Portnoy's Complaint," Kurt Vonnegut, Jr.'s "Slaughterhouse-Five," John Le Carre's "A Small Town in Germany," Louis Auchincloss's "A World of Profit." One of the year's fiction bestsellers, "Naked Came the Stranger," turned out to be a literary hoax. Purportedly written by a Long Island housewife, Penelope Ashe, the book was actually hatched up by a group of 13 newspapermen, each of whom was assigned to write a chapter which, if found to have any literary merit, had to be rewritten.

Top non-fiction included Andre Malraux's "Anti-Memoirs," William Manchester's "The Arms of Krupp," Bruce Catton's "Grant Takes Command," Jerry Kramer's "Instant Replay," Ralph G. Martin's "Jennie," Leo Rosten's "The Joys of Yiddish," Laurence J. Peter and Raymond Hull's "The Peter Principle," Peter Maas's "The Valachi Papers."

"The Love Bug" (Dean Jones) was the top money-making film of 1969. Other major films of the year were "Funny Girl" (Barbra Streisand), "Bullitt" (Steve McQueen), "Butch Cassidy and the Sundance Kid" (Paul Newman, Robert Redford), "Romeo and Juliet" (Leonard Whiting, Olivia Hussey), "True Grit" (John Wayne), "Midnight Cowboy" (Dustin Hoffman, Jon Voight), "Oliver" (Mark Lester, Oliver Reed), "Goodbye Columbus" (Richard Benjamin, Ali McGraw), "Chitty Chitty Bang Bang" (Dick Van Dyke, Sally Anne Howes), "Easy Rider" (Peter Fonda, Dennis Hopper), "Where Eagles Dare" (Richard Burton, Clint Eastwood), "Lion in Winter" (Katharine Hepburn, Peter O'Toole), "Winning" (Paul Newman, Joanne Woodward), "Impossible Years" (David Niven, Lola Albright), "Three in the Attic" (Christopher Jones, Yvette Mimieux), "Finian's Rainbow" (Fred Astaire, Petula Clark), "Support Your Local Sheriff" (James Garner), "The April Fools" (Jack Lemmon, Catherine Deneuve), "The Undefeated" (John Wayne, Rock Hudson), "The Wild Bunch" (William Holden, Ernest Borgnine), "Star" (Julie Andrews), "Alice's Restaurant" (Arlo Guthrie), "The Arrangement" (Kirk Douglas, Deborah Kerr, Faye Dunaway), "100 Rifles" (Jim Brown, Raquel Welch). A Swedish film, "I Am Curious (Yellow)" broke box office records and also broke prior standards for dealing with sex in films.

Longest-running shows On-Broadway at the end of the year were "Hello Dolly," "Fiddler on the Roof," "Man of La Mancha" and "Mame." Off-Broadway, the longest-running shows were "The Fantasticks," "This Was Burlesque," "The Premise," "You're a Good Man, Charlie Brown," "Curley McDimple," "Your Own Thing," "Jacques Brel Is Alive and Well and Living in Paris" and "The Boys in the Band." Among the major new productions of the season were "In the Matter of J. Robert Oppenheimer," "Red, White and Maddox," "We Bombed in New Haven," "Hadrian VII," and Nicole Williamson's version of "Hamlet." Howard Sackler's "The Great White Hope' won the Pulitzer drama award.

Deaths during the year included Irene Castle, 75 (Jan. 25) in Eureka Springs, Ark.; Sen. Everett McKinley Dirksen, 73 (Sept. 7) in Washington, D. C.; Judy Garland, 47 (June 22) in London; Sonja Henie, 57 (Oct. 12) on a plane en route to Oslo; Boris Karloff, 81 (Feb. 2) in Midhurst, England; Frank Loesser, 59 (July 28) in New York; Rocky Marciano, 45 (Aug. 31) in an airplane crash at Newton, Iowa; Josh White, 61 (Sept. 5) in Manhasset, N. Y.

Appendix: Some Late-Blooming Perennials*

Down Yonder. w., m., L. Wolfe Gilbert. La Salle Music Publishers, Inc., cop. 1921.

There'll Be Some Changes Made. w., Billy Higgins. m., W. Benton Overstreet. Edward B. Marks Music Corp., cop. 1921.

Nobody Knows You When You're Down and Out. w., m., Jimmy Cox. MCA, Inc., cop. 1923.

Hard-Hearted Hannah, the Vamp of Savannah. w., m., Jack Yellen, Bob Bigelow, and Charles Bates. Warner Bros. Music, cop. 1924.

It Had to Be You. w., Gus Kahn., m., Isham Jones. Warner Bros. Music, cop. 1924.

You Were Meant for Me. w., m., Noble Sissle and Eubie Blake. Warner Bros. Music, cop. 1924.

Love Me Tonight. w., Brian Hooker. m., Rudolf Friml. Famous Music Corp., cop. 1925.

My Yiddishe Momme. w., Jack Yellen. m., Yellen and Lew Pollack. Chappell & Co., cop. 1925.

Squeeze Me. w., m., Thomas (Fats) Waller and Clarence Williams. MCA, Inc., cop. 1925.

Muskrat Ramble. w., Ray Gilbert., m., Edward (Kid) Ory. George Simon, Inc., cop. 1926.

Reaching for the Moon. w., m., Benny Davis and Jesse Greer. Edward B. Marks Music Corp., cop. 1926.

* Songs which later became standards or enjoyed successful revival.

Sugar Foot Stomp, also known as **Dipper Mouth Blues.** w., Walter Melrose. m., Joe (King) Oliver. Melrose Music Corp., International Music, Inc., cop. 1926.

What Can I Say Dear After I Say I'm Sorry? w., m., Walter Donaldson and Abe Lyman. Miller Music Corp., cop. 1926.

Black and Tan Fantasy. m., Bubber Miller and Edward Kennedy (Duke) Ellington. Mills Music, Inc., cop. 1927.

Wild Man Blues. m., Louis Armstrong and Ferdinand (Jelly Roll) Morton. Melrose Music Corp., cop. 1927.

Alabama Song, also known as **Moon of Alabama (The Rise and Fall of the City of Mahagonny).** w., Bertolt Brecht. m., Kurt Weill. Weill-Brecht-Harms Co., cop. 1928.

How Long, How Long Blues. w., Ann Engberg. m., Leroy Carr. MCA, Inc., cop. 1929.

Mean to Me. w., m., Roy Turk and Fred E. Ahlert. Fred Ahlert Music Corp., Cromwell Music, Inc., cop. 1929.

You Were Meant for Me. w., Arthur Freed. m., Nacio Herb Brown. Robbins Music Corp., cop. 1929.

Falling in Love Again (Can't Help It) (film: The Blue Angel). w., Sammy Lerner. m., Frederick Hollander. Famous Music Corp., cop. 1930.

Reaching for the Moon (film: Reaching for the Moon). w., m., Irving Berlin. Irving Berlin Music Corp., cop. 1930.

As Times Goes By. w., m., Herman Hupfeld. Harms, Inc., cop. 1931.

I'm Through with Love. w., Gus Kahn. m., Matt Melneck and Fud Livingston. Robbins Music Corp., cop. 1931.

Kickin' the Gong Around. w., Ted Koehler. m., Harold Arlen. Arko Music Corp., cop. 1931.

Paradise. w., Gordon Clifford and Nacio Herb Brown. m., Brown. Leo Feist, Inc., cop. 1931.

That's My Desire. w., m., Carroll Loveday and Helmy Kress. Mills Music, Inc., cop. 1931.

When It's Sleepy Time Down South. w., m., Leon Rene, Otis Rene and Clarence Music. Mills Music, Inc., cop. 1931.

(I'd Love to Spend) One Hour with You. w., Leo Robin. m., Richard A. Whiting. Famous Music Corp., cop. 1932.

Try a Little Tenderness. w., m., Harry Woods, Jimmy Campbell, and Reg Connelly. Robbins Music Corp., cop. 1932.

Basin Street Blues. w., m., Spencer Williams. Mayfair Music Corp., cop. 1933.

Miss Otis Regrets. w., m., Cole Porter. Harms, Inc., cop. 1934.

The Glory of Love. w., m., Billy Hill. Shapiro, Bernstein & Co., Inc., cop. 1936.

In the Chapel in the Moonlight. w., m., Billy Hill. Shapiro, Bernstein & Co., Inc., cop. 1936.

Poinciana. English words, Buddy Bernier. Spanish words, Manuel Lliso. m., Nat Simon. Edward B. Marks Music Corp., Anne-Rachel Music Corp., cop. 1936.

Slaughter on Tenth Ave. m., Richard Rodgers. Chappell & Co., Inc., cop. 1936.

Caravan. w., Irving Mills. m., Juan Tizol and Duke Ellington. American Academy of Music, Inc., cop. 1937.

Once in a While. w., Bud Green. m., Michael Edwards. Miller Music Corp. cop. 1937.

Jumpin' at the Woodside. m., William (Count) Basie. Bregman, Vicco & Conn., Inc., cop. 1938.

One O'Clock Jump. m., Count Basie. Leo Feist, Inc., cop. 1938.

Strange Fruit. w., m., Lewis Allan. Edward B. Marks Corp., cop. 1939.

Tuxedo Junction. w., Buddy Feyne. m., Erskine Hawkins, William Johnson, and Julian Dash. Lewis Music Publishing Co., Inc., cop. 1940.

Take the "A" Train. w., m., Billy Strayhorn. Tempo Music, Inc., cop. 1941.

Happiness Is Just a Thing Called Joe (film: Cabin in the Sky). w., E. Y. Harburg. m., Harold Arlen. Leo Feist, Inc., cop. 1942.

Perdido. w., H. J. Lengsfelder and Ervin Drake. m., Juan Tizol. Tempo Music, Inc., cop. 1942.

See See Rider. w., m., Ma Rainey. Leeds Music Corp., cop. 1943.

Nancy (With the Laughing Face). w., Phil Silvers. m., Jimmy Van Heusen. Barton Music Corp., cop. 1944.

You Always Hurt the One You Love. w., m., Allan Roberts and Doris Fisher. Pickwick Music Corp., cop. 1944.

(Get Your Kicks on) Route 66. w., m., Bob Troup. Burke & Van Heusen, Inc., cop. 1946.

Puttin' on The Ritz (film: Puttin' on The Ritz). w., m., Irving Berlin. Irving Berlin Music Corp., cop. 1946.

La Vie En Rose. English words, Mack David. French words, Edith Piaf. m., Louiguy. Harms, Inc., cop. 1946.

Every Day I Have the Blues. w., m., Peter Chatman. Arc Music Corp.; Golden State Songs, cop. 1950.

If You Go. English words, Geoffrey Parsons. French words and music, Michel Emer. Original titled "Si Tu Partais." Pickwick Music Corp., cop. 1951.

Lullaby of Birdland. w., B. Y. Forster. m., George Shearing. Patricia Music Publishing Corp., cop. 1952.

He's Got the Whole World in His Hands. w., m., Geoff Love. Chappell & Co., cop. 1957.

Satin Doll. w., Johnny Mercer. m., Billy Strayhorn and Duke Ellington. Tempo Music, Inc., cop. 1958.

MUSICAL NUMBERS BY TITLE

*Numbers given after musical titles refer to
years under which they may be found in text.*

A hubba-hubba-hubba. *See* Dig you later, 1945
"A"—you're adorable, 1948
Aba daba honeymoon, The, 1914
Abraham, Martin and John, 1968
Abide with me, [1861]
Abilene, 1963
About a quarter to nine, 1935
Absence makes the heart grow fonder, 1900
Absent, 1899
Absinthe frappé, 1904
Accent on youth, 1935
Ac-cent-tchu-ate the positive, 1944
Accidently on purpose, 1940
Ach wie ist's moeglich. *See* How can I leave thee!, 1851
Actions speak louder than words, 1891
Adams and liberty, [1798]
Addio, addio, 1962
Addio, mia bella Napoli [1868]
Affair to remember, An, 1957
After all that I've been to you, 1912
After all you're all I'm after, 1933
After I say I'm sorry, 1926
After the ball, 1892
After the roses have faded away, 1914
After you're gone, 1918
Afternoon of a faun, The, [1895]
Aggravatin' papa, 1922
Ah, but is it love, 1933
Ah! sweet mystery of life, 1910
Ain't it a shame, 1922
Ain't it funny what a difference just a few hours make, 1903
Ain't misbehavin', 1929
Ain't that a shame!, 1955
Ain't we got fun, 1921
Airy, fairy Lillian, 1894
Al fresco, 1904
Alabama blossoms, The, 1874
Alabama Song, App. (1928)

Alabamy bound, 1925
Alexander, don't you love your baby no more, 1904
Alexander's ragtime band, 1911
"Algy," the Piccadilly Johnny with the little glass eye, 1895
Alknomook, [1799-1801]
Alice blue gown. *See* In my sweet little Alice blue gown, 1919
Alice, where art thou, 1861
All, 1967
All aboard for Blanket Bay, 1910
All alone (Von Tilzer), 1911
All alone (Berlin), 1924
All alone Monday, 1926
All at once you love her, 1955
All coons look alike to me, 1896
All for love of you, 1908
All for you, 1915
All I ask of you is love, 1910
All I do is dream of you, 1934
All I have to do is dream, 1958
All I really want to do, 1964
All in down and out, 1906
All my life, 1936
All my love, 1950
All of God's children got shoes. *See* Heav'n, heav'n, 1921
All of me, 1931
All of you, 1954
All on account of Liza, [1881]
All or nothing at all, 1940
All over nothing at all, 1922
All quiet along the Potomac tonight, 1864
All saints new. *See* The Son of God goes forth to war, 1877
All she'd say was "Umh hum," 1920
All shook up!, 1957
All that I ask of you is love, 1910
All the king's horses, 1930
All the Quakers are shoulder shakers —down in Quaker Town, 1919
All the things you are, 1939

715

Dark eyes. *See* Black eyes, 1926
Dark moon, 1957
Darkest the hour, 1886
Darktown strutters' ball, The, 1917
Darling Nelly Gray, 1856
Darling Sue. *See* I love you in the same old way, 1896
Darn that dream, 1939
Dashing white sergeant, The, 1826
Daughter of Rosie O'Grady, The, 1918
[Dawes' melody.] *See* Melody, 1912
Day tripper, 1966
Davy Jones' locker, 1901
Day dreaming, 1941
Day dreams, 1910
Day that you grew colder. The, 1905
Day the rains came, The, 1957
Daydream, 1966
Daydream believer, 1967
Days of wine and roses, 1962
Dear eyes that haunt me, 1927
Dear heart, 1964
Dear hearts and gentle people, 1949
Dear John letter, A, 1953
Dear little boy of mine, 1918
Dear mother, in dreams I see her, 1886
Dear old girl, 1903
Dear old pal of mine, 1918
Dear old Rose, 1912
Dear old Southland, 1921
Dearest, you're the nearest to my heart, 1922
Dearie (Kummer), 1905
Dearie (Hilliard and Mann), 1950
Dearly beloved, 1942
Death and transfiguration, [1891]
Death of Nelson, The, 1811
December and May, 1893
Decoration Day. *See* I was looking for my boy, she said, 1895
Dedicated to the one I love, 1967
Deep in my heart, dear, 1924
Deep in the heart of Texas, 1941
Deep in your eyes, 1920
Deep night, 1929
Deep purple, 1934
Deep river, 1917
Deitcher's dog, Der, 1864
Delicado, 1952
Delishious, 1931
Dennis, 1845
Desafinado, 1962
Desert song, The, 1926

Dew-dew-dewy day. *See* What do we do on a dew-dew-dewy day, 1927
Diamonds are a girl's best friend, 1949
Diane, 1927
Dichter und Bauer. *See* Poet and peasant, [1854]
Did I remember, 1936
Did you close your eyes when we kissed, 1957
Did you ever see a dream walking?, 1933
Dig you later, 1945
Diga diga doo, 1928
Dinah, 1925
Dinner at eight, 1933
Dipsy doodle, 1937
Dixie's land, 1860
Dizzy, 1969
Dizzy fingers, 1923
Do-do-do, 1926
Do, do, my huckleberry, do, 1893
Dock of the bay, The, 1968
Does the spearmint lose its flavor on the bedpost overnight?, 1924
Do I love you? (Christiné and Goetz), 1925
Do I love you? (Porter), 1939
Do it again, 1922
Do nothin' till you hear from me, 1943
Do the New York, 1931
Do they miss me at home?, 1852
Do wah diddy diddy, 1964
Do you believe in magic?, 1964
Do your own thing, 1969
Do you love me?, 1946, 1962
Do you take this woman for your lawful wife? I do, I do, 1913
Dominique, 1963
Don't be angry, 1955
Don't be cruel, 1956
Don't bite the hand that's feeding you, 1915
Don't blame it all on Broadway, 1913
Don't blame me, 1933
Don't bring Lulu, 1925
Don't cry, Frenchy, don't cry, 1919
Don't cry, Joe, 1949
Don't ever leave me, 1929
Don't fence me in, 1944
Don't forbid me, 1956
Don't get around much anymore, 1942

High and the mighty, The, 1954
High hopes, 1959
High noon, 1952
High up on a hill top, 1928
Hi-heel sneakers, 1964
Hi-lili, hi-lo, [1953]
Hills of home, The, 1925
Hindustan, 1918
Hinky dinky parlay voo, 1924
His last thoughts were of you, 1894
Hitchy koo, 1912
Hold me, 1920
Holiday for strings, 1943
Holy City, The (Adams), 1892
Holy City, The (Gaul), 1882
Holy, holy, holy! Lord God
  Almighty, [1861]
Home, 1931
Home again, 1851
Home for the holidays, 1954
Home of my youth, 1852
Home, sweet home, [1823]
Homeward bound, 1966
Homing, 1917
Honey, 1928, 1968
Honey babe, 1955
Honey boy, 1907
Honeycomb, [1957]
Honey-love, 1911
Honeymoon march, The, 1894
Honeysuckle Rose, 1929
Honky tonk, 1956
Honky tonk women, 1969
Hoo-oo!—Ain't you coming out to-
  night, 1907
Hooked on a feeling, 1969
Hoop-dee-doo, 1950
Hootchy-kootchy. See The streets of
  Cairo, 1895
Hope told a flattering tale, [1793]
Hop-scotch polka, 1949
Hora staccato, 1930
Horses, 1926
Hosanna (Granier), 1891
Hospodi pomiloi, 1930
Hot canary, The, 1949
Hot diggity, 1956
Hot lips, 1922
Hot fun in the summertime, 1969
Hot time in the old town, A, 1896
Hound dog, 1956
House by the side of the road, The,
  1927
House of the rising sun, The, 1964
How about me?, 1926

How about you?, 1941
How are things in Glocca Morra?,
  1946
How beautiful upon the mountains,
  1910
How blue the night, 1944
How can I leave thee!, 1851
How can you tell?, 1918
How come you do me like you do?,
  1924
How deep is the ocean?, 1932
How do you speak to an angel?, 1952
How dry I am. See O happy day,
  1891
How high the moon, 1940
How I love you, 1926
How important can it be?, 1955
How insensitive, 1963
How it lies, how it lies, how it lies!,
  1949
How's every little thing in Dixie?,
  1916
How long, how long blues, App.
  (1929)
How lovely are Thy dwellings, 1908
How many hearts have you broken?,
  1943
How sweet you are, 1943
How'd you like to be my daddy?,
  1918
How'd you like to spoon with me?,
  1915
How 'ya gonna keep 'em down on
  the farm?, 1919
Hubba-hubba-hubba. See Dig you
  later, 1945
Huckle-buck, 1949
Huckleberry Finn, 1917
Hummingbird, 1955
Humoresque, (Dvorak), 1894
100 pounds of clay, A, 1961
Hungarian dances (Brahms), [1869]
Hungarian rhapsody No. 2 (Liszt),
  [1851]
Hunters of Kentucky, The, 1826
Hurdy gurdy man, 1968
Hurt, [1961]
Hurt so bad, 1969

I ain't down yet, 1960
I ain't got nobody, 1916
I ain't nobody's darling, 1921
I almost lost my mind, [1956]
I'm a believer, 1966